12th International Natural Language Generation Conference (INLG 2019)

Tokyo, Japan
29 October – 1 November 2019

ISBN: 978-1-7138-0066-8

INLG 2019

**The 12th International Conference
on Natural Language Generation**

Proceedings of the Conference

Oct 29 - Nov 1, 2019
Tokyo, Japan

Preface

We are pleased to present the Proceedings of the 12th International Natural Language Generation Conference (INLG 2019), the first to be organised in Asia. The INLG conference is the main international forum for the discussion of all aspects of Natural Language Generation (NLG), including data-to-text, concept-to-text, text-to-text and vision-to-text approaches. This year, we decided to reach out to a number of neighbouring research communities (including Machine Translation, Dialogue Systems, and Psycholinguistics, among others) by inviting a broad range of workshops, and by inviting keynote speakers from neighbouring communities as well.

INLG 2019 was organised by the Artificial Intelligence Research Center of Japan (AIRC, AIST), the University of Aberdeen, and Utrecht University. The event took place under the auspices of the Special Interest Group on Natural Language Generation (SIGGEN) of the Association for Computational Linguistics (ACL) and the International Speech Communication Association (ISCA).

We were very pleased to hear keynote presentations from the following experts:

- Philipp Koehn (Johns Hopkins University, USA)

- Kazunori Komatami (Osaka University, Japan)

- Roger van Gompel (University of Dundee, UK)

- Anya Belz (University of Brighton, UK)

In addition to the main conference, a number of workshops were accepted following an open Call for Workshop Proposals:

- 1st Workshop on Interactive Natural Language Technology for Explainable Artificial Intelligence

- 1st Workshop on AI Werewolf and Dialog System

- 4th Workshop on Computational Creativity in Language Generation

- 1st Workshop on Discourse Structure in Neural NLG

The rising trend in the number of submitted papers that we have seen for Natural Language Generation in the last few years continued strongly this year, so the main conference was extended to take up two and a half days. For the main conference, we received a record number of 147 submissions, of which 36 were accepted as long papers, 30 as short papers, 4 as demo papers, and 3 as generation challenge papers. All accepted papers for the main conference are included in these proceedings.

We received financial support from the following sponsors:

- ARRIA NLG

- Megagon Labs

- DENSO IT Lab

- Yahoo Japan

- Fuji Xerox

- The Association for Natural Language Processing

- Google

- Facebook

We would like to thank all our sponsors for their support, and we extend our gratitude to all speakers and reviewers for their excellent work.

Kees van Deemter
Chenhgua Lin
Hiroya Takamura

INLG 2019 Programme Chairs

Programme Chairs:

Kees van Deemter (Utrecht University, The Netherlands)
Chenghua Lin (University of Sheffield, UK)
Hiroya Takamura (AIST/Tokyo Institute of Technology, Japan)

Invited Speakers:

Philipp Koehn (Johns Hopkins University, USA)
Kazunori Komatami (Osaka University, Japan)
Roger van Gompel (University of Dundee, UK)
Anya Belz (University of Brighton, UK)

Workshop Chairs:

Wenge Rong (Beihang University, China)
Sho Takase (Tokyo Institute of Technology, Japan)

Tutorial and Invited Speaker Chair:

Riza Batista (University of Manchester, UK)

Publicity Chair:

Sebastian Gehrmann (Harvard University, US)

Publication Chair:

Xiao Li (University of Aberdeen, UK)

Local Organization Committee:

Takenobu Tokunaga (**Chair**, Tokyo Institute of Technology, Japan)
Ichiro Kobayashi (Ochanomizu University, Japan)
Hitoshi Nishikawa (Tokyo Institute of Technology, Japan)
Hiroya Takamura (AIST/Tokyo Institute of Technology, Japan)
Sho Takase (Tokyo Institute of Technology, Japan)
Hikaru Yokono (Fujitsu Laboratories, Japan)

Area Chairs:

Albert Gatt (University of Malta)
Guanyi Chen (Utrecht University)
David Schlangen (University of Potsdam)
David McDonald (Smart Information Flow Technologies (dba SIFT, LLC))
Dimitra Gkatzia (Edinburgh Napier University)
Emiel Krahmer (Tilburg University)

Alberto Bugarín Diz (Univ. Santiago de Compostela)
Ehud Reiter (University of Aberdeen)
Kathy McKeown (Columbia University)
Keith VanderLinden (Calvin College)
Michael White (The Ohio State University)
Pablo Duboue (Textualization Software Ltd.)
François Portet (Laboratoire d'Informatique de Grenoble)
Saad Mahamood (trivago N.V)
Kristina Striegnitz (Union College)
Mariët Theune (University of Twente)

Program Committee:

Manex Agirrezabal (University of Copenhagen)
Malihe Alikhani (Rutgers University)
Jose Alonso (University of Santiago de Compostela)
Jun Araki (Bosch Research)
Anja Belz (University of Brighton)
Jennifer Biggs (Defence Science and Technology Group)
Nadjet Bouayad-Agha (NLP Consultant)
Jan Buys (University of Washington)
Deng Cai (The Chinese University of Hong Kong)
Thiago Castro Ferreira (Tilburg University)
PohLian Choong (Commonwealth of Australia)
Yagmur Gizem Cinar (Naver Labs Europe)
Elizabeth Clark (University of Washington)
Brian Davis (Dublin City University)
Nina Dethlefs (University of Hull)
Ondřej Dušek (Charles University)
Zhenxin Fu (Peking University)
Lorenzo Gatti (Human Media Interaction, University of Twente)
Kim Gerdes (Sorbonne Nouvelle)
Martijn Goudbeek (Tilburg University)
Ting Han (National Institute of Advanced Industrial Science and Technology)
Wenjuan Han (ShanghaiTech University)
Aki Harma (Philips Research)
Sadid A. Hasan (Philips Research North America)
Hiroaki Hayashi (Carnegie Mellon University)
David M. Howcroft (Heriot-Watt University)
Wenpeng Hu (School of Mathematical Sciences, Peking University)
Amy Isard (University of Hamburg)
Feng Ji (Alibaba Group)
Aditya Joshi (CSIRO)
Natthawut Kertkeidkachorn (National Institute of Advanced Industrial Science and Technology)
Cyril Labbe (UGA)
Gerasimos Lampouras (University of Cambridge)
Hoa T. LE (Loria)
Chu-Cheng Lin (Johns Hopkins University)
Tianyu Liu (Peking University)
Elena Lloret (University of Alicante)
Pablo Loyola (IBM Research)

Edison Marrese-Taylor (The University of Tokyo)
Prashant Mathur (Amazon)
Kathy McCoy (University of Delaware)
Antonio Valerio Miceli Barone (The University of Edinburgh)
Simon Mille (Pompeu Fabra University)
Diego Moussallem (Paderborn Univerisity)
Ryo Nagata (Konan University)
Jianmo Ni (University of California San Diego)
Xing Niu (University of Maryland)
Avinesh P.V.S (UKP Lab, Technische Universität Darmstadt)
Suraj Pandey (The Open University)
Cecile Paris (CSIRO)
Steffen Pauws (Philips Research)
Baolin Peng (The Chinese University of Hong Kong)
Minlong Peng (Fudan University)
Laura Perez-Beltrachini (School of Informatics, University of Edinburgh)
Paul Piwek (The Open University)
Shrimai Prabhumoye (Carnegie Mellon University)
Raheel Qader (Université Grenoble Alpes)
Alejandro Ramos Soto (CiTIUS, Universidade de Santiago de Compostela)
Wenge Rong (Beihang University)
Daniel Sanchez (University of Granada)
Mingyue Shang (Peking University)
Dinghan Shen (Duke University)
Lei Shu (Department of Computer Science, University of Illinois at Chicago)
Advaith Siddharthan (The Open University)
Linfeng Song (University of Rochester)
Balaji Vasan Srinivasan (Adobe Research)
Somayajulu Sripada (Arria NLG Plc and University of Aberdeen)
Shahbaz Syed (Leipzig University)
Hiroya Takamura (Tokyo Institute of Technology)
Hao Tan (The University of North Carolina at Chapel Hill)
Craig Thomson (University of Aberdeen)
Son Tran (University of Tasmania)
Lifu Tu (Toyota Technological Institute at Chicago)
Chris van der Lee (Tilburg University)
Emiel van Miltenburg (Tilburg University)
Tu Vu (University of Massachusetts Amherst)
Michael Völske (Bauhaus-Universität Weimar)
Stephen Wan (CSIRO)
Qingyun Wang (University of Illinois at Urbana-Champaign)
Di Wang (School of Computer Science, Carnegie Mellon University)
Wenlin Wang (Duke University)
Leo Wanner (ICREA and Pompeu Fabra University)
Sander Wubben (Flow.ai / Tilburg University)
Qiongkai Xu (The Australian National University and Data61)
Chang Xu (Data61, CSIRO, Australia)
Pengcheng Yang (Peking University)
Jin-ge Yao (Peking University)
Sina Zarrieß (University of Jena)
Zhirui Zhang (University of Science and Technology of China)

Zaixiang Zheng (National Key Laboratory for Novel Software Technology, Nanjing University)
Yinhe Zheng (Tsinghua University)
Qingyu Zhou (Harbin Institute of Technology)
Qile Zhu (University of florida)

Table of Contents

Conference Program

29 Oct 2019

10:30–13:30 **Workshop 1: Interactive Natural Language Technology for Explainable Artificial Intelligence (NL4XAI2019)**

10:30–13:10 **Workshop 2: AI Werewolf and Dialog System (AIWolfDial2019)**

14:30–14:45 **Opening of INLG 2019**

14:45–15:35 *Tutorial 2: Deepfake News Generation: Methods, Detection and Wider Implications*
Anya Belz

15:50–16:50 **Oral Session 1: Referring Expression Generation**

Talking about what is not there: Generating indefinite referring expressions in Minecraft
Arne Köhn and Alexander Koller

Generating Quantified Referring Expressions with Perceptual Cost Pruning
Gordon Briggs and Hillary Harner

A case study on context-bound referring expression generation
Maurice Langner

12:25–13:50 **Poster Session 1**

A Tree-to-Sequence Model for Neural NLG in Task-Oriented Dialog
Jinfeng Rao, Kartikeya Upasani, Anusha Balakrishnan, Michael White, Anuj Kumar and Rajen Subba

Multiple News Headlines Generation using Page Metadata
Kango Iwama and Yoshinobu Kano

Neural Question Generation using Interrogative Phrases
Yuichi Sasazawa, Sho Takase and Naoaki Okazaki

Generating Text from Anonymised Structures
Emilie Colin and Claire Gardent

MinWikiSplit: A Sentence Splitting Corpus with Minimal Propositions
Christina Niklaus, André Freitas and Siegfried Handschuh

QTUNA: A Corpus for Understanding How Speakers Use Quantification
Guanyi Chen, Kees van Deemter, Silvia Pagliaro, Louk Smalbil and Chenghua Lin

KPTimes: A Large-Scale Dataset for Keyphrase Generation on News Documents
Ygor Gallina, Florian Boudin and Beatrice Daille

Sketch Me if You Can: Towards Generating Detailed Descriptions of Object Shape by Grounding in Images and Drawings
Ting Han and Sina Zarrieß

An Encoder with non-Sequential Dependency for Neural Data-to-Text Generation
Feng Nie, Jinpeng Wang, Rong Pan and Chin-Yew Lin

On Leveraging the Visual Modality for Neural Machine Translation
Vikas Raunak, Sang Keun Choe, Quanyang Lu, Yi Xu and Florian Metze

Tell Me More: A Dataset of Visual Scene Description Sequences
Nikolai Ilinykh, Sina Zarrieß and David Schlangen

13:50–15:20   GenChal

15:40–17:00   Oral Session 4: Generation Techniques 2

Privacy-Aware Text Rewriting
Qiongkai Xu, Lizhen Qu, Chenchen Xu and Ran Cui

Personalized Substitution Ranking for Lexical Simplification
John Lee and Chak Yan Yeung

Revisiting the Binary Linearization Technique for Surface Realization
Yevgeniy Puzikov, Claire Gardent, Ido Dagan and Iryna Gurevych

Head-First Linearization with Tree-Structured Representation
Xiang Yu, Agnieszka Falenska, Ngoc Thang Vu and Jonas Kuhn

17:10–18:30   Oral Session 5: Creative and Controllable Text Generation

Let's FACE it. Finnish Poetry Generation with Aesthetics and Framing
Mika Hämäläinen and Khalid Alnajjar

Generation of Hip-Hop Lyrics with Hierarchical Modeling and Conditional Templates
Enrique Manjavacas, Mike Kestemont and Folgert Karsdorp

Revisiting Challenges in Data-to-Text Generation with Fact Grounding
Hongmin Wang

Controlling Contents in Data-to-Document Generation with Human-Designed Topic Labels
Kasumi Aoki, Akira Miyazawa, Tatsuya Ishigaki, Tatsuya Aoki, Hiroshi Noji, Keiichi Goshima, Ichiro Kobayashi, Hiroya Takamura and Yusuke Miyao

31 Oct 2019

10:00–10:50   *Tutorial 3: New Challenges for Neural Sequence Generation Models - Insights from Machine Translation*
Philipp Koehn

11:05–12:25   **Oral Session 6: Evaluation and Language Resources**

A Large-Scale Multi-Length Headline Corpus for Analyzing Length-Constrained Headline Generation Model Evaluation
Yuta Hitomi, Yuya Taguchi, Hideaki Tamori, Ko Kikuta, Jiro Nishitoba, Naoaki Okazaki, Kentaro Inui and Manabu Okumura

Agreement is overrated: A plea for correlation to assess human evaluation reliability
Jacopo Amidei, Paul Piwek and Alistair Willis

Best practices for the human evaluation of automatically generated text
Chris van der Lee, Albert Gatt, Emiel van Miltenburg, Sander Wubben and Emiel Krahmer

Automatic Quality Estimation for Natural Language Generation: Ranting (Jointly Rating and Ranking)
Ondřej Dušek, Karin Sevegnani, Ioannis Konstas and Verena Rieser

12:25–13:50   **Poster Session 2**

Improving Quality and Efficiency in Plan-based Neural Data-to-text Generation
Amit Moryossef, Yoav Goldberg and Ido Dagan

Toward a Better Story End: Collecting Human Evaluation with Reasons
Yusuke Mori, Hiroaki Yamane, Yusuke Mukuta and Tatsuya Harada

Hotel Scribe: Generating High Variation Hotel Descriptions
Saad Mahamood and Maciej Zembrzuski

The use of rating and Likert scales in Natural Language Generation human evaluation tasks: A review and some recommendations
Jacopo Amidei, Paul Piwek and Alistair Willis

On task effects in NLG corpus elicitation: a replication study using mixed effects modeling
Emiel van Miltenburg, Merel van de Kerkhof, Ruud Koolen, Martijn Goudbeek and Emiel Krahmer

DisSim: A Discourse-Aware Syntactic Text Simplification Framework for English and German
Christina Niklaus, Matthias Cetto, André Freitas and Siegfried Handschuh

Real World Voice Assistant System for Cooking
Takahiko Ito, Shintaro Inuzuka, Yoshiaki Yamada and Jun Harashima

VAE-PGN based Abstractive Model in Multi-stage Architecture for Text Summarization
Hyungtak Choi, Lohith Ravuru, Tomasz Dryjanski, Sunghan Rye, Donghyun Lee, Hojung Lee and Inchul Hwang

Generating Abstractive Summaries with Finetuned Language Models
Sebastian Gehrmann, Zachary Ziegler and Alexander Rush

Towards Summarization for Social Media - Results of the TL;DR Challenge
Shahbaz Syed, Michael Völske, Nedim Lipka, Benno Stein, Hinrich Schütze and Martin Potthast

13:50–14:30   Oral Session 7: Describnig Visual Scenes

Generating Quantified Descriptions of Abstract Visual Scenes
Guanyi Chen, Kees van Deemter and Chenghua Lin

What goes into a word: generating image descriptions with top-down spatial knowledge
Mehdi Ghanimifard and Simon Dobnik

14:30–15:20   *Tutorial 4: Developing Psychologically Plausible NLG Models of Human Reference Production*
Roger van Gompel

14:30–15:45   **Workshop 5: Discourse Structure in Neural NLG**

14:30–15:45   **workshop 6: Computational Creativity in Language Generation**

Talking about what is not there:
Generating indefinite referring expressions in Minecraft

Arne Köhn and **Alexander Koller**
Department of Language Science and Technology
Saarland University
{koehn|koller}@coli.uni-saarland.de

Abstract

When generating technical instructions, it is often necessary to describe an object that does not exist yet. For example, an NLG system which explains how to build a house needs to generate sentences like "build *a wall of height five to your left*" and "now build *a wall on the other side*." Generating (indefinite) referring expressions to objects that do not exist yet is fundamentally different from generating the usual definite referring expressions, because the new object must be distinguished from an infinite set of possible alternatives. We formalize this problem and present an algorithm for generating such expressions, in the context of generating building instructions within the Minecraft video game.

1 Introduction

Everyone who has ever had to assemble a piece of furniture knows the importance of clearly worded technical instructions. Ideally, such instructions should be personalized to the current user and their level of expertise, and should be rephrased if the user has trouble with some instruction.

In this paper, we explore the challenge of automatically generating personalized building instructions in the context of the video game "Minecraft". Minecraft is a game in which players can explore an open world, mine materials, and build complex structures such as houses and technical devices. By situating the NLG task in Minecraft, we retain the challenge of generating complex technical instructions, within the context of a fully observable virtual environment. Minecraft is an extremely popular game, with 50 million active users, which facilitates access to experimental subjects for evaluation. There are currently about 130 million Minecraft-related videos on YouTube, many of which have humans explain how to construct complex objects;

thus there is a clear interest in building instructions for Minecraft.

One challenge in generating building instructions for Minecraft is to refer to objects that do not exist yet. For instance, in order to instruct the player to build the left railing of the bridge in Fig. 2c, the NLG system might say "build *a railing on the left side of the bridge*". When this instruction is uttered, there is no left railing yet; thus one uses the indefinite referring expression (RE) in italics to refer to a non-existing object. Generating such indefinite NPs is a fundamentally different task than the more established task of generating definite NPs, in which the target referent only needs to be distinguished from a finite set of distractors. In generating indefinite REs, the target referent needs to be distinguished from an infinite set of alternatives, such as railings of different lengths and in different locations. This makes it infeasible to use existing generation algorithms for definite REs.

In this paper, we show how to generate indefinite REs for objects in Minecraft which do not exist yet. We proceed in two steps. First, we will show how to generate definite and indefinite REs to individual blocks in Minecraft, in a way which makes it possible to generate REs for locations in the environment, in addition to REs for objects. We will then build a method for generating definite and indefinite REs to complex objects (such as railings) upon this. The basic idea is to precompute possible sets of features which will uniquely identify the complex object by specifying all of its relevant attributes. We implement our RE generation method in terms of Semantically Interpreted Grammars (SIGs) (Koller and Engonopoulos, 2017) and use their chart-based sentence generator to perform the actual RE generation.

Plan of the paper. We will introduce the task and discuss some related work in Section 2 and

Proceedings of The 12th International Conference on Natural Language Generation, pages 1–10,
Tokyo, Japan, 28 Oct - 1 Nov, 2019. ©2019 Association for Computational Linguistics

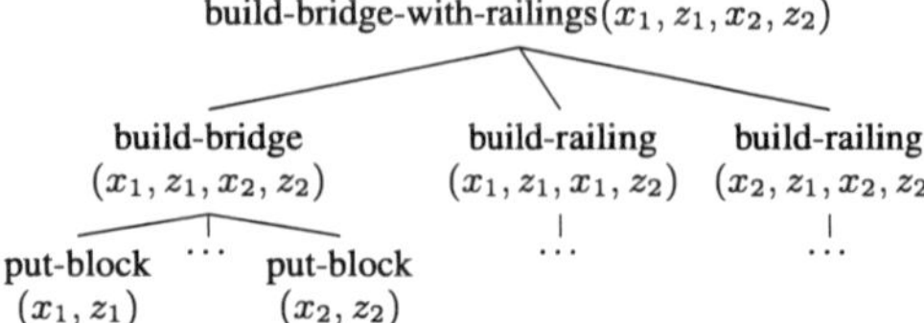

Figure 1: A construction plan.

sketch chart generation with SIGs in Section 3. We will then show how to refer to individual blocks in Section 4 and to complex objects in Section 5. Section 6 concludes and discusses future work.

2 Background

There is an extensive literature on the generation of definite REs to objects which exist in the environment. These algorithms typically aim to distinguish the target referent from the other existing objects, and can thus assume that the denotations of all properties are subsets of the (finite) set of existing objects. They then intersect denotations of properties in some way, keeping track of the (finite) set of possible referents in the intersection, until the set of referents becomes singleton. The classical reference for this approach is the Incremental Algorithm of Dale and Reiter (1995); other methods for generating definite REs follow the same perspective (Krahmer et al., 2003). See (Krahmer and van Deemter, 2012; van Deemter, 2016) for an overview. To our knowledge, there is no accepted method for systematically generating indefinite REs.

There is also an extensive literature on the meaning of indefinites in theoretical semantics. Classical theories (Heim, 1982; Kamp and Reyle, 1993) focus on the ability of indefinites to update the discourse context with new referents; their ability to refer to objects in the world is only a byproduct of this. von Heusinger (2000) describes the referential potential of indefinites in terms of choice functions, i.e. the referent of "a bridge" is an arbitrary bridge. In either case, there is no requirement that an indefinite noun phrase should refer uniquely, as we require in Minecraft building instructions.

2.1 Instruction generation in Minecraft

Generating indefinite referring expressions is a sub problem of instruction generation, for which we

first sketch the overall setting. In the instruction giving task, an *architect* observes the actions of a (human) builder and sends real-time instructions to the builder. The architect has to solve several tasks: First, it needs to generate a *construction plan* which describes the actions the player needs to take in the Minecraft environment in order to construct the goal object (see Wichlacz et al. (2019)). For instance, a possible construction plan for the bridge in Fig. 2 is shown in Fig. 1. Observe that the construction plan is *hierarchical*: Higher-level actions such as "build bridge with railings" are recursively decomposed into lower-level actions; this hierarchical decomposition is present an most instruction giving tasks. At the lowest level of abstraction, each action consists of the placement of individual blocks. As the actions become more fine-grained, so do the types of objects they manipulate (the complete bridge down to the individual blocks). This construction plan can be computed by a hierarchical planner.

The architect then decides at which level of abstraction each construction step should be described; for instance, it might decide to describe the construction in terms of the individual blocks, or it might decide to instruct the player to build a bridge and then the two railings. This decision depends on whether the architect can assume that the builder understands the concept "railing" in the same way the architect intends it: as a single row of blocks along the bridge. The result is an *instruction plan*. Finally, a *sentence generator* translates each step of the instruction plan to a natural-language sentence. For instance, it might map the instruction step 'build-railing(x_2, z_1, x_2, z_2)' to the sentence "build a railing on the other side of the bridge". This paper is concerned with this sentence generation task – more precisely, with the referring expression part.

2.2 Reference in the Minecraft environment

We distinguish two types of objects in a Minecraft environments: individual blocks and *complex objects (COs)* such as bridges, railings, or houses. Each type of object has a set of *features*: bridges for example can be described by the features (type, corner$_1$, corner$_2$, corner$_3$, corner$_4$, width, length), where the corners define the coordinates of each corner in space and type defines what kind of object this is (in this case, a bridge). A concrete object has a specific value for each feature and we

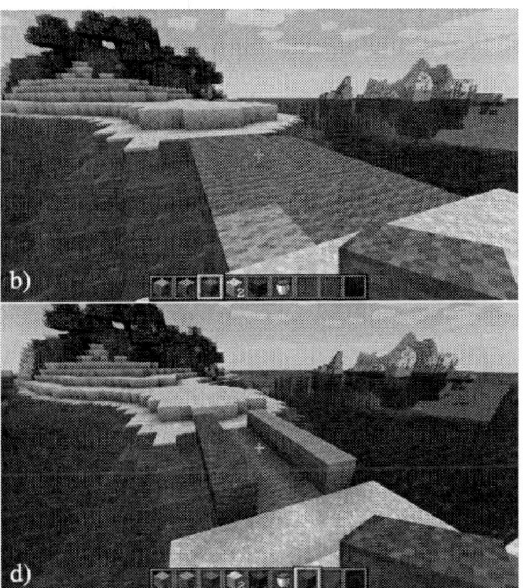

Figure 2: Instructing a user to build a bridge. Left: current state, right: target state. For the first task, the user could be instructed by saying "build a bridge from the blue block to the red block", for the second by "build a railing on the other side of the bridge".

will call a value associated with a feature a *property*. Each object – whether it already exists or not – has a property $p(f)$ for each feature f of its type.[1] For instance, a block b at the location $(1, 1, 1)$ has the two properties [position $= (1, 1, 1)$] and [type $= block$].

These properties are not necessarily independent: the width and length of a bridge are determined uniquely by the positions of the corners. Features are modeled in such a way that there is only one possible object of each type with a certain property tuple, and we identify the objects with their property tuples.

We follow the mainstream literature on RE generation by assuming that the purpose of a referring expression is to uniquely distinguish an object from all alternatives. Technically, we assume a set $\mathcal{P}$ of properties; each property $p \in \mathcal{P}$ denotes a subset $\mathcal{R}(p)$ of objects in the world. For example, the property [width $= 3$] denotes only those objects whose width is 3; the property [type $= bridge$] only those objects which are bridges; and so on. When generating a referring expression, we can keep track of which features are specified by describing the corresponding property of the target object. While it might seem unintuitive to keep

track of the features and not of the corresponding properties, but this approach will come in handy when generating indefinite REs. We denote the properties of an object o corresponding to a specific set of features F as $P_o(F)$. For the block b introduced above, $P_b(\{\text{location}, \text{type}\})$ would be $\{[\text{position} = \{1, 1, 1\}], [\text{type} = block]\}$. When trying to refer to an object o, we need to find a set of features which together distinguish this object from all other objects. We say that a finite set F of features is *distinguishing* for a specific target object t if t is the only object with all the properties $D = P_t(F)$, i.e. $\bigcap_{p \in D} \mathcal{R}(p) = \{t\}$.

2.3 Referring to objects that do not exist

The starting point of this paper is the observation that indefinite reference to objects which do not exist yet differs fundamentally from definite reference to existing objects. In the extensive literature on generation of definite REs, it is customary to limit the denotation of each property to objects which already exist in the environment. This makes these denotations finite, and thus a definite RE can be computed by keeping explicit track of (finite) sets of possible referents and intersecting properties until the set becomes singleton.

By contrast, a unique indefinite RE to an object which does not exist yet must distinguish it from

---

[1] Note that type itself is also a feature to distinguish objects of different types.

type	distinguishing features
bridge	$\{\text{type}, \text{corner}_1, \text{corner}_3\}$
	$\{\text{type}, \text{corner}_1, \text{width}, \text{length}\}$
railing	$\{\text{type}, \text{corner}_1, \text{corner}_2\}$
	$\{\text{type}, \text{corner}_1, \text{length}, \text{orientation}\}$

Figure 3: Examples for distinguishing feature sets.

the entire infinite set of other objects which do not exist yet. For instance, in the example of Fig. 2a, it would be insufficient to say "build a bridge": There are infinitely many places at which a bridge could be built, and it could potentially point in an arbitrary direction[2]. Thus, algorithms which are based on intersecting denotations of properties will not generalize to indefinites.

We therefore choose a different approach. We predefine, for each type of object, a number of distinguishing sets of features (see Figure 3). By definition, if an RE realizes such a feature set by describing the corresponding properties of the target object, the target referent will be described uniquely, even among a potentially infinite set of alternative referents. For instance, "a bridge from the blue block to the red block" is a unique RE because it expresses the feature set $\{\text{type}, \text{corner}_1, \text{corner}_3\}$, which is distinguishing. Similarly, "a bridge of width three and length five, starting at the blue block" is also a unique RE.

There is one way in which generating indefinite REs is easier than generating definite ones: Because there is always an infinite set of alternative referents, no matter what the actual Minecraft world looks like, the distinguishing feature sets are always the same. Thus, unlike in definite RE generation, we do not have to recalculate which feature sets are distinguishing for each world, but can simply reuse feature sets as in Fig. 3. This makes it feasible to shift some of the complexity of generating an indefinite RE from intersecting properties at sentence generation time to a preprocessing module.

---

[2]Even when considering saliency for an object's properties (bridges are usually built over water, walls on the ground), there is still no straight-forward way to distinguish the (possibly finite) set of plausible property tuples from the implausible ones.

3 Semantically Interpreted Grammars

In this paper, we build upon the chart generation algorithm of (Koller and Engonopoulos, 2017) for Semantically Interpreted Grammars (SIGs, (Engonopoulos and Koller, 2014)). SIGs are synchronous grammars which compositionally relate natural-language expressions with their possible referents; they are a special case of IRTGs (Koller and Kuhlmann, 2011). The K&E algorithm performs surface realization together with the generation of definite REs; we extend it to indefinites here.

At the core of a SIG is a regular tree grammar (RTG, (Comon et al., 2007)) which generates a language of *derivation trees*. These derivation trees represent the underlying

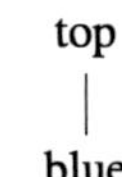

Figure 4: Derivation tree t for "The block on top of the blue block".

structure of the referring expression; Fig. 4 shows such a derivation tree. Derivation trees are built by repeatedly replacing nonterminal symbols using the production rules of the RTG (see the first lines in the toy grammar in Fig. 5), starting from a designated start symbol. For instance, the rule RefBlock $\rightarrow$ *top*(RefBlock) replaces an occurrence of the nonterminal RefBlock by a node which has the label *top* and a child labeled with the nonterminal RefBlock. This new nonterminal occurrence will again be replaced by the right-hand side of a production rule, and so on until no nonterminals are left. We write $L_S(G)$ for the set of derivation trees which can be derived from the start symbol S. If we assume that RefBlock is the start symbol, the tree in Fig. 4 is in the language $L_{\text{RefBlock}}(G)$ of the toy grammar.

Interpretations SIGs describe k-ary relations by taking the derivation trees t described by the RTG and *interpreting* each t in k different ways. Technically, if the derivation trees have node labels in the ranked signature Σ, we say that an interpretation $\mathcal{I}$ consists of a domain $\Delta_\mathcal{I}$, a set of functions $\Sigma_\mathcal{I}$ over this domain ($\Delta_\mathcal{I}^n \rightarrow \Delta_\mathcal{I}$), and a homomorphism from Σ to these functions. By evaluating these functions recursively along t, we obtain a value $[\![t]\!]_\mathcal{I} \in \Delta_\mathcal{I}$ of t in the interpretation $\mathcal{I}$.

String interpretation Basic SIGs focus on two specific interpretations. The *string interpretation* $\mathcal{S}$ generates natural-language expressions from t. The

RefBlock $\to top$(RefBlock)
$\mathcal{I}_S(top)(A) =$ The block on top of $\bullet A$
$\mathcal{I}_R(top)(A) = [\text{topof} \cap_2 A]_1$
$\mathcal{I}_F(top)(A) = \{\text{location}\} \cup A$

RefBlock $\to blue$
$\mathcal{I}_S(blue) =$ the blue block
$\mathcal{I}_R(blue) = uniq(\text{blue})$
$\mathcal{I}_F(blue) = \{\text{location}\}$

Figure 5: A grammar for referring to a block. The example is greatly simplified, see Figures 7 and 9 and Engonopoulos and Koller (2014) for more realistic grammars.

domain Δ_S consists of strings such as "the" and "the block". The functions Σ_s only use string concatenation $\bullet$ and string literals. In our toy example, $[\![t]\!]_S$ is computed by first obtaining a value for $blue$: $\mathcal{I}_S(blue) =$ "the blue block" and based on that obtaining the value of the whole tree: $\mathcal{I}_S(top)($"the blue block"$) =$ "the block on top of" $\bullet$ "the blue block" = "the block on top of the blue block".

Referential interpretation Second, the *referential interpretation* $\mathcal{R}$ maps (partial) derivation trees t to sets of objects to which t might refer.

The definition of the referential interpretation relies on a *model m* of the current world state. We take a model to be a relational structure which maps names of relations to n-ary relations over some universe W. For the toy example, let's assume a model with two relations: the unary relation blue $\subseteq W^1$ and the binary relation topof $\subseteq W^2$; we will work with the model $m = \{\text{blue}: \{(b1)\}; \text{topof}: \{(b2, b1)\}\}$.

The domain of the referential interpretation is the set of tuples of objects in the universe, i.e. W^*. The functions Σ_r perform set operations utilizing the model of the world. Constants such as blue denote the corresponding set of tuples of the model. $uniq(A)$ returns A if the set A contains exactly one tuple, and the empty set otherwise. Its use in the second rule ensures that one can only say "the blue block" to refer to a block if there is exactly one blue block in the world: $[\![blue]\!]_{\mathcal{R}} = uniq(\text{blue}) = uniq(\{(b1)\}) = \{(b1)\}$.

$A \cap_2 B$ filters A: $A \cap_i B := \{a \in A : (a[i]) \in B\}$, i.e. only those tuples of A are retained for

which the i-th element is an element of B. The operator $[A]_i$ projects all tuples of A to their i-th element: $[A]_i := \{(a[i]) \mid a \in A\}$. The interpretation of t is thus

$$
\begin{aligned}
[\![t]\!]_{\mathcal{R}} &= [\text{topof} \cap_2 \{(b1)\}]_1 \\
&= [\{(b2, b1)\} \cap_2 \{(b1)\}]_1 \\
&= [\{(b2, b1)\}]_1 \\
&= \{(b2)\}
\end{aligned}
$$

Note that because t denotes a singleton set of objects, it represents a unique RE for $b2$.

The language of a SIG A SIG G uses a string and a referential interpretation to define a relation between natural-language expressions and the objects they may denote. Given a start symbol S, we define

$$
L(G, S) = \{([\![t]\!]_S, [\![t]\!]_{\mathcal{R}}) \mid t \in L_S(G)\}.
$$

In the example outlined above, $L(G, \text{RefBlock})$ contains, among others, the pair ("the block on top of the blue block", $\{b2\}$).

In an NLG scenario, we assume that we are given a target referent b for which we should generate an RE. We can restrict the language to trees that evaluate to a specific value in certain interpretations and in this way define the language of derivation trees which refer to b:

$$
L(G, S, \mathcal{R}:\{b\}) = \{t \in L_S(G) \mid \{[\![t]\!]_{\mathcal{R}} = \{b\}\}\}.
$$

In the example, $L(G, \text{RefBlock}, \mathcal{R}:\{b2\})$ contains e.g. the derivation tree t in Fig. 4. We can read off the actual referring expression $[\![t]\!]_S$ via the string interpretation. The chart generation algorithm of Koller and Engonopoulos (2017) efficiently computes a compact representation of the language $L(G, S, \mathcal{R}:\{b\})$.

Feature interpretation In this paper, we add a third interpretation to SIGs, which maps derivation trees t to the set of features for which t determines a property value. In the toy example, there is only one feature: location. The domain of $\mathcal{F}$ are sets of features, and Σ_F are functions performing set union. For our toy example, this yields

$$
\begin{aligned}
[\![t]\!]_{\mathcal{F}} &= \{\text{location}\} \cup [\![\text{blue}]\!]_{\mathcal{F}} \\
&= \{\text{location}\} \cup \{\text{location}\} \\
&= \{\text{location}\}
\end{aligned}
$$

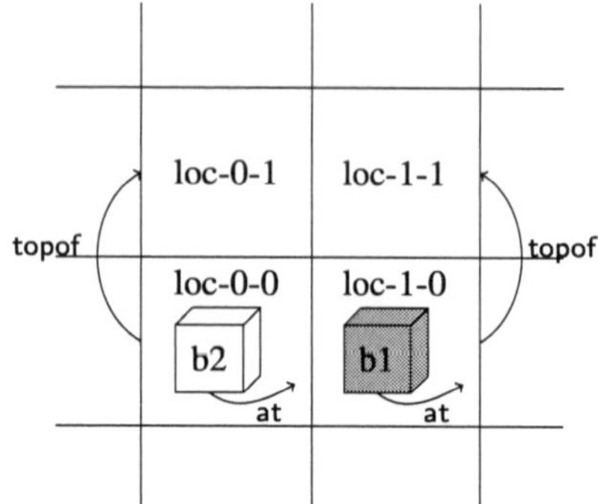

Figure 6: A small world model. The blocks are in an at relation to the locations, the locations are linked via spatial relations such as topof

Thus, we know that t expresses the location of its referent (it is on top of the blue button). We can extend the above definition to the set of derivation trees which refer to a given b and express a given set F of features:

$$L(G, S, \mathcal{R}{:}\{b\}, \mathcal{F}{:}F) =$$
$$\{t \in L_S(G) \mid [\![t]\!]_\mathcal{R} = \{b\} \wedge [\![t]\!]_\mathcal{F} = F\}.$$

The chart generation algorithm generalizes easily to computing $L(G, S, \mathcal{R}{:}\{b\}, \mathcal{F}{:}F)$ for a given G, b, and F.

4   Referring expressions for locations

When we want to instruct a user to place a block at the location loc-1-1 in Fig. 6, we can say

(1)   put a block on top of the blue block

which is a straightforward description of the intended action. This instruction uses the ditransitive verb "put" and the second argument to it subcategorizes a location, which is also the referring part of the instruction. In this section we will discuss how to generate these referring expressions to locations. However, the expressions still need to work with blocks to anchor the expression. We therefore model the world using a duality between blocks and locations; both blocks and locations are entities of the world. Consider these referring expressions in the world depicted in Figure 6:

(2)   the blue block

(3)   left of the blue block

$$\text{DetRefBlock} \to drb(\text{RefBlock})$$
$$\mathcal{I}_S(drb)(RefBlock) = \text{the} \bullet RefBlock$$
$$\mathcal{I}_R(drb)(RefBlock) = uniq(RefBlock)$$
$$\mathcal{I}_F(drb)(RefBlock) = \{\text{location}\} \cup RefBlock$$

$$\text{RefBlock} \to blue(\text{RefBlock})$$
$$\mathcal{I}_S(blue)(RefBlock) = \text{blue} \bullet RefBlock$$
$$\mathcal{I}_R(blue)(RefBlock) = \text{blue} \cap RefBlock$$
$$\mathcal{I}_F(blue)(RefBlock) = RefBlock \cup \text{color}$$

$$\text{RefBlock} \to block$$
$$\mathcal{I}_S(block) = \text{block}$$
$$\mathcal{I}_R(block) = \text{block}$$
$$\mathcal{I}_F(block) = \{\text{type}\}$$

$$\text{RefLoc} \to top(\text{DetRefBlock})$$
$$\mathcal{I}_S(top)(A) = \text{on top of} \bullet A$$
$$\mathcal{I}_R(top)(A) = [\text{topof} \cap_2 [\text{at} \cap_1 A]_2]_1$$
$$\mathcal{I}_F(top)(A) = \{\text{location}, \text{type}\}$$

$$\text{RefBlock} \to blockloc(\text{RefLoc})$$
$$\mathcal{I}_S(blockloc)(A) = \text{block} \bullet A$$
$$\mathcal{I}_R(blockloc)(A) = [\text{at} \cap_2 A]_1$$
$$\mathcal{I}_F(blockloc)(A) = \{\text{type}\}$$

Figure 7: A subset of the block laying grammar.

(4)   the block left of the blue block

Sentence 2 refers to the blue block $b1$, Sentence 3 to the location loc-0-0 to the left of $b1$, and Sentence 4 to the block at the location loc-0-0.

Locations are connected with spatial relations such as topof and blocks are anchored in the world by defining at which location they are using the at relation. While Figure 6 shows only a small 2D slice of a Minecraft world, the principles extend to a 3D Minecraft world and all these relations can be captured from a Minecraft world state.

4.1   Formalizing the block laying instruction

Section 3 introduced a simple SIG to refer to blocks in the world. To generate sentences such as the one in examples 1 to 4, the grammar has to encode the duality between blocks and locations. Figure 7 shows a subset of the grammar to generate these REs. The grammar reflects the duality of blocks and locations through the non-terminals DetRefBlock (which derive referring expressions to blocks) and RefLoc (which derive referring expressions to locations). This duality between locations and blocks is encoded in the at relation, as can be seen in the last two rules of the grammar in Fig. 7: $[\text{at} \cap_1 b]_2$ obtains the location of the block b and $[\text{at} \cap_2 l]_1$ obtains the block at the location l.

We will illustrate how this grammar works by generating a RE to refer to loc-1-1 in the world shown in Figure 6. A model is sketched with arrows in Figure 6; the relevant subset of the model is $\{\text{at}: \{(b1, \text{loc-1-0})\}; \text{block}: \{(b1)\}; \text{topof}: \{(\text{loc-1-1}, \text{loc-1-0})\}\}$. With this model, a RE to loc-1-1 can be obtained with the derivation tree $t = top(drb(blue(block)))$ because it is in $L(G, \text{RefLoc}, \mathcal{R}{:}\{\text{loc-1-1}\})$:

$$[\![block]\!]_\mathcal{R} = \{(b1), (b2)\}$$

$$\begin{aligned}[\![blue(\{(b1), (b2)\})]\!]_\mathcal{R} &= \text{blue} \cup \{(b1), (b2)\} \\ &= \{(b1)\}\end{aligned}$$

$$\begin{aligned}[\![drb(\{(b1)\})]\!]_\mathcal{R} &= uniq(\{(b1)\}) \\ &= \{(b1)\}\end{aligned}$$

$$\begin{aligned}[\![top(\{(b1)\})]\!]_\mathcal{R} &= [\text{topof} \cap_2 [\text{at} \cap_1 \{(b1)\}]_2]_1 \\ &= [\text{topof} \cap_2 [\{(b1,\text{loc-1-0})\}]_2]_1 \\ &= [\text{topof} \cap_2 \{(\text{loc-1-0})\}]_1 \\ &= [\{(\text{loc-1-1}, \text{loc-1-0})\}]_1 \\ &= \{(\text{loc-1-1})\}\end{aligned}$$

The referring expression to loc-1-1 is obtained by computing $[\![t]\!]_\mathcal{S}$, which is "on top of the blue block". On the feature interpretation, the features being described are collected. Note that when using a relation such as topof to switch the referent, the features from the sub-expression are discarded.

5 Indefinite REs to complex objects

Now we extend the RE generation to complex objects. The first step is to convert the coordinate-based representation which can be easily obtained from the 3D world to relations between the objects of the world similar to the one in the previous section. This step is more complex than for simple blocks as COs have no one-to-one correspondence to locations. To generate the instruction for building the second railing in Figure 2d, we want to generate the following model, with it denoting the salient object, i. e. the one that can be referred to as "it":

$$\begin{aligned}
&\{\text{bridge}: \{(b)\}; \\
&\quad \text{it}: \{(r1)\}; \\
&\quad \text{railing}: \{(r1), (r2)\}; \\
&\quad \text{block}: \{(bb), (rb)\}; \\
&\quad \text{from}: \{(b, bb)\}\}; \\
&\quad \text{to}: \{(b, rb)\}\}; \\
&\text{sameshape}: \{(r1, r2)\}\}; \\
&\text{otherside}: \{(r1, b, r2)\}\};
\end{aligned}$$

The object are the blocks rb (the red block) and bb (the blue one), the railings $r1$ and $r2$ ($r2$ is the railing that should be built) and the bridge b If the target object is a CO that does not exist yet, it is added to the objects from which the model is built so that relations between the target and the other objects are generated; this can be seen in the relations above containing $r2$.

We can assume that the input to the NLG system are descriptions of the COs in some fitting 3D description because the NLG system is embedded into an architect which reasons about construction plans containing these COs (compare Figure 1). Each object is described using properties in 3D space: the bridge b in Figure 2, for example, is described using the coordinates of its corners. In contrast to the simple block laying in Section 4, the relations can also be between several objects and not only between an object and a location. The type of relations expressed can be rather diverse: Besides basic spatial relations such as "left of" and unary relations such as the color, more complex relations were expressed when asked humans to instruct other humans in the Minecraft domain (Osmelak, 2018), such as "other side of" (with respect to an unnamed anchor object) or "same shape as" to express the shape of an object, modulo orientation.

To extract these relations from 3D space, a pre-processor iterates over all tuples of objects and checks which of these should be part of one or several relations. For example, each object is added to the unary relation with the name of its type; otherside is filled with all triples $\langle o_1, o_2, o_3 \rangle$ where o_1 and o_3 are on opposite sides of o_2 and both touch o_2. In our example, this is (r1, b, r2) because the two corners of r1 are right above the left corners of b and the corners of r2 are right above the right ones of b.

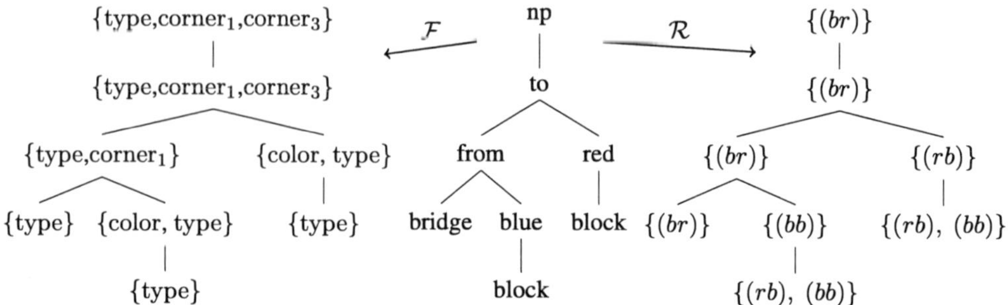

Figure 8: Derivation tree generating "a bridge from the blue block to the red block" (middle), values of the feature interpretation (left) and the referential interpretation (right). The model corresponds to the setting in Figure 2 a), br = bridge, bb = blue block, rb = red block.

5.1 Indefinite reference

As discussed in Section 2, when generating a referring expression for a given object, our aim is to find a set of features which distinguish this object from all other objects we currently *could* but do not want to refer to; for indefinite referents, this set is precomputed (cmp. Figure 3 and Section 2.2). With these distinguishing features sets $\mathcal{D}$, the feature sets that are admissible to be described are all supersets of each of these sets: $\hat{\mathcal{D}} = \{x | \exists d \in \mathcal{D}.x \supseteq d\}$, and the derivation trees for the indefinite REs to a target object o are:

$$L_o = \bigcup_{d \in \hat{\mathcal{D}}} L(G, \text{IndefNP}, \mathcal{R}{:}\{(o)\}, \mathcal{F}{:}d)$$

Internally, the languages do not have to be computed independently; the underlying SIG formalism allows to define a disjunction of target values for interpretations. As before, the REs describing o are the string interpretations of the derivation trees of L_o. Figure 8 shows a derivation tree to generate a RE to the bridge b to generate an instruction from Figure 2 a) to b).

In the SIG (Figure 9), the feature interpretation $\mathcal{F}$ keeps track of which features have been covered: in each rule, the feature interpretation performs a union of the currently described feature with the other features described in child nodes of the derivation tree. Therefore, in the interpretations for $from$, the features from the child noun node are incorporated, but not the features expressed for the blocks used as anchor, as can be seen in Figure 8 (left). $\mathcal{F}$ keeps track about which features are described but not whether their values actually correspond to the target object. Therefore, the referential interpretation $\mathcal{R}$ keeps track of what a

$\text{IndefNP} \rightarrow np(\text{N})$
$\mathcal{I}_S(np)(N) = \text{a} \bullet N$
$\mathcal{I}_R(np)(N) = N$
$\mathcal{I}_F(np)(N) = N$

$\text{DefNP} \rightarrow dnp(\text{N})$
$\mathcal{I}_S(np)(N) = \text{the} \bullet N$
$\mathcal{I}_R(np)(N) = uniq(N)$
$\mathcal{I}_F(np)(N) = N$

$\text{N} \rightarrow from(\text{N}, \text{DetRefBlock})$
$\mathcal{I}_S(from)(N, B) = N \bullet \text{from} \bullet B$
$\mathcal{I}_R(from)(N, B) = [\text{from} \cap_2 B]_1 \cap N$
$\mathcal{I}_F(from)(N, B) = N \cup \{\text{corner}_1\}$

$\text{N} \rightarrow to(\text{N}, \text{DetRefBlock})$
$\mathcal{I}_S(to)(N, B) = N \bullet \text{to} \bullet B$
$\mathcal{I}_R(to)(N, B) = [\text{to} \cap_2 B]_1 \cap N$
$\mathcal{I}_F(to)(N, B) = N \cup \{\text{corner}_3\}$

$\text{N} \rightarrow otherside(\text{N}, \text{DefNP})$
$\mathcal{I}_S(width)(N, P) = N \bullet \text{on the other side of} \bullet P$
$\mathcal{I}_R(width)(N, P) = [(\text{otherside} \cap_2 P) \cap_3 \text{it}]_1 \cap N$
$\mathcal{I}_F(width)(N, P) = N \cup \{\text{corner}_1, \text{corner}_2\}$

$\text{N} \rightarrow bridge$
$\mathcal{I}_S(bridge) = \text{bridge}$
$\mathcal{I}_R(bridge) = \text{bridge}$
$\mathcal{I}_F(bridge) = \{\text{type}\}$

$\text{N} \rightarrow railing$
$\mathcal{I}_S(railing) = \text{railing}$
$\mathcal{I}_R(railing) = \text{railing}$
$\mathcal{I}_F(railing) = \{\text{type}\}$

Figure 9: Excerpt of a grammar to describe a bridge or a railing.

sub-expression refers to when referring to objects in the world (i.e. when generating definite referring expressions such as "the blue block") and evaluates to the indefinite object if it describes a property of that object. On the referential interpretation, all sets of objects are intersected. If the referential interpretation of a derivation tree t is the target object ($[\![t]\!]_{\mathcal{R}} = \{(o)\}$), we can be sure that each feature described was a property of o as otherwise the interpretation would be empty. This can be observed in Figure 8 (right).

Finally, the RE to instruct the user to build the second railing (Figure 2 c) to d)) is defined by the following derivation tree:

$$t = np(otherside(railing, dnp(bridge)))$$

It refers to the correct object ($[\![t]\!]_{\mathcal{R}} = \{(r2)\}$) and describes a distinguishing set of features: $[\![t]\!]_{\mathcal{F}} = \{type, corner_1, corner_2\}$. The resulting RE is $[\![t]\!]_{\mathcal{S}} = $ "a railing on the other side of the bridge".

6 Conclusion

We have introduced a formalization for indefinite referring expressions and exemplified it in the Minecraft instruction giving domain. This formalization is able to generate definite referring expressions for locations and for objects, as well as indefinite referring expressions, which contain definite referring sub-expressions. For this, we have extended a system for generating REs based on SIGs to produce relational definite REs for objects in the world and uses these as building blocks for indefinite REs, as they anchor the target object into the world. The method proposed allows to both keep track of the properties described for the target object to generate indefinite REs and to generate definite REs by intersecting sets of possible referents until only one object is left.

The grammar itself only defines which REs are legal, it does not define any preferences. It is possible to define functions scoring certain rules applications and we implemented a preference for the smallest derivation tree, but this is clearly not sufficient. For example, "twenty blocks left of the blue block" and "to the right of the red block" might denote the same target and their derivation trees have the same size but using the first RE is probably less likely to succeed than one using the second. These differences can be captured by a scoring model for the grammar (Garoufi and Koller, 2014) and we

will work on learning one from interactions with players.

Our grammar and code is available at `https://minecraft-saar.github.io`.

Acknowledgments We would like to thank Paula Stadnikowa for working on early versions of these ideas. This work was supported by the German Research Foundation (DFG), SFB/CRC 1102 "Information density and linguistic encoding" (Project A7).

References

Hubert Comon, Max Dauchet, Rémi Gilleron, Florent Jacquemard, Denis Lugiez, Sophie Tison, Marc Tommasi, and Christof Löding. 2007. *Tree Automata techniques and applications.* published online - `http://tata.gforge.inria.fr/`.

Robert Dale and Ehud Reiter. 1995. Computational interpretations of the gricean maxims in the generation of referring expressions. *Cognitive Science*, 19(2):233 – 263.

Kees van Deemter. 2016. *Computational Models of Referring: A study in cognitive science.* MIT Press.

Nikos Engonopoulos and Alexander Koller. 2014. Generating effective referring expressions using charts. In *Proceedings of the 8th International Conference on Natural Language Generation (INLG)*, Philadelphia.

Konstantina Garoufi and Alexander Koller. 2014. Generation of effective referring expressions in situated context. *Language, Cognition, and Neuroscience*, 29(8):986–1001.

Irene Heim. 1982. *The semantics of definite and indefinite noun phrases.* Ph.D. thesis, University of Massachusetts, Amherst.

Klaus von Heusinger. 2000. The reference of indefinites. In Klaus von Heusinger and Urs Egli, editors, *Reference and Anaphoric Relations*, pages 247–265. Springer Netherlands, Dordrecht.

Hans Kamp and Uwe Reyle. 1993. *From Discourse to Logic.* Springer.

Alexander Koller and Nikos Engonopoulos. 2017. Integrated sentence generation with charts. In *Proceedings of the 10th International Conference on Natural Language Generation (INLG)*, Santiago de Compostela.

Alexander Koller and Marco Kuhlmann. 2011. A generalized view on parsing and translation. In *Proceedings of the 12th International Conference on Parsing Technologies (IWPT)*, Dublin.

Emiel Krahmer and Kees van Deemter. 2012. Computational generation of referring expressions: A survey. *Computational Linguistics*, 38(1):173–218.

Emiel Krahmer, Sebastiaan van Erk, and André Verleg. 2003. Graph-based generation of referring expressions. *Computational Linguistics*, 29(1):53–72.

Doreen Osmelak. 2018. Human experiments in minecraft. Master's thesis, Universität des Saarlandes.

Julia Wichlacz, Alvaro Torralba, and Jörg Hoffmann. 2019. Construction-planning models in minecraft. In *Proceedings of ICAPS workshop on Hierarchical Planning*.

Generating Quantified Referring Expressions with Perceptual Cost Pruning

Gordon Briggs[1] and **Hillary Harner**[2]
[1]Navy Center for Applied Research in Artificial Intelligence
[2]NRC Postdoctoral Fellow
U.S. Naval Research Laboratory, Washington, DC 20375 USA
{gordon.briggs,hillary.harner.ctr}@nrl.navy.mil

Abstract

We model the production of quantified referring expressions (QREs) that identify collections of visual items. To address this task, we propose a method of perceptual cost pruning, which consists of two steps: (1) determine what subset of quantity information can be perceived given a time limit t, and (2) apply a preference order based REG algorithm, such as the Incremental Algorithm (IA), to this reduced set of information. We demonstrate that this method successfully improves the human-likeness of the IA in the QRE generation task by successfully modeling human-generated language in most cases.

1 Introduction

Production of natural and human-like referring expressions in visual contexts is an ongoing challenge in natural language generation (NLG). What makes referring expression generation (REG) in visual contexts difficult is that it strongly depends on the dynamics of human perception (Clarke et al., 2013; Elsner et al., 2018). How to integrate REG algorithms with dynamic and incremental human-like perception is still an open problem. Starting with the Incremental Algorithm (IA) (Dale and Reiter, 1995), REG algorithms have sought to model factors of perceptual salience by considering a preferred ordering of visual attributes. Building off of the IA, the Visual Object Algorithm (VOA) favors certain visual attributes based on relative perceptual cost (Mitchell et al., 2013). However, these algorithms assume complete knowledge and model perceptual cost through preference orderings. In practice, some visual information is not just dis-preferred, but *impossible* to ascertain under time constraints.

In this paper, we investigate a more radical means to integrate perceptual cost in REG: pruning a knowledge base according to perceptual

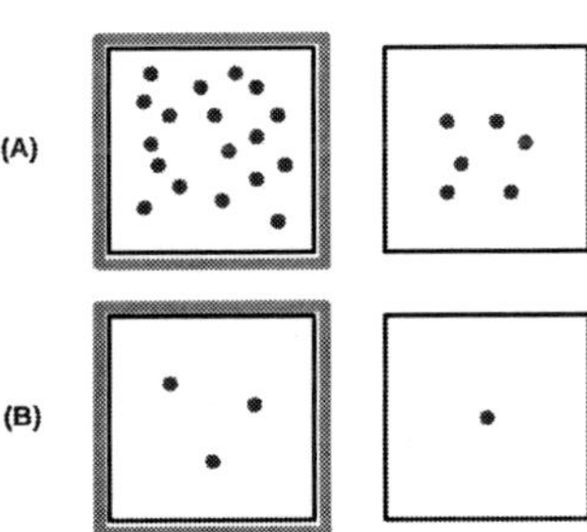

Figure 1: Examples of QRE generation tasks. Target referent collection highlighted in red.

costs. Specifically, we propose using only information in a preference-based REG algorithm (i.e., IA) that a psychological model suggests is plausible to have encoded under particular time constraints. To evaluate this proposed solution, we examine the problem of quantified referring expression (QRE) generation. First, we introduce QREs and give a brief overview of the psychology of numerical perception. Second, we detail a mathematical model of the time requirements of exact numerical perception and how we apply the proposed method of perceptual cost pruning (PCP) to the QRE task. We demonstrate that this method successfully improves the human-likeness of the IA in the quantified REG task by successfully modeling human-generated language in most cases.

2 The Case of QREs

In contrast to previous visual REG tasks based on identification of a single object (Mitchell et al., 2010, 2013), QRE tasks involve referring to *collections* of visual items. Two examples of QRE problems are found in Figure 1. Given that the items are homogeneous and randomly arranged,

Proceedings of The 12th International Conference on Natural Language Generation, pages 11–18,
Tokyo, Japan, 28 Oct - 1 Nov, 2019. ©2019 Association for Computational Linguistics

quantity becomes a salient means of describing a target set of items (indicated in red). For example, one could use an *exact number* expression (e.g., "the box with *eighteen* circles" (A) or "the box with *three* circles" (B)). One could also refer to *relative* quantity (e.g., "the box with *more* circles" (A&B)). Other forms of expression include *vague* expressions of quantity (e.g., "the box with *many* circles" (A) or "the box with *a few* circles" (B)) and *absolute* descriptions that refer to the presence of items (e.g., "the box with dots" (A&B)). The reader may find that the sort of expression he or she finds natural differs between problems A and B. It is likely the case that the reader finds it natural to describe the target in (B) with exact number, whereas the reader is more likely to describe the target in (A) in less precise terms. To account for this phenomenon, we turn to the psychophysics of human numerical perception.

The perception of quantity consists of multiple processes, each occurring at different rates and resulting in mental representations of varying precision. Explicit counting provides a slow, but precise, determination of number (Gelman and Gallistel, 1986), in which each visual item requires roughly 250–350 ms to enumerate (Trick and Pylyshyn, 1994). Estimation provides a rapid, but less precise, judgment of the quantity of a group of objects (Barth et al., 2003). A third process exists: subitizing, i.e. the rapid and precise judgment of numerosity for quantities from 1-4 (Kaufman et al., 1949). Within the subitizing range, each visual item requires only 40–100 ms to accurately enumerate (Trick and Pylyshyn, 1994). Thus, accurate *exact* numerical descriptions of small collections of items are fast and easy, whereas such descriptions require time and effort for larger quantities of items, so that *vague*, *relative*, or *absolute* descriptions are quicker and easier to produce for larger quantities.

Human subject experiments in QRE generation (Barr et al., 2013) show that this perceptual effort affects language usage even when there are no time limits in viewing the stimuli or generating QREs. The frequency of QRE types produced by subjects in Barr et al. (2013) study (for participants that gave more than one type of response) is plotted in the top portion of Figure 2. In the problem IDs, the number preceded by a 'T' indicates the target set quantity, while numbers preceded by 'D' indicate distractor set quantities. While the

data suggest a general tendency toward exact responses, it is clear that exact responses are significantly preferred in the subitizing range, while dispreferred outside the subitizing range.

One could propose that algorithms used to tackle QREs simply have a rule that treats quantities under four differently. However, studies have shown that common arrangements of visual items, such as the faces of six-sided dice, have been shown to be rapidly and accurately enumerated even beyond the traditional four-item subitizing limit (Mandler and Shebo, 1982) and that subitizing can be disrupted by attentional load (Railo et al., 2008). This suggests that a general solution in adapting current REG algorithms lies not in simple ad hoc rules, but rather in using more comprehensive models of human perception to inform what can or cannot be plausibly perceived given situational constraints, such as exogenous time limitations, or the desire to minimize perceptual effort or cost (self-imposed time limitations).

3 Approach

To apply perceptual cost pruning to QREs, our approach consists of two steps: (1) determine what quantified information can be perceived given a time limit t, and remove information that does not meet this threshold, and (2) apply the Incremental Algorithm to this reduced set of information, ignoring attributes that have been removed.

3.1 Time Cost of Exact Enumeration

Given that estimation occurs rapidly, we focus on modeling the time course of exact enumeration. The literature on numerical perception suggests that the time it takes to exactly enumerate n items follows a bilinear time function (Trick and Pylyshyn, 1994) that can be expressed as follows:

$$T_{exact}(n) \approx T_f \cdot min(r_s, n)$$

$$+ \prod_{max(r_s,n) \leq i \leq n} T_{subvocal}(i) + T_f$$

where T_f denotes the time necessary to attend to encode a single item into visual memory, r_s denotes the subitizing limit, and $T_{subvocal}(i)$ denotes the time necessary to subvocalize the i-th count word. Briggs et al. (2017) present a computational implementation of subitizing and counting that exhibits the above function for exact enumeration response time. In this paper, we draw from Briggs

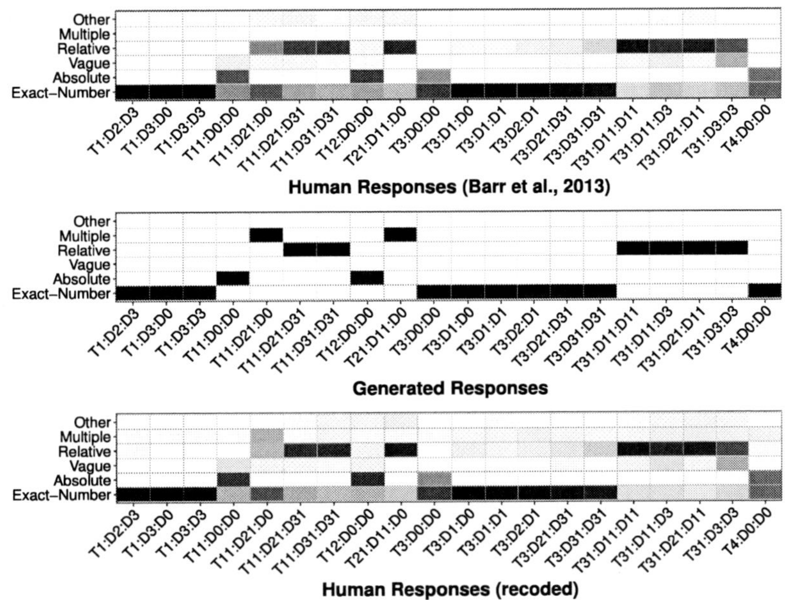

Figure 2: Graphical plot of frequency (darker shading indicates higher frequency) of each category of reference expression (y-axis) for each QRE problem (x-axis) for both human participants from (Barr et al., 2013) (above); the results of the best preference ordering for the Incremental Algorithm (IA_{NAR}) after perceptual cost adjustment of the knowledge base (middle); and recoded responses (bottom). In the problem names, the number preceded by a 'T' indicates the target set quantity, while numbers preceded by 'D' indicate distractor set quantities.

et al. (2017) to set the following values: $T_f = 50ms$, $r_s = 4$, $T_{subvocal}(i) = 250$ ms, which is shown to be a good fit with human response time data.

3.2 Factoring In Perceptual Cost

The first step in QRE generation is producing a knowledge base for a particular QREG trial. In this paper, we consider three types of quantified expression: absolute (A), exact number (N), and relative (R). The presented classification scheme is different from Barr et al. (2013)'s original scheme in that it consolidates the categories superlative and comparative into the category relative. We leave the production of *vague* quantified expression for future work. This is due in part to the relative infrequency of vague expressions in the human data.[1]

To demonstrate the application of perceptual

cost pruning, we consider an example from Barr et al. (2013), whose study was made up of 20 QREG tasks, each consisting of a target (T) and two distractors (D). Each QREG task is specified by the number of items in the target collection and in each distractor collection. Therefore, the exact number information is available without further processing. Absolute attributes are derived by a simple check as to whether or not the number of items in each collection is greater than or equal to zero. Relative attributes are derived by checking whether or not the target or distractor is the collection with the maximum or minimum number of items. If not, then the collection can be labeled as not having the most or least items.

To illustrate, let us consider the problem `T21:D11:D0`, in which the target collection has 21 items and the two distractors have 11 and 0 items, respectively. We can translate the information about each item into the following collection of quantity attributes:

- $Target$ = [A : "has items"; N : "has 21 items"; R : "has the most items"]

---

[1] Additionally, vague quantified expressions (such as "several" or "many") lack intensional definitions that would enable us to code simple rules to appropriately populate our knowledge base with the correct vague expressions. Additional human data is needed to inform an extensional definition of vague quantified expressions.

- $Distractor1$ = [A : "has items"; N : "has 11 items"; R : "does not have the most items"]

- $Distractor2$ = [A : "has no items"; N : "has 0 items"; R : "has the fewest items"]

Without perceptual cost pruning, the above knowledge base is passed to the REG algorithm as is. However, with perceptual cost pruning, we replace values that cannot be perceived under time constraints with null tokens. For example, if we assume only 0.5s are available to evaluate each collection (either through external time limitations or through deliberate choice to limit gaze time), our model of exact enumeration (above) would indicate that 21 and 11 items cannot be exactly enumerated and therefore would be pruned. This would result in the following modified knowledge base:

- $Target$ = [A : "has items"; N : $\emptyset$; R : "has the most items"]

- $Distractor1$ = [A : "has items"; N : $\emptyset$; R : "does not have the most items"]

- $Distractor2$ = [A : "has no items"; N : "has 0 items"; R : "has the fewest items"]

To handle a pruned knowledge base, we implemented a modified version of the IA, which we describe in the following section.

3.3 Modified IA

Given a target referent T, a set of distractors $D = D_1, ..., D_n$, and a preference ordering of attributes $A = [a_1, ..., a_m]$, the IA selects a subset of attributes to include in a referring expression (RE) by traversing the set of attributes in order of preference, adding the current attribute to the RE if it eliminates any of the remaining distractors (Krahmer and Van Deemter, 2012). Perceptual cost pruning can be accommodated by allowing the algorithm to skip an attribute if the target's value for the current attribute is equal to the null token.

Note that we also assume that if a distractor object's attribute value has been replaced by the null token, but the target's matching attribute value has not been replaced, then the speaker still represents this as a difference that allows for the elimination of that distractor. This can be justified under the simplifying assumption built into our knowledge base pruning method that people would devote equal time to perceive all collections. Therefore, if one collection's quantity was able to be

perceived exactly under t seconds, while the other was not, it is evidence against the two collections having the same quantity. However, as this is a preliminary idea, further investigation is needed to establish the limitations of this assumption.

4 Initial Evaluation

To evaluate the effectiveness of the IA with and without perceptual cost pruning, we rely on the Dice coefficient, commonly used in REG tasks, and defined below (Van Deemter, 2016):

$$Dice(H, A) = \frac{2 \times |H \cap A|}{|H| + |A|}$$

where H is the set of attributes found in a human-generated description and A is the set of attributes found in an algorithmically generated description. As previously mentioned, we consider here three types of quantified expression: absolute (A), exact number (N), and relative (R). Combining these three options into all possible orderings generates six preference orderings for the Incremental Algorithm. For example, an IA ordering of $A \succ N \succ R$ is denoted IA_{ANR}.

We calculated Dice scores for the IA for all possible orderings of these expression types. To test perceptual cost pruning, Dice scores were calculated for all six preference orderings for time limits between 0.5s ms and 10s (at 0.1s intervals). As originally reported by Barr et al. (2013), roughly 20% of participants only gave exact number responses. This could reflect different perceptual and generation strategies, specifically the difference between a *fixed* strategy, in which the speaker always takes time to count and reports an exact numerical description, and a *flexible* strategy, in which the speaker takes a more limited time to perceive each item and reports a description based on what was plausibly perceived in the limited timeframe. We predict that perceptual cost pruning will help account for participants that exhibit a flexible strategy. In our analysis, we calculate three Dice scores corresponding to the 20% of participants that exhibited the fixed strategy, the remaining participants that exhibited a flexible strategy, and the combined set of all participants. We report the results from the time ranges found to yield the highest Dice score for perceptual cost pruning in Table 1.

REG Algorithm	Subject Group	No PCP	PCP
IA_{ARN}	Flexible + Fixed (All)	0.300	0.300 $(2.2s \leq t \leq 4.4s)$
	Flexible Only	0.368	0.368 $(0.5s \leq t \leq 1.9s)$
	Fixed Only	0.0	0.0 $(t > 7.0s)$
IA_{ANR}	Flexible + Fixed (All)	0.571	0.635 $(2.2s \leq t \leq 4.4s)$
	Flexible Only	0.535	0.703 $(0.5s \leq t \leq 1.9s)$
	Fixed Only	0.730	0.734 $(t > 7.0s)$
IA_{RAN}	Flexible + Fixed (All)	0.235	0.235 $(2.2s \leq t \leq 4.4s)$
	Flexible Only	0.289	0.289 $(0.5s \leq t \leq 1.9s)$
	Fixed Only	0.0	0.0 $(t > 7.0s)$
IA_{RNA}	Flexible + Fixed (All)	0.235	0.235 $(2.2s \leq t \leq 4.4s)$
	Flexible Only	0.289	0.289 $(0.5s \leq t \leq 1.9s)$
	Fixed Only	0.0	0.0 $(t > 7.0s)$
IA_{NAR}	Flexible + Fixed (All)	0.649	0.706 $(2.2s \leq t \leq 4.4s)$
	Flexible Only	0.568	**0.752** $(0.5s \leq t \leq 1.9s)$
	Fixed Only	**1.0**	**1.0** $(t > 7.0s)$
IA_{NRA}	Flexible + Fixed (All)	0.649	**0.716** $(2.2s \leq t \leq 4.4s)$
	Flexible Only	0.568	0.713 $(0.5s \leq t \leq 1.9s)$
	Fixed Only	**1.0**	**1.0** $(t > 7.0s)$

Table 1: DICE scores for all IA preference orderings with no knowledge base adjustment (left) and with adjustment by perceptual cost pruning (right).

4.1 Naive IA

Because referring to the exact quantity of the target set was sufficient to eliminate distractors, instances of IA_{N**} *without* perceptual cost pruning simply produced all exact number responses. Given that exact number responses were found to be most common in the human data, these orderings were found to have the highest Dice scores. Including all participants, the Dice score of IA_{N**} was 0.649. This score decreased for the subset of participants that produced more than one type of response (Dice score of 0.568), showing that these participants expressed quantity non-exactly in some problems. In particular, these participants used non-exact quantified expressions a majority of the time in 9 out of 20 problems (see Figure 2).

4.2 IA with Perceptual Cost Pruning

Including all participants, the best Dice score (0.716) was found to be associated with a time limit of 2.2-4.4 seconds and the IA_{NRA} preference ordering. With the subset of flexible response participants, the IA_{NAR} preference ordering produced the best Dice score (0.752), during time limits of 0.5-2.0 seconds. In both cases, perceptual cost pruning increased the human-likeness of the IA relative to the baseline IA. As expected, perceptual cost pruning did not improve the similarity scores for subjects with fixed response strategies. More notable, however, is the fact that the IA with perceptual cost pruning would predict that at least 7.0 seconds are needed to view some target collections to obtain an exact numerical description and match the performance of the naive IA. The generated response types for these best runs IA_{NAR} with perceptual cost pruning are plotted in the middle chart of Figure 2. In these runs, the majority human response was correctly predicted 18 out of 20 times.

It is worth noting those instances where the predictions diverge from the human data. IA_{NAR} predicts an RE with both absolute and relative descriptors, (i.e., 'Multiple') on problems such as `T21:D11:D0` and `T11:D21:D0`. Because a brief perceptual time limit of less than two seconds is insufficient to exactly enumerate 21 or 11 dots, IA_{NAR} would predict that no exact descriptors would be used. However, because one of the distractors is empty and the other is non-empty, an absolute descriptor is added to the RE, but is still insufficient to eliminate all the distractors.

Our model's prediction for 'Multiple' expression types differs from Barr et al. (2013), as they did not originally annotate responses as having more than one type of quantified expression (so they could not have any aggregate 'Multiple' category for expressions with multiple types of descriptors) This additional category provides an opportunity to plot when our modified IA algorithm with perceptual cost pruning would predict more than one type of quantified descriptor. For example, some of the human-generated responses were consistent with a 'Multiple' coding, e.g., in problem `T11:D21:D0` with expressions such as "the square with some triangles but not the most triangles," and "the square containing the smaller number of symbols but not the blank square."[2] However, the majority of the human-generated responses for a task like `T21:D11:D0` were *not* consistent with a 'Multiple' coding; the majority response was simply a relative expression. Since our algorithm generated descriptions according to a scheme that did not match Barr et al. (2013)'s original coding, we re-examined and recoded a subset of their original data.

5 Recoding and Re-evaluation

After surveying the annotations from Barr et al. (2013), we decided to recode their data for two key reasons. First, as described above, the original coding marked responses as having only one expression type, whereas various expressions in the data were found to be plausibly ascribed two or more descriptor types. Second, the original coding was performed automatically by pattern-matching and had incorrectly labeled a significant portion of responses as exact number expressions (e.g., "the one with the most dots"). The patterns we identified for potential error and recoding are as follows: "one with", "other two', and "out of the three". In such cases, the numbers "one", "two", and "three" refer to the squares containing the collections of visual objects and not the quantity of items they contain. In addition, we verified the coding for all responses first marked OTH ("Other").

In total, we targeted for recoding 491 of the 1508 responses Barr et al. (2013) reported. Our recoding was performed by two annotators, who began by identifying expressions that contained multiple types of expressions. Agreement was calculated using Kendall's coefficient of concordance, which indicated high interannotator agreement ($W = .906$) regarding which expressions contained more than one type of expression. Au-

REG Algorithm	No PCP	PCP
IA_{ARN}	0.411	0.411
IA_{ANR}	0.536	0.732
IA_{RAN}	0.312	0.312
IA_{RNA}	0.312	0.312
IA_{NAR}	0.530	**0.773**
IA_{NRA}	0.530	0.717

Table 2: DICE scores under recoded data for all IA preference orderings with no perceptual cost pruning of the knowledge base (left) and with knowledge base adjustment by perceptual cost pruning (right).

tomated pattern matching was used to identify expressions that contained the template strings specified above. High interannotator agreement scores (Kendell's coefficient of concordance $W > .95$) were found across all expression types (ABS, NUM, BASE, and OTH).

5.1 Recoding Results

A plot of the recoded human responses can be found at the bottom of Figure 2. One major result the revised coding yielded was a revision of the number of participants that produced only one QRE type throughout the task. Barr et al. (2013) reported that 20% of participants only generated QREs with exact number descriptions. However, after recoding, only three participants (6% of all participants) were shown to exclusively use exact number descriptions, i.e., to rely on a fixed REG strategy.

Our recoding supported our initial observations regarding problem `T11:D21:D0`. Although exact number REs are still the plurality response for this problem, the plot in Figure 2 does indicate that the complex RE with multiple quantified expression types is the second most common response. As predicted by the IA_{NAR} preference ordering, nearly all of these complex REs use both absolute and relative descriptions. One possible reason that an exact number response is still frequent for this problem, but not for `T21:D11:D0`, is that the 11 visual items representing the target is at the threshold of what people can quickly judge to be "countable" (Mandler and Shebo, 1982). In contrast, 21 items are judged to not be easily "countable."

5.2 Naive IA

Because the revised number of respondents that used only one type of RE was significantly re-

---

[2]Data publicly available at: https://staff.fnwi.uva.nl/r.fernandezrovira/xprag/

duced, we do not report Dice scores for the different subsets of participants that used flexible or fixed REG strategies. Instead, we simply report the aggregate Dice score for all participants. As many previous instances of exact number responses were reexamined and revised, the Dice scores of IA_{N**} preference orderings are reduced from 0.649 to 0.530. Conversely, the smaller number of exact number expressions in the revised annotations improves the performance of the IA_{A**} and IA_{R**} preference orderings: their Dice scores increase with the new coding scheme. In contrast to the original coding, the best preference ordering without perceptual cost pruning is IA_{ANR}, with a Dice score of 0.536.

5.3 IA with Perceptual Cost Pruning

With perceptual cost pruning, the best Dice score (0.773) was found to be associated with a time limit of 0.2-1.9 seconds and the IA_{NAR} preference ordering. This reflects a better fit of the IA with perceptual cost pruning to the human data under the revised coding (compared with the best Dice score of 0.706 for the original coding). Additionally, the Dice score of the naive IA also improved under the new coding scheme. Under the original coding, the aggregate Dice score for all participants increased by only 0.057 for IA_{NAR} and 0.067 for IA_{NRA}. In contrast, the revised codings yield a Dice score improvement of 0.243 and 0.187 for IA_{NAR} and IA_{NRA}, respectively.

6 Discussion and Future Work

We have shown that the ability of a preference order based REG algorithm (IA) to produce human-like responses in QRE generation tasks can be significantly improved by integration of a model of perceptual cost. We believe this success can be attributed to the fact that our perceptual cost pruning approach captures the underlying tension in QRE generation between the desire to be as informative as possible and the desire to minimize perceptual effort, which reduces the precision of information (Barr et al., 2013). The desire to be informative is evidenced by the primacy of exact numbers in the best fit preference orderings, whereas the desire to minimize perceptual effort is evidenced by the fact that the time limit of the best fitting IAs is ≤ 2 seconds. The tradeoff between the desire to be as informative as possible and perceptual limitations has also been shown in recent work, where the precision of quantified descriptions of visual scenes decreases as presentation time decreases (Briggs et al., 2019).

Furthermore, our presented approach leads to a variety of predictions that we are testing. One such prediction involves the role of a set of items' spatial arrangement on QRE production. Findings in numerical perception indicate that common arrangements of visual items, often deemed canonical patterns, can be exactly enumerated more quickly than randomized patterns (Mandler and Shebo, 1982; Wender and Rothkegel, 2000). This would suggest that a greater amount of exact number REs would be produced for well-learned patterns (such as dice faces), since their enumeration is perceptually cheap. On the other hand, it is possible that canonical patterns would be described as canonical, without any reference to number (e.g., "the square with the dice pattern"). This raises the larger question of what attributes and descriptions of a group of visual items are preferred over one another.

Additionally, we wish to investigate how the psychophysics of approximate number representations may also limit what quantity information is available for REG. In the present study, large quantities were sufficiently different so that estimation easily yields valid relative comparisons. However, some numerosity differences are not so easy to assess by estimation (e.g., imagine attempting to tell the difference between 62 and 64 objects without counting). A complete account of QREG must include both the limitations of exact and inexact numerical representation.

Finally, if additional experiments are designed such that the quantity of the total number of individuals in a collection does not provide a clear differentiating attribute, we would predict that other properties of visual groups would be referenced. Specifically, our predictions are that the following properties could be used:

Spatial descriptions of the group - groups of visual items can be described across a variety of spatial dimensions that are unrelated to the quantity of items in the group. Examples of types of spatial descriptions could include: area, shape, and density of the cluster of visual items.

Number of subgroups - people have the ability to group visual items together based on proximity (Im et al., 2016). In other words, people can not only refer to the total number of individuals in a collection, but also to the number of subgroups within a collection or the size of these subgroups.

Further data collection is needed to determine which forms of these visual group properties are commonly generated and which are preferred over one another.

7 Conclusion

In this paper, we investigated the problem of generating referring expressions in visual contexts based on differences in the quantity of a target collection and distractor collections. Given the low performance of a traditional, preference ordering based REG algorithm in this task, we have demonstrated the importance of factoring in perceptual cost in REG. We have also proposed and validated a novel method, called perceptual cost pruning, of factoring in perceptual cost by ablating a knowledge base according to models of human psychophysical limits. Future work is needed to further refine this proposed method and explore REG in the context of differentiating collections of visual items with varying spatial arrangements.

Acknowledgments

This work was supported by an NRL Karles Fellowship awarded to the first author, an NRC Postdoctoral Fellowship awarded to the second author, and AFOSR MIPR grant F4FGA07074G001. The views expressed in this paper are solely those of the authors and should not be taken to reflect any official policy or position of the United States Government or the Department of Defense.

References

Dale Barr, Kees van Deemter, and Raquel Fernández. 2013. Generation of quantified referring expressions: evidence from experimental data. In *Proceedings of the 14th European Workshop on Natural Language Generation*, pages 157–161.

Hilary Barth, Nancy Kanwisher, and Elizabeth Spelke. 2003. The construction of large number representations in adults. *Cognition*, 86:201–221.

Gordon Briggs, Will Bridewell, and Paul F. Bello. 2017. A computational model of the role of attention in subitizing and enumeration. In *Proceedings of the 39th Annual Meeting of the Cognitive Science Society*, pages 1672–1677, London, UK.

Gordon Briggs, Christina Wasylyshyn, and Paul F. Bello. 2019. Elicitation of Quantified Description Under Time Constraints. In *Proceedings of the 41st Annual Meeting of the Cognitive Science Society*, pages 1436–1442, Montreal, Canada.

Alasdair Clarke, Daniel Francis, Micha Elsner, and Hannah Rohde. 2013. Where's wally: the influence of visual salience on referring expression generation. *Frontiers in Psychology*, 4:329.

Robert Dale and Ehud Reiter. 1995. Computational interpretations of the gricean maxims in the generation of referring expressions. *Cognitive Science*, 19:233–263.

Micha Elsner, Alasdair Clarke, and Hannah Rohde. 2018. Visual complexity and its effects on referring expression generation. *Cognitive Science*, 42:940–973.

Rochel Gelman and Charles R Gallistel. 1986. *The child's understanding of number*. Harvard University Press, Cambridge, MA.

Hee Yeon Im, Sheng-hua Zhong, and Justin Halberda. 2016. Grouping by proximity and the visual impression of approximate number in random dot arrays. *Vision Research*, 126:291–307.

Edna L Kaufman, Miles W Lord, Thomas Whelan Reese, and John Volkmann. 1949. The discrimination of visual number. *The American Journal of Psychology*, 62:498–525.

Emiel Krahmer and Kees Van Deemter. 2012. Computational generation of referring expressions: A survey. *Computational Linguistics*, 38:173–218.

George Mandler and Billie J Shebo. 1982. Subitizing: An analysis of its component processes. *Journal of Experimental Psychology: General*, 111:1–22.

Margaret Mitchell, Kees van Deemter, and Ehud Reiter. 2010. Natural reference to objects in a visual domain. In *Proceedings of the 6th International Natural Language Generation Conference*, pages 95–104. Association for Computational Linguistics.

Margaret Mitchell, Kees Van Deemter, and Ehud Reiter. 2013. Generating expressions that refer to visible objects. In *Proceedings of the Conference of the North American Chapter of the Association for Computational Linguistics*. Association for Computational Linguistics (ACL).

Henry Railo, Mika Koivisto, Antti Revonsuo, and Minna M Hannula. 2008. The role of attention in subitizing. *Cognition*, 107:82–104.

Lana M Trick and Zenon W Pylyshyn. 1994. Why are small and large numbers enumerated differently? a limited-capacity preattentive stage in vision. *Psychological Review*, 101:80–102.

Kees Van Deemter. 2016. *Computational Models of Referring: A Study in Cognitive Science*. MIT Press, Cambridge, MA.

Karl F Wender and Rainer Rothkegel. 2000. Subitizing and its subprocesses. *Psychological Research*, 64:81–92.

A case study on context-bound referring expression generation

Maurice Langner
Sprachwissenschaftliches Institut
Ruhr-Universität Bochum

`Maurice.Langner@rub.de`

Abstract

This paper describes and discusses the results of an empirical study on the production of referring expressions in visual fields with different object configurations of varying complexity and different contextual premises for using a referring expression. The visual fields are set up using data from the TUNA experiment with plain random or pragmatically enriched configurations which allow for target inference. Different categories of the situational contexts, in which the referring expressions are produced, provide different degrees of cooperativeness, so that generation quality and its relations to contextual user intention can be observed. The results of the study suggest that algorithms for REG must integrate individual generation preference and the cooperativeness of the situational task in order to model the broad variance between speakers more adequately.

1 Introduction

In the past, experiments on the production of referring expressions (REs) produced corpora on domains of different complexity, among those the TUNA corpus (van der Sluis, Gatt, van Deemter, 2006; 2006 online manual), GRE3D3 and GRE3D7 (Viethen & Dale, 2008;2011), ReferIT (Kazemzadeh et al., 2014), Wally (Clarke et al.,2013) and some interlingual experiments revealing that the basic concepts of reference are independent from language expertise (e.g. Khan & Siddiqui, 2015). Da Silva Rocha & Paraboni (2018) distinguish two general experimental designs in the REG task, related to the speaker-listener configuration: monologue and dialogue. The authors remark that "both dialogue and monologue are of course instances of real language use but, at least from these studies, it is not entirely clear whether the two situations are truly comparable" (p.2994). Questionable is still, whether or

not content determination and the resulting generation quality, i.e. underspecification, minimality or overgeneration, may differ not only according to the speaker-listener configuration but also according to the context in which the REG task is situated. This question also includes variance between speakers. The experiment described in this paper builds on its predecessors, focusing on the technical and contextual parameters that may trigger differences in generation quality and content determination during production. The goal is to provide empirical data clarifying the influence of the situational context on the generation quality of referring expressions.

2 Methods

The experiment is designed using the TUNA furniture corpus and a subset of the TUNA people corpus that has been selected in a balanced way, making each feature value combination unique. It is conducted as a web-based experiment. Data from native speakers of English is collected using the crowdsourcing platform Amazon Mturk. The compiled corpus consists of 1029 production sessions from 50 participants.

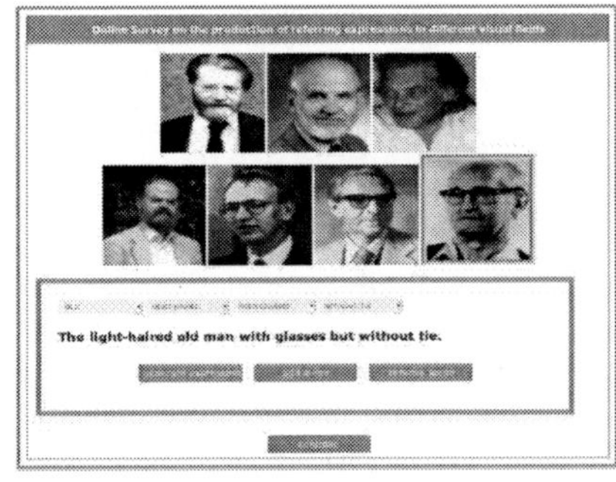

Figure 1: Web application: a production session

Proceedings of The 12th International Conference on Natural Language Generation, pages 19–23,
Tokyo, Japan, 28 Oct - 1 Nov, 2019. ©2019 Association for Computational Linguistics

category	context formulation (furniture)
+	You want to buy a very rare and valuable piece of furniture that you have been looking for for a long time. Please describe to the salesman which piece of furniture in his showroom you long for.
−	You are talking to friends about the design of your living room. They want to know which piece of furniture you recently sold on the internet. Please tell them.
o	You rearrange your living room. Tell your friend which piece of furniture you want to move to the free space below the windows.
category	context formulation (people)
+	You are the victim of a crime. Please describe to the police officer who of the suspects in the interrogation room is the criminal.
−	You want to buy a car and the sales agent wants to know who of his colleagues in the salesroom gave you advise at your previous visit. Please give a description.
o	You work as a waiter. You tell your colleague whom of the guests you still have to bring the bill. Please describe the guest.

Table 1: Situational contexts used in production sessions

domain/ID	furniture/A1IV1O890FN1QA-1
context	-
distractors	{ desk, front, grey, large }, { chair, left, green, small }, { fan, left, blue, large }
target	{sofa, left, green, small}
RE	*The sofa*
quality	minimality
domain/ID	furniture/AXQDSQGBC79S2-15
context	o
distractors	{fan, front, red, large}, { chair, left, red, large }, { sofa, front, green, large }
target	{ desk, back, blue, large}
RE	*The blue desk*
quality	overgeneration
domain/ID	people/A1TUI63TLCHYMR-12
context	-
distractors	{old, beard+, glasses-, hair-, front, shirt-, suit+, tie+}, {old, beard-, glasses-, hair+, front, shirt-, suit+, tie+}
target	{old, beard-, glasses-, hair+, front, shirt-, suit+,tie-}
RE	*the old front man with suit but without tie, shirt or glasses*
quality	overgeneration

Table 2: Examples from the experimental data

Production sessions were associated with different contexts which are representative of different communicative intents of the dialogue. Contexts are given in table 1. Either no contextual text was given and the participants were asked to generate expressions to their liking, or the context type was randomly chosen according to the domain type of the production session.

The contexts marked with + are designed with focus on the speaker's interest. In these contexts, the speaker envisages some personal intention for which it is important to convey to the listener which object he/she refers to. Correct identification is important to the speaker. The contexts marked with o are designed as rather neutral, where correct identification is of equal importance for both speaker and hearer in a collaborative task. The - marker indicates that these contexts focus on the hearer's interest, implied by the fact that the production task is the answer to the hearer's question. Correct identification is more important to the hearer than to the speaker.

3 Results

In this experiment, the main parameter of potential influence on the generation quality is the situational context. Consequently, all context conditions need to be evaluated in regard to overgeneration, minimality and underspecification. Examples of referring expressions produced by the participants and the corresponding context condition as well as the general session configuration are given in table 2.

The absence of a situational context (NONE condition) results in a nearly equal distribution of overgeneration and minimality (36.3% and 34.2%), while underspecification is slightly lower with a percentage of 29.5% (compare figure 2).

In contrast to this, the neutral context marked with o has a significantly higher ratio of minimal expressions, while overgeneration is close to equal in comparison. Underspecification occurs much less frequently (19.8%) than in sessions without situational context. The resulting difference between o and NONE is significant (χ^2 :5.66; p < 0.05). The + marked context shows a nearly equal distribution of overgeneration and minimality (32.0% and 31.0%), while there is a slight tendency towards underspecification (36.9%). The results for sessions with - marked contexts are diametrical to the + contexts (not significantly, though), revealing an approximately mirrored distribution of underspecification and minimality (32.4% and 30.0%), while overgeneration is slightly ahead with a ratio of 37.6%. Neither + nor - are significantly different from the sessions without context (NONE condition) but both are significantly different from the neutral o context (χ^2: 11.37/10.15, p : 0.003/0.006).

The positive and negative contexts show tendencies towards overgeneration and underspecification respectively, but in opposite relation to the prior expectation. Contexts marked with +, in contradiction to intuitive assumptions, trigger more underspecification. A possible explanation for this is that the speaker may pay less attention to unique identification because it is only important to him-

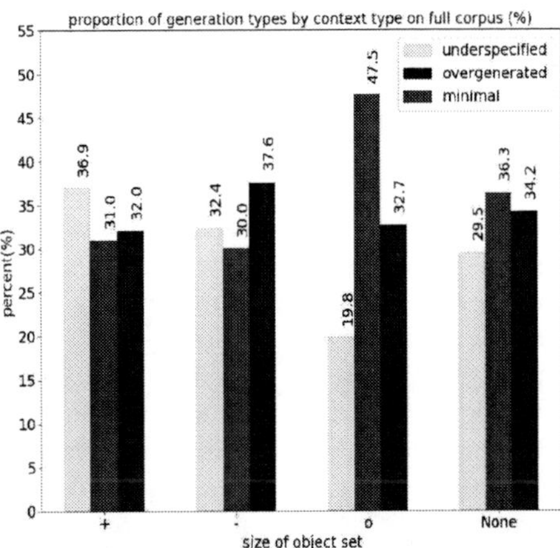

Figure 2: percentage of generation qualities by context condition

self/herself and not to the listener. In consideration of realistic settings of the REG task within dialogue speakers may be accustomed to the ability of correcting a referring expression after hearer feedback (installment noun phrases) in case that unique identification is not yet possible (Clark and Bangerter 2004, p.37). This would correlate with the tendency found by Paraboni & da Silva Rocha (2018) that dialogue settings trigger less overgeneration than monologue settings. Contexts marked with - provide a reversed balance of importance. The speaker may anticipate the listener's inability to infer the target, overgeneration being the consequence of guaranteeing the ability to correctly identify the target in consideration of its importance to the listener (Goodman & Frank, 2016). There is no reliable evidence for these assumptions due to data sparseness, but further research on larger data sets may reveal whether this relation is stochastically significant, resulting in a modelling of the REG task implementing context as pragmatic factors of cooperative dialogue.

For the neutral contexts, a cooperative task may result in a higher ratio of minimality for two reasons. Firstly, importance of correct identification prevails for both speaker and listener. Consequently, underspecification would be uncooperative, therefore being the disfavoured generation quality. This is mirrored by the low ratio of 19.8% for underspecified phrases. The second reason limiting the usage of overspecification may be not

to give redundant information, which may cause the listener to reason about why the speaker violated Gricean Maximes of relevance, resulting in unnecessary cognitive effort prolonging the identification process or even in erroneous target inference (Paraboni et al., 2017). The data proves that situational contexts trigger significant differences in generation qualities. This depends on cooperativeness as much as on the quality and personal concern with the contexts, as well as the character of and relation to the listener.

3.1 Variance between speakers

For individual participants, the ratio of significantly different balances of generation qualities across context conditions is 8.16% (Fisher's exact test). This result for the variance within speakers is hardly reliable due to data sparseness [1]. Further studies with more sessions per participant will permit a valid evaluation of variance within speakers.

Nevertheless the experimental data gives rise to the assumption that variance between speakers is large. For each participant, sessions are counted according to the generation quality. The scatter plot reveals some interesting relations (see figure 3).

Every data point represents a single participant, its coordinates the counts of sessions where a minimal, overgenerated or underspecified expression has been produced. The data points are all arranged on a triangular surface. Each tip of the triangle represents a different group of participants with a specific preference to one generation type. The threshold used for the markers is a proportion of 0.6 of the preferred quality, 0.4 the combined occurrence of the residual qualities. As the plot already visualizes there is a huge variance between speakers. Comparing the group of participants preferring minimality (blue dots) with the group producing mainly overspecified phrases (dark blue triangles pointing upwards), the groups are highly significantly different (ANOVA, $f :> 100, p :< 5e^{-10}$). The groups preferring underspecification (light blue triangles pointing downwards) are even more significantly different from overgeneration and minimality with f-scores of 248.01 / 165.66 and a residual p-value of $4.19e^{-13}$ / $5.93e^{-12}$. The balanced group marked by black diamonds is

---

[1] With 20 sessions per participant and four context conditions, each context condition occurred five times on average. The values for generation qualities for each context condition are therefore too small for reliable significance tests.

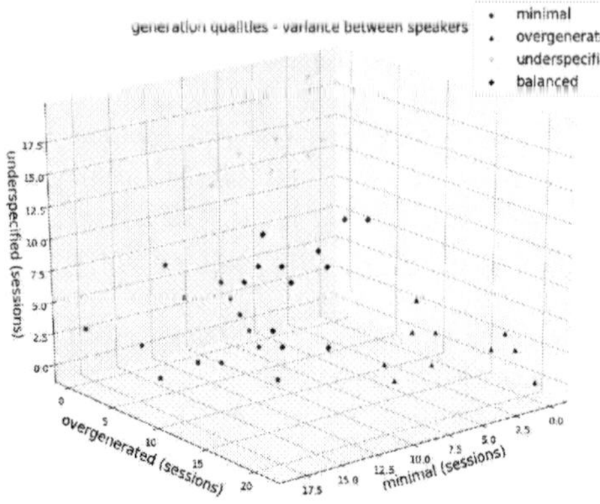

Figure 3: speaker variance

significantly different from all three groups with stronger preference towards a specific generation type, though f-scores range about 60 to 100 with p-values about $1e^{-8}$.

The graphs and the significant variance emphasize clearly that different speakers use different strategies in REG tasks (Viethen & Dale, 2011; Paraboni & Ferreira, 2014; van Deemter et al., 2010). The group preferring minimality is the largest with about 13 instances, overgeneration and underspecification each comprise about 10 participants. The least distinguished group shows a balanced use of generation qualities, representing a large amount of variance within speakers (van Deemter et al., 2010), since no clear tendency towards a strategy is visible. Further studies with more participants may probably allow for a Machine Learning approach (Janarthanam & Lemon, 2010, for further information on their Reinforcement Learning System for reference policies) in order to classify speakers according to instances of referring expressions produced during REG tasks. Another intriguing fact is that Goudbeek et al. (2011) were able to prove that the usage of dispreferred attributes as much as overgeneration can be primed in mixed comprehension and production sessions, showing that speakers may adjust even more to one another in real dialogue settings. For future work on reference in dialogue it is therefore crucial to control the parameter of strategical alignment and the mutual adjustment in cooperative reference tasks.

4 Discussion

The context condition triggers significant differences on the data gathered in this experiment. The neutral context entails a significantly higher ratio of minimality, proving that for the accomplishment of a cooperative task, participants tend to produce expressions by which the listener is able to identify the target unambiguously. The differences between the + and - contexts may be insignificant, but the existing tendency points in the opposite direction of the prior expectation. Participants produced slightly more overgenerated phrases in situations where target identification was more important to the listener, while underspecifying more in contexts where identification was more important for themselves. This indicates that speakers tend to value the listener's interests much higher than their own (van Deemter, 2016, p. 58). This needs to be considered since underspecification may be a symptom of habitual reference in realistic communication where correction and incremental reference is possible. Apart from the obvious fact that the experiment provided some evidence that contexts influence the REG task, the quality of formulations of exactly these contexts may not have been optimal. Further studies on more elaborated contexts integrating more factors of personal relationship towards the listener, dialogue settings, common ground and cooperativeness may show whether and to what degree the different parameters influence the content determination and the generation quality in context-bound REG tasks. Strategies are besides salience the most individual influence on the production of referring expressions. The variance between speakers clearly gave evidence for the existence of different generation strategies and preferences towards a specific generation quality. The distribution of instances of overgenerating and underspecifying instances are well balanced. Besides these there is a group of participants with balanced proportion of all three qualities giving empirical proof for the large variance within speakers. In a probabilistic approach to REG, the strategy of the listener and the speaker may be an important parameter the model has to integrate in order to adjust production and comprehension more elaborately to the relation between the interlocutors and their strategic alignment.

References

H. Rohde A. D. F. Clarke, M. Elsner. 2013. Wheres wally: the influence of visual salience on referring expression generation. *Frontiers in Psychology*, 4.

A. Gatt K. van Deemter, I. van der Sluis. 2006a. Building a semantically transparent corpus for the generation of referring expressions. In *Proceedings of the 4th International Conference on Natural Language Generation, INLG-04*, pages 130–132, Sydney, Australia.

A. Gatt K. van Deemter, I. van der Sluis. 2006b. Manual for tuna corpus: Referring expressions in two domains.

A. Gatt K. van Deemter, I. van der Sluis. 2007. Evaluating algorithms for the generation of referring expressions: Going beyond toy domains. In *Proceedings of the International Conference on Recent Advances in Natural Language Processing, RANLP-07*.

A. Gatt K. van Deemter, I. van der Sluis. 2010. Speaker- dependent variation in content selection for referring expression generation. In *Proceedings of the 8th Australasian Language Technology Workshop*, pages 81–89.

K. van Deemter. 2016. *Computational Models of Referring*. MIT Press, Cambridge, UK.

A. Bangerter H. H. Clark. 2004. Changing ideas about reference. In D. Sperber I.Noveck, editor, *Experimental Pragmatics*, pages 25–49. Springer.

M. Siddiqui I. Khan. 2015. Do speakers produce different referring expressions in their native language than a non-native language? *International Journal of Computational Linguistics Research*, 6(2):41–47.

D. da Silva Rocha I. Paraboni. 2018. Reference production in human-computer interaction: Issues for corpus-based referring expression generation. In *Proceedings of the 11th Language Resources and Evaluation Conference*.

M. de Sant'Ana F. Coutinho I. Paraboni, A. Lan. 2017. Effects of cognitive effort on the resolution of over-specified descriptions. *Computational Linguistics*, 43(2):451–459.

T. C. Ferreira I. Paraboni. 2014. Referring expression generation: Taking speakers' preferences into account. In I. Kopecek K. Pala P. Spjka, A. Horák, editor, *Text, Speech and Dialogue. 17th International Conference, TSD 2014*, pages 539–546. Springer International Publishing, Schweiz.

R. Dale J. Viethen. 2008. Generating relational references: What makes a difference? In *Proceedings of the Australasian Language Technology Association Workshop 2008*, pages 160–168.

R. Dale J. Viethen. 2011. Gre3d7: A corpus of distinguishing descriptions for objects in visual scenes. In *Proceedings of the UCNLG+Eval: Language Generation and Evaluation Workshop*, pages 12–22.

M. C. Frank N. Goodman. 2016. Pragmatic language interpretation as probabilistic inference. *Trends in Cognitive Sciences*, 20(11):818–829.

O. Lemon S. Janarthanam. 2010. Adaptive referring expression generation in spoken dialogue systems: Evaluation with real users. In *Proceedings of Sigdial 2010: the 11th Annual Meeting of the special Interest Group on Discourse and Dialogue*, pages 124–131.

M. Matten T. Berg S. Kazemzadeh, V. Ordonez. 2014. Referitgame: Referring to objects in photographs of natural scenes. In *Proceedings of the 2014 Conference on Empirical Methods in Natural Language Processing (EMNLP)*, pages 787–798.

Rethinking Text Attribute Transfer: A Lexical Analysis

Yao Fu[*1], Hao Zhou[2], Jiaze Chen[2], Lei Li[2]
[1]Columbia University
[2]Bytedance AI Lab
yao.fu@columbia.edu, zhouhao.nlp@bytedance.com
teoyde@gmail.com, lileilab@bytedance.com

Abstract

Text attribute transfer is modifying certain linguistic attributes (e.g. sentiment, style, authorship, etc.) of a sentence and transforming them from one type to another. In this paper, we aim to analyze and interpret what is changed during the transfer process. We start from the observation that in many existing models and datasets, certain words within a sentence play important roles in determining the sentence attribute class. These words are referred to as *the Pivot Words*. Based on these pivot words, we propose a lexical analysis framework, *the Pivot Analysis*, to quantitatively analyze the effects of these words in text attribute classification and transfer. We apply this framework to existing datasets and models, and show that: (1) the pivot words are strong features for the classification of sentence attributes; (2) to change the attribute of a sentence, many datasets only requires to change certain pivot words; (3) consequently, many transfer models only perform the lexical-level modification, while leaving higher-level sentence structures unchanged. Our work provides an in-depth understanding of linguistic attribute transfer and further identifies the future requirements and challenges of this task[1].

1 Introduction

The task of text attribute transfer (or text style transfer [2]) is to transform certain linguistic attributes (sentiment, style, authorship, rhetorical devices, etc.) from one type to another (Ficler and Goldberg, 2017; Fu et al., 2018; Hu et al., 2017; Li et al., 2018; Shen et al., 2017). The state-of-the-art

---

[*] Work done when Yao was an intern at Bytedance AI Lab.

[1]Our code can be found at https://github.com/FranxYao/pivot_analysis

[2]Many existing works also call this task style transfer(Fu et al., 2018), our work view style as one of the linguistic attributes, and use the term style or attribute according to the context.

	Before	After
negative to positive	service is trashy rude	service is pretty good
positive to negative	go to place for client visits with gorgeous views	go to place for client visits with terrible views

Figure 1: Examples of pivot words in sentiment transfer. Certain words are strongly correlated with the sentiment such that a transfer model only need to modify these words to accomplish the transfer task while leaving the higher level sentence structure unchanged.

(SOTA) models have achieved inspiring transfer success rates (Zhao et al., 2018; Zhang et al., 2018; Prabhumoye et al., 2018; Yang et al., 2018). However, it is still unclear in current literature about what is transferred and what remains to be unchanged during the transfer process. To answer this question, we perform an in-depth investigation of the linguistic attribute transfer datasets and models.

Our investigation starts from a simple observation: in many transfer datasets and models, certain class-related words play very important roles in attribute transfer (Li et al., 2018; Prabhumoye et al., 2018). Figure 1 gives a sentiment transfer example from the controllable generation (CG) model (Hu et al., 2017) on the Yelp dataset. In this example, *rude* is strongly related to the *negative* sentiment and *good* is strongly related to the *positive* sentiment, thus simply substituting *rude* with *good* will transfer the sentence from negative to positive. In this work, We name these words the *pivot words* for a class. We use the term *the pivot effect* to refer the effect that certain strong words may be able to determine the class of a sentence.

Based on the observation of the pivot effect, our research questions are: (1) which words are pivot words and how do they influence the attribute class of a sentence in different datasets? (2) does the model only need to modify the pivot words to per-

Proceedings of The 12th International Conference on Natural Language Generation, pages 24–33,
Tokyo, Japan, 28 Oct - 1 Nov, 2019. ©2019 Association for Computational Linguistics

form the attribute transfer or it may change higher-level sentence compositionality like syntax?

To answer question (1), we propose the *pivot analysis*, a series of simple yet effective text mining algorithms, to quantitatively examine the pivot effects in different datasets. The basics of the datasets we investigate are listed in Table 1. We first give the algorithm to extract pivot words (Sec 3). We statistically show the stronger the pivot effect is on a dataset, the easier for a model to transfer its sentences. To further analyze the fine-grained distributional structure of these pivot words, we propose the *precision-recall histogram* to show to what extent the datasets may be influenced by their pivot words (Sec 4.2).

To answer question (2) and discover what is changed during the transfer process, we use the pivot words to analyze the transfer results of two SOTA models: the Controllable Generation (CG) model(Hu et al., 2017) and the Cross Alignment (CA) model (Shen et al., 2017). We show that although equipped with sophisticated modeling techniques, in many datasets, these models tend to change only a few words and most of these modified words are pivot words. When we mask out the modified words (to eliminate the lexical changes) and compare the Levenshtein string edit distance (Levenshtein, 1966) of the sentence stems before and after the transfer, we find out many of the sentence stems are the same (the distance of the masked sentences equals to 0). This means that in transfer, the model only modifies few pivot words while leaving the syntactical structure of the sentence unchanged (Sec 5).

To sum up, we show that: (1) in many datasets, words are important features in classification and transfer. But still, certain hard cases require a higher level of understanding of the sentence structures. (2) SOTA models tend to perform the transfer at the lexical level, the syntax of a sentence is generally unchanged. The understanding and modification of higher-level sentence compositionality (syntax trees and dependency graphs) is still a challenging problem.

2 Background

Inspired by the image style transfer task (Gatys et al., 2016; Zhu et al., 2017), the goal of text attribute(style) transfer is to transfer the stylistic attributes of the sentence from one class to another while maintaining the content of the sentence unchanged (Fu et al., 2018; Ficler and Goldberg, 2017; Hu et al., 2017). Because of the lack of parallel datasets, most models focus on the unpaired transfer. Although plenty of sophisticated techniques are used in this task, such as adversarial learning (Zhao et al., 2018; Chen et al., 2018), latent representations (Li and Mandt, 2018; Dai et al., 2019; Liu et al., 2019), and reinforcement learning (Luo et al., 2019; Gong et al., 2019; Xu et al., 2018), there is little discussion about what is changed and what remains unchanged.

Because of the lack of transparency and interpretability, there is some retrospection on this topic. Such as the definition of text style (Tikhonov and Yamshchikov, 2018), and the evaluation metrics (Li et al., 2018; Mir et al., 2019). Our proposed pivot analysis aligns with these works and provides a new tool to probe the transfer datasets and models. The de facto metrics is to use a pretrained classifier to classify if the transferred sentence is in the target class. So our pivot analysis starts from the classification task and mines the words with strong predictive performance.

While many previous works focus on one-to-one transfer, many recent works extend this task to one-to-many transfer (Logeswaran et al., 2018; Liao et al., 2018; Subramanian et al., 2019). For simplicity, we focus on the one-to-one setting. But it is also easy to extend the pivot analysis into one-to-many transfer settings.

3 Pivot Words Discovery

To study the factors influencing attribute transfer, we start from mining words strongly correlated with the attribute class i.e. pivot words. Algorithm 1 shows the procedure of mining pivot words. This algorithm is based on a simple intuition: if one single word is strong enough to determine the sentence attributes, then when we use the existence of this word to classify the attribute, we should achieve very high precision. Consider two extreme examples: when a word only exists in one class, it should achieve 100% classification precision. When a word exists evenly in two different classes, its precision is 50%. The reason we use precision instead of recall or accuracy is that only precision reveals the influence of a single word: suppose the word "awesome" only exists in 100 positive sentences, and the whole dataset size is 100K. In this case, "awesome" will have low recall and accuracy, but high precision. This algorithm

	Yelp	Amazon	Caption	Paper	Gender	Politics	Reddit	Twitter
Source	Hu et al. (2017)	Li et al. (2018)	Li et al. (2018)	Fu et al. (2018)	Prabhumoye et al. (2018)	Prabhumoye et al. (2018)	dos Santos et al. (2018)	dos Santos et al. (2018)
Class	Positive Negative	Positive Negative	Romantic Humorous	Academic Journalism	Male Female	Democratic Republican	Polite Impolite	Polite Impolite
Size(train/ dev/test)	444K/ 63K/126K	554K/ 2K/1K	12K/ -/1K	392K/ 20K/20K	2M/ 4K/534K	537K/ 4K/56K	10M/ 19K/47K	3M/ 18K/18K

Table 1: The text attribute transfer datasets we investigate.

Yelp	Positive	Negative
pivot words	great, perfection, local, nice, good, thanks, ambiance, incredible, amazing, fair	sadly, kidding, never, sucks, disappointed, terrible, slow, frustrated, overpriced, waste
sentences w. pivots	the owner was super nice and welcoming / thanks for always satisfying ! / great prices , outstanding food , quick and polite service .	the service sucks , management is terrible . / we completely wasted an hour of our time and left . / unfortunately we left over 3/4 of our food in the trash .
sentences w/o. pivots	now it 's our weekly treat . / first time going today and i got the new york pastrami . / i will be back !	do yourself a favor and just stay away . / this place is large enough for everything . / i am not exaggerating .
Amazon	**Positive**	**Negative**
pivot words	great, easy, attractive, nicely, compact, wonderful, love, fancy, happy, fits	worst, disapointed, horrible, refused, poor, waste, uncomfortable, worse, insult, dissapointed
sentences w. pivots	nice pan ! this pizza pan is a great size / it works perfectly ! i m very happy with the price / it is easy to use and fits the iphone great	that s what makes this game so damn frustrating and boring / incredibly worthless and complex drm that ruins the point / the taste was bitter and sharp , not smooth and had a yucky fake taste
sentences w/o. pivots	it really just sits lightly over your ear / give it a chance , you won t be disappointed / i hastily ordered her another one and it arrived on time	this kettle looks pretty but doesn t turn off once it boils / no instructions are included , although it s possible to google / on my scale , it weighs over num_num ounces with batteries
Gender	**Female**	**Male**
pivot words	love, smoothie, massage, lattes, yoga, spa, chocolate, pillows, grateful, gorgeous	builds, value, wife, failure, respectable, roaster, competition, vehicle, beers, workmanship
sentences w. pivots	my favorite cupcake is the strawberry shortcake / best of luck ,love this hidden gem ! hits the spot every time !	their drink selection is simple with many local brews and mass produced american beers / great stadium the best setting for a ballpark anywhere in the us
sentences w/o. pivots	we had a great experience and will go back / i strongly recommend this animal hospital for your pets	the managers seemed to be running a nice place / the desserts are another shining feature of this place

Figure 2: The pivot words and sentence examples in three example datasets. The vocabulary of pivot words is large so we only list typical words. Sentences without pivot words are intuitively harder to classify and transfer.

calculates the precision for each word-class pair, and choose pivot words with a predefined threshold p_0.

For simplicity, we only consider binary classification in Algorithm 1, but one could easily extend it to multi-class settings. Also, we only consider unigrams(words), while it is also straightforward to extend it to ngrams. In practice, we find the unigram version performs quite good, as is shown in Table 2. As for the parameters in the algorithm, the precision threshold p_0 controls the confidence of a word to be a pivot, and the occurrence threshold f_0 prevents overfitting. We tune these parameters based on the classification performance on the validation set. Specifically, to get better classification performance, f_0 and p_0 should be lower to allow more vote (e.g. $f_0 \leq 10, p_0 \in [0.5, 0.7]$). To get more confidence and filter out stronger pivot

---

Algorithm 1 Pivot Words Discovery

Input: The vocabulary $\mathcal{V}$, the sentences $\mathcal{S}$ and the labels $\mathcal{Y}$, the frequency threshold f_0, the precision threshold p_0
Output: The pivot words Ω_y for each class $y \in \{0, 1\}$. The word-class precision matrix $p(x, y)$

1: **procedure** PIVOT WORDS DISCOVERY
2:     Balance the dataset by down-sampling the majority class.
3:     **for** each sentence s, each class y, and each word x in the vocabulary $\mathcal{V}$ with frequency higher than f_0 **do**
4:         Consider the class of s is y or $1 - y$
5:         Use *the existence of* x to classify:
6:         **if** x is in s **then**
7:             Classify s to be y
8:         **else**
9:             Classify s to be $1 - y$
10:     Calculate the classification precision $p(x, y)$ of word x for label y over all sentences $\mathcal{S}$.
11:         **if** $p(x, y) > p_0$ **then**
12:             x is a pivot word for class y i.e. $x \in \Omega_y$
13:     **return** $\Omega_y, p(x, y)$

Algorithm 2 The Pivot Classifier

Input: sentence s, the pivot words Ω_y for class $y \in \{0, 1\}$
Output: The class $y(s)$ of sentence s
1: **procedure** PIVOT CLASSIFICATION
2:     View s as bag of words
3:     For each $y \in \{0, 1\}$, calculate $s_y = ||s \cap \Omega_y||$
4:     Predict the class of s to be $y(s) = \text{argmax}_y\{s_y\}$.
    Break tie randomly.
5:     **return** $y(s)$
---

words, f_0 and p_0 should be higher (e.g. $f_0 \geq 100, p_0 \geq 0.7$).

Figure 2 shows the mined pivot words in different datasets. For sentences that contain pivot words, it is clear that these words are strong features for classification. Intuitively, to transfer the class of these sentences, one could directly modify these words. But there are also cases that contain no pivot words, e.g. *i will be back* in the Yelp dataset. To modify the sentiment of these sentences, a model needs to understand a broader context and common sense. In general, the existence of pivot words gives us a method to understand in attribute transfer, what cases are easier and what cases are more difficult.

The intuition that the existence of single words is enough to determine the linguistic attribute does not necessarily hold on all datasets. But empirically, we find out many transfer datasets tend to contain strong pivot words (Figure 5). One could compare our pivot analysis with other methods that mine the word importance, such as the weights of a logistic classifier, or more sophisticated Bayesian methods like the log-odds ratio informative Dirichlet prior (Monroe et al., 2008). Our method is more straightforward and interpretable. We further develop this method as a simple yet strong classification baseline to indicate the transfer difficulty of different datasets and use the pivot words as a tool to analyze, interpret, and visualize the text attribute transfer models.

4   Analysing Datasets with Pivot Analysis

In this section, we use the pivot words to analyze the transfer datasets. We first reveal the mechanisms of how pivot words affect classification and transfer by using the pivot words as the classification boundary. Then we use the precision-recall histogram to demonstrate the distributional structure of the pivot words in different portions of the datasets.

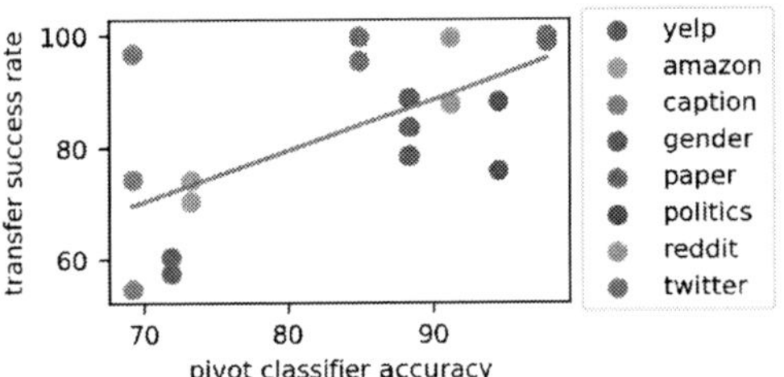

Figure 3: Pivot classification accuracy v.s. transfer success rate (correlation = 0.64, p-value = 0.003). The stronger the pivot effect is, the easier to transfer.

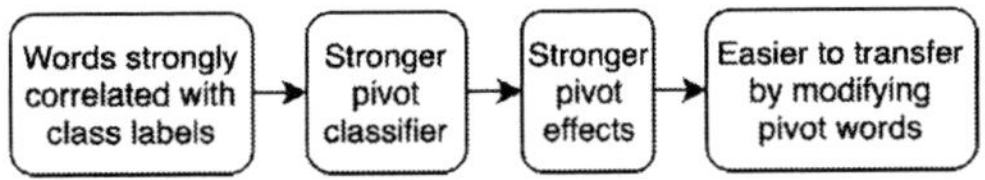

Figure 4: The mechanism of the pivot effect on classification and transfer.

4.1   The Pivot Classifier

Algorithm 2 gives a simple method to classify a sentence based on the pivot words output from Algorithm 1. This is essentially a voting based classifier. This classifier holds strong independence assumption that the label of a sentence is only related to the bag of words, but ignore the word orders. This is to say, the decision boundary only stays at the lexical level, and does not go to the syntax level. Then it counts the pivot words of different classes contained by the sentence and predicts the label to be one of the largest pivot words overlap. Intuitively, this algorithm classifies a sentence only based on the existence of strong attribute-related words.

The pivot classifier is a simple yet strong classification baseline, as is shown in Table 2. We use it to study different datasets and compare it with (1) a logistic classifier, (2) a SOTA CNN classifier (Kim, 2014). We have balanced the test sets so the random baseline is 50%. This voting based classifier achieves comparable performance with the two models in 4 datasets (Amazon, Gender, Paper, Politics), and only loses small margins in 2 datasets (Yelp, Caption). Although the independence assumption from our pivot classifier does not necessarily hold for all datasets, empirically it performs very well. This means that these pivot words are a meaningful approximation of the true decision boundary.

If the decision boundary of a linguistic attribute stays at the lexical level, then one could cross the

Validation	Yelp	Amazon	Caption	Gender	Paper	Politics	Reddit	Twitter
Pivot	88.00	75.85	-	72.02	97.82	98.32	90.00	85.25
Logistic	91.83	76.75	-	72.77	98.39	99.82	98.05	98.20
CNN	92.87	77.93	-	74.20	98.36	98.85	99.45	99.55
Test	Yelp	Amazon	Caption	Gender	Paper	Politics	Reddit	Twitter
Pivot	88.35	73.30	69.20	71.91	98.07	94.60	91.15	85.05
Logistic	91.97	73.80	75.20	72.91	98.67	96.83	98.05	98.05
CNN	92.96	75.80	76.10	74.29	98.66	87.91	99.65	99.45

Table 2: Classification accuracy. The voting based pivot classifier is a strong classification baseline compared with the state of art CNN classifier, indicating that in many datasets, words are strong features for class labels.

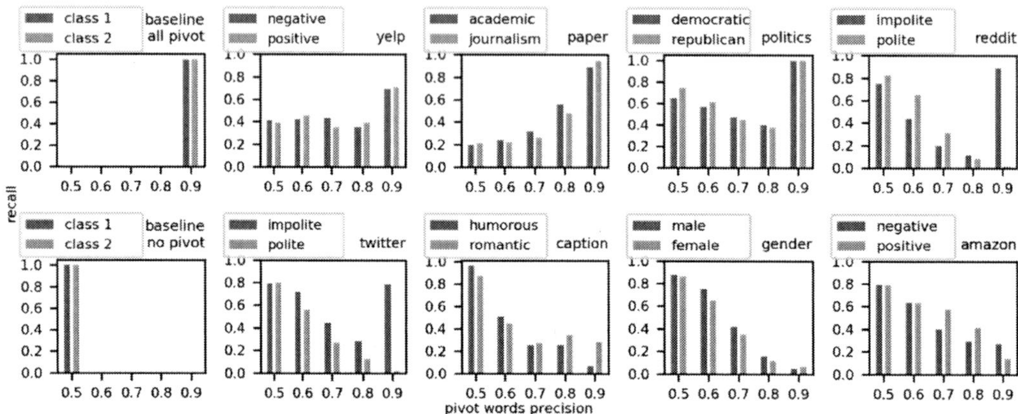

Figure 5: The precision-recall histogram. The high right bars in Yelp, Paper, Politics, Reddit, and Twitter datasets reveal the existence of strong pivot words, Each bar at location (x, y) should be interpreted as: if use pivot words with precision x to classify the sentence, the recall will be y. The higher the right bars are, the more sentences can be classified by words accurately, the stronger the pivot effect is, the easier to transfer. The baseline cases where the dataset is full of/ has no pivot words are show on the left.

boundary by simply substituting the pivot words of one class to another, thus achieving text class transfer. Intuitively, the more pivot words a dataset contains, the stronger the pivot effect is, the easier for the pivot classifier to classify, and the easier to transfer the attribute. This intuition is demonstrated in Figure 3. The pivot effect (shown by pivot classification accuracy) and the transfer difficulty (shown by the transfer success rate reported from previous models) has a strong positive correlation and is statistically significant. This mechanism is demonstrated in Figure 4. The stronger the pivot effect is, the easier to transfer.

4.2 The Precision-Recall Histogram

Now we go one step further to reveal how the pivot effect distributes in different portions of the datasets. We propose a new tool, *the precision-recall* histogram based on the results from Algorithm 1 and 2. As is shown in Algorithm 3, essentially, this algorithm use pivot words with differ-

ent level of confidence (precision) to classify the dataset, and output the recall. For better visualization, we set the precision interval gap to be 0.1, but it is also possible to use smaller or larger gaps. It is also important to balance the dataset in Algorithm 1 to make the baseline precision 0.5.

The histogram for all datasets gives a fine-grained illustration of the pivot effect (Figure 5). We first look at the two baseline cases: a dataset with no pivot words, and a dataset full of pivots. If a dataset is full of pivots, i.e. the vocabulary of the two classes have no overlap, then all words should have precision 1.0 and they should achieve 1.0 recall, so the right-most bars are the highest. If a dataset has no pivot words, i.e. all words are distributed evenly in two classes, then all words have precision 0.5 and they should achieve 1.0 recall, so the left-most bars are the highest. The higher the right bars are, the stronger the pivot effect is.

The histograms of the datasets are somewhere between the two baseline cases. Generally, we

Algorithm 3 The Precision-Recall Histogram

Input: The sentences S, the labels $\mathcal{Y}$, the pivot words for each class $\Omega_y, y \in \mathcal{Y}$, the precision matrix $p(x,y), x \in \mathcal{V}, y \in \mathcal{Y}$
Output: The precision-recall histogram

1: **procedure** THE PRECISION-RECALL HISTOGRAM
2:    **for** The precision range pair $(p_i, p_{i+1}) \in [(0.5, 0.6), (0.6, 0.7)...(0.9, 1.0)]$ **do**
3:       For each class y, gather all pivot words of the precision in the given range: $\Omega_y^{(i)} = x : p(x,y) \in [p_i, p_{i+1}]$
4:       Use $\Omega_y^{(i)}$ to form a pivot classifier and classify the dataset S. Calculate the recall r_i.
5:       Store (p_i, r_i)
6:    **return** The list of (p_i, r_i)

	Yelp	Amazon	Gender
CG - # modified	1.66	0.56	0.79
- percentage	18%	4%	5%
CA - # modified	1.61	3.54	5.60
- percentage	18%	23%	33%
sentence length	8.89	14.82	17.01

Table 3: Average number of modified words and their percentage in the sentence length. The transfer models tend to modify only a few attribute-related words.

	Yelp	Amazon	Gender
CG	91.25	94.77	94.17
CA	72.33	74.04	56.09

Table 4: Percentage of modified words that are pivot words. A large portion of the modified words are pivots.

see two different shape distributions. In the Yelp, Paper, Politics, Reddit, and Twitter datasets, the right-most bars are the highest, meaning that in these datasets, strong pivot words exist in a large portion of the dataset. These are close to the all-pivot baseline. Specially, we see that in the Reddit and Twitter dataset, the pivot effect only exists in the *impolite* class, while in other datasets, the pivot effect exists in both classes. Note that this phenomenon cannot be discovered simply from the overall classification accuracy. After manual inspection, we find out since the attribute of these two datasets is politeness, the pivot words for the impolite class are the common swearwords in English. These words dominate the impolite sentences.

In the Caption, Gender, and Amazon dataset, we see a decreasing height from left to right, indicating a weaker pivot effect. Highest bars exist in the 0.5 precision bars, meaning that for each class, most of them can be classified by 0.5 precision (= random guessing). This is close to the no-pivot baseline. The high-precision words still exist, but they cannot dominate the whole class. In conclusion, the precision-recall histograms give a structural examination for each class. The existence of pivots and the determination power of pivots differ from class to class, and from datasets to datasets.

5 Analysing Transfer Models with Pivot Analysis

In this section, we aim to analyze what is changed and what remains in linguistic attribute transfer systems. We perform our experiments from two perspectives: the lexical structures, and the syntactical structures. For the lexical structures, we show what words are modified by the transfer model. For the syntactical structures, we mask out the modified pivot words and compare the resulting sentence stems.

We use the two most common SOTA models, the Controllable Generation (CG) model from Hu et al. (2017), and the Cross Aligned Autoencoder (CA) model from Shen et al. (2017). The CG model uses a conditional VAE with style-discriminator and trained with a wake-sleep algorithm. The CA model uses a cross-alignment mechanism to guide the transfer process. These are two strong models in many datasets compared to many other models. We direct the readers to the original papers for more details.

We test the models on three datasets: Yelp, Amazon, and Gender. The Yelp dataset is the most widely used benchmark in the text style transfer task. As is shown in the previous sections, it exists strong pivot effects. There are many sentiment words in this dataset. For the Amazon and the Gender dataset, there is less pivot effect. So our experiments give a minimum cover of different types of datasets. We use the released implementation for our experiments [3]. All hyper-parameters are followed by their official instructions. Both models are trained until the simultaneous convergence of the reconstruction loss and the adversarial loss. We refer the readers to the implementation repositories for more details.

---

[3]The CG model: `https://github.com/asyml/texar/tree/master/examples/text_style_transfer`
the CA model: `https://github.com/shentianxiao/language-style-transfer`

CG	0	1	2	3	4	5	6	>6
Yelp	74.65	5.05	10.68	5.71	1.84	0.72	0.66	0.69
Amazon	94.20	0.00	0.90	4.00	0.80	0.10	0.00	0.00
Gender	90.96	0.04	6.60	0.45	0.89	0.43	0.16	0.48
CA	0	1	2	3	4	5	6	>6
Yelp	41.30	1.98	13.63	10.01	8.76	7.49	6.17	10.66
Amazon	37.60	1.85	9.95	9.25	6.15	6.15	4.65	24.40
Gender	37.89	0.27	2.27	3.36	1.60	1.40	2.03	51.18

Table 5: Masked edit distance percentage distributions. For the CG model, in most of the cases($> 74\%$), the masked edit distance is 0, meaning that only few words are changed while the sentence structures are exactly the same. For the CA model, still a large portion of the sentence structures are unchanged ($> 37\%$)

Yelp	
Before	After
but not worth _num_ bucks .	but consistently worth incredible bucks
i 'm the wrong person to ask .	i 'm adds fantastic person to ask .
food is acceptable , service is terrible	food is acceptable , service is nice .

Amazon	
Before	After
this product is a ripoff on consumers	this product is a reasonable on consumers
this is a worthless item	this is a sturdy item
for me this was a disappointing product	for me this was a great product .

Gender	
Before	After
my boyfriend and i chose this restaurant	my buddy and i chose this restaurant
really do love the animals	really do love the milkshakes
you get to wait in a recreation room	you get to wait in a bathing room

Figure 6: The transfer cases. Many of the transfered words are pivot words. The model tend to transfer only a few words while leaving the higher level sentence structure unchanged.

	Before	After
original	service is trashy rude	service is pretty good
masked	service is [mask] [mask]	service is [mask] [mask]

Figure 7: An example of the masked sentences. Edit distance = 0 after masking.

	Yelp	Amazon	Gender
CG - distance	0.65	0.17	0.26
- percentage	7.3%	1.4%	1.5%
CA - distance	2.63	4.56	9.95
- percentage	29%	31%	58%
sentence length	8.89	14.82	17.01

Table 6: Edit distance after masking out the pivot words. In the CG model, only words are modified, while the higher-level sentence structures remain to be the same. For the CA model, it tries to modify more sentence structures.

5.1 Lexical Structures

We show that the two models tend to modify only a few words in a given sentence, and a large portion of these words are pivot words. The results are shown in Table 3 and 4. On the Yelp dataset, the CG model and the CA model only modify 1.66 and 1.61 words on average. The portion of pivot words is 91% and 72% respectively. This means on this dataset, both two models focus on word substitutions to change the sentence style. On the Amazon and the Gender dataset, the models take different transfer strategies. For the CG model, it concentrates on fewer words to modify (0.56 on Amazon and 0.79 on Gender). For the CA model, it tends to modify more words (3.54 on Amazon and 5.60 on Gender). Still, both models tend to modify the pivot words for class transfer. In general, a small portion of the sentences are modified ($< 30\%$ approximately), and a large portion of the modified words are pivots ($> 60\%$ approximately).

5.2 Syntactic Structures

If we eliminate the lexical differences by masking out the modified words, what is changed in the resulting sentence stems? We use the Levenshtein string edit distance (Levenshtein, 1966) to measure the distances of the masked sentences as an approximation to the distances of syntactic structures. Figure 7 gives an example of masked sentences. One could also consider more sophisticated metrics to measure the syntactic distances with parsing trees (Shen et al., 2018; Zhang and Shasha, 1989). Here we use the string edit distance for simplicity. In practice, it is informative enough to demonstrate the change of sentence structures.

Table 6 shows the edit distances after masking the pivot words. We see clear differences between the two models. For the CG model, it barely changes the sentence structures (0.1+ distances). This indicates that it takes the strategy to focus more on the substitution of pivot words. For the CA model, it takes the strategy that not only to modify the words, but also a portion of the sentence structures. We see a moderate percentage of the sentence structure modified on the Yelp and Amazon dataset (about 30%), and a large syntactic modification (58%) on the Gender dataset. Compared with the CG model, the CA model tries to modify the sentences more radically.

To show a fine-grained distribution of the distances among different cases, we list the distribution statistics in Table 5. We see that for the CG model, most of the cases > 74%) sentence stems are unchanged. For the CA model, although its average edit distance is larger, in a large portion of the cases (> 37%), the distance is still 0. In conclusion, both models tend to retain the sentence structures in a large portion of the datasets.

5.3 Qualitative Analysis

Now we examine the transfer cases qualitatively in Figure 6. These are cases from the CG model on the three datasets. The pivot words are highlighted. When the model tries to change the class of a sentence, it first identifies the pivot words, then substitutes them with the pivots from another class. If we mask out the highlighted pivot words, the resulting sentence stems are the same, indicating that the syntactic structures remain unchanged. Although this is not all the case, the models tend to focus on words in a large portion of the datasets.

6 Discussion

Implications: Our pivot classifier reveals that to a certain extent, in many transfer datasets, the decision boundary stays at the lexical level. Consequently, to cross the boundary and transfer the text class, many instances in the dataset only requires to modify certain pivot words. But still, there are cases with no pivot words. The decision boundary in such cases is higher than the word level. To transfer these cases, the model needs a

deeper understanding of the sentence structures, which may include syntax, semantics, and common sense (Figure 2).

Considerations: In our experiments, we find out the two models are both quite unstable during training. The balance between the reconstruction loss and the adversarial loss will significantly influence the convergence point. Our pivot analysis framework requires the model to converge to a meaningful local optimum with reasonable content preservation and transfer strength at the same time(Fu et al., 2018). For our pivot algorithms, it is important to balance the datasets (both training and testing) for a reasonable precision baseline(0.5). Our algorithm is mostly sensitive to the precision threshold p_0 i.e. the confidence of how *pivot* a word is. We tune this parameter based on the development set performance.

Limitations: All of our pivot algorithms stays at *the lexical level*. These algorithms hold strong Independence assumption that the class of a sentence is independent of the order of words. So this method may not be able to capture certain linguistical phenomenons, such as anastrophe [4]. One could also consider an extreme example where the pivot analysis *does not work*: suppose we have a corpus of sentences, we label all of them to be 0, then we *reverse all sentences*, and label the reversed sentences to be 1. In this dataset, both classes share the same vocabulary, and the precision of any word will be 0.5. This is an example where only the order determines the class. Further, in our work, we only consider lexical changes, and do not consider other issues with regard to more rigorous definition of linguistic style(Tikhonov and Yamshchikov, 2018), the evaluation metrics (Mir et al., 2019), and the causality in text classification(Wood-Doughty et al., 2018). These topics will be the future directions.

7 Conclusion

In this work, we present *the Pivot Analysis*, a lexical analysis framework for the examination and inspection of text style transfer datasets and models. This analysis framework consists of three text mining algorithms, *pivot words discovery, the pivot classifier, and the precision-recall histograms*. With these algorithms, we reveal what are the important words that influence the class

---

[4]To change the order of certain words

of a sentence, how these words are distributed in a dataset, the mechanisms through which these words interact with a transfer model, and how the models perform the transfer. Our method serves as a probe for the transparency and the interpretability of the datasets and the transfer models. We show that a large portion of the transfer cases stays at the lexical level, while the syntactic structures are unchanged.

Since our methods stay at the lexical level, it has its own limitations in understanding higher-level sentence compositionality. These limitations are also shared by the SOTA transfer models: to understand the syntax and semantics (i.e. the structures of the sentence), and the common sense (i.e. the background and implications of the surface words). These limitations are also directions for future challenges. In the future, we need to use better inductive bias and use more powerful models towards higher-level sentence compositionality.

Acknowledgments

We thank the reviewers for their informative reviews. We thank Yansong Feng, Bingfeng Luo, and Zhenxin Fu for the helpful discussions. This work is supported by the China Scholarship Council.

References

Liqun Chen, Shuyang Dai, Chenyang Tao, Haichao Zhang, Zhe Gan, Dinghan Shen, Yizhe Zhang, Guoyin Wang, Ruiyi Zhang, and Lawrence Carin. 2018. Adversarial text generation via feature-mover's distance. In *NeurIPS*.

Ning Dai, Jianze Liang, Xipeng Qiu, and Xuanjing Huang. 2019. Style transformer: Unpaired text style transfer without disentangled latent representation. In *Proceedings of the 57th Annual Meeting of the Association for Computational Linguistics*, pages 5997–6007, Florence, Italy. Association for Computational Linguistics.

Jessica Ficler and Yoav Goldberg. 2017. Controlling linguistic style aspects in neural language generation. In *Proceedings of the Workshop on Stylistic Variation*, pages 94–104, Copenhagen, Denmark. Association for Computational Linguistics.

Zhenxin Fu, Xiaoye Tan, Nanyun Peng, Dongyan Zhao, and Rui Yan. 2018. Style transfer in text: Exploration and evaluation. In *AAAI*.

Leon A. Gatys, Alexander S. Ecker, and Matthias Bethge. 2016. Image style transfer using convolutional neural networks. *2016 IEEE Conference on Computer Vision and Pattern Recognition (CVPR)*, pages 2414–2423.

Hongyu Gong, Suma Bhat, Lingfei Wu, Jinjun Xiong, and Wen mei W. Hwu. 2019. Reinforcement learning based text style transfer without parallel training corpus. In *NAACL-HLT*.

Zhiting Hu, Zichao Yang, Xiaodan Liang, Ruslan Salakhutdinov, and Eric P. Xing. 2017. Toward controlled generation of text. In *Proceedings of the 34th International Conference on Machine Learning*, volume 70 of *Proceedings of Machine Learning Research*, pages 1587–1596, International Convention Centre, Sydney, Australia. PMLR.

Yoon Kim. 2014. Convolutional neural networks for sentence classification. In *EMNLP*.

Vladimir I Levenshtein. 1966. Binary codes capable of correcting deletions, insertions, and reversals. *Soviet physics doklady*, 10(8):707–710.

Juncen Li, Robin Jia, Hua He, and Percy S. Liang. 2018. Delete, retrieve, generate: A simple approach to sentiment and style transfer. In *NAACL-HLT*.

Yingzhen Li and Stephan Mandt. 2018. Disentangled sequential autoencoder. In *ICML*.

Yi Liao, Lidong Bing, Piji Li, Shuming Shi, Wai Lam, and Tong Zhang. 2018. Quase: Sequence editing under quantifiable guidance. In *EMNLP*.

Dayiheng Liu, Jie Fu, Yidan Zhang, Chris Pal, and Jiancheng Lv. 2019. Revision in continuous space: Fine-grained control of text style transfer. *ArXiv*, abs/1905.12304.

Lajanugen Logeswaran, Honglak Lee, and Samy Bengio. 2018. Content preserving text generation with attribute controls. In *Advances in Neural Information Processing Systems*, pages 5103–5113.

Fuli Luo, Peng Li, Jie Zhou, Pengcheng Yang, Baobao Chang, Zhifang Sui, and Xu Rui Sun. 2019. A dual reinforcement learning framework for unsupervised text style transfer. In *IJCAI*.

Remi Mir, Bjarke Felbo, Nick Obradovich, and Iyad Rahwan. 2019. Evaluating style transfer for text. In *NAACL-HLT*.

Burt L. Monroe, Michael Colaresi, and Kevin M. Quinn. 2008. Fightin' words: Lexical feature selection and evaluation for identifying the content of political conflict. *Political Analysis*, 16(4):372–403.

Shrimai Prabhumoye, Yulia Tsvetkov, Ruslan R. Salakhutdinov, and Alan W. Black. 2018. Style transfer through back-translation. In *ACL*.

Cícero Nogueira dos Santos, Igor Melnyk, and Inkit Padhi. 2018. Fighting offensive language on social media with unsupervised text style transfer. In *ACL*.

Tianxiao Shen, Tao Lei, Regina Barzilay, and Tommi S. Jaakkola. 2017. Style transfer from non-parallel text by cross-alignment. In *NIPS*.

Yikang Shen, Zhouhan Lin, Athul Paul Jacob, Alessandro Sordoni, Aaron Courville, and Yoshua Bengio. 2018. Straight to the tree: Constituency parsing with neural syntactic distance. In *ACL*.

Sandeep Subramanian, Guillaume Lample, Eric Michael Smith, Ludovic Denoyer, Marc'Aurelio Ranzato, and Y-Lan Boureau. 2019. Multiple-attribute text style transfer. In *ICLR*.

Alexey Tikhonov and Ivan P. Yamshchikov. 2018. What is wrong with style transfer for texts? *ArXiv*, abs/1808.04365.

Zach Wood-Doughty, Ilya Shpitser, and Mark Dredze. 2018. Challenges of using text classifiers for causal inference. *arXiv preprint arXiv:1810.00956*.

Jingjing Xu, Xu Sun, Qi Zeng, Xuancheng Ren, Xiaodong Zhang, Houfeng Wang, and Wenjie Li. 2018. Unpaired sentiment-to-sentiment translation: A cycled reinforcement learning approach. In *ACL*.

Zichao Yang, Zhiting Hu, Chris Dyer, Eric P. Xing, and Taylor Berg-Kirkpatrick. 2018. Unsupervised text style transfer using language models as discriminators. In *NeurIPS*.

Kaizhong Zhang and Dennis Shasha. 1989. Simple fast algorithms for the editing distance between trees and related problems. *SIAM journal on computing*, 18(6):1245–1262.

Ye Zhang, Nan Ding, and Radu Soricut. 2018. Shaped: Shared-private encoder-decoder for text style adaptation. In *NAACL-HLT*.

Junbo Jake Zhao, Yoon Kim, Kelly Zhang, Alexander M. Rush, and Yann LeCun. 2018. Adversarially regularized autoencoders. In *ICML*.

Jun-Yan Zhu, Taesung Park, Phillip Isola, and Alexei A. Efros. 2017. Unpaired image-to-image translation using cycle-consistent adversarial networks. *2017 IEEE International Conference on Computer Vision (ICCV)*, pages 2242–2251.

Choosing between Long and Short Word Forms in Chinese

Lin Li[♠△★]**, Kees van Deemter**[♠♡]**, Denis Paperno**[◇]**, Jinyu Fan**[♣]**, Zewangkuanzhuo**[△]
[♠]Department of Information and Computing Sciences, Utrecht University
[△]Department of Computer Science, Qinghai Normal University
[★]CMLI Research Center, Minzu University of China
[♡]Department of Computing Science, University of Aberdeen
[◇]Department of Languages, Literature and Communication, Utrecht University
[♣]Department of Physics and Information , Qinghai Normal University
{l.li1, c.j.vandeemter, d.paperno}@uu.nl
{2104439819, 2497138704}@qq.com

Abstract

Between 80% and 90% of all Chinese words have long and short form such as 老虎/虎 *(laohu/hu , tiger)* (Duanmu, 2013). Consequently, the choice between long and short forms is a key problem for lexical choice across NLP and NLG in Chinese.

Following on from earlier work on abbreviations in English (Mahowald et al., 2013), we bring a probabilistic perspective to word length choice, using both a behavioural and a corpus-based approach. Thus, we hypothesise that, in Chinese, short forms are likelier in supportive than in neutral contexts. Our corpus and behavioral study supported this hypothesis, but a closer analysis revealed striking differences between different types of Chinese words.

1 Introduction

Choosing words is an important task for both Natural Language Generation (Gatt and Krahmer, 2018; Reiter et al., 2005; Stede, 1994; Polguère, 2000; Wanner, 1996) and systems that perform summarisation and machine translation. Many Chinese words can be expressed by either a short form or a long form. These words are known as *elastic* words (Guo, 1938; Duanmu, 2013; Qin and Duanmu, 2017). For instance, one Chinese sentence in Table 1[1] contains three elastic words, 学习/学*(xue-xi/xue, to study)*, 养殖/养*(yang-zhi/yang, to cultivate)*, and 蜜蜂/蜂*(mi-feng/feng, bee)*. Such long and short form pairs are interchangeable in some contexts with little difference in meaning. Choosing between a long and a short form of the same word is an important problem for any NLG system that produces Chinese text.

Various theories have sought to address the issue of elastic words. Speech rate theory (Guo,

---

[1]This sentence contains 3 elastic words, which has 8 varied-length sentences. * indicates degraded sentences.

他	想	学习	养殖	蜜蜂。
ta	*xiang*	*xue-xi*	*yang-zhi*	*mi-feng*
He	*want*	*learn*	*cultivate*	*bee.*
他	想	学习	养	蜜蜂。
他	想	学习	养	蜂。
他	想	学	养	蜂。
他	想	学	养	蜜蜂。
他	想	学	养殖	蜜蜂。
*他	想	学	养殖	蜂。
*他	想	学习	养殖	蜂。

He wants to lean how to cultivate bee.

Table 1: Example of an ordinary sentence with elastic words.

1938) proposed that speakers control their speech rate by alternating between long and short forms. And processing need theory (Pan, 1997) suggests (without offering computational detail) that the choice between long and short forms can help to decrease information density, thus aiding listeners' understanding.

In this paper, we adopt a similar perspective, informed by work in information theory (Shannon, 1948). The information content of a word depends on its context, that is, a word conveys more information content in unpredictable contexts than in predictive ones. More specifically, we follow the study design of Mahowald et al. (2013), who test the hypothesis that short forms should convey less information than their longer counterparts, given that language is designed to be information-theoretically optimal.

2 Related work

Our work in Chinese builds on previous studies on other languages (Mahowald et al., 2013; Piantadosi et al., 2011; Willems et al., 2015; Seyfarth, 2014; Jaeger and Buz, 2017; Lewis and Frank, 2016). Piantadosi et al. (2011) investigated

Proceedings of The 12th International Conference on Natural Language Generation, pages 34–39,
Tokyo, Japan, 28 Oct - 1 Nov, 2019. ©2019 Association for Computational Linguistics

the correlation between word length and information content across 11 languages (not including Chinese) and suggested that information content (specifically, surprisal) is a good predictor of word length.

Mahowald et al. (2013) hypothesised that *when an English word w has a long and a short form, then the choice between the two is affected by the extent to which the occurrence of w is "predictable": in contexts where w has high probability, the short form is more preferred than in contexts where w has low probability*. They used two approaches to testing this idea: a corpus study and a behavioural one. Both these studies made use of word pairs w_1, w_2 , where w_1 and w_2 have nearly identical meanings but different length; for instance, *math/mathematics*, *chimp/chimpanzee*, *dorm/dormitory*, etc.

Corpus Study *Surprisal* (Shannon, 1948) quantifies the information content conveyed by a word in a given context. Surprisal values of 22 word pairs were obtained from Google N-gram corpus of English (Mahowald et al., 2013). The mean surprisal for long forms was significantly higher than short forms, confirming the authors' expectations. For all 22 word pairs, the long forms of 18 word pairs showed higher surprisal than short forms.

Behavioural Study Mahowald et al. (2013)'s behavioural study asked participants to complete a sentence whose final word w was missing. Participants were offered a choice between the long and short form of w. Half the context sentences described a situation that made w highly probable (*supportive contexts*), the other half made w not very probable (*neutral contexts*).

A validation experiment ensured that suitable contexts had been chosen as supportive and neural contexts: Participants were asked to complete a sentence by filling in one word. The validation experiment showed that in supportive contexts, the target word (i.e., either its long or its short form) was chosen 33 times as often as in neutral contexts, suggesting that suitable contexts had been chosen.

For their main behavioural study, the authors hypothesised that in supportive contexts, a larger proportion of short forms is chosen than in neutral contexts. This hypothesis was confirmed, with short forms being 11% more frequent in supportive than in neutral contexts.

We decided to replicate the two studies by (Mahowald et al., 2013) as precisely as possible, but focusing on Chinese instead, to see how the choice between long and short word forms might differ across the two languages.

3 Experiments and results

We planed to find out whether the findings of Mahowald et al. (2013) in English can be replicated for Chinese. Our main goal was to test whether predictiveness of context affects the form choice for elastic words. We focus on *nominal* elastic words because these are particularly plentiful, and particularly varied in terms of their form (Duanmu, 2013). As our elastic words, we used the list of elastic words in the appendix of Dong (2015), focusing on those cases in which (1) the part-of-speech is Noun, and (2) the short form is a free morpheme (i.e., a morpheme that can occur as a complete word).

3.1 Corpus study

In the corpus study, the predictiveness of a context was assessed as a continuous measure using surprisal. The surprisal of w is high if it's very unpredictable in a given context. For instance, consider
我的包坏了，我要去买新包。
wo-de-bao-huai-le, wo-yao-qu-mai-xin-bao.
My bag is torn out, I want to buy a new bag.
The last word 包 *(bao, bag)* is highly predictable, so its surprisal would be very small in this context.

We made use of the simplified Chinese corpora of Google Ngram corpus[2]. And we focused on the 442 word pairs from Dong (2015) that meet the criteria above. First, we trained a trigram language model on Google Ngram corpus. Then for each word occurrence, we calculated the surprisal using a trigram language model to estimate word occurrence probability. Surprisal of the occurrence of w is defined as

$$-\frac{1}{N}\sum_{i=1}^{n} \log P(W = w | C = c_i),$$

where N is the total frequency of word w and c_i indicates the ith occurrence context of word w in the corpus. We tested whether short forms tend to have lower mean surprisal than the corresponding long forms using Student's t-test.

---

[2] https://books.google.com/ngrams

3.2 Behavioural study

In the behavioral study, context predictiveness was a binary variable. For each word, two contexts, supportive and neutral, were presented to experimental participants. In our work, a context is *supportive* if it makes the target word has a very high probability of occurrence; a context is *neutral* if docs not.

Following Mahowald et al. (2013), we recruited two disjoint groups of native speakers of Chinese. Each group contained 52 undergraduates at Qinghai Normal University. One group of speakers was given the main behavioural study and the second group was presented with a validation experiment (described below).

Main experiment As target (elastic) words, we chose 42 word pairs from Dong (2015)'s list. To avoid complications that could be caused by abstract nouns, we ensured that all target words describe physical objects.[3] We constructed supportive and neutral contexts for each of these words. Like Mahowald et al. (2013) before us, we ensured that the length of the supportive context and neutral context was always approximately the same. A comprehension question followed each item. For instance, a (supportive) context sentence might be

大蒜素能抗癌，所以我妈做菜时会放很多....

da-suan-neng-kang-ai,suo-yi-wo-ma-zuo-cai-shi-hui-fang-hen-duo...

Garlic allicin is helpful for anti-cancer, so my mom cooks dishes with ...

where participants could fill in the dots by choosing between 大蒜*(da-suan, garlic)* and 蒜*(suan, garlic)*.

This was followed by a question saying
大蒜素是不是能抗癌？

da-suan-su-shi-bu-shi-neng-kang-ai?

Is Garlic allicin helpful for anti-cancer?

The follow up questions were included to make sure the participants had read and understood the sentences.

Validation experiment In our work, we performed a validation experiment analogous to that of Mahowald et al. (2013). Its goal was to ensure that the target word is more likely in the context we had constructed as supportive. Indeed, in supportive contexts, the target word was chosen 38 times as often as in neutral contexts; this figure is

quite similar to Mahowald et al. (2013) and shows that our choice of supportive and neutral sentence contexts was appropriate.

3.3 Results

The results of the two studies confirm our initial hypothesis. In the corpus study, we found that the mean surprisal for long forms (11.78) was higher than that for short forms (10.87). In 324 (73.30%) of the 442 cases, long forms showed significant higher mean surprisal than its short counterpart. The difference between mean surprisal of short and long forms is statistically significant (t=11.66, p<0.01 by paired-sample *t*-test), confirming our hypothesis.

In the behavioural study, we found that the short form was more often chosen in supportive context (51.73%) than in neutral context (48.27%); the difference is significant under a paired-samples *t*-test (t = 3.04, p < 0.05).

Our two studies about Chinese suggest that the probability of occurrence of a word (more precisely: of a word pair) in a given context, as defined in two very different types of study, affects the choice between the long and the short version of the word, in accordance with our hypotheses. On the other hand, this effect was not as strong as it had been in the work of Mahowald et al. (2013).

4 Distinguishing between types of words

We analysed our data by distinguishing between different types of elastic words. We classified elastic words into seven categories, according to the relation between two morphemes in the long form. The following notation for different types of morphemes is used in characterising types of elastic words. Before explaining what these categories are, we define a few linguistic terms.

Affixes are bound and functional morphemes (Liao, 2014), denoted by 0 in what follows; they are members of a closed set (Wang et al., 2015), for instance, 老 in 老虎*(lao-hu, tiger)*, 头 in 骨头*(gu-tou, bone)*, etc. **Pseudo-affixes** are very similar to affixes, but they are not a member of the closed set; they are free morphemes that can be used separately (i.e., as a separate word) but also as part of a multi-syllabic word, in which case they lose their original meaning. Pseudo-affixes will be denoted by $0'$. For example, 蜂蜜*(feng-mi, honey)* starts with the pseudo-affix 蜂*(feng, bee)*, followed by the short form 蜜*(mi, honey)* (Note

---

[3] All 7 categories of elastic words discussed in section 4 were represented by 6 long-short word pairs.

that 蜂*(bee)* can also be used separately, which means 'bee'. A **free morpheme** can occur as an independent word and can also combine with other morphemes to form a new word. Free morphemes will be denoted by the symbols X, X', and Y such as 树*(shu, tree) and* 井*(jing, well).* The word 谎话*(huang-hua, lie),* by contrast, starts with the word 谎*(lie),* followed by the pseudo-affix 话*(hua, talk)* (Note that 话*(talk)* can be used separately.)

Using the terminology above, Duanmu (2015) distinguished the following categories:[4] (1) $X\text{-}0X$, (2) $X\text{-}0'X$, (3) $X\text{-}X0$, (4) $X\text{-}X0'$, (5) $X\text{-}XX$, (6) $X\text{-}X'X/XX'$. We add another category, namely (7) $X\text{-}YX/XY$, where the long form adds a free morpheme Y that has a different meaning from X. Most of the long and short form pairs of category (7) have hyponymy relations such as 手表/表 *(shou-biao/biao, watch)* and 台灯/灯 (tai-deng/deng, lamp). Moreover, they have identical meaning in some contexts, thus are interchangeable in these contexts. We take this category into consideration because $X\text{-}YX/XY$ is in generally consistent with the definition of elastic words and is very common in Chinese.

Post-hoc analysis of our corpus study Fig.1 shows average surprisal of long and short word forms investigated in our corpus study grouped by category. One category $X\text{-}XX$ showed a reverse trend with our hypothesis. If the category $X\text{-}XX$ is ignored, then in the words of remaining 6 categories together, the surprisal for long forms (11.83) is much higher than that for short forms (10.51). In 322 (74.02%) of the 435 cases, long forms showed higher mean surprisal than its short counterpart (t=11.78, p<0.01).

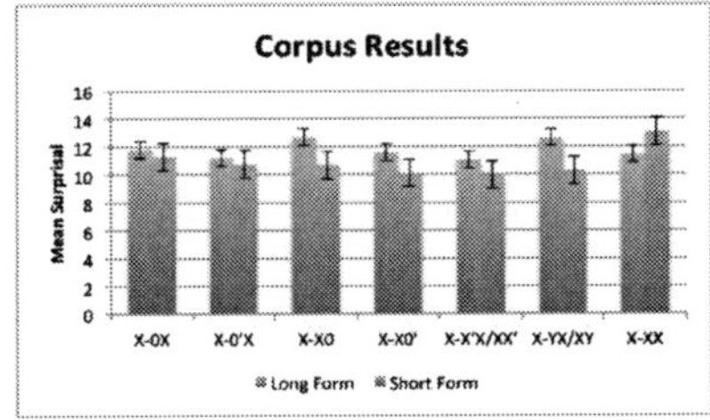

Figure 1: The y-axis is the mean surprisal of the long and short form. The x-axis shows the 7 categories of long and short forms. The blue bar indicates the long form, and the red bar is the short form.

Post-hoc analysis of our behavioural study

<hr>

[4]Dashes denote separation between long and short forms; slashes denote alternatives.

Fig.2 shows that the frequency of short forms in supportive and neutral contexts. Using the classification above, 5 of 7 categories indicated results that are consistent with our prediction. For the categories $X\text{-}0X$ and $X\text{-}XX$ we found the reverse, suggesting that the short form is *more* probable in a neutral context than in a supportive context.

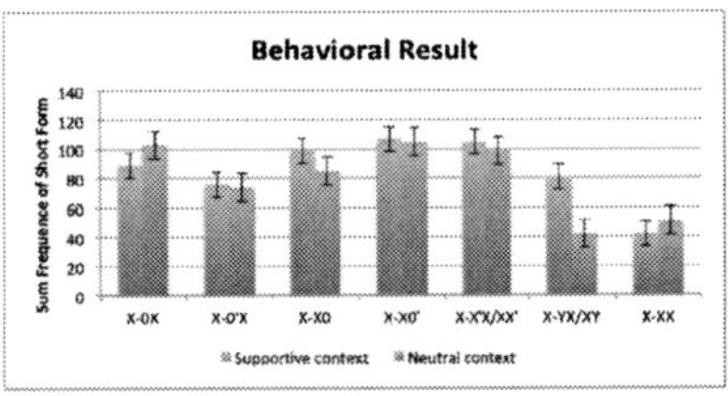

Figure 2: The y-axis indicates the frequency of the short form being chosen by speakers in supportive vs. neutral contexts. The x-axis shows the category of elastic word.

This post-hoc analysis suggests that a revised definition of elastic words in Chinese might be considered. In particular, it might be better not to adopt the same strategy to choose the long and short form of category $X\text{-}XX$. Not only because the words in this category show contrary results with all other categories in both studies, but they arguably play a different role in the language: whereas the long forms of elastic words in the other categories may be seen as adding more information in an extra morpheme (thus aiding the hearer's understanding), words in the $X\text{-}XX$ category merely reduplicate the same morpheme.

5 Discussion

Lexical choice – in automatic summarisation and machine translation as well as NLG – is not just mapping concept into words, because the choice of words depends on linguistic context. We investigated the correlation between the degree to which a concept (or word pair) is predictable, on the one hand, and the length of the word on the other. We hypothesized that speakers use short forms more often in supportive contexts than in neutral contexts. The results of our two studies were consistent with this hypothesis. And the result confirmed the idea that the information-theoretic factors (i.e., factors related to the probability of expressing a given concept (or word pair)) that influence the choice between long and short forms of elastic words in Chinese.

We investigated the occurrence probability of long and short form in supportive and neutral contexts by means of Deep Neural Network language model[5]. The result shows that the probability of short form in supportive contexts (2.96%) is much higher than in neutral contexts(0.11%), which is consistent with our prediction (t=3.15, $p < 0.05$) again.

Our findings are broadly consistent with the view that the choice between long and short form of the same word in Chinese works the same way as the analogous choice in English. However, our post-hoc analysis suggests that this simple picture is complicated by differences between types of elastic words. In particular, the reduplicative X-XX category showed a trend that is opposite to what is seen in the other categories, with the longer version of the word *more* (not less) frequent than the shorter version in supportive contexts. Most reduplicative nouns are appellations that are used among family relatives, such as 妈妈/妈 (ma-ma/ma, mother) and 叔叔/叔(shu-shu/shu, uncle). This suggests that surprisal is not the only factor that influences the choice on which our study has focused.

Our research has obvious applications for lexicalization in Chinese NLG: Following findings in this work, a NLG system might implement the choice of word length based on its surprisal. However, this cannot be a universal strategy applied to the whole vocabulary without exception. At least the words of the X-XX category should have a different generation strategy. Furthermore, while we establish surprisal as a significant predictor of word form choice in Chinese, it might also be influenced by other factors, including, for instance, ambiguity avoidance (Khan et al., 2012), prosody (Duanmu et al., 2018; Duanmu, 2013), and style (Feng, 2016). We leave the investigation of these factors and their interaction to further study.

Acknowledgements

The first author of this paper received support from Qinghai Natural Science Foundation under Grant 2016-ZJ-931Q, Qinghai Major R&D Transformation Foundation under Grant 2019-GX-162, and National Natural Foundation under Grant 61862055, which is gratefully acknowledged.

---

[5]https://developer.baidu.com/platform/s91

References

Yan Dong. 2015. *The prosody and morphology of elastic words in Chinese: annotations and analyses.* Ph.D. thesis, University of Michigan.

San Duanmu. 2013. How many chinese words have elastic length. *Eastward flows the Great river: Festschrift in honor of Prof. William S.-Y. Wang on his 80th birthday*, pages 1–14.

San Duanmu. 2015. A study of elastic word length of monomorphemic nouns in chinese:'monosyllabic-only'nouns in the lexicon and in actual use.

San Duanmu, Shengli Feng, Yan Dong, and Yingyue Zhang. 2018. A judgment study of length patterns in chinese: Prosody, last resort, and other factors. *Journal of Chinese Linguistics*, 46(1):42–68.

Shengli Feng. 2016. Modern chinese: Written chinese. *The Routledge Encyclopedia of the Chinese Language*, pages 645–663.

Albert Gatt and Emiel Krahmer. 2018. Survey of the state of the art in natural language generation: Core tasks, applications and evaluation. *Journal of Artificial Intelligence Research*, 61:65–170.

Shaoyu Guo. 1938. 中国语词之弹性作用(the function of elastic word length in chinese). *Yen Ching Hsueh Pao*, 24:1–34.

T Florian Jaeger and Esteban Buz. 2017. Signal reduction and linguistic encoding. *Handbook of psycholinguistics*, pages 38–81.

Imtiaz H Khan, Kees van Deemter, and Graeme Ritchie. 2012. Managing ambiguity in reference generation: the role of surface structure. *Topics in Cognitive science*, 4(2):211–231.

Molly L Lewis and Michael C Frank. 2016. The length of words reflects their conceptual complexity. *Cognition*, 153:182–195.

Wei-Wen Roger Liao. 2014. *Morphology*, chapter 1. John Wiley Sons, Ltd.

Kyle Mahowald, Evelina Fedorenko, Steven T Piantadosi, and Edward Gibson. 2013. Info/information theory: Speakers choose shorter words in predictive contexts. *Cognition*, 126(2):313–318.

Guowe Pan. 1997. 汉英语对比纲要(an outline comparison of chinese and english).

Steven T Piantadosi, Harry Tily, and Edward Gibson. 2011. Word lengths are optimized for efficient communication. *Proceedings of the National Academy of Sciences*, 108(9):3526–3529.

Alain Polguère. 2000. A "natural" lexicalization model for language generation. In *Proceedings of the Fourth Symposium on Natural Language Processing (SNLP2000). Chiangmai, Thailand*, pages 37–50. Citeseer.

Zuxuan Qin and San Duanmu. 2017. A judgment study of word-length preferences in chinese nn compounds. *Lingua*, 198:1–21.

Ehud Reiter, Somayajulu Sripada, Jim Hunter, Jin Yu, and Ian Davy. 2005. Choosing words in computer-generated weather forecasts. *Artificial Intelligence*, 167(1-2):137–169.

Scott Seyfarth. 2014. Word informativity influences acoustic duration: Effects of contextual predictability on lexical representation. *Cognition*, 133(1):140–155.

Claude Elwood Shannon. 1948. A mathematical theory of communication. *Bell system technical journal*, 27(3):379–423.

Manfred Stede. 1994. Lexicalization in natural language generation: A survey. *Artificial Intelligence Review*, 8(4):309–336.

William S-Y. Wang, Chaofen Sun, and Jerome L. Packard. 2015. Morphology morphemes in chinese.

Leo Wanner. 1996. Lexical choice in text generation and machine translation. *Machine Translation*, 11(1-3):3–35.

Roel M Willems, Stefan L Frank, Annabel D Nijhof, Peter Hagoort, and Antal Van den Bosch. 2015. Prediction during natural language comprehension. *Cerebral Cortex*, 26(6):2506–2516.

Diamonds in the Rough: Generating Fluent Sentences from Early-Stage Drafts for Academic Writing Assistance

Takumi Ito[*,1,2] , **Tatsuki Kuribayashi**[*,1,2], **Hayato Kobayashi**[3,4],
Ana Brassard[4,1], **Masato Hagiwara**[5], **Jun Suzuki**[1,4], **and Kentaro Inui**[1,4]

[1]Tohoku University [2]Langsmith Inc. [3]Yahoo Japan Corporation [4]RIKEN [5]Octanove Labs LLC

{t-ito, kuribayashi, jun.suzuki, inui}@ecei.tohoku.ac.jp
hakobaya@yahoo-corp.jp, ana.brassard@riken.jp
masato@octanove.com

Abstract

The writing process consists of several stages such as drafting, revising, editing, and proof-reading. Studies on writing assistance, such as grammatical error correction (GEC), have mainly focused on sentence *editing* and *proofreading*, where surface-level issues such as typographical, spelling, or grammatical errors should be corrected. We broaden this focus to include the earlier *revising* stage, where sentences require adjustment to the information included or major rewriting and propose *Sentence-level Revision (SentRev)* as a new writing assistance task. Well-performing systems in this task can help inexperienced authors by producing fluent, complete sentences given their rough, incomplete drafts. We build a new freely available crowdsourced evaluation dataset consisting of incomplete sentences authored by non-native writers paired with their final versions extracted from published academic papers for developing and evaluating SentRev models. We also establish baseline performance on SentRev using our newly built evaluation dataset.

1 Introduction

Academic writing can be a daunting task, even for experienced writers with a native or near-native command of English. Inexperienced, non-native speakers find themselves in an even more difficult situation—in addition to grammatical or spelling errors, their sentences may lack fluidity, have an awkward style, contain collocation errors, or have missing words where they could not remember or did not know the appropriate expressions. Such authors, especially students with insufficient academic experience, may often have difficulty putting their ideas and findings into words, even if the ideas are sound and contribute to the research community. Improving writing quality is

---

* The authors contributed equally

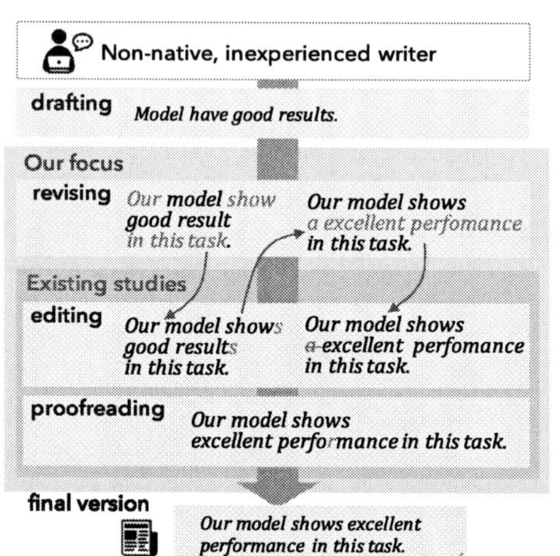

Figure 1: Overview of the estimated process of writing a sentence *Our model shows excellent performance in this task.*. Writing activity consists of four stages: (i) drafting, (ii) revising, (iii) editing, and (iv) proofreading.

thus a concern for both individual researchers and the academic community.

Writing assistance technologies have been extensively studied in the natural language processing (NLP) field (Brill and Moore, 2000; Ng et al., 2014; Grangier and Auli, 2018). We focus on helping inexperienced authors in writing fluent grammatical sentences.

Models developed for academic writing assistance using existing datasets can serve as a support system during the final stages by editing a nearly finished version of the draft. For example, Daudaravicius (2015) collects scientific papers before and after professional editing from publishing companies, and Dale and Kilgarriff (2011) extract already published papers that still contain errors and correct the errors to obtain target fragments of text.

Proceedings of The 12th International Conference on Natural Language Generation, pages 40–53,
Tokyo, Japan, 28 Oct - 1 Nov, 2019. ©2019 Association for Computational Linguistics

Process-writing pedagogy, however, asserts that writing comprises several processes (Susser, 1994; Seow, 2002; Buchman et al., 2000) as shown in Figure 1. This study takes on the challenge of automatic assistance in both the final checking process (*proofreading* and *editing*) and the earlier stages of writing (*revising*). In the revising stage, authors may drastically modify the wording and supplement some words, a highly demanding task for non-native or less experienced writers. Assistance in this stage has been less explored in NLP.

In this study, we design a new type of academic writing assistance task, Sentence-level Revision (SentRev), where a system receives an early draft of a sentence, and generates a revised, error-free, proofread version.

A critical issue in tackling this type of assistance task is that evaluation resources are scarce since early-stage draft sentences are not usually publicly available. To overcome this limitation, we release an evaluation dataset of pairs of draft sentences and their final versions, the *Set of Modified Incomplete TecHnical paper sentences* (SMITH), that we created using crowdsourcing techniques. Additionally, we evaluate the quality of our dataset and extensively analyze the characteristics of the obtained drafts. Finally, we train unsupervised models and report the baseline performance for our task on the SMITH evaluation dataset.

Our contribution is fourfold:

- We propose a new task—SentRev.
- We create an evaluation dataset, SMITH, for SentRev using a new crowdsourcing approach and release it.[1]
- We compare the characteristics of our dataset with major corpora and analyze the obtained draft sentences.
- We establish baseline scores for SentRev.

2   The Sentence-level Revision task

The proposed task, SentRev, is revising and editing incomplete draft sentences to create final versions. Examples of sentence-level revision are shown in Table 1.

A draft sentence, x, may have several types of problems. Surface-level problems such as typographical errors, spelling errors, or grammatical

---

[1] https://github.com/taku-ito/INLG2019_SentRev

Draft	*However, the F1 score of KBP 2017 coupus <*> decreased by the sub event base rule.*
Reference	*However, subevent based constraints slightly reduced the F1 scores on KBP 2017 corpus.*
Draft	*But, there are some important difference to <*> our work unique.*
Reference	*However, there exist several key differences that make our work unique.*

Table 1: Examples of sentence-level revisions in our SMITH dataset. Our task is to transform the draft sentences into their corresponding reference sentences.

errors are a common occurrence. Wording problems, such as collocation errors or expressions being stylistically odd or inappropriate for the academic domain, are also typical of rough sentences written by non-native, inexperienced writers. The third type of error is *information gaps*. Information gaps are cases where the author likely could not find the appropriate wording for the idea he or she wanted to convey, such as a specific expression common in the academic domain or a technical term. In addition, a draft sentence may be missing sections without the author being aware of this. Solving the aforementioned problems in a draft sentence would elevate the draft sentence x to its final or nearly final version y with greatly improved correctness and fluency. Ideally, a single error-free and correctly filled-in final version should be generated while considering the context of the sentence. However, as a first step, an assistance system may output a set of *likely candidates* for the user to choose from or be inspired by, which would be realistic for a real-world application.

Our proposed task is, therefore, to generate likely final versions y from early-draft sentences x. For this purpose, we provide an evaluation dataset, SMITH, comprising pairs of drafts and their final versions (X, Y).

3   The SMITH dataset

3.1   Dataset creation

Process overview   Although we cannot collect "drafts" X from published papers, we can easily collect the "final versions" Y. We also have access to non-native, inexperienced writers through crowdsourcing services. Our test set creation process combines these two factors (Figure 2). The

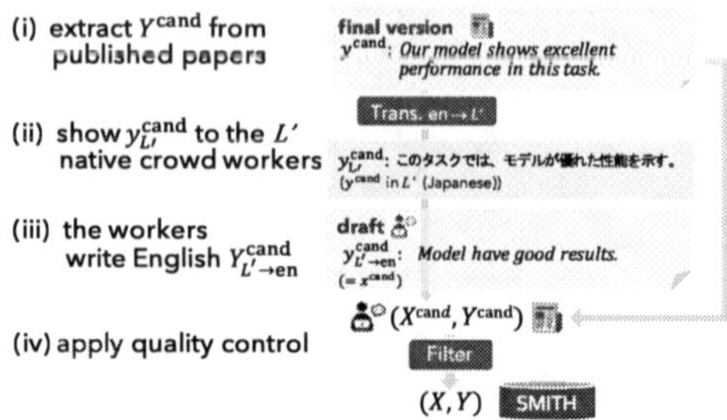

Figure 2: Overview of the crowdsourcing protocol for creating an evaluation dataset for the SentRev task.

protocol consists of the following four phases:

(i) Collecting a large number of sentences written by experts Y^{cand} from published papers.

(ii) Translating them into another language L', resulting in sentences $Y_{L'}^{\text{cand}}$.

(iii) Asking native speakers of L' to translate $Y_{L'}^{\text{cand}}$ back into English $Y_{L'\to\text{en}}^{\text{cand}}$ through crowdsourcing. Henceforth, we denote $Y_{L'\to\text{en}}^{\text{cand}}$ as X^{cand}.

(iv) Filtering the pairs of (X^{cand}, Y^{cand}) to ensure the quality of the dataset (X, Y).

This setting is analogous to the situation non-native writers face, as Cohen and Brooks-Carson (2001) report that non-native speakers tend to formulate in their native language and mentally translate to the target second language. We assume that most crowdworkers have never written an academic paper, and that the target users of SentRev-based systems also include this type of inexperienced writers.

To control the quality of the drafts, we first create many candidate pairs of drafts and reference sentences (X^{cand}, Y^{cand}) and then filter them to create the quality-controlled set (X, Y). The following subsections detail this process.

Collecting final version sentences We collected sentences Y^{cand} from the ACL Anthology Sentence Corpus (AASC).[2] We extracted the sentences that satisfied the following conditions from the AASC as Y^{cand}:

- accepted to ACL 2018,
- 70 to 120 characters long,
- does not include mathematical symbols, special tokens for citations, URLs, Greek letters, or other special symbols defined in AASC, and

---

[2]https://github.com/KMCS-NII/AASC

- free of clear conversion mistakes when automatically extracted from PDFs.

Creating draft sentences We used Japanese as L'. First, we translated Y^{cand} into Japanese using Google Translate.[3] We denote the Japanese versions of Y^{cand} by $Y_{\text{ja}}^{\text{cand}}$. To guarantee the quality of $Y_{\text{ja}}^{\text{cand}}$, two authors of this paper, who were native speakers of Japanese, inspected all the sentences from $Y_{\text{ja}}^{\text{cand}}$ and removed those that at least one speaker judged to be incorrect translations.

Next, we asked each Japanese crowdworker to translate three sentences from $Y_{\text{ja}}^{\text{cand}}$ into English $Y_{\text{ja}\to\text{en}}^{\text{cand}}$ within 15 minutes. The appropriate time limit and rules were determined based on several trial tasks.

The workers were allowed to insert the special symbol <*> in places where they could not think of a good expression for that position in their answer $Y_{\text{ja}\to\text{en}}^{\text{cand}}$. This instruction revealed the information gaps that the authors of the drafts consciously left empty. An author may also be unaware that a draft sentence is missing sections. 306 workers participated in our crowdsourcing task.

Quality control We designed thorough filtering criteria and applied them to the workers because Yahoo! crowdsourcing,[4] a Japanese crowdsourcing service, does not provide filtering based on the worker's writing skills or abilities. We filtered workers depending on their writing activities. We scored each worker using the three answers they produced by using the criteria detailed in Table 2. We accepted work from workers with score 0 or higher as valid. The hyperparameters were determined with trial experiments. We used spaCy-CLD[5] for language detection.

In addition, to remove instances with a too large gap, we automatically filtered out the obtained (x^{cand}, y^{cand}) $\in$ ($X^{\text{cand}}, Y^{\text{cand}}$) whose unigram overlap coefficient was considerably low:

$$\frac{|U(x_{\text{checked}}^{\text{cand}}) \cap U(y^{\text{cand}})|}{\min\{|U(x_{\text{checked}}^{\text{cand}})|, |U(y^{\text{cand}})|\}} < \alpha \, ,$$

where $U(\cdot)$ is the set of tokens excluding stopwords and special tokens (<*>). $x_{\text{checked}}^{\text{cand}}$ is the

---

[3]https://translate.google.com/
[4]https://crowdsourcing.yahoo.co.jp/
[5]https://github.com/nickdavidhaynes/spacy-cld

Criteria	Judgment
Working time is too short ($<$ 2 minutes)	Reject
All answers are too short ($<$ 4 words)	Reject
No answer ends with "." or "?"	Reject
Contain identical answers	Reject
Some answers have Japanese words	Reject
No answer is recognized as English	Reject
Some answers are too short ($<$ 4 words)	-2 points
Some answers use fewer than 4 kinds of words	-2 points
Too close to automatic translation (20 $<=$ L.D. $<=$ 30)	-0.5 points/ans
Too close to automatic translation (10 $<=$ L.D. $<=$ 20)	-1.5 points/ans
Too close to automatic translation (L.D. $<=$ 10)	Reject
All answers end with "." or "?"	+1 points
Some answers have <*>	+1 points
All answers are recognized as English	+1 points

Table 2: Criteria for evaluating workers. L.D denotes the Levenshtein distance.

spell-checked version[6] of x^{cand}. α is set to 0.4, which was determined in trial experiments.

We collected 10,804 pairs of draft and their final versions, which cost us approximately US\$4,200, including the trial rounds of crowdsourcing.

Unfortunately, works produced by unmotivated workers could have evaded the aforementioned filters and lowered the quality of our dataset. For example, workers could have bypassed the filter by simply repeating popular phrases in academic writing ("We apply we apply"). To estimate the frequency of such examples, we sampled 100 (x, y) pairs from (X, Y) and asked an NLP researcher (not an author of this paper) fluent in Japanese and English to check for examples where x was totally irrelevant to x_{ja}, which was shown to the crowdworkers when creating x. The expert observed no completely inappropriate examples, but noted a small number of clearly subpar translations. Therefore, 95% of sentence pairs were determined to be appropriate. This result shows that, overall, our method was suitable to create the dataset and confirms the quality of SMITH.

3.2 Statistics

Table 3 shows the statistics of our SMITH dataset and a comparison with major datasets for building a writing assistance system (Napoles et al., 2017; Mizumoto et al., 2011; Daudaravicius, 2015). The size of our dataset (10k sentence pairs) is six times greater than that of JFLEG, which contains both

---

⁶We corrected spelling errors using `https://github.com/barrust/pyspellchecker`

Dataset	size	w/mask	w/change	L.D.
Lang-8	2.1M	-	42%	3.5
AESW	1.2M	-	39%	4.8
JFLEG	1.5k	-	86%	12.4
SMITH	10k	33%	99%	47.0

Table 3: Comparison with existing datasets. w/mask and w/change denote the percentage of source sentences with mask tokens and the percentage where the source and target sentences differ, respectively. L.D. indicates the averaged character-level Levenshtein distance between the pairs of sentences.

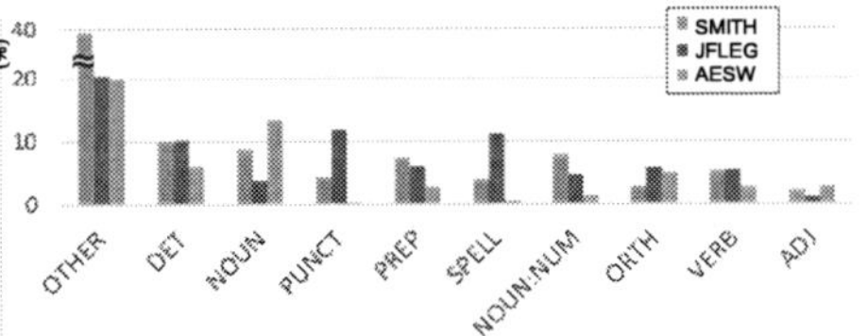

Figure 3: Comparison of the top 10 frequent errors observed in the 3 datasets.

grammatical errors and nonfluent wording. In addition, our dataset simulates significant editing— 99% of the pairs have some changes between the draft and its corresponding reference, and 33% of the draft sentences contain gaps indicated by the special token <*>. We also measured the amount of change from the drafts X to the references Y by using the Levenshtein distance between them. A higher Levenshtein distance between the X and Y sentences in our dataset indicated more significant differences between them compared with major GEC corpora. This finding implies that our dataset emulates more drastic rephrasing.

4 Analysis of the SMITH dataset

In this section, we run extensive analyses on the sentences written by non-native workers (*draft* sentences X), and the original sentences extracted from the set of accepted papers (*reference* sentences Y). We randomly selected a set of 500 pairs from SMITH as the development set for analysis.

4.1 Error type comparison

To obtain the approximate distributions of error types between the source and target sentences, we used ERRANT (Bryant et al., 2017; Felice et al., 2016). Next, we compared them with three datasets: SMITH, AESW (the same domain as SMITH), and JFLEG (has a relatively close Levenshtein distance to SMITH). To calculate the er-

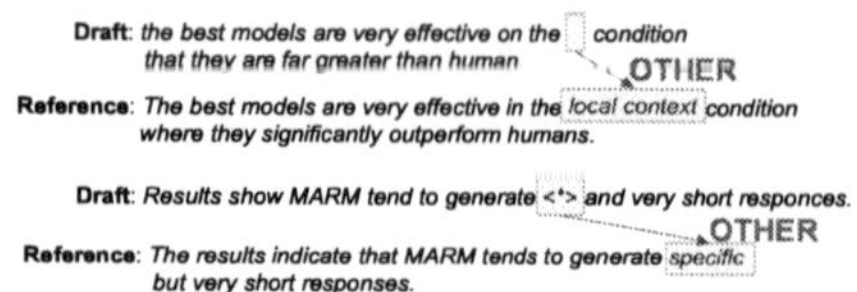

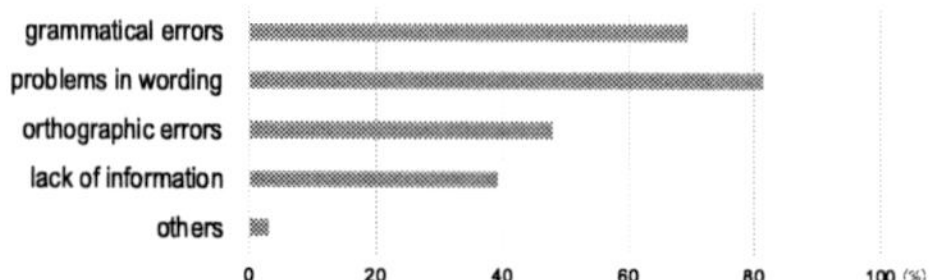

Figure 4: Examples of "OTHER" operations predicted by the ERRANT toolkit.

grammatical errors	
problems in wording	
orthographic errors	
lack of information	
others	

Figure 5: Result of the English experts' analyses of error types in draft sentences on our SMITH dataset. The scores show the ratio of sentences where the targeted type of errors occurred.

ror type distributions on AESW and JFLEG, we randomly sampled 500 pairs of source and target sentences from each corpus. Figure 3 shows the results of the comparison. Although all datasets contained a mix of error types and operations, the SMITH dataset included more "OTHER" operations than the other two datasets. Manual inspection of some samples of "OTHER" operations revealed that they tend to inject information missing in the draft sentence (Figure 4). This finding confirms that our dataset emphasizes a new, challenging "completion-type" task setting for writing assistance.

4.2 Human error type analysis

To understand the characteristics of our dataset in detail, an annotator proficient in English (not an author of this paper) analyzed the types of errors in the draft sentences (Figure 5). The most frequent errors were *fluency problems* (e.g., "In these *ways*" instead of "In these *methods*,")—characterized by errors in academic style and wording, which are out of the scope of traditional GEC. Another notable type of frequent error was *lack of information*, which further distinguishes this dataset from other datasets.

4.3 Human fluency analysis

We outsourced the scoring of the fluency of the given draft and reference sentence pairs to three annotators proficient in English. Nearly every draft x (94.8%) was marked as being less fluent than its corresponding reference y, confirming that

Data	FRE	passive voice (%)	word repetition (%)	PPL
Draft X	45.5	34.0	33.0	1373
Reference Y	40.0	29.6	28.6	147

Table 4: Comparison of the draft and reference sentences in SMITH. FRE and PPL scores were calculated once in each sentence and then averaged over all the sentences in the development set of SMITH.

obtaining high performance with our dataset requires the ability to transform rough input sentences into more fluent sentences.

4.4 Sentence-level linguistic characteristics

We computed some sentence-level linguistic measures over the dataset sentences: Flesch Reading Ease (FRE) (Flesch, 1948), passive voice[7], word repetition, and perplexity (PPL) (Table 4).

FRE measures the *readability* of a text, namely, how easy it is to understand (higher is easier). The draft sentences consistently demonstrated higher FRE scores than their reference counterparts, which may be attributed to the latter containing more sophisticated language and technical terms.

In addition, workers tended to use the passive voice and to repeat words within a narrow span, and both those phenomenon must be avoided in academic writing. We conducted further analyses on lexical tendencies between the drafts and references (Appendix A).

Finally, we analyzed the draft and the reference sentences using PPL calculated by a 5-gram language model trained on ACL Anthology papers.[8] The higher PPL scores in the draft sentences (Table 4) suggest that they have properties unsuitable for academic writing (e.g., less fluent wording).

5 Experiments

5.1 Baseline models

We evaluated three baseline models on the SentRev task.

5.1.1 Heuristic noising and denoising model

We can access a great deal of final version academic papers. Noising and denoising approaches

---

[7]https://github.com/armsp/active_or_passive

[8]PPL is calculated with the implementation available in the KenLM (https://github.com/kpu/kenlm), tuned on AASC (excluding the texts used for building the SMITH).

method	original	generated
Heuristic	Besides , the recognizer successfully rejected only 15 out of 42 negative sentences .	recognizer Besides successfully , the informativeness rejected of out < ⋆ >
Grammatical error generation	We plan to **analyze** these direct communications **and** interaction of sentiments **expressed** in these sequences of posts .	We plan to **analysis** the direct communication interaction of sentiments **express** in these sequence of posts .
Style removal	This experiment **suggested** that there were ambiguities in these pointing gestures and **led to a redesign** of the system .	This experiment **indicated** the ambiguity found in the pointing gestures and **caused a renewal** of the system .
Entailed sentence generation	Figure 2 **illustrates the effectiveness** of different features class.	There is different feature in figure 2 .

Table 5: Examples of generated training dataset.

have gained attention in the GEC and machine translation fields (Edunov et al., 2018; Xie et al., 2018; Lichtarge et al., 2019). We combined these two factors to train baseline models on noised final version sentences.

First, we collected 4,898,146 sentences Y^{aasc} from the AASC that satisfied the following conditions: (i) not included in the SMITH dataset, (ii) not too long or too short (between 5 and 35 tokens), (iii) over 50% of the characters were alphabetic. Next, we created a training dataset $(X^{\text{aasc}}_{\text{hrst}}, Y^{\text{aasc}})$ by adding noise to Y^{aasc}.

As the simplest approach for noising, we used a set of heuristic rules by randomly deleting, replacing, and swapping words in the reference sentences. Specifically, these rules included deleting words with a probability of 0.1, replacing words with a token that appeared over 10,000 times in Y_{aasc} with a probability of 0.1, and randomly shuffling the sentence while maintaining the originally adjacent words within three words apart. Next, we randomly replaced up to 50% of the words with a < ⋆ > token (see Appendix B for a more detailed algorithm). This method generated 4.8M heuristically noised sentences.

Subsequently, we trained a denoising model (a mapping function from $X^{\text{aasc}}_{\text{hrst}}$ to Y^{aasc}) by using Transformer (Vaswani et al., 2017) implemented in fairseq (Ott et al., 2019). We used an Adam optimizer (Kingma and Ba, 2015) with $\alpha = 0.0005$, $\beta_1 = 0.9$, $\beta_2 = 0.98$, and $\epsilon = 10e^{-8}$. We limited the maximum tokens per each minibatch to 3000, limited the maximum number of updates to 500,000, and used a dropout rate of 0.3. The input and output texts were tokenized and then segmented into character bigrams. We used a beam width of 5 in the decoding. This model is our first baseline model for the SentRev task (henceforth, H-ND).

5.1.2 Enc-Dec noising and denoising model

As an extension of the heuristic noising and denoising model, we changed the noising methods to better simulate the characteristics of X in SMITH than the heuristic rules in Section 5.1.1. As described in Section 4, the drafts tended to (i) contain grammatical errors, (ii) use stylistically improper wording, and (iii) lack certain words. We used the following three neural Encoder-Decoder (Enc-Dec) models to generate the synthetic draft sentences.

Grammatical error generation Here, we trained a model that introduces synthetic grammatical errors to "clean" sentences by using a "flipped" dataset from GEC (clean → erroneous). We used nonidentical (source, target) sentence pairs from the Lang-8, AESW, and JFLEG datasets.

Style removal To generate stylistically unnatural sentences in the academic domain, we used paraphrasing, which preserves a sentence's content while disregarding its style. We used the ParaNMT-50M dataset (Wieting and Gimpel, 2018), a paraphrase dataset automatically created using Enc-Dec translation. We extracted parallel sentences with annotated paraphrase scores between 0.7 and 0.95 from the ParaNMT-50M dataset and used swapped pairs of source and target sentences in the dataset.

Entailed sentence generation To simulate the missing words in the draft sentences, we trained a model that generated a sentence entailed with the given text. We extracted entailed sentence pairs

Model	BLEU	ROUGE-L	BERT-P	BERT-R	BERT-F	P	R	$F_{0.5}$	Gramm.	PPL
Draft X	9.8	46.8	75.9	78.2	77.0	-	-	-	92.9	1454
H-ND	8.2	45.0	77.0	76.1	76.5	5.4	2.9	4.6	94.1	406
ED-ND	**15.4**	**51.1**	**80.9**	**80.0**	**80.4**	21.8	**12.8**	**19.2**	96.3	236
GEC	11.9	49.0	80.8	79.1	79.9	**22.2**	6.2	14.6	**96.7**	414
Reference Y	-	-	-	-	-	-	-	-	96.5	147

Table 6: Results of quantitative evaluation. Gramm. denotes the grammaticality score.

Draft	The global modeling using the reinforcement learning in all documents is our work in the future .
H-ND	The global modeling **of** the reinforcement learning **using** all documents **in** our work **is** the future .
ED-ND	**In our future work , we plan to explore the use of** global modeling **for** reinforcement learning in all documents .
GEC	Global modelling using reinforcement learning in all documents is our work in the future .
Reference	The global modeling using reinforcement learning for a whole document is our future work .
Draft	Also , the above <*> efficiently calculated by dynamic programming .
H-ND	Also , the above **results are calculated** efficiently by dynamic programming .
ED-ND	Also , the above **probabilities are calculated** efficiently by dynamic programming .
GEC	Also , the above **is** efficiently calculated by dynamic programming .
Reference	Again , the above equation can be efficiently computed by dynamic programming .
Draft	Chart4 : relation model and gold % between KL and piason .
H-ND	**Table 1 : Charx-** relation between **gold and piason and KL** .
ED-ND	**Figure 2 : CharxDiff** relation between **model and gold standard and piason** .
GEC	Chart4 : relation model and gold % between KL and person .
Reference	Table 4 : KL and Pearson correlation between model and gold probability .

Table 7: Examples of the output from the baseline models. Bold text indicates tokens introduced by the model.

from the SNLI (Bowman et al., 2015) and the MultiNLI (Williams et al., 2018) datasets.

Random noising beam search As Xie et al. (2018) pointed out, a standard beam search often yields hypotheses that are too conservative. This tendency leads the noising models to generate synthetic draft sentences similar to their references. To address this problem, we applied the random noising beam search (Xie et al., 2018) on all three noising models. Specifically, during the beam search, we added $r\beta$ to the scores of the hypotheses, where r is a value sampled from a uniform distribution over the interval $[0, 1]$, and β is a penalty hyperparameter set to 5.

We obtained 14.6M sentence pairs of ($X^{\mathrm{aasc}}_{\mathrm{encdec}}$, Y^{aasc}) by applying these Enc-Dec noising models to Y^{aasc}. To train the denoising model, we used both data ($X^{\mathrm{aasc}}_{\mathrm{hrst}}$, Y^{aasc}) and ($X^{\mathrm{aasc}}_{\mathrm{encdec}}$, Y^{aasc}). The model architecture was the same as the heuristic model. This denoising model is our second baseline model (ED-ND). To facilitate research in the SentRev task, we released all the 19.6M synthetic data.[9]

Analysis of the synthetic drafts Finally, we analyzed the error type distribution of the synthetic data used for training Enc-Dec noising and denoising model with ERRANT (Figure 6). The error type distribution from the synthetic dataset had similar tendencies to the one from the development set in SMITH (real-draft). KullbackLeibler divergence between these error type distributions was 0.139. This result supports the validity of our assumption that the SentRev task is a combination of GEC, style transfer, and a completion-type task.

Table 5 shows examples of the training data generated by the noising models described in Section 5. Heuristic noising, the rule-based noising method, created ungrammatical sentences. The grammatical error generation model added grammatical errors (e.g., *plan to analyze* $\rightarrow$ *plan to analysis*). The style removal model generated stylistically unnatural sentences for the academic domain (e.g., *redesign* $\rightarrow$ *renewal*). The entailed

[9] https://github.com/taku-ito/INLG2019_SentRev

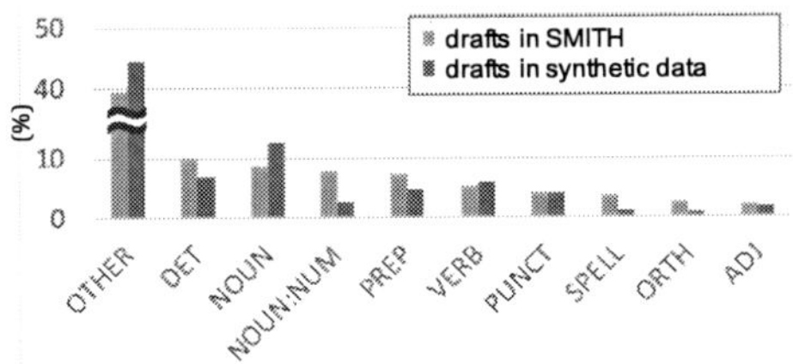

Figure 6: Comparison of the 10 most frequent error types in SMITH and synthetic drafts created by the Enc-Dec noising methods.

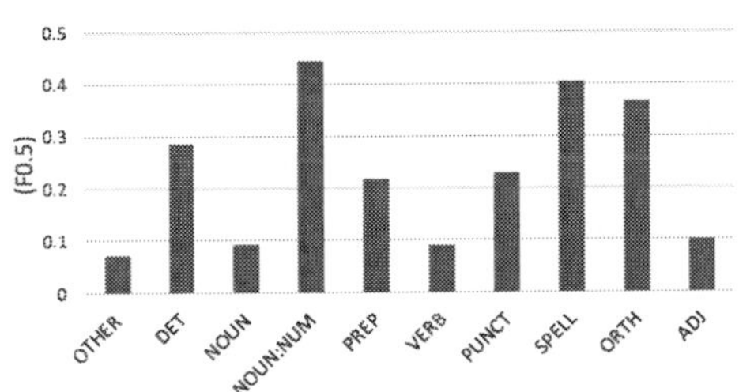

Figure 7: Performance of the ED-ND baseline model on top 10 most error types in SMITH.

sentence generation model caused a lack of information.

5.1.3 GEC model

The GEC task is closely related to SentRev. We examined the performance of the current state-of-the-art GEC model (Zhao et al., 2019) in our task. We applied spelling correction before evaluation following Zhao et al. (2019).

5.2 Evaluation metrics

The SentRev task has a very diverse space of valid revisions to a given context, which is challenging to evaluate. As one solution, we evaluated the performance from multiple aspects by using various reference and reference-less evaluation metrics. We used BLEU, ROUGE-L, and $F_{0.5}$ score, which are widely used metrics in related tasks (machine translation, style-transfer, GEC). We used nlg-eval (Sharma et al., 2017) to compute the BLEU and ROUGE-L scores and calculated $F_{0.5}$ scores with ERRANT. In addition, to handle the lexical and compositional diversity of valid revisions, we used BERT-score (Zhang et al., 2019), a contextualized embedding-based evaluation metric. Furthermore, we used two reference-less evaluation metrics: grammaticality score (Napoles et al., 2016) and PPL. Grammaticality was scored as

$1 - (N_{\text{errors in sentence}}/N_{\text{tokens in sentence}})$, where the number of grammatical errors in a sentence is obtained using LanguageTools.[10] By using a language model tuned to the academic domain, we expect PPL to evaluate the stylistic validity and fluency of a complemented sentence. We favored n-gram language models over neural language models for reproducibility and calculated the score in the same manner as described in Section 4.3.

6 Results

Table 6 shows the performance of the baseline models. We observed that the ED-ND model outperforms the other models in nearly all evaluation metrics. This finding suggests that the Enc-Dec noising methods induced noise closer to real-world drafts compared with the heuristic methods.

The current state-of-the-art GEC model showed higher precision but low recall scores in $F_{0.5}$. This suggests that the SentRev task requires the model to make a more drastic change in the drafts than in the GEC task. Furthermore, the GEC model, trained in the general domain, showed the worst performance in PPL. This indicates that the general GEC model did not reflect academic writing style upon revision and that SentRev requires academic domain-aware rewriting.

Table 7 shows examples of the models' output. In the first example, the ED-ND model made a drastic change to the draft. The middle example demonstrates that our models replaced the < * > token with plausible words. The last example is the case where our model underperformed by making erroneous edits such as changing *"Chart4"* to *"Figure2"*, and suggesting odd content (*"relation between model and gold standard and piason"*). This may be due to having inadvertently introduced noise while generating the training datasets. Appendix C shows more examples of generated sentences. Using ERRANT, we analyzed the performance of the ED-ND baseline model by error types. The results are shown in Figure 7. Overall, typical grammatical errors such as noun number errors or orthographic errors are well corrected, but the model struggles with drastic revisions ("OTHER" type errors).

---

[10]https://github.com/languagetool-org/languagetool/releases/tag/v3.2

7 Related work

7.1 Writing assistance in the academic domain

Several shared tasks for assisting academic writing have been organized. The Helping Our Own (HOO) 2011 Pilot Shared Task (Dale and Kilgarriff, 2011) aimed to promote the development of tools and techniques to assist authors in writing, with a specific focus on writing within the NLP community. The Automated Evaluation of Scientific Writing (AESW) Shared Task (Daudaravicius, 2015) was organized to promote tools to help write scientific papers. The HOO dataset was created by finding errors in published papers and editing the errors, and the AESW dataset contains a collection of text extracts from published journal articles before and after proofreading. Rather than adding finishing touches to almost completed sentences, our task is to convert unfinished, rough drafts into complete sentences. In addition, these studies tackled the task of the *identification* of errors while SentRev goes further by *rewriting* the drafts.

Other corpora for revisions are available in the academic domain (Lee and Webster, 2012; Tan and Lee, 2014; Zhang et al., 2017). Thus, we provide a notable contribution by exploring the methods to create a dataset of revisions with a scalable crowdsourcing approach. By contrast, Zhang et al. (2017) recruited 60 students over 2 weeks and Lee and Webster (2012) collected data from a language learning project where over 300 tutors reviewed academic essays written by 4500 students.

7.2 Grammatical error correction

GEC is the task of correcting errors in text such as spelling, punctuation, grammar, and word choice (Ng et al., 2014; Yuan and Briscoe, 2016). GEC falls within the *editing* and *proofreading* phases of the writing process, while SentRev subsumes GEC and a broader range of text generation (e.g., increasing the fluency of the sentence and complementing missing information). Napoles et al. (2017) and Sakaguchi et al. (2016) explored fluency edits to correct grammatical errors and to make a text more "native sounding." Although this direction is similar to SentRev, our task used sentences that required many more corrections.

7.3 Style transfer

Style transfer is the task of rephrasing the text to conform to specific stylistic properties while preserving the text's original semantic content (Logeswaran et al., 2018; Prabhumoye et al., 2018). From the perspective of automatic academic writing assistance, the assistance systems are required to convert nonacademic-style drafts into academic-style drafts. This type of transfer is regarded as a subproblem in the *revising* stage of the writing process.

7.4 Text completion

The drafts in the *revising* stage may contain gaps denoted with $<*>$. This setting is similar to *text infilling* (Zhu et al., 2019), masking-based language modeling (Fedus et al., 2018; Devlin et al., 2019), or the *sentence completion task* (Zweig et al., 2012), where the models are required to replace mask tokens with plausible words. Notably, SentRev differs from such tasks because systems for these tasks are expected to keep all the original tokens unchanged and only fill the $<*>$ token, with one or more other tokens.

8 Conclusion and future work

We proposed the SentRev task, where an incomplete, rough draft sentence is transformed into a more fluent, complete sentence in the academic writing domain. We created the SMITH dataset with crowdsourcing for development and evaluation of this task and established baseline performance with a synthetic training dataset. We believe that this task can increase the effectiveness of the process of academic writing. In future work, we plan to improve the information gap-filling aspect of revision by considering the surrounding context of target sentences. In addition, to develop a more holistic writing assistance tool, we plan to extend our system to be able to suggest diverse correction candidates, provide interactive assistance, and integrate translation systems.

9 Acknowledgements

We thank the Tohoku NLP laboratory members who provided us with their valuable advice. We are grateful to Benjamin Heinzerling and Marie-Josée Brassard for their feedback. We are also grateful to Masato Mita for advice on the experiments. The work of J. Suzuki was partly supported by JSPS KAKENHI Grant Number 19H04162.

References

Samuel R. Bowman, Gabor Angeli, Christopher Potts, and Christopher D. Manning. 2015. A Large Annotated Corpus for Learning Natural Language Inference. In *Proceedings of EMNLP*, pages 632–642.

Eric Brill and Robert C. Moore. 2000. An Improved Error Model for Noisy Channel Spelling Correction. In *Proceedings of ACL*, pages 286–293.

Christopher Bryant, Mariano Felice, and Ted Briscoe. 2017. Automatic Annotation and Evaluation of Error Types for Grammatical Error Correction. In *Proceedings of ACL*, pages 793–805.

Michael Buchman, Roberta Moore, Linda Stern, and Betsy Feist. 2000. *Power Writing: Writing with Purpose*, volume 4.

Andrew D Cohen and Amanda Brooks-Carson. 2001. Research on direct versus translated writing: Students' strategies and their results. *The Modern Language Journal*, 85(2):169–188.

Robert Dale and Adam Kilgarriff. 2011. Helping Our Own: The HOO 2011 Pilot Shared Task. In *Proceedings of ENLG*, pages 242–249.

Vidas Daudaravicius. 2015. Automated Evaluation of Scientific Writing: AESW Shared Task Proposal. In *Proceedings of the Tenth Workshop on Innovative Use of NLP for Building Educational Applications (BEA)*, pages 56–63.

Jacob Devlin, Ming-Wei Chang, Kenton Lee, and Kristina Toutanova. 2019. BERT: Pre-training of deep bidirectional transformers for language understanding. In *Proceedings of NAACL-HLT*, pages 4171–4186.

Sergey Edunov, Myle Ott, Michael Auli, and David Grangier. 2018. Understanding Back-Translation at Scale. In *Proceedings of EMNLP*, pages 489–500.

William Fedus, Ian Goodfellow, and Andrew M Dai. 2018. Maskgan: Better Text Generation via Filling in the _. In *Proceedings of ICLR*.

Mariano Felice, Christopher Bryant, and Ted Briscoe. 2016. Automatic Extraction of Learner Errors in ESL Sentences Using Linguistically Enhanced Alignments. In *Proceedings of COLING*, pages 825–835.

Rudolph Flesch. 1948. A new readability yardstick. *Journal of Applied Psychology*, 32(3):221 – 233.

David Grangier and Michael Auli. 2018. QuickEdit: Editing Text & Translations by Crossing Words Out. In *Proceedings of NAACL-HLT*, pages 272–282.

Jason S. Kessler. 2017. Scattertext: a Browser-Based Tool for Visualizing how Corpora Differ. In *Proceedings of ACL System Demonstrations*, pages 85–90.

Diederik P. Kingma and Jimmy Ba. 2015. Adam: A Method for Stochastic Optimization. In *Proceedings of ICLR*.

John Lee and Jonathan Webster. 2012. A corpus of textual revisions in second language writing. In *Proceedings of ACL*, pages 248–252.

Jared Lichtarge, Chris Alberti, Shankar Kumar, Noam Shazeer, Niki Parmar, and Simon Tong. 2019. Corpora generation for grammatical error correction. In *Proceedings of NAACL-HLT*, pages 3291–3301.

Lajanugen Logeswaran, Honglak Lee, and Samy Bengio. 2018. Content Preserving Text Generation with Attribute Controls. In *Proceedings of NeurIPS,*, pages 5103–5113.

Tomoya Mizumoto, Mamoru Komachi, Masaaki Nagata, and Yuji Matsumoto. 2011. Mining Revision Log of Language Learning SNS for Automated Japanese Error Correction of Second Language Learners. In *Proceedings of IJCNLP*, pages 147–155.

Courtney Napoles, Keisuke Sakaguchi, and Joel Tetreault. 2016. There's No Comparison: Reference-less Evaluation Metrics in Grammatical Error Correction. In *Proceedings of EMNLP*, pages 2109–2115.

Courtney Napoles, Keisuke Sakaguchi, and Joel Tetreault. 2017. JFLEG: A Fluency Corpus and Benchmark for Grammatical Error Correction. In *Proceedings of EACL*, pages 229–234.

Hwee Tou Ng, Siew Mei Wu, Ted Briscoe, Christian Hadiwinoto, Raymond Hendy Susanto, and Christopher Bryant. 2014. The CoNLL-2014 Shared Task on Grammatical Error Correction. In *Proceedings of CoNLL:Shared Task*, pages 1–14.

Myle Ott, Sergey Edunov, Alexei Baevski, Angela Fan, Sam Gross, Nathan Ng, David Grangier, and Michael Auli. 2019. fairseq: A fast, extensible toolkit for sequence modeling. In *Proceedings of NAACL-HLT*, pages 48–53.

Shrimai Prabhumoye, Yulia Tsvetkov, Ruslan Salakhutdinov, and Alan W. Black. 2018. Style Transfer Through Back-Translation. In *Proceedings of ACL*, pages 866–876.

Keisuke Sakaguchi, Courtney Napoles, Matt Post, and Joel Tetreault. 2016. Reassessing the Goals of Grammatical Error Correction: Fluency instead of Grammaticality. *TACL*, 4:169–182.

Anthony Seow. 2002. The writing process and process writing. *Methodology in language teaching: An anthology of current practice*, pages 315–320.

Shikhar Sharma, Layla El Asri, Hannes Schulz, and Jeremie Zumer. 2017. Relevance of Unsupervised Metrics in Task-Oriented Dialogue for Evaluating Natural Language Generation. *arXiv preprint arXiv:1706.09799*.

Bernard Susser. 1994. Process approaches in ESL/EFL writing instruction. *Journal of Second Language Writing*, 3(1):31–47.

Chenhao Tan and Lillian Lee. 2014. A corpus of sentence-level revisions in academic writing: A step towards understanding statement strength in communication. In *Proceedings of ACL*, pages 403–408.

Ashish Vaswani, Noam Shazeer, Niki Parmar, Jakob Uszkoreit, Llion Jones, Aidan N Gomez, Ł ukasz Kaiser, and Illia Polosukhin. 2017. Attention is All you Need. In *Proceedings of NIPS*, pages 5998–6008.

John Wieting and Kevin Gimpel. 2018. ParaNMT-50M: Pushing the Limits of Paraphrastic Sentence Embeddings with Millions of Machine Translations. In *Proceedings of ACL*, pages 451–462.

Adina Williams, Nikita Nangia, and Samuel Bowman. 2018. A Broad-Coverage Challenge Corpus for Sentence Understanding through Inference. In *Proceedings of NAACL-HLT*, pages 1112–1122.

Ziang Xie, Guillaume Genthial, Stanley Xie, Andrew Ng, and Dan Jurafsky. 2018. Noising and Denoising Natural Language: Diverse Backtranslation for Grammar Correction. In *Proceedings of NAACL-HLT*, pages 619–628.

Zheng Yuan and Ted Briscoe. 2016. Grammatical Error Correction using Neural Machine Translation. In *Proceedings of NAACL-HLT*, pages 380–386.

Fan Zhang, Homa B. Hashemi, Rebecca Hwa, and Diane Litman. 2017. A Corpus of Annotated Revisions for Studying Argumentative Writing. In *Proceedings of ACL*, pages 1568–1578.

Tianyi Zhang, Varsha Kishore, Felix Wu, Kilian Q. Weinberger, and Yoav. Artzi. 2019. BERTScore: Evaluating Text Generation with BERT. *arXiv preprint arXiv:1904.09675*.

Wei Zhao, Liang Wang, Kewei Shen, Ruoyu Jia, and Jingming Liu. 2019. Improving grammatical error correction via pre-training a copy-augmented architecture with unlabeled data. In *Proceedings of the NAACL-HLT*, pages 156–165.

Wanrong Zhu, Zhiting Hu, and Eric Xing. 2019. Text Infilling. *arXiv preprint arXiv:1901.00158*.

Geoffrey Zweig, John C. Platt, Christopher Meek, Christopher J. C. Burges, Ainur Yessenalina, and Qiang Liu. 2012. Computational Approaches to Sentence Completion. In *Proceedings of ACL*, pages 601–610.

A   Lexical tendencies

Certain words and phrases were more frequently
observed in the reference sentences than in the
draft sentences, and vice-versa. Figure 8 visualizes these biases, where words more often
observed in the draft sentences are plotted in
the upper-left corner, and words more often observed in the references are plotted in the lower-
right corner. Words observed more commonly
in the drafts were: *will*, *is not*, *if*, and *I*, versus *can be*, *no*, *when*, and *they*. The contrast
also includes a widely-used spelling (*data set* vs
dataset) and common plurality (*method* vs *methods*). The plot was generated using the scattertext
toolkit (Kessler, 2017).

B   Heuristic noising algorithm

Algorithm 1 shows the noising algorithm in the
heuristic noising method.

C   Examples from the SMITH dataset and generated sentences by Baseline models

Table 8 shows examples from the SMITH dataset
and the output of the baseline models. "Reference" is a sentence extracted from papers, "Draft"
is written by a crowdworker and is the input for
the baseline models.

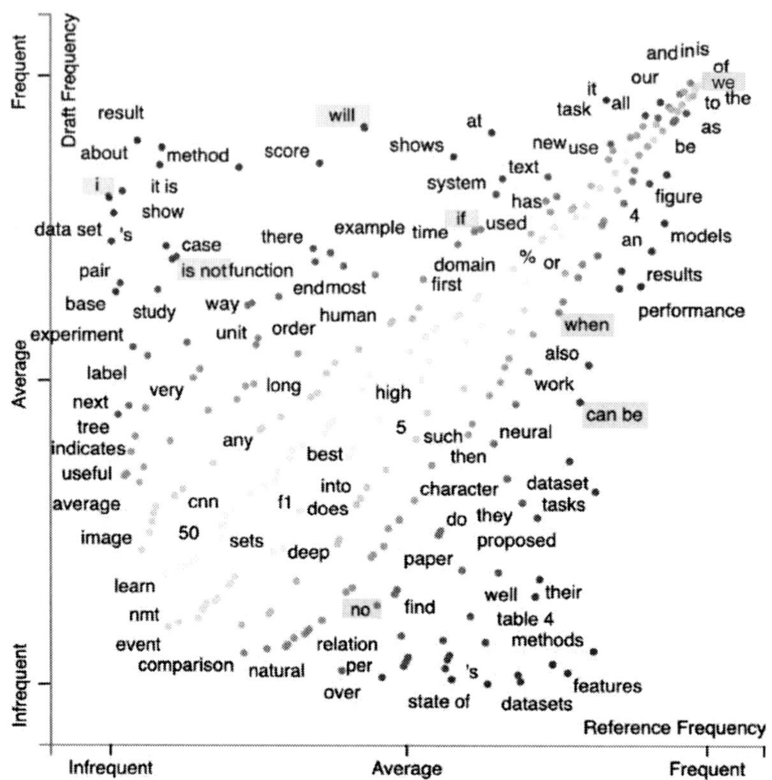

Figure 8: Characteristic words and phrases in draft sentences and reference sentences in the development set of SMITH.

Algorithm 1 Heuristic noising

INPUT: $x = \{w_0, w_1, \cdots, w_n\}$

1: $x = \text{delete}(x, 0.1)$
   # 10% of the tokens in x are deleted.
2: $x = \text{replace}(x, 0.1)$
   # 10% of the tokens in x are replaced with common terms in ACL.
3: $x = \text{permutate}(x)$
   # permutate the tokens in x.
4: $r \leftarrow \text{Uniform}(0, 0.5)$
5: $m = \text{int}(x.\text{length} * r)$
6: $c = 0$
7: **while** $c < m$ **do**
8:    $n \leftarrow \text{sample}(\{j \in \mathcal{N} \mid 1 \leq j \leq m - c\})$
9:    $(s, e) \leftarrow \text{sample}(\{n\text{-grams of } x\})$
10:   $x = \text{``}x_{:s-1} + \texttt{<*>} + x_{e+1:}\text{''}$
11:   $c = c + n$
12: **end while**
   # $r \times 100\%$ of the tokens in x are masked.

Draft	By this setting , the persona is acquired from a test set popl about both turker anad model .
H-ND	By this setting , the persona is acquired from a test set both about popl anad anad model .
ED-ND	In this setting , persona is obtained from the test set popl about both Turker and model .
GEC	By this setting , the persona is acquired from a test set pool about both turkey and models .
Reference	In this setting , for both the Turker and the model , the personas come from the test set pool .
Draft	In addition to results of study until now , we add two baseline to vindicate effectiveness on our flame work .
H-ND	In addition to the results of this study , we now add two baseline methods to vindicate effectiveness on our work .
ED-ND	In addition to the results of the study until now , we add two baselines to visualize the effectiveness of our framework .
GEC	In addition to the results of study until now , we added two baseline to vindicate effectiveness on our flame work .
Reference	In addition to results of previous work , we add two baselines to demonstrate the effectiveness of our framework .
Draft	Yhe input and output <*> are one - hot encoding of the center word and the context word , <*> .
H-ND	The input and output are one - hot encoding of the center word and the context word , respectively .
ED-ND	The input and output layers are one - hot encoding of the center word and the context word , respectively .
GEC	Yhe input and output are one - hot encoding of the center word and the context word , .
Reference	The input and output layers are centre word and context word one - hot encodings , respectively .
Draft	I registered the vocabulary sizes of encorder and decorder as 150 K and 50 K each other .
H-ND	I registered the vocabulary sizes of decorder and encorder as 150 K and each other .
ED-ND	We registered the vocabulary sizes of the encoder and decoder as 150 K and 50 K respectively .
GEC	I registered the vocabulary sizes of encoder and recorder as 150 K and 50 K for each other .
Reference	In this experiment , we set the vocabulary size on the encoder and decoder sides to 150 K and 50 K , respectively .
Draft	They add the new class image generated by generator and classfy them .
H-ND	They add the new image class generated by the generator and classfy them .
ED-ND	They add a new class of images generated by the generator and classify them .
GEC	They add a new class image generated by generator and classify them .
Reference	They add a new class of images that are generated by the generator and classify them .
Draft	The chart 3 shows performance of multi input correction against sub groups with different number of witnesses .
H-ND	Table 3 shows the performance of multi - chart correction against different input groups with different number of witnesses .
ED-ND	Figure 3 shows the performance of multiple input correction against subgraphs with different number of witnesses .
GEC	chart 3 shows performance of multi input correction against sub groups with different number of witnesses .
Reference	Figure 3 presents the performance of multi - input correction on subgroups with different number of witnesses .
Draft	It is vindicated that InferSent accomplishes the most <*> result regarding SentEval task .
H-ND	It is vindicated that InferSent accomplishes the most relevant result regarding the SentEval task .
ED-ND	It is vindicated that InferSent accomplishes the most important result regarding the SentEval task .
GEC	It is vindicated that InferSent accomplishes the most results regarding SentEval task .
Reference	InferSent has been shown to achieve state - of - the - art results on the SentEval tasks .
Draft	Our proposal model can get both long - term dependence and local information well .
H-ND	Our proposal can get both long - term and local information as well .
ED-ND	Our proposed model can capture both long - term dependencies and local information well .
GEC	Our proposal model can get both long - term dependence and local information well .
Reference	Our proposed model can both capture long - term dependencies and local information well .

Table 8: Further examples of draft, reference, and the baseline models' output.

Computational Argumentation Synthesis as a Language Modeling Task

Roxanne El Baff [1]   **Henning Wachsmuth** [2]   **Khalid Al-Khatib** [1]
Manfred Stede [3]   **Benno Stein** [1]

[1] Bauhaus-Universität Weimar, Weimar, Germany, `<first>{.<last>}`[+]`@uni-weimar.de`
[2] Paderborn University, Paderborn, Germany, `henningw@upb.de`
[3] University of Potsdam, Potsdam, Germany, `stede@uni-potsdam.de`

Abstract

Synthesis approaches in computational argumentation so far are restricted to generating claim-like argument units or short summaries of debates. Ultimately, however, we expect computers to generate whole new arguments for a given stance towards some topic, backing up claims following argumentative and rhetorical considerations. In this paper, we approach such an argumentation synthesis as a language modeling task. In our language model, argumentative discourse units are the "words", and arguments represent the "sentences". Given a pool of units for any unseen topic-stance pair, the model *selects* a set of unit types according to a basic rhetorical strategy (logos vs. pathos), *arranges* the structure of the types based on the units' argumentative roles, and finally *"phrases"* an argument by instantiating the structure with semantically coherent units from the pool. Our evaluation suggests that the model can, to some extent, mimic the human synthesis of strategy-specific arguments.

1 Introduction

Existing research on computational argumentation largely focuses on the *analysis* side. Various analysis tasks are widely studied including identifying the claims along with their supporting premises (Stab and Gurevych, 2014), finding the relation between argumentative units (Cocarascu and Toni, 2017), and assessing the persuasiveness of arguments (Habernal and Gurevych, 2016).

Diverse downstream applications, however, necessitate the development of argumentation *synthesis* technologies. For example, synthesis is needed to produce a summary of arguments for a given topic (Wang and Ling, 2016) or to build a debating system where new arguments are exchanged between the users and the system (Le et al., 2018).

As a result, a number of recent studies addresses the argumentation synthesis task. These studies have proposed different approaches to generating claims or reasons for a given topic, partly with a particular stance towards the topic (Bilu and Slonim, 2016; Hua and Wang, 2018). However, the next important synthesis step is still missing in the literature, namely, to generate complete texts including both argumentative and rhetorical considerations. With the latter, we refer to Aristotle's three means of persuasion: logos (providing logical arguments), ethos (demonstrating credibility), and pathos (evoking emotions). As discussed by Wachsmuth et al. (2018), following a rhetorical strategy is key to achieving persuasion with argumentative texts.

This paper proposes a new computational approach that synthesizes argumentative texts following a rhetorical strategy. We do not tackle this task immediately "in the wild", i.e., generating an entirely new argumentative text for a freely-chosen topic and a possibly complex strategy. Rather, we consider a "controlled" synthesis setting, with the goal of successively creating models that are able to deal with more complex settings later on.

In particular, given a pool of argumentative discourse units (ADUs), our approach generates arguments for any unseen pair of topic and stance (e.g., "con abortion") as well as a basic rhetorical strategy (i.e., logos-oriented vs. pathos-oriented).[1] To abstract from the arguments' topics during training, we first identify different ADU types using clustering. Our approach then learns to *select* unit types matching the given strategy and to *arrange* them according to their argumentative roles. Both steps are realized as a language model where ADUs represent words and arguments are sentences. Finally, our approach *"phrases"* an argument by predicting the best set of semantically related ADUs for the arranged structure using supervised regression. Thereby, we ensure that the synthesized texts are

---

[1] We consider a single argument to be a sequence of ADUs where each ADU has a specific role: thesis, con, or pro.

Proceedings of The 12th International Conference on Natural Language Generation, pages 54–64,
Tokyo, Japan, 28 Oct - 1 Nov, 2019. ©2019 Association for Computational Linguistics

composed of meaningful units, a property that neural generation methods barely achieve so far.

In our evaluation, we utilize the dataset of Wachsmuth et al. (2018). This dataset contains 260 argumentative texts on 10 topic-stance pairs, where each text composes five ADUs in a logos-oriented or pathos-oriented manner. In our experiments, we train our approach on nine topic-stance pairs and then generate an argument for the tenth. The results demonstrate that our approach successfully manages to combine pairs of ADUs, but its performance on longer sequences of ADUs is limited.

Altogether, our contribution is three-fold:

1. A new view of argumentation synthesis that represents argumentative and rhetorical considerations with language modeling.

2. A novel approach that selects, arranges, and phrases ADUs to synthesize strategy-specific arguments for any topic and stance.

3. First experimental evidence that arguments with basic rhetorical strategies can be synthesized computationally.[2]

2 Related Work

Recently, some researchers have tackled argumentation synthesis statistically with neural networks. For instance, Wang and Ling (2016) employed a sequence-to-sequence model to generate summaries of argumentative texts, and Hua and Wang (2018) did similar to generate counterarguments. Using neural methods in text generation, it is possible to achieve output that is on topic and grammatically (more or less) correct. However, when the desired text is to span multiple sentences, the generated text regularly suffers from incoherence and repetitiveness, as for instance discussed by Holtzman et al. (2018) who examine texts that were produced by RNNs in various domains. While these problems may be tolerable to some extent in some applications, such as chatbots, bad text cannot be accepted in an argumentative or debating scenario, where the goal is to convince or persuade a reader (rather than to merely inform or entertain).

Holtzman et al. (2018) propose to alleviate incoherence and repetitiveness by training a set of discriminators, which aim to ensure that a text respects the Gricean maxims of quantity, quality, relation, and manner (Grice, 1975). To this end, they

employ specific datasets, such as one that opposes authentic text continuation to randomly-sampled text. The discriminators learn optimal weightings for the various models and their combination, such that overall text quality is maximized. For argumentation, we hypothesize that one needs to go even further and eventually account for the author, implementing her underlying *intention* in the different parts of an argumentative text as well as in the relations between the parts.

In the past times of rule-based text generation, argumentation synthesis was a popular task (Zukerman et al., 2000). Approaches involved much handcrafted (linguistic and domain) knowledge and user modeling. For example, the system of Carenini and Moore (2006) compares attributes of houses (from a database) to desired target attributes (from a user model), to then recommend a house to the reader in a convincing text following the Gricean maxims. To this end, it selected house attributes potentially interesting to the user, arranged, and finally phrased them. The resulting texts resembled the arguments we work with here, which have been manually composed by experts (Wachsmuth et al., 2018) from the claims, evidence, and objections in the arg-microtext corpus (Peldszus and Stede, 2016). To achieve a similar level of output control, today's text-to-text generation models need to account for the various interdependencies between the text units to be combined.

Most related to our approach is the system of Sato et al. (2015), where a user can enter a claim-like topic along with a stance. The system then generates argumentative paragraphs on specific aspects of the topic by selecting sentences from 10 million news texts of the Gigaword corpus. Potentially relevant aspects are those that trigger evaluative judgment in the reader. The sentences are arranged so that the text starts with a claim sentence and is followed by support sentences, employing the approach of Yanase et al. (2015). The support sentences are ordered by maximizing the semantic connectivity between sentences. Finally, some rephrasing is done in terms of certain aspects of surface realization. In a manual evaluation, however, no text was seen as sounding natural, underlining the difficulty of the task. In contrast to Sato et al. (2015), we learn directly from input data what argumentative discourse units to combine and how to arrange them. We leave surface realization aside to keep the focus on the argument composition.

---

[2]The code for running the experiments is available here: https://github.com/webis-de/inlg19-argumentation-synthesis

Role	ID	Argumentative Discourse Unit
Thesis	t_1	German universities should on no account charge tuition fees
	t_2	the universities in Germany should not under any circumstances charge tuition fees
	t_3	tuition fees should not generally be charged by universities
	t_4	universities should not charge tuition fees in Germany
Con	c_1	one could argue that an increase in tuition fees would allow institutions to be better equipped
	c_2	those who study later decide this early on, anyway
	c_3	to oblige non-academics to finance others' degrees through taxes is not just
	c_4	unfortunately sponsoring can lead to disagreeable dependencies in some cases
Pro	p_1	education and training are fundamental rights which the state, the society must provide
	p_2	education must not be a question of money in a wealthy society such as Germany
	p_3	fees result in longer durations of studies
	p_4	funding-wise it ought to be considered how costs incurred by students from other (federal) states can be reimbursed
	p_5	if a university lacks the funds, sponsors must be found
	p_6	longer durations of studies are costly
	p_7	studying and taking higher degrees must remain a basic right for everyone
	p_8	there are other instruments to motivate tighter discipline while studying
	p_9	this would impede or prevent access to those who are financially weaker
	p_{10}	this would mean that only those people with wealthy parents or a previous education and a part-time job while studying would be able to apply for a degree programme in the first place
	p_{11}	universities are for all citizens, independent of their finances
	p_{12}	what is the good of a wonderfully outfitted university if it doesn't actually allow the majority of clever people to broaden their horizons with all that great equipment
Topic		Should all universities in Germany charge tuition fees? **Stance** Con

Table 1: The candidate thesis, con, and pro units for one topic-stance pair in the dataset of Wachsmuth et al. (2018).

Some other approaches have been proposed that recompose existing text segments in new arguments. In particular, Bilu and Slonim (2016) generated new claims by "recycling" topics and predicates that were found in a database of claims. Claim selection involves preferring predicates that are generally amenable to claim units and that are relevant for the target topic. Egan et al. (2016) created summaries of the main points in a debate, and Reisert et al. (2015) synthesized complete arguments from a set of manually curated topic-stance relations based on the fine-grained argument model of Toulmin (1958). However, we are not aware of any approach that synthesizes arguments fully automatically, let alone that follows rhetorical considerations in the synthesis process.

3 Data

To develop our model for argumentation synthesis, we exploit the dataset recently developed by Wachsmuth et al. (2018). The dataset comprises 260 *manually* generated argumentative texts. The generation of each text, for one topic-stance pair, has been conducted in a systematic fashion following the three canons of rhetoric (Aristotle, 2007):

1. *Inventio ~ Selecting* a subset of argumentative discourse units (ADUs) from a pool of given ADUs for a topic-stance pair.

2. *Dispositio ~ Arranging* the selected ADUs in a sequential order.

3. *Elocutio ~ Phrasing* the arranged ADUs by adding connectives at unit-initial or unit-final positions.

Specifically, Wachsmuth et al. (2018) selected a pool of 200 ADUs for 10 pairs of controversial topic and stance from the English version of the arg-microtexts corpus (Peldszus and Stede, 2016). As a preprocessing step, they "decontextualized" these ADUs manually by removing connectives, resolving pronouns, and similar. Each topic-stance pair comes with 20 such ADUs: four theses, four con units, and 12 pro units. Table 1 shows the ADU list for one topic-stance pair.

26 participants were asked by Wachsmuth et al. (2018) to create short argumentative texts for each topic-stance pair following one of two basic rhetorical strategies: (1) *logos-oriented*, i.e., arguing logically, and (2) *pathos-oriented*, i.e., arguing based on emotional appeals. For each topic-stance pair they created an argument by selecting one thesis, one con and three pro units that they thought could best form a persuasive argument following the given strategies. Table 2 shows two samples of generated arguments in the dataset.

The dataset contains 130 logos-oriented and 130

Strategy	ID	Text Manually Synthesized From Five Argumentative Discourse Units
Logos-oriented	c_1	one could argue that an increase in tuition fees would allow institutions to be better equipped,
	t_1	*however* German universities should on no account charge tuition fees.
	p_1	education and training are fundamental rights which the state, the society must provide,
	p_{12}	*because* what is the good of a wonderfully outfitted university if it doesn't actually allow the majority of clever people to broaden their horizons with all that great equipment.
	p_4	*Besides,* funding-wise it ought to be considered how costs incurred by students from other (federal) states can be reimbursed.
Pathos-oriented	p_1	education and training are fundamental rights which the state, the society must provide.
	t_2	*This is why* the universities in Germany should not under any circumstances charge tuition fees.
	c_1	one could argue that an increase in tuition fees would allow institutions to be better equipped,
	p_3	*however* fees result in longer durations of studies
	p_6	*and* longer durations of studies are costly.

Table 2: two sample arguments manually synthesized from the ADUs in Table 1, which are included in the dataset of Wachsmuth et al. (2018). The italiced connectives were added by the participants; they are *not* part of the ADUs.

pathos-oriented argumentative texts. We use these 260 texts to develop and evaluate our computational model for argumentation synthesis.

4 Approach

This section presents our computational approach to synthesize arguments for any pair of topic and stance, following one of two basic rhetorical strategies: arguing logically (*logos-oriented*) or arguing emotionally (*pathos-oriented*). A black-box view of the approach is shown in Figure 1.

As input, our approach takes a strategy as well as a pool of argumentative discourse units (ADUs) for any specific topic-stance pair x. Each ADU has the role of a *thesis* (in terms of claim with a stance on the topic), a *con* point (objecting the thesis), or a *pro* point (supporting the thesis). The approach then imitates the human selection, arrangement, and "phrasing" of a sequence of n ADUs, in order to synthesize an argument. Phrasing is done only in terms of picking semantically coherent ADUs for the arranged sequence; the addition of connectives between ADUs is left to future work.

Below, we detail how we realize each step (selection, arrangement, and phrasing) with a topic-independent model. For each step, we explain how it is trained (illustrated in Figure 2) and how it is applied to an unseen topic-stance pair (Figure 3).

4.1 Selection Language Model

This model handles the selection of a set of n ADUs for a topic-stance pair x and a rhetorical strategy. We approach the selection as a language modeling task where each ADU is a "word" of our language model and each argument a "sentence". To abstract from topic, the model actually selects ADU *types*, as explained in the following.

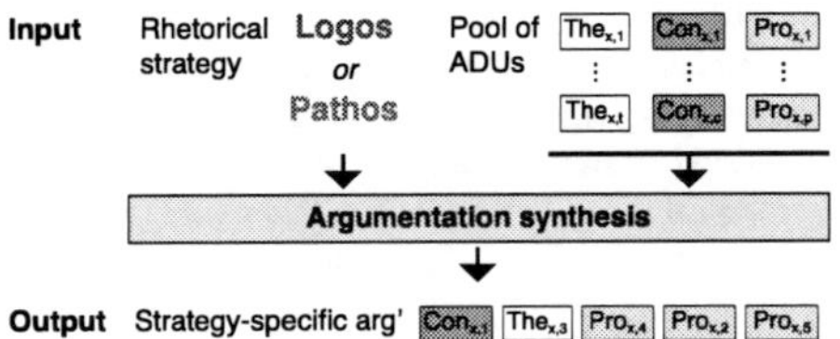

Figure 1: Black-box view of our argumentation synthesis approach. The input is a rhetorical strategy as well as a pool of thesis, con, and pro ADUs for some topic-stance pair x. The approach outputs a strategy-specific sequence of n ADUs as an argument for x (here, $n = 5$).

4.1.1 Training of the Model

We start from a training set of ADUs for a set of m topic-stance pairs. To generalize the language model beyond the covered topics, each ADU is represented using features that aim to capture general emotion-related and logic-related characteristics, accounting for the two given strategies.

In particular, we first cluster the pool of all training ADUs based on their feature representation. As a result, each ADU is represented by a cluster label (A–F in Figure 2), where each label represents one ADU type. Now, for each of the strategies, we map each manually-generated sequence of ADUs to a sequence of cluster labels. Using these sequences of labels, we train one separated selection language model for each strategy.

For clustering, we rely on topic-independent features that we expect to implicitly encode logical and emotional strategies: (1) psychological meaningfulness (Pennebaker et al., 2015), (2) eight basic emotions (Plutchik, 1980; Mohammad and Turney, 2013), and (3) argumentativeness (Somasundaran et al., 2007). In the following, we elaborate on the concrete features that we extract:

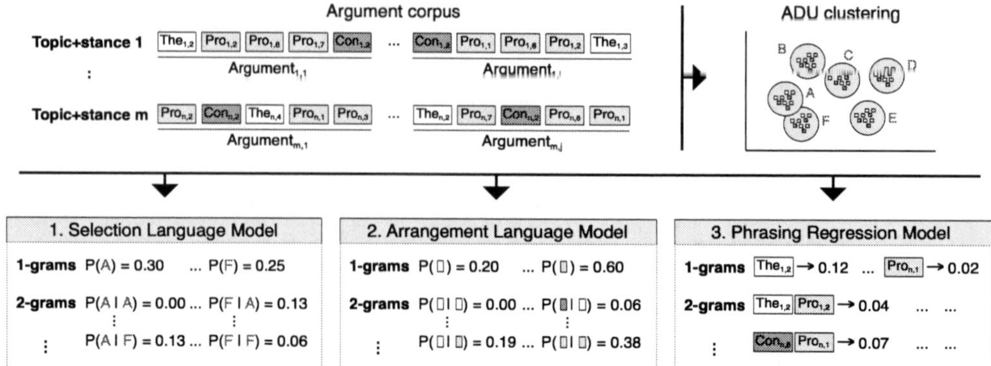

Figure 2: Illustration of training the three models of our argumentation synthesis approach. The input is a corpus of argumentative texts for m topic-stance pairs, each decomposed into a sequence of theses, con units, and pro units. Initially, the set of all these ADUs is clustered to obtain a set topic-independent ADU types, called *A–F* here. (1) *Selection language model*: Each argument is converted from a sequence of ADUs to a sequence of ADU types, where a language model is trained on these type sequences. (2) *Arrangement language model:* Each argument is converted from a sequence of ADUs to a sequence of ADU roles (thesis, pro, and con) where a language model is trained on these ADU role sequences. (3) *Phrasing regression model:* A linear regression model is trained which scores each ADU sequence with respect to its semantic coherence.

Linguistic Inquiry and Word Count (LIWC) LIWC is a lexicon-based text analysis that counts words in psychologically meaningful categories (Tausczik and Pennebaker, 2010). We use the version by Pennebaker et al. (2015), which contains the following 15 dimensions:

1. *Language metrics*, e.g., words per sentence.

2. *Function words*, e.g., pronouns and auxiliary verbs.

3. *Other grammar*, e.g., common verbs and comparisons.

4. *Affect words*, e.g., positive emotion words.

5. *Social words*, e.g., "family" and "friends".

6. *Cognitive processes*, e.g., "discrepancies" and "certainty".

7. *Perceptual processes*, e.g., "feeling".

8. *Biological processes*, e.g., "health".

9. *Core drives and needs*, e.g., "power" and "reward focused".

10. *Time orientation*, e.g., past-focused.

11. *Relativity*, e.g., "time" and "space".

12. *Personal concerns*, e.g., "work" and "leisure".

13. *Informal speech*, e.g., fillers and nonfluencies.

14. *Punctuation*, e.g., periods and commas.

15. *Summary variables*, as detailed below.

There are four summary variables, each of which is derived from various LIWC dimensions: (1) *analytical thinking* (Pennebaker et al., 2014), i.e., the degree to which people use narrative language (low value), or more logical and formal language (high); (2) *clout* (Kacewicz et al., 2014), i.e., the relative social status, confidence, and leadership displayed in a text; (3) *authenticity* (Newman et al., 2003), i.e., the degree to which people reveal themselves in an authentic way; and (4) *emotional tone* (Cohn et al., 2004), i.e., negative for values lower than 50 and positive otherwise.

NRC Emotional and Sentiment Lexicons We use the NRC lexicon of Mohammad and Turney (2013). The lexicon has been compiled manually using crowdsourcing and contains a set of English words and their associations with (1) *sentiment*, i.e., negative and positive polarities, and (2) *emotions*, i.e., the eight basic emotions defined by Plutchik (1980): anger, anticipation, disgust, fear, joy, surprise, sadness, and trust. These features are represented as the count of words associated with each category (e.g., the count of *sad words* in an ADU).

MPQA Arguing Lexicon Somasundaran et al. (2007) constructed a lexicon that includes the following arguing patterns: *assessments, doubt, authority, emphasis, necessity, causation, generalization, structure, conditionals, inconsistency, possibility, wants, contrast, priority, difficulty, inyour-*

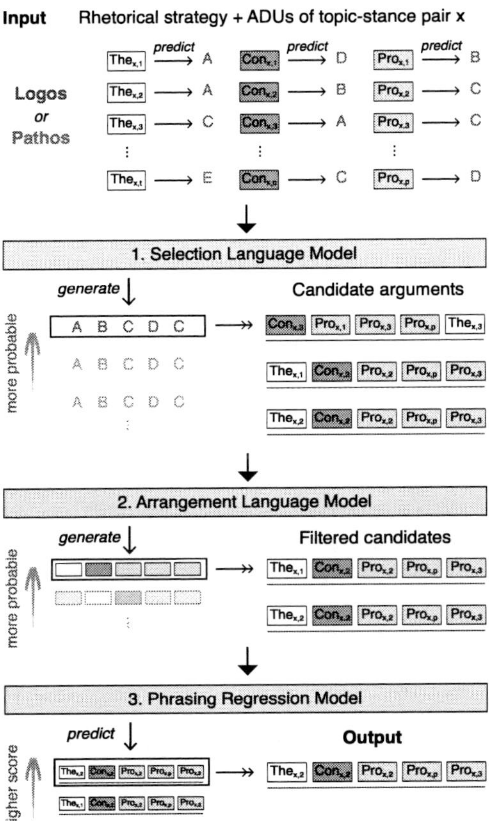

Figure 3: Illustration of applying our synthesis approach. Given the predicted type of each input ADU of the given topic-stance pair *x*, (1) the *selection* generates the most probable type sequence, (A, B, C, D, C). From the type sequence, a set of candidate arguments is decoded. (2) The *arrangement* filters out candidates not matching the most probable ADU role sequence, $(Thesis, Con, Pro, Pro, Pro)$. (3) *Phrasing* scores each remaining argument and outputs the top argument.

shoes, rhetorical question. We use the count of each arguing pattern in text as one feature (e.g., number of *assessments* patterns in an ADU).

4.1.2 Application of the Model

As shown in Figure 3, the selection language model takes the ADUs of an unseen topic-stance *x* as input. It then outputs a set of candidate arguments, in terms of sequences of ADUs. Each ADU is encoded into a cluster label (representing an ADU type). For example, one might have the following mappings, given the six labels *A–F* from Figure 2:

$$A \leftarrow \{The_{x,1}, The_{x,2}, Con_{x,3}\}$$
$$B \leftarrow \{Con_{x,2}, Pro_{x,1}\}$$

$$C \leftarrow \{The_{x,3}, Con_{x,c}, Pro_{x,2}, Pro_{x,3}\}$$
$$D \leftarrow \{Pro_{x,p}, Con_{x,1}\}$$
$$E \leftarrow \{The_{x,t}\}$$
$$F \leftarrow \{The_{x,4}, Con_{x,4}, Pro_{x,4}\}$$

The language model for either of the two rhetorical strategies generates a set of arguments where each argument is composed of n cluster labels, e.g., (A, B, C, D, C) for $n = 5$ in Figure 3. This set is ranked by probability of the associated sequence. For example, assume that (A, B, C, D, C) is most probable. Then we decode all possible ADU sequences for topic-stance x from (A, B, C, D, C) to a set of candidate arguments:

$$(A, B, C, D, C) \rightarrow$$
$$\{The_{x,1}, The_{x,2}, Con_{x,3}\}$$
$$\times \{Con_{x,2}, Pro_{x,1}\}$$
$$\times \{The_{x,3}, Con_{x,c}, Pro_{x,2}, Pro_{x,3}\}$$
$$\times \{Pro_{x,p}, Con_{x,1}\}$$
$$\times \{The_{x,3}, Con_{x,c}, Pro_{x,2}, Pro_{x,3}\}$$

The output of the model is a set of candidate arguments, which becomes the input of the arrangement language model.

4.2 Arrangement Language Model

In the arrangement process, we aim to imitate the human behavior of arranging ADUs for a specific topic-stance following a rhetorical strategy (here, *logos* or *pathos*). Again, we approach this problem as a language modeling task. Each ADU role (thesis, pro, or con) is a word of the language model and each argument a sentence.

4.2.1 Training of the Model

As sketched in Figure 2, we first convert the human-generated arguments from a sequence of ADUs to a sequence of ADU roles. Then, we use these sequences to train a language model for each strategy.

4.2.2 Application of the Model

As shown in Figure 3, the arrangement language model takes as input the candidate arguments that we get from the selection language model and outputs a set of filtered candidate arguments.

The language model for a specific strategy generates a set of argument structures where each such structure is a sequence of n ADU roles, e.g., $(Thesis, Con, Pro, Pro, Pro)$ for $n = 5$ in Figure 3. This set is ranked by the probability of the sequences. For example, assume that the most frequent sequence is $(Thesis, Con, Pro, Pro, Pro)$.

Using the output from the selection language model, we filter out all candidate arguments that do not match $(Thesis, Con, Pro, Pro, Pro)$, ending up with the following filtered arguments:

$$\{The_{x,1}, The_{x,2}\} \times \{Con_{x,2}\}$$
$$\times \{Pro_{x,2}, Pro_{x,3}\} \times \{Pro_{x,p}\}$$
$$\times \{Pro_{x,2}, Pro_{x,3}\}$$

The output of the model is a filtered set of candidate arguments, which becomes the input of the phrasing regression model.

4.3 Phrasing Regression Model

The set of arguments resulting from the selection and arrangement language models are based on topic-independent features. The missing step is to entail the topical relationship between the ADUs in each generated argument. We approach this task with supervised regression. As indicated above, our model does not really *phrase* an argument. Rather, it aims to choose the best among the given set of candidates in terms of semantic coherence.

4.3.1 Training of the Model

For each argument, we opt for a feature representation that embeds the content properties of ADUs in order to capture their content relationship. Concretely, we represent each argument by calculating the semantic similarities of each adjacent bigram in a human-generated argument. We train a linear regression model where each instance represents the features of one argument. To this end, we set a score to be the sum of the probabilities of ADU bigrams occurring in one argument.

The phrasing model scores each of the filtered arguments given as output by the arrangement model. The argument with the highest score is the final generated argument.

4.3.2 Application of the Model

At this point, the phrasing model is provided by the filtered arguments from the arrangement model. For each filtered argument, we extract the bigram features (semantic similarities). Next, using the phrasing model, we predict the score of each sequence. The sequence with the highest score is the generated argument. In Figure 3, this is:

$$(The_{x,2}, Con_{x,2}, Pro_{x,2}, Pro_{x,p}, Pro_{x,3})$$

5 Experiments

In this section, we report the results of evaluating the introduced approach to argumentation synthesis

Strategy	2-grams	3-grams
Logos-oriented	9,110.6	9,466.3
Pathos-oriented	7,939.5	10,279.6

Table 3: *Selection*. Perplexity of the 2-gram and 3-gram language models for each strategy, averaged over 10 leave-one-topic-out runs using Laplace smoothing.

based on the dataset described in Section 3.

5.1 Experimental Set-up

Our experiments are designed in leave-one-topic-out cross-validation setting: From the 10 topic-stance pairs in the dataset, we use nine for training and the last as the test fold, and we repeat this once for each possible fold. This way, no topic-specific knowledge can be used in the synthesis process.

For each given basic rhetorical strategy (*logos-oriented* and *pathos-oriented*), we train one model each for the selection, the arrangement, and the "phrasing" of argumentative discourse units (ADUs) on the nine training folds. The arguments synthesized by their combination are then evaluated against the human-generated arguments in the test folds. The evaluation covers all three models as well as the final generated argument for each strategy. We report the average accuracy across all ten folds for each of the models.

5.2 Training: Selection Language Model

In each training/test experiment for one of the two strategies, we first abstract all ADUs across all strategy-specific topic-stance pairs by extracting the LIWC, NRC, and MPQA features, as described in Section 4.1. Then, we cluster the given training set using standard k-means (Ostrovsky et al., 2012). After some initial experiments, we decide to set k to 6, because this best balanced the distribution of arguments over clusters, and showed clear strategy-specific differences.[3] Using the resulting clustering model, we predicted the type A–F of each ADU in the test set (the tenth topic).

Given the ADU types, we next converted the human-generated training and test arguments from a sequence of ADUs to a sequence of ADU types. After that, we trained one 2-gram and one 3-gram selection language.[4] In Table 3, we report the mean perplexity of the models for both strategies.

---

[3] A more thorough evaluation of k is left to future work.

[4] We did not consider 1-grams, because arguments are inherently relational, hence requiring at least two ADUs.

Strategy	2-grams	3-grams
Logos	54.5	33.5
Pathos	45.9	23.9

Table 4: *Arrangement.* Perplexity of the 2-gram and 3-gram language models for each strategy, averaged over 10 leave-one-topic-out runs using Laplace smoothing.

As shown, the 2-gram perplexity is lower than the 3-gram perplexity in both cases. We assume that the reason lies in the limited size of the dataset and the narrow setting: Only 117 sentences (ADUs) are given per strategy for training, with a vocabulary size of 6 (number of ADU types). Based on the results, we decided to use the 2-gram selection language model to generate candidate arguments.

5.3 Training: Arrangement Language Model

To train arrangement as described in Section 4.2, we took all arguments of the nine training topics in each experiment. We converted each argument from a sequence of ADUs to a sequence of ADU roles (thesis, pro, and con). After that, we trained a 2-gram and 3-gram language model for each strategy. Table 4 lists the mean perplexity values over the 10 folds.

Here, the perplexity is lower for 3-grams than for 2-grams, which can be expected to yield better performance. Therefore, we used the 3-gram language model to filter the set of candidate arguments.

5.4 Training: Phrasing Regression Model

For phrasing (in terms of choosing the best ADU sequence), we first extracted features from each candidate, as described in Section 4.3. Then, we calculated the semantic similarities between each pair of adjacent ADUs as follows:

1. We obtained a 300-dimensional word embedding for each word in an ADU using the pre-trained GloVe common-crawl model (Pennington et al., 2014).[5]

2. We averaged the embeddings of all words in an ADU, resulted in one vector representing the ADU.

3. For each adjacent pair of ADUs, we computed the cosine similarity of their vectors.

Figure 4 shows a histogram of the distribution of the cosine similarities of each adjacent pair of

[5]The used model can be found here: http://nlp.stanford.edu/data/glove.42B.300d.zip.

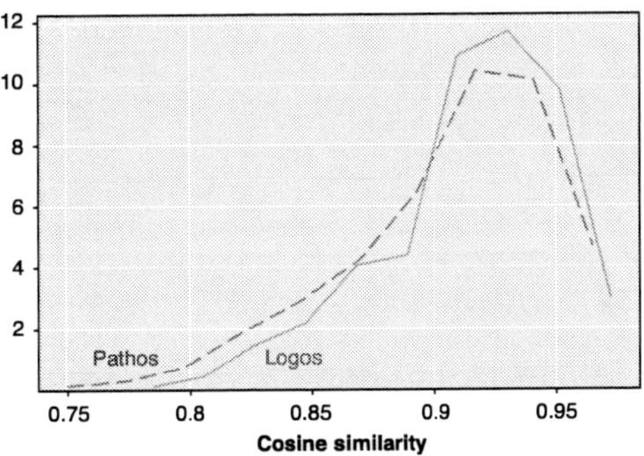

Figure 4: Histogram of the cosine similarity of the average word embeddings of adjacent pairs of ADUs in logos-oriented and in pathos-oriented arguments.

ADUs (i.e., each ADU 2-gram) in logos-oriented arguments and in pathos-oriented arguments. We observe a generally high similarity between neighboring ADUs for both strategies, with logos-oriented 2-grams being slightly more similar on average.

Given the ADU 2-grams, we train a linear regression model that predicts the sum of ADU 2-gram probabilities in each argument. In case of the logos strategy, the model has a mean squared error (MSE) of 0.05. In case of pathos the MSE is 0.03.

5.5 Results: Argumentation Synthesis

Up to this point, we trained all selection, arrangement, and phrasing models 10 times. Combining the three models for each strategy, we finally generated one argument per strategy for the topic-stance pair left out in each experiments. Hence, we ended up with 10 computationally synthesized arguments per strategy in total.

We evaluate each of these arguments by checking whether it matches any of the 13 human-generated ground-truth arguments given per topic-stance pair. The matching is quantified in terms of n-gram overlap with $n = \{1, \ldots, 5\}$.

For comparison, we consider a baseline that randomly generates arguments for each topic-stance pair as follows:

1. Select a random thesis unit from t_1 to t_4.

2. Select a random con unit from c_1 to c_4.

3. Select three random pro units from p_1 to p_{12}.

4. Randomly arrange the selected units.

Table 5 presents the accuracy of n-gram overlaps between each of the 13 human-generated arguments per topic-stance pair and the arguments computationally synthesized arguments by our model

		Sequential					Non-Sequential				
Strategy	**Approach**	1-gram	2-gram	3-gram	4-gram	5-gram	1-gram	2-gram	3-gram	4-gram	5-gram
Logos	Our model	**80.0%**	**15.0%**	0.0%	0.0%	0.0%	**80.0%**	**39.0%**	**9.0%**	0.0%	0.0%
	Baseline	76.0%	10.0%	**0.7%**	0.0%	0.0%	76.0%	3.1%	8.8%	**2.0%**	0.0%
Pathos	Our model	**88.0%**	**20.0%**	0.0%	0.0%	0.0%	**88.0%**	**48.0%**	**17.0%**	**4.0%**	0.0%
	Baseline	82.0%	11.5%	**0.7%**	0.0%	0.0%	82.0%	38.9%	10.7%	1.6%	0.0%

Table 5: Accuracy of n-gram overlaps between the human-generated arguments for each strategy and the arguments computationally synthesized by *our model* and the *baseline*. In the *sequential* case, the ordering is considered, in the *non-sequential* case, it is ignored. The better result in each experiment is marked bold, if any.

Strategy	**ID**	**Argument Computationally Synthesized from Five Argumentative Discourse Units**
Logos	t_4	**universities should not charge tuition fees in Germany.**
	c_3	to oblige non-academics to finance others' degrees through taxes is not just.
	p_9	this would impede or prevent access to those who are financially weaker.
	p_5	if a university lacks the funds, sponsors must be found.
	p_8	there are other instruments to motivate tighter discipline while studying.
Pathos	p_2	education must not be a question of money in a wealthy society such as Germany.
	c_1	one could argue that an increase in tuition fees would allow institutions to be better equipped.
	p_7	studying and taking higher degrees must remain a basic right for everyone.
	p_6	longer durations of studies are costly.
	t_2	**the universities in Germany should not under any circumstances charge tuition fees.**

Table 6: Comparison of two con arguments computationally synthesized with our model for the topic *Should all universities in Germany charge tuition fees?*, each being a sequence of five ADUs. A logos-oriented argument $(t_4, c_3, p_9, p_5, p_8)$ and a pathos-oriented argument $(p_2, c_1, p_7, p_6, t_2)$. The thesis of each argument is marked bold.

and by the baseline, with and without considering the ordering of ADUs. Our models outperform the baseline for 1-grams and 2-grams in all cases. For *sequential 3-grams*, however, it did not achieve any overlap with the human-generated arguments for either strategy. This may be explained by the fact that the employed selection and phrasing models are based on 2-grams only. For $n \geq 2$, the synthesis generally does not work well anymore. We believe that the small data size is a main cause behind this, although it may also point to the limitation of composing ADUs based on surface features. In the non-sequential case, though, our model performs comparably well for 3-grams, and it even manages to correctly synthesize some ADU 4-grams.

In Table 6, we exemplify the top-scored arguments for one topic-stance pair, synthesized by our approach for logos and for pathos respectively. They indicate that our model was able to learn strategy-specific differences.[6] In particular, the logos argument starts with the thesis (t_2), as argumentation guidelines suggest. It then reasons based on consequences and alternatives. Matching intu-

ition, the pathos argument appeals more to emotion, reflected in phrases such as "wealthy society" and "under any circumstances". Particularly the thesis (t_4) has a more intense tonality than t_2, and putting it at the end creates additional emphasis.

6 Conclusion

This paper has presented a topic-independent computational approach to imitate the process of selecting, arranging, and phrasing argumentative discourse units (ADUs) — so to speak, to synthesize arguments. We have proposed to operationalize the necessary synthesis knowledge in the form of a combined language and regression model that predicts ADU sequences. So far, we have evaluated our approach on a small dataset only that contains 260 argumentative texts following either of two rhetorical strategies. For a controlled experiment setting based on this data, we have reported preliminary results of medium effectiveness regarding the imitation of human-generated arguments.

A big challenge for the future is to move from such a controlled setting to a real-world scenario, where arguments have to be formed for a freely-chosen topic from material that is mined from the web. Still, our topic-independent approach defines a first substantial step in this direction.

---

[6]Notice that the coherence of the arguments may be optimized by inserting discourse markers, such as a "but" before p_7 in the pathos argument. As stated above, however, this is beyond the scope of the paper at hand.

References

Aristotle. 2007. *On Rhetoric: A Theory of Civic Discourse* (George A. Kennedy, Translator). Clarendon Aristotle series. Oxford University Press.

Yonatan Bilu and Noam Slonim. 2016. Claim synthesis via predicate recycling. In *Proceedings of the 54th Annual Meeting of the Association for Computational Linguistics (Volume 2: Short Papers)*, pages 525–530. Association for Computational Linguistics.

Giuseppe Carenini and Johanna D. Moore. 2006. Generating and evaluating evaluative arguments. *Artificial Intelligence*, 170(11):925–952.

Oana Cocarascu and Francesca Toni. 2017. Identifying attack and support argumentative relations using deep learning. In *Proceedings of the 2017 Conference on Empirical Methods in Natural Language Processing*, pages 1374–1379. Association for Computational Linguistics.

Michael A Cohn, Matthias R Mehl, and James W Pennebaker. 2004. Linguistic markers of psychological change surrounding September 11, 2001. *Psychological science*, 15(10):687–693.

Charlie Egan, Advaith Siddharthan, and Adam Wyner. 2016. Summarising the points made in online political debates. In *Proceedings of the Third Workshop on Argument Mining (ArgMining2016)*, pages 134–143, Berlin, Germany. Association for Computational Linguistics.

H. Paul Grice. 1975. Logic and conversation. In Peter Cole and Jerry L. Morgan, editors, *Syntax and Semantics, Vol. 3*, pages 41–58. Academic Press, New York.

Ivan Habernal and Iryna Gurevych. 2016. Which argument is more convincing? Analyzing and predicting convincingness of web arguments using bidirectional LSTM. In *Proceedings of the 54th Annual Meeting of the Association for Computational Linguistics (Volume 1: Long Papers)*, pages 1589–1599. Association for Computational Linguistics.

Ari Holtzman, Jan Buys, Maxwell Forbes, Antoine Bosselut, David Golub, and Yejin Choi. 2018. Learning to write with cooperative discriminators. Technical Report 1805.06087, arXiv.

Xinyu Hua and Lu Wang. 2018. Neural argument generation augmented with externally retrieved evidence. In *Proceedings of the 56th Annual Meeting of the Association for Computational Linguistics (Volume 1: Long Papers)*, pages 219–230. Association for Computational Linguistics.

Ewa Kacewicz, James W Pennebaker, Matthew Davis, Moongee Jeon, and Arthur C Graesser. 2014. Pronoun use reflects standings in social hierarchies. *Journal of Language and Social Psychology*, 33(2):125–143.

Dieu Thu Le, Cam-Tu Nguyen, and Kim Anh Nguyen. 2018. Dave the debater: a retrieval-based and generative argumentative dialogue agent. In *Proceedings of the 5th Workshop on Argument Mining*, pages 121–130, Brussels, Belgium. Association for Computational Linguistics.

Saif M Mohammad and Peter D Turney. 2013. Crowdsourcing a word–emotion association lexicon. *Computational Intelligence*, 29(3):436–465.

Matthew L Newman, James W Pennebaker, Diane S Berry, and Jane M Richards. 2003. Lying words: Predicting deception from linguistic styles. *Personality and social psychology bulletin*, 29(5):665–675.

Rafail Ostrovsky, Yuval Rabani, Leonard J Schulman, and Chaitanya Swamy. 2012. The effectiveness of lloyd-type methods for the k-means problem. *Journal of the ACM (JACM)*, 59(6):28.

Andreas Peldszus and Manfred Stede. 2016. An annotated corpus of argumentative microtexts. In *Argumentation and Reasoned Action: 1st European Conference on Argumentation (ECA 16)*. College Publications.

James W Pennebaker, Ryan L Boyd, Kayla Jordan, and Kate Blackburn. 2015. The Development and Psychometric Properties of LIWC2015.

James W Pennebaker, Cindy K Chung, Joey Frazee, Gary M Lavergne, and David I Beaver. 2014. When small words foretell academic success: The case of college admissions essays. *PloS one*, 9(12):e115844.

Jeffrey Pennington, Richard Socher, and Christopher D. Manning. 2014. Glove: Global vectors for word representation. In *Empirical Methods in Natural Language Processing (EMNLP)*, pages 1532–1543.

Robert Plutchik. 1980. A general psychoevolutionary theory of emotion. In *Theories of emotion*, pages 3–33. Elsevier.

Paul Reisert, Naoya Inoue, Naoaki Okazaki, and Kentaro Inui. 2015. A computational approach for generating Toulmin model argumentation. In *Proceedings of the 2nd Workshop on Argumentation Mining*, pages 45–55. Association for Computational Linguistics.

Misa Sato, Kohsuke Yanai, Toshinori Miyoshi, Toshihiko Yanase, Makoto Iwayama, Qinghua Sun, and Yoshiki Niwa. 2015. End-to-end argument generation system in debating. In *Proc. ACL-IJCNLP 2015 System Demonstrations*.

Swapna Somasundaran, Josef Ruppenhofer, and Janyce Wiebe. 2007. Detecting arguing and sentiment in meetings. In *Proceedings of the SIGdial Workshop on Discourse and Dialogue*, volume 6.

Christian Stab and Iryna Gurevych. 2014. Identifying argumentative discourse structures in persuasive essays. In *Proceedings of the 2014 Conference on Empirical Methods in Natural Language Processing (EMNLP)*, pages 46–56. Association for Computational Linguistics.

Yla R Tausczik and James W Pennebaker. 2010. The psychological meaning of words: LIWC and computerized text analysis methods. *Journal of language and social psychology*, 29(1):24–54.

Stephen E. Toulmin. 1958. *The Uses of Argument.* Cambridge University Press.

Henning Wachsmuth, Manfred Stede, Roxanne El Baff, Khalid Al Khatib, Maria Skeppstedt, and Benno Stein. 2018. Argumentation synthesis following rhetorical strategies. In *Proceedings of COLING 2018, the 27th International Conference on Computational Linguistics*. The COLING 2018 Organizing Committee. To appear.

Lu Wang and Wang Ling. 2016. Neural network-based abstract generation for opinions and arguments. In *Proceedings of the 2016 Conference of the North American Chapter of the Association for Computational Linguistics: Human Language Technologies*, pages 47–57. Association for Computational Linguistics.

Toshihiko Yanase, Toshinori Miyoshi, Kohsuke Yanai, Misa Sato, Makoto Iwayama, Yoshiki Niwa, Paul Reisert, and Kentaro Inui. 2015. Learning sentence ordering for opinion generation of debate. In *Proceedings of the 2nd Workshop on Argumentation Mining*, pages 94–103. Association for Computational Linguistics.

Ingrid Zukerman, Richard McConachy, and Kevin B. Korb. 2000. Using argumentation strategies in automated argument generation. In *First International Conference on Natural Language Generation (INLG 00)*, pages 55–62.

Towards Coherent and Engaging Spoken Dialog Response Generation Using Automatic Conversation Evaluators

Sanghyun Yi[1], Rahul Goel[2], Chandra Khatri[3], Alessandra Cervone[4], Tagyoung Chung[5],
Behnam Hedayatnia[5], Anu Venkatesh[5], Raefer Gabriel[5], Dilek Hakkani-Tur[5]
[1]Division of Humanities and Social Sciences, California Institute of Technology,
[2]Google, [3]Uber AI, [5]Alexa AI, Amazon
[4]Signals and Interactive Systems Lab, University of Trento
`syi@caltech.edu, goelrahul@google.com,`
`{tagyoung,behnam,anuvenk,raeferg,hakkanit}@amazon.com,`
`chdrak@uber.com, alessandra.cervone@unitn.it`

Abstract

Encoder-decoder based neural architectures serve as the basis of state-of-the-art approaches in end-to-end open domain dialog systems. Since most of such systems are trained with a maximum likelihood (MLE) objective they suffer from issues such as lack of generalizability and the *generic response problem*, i.e., a system response that can be an answer to a large number of user utterances, e.g., "Maybe, I don't know." Having explicit feedback on the relevance and interestingness of a system response at each turn can be a useful signal for mitigating such issues and improving system quality by selecting responses from different approaches. Towards this goal, we present a system that evaluates chatbot responses at each dialog turn for coherence and engagement. Our system provides explicit turn-level dialog quality feedback, which we show to be highly correlated with human evaluation. To show that incorporating this feedback in the neural response generation models improves dialog quality, we present two different and complementary mechanisms to incorporate explicit feedback into a neural response generation model: reranking and direct modification of the loss function during training. Our studies show that a response generation model that incorporates these combined feedback mechanisms produce more engaging and coherent responses in an open-domain spoken dialog setting, significantly improving the response quality using both automatic and human evaluation.

1 Introduction

Due to recent advances in spoken language understanding and automatic speech recognition, conversational interfaces such as Alexa, Cortana, and Siri have become increasingly common. While these interfaces are task oriented, there is an increasing interest in building conversational systems that can engage in more social conversations. Building systems that can have a general conversation in an open domain setting is a challenging problem, but it is an important step towards more natural human-machine interactions.

Recently, there has been significant interest in building chatbots (Sordoni et al., 2015; Wen et al., 2015) fueled by the availability of dialog data sets such as Ubuntu, Twitter, and Movie dialogs (Lowe et al., 2015; Ritter et al., 2011; Danescu-Niculescu-Mizil and Lee, 2011). However, as most chatbots are text-based, work on human-machine spoken dialog is relatively under-explored, partly due to lack of such dialog corpora. Spoken dialog poses additional challenges such as automatic speech recognition errors and divergence between spoken and written language.

Sequence-to-sequence (seq2seq) models (Sutskever et al., 2014) and their extensions (Luong et al., 2015; Sordoni et al., 2015; Li et al., 2015), which are used for neural machine translation (MT), have been widely adopted for dialog generation systems. In MT, given a source sentence, the correctness of the target sentence can be measured by semantic similarity to the source sentence. However, in open-domain conversations, a generic utterance such as "sounds good" could be a valid response to a large variety of statements. These seq2seq models are commonly trained on a maximum likelihood objective, which leads the models to place uniform importance on all user utterance and system response pairs. Thus, these models usually choose "safe" responses as they frequently appear in the dialog training data. This phenomenon is known as the *generic response problem*. These responses, while arguably correct, are bland and convey little information leading to short conversations and low user satisfaction.

Since response generation systems are trained by maximizing the average likelihood of the training data, they do not have a clear signal on how well the current conversation is going. We hypothesize that having a way to measure conversational success at every turn could be valuable information that can guide system response generation and help improving system quality. Such a measurement may also be useful for combining responses from various competing systems. To this end, we build a supervised conversational evaluator to assess two aspects of responses: engagement and coherence. The input to our evaluators are encoded conversations represented as fixed-length vectors as well as hand-crafted dialog and turn level features. The system outputs explicit scores on coherence and engagement of the system response.

We experiment with two ways to incorporate these explicit signals in response generation systems. First, we use the evaluator outputs as input to a reranking model, which are used to rescore the n-best outputs obtained after beam search decoding. Second, we propose a technique to incorporate the evaluator loss directly into the conversational model as an additional discriminatory loss term. Using both human and automatic evaluations, we show that both of these methods significantly improve the system response quality. The combined model utilizing re-ranking and the composite loss outperforms models using either mechanism alone.

The contributions of this work are two-fold. First, we experiment with various hand-crafted features and conversational encoding schemes to build a conversational evaluation system that can provide explicit turn-level feedback to a response generation system on the highly subjective task. This system can be used independently to compare various response generation systems or as a signal to improve response generation. Second, we experiment with two complementary ways to incorporate explicit feedback to the response generation systems and show improvement in dialog quality using automatic metrics as well as human evaluation.

2 Related Works

There are two major themes in this work. The first is building evaluators that allow us to estimate human perceptions of coherence, topicality, and interestingness of responses in a conversational context. The second is the use of evaluators to guide the generation process. As a result, this work is related to two distinct bodies of work.

Automatic Evaluation of Conversations: There are two major themes in this work. The

Learning automatic evaluation of conversation quality has a long history (Walker et al., 1997). However, we still do not have widely accepted solutions. Due to the similarity between conversational response generation and MT, automatic MT metrics such as BLEU (Papineni et al., 2002) and METEOR (Banerjee and Lavie, 2005) are widely adopted for evaluating dialog generation. ROUGE (Lin and Hovy, 2003), which is also used for chatbot evaluation, is a popular metric for text summarization. These metrics primarily rely on token-level overlap over a corpus (also synonymy in the case of METEOR), and therefore are not well-suited for dialog generation since a valid conversational response may not have any token-level or even semantic-level overlap with the ground truths. While the shortcomings of these metrics are well known for MT (Graham, 2015; Espinosa et al., 2010), the problem is aggravated for dialog generation evaluation because of the much larger output space (Liu et al., 2016; Novikova et al., 2017). However, due to the lack of clear alternatives, these metrics are still widely used for evaluating response generation (Ritter et al., 2011; Lowe et al., 2017). To ensure comparability with other approaches, we report results on these metrics for our models.

To tackle the shortcomings of automatic metrics, there have been efforts to build models to score conversations. Lowe et al. (2017) train a model to predict the score of a system response given a dialog context. However, they work with tiny data sets (around 4000 sentences) in a non-spoken setting. Tao et al. (2017) address the expensive annotation process by adding in unsupervised data. However, their metric is not interpretable, and the results are also not shown on a spoken setting. Our work differs from the aforementioned works as the output of our system is interpretable at each dialog turn.

There has also been work on building evaluation systems that focus on specific aspects of dialog. Li et al. (2016c) use features for information flow, Yu et al. (2016) use features for turn-level appropriateness. However, these metrics are based on a narrow aspect of the conversation and fail to capture broad ranges of phenomena that lead to a good dialog.

Improving System Response Generation: Seq2Seq models have allowed researchers to train dialog models without relying on handcrafted dialog acts and slot values. Using maximum mutual information (MMI) (Li et al., 2015) was one of the earlier attempts to make conversational responses more diverse (Serban et al., 2016b,a). Shao et al. (2017) use a segment ranking beam search to produce more diverse responses. Our method extends the strategy employed by Shao et al. (2017) utilizing a trained model as the reranking function and is similar to Holtzman et al. (2018) but with different kind of trained model.

More recently, there have been works which aim to alleviate this problem by incorporating conversation-specific rewards in the learning process. Yao et al. (2016) use the IDF value of generated sentences as a reward signal. Xing et al. (2017) use topics as an additional input while decoding to produce more specific responses. Li et al. (2016b) add personal information to make system responses more user specific.Li et al. (2017) use distillation to train different models at different levels of specificity and use reinforcement learning to pick the appropriate system response. Zhou et al. (2017) and Zhang et al. (2018) introduce latent factors in the seq2seq models that control specificity in neural response generation. There has been recent work which combines responses from multiple sub-systems (Serban et al., 2017; Papaioannou et al., 2017) and ranks them to output the final system response. Our method complements these approaches by introducing a novel learned-estimator model as the additional reward signal.

3 Data

The data used in this study was collected during the Alexa Prize (Ram et al., 2017) competition and shared with the teams who were participating in the competition. Upon initiating the conversation, users were paired with a randomly selected chatbot built by the participants. At the end of the conversation, the users were prompted to rate the chatbot quality, from 1–5, with 5 being the highest.

We randomly sampled more than 15K conversations (approximately 160K turns) collected during the competition. These were annotated for coherence and engagement (See Section 3.1) and used to train the conversation evaluators. For training the response generators, we selected highly-rated user conversations, which resulted in around 370K conversations containing 4M user utterances and their corresponding system response. One notable statistic is that user utterances are typically very short (mean: 3.6 tokens) while the system responses generally are much longer (mean: 23.2 tokens).

3.1 Annotations

Asking annotators to measure coherence and engagement directly is a time-consuming task. We observed that we could collect data much faster if we asked direct "yes" or "no" questions to our annotators. Hence, upon reviewing a user-chatbot interaction along with the entire conversation to the current turn, annotators[1] rated each chatbot response as "yes" or "no" on the following criteria:

- **The system response is comprehensible:** The information provided by the chatbot made sense with respect to the user utterance and is syntactically correct.

- **The system response is on topic:** The chatbot response was on the same topic as the user utterance or was relevant to the user utterance. For example, if a user asks about a baseball player on the LA Dodgers, then the chatbot mentions something about the baseball team.

- **The system response is interesting:** The chatbot response contains information which is novel and relevant. For example, the chatbot would provide an answer about a baseball player and give some additional information to create a fleshed-out response.

- **I want to continue the conversation:** Given the current state of the conversation and the system response, there is a natural way to continue the conversation. For example, this could be due to the system asking a question about the current conversation subject.

We use these questions as proxies for measuring coherence and engagement of responses. The answers to the first two questions ("comprehensible" and "on topic") are used as a proxy for coherence. Similarly, the answer to the last two questions ("interesting" and "continue the conversation") are used as a proxy for engagement.

4 Conversation Evaluators

We train conversational response evaluators to assess the state of a given conversation. Our models are trained on a combination of utterance and response pairs combined with context (past turn user utterances and system responses) along with other

---

[1] The data was collected through mechanical turk. Annotators were presented with the full context of the dialog up to the current turn.

Model	TREC	SUBJ	STS
Average Emb.	0.80	0.90	0.45
Transformer	0.83	0.91	0.48
BiLSTM	0.84	0.90	0.45

Table 1: Sentence embedding performance.

features, e.g., dialog acts and topics as described in Section 4.3. We experiment with different ways to encode the responses (Section 4.1) as well as with different feature combinations (Figure 1).

4.1 Sentence Embeddings

We pretrained models that produce sentence embeddings using the ParlAI chitchat data set (Miller et al., 2017). We use the Quick-Thought (QT) loss (Logeswaran and Lee, 2018) to train the embeddings. Our word embeddings are initialized with FastText (Bojanowski et al., 2016) to capture the sub-word features and then fine-tuned. We encode sentences into embeddings using the following methods:

a) Average of word embeddings (300 dim)

b) The Transformer Network (1 layer, 600 dim) (Vaswani et al., 2017)

c) Concatenated last states of a BiLSTM (1 layer, 600 dim)

The selected dimensions and network structures followed the original paper (Vaswani et al., 2017). All models were trained with a batch size of 400 using Adam optimizer with learning rate of 5e-4.

To measure the sentence embedding quality, we evaluate our models on a few standard classification tasks. The models are used to get sentence representation, which are passed through feedforward networks that are trained for the following classification tasks: (i) Semantic Textual Similarity (STS) (Marelli et al., 2014), (ii) Question Type Classification (TREC) (Voorhees and Dang, 2003), (iii) Subjectivity Classification (SUBJ) (Pang and Lee, 2004). Table 1 shows the different models' performances on these tasks. Based on this, we choose the Transformer as our sentence encoder as it was overall the best performing while being fast.

4.2 Context

Given the contextual nature of the problem we extracted the sentence embeddings of user utterances and responses for the past 5 turns and used a 1 layer LSTM with 256 hidden units to encode conversational context. The last state of LSTM is used to obtain the encoded representation, which is then concatenated with other features (Section 4.3) in a fully-connected neural network.

4.3 Features

Apart from sentence embeddings and context, the following features are also used:

- **Dialog Act:** Serban et al. (2017) show that dialog act (DA) features could be useful for response selection rankers. Following this, we use model (Khatri et al., 2018)-predicted DAs (Stolcke et al., 1998) of user utterances and system responses as an indicator feature.

- **Entity Grid:** Cervone et al. (2018); Barzilay and Lapata (2008) show that entities and DA transitions across turns can be strong features for assessing dialog coherence. Starting from a grid representation of the turns of the conversation as a matrix (DAs × entities), these features are designed to capture the patterns of topic and intent shift distribution of a dialog. We employ the same strategy for our models.

- **Named Entity (NE) Overlap:** We use named entity overlap between user utterances and their corresponding system responses as a feature. Our named entities are obtained using SpaCy[2]. Papaioannou et al. (2017) have also used similar NE features in their ranker.

- **Topic:** We use a one-hot representation of a dialog turn topic predicted by a conversational topic model (Guo et al., 2017) that classifies a given dialog turn into one of 26 pre-defined classes like Sports and Movies.

- **Response Similarity:** Cosine similarity between user utterance embedding and system response embedding is used as a feature.

- **Length:** We use the token-level length of the user utterance and the response as a feature.

The above features were selected from a large pool of features through significance testing on our development set. The effect of adding these features can be seen in Table 2. Some of the features such as **Topic** lack previous dialog context, which could be updated to include the context. We leave this extension for future work.

---

[2]https://spacy.io/

Evaluator	'Yes' Class Distr.	Accuracy	Precision	Recall	F-score	MCC
Comprehensible	0.80	0.84 (+3%)	0.83 (+1%)	0.85 (+15%)	0.84 (+8%)	0.37 (+107%)
On-topic	0.45	0.64 (+9%)	0.65 (+10%)	0.64 (+18%)	0.64 (+13%)	0.29 (+81%)
Interesting	0.16	0.83 (-1%)	0.77 (+10%)	0.80 (-5%)	0.78 (+2%)	0.12 (+inf%)
Cont. Conversation	0.71	0.75 (+4%)	0.73 (+5%)	0.72 (+31%)	0.72 (+17%)	0.32(+179%)

Table 2: Conversation Evaluators Performance. Numbers in parentheses denote relative changes when using our best model (all features) with respect to the baseline (no handcrafted features, only sentence embeddings). Second column shows the class imbalance in our annotations. Note that the baseline model had 0 MCC for Interesting

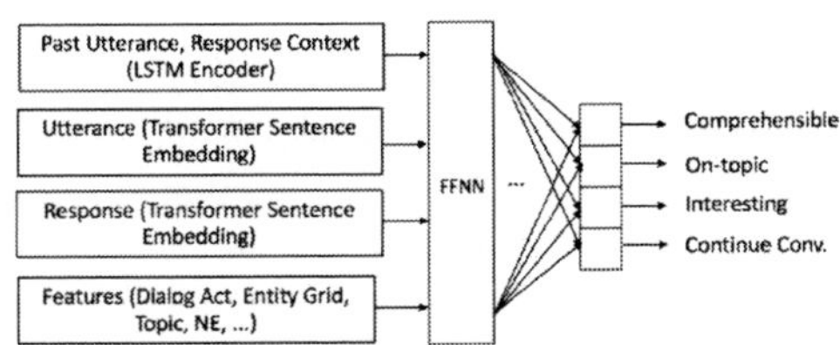

Figure 1: Conversation Evaluators

4.4 Models

Given the large number of features and their non-sequential nature, we train four binary classifiers using feedforward neural networks (FFNN). The input to these models is a dialog turn. Each output layer is a softmax function corresponding to a binary decision for each evaluation metric forming a four-dimensional vector. Each vector dimension corresponds to an evaluation metric (See Section 3.1). For example, one possible reference output would be [0,1,1,0], which corresponds to "not comprehensible," "on topic," "interesting," and "I don't want to continue."

We experimented with training the evaluators jointly and separately and found that training them jointly led to better performance. We suspect this is due to the objectives of all evaluators being closely related. We concatenate the aforementioned features as an input to a 3-layer FFNN with 256 hidden units. Figure 1 depicts the architecture of the conversation evaluators.

5 Response Generation System

To incorporate the explicit turn level feedback provided by the conversation evaluators, we augment our baseline response generation system with the softmax scores provided by the conversation evaluators. Our baseline response generation system is described in Section 5.1. We then incorporate evaluators outputs using two techniques: reranking and fine-tuning.

5.1 Base Model (S2S)

We extended the approach of Yao et al. (2016) where the authors used Luong's dot attention (Luong et al., 2015). In our experiments, the decoder uses the same attention (Figure 2a). As we want to observe the full impact of conversational evaluators, we do not incorporate inverse document frequency (IDF) or conversation topics into our objective. Extending the objective to include these terms can be a good direction for future work.

To make the response generation system more robust, we added user utterances and system responses from the previous turn as context. The input to the response generation model is previous-turn user utterance, previous-turn system response, and current-turn user utterance concatenated sequentially. We insert a special transition token (Serban et al., 2016c) between turns. We then use a single RNN to encode these sentences. Our word embeddings are randomly initialized and then fine-tuned during training. We used a 1-layer Gated Recurrent Neural network with 512 hidden units for both encoder and decoder to train the seq2seq model and MLE as our training objective.

5.2 Reranking (S2S_RR)

In this approach, we do not update the underlying encoder-decoder model. We maintain a beam to get 15-best candidates from the decoder. The top candidate out of the 15 candidates is equivalent to the output of the baseline model. Here, instead of selecting the top output, the final output response is chosen using a reranking model.

For our reranking model, we calculate BLEU scores for each of the 15 candidate responses against the ground truth response from the chatbot. We then sample two responses from the k-best list and train a pairwise response reranker. The response with the higher BLEU is placed in the positive class (+1) and the one with lower BLEU is placed in the negative class (-1). We do this for all possible candidate combinations from the 15-best

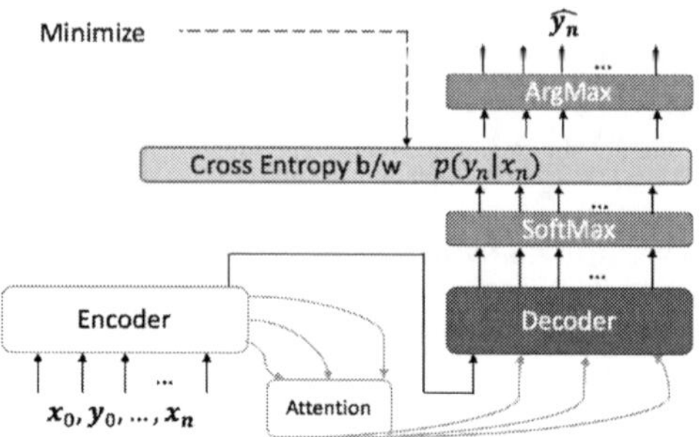

(a) Baseline Response Generator (Seq2Seq with Attention)

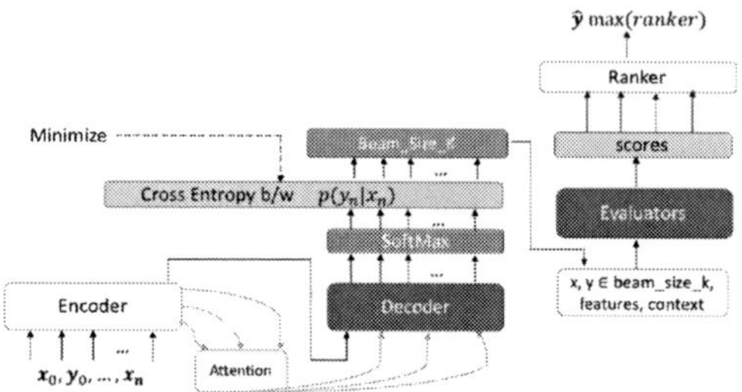

(b) Reranking Using Evaluators. Top 15 candidates from beam search are passed to the evaluators. The candidate that maximizes the reranker score is chosen as the output. Encoder-decoder remain unchanged.

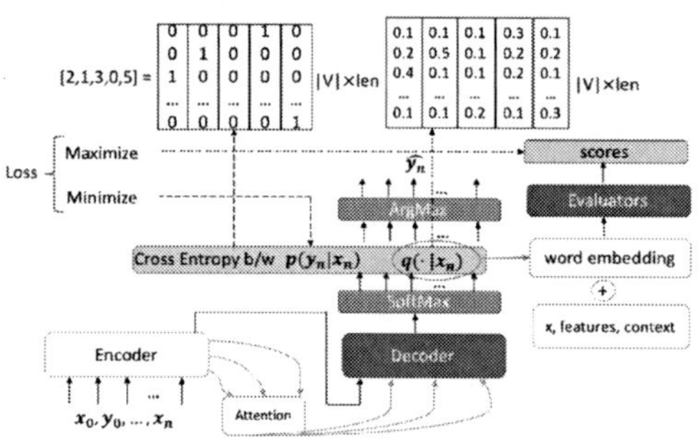

(c) Fine-tuning Using Evaluators. We minimize cross entropy loss and maximize discriminator loss. The output of softmax, i.e., likelihood over vocabulary for the length of output is passed to the evaluator along with the input (x and context). Evaluator generates the discriminative score over $|V| \times len$ generator output, which is subtracted from the loss. The updated loss is back-propagated to update encoder-decoder.

Figure 2: Response Model Configurations. The baseline is shown at the top. The terms x_n and y_n correspond to n^{th} utterance and response respectively.

responses. We use the max-margin ranking loss to train the model. The model is a three-layered FFNN with 16 hidden units.

The input to the pairwise reranker is the softmax output of the 4 evaluators as shown in Figure 1. The input to the evaluators are described in Section 4. The output of the reranker is a scalar,

which, if trained right, would give a higher value for responses with higher BLEU scores. Figure 2b depicts the architecture of this model.

5.3 Fine-tuning (S2S_FT)

In this approach, we use evaluators as a discriminatory loss to fine-tune the baseline encoder-decoder response generation system. We first train the baseline model and then, it is fine-tuned using the evaluator outputs in the hope of generating more coherent and engaging responses. One issue with MLE is that the learned models are not optimized for the final metric (e.g., BLEU). To combat this problem, we add a discriminatory loss in addition to the generative loss to the overall loss term as shown in Equation 1.

$$loss = \sum_{i=1}^{len} p(y_{ni}|z_n)log(q(\hat{y}_{ni}|z_n)) \tag{1}$$
$$- \lambda||Eval(x_n, q(.|z_n)||_1$$

where $z_n = x_n, y_{n-1}, \ldots, x_0, y_0$ is the conversational context where n is the context length. $q \in R^{|V| \times len}$ of the first term corresponds to the softmax output generated by the response generation model. The term $\hat{y}_{ni}$ refers to its corresponding decoder response at n_{th} conversation turn and i^{th} word generated. In the second term, the function $Eval$ refers to the evaluator score produced for a user utterance, x_n, and decoder softmax output, q.

In Equation 1, the first term corresponds to the cross-entropy loss from the encoder-decoder while the second term corresponds to the discriminative loss from the evaluator. In a standalone evaluation setting, the evaluator will take one hot representation of the user utterance as input, i.e., the input is len-tokens long which is passed through an embedding lookup layer which makes it $\mathbb{R}^{D \times len}$ input to rest of the network where D is the size of the word embeddings. To make the loss differentiable, instead of performing $argmax$ to get a decoded token, we use the output of the softmax layer (distribution of likelihood across entire vocabulary for output length, i.e., $\mathbb{R}^{|V| \times len}$) and use this to do a weighted embedding lookup across the entire vocabulary to get the same $\mathbb{R}^{D \times len}$ matrix as an input to rest of the evaluator network. Our updated evaluator input becomes the following:

$$\mathbb{R}^{D \times len} = \mathbb{R}^{D \times |V|} \times \mathbb{R}^{|V| \times len} \tag{2}$$

The evaluator score is defined as the sum of softmax outputs of all 4 models. We keep the rest of the input (context and features) for the evaluator as is.

We weight the discriminator score by λ, which is a hyperparameter. We selected λ to be 10 using grid search to optimize for final BLEU on our development set. Figure 2c depicts the architecture of this approach. The decoder is fine-tuned to maximize evaluator scores along while minimizing the cross-entropy loss. The evaluator model is trained on the original annotated corpus and parameters are frozen.

5.4 Reranking + Fine-tuning (S2S_RR_FT)

We also combined fine-tuning with reranking, where we obtained the 15 candidates from the fine-tuned response generator and then we select the best response using the reranker, which is trained to maximize the BLEU score.

6 Experiments and Results

6.1 Conversation Evaluators

The conversation evaluators were trained using cross-entropy loss. We used a batch size of 128, dropout of 0.3 and Adam optimizer with a learning rate of 5e-5 for our conversational evaluators. Sentence embeddings for user utterances and system responses are obtained using the fast-text embeddings and Transformer network.

Table 2 shows the evaluator performance compared with a baseline with no handcrafted features. We present precision, recall, and f-score measures along with the accuracy. Furthermore, since the class distribution of the dataset is highly imbalanced, we also calculate Matthews correlation coefficient (MCC)(Matthews, 1975), which takes into account true and false positives and negatives. It is a balanced measure which can be used even if the classes sizes are very different. With the proposed features we observe significant improvement across all metrics.

We also performed a correlation study between the model predicted scores and human annotated scores (1 to 5) on 2000 utterances. The annotators[3] were asked to answer a single question: "On a scale of 1–5, how coherent and engaging is this response given the previous conversation?" From Table 3, it can be observed that evaluator predicted scores has significant correlation (moderate to high) with the overall human evaluation score on this subjective

---

[3]Same setup as previously described

Metric	Pearson Corr	p-value
Comprehensible	0.2	$\ll 0.001$
On-topic	0.4	$\ll 0.001$
Interesting	0.25	$\ll 0.001$
Cont. Conversation	0.3	$\ll 0.001$

Table 3: Evaluators Correlation with Turn-level Ratings

task ($0.2 - 0.4$ Pearson correlation with turn-level ratings). Considering the substantial individual differences in evaluating open-domain conversations, we observe that our evaluators with moderate level of correlation can be used to provide turn-level feedback for a human-chatbot conversation.

6.2 Response Generation

We first trained the baseline model (S2S) on the conversational data set (4M utterance-response pairs from the competition. Section 3). The data were split into 80% training, 10% development, and 10% test sets. The baseline model was trained using Adam with learning rate of 1e-4 and batch size of 256 until the development loss converges. The vocabulary of 30K most frequent words were used. And the reranker was trained using the 20K number of beam outputs from the baseline model on the development set. Adam with learning rate of 1e-4 and batch size of 16 was used for the fine-tuning (S2S_FT).

Table 5 shows the performance comparison of different generation models (Section 5) on the Alexa Prize conversational data set. We observed that reranking n-best responses using the evaluator-based reranker (S2S_RR) provides nearly 100% improvement in BLEU-4 scores.

Fine-tuning the generator by adding evaluator loss (S2S_FT) does improve the performance but the gains are smaller compared to reranking. We suspect that this is due to the reranker directly optimizing for BLEU. However, using a fine-tuned model and then reranking (S2S_RR_FT) complements each other and gives the best performance overall. Furthermore, we observe that even though the reranker is trained to maximize the BLEU scores, reranking shows significant gains in ROUGE scores as well. We also measured different systems performance using Distinct-2 (Li et al., 2016a), which is the number of unique length-normalized bigrams in responses. The metric can be a surrogate for measuring diverse outputs. We see that our generators using reranking approaches

Conversation 1	Conversation 2
User: yes Chatbot: is there something specific you want to discuss User: fox news **Ground Truth**: my developers are working hard to get you recent news you can say topics to hear some topics **S2S(Base)**: I found **S2S_RR**: I heard about this **S2S_FT** : I heard of a man it may be interested in this news mentioned **S2S_RR_FT**: I heard about this news talked about this	User: cool Chatbot: back at you ok we could talk about movies or music User: movies **Ground Truth**: shall we chat about something else I love talking about music and movies **S2S(Base)**: so do you **S2S_RR**: who would you want to talk **S2S_FT** : what actor love most **S2S_RR_FT**: what actor

Table 4: Two randomly selected qualitative examples of responses

Metric	BLEU-4	ROUGE-2	Distinct-2
S2S (Base)	5.9	5.1	0.011
S2S_RR	11.6(+97%)	6.3(+24%)	**0.017(+54%)**
S2S_FT	6.2(+5%)	5.3(+4%)	0.011(-1%)
S2S_RR_FT	**12.2(+107%)**	**6.8(+33%)**	0.017(+53%)

Table 5: Generator performance on automatic metrics.

Metric	S2S(Base)	**S2S_RR**
BLEU-4	3.9	7.9 (+103%)
ROUGE-2	0.6	0.8 (+33%)
Distinct-2	0.0047	0.0086 (+82%)

Table 6: Response Generator on Reddit Conversations. Due to the size of the dataset we could not fine tune these models.

Metric	Coherence	Engagement
S2S(Base)	2.34	1.80
S2S_RR	2.42	2.16
S2S_FT	2.36	1.87
S2S_RR_FT	**2.55**	**2.31**

Table 7: Mean ratings for Qualitative and Human Evaluation of Response Generators

improve on this metric as well. Table 4 also shows 2 sampled responses from different models.

To further analyze the impact of reranker trained to optimize on BLEU score, we trained a baseline response generation system on a Reddit data set[4], which comprises of 9 million comments and corresponding response comments. All the hyperparameter setting followed the setting of training on the Alexa Prize conversational dataset.

We trained a new reranker for the Reddit data using the evaluator scores obtained from the models proposed in Section 4. We show in Table 6 that even though the evaluators are trained on a different data set, the reranker learns to select better responses nearly doubling the BLEU scores as well as improving on the Distinct-2 score. Thus, the evaluator generalizes in selecting more coherent and engaging responses in human-human interactions as well as human-computer interactions. As fine-tuning the evaluator is computationally expensive, we did not fine-tune it on the Reddit dataset.

The closest baseline that used BLEU scores for evaluation in open-domain setting is from Li et al. (2015) where they trained the models on Twitter data using Maximum Mutual Information (MMI) as the objective function. They obtained a BLEU score of 5.2 in their best setting on Twitter data (average length 23 chars), which is relatively less complex than Reddit (average length 75 chars).

6.3 Human Evaluation

As noted earlier, automatic evaluation metrics may not be the best way to measure chatbot response generation performance. Therefore, we performed human evaluation of our models. We asked annotators to provide ratings on the system responses from the models we evaluated, i.e., baseline model, S2S_RR, S2S_FT, and S2S_RR_FT. A rating was obtained on two metrics: coherence and engagement. Coherence measures how much the response is comprehensible and relevant to a user's request and engagement shows interestingness of the response (Venkatesh et al. (2018)). We asked the annotators to provide the rating based on a scale of 1–5, with 5 being the best. We had four annotators rate 250 interactions. Table 7 shows the performance of the models on the proposed metrics. Our inter-annotator agreement is 0.42 on Cohen's Kappa Coefficient, which implies moderate agreement. We believe this is because the task is relatively subjective and the conversations were performed in the challenging open-domain setting. The S2S_RR_FT model provides the best perfor-

---

[4]We use a publicly available data (Baumgartner, 2015).

mance across all the metrics, followed by S2S_RR, followed by S2S_FT.

7 Conclusion

Human annotations for conversations show significant variance, but it is still possible to train models which can extract meaningful signal from the human assessment of the conversations. We show that these models can provide useful turn-level guidance to response generation models. We design a system using various features and context encoders to provide turn-level feedback in a conversational dialog. Our feedback is interpretable on 2 major axes of conversational quality: engagement and coherence. We also plan to provide similar evaluators to the university teams participating in the Alexa Prize competition. To show that such feedback is useful in building better conversational response systems, we propose 2 ways to incorporate this feedback, both of which help improve on the baselines. Combining both techniques results in the best performance. We view this work as complementary to other recent work in improving dialog systems such as Li et al. (2015) and Shao et al. (2017). While such open-domain systems are still in their infancy, we view the framework presented in this paper to be an important step towards building end-to-end coherent and engaging chatbots.

References

Satanjeev Banerjee and Alon Lavie. 2005. Meteor: An automatic metric for mt evaluation with improved correlation with human judgments. In *Proceedings of the acl workshop on intrinsic and extrinsic evaluation measures for machine translation and/or summarization*, volume 29, pages 65–72.

Regina Barzilay and Mirella Lapata. 2008. Modeling local coherence: An entity-based approach. *Computational Linguistics*, 34(1):1–34.

Baumgartner. 2015. Reddit. https://archive. org/details/2015_reddit_comments_ corpus. [Accessed: 2018-07-01].

Piotr Bojanowski, Edouard Grave, Armand Joulin, and Tomas Mikolov. 2016. Enriching word vectors with subword information. *arXiv:1607.04606*.

Alessandra Cervone, Evgeny Stepanov, and Giuseppe Riccardi. 2018. Coherence models for dialogue. *Proc. Interspeech 2018*, pages 1011–1015.

Cristian Danescu-Niculescu-Mizil and Lillian Lee. 2011. Chameleons in imagined conversations: A new approach to understanding coordination of linguistic style in dialogs. In *Proceedings of the Workshop on Cognitive Modeling and Computational Linguistics, ACL 2011*.

Dominic Espinosa, Rajakrishnan Rajkumar, Michael White, and Shoshana Berleant. 2010. Further meta-evaluation of broad-coverage surface realization. In *EMNLP*, pages 564–574.

Yvette Graham. 2015. Accurate evaluation of segment-level machine translation metrics.

Fenfei Guo, Angeliki Metallinou, Chandra Khatri, Anirudh Raju, Anu Venkatesh, and Ashwin Ram. 2017. Topic-based evaluation for conversational bots. *arXiv:1801.03622*.

Ari Holtzman, Jan Buys, Maxwell Forbes, Antoine Bosselut, David Golub, and Yejin Choi. 2018. Learning to write with cooperative discriminators. *arXiv preprint arXiv:1805.06087*.

Chandra Khatri, Rahul Goel, Behnam Hedayatnia, Angeliki Metanillou, Anushree Venkatesh, Raefer Gabriel, and Arindam Mandal. 2018. Contextual topic modeling for dialog systems. In *2018 IEEE Spoken Language Technology Workshop (SLT)*, pages 892–899. IEEE.

Jiwei Li, Michel Galley, Chris Brockett, Jianfeng Gao, and Bill Dolan. 2015. A diversity-promoting objective function for neural conversation models. *arXiv:1510.03055*.

Jiwei Li, Michel Galley, Chris Brockett, Jianfeng Gao, and Bill Dolan. 2016a. A diversity-promoting objective function for neural conversation models. In *Proceedings of NAACL-HLT*, pages 110–119.

Jiwei Li, Michel Galley, Chris Brockett, Jianfeng Gao, and Bill Dolan. 2016b. A persona-based neural conversation model. *arXiv:1603.06155*.

Jiwei Li, Will Monroe, and Dan Jurafsky. 2017. Data distillation for controlling specificity in dialogue generation. *arXiv:1702.06703*.

Jiwei Li, Will Monroe, Alan Ritter, Dan Jurafsky, Michel Galley, and Jianfeng Gao. 2016c. Deep reinforcement learning for dialogue generation. In *EMNLP*, pages 1192–1202.

Chin-Yew Lin and Eduard Hovy. 2003. Automatic evaluation of summaries using n-gram co-occurrence statistics. In *NAACL-HLT*, pages 71–78.

Chia-Wei Liu, Ryan Lowe, Iulian V Serban, Michael Noseworthy, Laurent Charlin, and Joelle Pineau. 2016. How not to evaluate your dialogue system: An empirical study of unsupervised evaluation metrics for dialogue response generation. *arXiv:1603.08023*.

Lajanugen Logeswaran and Honglak Lee. 2018. An efficient framework for learning sentence representations. *arXiv:1803.02893*.

Ryan Lowe, Michael Noseworthy, Iulian V Serban, Nicolas Angelard-Gontier, Yoshua Bengio, and Joelle Pineau. 2017. Towards an automatic turing test: Learning to evaluate dialogue responses. *arXiv:1708.07149*.

Ryan Lowe, Nissan Pow, Iulian Serban, and Joelle Pineau. 2015. The ubuntu dialogue corpus: A large dataset for research in unstructured multi-turn dialogue systems. *arXiv:1506.08909*.

Minh-Thang Luong, Hieu Pham, and Christopher D Manning. 2015. Effective approaches to attention-based neural machine translation. *arXiv:1508.04025*.

Marco Marelli, Stefano Menini, Marco Baroni, Luisa Bentivogli, Raffaella Bernardi, Roberto Zamparelli, et al. 2014. A sick cure for the evaluation of compositional distributional semantic models. In *LREC*, pages 216–223.

Brian W Matthews. 1975. Comparison of the predicted and observed secondary structure of t4 phage lysozyme. *Biochimica et Biophysica Acta (BBA)-Protein Structure*, 405(2):442–451.

Alexander H Miller, Will Feng, Adam Fisch, Jiasen Lu, Dhruv Batra, Antoine Bordes, Devi Parikh, and Jason Weston. 2017. Parlai: A dialog research software platform. *arXiv:1705.06476*.

Jekaterina Novikova, Ondřej Dušek, Amanda Cercas Curry, and Verena Rieser. 2017. Why we need new evaluation metrics for nlg. *arXiv preprint arXiv:1707.06875*.

Bo Pang and Lillian Lee. 2004. A sentimental education: Sentiment analysis using subjectivity summarization based on minimum cuts. In *ACL*, page 271.

Ioannis Papaioannou, Amanda Cercas Curry, Jose L Part, Igor Shalyminov, Xinnuo Xu, Yanchao Yu, Ondrej Dušek, Verena Rieser, and Oliver Lemon. 2017. Alana: Social dialogue using an ensemble model and a ranker trained on user feedback. *Alexa Prize Proceedings*.

Kishore Papineni, Salim Roukos, Todd Ward, and Wei-Jing Zhu. 2002. Bleu: a method for automatic evaluation of machine translation. In *ACL*, pages 311–318.

Ashwin Ram, Rohit Prasad, Chandra Khatri, Anu Venkatesh, Raefer Gabriel, Qing Liu, Jeff Nunn, Behnam Hedayatnia, Ming Cheng, Ashish Nagar, Eric King, Kate Bland, Amanda Wartick, Yi Pan, Han Song, Sk Jayadevan, Gene Hwang, and Art Pettigrue. 2017. Conversational ai: The science behind the alexa prize. In *1st proceedings of Alexa Prize*.

Alan Ritter, Colin Cherry, and William B Dolan. 2011. Data-driven response generation in social media. In *Proceedings of the conference on empirical methods in natural language processing*, pages 583–593. ACL.

Iulian Serban, Alessandro Sordoni, Ryan Lowe, Laurent Charlin, Joelle Pineau, Aaron Courville, and Yoshua Bengio. 2016a. A hierarchical latent variable encoder-decoder model for generating dialogues. *arXiv:1605.06069*.

Iulian V Serban, Chinnadhurai Sankar, Mathieu Germain, Saizheng Zhang, Zhouhan Lin, Sandeep Subramanian, Taesup Kim, Michael Pieper, Sarath Chandar, Nan Rosemary Ke, et al. 2017. A deep reinforcement learning chatbot. *arXiv:1709.02349*.

Iulian V Serban, Alessandro Sordoni, Yoshua Bengio, Aaron Courville, and Joelle Pineau. 2016b. Building end-to-end dialogue systems using generative hierarchical neural network models. In *AAAI*.

Iulian V Serban, Alessandro Sordoni, Yoshua Bengio, Aaron Courville, and Joelle Pineau. 2016c. Building end-to-end dialogue systems using generative hierarchical neural network models. *arXiv:1507.04808*.

Louis Shao, Stephan Gouws, Denny Britz, Anna Goldie, Brian Strope, and Ray Kurzweil. 2017. Generating high-quality and informative conversation responses with sequence-to-sequence models. *arXiv:1701.03185*.

Alessandro Sordoni, Michel Galley, Michael Auli, Chris Brockett, Yangfeng Ji, Margaret Mitchell, Jian-Yun Nie, Jianfeng Gao, and Bill Dolan. 2015. A neural network approach to context-sensitive generation of conversational responses. *arXiv:1506.06714*.

Andreas Stolcke, Elizabeth Shriberg, Rebecca Bates, Noah Coccaro, Daniel Jurafsky, Rachel Martin, Marie Meteer, Klaus Ries, Paul Taylor, Carol Van Ess-Dykema, et al. 1998. Dialog act modelling for conversational speech.

Ilya Sutskever, Oriol Vinyals, and Quoc V Le. 2014. Sequence to sequence learning with neural networks. In *NIPS*, pages 3104–3112.

Chongyang Tao, Lili Mou, Dongyan Zhao, and Rui Yan. 2017. Ruber: An unsupervised method for automatic evaluation of open-domain dialog systems. *arXiv:1701.03079*.

Ashish Vaswani, Noam Shazeer, Niki Parmar, Jakob Uszkoreit, Llion Jones, Aidan N Gomez, Łukasz Kaiser, and Illia Polosukhin. 2017. Attention is all you need. In *NIPS*, pages 6000–6010.

Anu Venkatesh, Chandra Khatri, Ashwin Ram, Fenfei Guo, Raefer Gabriel, Ashish Nagar, Rohit Prasad, Ming Cheng, Behnam Hedayatnia, Angeliki Metallinou, et al. 2018. On evaluating and comparing open domain dialog systems. *arXiv preprint arXiv:1801.03625*.

Ellen M Voorhees and Hoa Trang Dang. 2003. Overview of the trec 2003 question answering track. In *TREC*, volume 2003, pages 54–68.

Marilyn A Walker, Diane J Litman, Candace A Kamm, and Alicia Abella. 1997. Paradise: A framework for evaluating spoken dialogue agents. In *EACL*, pages 271–280.

TH Wen, M Gašić, N Mrkšić, PH Su, D Vandyke, and S Young. 2015. Semantically conditioned lstm-based natural language generation for spoken dialogue systems. In *EMNLP*, pages 1711–1721.

Chen Xing, Wei Wu, Yu Wu, Jie Liu, Yalou Huang, Ming Zhou, and Wei-Ying Ma. 2017. Topic aware neural response generation. In *AAAI*, volume 17, pages 3351–3357.

Kaisheng Yao, Baolin Peng, Geoffrey Zweig, and Kam-Fai Wong. 2016. An attentional neural conversation model with improved specificity. *arXiv:1606.01292*.

Zhou Yu, Ziyu Xu, Alan W Black, and Alexander Rudnicky. 2016. Strategy and policy learning for non-task-oriented conversational systems. In *SIGDIAL*, pages 404–412.

Ruqing Zhang, Jiafeng Guo, Yixing Fan, Yanyan Lan, Jun Xu, and Xueqi Cheng. 2018. Learning to control the specificity in neural response generation. In *ACL*, volume 1, pages 1108–1117.

Ganbin Zhou, Ping Luo, Rongyu Cao, Fen Lin, Bo Chen, and Qing He. 2017. Mechanism-aware neural machine for dialogue response generation. In *AAAI*, pages 3400–3407.

Importance of Search and Evaluation Strategies
in Neural Dialogue Modeling

Ilia Kulikov
New York University
kulikov@cs.nyu.edu

Alexander H. Miller
Facebook AI Research

Kyunghyun Cho
New York University
Facebook AI Research
CIFAR Azrieli Global Scholar

Jason Weston
Facebook AI Research
New York University

Abstract

We investigate the impact of search strategies in neural dialogue modeling. We first compare two standard search algorithms, greedy and beam search, as well as our newly proposed iterative beam search which produces a more diverse set of candidate responses. We evaluate these strategies in realistic full conversations with humans and propose a model-based Bayesian calibration to address annotator bias. These conversations are analyzed using two automatic metrics: log-probabilities assigned by the model and utterance diversity. Our experiments reveal that better search algorithms lead to higher rated conversations. However, finding the optimal selection mechanism to choose from a more diverse set of candidates is still an open question.

1 Introduction

There are three high-level steps to building a neural autoregressive sequence model for dialog modeling, inspired by work of Vinyals and Le (2015). First, decide on a network architecture which will consume previous utterances as well as any extra information such as speaker identifiers. Second, choose a learning strategy. Finally, decide on a search algorithm, as neural autoregressive sequence models do not admit a tractable, exact approach for generating the most likely response.

Recent research in neural dialogue modeling has often focused on the first two aspects. A number of variants of sequence-to-sequence models (Sutskever et al., 2014; Cho et al., 2014; Kalchbrenner and Blunsom, 2013) have been proposed for dialogue modeling in recent years, including hierarchical models (Serban et al., 2016) and transformers (Mazaré et al., 2018; Yang et al., 2018). These advances in network architectures have often been accompanied by advanced learning algorithms. Serban et al. (2017) introduce latent variables to their earlier hierarchical model and train it to maximize the variational lower bound, similar to Zhao et al. (2017) who propose to build a neural dialogue model as a conditional variational autoencoder. Xu et al. (2017) and Li et al. (2017b) train a neural dialogue model as conditional generative adversarial networks (Mirza and Osindero, 2014). These two learning algorithms, variational lower-bound maximization and adversarial learning, have been combined into a single model by Shen et al. (2018), which has been followed by Gu et al. (2018).

Despite abundant endeavors on modeling and learning, search has received only a little attention (Dinan et al., 2019). Most of the work on search has focused on training an additional neural network that provides a supplementary score to guide either greedy or beam search. Li et al. (2015) propose a maximum mutual information criterion for decoding using a reverse model. This has been extended by Li et al. (2017a), where an extra neural network is trained to predict an arbitrary reward given a partial hypothesis and used during decoding. Similarly, Zemlyanskiy and Sha (2018) train a neural network that predicts the other participant's personality given a partial conversation and use its predictability as an auxiliary score for re-ranking a set of candidate responses. None of these approaches study how the choice of the underlying search algorithm, rather than its scoring function, affects the quality of the neural dialogue model.

In this paper, we investigate the effects of varying search and selection strategies on the quality of generated dialogue utterances. We start with an attention-based sequence-to-sequence model (Bahdanau et al., 2014) trained on the recently-released PersonaChat dataset (Zhang et al., 2018). We evaluate three search algorithms: greedy search, beam search and iterative beam search, the last of which we design based on ear-

Proceedings of The 12th International Conference on Natural Language Generation, pages 76–87,
Tokyo, Japan, 28 Oct - 1 Nov, 2019. ©2019 Association for Computational Linguistics

lier works by Batra et al. (2012). These algorithms are qualitatively different from each other in the size of subspace over which they search for the best response.

We compare all of these alternatives using two families of metrics. First, we use human evaluation of full, multi-turn conversation. The resulting distribution of annotator's scores has huge variance that is rarely discussed nor analyzed by other groups. This variance comes from each annotator's individual attitude towards and understanding of the task, which we call annotator bias. In order to address this bias, we propose model-based Bayesian calibration that explicitly factors in each annotator's bias and the algorithm's underlying score, and report the posterior mean and variance of each algorithm's score. Additionally, we also compare automatic metrics that capture the model's intrinsic preference (log-probability) and the diversity of responses (distinct-n).

We make two key observations from the experiments. A better search strategy can indeed generate responses that are both intrinsically preferred by the underlying model and diverse, without re-designing or re-training the neural dialogue model. However, this observation does not necessarily carry over to human evaluation, as the best performing strategy according to these automatic metrics was not the best strategy according to human annotators. These results highlight both the importance of search algorithms as well as the difficulty in evaluating neural dialogue systems in a realistic, full conversation setup.

We will make trained models, code and human evaluation transcripts publicly available. Randomly sampled transcripts for each strategy are available in 2 additional pages of examples. All transcripts are given in additional materials and we encourage everyone to read it.

2 Neural dialogue modeling

Since Vinyals and Le (2015), a neural autoregressive sequence model based on sequence-to-sequence models Sutskever et al. (2014); Cho et al. (2014) have become one of the most widely studied approaches to dialogue modeling (see, e.g., Serban et al., 2016, 2017; Zhao et al., 2017; Xu et al., 2017; Li et al., 2016, 2017a,b; Zemlyanskiy and Sha, 2018; Zhang et al., 2018; Miller et al., 2017; Shen et al., 2018; Gu et al., 2018). In this approach, a neural sequence model is used to model

a conditional distribution over responses given a context which consists of previous utterances by both itself and a partner in the conversation as well as any other information about the speaker.

2.1 Neural autoregressive sequence modeling

A neural autoregressive sequence model learns the conditional distribution over all possible responses given the context. Each conditional distribution is modelled by a neural network, and popular choices include recurrent neural networks (Mikolov et al., 2010; Sutskever et al., 2014; Cho et al., 2014; Bahdanau et al., 2014), convolutional networks (Dauphin et al., 2016; Gehring et al., 2017) and self-attention (Sukhbaatar et al., 2015; Vaswani et al., 2017). We explore search strategies and fix the model to a recurrent neural network.

Learning: Maximum Likelihood Each example in a training set D consists of auxiliary information or context U (such as a persona profile or external knowledge context) and a sequence of utterances, each of which is marked with a speaker tag, i.e., $C = (U, (Y_1^a, Y_1^b, \ldots, Y_L^a, Y_L^b) \in D$, where Y_l^s is the utterance from the l-th turn by a speaker s. The conditional log-probability assigned to this example given by a neural sequence model is then written as

$$\log p(C) = \sum_{s \in \{a,b\}} \sum_{l=1}^{L} \log p(Y_l^s | Y_{<l}^s, Y_{\leq l}^{\bar{s}}, U),$$

$$(1)$$

where $\bar{s} = a$ if $s = b$ and otherwise $\bar{s} = b$.

Learning maximizes the log-probabilities of all the conversations in the training set:

$$L = \frac{1}{|D|} \sum_{C \in D} \log p(C), \qquad (2)$$

often done using stochastic gradient descent with backpropagation (Rumelhart et al., 1985).

2.2 Inference (generation)

In this paper, we generate a response to the current state of the conversation (but do not attempt to plan ahead to future exchanges), maximizing

$$p(Y | Y_{<l}^s, Y_{<l}^{\bar{s}}, U) = \prod_{t=1}^{T} \log p(y_t | y_{<t}, Y_{<l}^s, Y_{<l}^{\bar{s}}, U).$$

Unfortunately, it is intractable to solve this problem due to the exponentially-growing space of all possible responses w.r.t. the maximum length T. It is thus necessary to resort to approximate search algorithms.

Greedy search Greedy search has been the search algorithm of choice among the recent papers on neural dialogue modeling (Gu et al., 2018; Zhao et al., 2017; Xu et al., 2017; Weston et al., 2018; Zhang et al., 2018). It moves from left to right selecting one token at a time, simply choosing the most likely token at the current time step:

$$\hat{y}_t = \arg\max_{v \in V} \log p(y_t = v | \hat{y}_{<t}, Y^s_{<l}, Y^{\bar{s}}_{<l}, U).$$

Greedy search has been found significantly suboptimal within the field of machine translation (see, e.g., Table 1 in Chen et al., 2018), where similar neural sequence models are frequently used.

Beam search Instead of maintaining a single hypothesis at a time, as in greedy search above, at time step t beam search maintains a set of K hypotheses $\mathcal{H}_t$:

$$\mathcal{H}_t = \{(y_1^1, \ldots, y_t^1), \ldots, (y_1^K, \ldots, y_t^K)\}. \quad (3)$$

Each hypothesis $h_{y_t^i}^i, i \in \{1, \ldots, K\}$ from $\mathcal{H}_t$ is expanded with all possible next tokens v from the vocabulary V to form candidate hypotheses. Each candidate is in the form of

$$\tilde{h}_v^i = h_{y_t^i}^i \| (v) = (y_1^i, \ldots, y_t^i, v), \quad (4)$$

and is assigned a score:

$$s(\tilde{h}_v^i) = s(h_{y_t^i}^i) + \log p(v | y_{\leq t}^i). \quad (5)$$

The new hypothesis set of K hypotheses is then constructed as

$$\mathcal{H}_{t+1} = \arg\text{-top-}k_{i,v}\ s(\tilde{h}_v^i). \quad (6)$$

From the new hypothesis set, we find and copy *finalized* hypotheses (sequences ending with the special token $\langle \text{eos} \rangle$ for "end of sequence") to a candidate sequence set $\mathcal{M}_t$. That is,

$$\mathcal{M}_t = \left\{ h_v^i \in \mathcal{H}_{t+1} | v = \langle \text{eos} \rangle \right\}.$$

Beam search terminates when $|\cup_{t'=1}^t \mathcal{M}_t| \geq K'$, where K' is the maximum number of candidate sequences to be returned, or when $t \geq L_{\max}$, where $L_{\max}$ is the maximum length allowed for each candidate sequence. When terminated, beam search returns all the candidate sequences in $\mathcal{M} = \cup_{t'=1}^t \mathcal{M}_t$.

One can increase the size of the subspace over which beam search searches for a response and size of $\mathcal{M}$ by changing hyper-parameters $K, K', L_{\max}$. However, beam search is known to suffer from the problem that most of the hypotheses discovered in $\mathcal{M}$ are near each other in the response space (Li et al., 2016, 2015). For tasks such as dialogue modeling, which are much more open-ended than e.g. machine translation, this is particularly troublesome as many high quality responses may be missing in the beam.

Final sequence selection We consider search strategies to produce a set of candidate responses for the model to choose from. While greedy search provides only a single possible sequence, beam search generates a candidate set of size $|\mathcal{M}|$. It is usual practice to use the score $s(h)$ used during the search to select the final sequence, but it is an open question whether there are better selection strategies for choosing between these final candidate responses.

Avoiding repeating n-grams Although this has not been reported in a formal publication in the context of neural dialogue modeling to our knowledge, Paulus et al. (2017) and Klein et al. (2017) implement so-called n-gram blocking. In n-gram blocking, a hypothesis in a beam $\mathcal{H}_t$ is discarded if there is an n-gram that appears more than once within it.

3 Uncovering hidden responses

We now propose an improved search strategy. To address the locality issue in beam search, we propose an iterative beam search to radically increase the size of search space without introducing much computational overhead, inspired by earlier work on diverse beam search (Vijayakumar et al., 2018; Batra et al., 2012; Li et al., 2016).

3.1 Iterative beam search

The search space over which beam search has operated can be characterized by the union of all partial hypothesis sets $\mathcal{H}_t$ in Eq. (3): $\mathcal{S}_0 = \cup_{t=1}^T \mathcal{H}_t$, where we use the subscript 0 to indicate that beam search has been done without any other constraint. Re-running beam search with an increased beam width K would result in the search space that overlaps significantly with $\mathcal{S}_0$, and would not give us much of a benefit with respect to the increase in computation.

Instead, we keep the beam size K constant but run multiple iterations of beam search while ensuring that any previously explored space $\bar{S}_{<l} = \cup_{l'=0}^{l-1} S_{l'}$ is *not* included in a subsequent iteration of beam search. This is done by setting the score of each candidate hypothesis $s(\tilde{h}_{t+1}^i)$ in Eq. (5) to negative infinity, when this candidate is included in $\bar{S}_{<l}$. We relax this inclusion criterion by using a non-binary dissimilarity metric, and say that the candidate is included in $\bar{S}_{<l}$, if

$$\min_{h \in \bar{S}_{<l}} \Delta(\tilde{h}_{t+1}^i, h) < \epsilon, \tag{7}$$

where Δ is a string dissimilarity measure, such as Hamming distance used in this work, and ϵ is a similarity threshold.

This procedure ensures that a new partial hypothesis set of beam search in the l-th iteration minimally overlaps with any part of the search space explored earlier during the first $l - 1$ iterations of beam search. By running this iteration multiple times, we end up with a set of top hypotheses from each iteration of beam search, from which the best one is selected according to for instance the log-probability assigned by the model. We build a final candidate set $\mathcal{M}$ as a set of all these best hypotheses from beam search iterations.

Practical implementation A major issue with iterative beam search in its naive form is that it requires running beam search multiple times, when even a single run of beam search can be prohibitively slow in an interactive environment, such as in dialogue generation. We address this computational issue by performing these many iterations of beam search in parallel simultaneously. At each time step in the search, we create sets of candidate hypotheses for all iterations in parallel, and go through these candidate sets in sequence from the $(l = 0)$-th iteration down to the last iteration, while eliminating those candidates that satisfy the criterion in Eq. (7). We justify this parallelized approach by defining the similarity measure Δ to be always larger than the threshold ϵ when the previous hypothesis h is longer than $\tilde{h}_{t+1}^i$ in Eq. (7).

4   Dialogue evaluation

Broadly there are two ways to evaluate a neural dialogue model. The first approach is to use a set of (often human generated) reference responses and compare a single generated response against them (Serban et al., 2015; Liu et al., 2016). There are several methods for this comparison: (1) measure the perplexity of reference responses using the neural dialogue model, (2) compute a string match-based metric of a generated response against reference responses, and (3) use human annotators to compare model generated responses against reference or other models' responses. None of these approaches capture the effectiveness of a neural sequence model in conducting a full conversation, because the model responses are computed given a human-written context, i.e., it does not see its own responses in the dialogue history, but gold responses only.

We concentrate on a second approach for evaluation where a neural dialogue model has a multi-turn conversation with a human partner (or annotator) (Zhang et al., 2018; Zemlyanskiy and Sha, 2018; Weston et al., 2018; Dinan et al., 2019). Unlike other approaches, it requires active human interaction, as a conversation almost always deviates from a previously collected data even with the same auxiliary information (U in Eq. (1)). This evaluation strategy reflects both how well a neural dialogue model generates a response given a correct context as well as how well it adapts to a dynamic conversation—the latter was not measured by the first strategy, where the model only had to generate a single response.

4.1   Human evaluation of a full conversation

An annotator is asked to make a conversation with a randomly selected model (search strategy) for at least five turns. At the end of the conversation, we ask the annotator three sets of questions:

1. Overall score ($\{1, 2, 3, 4\}$)
2. Marking of each *good* utterance-pair ($\{0, 1\}$)
3. Marking of each *bad* utterance-pair ($\{0, 1\}$)

The first overall score allows us to draw a conclusion on which algorithm makes a better conversation overall. We use a 4 point scale in order to avoid having a "catch-all" category in the answer (Dalal et al., 2014). The latter two questions are collected to investigate the relationship between the overall impression and the quality of each utterance-pair.

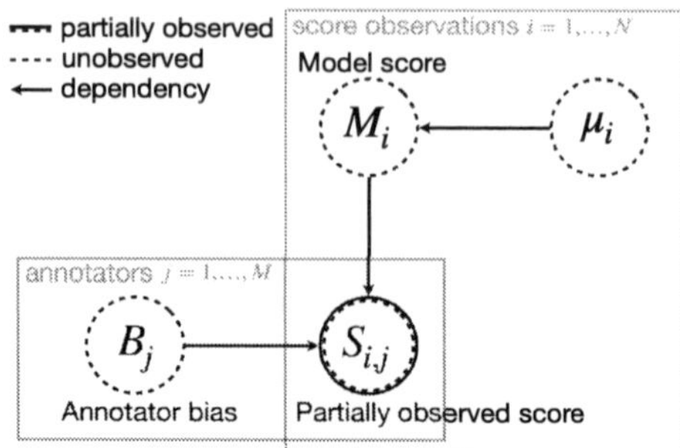

Figure 1: Graphical model used for Bayesian Calibration. M annotators participated such that in total N observed scores are presented.

4.2 Bayesian calibration

Although human evaluation is desirable, raw scores collected by annotators are difficult to use directly due to the annotator bias. Some are more generous while others are quite harsh, as recently reported in Zhang et al. (2018); Zemlyanskiy and Sha (2018). We propose using Bayesian inference as a framework to account for the bias of each annotator, and describe two instances of this framework below.

1-4 star rating of a conversation We treat both the unobserved score M_i of each model, in our case each search algorithm, and the unobserved bias B_j of each annotator as latent variables. The score of the i-th model follows the following distribution: $\mu_i \sim \mathcal{U}(1, 4)$ and $M_i \sim \mathcal{N}(\mu_i, 1^2)$, where $\mathcal{U}$ and $\mathcal{N}$ are uniform and normal distributions. It states that *a priori* each model is likely to be uniformly good or bad. The annotator bias B_j follows $B_j \sim \mathcal{N}(0, 1^2)$, where we are assuming that each annotator does not have any bias *a priori*.

Given the model score M_i and annotator bias B_j, the conditional distribution over an observed score S_{ij} given by the j-th annotator to the i-th model is then:

$$S_{ij} \sim \mathcal{N}(M_i + B_j, 1^2).$$

Due to the nature of human evaluation, only a few of S_{ij}'s are observed. Figure 1 shows the graphical model described above.

The goal of inference in this case is to infer the

posterior mean and the variance:

$$\mathbb{E}[M_i| \{S_{ij}|S_{ij} \in \mathcal{O}\}], \qquad (8)$$
$$\mathbb{V}[M_i| \{S_{ij}|S_{ij} \in \mathcal{O}\}],$$

where $\mathcal{O}$ is a set of observed scores.

Binary rating of an utterance When an annotator labels pairs of utterances from the conversation with a binary score $\{0, 1\}$ (such as whether that pair was a "good" exchange), we need to further take into account the turn bias T_k: $T_k \sim \mathcal{N}(0, 1^2)$. As we will use a Bernoulli distribution for each observed score rather than a 1-4 rating, we modify the prior of the model scores accordingly: $M_i \sim \mathcal{N}(0, 1^2)$.

The distribution of an observed utterance-pair score is then $S_{ijk} \sim \mathcal{B}(\text{sigmoid}(M_i + B_j + T_k))$, where $\mathcal{B}$ is a Bernoulli distribution. The goal of inference is then to compute

$$\mathbb{E}_{M_i| \{S_{ijk}|S_{ijk} \in \mathcal{O}\}} [\text{sigmoid}(M_i)], \qquad (9)$$
$$\mathbb{V}_{M_i| \{S_{ijk}|S_{ijk} \in \mathcal{O}\}} [\text{sigmoid}(M_i)],$$

which estimate the average number of positively labelled utterance-pairs given the i-th model and the uncertainty in this estimate, respectively.

Inference We use no-u-turn (NUTS) sampler (Hoffman and Gelman, 2014) for posterior inference in Pyro (Bingham et al., 2018).

5 Experiment Settings

5.1 Data: Persona-Chat

We use Persona-Chat, released recently by Zhang et al. (2018) and the main dataset for the Conversational Intelligence Challenge 2 (ConvAI2),[1] to train a neural dialogue model. The dataset contains dialogues between pairs of speakers randomly assigned personas from a set of 1,155, each consisting of 4-5 lines of description about the part they should play, e.g. *"I have two dogs"* or *"I like taking trips to Mexico"*. The training set consists of 9,907 such dialogues where pairs of partners play their roles, and a validation set of 1,000 dialogues. The ConvAI2 test set has not been released. Each dialogue is tokenized into words, resulting in a vocabulary of 19,262 unique tokens. See Zhang et al. (2018) for more details.

---

[1] http://convai.io/

5.2 Neural dialogue modeling

Model   We closely follow Bahdanau et al. (2014) in building an attention-based neural autoregressive sequence model. The encoder has two bidirectional layers of 512 LSTM (Hochreiter and Schmidhuber, 1997) units each direction-layer, and the decoder has two layers of 512 LSTM units each. We use global general attention as described by Luong et al. (2015). We use the same word embedding matrix for both the encoder and decoder, which is initialized from 300-dimensional pretrained GloVe vectors (Pennington et al., 2014) for the 97% of the vocabulary which overlaps with GloVe. We allow word embedding weights to be updated during the training.

Learning   We use Adam (Kingma and Ba, 2014) with the initial learning rate set to 0.001. We apply dropout (Srivastava et al., 2014) between the LSTM layers with the dropout rate of 0.5 to prevent overfitting. We train the neural dialogue model until it early-stops on the validation set.[2]

The perplexity of trained model on the ConvAI2 validation set is 24.84, which is competitive compared to the other entries on the competition's leaderboard.[3] Our model serves well as an underlying system for investigating the effect of search algorithms.

5.3 Search Strategies

We test three search strategies; **greedy** and **beam** search from §2.2, and iterative beam search (**iter-beam**) from §3.1.

Beam search (**beam**) uses beam size $K = 5$ and $K' = 15$. This decision is based on preliminary experiments where we found that smaller beam sizes work better than larger ones do. We use the length penalty, described by Wu et al. (2016) and n-gram blocking from §2.2.

Iterative beam search (**iter-beam**) uses 15 iterations of beam search with beam size 5 resulting in a candidate set of size 15. We use the same length penalty and n-gram blocking as in beam search (**beam**). Given the hyper-parameters above both **beam** and **iter-beam** produce 15 candidates and selects the final response based on log-probability.

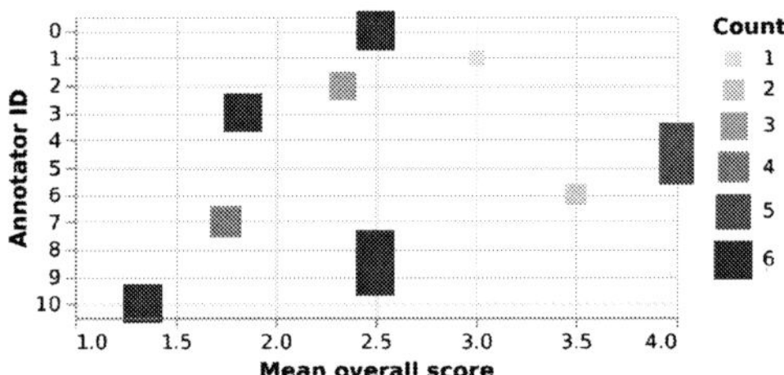

Figure 2: The distribution of averaged overall scores given by annotators to greedy search (**greedy**). Each row plots scores given by a single annotator over multiple conversations. Counts show how many dialogues each annotator performed.

5.4 Evaluation

Human evaluation   We use ParlAI (Miller et al., 2017) which provides seamless integration with Amazon Mechanical Turk (MTurk) for human evaluation. A human annotator is paired with a model with a specific search strategy, and both are randomly assigned personas out of a set of 1,155, and are asked to make a conversation of at least either five or six turns (randomly decided). We allow each annotator to participate in at most six conversations per search strategy and collect approximately 50 conversations per search strategy and additional human-human test.[4] Each conversation is given a single overall score and two sequences of binary utterance pairs flags, as described in §4.1.

Bayesian calibration   In order to remove annotator bias, or inter-annotator variability, we use Bayesian calibration from §4.2. We take 50 warm-up steps and collect 150 samples using NUTS sampler for inferring the posterior mean and variance of the model score in Eq. (8). We use 30 warm-up steps and 100 samples for inferring the mean and variance of the average portion of positively or negatively labelled utterance-pairs in Eq. (9).[5]

Automatic metrics   In addition to human evaluation, we compute automatic metrics to quantitatively characterize each search algorithm. First, we report the **log-p**robability of a generated response assigned by the model which is a direct

---

[2] When the validation loss does not improve for twelve epochs, we early-stop.

[3] https://github.com/DeepPavlov/convai/blob/master/leaderboards.md

[4] Some conversations were dropped due to technical errors, resulting in total 50, 51, 49 and 53 conversations for **greedy, beam, iter-beam** and **humans**, respectively.

[5] Variances of inferred posterior distribution and original data distribution are not comparable, as the former reflects the uncertainty in posterior inference rather than the spread of scores.

Search strategy	log-p↑	Overall Score (1-4)↑		% Good Pairs↑		% Bad Pairs↓	
		Raw	Calibrated	Raw	Calibrated	Raw	Calibrated
greedy	-9.66±2.73	2.56±0.98	2.30±0.24	0.45	0.28±0.07	0.38	0.54±0.07
beam	-7.26±2.28	2.67±0.86	2.70±0.27	0.58	0.44±0.08	0.35	0.27±0.01
iter-beam	**-5.95±1.35**	2.80±0.90	2.67±0.23	0.58	0.45±0.08	0.31	0.32±0.03
human	-42.95±18.87	3.62±0.71	3.37±0.22	0.76	0.76±0.06	0.07	0.04±0.003

Table 1: The average log-probabilities and model scores (average±standard deviation) assigned to the responses during human evaluation. Better search algorithms find responses with higher log-probabilities according to the model. Without observing standard deviations and calibrated scores one can make erroneous conclusions.

indicator of the quality of a search algorithm. Second, we compute the average number of unique n-grams generated per conversation normalized by the number of generated tokens in the conversation, called **distinct-n** from (Li et al., 2015), with $n = 1, 2, 3$.

We compute distinct-n in two different settings. First, we compute distinct-n over the candidate set $\mathcal{M}$ given by the search algorithm. Second, we compute distinct-n over the final selected responses for each search strategy. The former shows diversity within the possible response candidates, while the latter shows diversity among the actual selected dialogue outputs.

6 Result

6.1 Human Evaluation

Annotator bias In Fig. 2, we plot the averaged scores provided by the human annotators for one search strategy (**greedy**), where each row corresponds to each annotator. Consider the three annotators with id $3, 4, 10$. Their means are clearly separated from each other, which points to the existence of annotator bias. This observation supports the necessity of the Bayesian calibration described in §4.2.

Human evaluation In Table 1, we present the scores from human evaluation. In total 41 unique annotator participated within 201 collected conversations. We make a major observation which is that greedy search (**greedy**), which has been the search algorithm of choice in neural dialogue modeling, significantly lags behind the variants of beam search (**beam, iter-beam**) in all metrics. This stark difference is worth our attention, as this difference is *solely* due to the choice of a search algorithm and is not the result of different network architectures nor learning algorithms. In fact, this cannot even be attributed to different parameter initialization, as we use only *one* trained model for all of these results.

The model scores assigned to human conversations (**humans**) are far superior to all search strategies. It is clear with both overall score and utterance pairs proportion scores. This tells us that there are many open questions how to improve neural dialogue models.

6.2 Automatic Metrics

Search quality: log probability (log-p) Better search algorithms find responses with higher log-probability according to the model, as shown in Table 1. This is a natural consequence from exploring a larger subset of the search space.

A notable observation from Table 1 is that the neural sequence model assigns very low log-probabilities to human response. This implies that there is a limit to improving this specific neural dialogue model by using a better search algorithm and instead there is more room to improve the models and learning algorithms to place a high probability on human responses. It is necessary to test the proposed search strategies with new models and we leave this for the future.

Diversity: distinct-n The diversity metric is measured before (pre) and after (post) selecting the final response from the candidate set $\mathcal{M}$ for both **beam** search and **iter-beam** search. Since **greedy** and **humans** produce only single response, we compute the diversity metric only using those final responses for both greedy search and humans. In both pre and post settings, the normalization is done per each conversation.

As well as in human evaluation, **greedy** has lower diversity compared to all the other strategies as shown in Table 2. We see large gap in pre-selection distinct-n for all n between **beam** and **iter-beam** while the difference is small in post-selection distinct-n. In other words, while providing more diverse set of candidates, the final selected output response with **iter-beam** is not

Search	distinct-n $\uparrow$					
	$n = 1$		$n = 2$		$n = 3$	
strategy	post	pre	post	pre	post	pre
greedy	0.47	-	0.61	-	0.62	-
beam	0.56	0.06	**0.69**	0.12	**0.63**	0.18
iter-beam	**0.59**	**0.18**	0.68	**0.41**	0.60	**0.58**
human	0.66	-	0.85	-	0.82	-

Table 2: Measuring the diversity of different search and selection strategies. Both **beam** and **iter-beam** produce up to 15 hypotheses each. Column **post** is distinct-n measured over the final selected output responses given by the model and allows us to compare the diversity of the best responses each search procedure produces. Column **pre** is distinct-n measured over the candidate set $\mathcal{M}$ given by the search algorithm and allows us compare diversity generated within the search.

Beam search	Iterative beam search
do you have any pets ?	that ' s cool , what do you like to eat ?
what is your favorite animal ?	do you have a favorite color ? mine is pink .
i like to talk about strangers .	what do you like to eat ?
do you like animals ?	i don ' t like fish , but my favorite color is pink .
do you like animals ? i want to live at the beach .	what color is your hair ?
do you like animals ? i ' ve a pet .	that does sound good , i like to go alone .
do you like animals ? i want to live on the beach .	i would love to eat fish .
do you like animals ? i want to live at the beach	that makes sense , do you have any hobbies ?
do you like animals ? i ' ve a monkey .	i hear you , my favorite color is pink .
do you like animals ? i want to be a monkey .	i want to be a yoga instructor .
do you like animals ? i want to live at the beach , but love it .	i did not eat meat , but my favorite color is pink .
do you like animals ? i want to live at the beach , but love monkeys .	what are your favorite foods ? mine is pink .
do you like animals ? i want to live at the beach , but they are my favorite .	what does your favorite color ? mine is pink .
do you like animals ? i want to live at the beach , but have a monkey .	what type of food do you like ?
do you like animals ? i want to live at the beach , but they are my favorite	i spend a lot of time alone .

Table 3: **beam** and **iter-beam** candidate sets $\mathcal{M}$. These are from one turn of one randomly selected conversation from human evaluation. **iter-beam** produces more diverse responses.

particularly diverse. This agrees well with human evaluation, where both **iter-beam** and **beam** model scores were indistinguishable, as annotators could only see the final response after selecting from the candidate set. Table 3 shows pre-selection candidate sets for both beam search and iterative beam search.

Finally, we observe a significant gap between the best search strategy and humans in these diversity metrics. Together with the gap we observed in human evaluation scores, we suspect that the lack of diversity in the output responses is a major factor behind the low performance of the tested neural dialogue model in the human evaluation.

7 Conclusion and Discussion

We have performed realistic human evaluation of the neural dialogue model to validate the importance of exploring better search strategies. We observed that careful design of human evaluation is necessary to properly evaluate the ability of the neural dialogue model to conduct a conversation with a human. The proposed Bayesian calibration of model scores helps to account the annotator bias observed in human evaluation.

Extensive analysis reveals that greedy search, which has been the inference algorithm of choice in neural dialogue modeling, significantly lags behind more sophisticated search strategies such as beam search and iterative beam search.

We have proposed the iterative beam search which produces more diverse set of candidate responses w.r.t. pre-selection distinct-n metric. Post-selection final responses with iterative beam search have higher log-probability compared to other search strategies. In spite of this, there is only a marginal difference between iterative beam search and beam search w.r.t. scores from human evaluation and post-selection distinct-n. This suggests that final response selection strategy is as important as the search strategy being used and can be a major factor in the inference pipeline of the neural dialogue model. We leave improving this strategy to future work.

Finally, the model assigns lower probability to reference responses, which implies suboptimality in the current neural dialogue model . It is necessary in the future to test the proposed search strategies with new models.

Acknowledgments

KC is partly supported by Samsung Advanced Institute of Technology (Next Generation Deep Learning: from Pattern Recognition to AI) and Samsung Electronics (Improving Deep Learning using Latent Structure).

References

Dzmitry Bahdanau, Kyunghyun Cho, and Yoshua Bengio. 2014. Neural machine translation by jointly learning to align and translate. *arXiv preprint arXiv:1409.0473*.

Dhruv Batra, Payman Yadollahpour, Abner Guzman-Rivera, and Gregory Shakhnarovich. 2012. Diverse m-best solutions in markov random fields. In *European Conference on Computer Vision*, pages 1–16. Springer.

Eli Bingham, Jonathan P. Chen, Martin Jankowiak, Fritz Obermeyer, Neeraj Pradhan, Theofanis Karaletsos, Rohit Singh, Paul Szerlip, Paul Horsfall, and Noah D. Goodman. 2018. Pyro: Deep Universal Probabilistic Programming. *arXiv preprint arXiv:1810.09538*.

Yun Chen, Victor OK Li, Kyunghyun Cho, and Samuel R Bowman. 2018. A stable and effective learning strategy for trainable greedy decoding. *arXiv preprint arXiv:1804.07915*.

Kyunghyun Cho, Bart Van Merriënboer, Caglar Gulcehre, Dzmitry Bahdanau, Fethi Bougares, Holger Schwenk, and Yoshua Bengio. 2014. Learning phrase representations using rnn encoder-decoder for statistical machine translation. *arXiv preprint arXiv:1406.1078*.

Dev K Dalal, Nathan T Carter, and Christopher J Lake. 2014. Middle response scale options are inappropriate for ideal point scales. *Journal of Business and Psychology*, 29(3):463–478.

Yann N Dauphin, Angela Fan, Michael Auli, and David Grangier. 2016. Language modeling with gated convolutional networks. *arXiv preprint arXiv:1612.08083*.

Emily Dinan, Varvara Logacheva, Valentin Malykh, Alexander Miller, Kurt Shuster, Jack Urbanek, Douwe Kiela, Arthur Szlam, Iulian Serban, Ryan Lowe, et al. 2019. The second conversational intelligence challenge (convai2). *arXiv preprint arXiv:1902.00098*.

Jonas Gehring, Michael Auli, David Grangier, Denis Yarats, and Yann N Dauphin. 2017. Convolutional sequence to sequence learning. *arXiv preprint arXiv:1705.03122*.

Xiaodong Gu, Kyunghyun Cho, Jungwoo Ha, and Sunghun Kim. 2018. Dialogwae: Multimodal response generation with conditional wasserstein auto-encoder. *arXiv preprint arXiv:1805.12352*.

Sepp Hochreiter and Jürgen Schmidhuber. 1997. Long short-term memory. *Neural computation*, 9(8):1735–1780.

Matthew D Hoffman and Andrew Gelman. 2014. The no-u-turn sampler: adaptively setting path lengths in hamiltonian monte carlo. *Journal of Machine Learning Research*, 15(1):1593–1623.

Nal Kalchbrenner and Phil Blunsom. 2013. Recurrent continuous translation models. In *Proceedings of the 2013 Conference on Empirical Methods in Natural Language Processing*, pages 1700–1709.

Diederik P Kingma and Jimmy Ba. 2014. Adam: A method for stochastic optimization. *arXiv preprint arXiv:1412.6980*.

Guillaume Klein, Yoon Kim, Yuntian Deng, Jean Senellart, and Alexander M. Rush. 2017. OpenNMT: Open-source toolkit for neural machine translation. In *Proc. ACL*.

Jiwei Li, Michel Galley, Chris Brockett, Jianfeng Gao, and Bill Dolan. 2015. A diversity-promoting objective function for neural conversation models. *arXiv preprint arXiv:1510.03055*.

Jiwei Li, Will Monroe, and Dan Jurafsky. 2016. A simple, fast diverse decoding algorithm for neural generation. *arXiv preprint arXiv:1611.08562*.

Jiwei Li, Will Monroe, and Dan Jurafsky. 2017a. Learning to decode for future success. *arXiv preprint arXiv:1701.06549*.

Jiwei Li, Will Monroe, Tianlin Shi, Sébastien Jean, Alan Ritter, and Dan Jurafsky. 2017b. Adversarial learning for neural dialogue generation. *arXiv preprint arXiv:1701.06547*.

Chia-Wei Liu, Ryan Lowe, Iulian V Serban, Michael Noseworthy, Laurent Charlin, and Joelle Pineau. 2016. How not to evaluate your dialogue system: An empirical study of unsupervised evaluation metrics for dialogue response generation. *arXiv preprint arXiv:1603.08023*.

Minh-Thang Luong, Hieu Pham, and Christopher D Manning. 2015. Effective approaches to attention-based neural machine translation. *arXiv preprint arXiv:1508.04025*.

Pierre-Emmanuel Mazaré, Samuel Humeau, Martin Raison, and Antoine Bordes. 2018. Training millions of personalized dialogue agents. *arXiv preprint arXiv:1809.01984*.

Tomáš Mikolov, Martin Karafiát, Lukáš Burget, Jan Černocký, and Sanjeev Khudanpur. 2010. Recurrent neural network based language model. In *Eleventh Annual Conference of the International Speech Communication Association*.

Alexander H Miller, Will Feng, Adam Fisch, Jiasen Lu, Dhruv Batra, Antoine Bordes, Devi Parikh, and Jason Weston. 2017. ParlAI: A dialog research software platform. *arXiv preprint arXiv:1705.06476*.

Mehdi Mirza and Simon Osindero. 2014. Conditional generative adversarial nets. *arXiv preprint arXiv:1411.1784*.

Romain Paulus, Caiming Xiong, and Richard Socher. 2017. A deep reinforced model for abstractive summarization. *arXiv preprint arXiv:1705.04304*.

Jeffrey Pennington, Richard Socher, and Christopher Manning. 2014. Glove: Global vectors for word representation. In *Proceedings of the 2014 conference on empirical methods in natural language processing (EMNLP)*, pages 1532–1543.

David E Rumelhart, Geoffrey E Hinton, and Ronald J Williams. 1985. Learning internal representations by error propagation. Technical report, California Univ San Diego La Jolla Inst for Cognitive Science.

Iulian Vlad Serban, Ryan Lowe, Peter Henderson, Laurent Charlin, and Joelle Pineau. 2015. A survey of available corpora for building data-driven dialogue systems. *arXiv preprint arXiv:1512.05742*.

Iulian Vlad Serban, Alessandro Sordoni, Yoshua Bengio, Aaron C Courville, and Joelle Pineau. 2016. Building end-to-end dialogue systems using generative hierarchical neural network models. In *AAAI*, volume 16, pages 3776–3784.

Iulian Vlad Serban, Alessandro Sordoni, Ryan Lowe, Laurent Charlin, Joelle Pineau, Aaron C Courville, and Yoshua Bengio. 2017. A hierarchical latent variable encoder-decoder model for generating dialogues. In *AAAI*, pages 3295–3301.

Xiaoyu Shen, Hui Su, Shuzi Niu, and Vera Demberg. 2018. Improving variational encoder-decoders in dialogue generation. *arXiv preprint arXiv:1802.02032*.

Nitish Srivastava, Geoffrey Hinton, Alex Krizhevsky, Ilya Sutskever, and Ruslan Salakhutdinov. 2014. Dropout: a simple way to prevent neural networks from overfitting. *The Journal of Machine Learning Research*, 15(1):1929–1958.

Sainbayar Sukhbaatar, Jason Weston, Rob Fergus, et al. 2015. End-to-end memory networks. In *Advances in neural information processing systems*, pages 2440–2448.

Ilya Sutskever, Oriol Vinyals, and Quoc V Le. 2014. Sequence to sequence learning with neural networks. In *Advances in neural information processing systems*, pages 3104–3112.

Ashish Vaswani, Noam Shazeer, Niki Parmar, Jakob Uszkoreit, Llion Jones, Aidan N Gomez, Łukasz Kaiser, and Illia Polosukhin. 2017. Attention is all you need. In *Advances in Neural Information Processing Systems*, pages 5998–6008.

Ashwin K Vijayakumar, Michael Cogswell, Ramprasaath R Selvaraju, Qing Sun, Stefan Lee, David J Crandall, and Dhruv Batra. 2018. Diverse beam search for improved description of complex scenes. In *AAAI*.

Oriol Vinyals and Quoc Le. 2015. A neural conversational model. *arXiv preprint arXiv:1506.05869*.

Jason Weston, Emily Dinan, and Alexander H Miller. 2018. Retrieve and refine: Improved sequence generation models for dialogue. *arXiv preprint arXiv:1808.04776*.

Yonghui Wu, Mike Schuster, Zhifeng Chen, Quoc V Le, Mohammad Norouzi, Wolfgang Macherey, Maxim Krikun, Yuan Cao, Qin Gao, Klaus Macherey, et al. 2016. Google's neural machine translation system: Bridging the gap between human and machine translation. *arXiv preprint arXiv:1609.08144*.

Zhen Xu, Bingquan Liu, Baoxun Wang, Chengjie SUN, Xiaolong Wang, Zhuoran Wang, and Chao Qi. 2017. Neural response generation via gan with an approximate embedding layer. In *Proceedings of the 2017 Conference on Empirical Methods in Natural Language Processing*, pages 617–626. Association for Computational Linguistics.

Yinfei Yang, Steve Yuan, Daniel Cer, Sheng-yi Kong, Noah Constant, Petr Pilar, Heming Ge, Yun-Hsuan Sung, Brian Strope, and Ray Kurzweil. 2018. Learning semantic textual similarity from conversations. *arXiv preprint arXiv:1804.07754*.

Yury Zemlyanskiy and Fei Sha. 2018. Aiming to know you better perhaps makes me a more engaging dialogue partner. *arXiv preprint arXiv:1808.07104*.

Saizheng Zhang, Emily Dinan, Jack Urbanek, Arthur Szlam, Douwe Kiela, and Jason Weston. 2018. Personalizing dialogue agents: I have a dog, do you have pets too? *arXiv preprint arXiv:1801.07243*.

Tiancheng Zhao, Ran Zhao, and Maxine Eskenazi. 2017. Learning discourse-level diversity for neural dialog models using conditional variational autoencoders. *arXiv preprint arXiv:1703.10960*.

A Selected dialogue transcripts from the evaluation

We publish dialogue transcripts from human evaluation for reader's analysis. We randomly select a transcript per each search strategy. Formatted representations are printed in tables from Table 4 to Table 6. The second row refers to personalized context from PersonaChat dataset (Zhang et al., 2018). The third row prints the whole dialogue where each turn is bounded with a box. Left column named Annotator contains responses written by the annotator. Middle column prints positional ordering of turns. Right column named Model contains responses generated by the model. The caption contains the search type and the score given by the annotator. We have prepared all evaluation scripts for reader in additional materials and we encourage everyone to read it.

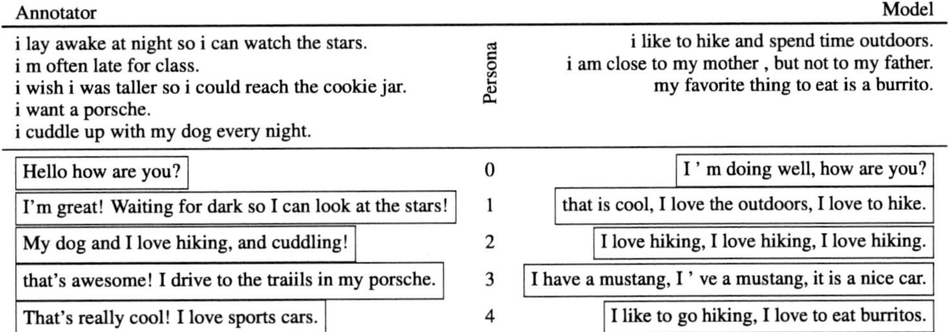

Annotator	Persona	Model
i lay awake at night so i can watch the stars. i m often late for class. i wish i was taller so i could reach the cookie jar. i want a porsche. i cuddle up with my dog every night.		i like to hike and spend time outdoors. i am close to my mother , but not to my father. my favorite thing to eat is a burrito.
Hello how are you?	0	I ' m doing well, how are you?
I'm great! Waiting for dark so I can look at the stars!	1	that is cool, I love the outdoors, I love to hike.
My dog and I love hiking, and cuddling!	2	I love hiking, I love hiking, I love hiking.
that's awesome! I drive to the traiils in my porsche.	3	I have a mustang, I ' ve a mustang, it is a nice car.
That's really cool! I love sports cars.	4	I like to go hiking, I love to eat burritos.

Table 4: Search strategy: **greedy**. Annotator score: **3**

Annotator	Persona	Model
my father died when i was 2. i have blue eyes. i love fishing. my favorite season is spring.		i believe in aliens. to free my mind from feeling depressed i look up at the stars at night. i cannot choose between lollipops and rainbows. i would love to be a professional eater and not get fat. i hate cleaning up after my husband and children.
Hey there, how are you?	0	I ' m good. how are you?
pretty good. I'm planning my next fishing trip!	1	that sounds fun. I ' m going to be a professional eater
that sounds amazing! I would love that.	2	do you have any hobbies?
I really like going fishing, especially in the spring time.	3	I like to stay at night with my husband and kids
That is nice! I wish I had a family, my dad died when I was really little.	4	I ' m sorry to hear that

Table 5: Search strategy: **beam**. Annotator score: **4**

Annotator	Persona	Model
i eat tuna fish salad at least every day. my favorite music is two steps from hell and rock opera genre. i have sandy brown hair and green eyes. i can t get enough gummy worms to satisfy my sweet tooth. i read sci fi space adventures with a passion.		i am a yoga instructor. i married my highschool sweetheart. pink is my favorite color. i enjoy being alone.
hello there friend!	0	hello, how are you?
I'm great. how are you?	1	I ' m doing well, thank you.
What's your favorite food?	2	I love pizza, what about you?
tuna fish salad is my favorite. i eat it every day.	3	do you have a favorite color? mine is pink.
I like all of the colors, but my eyes are green. do you have any hobbies?	4	I like to go alone.
ah, I enjoy reading sci-fi. that's something you do alone.	5	do you have any hobbies?
reading. I also really like rock operas.	6	what is your favorite genre?
rock opera. but my favorite band is two steps from hell. what about you?	7	I like all kinds of music.
is there any food you can't get enough of?	8	I do not have a lot of free time.
ah, sorry to hear that. It was nice chatting with you, though!	9	it was nice talking to you too!

Table 6: Search strategy: **iter-beam**. Annotator score: **3**

Towards Best Experiment Design for Evaluating Dialogue System Output

Sashank Santhanam and Samira Shaikh
Computer Science
University of North Carolina at Charlotte
Charlotte, NC, USA
{ssanthal,sshaikh2}@uncc.edu

Abstract

To overcome the limitations of automated metrics (e.g. BLEU, METEOR) for evaluating dialogue systems, researchers typically use human judgments to provide convergent evidence. While it has been demonstrated that human judgments can suffer from the inconsistency of ratings, extant research has also found that the *design* of the evaluation task affects the consistency and quality of human judgments. We conduct a between-subjects study to understand the impact of four experiment conditions on human ratings of dialogue system output. In addition to discrete and continuous scale ratings, we also experiment with a novel application of Best-Worst scaling to dialogue evaluation. Through our systematic study with 40 crowdsourced workers in each task, we find that using continuous scales achieves more consistent ratings than Likert scale or ranking-based experiment design. Additionally, we find that factors such as time taken to complete the task and no prior experience of participating in similar studies of rating dialogue system output *positively* impact consistency and agreement amongst raters.

1 Introduction and Related Work

A tremendous amount of recent research has focused on approaches towards generating responses for conversations in an open-domain setting (Radford et al., 2019; Xing et al., 2018; Wolf et al., 2019). An equally challenging task for natural language generation systems is evaluating the quality of the generated responses. Evaluation of generated output is typically conducted using a combination of crowdsourced human judgments and automated metrics adopted from machine translation and text summarization (Liu et al., 2016; Novikova et al., 2017). However, studies conducted by Liu *et al.*(2016) and Novikova *et al.* (2017) show that the automated metrics have poor correlation with human judgments. Despite their shortcomings, automated metrics like BLEU, ROUGE, and METEOR are used due to a lack of alternative metrics. This puts a major imperative on obtaining high-quality crowdsourced human judgments. Previous research which employs crowdsourced judgments has focused on metrics including *ease of answering, information flow* and *coherence* (Li et al., 2016; Dziri et al., 2018), *naturalness* (Asghar et al., 2018), *interestingness* (Asghar et al., 2017; Santhanam and Shaikh, 2019), *fluency* or *readability* (Zhang et al., 2018), *engagement* (Venkatesh et al., 2018). While experiment designs primarily use Likert scales, Belz and Kow (2010) argue that discrete scales, such as the Likert scales, can be unintuitive and certain individuals may avoid extreme values in their judgments. Prior research has also shown that use of continuous scales is more viable for language evaluation (Novikova et al., 2018; Belz and Kow, 2011). Such evidence places more emphasis on a careful study towards obtaining reliable and consistent human ratings for dialogue evaluation.

To address this research problem, we focus on a systematic comparison of four experimental conditions by incorporating **continuous, relative** and **ranking scales** for obtaining crowdsourced human judgments. In this initial study, we evaluate the use of two metrics: **Readability** and **Coherence**.

Our key findings are:

1. Use of Likert scales results in the lowest inter-rater consistency and agreement when compared to other experiment conditions

2. Use of continuous scales results in higher inter-rater consistency and agreement

3. Raters who have no prior experience in evaluating dialogue system output have greater inter-rater consistency and agreement than do those who have previously participated in such rating tasks.

Proceedings of The 12th International Conference on Natural Language Generation, pages 88–94,
Tokyo, Japan, 28 Oct - 1 Nov, 2019. ©2019 Association for Computational Linguistics

Our findings have the potential to help the research community in the design of their evaluation tasks to obtain higher quality human judgments for natural language generation output.

2 Data and Models

We used the Reddit conversation corpus to train our models. The Reddit conversation corpus, made available by Dziri *et al.* (2018), consists of data extracted from 95 top-ranked subreddits that discuss various topics such as sports, news, education and politics. The corpus contains 9M training examples, 500K development dialogues and 400K dialogues as test data.[1] We trained three models on the Reddit conversational dataset described below. All the pre-trained models and supporting analysis code along with user study data are available at `https://www.github.com/sashank06/INLG_eval`. The models trained for this study include:

- **Seq2Seq:** Simple encoder-decoder model with attention mechanism (Bahdanau et al., 2014)
- **HRED:** *Hierarchical Encoder-Decoder* (Serban et al., 2016) which incorporates an utterance and intra-utterance layer to model context.
- **THRED:** *Topic Augmented Hierarchical Encoder-Decoder* (Dziri et al., 2018) which uses topic words along with a hierarchical encoder-decoder to produce a response.

3 Metrics

For this initial study, we focus on two metrics, readability and coherence. These metrics are among those essential to evaluate the quality of generated responses (Novikova et al., 2017; Dziri et al., 2019). We describe an automated method to compute each metric.

Readability or Fluency measures the linguistic quality of text and helps quantify the difficulty of understanding the text for a reader (Gatt and Krahmer, 2018; Novikova et al., 2017). We use the Flesch Reading Ease (FRE) (Kincaid et al., 1975) that counts the number of words, syllables and sentences in the text.[2] Higher readability scores indicate that utterance is easier to read and comprehend.

Coherence measures the ability of the dialogue system to produce responses consistent with the topic of conversation (Venkatesh et al., 2018). To calculate coherence, we use the method proposed by Dziri *et al.* (2018). This metric computes the cosine similarity on embedding vectors of generated response and target while accounting for dull and generic responses through a penalty factor.

To overcome the issue of dull and generic responses, Dziri *et al.* (2018) induce a penalty factor which takes into account

$$P = 1 + \log \frac{2 + L'}{2 + L''} \qquad (1)$$

where L' indicates the length of response after dropping stop words and punctuation and L'' indicates the length of non-dull parts of the response after dropping stop words. The penalized semantic similarity (SS) score is then calculated as:

$$SS(utt_{i,j}, resp_i) = P \times (1 - cos(utt_{i,j}, resp_i)) \qquad (2)$$

where i represents the index of the dialogue in the dataset and j denotes index of the utterance in the conversation history.

4 Experiment Designs

In our study, we use three well-known question types of Likert Scale, Magnitude Estimation and Best-Worst Ranking. We chose these questions types to investigate as these are commonly used across various language evaluation tasks (Belz and Kow, 2011; Asghar et al., 2018; Novikova et al., 2018; Kiritchenko and Mohammad, 2017) . With the help of these three types of questions, we design four rating procedures that are explained below.

Likert Scale (LS): is typically used in experiments for crowdsourcing human evaluation of dialogue systems (Asghar et al., 2018; Lowe et al., 2017). In our experiment, we ask the raters to rate the generated responses on a 6-point scale, following Novikova *et al.* (2018) (where 1 is the lowest and 6 is the highest on the metrics of readability and coherence).

Rank-Based Magnitude Estimation (RME): Prior research by Belz and Kow (2011) demonstrates through six separate experiments that continuous scales are more viable and offer distinct advantages over discrete scales in evaluation tasks. Recently, Novikova *et al.* (2018) adopted magnitude estimation by providing the rater with a *standard value* for a reference sentence to evaluate output from goal-oriented systems. Following Novikova *et al.* (2018), we also set the value of the

---

[1] `https://github.com/nouhadziri/THRED`
[2] `https://bit.ly/1IZ0FG4`

standard (reference utterance) as 100 since the reference utterance was produced by humans and is considered as gold-standard. The crowd-sourced workers are asked to provide a score relative to 100 (from 0 to 999) for three system-generated outputs.

Biased Magnitude Estimation (BME): Our third experiment design is biased magnitude estimation (BME). The main difference between RME and BME method is that the standard value we provide for the reference utterance is not uniformly set to 100 for all examples, but instead calculated by automated methods (explained in Section 3). Our motivation to do so is to understand if **anchoring bias** may affect the ratings when judgments are made relative to a fixed value (100) or relative to a value calculated by automated means. Anchoring bias is the tendency to rely too heavily on one piece of information offered (the "anchor", in this case, the number 100) when making decisions (Kahneman, 2016).

Best-Worst Scaling (BWS): Our last experiment condition is best-worst scaling (BWS) in which raters are asked to rank the generated responses in order of best to worst on both metrics (readability and coherence). This approach has previously been used to estimate emotion intensity and has been demonstrated to produce high quality and consistent judgments from humans (Kiritchenko and Mohammad, 2017).

Each task includes 50 randomly sampled conversations from the test set in our corpus along with generated responses from the three models and the ground truth (reference utterance). For each task, we collected ratings from 40 workers with Master qualifications through Amazon Mechanical Turk.

5 Experiment Results

We organize our findings along five main research questions (RQs) outlined in this section. In the following section, we report on statistical significance using two-way ANOVAs on the between-subject ratings across the four experiment conditions (Tables 1–7).

RQ1: What is the effect of experiment design on the reliability on human ratings? We use intra-class correlation (ICC) to measure the reliability across multiple raters (Shrout and Fleiss, 1979; Landis and Koch, 1977). To compare the scores obtained from magnitude estimation ex-

		Likert	RME	BME	BWS
ICC-C	Readability	0.75	0.95†	0.83	0.75
	Coherence	0.83	0.92	0.81	0.80
ICC-A	Readability	0.59	0.95†	0.83	0.75
	Coherence	0.77	0.92	0.81	0.80

Table 1: ICC scores on the metrics of readability and coherence for each experiment design. All values are statistically significant p-value<0.001 except those indicated by †. n=40 for all four designs.

periments to the ratings from the task using discrete Likert scales, we perform a normalization of the magnitude estimation scores on a logarithmic scale as suggested by Bard *et al.* (1996).

Table 1 represents the ICC scores on consistency (ICC-C) and agreement (ICC-A) for our four experiment tasks. We observe that use of Magnitude Estimation with anchors (RME or BME) results in more reliable ratings than using Likert Scale or using Best-Worst ranking (BWS). This result is consistent with prior research by Novikova *et al.* (2018) and Belz and Kow (2011).

RQ2: Does time taken to complete the survey influence reliability of the rankings? To analyze RQ2, we calculated the total time spent by each participant from the start to the end of the experiment. We found that BME task had longest on average time to completion (43 minutes), followed by RME (42.8 minutes) and Likert scale (33 minutes; Best-Worst ranking had shortest average completion time (32.5 minutes). We then test the hypothesis that raters who spent longer than average time on the task would be more reliable in their ratings than those who completed in less than average time. Table 2 represents the ICC scores for raters who spent higher than average time for the task, while Table 3 represents scores for raters who spent less than average time. Surprisingly, we find that consistency and agreement among raters who spend less than average time is higher than those who spend more time, for the Likert, BME or BWS experiment designs. When using the RME design, raters who spend more time have higher consistency and agreement.

RQ3: Does prior experience of evaluating dialogue system output or engaging with conversational agents affect reliability of rankings? We asked each rater two additional questions at the end of the task. The questions asked raters to indicate whether or not they had prior experi-

		Likert (n=15)	RME (n=16)	BME (n=15)	BWS (n=16)
ICC-C	Readability	0.58	0.93	0.51	0.62
	Coherence	0.74	0.85	0.55	0.64
ICC-A	Readability	0.52	0.93	0.51	0.62
	Coherence	0.69	0.86	0.56	0.64

Table 2: ICC scores when participants spend **above average time**. All values in this table are statistically significant with p-value<0.001

		Likert (n=25)	RME (n=24)	BME (n=25)	BWS (n=24)
ICC-C	Readability	0.61	0.88	0.81	0.65
	Coherence	0.66	0.85	0.75	0.76
ICC-A	Readability	0.36	0.88	0.81	0.66
	Coherence	0.55	0.85	0.75	0.76

Table 3: ICC scores when participants spend **below average time**. All values in this table are statistically significant with p-value<0.001

ence taking part in studies (a) to evaluate dialogue system output; and (b) to engage with a conversational agent.

Tables 4 and 5 show how reliable the ratings from the participants based on their prior experience of taking part in studies about evaluating conversational response. We find that participants who have not taken part in prior studies are more consistent and have a higher agreement score than participant who have prior experience. These results are also validated by Tables 6 and 7 which shows that participants with no prior experience of engaging with conversational agents are more consistent and reliable.

		Likert (n=15)	RME (n=7)	BME (n=18)	BWS (n=13)
ICC-C	Readability	0.45	0.37	0.51	0.54
	Coherence	0.38	0.48	0.55	0.63
ICC-A	Readability	0.35	0.38	0.52	0.55
	Coherence	0.32	0.49	0.55	0.63

Table 4: ICC scores when participants **have** prior experience evaluating dialogue system output. All values statistically significant at p-value<0.001.

RQ4: How well do automated methods to calculate readability and coherence correlate with human ratings? We report on correlation between readability and coherence scores that are

		Likert (n=25)	RME (n=33)	BME (n=22)	BWS (n=27)
ICC-C	Readability	0.71	0.95†	0.83	0.70
	Coherence	0.82	0.92	0.76	0.72
ICC-A	Readability	0.50	0.95†	0.83	0.70
	Coherence	0.75	0.92	0.77	0.72

Table 5: ICC scores when participants **do not have** prior experience evaluating dialogue system output. All values statistically significant at p-value<0.001 except those indicated by †.

		Likert (n=18)	RME (n=11)	BME (n=23)	BWS (n=18)
ICC-C	Readability	0.46	0.69	0.60	0.57
	Coherence	0.44	0.65	0.62	0.67
ICC-A	Readability	0.37	0.69	0.61	0.57
	Coherence	0.38	0.65	0.62	0.67

Table 6: ICC scores when participants **have** prior experience engaging with conversational agents. All values statistically significant at p-value<0.001.

		Likert (n=22)	RME (n=29)	BME (n=17)	BWS (n=22)
ICC-C	Readability	0.70	0.95†	0.84	0.67
	Coherence	0.82	0.91	0.76	0.68
ICC-A	Readability	0.48	0.95†	0.84	0.67
	Coherence	0.75	0.91	0.76	0.68

Table 7: ICC scores when participants **do not have** prior experience engaging with conversational agents. All values statistically significant at p-value<0.001 except those indicated by †.

calculated using automated methods (outlined in Section 3) with the human ratings in Table 8. Readability scores were computed using the Flesh Reading Ease (Kincaid et al., 1975) and coherence scores were computed based on method proposed by Dziri *et al.* (2018). We observe that the automated metrics for Readability (Kincaid et al., 1975) and Semantic Similarity (Dziri et al., 2018) show low correlation to human judgments ratings.

	Likert	RME	BME	BWS
	Automated Metric			
Readability	0.26	-0.11	-0.12	-0.06
Coherence	-0.12	-0.13	-0.11	0.01

Table 8: Spearman correlation between the ratings obtained from the automated metrics to human ratings.

RQ5: Is there any correlation between ratings of readability and coherence for each of the four experiment conditions? To evaluate whether there is any correlation between the ratings obtained for readability and coherence through of four experimental designs, we report the Spearman correlation values in Table 9. We find that there is high correlation between the human ratings of readability and coherence obtained through RME and BME (statistically significant). One likely factor affecting correlation may be anchoring bias towards the fixed value of the standard utterance provided in RME (100) and reference value provided in BME. We aim to investigate this further in future work.

	Likert	RME	BME	BWS
		Readability		
Coherence	0.1	0.79***	0.77***	0.5***

Table 9: Spearman correlation between the ratings of readability and coherence obtained on four different experiment designs. *** p-value<0.001

6 Conclusion and Future Work

In this paper, we present our work on designing a systematic experiment with four experiment conditions to evaluate the output of dialogue systems. Different from prior work where a similar study was conducted with output from goal-oriented systems (Novikova et al., 2018), our study focuses on evaluating output in open-domain situations. Consistent with prior findings, metrics calculated using automated methods (Dziri et al., 2019) were found to have a negative correlation with human judgments (c.f. Table 8). This finding points to the need for more effective automated metrics.

We find that that use of continuous scales to obtain crowdsourced ratings provides more consistent and reliable ratings than ratings obtained through Likert scales or Best-Worst scaling. This finding is consistent with prior work conducted by Novikova *et al.* (2018). Novel in our study was the testing of the Best-Worst scaling method to evaluate responses against one another. Although the Best-Worst scaling method has been shown to be effective in obtaining crowdsourced ratings of emotions (Kiritchenko and Mohammad, 2017), we did not find it to be effective in this study. We aim to investigate further whether this finding can be reproduced in a different experiment.

Further, we were able to identify the effects of time taken to complete the task on rating reliability. We find that workers who spent less than average time on the task had higher consistency (for the Likert, BME and BWS experiment conditions) than did the workers who spent more than average time. This finding is counter-intuitive, we expect that spending more time would positively impact inter-rater consistency. Our first step in the analysis of the effects of time taken on reliability included analyzing data from workers who spent more or less than average time, which offers admittedly a limited perspective; an interesting next step would be to more thoroughly study the effects of time taken on reliability by taking into account the full distribution of the time spent data.

We also find that *lack of* prior experience of evaluating open-domain dialogue system output results in more reliable ratings. One potential explanation for this could be that workers may have pre-conceived notions based on their past experience. One limitation of our current study is that although we had output from three separate models, we conducted the study using data from one corpus. Reproducing our findings across additional corpora, additional metrics and other experiment designs would help substantiate these findings further. An analysis of the interaction effects between independent variables such as time taken and prior experience would also help strengthen the findings of our study.

By using a larger sample size (n=40), we are able to make claims about statistical significance across experiment conditions. In future work, we plan to evaluate the impact of cognitive biases such as anchoring and confirmation bias in-depth and how it affects consistency and reliability along with testing continuous scale ratings with no reference value.

Acknowledgments

This work was supported by the Defense Advanced Research Projects Agency (DARPA) under Contract No FA8650-18-C-7881. All statements of fact, opinion or conclusions contained herein are those of the authors and should not be construed as representing the official views or policies of AFRL, DARPA, or the U.S. Government. We thank the anonymous reviewers for the helpful feedback.

References

Nabiha Asghar, Pascal Poupart, Jesse Hoey, Xin Jiang, and Lili Mou. 2018. Affective neural response generation. In *European Conference on Information Retrieval*, pages 154–166. Springer.

Nabiha Asghar, Pascal Poupart, Xin Jiang, and Hang Li. 2017. Deep active learning for dialogue generation. In *Proceedings of the 6th Joint Conference on Lexical and Computational Semantics (*SEM 2017)*, pages 78–83, Vancouver, Canada. Association for Computational Linguistics.

Dzmitry Bahdanau, Kyunghyun Cho, and Yoshua Bengio. 2014. Neural machine translation by jointly learning to align and translate. *arXiv preprint arXiv:1409.0473*.

Ellen Gurman Bard, Dan Robertson, and Antonella Sorace. 1996. Magnitude estimation of linguistic acceptability. *Language*, pages 32–68.

Anja Belz and Eric Kow. 2010. Comparing rating scales and preference judgements in language evaluation. In *Proceedings of the 6th International Natural Language Generation Conference*, pages 7–15. Association for Computational Linguistics.

Anja Belz and Eric Kow. 2011. Discrete vs. continuous rating scales for language evaluation in nlp. In *Proceedings of the 49th Annual Meeting of the Association for Computational Linguistics: Human Language Technologies: short papers-Volume 2*, pages 230–235. Association for Computational Linguistics.

Nouha Dziri, Ehsan Kamalloo, Kory Mathewson, and Osmar Zaiane. 2019. Evaluating coherence in dialogue systems using entailment. In *Proceedings of the 2019 Conference of the North American Chapter of the Association for Computational Linguistics: Human Language Technologies, Volume 1 (Long and Short Papers)*, pages 3806–3812, Minneapolis, Minnesota. Association for Computational Linguistics.

Nouha Dziri, Ehsan Kamalloo, Kory W Mathewson, and Osmar Zaiane. 2018. Augmenting neural response generation with context-aware topical attention. *arXiv preprint arXiv:1811.01063*.

Albert Gatt and Emiel Krahmer. 2018. Survey of the state of the art in natural language generation: Core tasks, applications and evaluation. *Journal of Artificial Intelligence Research*, 61:65–170.

Daniel Kahneman. 2016. 36 heuristics and biases. *Scientists Making a Difference: One Hundred Eminent Behavioral and Brain Scientists Talk about Their Most Important Contributions*, page 171.

J Peter Kincaid, Robert P Fishburne Jr, Richard L Rogers, and Brad S Chissom. 1975. Derivation of new readability formulas (automated readability index, fog count and flesch reading ease formula) for navy enlisted personnel.

Svetlana Kiritchenko and Saif Mohammad. 2017. Best-worst scaling more reliable than rating scales: A case study on sentiment intensity annotation. In *Proceedings of the 55th Annual Meeting of the Association for Computational Linguistics (Volume 2: Short Papers)*, pages 465–470, Vancouver, Canada. Association for Computational Linguistics.

J Richard Landis and Gary G Koch. 1977. The measurement of observer agreement for categorical data. *biometrics*, pages 159–174.

Jiwei Li, Will Monroe, Alan Ritter, Dan Jurafsky, Michel Galley, and Jianfeng Gao. 2016. Deep reinforcement learning for dialogue generation. In *Proceedings of the 2016 Conference on Empirical Methods in Natural Language Processing*, pages 1192–1202. Association for Computational Linguistics.

Chia-Wei Liu, Ryan Lowe, Iulian Serban, Mike Noseworthy, Laurent Charlin, and Joelle Pineau. 2016. How not to evaluate your dialogue system: An empirical study of unsupervised evaluation metrics for dialogue response generation. In *Proceedings of the 2016 Conference on Empirical Methods in Natural Language Processing*, pages 2122–2132. Association for Computational Linguistics.

Ryan Lowe, Michael Noseworthy, Iulian Vlad Serban, Nicolas Angelard-Gontier, Yoshua Bengio, and Joelle Pineau. 2017. Towards an automatic Turing test: Learning to evaluate dialogue responses. In *Proceedings of the 55th Annual Meeting of the Association for Computational Linguistics (Volume 1: Long Papers)*, pages 1116–1126, Vancouver, Canada. Association for Computational Linguistics.

Jekaterina Novikova, Ondřej Dušek, Amanda Cercas Curry, and Verena Rieser. 2017. Why we need new evaluation metrics for NLG. In *Proceedings of the 2017 Conference on Empirical Methods in Natural Language Processing*, pages 2241–2252, Copenhagen, Denmark. Association for Computational Linguistics.

Jekaterina Novikova, Ondřej Dušek, and Verena Rieser. 2018. RankME: Reliable human ratings for natural language generation. In *Proceedings of the 2018 Conference of the North American Chapter of the Association for Computational Linguistics: Human Language Technologies, Volume 2 (Short Papers)*, pages 72–78, New Orleans, Louisiana. Association for Computational Linguistics.

Alec Radford, Jeff Wu, Rewon Child, David Luan, Dario Amodei, and Ilya Sutskever. 2019. Language models are unsupervised multitask learners.

Sashank Santhanam and Samira Shaikh. 2019. A survey of natural language generation techniques with a focus on dialogue systems-past, present and future directions. *arXiv preprint arXiv:1906.00500*.

Iulian V Serban, Alessandro Sordoni, Yoshua Bengio, Aaron Courville, and Joelle Pineau. 2016. Building end-to-end dialogue systems using generative hierarchical neural network models. In *Thirtieth AAAI Conference on Artificial Intelligence*.

Patrick E Shrout and Joseph L Fleiss. 1979. Intraclass correlations: uses in assessing rater reliability. *Psychological bulletin*, 86(2):420.

Anu Venkatesh, Chandra Khatri, Ashwin Ram, Fenfei Guo, Raefer Gabriel, Ashish Nagar, Rohit Prasad, Ming Cheng, Behnam Hedayatnia, Angeliki Metallinou, et al. 2018. On evaluating and comparing conversational agents. *arXiv preprint arXiv:1801.03625*.

Thomas Wolf, Victor Sanh, Julien Chaumond, and Clement Delangue. 2019. Transfertransfo: A transfer learning approach for neural network based conversational agents. *arXiv preprint arXiv:1901.08149*.

Chen Xing, Yu Wu, Wei Wu, Yalou Huang, and Ming Zhou. 2018. Hierarchical recurrent attention network for response generation. In *Thirty-Second AAAI Conference on Artificial Intelligence*.

Saizheng Zhang, Emily Dinan, Jack Urbanek, Arthur Szlam, Douwe Kiela, and Jason Weston. 2018. Personalizing dialogue agents: I have a dog, do you have pets too? In *Proceedings of the 56th Annual Meeting of the Association for Computational Linguistics (Volume 1: Long Papers)*, pages 2204–2213, Melbourne, Australia. Association for Computational Linguistics.

A Tree-to-Sequence Model for Neural NLG in Task-Oriented Dialog

Jinfeng Rao, Kartikeya Upasani, Anusha Balakrishnan,
Michael White, Anuj Kumar, Rajen Subba
Facebook Assistant
{raojinfeng,kart,anushabala,,mwhite14850,anujk,rasubba}@fb.com

Abstract

Generating fluent natural language responses from structured semantic representations is a critical step in task-oriented conversational systems. Sequence-to-sequence models on flat meaning representations (MR) have been dominant in this task, for example in the E2E NLG Challenge. Previous work has shown that a tree-structured MR can improve the model for better discourse-level structuring and sentence-level planning. In this work, we propose a tree-to-sequence model that uses a tree-LSTM encoder to leverage the tree structures in the input MR, and further enhance the decoding by a structure-enhanced attention mechanism. In addition, we explore combining these enhancements with constrained decoding to improve semantic correctness. Our method not only shows significant improvements over standard seq2seq baselines, but also is more data-efficient and generalizes better to hard scenarios.

1 Introduction

Generating fluent natural language responses from structured semantic representations is crucial to building engaging and effective task-oriented dialog systems. Neural approaches for natural language generation (NNLG), particularly sequence-to-sequence approaches, have achieved promising results and were dominant in the recent E2E Challenge. Most of these approaches are built on flat meaning representations (MR) that use key-value pairs to capture attributes to be conveyed in responses. However, coupled with such flat MRs, current NNLG methods still struggle with 1) reliably performing sentence-level planning and discourse-level structuring (Reed et al., 2018); 2) avoiding generating semantic errors like hallucinated content (Dušek et al., 2018, 2019); and 3) generalizing to hard inputs (Wiseman et al., 2017).

To help overcome these drawbacks, Balakrishnan et al. (2019) propose a novel tree-structured meaning representation to gain better control of the discourse structure and content in generated utterances. Their proposed tree-structured MRs consist of three sets of non-terminal tokens: argument, dialog act and discourse act. A dialog act is a minimum atomic unit that contains a few arguments to be expressed in an utterance, while discourse acts define the relationship between dialog acts.

An example of their tree-structured MR for the weather domain is provided in Table 1, along with a flat MR and human reference. We also add a reference annotated with the tree-structured MR in the last row. The tree-structured MR provides much better controllability to a live task-oriented dialog system, where developers can easily inject external knowledge into a rule-based response planner to specify the relationship between multiple dialog acts (e.g., rainy is the opposite to sunny), and the grouping of arguments in a dialog act is possible. These consideration have been shown to be critical to user perceptions of quality and naturalness (Lemon et al., 2004; Carenini and Moore, 2006; Walker et al., 2007; White et al., 2010; Demberg et al., 2011).

In their Seq2Seq model, Balakrishnan et al. (2019) treat the tree-structured MR as just a sequence of tokens, ignoring the inherent tree structure (though this structure is taken into account in constrained decoding). We aim to examine the hypothesis that a better representation of the input tree structures could lead to better generalizability of the model and enhance semantic correctness. Therefore, we propose a tree-to-sequence model that uses a tree-based encoder to better represent the tree-structured MRs, and a structure-enhanced decoder to further incorporate contextual information in decoding.

Our contributions are summarized as follows:

Proceedings of The 12th International Conference on Natural Language Generation, pages 95–100,
Tokyo, Japan, 28 Oct - 1 Nov, 2019. ©2019 Association for Computational Linguistics

Reference	It'll be sunny throughout this weekend. The high will be in the 60s, but expect temperatures to drop as low as 43 degrees by Sunday evening. There's also a chance of strong winds on Saturday morning.
Flat MR	`condition1[sunny] date_time1[this weekend] avg_high1[60s] low2[43] date_time2[Sunday evening] chance3[likely] wind_summary3[strong] date_time3[Saturday morning]`

Our MR	`INFORM [ condition[sunny], date_time_range[ colloquial[this weekend ] ] ]`
	 `CONTRAST [`
	 `    INFORM [ avg_high[60s] date_time[ [colloquial this weekend ] ] ]`
	 `    INFORM [ low[43] date_time[ week_day[Sunday] colloquial[evening] ] ]`
	 `]`
	 `INFORM [ chance[likely], wind_summary[heavy], date_time[ week_day[Saturday] colloquial[morning] ] ]`

Annotated Reference	[INFORM It'll be [condition sunny] throughout [date_time_range colloquial[this weekend]]. [CONTRAST [INFORM The high will be in the [avg_high 60s]]], [INFORM but expect temperatures to drop as low as [avg_low 43 degrees] by [date_time [week_day Sunday] [colloquial evening]]]. [INFORM There's also [chance a chance of] [wind_summary strong winds] on [date_time [week_day Saturday] [colloquial morning]] .]

Table 1: Sample flat MR with reference compared against tree-structured MR. The last row shows an annotated reference with the tree-structured MR. Nodes in blue are all children of the root node of the tree.

- We propose a tree-to-sequence (tree2seq) model to better leverage the inherent structures in the tree-based MRs. Coupled with the constrained decoding technique from (Balakrishnan et al., 2019), we explore whether combining better learning and decoding methods yields the best performance.

- Extensive evaluations on conversational weather and E2E datasets (Dušek et al., 2019) show that the tree2seq model can significantly improve semantic correctness. Analysis further shows that tree2seq is more data-efficient and generalizes better to hard scenarios.

2 Related Work

Several previous works have focused on adding planning steps to neural NLG architectures or employed non-sequential encoders. Puduppully et al. (2019) add a content planning step where a set of input database records are mapped to an ordered list of selected records; however, their approach does not employ hierarchical content plans as in our approach. Moryossef et al. (2019) add a symbolic text planning step where facts are grouped and ordered in the input; in contrast to our work though, their approach uses standard Seq2Seq models for realization and leaves no ordering choices to the model. Previous work on AMR and WebNLG (Beck et al., 2018; Song et al., 2018; Marcheggiani and Perez-Beltrachini, 2018) has demonstrated improvements over Seq2Seq models by using graph-to-sequence models; while similar in principle, these works do not explore the use of hierarchical content plans as intermediate structures and do not experiment with constrained decoding.

Elder et al. (2019) propose using an intermediate representation motivated by a universal dependency tree, and find that this greatly improves performance. However, their approach is still Seq2Seq-based and can't explicitly model the tree structures. Similar to our approach, Eriguchi et al. (2016) use a tree-to-sequence model for machine translation, but here we focus on NLG and use different tree encoder and constrained decoding techniques.

3 Tree-to-Sequence Model

3.1 Tree-Based Encoder

The input to our model is a tree-structured MR, and the output is an annotated reference, e.g., the last row in Table 1. Having annotated non-terminal tokens in the output allows us to check whether all arguments are expressed in output following the input tree structures.

We represent each token in the input MR as a tree node, using the tree structure to compute the hidden state of the k-th parent node $\mathbf{h}_k^p$ as a function of its child states $\{\mathbf{h}_k^{c_1}, ..., \mathbf{h}_k^{c_N}\}$:

$$\mathbf{h}_k^p = f_{\text{tree}}(\{\mathbf{h}_k^{c_1}, ..., \mathbf{h}_k^{c_N}\})$$

where N is the number of children for k-th node and f_{tree} is a non-linear function. We implemented a variant of the N-ary TreeLSTM by (Tai et al., 2015) as our tree encoder.

Since trees can have completely different layouts, it's hard to train and do inference with tree inputs in parallel. We propose an iterative bottom-up traversal algorithm to support batch forward and backward with tree inputs. Given a batch of trees, we first extract all the leaf nodes and update their states in a batch manner. Then we iteratively update the states of non-leaf nodes if all of their children nodes have been processed. As nodes can have different number of children nodes, we padded non-leaf nodes to have the same number of children nodes (i.e., N) for batch processing. Overall, the batch calculation ends up with 5-10X speedup compared to single-tree forward, allowing us to train on large datasets.[1]

3.2 Structure-Enhanced Decoder

The tree-based encoder returns a list of hidden states $\{\mathbf{h}_1, ..., \mathbf{h}_K\}$, where K is the length of source sequence. We first initialize the initial decoder state $\mathbf{s}_1$ as its root hidden state:

$$\mathbf{s}_1 = \mathbf{h}_{\text{root}}$$

In a standard attentional seq2seq (Bahdanau et al., 2014), $\alpha_j(k)$ denotes the attention score between j-th target state $\mathbf{s}_j$ and k-th source state $\mathbf{h}_k$. Then a weighted sum over source hidden states are calculated as $\mathbf{d}_j = \sum_k \alpha_j(k)\mathbf{h}_k$, and is used for updating the context state as follows:

$$\hat{\mathbf{s}}_j = \tanh(\mathbf{W}_d \cdot [\mathbf{s}_j; \mathbf{d}_j] + \mathbf{b}_d) \qquad (1)$$

where $[\mathbf{s}_j; \mathbf{d}_j]$ is a concatenation of hidden state $\mathbf{s}_j$ and $\mathbf{d}_j$. Next $\hat{\mathbf{s}}_j$ is used for predicting the j-th target token:

$$P(y_j|\mathbf{y}_{<j}, x) = \text{softmax}(\mathbf{W}_s \cdot \hat{\mathbf{s}}_j + \mathbf{b}_s)$$

However, the above decoding procedure doesn't take the tree structures into account. We adopted the input feeding approach (Eriguchi et al., 2016) by modifying equation (1) to feed the previous unit $\mathbf{s}_{j-1}$ to update the j-th context state:

$$\hat{\mathbf{s}}_j = \tanh(\mathbf{W}_d \cdot [\mathbf{s}_j; \mathbf{d}_j; \hat{\mathbf{s}_{j-1}}] + \mathbf{b}_d)$$

The input feeding approach allows us to enrich the contextual information when predicting the current token, in particular because $\hat{\mathbf{s}_{j-1}}$ is often the parent state of j-th node (given that the output tree structures are linearized to a sequence of words).

3.3 Constrained Decoding

Balakrishnan et al. (2019) propose a constrained decoding approach that derives constraints from the input tree structure to be enforced during decoding. In the beam search process, if a predicted non-terminal token violates the input MR structure, then the token is rejected. This allows beam search to explore more valid hypotheses with the same beam size. Their experiments show that constrained decoding can significantly improve the semantic correctness of generated responses by avoiding missing/repeating arguments and reducing hallucinated content while also enforcing desired groupings. (See their paper for further details on how the constraints are enforced.)

Though constrained decoding yields promising results in Balakrishnan et al.'s experiments, it's worth observing that constrained decoding does not affect the training process, which means that it doesn't help with generalization and relies on a strong base model. Therefore, we experiment with combining our tree-to-sequence model with constrained decoding, in order to determine whether the two methods work better in combination.

4 Experiments

4.1 Setup

Datasets: We conducted experiments on both the enriched E2E dataset and the weather dataset from (Balakrishnan et al., 2019).

Models We consider both Seq2Seq-based models and our proposed Tree2Seq models in our experiments. All Seq2Seq models use an LSTM-based encoder and decoder, with attention, while the Tree2Seq models have the architecture described in Section 3.

- **S2S**: Standard S2S-Tree model proposed in (Balakrishnan et al., 2019). This is a Seq2Seq model in which the input is a linearized text representation of the MR, while the output is an annotated response (example in Table 1).
- **S2S-Constr**: This is the S2S-Constr model proposed in (Balakrishnan et al., 2019). This is identical in architecture to the S2S model, and differs only in the decoding step, where constrained decoding is applied to ensure semantic correctness.
- **T2S**: Our proposed model, with tree-based encoding and structure-enhanced decoding.
- **T2S-Constr**: Has the same architecture as T2S, but with constrained decoding applied to the decoder to ensure semantic correctness.

Metrics We consider both automatic metrics and human evaluation results. For automatic metrics, we evaluate on following automatic metrics:

---

[1]On the E2E dataset, the batchized tree2seq model takes 20 and 2 minutes every epoch in training and testing.

Model	E2E					Weather				
Metric	BLEU	TreeAcc		Gram.	Corr.	BLEU	TreeAcc		Gram.	Corr.
	-	NoDisc	Disc	-	-	-	NoDisc	Disc	-	-
S2S	74.58	99.68	95.28	93.59	83.85	76.75	96.62	83.30	94.17	87.40
S2S-Constr	74.69	**99.89**	97.78	94.33	**85.89**	77.45	98.52	91.61	94.20	90.40
Our Approaches										
T2S	**74.75**	**99.89**	96.96	94.83	84.66	**77.86**	97.1	88.80	**94.55**	89.75
T2S-Constr	74.63	99.84	**98.60**	**94.68**	85.68	77.82	**99.11**	**94.13**	94.14	**91.84**

Table 2: Results on E2E and Weather datasets. All metrics are percentages.

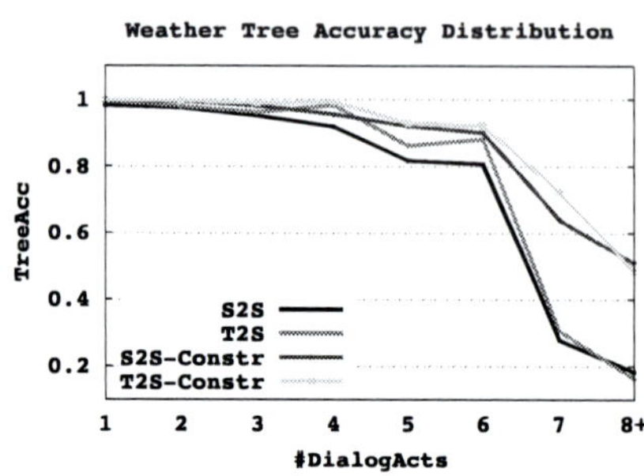

Figure 1: Tree Accuracy Distribution on Weather

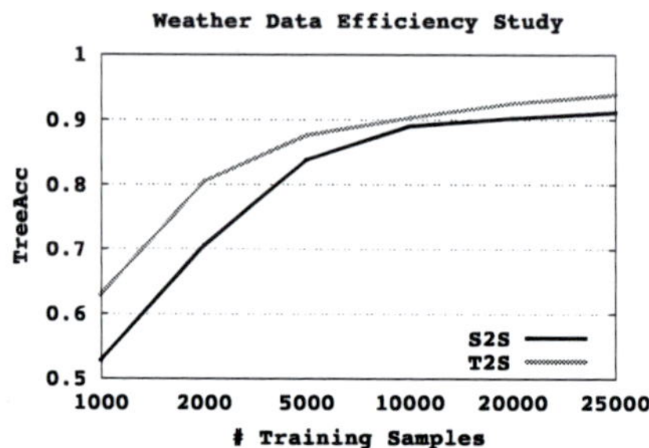

Figure 2: Data Efficiency Study on Weather

1) **BLEU-4** (Papineni et al., 2002); 2) **Tree accuracy** (Balakrishnan et al., 2019), which is a binary metric to indicate whether the tree structure in the prediction matches that of the input MR exactly.

For human evaluation, annotators rate model responses in a **binary** scale on two dimensions:

- **Grammaticality** (`Gram`): Our evaluation guidelines included considerations for proper subject-verb agreement, word order, grammatical completeness, etc..

- **Correctness** (`Corr`): Measures *semantic correctness* of the responses. Our guidelines considered sentence structure, contrast, hallucinations (incorrectly included attributes), and missing attributes. We asked annotators to evaluate model predictions against the reference rather than the MR.

Our human evaluation was conducted in a double-blind setting, in which two annotators independently provide ratings for each response, and a third annotator resolves any disagreements between the two. The disagreement rate is 20.7% for the weather dataset and 23.2% for the E2E dataset.

4.2 Main Results

Table 2 shows the main results. For the tree accuracy metric, we report the numbers on two disjoint subsets: discourse subset (column Disc), which contains inputs with 1+ discourse acts, and no-discourse subset (column NoDisc), which includes inputs without any discourse acts. The discourse subset is expected to be more challenging as it contains longer and more complex inputs.

From the table, we can see that all approaches are roughly comparable on BLEU scores. With tree accuracy, T2S consistently outperforms S2S in on both the discourse and no-discourse subsets, with the exception of the NoDisc subset of the E2E data, where all models are close to 100% accuracy. The margins of improvement from T2S are higher on the discourse subset, suggesting T2S is more effective on hard inputs. S2S-Constr consistently outperforms S2S and T2S, affirming the effectiveness of constrained decoding. Overall, combining the enhanced encoding and decoding methods, T2S-Constr achieves the best performance on all subsets (again, except with NoDisc tree accuracy for E2E, where ceiling performance is effectively reached).

For grammaticality, we see all approaches are comparable in E2E and Weather. Analysis show above 90% grammatical errors are because models tend to generate run-on responses that group many arguments in one sentence, without appropriate punctuation (e.g., commas). Consistent with Balakrishnan et al. (2019), we found higher tree accuracy usually corresponds to higher human judgements of semantic correctness (except with S2S-Constr and T2S-Constr for E2E). We also note that there's a noticeable gap in the E2E dataset

Column	G/T/C	Text

MR Input	-	`Join [`
		`  INFORM [ area[riverside] name[_name_] price_range[high]`
		`           eat_type[restaurant] [near _near_ ] ]`
		`  CONTRAST [`
		`    INFORM [ rating[1 out of 5] family_friendly_no[no] ]`
		`    INFORM [ food_italian[_food_italian_] ]`
		`  ] ]`

Annotated Reference	-	[Join [**INFORM** There is a [price_range high] price range [eat_type restaurant] [name name] in [area riverside] near [_near_]] [**CONTRAST** [INFORM It is [family_friendly not kids friendly] and [rating has low] customer ratings] but [INFORM they serve [food_italian Italian food] .]]]
S2S	1/0/0	[Join [**INFORM** [name _name_] is a [price_range high] priced [eat_type restaurant] in the [area riverside] area near [near _near_] .] [**CONTRAST** [INFORM is [family_friendly_no not children friendly] ,] but [INFORM it has a customer rating of [rating 1 out of 5] .]]]
T2S	1/0/0	[Join [**INFORM** [name _name_] is a [price_range high] priced [eat_type restaurant] in the [area riverside] area near [near _near_] .] [**CONTRAST** [INFORM it has a customer rating of [rating 1 out of 5] ,] but [INFORM is [family_friendly_no not children friendly] and serves [food_italian Italian] food.]]]
T2S-Constr	1/1/1	[Join [**INFORM** [name _name_] is a [price_range high] priced [eat_type restaurant] in the [area riverside] area near [near _near_] .] [**CONTRAST** [INFORM it is [family_friendly not children friendly] and has a [rating 1 out of 5] rating] but [INFORM it serves [food_italian Italian] food.]]]

Table 3: Sample model responses. Row 'Annotated Reference' is human-annotated reference. Column 'G/T/C' represents the value of grammaticality/tree accuracy/correctness of model predicted response.

where the tree accuracy doesn't align with the correctness numbers from human evaluation (the gap on weather is smaller). Our analysis show most correctness errors are mainly due to: 1) the compositional MR inputs were missing information in the reference which was caused by the noisy dataset creation by Balakrishnan et al. (2019); 2) some attributes caused confusions to human annotators, e.g., "20-30 pounds" can imply "a mid-priced restaurant"; 3) a legitimate amount of content hallucinations, especially in hard inputs and unseen attributes.

We also plot the tree accuracy distribution against the number of dialog acts in Figure 1. (We skip this figure for E2E dataset for space reasons, as it shows similar pattern to weather dataset.) Clearly, for smaller numbers of dialog acts (#DialogActs <= 3), all models perform roughly the same and almost hit 100% accuracy. But the gains of T2S is much more clear when the number of dialog acts is larger than 3. T2S-Constr is also generally better than S2S-Constr in most cases, and both are more effective for complex MRs (7 or 8+ dialog acts), where there are very few MRs (less than 0.5%) in the training set.

Data Efficiency. We set up a data efficiency experiment, in which we trained each model on increasingly larger subsets of our training set (while keeping the test set constant). Figure 2 shows the results of this experiment. Overall T2S consistently outperforms S2S, and the difference is larger with fewer training samples. This suggests that structure awareness leads to better representa-tions and improves data efficiency.

4.3 Sample Analysis

We also provide some sample responses on E2E in Table 3. Column 'G/T/C' stands for the value of grammaticality, tree accuracy and correctness of model prediction. We obviate S2S-Constr response here as it is similar to T2S-Constr.

From the example, we can see that T2S mistakenly contrasted the family friendly and customer rating attributes, largely due to the overwhelming contrast patterns between family friendly and customer rating in training data. In addition to the contrast mistake, S2S completely ignores the attribute of serving Italian food, suggesting its poor generalization ability to rare argument (i.e., `food_italian`). T2S-Constr shared the first sentence with the T2S approach, but was able to correct the constrast mistake by adding structure constraints during beam search.

5 Conclusion

In this paper, we have demonstrated via experiments on two datasets that a tree-to-sequence model that leverages the inherent tree structures in input MRs can improve semantic correctness over a sequence-to-sequence model and is more data-efficient. Moreover, we have shown that the tree-to-sequence model can be coupled with a better constrained decoding method to achieve better semantic correctness than either method alone.

References

Dzmitry Bahdanau, Kyunghyun Cho, and Yoshua Bengio. 2014. Neural machine translation by jointly learning to align and translate. *arXiv preprint arXiv:1409.0473*.

Anusha Balakrishnan, Jinfeng Rao, Kartikeya Upasani, Michael White, and Rajen Subba. 2019. Constrained decoding for neural NLG from compositional representations in task-oriented dialogue. In *Proceedings of the 57th Annual Meeting of the Association for Computational Linguistics*. To appear.

Daniel Beck, Gholamreza Haffari, and Trevor Cohn. 2018. Graph-to-sequence learning using gated graph neural networks. In *Proceedings of the 56th Annual Meeting of the Association for Computational Linguistics (Volume 1: Long Papers)*, pages 273–283, Melbourne, Australia. Association for Computational Linguistics.

Giuseppe Carenini and Johanna D. Moore. 2006. Generating and evaluating evaluative arguments. *Artificial Intelligence*, 170:925–952.

Vera Demberg, Andi Winterboer, and Johanna D Moore. 2011. A strategy for information presentation in spoken dialog systems. *Computational Linguistics*, 37(3):489–539.

Ondřej Dušek, Jekaterina Novikova, and Verena Rieser. 2018. Findings of the E2E NLG challenge. In *Proceedings of the 11th International Conference on Natural Language Generation*, pages 322–328. Association for Computational Linguistics.

Ondřej Dušek, Jekaterina Novikova, and Verena Rieser. 2019. Evaluating the state-of-the-art of end-to-end natural language generation: The E2E NLG Challenge. *arXiv preprint arXiv:1901.11528*.

Henry Elder, Jennifer Foster, James Barry, and Alexander OConnor. 2019. Designing a symbolic intermediate representation for neural surface realization. In *Proceedings of the Workshop on Methods for Optimizing and Evaluating Neural Language Generation*, pages 65–73.

Akiko Eriguchi, Kazuma Hashimoto, and Yoshimasa Tsuruoka. 2016. Tree-to-sequence attentional neural machine translation. *the 54th Annual Meeting of the Association for Computational Linguistics*.

Oliver Lemon, Johanna Moore, Mary Ellen Foster, and Michael White. 2004. Generating tailored, comparative descriptions in spoken dialogue. In *Proc. of FLAIRS*. AAAI.

Diego Marcheggiani and Laura Perez-Beltrachini. 2018. Deep graph convolutional encoders for structured data to text generation. In *Proceedings of the 11th International Conference on Natural Language Generation*, pages 1–9, Tilburg University, The Netherlands. Association for Computational Linguistics.

Amit Moryossef, Yoav Goldberg, and Ido Dagan. 2019. Step-by-step: Separating planning from realization in neural data-to-text generation. In *Proceedings of the 2019 Conference of the North American Chapter of the Association for Computational Linguistics: Human Language Technologies, Volume 1 (Long and Short Papers)*, pages 2267–2277, Minneapolis, Minnesota. Association for Computational Linguistics. ArXiv preprint arXiv:1904.03396.

Kishore Papineni, Salim Roukos, Todd Ward, and Wei-Jing Zhu. 2002. BLEU: a method for automatic evaluation of machine translation. In *Proc. ACL-02*.

Ratish Puduppully, Li Dong, and Mirella Lapata. 2019. Data-to-text generation with content selection and planning. In *Proceedings of AAAI*. ArXiv preprint arXiv:1809.00582.

Lena Reed, Shereen Oraby, and Marilyn Walker. 2018. Can neural generators for dialogue learn sentence planning and discourse structuring? In *Proceedings of the 11th International Conference on Natural Language Generation*, pages 284–295. Association for Computational Linguistics.

Linfeng Song, Yue Zhang, Zhiguo Wang, and Daniel Gildea. 2018. A graph-to-sequence model for AMR-to-text generation. In *Proceedings of the 56th Annual Meeting of the Association for Computational Linguistics (Volume 1: Long Papers)*, pages 1616–1626, Melbourne, Australia. Association for Computational Linguistics.

Kai Sheng Tai, Richard Socher, and Christopher D Manning. 2015. Improved semantic representations from tree-structured long short-term memory networks. In *Proceedings of the 53rd Annual Meeting of the Association for Computational Linguistics and the 7th International Joint Conference on Natural Language Processing (Volume 1: Long Papers)*, pages 1556–1566.

Marilyn Walker, Amanda Stent, Francois Mairesse, and Rashmi Prasad. 2007. Individual and domain adaptation in sentence planning for dialogue. *Journal of Artificial Intelligence Research (JAIR)*, 30:413–456.

Michael White, Robert A. J. Clark, and Johanna D. Moore. 2010. Generating tailored, comparative descriptions with contextually appropriate intonation. *Computational Linguistics*, 36(2):159–201.

Sam Wiseman, Stuart Shieber, and Alexander Rush. 2017. Challenges in data-to-document generation. In *Proceedings of the 2017 Conference on Empirical Methods in Natural Language Processing*, pages 2253–2263. Association for Computational Linguistics.

Multiple News Headlines Generation using Page Metadata

Kango Iwama, Yoshinobu Kano

Faculty of Informatics, Shizuoka University, Japan

`kiwama@kanolab.net, kano@inf.shizuoka.ac.jp`

Abstract

Multiple headlines of a newspaper article have an important role to express the content of the article accurately and concisely. A headline depends on the content and intent of their article. While a single headline expresses the whole corresponding article, each of multiple headlines expresses different information individually. We suggest an automatic generation method of such diverse multiple headlines in a newspaper. Our generation method is based on the Pointer-Generator Network, using page metadata on a newspaper which can change headline generation behavior. We conducted automatic evaluations for generated headlines. The results show that our method improved ROUGE-1 score by 4.32 points compared to a baseline system. This is the first trial to evaluate such multiple headlines generation as far as we know. These results suggest that our model using page metadata can generate various multiple headlines for an article with better performance.

1 Introduction

Headlines of newspaper articles have a role to express the content accurately and concisely. Newspapers have *pages*, by which the importance of an article, and sometimes an article's genre, is determined. Therefore, a headline depends on the *page* metadata. For example, the first (front) *page* is normally most important; the literary style of headlines is different depending on genres such as national current affairs and local news. The contents and corresponding headlines of articles are different by the *page*.

Generation of newspaper article headlines is a kind of summarization tasks of articles. There have been a variety of previous works of headline

Figure 1: Example of multiple headlines in newspaper. (The Chunichi Shimbun, 2017)

generation and document summarization: neural headline generation by AMR (Takase et al., 2016); Japanese news articles compression using the Dependency Tree (Hasegawa et al., 2017); summary generation by Attention-based model (Rush et al., 2015); readable summary generation by GAN (Wang and Lee, 2018). These methods normally generate a single summary from a single given document. However, a news article could have multiple headlines. Multiple headlines could have a sub headline(s) in addition to its main headline. Headlines do not share same information; main and sub headlines supplement the content of an article each other (Figure 1). Therefore, multiple headline generation requires a variety of headlines with different contents from the same article.

Wang et al. (2016) generated multiple headlines, then scored them to filter candidates out. They aimed to provide candidates of main headlines rather than to provide main and sub headlines. They used three generation models, where a single headline is generated from each model.

Proceedings of The 12th International Conference on Natural Language Generation, pages 101–105,
Tokyo, Japan, 28 Oct - 1 Nov, 2019. ©2019 Association for Computational Linguistics

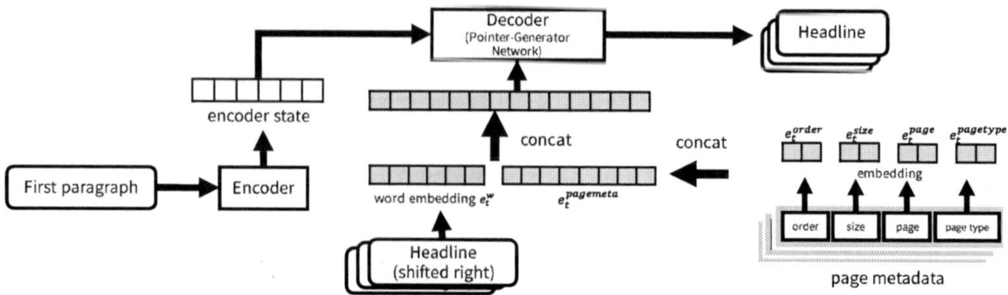

Figure 2: Our method overview.

We suggest a method to generate such a variety of multiple headlines using page metadata. In contrast to the previous work (Wang et al., 2016), we use a single model to generate multiple headlines. Our system generates individual main/sub headlines separately, which allows partial re-generation upon users' requests e.g. when users wish to change a generated headline and/or its style. Our generation method is based on the Pointer-Generator Network, using page metadata on a newspaper which can change headline generation behavior. This is the first trial to evaluate such multiple headlines generation as far as we know. Our evaluation results show better ROUGE-1 score in 4.32 points than a baseline.

2 Model

A news article often picks up new topics which include new named entities such as person names, requiring unknown word processing. Pointer-Generator Network (See et al., 2017) is a hybrid model of Attention-based Seq2Seq (Nallapati et al., 2016) and Pointer Networks (Vinyals et al., 2015) for automatic summarization. Pointer-Generator Network temporarily gives a word ID to an unknown word, outputs a probabilistic distribution of its given lexicon including the unknown words. Our method is based on Pointer-Generator Network, using page metadata as one of its inputs. This page metadata includes a headline *order* within multiple headlines for an article, a headline *size* indicating the font size, an article's page number, and an article's page type. We explain details of these metadata in the Dataset section later. We describe our model assuming that the input is in the Japanese language, but the system architecture can be applied to any other languages.

Our method overview is shown in Figure 2. Given a target article's body text, we use words of the first paragraph with the article's page metadata as inputs to our model. Our encoder takes morphemes (tokens) w_i of the first paragraph, then we obtain the hidden state of our encoder. We define the input x_t to our decoder LSTM at time step t as follows:

$$x_t = e_t^w \oplus e^{pagemeta}$$
$$e^{pagemeta} = e^{order} \oplus e^{size} \oplus e^{page} \oplus e^{pagetype}$$

where $\oplus$ indicates concatenation. CLSTM (Contextual LSTM) (Ghosh et al., 2016) generates sentences which are related to input topics, using concatenation of a word vector and a topic vector as an input to LSTM. We input an input vector x_t to the decoder LSTM, which is a concatenation of a word vector e_t^w and a vector of page metadata $e^{pagemeta}$. We define e^{order}, e^{size}, e^{page}, and $e^{pagetype}$ as vectors in which the order of the headline, the headline's *size*, the page number, and the page type is embedded, respectively.

Final word distribution P(w) is calculated as follows:

$$P(w) = P_{vocab}(w) + (1 - P_{gen}) \sum_{i:w_i=w} a_i^t$$

P_{vocab} is calculated by feeding a vector that concatenates a decoder state s_t and a context vector h_t^*, through linear layers. P_{gen} is calculated by feeding a vector that sums h_t^*, s_t, x_t, through sigmoid function. a_i^t indicates attention distribution. During training, the loss at the time step t is a negative log likelihood of a target word, and an entire loss is an average of these losses.

3 Dataset

We use a newspaper corpus provided by Chunichi Shimbun, which is one of the major Japanese newspaper companies. This newspaper article

Model type	ROUGE			distinct-n	
	1	**2**	**L**	**1**	**2**
(1) word (baseline)	19.52	8.18	17.70	0.0135	0.1740
(2) + order	22.45	9.57	20.24	0.0145	0.1669
(3) + order + size	23.77	10.13	21.55	0.0141	0.1660
(4) + order + size + page	23.74	**10.19**	21.51	0.0143	0.1672
(5) + order + size + page + page type	**23.84**	10.17	**21.60**	0.0142	0.1651

Table 1: ROUGE F1 and distinct-n(n=1,2) scores on the test set.

Page type	Data size	ROUGE			distinct-n	
		1	**2**	**L**	**1**	**2**
Variable page	2473k	24.09	8.87	22.01	0.0234	0.2133
Local page	3425k	**26.68**	**12.49**	**24.05**	0.0173	0.1755
Special page	537k	22.63	9.01	20.40	0.0638	0.3292

Table 2: ROUGE F1 and distinct-n(n=1,2) scores on the test set by page type (model (5)).

corpus includes almost all of the published articles for 30 years. An article in this corpus includes a page number, a page type, a body text of the article, and corresponding multiple headlines. A page type is one of *variable page, local page, special page, radio page, or additional page*. Each headline has *size* information of that headline. Size information indicates the physical size in five grades. The smaller the value, the larger the physical size. Size information normally shows the importance of the article and headlines.

We used about 15 years from the original corpus because older data does not include the size information. In order to exclude headlines which are fixed regardless of the article content, e.g. the "editorial" and "column", we excluded the top 200 frequent headlines from the data. Then we excluded articles of which the number of words in the first paragraph is more than 10 and less than 150, also excluded articles which headlines include more than 10 words. We finally excluded articles with headlines which *order*, i.e. the number of appearances among multiple headlines for an article, is fifth or after. The final dataset used in our experiments include 6,435,774 articles.

4   Experiments

We compared five models which use different page metadata. Our evaluation was performed by 3-fold cross validation, using ROUGE and distinct-n (Li et al., 2016), which is a metric to evaluate diversity

Page Type	distinct-n	
	1	**2**
Variable page	0.0333	0.3511
Local page	0.0320	0.3164
Special page	0.0465	0.3562

Table 3: distinct-n(n=1,2) scores on true data.

of outputs. We used ROUGE-1, ROUGE-2, ROUGE-L and distinct-n (n=1, 2) scores.

We used MeCab 0.996[1] with the mecab-ipadic-NEologd[2] dictionary to tokenize sentences. We implemented our model using PyTorch 1.0.1[3]. Dimensions of each embedding vector were set to 128. Each layer of our encoder LSTM and our decoder LSTM has 256 dimensions. The vocabulary size was 50,000. Word vector representations are same between the encoder and the decoder. Adam as an optimizer, batch size was 64. All numerals were regarded as unknown words. Japanese letters of numerals in the first paragraph were converted into Arabic numerals. Consecutive numerals were concatenated into a single word.

We used an early stopping to avoid overfitting in our training. Our validation data was 2.5% of the training data, randomly extracted. The remaining of the data was used as our training data. The loss for the validation data was calculated for every 1000 iterations, and training was stopped if the loss did not decrease within 1 epoch at the longest.

5   Results

Table 1 shows our results of the automatic evaluation. *word, order, size, page*, and *page type*

---

[1] https://taku910.github.io/mecab/
[2] https://github.com/neologd/mecab-ipadic-neologd
[3] https://pytorch.org/

F: 年金記録不備問題で社会保険庁は十一日、二十四時間態勢でオペレーターが対応する電話相談「ねんきんあんしんダイヤル」を始めたが、午前八時半から電話が殺到。午後になってもほとんどつながらない状態で、同庁担当者は「ご不便をおかけして申し訳ない。今後はスタッフを増員したい」と、前日のシステム障害に続く不手際に平謝りだった。(The Social Insurance Agency started working on a telephone call "Pension Relief Dial", which the operator responded in 24 hours on Monday, due to the problem of inadequate pension record, but the telephone was flooded at 8:30 am. With no connection in the afternoon, the agency official said, "I am sorry for the inconvenience. We would like to increase the number of staff in the future," they said sorry for the trouble following the system failure the day before.)
H: 年金記録　フリーダイヤル相談 (Pension record, Free dial consultation)
　『不安』鳴りっぱなし ("anxiety" ringing)
B: 社保庁 (Social Insurance Agency)
　『ねんきんあんしんダイヤル』 ("Pension Relief Dial")
P: 社保庁 (Social Insurance Agency)
　社保庁　『ねんきん』 (Social Insurance Agency, Pension)
PA: 社保庁　年金電話相談 (Social Insurance Agency, Pension telephone consultation)
　電話殺到 (a flood of calls)
　年金電話相談　電話殺到(Pension telephone consultation, a flood of calls)
　『今後はスタッフ増員』 ("We will increase the number of staff in the future.")
　年金記録不備 (Pension record deficiencies)
　どうなる年金(Whither Pension?)

Figure 3: Example of automatically generated headlines by our method. **F:** first paragraph, **H:** human written original headlines, **B:** baseline (word), **P:** word + all page metadata, **PA:** all parameters combinations of all page metadata (Excerpts)

indicate the word vector, e^{order}, e^{size}, e^{page}, and $e^{pagetype}$, respectively. Model (1) outputs words that concatenate multiple headlines, but the outputs are subdivided into individual headlines when in the evaluation. Model (5) used all of page metadata. Comparing with the baseline, Model (5) performed better 4.32 points in ROUGE-1, 1.99 points in ROUGE-2, 3.9 points in ROUGE-L. ROUGE-1 and ROUGE-L scores were the highest in model (5). Regarding the distinct-1 score, which is the metric to evaluate diversity of outputs, any model using page metadata performed better than model (1) that uses words only.

6 Discussion

The result of the automatic evaluation shows that page metadata improves ROUGE scores. Table 2 shows the results for each page type. We discarded page types of *radio page* and *additional page* because articles of these types were 0.01% of the entire data. Among these page types, *local page* was the best (ROUGE-1 and ROUGE-2 are p<0.001).

Table 3 shows the distinct-n scores that are calculated from the original headlines of the newspaper articles for each page type. We used 500,000 headlines extracted randomly to calculate scores in Table 3. The distinct-n scores of *local page*s are lower than the other page types. The ROUGE scores of *local page*s would have been higher than other page types because the vocabulary patterns in *local page* type were limited.

Figure 3 shows a part of a generated headline example of using all of page metadata. Our model generated more variety of headlines than original human written headlines and the baseline headlines. On the other hand, while the same information does not appear repeatedly in multiple headlines of an article in the original newspaper, our model sometimes generated headlines with the same information. The distinct-n scores in Table 1 do not show an increase in the diversity of the vocabulary. We currently assume that humans will select final candidates from our system output, but automatic selection excluding information overlaps would be our future work.

Using other evaluation metrics could be another future work. Even if a generated headline is different from with a corresponding human written headline, some of such headlines are acceptable because the human written headlines are not the unique available gold standard. Therefore, manual evaluations to measure quality of the headlines are also meaningful. Because larger vocabulary is required to generate diverse headlines, we would like to handle omitted words and unknown words which even do not appear in articles in future.

7 Conclusion

We suggested an automatic generation method of multiple headlines of news articles. We can control generated headlines by configuring page metadata manually if needed. While we used newspaper corpus, our method can be applied to any other media e.g. journals and electronic articles that could have multiple headlines. This is the first trial to generate such multiple articles as far as we know. Our model using page metadata performed better than the baseline 4.32 points in ROUGE-1 score.

References

The Chunichi Shimbun, The Chunichi Shimbun (Shizuoka) on July 31, 2017. page 12.

Shalini Ghosh, Oriol Vinyals, Brian Strope, Scott Roy, Tom Dean, Larry Heck, 2016. Contextual LSTM (CLSTM) models for Large scale NLP tasks. arXiv preprint arXiv:1602.06291.

Shun Hasegawa, Yuta Kikuchi, Hiroya Takamura, Manabu Okumura, 2017. Japanese Sentence Compression with a Large Training Dataset. *In Proceedings of the 55th Annual Meeting of the Association for Computational Linguistics*, pages 281-286.

Jiwei Li, Michel Galley, Chris Brockett, Jianfeng Gao, Bill Dolan, 2016. A Diversity-Promoting Objective Function for Neural Conversation Models. *In Proceedings of NAACL-HLT 2016*, pages 110-119.

Ramesh Nallapati, Bowen Zhou, Cicero Nogueira dos Santos, Caglar Gulcehre, Bing Xiang, 2016. Abstractive Text Summarization Using Sequence-to-Sequence RNNs and Beyond. *In Proceedings of the 20th SIGNLL Conference on Computational Natural Language Learning (CoNLL)*, pages 280-290.

Alexander M. Rush, Sumit Chopra, Jason Weston, 2015. A Neural Attention Model for Abstractive Sentence Summarization. *In Proceedings of the 2015 Conference on Empirical Methods in Natural Language Processing*, pages 379-389.

Abigail See, Peter J. Liu, Christopher D. Manning, 2017. Get To The Point: Summarization with Pointer-Generator Networks. *In Proceedings of the 55th Annual Meeting of the Association for Computational Linguistics*, pages 1073-1083.

Sho Takase, Jun Suzuki, Naoaki Okazaki, Tsutomu Hirao, Masaaki Nagata, 2016. Neural Headline Generation on Abstract Meaning Representation. *In Proceedings of the 2016 Conference on Empirical Methods in Natural Language Processing.* pages 1054-1059.

Oriol Vinyals, Meire Fortunato, Navdeep Jaitly, 2015. Pointer Networks. *Neural Information Processing Systems*.

Shuguang Wang, Eui-Hong (Sam) Han, Alexander M. Rush, 2016. Headliner: An integrated headline suggestion system. *Computation + Journalism Symposium*.

Yau-Shian Wang, Hung-Yi Lee, 2018. Learning to Encode Text as Human-Readable Summaries using Generative Adversarial Networks. *In Proceedings of the 2018 Conference on Empirical Methods in Natural Language Processing*, pages 4187-4195.

Neural Question Generation using Interrogative Phrases

Yuichi Sasazawa   **Sho Takase**   **Naoaki Okazaki**
Tokyo Institute of Technology
{yuichi.sasazawa, sho.takase} at nlp.c.titech.ac.jp
okazaki at c.titech.ac.jp

Abstract

Question Generation (QG) is the task of generating questions from a given passage. One of the key requirements of QG is to generate a question such that it results in a target answer. Previous works used a target answer to obtain a desired question. However, we also want to specify how to ask questions and improve the quality of generated questions. In this study, we explore the use of interrogative phrases as additional sources to control QG. By providing interrogative phrases, we expect that QG can generate a more reliable sequence of words subsequent to an interrogative phrase. We present a baseline sequence-to-sequence model with the attention, copy, and coverage mechanisms, and show that the simple baseline achieves state-of-the-art performance. The experiments demonstrate that interrogative phrases contribute to improving the performance of QG. In addition, we report the superiority of using interrogative phrases in human evaluation. Finally, we show that a question answering system can provide target answers more correctly when the questions are generated with interrogative phrases.[1]

1   Introduction

Question Generation (QG) is the task of generating questions from a given passage. It has several applications: (1) In the area of the education, QG can help to generate questions for reading comprehension materials (Heilman and Smith, 2010). (2) QG can aid development of conversational chatbots, which ask questions (Mostafazadeh et al., 2016). (3) QG is useful for development of question answering datasets (Duan et al., 2017; Tang et al., 2018).

One of the key requirements of QG is to generate a question such that it asks a target answer. For example, the sentence "Bob went to the airport yesterday." can have various candidate questions such as "When did Bob go to the airport?," "Where did Bob go yesterday?," and "Who went to the airport yesterday?" It is necessary for QG to specify a desired question from among multiple possibilities. Du et al. (2017) and Chali et al. (2018) used the sequence-to-sequence model (Bahdanau et al., 2015), which takes only a passage as the input. Thus, only one question is generated from multiple possibilities at random. Most recent studies tried to generate a desired question using a target answer as the input. Zhou et al. (2017) and Song et al. (2018) incorporated the target answer using the answer position feature. Kim et al. (2018) separated target answer words from the original passages to address the problem of many generated questions including the target answer words.

However, we also want to specify how questions should be asked and improve the quality of the generated questions. The existing method sometimes generates inappropriate questions whose interrogative phrases do not match the target answers. For example, we specify a target answer, "in 1920," but an interrogative phrase of the generated question is "how much." Sun et al. (2018) proposed the answer-focused model to address this problem. Heilman and Smith. (2010) extracted target answers from passages and automatically converted them into interrogative phrases by a sequence of general rules.

In this study, we explore the use of interrogative phrases as additional sources to control QG. Using appropriate interrogative phrases that match the target answers is important for generating questions. Unlike Heilman and Smith (2010) or Sun et al. (2018), we directly input the correct interrogative phrases. Selecting correct interrogative

---

[1]Our code is available at https://github.com/WERimagin/NQG_Interrogative_Phrases.

Proceedings of The 12th International Conference on Natural Language Generation, pages 106–111,
Tokyo, Japan, 28 Oct - 1 Nov, 2019. ©2019 Association for Computational Linguistics

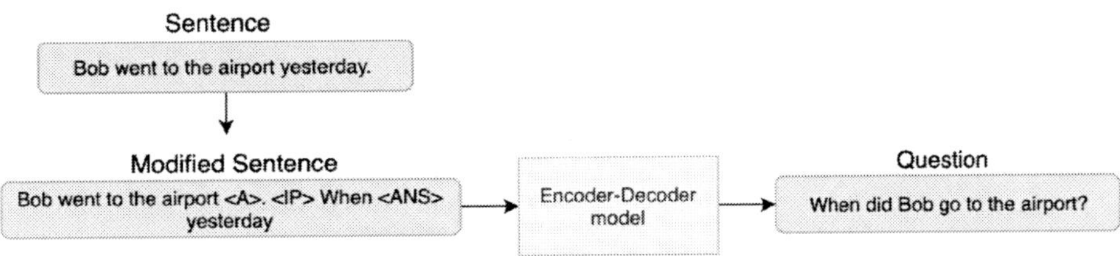

Figure 1: Overview of the proposed method. We concatenate an answer and interrogative phrase at the end of the passage using the special tokens <IP> and <ANS>. Also, we replace the answer phrase with the special token <A>. We use this modified passage as the input and generate a question.

phrases manually is not so difficult; thus, using the correct interrogative phrases as inputs is an expected experimental setting. We investigate to what extent using proper interrogative phrases as inputs contributes to the quality of the questions. To the best of our knowledge, this is the first study that studies the use of interrogative phrases as inputs to improve the quality of questions in QG.

We test our method on the SQuAD dataset (Rajpurkar et al., 2016). We demonstrate that the use of interrogative phrases contributes to improving the performance of QG by automatic metrics and human evaluation. We also conduct a question answering experiment. We show that it is easier for a question answering system to provide the correct target answers when questions are generated using interrogative phrases.

2 Method

In this work, we generate a question from a passage, a target answer, and an interrogative phrase. An outline of our method is shown in Figure 1.

We use the Encoder-Decoder model with an attention mechanism (Bahdanau et al., 2015) for generating questions. In order to obtain a question that depends on a passage, a target answer and an interrogative phrase, we concatenate the target answer and the interrogative phrase at the end of the passage using the special tokens <IP> and <ANS>. This treatment can inform the model about the target answer and the interrogative phrase that should be considered in the generated questions. In addition, we replace the span of the target answer in the passage with the special token <A>. This treatment helps the model to focus on the words present near the answer in the passage when generating a question.

Because a question is expected to use the words appearing in the passage, we incorporate the copy mechanism (See et al., 2017) into the model. By copying the words in the passage while generating the question, this mechanism reduces the risk of generating words not included in the passage. We also explore the use of the coverage mechanism (Tu et al., 2016) to avoid generating an inappropriate question. This mechanism can also prevent the model from generating the same word repeatedly.

Although this model is simpler than other QG models, it achieves the surprisingly good performance on the SQuAD v1.1 dataset, as described in Sections 3.4 and 3.5.

3 Experiments

3.1 Dataset

We use the SQuAD v1.1 dataset (Rajpurkar et al., 2016) in this study. The SQuAD dataset is a question answering dataset containing 107,785 questions with 536 articles. We lowercase all the data. We extract a sentence containing an answer phrase. Then, we use it as the input passage. If the answer phrase spans multiple sentences, we extract these sentencese and use the concatenation of them as the input passage. We use Stanford CoreNLP (Manning et al., 2014) to extract the interrogative phrases from the questions. If the CoreNLP detects multiple words as the interrogative phrases (e.g., "how many", "in what year" or "what country"), we use all the word as the interrogative phrase. We remove the sentence-question pairs whose questions do not contain an interrogative phrase. For instance, Yes/No questions (e.g., "Did you go to the school?") or questions whose interrogative phrase is located in the middle of the question, which Stanford CoreNLP cannot detect accurately (e.g., "Bob went to the airport how many times?"). We remove passage-question pairs that have no content (non-stop) word in common.

These pairs are unsuitable for the QG dataset because the passage is not related to the question. We thus obtain 74,863, 4,658, and 4,658 pairs for training, development, and test, respectively.

3.2 Experiment setting

We use the OpenNMT system (Klein et al., 2017). We retain 45,000 of the most frequent words on the source side and 28,000 of the most frequent words on the target side. All the other words are replaced by the <UNK> token. We use 300 dimensions pretrained glove.840B.300d (Pennington et al., 2014) embeddings for initialization, and we fix them during training. We use 2-layer long short-term memory in both the encoder and the decoder. The size of the hidden state is 600. The dropout rate is 0.3. We use stochastic gradient descent for optimization. The initial learning rate is 1.0. We halve the learning rate every 2,500 steps from 20,000 steps onwards. We finish the training at 50,000 steps. We adopt the model that achieves the highest accuracy in the development set.

During inference, we conduct the beam search with a beam width of 2. Decoding stops when the model generates the <EOS> token. All hyperparameters are tuned using the development set, and the results are reported using the test set.

We use two models for comparisons.

ASs2s This model is the state-of-the-art of the neural QG model for the SQuAD dataset (Kim et al., 2018). Based on the Encoder-Decoder architecture, this model incorporates a target answer using answer-separated seq2seq and the keyword-net module. This model need to use a target answer. We compare the accuracy of using interrogative phrases as inputs. When we use an interrogative phrase as the input, we concatenate it at the end of the passage using the special token <IP>.

Seq2Seq This is our baseline model. We use the RNN-based Encoder-Decoder model with the attention, copy, and coverage mechanisms. We compare the accuracy of using interrogative phrases or target answers as inputs. When we use an interrogative phrase as the input, we concatenate it at the end of the passage using the special token <IP>. When we use a target answer as the input, we concatenate it at the end of the passage using the special token <ANS> and replace the span of the target answer in the passage with special token <A>.

To check the contributions of the components in our model, we conduct ablation tests. We remove each component from the Seq2Seq + Answer + Interrogative method.

-Copy: Without the copy mechanism.

-Coverage: Without the coverage mechanism.

-Answer: Without concatenating the target answer at the end of the passage. We use the target answer by replacing it in the passage.

-Answer separation: Without replacing the target answer in the passage. We use the target answer by concatenating it at the end of the passage.

3.3 Evaluation

Following other QG studies, we use three evaluation metrics: BLEU, METEOR, and $ROUGE_L$ similar to other QG studies (Du et al., 2017; Kim et al., 2018). In the SQuAD dataset, a passage sometimes has multiple gold questions. Other studies used all these questions as references. In this research, we use one gold question that is a pair of the source passage and the target answer, as a reference. The score apparently decreases using this evaluation method. This method is more accurate to evaluate generated questions using target answers as inputs.

In addition, the evaluation method has one limitation. As we use interrogative phrases that form part of the questions, the score increases considerably because the model knows parts of the questions (interrogative phrases) to be generated. For this reason, we also evaluate the generated questions excluding the interrogative phrases. This treatment helps us verify whether the whole generated questions will lead to the target answers.

3.4 Result of the experiment

Table 1 shows the main result. Seq2Seq + Answer + Interrogative outperforms other methods by a large margin. Even when we evaluate questions excluding interrogative phrases, Seq2Seq + Answer + Interrogative still outperforms Seq2Seq + Answer. This result demonstrates that interrogative phrases help to improve the performance of QG. Furthermore, it is noteworthy that our simple Seq2Seq model outperforms the state-of-the-art model ASs2s. The results of the ablation test show that our components help to increase the accuracy. Notably, the copy mechanism increases the accuracy to a considerable extent, showing that it is very useful for the QG task. With regard to the answers, replacing target answers contributes

Model	Answer	Interrogative	Normal Evaluation			Excluding Interrogative Phrases		
			BLEU	METEOR	$ROUGE_L$	BLEU	METEOR	$ROUGE_L$
ASs2s	✓		14.6	19.1	43.0	13.7	17.7	40.8
	✓	✓	21.6	23.0	51.2	14.4	17.8	41.8
Seq2Seq		✓	12.1	16.4	39.0	11.8	15.5	37.9
		✓	22.8	23.1	51.6	14.4	17.4	41.6
	✓		18.7	21.8	47.5	17.9	20.4	45.2
	✓	✓	**26.4**	**26.2**	**55.9**	**18.6**	**20.9**	**46.9**
Ablation Tests								
- Copy	✓	✓	22.0	23.3	52.1	14.2	17.9	42.8
- Coverage	✓	✓	26.4	26.1	56.0	18.5	20.8	46.9
- Answer	✓	✓	26.1	25.9	55.5	18.3	20.5	46.3
- Answer Sep	✓	✓	23.5	23.5	52.2	15.2	17.9	42.4

Table 1: Result of the QG. We use three evaluation metrics: BLEU, METEOR, and $ROUGE_L$. We also evaluate questions excluding interrogative phrases. In addition, we do four ablation tests.

	Seq2Seq+Answer	Seq2Seq+Answer +Interrogative
Interrogative Phrase		
Same as Gold	51%	100%
Appropriate	43%	0%
Inappropriate	6%	0%
Answer		
Correct	61%	74%
Incorrect	39%	26%

Table 2: Human evaluations of QG. We check the questions according to two criteria: (1) Do the interrogative phrases match the target answers? (2) Can the questions provide the target answers?

to increasing the accuracy compared to concatenating the target answers at the end of the passage.

Human evaluation We conduct human evaluation to check whether the generated questions are appropriate. We randomly extract 100 generated questions from the test set. We check the questions according to two criteria: (1) Do the interrogative phrases match the target answers? We classify the generated questions as follows: the same interrogative phrase as one of the gold questions, different from one of the gold questions but an appropriate interrogative phrase that matches the target answer, and inappropriate interrogative phrase that do not match the target answer. (2) Can the questions provide the target answers?

Table 2 shows the result. Seq2Seq + Answer + Interrogative always generates questions that include the same interrogative phrase as one of the gold questions. Seq2Seq2 + Answer often uses simpler interrogative phrases than Seq2Seq + Answer + Interrogative, and thus, the questions become abstractive. For example, while the gold interrogative phrase is "what year", Seq2Seq + Answer generates "when". With regard to the an-

Passage: A regulation of the Rhine was called for, with an upper canal near Diepoldsau and a lower canal at Fuach, in order to counteract the constant flooding and strong sedimentation in the western Rhine Delta.
Target Answer: constant flooding
Gold Question: Why was the Rhine regulated?
ASs2s: What is a lower canal by a lower canal at the western Rhine Delta?
Seq2Seq+Answer: What was the regulation of the Rhine called for ?
Seq2Seq+Answer+Interrogative: Why was a regulation of the Rhine called ?
Passage: [note 6] In 1978 a disco version of the theme was released in the UK, Denmark and Australia by the group Mankind, which reached number 24 in the UK charts.
Target Answer: number 24
Gold Question: How high on the charts did the Mankind version of the theme go?
ASs2s: What was the group of the theme ballad released by the group?
Seq2Seq+Answer: How many number of the UK charts did the group Mankind reach in the UK charts?
Seq2Seq+Answer+Interrogative: How high on the charts did the group Mankind reach?

Table 3: Examples of the generated questions. This shows questions generated by three models: ASs2S, Seq2Seq + Answer, and Seq2Seq + Answer + Interrogative.

swers, Seq2Seq + Answer + Interrogative outperforms Seq2Seq + Answer. This implies that using interrogative phrases as inputs makes the questions more informative and answerable.

Case study Table 3 shows two examples generated by our model. In the first example, ASs2s and Seq2Seq + Answer use an inappropriate interrogative word "what", and passages become unnatural. This is probably because the target answer is a short noun phrase, so the system decided to use it without considering the context. However, Seq2Seq + Answer + Interrogative uses the cor-

Passage: In July 1977, General Zia-ul-Haq overthrew Prime Minister Zulfiqar Ali Bhutto's regime in Pakistan .
Interrogative Phrase: What Generated Question: What was the name of the Prime Minister who overthrew Pakistan in 1977?
Interrogative Phrase: Who Generated Question: Who overthrew Prime Minister in 1977?
Interrogative Phrase: When Generated Question: When was Zulfiqar Ali Bhutto elected?
Interrogative Phrase: Where Generated Question: Where was Zulfiqar Ali Bhutto from?
Interrogative Phrase: How Generated Question: How did Zulfiqar Ali Bhutto respond to the Prime Minister?
Interrogative Phrase: Why Generated Question: Why was Zulfiqar Ali Bhutto elected?
Interrogative Phrase: In what year Generated Question: In what year was Zulfiqar Ali Bhutto elected?
Interrogative Phrase: How many Generated Question: How many Prime Minister did Zulfiqar Ali Bhutto have in pakistan?

Table 4: Example of the question generated by the Seq2Seq + Interrogative model. This model does not use an answer phrase. Thus, it can generate various questions only from passages and interrogative phrases.

rect interrogative phrase and the generated question can thus provide the target answer.

In the second example, a similar phenomenon appears. ASs2s use "what" and Seq2Seq + Answer use "how many number of the UK charts" as interrogative phrases for the target answer "number 24". They are inappropriate for context, and the passage become unnatural.

Table 4 shows an example generated by Seq2Seq + Interrogative model. This example comprises a passage and eight questions generated from eight frequently interrogative phrases. This model does not use answer phrases. Thus, it can generate various questions only from passages and interrogative phrases. They can also generate questions where the answer phrase is not in the passage although all questions in the train data include answer phrases in the passage.

3.5 Question answering using generated questions

We also examine the quality of the generated questions in the question answering experiments. We verify whether the generated questions can provide the target answers. We apply BERT (Devlin et al., 2019) for the question answering model on

Method	Answer	Interrogative	EM	F1
ASs2s	✓		68.9	78.7
	✓	✓	71.7	80.1
Seq2Seq		✓	34.1	43.4
		✓	58.7	69.0
	✓		72.6	82.2
	✓	✓	**75.3**	**84.2**
Human			81.2	88.9

Table 5: Result of question answering using generated questions. We use two evaluation metrics: Exact Match and F1 score.

the SQuAD dataset. We train and test the question answering model using the generated questions. We also train and test original passages created by a human in the SQuAD dataset as the upper bound. We use two evaluation metrics: Exact Match and F1 score.

Table 5 shows the result. This demonstrates that using interrogative phrases helps the question answering system to reach the target answers. The score of Seq2Seq + Answer + Interrogative is a little lower than the one associated with the human-generated questions (by 4.7 F1 points). This shows that for the question answering model, the system-generated questions are close to those created by a human.

4 Conclusion and Future Work

In this study, we explore the use of interrogative phrases as additional sources to control QG. The results of the experiment show that using interrogative phrases contributes to improving the performance of QG. The question answering experiment demonstrates that using interrogative phrases helps the question answering system to provide target answers.

Future studies on QG will focus on the following aspects. (1) We directly input the interrogative phrases in this study. However, we also consider automatic selection of appropriate interrogative phrases such that the answerers can reach the target answer easily. (2) The model sometimes generates questions that contradict the source passages. To reduce that risk, we will use textual entailment to verify whether the generated questions are consistent with the source passages.

Acknowledgments

We thank the laboratory members for their useful comments. This work was supported by JSPS KAKENHI Grant Number 19H01118.

References

Dzmitry Bahdanau, Kyunghyun Cho, and Yoshua Bengio. 2015. Neural machine translation by jointly learning to align and translate. In *Proceedings of the International Conference on Learning Representations*.

Yllias Chali and Tina Baghaee. 2018. Automatic opinion question generation. In *Proceedings of the 11th International Conference on Natural Language Generation*, pages 152–158.

Jacob Devlin, Ming-Wei Chang, Kenton Lee, and Kristina Toutanova. 2019. BERT: Pre-training of deep bidirectional transformers for language understanding. In *Proceedings of the 2019 Conference of the North American Chapter of the Association for Computational Linguistics*, pages 4171–4186.

Xinya Du, Junru Shao, and Claire Cardie. 2017. Learning to Ask: Neural Question Generation for Reading Comprehension. In *Proceedings of the 55th Annual Meeting of the Association for Computational Linguistics*, pages 1342–1352.

Nan Duan, Duyu Tang, Peng Chen, and Ming Zhou. 2017. Question generation for question answering. In *Proceedings of the 2017 Conference on Empirical Methods in Natural Language Processing*, pages 866–874.

Michael Heilman and Noah A. Smith. 2010. Good Question! Statistical Ranking for Question Generation. In *Human Language Technologies: The 2010 Annual Conference of the North American Chapter of the Association for Computational Linguistics*, pages 609–617.

Yanghoon Kim, Hwanhee Lee, Joongbo Shin, and Kyomin Jung. 2018. Improving Neural Question Generation using Answer Separation. In *Proceedings of the Thirty-Third AAAI Conference on Artificial Intelligence*.

Guillaume Klein, Yoon Kim, Yuntian Deng, Jean Senellart, and Alexander Rush. 2017. OpenNMT: Open-source toolkit for neural machine translation. In *Proceedings of the 55th annual meeting of the Association for Computational Linguistics*, pages 67–72.

Christopher Manning, Mihai Surdeanu, John Bauer, Jenny Finkel, Steven Bethard, and David McClosky. 2014. The Stanford CoreNLP natural language processing toolkit. In *Proceedings of the the 52nd Annual Meeting of the Association for Computational Linguistics*, pages 55–60.

Nasrin Mostafazadeh, Ishan Misra, Jacob Devlin, Margaret Mitchell, Xiaodong He, and Lucy Vanderwende. 2016. Generating natural questions about an image. In *Proceedings of the 54th Annual Meeting of the Association for Computational Linguistics*, pages 1802–1813.

Jeffrey Pennington, Richard Socher, and Christopher Manning. 2014. Glove: Global vectors for word representation. In *Proceedings of the 2014 Conference on Empirical Methods in Natural Language Processing*, pages 1532–1543.

Pranav Rajpurkar, Jian Zhang, Konstantin Lopyrev, and Percy Liang. 2016. SQuAD: 100,000+ Questions for Machine Comprehension of Text. In *Proceedings of the 2016 Conference on Empirical Methods in Natural Language Processing*, pages 2383–2392.

Abigail See, Peter J. Liu, and Christopher D. Manning. 2017. Get to the point: Summarization with pointer-generator networks. In *Proceedings of the 55th Annual Meeting of the Association for Computational Linguistics*, pages 1073–1083.

Linfeng Song, Zhiguo Wang, Wael Hamza, Yue Zhang, and Daniel Gildea. 2018. Leveraging Context Information for Natural Question Generation. In *Proceedings of the 2018 Conference of the North American Chapter of the Association for Computational Linguistics*, pages 569–574.

Xingwu Sun, Jing Liu, Yajuan Lyu, Wei He, Yanjun Ma, and Shi Wang. 2018. Answer-focused and position-aware neural question generation. In *Proceedings of the 2018 Conference on Empirical Methods in Natural Language Processing*, pages 3930–3939.

Duyu Tang, Nan Duan, Zhao Yan, Zhirui Zhang, Yibo Sun, Shujie Liu, Yuanhua Lv, and Ming Zhou. 2018. Learning to collaborate for question answering and asking. In *Proceedings of the 2018 Conference of the North American Chapter of the Association for Computational Linguistics*, pages 1564–1574.

Zhaopeng Tu, Zhengdong Lu, Yang Liu, Xiaohua Liu, and Hang Li. 2016. Modeling coverage for neural machine translation. In *Proceedings of the 54th Annual Meeting of the Association for Computational Linguistics*, pages 76–85.

Qingyu Zhou, Nan Yang, Furu Wei, Chuanqi Tan, Hangbo Bao, and Ming Zhou. 2017. Neural Question Generation from Text: A Preliminary Study. In *National CCF Conference on Natural Language Processing and Chinese Computing*, pages 662–671. Springer.

Generating Text from Anonymised Structures

Émilie Colin
Université de Lorraine / LORIA
Nancy, France
emilie.colin@loria.fr

Claire Gardent
CNRS / LORIA
Nancy, France
claire.gardent@loria.fr

Abstract

Surface realisation maps a meaning representation (MR) to a text, usually a single sentence. In this paper, we introduce a new parallel dataset of deep meaning representations and French sentences and we present a novel method for MR-to-text generation which seeks to generalise by abstracting away from lexical content. Most current work on natural language generation focuses on generating text that matches a reference using BLEU as evaluation criteria. In this paper, we additionally consider the model's ability to reintroduce the function words that are absent from the deep input meaning representations. We show that our approach increases both BLEU score and the scores used to assess function words generation.

1 Introduction

Surface realisation (SR), the ability to generate text from meaning representations (MR), is a key component of data-to-text generation. In this paper, we focus on surface realisation for French. We make two contributions.

First, we present a method for automatically creating a parallel dataset of sentences and their meaning representations[1].

Second, we propose a novel surface realisation approach which differs from previous work in that it relies on an extensive anonymization of the data. The underlying intuition behind our approach is that abstracting away from lexical content reduces data sparsity which in turn, should facilitate the learning of linguistic structure. We show that extensive anonymization indeed improves performance. To further assess the degree to which our model learns linguistic structure, we provide an analysis of the extent to which it handles the rein-

troduction in the generated sentence of the function words that are absent from the input.

2 Related Work

SR Corpora Various datasets have been introduced to support the learning of surface realisers.

The 2017 AMR SemEval generation shared task (May and Priyadarshi, 2017) provides a parallel corpus where the input semantic representations are AMRs (Abstract Meaning Representation, (Banarescu et al., 2013)) and the task is to generate a sentence verbalising that AMR.

Mille et al. (2018) derived multilingual MR-to-Text datasets from the UD (Universal Dependencies) treebanks[2] creating two types of input, shallow and deep. In the shallow input, the nodes of the UD dependency tree are scrambled to remove word order information and words are replaced by their lemmas. The generation task consists in ordering and inflecting the lemmas decorating the input tree. The deep input is closer to an applicative context. It abstracts away from the surface form by removing additional information from the UD tree and replacing syntactic edge labels with ProbBank/NomBank labels.

Finally, (Novikova et al., 2017) introduce a dataset where the input MRs are dialog moves.

All these datasets were expensive to build as they require extensive human intervention. The AMR datasets were built by manually annotating sentences with AMRs, the SR datasets were derived from hand-annotated treebanks and (Novikova et al., 2017)'s dialog moves were associated with text using crowdsourcing. Moreover, except for the SR task, these datasets all focus on English. In short, we depart from previous work in that we introduce a new dataset for French which is automatically derived from text using parsers.

---

[1]The corpus is available by simple request to the authors.

[2]http://universaldependencies.org

Proceedings of The 12th International Conference on Natural Language Generation, pages 112–117,
Tokyo, Japan, 28 Oct - 1 Nov, 2019. ©2019 Association for Computational Linguistics

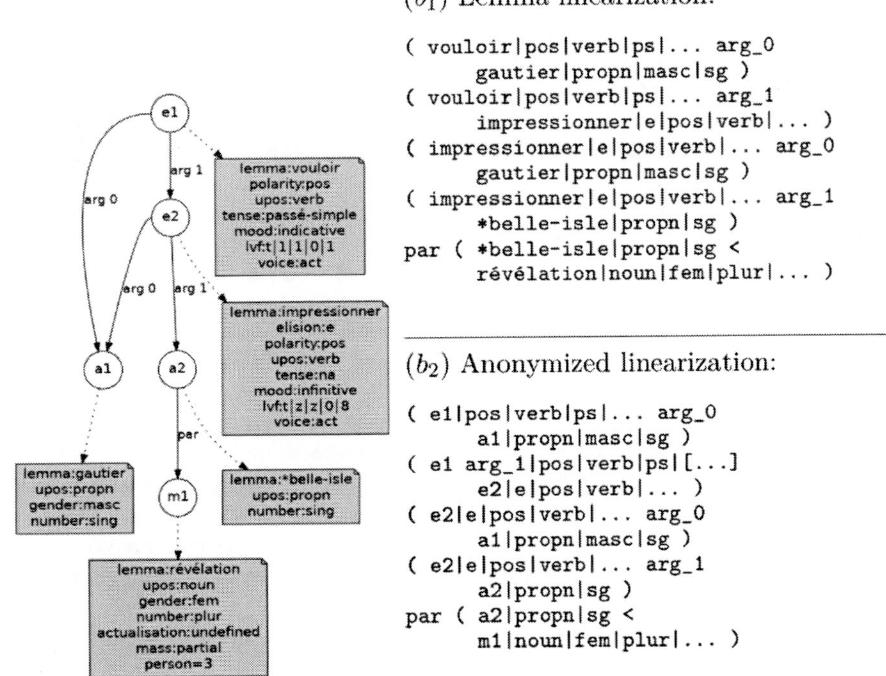

Figure 1: Example Input Meaning Representation and Linearizations for the sentence *Gautier voulut impressionner Belles-Isle par des révélations (Gautier wanted to impress Belles-Isle by some revelations)*

SR Models. Using the parallel MR-to-text corpora just described, various SR models have been proposed. We focus here on SR from deep meaning representations (AMRs and SR'18 deep track MRs) as this is closest to our proposal.

Early work on MR-to-text generation linearise the input graph and use various statistical methods to generate text (Flanigan et al., 2016; Song et al., 2017; Pourdamghani et al., 2016; Bohnet et al., 2010). Similarly, early neural approaches linearise the input graph and use a sequence-to-sequence (S2S) model. Konstas et al. (2017) achieve strong results on the AMR-to-text task by using data expansion and anonymising data entities while Cao and Clark (2019) additionally leverages syntactic information to improve performance. On the deep SR data, (Elder and Hokamp, 2018) uses data expansion and a factored S2S model.

Graph-to-sequence models have also been proposed using various graph encoders and testing on different datasets Marcheggiani and Perez-Beltrachini (2018); Song et al. (2018); Beck et al. (2018); Koncel-Kedziorski et al. (2019); Veličković et al. (2018).

Our approach is closest to the S2S model used by Elder and Hokamp (2018) in that it uses a factored S2S model to create rich node embeddings capturing the structure of the graph. We differ from that work in that we use full anonymization on input and output data.

3 Data

Instead of relying on hand annotations, we automatically create a silver corpus using syntactic parsing and post-processing. Creating the dataset consists of two main steps. First, we compare the output of three syntactic dependency parsers and keep only those sentences for which there is a strong consensus. Second, we derive a meaning representation from the syntactic parse.

The three parsers used are Grew[3] (Guillaume et al., 2012), Talismane[4] and the Stanford Dependency Parser[5]. As the parsers have different tokenization strategies (for instance, *"entre autres"* is treated by Talismane and Stanford as two tokens but analysed as one token *entre_autres* by Grew), the largest tokens (e.g., *entre_autres*) are used as

basis for the alignment. For POS tags and dependency relations, the alignment is neither one-to-one nor one-to-many. We only keep those mappings whose frequency is above 95% for POS tags and 94% for dependency relations. Grew is used as a reference and a POS tag/Dependency relation from Talismane and the Stanford parser is judged compatible if it matches one of these mappings. We only keep those sentences for which a mapping could be found for all three parsers (for both POS tags and dependency relations) and which contain less than 70 tokens[6].

We then derive deep meaning representations from the parse tree by mapping grammatical functions (subject, etc) to semantic ones (arg0, arg1, etc.), removing function words (determiners, auxiliaries, relative pronouns, complementizers, non subcategorised prepositions), lemmatizing word forms and keeping only those features which cannot be learned e.g., the number and gender of a noun and the tense of a verb. Since determiners and auxiliary are removed from the meaning representations their number must be learned by the model or more generally, agreement constraints (between verb and subject and between noun, determiners and adjectives) must be learned. The mapping from syntactic to semantic relations makes use of a verb lexicon[7] which permits identifying which phrases are arguments (rather than modifiers). The arg0 relation is assigned to the subject of verbs in the active voice, arg1 the object and arg2 is used for prepositional arguments.

Figure 1 shows an example meaning representation.

We download 2,835 french books (3,806,889 sentences) from the Gutenberg website[8]. We filter out sentences that do not contain at least one noun and a verb or which contain incorrect bracketing or foreign (non-French) material. This yields a total of 1,700,000 sentences. We then apply the alignment procedure described above and filter out sentences with more than 70 tokens reducing the dataset further to a total of roughly 500K sentences[9]

---

[3]Version 0.48.0 `http://grew.fr/`

[4]Version 5.1.2, `http://redac.univ-tlse2.fr/applications/talismane.html`

[5]Version 2018-02-27, `https://nlp.stanford.edu/software/lex-parser.shtml`

[6]An example alignment is shown in the supplementary material.

[7]We use the LVF ("Les verbes français", the French verbs) by Jean Dubois and Françoise Dubois-Charlier, version LVF+1, `http://rali.iro.umontreal.ca/rali/?q=fr/lvf`.

[8]`http://www.gutenberg.org/`

[9]More descriptive statistics for the created corpus are given in the supplementary material.

4 Model

Model	BLEU-4	C-R	FW-F1
BL	64.35	0.59	0.906
Dual (Test:Non Anon.)	66.55	0.62	0.910
Anonymised	66.87	0.87	0.933
Dual (Test:Anon.)	68.31	0.87	0.937

Table 1: Results

Our approach extends a standard S2S model with full anonymization and factored token embeddings which capture the linguistic and structural information associated with each node in the input graph.

Full Anonymization. Anonymisation (also often dubbed, delexicalisation) has frequently been used in neural NLG to help handle unknown or rare words (Wen et al., 2015; Dušek and Jurcicek, 2015; Chen et al., 2018). Rare items are replaced by placeholders both in the input data or MR and in the output sentence or text. Models are trained on the anonymized data. Finally, a post-processing step ensures that the generated text is relexicalised using the placeholders original value. In these approaches, anonymization is restricted to rare items (named entities) and replaces them with a simple identifier. In contrast, we apply anonymization to all lemmatized content words, adverbs excepted. As we derive the input MR from the sentence parse tree (cf. Section 3), we keep track of which word form in the target sentence matches which lemma in the input MR and use this at post-processing time to relexicalise the anonymous output structure.

Factored Sequence-to-Sequence model. We use OpenNMT factored S2S model with attention. Each input token is represented by the concatenation of 18 embeddings whereby each embedding represents a distinct feature type (part-of-speech, gender, number, tense etc) (Alexandrescu and Kirchhoff, 2006). We focus on word ordering and use a table lookup to match output lemmas to word forms.

5 Experimental Settings

Evaluation Metrics. Following common practice in NLG, we evaluate our model using BLEU-4[10]. To further assess the ability of the model to learn linguistic structure, we also evaluate recall on content words (C-R) and F1 on function words (FW-F1). We define content words to be the lemmas present in the input meaning representation. Function words are the words in the (lemmatized) output sentence that are not content words.

Models. The baseline is a factored S2S model with attention trained on the original data (no anonymization). We compare this baseline with the same model trained on anonymised data (Anonymised) and with two models trained on a corpus consisting of both the original and the anonymised data. The intuition behind used both anonymised and non anonymised data for training is to see whether the combination of both sources of information can help. The first model (Dual Lexicalised) is tested on lexicalised data (does the adjunction of anonymised training data help improve generation from non anonymised meaning representations?) while the second (Dual Anonymised) is tested on anonymised data (does the adjunction of non anonymised training data help improve generation from anonymised meaning representations?). We did never anonymised adverbs, having them in outputs, waiting them in outputs.

Results. The results are shown in Table 1. The BLEU scores show that training on anonymised structures yields better results (+2.52 BLEU). Using both lexicalised and anonymised data for training further improves results which is not surprising given that the size of the training data has doubled. Interestingly, the delta is slightly better when testing on anonymised data (+3.96 vs. +2.2) which suggests that adding lexical information to the training data is more beneficial to anonymised generation than vice versa.

A similar trend can be observed concerning the handling of function words although the increase is much less.

Qualitative Analysis. On the whole test corpus (49,026 sentences), an automatic analysis of the results shows that (i) 34.76% of the generated sentences are the same as the reference sentence, (ii) relexicalisation fails for some input token for 34.07 % of cases and (iii) in total, 94.8% of the input content words are present in the output.

We also manually examined 50 randomly selected sentences[11] generated by our model. 34%

---

[10]We use sacrebleu (Post, 2018)

[11]The selected sentences are given in the supplementary

of these are exactly the same as the reference. 58% are both grammatically and semantically correct. 78% are grammatically correct. All verbs were found to be in the correct form (agreement and tense). We detected only one agreement error between a noun and its determiner. A detailed analysis of the errors found can be found in the supplementary material.

6 Conclusion

We introduced a new MR-to-text dataset for French and showed that full anonymization helps improve surface realisation. The automatic construction of parallel data using parsing makes available a detailed linguistic description of the target sentences to be generated. We are currently exploring how to extend the data creation method described in section 3 to better evaluate the ability of neural models to generate under syntactic constraints.

Acknowledgments

The research presented in this paper was partially supported by the E-FRAN Program (Espaces de Formation, de Recherche et d'Animation Numérique) within the framework of the METAL Project (Modèles et Traces au Service de l'Apprentissage des Langues).

References

Andrei Alexandrescu and Katrin Kirchhoff. 2006. Factored neural language models. In *Proceedings of the Human Language Technology Conference of the NAACL, Companion Volume: Short Papers*, pages 1–4. Association for Computational Linguistics.

Laura Banarescu, Claire Bonial, Shu Cai, Madalina Georgescu, Kira Griffitt, Ulf Hermjakob, Kevin Knight, Philipp Koehn, Martha Palmer, and Nathan Schneider. 2013. Abstract meaning representation for sembanking. In *Proceedings of the 7th Linguistic Annotation Workshop and Interoperability with Discourse*, pages 178–186. Association for Computational Linguistics.

Daniel Beck, Gholamreza Haffari, and Trevor Cohn. 2018. Graph-to-sequence learning using gated graph neural networks. In *Proceedings of the 56th Annual Meeting of the Association for Computational Linguistics (Volume 1: Long Papers)*, pages 273–283, Melbourne, Australia. Association for Computational Linguistics.

Bernd Bohnet, Leo Wanner, Simon Mille, and Alicia Burga. 2010. Broad coverage multilingual deep sentence generation with a stochastic multi-level realizer. In *Proceedings of the 23rd International Conference on Computational Linguistics*, pages 98–106. Association for Computational Linguistics.

Kris Cao and Stephen Clark. 2019. Factorising amr generation through syntax. In *Proceedings of the 2019 Conference of the North American Chapter of the Association for Computational Linguistics: Human Language Technologies (NAACL-HLT)*.

Mingje Chen, Gerasimos Lampouras, and Andreas Vlachos. 2018. Sheffield at e2e: structured prediction approaches to end-to-end language generation. Technical report, E2E Challenge System Descriptions.

Ondřej Dušek and Filip Jurcicek. 2015. Training a natural language generator from unaligned data. In *Proceedings of the 53rd Annual Meeting of the Association for Computational Linguistics and the 7th International Joint Conference on Natural Language Processing (Volume 1: Long Papers)*, pages 451–461. Association for Computational Linguistics.

Henry Elder and Chris Hokamp. 2018. Generating high-quality surface realizations using data augmentation and factored sequence models. In *Proceedings of the First Workshop on Multilingual Surface Realisation*, pages 49–53. Association for Computational Linguistics.

Jeffrey Flanigan, Chris Dyer, Noah A Smith, and Jaime Carbonell. 2016. Generation from abstract meaning representation using tree transducers. In *Proceedings of the 2016 Conference of the North American Chapter of the Association for Computational Linguistics: Human Language Technologies*, pages 731–739.

Bruno Guillaume, Guillaume Bonfante, Paul Masson, Mathieu Morey, and Guy Perrier. 2012. Grew: un outil de réécriture de graphes for le tal (grew: a graph rewriting tool for nlp). In *Proceedings of the Joint Conference JEP-TALN-RECITAL 2012, volume 5: Software Demonstrations*, pages 1–2.

Rik Koncel-Kedziorski, Dhanush Bekal, Yi Luan, Mirella Lapata, and Hannaneh Hajishirzi. 2019. Text generation from knowledge graphs with graph transformers. In *Proceedings of the 2019 Conference of the North American Chapter of the Association for Computational Linguistics: Human Language Technologies (NAACL-HLT)*.

Ioannis Konstas, Srinivasan Iyer, Mark Yatskar, Yejin Choi, and Luke Zettlemoyer. 2017. Neural amr: Sequence-to-sequence models for parsing and generation. In *Proceedings of the 55th Annual Meeting of the Association for Computational Linguistics (Volume 1: Long Papers)*, pages 146–157. Association for Computational Linguistics.

---

material together with some statistics about their length.

Diego Marcheggiani and Laura Perez-Beltrachini. 2018. Deep graph convolutional encoders for structured data to text generation. In *Proceedings of the 11th International Conference on Natural Language Generation*, pages 1–9, Tilburg University, The Netherlands. Association for Computational Linguistics.

Jonathan May and Jay Priyadarshi. 2017. Semeval-2017 task 9: Abstract meaning representation parsing and generation. In *Proceedings of the 11th International Workshop on Semantic Evaluation (SemEval-2017)*, pages 536–545. Association for Computational Linguistics.

Simon Mille, Anja Belz, Bernd Bohnet, Yvette Graham, Emily Pitler, and Leo Wanner. 2018. The first multilingual surface realisation shared task (sr'18): Overview and evaluation results. In *Proceedings of the First Workshop on Multilingual Surface Realisation*, pages 1–12. Association for Computational Linguistics.

Jekaterina Novikova, Ondřej Dušek, and Verena Rieser. 2017. The e2e dataset: New challenges for end-to-end generation. In *Proceedings of the 18th Annual SIGdial Meeting on Discourse and Dialogue*, pages 201–206. Association for Computational Linguistics.

Matt Post. 2018. A call for clarity in reporting BLEU scores. In *Proceedings of the Third Conference on Machine Translation: Research Papers*, pages 186–191, Belgium, Brussels. Association for Computational Linguistics.

Nima Pourdamghani, Kevin Knight, and Ulf Hermjakob. 2016. Generating english from abstract meaning representations. In *Proceedings of the 9th International Natural Language Generation conference*, pages 21–25.

Linfeng Song, Xiaochang Peng, Yue Zhang, Zhiguo Wang, and Daniel Gildea. 2017. Amr-to-text generation with synchronous node replacement grammar. *arXiv preprint arXiv:1702.00500*.

Linfeng Song, Yue Zhang, Zhiguo Wang, and Daniel Gildea. 2018. A graph-to-sequence model for AMR-to-text generation. In *Proceedings of the 56th Annual Meeting of the Association for Computational Linguistics (Volume 1: Long Papers)*, pages 1616–1626, Melbourne, Australia. Association for Computational Linguistics.

Petar Veličković, Guillem Cucurull, Arantxa Casanova, Adriana Romero, Pietro Liò, and Yoshua Bengio. 2018. Graph Attention Networks. *International Conference on Learning Representations*. Accepted as poster.

Tsung-Hsien Wen, Milica Gasic, Nikola Mrkšić, Pei-Hao Su, David Vandyke, and Steve Young. 2015. Semantically conditioned lstm-based natural language generation for spoken dialogue systems. In *Proceedings of the 2015 Conference on Empirical Methods in Natural Language Processing*, pages 1711–1721. Association for Computational Linguistics.

MinWikiSplit: A Sentence Splitting Corpus with Minimal Propositions

Christina Niklaus[13], André Freitas[2], and Siegfried Handschuh[13]

[1] University of St.Gallen

{christina.niklaus, siegfried.handschuh}@unisg.ch

[2] University of Manchester

andre.freitas@manchester.ac.uk

[3] University of Passau

{christina.niklaus, siegfried.handschuh}@uni-passau.de

Abstract

We compiled a new sentence splitting corpus that is composed of 203K pairs of aligned complex source and simplified target sentences. Contrary to previously proposed text simplification corpora, which contain only a small number of split examples, we present a dataset where each input sentence is broken down into a set of minimal propositions, i.e. a sequence of sound, self-contained utterances with each of them presenting a minimal semantic unit that cannot be further decomposed into meaningful propositions. This corpus is useful for developing sentence splitting approaches that learn how to transform sentences with a complex linguistic structure into a fine-grained representation of short sentences that present a simple and more regular structure which is easier to process for downstream applications and thus facilitates and improves their performance.

1 Introduction

Sentences that present a complex linguistic structure can be *hard to comprehend by human readers*, as well as *difficult to analyze by semantic applications* (Saggion, 2017). Identifying such grammatical complexities in a sentence and transforming them into simpler structures, using a set of text-to-text rewriting operations, is the goal of syntactic text simplification (TS). One of the major types of operations that are used to perform this rewriting step is *sentence splitting*: it divides a sentence into several shorter components, with each of them presenting a simpler and more regular structure that is easier to process by both humans and machines (see Table 1).

Syntactic TS with a focus on the task of sentence splitting has been attracting growing interest in the natural language processing (NLP) community within the past few years. One line of work targets reader populations with reading difficulties, such as people suffering from dyslexia, aphasia or deafness (Siddharthan and Mandya, 2014; Saggion et al., 2015; Ferrés et al., 2016), while the second line of work aims at generating an intermediate representation that is easier to process for downstream semantic tasks whose predictive quality deteriorates with sentence length and complexity. Prior work has established that applying syntactic TS as a preprocessing step can improve the performance of a variety of applications, including Machine Translation (Štajner and Popovic, 2016, 2018), Open Information Extraction (Cetto et al., 2018), or Text Summarization (Siddharthan et al., 2004; Bouayad-Agha et al., 2009).

2 Limitations of Existing Sentence Splitting Corpora

All of the TS approaches mentioned above make use of a set of *hand-crafted transformation rules* to decompose complex sentences into a sequence of structurally simplified components, requiring a complex rule engineering process. To overcome this expensive manual effort, Narayan et al. (2017) presented a first attempt at modelling a data-driven sentence splitting approach where simplification rewrites are learned automatically from examples of aligned complex source and simplified target sentences. Since previously compiled TS corpora (PWKP (Zhu et al., 2010), EW-SEW (Coster and Kauchak, 2011), and Newsela (Xu et al., 2015)) contain only a small number of split examples, they are ill-suited for learning to decompose sentences into shorter, syntactically simplified components. Therefore, Narayan et al. (2017) gathered a new dataset, WEBSPLIT, which is the first TS corpus that explicitly addresses the task of sentence splitting, while abstracting away from deletion-based and lexical simplification opera-

Proceedings of The 12th International Conference on Natural Language Generation, pages 118–123,
Tokyo, Japan, 28 Oct - 1 Nov, 2019. ©2019 Association for Computational Linguistics

Complex source	The house was once part of a plantation and it was the home of Josiah Henson, a slave who escaped to Canada in 1830 and wrote the story of his life.
MINWIKISPLIT	**The house was once part of a plantation. It was the home of Josiah Henson. Josiah Henson was a slave. This slave escaped to Canada. This was in 1830. This slave wrote the story of his life.**
Complex source	Gary Goddard, founder of Gary Goddard Entertainment, a company that designs theme parks, attractions and upscale resorts, estimated that about half his work in the last few years has been in Asia and the Middle East.
MINWIKISPLIT	**About half his work in the last few years has been in Asia. This was what Goddard estimated. About half his work in the last few years has been in the Middle East. This was what Gary Goddard estimated. Gary Goddard was founder of Gary Goddard Entertainment. Gary Goddard Entertainment was a company. This company designs theme parks. This company designs attractions. This company designs upscale resorts.**
Complex source	The film is a partly fictionalized presentation of the tragedy that occurred in Kasaragod District of Kerala in India, as a result of endosulfan, a pesticide used on cashew plantations owned by the government.
MINWIKISPLIT	**The film is a partly fictionalized presentation of the tragedy. This tragedy occurred in Kasaragod District of Kerala in India. This was as a result of endosulfan. Endosulfan is a pesticide. This pesticide is used on cashew plantations. These cashew plantations are owned by the government.**

Table 1: Example instances from MINWIKISPLIT. A complex source sentence is broken down into a set of syntactically simplified sentences by decomposing clausal and phrasal elements and transforming them into self-contained propositions that present a simple structure in the form of a sequence of subject, predicate, and optionally an object, adverbial or complement (or simple combination thereof).

tions. It is composed of over one million tuples that map a single complex sentence to a sequence of structurally simplified sentences.

Aharoni and Goldberg (2018) criticized the data split proposed by Narayan et al. (2017). They observed that 99% of the simple sentences (which make up for more than 89% of the unique ones) contained in the validation and test sets also appear in the training set. Consequently, instead of learning to split and rephrase complex sentences, models that are trained on this dataset will be prone to learn to memorize entity-fact pairs. Hence, this split is not well suited for measuring a model's ability to generalize to unseen input sentences. To fix this issue, Aharoni and Goldberg (2018) present a new train-development-test data split where nearly no simple sentence that is contained in the development or test set occurs verbatim in the training set.

Lately, Botha et al. (2018) discovered that the sentences from the WEBSPLIT corpus contain fairly *unnatural linguistic expressions* over only a *small vocabulary* and a rather *uniform sentence structure*, which is predominantly composed of a sequence of coordinate clauses, occasionally augmented with a relative or adverbial clause (see Table 2). To overcome these limitations, they present WIKISPLIT, a dataset of one million sentences that were mined from Wikipedia edit histories. This corpus provides a rich and varied vocabulary over naturally expressed sentences showing a diverse linguistic structure, and their extracted splits. However, there is only a single split per source sentence in the training set (see Table 3). Accordingly, when a model is trained on this dataset, it is susceptible to exhibiting a *strong conservatism*, splitting each input sentence into exactly two output sentences only. Consequently, the resulting simplified sentences are still comparatively long and complex, mixing multiple, potentially semantically unrelated propositions that are difficult to analyze for downstream tasks.

3 MINWIKISPLIT Corpus

We improve on previously compiled sentence splitting corpora and present MINWIKISPLIT,[1] a

---

[1] The MINWIKISPLIT dataset is publicly released under `https://github.com/Lambda-3/MinWikiSplit`.

(1) A Loyal Character Dancer was published by Soho Press, in the United States, where some Native Americans live.
(2) Dead Man's Plack is in England and one of the ethnic groups found in England is the British Arabs.

Table 2: Characteristic example source sentences from the WEBSPLIT corpus.

Complex source	Starring Meryl Streep, Bruce Willis, Goldie Hawn and Isabella Rossellini, the film focuses on a childish pair of rivals who drink a magic potion that promises eternal youth.
Simplified output	Starring Meryl Streep, Bruce Willis, Goldie Hawn and Isabella Rossellini. The film focuses on a childish pair of rivals who drink a magic potion that promises eternal youth.
Complex source	The Assistant Attorney in Orlando investigated the modeling company, and decided that they were not doing anything wrong, and after Pearlman's bankruptcy, the company emerged unscathed and was sold to a Canadian company.
Simplified output	The Assistant Attorney in Orlando investigated the modeling company, and decided that they were not doing anything wrong. After Pearlman's bankruptcy, the modeling company emerged unscathed and was sold to a Canadian company.

Table 3: Pairs of aligned complex source and simplified target sentences from WIKISPLIT.

new dataset that can be used to train models for the task of decomposing sentences with a complex linguistic structure into a simplified representation that presents a more regular structure which is easier to process for downstream semantic applications and may support a faster generalization in machine learning tasks. This output may serve as an intermediate representation to facilitate and improve the performance of a wide range of artificial intelligence (AI) tasks.

Since shorter sentences are generally better processed by NLP systems (Narayan et al., 2017), we aimed at gathering a corpus where **each complex source sentence is broken down into a set of minimal propositions**, i.e. a sequence of sound, self-contained utterances, with each of them presenting a minimal semantic unit that cannot be further decomposed into meaningful propositions (Bast and Haussmann, 2013). Thus, we augment the Split-and-Rephrase task that was originally defined in Narayan et al. (2017) by the notion of *minimality*. In that way, we intend to overcome the conservatism exhibited by state-of-the-art structural TS approaches, which tend to retain the input rather than transforming it, and expect to improve the performance of a wide range of AI tasks.

4   Corpus Construction

MINWIKISPLIT is a large-scale sentence splitting corpus consisting of 203K complex source sentences and their simplified counterparts in the form of a sequence of minimal propositions. It was created by running DISSIM (Niklaus et al., 2019), a syntactic TS framework, over the one million complex input sentences from the WIKISPLIT corpus. DISSIM applies a small set of 35 hand-written transformation rules to decompose a wide range of linguistic constructs, including both clausal components (coordinations, adverbial clauses, relative clauses and reported speech) and phrasal elements (appositions, prepositional phrases, adverbial/adjectival phrases and coordinate noun phrases). In that way, a fine-grained output in the form of a sequence of minimal, self-contained propositions is produced. Some example instances are shown in Table 1.

To ensure that the resulting dataset is of high quality, we defined a set of dependency parse and part of speech based heuristics to filter out sequences that contain *grammatically incorrect* sentences, as well as sentences that *mix multiple semantic units* and, thus, are violating the specified minimality requirement. For instance, in order to verify that the simplified sentences are grammatically sound, we check whether the root node of the output sentence is a verb and whether one of its child nodes is assigned a dependency label that denotes a subject component. To test if the simplified sentences represent minimal propositions, we check whether the output does not contain a clausal modifier, such as a relative clause modifier,

	#T/S	#S/C	%SAME	LD_{SC}	SAMSA	$SAMSA_{abl}$
Complex	30.75	1.18	100	0.00	0.36	0.94
MINWIKISPLIT	12.12	3.84	0.00	17.73	0.40	0.48

Table 4: Results of the automatic evaluation procedure on a random sample of 1000 sentences.

adverbial clause modifier or a clausal modifier of a noun. Moreover, we ensure that no conjunction is included in the simplified output sentences. In the future, we will implement some further heuristics to *avoid uniformity* in the structure of the source sentences. In that way, we aim at guaranteeing a great structural variability in the input in order to enable systems that are trained on the MINWIKI-SPLIT corpus to learn splitting rewrites for a wide range of linguistic constructs.

After running the sentence simplification framework DISSIM over the sentences from the WIKI-SPLIT corpus and applying the set of heuristics that we defined to ensure grammaticality and minimality of the output, 203K pairs of input and corresponding output sequences were left.

5 Experiments

We performed both a manual analysis and an automatic evaluation to assess the quality of the produced corpus.

5.1 Automatic Metrics

To estimate the quality of the simplified target sentences of the MINWIKISPLIT corpus, we computed some basic statistics, including (i) the average sentence length of the simplified sentences in terms of the average number of tokens per output sentence (#T/S); (ii) the average number of simplified output sentences per complex input (#S/C); (iii) the percentage of sentences that are copied from the source without performing any simplification operation (%SAME), serving as an indicator for conservatism, i.e. the tendency to retain the input rather than transforming it; and (iv) the averaged word-based Levenshtein distance from the input (LD_{SC}), which provides further evidence for how reluctant the underlying system is in splitting the input into minimal semantic units.

Moreover, to measure the structural simplicity of the instances contained in MINWIKISPLIT, we calculated the SAMSA and $SAMSA_{abl}$ scores of both the complex source and the simplified output sentences (Sulem et al., 2018b). They are the first metrics that explicitly target syntactic aspects

of TS. The SAMSA metric is based on the idea that an optimal split of the input is one where each predicate-argument structure is assigned its own sentence in the simplified output and measures to what extent this assertion holds for the input-output pair under consideration. Accordingly, the SAMSA score is maximized when each split sentence represents exactly one semantic unit in the input. $SAMSA_{abl}$ does not penalize cases where the number of sentences in the simplified output is lower than the number of events contained in the input, indicating separate semantic units that should be split into individual target sentences for obtaining minimal propositions.[2]

These computations were carried out on a random sample of 1000 sentences from MINWIKI-SPLIT. The results are provided in Table 4. The scores demonstrate that on average our proposed sentence splitting corpus contains four simplified target sentences per complex source sentence, with every target proposition consisting of 12 tokens. Moreover, no input is simply copied to the output, but split into smaller components. Both the high averaged Levenshtein distance of almost 18 and the SAMSA score (0.40) confirm previous findings. The latter is highly correlated with structural simplicity and grammaticality, indicating that the output sentences contained in our corpus are grammatically sound and present a simpler syntax than the input. With 0.48, we reach a decent score for the simplified target sentences with regard to $SAMSA_{abl}$, too, which has a high correlation with meaning preservation.

5.2 Manual Analysis

In a second step, we randomly selected a subset of 300 sentences from MINWIKISPLIT, on which we conducted a manual analysis in order to get some deeper insights into the quality of the simplified sentences. Each input-output pair was rated by

---

[2]Prior work on syntactic TS commonly also reports average BLEU (Papineni et al., 2002) scores. However, Sulem et al. (2018a) recently demonstrated that this score is inappropriate for the evaluation of TS approaches when sentence splitting is involved. Therefore, we refrain from calculating BLEU scores.

2 non-native, but fluent English speakers according to three parameters: grammaticality, meaning preservation and structural simplicity (see Table 5).

G	Is the output fluent and grammatical?
M	Does the output preserve the meaning of the input?
S	Is the output simpler than the input, ignoring the complexity of the words?

Table 5: Questions for the human evaluation.

The inter-annotator agreement was computed using Cohens quadratic weighted κ (Cohen, 1968). The obtained rates were 0.24, 0.25 and 0.75 for grammaticality, meaning preservation and structural simplicity, respectively. System scores were calculated by averaging over the annotators' scores and the 300 sentences.

G	M	S
4.36	**4.10**	**3.43**

Table 6: Averaged human evaluation ratings on a random sample of 300 sentences from MINWIKISPLIT. Grammaticality (G), meaning preservation (M) and structural simplicity (S) are measured using a 1 (very bad) to 5 (very good) scale.

The results of the human evaluation are displayed in Table 6. These scores show that we succeed in producing output sequences that reach a high level of grammatical soundness and almost always perfectly preserve the original meaning of the input. The third dimension under consideration, structural simplicity, which captures the degree of minimality in the simplified sentences, scores high values, too. However, our manual analysis revealed some room for improvement. Consequently, in the future, we plan to implement stricter heuristics for sorting out output sequences that still mix multiple semantically unrelated propositions.

6 Conclusion

We compiled MINWIKISPLIT, a sentence splitting corpus consisting of 203K complex source sentences and their split counterparts. This dataset can be used to train natural language generation applications that perform a syntactic TS, simplifying sentences with a complex linguistic structure into a fine-grained representation of short sentences that present a simple and more regular structure. The thus generated output may serve as an intermediate representation that is easier to process for downstream semantic applications and may thus lead to a better performance of those tools. We intend to train a sentence simplification model on MINWIKISPLIT and compare it to previously proposed systems trained on the WEBSPLIT and WIKISPLIT corpora.

Moreover, we plan to improve the quality of the simplified target sentences in our corpus in accordance with the insights we gained through the analyses described above. First of all, we will perform a detailed error analysis of the output to determine the most common types of mistakes and get some starting points for further improving our heuristics for filtering out malformed simplifications. To enhance the syntactic correctness of the output, we will train a classifier on the recently proposed CoLA dataset (Warstadt et al., 2018) to eliminate instances with ungrammatical target sentences from our corpus. In addition, special attention will be given to improving the heuristics that ensure that each simplified target sentence represents a single semantic unit.

References

Roee Aharoni and Yoav Goldberg. 2018. Split and rephrase: Better evaluation and stronger baselines. In *Proceedings of the 56th Annual Meeting of the Association for Computational Linguistics (Volume 2: Short Papers)*, pages 719–724. Association for Computational Linguistics.

Hannah Bast and Elmar Haussmann. 2013. Open information extraction via contextual sentence decomposition. In *2013 IEEE Seventh International Conference on Semantic Computing*, pages 154–159. IEEE.

Jan A. Botha, Manaal Faruqui, John Alex, Jason Baldridge, and Dipanjan Das. 2018. Learning to split and rephrase from wikipedia edit history. In *Proceedings of the 2018 Conference on Empirical Methods in Natural Language Processing*, pages 732–737. Association for Computational Linguistics.

Nadjet Bouayad-Agha, Gerard Casamayor, Gabriela Ferraro, Simon Mille, Vanesa Vidal, and Leo Wanner. 2009. Improving the comprehension of legal documentation: the case of patent claims. In *Proceedings of the 12th International Conference on Artificial Intelligence and Law*, pages 78–87. ACM.

Matthias Cetto, Christina Niklaus, André Freitas, and Siegfried Handschuh. 2018. Graphene:

This Page Intentionally Left Blank.

QTUNA: A Corpus for Understanding How Speakers Use Quantification

Guanyi Chen♠, Kees van Deemter♠♡, Silvia Pagliaro♠, Louk Smalbil♠, Chenghua Lin♣
♠Department of Information and Computing Sciences, Utrecht University
♡Department of Computing Science, University of Aberdeen
♣Department of Computer Science, University of Sheffield
{g.chen, c.j.vandeemter}@uu.nl, s.pagliaro@students.uu.nl
l.smalbil@students.uu.nl, c.lin@sheffield.ac.uk

Abstract

A prominent strand of work in formal semantics investigates the ways in which human languages quantify over the elements of a set, as when we say *"All A are B"*, *"All except two A are B"*, *"Only a few of the A are B"* and so on. Our aim is to build Natural Language Generation algorithms that mimic humans' use of quantified expressions. To inform these algorithms, we conducted on a series of elicitation experiments in which human speakers were asked to perform a linguistic task that invites the use of quantified expressions. We discuss how these experiments were conducted and what corpora they gave rise to. We conduct an informal analysis of the corpora, and offer an initial assessment of the challenges that these corpora pose for Natural Language Generation. The dataset is available at: `https://github.com/a-quei/qtuna`.

1 Introduction

A long tradition of research in the formal semantics of natural language asks how speakers quantify, as when we say *"Some A are B"*, *"All except two A are B"*, *"Only a few of the A are B"* and so on. This area of work is known as the theory of "Generalised Quantifiers" (GQ) (Peters and Westerstahl, 2006, GQ), because it generalises the idea of quantification beyond the standard logical quantifiers of $\forall$ and $\exists$, even including quantifiers like *"most"* or *"many"*, which are not expressible in First-Order Logic (Mostowski, 1957; Barwise and Cooper, 1981; Van Benthem et al., 1986; Peters and Westerstahl, 2006). Since definite NPs can also be understood in these terms, GQ theory comprises, at least in principle, all Noun Phrases (NPs): the study of quantifiers in natural language is essentially the study of Noun Phrases.

There exists some work that can help to give this theoretical work an empirical basis. For example, there is psycholinguistic work on people's use of vague quantifiers (Moxey and Sanford, 1993), and work that investigates the links between quantifiers' logical types and human processing of quantified expressions (Szymanik and Zajenkowski, 2010; Szymanik et al., 2016, QEs). Yet there is a dearth of knowledge about human usage of QEs. For instance, what QEs, and what combinations of QEs, are uttered by a speaker in a given situation, to accomplish a given task? And, if a given NP is uttered, what information does it convey? Some questions are starting to be addressed, for example, Sorodoc et al. (2016) looked at speakers' choice between "all", "some", and "no" (see also Grefenstette (2013) and Herbelot and Vecchi (2015)). Yildirim et al. (2013) studied speakers' use (and hearers' interpretation) of the quantifiers "some" and "many", as in "Many of the candies are green". Barr et al. (2013) investigated referring expressions in which a quantifier is embedded (e.g., "the square with 11 black dots", "the square with lots of dark dashes"). Yet there has been few attempts to chart how the wider class of generalised quantifiers are used by human speakers. The present paper lies the basis for such a study, with the ultimate aim of modelling the human production of quantifiers computationally.

In the computational modelling of language production, one class of NPs has been studied widely, namely *referring* NPs (Krahmer and van Deemter, 2012), and van Deemter (2016). One line of work focuses on corpora of referring expressions (REs) that were elicited under experimentally controlled conditions (e.g., the TUNA corpus (Gatt et al., 2007; van Deemter et al., 2012a)). Such corpora were used as a gold standard for a sequence of evaluation campaigns in which generation algorithms that produce referring expressions were compared with the gold standard (Gatt and Belz, 2010). This systematic

Proceedings of The 12th International Conference on Natural Language Generation, pages 124–129,
Tokyo, Japan, 28 Oct - 1 Nov, 2019. ©2019 Association for Computational Linguistics

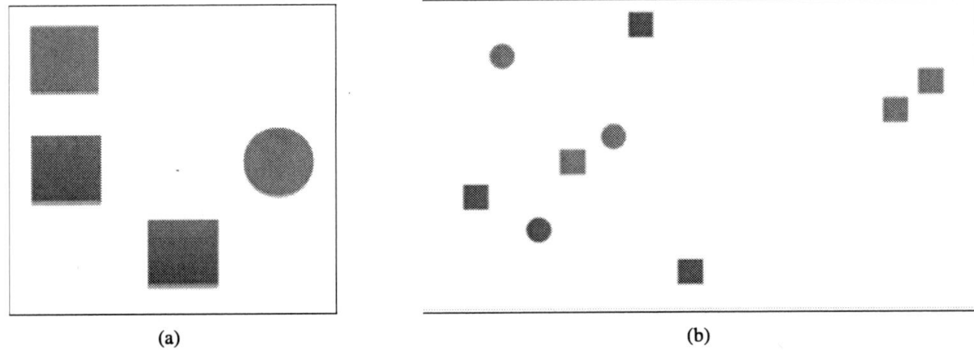

(a)   (b)

Figure 1: Examples from (a) the $n = 4$ experiment; (b) the $n = 9$ experiment.

comparison allowed researchers to know which algorithms worked best, and to develop new algorithms that match human language production. Inspired by this line of work on referring expressions, but aiming this time to gain insights into quantified NPs, we conducted a new series of elicitation experiments, called the QTUNA experiments (where Q stands for quantification). We report on these elicitation experiments, on the resulting corpus, and on an initial analysis of the corpus.

We set up the experiments in such a way that they would tell us how quantified NPs are employed to describe an abstract visual scene. We were curious what NPs would be used, what they meant, and how they were used (e.g., how correctly and how completely did speakers manage to describe the different scenes?). We were keen to look at tasks of different difficulty levels, curious how these levels affected the use of quantifiers.

2 The QTUNA Experiment

We wanted to find out how a wide range of quantified NPs are used as part of a wider communicative task. So, instead of showing our subjects a scene and asking them how they would describe the number of so-and-so's (e.g., circles) that are red (e.g., "Many circles are red"), we asked them to describe the scene as a whole, hoping that they would use quantifiers to do this. Moreover, we made the scenes complex enough that one simple Quantified Expression would never suffice. Let's explain in more detail how we proceeded.

Each participant presented with a series of abstract visual scenes. We asked them to try to produce a description that would allow a reader to *reconstruct* the situation, except for the location of

We'd like you to describe each situation in one or more grammatically correct English sentences. (...)

*1 Based on your description, a reader will try to "reconstruct" the situation. We use the word "reconstruct" loosely here, because the only thing that matters is the different types of objects that the sheet contains. Therefore, please do not say *where* in the grid a particular object is located (e.g., "top left", "in the middle", "on the diagonal").*

2 Each object is a circle or a square, and either red or blue. Your reader knows this.

3 Please do not "enumerate the different types of objects. For example, do not say "There is a red circle, two blue circles, and ...".

4 Every situation contain four objects. Your reader knows this in advance, and he/she will take this information into account when interpreting your description.

Figure 2: The sketch of how a instruction looks like, taking $n = 4$ as an example. A full version of the instruction can be found in the supplementary material.

the objects. Each scene contains a certain number of objects, which is either a circle or a square and either red or blue. In order to gain insight into the question of how domain size impacts the production of QEs, we conducted three experiments, with domain size (n) of 4, 9, and 20 respectively, each containing 10 different scenes. Figure 1(a) and Figure 1(b) show two examples from the $n = 4$ and $n = 9$ experiment respectively; Figure 2 depicts how the instruction looks like.

We conducted a number of pilot experiments for each of the three experiments. These taught us that if no further instructions were offered,

$n = 4$	*There are 4 squares. Every object is blue.*
$n = 4$	*More than half of the objects are blue squares. Less than half are blue circles.*
$n = 4$	*There is one red square and the rest are blue circles.*
$n = 4$	*All possible objects are shown.*
$n = 9$	*Most of the items are red circles, but there are a couple of blue squares.*
$n = 9$	*Most of the objects are blue squares. A few objects are blue circles.*
$n = 20$	*All the objects in the picture are circles and majority of them is blue.*
$n = 20$	*Both circles and squares appear in either red or blue.*

Table 1: List of example descriptions from QTUNA corpus; n indicates domain size.

then only a small range of existentially quantified sentence patterns would be used. For example, for Figure 1(a), a description like *"There are two blue squares, one red square and one red circle."* would tend to be given. To nudge participants into using a wider range of quantified statements, we asked participants not to use *enumerations*, followed by an example. This request may have diminished the ecological validity (Schmuckler, 2001) of our experiment, but we believe that this is more than outweighed by the increased richness of the resulting descriptions.

Participants were students at the Computing department of Utrecht University. Data from 66, 63, and 58 participants were collected for the three experiments. We manually filtered out all descriptions from subjects who showed a misunderstanding of the task by committing at least 3 (what we considered to be) errors, namely by writing gibberish, by using enumerations, or by expressing locations (e.g., ".. in the top left"). The resulting corpus contains 656, 380, and 378 valid descriptions for the three domain sizes. Examples are shown in Table 1. The larger the domain size, the smaller was the proportion of valid descriptions in it, presumably because the difficulty of producing descriptions increases with domain size.

We annotated each description with a formula that encodes its semantic content. Following Barwise and Cooper (1981), we used a form in which each k-ary quantifier is a relation between 2 or more set terms as arguments. For example, *"All the objects are blue. Half of them are squares."* is labelled as $\text{All}(O, B) \wedge \text{Half}(O, S)$, where O, B, and S stand for the set of all objects in the situation, blue objects, and squares, respectively.

3 Analysis

The corpus was analysed on the basis of hypotheses formulated before we looked into the corpus.

Annotations were done by the first two authors, who discussed their initial judgements and made final decisions together. All hypotheses focus on generation, that is, on the choices that speakers made between different possible utterances.

Vague quantifiers. The larger a domain, the harder it is to see at a glance how many objects there are in each of its set-theoretic regions (A, B, $A \cup B$, $A \cap B$, $A - B$, $B - A$, and the domain of objects O as a whole). We therefore hypothesised ($\mathcal{H}_1$) that, as our 3 domains grew larger, more vague quantifiers would occur. To test this idea, we counted the number of QEs that use vague quantifiers (e.g., *many*, and *few*, which permit so-called borderline cases, where it is unclear whether the QE is true or false, see e.g., Keefe and Smith (1996)) in each sub-corpus.[1] The number of vague QEs was compared with the total number of QEs (Table 2). Chi-Square suggests an affirmative answer ($\chi^2(2) = 471.55, p < .001$).[2]

How often do speakers describe a situation completely and correctly?

We considered a description to be complete if the described situation was the only one (modulo location) that fits the description. Since producing a complete description requires more work in a larger domain, we hypothesised that larger domains would give rise to a smaller proportion of complete descriptions than smaller ones.

This hypothesis is challenging to test because speakers frequently relied on inference when describing a scene. Consider *"half of the objects are blue"*. Given there are only two colours (blue and red), we infer that the other half are red. Or consider, *"Everything is blue. Most things are*

---

[1] A list of all the vague quantifiers in our corpora can be found in the supplementary material.

[2] As we had 6 hypotheses, all the p-values reported in this paper are those after Bonferroni correction, i.e., multiplicated by 6.

Hypothesis	$n = 4$	$n = 9$	$n = 20$
$\mathcal{H}_1$: #(Vague Quantifier)/#(QE)	57/1401	201/638	234/543
$\mathcal{H}_2$: #(Incompleteness)/#(Description)	46/656	137/380	261/378
$\mathcal{H}_3$: #(Wrong Description)/#(Description)	7/656	11/380	29/378
$\mathcal{H}_4$: #(Word) per description	13.02	12.75	9.53
$\mathcal{H}_4$: #(QE) per description	2.13	1.67	1.43

Table 2: Statistics with respected to some of the hypotheses in §3, where #(·) means "the number of".

square". If "*most*" means not just "more than half" but also "not all", then the above description *completely* describes a situation with 3 blue squares and 1 blue circle, despite not saying this explicitly. Instead of relying on our formalisation of the meaning of quantifiers,[3] we tackled the issue by asking annotators to say directly, for each description in each sub-corpus, whether they considered the description to be logically complete.

We likewise hypothesised ($\mathcal{H}_2$) that smaller domains would give rise to a larger proportion of logically complete descriptions (because this is easier in a smaller domain). The results in Table 2 confirm ($\chi^2(2) = 443.60, p < .001$) this.

For the same reason, we expected ($\mathcal{H}_3$) that, in larger domains, there will be more descriptions that convey *incorrect* information, because counting mistakes becomes more likely. For example, we would mark a description "*all objects are blue*" as incorrect if it describes a situation where all objects are actually red. Chi-square shows an overall association between domain size and error frequency ($\chi^2(2) = 32.85, p < .001$). The association also held between each subsequent level of size, but although the proportion of errors went up from $n = 9$ to $n = 20$ ($\chi^2(1) = 8.65, p < .01$), from $n = 4$ to $n = 9$ it fell, perhaps because *vague* QEs are used (as is frequently the case in $n = 9$ and $n = 20$, but not in $n = 4$). This reduces the proportion of QEs that are downright incorrect (e.g., annotators in most situations will have been understandably reluctant to describe a QEs of the form "many/few A are B" as incorrect).

Are larger scenes described more elaborately? We expected ($\mathcal{H}_4$) participants to produce longer descriptions in larger scenes, because there is more to describe. To test this, we calculated the length, as defined by both the number of words and the number of QEs, of each description. The

	First	Later
Shape	489	121
Colour	112	514

Table 3: The number of QEs that put shape/colour in the first/later place.

results in Table 2 show the opposite of what we expected: the length of descriptions *decreased* with domain size. A plausible explanation lies in the fact that (hypothesis $\mathcal{H}_2$), speakers produced fewer *complete* descriptions in larger domains.

Ordering of QEs. We noticed during our pilots that speakers tended to employ two discourse structures. The first starts by describing the whole scene, e.g., "*all objects are blue*", followed by a more detailed statement, e.g., "*half of them are squares*". The second discourse structure cuts the set of objects into two parts, each of which is described separately. We hypothesised ($\mathcal{H}_5$) that when a scene is described in two parts, where one part is larger than the other, then the larger part if described before the smaller part, because this strategy lets more important information be followed by less important information. For instance, "*3/4 of A are B, 1/4 are C.*" occurs more often than "*1/4 of A are C, 3/4 are B.*". We counted the number of descriptions that describe the larger part first, and those that describe the smaller part first, obtaining the numbers of 367 and 136 descriptions respectively. This confirmed ($\chi^2(1) = 212.17, p < .001$) the hypothesis.

Differences between colour and shape. Given the well-documented primacy of colour over shape in referring expressions (Pechmann, 1989; van Deemter et al., 2012b), it seemed plausible to us that colour and shape play different roles in quantification too. Based on our pilot experiments, our last hypothesis ($\mathcal{H}_6$) was: in k-ary QEs (i.e., QEs with quantifiers that describe relations between k sets), shape occurs more often in the first argument

---

[3]See e.g. Coventry et al. (2010) for problems assessing the meaning of "most".

place (i.e., the A position in $Q(A, B)$) and colour in the second argument place (the B position). For example, we expect to see sentences like *"all circles are blue"* more often than ones like *"all blue objects are circular"*. The results in Table 3 confirm this hypothesis ($\chi^2(1) = 479.59, p < .001$).

4 Discussion

The corpus also gave rise to a number of interesting *post hoc* observations. For example, we found a substantial number of 3-ary quantifiers, such as *"half of A are B, and the other half are C"*, which should not be confused with *"half of A are B and half of A are C"*; the latter allows B and C have a non-empty intersection, while the former means 1/2 of A are B and $(A - B) \subseteq C$. A similar example is *"Most A are B, the others are C"*

Another unanticipated feature is the existence of higher-order quantifiers. For instance, in the $n = 4$ experiment, when all the objects were different, many participants used QEs such as *"All possible types of objects are shown"*, a strikingly brief and complete description which quantifies over the Cartesian product of the colours and the shapes.

In future, two issues will be addressed: 1) What descriptions will be produced if the domain size is further increased? One might expect that, similar to the findings of this paper, the participants would produce even more vague quantifiers, more incompleteness, etc.; 2) What types of QEs are produced in other languages? We are particularly curious about Chinese, since previous corpus study for machine translation suggests there is much more variations in QEs in Chinese than in English (Wang and Piao, 2007).

Computational modelling of the human production of QEs is one major goal of building QTUNA corpus. The idea is to work analogously to the generation of *referring* expressions, where corpora of experimentally elicited descriptions (such as the TUNA corpus (Gatt et al., 2007)) have guided the construction and evaluation of Referring Expressions Generation algorithms. In the same way, the QTUNA corpus can guide the construction of algorithms that mimic the human production of *quantified* descriptions. (For example, the corpus can help us understand which quantifiers and QE patterns are most frequently used, and how elaborate a description needs to be – for example, when should the generator stop adding further QEs, be-cause it has provided enough information already, whether or not the scene has been described completely.) Examples of such a generation algorithm, based on the corpus of the present paper, can be found in Chen et al. (2019).

Acknowledgements

We thank the anonymous reviewers for their helpful comments. We thank Larry Moss, Jakub Szymanik, and Camilo Thorne for suggestions that helped shape our work. Guanyi Chen is supported by China Scholarship Council (No.201907720022).

References

Dale Barr, Kees van Deemter, and Raquel Fernández. 2013. Generation of quantified referring expressions: Evidence from experimental data. In *Proceedings of the 14th European Workshop on Natural Language Generation*, pages 157–161, Sofia, Bulgaria. Association for Computational Linguistics.

Jon Barwise and Robin Cooper. 1981. Generalized quantifiers and natural language. In *Philosophy, language, and artificial intelligence*, pages 241–301. Springer.

Guanyi Chen, Kees van Deemter, and Chenghua Lin. 2019. Generating quantified descriptions of abstract visual scenes. In *Proceedings of the 12th International Conference on Natural Language Generation*.

Kenny R Coventry, Angelo Cangelosi, Stephen E Newstead, and Davi Bugmann. 2010. Talking about quantities in space: Vague quantifiers, context and similarity. *Language and Cognition*, 2(2):221–241.

Kees van Deemter. 2016. *Computational models of referring: a study in cognitive science*. MIT Press.

Kees van Deemter, Albert Gatt, Ielka van der Sluis, and Richard Power. 2012a. Generation of referring expressions: Assessing the incremental algorithm. *Cognitive science*, 36(5):799–836.

Kees van Deemter, Albert Gatt, Ielka van der Sluis, and Richard Power. 2012b. Generation of referring expressions: Assessing the incremental algorithm. *Cognitive Science*, 36(5):799–836.

Albert Gatt and Anja Belz. 2010. Introducing shared tasks to nlg: The tuna shared task evaluation challenges. In *Empirical methods in natural language generation*, pages 264–293. Springer.

Albert Gatt, Ielka van der Sluis, and Kees van Deemter. 2007. Evaluating algorithms for the generation of referring expressions using a balanced corpus. In *Proceedings of the Eleventh European Workshop on Natural Language Generation (ENLG 07)*, pages 49–56, Saarbrücken, Germany. DFKI GmbH.

Edward Grefenstette. 2013. Towards a formal distributional semantics: Simulating logical calculi with tensors. In *Second Joint Conference on Lexical and Computational Semantics (*SEM), Volume 1: Proceedings of the Main Conference and the Shared Task: Semantic Textual Similarity*, pages 1–10, Atlanta, Georgia, USA. Association for Computational Linguistics.

Aurélie Herbelot and Eva Maria Vecchi. 2015. Building a shared world: mapping distributional to model-theoretic semantic spaces. In *Proceedings of the 2015 Conference on Empirical Methods in Natural Language Processing*, pages 22–32, Lisbon, Portugal. Association for Computational Linguistics.

Rosanna Keefe and Peter Smith. 1996. *Vagueness: A reader*. MIT press.

Emiel Krahmer and Kees van Deemter. 2012. Computational generation of referring expressions: A survey. *Computational Linguistics*, 38(1):173–218.

Andrzej Mostowski. 1957. On a generalization of quantifiers. *Fundamenta Mathematicae*, 44(2):12–36.

Linda M Moxey and Anthony J Sanford. 1993. *Communicating quantities: A psychological perspective*. Lawrence Erlbaum Associates, Inc.

Thomas Pechmann. 1989. Incremental speech production and referential overspecification. *Linguistics*, 27(1):89–110.

Stanley Peters and Dag Westerstahl. 2006. *Quantifiers in language and logic*. Oxford University Press.

Mark A Schmuckler. 2001. What is ecological validity? a dimensional analysis. *Infancy*, 2(4):419–436.

Ionut Sorodoc, Angeliki Lazaridou, Gemma Boleda, Aurélie Herbelot, Sandro Pezzelle, and Raffaella Bernardi. 2016. "look, some green circles!": Learning to quantify from images. In *Proceedings of the 5th Workshop on Vision and Language*, pages 75–79, Berlin, Germany. Association for Computational Linguistics.

Jakub Szymanik and Marcin Zajenkowski. 2010. Comprehension of simple quantifiers: Empirical evaluation of a computational model. *Cognitive Science*, 34(3):521–532.

Jakub Szymanik et al. 2016. *Quantifiers and cognition: Logical and computational perspectives*, volume 96. Springer.

JFAK Van Benthem et al. 1986. *Essays in logical semantics*. Springer.

Amy Y Wang and Scott Piao. 2007. Translating vagueness? a study on translations of vague quantifiers in an english-chinese parallel corpus. In *Proceedings of the Corpus Linguistics Conference*.

Ilker Yildirim, Judith Degen, Michael K. Tanenhaus, and T. Florian Jaeger. 2013. Linguistic variability and adaptation in quantifier meanings. In *Proceedings of the 35th Annual Meeting of the Cognitive Science Society*.

KPTimes: A Large-Scale Dataset for Keyphrase Generation on News Documents

Ygor Gallina   **Florian Boudin**   **Beatrice Daille**

LS2N, Université de Nantes, France
`firstname.lastname@univ-nantes.fr`

Abstract

Keyphrase generation is the task of predicting a set of lexical units that conveys the main content of a source text. Existing datasets for keyphrase generation are only readily available for the scholarly domain and include non-expert annotations. In this paper we present *KPTimes*, a large-scale dataset of news texts paired with editor-curated keyphrases. Exploring the dataset, we show how editors tag documents, and how their annotations differ from those found in existing datasets. We also train and evaluate state-of-the-art neural keyphrase generation models on *KPTimes* to gain insights on how well they perform on the news domain. The dataset is available online at `https://github.com/ygorg/KPTimes`.

1 Introduction

Keyphrases are single or multi-word lexical units that best summarise a document (Evans and Zhai, 1996). As such, they are of great importance for indexing, categorising and browsing digital libraries (Witten et al., 2009). Yet, very few documents have keyphrases assigned, thus raising the need for automatic keyphrase generation systems. This task falls under the task of automatic keyphrase extraction which can also be the subtask of finding keyphrases that only appear in the input document. Generating keyphrases can be seen as a particular instantiation of text summarization, where the goal is not to produce a well-formed piece of text, but a coherent set of phrases that convey the most salient information. Those phrases may or may not appear in the document, the latter requiring some form of abstraction to be generated. State-of-the-art systems for this task rely on recurrent neural networks (Meng et al., 2017; Chen et al., 2018, 2019), and hence require large amounts of annotated training data to achieve good performance. As gold anno-tated data is expensive and difficult to obtain (Mao and Lu, 2017), previous works focused on readily available scientific abstracts and used author-assigned keyphrases as a proxy for expert annotations. However, this poses two major issues: 1) neural models for keyphrase generation do not generalize well across domains, thus limiting their use in practice; 2) author-assigned keyphrases exhibit strong consistency issues that negatively impacts the model's performance. There is therefore a great need for annotated data from different sources, that is both sufficiently large to support the training of neural-based models and that comprises gold-standard labels provided by experts. In this study, we address this need by providing *KPTimes*, a dataset made of 279 923 news articles that comes with editor-assigned keyphrases.

Online news are particularly relevant to keyphrase generation since they are a natural fit for faceted navigation (Tunkelang, 2009) or topic detection and tracking (Allan, 2012). Also, and not less importantly, they are available in large quantities and are sometimes accompanied by meta-data containing human-assigned keyphrases initially intended for search engines. Here, we divert these annotations from their primary purpose, and use them as gold-standard labels to automatically build our dataset. More precisely, we collect data by crawling selected news websites and use heuristics to draw texts paired with gold keyphrases. We then explore the resulting dataset to better understand how editors tag documents, and how these expert annotations differ from author-assigned keyphrases found in scholarly documents. Finally, we analyse the performance of state-of-the-art keyphrase generation models and investigate their transferability to the news domain and the impact of domain shift.

Proceedings of The 12th International Conference on Natural Language Generation, pages 130–135,
Tokyo, Japan, 28 Oct - 1 Nov, 2019. ©2019 Association for Computational Linguistics

> **Muslim Women in Hijab Break Barriers: 'Take the Good With the Bad'**
>
> When Ginella Massa, a Toronto-based TV reporter, recently accepted a request to host an evening newscast, she was not planning or expecting to make history for wearing a hijab. She was just covering for a colleague who wanted to go to a hockey game. And that's how Ms. Massa, who works at CityNews in Toronto, became the first Canadian woman to host a newscast from a large media company while wearing the head scarf. [...] This new trend of inclusion occurs amid a more sinister one, as reported hate crimes against Muslims are on the rise in the United States and Canada. The F.B.I. says that a surge in hate crimes against Muslims has led to an overall increase in hate crimes in the United States; Muslims have borne the brunt of the increase with 257 recorded attacks. [...] In Canada, where Ms. Massa has lived since she was a year old, the number of reported hate crimes has dropped slightly overall, but the number of recorded attacks against Muslims has grown: 99 attacks were reported in 2014, according to an analysis by the news site Global News of data from Statistics Canada, a government agency. [...]
>
> **keywords:** US; Islam; Fashion; Muslim Veiling; Women and Girls; (News media, journalism); Hate crime; Canada

Figure 1: Sample document from *KPTimes* (id: 0296216). Keyphrases (or part of) appearing in the document are colored.

2   Existing datasets

Frequently used datasets for keyphrase generation have a common characteristic that they are, by and large, made from scholarly documents (abstracts or full texts) paired with non-expert (mostly from authors) annotations. Notable examples of such datasets are SemEval-2010 (Kim et al., 2010) and KP20k (Meng et al., 2017), which respectively comprises scientific articles and paper abstracts, both about computer science and information technology. Detailed statistics are listed in Table 1. Only two publicly available datasets, that we are aware of, contain news documents: DUC-2001 (Wan and Xiao, 2008) and KPCrowd (Marujo et al., 2012). Originally created for the DUC evaluation campaign on text summarization (Over, 2001), the former is composed of 308 news annotated by graduate students. The latter includes 500 news annotated by crowdsourcing. Both datasets are very small and contain newswire articles from various online sources labelled by non-expert annotators, in this case readers, which is not without issues.

Thus, unlike author annotations, those produced by readers exhibit significantly lower missing keyphrases, that is, gold keyphrases that do not occur in the content of the document. In the DUC-2001 dataset for example, more than 96% of the gold keyphrases actually appear in the documents. This confirms previous observations that readers tend to assign keyphrases in an extractive fashion (Wang et al., 2015), which

makes these datasets less suitable for the task at hand (keyphrase generation) but rather relevant for a purely extractive task (keyphrase extraction). Yet, author-assigned keyphrases commonly found in scientific paper datasets are not perfect either, as they are less constrained (Sood et al., 2007) and include seldom-used variants or misspellings that negatively impact performance. One can see there is an apparent lack of sizeable expert-annotated data that enables the development of neural keyphrase generation models in a domain other than scholarly texts. Here, we fill this gap and propose a large-scale dataset that includes news texts paired with manually curated gold standard annotations.

3   Building the *KPTimes* dataset

To create the *KPTimes* dataset, we collected over half a million newswire articles by crawling selected online news websites. We applied heuristics to identify the content (title, headline and body) of each article and regarded the keyphrases provided in the HTML metadata as the gold standard. A cherry-picked sample document is showcased in Figure 1, it allows to show present and absent keyphrases, as well as keyphrase variants (in this example `News media` and `journalism`).

We use the New York Times[1] as our primary source of data, since the content tagging policy that it applies is rigorous and well-

---

[1]`https://www.nytimes.com/`

	Dataset	Ann.	#Train	#Dev	#Test	#words	#kp	len kp	%abs
Scholar	SemEval-2010	$A \cup R$	144	-	100	7 961	14.7	2.2	19.7
Scholar	KP20k	A	530K	20K	20K	176	5.3	2.6	42.6
News	DUC-2001	R	-	-	308	847	8.1	2.0	3.7
News	KPCrowd	R	450	-	50	465	46.2	1.1	11.2
News	*KPTimes* (this work)	E	260K	10K	10K	921	5.0	1.5	54.7
News	*JPTimes* (this work)	A	-	-	10K	648	5.3	1.3	28.2

Table 1: Statistics of available datasets for keyphrase generation. Gold annotation is performed by authors (A), readers (R) or editors (E). The number of documents in the training (#Train), validation (dev) and testing (#Test) splits are shown. The average number of keyphrases (#kp) and words (#words) per document, the average length of keyphrases (len kp) and the ratio of keyphrases in the reference that do not appear in the document (%abs) are computed on the test set.

documented[2]. The news articles are annotated in a semi-automatic way, first the editors revise a set of tags proposed by an algorithm. They then provide additional tags which will be used by a taxonomy team to improve the algorithm.

We first retrieved the URLs of the free-to-read articles from 2006 to 2017[3], and collected the corresponding archived HTML pages using the Internet Archive[4]. Doing so allows the distribution of our dataset using a thin, URL-only list. We then extracted the HTML body content using `beautifulsoup`[5] and devised heuristics to extract the main content and title of each article while excluding extraneous HTML markup and inline ads. Gold standard keyphrases are obtained from the metadata (field types `news_keywords` and `keywords`[6]) available in the HTML page of each article. Surface form variants of gold keyphrases (e.g. "*AIDS*; *HIV*", "*Driverless Cars*; *Self-Driving Cars*" or "*Fatalities*; *Casualties*"), which are sometimes present in the metadata, are kept to be used for evaluation purposes.

We further cleansed and filtered the dataset by removing duplicates, articles without content and those with too few (less than 2) or too many (more than 10) keyphrases. This process resulted in a set of 279 923 article-keyphrase pairs. We randomly divided this dataset into training (92.8%), development (3.6%) and test (3.6%) splits.

Restricting ourselves to one source of data ensures the uniformity and consistency of annotation that is missing in the other datasets, but it may also make the trained model source-dependent and harm generalization. To monitor the model's ability to generalize, we gather a secondary source of data. We collected HTML pages from the Japan Times[7] and processed them the same way as described above. 10K more news articles were gathered as the *JPTimes* dataset.

Although in this study we concentrate only on the textual content of the news articles, it is worth noting that the HTML pages also provide additional information that can be helpful in generating keyphrases such as text style properties (e.g. bold, italic), links to related articles, or news categorization (e.g. politics, science, technology).

4 Data analysis

We explored the *KPTimes* dataset to better understand how it stands out from the existing ones. First, we looked at how editors tag news articles. Figure 2 illustrates the difference between the annotation behaviour of readers, authors and editors through the number of times that each unique keyphrase is used in the gold standard. We see that non-expert annotators use a larger, less controlled indexing vocabulary, in part because they lack the higher level of domain expertise that editors have. For example, we observe that frequent keyphrases in *KPTimes* are close to topic descriptors (e.g. "*Baseball*", "*Politics and Government*") while those appearing only once are very precise (e.g. "*Marley's Cafe*", "*Catherine E. Connelly*").

[2]https://lac-group.com/rules-based-tagging-metadata/

[3]https://spiderbites.nytimes.com/

[4]https://archive.org/

[5]https://www.crummy.com/software/BeautifulSoup/

[6]The change of field name correspond to the introduction of the *keywords* tag as a W3C standard.

[7]https://www.japantimes.co.jp/

Annotations in *KPTimes* are arguably more uniform and consistent, through the use of tag suggestions, which, as we will soon discuss in §5.3, makes it easier for supervised approaches to learn a good model.

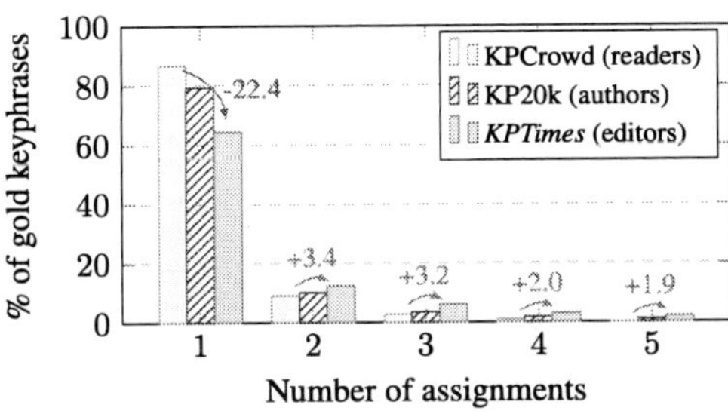

Figure 2: Distributions of gold keyphrase assignments.

Next, we further looked at the characteristics of the gold keyphrases in *KPTimes*. Table 1 shows that the number of gold keyphrases per document is similar to the one observed for KP20k while the number of missing keyphrases is higher. This indicates that editors are more likely to generalize and assign keyphrases that do not occur in the document ($\approx 55\%$). It is therefore this ability to generalize that models should mimic in order to perform well on *KPTimes*. We also note that keyphrases are on average shorter in news datasets (1.5 words) than those in scientific paper datasets (2.4 words). This may be due to the abundant use of longer, more specific phrases in scholarly documents (Jin et al., 2013).

Variants of keyphrases recovered from the metadata occur in 8% of the documents and represent 810 sets of variants in the *KPTimes* test split. These variants often refer to the same concept (e.g. "*Marijuana; Pot; Weed*"), but can sometimes be simply semantically related (e.g. "*Bridges; Tunnels*"). Thereafter, keyphrase variants will be used during model evaluation for reducing the number of mismatches associated with commonly used lexical overlap metrics.

5 Performance of existing models

We train and evaluate several keyphrase generation models to understand the challenges of *KPTimes* and its usefulness for training models.

5.1 Evaluation metrics

We follow the common practice and evaluate the performance of each model in terms of f-measure (F_1) at the top $N = 10$ keyphrases, and apply stemming to reduce the number of mismatches. We also report the Mean Average Precision (MAP) scores of the ranked lists of keyphrases.

5.2 Models

Baseline: FirstPhrase

Position is a strong feature for keyphrase extraction, simply because texts are usually written so that the most important ideas go first (Marcu, 1997). In news summarization for example, the lead baseline –that is, the first sentences from the document–, while incredibly simple, is still a competitive baseline (Kedzie et al., 2018). Similar to the lead baseline, we compute the **FirstPhrases** baseline that extracts the first N keyphrase candidates[8] from a document.

Baseline, unsupervised: MultipartiteRank

The second baseline we consider, **MultipartiteRank** (Boudin, 2018), represents the state-of-the-art in unsupervised graph-based keyphrase extraction. It relies on a multipartite graph representation to enforce topical diversity while ranking keyphrase candidates. Just as FirstPhrases, this model is bound to the content of the document and cannot generate missing keyphrases. We use the implementation of MultipartiteRank available in `pke`[9] (Boudin, 2016).

State-of-the-art, supervised: CopyRNN

The generative neural model we include in this study is **CopyRNN** (Meng et al., 2017), an encoder-decoder model that incorporates a copying mechanism (Gu et al., 2016) in order to be able to generate phrases that rarely occur. When properly trained, this model was shown to be very effective in extracting keyphrases from scientific abstracts. CopyRNN has been further extended by (Chen et al., 2018) to include correlation constraints among keyphrases which we do not include here as it yields comparable results.

Two models were trained to bring evidence on the necessity to have datasets from multiple domains. CopySci was trained using scientific abstracts (KP20k) and CopyNews using newspaper articles (*KPTimes*), the two models use the same architecture.

---

[8] Sequences of adjacent nouns with one or more preceding adjectives of length up to five words.
[9] `https://github.com/boudinfl/pke`

	KPCrowd		DUC		KPTimes		JPTimes		SemEval		KP20k	
	F@10	MAP	F@10	MAP	F@10	MAP	F@10	MAP	F@10	MAP	F@10	MAP
FirstPhrases	17.1	16.5	24.6	22.3	9.2	8.4	13.5	13.1	13.8	10.5	13.5	12.6
MultipartiteRank	18.2	17.0	25.6	24.9	11.2	10.1	16.9	16.5	14.3	10.6	13.6	13.3
CopySci	15.5	11.1	12.7	9.7	11.0	10.6	18.9	19.8	20.3	13.8	25.4	28.7
CopyNews	8.4	4.2	10.5	7.2	39.3	50.9	24.6	26.5	7.0	3.5	6.6	5.1

Table 2: Performance on benchmark datasets composed of newspaper article, full scientific article and scientific article abstract. The generation models CopySci and CopyNews were trained respectively on KP20k and *KPTimes*. The dataset presented in this work are written in italic.

5.3 Results

Model performances for each dataset are reported in Table 2. Extractive baselines show the best results for KPCrowd and DUC-2001 which is not surprising given that these datasets exhibit the lowest ratio of absent keyphrases. Neural-based models obtain the greatest performance, but only for the dataset on which they were trained. We therefore see that these models do not generalize well across domains, confirming previous preliminary findings (Meng et al., 2017) and exacerbating the need for further research on this topic. Interestingly, CopyNews outperforms the other models on *JPTimes* and achieves very low scores for KPCrowd and DUC-2001, although all these datasets are from the same domain. This emphasizes the differences that exist between the reader- and editor-assigned gold standard. The score difference may be explained by the ratio of absent keyphrases that differs greatly between the reader-annotated datasets and *JPTimes* (see Table 1), and thus question the use of these rather extractive datasets for evaluating keyphrase generation.

Finally, we note that the performance of Copy-News on *KPTimes* is significantly higher than that of CopySci on KP20k, proving that a more uniform and consistent annotation makes it easier to learn a good model.

6 Conclusion

In this paper we presented *KPTimes*, a large-scale dataset of newswire articles to train and test deep learning models for keyphrase generation. The dataset and the code are available at `https://github.com/ygorg/KPTimes`. Large datasets have driven rapid improvement in other natural language generation tasks, such as machine translation or summarization. We hope that *KPTimes* will play this role and help the community in devising more robust and generalizable neural keyphrase generation models.

References

James Allan. 2012. *Topic detection and tracking: event-based information organization*, volume 12. Springer Science & Business Media.

Florian Boudin. 2016. pke: an open source python-based keyphrase extraction toolkit. In *Proceedings of COLING 2016, the 26th International Conference on Computational Linguistics: System Demonstrations*, pages 69–73, Osaka, Japan. The COLING 2016 Organizing Committee.

Florian Boudin. 2018. Unsupervised keyphrase extraction with multipartite graphs. In *Proceedings of the 2018 Conference of the North American Chapter of the Association for Computational Linguistics: Human Language Technologies, Volume 2 (Short Papers)*, pages 667–672, New Orleans, Louisiana. Association for Computational Linguistics.

Jun Chen, Xiaoming Zhang, Yu Wu, Zhao Yan, and Zhoujun Li. 2018. Keyphrase generation with correlation constraints. In *Proceedings of the 2018 Conference on Empirical Methods in Natural Language Processing*, pages 4057–4066, Brussels, Belgium. Association for Computational Linguistics.

Wang Chen, Hou Pong Chan, Piji Li, Lidong Bing, and Irwin King. 2019. An integrated approach for keyphrase generation via exploring the power of retrieval and extraction. In *Proceedings of the 2019 Conference of the North American Chapter of the Association for Computational Linguistics: Human Language Technologies, Volume 1 (Long and Short Papers)*, pages 2846–2856, Minneapolis, Minnesota. Association for Computational Linguistics.

David A. Evans and Chengxiang Zhai. 1996. Noun phrase analysis in large unrestricted text for information retrieval. In *Proceedings of the 34th Annual Meeting of the Association for Computational Linguistics*, pages 17–24, Santa Cruz, California, USA. Association for Computational Linguistics.

Jiatao Gu, Zhengdong Lu, Hang Li, and Victor O.K. Li. 2016. Incorporating Copying Mechanism in Sequence-to-Sequence Learning. In *Proceedings of the 54th Annual Meeting of the Association for Computational Linguistics (Volume 1: Long Papers)*, pages 1631–1640, Berlin, Germany. Association for Computational Linguistics.

Yiping Jin, Min-Yen Kan, Jun-Ping Ng, and Xiangnan He. 2013. Mining scientific terms and their definitions: A study of the ACL anthology. In *Proceedings of the 2013 Conference on Empirical Methods in Natural Language Processing*, pages 780–790, Seattle, Washington, USA. Association for Computational Linguistics.

Chris Kedzie, Kathleen McKeown, and Hal Daum III. 2018. Content Selection in Deep Learning Models of Summarization. In *Proceedings of the 2018 Conference on Empirical Methods in Natural Language Processing*, pages 1818–1828, Brussels, Belgium. Association for Computational Linguistics.

Su Nam Kim, Olena Medelyan, Min-Yen Kan, and Timothy Baldwin. 2010. Semeval-2010 task 5 : Automatic keyphrase extraction from scientific articles. In *Proceedings of the 5th International Workshop on Semantic Evaluation*, pages 21–26, Uppsala, Sweden. Association for Computational Linguistics.

Yuqing Mao and Zhiyong Lu. 2017. Mesh now: automatic mesh indexing at pubmed scale via learning to rank. *Journal of Biomedical Semantics*, 8(1):15.

Daniel Marcu. 1997. The rhetorical parsing of unrestricted natural language texts. In *35th Annual Meeting of the Association for Computational Linguistics*, pages 96–103.

Lus Marujo, Anatole Gershman, Jaime Carbonell, Robert Frederking, and Joao P. Neto. 2012. Supervised topical key phrase extraction of news stories using crowdsourcing, light filtering and co-reference normalization. In *Proceedings of the Eight International Conference on Language Resources and Evaluation (LREC'12)*, Istanbul, Turkey. European Language Resources Association (ELRA).

Rui Meng, Sanqiang Zhao, Shuguang Han, Daqing He, Peter Brusilovsky, and Yu Chi. 2017. Deep keyphrase generation. In *Proceedings of the 55th Annual Meeting of the Association for Computational Linguistics (Volume 1: Long Papers)*, pages 582–592. Association for Computational Linguistics.

Paul Over. 2001. Introduction to duc-2001: an intrinsic evaluation of generic news text summarization systems.

Sanjay Sood, Sara Owsley, Kristian J. Hammond, and Larry Birnbaum. 2007. Tagassist: Automatic tag suggestion for blog posts. In *Proceedings of the First International Conference on Weblogs and Social Media, ICWSM 2007, Boulder, Colorado, USA, March 26-28, 2007.*

Daniel Tunkelang. 2009. Faceted search. *Synthesis lectures on information concepts, retrieval, and services*, 1(1):1–80.

Xiaojun Wan and Jianguo Xiao. 2008. Single document keyphrase extraction using neighborhood knowledge. In *Proceedings of the 23rd National Conference on Artificial Intelligence - Volume 2*, AAAI'08, pages 855–860. AAAI Press.

Rui Wang, Wei Liu, and Chris McDonald. 2015. Using word embeddings to enhance keyword identification for scientific publications. In *Databases Theory and Applications*, pages 257–268, Cham. Springer International Publishing.

Ian H Witten, David Bainbridge, and David M Nichols. 2009. *How to build a digital library*. Morgan Kaufmann.

Sketch Me if You Can: Towards Generating Detailed Descriptions of Object Shape by Grounding in Images and Drawings

Ting Han
Artificial Intelligence Research Center
Tokyo, Japan
`ting.han@aist.go.jp`

Sina Zarrieß
Friedrich-Schiller-Universität Jena
Jena, Germany
`sina.zarriess@uni-jena.de`

Abstract

A lot of recent work in Language & Vision has looked at generating descriptions or referring expressions for objects in scenes of real-world images, though focusing mostly on relatively simple language like object names, color and location attributes (e.g., brown chair on the left). This paper presents work on Draw-and-Tell, a dataset of detailed descriptions for common objects in images where annotators have produced fine-grained attribute-centric expressions distinguishing a target object from a range of similar objects. Additionally, the dataset comes with hand-drawn sketches for each object. As Draw-and-Tell is medium-sized and contains a rich vocabulary, it constitutes an interesting challenge for CNN-LSTM architectures used in state-of-the-art image captioning models. We explore whether the additional modality given through sketches can help such a model to learn to accurately ground detailed language referring expressions to object shapes. Our results are encouraging.

1 Introduction

Recent work in referring expression generation (REG) has focused more and more on large-scale image datasets (Kazemzadeh et al., 2014; Mao et al., 2016; Yu et al., 2016) and models that incorporate a state-of-the-art vision component (Mao et al., 2016; Yu et al., 2017; Zarrieß and Schlangen, 2018). As compared to traditional REG settings (Dale and Reiter, 1995; Krahmer and Van Deemter, 2012), these works have led to substantial advances in terms of the complexity of visual inputs that can be processed and the visual object categories that can be covered. At the same time, it is questionable whether these recent benchmarks for real-world REG constitute an equally big step forward in terms of the language that needs to be modeled. As noted

(a)   (b)

Figure 1:   (a) Photo of a starfish; (b) Sketch of the starfish in (a). Starfish attribute description: *Top view, legs bend, thin legs, on sand.*

by Achlioptas et al. (2019), the vocabulary and attributes learnt by state-of-the-art REG models is linguistically and lexically relatively constrained, and does not cover language that can be used to describe fine-grained differences between object parts and shapes (see Section 2) . Thus, Achlioptas et al. (2019) propose to go back to carefully designed datasets with graphical, abstract objects in order to elicit complex descriptions of object attributes and also to have access to more fine-grained representations of an object's geometry and topology.

We explore modeling of fine-grained attribute descriptions of objects in real-world images, based on the *Draw-and-Tell* dataset introduced by Han and Schlangen (2017). This dataset was collected in a controlled procedure akin to traditional REG set-ups, resulting in fine-grained attribute descriptions and a rich vocabulary, see Figure 1 for an example. As the *Draw-and-Tell* data was originally designed for sketch-based image retrieval (Eitz et al., 2012; Sangkloy et al., 2016), each image is paired with hand-drawn sketches depicting the object in it. As illustrated in Figure 1(b), these sketches are somewhat distorted and abstract away from many visual properties of the complex real-world objects (e.g. colour). Yet they provide a clear outline of the object's shape. In this paper, we explore whether this

Proceedings of The 12th International Conference on Natural Language Generation, pages 136–140,
Tokyo, Japan, 28 Oct - 1 Nov, 2019. ©2019 Association for Computational Linguistics

form of visual abstraction is useful for modeling and generating fine-grained attribute descriptions of objects. We investigate whether object sketches lead to improvements in neural generation of descriptions of real-world objects, especially for attributes related to shape and orientation.

In the following, we present our ongoing work on generating detailed attribute descriptions of object by grounding in images and hand-drawn sketches. We first introduce the Draw-and-Tell dataset (Section 3), then describe a basic recurrent neural network architecture for generating attribution descriptions (Section 4). We carry out an automatic evaluation based on measures like BLEU (Papineni et al., 2002), vocabulary size, and the average length of generated descriptions. In addition, we provide a qualitative analysis and discussion on how incorporating sketches can benefit the task of generating fine-grained attribute descriptions.

2 Related Work

Visual language grounding and REG Foundational work in REG has often followed the well-known attribute selection paradigm established by (Dale and Reiter, 1995). Here, visual scenes have usually been carefully created and controlled so that the target and distractor referents and distractors would have similarities in their set of annotated attributes (e.g. type, position, size, color and so on), see Krahmer and Van Deemter (2012). In recently used image benchmarks for REG, the visual scene is typically given through a real-world image (Kazemzadeh et al., 2014; Yu et al., 2016), which makes it very difficult to systematically control the underlying attributes of a target referent and to what extent it resembles its distractors in the scene. At the same time, Yu et al. (2016) found that, in the standard version of the RefCOCO benchmark, many participants simply used location attributes like *left, right* relying on the 2D layout of the scene. As a remedy, they propose to introduce "taboo words" into the reference task in order to elicit "appearance-based" attributes. Achlioptas et al. (2019) adopt a different approach and suggest to collect data based on more abstract objects. They collect a dataset of referring expressions to chairs where various properties and parts of targets and distractors are controlled in terms of their visual similarity. Our work combines ideas from both paradigms: we use real-world images of objects paired with hand-drawn sketches, which allows us to integrate realistic and abstract visual inputs.

Multimodal Embedding Space For being able to model REG with multiple input modalities (images and sketches), we need to be able to represent these inputs as visual embeddings or features transferred from a CNN. Here, we rely on previous work that has mapped different modalities into joint vector spaces, as in text- or sketch-based image retrieval (Kiros et al., 2016; Sangkloy et al., 2016; Liu et al., 2017). We adopt (Sangkloy et al., 2016)'s Siamese network to project sketches and images into a joint space, and use the projections as inputs to a basic recurrent neural network for REG. It is noteworthy that this joint image-sketch space is designed to capture similarities across modalities, rather than complementary information expressed in different modalities. We leave the exploration of other modes of representation for future work.

3 The Draw-and-Tell Dataset

The **Draw-and-Tell** dataset (Han and Schlangen, 2017) includes 10,804 photographs of objects (referred to as target objects below), spread across 125 categories. Each image is paired with around 5 hand-drawn sketches and a description of the object's attributes, as shown in Figure 1.

The photos and sketches were selected from the Sketchy Database[1] (Sangkloy et al., 2016). Han and Schlangen (2017) augmented part of the Sketchy Database with object attribute descriptions which were collected from English speakers using a Crowdsourcing service. In each description task, workers were presented with 6 photos of objects from the same category. They were instructed to describe attributes of the target object, so that another person can distinguish the target object from distractor objects. Hence, this resembles classical settings in REG where distractors are controlled for being similar to the target reference. Attributes such as *shape*, *color* and *orientation* were suggested as examples to the workers, but they were also encouraged to list all attributes that they consider useful. Attribute phrases in the descriptions were typically separated by ",". As all the distractor images were in the same category and in separate images, workers were suggested not to use non-discriminative words such as category names or spatial relations in the descriptions.

---

[1] http://sketchy.eye.gatech.edu/

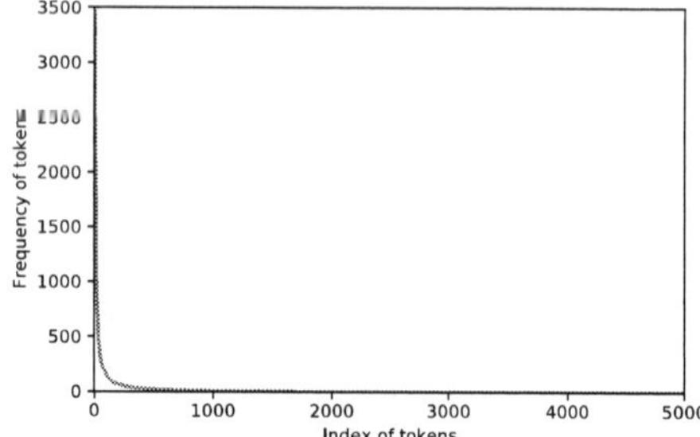

Figure 2: Word frequency in the corpus.

Sets	Token No.	Vocab size	Overlap
Train	85974	4621	-
Validation	4698	1099	962
Test	9948	1601	1370

Table 1: Data statistics. **Overlap** column shows vocabulary overlaps between the training set and validation/test sets.

Data Statistics On average, each object description includes 3 attribute phrases. In total, there are 100620 tokens in all the descriptions. The vocabulary size is 4982. 2893 of all the words in the vocabulary appear less than 3 times, as shown in Figure 2. We split the dataset into train (9233), validation (500) and test (1071) sets. Table 1 shows the token numbers, vocabulary size of each data split, and vocabulary overlaps with the training set.

Image and Sketch Joint Embedding Space Along with the Sketchy Database, Sangkloy et al. (2016) published a Siamese network model that embeds images and sketches into a joint vector space. The Siamese network is composed of two separate networks with the same architecture, the sketch-net and the image-net. The image-net encodes photographs into image feature vectors. Similarly, the sketch-net encodes sketch images into feature vectors. The Siamese network was trained and optimized to project photo vectors as close as possible to corresponding sketch vectors, while in the mean time, as distinguishable as possible from other photo vectors. In this work, we used the pre-trained models and took the output vector from the last fully connected layers as feature vectors (in 1024 dimension) to represent images and sketches. Next, we describe how we train a natural language generation model with the extracted vectors.

4 The RNN Caption Generator

Considering the small size of the *Draw-and-Tell* dataset, we built a basic Recurrent Neural Network model for the generation task (Tanti et al., 2017). The model takes a text vector and a visual feature vector as inputs, and predicts a sequence of tokens to describe the target object in the input visual vector. Therefore, the generated tokens are conditioned on the input visual feature vector.

The network includes an embedding layer, an LSTM layer, and a softmax layer. We encode word tokens as a one-hot vector, and concatenate the vector with image feature vectors (i.e., injecting image information into the network). An embedding layer takes the concatenated vector as input. The size of the LSTM layer is 512. The model was implemented using Tensorflow[2]. Training of the model is performed using the Adam optimizer and the cross entropy loss function.

When applying the model to generate object descriptions, the model first takes an image vector as input, then predicts each token conditioned on the image vector and previously predicted tokens until an end token EOS is predicted. We used a beam search method to predict the tokens. The bandwidth of the beam search algorithm is 3.

Note that in the current set-up, we do not include context or distractor images to generate discriminative descriptions, but focus on exploring the modality aspect in the generation task. See Zarrieß and Schlangen (2018) for a detailed discussion of the benefit of context features in image-based REG.

5 Experiments

We conducted ablation experiments by altering the input visual feature vectors. In the **Image Only** setup, we trained a model with *(object description, image feature)* pairs as input. This results in training set of 9233 description-image pairs. In the **Sketch Only** setup, we trained a model with *(object description, sketch feature)* pairs, using training data of the same size as in the Image Only setup. In the **Multimodal** setup, we use both *(object description, image feature)* and *(object description, sketch feature)* pairs to train the RNN. That is, we doubled the size of the training data. Therefore, the model does not only learn to generate expressions conditioned on image features, but also conditioned on sketch features.

---

[2]https://www.tensorflow.org/

(a)

(b)

(c)

(d)

(e)

(f)

Figure 3: Samples of generated descriptions. Grey utterances are attribute annotations from humans; Red utterances are generated using both sketch and image features. Blue utterances are from the sketch feature only model; Green utterances are from the image feature only model.

During training, the data was randomly shuffled, with a mini batch size of 50. The maximum epochs is 100. Words appearing less than 3 times were removed.

All the models were evaluated with image features in the test set as input to resemble the task of object description from images. Figure 2 shows the evaluation results.

Metrics We evaluated the generated attribute descriptions with **BLEU1** score. We also report vocabulary size, average number of tokens in each generated object description to show the word capacity of the models.

Table 2 shows the evaluation results. The *Multimodal* model achieved a slightly higher BLEU1 score. It also results in a slightly larger vocabulary of the generated descriptions.

As sketch vectors are expected to encode iconic information, we analyze *color*, *shape*, and *orientation words* in the generated descriptions in the Qualitative analysis section below.

5.1 Qualitative Analysis

Figure 3 shows some examples for generated referring expressions. We observed that, given only sketch vectors in the training data, the model still

Experiments	BLEU1	BLEU2	Vocab. size	Token Number
Sketch only	0.58	0.43	310	8.24
Image only	0.61	0.43	325	8.42
Multimodal	**0.64**	0.44	331	8.90

Table 2: BLEU scores, vocabulary size and average length of object descriptions in the experiments.

generates color words, but less accurate than Image Only and Multimodal models. For instance, in Figure 3 (a), the Sketch Only model describes a *brown* starfish as *red and yellow*. As shown in Figure 3 (b), the Multimodal model used *red comb* to describe the chicken, while the other two models only used color and orientation words. We conjecture that this could be due to the combination of sketch and image features in the training set. In Figure 3 (e) and (f), the descriptions of the Sketch Only model correctly describe the directions, while missing other attributes such as color or adding wrong attributes (e.g., grass).

6 Conclusion & Discussion

We have presented our ongoing work on generating fine-grained attribute descriptions of objects in real-life images by grounding in images and hand-drawn sketches. Given a medium-sized dataset with many low frequency words, we deployed sketch vectors from a joint sketch-image embedding space to improve the generation results. We show that by training a basic recurrent neural network with both sketch and image features, the model is able to capture more fine-grained attribute descriptions. Moreover, even when training only with sketch feature vectors, the model still achieves a satisfactory performance according to automatic evaluation with a BLEU.

In future work, we plan to add human evaluation results to show how humans perceive the generated descriptions in terms of naturalness and accuracy. We plan to further explore the multimodal joint embedding space for fine-grained object description generation tasks such as shape and orientation description generation.

Acknowledgments

This paper is based on results obtained from a project commissioned by the New Energy and Industrial Technology Development Organization (NEDO).

References

Panos Achlioptas, Judy Fan, X.D. Robert Hawkins, D. Noah Goodman, and J. Leonidas Guibas. 2019. ShapeGlot: Learning language for shape differentiation. *CoRR*, abs/1905.02925.

Robert Dale and Ehud Reiter. 1995. Computational interpretations of the gricean maxims in the generation of referring expressions. *Cognitive Science*, 19(2):233–263.

Mathias Eitz, James Hays, and Marc Alexa. 2012. How do humans sketch objects? *ACM Trans. Graph. (Proc. SIGGRAPH)*, 31(4):44:1–44:10.

Ting Han and David Schlangen. 2017. Draw and tell. multimodal descriptions outperform verbal-or sketch-only descriptions in an image retrieval task. In *The 8th International Joint Conference on Natural Language Processing. Proceedings of the Conference. Vol. 2: Short Papers*.

Sahar Kazemzadeh, Vicente Ordonez, Mark Matten, and Tamara Berg. 2014. Referitgame: Referring to objects in photographs of natural scenes. In *Proceedings of the 2014 conference on empirical methods in natural language processing (EMNLP)*, pages 787–798.

Ryan Kiros, Ruslan Salakhutdinov, and Richard S. Zemel. 2016. Unifying visual-semantic embeddings with multimodal neural language models. In *Proceedings of the IEEE conference on computer vision and pattern recognition*, pages 11–20.

Emiel Krahmer and Kees Van Deemter. 2012. Computational generation of referring expressions: A survey. *Computational Linguistics*, 38(1):173–218.

Li Liu, Fumin Shen, Yuming Shen, Xianglong Liu, and Ling Shao. 2017. Deep sketch hashing: Fast freehand sketch-based image retrieval. In *Proceedings of the IEEE conference on computer vision and pattern recognition*, pages 2862–2871.

Junhua Mao, Jonathan Huang, Alexander Toshev, Oana Camburu, Alan L Yuille, and Kevin Murphy. 2016. Generation and comprehension of unambiguous object descriptions. In *Proceedings of the IEEE conference on computer vision and pattern recognition*, pages 11–20.

Kishore Papineni, Salim Roukos, Todd Ward, and Wei-Jing Zhu. 2002. Bleu: a method for automatic evaluation of machine translation. In *Proceedings of the 40th annual meeting on association for computational linguistics*, pages 311–318. Association for Computational Linguistics.

Patsorn Sangkloy, Nathan Burnell, Cusuh Ham, and James Hays. 2016. The sketchy database: Learning to retrieve badly drawn bunnies. *ACM Transactions on Graphics (proceedings of SIGGRAPH)*.

Marc Tanti, Albert Gatt, and Kenneth Camilleri. 2017. What is the role of recurrent neural networks (rnns) in an image caption generator? In *Proceedings of the 10th International Conference on Natural Language Generation*, pages 51–60.

Licheng Yu, Patrick Poirson, Shan Yang, Alexander C. Berg, and Tamara L. Berg. 2016. *Modeling Context in Referring Expressions*, pages 69–85. Springer International Publishing, Cham.

Licheng Yu, Hao Tan, Mohit Bansal, and Tamara L Berg. 2017. A joint speaker-listener-reinforcer model for referring expressions. In *Proceedings of the IEEE Conference on Computer Vision and Pattern Recognition*, pages 7282–7290.

Sina Zarrieß and David Schlangen. 2018. Decoding strategies for neural referring expression generation. In *Proceedings of the 11th International Conference on Natural Language Generation*, pages 503–512, Tilburg University, The Netherlands. Association for Computational Linguistics.

An Encoder with non-Sequential Dependency for Neural Data-to-Text Generation

Feng Nie[1]* **Jinpeng Wang**[2] **Rong Pan**[1] **Chin-Yew Lin**[2]
[1]Sun Yat-Sen University [2]Microsoft Research Asia
[1]fengniesysu@gmail.com, [1]panr@sysu.edu.cn
[2]{jinpwa, cyl}@microsoft.com

Abstract

Data-to-text generation aims to generate descriptions given a structured input data (i.e., a table with multiple records). Existing neural methods for encoding input data can be divided into two categories: a) pooling based encoders which ignore dependencies between input records or b) recurrent encoders which model only sequential dependencies between input records. In our investigation, although the recurrent encoder generally outperforms the pooling based encoder by learning the sequential dependencies, it is sensitive to the order of the input records (i.e., performance decreases when injecting the random shuffling noise over input data). To overcome this problem, we propose to adopt the self-attention mechanism to learn dependencies between arbitrary input records. Experimental results show the proposed method achieves comparable results and remains stable under random shuffling over input data.

1 Introduction

Data-to-text generation, one classic task of natural language generation, aims to produce a piece of texts that adequately and fluently describes its structured input data (i.e., tables) (Kukich, 1983; Reiter and Dale, 1997; Barzilay and Lapata, 2005; Angeli et al., 2010; Kim and Mooney, 2010; Perez-Beltrachini and Gardent, 2017). Traditionally, it is divided into two subtasks: content selection (i.e., *what to say*) and the surface realization (i.e., *how to say*) (Reiter and Dale, 1997; Gatt and Krahmer, 2018). Recent neural generation systems ignore the distinction of these two subtasks using a single encoder-decoder model (Sutskever et al., 2014) with attention mechanism (Bahdanau et al., 2015; Mei et al., 2016; Dušek and Jurcicek, 2016; Kiddon et al., 2016; Chisholm et al., 2017).

Input	
Birth name	Johnny Allen Hendrix
Born	November 27, 1942 Seattle, Washington, U.S.
Genres	Rock, psychedelic rock, hard rock, blues, R&B
Occupation	Musician, songwriter, producer
Instruments	Guitar, vocals
Reference	
James Marshall Hendrix ... was an American rock guitarist, singer and songwriter.	

Table 1: An example of generating descriptions from the input data.

The encoder-decoder architecture first encodes the input data (e.g., a table) into a dense representation, where the input contains a set of records. Then descriptions are produced based on the input representation. The appropriate encoding method of input structured data remains an open question. Existing encoding methods for an input table can be decomposed into two stages: 1) converting each record in the table to a record vector, 2) combining the record vectors using a pooling method or a recurrent neural network (RNN) to represent the input table. In this paper, we investigate these two types of neural encoding methods over several data-to-text datasets. The empirical results show that RNN based methods outperform simple pooling methods in terms of BLEU evaluation.

The major difference between pooling and RNN based methods lies in the fact that pooling methods treat records in the input table independently while RNN based methods model the relationships among the records by treating the input records as a sequence. As a result, it is common that two records in the input data are relevant. For example, as shown in Table 1, the input record "Instruments: Guitar, vocals" is related to "Occupation: Musician, songwriter, producer".

The improvements of RNN based methods over

---

*Contribution during internship at Microsoft.

Proceedings of The 12th International Conference on Natural Language Generation, pages 141–146,
Tokyo, Japan, 28 Oct - 1 Nov, 2019. ©2019 Association for Computational Linguistics

pooling methods suggest that capturing dependencies among the input records is helpful. However, RNN based methods capture only the sequential relationships among the input data, which is sensitive to its input order. Given an input table, intuitively, permutations over the records should make no change to input representations, while we observe large performance decrease of RNN based methods when injecting the random shuffling noise over input data. To address this undesired nature of RNN, we propose using a self-attention mechanism to capture the dependency and enable the encoding to be less sensitive to any permutation noise. The experimental results on several datasets show self-attention based encoder achieves comparable results than RNN based methods and is more robust handling the input shuffling noise.

2 Method

The neural data-to-text generation is based on the encoder-decoder architecture. As shown in Figure 1 , there are multiple choices of table encoding that affect the generation decoder. We briefly introduce the backbone of the neural generation method in Section 2.1 and then introduce the details of three types of table encoders in Section 2.2.

2.1 Base Model

Given a set of records $S = \{r_j\}_{j=1}^K$, the goal of data-to-text generation is to produce a description $y = y_1, ..., y_T$. Usually, the encoder-decoder architecture consist of a table encoder and a recurrent neural network based decoder segmented with attention (Bahdanau et al., 2015) and conditional copy (See et al., 2017) mechanism. Firstly, each input record r_j is encoded into a hidden vector $\mathbf{h}_j$ using a specified table encoder, which is the focus of this paper and three encoders will be introduced in Section 2.2. Then, for the generated description y, the decoder generates the word y_t at the t-th time step based on the previously generated words $y_{<t}$ and the input hidden vectors $\mathbf{H} = \{\mathbf{h}_j\}_{j=1}^K$. Specifically,

$$P(y_t|y_{<t}, \mathbf{H}) = \mathrm{softmax}(f(\mathbf{d}_t, y_{t-1}, \mathbf{c}_t)) \quad (1)$$

where $f(.)$ is a tanh function and $\mathbf{d}_t = \mathrm{LSTM}(\mathbf{d}_{t-1}, y_{t-1}, \mathbf{c}_{t-1})$ is the hidden state of the decoder at step t. $\mathbf{c}_t$ in Eq. 1 is the context vector at timestep t, computed as a weighted sum

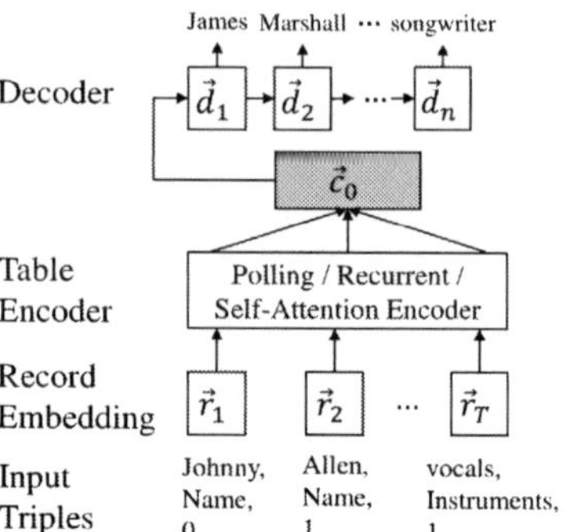

Figure 1: Overview of encoder-decoder architecture with different encoding methods.

of input hidden vectors $\mathbf{h}_j$:

$$\mathbf{c}_t = \sum_{j=1}^K \alpha_{t,j} \mathbf{h}_j \quad (2)$$

where we use the attention model introduced in (Bahdanau et al., 2015) to compute the attention weight $\alpha_{t,j}$.

2.2 Table Encoder

Record Vectors: The input table can be viewed as a set of field-value records, where values are sequences of words corresponding to a certain field (Liang et al., 2009; Lebret et al., 2016; Yang et al., 2017). For instance, in the Table 1, the word "William" has the field "Birth name" and it is the first word in this field. Every word in the field is a record r and is presented as triple (r^v, r^f, r^{pos}), where r^v, r^f and r^{pos} refer to the value (e.g., William), the field name (e.g., Birth name), the relative position in its field (e.g., 0). We map each record $r \in S$ into a vector $\mathbf{r}$ by concatenating the embedding of r^v, r^f and r^{pos}, denoted as $\mathbf{r} = [\mathbf{e}^v, \mathbf{e}^f, \mathbf{e}^{pos}]$, where $\mathbf{e}^v$, $\mathbf{e}^f$, $\mathbf{e}^{pos}$ are trainable word embeddings of r^v, r^f and r^{pos}.

Pooling Based Encoders: The pooling based encoder treats input records independently, therefore, it first applies a feed forward neural network layer over every record vector $\mathbf{r}_j$ and yields the input hidden vector $\mathbf{h}_j = \tanh(W\mathbf{r}_j)$, where W is a trainable parameter. The initial context vector $\mathbf{c}_0$ in Eq. 1 is calculated by the following max-pooling layer.

$$\mathbf{c}_0 = \max([\mathbf{h}_0, ..., \mathbf{h}_T]^T) \quad (3)$$

Recurrent Encoders: Different from pooling based encoder, the recurrent encoder captures the

	E2E	WIKIBIO
#Train	42061	582695
#Validation	4672	72831
#Test	4693	72831
Average field number	5.4	19.7
Average input length	20.1	53.1

Table 2: Statistics of two datasets.

Method	E2E	WIKIBIO
Template	-	19.8
StructAware	-	44.89
Slug2Slug	66.19	-
MaxEnc	66.05	43.19
RnnEnc	66.11	44.93
SelfAtt	66.29	45.02

Table 3: Experimental results of different encoding methods and other systems over three datasets.

dependency among the records by treating the set of record vectors $\mathbf{r}_1, ..., \mathbf{r}_T$ as a sequence. The sequence of records are fed into a RNN yielding a sequence of input hidden vectors $\mathbf{h}_1, ...\mathbf{h}_T$. We adopt a bidirectional LSTM by following (Mei et al., 2016). The initial context vector is set as the last hidden vector of the sequence $\mathbf{c}_0 = \mathbf{h}_T$.

Self-Attention Encoders: For data-to-text generation, input records are order invariant as input data should convey the same information regardless of the order of input records. The input records is a set, while the recurrent encoder makes strong hypothesis and treats it as a sequence.

Therefore an ideal table encoder has two desired properties: a) enable to capture relationships among the input records and b) is also order invariant. Recently proposed self-attention mechanism (Vaswani et al.; Wang et al., 2017) is able to learn interactions between arbitrary records and therefore is also irrelevant to the order of the records. For this purpose, we adapt the multi-layer self-attention mechanism for the encoding. Each layer has two sub-layers: one layer is for multi-head self-attention and the other one is a position wise feed-forward neural network with layer normalization (Vaswani et al.). Specifically,

$$s_{i,j} = \frac{Q_i^l \mathbf{h}_i^l (K_j^l \mathbf{h}_j^l)^T}{\sqrt{d_k}}; \beta_{i,j} = \frac{e^{s_{i,j}}}{\sum_{n=1}^{T} e^{s_{i,n}}} \quad (4)$$

$$\mathbf{h}_i^l = \sum_{j=0}^{T} \beta_{i,j}(V_j^l \mathbf{h}_j^l); \mathbf{h}_i^{l+1} = f(\mathbf{h}_i^l + g(\mathbf{h}_i^l)) \quad (5)$$

where Q^l, K^l, V^l are trainable parameters for layer l, d_k is the dimension of K, and the first layer of the hidden vector $\mathbf{h}_i^0$ refers to the record vector $\mathbf{r}_i$. To represent the full table, we apply max-pooling in Eq.3 using the last layer of hidden vectors similarly.

3 Experiments

3.1 Datasets and Evaluation Metrics

We conduct experiments on two datasets. E2E (Novikova et al., 2017) is a dataset for task-oriented language generation in the restaurant domain with 50,000 samples, the validation and test data are multi-reference; WIKIBIO (Lebret et al., 2016) contains 728,321 articles from English Wikipedia. It uses the first sentence of each article as the description of the corresponding infobox. The detailed statics of two datasets are listed in Table 2.

For evaluation metrics, we use BLEU-4 (Papineni et al., 2002) to assess the generation quality automatically.

3.2 Implementation Details

We tune all hyper-parameters according to the performance on the separated validation set. The dimension of trainable embeddings and hidden units in LSTMs are all set to 600. For the multi-layer and multi-head architecture, 3 layers and 4 multi-attention heads are used. During training, we regularize all layers with a dropout 0.1. For optimization, we use Adam with learning rate 0.0002. The gradient is truncated by 1. All experiments use beam size of 5 in decoding. We use pytorch version of OpenNMT (Klein et al., 2017) for implementation.

3.3 Performance

The results of different input encoding methods along with other competing systems on the test sets of three datasets are shown in Table 3. We compare three types of encoders (i.e., Pooling based encoders refer to MaxEnc, Recurrent encoders refer to RnnEnc, and self-attention encoders refer SelfAtt) introduced in Section 2.2 with the following generation systems: (1)

Methods	Training	E2E		WIKIBIO	
		Original	Shuffle	Original	Shuffle
MaxEnc	Original	66.05	66.05	43.19	43.19
	Shuffle	66.17	66.17	43.21	43.21
RnnEnc	Original	66.11	42.74	44.93	28.56
	Shuffle	64.08	65.40	43.95	43.59
SelfAtt	Original	66.29	66.29	45.02	45.02
	Shuffle	66.29	66.29	44.47	44.47

Table 4: Experimental results of different encoding methods trained and tested on different input settings

	MaxEnc	RnnEnc	SelfAtt	ReSAtt
ESPN	14.01	16.32	13.93	16.43

Table 5: Results of different encoding methods over ESPN dataset

Template is a method that replaces the words occurring in both the table and the training sentences with a special token reflecting its field. (2) StructAware (Liu et al., 2018) is a structure-aware encoder-decoder architecture which using a modified LSTM unit and a specific attention mechanism to incorporate the attribute information. (3) Slug2Slug is an ensemble neural method that re-ranks several neural outputs during inference.

From table 3, the results show that three encoders achieves comparable results on E2E dataset, as the input of E2E is relatively short and simple. For WIKIBIO, the simple max-pooling encoder MaxEnc performs worse than the bidirectional LSTM encoder RnnEnc. The proposed method SelfAtt which capture the dependencies between arbitrary records yields better results compared to MaxEnc, and achieves comparable results with respect to RnnEnc. The result suggests modeling the dependencies among input records can yield better performance when the input is long and complex. More importantly, recurrent encoders only capture sequential dependencies, which is sensitive to the order of input records. To investigate the robustness of different table encoders, we design random shuffling noise over input data. For example, the original order of the input is "Birth name; Genres; Occupation; Associated Acts", and the order after random shuffling can be "'Geners; Birth name; Associated Acts; Occupation'. Note that we do not change the order of content inside a field. We apply such random shuffling noise on both training and testing stages. For model training, there are two choices: training on original input data Original or data with input random shuffling noise Shuffle. For testing, the trained model can be applied to the original input data or the shuffled version.

From the Table 4, We observe that the per-formance of RnnEnc drops dramatically when the input ordering information during training is different from the testing (i.e., the model trained on the original drops more than 15 BLEU scores when testing on input with random shuffling noise). In a slight difficult setting compared to original input, where both the input of training and testing are randomly shuffled, the performance of RnnEnc also decreases (i.e., 0.71 and 1.34 BLEU score decrease on E2E and WIKIBIO respectively). On the contrary, both MaxEnc and SelfAtt are less sensitive to the change of record ordering information, and the performance of both models under different shuffling noise are more stable than RnnEnc. The experimental results further confirms that using order invariant encoding SelfAtt is stable and suitable for table encoder.

3.4 Limitations of Self-Attention Mechanism

The self-attention table encoder achieves comparable performance with respect to recurrent table encoders on E2E and WIKIBIO datasets. However, the input of these two datasets are relatively short. To investigate the performance of self-attention mechanism on capturing long range dependencies, we conduct SelfAtt on a recently proposed NBA dataset ESPN (Nie et al., 2018), where the average input length 165.9 and average field number is 134.2. The results on ESPN are shown in Table 5. The SelfAtt has difficulty in learning such long range dependencies and performs worse than RnnEnc. When applying a restricted self-attention ReSAtt (Wang et al., 2018), where we limit the self-attention mechanism to capture dependencies within a fixed window size (set to 10 in the experiments), the result of `ReSAtt` performs comparable with respect to `RnnEnc`, despite this type of method is not order invariant. Handling long range dependencies for input data that is non-sensitive to the order of input data is a potential future work.

4 Conclusion

In this paper, we analyze several existing encoding methods for neural data-to-text generation. We find that modeling the dependency among the input records can yield better generation results. However, current recurrent table encoders can only model the sequential dependencies which is sensitive to the input order. We propose using self-attention for table encoder that can capture the dependencies and remains stable at the same time. In the future, we will analyze the explicit dependencies that lies in the input data, and improve the performance of encoding methods.

5 Acknowledgement

We thank the anonymous reviewers for helpful comments. The contact author of this paper, according to the meaning given to this role by Sun Yat-Sen University, is Rong Pan.

References

Gabor Angeli, Percy Liang, and Dan Klein. 2010. A simple domain-independent probabilistic approach to generation. In *EMNLP*, pages 502–512.

Dzmitry Bahdanau, Kyunghyun Cho, and Yoshua Bengio. 2015. Neural machine translation by jointly learning to align and translate. *ICLR*.

Regina Barzilay and Mirella Lapata. 2005. Collective content selection for concept-to-text generation. In *EMNLP*, pages 331–338.

Andrew Chisholm, Will Radford, and Ben Hachey. 2017. Learning to generate one-sentence biographies from wikidata. *CoRR*, abs/1702.06235.

Ondřej Dušek and Filip Jurcicek. 2016. Sequence-to-sequence generation for spoken dialogue via deep syntax trees and strings. In *ACL*.

Albert Gatt and Emiel Krahmer. 2018. Survey of the state of the art in natural language generation: Core tasks, applications and evaluation. *J. Artif. Intell. Res.*, 61:65–170.

Chloé Kiddon, Luke Zettlemoyer, and Yejin Choi. 2016. Globally coherent text generation with neural checklist models. In *EMNLP*, pages 329–339.

Joohyun Kim and Raymond J. Mooney. 2010. Generative alignment and semantic parsing for learning from ambiguous supervision. In *COLING*, pages 543–551.

Guillaume Klein, Yoon Kim, Yuntian Deng, Jean Senellart, and Alexander M. Rush. 2017. OpenNMT: Open-source toolkit for neural machine translation. In *Proc. ACL*.

Karen Kukich. 1983. Design of a knowledge-based report generator. In *ACL*, pages 145–150.

Rémi Lebret, David Grangier, and Michael Auli. 2016. Neural text generation from structured data with application to the biography domain. In *EMNLP*, pages 1203–1213.

Percy Liang, Michael I. Jordan, and Dan Klein. 2009. Learning semantic correspondences with less supervision. In *ACL*, pages 91–99.

Tianyu Liu, Kexiang Wang, Lei Sha, Baobao Chang, and Zhifang Sui. 2018. Table-to-text generation by structure-aware seq2seq learning. In *AAAI*, pages 4881–4888. AAAI Press.

Hongyuan Mei, Mohit Bansal, and Matthew R. Walter. 2016. What to talk about and how? selective generation using lstms with coarse-to-fine alignment. In *NAACL*, pages 720–730.

Feng Nie, Jinpeng Wang, Jin-Ge Yao, Rong Pan, and Chin-Yew Lin. 2018. Operation-guided neural networks for high fidelity data-to-text generation. In *EMNLP*, pages 3879–3889. Association for Computational Linguistics.

Jekaterina Novikova, Ondřej Dušek, and Verena Rieser. 2017. The E2E dataset: New challenges for end-to-end generation. In *Proceedings of the 18th Annual Meeting of the Special Interest Group on Discourse and Dialogue*, Saarbrücken, Germany. ArXiv:1706.09254.

Kishore Papineni, Salim Roukos, Todd Ward, and Wei-Jing Zhu. 2002. Bleu: a method for automatic evaluation of machine translation. In *ACL*, pages 311–318.

Laura Perez-Beltrachini and Claire Gardent. 2017. Analysing data-to-text generation benchmarks. In *INLG*, pages 238–242.

Ehud Reiter and Robert Dale. 1997. Building applied natural language generation systems. *Natural Language Engineering*, 3(1):57–87.

Abigail See, Peter J. Liu, and Christopher D. Manning. 2017. Get to the point: Summarization with pointer-generator networks. In *ACL*, pages 1073–1083. Association for Computational Linguistics.

Ilya Sutskever, Oriol Vinyals, and Quoc V. Le. 2014. Sequence to sequence learning with neural networks. In *NIPS*, pages 3104–3112.

Ashish Vaswani, Noam Shazeer, Niki Parmar, Jakob Uszkoreit, Llion Jones, Aidan N Gomez, Ł ukasz Kaiser, and Illia Polosukhin. Attention is all you need. In *Advances in Neural Information Processing Systems 30*.

Wenhui Wang, Nan Yang, Furu Wei, Baobao Chang, and Ming Zhou. 2017. Gated self-matching networks for reading comprehension and question answering. In *Proceedings of the 55th Annual Meeting of the Association for Computational Linguistics (Volume 1: Long Papers)*, pages 189–198. Association for Computational Linguistics.

Yizhong Wang, Sujian Li, and Jingfeng Yang. 2018. Toward fast and accurate neural discourse segmentation. In *Proceedings of the 2018 Conference on Empirical Methods in Natural Language Processing*, pages 962–967. Association for Computational Linguistics.

Zichao Yang, Phil Blunsom, Chris Dyer, and Wang Ling. 2017. Reference-aware language models. In *EMNLP*, pages 1850–1859.

On Leveraging the Visual Modality for Neural Machine Translation

Vikas Raunak[*] **Sang Keun Choe**[*] **Quanyang Lu**[*] **Yi Xu**[*] **Florian Metze**
Carnegie Mellon University
`{vraunak, sangkeuc, qlv, yx2, fmetze}@andrew.cmu.edu`

Abstract

Leveraging the visual modality effectively for Neural Machine Translation (NMT) remains an open problem in computational linguistics. Recently, Caglayan et al. posit that the observed gains are limited mainly due to the very simple, short, repetitive sentences of the Multi30k dataset (the only multimodal MT dataset available at the time), which renders the source text sufficient for context. In this work, we further investigate this hypothesis on a new large scale multimodal Machine Translation (MMT) dataset, How2, which has 1.57 times longer mean sentence length than Multi30k and no repetition. We propose and evaluate three novel fusion techniques, each of which is designed to ensure the utilization of visual context at different stages of the Sequence-to-Sequence transduction pipeline, even under full linguistic context. However, we still obtain only marginal gains under full linguistic context and posit that visual embeddings extracted from deep vision models (ResNet for Multi30k, ResNext for How2) do not lend themselves to increasing the discriminativeness between the vocabulary elements at token level prediction in NMT. We demonstrate this qualitatively by analyzing attention distribution and quantitatively through Principal Component Analysis, arriving at the conclusion that it is the quality of the visual embeddings rather than the length of sentences, which need to be improved in existing MMT datasets.

1 Introduction

A number of works have explored integrating the visual modality for Neural Machine Translation (NMT) models, though, there has been relatively modest gains or no gains at all by incorporating the visual modality in the translation pipeline (Caglayan et al., 2019). In particular, Elliott and Kádár (2017) leverage multi-task learning,

Sanabria et al. (2018a) use visual adaptive training, while Caglayan et al. (2016); Libovický and Helcl (2017); Huang et al. (2016) use a number of fusion techniques to incorporate features obtained from the visual modality.

Regarding the seemingly low utility of visual modality in machine translation, Lazaridou et al. (2014) hypothesize that the highly relevant visual properties are often not represented by linguistic models because they are too obvious to be explicitly mentioned in text (e.g., birds have wings, violins are brown). Similarly, Louwerse (2011) argue that perceptual information is already sufficiently encoded in textual cues. However, recently Caglayan et al. (2019) have demonstrated that neural models are capable of leveraging the visual modality for translations, and posit that it is the nature of the Multi30k dataset (the only multimodal machine translation dataset at the time) which is inhibiting gains from the visual modality to emerge, due to the presence of short, simple and repetitive sentences, which renders the source text as sufficient context for translation. In this work, we further investigate this hypothesis on a large-scale multimodal machine translation (MMT) dataset, named How2 (Sanabria et al., 2018a), which has 1.57 times longer sentences, in terms of the mean sentence length, when compared to Multi30k [1].

To this end, we restrict ourselves to the Sequence-to-Sequence (Seq2Seq) framework and propose three simple but novel fusion techniques to ensure the utilization of visual context during different stages (Input Context Encoding, Attention and Supervision) of the Sequence-to-Sequence transduction pipeline. We then evaluate and ana-

---

[1]Mean Sentence Lengths (in terms of words) are computed post tokenization on the training set for the English language. How2 has a mean sentence length of 20.6, a median of 17, when compared to the mean sentence length of 13 and a median length of 12 for Multi30k
[*] Equal Contribution

Proceedings of The 12th International Conference on Natural Language Generation, pages 147–151,
Tokyo, Japan, 28 Oct - 1 Nov, 2019. ©2019 Association for Computational Linguistics

lyze the results for further insights, with the goal of testing the utility of visual modality for NMT under full source-side linguistic context.

2 Proposed Fusion Techniques

In this section, we describe three additions to the Seq2Seq model to ensure that the visual context is utilized at different stages, namely when computing context during each step of the decoder, during attention as well as when computing the supervision signal in the Sequence-to-Sequence pipeline. This is done to encourage the Seq2Seq NMT model to make use of the visual features under full linguistic context. In each case, we assume that the visual features are fine-tuned using a visual encoder, which is trained jointly alongside the Seq2Seq model.

2.1 Step-Wise Decoder Fusion

Our first proposed technique is the step-wise decoder fusion of visual features during every prediction step i.e. we concatenate the visual encoding as context at each step of the decoding process. This differs from the usual practice of passing the visual feature only at the beginning of the decoding process (Huang et al., 2016).

2.2 Multimodal Attention Modulation

Similar to general attention (Luong et al., 2015), wherein a variable-length alignment vector $a_{th}(s)$, whose size equals the number of time steps on the source side, is derived by comparing the current target hidden state h_t with each source hidden state $\overline{h_s}$; we consider a variant wherein the visual encoding v_t is used to calculate an attention distribution $a_{tv}(s)$ over the source encodings as well. Then, the true attention distribution $a_t(s)$ is computed as an interpolation between the visual and text based attention scores. The score function is a content based scoring mechanism as usual.

$$a_{tv}(s) = \text{align}\left(v_t, \overline{h}_s\right)$$

$$a_{tv}(s) = \frac{\exp\left(\text{score}\left(v_t, \overline{h}_s\right)\right)}{\sum_{s'} \exp\left(\text{score}\left(v_t, \overline{h}_{s'}\right)\right)}$$

$$\text{score}\left(v_t, \overline{h}_s\right) = v_t^\top W_v \overline{h}_s$$

$$a_t(s) = (1 - \gamma) \cdot a_{th}(s) + \gamma \cdot a_{tv}(s)$$

This formulation differs from Caglayan et al. (2016) in that we use both the natural language as well as the visual modality to compute attention over the source sentence, rather than having

attention over images. Since attention is computed over the same source embeddings (arising from a single encoder) using two different modalities, our approach also differs from Libovický and Helcl (2017), which focuses on combining the attention scores of multiple source encoders.

2.3 Visual-Semantic (VS) Regularizer

In terms of leveraging the visual modality for supervision, Elliott and Kádár (2017) use multi-task learning to learn grounded representations through image representation prediction. However, to our knowledge, visual-semantic supervision hasn't been much explored for multimodal translation in terms of loss functions.

Our proposed technique is the inclusion of visual-semantic supervision to the machine translation model. Recently, Chen et al. (2019) proposed an optimal transport based loss function which computes the distance between the word embeddings [2] of the predicted sentence and the target sentence and uses it as a regularizer $L_{\text{ot}}^{\text{tgt}}$. The purpose of this term is to provide the model with sequence level supervision. We leverage this idea by including a Cosine distance term, $L_{\text{cosine}}^{\text{visual}}$, between the visual encoding (which is at the sentence level) and the target/predicted sentence embeddings (computed as the average of the target/predicted word embeddings). The purpose of this distance term is to provide sequence level supervision by aligning the visual and text embeddings. In practice, as in Chen et al. (2019), we introduce a hyperparameter in the loss function:

$$L = (1 - \gamma) \cdot L_{\text{mle}} + \gamma \cdot (L_{\text{ot}}^{\text{tgt}} + L_{\text{cosine}}^{\text{visual}}),$$

where γ is a hyper-parameter balancing the effect of loss components (a separate hyperparameter than in Section 2.2).

3 Results and Analysis

Throughout our experiments, we use the 300 hours subset of How2 [3] dataset (Sanabria et al., 2018b), which contains 300 hours of videos, sentence-level time alignments to the ground-truth English subtitles, and Portuguese translations of English subtitles. The How2 dataset has 2048 dimensional pre-trained ResNeXt embeddings (Xie et al., 2017)

---

[2] The embeddings are obtained from the Decoder's embedding layer.

[3] https://github.com/srvk/how2-dataset

Methods	BLEU	Improvement
Baseline (En-Pt)	51.32	
+ Decoder Fusion (En-Pt)	51.79	**+0.47**
+ Multimodal Attention (En-Pt)	51.85	**+0.53**
+ VS Regularization (En-Pt)	52.00	**+0.68**

Table 1: BLEU Score Comparison of the proposed methods

Methods	BLEU	Improvement
Baseline (Pt-En)	49.12	
+ Decoder Fusion (Pt-En)	49.68	**+0.56**
+ Multimodal Attention (Pt-En)	49.49	**+0.37**
+ VS Regularization (Pt-En)	49.31	**+0.19**

Table 2: BLEU Score Comparison of the proposed methods

available for each of the video clips aligned to the sentences.

Further, our baseline model is the canonical Seq2Seq model (Sutskever et al., 2014) consisting of bidirectional LSTM as encoder and decoder, general attention (Luong et al., 2015) and length normalization (Wu et al., 2016). In all cases, we use the embedding size of 300 and the hidden size of 512. Whenever the visual modality is used, we encode each of the visual features to 300 dimensional vectors through an encoder (consisting of a Linear layer followed by Batch Normalization and ReLU non-linearity) which is also trained end-to-end with the Seq2Seq model. Further, to integrate sequence level supervision as in Chen et al. (2019), we utilize the Geomloss library [4], which provides a batched implementation of the Sinkhorn algorithm for the Optimal Transport computation. For all the translation experiments, we preprocess the data by lowercasing and removing the punctuations (Sanabria et al., 2018a), and construct vocabulary at word level. Adam optimizer with a learning rate of 0.001 and a learning rate decay of 0.5 is used throughout to train our models.

3.1 Experimental Results

The performances of the models are summarized in Table 1, along with the gains in BLEU points. From Table 1, we can make a few observations:

1. The visual modality leads to modest gains in BLEU scores. The proposed VS regularizer leads to slightly higher gain when compared to Decoder-Fusion and Attention modulation techniques for the En-Pt language pair.

[4]https://github.com/jeanfeydy/geomloss

2. Further, the gains from incorporating the visual modality are less for Multimodal Attention and VS Regularization in the case of the reversed language pair of Pt-En (Table 2), even though the visual modality is common to both the languages. This can possibly be attributed to the How2 dataset creation process wherein first the videos were aligned with English sentences and then the Portuguese translations were created, implying a reduction in correspondence with the visual modality due to errors introduced in the translation process.

3.2 Discussion

To analyze the reasons for modest gains, despite incorporating multiple techniques to effectively leverage the visual modality for machine translation, we inspect the dataset as well as the proposed mechanisms.

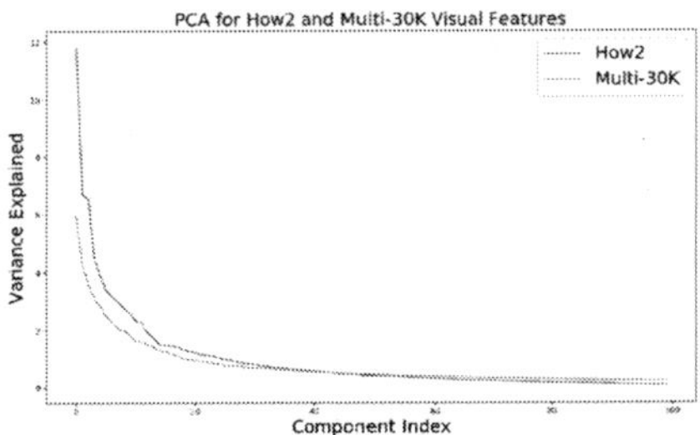
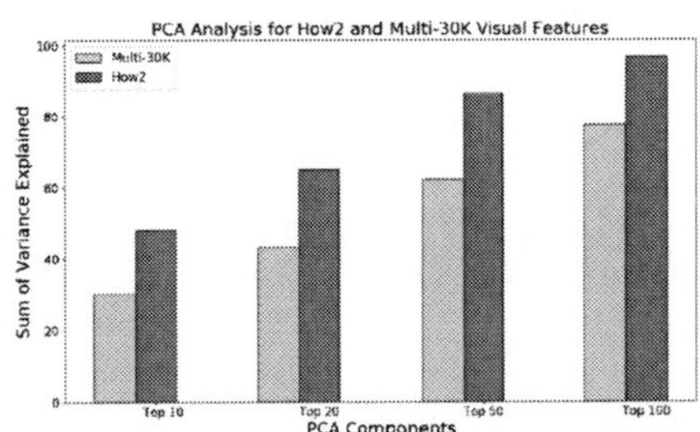

Figure 1: **Top**: Variance Explained by the Top 100 Components. **Bottom**: Cumulative Variance Explained by the Top Components.

3.2.1 PCA of Visual Features

We first investigate and compare the visual feature quality of the How2 dataset with respect to that of the Multi30k dataset [5]. To analyze the discriminativeness of the visual features for both of these datasets, we leverage an analysis mechanism used

[5]https://github.com/multi30k/dataset

in Mu and Viswanath (2018) in the context of analyzing word embedding discriminativeness. We analyze the variance of the visual features corresponding to each sentence in the training set. Since the visual features semantically represent the sentence as well, we could analyze how well the features are able to discriminate between the sentences and consequently between the individual words, as a measure of their utility for NMT.

Figure 1 (Top) shows the variance explained by the Top 100 principal components, obtained by applying PCA on the How2 and Multi30k training set visual features. The original feature dimensions are 2048 in both the cases. It is clear from the Figure 1 that most of the energy of the visual feature space resides in a low-dimensional subspace (Mu and Viswanath, 2018). In other words, there exist a few directions in the embedding space which disproportionately explain the variance. These "common" directions affect all of the embeddings in the same way, rendering them less discriminative. Figure 1 also shows the cumulative variance explained by Top 10, 20, 50 and 100 principal components respectively. It is clear that the visual features in the case of How2 dataset are much more dominated by the "common" dimensions, when compared to the Multi30k dataset. Further, this analysis is still at the sentence level, i.e. the visual features are much less discriminative among individual sentences, further aggravating the problem at the token level. This suggests that the existing visual features aren't sufficient enough to expect benefits from the visual modality in NMT, since they won't provide discriminativeness among the vocabulary elements at the token level during prediction. Further, this also indicates that under subword vocabulary such as BPE (Sennrich et al., 2015) or Sentence-Piece (Kudo and Richardson, 2018), the utility of such visual embeddings will only aggravate.

3.2.2 Comparison of Attention Components

In this section, we analyze the visual and text based attention mechanisms. We find that the visual attention is very sparse, in that just one source encoding is attended to (the maximum visual attention over source encodings, across the test set, has mean 0.99 and standard deviation 0.015), thereby limiting the use of modulation. Thus, in practice, we find that a small weight ($\gamma = 0.1$) is necessary to prevent degradation due to this sparse visual attention component. Figure 2 & 3 shows the comparison of visual and text based attention for two sentences,

one long source sentence of length 21 and one short source sentence of length 7. In both cases, we find that the visual component of the attention hasn't learnt any variation over the source encodings, again suggesting that the visual embeddings do not lend themselves to enhancing token-level discriminativess during prediction. We find this to be consistent across sentences of different lengths.

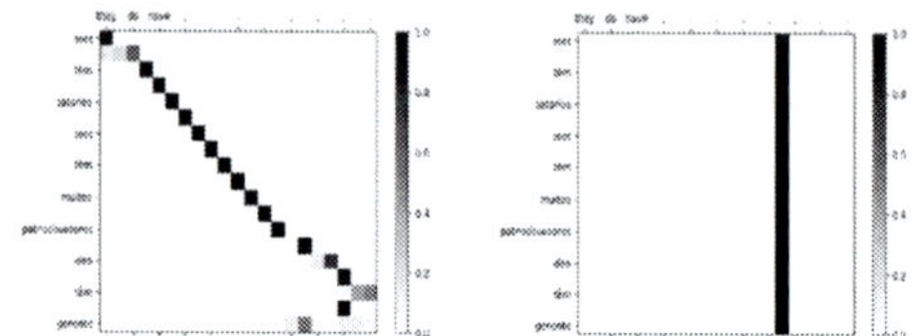

Figure 2: **Left**: Text Based Attention (Horizontal Direction Represents the Source Sentence) **Right**: Visual Attention for a 21 word Source Sentence (Labels omitted to avoid cluttering).

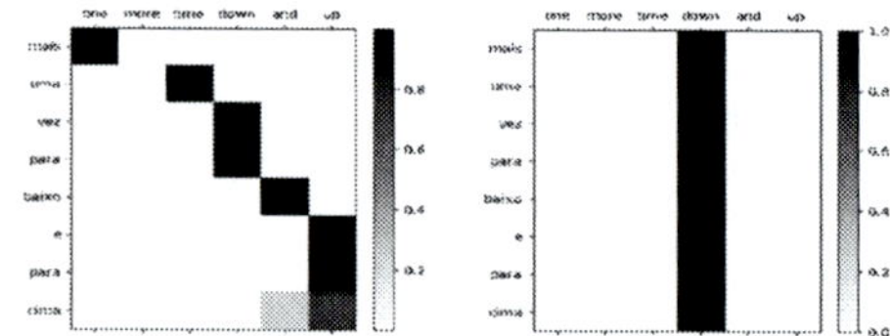

Figure 3: **Left**: Text Based Attention (Horizontal Direction Represents the Source Sentence) **Right**: Visual Attention for a 7 word Source Sentence.

4 Conclusions and Future Work

To conclude, we investigated the utility of visual modality for NMT, under full linguistic context on a new large-scale MMT dataset named How2. Our results on the How2 dataset confirm the general consensus that the visual modality does not lead to any significant gains for NMT, however, unlike Caglayan et al. (2019) we attribute the relatively modest gains to the limited discriminativeness offered by the existing visual features, rather than the length of the sentences in the dataset. We validate this hypothesis quantitatively through a PCA based analysis of the visual features as well as qualitatively by analyzing attention components. We hope that our work would lead to more useful techniques and better visual features for MMT. An immediate future direction to explore would be to construct more discriminative features for utilizing the visual modality in NMT.

References

Ozan Caglayan, Loïc Barrault, and Fethi Bougares. 2016. Multimodal attention for neural machine translation. *arXiv preprint arXiv:1609.03976*.

Ozan Caglayan, Pranava Madhyastha, Lucia Specia, and Loïc Barrault. 2019. Probing the need for visual context in multimodal machine translation. *arXiv preprint arXiv:1903.08678*.

Liqun Chen, Yizhe Zhang, Ruiyi Zhang, Chenyang Tao, Zhe Gan, Haichao Zhang, Bai Li, Dinghan Shen, Changyou Chen, and Lawrence Carin. 2019. Improving sequence-to-sequence learning via optimal transport. *arXiv preprint arXiv:1901.06283*.

Desmond Elliott and Akos Kádár. 2017. Imagination improves multimodal translation. *arXiv preprint arXiv:1705.04350*.

Po-Yao Huang, Frederick Liu, Sz-Rung Shiang, Jean Oh, and Chris Dyer. 2016. Attention-based multimodal neural machine translation. In *Proceedings of the First Conference on Machine Translation: Volume 2, Shared Task Papers*, volume 2, pages 639–645.

Taku Kudo and John Richardson. 2018. Sentencepiece: A simple and language independent subword tokenizer and detokenizer for neural text processing. *arXiv preprint arXiv:1808.06226*.

Angeliki Lazaridou, Elia Bruni, and Marco Baroni. 2014. Is this a wampimuk? cross-modal mapping between distributional semantics and the visual world. In *Proceedings of the 52nd Annual Meeting of the Association for Computational Linguistics (Volume 1: Long Papers)*, volume 1, pages 1403–1414.

Jindřich Libovický and Jindřich Helcl. 2017. Attention strategies for multi-source sequence-to-sequence learning. *arXiv preprint arXiv:1704.06567*.

Max M Louwerse. 2011. Symbol interdependency in symbolic and embodied cognition. *Topics in Cognitive Science*, 3(2):273–302.

Minh-Thang Luong, Hieu Pham, and Christopher D Manning. 2015. Effective approaches to attention-based neural machine translation. *arXiv preprint arXiv:1508.04025*.

Jiaqi Mu and Pramod Viswanath. 2018. All-but-the-top: Simple and effective postprocessing for word representations. In *International Conference on Learning Representations*.

Ramon Sanabria, Ozan Caglayan, Shruti Palaskar, Desmond Elliott, Loïc Barrault, Lucia Specia, and Florian Metze. 2018a. How2: A large-scale dataset for multimodal language understanding. *CoRR*, abs/1811.00347.

Ramon Sanabria, Ozan Caglayan, Shruti Palaskar, Desmond Elliott, Loïc Barrault, Lucia Specia, and Florian Metze. 2018b. How2: A large-scale dataset for multimodal language understanding. *CoRR*, abs/1811.00347.

Rico Sennrich, Barry Haddow, and Alexandra Birch. 2015. Neural machine translation of rare words with subword units. *arXiv preprint arXiv:1508.07909*.

Ilya Sutskever, Oriol Vinyals, and Quoc V Le. 2014. Sequence to sequence learning with neural networks. In *Advances in neural information processing systems*, pages 3104–3112.

Yonghui Wu, Mike Schuster, Zhifeng Chen, Quoc V Le, Mohammad Norouzi, Wolfgang Macherey, Maxim Krikun, Yuan Cao, Qin Gao, Klaus Macherey, et al. 2016. Google's neural machine translation system: Bridging the gap between human and machine translation. *arXiv preprint arXiv:1609.08144*.

Saining Xie, Ross Girshick, Piotr Dollár, Zhuowen Tu, and Kaiming He. 2017. Aggregated residual transformations for deep neural networks. In *Proceedings of the IEEE conference on computer vision and pattern recognition*, pages 1492–1500.

Tell Me More: A Dataset of Visual
Scene Description Sequences

Nikolai Ilinykh
Dialogue Systems Group
Bielefeld University
nikolai.ilinykh@uni-bielefeld.de

Sina Zarrieß *
Digital Humanities
University of Jena
sina.zarriess@uni-jena.de

David Schlangen *
Computational Linguistics
University of Potsdam
david.schlangen@uni-potsdam.de

Abstract

We present a dataset consisting of what we call *image description sequences*. These multi-sentence descriptions of the contents of an image were collected in a pseudo-interactive setting, where the describer was told to describe the given image to a listener who needs to identify the image within a set of images, and who successively asks for more information. As we show, this setup produced nicely structured data that, we think, will be useful for learning models capable of planning and realising such description discourses.

1 Introduction

Talking about what one sees brings together several core competences of situated agents: to *understand* the world in terms of objects and their attributes and mutual relations, and to be able to *name* these objects, attributes, and relations, and to *compose* linguistic expressions from that, for the given addressee and under the constraints of the given communicative intention.

Many of the decisions involved in this do not only require general visual and linguistic competences, but are well-known to be affected by the task, the context and the intended addressee. Consequently, recent progress in the area of NLG, Language & Vision has been made by moving from generic settings like image captioning (Lin et al., 2014; Chen et al., 2015; Hodosh et al., 2013; Plummer et al., 2015) to *task-oriented* settings like referring expression generation (Kazemzadeh et al., 2014; Yu et al., 2016) or interactive visual question answering (Das et al., 2017; De Vries et al., 2017). As shown by Ilinykh et al. (2018), task-based image descriptions substantially differ in terms of their linguistic properties (e.g. occurrence of referring expressions, attribute types) from their "neutral" counterparts.

An orthogonal development has been to move towards longer units of text as the desired output. A few datasets exist that pair longer natural language texts (like full *paragraphs*) with single images that they are meant to describe (Krause et al., 2017; Lin et al., 2015). These constitute a challenging testbed for state-of-the-art models in NLG where common tasks from Language & Vision need to be connected to core aspects of text generation such as content selection, text structuring, or aggregation.[1] On the "interactivity" dimension, however, these datasets constitute a step back to a monological setting. While the instructions to the annotators were to imagine that they describe an image for an imagined partner, they were allowed to edit the paragraph in the usual way, thus creating something that is more akin to a text than to a task-oriented contribution to an interaction.

We present a task and a dataset that is meant to combine aspects of those mentioned above. We have collected *image description sequences*, which are sequences of expressions that collectively are meant to single out one image from an (imagined) set of other similar images. These sequences were produced in a monological setting, but with the instruction to imagine they were provided to a partner who successively asked for more information (hence, "tell me more").[2] We believe that such setting at least partially resembles dialogical interaction between humans, and, therefore, we refer to a single expression in a sequence as *a turn*. In the user interface, this sequential / incremental aspect was stressed by offering separate text input fields, rather than one block.

---

[1] See (Gatt and Krahmer, 2018) for a survey on this traditional area in NLG.

[2] This setting is somewhat similar to that of Lin et al. (2015), who collected texts meant to describe a scene to someone who can't see it, but it is tuned even more towards (imagined) interaction. We also collected data for about 4 times as many images.

*Work done while at Bielefeld University.

Proceedings of The 12th International Conference on Natural Language Generation, pages 152–157,
Tokyo, Japan, 28 Oct - 1 Nov, 2019. ©2019 Association for Computational Linguistics

1: *This is a large bedroom with two large windows, a bed, and a two person chaise lounge.*

2: *The windows have striped curtains in front of them and a curtain rod that goes over both windows.*

3: *There is a ceiling light and fan in the center of the room.*

4: *There are two large pictures above the bed and dark colored nightstands on both sides.*

5: *There are table lights on the nightstands and several plants throughout the room.*

Figure 1: An image / description sequence pair

As the example in Figure 1 illustrates, the sequences bring together higher level summarising descriptions ("a large bedroom") with more detailed descriptions of individual objects in the scene and their relations (e.g., "a curtain rod that goes over both windows"), and they form mini-*discourses* that are cohesive (co-references, e.g. "a bed" – "the bed") and coherent (elaborations of descriptions of individual objects followed by descriptions of other objects). The sequence as a whole can be seen as providing a single fine-grained description which is delivered in *installments* (Clark, 1996).[3]

The research questions to which we aim to contribute are: How is the selection made of objects, attributes, and relations that are to be mentioned? How is the selection serialised and prioritized to form the sequence, and how are later turns in the sequence influenced by earlier ones? Ultimately, we want models derived from this dataset to also contribute to interactive description generation where parts of the sequence may come from different participants. More immediately, however, the combination of visual grounding and successive discourse planning seems already challenging.

---

[3]But note that this is just an approximation, for the sake of allowing for a more controlled data collection. A truly interactive setting, such as in Ilinykh et al. (2019), will turn up additional phenomena like clarification requests and corrections, from which we wanted to abstract away here.

2   The Dataset

2.1   Data Collection

Images   As our material on the visual side, we used a part of the ADE20k corpus (Zhou et al., 2017), which consists of images of indoor and outdoor environmental scenes that come with pixel-level object labels. We chose visual scenes as image subject matter, rather than the more event or single-object oriented settings that dominate other corpora, because scenes afford a natural high-level categorisation (e.g., "a bathroom") that triggers expectations about objects that are present (e.g., "a sink"), while at the same time still allowing for a wide variety in how they are composed (e.g., what shape or colour the sink has, what material it is made of, where it is placed). This turns the task into a fine-grained classification task, where unlike in other such settings— e.g., the CUB corpus of images of bird species, (Wah et al., 2011)—there is no single label that fully categorises the instance. To further reinforce this, we used only such images which belong to one of the 35 house-related image categories specified in the 'indoor/home or hotel' section of the SUN image hierarchy (Xiao et al., 2016), which this corpus follows; the corpus as a whole contains also more esoteric scene categories where these expectations may not hold.

We have noticed that the first largest category ("bedroom") is oversampled with nearly twice as many images as the second largest category in each scene set; we hence reduced this to the same size as the next largest categories (bathroom, living room, kitchen). In total, we selected 4,410 images of house indoor and outdoor visual scenes, for which the corpus provides 165,088 annotated objects (for an average of 37 objects per image). The data has been divided into three disjoint subsets: 3528 images in the train set, 441 in the validation and test sets (80/10/10).

Crowd-sourcing   The data collection has been conducted on Amazon Mechanical Turk (AMT). We created a task (according to AMT terminology, a HIT), in which workers were presented with an image that they could zoom into, a set of instructions, and 5 text fields in which to enter the subsequent turns. Providing separate text fields was meant to encourage the workers to indeed treat the turns as separate, and set up a small obstacle discouraging editing of earlier turns.

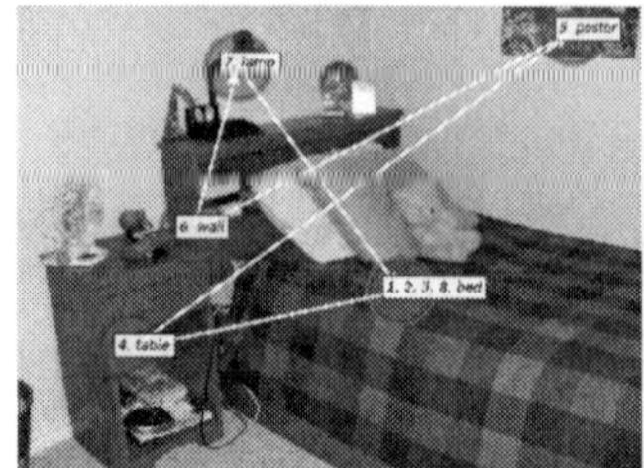

1: This is a boys bedroom with a teddy bear on the *bed*[1].
2: The *bed*[2] has a plaid blue *bed*[3] spread.
3: The head board and side *table*[4] are painted blue.
4: There is a *poster*[5] on the *wall*[6].
5: A *lamp*[7] is situated over the *bed*[8] to read with.

(a) Scene type: kids' room

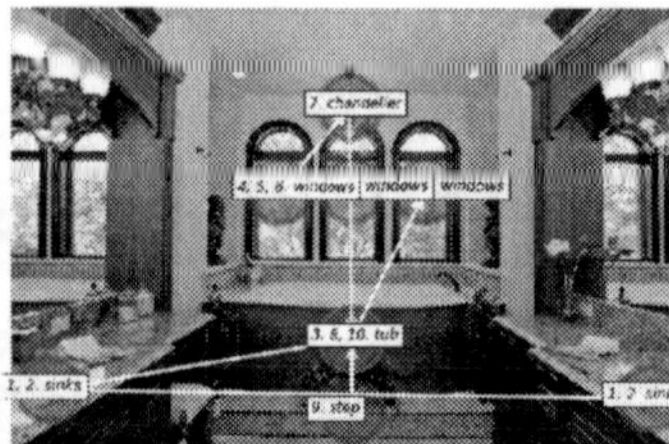

1: It is a very fancy bathroom.
2: There are twin *sinks*[1,2] across from each other.
3: There is a deep soaking *tub*[3] in front of 3 domed *windows*[4,5,6].
4: There is a very fancy *chandelier*[7] over the *bathtub*[8] and everything is done in brown woods and granite.
5: There is a *step*[9] up to the *bathtub*[10].

(b) Scene type: bathroom

1: there is a *couch*[1] white striped brown
2: there is a *window*[2] behind the *couch*[3] the view outside is beautiful
3: there is a side *table*[4] beside the *couch*[5]
4: there is a *statue*[6] on the side *table*[7]
5: there is a *plant*[8] behind the *couch*[9]

(c) Scene type: living room

Figure 2: Examples of visual scenes with corresponding IDS. The results of the linking are superimposed on the images, with the numbers indicating the position in the sequence and the nouns shown in italics. Nouns where a (correct) link could not be established are shown in red.

For each image, we collected a single description sequence. Table 1 in Appendix A gives the set of instructions that the workers were presented with when working on the HIT. We restricted the worker's location to English-speaking countries only and only used workers who had previously successfully completed more than 3000 HITs. For each sequence, we payed $0.15. In total, 297 workers submitted HITs with the top five participants completing over 80 tasks each. For comparison, in a separate task, we randomly chose almost 10% of the images in our subcorpus and collected traditional captions for them, using the COCO instructions (Chen et al., 2015) (at least 8 words, don't start with "there is", don't mention things that can't be seen).

General statistics Overall, we collected a sequence for each of the 4,410 images in our set, with a fixed number of 5 turns each and consequently resulting in 22,050 collected turns. A few turns contained more than one sentence, as indicated by using the nltk sentence splitter (Bird et al., 2009), yielding an average of 1.01 sentences per turn. There are 208,778 tokens altogether in the corpus, realising 5,124 token types. On average, each turn contains 9 tokens.

Preprocessing While there are various methods for unsupervised learning to ground phrases in images (e.g., Rohrbach et al., 2015; Wang et al., 2016), for now we went a simpler route and made use of the object level annotations provided by the ADE corpus. More specifically, we tried to link nouns in the sequences with labels of objects in the corpus, going first by string matches and then by similarity in a vector space (where we used the GoogleNews vectors provided by Mikolov et al. (2013)). For plural nouns, we took their singular form; if the image had a set of objects marked with the same label, a matching noun would be linked to all of them. If singular nouns matched more than one object, we selected the one with the biggest bounding box. Out of all noun candidates for linking, 30,198 nouns were linked with 45,324 annotated objects (that is, on average each noun was linked to 1.5 objects). On a manually annotated small set (44 sequences), the best linking method (testing various weightings and similarity thresholds) reached a precision of 0.77, recall 0.64, and 0.70 f-score; the numbers provided next are hence somewhat noisy. We note that our linking method ignores any adnominal dependents (determiners, adjectives, etc.), and, therefore, has no capability to resolve ambiguity between objects of the same type, but with different attributes ("red chair" vs. "blue chair"). We leave this for the future work. Some examples with the computed links are shown in Figure 2.

3 Data Analysis

Sequence Structure Looking at the validation set, we noticed that there is a characteristic structure to the sequences. Typically, the first turn provides a classification of the scene using the expected labels ("a bathroom", "a boys bedroom", as in Figure 2), with subsequent turns providing additional information about selected objects. Figure 3 shows the frequency distribution of initial 3-grams for the first turn (left) and for the remaining turns together, confirming this impression.

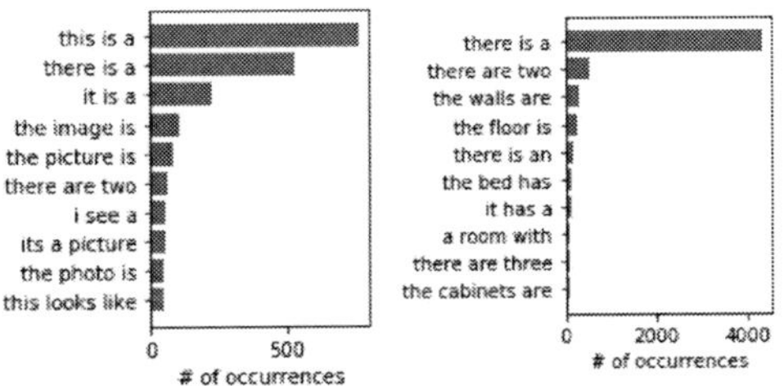

Figure 3: Frequency distribution of the first 10 trigram prefixes of the first sentences in first turn (left) compared to those in other sequence positions (right).

Our elicitation method enforced a natural split into discourse segments, by providing 5 separate text fields. We expect that the intentional structure, in the sense of Grosz and Sidner (1986), is flat, i.e. the whole sequence only serves the purpose of describing the image. The attentional structure of which object is in the center of attention, however, can be expected to be richer, as we discuss next.

What gets mentioned? Using the linking method described above, we associate on average 10 objects in each scene to nouns in the description sequence. The ADE annotation contains on average 37 objects per image. This indicates that the describers did not simply describe the images exhaustively.

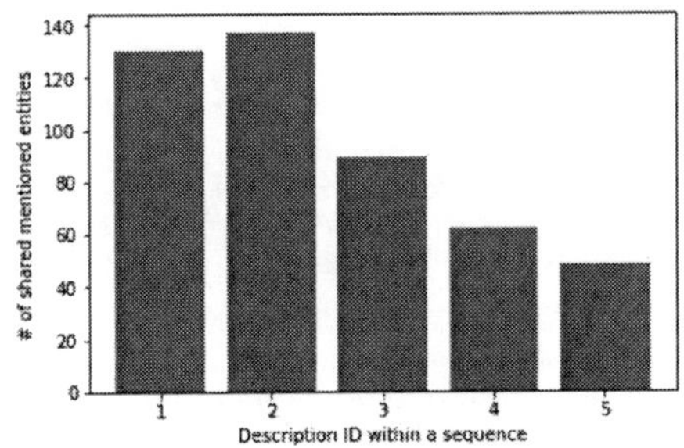

Figure 4: Position in the sequence of objects mentioned both in sequence and caption.

To investigate whether the sequences tend to mention salient objects first, we compared them to the captions that we collected for a subset of the corpus. In the collected captions, on average 3.7 links to image objects were found.

65% of all objects mentioned in all captions were also mentioned in the sequences, but only 32% of the objects mentioned in the sequences were mentioned in the captions. Figure 4 shows that objects mentioned in both caption and sequence tend to occur early in the sequence.

Co-reference We expected that this dataset would also provide interesting data for learning to co-refer, see e.g. Lin et al. (2015). The examples in Figure 2 illustrate the phenomenon. In each of the sequences, there is an object that is referred to repeatedly, and in all of them, it is the central or most salient one (the bed, the bathtub, the couch). As it should be, first mentions are indefinite NPs ("a deep soaking tub") and repeated mentions definite NPs ("the bathtub"). The exceptions are interesting as well: In Figure 2a, the definite "the bed" can be resolved as given with a bridging inference (Clark, 1977) linking it to "bedroom", and "the headboard" to "the bed". Pronominal co-reference occurs as well, with at least one pronoun, as determined via their POS tag as assigned by SpaCy (Honnibal and Montani, 2017), occurring in 42% of the sequences. We leave to future work an analysis of a larger part of the corpus in terms of the *centering* process assumed by Grosz et al. (1995) to underlie local coherence.

4   Conclusions

We have presented a dataset of in-depth descriptions of images of typical domestic scene types. The description sequences were elicited in a pseudo-interactive setting under the pretense of helping an imagined addressee to do a task, namely to identify the described image within a set of similar images. We have shown that the resulting data is rich in referring expressions, and poses interesting discourse planning challenges from the perspective of natural language generation. We hope that the data will be useful for training models that can perform in actual interactive settings and can realise descriptions of scenes in *installments*, similar to previous work on collaborative reference to objects (Fang et al., 2014; Zarrieß and Schlangen, 2016). Whether that is the case remains to be seen in future work.

References

Steven Bird, Ewan Klein, and Edward Loper. 2009. *Natural Language Processing with Python*, 1st edition. O'Reilly Media, Inc.

Xinlei Chen, Hao Fang, Tsung-Yi Lin, Ramakrishna Vedantam, Saurabh Gupta, Piotr Dollár, and C. Lawrence Zitnick. 2015. Microsoft COCO captions: Data collection and evaluation server. *CoRR*, abs/1504.00325.

Herbert Clark. 1977. Bridging. In Phillip N. Johnson-Laird and P. C. Wason, editors, *Thinking: Readings in Computer Science*, pages 411–420. Cambridge University Press, Cambridge, UK.

Herbert H. Clark. 1996. *Using Language*. Cambridge University Press, Cambridge.

Abhishek Das, Satwik Kottur, Khushi Gupta, Avi Singh, Deshraj Yadav, José MF Moura, Devi Parikh, and Dhruv Batra. 2017. Visual dialog. In *Proceedings of the IEEE Conference on Computer Vision and Pattern Recognition*, volume 2.

Harm De Vries, Florian Strub, Sarath Chandar, Olivier Pietquin, Hugo Larochelle, and Aaron Courville. 2017. Guesswhat?! visual object discovery through multi-modal dialogue. In *Proc. of CVPR*.

Rui Fang, Malcolm Doering, and Joyce Y Chai. 2014. Collaborative models for referring expression generation in situated dialogue. In *Twenty-Eighth AAAI Conference on Artificial Intelligence*.

Albert Gatt and Emiel Krahmer. 2018. Survey of the state of the art in natural language generation: Core tasks, applications and evaluation. *Journal of Artificial Intelligence Research*, 61:65–170.

Barbara Grosz, Aravind K. Joshi, and Scott Weinstein. 1995. Centering: A framework for modelling the local coherence of discourse. *Computational Linguistics*, 21(2):203–225.

Barbara J. Grosz and Candace L. Sidner. 1986. Attention, intentions, and the structure of discourse. *Comput. Linguist.*, 12(3):175–204.

Micah Hodosh, Peter Young, and Julia Hockenmaier. 2013. Framing image description as a ranking task: Data, models and evaluation metrics. *J. Artif. Int. Res.*, 47(1):853–899.

Matthew Honnibal and Ines Montani. 2017. spacy 2: Natural language understanding with bloom embeddings, convolutional neural networks and incremental parsing. *To appear.*

Nikolai Ilinykh, Sina Zarrieß, and David Schlangen. 2018. The task matters: Comparing image captioning and task-based dialogical image description. In *Proceedings of the 11th International Conference on Natural Language Generation*, pages 397–402, Tilburg University, The Netherlands. Association for Computational Linguistics.

Nikolai Ilinykh, Sina Zarrieß, and David Schlangen. 2019. Meetup! a corpus of joint activity dialogues in a visual environment. In *Proceedings of the 23rd Workshop on the Semantics and Pragmatics of Dialogue (SemDial 2019 / LondonLogue)*, London, UK.

Sahar Kazemzadeh, Vicente Ordonez, Mark Matten, and Tamara L Berg. 2014. ReferItGame: Referring to Objects in Photographs of Natural Scenes. In *Proceedings of the Conference on Empirical Methods in Natural Language Processing (EMNLP 2014)*, pages 787–798, Doha, Qatar.

Jonathan Krause, Justin Johnson, Ranjay Krishna, and Li Fei-Fei. 2017. A hierarchical approach for generating descriptive image paragraphs. In *Computer Vision and Pattern Recognition (CVPR)*.

Dahua Lin, Sanja Fidler, Chen Kong, and Raquel Urtasun. 2015. Generating multi-sentence natural language descriptions of indoor scenes. In *Proceedings of the British Machine Vision Conference (BMVC)*, pages 93.1–93.13. BMVA Press.

Tsung-Yi Lin, Michael Maire, Serge Belongie, James Hays, Pietro Perona, Deva Ramanan, Piotr Dollár, and C.Lawrence Zitnick. 2014. Microsoft coco: Common objects in context. In *Computer Vision – ECCV 2014*, volume 8693, pages 740–755. Springer International Publishing.

Tomas Mikolov, Kai Chen, Gregory S. Corrado, and Jeffrey Dean. 2013. Efficient estimation of word representations in vector space. *CoRR*, abs/1301.3781.

Bryan A. Plummer, Liwei Wang, Chris M. Cervantes, Juan C. Caicedo, Julia Hockenmaier, and Svetlana Lazebnik. 2015. Flickr30k entities: Collecting region-to-phrase correspondences for richer image-to-sentence models. *CoRR*, abs/1505.04870.

Anna Rohrbach, Marcus Rohrbach, Ronghang Hu, Trevor Darrell, and Bernt Schiele. 2015. Grounding of textual phrases in images by reconstruction. *CoRR*, abs/1511.03745.

C. Wah, S. Branson, P. Welinder, P. Perona, and S. Belongie. 2011. The Caltech-UCSD Birds-200-2011 Dataset. Technical Report CNS-TR-2011-001, California Institute of Technology.

Mingzhe Wang, Mahmoud Azab, Noriyuki Kojima, Rada Mihalcea, and Jia Deng. 2016. Structured matching for phrase localization. In *Computer Vision – ECCV 2016*, pages 696–711, Cham. Springer International Publishing.

Jianxiong Xiao, Krista A. Ehinger, James Hays, Antonio Torralba, and Aude Oliva. 2016. Sun database: Exploring a large collection of scene categories. *Int. J. Comput. Vision*, 119(1):3–22.

L. Yu, P. Poirson, S. Yang, A.C. Berg, and Berg T.L. 2016. Modeling context in referring expressions. In *Computer Vision – ECCV 2016*, volume 9906 of *Lecture Notes in Computer Science*. Springer.

Sina Zarrieß and David Schlangen. 2016. Easy things first: Installments improve referring expression generation for objects in photographs. In *Proceedings of the 54th Annual Meeting of the Association for Computational Linguistics (Volume 1: Long Papers)*, pages 610–620, Berlin, Germany. Association for Computational Linguistics.

Bolei Zhou, Hang Zhao, Xavier Puig, Sanja Fidler, Adela Barriuso, and Antonio Torralba. 2017. Scene parsing through ade20k dataset. In *Proceedings of the IEEE Conference on Computer Vision and Pattern Recognition*.

A   Instructions

Imagine that you are talking to someone over the phone, who sees a set of images of places. What you see is one image from this set. Your partner has to pick out the image that you see out of the set that they see.
What would you say?
Imagine that is a game and the both of you want to do this as quickly as possible. There are several text fields here. Imagine that your partner can't immediately find the image, and you want to offer more information, or phrase what you've said differently, until they find the image.
We will pay you (and accept your results) only if you (a) fill our all the text fields with descriptions, (b) provide reasonable descriptions, (c) properly follow the instructions. You can get an image zoomed in by clicking on it.

Table 1: The set of instructions for the non-interactive data collection. Workers additionally saw an image and five text fields that they were supposed to fill with descriptions.

A Closer Look at Recent Results of Verb Selection for Data-to-Text NLG

Guanyi Chen[*]
Utrecht University
`g.chen@uu.nl`

Jin-Ge Yao
Microsoft Research Asia
$jinge \cdot yao@microsoft \cdot com$

Abstract

Automatic natural language generation systems need to use the contextually-appropriate verbs when describing different kinds of facts or events, which has triggered research interest on verb selection for data-to-text generation. In this paper, we discuss a few limitations of the current task settings and the evaluation metrics. We also provide two simple, efficient, interpretable baseline approaches for statistical selection of trend verbs, which give a strong performance on both previously used evaluation metrics and our new evaluation.

1 Introduction

The authors of financial headlines often need to use appropriate verbs to describe a percentage change, sometimes also revealing its intensity. For instance, the verb *climb* in the headline *Microsoft's profit climbed 28%* expresses an upward direction, as well as the magnitude, of a percentage change. Likewise, an automatic natural language generation systems for data-to-text generation under similar scenarios should also properly select verbs as well. In earlier systems, neutral verbs such as *increase* and *decrease* that only describes the direction of changes were preferred for simplicity. However, the generated sentences can be more natural if automatic NLG systems could use a more diverse set of verb choices suitable in the context like human writers could do.

Due to the vagueness of word meaning and variations in word usage, data-driven methods are believed to be a reasonable choice for automatic systems (Reiter, 2018). Recently, there indeed exist several studies working towards this direction, with a special focus on statistical or probabilistic methods for selecting verbs to describe trends in percentages. In the most typical task settings,

a dataset is extracted from some sentences in a corpora describing percentage changes, with the form of $\mathcal{D} = \{(x_1, v_1), ..., (x_N, v_N)\}$, where x_i is the numeric value of the percentage change (e.g. 12.5%) and v_i is the verb used by human writers in the original sentence to describe the percentage change. Rising trends and falling trends were typically collected separately. The task is to train a verb selector $f(\cdot)$ aiming at mapping a new input percentage x_* to a verb v_*, or a distribution of appropriate verbs from which a verb could be randomly selected to form an utterance.

Thomson Reuters' NLG system (Plachouras et al., 2016) for macro-economic indicator and merger-and-acquisition deals data includes a submodule for trend verb selection (Smiley et al., 2016). For each verb, their system estimates the interquartile range (IQR) of its associated percentage changes from the corpus. Given a new percentage change, their method randomly selects a verb from those verbs whose IQRs could cover the specified percentage value.

One more recent work (Zhang et al., 2018) proposed a Bayesian probabilistic model by estimating the prior probability of each verb as well as the likelihood of seeing the percentage change given the verb. Their evaluation based on the mean reciprocal ranking (MRR) of the human-written verb suggests significant superiority over the Thomson Reuters' approach.

However, we notice that naively outputing the most frequently used verbs for upward / downward direction can perform surprisingly high in terms of a few automatic metrics on the dataset used by Zhang et al. (2018). In this paper, we try to point out a few limitations of currently used evaluation metrics, and provide two simple, efficient and interpretable baseline approaches that achieve results competitive to prior approaches in both previous metrics and our new evaluation strategies.

---

[*] Work done during internship at MSRA.

Proceedings of The 12th International Conference on Natural Language Generation, pages 158–163,
Tokyo, Japan, 28 Oct - 1 Nov, 2019. ©2019 Association for Computational Linguistics

2   Systems in Comparison

The scope of this study is mainly a slightly closer investigation of approaches compared in the recent study by Zhang et al. (2018). For self-containedness, we briefly describe the systems in comparison. The datasets we used to derive or train these systems are those collected and reported by Zhang et al. (2018). [1]

Thomson Reuters: The method adopted by Smiley et al. (2016) as aforementioned.

Neural Networks: A feed-forward neural network with hidden layers and rectified linear unit activations, trained with ℓ_2 regularization. Detailed settings were following Zhang et al. (2018).

Bayesian Models: The method proposed by Zhang et al. (2018), which is a generative model of the posterior $P(v|x)$ inferred by the Bayes rule:

$$P(v|x) \propto P(x|v)P(v), \qquad (1)$$

where the likelihood $P(x|v)$ (conditioned on a given verb v) and the verb prior $P(v)$ are estimated from corpus statistics. Zhang et al. (2018) formulated the likelihood model using either kernel density estimation (KDE) or a Beta distribution, while the prior was estimated by frequency ratio with the Jelinek-Mercer smoothing (Jelinek, 1980) on a uniform distribution over all verbs $\mathcal{V}$:

$$P(w) = \lambda \frac{freq(v)}{\sum_{v'} freq(v')} + (1 - \lambda)\frac{1}{|\mathcal{V}|}. \qquad (2)$$

The choice of λ dictates the trade-off between accuracy and diversity.

In our study, we also introduce two more straightforward baseline approaches that are simpler, more efficient, and more interpretable than non-parametric estimators such as KDE.

The Frequency Baseline: The simplest baseline that directly samples a verb based on the overall frequency distribution was ignored in previous studies when calculating the metrics. In our study, we would like to investigate how different the previous systems perform when compared with this baseline in metrics.

Decision Tree Baseline: One simple improvement of the frequency baseline is segmenting the range of x into groups, and separately calculate frequency distributions within each group. To keep the baseline simple, we only split the range

---

[1]Retrieved from: https://goo.gl/gkj8Fa ; We only use the WSJ and Reuters subsets in English in this study.

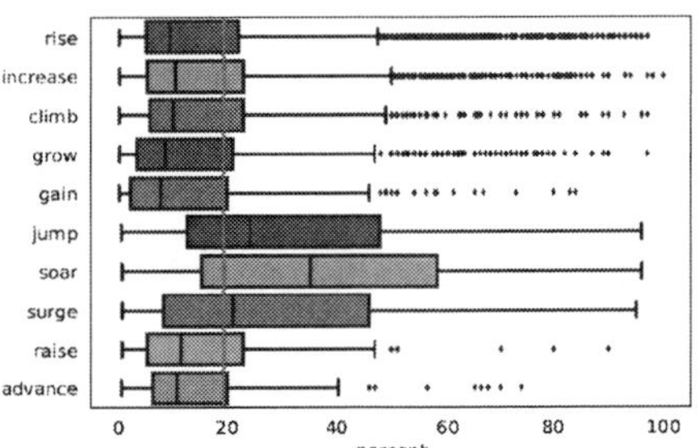

Figure 1: Box plot for the top-10 frequent verbs describing upward trends, with the red line denoting the decision tree split

into two groups, which is equivalent to a decision tree with a depth of one. We use information gain as the splitting criterion (Safavian and Landgrebe, 1991). See Figure 1 for a visualization of the split point, which roughly depicts a group of moderate changes versus another group for larger changes.

3   Experiments

3.1   The Original Automatic Metrics

The automatic metrics reported by Zhang et al. (2018) aim at evaluating accuracy and diversity. The accuracy for verb selection is reflected by the Mean Reciprocal Rank (Voorhees et al., 1999; Radev et al., 2002, MRR) of the reference verb:

$$\text{MRR} = \frac{1}{|\mathcal{T}|} \sum_{(x'_i, v'_i) \in \mathcal{T}} \frac{1}{rank(v'_i)}, \qquad (3)$$

where T denotes the held-out test set: $\mathcal{T} = \{(x'_1, v'_1), .., (x'_M, v'_M)\}$. For diversity, the number of distinct verbs (*richness*) and the relative abundance (*evenness*) in the selected outputs are reported, along with the well-known Inverse Simpson Index aka Simpsons Reciprocal Index (Simpson, 1949) that takes both aspects into account: $D = (\sum_{i=1}^{R} p_i^2)^{-1}$, where R is the total number of distinct selected verbs. Evenness is calculated as D/R.

Table 1 listed the MRR results along with the difference of top-1 system output with the most frequent baseline. We also calculate the Jensen-Shannon Divergence (Wong and You, 1985; Osterreicher and Vajda, 2003, JSD), which is defined to be the mean of KL divergences in two directions, to measure how different the probability distributions are compared with the frequency distribution. We mostly reproduce the results from (Zhang

corpus	Model	upward verbs			downward verbs		
		MRR(%)	Diff.(%)	JSD	MRR(%)	Diff.(%)	JSD
WSJ	Thomson Reuters	11.92 ± 0.16	-	-	10.55 ± 0.34	-	-
	Neural Network	72.33 ± 1.14	0	0.01	68.48 ± 1.46	0	0.11
	Frequency	72.27 ± 1.18	-	-	68.32 ± 1.66	-	-
	Decision Tree	72.40 ± 1.14	0	0.08	68.56 ± 1.60	0	0.09
	Bayesian ($\lambda = 1$, KDE)	72.41 ± 1.14	0	0.12	68.61 ± 1.56	1.3	0.14
	Bayesian ($\lambda = 1$, Beta)	72.30 ± 1.14	13.20	0.17	68.54 ± 1.53	13	0.18
	Bayesian ($\lambda = 0.05$, KDE)	53.32 ± 1.82	88	0.49	51.57 ± 0.31	84.3	0.51
	Bayesian ($\lambda = 0.05$, Beta)	52.68 ± 1.16	87.6	0.51	53.19 ± 1.08	69.7	0.52
Reuters	Thomson Reuters	37.01 ± 3.33	-	-	33.86 ± 2.27	-	-
	Neural Network	88.91 ± 3.65	0	0.13	88.58 ± 3.52	0	0.09
	Frequency	88.55 ± 3.85	-	-	88.34 ± 3.85	-	-
	Decision Tree	88.76 ± 3.76	0	0.14	88.38 ± 3.52	0	0.18
	Bayesian ($\lambda = 1$, KDE)	88.70 ± 3.80	0	0.15	88.10 ± 3.61	1.9	0.26
	Bayesian ($\lambda = 1$, Beta)	88.67 ± 4.46	15.1	0.19	87.16 ± 3.82	28.9	0.26
	Bayesian ($\lambda = 0.05$, KDE)	72.87 ± 5.97	87.9	0.52	79.91 ± 3.60	73.2	0.54
	Bayesian ($\lambda = 0.05$, Beta)	72.11 ± 6.95	89.1	0.54	69.52 ± 5.36	84.1	0.57

Table 1: MRR along with the top-1 difference and the Jensen-Shannon Divergence with the frequency baseline

et al., 2018) with a difference in the neural network baseline, which appears to be equally competitive against other systems in our experiments when running their implementation. [2] Additionally, we have two more interesting observations:

1. The frequency baseline is not distinguishable from the Bayesian methods in terms of MRR;

2. Systems achieving high MRR in fact yield neglectable difference with the frequency baseline in terms of the top-1 output and JSD.

For automatic metrics measuring diversity, we list the results in Table 2. By correcting an error in the codes from Zhang et al. (2018) where they amplified the differences between two systems by dropping cases that both yield the same verbs, the results are slightly different from what was originally reported. Bayesian models with low smoothing factor (λ) now defeat (not significantly) the Thomson Reuters in the sense of both richness and evenness. Other systems, including the neural network, our two new baselines, and Bayesian models with high smoothing factor has lower diversity, but not goes to zero as stated by Zhang et al. (2018). Almost all the models have

exactly the same level of richness. This said, diversity metrics alone cannot reflect quality in selection, as a system could always select every candidate verb with equal probabilities for maximal diversity. We need better ways to simultaneously evaluate appropriateness and comprehensiveness.

3.2 Alternative Evaluation

Our observation of the frequency baseline is reasonable in the sense that it in theory minimises the Bayes risk (Berger, 2013) if the conditional likelihood has tiny subtle differences and is overwhelmed by an overall prior of verb choice, and a number of systems in comparison with high MRR in fact reduce to this baseline by certain degree. More intuitively, the most frequently used verbs in the corpora are *rise* and *fall*, which are often correct but less informative. For each numerical value of percentage, there could be multiple verb choices that are plausible to human writers, while some verbs may not be appropriate. Since neither MRR nor diversity metrics could address this point, we conduct some alternative evaluations by collecting a gold-standard set of multiple plausible candidate verbs on Amazon Mechanical Turk (AMT), using the WSJ subset of the original dataset. Following Smiley et al. (2016), we restricted raters to those located in the United States, with an approval rating above 95% and 1,000 or more HITs approved.

corpus	Model	upward verbs			downward verbs		
		richness	evenness	diversity	richness	eveness	diversity
WSJ	Thomson Reuters	11	0.8555	9.4107	14	0.9485	13.2787
	Neural Network	11	0.2303	2.5330	14	0.1916	2.6819
	Frequency	11	0.2345	2.5799	14	0.2555	3.5770
	Decision Tree	11	0.2461	2.7077	14	0.2361	3.3065
	Bayesian ($\lambda = 1$, KDE)	11	0.2435	2.6789	13	0.2294	2.9822
	Bayesian ($\lambda = 1$, Beta)	11	0.2589	2.8489	14	0.2187	3.0619
	Bayesian ($\lambda = 0.05$, KDE)	11	0.9623	10.8046	14	0.8866	12.4126
	Bayesian ($\lambda = 0.05$, Beta)	11	0.9522	10.5855	14	0.9700	13.5797
Reuters	Thomson Reuters	4	0.9036	3.6142	4	0.8409	3.3635
	Neural Network	4	0.3730	1.4919	4	0.3955	1.5820
	Frequency	4	0.3496	1.3985	4	0.3573	1.4292
	Decision Tree	4	0.3699	1.4797	4	0.3741	1.4962
	Bayesian ($\lambda = 1$, KDE)	4	0.3590	1.4360	4	0.3411	1.3642
	Bayesian ($\lambda = 1$, Beta)	4	0.3668	1.4672	4	0.3623	1.4493
	Bayesian ($\lambda = 0.05$, KDE)	4	0.9129	3.6516	4	0.9262	3.7047
	Bayesian ($\lambda = 0.05$, Beta)	4	0.9705	3.8818	4	0.9175	3.6699

Table 2: The diversity of verb selection measured by the Inverse Simpson Index.

We construct natural language utterances using uniformly sampled percentage values and all the verbs in the dataset (11 verbs describing upward changes and 14 for downward changes in total), and using one consistent subject (*Net Profits*) to reduce the potential variance brought by different subjects which is beyond the scope of this study. AMT workers will try to annotate each sentence with one of the three degrees of appropriateness:

- 3 (Appropriate): The verb is among the most suitable ones to describe the percentage

- 2 (Okay): The verb could be used to describe the percentage, although it might not be one of the most appropriate choices

- 1 (Not Appropriate): The verb is not naturally used to describe the percentage

See supplementary notes for a screenshot of the annotation interface. For either upward and downward verbs, we uniformly random sampled 100 different percentage changes from the interval $[0, 100]$, which results in 12,500 judges in total.

The resulting corpus has the format that each percentage change is paired with a list of candidate verbs, each of which has five judges from five different workers. We treat any verb with more than three judges rated 3 as one appropriate verb. This crowdsourced dataset could be used to evaluate each system on the ability to select multiple plausible verbs, treating verb selection as an ordinary classification task. We randomly leave out 20% of this dataset as the development set, and the rest for the final test set evaluation. For systems giving probability distributions on verbs (as opposed to deterministic selections), it is natural to threshold the accumulated value to decide which verbs to include as the finally selected candidates, with the threshold determined on the development set. We calculate the performance in terms of the precision, recall and F1 measure of all the annotated appropriate verbs, and the results are displayed in Table 3. The values of the cross-entropy loss as we calculated follow similar trends, as included in the supplementary notes.

We can observe that under the new evaluation protocol, the results from the two baseline approaches are more competitive than those reflected by MRR. The frequency baseline is surprisingly strong, indicating that authors of the standard corpora might favor more neutral verbs that could be applicable for almost all percentage values. A slightly more crafted decision tree marginally brings further performance increase. Meanwhile, we can also notice that models achieving higher diversity scores (cf. Table 2) have comparatively lower recall when all of them have precision vary-

Model	upward verbs				downward verbs			
	l	Precision	Recall	F1	l	Precision	Recall	F1
Thomson Reuters	5.67	48.98	51.35	48.22	7.34	39.23	51.04	41.81
Neural Network	9.15	50.10	84.94	61.96	12.29	40.97	89.12	53.45
Frequency	10	47.07	90.91	60.38	13	39.19	**92.86**	52.09
Decision Tree	10	50.58	**92.52**	**62.53**	11.94	45.48	86.59	53.73
Bayesian ($\lambda = 1$, KDE)	7.87	52.13	73.25	57.48	11.56	42.31	85.30	**54.10**
Bayesian ($\lambda = 1$, Beta)	7.62	**52.28**	71.85	56.95	11.01	44.97	80.05	52.64
Bayesian ($\lambda = 0.05$, KDE)	4.29	52.06	43.03	40.85	4.95	48.96	36.51	35.20
Bayesian ($\lambda = 0.05$, Beta)	3.77	44.66	38.38	36.93	3.54	**50.40**	31.08	34.29

Table 3: Results of viewing verb section as a classification task. Precision, recall, and F1 reported here are macro-averaged.; l stands for the average number of verbs each system has selected for each specified percentage.

ing around 50. This suggests that models may have learned rather flat distributions over verbs, with an implication that although these models have higher diversity on selecting verbs, they actually have lower diversity on selecting *appropriate* verbs. Given the current F1 values around 50 to 60, there still exists room for improvements over simple baselines for more precise selection.

4 Discussion

For the task of trend verb selection for data-to-text generation, our observations suggest that the evaluation results for current automatic metrics should be interpreted with caveats. Automatic verb selection systems that achieves good accuracy as reflected by high mean reciprocal ranks could in fact hardly yield real difference compared with just outputting the most frequently used verbs in overall statistics. More complex likelihood modelling using kernel density estimation could not produce more diverse selection of all plausible verbs as it behaves similar to a frequency baseline, while being slightly less interpretable compared with simpler frequency based approaches such as a shallow decision tree. One source of this issue should be the lack of good definition of appropriateness, as the difference in various verbs is often vague (see Figure 1 for an instance, where the used range for a number of verbs could almost span the entire range of the percentages). It also remains an open problem for a more thorough, rigorous, systematic treatment in terms of experimental design and evaluation protocol, given that this work and previous relevant studies have all just temporarily ignored the potential impact of different subjects in a sentence on verb selection for the simplicity of problem settings.

In this study, we focus on a few issues with recent work on trend verb selection in describing various kinds of percentages, with experiments conducted on samples collected from financial news data. We believe that similar caveats should exist in lexical choice problems appeared in other domains as well, such as various kinds of phrases in weather forecasts (Reiter et al., 2005; Ramos-Soto et al., 2014; Li et al., 2016) and in sports match reports (van der Lee et al., 2017; Wiseman et al., 2017; Qin et al., 2018), and hopefully the field will be exploring on some more principled, domain-agnostic approaches in the future.

Acknowledgments

We thank all three anonymous reviewers for helpful comments on our submitted draft.

References

James O Berger. 2013. *Statistical decision theory and Bayesian analysis.* Springer Science & Business Media.

Frederick Jelinek. 1980. Interpolated estimation of markov source parameters from sparse data. In *Proc. Workshop on Pattern Recognition in Practice, 1980.*

Chris van der Lee, Emiel Krahmer, and Sander Wubben. 2017. PASS: A Dutch data-to-text system for soccer, targeted towards specific audiences. In *Proceedings of the 10th International Conference on Natural Language Generation*, pages 95–104, Santiago de Compostela, Spain. Association for Computational Linguistics.

Xiao Li, Kees van Deemter, and Chenghua Lin. 2016. Statistics-based lexical choice for NLG from quantitative information. In *Proceedings of the 9th International Natural Language Generation conference*, pages 104–108, Edinburgh, UK. Association for Computational Linguistics.

Ferdinand Osterreicher and Igor Vajda. 2003. A new class of metric divergences on probability spaces and its applicability in statistics. *Annals of the Institute of Statistical Mathematics*, 55(3):639–653.

Vassilis Plachouras, Charese Smiley, Hiroko Bretz, Ola Taylor, Jochen L Leidner, Dezhao Song, and Frank Schilder. 2016. Interacting with financial data using natural language. In *Proceedings of the 39th International ACM SIGIR conference on Research and Development in Information Retrieval*, pages 1121–1124. ACM.

Guanghui Qin, Jin-Ge Yao, Xuening Wang, Jinpeng Wang, and Chin-Yew Lin. 2018. Learning latent semantic annotations for grounding natural language to structured data. In *Proceedings of the 2018 Conference on Empirical Methods in Natural Language Processing*, pages 3761–3771, Brussels, Belgium. Association for Computational Linguistics.

Dragomir R Radev, Hong Qi, Harris Wu, and Weiguo Fan. 2002. Evaluating web-based question answering systems. In *LREC*.

Alejandro Ramos-Soto, Alberto Jose Bugarin, Senén Barro, and Juan Taboada. 2014. Linguistic descriptions for automatic generation of textual short-term weather forecasts on real prediction data. *IEEE Transactions on Fuzzy Systems*, 23(1):44–57.

Ehud Reiter. 2018. Lexical choice needs machine learning!

Ehud Reiter, Somayajulu Sripada, Jim Hunter, Jin Yu, and Ian Davy. 2005. Choosing words in computer-generated weather forecasts. *Artificial Intelligence*, 167(1-2):137–169.

S Rasoul Safavian and David Landgrebe. 1991. A survey of decision tree classifier methodology. *IEEE transactions on systems, man, and cybernetics*, 21(3):660–674.

Edward H Simpson. 1949. Measurement of diversity. *Nature*, 163(4148):688.

Charese Smiley, Vassilis Plachouras, Frank Schilder, Hiroko Bretz, Jochen Leidner, and Dezhao Song. 2016. When to plummet and when to soar: Corpus based verb selection for natural language generation. In *Proceedings of the 9th International Natural Language Generation conference*, pages 36–39, Edinburgh, UK. Association for Computational Linguistics.

Ellen M Voorhees et al. 1999. The trec-8 question answering track report. In *Trec*, volume 99, pages 77–82. Citeseer.

Sam Wiseman, Stuart Shieber, and Alexander Rush. 2017. Challenges in data-to-document generation. In *Proceedings of the 2017 Conference on Empirical Methods in Natural Language Processing*, pages 2253–2263, Copenhagen, Denmark. Association for Computational Linguistics.

Andrew KC Wong and Manlai You. 1985. Entropy and distance of random graphs with application to structural pattern recognition. *IEEE Transactions on Pattern Analysis and Machine Intelligence*, (5):599–609.

Dell Zhang, Jiahao Yuan, Xiaoling Wang, and Adam Foster. 2018. Probabilistic verb selection for data-to-text generation. *Transactions of the Association for Computational Linguistics*, 6:511–527.

ViGGO: A Video Game Corpus for Data-To-Text Generation in Open-Domain Conversation

Juraj Juraska, Kevin K. Bowden and **Marilyn Walker**
Natural Language and Dialogue Systems Lab
University of California, Santa Cruz
{jjuraska,kkbowden,mawalker}@ucsc.edu

Abstract

The uptake of deep learning in natural language generation (NLG) led to the release of both small and relatively large parallel corpora for training neural models. The existing data-to-text datasets are, however, aimed at task-oriented dialogue systems, and often thus limited in diversity and versatility. They are typically crowdsourced, with much of the noise left in them. Moreover, current neural NLG models do not take full advantage of large training data, and due to their strong generalizing properties produce sentences that look template-like regardless. We therefore present a new corpus of 7K samples, which (1) is clean despite being crowdsourced, (2) has utterances of 9 generalizable and conversational dialogue act types, making it more suitable for open-domain dialogue systems, and (3) explores the domain of video games, which is new to dialogue systems despite having excellent potential for supporting rich conversations.

1 Introduction

The recent adoption of deep learning methods in natural language generation (NLG) for dialogue systems resulted in an explosion of neural data-to-text generation models, which depend on large training data. These are typically trained on one of the few parallel corpora publicly available, in particular the E2E (Novikova et al., 2017) and the WebNLG (Gardent et al., 2017) datasets. Crowdsourcing large NLG datasets tends to be a costly and time-consuming process, making it impractical outside of task-oriented dialogue systems. At the same time, current neural NLG models struggle to replicate the high language diversity of the training sentences present in these large datasets, and instead they learn to produce the same generic type of sentences as with considerably less training data (Deriu and Cieliebak, 2018; Juraska and Walker, 2018; Dušek et al., 2019).

give_opinion(NAME [**SpellForce 3**], RATING [**poor**], GENRES [**real-time strategy, role-playing**], PLAYER_PERSPECTIVE [**bird view**])
I think that **SpellForce 3** is **one of the worst games** I've ever played. Trying to combine the **real-time strategy** and **role-playing** genres just doesn't work, and the **bird's eye view** makes it near impossible to play.
verify_attribute(NAME [**Little Big Adventure**], RATING [**average**], HAS_MULTIPLAYER [**no**], PLATFORMS [**PlayStation**])
I recall that you were **not that fond** of **Little Big Adventure**. Does **single-player** gaming on the **PlayStation** quickly get boring for you?

Table 1: Examples of MRs and corresponding reference utterances in the ViGGO dataset. The DA of the MRs is indicated in italics, and the slots in small caps. The slot mentions in the utterances are bolded.

Motivated by the rising interest in open-domain dialogue systems and conversational agents, we present ViGGO – a smaller but more comprehensive dataset in the video game domain, introducing several generalizable dialogue acts (DAs), making it more suitable for training versatile and more conversational NLG models.[1] The dataset provides almost 7K pairs of structured meaning representations (MRs) and crowdsourced reference utterances about more than 100 video games. Table 1 lists three examples.

Video games are a vast entertainment topic that can naturally be discussed in a casual conversation, similar to movies and music, yet in the dialogue systems community it does not enjoy popularity anywhere close to that of the latter two topics (Fazel-Zarandi et al., 2017; Li et al., 2017; Moghe et al., 2018; Shah et al., 2018; Khatri et al., 2018). Restaurants have served as the go-to topic in data-to-text NLG for decades, as they offer a sufficiently large set of various attributes and cor-

---

[1] The ViGGO corpus is available for download at: https://nlds.soe.ucsc.edu/viggo

Proceedings of The 12th International Conference on Natural Language Generation, pages 164–172,
Tokyo, Japan, 28 Oct - 1 Nov, 2019. ©2019 Association for Computational Linguistics

responding values to talk about. While they certainly can be a topic of a casual conversation, the existing restaurant datasets (Stent et al., 2004; Gašić et al., 2008; Mairesse et al., 2010; Howcroft et al., 2013; Wen et al., 2015a; Nayak et al., 2017) are geared more toward a task-oriented dialogue where a system tries to narrow down a restaurant based on the user's preferences and ultimately give a recommendation. Our new video game dataset is designed to be more conversational, and to thus enable neural models to produce utterances more suitable for an open-domain dialogue system.

Even the most recent addition to the publicly available restaurant datasets for data-to-text NLG, the E2E dataset (Novikova et al., 2017), suffers from the lack of a conversational aspect. It has become popular, thanks to its unprecedented size and multiple reference utterances per MR, for training end-to-end neural models, yet it only provides a single DA type. In contrast with the E2E dataset, ViGGO presents utterances of 9 different DAs.

Other domains have been represented by task-oriented datasets with multiple DA types, for example the Hotel, Laptop, and TV datasets (Wen et al., 2015b, 2016). Nevertheless, the DAs in these datasets vary greatly in complexity, and their distribution is thus heavily skewed, typically with two or three similar DAs comprising almost the entire dataset. In our video game dataset, we omitted simple DAs, in particular those that do not require any slots, such as greetings or short prompts, and focused on a set of substantial DAs only.

The main contribution of our work is thus a new parallel data-to-text NLG corpus that (1) is more conversational, rather than information seeking or question answering, and thus more suitable for an open-domain dialogue system, (2) represents a new, unexplored domain which, however, has excellent potential for application in conversational agents, and (3) has high-quality, manually cleaned human-produced utterances.

2 The ViGGO Dataset

ViGGO features more than 100 different video game titles, whose attributes were harvested using free API access to two of the largest online video game databases: IGDB[2] and GiantBomb[3]. Using these attributes, we generated a set of 2,300 structured MRs. The human reference utterances

[2]https://www.igdb.com/
[3]https://www.giantbomb.com/

DA	Slot range	Mandatory slots	Additional common slots
inform	3-8	NAME, GENRES	RELEASE_YEAR, DEVELOPER, ESRB, GENRES, PLAYER_PERSPEC- TIVE, HAS_MULTI- PLAYER, PLATFORMS, AVAIL- ABLE_ON_STEAM, HAS_LINUX_RE- LEASE, HAS_MAC_RELEASE
confirm	2-3	NAME	
give_opin- ion	3-4	NAME, RATING	
recommend	2-3	NAME	
request	1-2	SPECIFIER	
request_at- tribute	1		
request_ex- planation	2-3	RATING	
suggest	2-3	NAME	
verify_at- tribute	3-4	NAME, RATING	

Table 2: Overview of mandatory and common possible slots for each DA in the ViGGO dataset. There is an additional slot, EXP_RELEASE_DATE, only possible in the *inform* and *confirm* DAs. Moreover, RATING is also possible in the *inform* DA, though not mandatory.

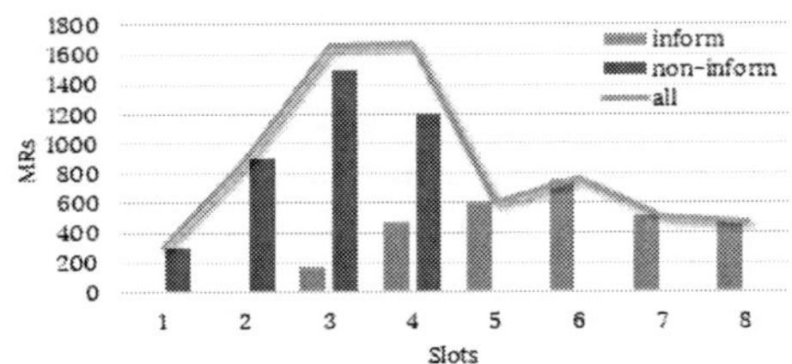

Figure 1: Distribution of the number of slots across all types of MRs, as well as the *inform* slot separately, and non-*inform* slots only.

for the generated MRs were then crowdsourced using vetted workers on the Amazon Mechanical Turk (MTurk) platform (Buhrmester et al., 2011), resulting in 6,900 MR-utterance pairs altogether. With the goal of creating a clean, high-quality dataset, we strived to obtain reference utterances with correct mentions of all slots in the corresponding MR through post-processing.

2.1 Meaning Representations

The MRs in the ViGGO dataset range from 1 to 8 slot-value pairs, and the slots come from a set of 14 different video game attributes. Table 2 details how these slots may be distributed across the 9 different DAs. The *inform* DA, represented by 3,000 samples, is the most prevalent one, as the average number of slots it contains is significantly higher than that of all the other DAs. Figure 1 visualizes the MR length distribution across the entire dataset.

The slots can be classified into 5 general categories covering most types of information MRs typically convey in data-to-text generation scenarios: *Boolean*, *Numeric*, *Scalar*, *Categorical*, and *List*. The first 4 categories are common in other NLG datasets, such as E2E, Laptop, TV, and Hotel, while the *List* slots are unique to ViGGO. *List* slots have values which may comprise multiple items from a discrete list of possible items.

2.2 Utterances

With neural language generation in mind, we crowdsourced 3 reference utterances for each MR so as to provide the models with the information about how the same content can be realized in multiple different ways. At the same time, this allows for a more reliable automatic evaluation by comparing the generated utterances with a set of different references each, covering a broader spectrum of correct ways of expressing the content given by the MR. The raw data, however, contains a significant amount of noise, as is inevitable when crowdsourcing. We therefore created and enforced a robust set of heuristics and regular expressions to account for typos, grammatical errors, undesirable abbreviations, unsolicited information, and missing or incorrect slot realizations.

2.3 Data Collection

The crowdsourcing of utterances on MTurk took place in three stages. After collecting one third of the utterances, we identified a pool of almost 30 workers who wrote the most diverse and natural-sounding sentences in the context of video games. We then filtered out all utterances of poor quality and had the qualified workers write new ones for the corresponding inputs. Finally, the remaining two thirds of utterances were completed by these workers exclusively.

For each DA we created a separate task in order to minimize the workers' confusion. The instructions contained several different examples, as well as counter-examples, and they situated the DA in the context of a hypothetical conversation. The video game attributes to be used were provided for the workers in the form of a table, with their order shuffled so as to avoid any kind of bias. Further details on the data collection and cleaning are included in the Appendix.

2.4 Train/Validation/Test Split

Despite the fact that the ViGGO dataset is not very large, we strived to make the test set reasonably challenging. To this end, we ensured that, after delexicalizing the NAME and the DEVELOPER

Figure 2: Distribution of the DAs across the train/validation/test split. For each partition the total count of DAs/MRs is indicated.

slots, there were no common MRs between the train set and either of the validation or test set. We maintained a similar MR length and slot distribution across the three partitions. The distribution of DA types, on the other hand, is skewed slightly toward fewer *inform* DA instances and a higher proportion of the less prevalent DAs in the validation and test sets (see Figure 2). With the exact partition sizes indicated in the diagram, the final ratio of samples is approximately 7.5 : 1 : 1.5.

2.5 ViGGO vs. E2E

Our new dataset was constructed under different constraints than the E2E dataset. First, in ViGGO we did *not* allow any omissions of slot mentions, as those are not justifiable for data-to-text generation with no previous context, and it makes the evaluation ambiguous. Second, the MRs in ViGGO are grounded by *real* video game data, which can encourage richer and more natural-sounding reference utterances.

While ViGGO is only 13% the size of the E2E dataset, the lexical diversity of its utterances is 77% of that in the E2E dataset, as indicated by the "delexicalized vocabulary" column in Table 3. Part of the reason naturally is the presence of additional DAs in ViGGO, and therefore we also indicate the statistics in Table 3 for the *inform* samples only. The average *inform* utterance length in ViGGO turns out to be over 30% greater, in terms of both words and sentences per utterance.

Finally, we note that, unlike the E2E dataset, our test set does not place any specific emphasis on longer MRs. While the average number of slots per MR in the *inform* DAs are comparable to the E2E dataset, in general the video game MRs are significantly shorter. This is by design, as shorter, more focused responses are more conversational than consistently dense utterances.

	Instances	Unique MRs	Unique delex. MRs	Vocab	Delex. vocab	Avg. 3-gram freq.	Refs/ MR	Slots/ MR	W/ Ref	W/ Sent	Sents/ Ref
E2E	51,426	6,039	5,963	2,878	2,818	18.70	8.1	5.43	22.41	14.36	1.56
ViGGO$_{inf}$	3,000	1,000	997	1,378	1,102	8.33	3	5.81	30.62	15.01	2.04
ViGGO	6,900	2,253	2,066	2,427	2,178	6.91	3	4.18	25.01	15.04	1.66

Table 3: Dataset statistics comparing the ViGGO dataset, as well as its subset of *inform* DAs only (ViGGO$_{inf}$), with the E2E dataset. The average trigram frequency was calculated on trigrams that appear more than once.

	BLEU	METEOR	ROUGE	CIDEr	SER
Ao3	0.519	0.388	0.631	2.531	2.55%
Bo3	0.521	0.391	0.638	2.545	2.48%

Table 4: Baseline system performance on the ViGGO test set. Despite individual models (Bo3 – best of 3 experiments) often having better overall scores, we consider the Ao3 (average of 3) results the most objective.

	Naturalness		Coherence	
	Ref.	Gen. utt.	Ref.	Gen. utt.
E2E	4.48	4.67	4.57	4.77
ViGGO$_{inf}$	4.85	4.83	4.85	4.93
ViGGO	4.68	4.74	4.78	4.84

Table 5: Naturalness and coherence scores of our model's generated outputs compared to the reference utterances, as per the human evaluation. ViGGO$_{inf}$ corresponds to the subset of *inform* DAs only.

3 Baseline System Evaluation

The NLG model we use to establish a baseline for this dataset is a standard Transformer-based (Vaswani et al., 2017) sequence-to-sequence model. For decoding we employ beam search of width 10 ($\alpha = 1.0$). The generated candidates are then reranked according to the heuristically determined slot coverage score. Before training the model on the ViGGO dataset, we confirmed on the E2E dataset that it performed on par with, or even slightly better than, the strong baseline models from the E2E NLG Challenge[4], namely, TGEN (Dušek and Jurčíček, 2016) and SLUG2SLUG (Juraska et al., 2018).

Automatic Metrics We evaluate our model's performance on the ViGGO dataset using the following standard NLG metrics: BLEU (Papineni et al., 2002), METEOR (Lavie and Agarwal, 2007), ROUGE-L (Lin, 2004), and CIDEr (Vedantam et al., 2015). Additionally, with our heuristic slot error rate (SER) metric we approximate the percentage of failed slot realizations (i.e., missed, incorrect, or hallucinated) across the test set. The results are shown in Table 4.

Human Evaluation We let two expert annotators with no prior knowledge of the ViGGO dataset evaluate the outputs of our model. Their task was to rate 240 shuffled utterances (120 generated utterances and 120 human references) each on *naturalness* and *coherence* using a 5-point Likert scale. We define naturalness as a measure of how much one would expect to encounter an utterance in a conversation with a human, as opposed to sounding robotic, while coherence measures its grammaticality and fluency. Out of the 120 MRs in each partition, 40 were of the *inform* type, with the other 8 DAs represented by 10 samples each. In addition to that, we had the annotators rate a sample of 80 utterances from the E2E dataset (40 generated and 40 references) as a sort of a baseline for the human evaluation.

With both datasets, our model's outputs were highly rated on both naturalness and coherence (see Table 5). The scores for the ViGGO utterances were overall higher than those for the E2E ones, which we understand as an indication of the video game data being more fluent and conversational. At the same time, we observed that the utterances generated by our model tended to score higher than the reference utterances, though significantly more so for the E2E dataset. This is likely a consequence of the ViGGO dataset being cleaner and less noisy than the E2E dataset.

In an additional evaluation of ViGGO, we asked the annotators to classify the utterance samples into the 9 DA groups. For this task they were provided with a brief description of each DA type. The annotators identified the DA incorrectly in only 7% of the samples, which we interpret as a confirmation that our DAs are well-defined. Most of the mistakes can be ascribed to the inherent similarity of the *recommend* and the *suggest* DA, as

[4]http://www.macs.hw.ac.uk/InteractionLab/E2E/

well as to our model often generating *give_opinion* utterances that resemble the *inform* ones.

Qualitative Analysis Among all 9 DAs, the one posing the greatest challenge for our model was *give_opinion*, due to its high diversity of reference utterances. Despite the occasional incoherence, it learned to produce rich and sensible utterances, for instance "Little Nightmares is a pretty good game. Tarsier Studios is a talented developer and the side view perspective makes it easy to play.".

Since our baseline model does not implement any form of a copy mechanism, it fails on instances with out-of-vocabulary terms, such as the values of the SPECIFIER slot in the test set. These, in fact, account for almost half of the errors indicated by the SER metric in Table 4. Therefore, more robust models have good potential for improving on our scores.

4 Discussion

In Table 6 we demonstrate how the 9 DAs of the ViGGO dataset can support a natural multi-turn exchange on the topic of video games, as a part of a longer casual conversation on different topics. One caveat of using a language generator trained on this dataset in a dialogue system as-is is that multiple subsequent turns discussing the same video game would be repeating its full name. ViGGO was designed for grounded generation but without context, and therefore it is up to the dialogue manager to ensure that pronouns are substituted for the names whenever it would sound more natural in a dialogue. Alternately, the dataset can easily be augmented with automatically constructed samples which omit the NAME slot in the MR and replace the name with a pronoun in the reference utterance.

5 Conclusion

In this paper we presented a new parallel corpus for data-to-text NLG, which contains 9 dialogue acts, making it more conversational than other similar datasets. The crowdsourced utterances were thoroughly cleaned in order to obtain high-quality human references, which we hope will support the recent trend in research to train neural models on small but high-quality data, like humans can. This could possibly be achieved by transferring fundamental knowledge from larger available corpora, such as the E2E dataset, but perhaps by other, completely new, methods.

S:	. . . What about video games?
U:	Totally, I spend my entire evenings in front of my PC ? .
S:	What is your favorite **genre** of video games? *request_attribute*(GENRES [])
U:	I guess I play a lot of shooter games.
S:	Have you played any **interesting** games lately? *request*(SPECIFIER [**interesting**])
U:	Tomb Raider is pretty good.
S:	Do you mean **Tomb Raider** from **2013**? *confirm*(NAME [**Tomb Raider**], RELEASE_YEAR [**2013**])
U:	Yes, that one with the epic E3 trailer.
S:	Do you also enjoy playing **first-person shooters**, such as **Half-Life 2**? *suggest*(NAME [**Half-Life 2**], GENRES [**shooter**], PLAYER_PERSPECTIVE [**first person**])
U:	I haven't played that one in a while. Would you recommend something else?
S:	Well, since you seem to be a fan of **M-rated PlayStation** games, I thought you would perhaps like **Max Payne 3**. Have you heard about that game? *recommend*(NAME [**Max Payne 3**], ESRB [**M (for Mature)**], PLATFORMS [**PlayStation**])
U:	No.
S:	**Max Payne 3** is a **multiplayer action-adventure shooter** from **2012**. *inform*(NAME [**Max Payne 3**], RELEASE_YEAR [**2012**], GENRES [**action-adventure; shooter**], MULTIPLAYER [**yes**])
U:	I see. So, you enjoyed it?
S:	Oh, I **love Max Payne 3**. When I see a game developed by **Rockstar Games**, I buy it without thinking. *give_opinion*(NAME [**Max Payne**], RATING [**excellent**], DEVELOPER [**Rockstar Games**])
U:	That sounds cool.
S:	Previously you told me that you **enjoyed Tomb Raider**. Is that the case with all games developed by **Crystal Dynamics**? *verify_attribute*(NAME [**Tomb Raider**], RATING [**good**], DEVELOPER [**Crystal Dynamics**])
U:	You bet.
S:	What is it that you **like** about **Crystal Dynamics** games? *request_explanation*(RATING [**good**], DEVELOPER [**Crystal Dynamics**])
U:	They usually have really good stories.
S:	. . .

Table 6: An example of a chit-chat about video games comprising utterances of DAs defined in ViGGO. "S" denotes the system and "U" the user turns.

References

Michael Buhrmester, Tracy Kwang, and Samuel D Gosling. 2011. Amazon's mechanical turk: A new source of inexpensive, yet high-quality, data? *Perspectives on psychological science*, 6(1):3–5.

Jan Milan Deriu and Mark Cieliebak. 2018. Syntactic manipulation for generating more diverse and interesting texts. In *11th International Conference on Natural Language Generation (INLG 2018), Tilburg, The Netherlands, 05-08 November 2018*, pages 22–34. Association for Computational Linguistics.

Ondřej Dušek and Filip Jurčíček. 2016. Sequence-to-sequence generation for spoken dialogue via deep syntax trees and strings.

Ondřej Dušek, Jekaterina Novikova, and Verena Rieser. 2019. Evaluating the state-of-the-art of end-to-end natural language generation: The e2e nlg challenge. *CoRR*.

Maryam Fazel-Zarandi, Shang-Wen Li, Jin Cao, Jared Casale, Peter Henderson, David Whitney, and Alborz Geramifard. 2017. Learning robust dialog policies in noisy environments. *NIPS 2017 Workshop on Conversational AI*.

Claire Gardent, Anastasia Shimorina, Shashi Narayan, and Laura Perez-Beltrachini. 2017. Creating training corpora for micro-planners. In *Proceedings of the 55th Annual Meeting of the Association for Computational Linguistics (Volume 1: Long Papers)*, Vancouver, Canada. Association for Computational Linguistics.

Milica Gašić, Simon Keizer, Francois Mairesse, Jost Schatzmann, Blaise Thomson, Kai Yu, and Steve Young. 2008. Training and evaluation of the HIS POMDP dialogue system in noise. In *Proceedings of the 9th SIGDIAL Workshop on Discourse and Dialogue*, pages 112–119. Association for Computational Linguistics.

David Howcroft, Crystal Nakatsu, and Michael White. 2013. Enhancing the expression of contrast in the SPaRKy restaurant corpus. In *Proceedings of the 14th European Workshop on Natural Language Generation*, pages 30–39.

Juraj Juraska, Panagiotis Karagiannis, Kevin Bowden, and Marilyn Walker. 2018. A deep ensemble model with slot alignment for sequence-to-sequence natural language generation. In *Proceedings of the 2018 Conference of the North American Chapter of the Association for Computational Linguistics: Human Language Technologies, Volume 1 (Long Papers)*, pages 152–162.

Juraj Juraska and Marilyn Walker. 2018. Characterizing variation in crowd-sourced data for training neural language generators to produce stylistically varied outputs. In *Proceedings of the 11th International Conference on Natural Language Generation*, pages 441–450.

Chandra Khatri, Behnam Hedayatnia, Anu Venkatesh, Jeff Nunn, Yi Pan, Qing Liu, Han Song, Anna Gottardi, Sanjeev Kwatra, Sanju Pancholi, et al. 2018. Advancing the state of the art in open domain dialog systems through the alexa prize. In *2018 Alexa Prize Proceedings*.

Alon Lavie and Abhaya Agarwal. 2007. Meteor: An automatic metric for mt evaluation with high levels of correlation with human judgments. In *Proceedings of the Second Workshop on Statistical Machine Translation*, pages 228–231. Association for Computational Linguistics.

Xiujun Li, Yun-Nung Chen, Lihong Li, Jianfeng Gao, and Asli Celikyilmaz. 2017. End-to-end task-completion neural dialogue systems. In *Proceedings of the Eighth International Joint Conference on Natural Language Processing (Volume 1: Long Papers)*, pages 733–743.

Chin-Yew Lin. 2004. Rouge: A package for automatic evaluation of summaries. *Text Summarization Branches Out*.

François Mairesse, Milica Gašić, Filip Jurčíček, Simon Keizer, Blaise Thomson, Kai Yu, and Steve Young. 2010. Phrase-based statistical language generation using graphical models and active learning. In *ACL*.

Nikita Moghe, Siddhartha Arora, Suman Banerjee, and Mitesh M Khapra. 2018. Towards exploiting background knowledge for building conversation systems. In *Proceedings of the 2018 Conference on Empirical Methods in Natural Language Processing*, pages 2322–2332.

Neha Nayak, Dilek Hakkani-Tür, Marilyn Walker, and Larry Heck. 2017. To plan or not to plan? discourse planning in slot-value informed sequence to sequence models for language generation. In *INTERSPEECH*.

Jekaterina Novikova, Ondřej Dušek, and Verena Rieser. 2017. The E2E NLG shared task.

Kishore Papineni, Salim Roukos, Todd Ward, and Wei-Jing Zhu. 2002. Bleu: a method for automatic evaluation of machine translation. In *ACL*.

Pararth Shah, Dilek Hakkani-Tür, Gokhan Tür, Abhinav Rastogi, Ankur Bapna, Neha Nayak, and Larry Heck. 2018. Building a conversational agent overnight with dialogue self-play. *CoRR*.

Amanda Stent, Rashmi Prasad, and Marilyn Walker. 2004. Trainable sentence planning for complex information presentation in spoken dialog systems. In *Proceedings of the 42nd annual meeting on association for computational linguistics*, page 79. Association for Computational Linguistics.

Ashish Vaswani, Noam Shazeer, Niki Parmar, Jakob Uszkoreit, Llion Jones, Aidan N Gomez, Łukasz Kaiser, and Illia Polosukhin. 2017. Attention is all you need. In *Proceedings of the 31st International*

Conference on Neural Information Processing Systems, pages 6000–6010. Curran Associates Inc.

Ramakrishna Vedantam, C Lawrence Zitnick, and Devi Parikh. 2015. Cider: Consensus-based image description evaluation. In *Proceedings of the IEEE conference on computer vision and pattern recognition*, pages 4566–4575.

Tsung-Hsien Wen, Milica Gašić, Dongho Kim, Nikola Mrkšić, Pei hao Su, David Vandyke, and Steve Young. 2015a. Stochastic language generation in dialogue using recurrent neural networks with convolutional sentence reranking. In *SIGDIAL Conference*.

Tsung-Hsien Wen, Milica Gašić, Nikola Mrkšić, Lina M. Rojas-Barahona, Pei-Hao Su, David Vandyke, and Steve Young. 2016. Multi-domain neural network language generation for spoken dialogue systems. In *NAACL*.

Tsung-Hsien Wen, Milica Gašić, Nikola Mrkšić, Pei-Hao Su, David Vandyke, and Steve Young. 2015b. Semantically conditioned lstm-based natural language generation for spoken dialogue systems. In *EMNLP*.

A Appendix

A.1 Additional ViGGO Dataset Examples

In Table 7 we present one example of each DA in the ViGGO dataset, including the examples given in Table 1.

A.2 Slot Categories

In Section 2.1 we mentioned that the slots in the ViGGO dataset can be classified into 5 general categories. Here we provide more detailed descriptions of the categories:

1. *Boolean* – binary value, such as "yes"/"no" or "true"/"false" (e.g., HAS_MULTIPLAYER or AVAILABLE_ON_STEAM),
2. *Numeric* – value is a number or contains number(s) as the salient part (e.g., RELEASE_YEAR or EXP_RELEASE_DATE),
3. *Scalar* – values are on a distinct scale (e.g., RATING or ESRB),
4. *Categorical* – takes on virtually any value, typically coming from a certain category, such as names or types (e.g., NAME or DEVELOPER),
5. *List* – similar to categorical, where the value can, however, consist of multiple individual items (e.g., GENRES or PLAYER_PERSPECTIVE).

inform(NAME [**God of War**], RELEASE_YEAR [**2018**], DEVELOPER [**SIE Santa Monica Studio**], RATING [**excellent**], GENRES [**action-adventure, platformer, role-playing**], PLAYER_PERSPECTIVE [**third person**], HAS_MULTIPLAYER [**no**], PLATFORMS [**PlayStation**])
Developed by **SIE Santa Monica Studio** in **2018**, **God of War** is an **excellent single-player third person platformer** made exclusively for **PlayStation**. The **action-adventure** storyline involves **role-playing** as one of the dynamic characters.
confirm(NAME [**Hellblade: Senua's Sacrifice**], RELEASE_YEAR [**2017**], DEVELOPER [**Ninja Theory**])
Oh, do you mean the **2017** game from **Ninja Theory**, **Hellblade: Senua's Sacrifice**?
give_opinion(NAME [**SpellForce 3**], RATING [**poor**], GENRES [**real-time strategy, role-playing**], PLAYER_PERSPECTIVE [**bird view**])
I think that **SpellForce 3** is **one of the worst games** I've ever played. Trying to combine the **real-time strategy** and **role-playing** genres just doesn't work, and the **bird's eye view** makes it near impossible to play.
recommend(NAME [**Call of Duty: Advanced Warfare**], DEVELOPER [**Sledgehammer Games**], ESRB [**M (for Mature)**])
Speaking of **M rated** games developed by **Sledgehammer Games**, have you tried **Call of Duty: Advanced Warfare**?
request(DEVELOPER [**Guerrilla Games**], SPECIFIER [**overrated**])
What would you say is the most **overrated** game made by **Guerrilla Games**?
request_attribute(AVAILABLE_ON_STEAM [])
Do you prefer playing games that you can get on **Steam**?
request_explanation(RATING [**poor**], HAS_MAC_RELEASE [**yes**])
What is it about **Mac** games that you find **so disappointing**?
suggest(NAME [**Rocket League**], GENRES [**sport, vehicular combat**], PLAYER_PERSPECTIVE [**third person**])
Are you into **third person sport** games with **vehicular combat** like **Rocket League**?
verify_attribute(NAME [**Little Big Adventure**], RATING [**average**], HAS_MULTIPLAYER [**no**], PLATFORMS [**PlayStation**])
I recall that you were **not that fond** of **Little Big Adventure**. Does **single-player** gaming on the **PlayStation** quickly get boring for you?

Table 7: Examples of MRs and corresponding reference utterances in the ViGGO dataset. The DA of the MRs is indicated in italics, and the slots in small caps. The slot mentions in the utterances are bolded.

Note that in ViGGO the items in the value of a *List* slot are comma-separated, and therefore the individual items must not contain a comma. There are no restrictions as to whether the values are single-word or multi-word in any of the categories.

A.3 Data Collection

When generating the MRs for the *inform* DA, we fixed the slot ratios: the NAME and GEN-RES slots were mandatory in every MR, the PLAYER_PERSPECTIVE and RELEASE_YEAR were enforced in about half of the MRs, while the remaining slots are present in about 25% of the MRs. At the same time we imposed two constraints on the slot combinations: (1) whenever one of the Steam, Linux or Mac related boolean slots is present in an MR, the PLATFORMS slot must be included too, and (2) whenever either of the Linux or Mac slots was picked for an MR, the other one was automatically added too. These two constraints were introduced so as to encourage reference utterances with natural aggregations and contrast relations.

The remaining 8 DAs, however, contain significantly fewer slots each (see Table 2). We therefore decided to have the MTurk workers select 5 unique slot combinations for each given video game before writing the corresponding utterances. Since for these DAs we collected less data, we tried to ensure in this way that we have a sufficient number of samples for those slot combinations that are most natural to be mentioned in each of the DAs. While fixing mandatory slots for each DA, we instructed the workers to choose 1 or 2 additional slots depending on the task. The data collection for MRs with only 1 additional slot and for those with 2 was performed separately, so as to prevent workers from taking the easy way out by always selecting just a single slot, given the option.

Leaving the slot selection to crowdworkers yields a frequency distribution of all slot combinations, which presumably indicates the suitability of different slots to be mentioned together in a sentence. This meta-information can be made use of in a system's dialogue manager to sample from the observed slot combination distributions instead of sampling randomly or hard-coding the combinations. Figure 3 shows the distributions of the 8 slot pairs most commonly mentioned together in different DAs. These account for 53% of the selections among the 6 DAs that can take 2 additional

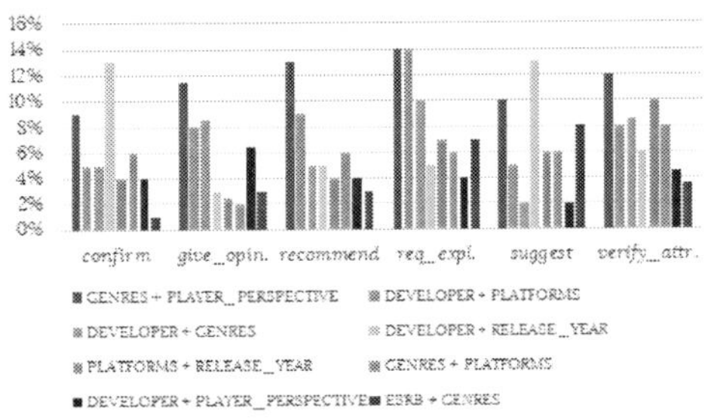

Figure 3: Distribution of the 8 most frequently selected slot combinations across different DAs.

slots besides the mandatory ones. We can observe some interesting trends in the distributions, such as that the DEVELOPER + RELEASE_YEAR combination was the most frequent one in the *confirm* DA, while fairly rare in most of the other DAs. This might be because this pair of a game's attributes is arguably the next best identifier of a game after its name.

A.4 Dataset Cleaning

A large proportion of the raw data collected contained typos and various errors, as is inevitable when crowdsourcing. We took the following three steps to clean the data.

First, we used regular expressions to enforce several standardization policies regarding special characters, punctuation, and the correction of undesired abbreviations/misspellings of standard domain-specific terms (e.g., we would change terms like "Play station" or "PS4" to the uniform "PlayStation"). At the same time, we removed or enforced hyphens uniformly in certain terms, for example, "single-player". Although phrases such as "first person" should correctly have a hyphen when used as adjective, the turkers used this rule very inconsistently. In order to avoid model outputs being penalized during the evaluation by the arbitrary choice of a hyphen presence or absence in the reference utterances, we decided to remove the hyphen in all such phrases regardless of the noun/adjective use.

Second, we developed an extensive set of heuristics to identify slot-related errors. This process revealed the vast majority of missing or incorrect slot mentions, which we subsequently fixed according to the corresponding MRs. Turkers would sometimes also inject a piece of information which was not present in the MR, some of

which is not even represented by any of the slots,
e.g., plot or main characters. We remove this extraneous information from the utterances so as to
avoid confusing the neural model. This step thus
involved certain manual work and was thus performed jointly with the third step.

Finally, we further resolved the remaining typos, grammatical errors, and unsolicited information.

A.5 Model Parameters

Even though on the small datasets we work with
we do not necessarily expect the Transformer
model to perform better than recurrent neural
networks, we chose this model for its significantly faster training, without sacrificing the performance. For our experiments a small 2-layer
Transformer with 8 heads proved to be sufficient.
The input tokens are encoded into embeddings of
size 256, and the target sequences were truncated
to 60 tokens. The model performed best with
dropout values of 0.2. For training of the Transformer models we used the Adam optimizer with
a custom learning rate schedule including a brief
linear warm-up and a cosine decay.

BERT for Question Generation

Ying-Hong Chan
Department of Computer Science
National Chung Hsing University
Taichung, Taiwan
harry831120@gmail.com

Yao-Chung Fan
Department of Computer Science
National Chung Hsing University
Taichung, Taiwan
yfan@nchu.edu.tw

Abstract

In this study, we investigate the employment of the pre-trained BERT language model to tackle question generation tasks. We introduce two neural architectures built on top of BERT for question generation tasks. The first one is a straightforward BERT employment, which reveals the defects of directly using BERT for text generation. And, the second one remedies the first one by restructuring the BERT employment into a sequential manner for taking information from previous decoded results. Our models are trained and evaluated on the question-answering dataset SQuAD. Experiment results show that our best model yields state-of-the-art performance which advances the BLEU 4 score of existing best models from 16.85 to 21.04.

1 Introduction

Question generation (QG) task, which takes a context and an answer as input and generates a question that targets the given answer, have received tremendous interests in recent years from both industrial and academic communities (Zhao et al., 2018)(Zhou et al., 2017)(Du et al., 2017). The state-of-the-art models mainly adopt neural approaches by training a neural network based on the sequence-to-sequence framework. So far, the best performing result is reported in (Zhao et al., 2018), which advances the state-of-the-art results from 13.9 to 16.8 (BLEU 4).

The existing QG models mainly rely on recurrent neural networks (RNN) augmented by attention mechanisms. However, the inherent sequential nature of the RNN models suffers from the problem of handling long sequences. As a result, the existing QG models (Du et al., 2017)(Zhou et al., 2017) mainly use only sentence-level information as context. When applied to a paragraph-level context, the existing models show significant performance degradation. However, as indicated by (Du et al., 2017), providing paragraph-level information can improve QG performance. For handling long context, the work (Zhao et al., 2018) introduces a maxout pointer mechanism with gated self-attention encoder for processing paragraph-level input. The work reports state-of-the-art performance for QG tasks.

Recently, the NLP community has seen excitement around neural learning models that make use of pre-trained language models (Devlin et al., 2018)(Radford et al., 2018). The latest development is BERT, which has shown significant performance improvement over various natural language understanding tasks, such as document summarization, document classification, etc. In this study, we investigate the employment of the pre-trained BERT language model to tackle question generation tasks. We introduce two neural architectures built on top of BERT for question generation tasks. The first one is a straightforward BERT employment, which reveals the defects of directly using BERT for text generation. As will be shown in the experiment, naive employment of BERT offers poor performance, as, by construction, BERT produces all tokens at a time without considering decoding results in previous steps. Thus, we propose a sequential question generation model based on BERT as our second model for taking information from previous decoded results. Our model is simple but effective. We think this is a feature of BERT, as the power of BERT is able to simplify neural architecture design for natural language processing tasks. Our model outperforms the existing best models (Zhao et al., 2018) and pushes the state-of-the-art result from 16.85 to 21.04 (BLEU 4).

The rest of this paper is organized as follows. First, in Section 2, we review the BERT model which is the building block for our models. In Sec-

Proceedings of The 12th International Conference on Natural Language Generation, pages 173–177,
Tokyo, Japan, 28 Oct - 1 Nov, 2019. ©2019 Association for Computational Linguistics

tion 3, we introduce two BERT adaptions for QG tasks. Section 4 provides the performance evaluation and Section 5 concludes our findings and discuss future works.

2 BERT Overview

The BERT model is built by a stack of multi-layer bidirectional Transformer encoder (Vaswani et al., 2017). The BERT model has three architecture parameter settings: the number of layers (i.e., transformer blocks), the hidden size, and the number of self-attention heads in a transformer block. There are two BERT models with different model size released.

- **BERT$_{base}$**: 12 layers, 768 hidden dimensions and 12 attention heads (in transformer) with the total number of 110M parameters.

- **BERT$_{large}$**: 24 layers, 1024 hidden dimensions and 16 attention heads (in transformer) with the total number of 340M parameters.

For using BERT model, the input is required to be aligned as the BERTs specific input sequence. In general, a special token [CLS] is inserted as the first token for BERT's input sequence. The final hidden state of the [CLS] token is designed to be used as a final sequence representation for classification tasks. The input token sequence can be a pack of multiple sentences. To distinguish the information from different sentences, a special token [SEP] is added between the tokens of two consecutive sentences. In addition, a learned embedding is added to every token to denote whether it belongs to sentence A or sentence B. For example, given a sentence pair (s_i, s_j) where s_i contains $|s_i|$ tokens and s_j contains $|s_j|$ tokens, the BERT input sequence is formulated as a sequence in the following form:

$$X = ([\text{CLS}], t_{i,1}, ..., t_{i,|s_i|}, [\text{SEP}], t_{j,1}..., t_{j,|s_j|})$$

The input representation of a given token is the sum of three embeddings: the token embeddings, the segmentation embeddings, and the position embeddings. Then the input representation is fed forward into extra layers to perform a fine-tuning procedure. BERT can be employed in three language modeling tasks: sequence-level classification, span-level prediction, and token-level prediction tasks. The fine-tuning procedure is performed

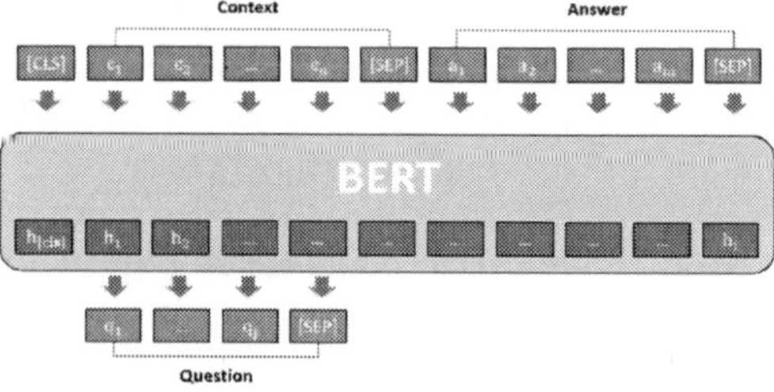

Figure 1: The BERT-QG architecture

in a task-specific manner. The details of our fine-tuning procedure are introduced in the later subsections.

3 BERT for Question Generation

3.1 BERT-QG

As an initial attempt, we first adapt the BERT model for QG as follows. First, for a given context paragraph $C = [c_1, ..., c_{|C|}]$ and an answer phase $A = [a_1, ..., a_{|A|}]$, the input sequence X is aligned as

$$X = ([\text{CLS}], C, [\text{SEP}], A, [\text{SEP}])$$

Let BERT() be the BERT model. We first obtain the hidden representation $\mathbf{H} \in \mathbb{R}^{|X| \times h}$ by $\mathbf{H} = \text{BERT}(X)$, where $|X|$ is the length of the input sequence and h is the size of the hidden dimension. Then, $\mathbf{H}$ is passed to a dense layer $\mathbf{W} \in \mathbb{R}^{h \times |V|}$ followed by a softmax function as follows.

$$Pr(w|x_i) = softmax(\mathbf{H} \cdot \mathbf{W} + \mathbf{b}), \forall x_i \in X$$

$$\hat{q}_i = \text{argmax}_w Pr(w|x_i)$$

The softmax is applied along the dimension of the sequence. All the parameters are fine-tuned jointly to maximize the log-probability of the correct token q_i. The model architecture is illustrated in Figure 1. As shown in the figure, we align a given context paragraph and a given answer as the input sequence and feed the input sequence into the BERT model to generate a sequence of tokens as a generated question.

3.2 BERT-SQG

In text generation tasks, as suggested by (Sutskever et al., 2014), considering the previous decoded results has significant impacts on the

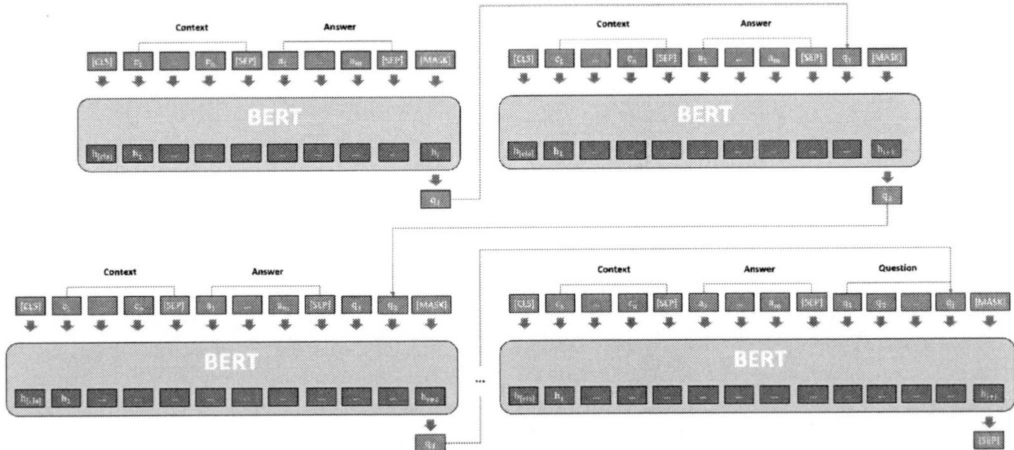

Figure 2: The BERT-SQG architecture

quality of the generated text. However, in BERT-QG, the token generation is performed without previously decoded result information. Due to this consideration, we propose a sequential question generation model based on BERT (called BERT-SQG).

In BERT-SQG, we take into consideration the previous decoded results for decoding a token. We adapt the BERT model for question generation as follows. First, for a given context paragraph $C = [c_1, ..., c_{|C|}]$ and an answer phase $A = [a_1, ..., a_{|A|}]$, and $\hat{Q} = [\hat{q}1, ..., \hat{q}_i]$ the input sequence X_i is formulated as

$$X_i = (\texttt{[CLS]}, C, \texttt{[SEP]}, A, \texttt{[SEP]}, \hat{q}_1,$$
$$..., \hat{q}_i, \texttt{[MASK]})$$

Then, the input sequence X_i is represented by the BERT embedding layers and then travel forward into the BERT model. After that, we take the final hidden state of the last token $\texttt{[MASK]}$ in the input sequence. We denote the final hidden vector of $\texttt{[MASK]}$ as $\mathbf{h}_{\texttt{[MASK]}} \in \mathbb{R}^h$. We adapt BERT model by adding an affine layer $\mathbf{W}_{\text{SQG}} \in \mathbb{R}^{h \times |V|}$ to the output of the $\texttt{[MASK]}$ token. We compute the probabilities $Pr(w|X_i) \in R^{|V|}$ by a softmax function as follows.

$$Pr(w|X_i) = softmax(\mathbf{h}_{\texttt{[MASK]}} \cdot \mathbf{W}_{\text{SQG}} + \mathbf{b}_{\text{SQG}})$$
$$\hat{q}_i = \text{argmax}_w Pr(w|X_i)$$

Subsequently, the newly generated token $\hat{q}_i$ is appended into X and the question generation process is repeated (as illustrated in Figure 2) with the new X until $\texttt{[SEP]}$ is predicted. We report the generated tokens as the predicted question.

4 Performance Evaluation

4.1 Datasets

The SQuAD dataset contains 536 Wikipedia articles and around 100K reading comprehension questions (and the corresponding answers) posed about the articles. Answers of the questions are text spans in the articles.

We follow the same data split settings as previous work on the QG tasks (Du et al., 2017)(Zhao et al., 2018) to directly compare the state-of-the-art results on QG tasks. Table 1 summarizes some statistics for the compared datasets.

- **SQuAD 73K** In this set, we follow the same setting as (Du et al., 2017); the accessible parts of the SQuAD training data are randomly divided into a training set (80%), a development set (10%), and a test set (10%). We report results on the 10% test set.

- **SQuAD 81K** In this set, we follow the same setting as (Zhao et al., 2018); the accessible SQuAD development data set is divided into a development set (50%), and a test set (50%).

4.2 Implementation Details

We use the PyTorch version of BERT [1] to train our BERT-QG and BERT-SQG models. The

---

[1] https://github.com/huggingface/pytorch-pretrained-BERT

Table 1: Dataset statistics: SQuAD 73K is the setting of (Du et al., 2017), and SQuAD 81K is the setting of (Zhao et al., 2018).

	Train	Test	Dev
SQuAD 73K	73240	11877	10570
SQuAD 81K	81577	8964	8964

pre-trained model uses the officially provided **BERT**$_{base}$ model (12 layers, 768 hidden dimensions, and 12 attention heads.) with a vocab of 30522 words. Dropout probability is set to 0.1 between transformer layers. The Adamax optimizer is applied during the training process, with an initial learning rate of 5e-5. The batch size for the update is set at 28. All our models use two TITAN RTX GPUs for 5 epochs training. We use Dev. data for epoch model to make predictions and select the highest accuracy rate as our score evaluation model. Also, in our BERT-SQG model, we use the Beam Search strategy for sequence decoding. The beam size is set to 3.

4.3 Model Comparison

In this paper, we compare our models with the best performing models (Du et al., 2017)(Zhao et al., 2018) in the literature. The compared models in the experiment are:

- **NQG-RC** (Du et al., 2017): A seq2seq question generation model based on bidirectional LSTM.

- **PLQG** (Zhao et al., 2018): A seq2seq network which contains a gated self-attention encoder and a maxout pointer decoder to enable the capability of handling long text input. PLQG model is the state-of-the-art models for QG tasks.

4.4 Evaluation Results

Table 2 shows the comparison results using sentence-level context and Table 3 shows the results on paragraph level context. We compare the models using standard metric BLEU and ROUGE-L ((Papineni et al., 2002)).

We have the following findings to note about the results. First, as can be observed, BERT-QG offers poor performance. In fact, the performance of BERT-QG is far from the results by other models. This result is expected as BERT-QG generates the sentences without considering the previous decoded results. However, when taking into account

the previous decoded results (BERT-SQG), we effectively utilize the power of BERT and yield the state of the art result compared with the existing RNN variants for QG. As shown in Table 2, BERT-SQG outperforms the existing best performing model by 2% on both benchmark datasets.

Second, the results in Table 3 further show that BERT-SQG successfully processes the paragraph-level contexts and further push the state-of-the-art from 16.85 to 21.04 in terms of BLEU 4 score. Note that NQG-RC and PLQG both use the RNN architecture, and the RNN-based models all suffer from the issue of consuming long text input. We see that the BERT model based on transformer blocks effectively addresses the issue of processing long text. The results of our BERT-SQG model are consistent in two data set and have achieved the best score at the paragraph level.

5 Conclusion

In this paper, we demonstrate that BERT can be adapted to question generation tasks. We concede that our BERT-SQG model is simple. However, we think this is a feature of BERT, as the power of BERT is able to simplify neural architectures design for specific tasks. While our model is simple, our model achieves state-of-the-art performance at both sentence-level and paragraph-level input and provides strong baselines for future research.

Acknowledgments

This work is supported in part by the Ministry of Science and Technology, Taiwan, under grant No: 107-2221-E-005-064-MY2.

References

Jacob Devlin, Ming-Wei Chang, Kenton Lee, and Kristina Toutanova. 2018. Bert: Pre-training of deep bidirectional transformers for language understanding. *arXiv preprint arXiv:1810.04805*.

Xinya Du, Junru Shao, and Claire Cardie. 2017. Learning to ask: Neural question generation for reading comprehension. *arXiv preprint arXiv:1705.00106*.

Kishore Papineni, Salim Roukos, Todd Ward, and Wei-Jing Zhu. 2002. Bleu: a method for automatic evaluation of machine translation. In *Proceedings of the 40th annual meeting on association for computational linguistics*, pages 311–318. Association for Computational Linguistics.

Alec Radford, Karthik Narasimhan, Tim Salimans, and Ilya Sutskever. 2018. Improving language under-

Table 2: Comparison between our model and the published methods using sentence level context

	Model	BLEU 1	BLEU 2	BLEU 3	BLEU 4	METEOR	ROUGE-L
SQuAD 73K	NQG-RC	43.09	25.96	17.50	12.28	16.62	39.75
	PLQG	43.47	28.23	20.40	15.32	19.29	43.91
	BERT-QG	34.17	15.52	8.36	4.47	14.78	37.60
	BERT-SQG	**48.38**	**33.15**	**24.75**	**19.08**	**22.43**	**46.94**
SQuAD 81K	PLQG	44.51	29.07	21.06	15.82	19.67	44.24
	BERT-QG	34.18	15.51	8.57	4.97	14.57	37.65
	BERT-SQG	**50.18**	**35.03**	**26.60**	**20.88**	**23.84**	**48.37**

Table 3: Comparison between our model and the published methods using paragraph level context

	Model	BLEU 1	BLEU 2	BLEU 3	BLEU 4	METEOR	ROUGE-L
SQuAD 73K	NQG-RC	42.54	25.33	16.98	11.86	16.28	39.37
	PLQG	45.07	29.58	21.60	16.38	20.25	44.48
	BERT-QG	37.49	18.32	10.47	6.10	16.80	41.01
	BERT-SQG	**50.00**	**34.54**	**25.98**	**20.11**	**23.88**	**48.12**
SQuAD 81K	PLQG	45.69	30.25	22.16	16.85	20.62	44.99
	BERT-QG	32.61	14.50	7.70	4.08	14.18	37.94
	BERT-SQG	**50.89**	**35.49**	**26.87**	**21.04**	**24.25**	**48.66**

standing by generative pre-training. *URL https://s3-us-west-2. amazonaws. com/openai-assets/research-covers/languageunsupervised/language understanding paper. pdf.*

Ilya Sutskever, Oriol Vinyals, and Quoc V Le. 2014. Sequence to sequence learning with neural networks. In *Advances in neural information processing systems*, pages 3104–3112.

Ashish Vaswani, Noam Shazeer, Niki Parmar, Jakob Uszkoreit, Llion Jones, Aidan N Gomez, Łukasz Kaiser, and Illia Polosukhin. 2017. Attention is all you need. In *Advances in neural information processing systems*, pages 5998–6008.

Yao Zhao, Xiaochuan Ni, Yuanyuan Ding, and Qifa Ke. 2018. Paragraph-level neural question generation with maxout pointer and gated self-attention networks. In *Proceedings of the 2018 Conference on Empirical Methods in Natural Language Processing*, pages 3901–3910.

Qingyu Zhou, Nan Yang, Furu Wei, Chuanqi Tan, Hangbo Bao, and Ming Zhou. 2017. Neural question generation from text: A preliminary study. In *National CCF Conference on Natural Language Processing and Chinese Computing*, pages 662–671. Springer.

Visually grounded generation of entailments from premises

Somaye Jafaritazehjani
IRISA, Université de Rennes I, France
`somayeh.jafaritazehjani@irisa.fr`

Albert Gatt
LLT, University of Malta
`albert.gatt@um.edu.mt`

Marc Tanti
LLT, University of Malta
`marc.tanti@um.edu.mt`

Abstract

Natural Language Inference (NLI) is the task of determining the semantic relationship between a premise and a hypothesis. In this paper, we focus on the *generation* of hypotheses from premises in a multimodal setting, to generate a sentence (hypothesis) given an image and/or its description (premise) as the input. The main goals of this paper are (a) to investigate whether it is reasonable to frame NLI as a generation task; and (b) to consider the degree to which grounding textual premises in visual information is beneficial to generation. We compare different neural architectures, showing through automatic and human evaluation that entailments can indeed be generated successfully. We also show that multimodal models outperform unimodal models in this task, albeit marginally.

1 Introduction

Natural Language Inference (NLI) or Recognizing Textual Entailment (RTE) is typically formulated as a classification task: given a pair consisting of premise(s) P and hypothesis Q, the task is to determine if Q is entailed by P, contradicts it, or whether Q is neutral with respect to P (Dagan et al., 2006). For example, in both the left and right panels of Figure 1, the premise P in the caption entails the hypothesis Q.

In classical (i.e. logic-based) formulations (e.g., Cooper et al., 1996), P is taken to entail Q if Q follows from P in all 'possible worlds'. Since the notion of 'possible world' has proven hard to handle computationally, more recent approaches have converged on a probabilistic definition of the entailment relationship, relying on data-driven classification methods (cf. Dagan et al., 2006, 2010). In such approaches, P is taken to entail Q if, 'typically, a nhuman reading P would infer that Q is most likely true' (Dagan et al., 2006). Most approaches to RTE seek to identify the semantic relationship between P and Q based on their textual features.

With a few exceptions (Xie et al., 2019; Lai, 2018; Vu et al., 2018), NLI is defined in unimodal terms, with no reference to the non-linguistic 'world'. This means that NLI models remain trapped in what Roy (2005) described as a 'sensory deprivation tank', handling symbolic meaning representations which are ungrounded in the external world (cf. Harnad, 1990). On the other hand, the recent surge of interest in NLP tasks at the vision-language interface suggests ways of incorporating non-linguistic information into NLI. For example, pairing the premises in Figure 1 with their corresponding images could yield a more informative representation from which the semantic relationship between premise and hypothesis could be determined. This would be especially useful if the two modalities contained different types of information, effectively making the textual premise and the corresponding image complementary, rather than redundant with respect to each other.

While NLI is a classic problem in Natural Language Understanding, it also has considerable relevance for generation. Many text generation tasks, including summarisation (Nenkova and McKeown, 2011), paraphrasing (Androutsopoulos and Malakasiotis, 2010), text simplification (Siddharthan, 2014) and question generation (Piwek and Boyer, 2012), depend on the analysis and understanding of an input text to generate an output that stands in a specific semantic relationship to the input.

In this paper, we focus on the task of *generating* hypotheses from premises. Here, the challenge is to produce a text that follows from ('is entailed by') a given premise. Arguably, well-established tasks such as paraphrase generation and text sim-

Proceedings of The 12th International Conference on Natural Language Generation, pages 178–188,
Tokyo, Japan, 28 Oct - 1 Nov, 2019. ©2019 Association for Computational Linguistics

(a) *P*: Four guys in wheelchairs on a basketball court two
are trying to grab a ball in midair
Q: Four guys are playing basketball.

(b) *P*: A little girl walking down a dirt road behind a
group of other walkers
Q: The girl is not at the head of the pack of people

Figure 1: Images with premises and hypotheses

plification are specific instances of this more general problem. For example, in paraphrase generation, the input-output pair should be in a relationship of meaning preservation.

In contrast to previous work on entailment generation (Kolesnyk et al., 2016; Starc and Mladenić, 2017), we explore the additional benefits derived from grounding textual premises in image data. We therefore assume that the data consists of triples $\langle P, I, Q \rangle$, such that premises are accompanied by their corresponding images (I) as well as the hypotheses, as in Figure 1. We compare multimodal models to a unimodal setup, with a view to determining to what extent image data helps in generating entailments.

The rest of this paper is structured as follows. In Section 2 we discuss further motivations for viewing NLI and entailment generation as multimodal tasks. Section 3 describes the dataset and architectures used; Section 4 presents experimental results, including a human evaluation. Our conclusion (Section 5) is that it is feasible to frame NLI as a generation task and that incorporating non-linguistic information is potentially profitable. However, in line with recent research evaluating Vision-Language (VL) models (Shekhar et al., 2017; Wang et al., 2018; Vu et al., 2018; Tanti et al., 2019), we also find that current architectures are unable to ground textual representations in image data sufficiently.

2 NLI, Multimodal NLI and Generation

Since the work of Dagan et al. (2006), research on NLI has largely been data-driven (see Sammons et al., 2012, for an overview). Most recent approaches rely on neural architectures (e.g. Rocktäschel et al., 2015; Chen et al., 2016; Wang et al., 2017), a trend which is clearly evident in the submissions to recent RepEval challenges (Nangia et al., 2017).

Data-driven NLI has received a boost from the availability of large datasets such as SICK (Marelli et al., 2014), SNLI (Bowman et al., 2015) and MultiNLI (Williams et al., 2018). Some recent work has also investigated multimodal NLI, whereby the classification of the entailment relationship is done on the basis of image features (Xie et al., 2019; Lai, 2018), or a combination of image and textual features (Vu et al., 2018). In particular, Vu et al. (2018) exploited the fact that the main portion of SNLI was created by reusing image captions from the Flickr30k dataset (Young et al., 2014) as premises, for which entailments, contradictions and neutral hypotheses were subsequently crowdsourced via Amazon Mechanical Turk (Bowman et al., 2015). This makes it possible to pair premises with the images for which they were originally written as descriptive captions, thereby reformulating the NLI problem as a Vision-Language task. There are at least two important motivations for this:

1. The inclusion of image data is one way to bring together the classical and the probabilistic approaches to NLI, whereby the image can be viewed as a (partial) representation of the 'world' described by the premise, with the entailment relationship being determined jointly from both. This is in line with the suggestion by Young et al. (2014), that images be considered as akin to the 'possible worlds' in which sentences (in this case, captions) receive their denotation.

2. A multimodal definition of NLI also serves as a challenging testbed for VL NLP models, in which there has been increasing interest in recent years. This is especially the case since neural approaches to fundamental computer vision (CV) tasks have yielded significant improvements (LeCun et al., 2015), while also making it possible to use pretrained CV models in multimodal neural architectures, for example in tasks such as image captioning (Bernardi et al., 2016). However, recent work has cast doubt on the extent to which such models are truly exploiting image features in a multimodal space (Shekhar et al., 2017; Wang et al., 2018; Tanti et al., 2019). Indeed, Vu et al. (2018) also find that image data contributes less than expected to determining the semantic relationship between premise-hypothesis pairs in the classic RTE labelling task.

There have also been a few approaches to entailment generation, which again rely on the SNLI dataset. Kolesnyk et al. (2016) employed a sequence-to-sequence architecture with attention (Sutskever et al., 2014; Bahdanau et al., 2015) to generate hypotheses from premises. They extended this framework to the generation of inference chains by recursively feeding the model with the generated hypotheses as the input. Starc and Mladenić (2017) proposed different generative neural network models to generate a stream of hypotheses given ⟨premise, Label⟩ pairs as the input.

In seeking to reframe NLI as a generation task, the present paper takes inspiration from these approaches. However, we are also interested in framing the task as a multimodal, VL problem, in line with the two motivations noted at the beginning of this section. Given that recent work has suggested shortcomings in the way VL models adequately utilise visual information, a focus on multimodal entailment generation is especially timely, since it permits direct comparison between models utilising unimodal and multimodal input.

As Figure 1 suggests, given the triple $\langle P, I, Q \rangle$, the hypothesis Q could be generated from the premise P only, from the image I, or from a combination of $P + I$. Our question is whether we can generate better entailments from a combination of both, compared to only one of these input modalities.

3 Methodology

3.1 Data

We focus on the subset of entailment pairs in the SNLI dataset (Bowman et al., 2015). The majority of instances in SNLI consist of premises that were originally elicited as descriptive captions for images in Flickr30k (Young et al., 2014; ands Liwei Wang et al., 2015).[1]

In constructing the SNLI dataset, Amazon Mechanical Turk workers were shown the captions/premises without the corresponding images, and were asked to write a new caption that was (i) true, given the premise (entailment); (ii) false, given the premise (contradiction); and (iii) possibly true (neutral).

Following Vu et al. (2018), we use a multimodal version of SNLI, which we refer to as V-SNLI, which was obtained by mapping SNLI premises to their corresponding Flickr30k images (Xie et al., 2019, use a similar approach). The resulting V-SNLI therefore contains premises which are assumed to be true of their corresponding image. Since we focus exclusively on the entailment subset, we also assume, given the instructions given to annotators, that the hypotheses are also true of the image. Figure 1 shows two examples of images with both premises and hypotheses.

Each premise in the SNLI dataset includes several reference hypotheses by different annotators. In the original SNLI train/dev/test split, some premises show up in both train and test sets, albeit with different paired hypotheses. For the present work, once premises were mapped to their corresponding Flickr30k images, all premises corresponding to an image were grouped, and the

---

[1] A subset of 4000 cases in SNLI was extracted from the VisualGenome dataset (Krishna et al., 2017). Like Vu et al. (2018), we exclude these from our experiments.

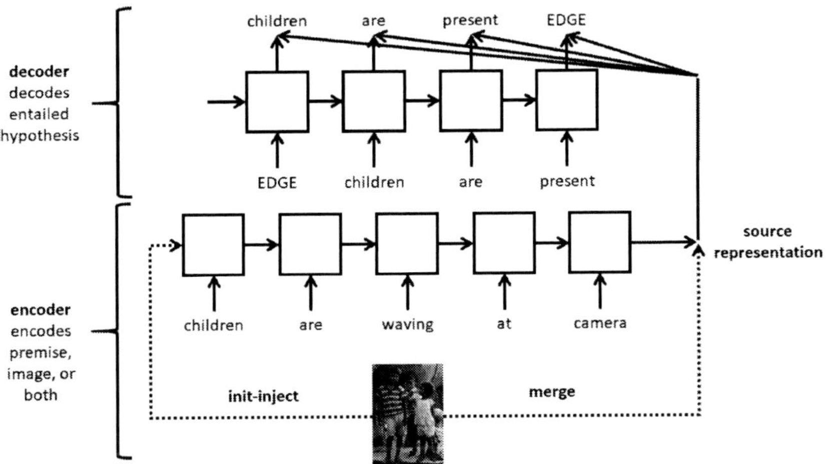

Figure 2: Architecture schema that is instantiated in the different models. The encoder returns a source representation which conditions the decoder into generating the entailed hypothesis. The encoder of multimodal models either (1) initialises the encoder RNN with the image features (init-inject) and returns the final state; or (2) concatenates the encoder RNN's final state with the image features (merge) and returns the result; or (3) returns the image features as is without involving the encoder RNN. The unimodal model encoder returns the encoder RNN's final state as is. The source representation is concatenated to the decoder RNN's states prior to passing them to the softmax layer.

dataset was resplit so that the train/test partitions had no overlap, resulting in a split of 182,167 (train), 3,291 (test) and 3,329 (dev) entailment pairs. This also made it possible to use a multi-reference approach to evaluation (see Section 3.3).

Prior to training, all texts were lowercased and tokenized.[2] Vocabulary items with frequency less than 10 were mapped to the token $\langle UNK \rangle$. The unimodal model (see Section 3.2) was trained on textual P-Q pairs from the original SNLI data, while the multimodal models were trained on pairs from V-SNLI where the input consisted of P+I (for the multimodal text+image model), or I only (for the image-to-text model), to generate entailments.

3.2 Models

Figure 2 is an illustration of the architecture schema that is employed for both multimodal and unimodal architectures. A sequence-to-sequence encoder-decoder architecture is used to predict the entailed hypothesis from the source. The source can be either a premise sentence, an image, or both.

Both the encoder and the decoder use a 256D GRU RNN and both embed their input words using a 256D embedding layer. In multimodal

models, the encoder either produces a multimodal source representation that represents the sentence-image mixture or produces just an image representation. In the unimodal model, the encoder produces a representation of the premise sentence only.

This encoded representation (multimodal or unimodal) is then concatenated to every state in the decoder RNN prior to sending it to the softmax layer, which will predict the next word in the entailed hypothesis.

All multimodal models extract image features from the penultimate layer of the pre-trained VGG-19 convolutional neural network (Simonyan and Zisserman, 2014). All models were implemented in Tensorflow, and trained using the the Adam optimizer (Kingma and Ba, 2014) with a learning rate of .0001 and a cross-entropy loss.

The models compared are as follows:

1. **Unimodal** model: A standard sequence-to-sequence architecture developed for neural machine translation (NMT). It uses separate RNNs for encoding the source text and for decoding the target text. This model encodes the premise sentence alone and generates the entailed hypothesis. In the unimodal architecture, the final state of the encoder RNN is

---

[2]Experiments without lowercasing showed only marginal differences in the results.

used as the representation of the premise P.

2. Multimodal, text+image input, init-inject (**T+I-Init**): A multimodal model in which the image features are incorporated at the encoding stage, that is, image features are used to initialise the RNN encoder. This architecture, which is widely used in image captioning (Devlin et al., 2015; Liu et al., 2016) is referred to as *init-inject*, following Tanti et al. (2018), on the grounds that image features are directly injected into the RNN.

3. Multimodal, text+image input, merge (**T+I-Merge**): A second multimodal model in which the image features are concatenated with the final state of the encoder RNN. Following Tanti et al. (2018), we refer to this as the *merge* model. This too is adapted from a widely-used architecture in image captioning (Mao et al., 2014, 2015a,b; Hendricks et al., 2016). The main difference from *init-inject* is that here, image features are combined with textual features immediately prior to decoding at the softmax layer, so that the RNN does not encode image features directly.

4. Multimodal, image input only (**IC**): This model is based on a standard image captioning setup (Bernardi et al., 2016) in which the entailed hypothesis is based on the image features only, with no premise sentence. This architecture leaves out the encoder RNN completely. Note that, while this is a standard image captioning setup, it is put to a somewhat different use here, since we do not train the model to generate captions (which correspond to the premises in V-SNLI) but the hypotheses (which are taken to follow from the premises).

3.3 Evaluation metrics

We employed the evaluation metrics BLEU-1 (Papineni et al., 2002), METEOR (Lavie and Agarwal, 2007) and CIDEr (Vedantam et al., 2015) to compare generated entailments against the gold outputs in the model. We also compare the model perplexity on the test set.

As noted earlier, we adopted a multi-reference approach to evaluation, exploiting the fact that in our dataset we grouped all reference hypotheses corresponding to each premise (and its corresponding image). Thus, evaluation metrics are calculated by comparing the generated hypotheses to a group of reference hypotheses. This is advantageous, since n-gram based metrics such as BLEU and METEOR are known to yield more reliable results when multiple reference texts are available.

4 Results

4.1 Metric-based evaluation

The results obtained by all models are shown in Table 1. The T+I-Merge architecture outperforms all other models on CIDEr and METEOR, while the unimodal model, relying only on textual premises, is marginally better on BLEU and has slightly lower perplexity.

The lower perplexity of the unimodal model is is unsurprising given that in the unimodal model, the decoder is only conditioned on textual features without images. However, it should also be noted that the unimodal model also fares quite well on the other two metrics, and is only marginally worse than T+I-Merge. Its score on BLEU-1 is also competitive with that reported by Kolesnyk et al. (2016) for their seq2seq model, which obtained a BLEU score of 0.428. Note, however, that this score was not obtained using a multi-reference approach, that is, each generated candidate was compared to each reference candidate, rather than the set of references together. Recomputing our BLEU-1 score for the Unimodal model in this way, we obtain a score of 0.395, which is marginally lower than that reported by Kolesnyk et al. (2016).

The IC model, which generates entailments exclusively from images, ranks lowest on all metrics. This is probably due to the fact that, contrary to the usual setup for image caption generation, this model was trained on image-entailment pairs rather than directly on image-caption pairs. Although, based on the instructions given to annotators (Bowman et al., 2015), entailments in SNLI are presumed to be true of the image, it must be noted that the entailments were not elicited as descriptive captions with reference to an image, unlike the premises.

We discuss these results in more detail in Section 4.3, after reporting on a human evaluation.

4.2 Human evaluation

We conducted a human evaluation experiment, designed to address the question whether better en-

Model	BLEU-1	METEOR	CIDEr	Perplexity
Unimodal	**0.695**	0.267	0.938	**7.23**
T+I-Init	0.634	0.239	0.763	10.73
T+I-Merge	0.686	**0.271**	**0.955**	7.26
IC	0.474	0.16	0.235	13.7

Table 1: Automatic evaluation results for unimodal and multimodal models

tailments are generated from textual premises, images, or a combination of the two. In the metric-based evaluation (Section 4.1), the best multimodal model was T+I-Merge; hence, we use the outputs from this model, comparing them to the outputs from the unimodal and the image-only IC model.

Participants Twenty self-reported native or fluent speakers of English were recruited through social media and the authors' personal network.

Materials A random sample of 90 instances from the V-SNLI test set was selected. Each consisted of a premise, together with an image and three entailments generated using the Unimodal, IC and I+T-Merge models, respectively. The 90 instances were randomly divided into three groups. Participants in the evaluation were similarly allocated to one of three groups. The groups were rotated through a latin square so that each participant saw each of the 90 instances, one third in each of the three conditions (Unimodal, IC or I+T-Merge). Equal numbers of judgments were thus obtained for each instance in each condition, while participants never saw a premise more than once.

Procedure Participants conducted the evaluation online. Test items were administered in blocks, by condition (text-only, image-only or text+image) and presented in a fixed, randomised order to all participants. However, participants evaluated items in the three conditions in different orders, due to the latin square rotation. Each test case was presented with an input consisting of textual premise, an image, or both. Participants were asked to judge to what extent the generated sentence followed from the input. Answers were given on an ordinal scale with the following qualitative responses: *totally*; *partly*; *not clear* or *not at all*. Figure 3 shows an example with a generated entailment in the text+image condition.

Figure 3: Example of an evaluation test item, with a sentence generated from both text and image.

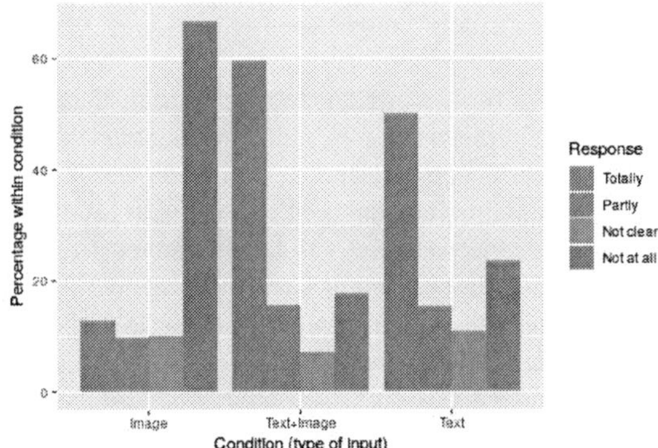

Figure 4: Proportion of responses in each category for each input condition.

Results Figure 4 shows the proportion of responses in each category for each of the three conditions. The figure suggests that human judgments were in line with the trends observed in Section 4.1. More participants judged the generated entailments as following totally or partly from the input, when the input consisted of text and image together (T+I-Merge), followed closely by the case where the input was text only (Unimodal). By contrast, in the case of the image-only (IC) condition, the majority of cases were judged as not following at all.

Possible reasons for these trends are discussed in the following sub-section in light of further analysis. First, we focus on whether the advantage of incorporating image features with text is statistically reliable. We coded responses as a binomial variable, distinguishing those cases where participants responded with 'totally' (i.e. the generated entailment definitely follows from the input) from all others. Note that this makes the evaluation conservative, since we focus only on the odds of receiving the most positive judgment in a given condition.

We fitted logit mixed-effects models. All models included random intercepts for participants and items (premise IDs) and random slopes for participants and items by condition. Where a model did not converge, we dropped the by-items random slope term. All models were fitted and tested using the `lme4` package in R (Bates et al., 2014).

The difference between the three types of input Condition significantly affected the odds of a positive ('totally') response ($z = 8.06, p < .001$).

We further investigated the impact of incorporating image features with or without text through planned comparisons. A mixed-effects model comparing the image-only to the text+image condition showed that the latter resulted in significantly better output as judged by our participants ($z = 7.80, p < .001$). However, the text+image model did not significantly outperform the text-only unimodal model, despite the higher percentage of positive responses in Figure 4 ($z = 1.61, p > .1$). This is consistent with the CIDEr and METEOR scores, which show that T+I-Merge outperforms the Unimodal model, but only marginally.

4.3 Analysis and discussion

Two sets of examples of the outputs of different models are provided in Table 2, corresponding to the images with premises and entailments shown in Figure 1a.

These examples, which are quite typical, suggest that the IC model is simply generating a descriptive caption which only captures some entities in the image. We further noted that in a number of cases, the IC model also generates repetitive sentences that are not obviously related to the image. These are presumably due to predictions relying extensively on the language model itself, yielding stereotypical 'captions' which reflect frequent patterns in the data. Together, these reasons may account for the poor performance of the IC model on both the metric-based and the human evaluations.

The main difference between the Unimodal and the multimodal T+I models seems to be that they generate texts that correspond to different, but arguably valid, entailments of the premise. However, the fact remains that the ungrounded Unimodal model yields good results that are close to those of T+I-Merge. While humans judged the T+I-Merge entailments as better than the unimodal ones overall, this is not a significant difference, at least as far as the highest response category ('totally') is concerned.

These limitations of multimodal models echo previous findings. In image captioning, for example, it has been shown that multimodal models are surprisingly insensitive to changes in the visual input. For instance Shekhar et al. (2017) found that VL models perform poorly on a task where they are required to distinguish between a 'correct' image (e.g. one that corresponds to a caption) and a completely unrelated foil image (Shekhar et al., 2017). Similarly, Tanti et al. (2019) find that image captioning models exhibit decreasing sensitivity to the input visual features as more of the caption is generated. In their experiments on multimodal NLI, Vu et al. (2018) also found that image features contribute relatively little to the correct classification of pairs as entailment, contradiction or neutral. These results suggest that current VL architectures do not exploit multimodal information effectively.

Beyond architectural considerations, however, there are also properties of the dataset which may account for why linguistic features play such an

Source	Sentence
P (Figure 1a)	Four guys in wheelchairs on a basketball court two are trying to grab a ball in midair.
Q (ref)	Four guys are playing basketball.
IC	A man is playing a game.
T+I-Init	Two men are jumping.
T+I-Merge	The basketball players are in the court.
Unimodal	The men are playing basketball.
P (Figure 1b)	A little girl walking down a dirt road behind a group of other walkers.
Q (ref)	The girl is not at the head of the pack of people.
IC	A man is wearing a hat.
T+I-Init	A young girl is walking down a path.
T+I-Merge	A group of people are walking down a road.
Unimodal	A girl is walking .

Table 2: Premises and reference captions, with output examples. These test cases correspond to the images in Figure 1.

important role in generating hypotheses. We discuss two of these in particular.

V-SNLI is not (quite) multimodal SNLI hypotheses were elicited from annotators in a unimodal setting, without reference to the images. Although we believe that our assumption concerning the truth of entailments in relation to images holds (see Section 3.1), the manner in which the data was collected potentially results in hypotheses which are in large measure predictable from linguistic features, accounting for the good performance of the unimodal model. If correct, this also offers an explanation for the superior performance of the T+I-Merge model, compared to T+I-Init. In the former, we train the encoder language model separately, mixing image features at a late stage, thereby allocating more memory to linguistic features in the RNN, compared to T+I-Init, where image features are used to initialise the encoder. Apart from yielding lower perplexity (see Table 1), this allows the T+I-Merge model to exploit linguistic features to a greater extent than is possible in T+I-Init.

Linguistic biases Recently, a number of authors have expressed concerns that NLI models may be learning heuristics based on superficial syntactic features rather than classifying entailment relationships based on a deeper 'understanding' of the semantics of the input texts (McCoy et al., 2019). Indeed, studies on the SNLI dataset have shown that it contains several linguistic biases (Gururangan et al., 2018), such that the semantic relationship (entailment/contradiction/neutral) becomes predictable from textual features of the hypotheses alone, without reference to the premise. Gururangan et al. (2018) identify a 'hard' subset of SNLI where such biases are not present.

Many of these biases are due to a high degree of similarity between a premise and a hypothesis. For example, contradictions were often formulated by annotators by simply including a negation, while entailments are sometimes substrings of the premises, as in the following pair:

P : A bicyclist riding down the road wearing a helmet and a black jacket.

Q : A bicyclist riding down the road.

Such biases could also account for the non-significant difference in performance between the two best models, Unimodal and T+I-Merge (which also allocates all RNN memory to textual features, unlike T+I-Init). In either case, it is possible that a hypothesis is largely predictable from the textual premise, irrespective of the image, and generation boils down to 'rewriting' part of the premise to produce a similar string (see, e.g., the last example in Table 2).

If textual similarity is indeed playing a role, then we would expect a model to generate entailments (Q_{gen}) with a better CIDEr score, in those cases where there is a high degree of overlap between the premise and the reference hypothesis (Q_{ref}).

We operationalised overlap in terms of the Dice

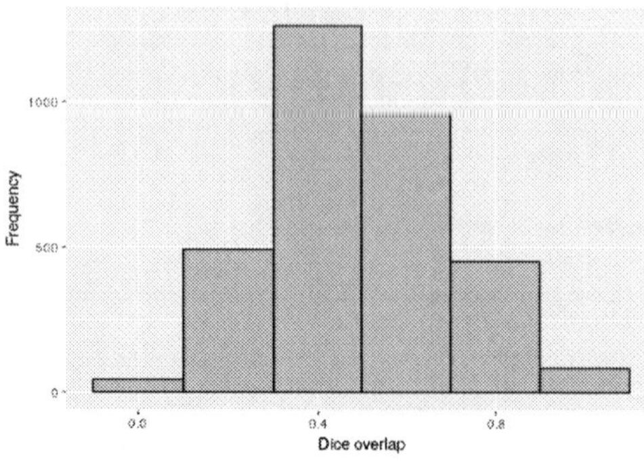

(a) Histogram of Dice overlap values

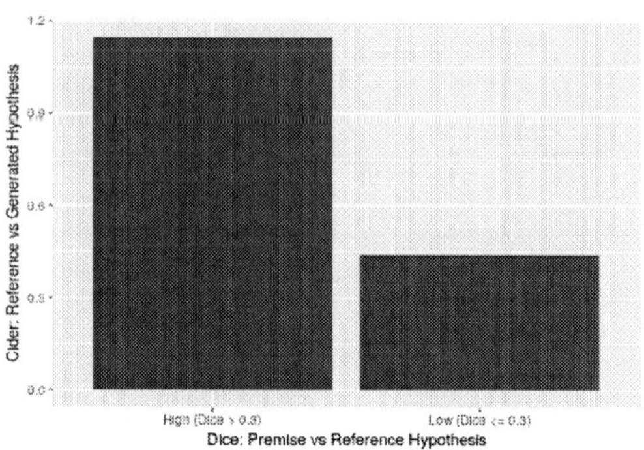

(b) CIDEr scores for Low vs High overlap test cases

Figure 5: Dice overlap vs CIDEr scores (T+I-Merge)

coefficient[3], computed over the sets of words in P or Q_{ref}, after stop word removal.[4] As shown by the histogram in Figure 5a, a significant proportion of the P-Q_{ref} pairs have a relatively high Dice coefficient ranging from 0.4 to 0.8. We divided test set instances into those with 'low' overlap (Dice $\leq$ 0.3; $n = 536$) and those with high overlap (Dice > 0.3; $n = 2755$). Figure 5b displays the mean CIDEr score between entailments generated by the T+I-Merge model, and reference entailments, as a function of whether the reference entailment had high overlap with the hypothesis.

Clearly, for those cases where the overlap between P and Q_{ref} was high, the T+I-Merge model obtains a higher CIDEr score between generated and reference outputs. This is confirmed by Pearson correlation coefficients between Dice coefficient and CIDEr, computed for each of the high/low overlap subsets: On the subset with high Dice overlap, we obtain a significant positive correlation ($r = 0.20, p < .001$); on the subset with low overlap, the correlation is far lower and does not reach significance ($r = .06, p > .1$).

5   Conclusion

This paper framed the NLI task as a generation task and compared the role of visual and linguistic features in generating entailments. To our knowledge, this was the first systematic attempt to compare unimodal and multimodal models for entailment generation.

---

[3]
$$Dice(P, Q_{ref}) = \frac{2 \times |P \cap Q_{ref}|}{|P| + |Q_{ref}|}$$

[4]Stopwords were removed using the built-in English stopword list in the Python NLTK library.

We find that grounding entailment generation in images is beneficial, but linguistic features also play a crucial role. Two reasons for this may be adduced. On the one hand, the data used was not elicited in a multimodal setting, despite the availability of images. It also contains linguistic biases, including relatively high degrees of similarity between premise and hypothesis pairs, which may result in additional image information being less important. On the other hand, it has become increasingly clear that Vision-Language NLP models are not grounding language in vision to the fullest extent possible. The present paper adds to this growing body of evidence.

Several avenues for future work are open, of which three are particularly important. First, in order to properly assess the contribution of grounded language models for entailment generation, it is necessary to design datasets in which the textual and visual modalities are complementary, rather than redundant with respect to each other. Second, while the present paper focused exclusively on entailments, future work should also consider generating contradictions. Finally, further research should investigate more sophisticated Vision-Language architectures, especially incorporating attention mechanisms.

Acknowledgments

The first author worked on this project while at the University of Malta, on the Erasmus Mundus European LCT Master Program. The third author was supported by the Endeavour Scholarship Scheme (Malta). We thank Raffaella Bernardi, Claudio Greco and Hoa Vutrong and our anonymous reviewers for their helpful comments.

References

Ion Androutsopoulos and Prodromos Malakasiotis. 2010. A survey of paraphrasing and textual entailment methods. *Journal of Artificial Intelligence Research*, 38:135–187.

Dzmitry Bahdanau, Kyunghyun Cho, and Yoshua Bengio. 2015. Neural Machine Translation By Jointly Learning To Align and Translate. In *Proc. ICLR'15*.

Douglas Bates, Martin Maechler, and Ben Bolke. 2014. lme4: Linear mixed-effects models using S4 classes.

Raffaella Bernardi, Ruket Cakici, Desmond Elliott, Aykut Erdem, Erkut Erdem, Nazli Ikizler-Cinbis, Frank Keller, Adrian Muscat, and Barbara Plank. 2016. Automatic description generation from images: A survey of models, datasets, and evaluation measures. *Journal of Artificial Intelligence Research*, 55(1):409–442.

Samuel R Bowman, Gabor Angeli, Christopher Potts, and Christopher D Manning. 2015. A large annotated corpus for learning natural language inference. In *Proc. EMNLP'15*.

Qian Chen, Xiaodan Zhu, Zhenhua Ling, Si Wei, Hui Jiang, and Diana Inkpen. 2016. Enhanced LSTM for Natural Language Inference. *arXiv*, 1609.06038(2016).

Robin Cooper, Dick Crouch, Jan Van Eijck, Chris Fox, Johan Van Genabith, Jan Jaspars, Hans Kamp, David Milward, Manfred Pinkal, Massimo Poesio, and Steve Pulman. 1996. Using the framework. Technical Report Technical Report LRE 62-051 D-16, The FraCaS Consortium.

Ido Dagan, Bill Dolan, Bernardo Magnini, and Dan Roth. 2010. The fourth pascal recognizing textual entailment challenge. *Natural Language Engineering*.

Ido Dagan, Oren Glickman, Bernardo Magnini, and Ramat Gan. 2006. The PASCAL Recognising Textual Entailment Challenge. In J. Quinonero-Candela, I. Dagan, B. Magnini, and F D'Alche-Buc, editors, *Machine Learning Challenges*, pages 177–190. Springer, Berlin and Heidelberg.

Jacob Devlin, Hao Cheng, Hao Fang, Saurabh Gupta, Li Deng, Xiaodong He, Geoffrey Zweig, and Margaret Mitchell. 2015. Language models for image captioning: The quirks and what works. In *Proc. ACL'15*.

Suchin Gururangan, Swabha Swayamdipta, Omer Levy, Roy Schwartz, Samuel R. Bowman, and Noah A. Smith. 2018. Annotation Artifacts in Natural Language Inference Data. *ArXiv*, 1803.02324.

Stevan Harnad. 1990. The symbol grounding problem. *Physica*, D42:335–346.

Lisa Anne Hendricks, Subhashini Venugopalan, Marcus Rohrbach, Raymond Mooney, Kate Saenko, and Trevor Darrell. 2016. Deep Compositional Captioning: Describing Novel Object Categories without Paired Training Data. In *Proc. CVPR'16*.

Diederik P. Kingma and Jimmy Lei Ba. 2014. Adam: A method for stochastic optimization. *arXiv*, abs/1412.6980.

Vladyslav Kolesnyk, Tim Rocktäschel, and Sebastian Riedel. 2016. Generating natural language inference chains. *arXiv*, abs/1606.01404.

Ranjay Krishna, Yuke Zhu, Oliver GrothJustin, Johnson Kenji Hata, Joshua Kravitz, Stephanie Chen, Yannis Kalantidis, Li-Jia Li, David A. Shamma, Michael S. Bernstein, and Li Fei-Fei. 2017. Visual genome: Connecting language and vision using crowdsourced dense image annotations. *International Journal of Computer Vision*, 123(1):32–73.

Alice Yingming Lai. 2018. *Textual entailment from image caption denotation*. Phd thesis, University of Illinois at Urbana-Champaign.

Alon Lavie and Abhaya Agarwal. 2007. METEOR: An Automatic Metric for MT Evaluation with Improved Correlation with Human Judgments. In *Proc. ACL Workshop on Intrinsic and Extrinsic Evaluation Measures for Machine Translation and/or Summarization*, Ann Arbor, Michigan.

Yann LeCun, Yoshua Bengio, and Geoffrey Hinton. 2015. Deep learning. *Nature*, 521(7553):436–444.

Siqi Liu, Zhenhai Zhu, Ning Ye, Sergio Guadarrama, and Kevin Murphy. 2016. Optimization of image description metrics using policy gradient methods. *ArXiv*, 1612.00370.

Bryan A. Plummer ands Liwei Wang, Chris M. Cervantes, Juan C. Caicedo, Julia Hockenmaier, and Svetlana Lazebnik. 2015. Flickr30k entities: Collecting region-to-phrase correspondences for richer image-to-sentence models. *arXiv*, abs/1505.04870.

Junhua Mao, Wei Xu, Yi Yang, Jiang Wang, Zhiheng Huang, and Alan Yuille. 2015a. Deep Captioning with Multimodal Recurrent Neural Networks (m-RNN). *Proc. ICLR'15*.

Junhua Mao, Wei Xu, Yi Yang, Jiang Wang, Zhiheng Huang, and Alan Yuille. 2015b. Learning like a Child: Fast Novel Visual Concept Learning from Sentence Descriptions of Images. In *Proc. ICCV'15*.

Junhua Mao, Wei Xu, Yi Yang, Jiang Wang, and Alan L. Yuille. 2014. Explain images with multimodal recurrent neural networks. *Proc. NIPS'14*.

Marco Marelli, Stefano Menini, Marco Baroni, Luisa Bentivogli, Raffaella bernardi, and Roberto Zamparelli. 2014. A SICK cure for the evaluation of compositional distributional semantic models. In *Proc. LREC'14*.

R. Thomas McCoy, Ellie Pavlick, and Tal Linzen. 2019. Right for the Wrong Reasons: Diagnosing Syntactic Heuristics in Natural Language Inference. In *Proc. ACL'19*.

Nikita Nangia, Adina Williams, Angeliki Lazaridou, and Samuel R Bowman. 2017. The RepEval 2017 Shared Task: Multi-Genre Natural Language Inference with Sentence Representations. In *Proc. 2nd Workshop on Evaluating Vector Space Representations for NLP*.

Ani Nenkova and Kathleen R McKeown. 2011. Automatic Summarization. *Foundations and Trends in Information Retrieval*, 5(2-3):103–233.

Kishore Papineni, Salim Roukos, Todd Ward, and Wei-jing Zhu. 2002. BLEU : a Method for Automatic Evaluation of Machine Translation. In *Proc. ACL'02)*, Philadelphia, PA.

Paul Piwek and Kristy Elizabeth Boyer. 2012. Varieties of question generation: Introduction to this special issue. *Dialogue and Discourse*, 3(2):1–9.

Tim Rocktäschel, Edward Grefenstette, Karl Moritz Hermann, Tomás Kociský, and Phil Blunsom. 2015. Reasoning about entailment with neural attention. *arXiv*, abs/1509.06664.

Deb Roy. 2005. Semiotic schemas: A framework for grounding language in action and perception. *Artificial Intelligence*, 167(1-2):170–205.

Mark Sammons, Vinod Vydiswaran, and Dan Roth. 2012. Recognising Textual Entailment. In Daniel M. Bikel Zitouni and Imed, editors, *Multilingual Natural Language Processing*, pages 209–281. IBM Press, Westford, MA.

Ravi Shekhar, Sandro Pezzelle, Yauhen Klimovich, Aurelie Herbelot, Moin Nabi, Enver Sangineto, and Raffaella Bernardi. 2017. FOIL it! Find One mismatch between Image and Language caption. In *Proc. ACL'17*.

Advaith Siddharthan. 2014. A survey of research on text simplification. *International Journal of Applied Linguistics*, 165(2):259–298.

Karen Simonyan and Andrew Zisserman. 2014. Very Deep Convolutional Networks for Large-Scale Image Recognition. *arXiv*, 1409.1556.

Janez Starc and Dunja Mladenić. 2017. Constructing a Natural Language Inference dataset using generative neural networks. *Computer Speech and Language*, 46:94–112.

Ilya Sutskever, Oriol Vinyals, and Quoc V Le. 2014. Sequence to sequence learning with neural networks. In *Proc. NIPS'14*.

M Tanti, A Gatt, and K Camilleri. 2018. Where to put the image in an image caption generator. *Natural Language Engineering*, 24:467–489.

M Tanti, A Gatt, and K Camilleri. 2019. Quantifying the amount of visual information used by neural caption generators. In *Proc. Workshop on Shortcomings in Vision and Language*, pages 124–132.

Ramakrishna Vedantam, C. Lawrence Zitnick, and Devi Parikh. 2015. CIDEr: Consensus-based image description evaluation. In *Proc. CVPR'15*.

Hoa Trong Vu, Claudio Greco, Aliia Erofeeva, Somayeh Jafaritazehjani, Guido Linders, Marc Tanti, Alberto Testoni, Raffaella Bernardi, and Albert Gatt. 2018. Grounded textual entailment. In *Proc. COLING'18*.

Josiah Wang, Pranava Madhyastha, and Lucia Specia. 2018. Object Counts! Bringing Explicit Detections Back into Image Captioning. In *Proc. NAACL-HLT'18*.

Zhiguo Wang, Wael Hamza, and Radu Florian. 2017. Bilateral Multi-Perspective Matching for Natural Language Sentences. In *Proc. IJCAI'17*.

Adina Williams, Nikita Nangia, and Samuel R. Bowman. 2018. A Broad-Coverage Challenge Corpus for Sentence Understanding through Inference. In *Proc. NAACL-HLT'18*.

Ning Xie, Farley Lai, Derek Doran, and Asim Kadav. 2019. Visual Entailment: A Novel Task for Fine-Grained Image Understanding. *ArXiv*, 1901.06706v1.

Peter Young, Alice Lai, Micah Hodosh, and Julia Hockenmaier. 2014. From image descriptions to visual denotations: New similarity metrics for semantic inference over event descriptions. *Transactions of the Association for Computational Linguistics*, 2:67–78.

Detecting Machine-Translated Text using Back Translation

Hoang-Quoc Nguyen-Son[1], Tran Phuong Thao[2], Seira Hidano[1], and Shinsaku Kiyomoto[1]

[1]KDDI Research, Inc.

2-1-15, Ohara, Fujimino, Saitama, 356-8502, Japan

{ho-nguyen, se-hidano, kiyomoto}@kddi-research.jp

[2]The University of Tokyo

7-3-1, Hongo, Bunkyo, Tokyo, 113-8656, Japan

tpthao@yamagula.ic.i.u-tokyo.ac.jp

Abstract

Machine-translated text plays a crucial role in the communication of people using different languages. However, adversaries can use such text for malicious purposes such as plagiarism and fake review. The existing methods detected a machine-translated text only using the text's intrinsic content, but they are unsuitable for classifying the machine-translated and human-written texts with the same meanings. We have proposed a method to extract features used to distinguish machine/human text based on the similarity between the intrinsic text and its back-translation. The evaluation of detecting translated sentences with French shows that our method achieves 75.0% of both accuracy and F-score. It outperforms the existing methods whose the best accuracy is 62.8% and the F-score is 62.7%. The proposed method even detects more efficiently the back-translated text with 83.4% of accuracy, which is higher than 66.7% of the best previous accuracy. We also achieve similar results not only with F-score but also with similar experiments related to Japanese. Moreover, we prove that our detector can recognize both machine-translated and machine-back-translated texts without the language information which is used to generate these machine texts. It demonstrates the persistence of our method in various applications in both low- and rich-resource languages.

1 Introduction

Nowadays, cross-language communication among people plays an important role in modern life. It opens great opportunities in various fields such as entertainment, e-commerce, career, etc. In this communication, a machine translator is an essential component. Moreover, the translator can also support other mutual interactions among machines and between a human with a machine. For example, a new AI system can be built from the other mature systems, which are operated in another language. In another example, the cutting-edge smart devices such as Apple Siri and Google Home have already supported multiple languages via translators.

However, the main problem of using translation is that it can lead to misunderstanding due to the diversity of language usages such as slang, idiom, dialect, etc. In another problem, adversaries can take advantage of translators to generate paraphrasing texts for malicious purposes, for example, plagiarism (Jones and Sheridan, 2015) and style transfer (Prabhumoye et al., 2018). Spreading such artificial texts can seriously reduce the reputation of the original texts which are created from human society. Therefore, it is crucial to develop a detector for determining whether a text is written by a human or generated by a translator.

Many researchers have interested in detecting machine-translated text. The most common methods are based on the N-gram model (Aharoni et al., 2014; Arase and Zhou, 2013; Nguyen-Son and Echizen, 2017) to measure the fluency of text. On the other hand, the structure of the parsing tree is exploited to recognize the machine-generated texts (Li et al., 2015). Moreover, the different word usages in human and machine texts lead to the differences in their word distributions (Nguyen-Son et al., 2017). Other researchers prove that the coherence of the human-written text is better than the machine-translated one (Nguyen-Son et al., 2018, 2019). Beyond detecting machine-translated text, artificial fake reviews and papers are also recognized by readability (Juuti et al., 2018) and duplicate patterns (Labbé and Labbé, 2013), respectively. The limitation in all existing methods above is that they only analyze the intrinsic contents of machine-generated texts but ignore the original processes which are used to produce the texts.

Proceedings of The 12th International Conference on Natural Language Generation, pages 189–197,
Tokyo, Japan, 28 Oct - 1 Nov, 2019. ©2019 Association for Computational Linguistics

> h_0: *"When we have finalised our proposal on the new rules and decided on the most suitable legal form, I will be happy to present our viewpoint to you."*
>
> h_2: *"**Once** we have **finalized** our proposal on the new rules and decided on the most **appropriate** legal form, I will be **pleased** to present our **<u>point of view</u>.**"*
>
> h_4: *Once we have finalized our proposal on the new rules and decided on the most appropriate legal form, I will be **happy** to present our point of view.*
>
> h_6: *Once we have finalized our proposal on the new rules and decided on the most appropriate legal form, I will be happy to present our point of view.*

Figure 1: The variants of repeatedly using back-translations.

Our idea based on the fact that the processing on original data often produces more variations than that on modified data. For example, in the field of image, equalizing histogram on an original image makes the much larger change than that on a balanced image, which has already equalized before. In the field of text, we also have a similar phenomenon. More particularly, we conduct a random example on an original sentence h_0 from European parallel corpus[1] as shown in Figure 1. h_0 is translated to French and then re-translated to English to create the back-translation denoted as h_2 where the subscript 2 represents to the number times of transitions applied from h_0. The other back-translations h_4 and h_6 are generated in the same manner of h_2. The variation between a back-translation with its origin is highlighted in bold with word usage and in underline with structure. The back-translation reach the saturation in h_6 with no change. Among back-translations, h_2 has the largest variations with seven positions in the word usage and three positions in the structure. The variations are remarkably reduced in the next back-translation h_4 with only one position in the word usage and nothing in h_6. The example demonstrates that the earlier generations have a higher number of variations than the latter ones.

We check our findings on machine-translated text detection. More particularly, we picked up the English-French pair $\{h_0, m_0\}$ in the parallel corpus in which h_0 is analyzed above. While h_0 is considered as the human-written sentence, m_0 is translated to English by Google for generating a machine sentence m_1 as shown in Figure 2. We then generate the two back-translation versions h_2 and m_3 using French as the intermediate language. While h_2 is translated in two times from the origin h_0, m_3 is generated after three from m_1. At the result, h_2 has more variations with h_0 in word usage than m_3 with m_1. Moreover, the structure in h_2 is slightly changed whereas in m_3 is preserved. It demonstrates that the differences in back-translation can be used to distinguish human-written with machine-translated text.

In this paper, we have proposed a method using back-translation to detect machine-translated text. Our contributions are listed as below:

- We explore the variant of a text when repeatedly back-translated in the same translator. In particular, the text is invariant after certain times of back-translating. Moreover, the earlier back-translations produce the larger variants than the later ones.

- We measure the variant by calculating the similarity between the text and its back-translation using BLEU scores.

- We suggest using a classifier with these scores to determine whether the text is translated by a machine or written by a human.

We randomly selected 2000 English-French sentence pairs from the European corpus for evaluation. While the English was considered as the human-written text, the French was translated to English using Google and is represented for the machine-translated text. Our method achieves both accuracy and F-score as 75.0%. It outperforms previous methods with the best accuracy as 62.8% and F-score as 62.7%. The similar experiment was conducted with back-translation detection. More specifically, we randomly chose 2000 sentiment sentences including 1000 positives and 1000 negatives from a Stanford Treebank corpus[2]. We then generated the machine back-translated text using French as the intermediate language. Our performance gives 83.4% of both accuracy

[1]https://www.statmt.org/europarl/

[2]http://nlp.stanford.edu/~socherr/stanfordSentimentTreebank.zip

	$\boldsymbol{m_0}$: *"Quand nous aurons mis au point notre proposition sur les nouvelles règles et choisi la forme juridique la plus adaptée, je me ferai un plaisir de vous exposer nos vues."*
$\boldsymbol{h_0}$ **(human-written text):** *"**When** we have **finalised** our proposal on the new rules and decided on the most **suitable** legal form, I will be **happy** to present our **<u>viewpoint to you</u>**."*	$\boldsymbol{m_1}$ **(machine-translated text):** *"**When** we have finalized our proposal on the new rules and chosen the most appropriate legal form, I will be happy to share our views."*
$\boldsymbol{h_2}$: *"**Once** we have **finalized** our proposal on the new rules and decided on the most **appropriate** legal form, I will be **pleased** to present our **<u>point of view</u>**."*	$\boldsymbol{m_3}$: *"**Once** we have finalized our proposal on the new rules and chosen the most appropriate legal form, I will be happy to share our views."*

Figure 2: Human-written vs machine-translated text.

and F-score that is better than the best previous work's accuracy and F-score as 66.7% and 63.7%, respectively. We conducted further experiments with Japanese and reach similar results. It demonstrates the persistence of the proposed method in various tasks in both low- and rich-resource languages.

The rest of the paper is organized as follow. Section 2 describes some main previous methods of detecting machine-translated and other machine-generated texts. The proposed method is presented in Section 3. The experimental results are shown in Section 4. Finally, we summarize some main key points and mention future work in Section 5.

2 Related Work

2.1 Machine Translation Detection

The previous methods for detecting machine-translated text can be split into four groups.

N-gram model This model is commonly used to estimate the fluency of continuous words. Researchers have suggested additional features to support the original model. For example, Arase and Zhou (2013) estimated the fluency of non-continuous words by sequential pattern mining. They can extract fluent human patterns (e.g., *"not only * but also,"* and *"more * than"*) comparing with weird machine patterns (e.g., *"after * after the,"* *"and also * and"*). On the other hand, Aharoni et al. (2014) combined the POS N-gram model with functional words, which abundantly occur in the machine-translated text. Nguyen-Son and Echizen (2017) also integrated the word

N-gram model with noise features for detecting translation in online social networking (OSN) messages. Such specific features often occur in human messages such as misspelling and spoken words or in machine messages, for example, untranslated words. However, these noises frequently appear in the OSN messages more than others.

Parsing tree Li et al. (2015) used the syntactic parsing tree for classifying human and machine sentences. They claim that the structure of a human parsing is more balancing than that of a machine. They thus extracted balancing-based features such as the ratio between left and right nodes in both general and main continents. The limitation of this approach is that it ignores the semantic meaning of the text.

Word distribution The usage of words in the human text often complies the Zipfian law, which indicates the topmost frequent words double the second, three times the third, etc. Nguyen-Son et al. (2017) use this law for detecting machine translated document. Furthermore, they extracted useful humanity text including idiom, cliché, ancient, and dialect phrases. They also estimated the relationships among certain phrases based on co-reference resolutions. These features only work well on a large text in which the word distribution is more stable and additional features appear more.

Coherence Although the machine-translated text can preserve the meaning, the coherence of such text is still low. Some researchers have measured the coherence to distinguish the ma-

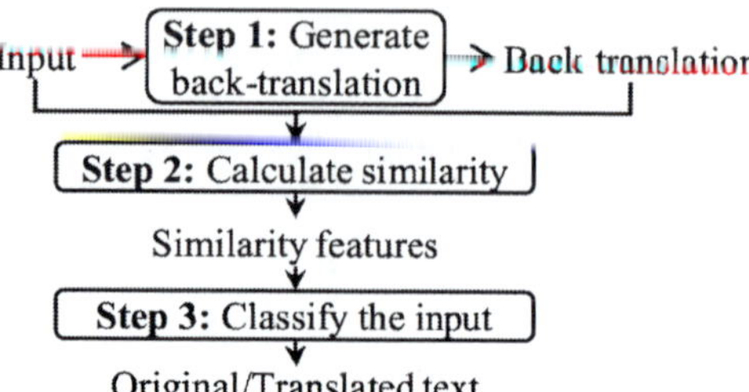

Figure 3: The proposed schema for detecting machine-translated text.

chine text with the human text. For example, Nguyen-Son et al. (2018) matched similar words between two sentences in a paragraph. The similarity between two matched words is used to estimate the coherence. In another work, Nguyen-Son et al. (2019) broadened the matching on any words in the paragraph in both within and across sentences. However, the coherence is tight in a paragraph but is downgraded in other levels such as sentence and document.

2.2 Other Machine-Generated Text Detection

Many other machine-generated texts support for malicious purposes such as paper generation and fake review. Labbé and Labbé (2013) prove that artificial papers are produced by using abundant duplicated words and phrases. Therefore, they suggested an inter-textual distance to estimate the similarity between two word distributions and used the distance to recognize the machine-generated text. In fake review detection, Juuti et al. (2018) extracted features from thirteen readability metrics. Moreover, they used N-gram models for various text components including words, simple POS, detailed POS and syntactic dependency. The duplicated usages of word distribution and N-gram model indicate high relevant between machine-translated and other machine-generated texts detection.

3 Proposed Method

The schema of the proposed method includes three steps as shown in Figure 3:

- **Step 1 (*Generate back-translation*)**: The Google Translation is used to generate the back-translation of the input text.

- **Step 2 (*Calculate similarity*)**: The similarity between the input text and its back-

translation is measured on the basis of BLEU scores.

- **Step 3 (*Classify the input*)**. The similarity features are used to determine whether the input text is written by a human or generated by a machine.

The following subsections describe the step-by-step of the proposed method.

3.1 Generating Back-Translation (Step 1)

The input text in the original language is translated into an intermediate language, which is different from the original one. The translated version is then re-translated back to the original language. The final translation is called as back-translation. In this paper, we use Google as a translator. In Figure 2, the back-translations h_2 and m_3 are generated from the human text h_0 and machine text m_1 respectively with the intermediate language, French.

Figure 4 shows an example of back-translation detection. In particular, we use Japanese for generating the machine-translated text m_2' from the original text m_0'. For distinguishing the two input texts h_0' and m_2', we create their back-translated texts h_2' and m_4' respectively with Chinese. Like Figure 2, we highlight the variants between the input texts and their back-translations with bold for word usages and underline for structures. Although using different languages in the generator and the detector, h_2' still makes more variants than m_4'. Again, the translation with four times in m_4' causes fewer changes than that with two times in h_2'.

3.2 Calculating Similarity (Step 2)

This step aims to estimate the similarity between the input and its back-translation. Due to the high relevance with machine translated-text measurement, we use BLEU scores (Papineni et al., 2002) for this step. There are two groups of the BLEU including individual N-gram and cumulative N-gram scores. While the individuals estimate phrases in the text independently, the later scores cumulate the measurements of the phrases with various lengths. Because the individual unigram score equals to the cumulative uni-gram, we only use one of them. The BLEU scores B for both translation and back-translation detection are listed in Figure 5. The first four values indicate the

	m'_0 (English)=h'_0: *"One of the best examples of how to treat a subject, you're not fully aware is being examined, much like a photo of yourself you didn't know was being taken."*
	m'_1 **(Japanese):** *"被写体をどのように扱うかの最も良い例の1つは、あなたが完全に気付いていないということです。"*
h'_0 **(English)=**m'_0: *"One of the best examples of how to treat a **subject**, you**'re** not **fully aware is being** examined, **much** like a photo **of yourself** you **didn't** know **was being taken.**"*	m'_2 **(English):** *"One of the best examples of how to deal with **the subject** is that you are not completely **aware.**"*
h'_1 **(Chinese):** *"关于如何治疗某个主题的最好例子之一，你还没有完全清楚地被检查，就像你自己不知道的照片一样。"*	m'_3 **(Chinese):** *"如何处理这个问题的最好例子之一是你并不完全清楚。"*
h'_2 **(English):** *"One of the best examples of how to treat a **topic** **is that** you **have** not **been completely** examined, **just** like a photo you **don't** know."*	m'_4 **(English):** *"One of the best examples of how to deal with **this problem** is that you are not completely **clear.**"*

Figure 4: Human vs machine text in back-translation detection.

Translation detection (Figure 2)
$B(h_0, h_2)$:0.73;0.67;0.61;0.55;0.62;0.50;0.41
$B(m_1, m_3)$:0.96;0.96;0.96;0.96;0.95;0.96;0.96
Back-translation detection (Figure 4)
$B(h'_0, h'_2)$:0.62;0.48;0.40;0.34;0.37;0.27;0.22
$B(m'_2, m'_4)$:0.85;0.79;0.75;0.70;0.73;0.67;0.58

Figure 5: BLEU scores B of the human and machine texts with their back-translations.

individual N-gram with N within 1 and 4; the remaining values are represented for the cumulative N-gram with N from 2 to 4.

The results show that the BLEU scores between machine texts and their back-translations are all higher than those of machine texts in both translation and back-translation detection. It demonstrates that the more times use a translator, the higher similarity is taken. This significant information can be used to distinguish the human with machine text.

3.3 Classifying the Input (Step 3)

The seven BLEU scores extracted from the previous step are run with a classifier to determine whether the input text is translated by a machine or is written by a human. We examine with four best classifiers, chosen from previous work, including linear classification (Fan et al., 2008), adap-

tive boosting, support vector machine (SVM) optimized by sequential minimal optimization, and SVM optimized by stochastic gradient descent. All of the classifiers achieve nearly similar results, so we can use any of them for this step.

4 Evaluation

4.1 Translation Detection

4.1.1 Dataset

We randomly selected 2000 English-French sentence pairs from the European parallel corpus[3]. While the English was used as human-written texts, the French was translated to English by Google for producing machine texts. The 4000 sentences are merged together; the integrated dataset contains 26.2 words per sentence on average. The dataset then is split into two parts: 2800 sentences for a train set and the remaining for the test set. To balance between human and machine texts in each set, we distribute both human and corresponding machine sentences into the same set.

4.1.2 Comparison

We evaluated the dataset on previous methods which detect machine-translated texts and machine-generated reviews. The train set was learned with four machine learning classifiers,

---

[3] https://statmt.org/europarl/

which were chosen as the best classifiers in the previous methods. The topmost classifiers, which are mentioned in each method, are marked in underline as shown in Table 1. They include linear classification (LINEAR) (Fan et al., 2008), adaptive boosting (ADABOOST), support vector machine optimized by sequential minimal optimization SVM(SMO), and SVM optimized by stochastic gradient descent SVM(SGD). Two standard metrics are used to evaluate the classifiers including accuracy (ACC) and F-score (F1) whose best performances are highlighted in bold. The two last columns calculate the average and the two last rows show the results of our detectors. The first one chooses Spanish for extracting back-translation information that is different from the language of the generator. The second detector uses the same generator language, i.e. French.

Surprisingly, both accuracy and F-score of most previous methods are nearly the randomize approach which is around 50%. It demonstrates the balanced pairs in the dataset with mostly the same meanings and word usages between human and machine texts make the existing methods confused. The best results are identical or comparative with the topmost performances mentioned in corresponding previous methods. The huge difference comes from the Juuti et al. (2018)'s method because it is originally targeted on detecting another machine-generated text, namely fake reviews. Among them, the method based on word distribution (Nguyen-Son et al., 2017) has the lowest results. It indicates that the limited number of words within a sentence is insufficient to form a stable distribution. The coherence-based method (Nguyen-Son et al., 2019) appropriately targets on paragraph level but not in sentence level. On the other hand, the method based on the parsing tree (Li et al., 2015) can slightly improve the outcome but the structures of human and machine pairs seem to be similar in this balanced dataset. The most reasonable methods (Aharoni et al., 2014; Juuti et al., 2018) are to use N-gram model for measuring the text fluency. However, the performances are unstable among classifiers especially in Juuti et al. (2018)'s work. It indicates that the current neural translator has already improved, so the only use of internal text information is insufficient to recognize machine-translated texts.

Our method uses additional information from back-translation improving the overall performances. Even using the different language with machine generator, the Spanish-based method achieves higher performance in all classifiers. It demonstrates that our method can efficiently detect machine-translated text without information of the translation language. Moreover, the use of the same language reaches the best performances in both accuracy and F-score. Our method also gives a more balancing results not only between accuracy and F-score but also among classifiers.

4.2 Back-translation Detection

4.2.1 Dataset

We check the capability of the proposed method on another task, namely back-translation detection. The back-translation can be easily used to generating paraphrasing texts for supporting malicious purposes such as fake reviews or political posts. The generation needs only an original text and using back-translation with various languages for generating many paraphrasing versions. For simulating this scenario, we randomly picked up 2000 sentiment sentences from Stanford Treebank corpus[4]. Half of them is positive while the remaining one is negative. We then generated the back-translated texts which are considered as machine sentences using French as the intermediate language. The machine sentences were integrated with the original ones into 4000 sentence dataset that averagely has 17.3 words per sentence. It is obviously smaller than the translation dataset above due to short sentences such as "*Imperfect?*" and "*Cool.*" The dataset was also split into train and test sets with balancing human and machine sentences in the same manner with the section 4.1.1.

4.2.2 Comparison

We conducted similar experiments with the previous methods on this back-translation dataset. For evaluating our detectors, we also use two languages including Spanish and French. The first language is different from the generator while the last is the same. The results are shown in Table 2.

The performances on most previous methods are slightly increased. The main reason is that the back-translation machine texts are generated after using the translator in two times. Therefore, the quality is downgraded and this text is more

---

Method	LINEAR		ADABOOST		SVM(SMO)		SVM(SGD)		AVERAGE	
	ACC	F1	ACC	F1	ACC	F1	ACC	F1	ACC	F1
Word distribution (Nguyen-Son et al., 2017)	**54.8%**	**54.8%**	53.8%	53.0%	52.8%	52.6%	<u>52.0%</u>	<u>51.2%</u>	53.4%	52.9%
Coherence (Nguyen-Son et al., 2019)	55.0%	53.3%	53.8%	41.6%	**56.9%**	**56.8%**	50.2%	50.0%	54.0%	50.4%
Parsing tree (Li et al., 2015)	**55.2%**	**55.0%**	53.7%	52.4%	54.8%	54.2%	54.2%	54.2%	54.5%	54.0%
N-gram & functional words (Aharoni et al., 2014)	56.9%	56.9%	56.0%	55.2%	**58.2%**	**58.2%**	50.3%	50.2%	55.3%	55.1%
N-gram & readability (Juuti et al., 2018)	**62.8%**	**62.7%**	<u>52.1%</u>	<u>37.8%</u>	61.5%	61.5%	55.1%	55.1%	57.9%	54.3%
Our using Spanish	64.8%	64.7%	**65.6%**	**65.5%**	64.1%	64.1%	63.8%	63.8%	64.6%	64.5%
Our using French	73.9%	73.9%	72.8%	72.7%	74.1%	74.1%	**75.0%**	**75.0%**	73.9%	73.9%

Table 1: Comparison with other methods on machine-translation detection.

Method	LINEAR		ADABOOST		SVM(SMO)		SVM(SGD)		AVERAGE	
	ACC	F1	ACC	F1	ACC	F1	ACC	F1	ACC	F1
Word distribution (Nguyen-Son et al., 2017)	53.8%	53.5%	**54.3%**	**53.8%**	53.6%	52.8%	<u>51.4%</u>	<u>50.4%</u>	53.3%	52.6%
Coherence (Nguyen-Son et al., 2019)	51.2%	37.1%	58.3%	57.4%	**59.4%**	**59.4%**	49.3%	49.3%	54.5%	50.8%
Parsing tree (Li et al., 2015)	<u>56.2%</u>	<u>56.2%</u>	54.8%	54.8%	**56.6%**	**56.6%**	54.8%	54.1%	55.6%	55.4%
N-gram & functional words (Aharoni et al., 2014)	57.7%	57.7%	55.9%	52.5%	**58.3%**	**58.3%**	45.4%	45.3%	54.3%	53.5%
N-gram & readability (Juuti et al., 2018)	61.9%	57.5%	**66.7%**	<u>62.5%</u>	63.8%	**63.7%**	56.3%	56.3%	62.2%	60.0%
Our using Spanish	70.7%	70.7%	70.6%	70.6%	**71.0%**	**71.0%**	68.3%	68.3%	70.1%	70.1%
Our using French	83.0%	83.0%	83.1%	83.0%	83.1%	83.0%	**83.4%**	**83.4%**	83.1%	83.1%

Table 2: Back-translation detection with rich-resource language.

easily distinguishable. The most changing comes from Juuti et al. (2018)'s work in which the ADABOOST reaches the best accuracy contrasting with the result from the previous task in Table 1. Moreover, the best F-score places in another classifier, i.e., SVM(SMO). The differences with other classifiers are also remarkable that exploits the inconsistent of this work on detecting various kinds of translated texts. On the other hand, our methods achieve the highest performances in both Spanish and French. The improvements are even larger compared with the previous task. In this task, the back translations of machine texts are created after using the translator in four times while the previous task is only three, so we can exploit more differences comparing with the back-translations

created by human texts in the same two times. The proposed method again demonstrates the high consistent results among classifiers. Furthermore, the accuracy and F-scores are almost identical. It shows the persistent of our method on various tasks even without language information from the generator.

4.2.3 Low-resource language

We examined similar experiments with low-resource languages. With the same dataset of 2000 human sentiment sentences, we choose Japanese for generating machine back-translated texts. For detectors, we use two languages as intermediate languages for generating back-translation. They include Chinese, different from the generator, and the same language, i.e Japanese. The results of

Method	LINEAR		ADABOOST		SVM(SMO)		SVM(SGD)		AVERAGE	
	ACC	F1	ACC	F1	ACC	F1	ACC	F1	ACC	F1
Word distribution (Nguyen-Son et al., 2017)	**52.4%**	**52.3%**	52.4%	51.4%	50.8%	49.9%	<u>51.3%</u>	<u>50.7%</u>	51.7%	51.1%
Coherence (Nguyen-Son et al., 2019)	51.5%	39.1%	**58.8%**	**58.8%**	**<u>58.8%</u>**	**<u>58.8%</u>**	53.1%	52.8%	55.6%	52.4%
Parsing tree (Li et al., 2015)	<u>57.8%</u>	<u>57.7%</u>	57.6%	57.6%	**58.4%**	**58.4%**	54.6%	54.5%	57.1%	57.1%
N-gram & functional words (Aharoni et al., 2014)	55.6%	55.6%	53.5%	43.0%	**<u>56.9%</u>**	**<u>56.9%</u>**	47.4%	47.4%	53.4%	50.7%
N-gram & readability (Juuti et al., 2018)	**66.1%**	**65.6%**	<u>55.8%</u>	<u>45.0%</u>	65.6%	65.5%	58.0%	58.0%	61.4%	58.5%
Our using Chinese	**65.2%**	**65.2%**	64.6%	64.2%	63.9%	63.9%	63.3%	63.3%	64.2%	64.1%
Our using Japanese	**80.6%**	**80.6%**	78.9%	78.5%	79.8%	79.7%	78.7%	78.6%	79.5%	79.3%

Table 3: Back-translation detection with low-resource language.

comparison with other methods are listed in Table 3.

In the previous methods, the results are quite similar to detecting back-translation with the rich-resource language. The most difference again lays in Juuti et al. (2018)'s work. The best performances come back to LINEAR while AD-ABOOST is dropped down to the lowest. It indicates the inconsistent of this method not only on different tasks but also on the same task with different resource languages. Comparing Figure 2 and Figure 4, the translated texts from rich-resource have still higher qualities than those from low-resource. Therefore, it affects the back-translation information which is used in our method. Especially with Chinese, our detector is slightly lower than some classifiers of the previous work, but the stable outcome still demonstrates via average, which is better than the state-of-the-art methods. Moreover, the experiment with Japanese outperforms in all classifiers with significant improvements of both accuracy as 14.5% and F-score as 15.0%.

5   Conclusion

In this paper, we have exploited that when using machine translators many times, the translated text is converged. Moreover, the variant between two consecutive usages gets to be smaller. We then propose a method for estimating the variant by using BLEU scores and use them for detecting two types machine-generated text: machine translation and machine back-translation. In machine transla-

tion detection, the evaluation of French sentences on best classifiers, which are mentioned on previous methods, shows that our method can detect translated text with 75.0% of both accuracy and F-score. It outperforms the previous methods with the best accuracy as 62.8% and F-score as 62.7%. In back-translated text detection, the performance is even significantly improved from 66.7% to 83.4% of accuracy and from 63.7% to 83.4% of F-score. The experiments on low-resource language, i.e., Japanese, achieve similar results. Moreover, we conduct similar experiments with different languages between generators and detectors. Although the performances are lower than the same language experiments, our detectors still are better than the existing work in all classifiers related to rich-resource languages and are higher on average performances of the classifiers with low-resource. It demonstrates our detectors work well even without language information of the generators.

In future work, we will investigate the effect of our findings on various translators such as neural-network-based and phrase-based translators. Moreover, we will verify the use of the same translator but trained on different corpora. We also analyze other machine generators for detecting other malicious texts such as adversarial texts, artificial fake news, etc. Beyond text, the applications using our hypothesis for detecting other machine-generated data (e.g., image, video, sound, and structured data) will be considered.

References

Roee Aharoni, Moshe Koppel, and Yoav Goldberg. 2014. Automatic detection of machine translated text and translation quality estimation. In *Proceedings of the 52nd Annual Meeting of the Association for Computational Linguistics (ACL)*, pages 289–295.

Yuki Arase and Ming Zhou. 2013. Machine translation detection from monolingual web-text. In *Proceedings of the 51st Annual Meeting of the Association for Computational Linguistics (ACL)*, pages 1597–1607.

Rong-En Fan, Kai-Wei Chang, Cho-Jui Hsieh, Xiang-Rui Wang, and Chih-Jen Lin. 2008. LIBLINEAR: A library for large linear classification. *Journal of machine learning research*, 9(Aug):1871–1874.

Michael Jones and Lynnaire Sheridan. 2015. Back translation: an emerging sophisticated cyber strategy to subvert advances in digital ageplagiarism detection and prevention. *Assessment and Evaluation in Higher Education*, 40(5):712–724.

Mika Juuti, Bo Sun, Tatsuya Mori, and N Asokan. 2018. Stay on-topic: Generating context-specific fake restaurant reviews. In *Proceedings of the European Symposium on Research in Computer Security (ESORICS)*, pages 132–151.

Cyril Labbé and Dominique Labbé. 2013. Duplicate and fake publications in the scientific literature: how many scigen papers in computer science? *Scientometrics*, 94(1):379–396.

Yitong Li, Rui Wang, and Hai Zhao. 2015. A machine learning method to distinguish machine translation from human translation. In *Proceedings of the 29th Pacific Asia Conference on Language, Information and Computation (PACLIC)*, pages 354–360.

Hoang-Quoc Nguyen-Son and Isao Echizen. 2017. Detecting computer-generated text using fluency and noise features. In *Proceedings of the International Conference of the Pacific Association for Computational Linguistics (PACLING)*, pages 288–300.

Hoang-Quoc Nguyen-Son, Tran Phuong Thao, Seira Hidano, and Shinsaku Kiyomoto. 2019. Detecting machine-translated paragraphs by matching similar words. In *ArXiv Preprint arXiv:1904.10641*.

Hoang-Quoc Nguyen-Son, Ngoc-Dung T Tieu, Huy H Nguyen, Junichi Yamagishi, and Isao Echizen. 2017. Identifying computer-generated text using statistical analysis. In *2017 Asia-Pacific Signal and Information Processing Association Annual Summit and Conference (APSIPA ASC)*, pages 1504–1511.

Hoang-Quoc Nguyen-Son, Ngoc-Dung T Tieu, Huy H Nguyen, Junichi Yamagishi, and Isao Echizen. 2018. Identifying computer-translated paragraphs using coherence features. *ArXiv Preprint arXiv:1812.10896*.

Kishore Papineni, Salim Roukos, Todd Ward, and Wei-Jing Zhu. 2002. BLEU: a method for automatic evaluation of machine translation. In *Proceedings of the 40th Annual Meeting on Association for Computational Linguistics (ACL)*, pages 311–318.

Shrimai Prabhumoye, Yulia Tsvetkov, Ruslan Salakhutdinov, and Alan W Black. 2018. Style transfer through back-translation. In *Proceedings of the 56th Annual Meeting of the Association for Computational Linguistics (ACL)*, pages 866–876.

Neural Conversation Model Controllable by Given Dialogue Act Based on Adversarial Learning and Label-aware Objective

Seiya Kawano, Koichiro Yoshino and Satoshi Nakamura

Devision of Information Science, Graduate School of Science and Technology
Nara Institute of Science and Technology, Nara 630-0192, Japan
{kawano.seiya.kj0, koichiro, s-nakamura}@is.naist.jp

Abstract

Building a controllable neural conversation model (NCM) is an important task. In this paper, we focus on controlling the responses of NCMs by using dialogue act labels of responses as conditions. We introduce an adversarial learning framework for the task of generating conditional responses with a new objective to a discriminator, which explicitly distinguishes sentences by using labels. This change strongly encourages the generation of label-conditioned sentences. We compared the proposed method with some existing methods for generating conditional responses. The experimental results show that our proposed method has higher controllability for dialogue acts even though it has higher or comparable naturalness to existing methods.

1 Introduction

A dialogue act is defined as the intention or the function of an utterance in dialogues. Dialogue act labels are defined as unique classes to distinguish between kinds of dialogue acts (Boyer et al., 2010; Bunt et al., 2012). Some existing studies have exploited the dialogue act as a component in modeling the dialogue strategy of dialogue systems (Meguro et al., 2010; Yoshino and Kawahara, 2015; Shibata et al., 2016; Keizer and Rieser, 2017).

Neural conversation models (NCMs), which learn a direct mapping between a dialogue history and a response utterance, are widely researched as a scalable approach to building non-task oriented dialogue systems (Vinyals and Le, 2015; Serban et al., 2016). However, it is difficult to control their responses on the basis of actual constraints such as dialogue act classes. Some existing studies have tackled this problem to control responses from

NCMs by using actual labels; however, these models still had some limitations (Wen et al., 2015; Li et al., 2016; Sun et al., 2017; Zhao et al., 2017; Huang et al., 2018; Zhou et al., 2018). One crucial issue was that they do not have any explicit training objectives to guarantee that a generation has a discriminability for a given condition.

We extend a framework of the generative adversarial network for sequential generation (Yu et al., 2017) for improving the controllability of NCMs under the constraint of a given dialogue act condition. We propose an adversarial learning framework that alternatively trains between conditioned generator and a conditioned discriminator. The discriminator has a multi-class objective that explicitly classifies a generated response into an appropriate dialogue act class. This improves the discriminability of generation.

In this paper, we first describe the task of conditional response generation given a dialogue act label and its existing approaches (Section 3). Second, we introduce an adversarial learning framework and extend its architecture and objective to fit the problem of conditional generation (Section 4). In experiments, we use metrics to evaluate the controllability and naturalness of responses (Section 5). The experimental results show that our proposed model achieved the best controllability score in both automatic and human subjective evaluations even if it achieves better or comparable naturalness to existing methods (Section 6).

2 Related Work

Dialogue systems that have dialogue management modules determine a dialogue act or dialogue state of a system response by using statistical methods such as reinforcement learning (Young et al., 2010; Meguro et al., 2010; Yoshino and Kawahara, 2015; Keizer and Rieser, 2017). Response generation modules generate responses according to these dialogue acts or dialogue states on the basis of the rules, templates, agendas or other statistical models (Oh and Rudnicky, 2000; Xu and Rudnicky, 2000). Recently, neural network based generation modules have been widely used.

Wen et al. (2015) proposed a conditional language model (Semantically Conditioned Long Short-Term Memory; SC-LSTM) for task-oriented systems, which generates utterances on the basis of any dialogue acts and frames in the domain of restaurant navigation dialogue by using gating mechanism. However, the training framework of SC-LSTM requires state frames that express the function and the contents of target utterances entirely. Thus, it is not realistic to apply this method to building an open-domain dialogue system. Zhao et al. (2017) proposed an NCM based on a variation of the conditional variational autoencoder (CVAE), which generates responses that have high diversity in discourse level by using latent variables as dialogue acts. However, this model has no mechanism to guarantee for generating discriminable responses for given dialogue acts.

There is another research trend in controlling NCMs with a given condition, such as speaker or emotion labels (Li et al., 2016; Sun et al., 2017; Huang et al., 2018; Zhou et al., 2018). These NCMs are optimized by softmax cross-entropy loss (SCE-loss), which calculates a loss word-by-word. However, such existing training objectives do not necessarily guarantee that a generated response has high discriminability to for a given class label. In other words, SCE-loss is not an appropriate objective that explicitly evaluates whether a generated response reflects the property of the given class label or not. Therefore, the generated response will be biased by majority class labels.

To prevent these problems, we introduce the

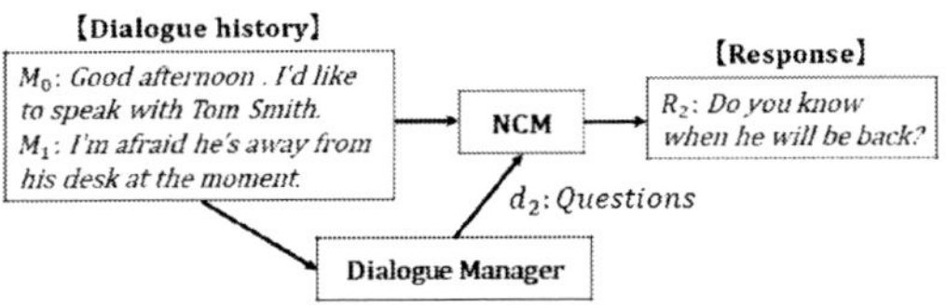

Figure 1: Task of response generation conditioned by dialogue act labels.

framework of the generative adversarial network (Yu et al., 2017; Li et al., 2017a; Tuan and Lee, 2019). This framework makes it possible to consider the total quality of generated sequences unlike SCE-loss, which is optimized for each token. We extend adversarial networks to generate qualified and controlled sentences given a condition, especially dialogue act labels.

3 Response Generation Conditioned by Dialogue Act Label

3.1 Task Settings

The task we focus on is building a controllable NCM with a given condition, typically dialogue act labels. The problem is defined as generating the ith response word sequence $R_i = \{w_1, w_2, \cdots, w_T\}$ given a dialogue history $M = \{M_{i-1}, M_{i-2}, \ldots, M_{i-n}\}$ and dialogue act label d_i. Here, n is the length of a dialogue, and T is the number of words in an utterance. As shown in Figure 1, a response R_i is required to satisfy not only the behavioral characteristic of a given dialogue act but also the appropriateness in the dialogue context (=history).

One of the simplest approaches to building such a conditional generation system given a class label in NCM is adding the class label to the input of a decoder (Li et al., 2016; Zhao et al., 2017; Sun et al., 2017). We describe this baseline in the following section.

3.2 Conditional NCM with Dialogue Acts

We introduce a general conditional NCM that is conditioned by dialogue act labels as a baseline. We built an NCM on the basis of a hierarchical encoder-decoder model that explicitly gives labels to the decoder at any of the steps of decoding as

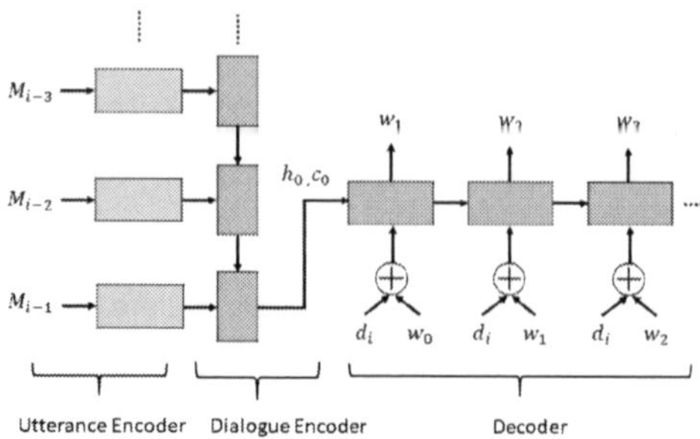

Figure 2: Conditional-NCM with dialogue acts.

shown in Figure 2.

Recurrent neural networks (RNNs) such as long short-term memory (LSTM) are generally used to model a sequential generation of responses in NCMs (Hochreiter and Schmidhuber, 1997; Vinyals and Le, 2015; Serban et al., 2016). The encoder receives a word at each time step by using forward RNNs to encode an utterance into a fixed length vector (utterance encoder). Utterance vectors of a dialogue are input to another fixed length vector according to their time sequence to encode the dialogue context (dialogue encoder). The resultant vector is fed into the decoder to generate a response sentence (word sequence). We used the same encoder architecture as Tian et al. (2017).

In the decoding steps of the NCMs, the decoder receives a previous hidden vector h_{t-1}, memory cell c_{t-1}, and generated word w_{t-1} to generate a word w_t. Here, t is an actual time-step of generation. The model has been changed to receive not only the previous word w_{t-1} but also the dialogue act label d in conditional generation. The vector representations of d and w_t are concatenated and used as the input of the decoder at time-step t.[1] The decoder itself also predicts the vector representation of words. This architecture is also the same as those of the models proposed by Zhao et al. (2017).

Softmax cross-entropy loss (SCE-loss) is widely used to train the model.

$$loss_{sce} = -\log \frac{\exp(x_c)}{\sum_k^{|\mathcal{V}|} \exp(x_k)}. \quad (1)$$

---

[1] w_t and d are converted into vector representation and then concatenated.

Here, $|\mathcal{V}|$ indicates the vocabulary size, $x \in \mathbb{R}^{|\mathcal{V}|}$ indicates the output of the projection layer in the decoding steps, and $x_k \in \mathbb{R}^{|\mathcal{V}|}$ indicates the kth element of x. x_c is the target word. SCE-loss optimizes the prediction of words at each decoding step. However, it does not use the information of a given dialogue act label in the loss calculation during training. Thus, the resultant model often generates a response that does not consider a given dialogue act label or a biased response by using the majority dialogue act labels in the training data. We tackle this problem by introducing an explicit training objective to generate a conditioned word sequence in adversarial learning.

4 Conditional Response Generation Based on Adversarial Learning

We introduce sequential generative adversarial networks (SeqGANs) (Yu et al., 2017; Li et al., 2017a; Tuan and Lee, 2019) to improve the controllability and quality of conditional response generation. SeqGAN is a prospective approach to preventing the problems caused by SCE-loss based training because it can evaluate not only the word prediction of each decoding step but also the whole quality of a generated sequence. In this section, we first describe the architecture of SeqGAN (Section 4.1) and then propose our extension of SeqGAN to realize conditional response generation by using given dialogue act labels (Section 4.2).

4.1 SeqGAN for Response Generation

The generation process in SeqGAN is formalized as a Markov decision process (MDP) and optimized with reinforcement learning (RL) (Li et al., 2017a; Tuan and Lee, 2019). The problem of response generation in NCMs is generating response word sequence $R = \{w_1, \cdots, w_T\}$ given a dialogue context M. Such a word selection process in the generation is defined as an action sequence, which is generated by an actual policy in MDP. In SeqGAN, the generator generates a sentence according to the current policy. The discriminator gives an evaluation score to the generated sentence after the generation. The evaluation score is fed as a reward to update the policy of the generator in RL. We use a policy gradient (Williams, 1992) to train the policy. The objective function and its gradient of the policy gradient are defined as follows[2].

$$J(\theta) = \sum_{w_{1:T}} G_\theta(w_t|w_{1:t-1}, M) \cdot Q_{D_\phi}^{G_\theta}((w_{1:t-1}, M), w_t) \tag{2}$$

$$\nabla J(\theta) \simeq \frac{1}{T} \sum_{t=1}^{T} \sum_{w_t \in \mathcal{V}} Q_{D_\phi}^{G_\theta}((w_{1:t-1}, M), w_t)$$
$$\cdot \nabla_\theta G_\theta(w_t|w_{1:t-1}, M) \tag{3}$$
$$= \frac{1}{T} \sum_{t=1}^{T} \mathbb{E}_{w_t \sim G_\theta}[Q_{D_\phi}^{G_\theta}((w_{1:t-1}, M), w_t)$$
$$\cdot \nabla_\theta \log p(w_t|w_{1:t-1}, M)] \tag{4}$$

Here, θ is a parameter of the policy. $w_{1:t-1}$ indicates a word sequence, $\mathcal{V}$ is a vocabulary, and p is the generative probability of word $w_t \in \mathcal{V}$. $Q_{D_\phi}^{G_\theta}((w_{1:t-1}, M), w_t)$ is an action-value function that gives an expected future reward when the system takes the action of generating word w_t given the state: already generated word sequence $w_{1:t-1}$ and dialogue context M. ϕ is a parameter of the discriminator. The discriminator only outputs the reward after the whole generation of the sequence. Thus, the value of the action-value function $Q_{D_\phi}^{G_\theta}((w_{1:t-1}, M), w_t)$ for each step is calculated by using a Monte Carlo tree search (MCTS) under the current policy and its parameter θ (Browne et al., 2012).

The discriminator is trained to classify a generated sentence (fake) and sentence in training data (real). Its training objective is defined as,

$$\min_\phi -\mathbb{E}_{R \sim p_{data}(\cdot|M)}[\log D_\phi(R, M)]$$
$$-\mathbb{E}_{R \sim G_\theta(\cdot|M)}[\log(1 - D_\phi(R, M))]. \tag{5}$$

The generator and the discriminator are trained alternatively to train their network adversarially.

4.2 SeqGAN for Conditional Response Generation with Dialogue Acts

The generator and the discriminator in SeqGAN are extended to produce responses according to given dialogue acts. The adversarial framework is extended for jointly optimizing both networks: a generator network to produce response utterances under specified dialogue acts, and a discriminator network to distinguish between generation (fake) and training data (real) that reflect their conditions.

As the generator network, we applied the conditional-NCM described in Section 3.2. Equations (2) - (4) are changed as follows.

$$J(\theta) = \sum_{w_{1:T}} G_\theta(w_t|w_{1:t-1}, M, d) \cdot Q_{D_\phi}^{G_\theta}((w_{1:t-1}, M, d), w_t) \tag{6}$$

$$\nabla J(\theta) \simeq \frac{1}{T} \sum_{t=1}^{T} \sum_{w_t \in \mathcal{V}} Q_{D_\phi}^{G_\theta}((w_{1:t-1}, M, d), w_t)$$
$$\cdot \nabla_\theta G_\theta(w_t|w_{1:t-1}, M, d) \tag{7}$$
$$= \frac{1}{T} \sum_{t=1}^{T} \mathbb{E}_{w_t \sim G_\theta}[Q_{D_\phi}^{G_\theta}((w_{1:t-1}, M, d), w_t)$$
$$\cdot \nabla_\theta \log p(w_t|w_{1:t-1}, M, d)] \tag{8}$$

As the discriminator network, we incorporated dialogue act labels in the classification model (Figure 3). In the discriminator model, the utterance encoder converts dialogue contexts into fixed length vectors and uses them as features of discrimination. We propose to use two discriminators for incorporating dialogue act label information in the discriminator: implicit and explicit. Each method is described below in respective sections.

4.2.1 Binary Objective; Implicit-Discriminator

We built a simple extension for the discriminator that incorporates dialogue acts in the feature vectors of the discriminator. We call this architecture "implicit." This discriminator is defined as,

$$\min_\phi -\mathbb{E}_{R \sim p_{data}(\cdot|M,d)}[\log D_\phi(R, M, d)]$$
$$-\mathbb{E}_{R \sim G_\theta(\cdot|M,d)}[\log(1 - D_\phi(R, M, d))]. \tag{9}$$

We expect that the implicit discriminator can use the information of dialogue acts as a feature and discriminate generated results as fakes if they do not follow a given dialogue act (Figure 3, lower-right). There are some works that have similar approaches in emotional response generation (Sun et al., 2018; Kong et al., 2019). However, this discriminator is still a simple extension of the standard discriminator, which classifies response in two classes. In other words, the objective is not changed; thus it probably has difficulty in distinguishing the class (dialogue act label) of

---

[2]Detailed derivation is shown in (Yu et al., 2017).

responses. We propose another discriminator to solve this problem in the next section.

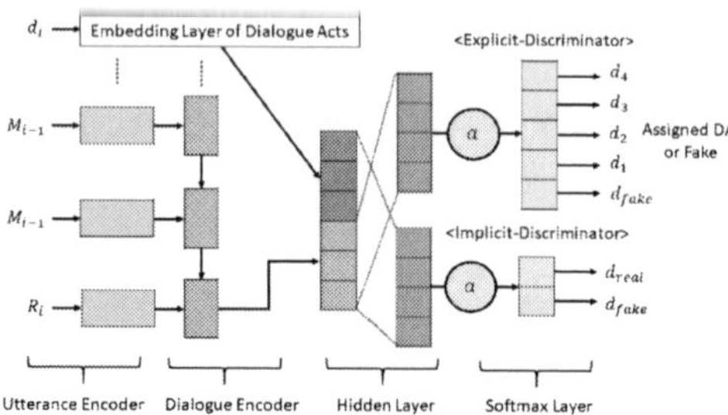

Figure 3: Implicit & Explicit-Discriminator.

4.2.2 Multi-class Objective; Explicit-Discriminator

We propose an approach extending the classification problem of the discriminator from the binary classification of fake/real to multi-class classification to distinguish target dialogue act classes (Figure 3 upper-right). This discriminator has a multi-class objective for $N+1$ class classification. Here, N is the number of unique dialogue act classes; another one is a fake class for categorizing the responses as generated. We call this architecture "explicit." Its objective function is defined as,

$$\min_{\phi} -\sum_{i=1}^{N} \mathbb{E}_{R \sim p_{data}(\cdot|M,d)}[\log D_{\phi}(d_i|R,M)]$$
$$-\mathbb{E}_{R \sim G_{\theta}(\cdot|M,d)}[\log D_{\phi}(d_{fake}|R,M)]. \quad (10)$$

We used the posterior probability $D_{\phi}(d|R,M)$ estimated by the discriminator as the reward of the generator. We expect that this discriminator will encourage training the generator to generate discriminative sentences with dialogue acts because generations that follow different dialogue act manners are penalized even if they are natural. Odena (2016) proposed a similar idea to use multi-class objective in GAN for the image generation task.

4.3 Speeding Up Adversarial Learning Using Simple Recurrent Unit

Using LSTM or GRU as an encoder and decoder is a general method for building NCMs (Vinyals and Le, 2015; Serban et al., 2016). LSTM is also often used for classification problems to encode a hierarchical structure, such as the discriminators of

GANs (Tran et al., 2017). However, the training speed of LSTM is much slower than other types of networks, although LSTM has dominant performance (Lei et al., 2017). This characteristic is critical for adversarial learning, which requires a large number of iterations.

We used the policy gradient in this research to update the parameters of the generator, which is based on expected reward calculation by MCTS. However, MCTS requires enormous calculation costs because it requires scanning the discriminator and generator $r \times w$ times per one update of generator, where r is the number of rollouts and w is the number of words in a response each time step. Thus, we propose to use a simple recurrent unit (SRU) (Lei et al., 2018) in our generator and discriminator. SRU is known as an extension of RNN, which has comparable performance to LSTM even if it works at significantly higher speed. SRU is defined as follows.

$$\tilde{v}_t = W v_t \quad (11)$$
$$f_t = \sigma(W_f v_t + b_f) \quad (12)$$
$$r_t = \sigma(W_r v_t + b_r) \quad (13)$$
$$c_t = f_t \odot c_{t-1} + (1 - f_t) \odot \tilde{v}_t \quad (14)$$
$$h_t = r_t \odot g(c_t) + (1 - r_t) \odot v_t \quad (15)$$

Here, v_t is the input vector at time-step t, f_t is the forgetting gate, r_t is the input gate, c_t is the memory cell, and h_t is the hidden vector. The key idea of SRU is minimizing the number of vectors and gates affected by previous states. Under this definition, only c_t is affected by the previous state c_{t-1}. Furthermore, c_t and h_t are calculated only by the element-wise production and summation of a vector for easy speed up. It was reported that forward and backward propagations in SRU are 10-16 times faster than LSTM (Lei et al., 2018). SRU leads to computational advantage compared with another type of RNNs including GRU as well. We expect to have a significant improvement in speeding up adversarial learning by using SRU instead of LSTM. However, applying SRU to NCM has no track record; thus, we introduce SRU to both the existing methods and our proposed adversarial network; however, we also perform a comparison with another baseline implemented by LSTM.

5 Experimental Settings

5.1 Dataset

We used the DailyDialog corpus that covers ten categories from a wide variety of topics (Li et al., 2017b). The corpus contains 13,118 dialogues, with a total of 102,979 utterances annotated with dialogue act labels: inform (46,532 utterances), questions (29,428 utterances), directives (17,295 utterances) and commissive (9,724 utterances). We divided the corpus into training/validation/test sets with 11,118/1,000/1,000 dialogues according to the work of Li et al. (2017b). In all experiments, the vocabulary size was set to 25,000, and all the OOV words were replaced by "UNK" symbol.

5.2 Training Settings

We used the same setting for embedding: words, 256, dialogue acts, 100. The mini-batch size was 32. In the training for conditional-NCM, we set two-layers RNNs in both the encoder and the decoder and used the Adam optimizer with a learning rate of 1e-5.

In the proposed adversarial learning, we followed the training procedure proposed by Li et al. (2017a). The training algorithm that we used is shown as follows.

Algorithm 1 Training procedure

1: **for** number of iterations **do**
2:     $G' \leftarrow G$
3:     **for** number of G-steps **do**
4:         sample (M_G, R_G, d_G) from training data
5:         generate response $\hat{R}_G$ by using G' on (M_G, d_G)
6:         compute reward r_{R_G} for $(M_G, \hat{R}_G, d_G)$ by using D
7:         update G on $(M_G, \hat{R}_G, d_G)$ using r_{R_G}
8:     **for** number of D-steps **do**
9:         sample (M_D, R_D, d_D) from training data
10:        generate response $\hat{R}_D$ by using G on (M_D, d_D)
11:        update D using $(M_D, \hat{R}_D, d_D)$ and (M_D, R_D, d_D)

In the training of SeqGAN for conditional response generation based on dialogue acts, we prepare well pre-trained conditional generator and a discriminator in advance. After initializing parameters by pre-trained models, G-steps for the generator G and D-steps for the discriminator D are applied alternatively to train them. In G-steps, a generated response $\hat{R}_G$ is sampled by using a dialogue history M_G and dialogue act d_G, and then the reward $r_{\hat{R}_G}$ for the generation is calculated by the discriminator D. By using the calculated reward $r_{\hat{R}_G}$, parameters of G are updated. In D-steps, a real response R_D, given a dialogue history M_D and a dialogue act label d_D, is sampled from the training data. A fake response $\hat{R}_D$ is generated from the generator G by using the dialogue history M_D and the dialogue act label d_D. Parameters of the discriminator D is updated by using the real sample and the fake sample.

We set the number of G-steps to 4 and D-steps to 20. In the generator, we used two-layers SRUs in both the encoder and the decoder as 1024 hidden units. We used the Adam optimizer with a learning rate of 1e-5. For the discriminator, we used a one-layer SRU, 1024 hidden units, and the SGD optimizer with a learning rate of 1e-3. We set the number of rollout to 5 in MCTS.

5.3 Automatic Evaluation Metrics

We automatically evaluated generation results by comparing with references in the test-set. As the automatic evaluation, we used three different types of metrics: perplexity, relevance scores, and controllability.

Perplexity is a metric for evaluating a language model performance. Likelihoods of models for reference responses are calculated as perplexities. Note that the perplexity score does not directly reflect the quality of generation; dull responses also have good perplexity scores.

Relevance scores are similarities between references and generated results. We used NIST, a variation of BLEU, which focuses on content words more than BLEU (Doddington, 2002). However, using count-based metrics such as BLEU and NIST are not appropriate, because they have small correlations with human judgment score in response generation tasks (Liu et al., 2016). Thus, we also used three different relevance scores proposed by Liu et al. (2016): embedding average ("Average"), greedy matching ("Greedy") and vector extrema ("Extrema")[3]. "Average" calculates a cosine similarity between the reference sentence vector and the generated sentence vector. Each sentence vector is calculated by an average of word embedding vectors in the sentence. "Extrema" also calculates a cosine similarity between sentence vectors; however, the sentence vector is constructed in a different way. Each dimension of the sentence vector is selected from the same dimension of a word embedding vector, which has the highest absolute value in the sentence. "Greedy" calculates cosine similarities of word pairs in the reference and the generated sentence, which is paired by alignment, and then averages these similarities.

The last automatic metric we used is "controllability", which is given by the classification result of the pre-trained dialogue act classifier by using the training set. We connected our encoder for conditional-NCM (Figure 2 left side) to a multi-class softmax layer to build the classifier.[4] Any generated sentences are labeled by the classifier and then compared with the given condition label to calculate the label accuracy.

5.4 Human Subjective Evaluation Metrics

The automatic evaluation scores still have a problem in that they do not have high correlations with human subjective evaluation results (Liu et al., 2016). Thus, we also evaluated systems with a human subjective evaluation to confirm the naturalness and controllability of responses.

In the evaluation of naturalness, we used a 3-point scale score in accordance with the existing work (Li et al., 2019). Thirty generated responses were randomly selected from each dialog act (120 in total) and human annotators selected an evaluation for the sample in following instructions.

- 2: The response can be used as a reply and it is informative and interesting; the response is natural and can make the conversation continue.

- 1: The response can be used as a reply, but it is too generic like " I don't know. "

- 0: The response cannot be used as a reply to the given dialogue history. It is either semantically irrelevant or disfluent.

Each sample was evaluated by three annotators, and the final score was decided by majority voting. If the evaluation was completely separated (0, 1 and 2), the example was evaluated as 1.

In the controllability evaluation, we requested one annotator to annotate dialogue acts for generated responses, who had two years experience in dialogue act annotation. The annotator was trained by using training data of DailyDialog corpus before the evaluation.

6 Experimental Results

6.1 Results of Automatic Evaluation

Table 1 shows the results of the automatic objective evaluation. We compared our proposed SeqGAN based on explicit-discriminator (Adversarial-Explicit) with the following baselines. "Vanilla-NCM" shows performances of vanilla LSTM, which has no mechanism to receive condition labels. These scores indicate a general performance of systems in DailyDialog corpus. "Conditional-NCMs" show performances of NCMs that receives condition labels on its decoder as proposed by Zhao et al. (2017). We compared two variations of "Conditional-NCMs", LSTM and SRU, to check the performance of SRU compared with LSTM. "Adversarial-Implicit" shows performances of SeqGAN that has implicit discriminator, which is proposed by Sun et al. (2018) and Kong et al. (2019). "Adversarial-Explicit" indicates the proposed model that has a multi-class discriminator on its SeqGAN. The table shows both results of beam search (width=5) and random sampling in the decoding process.

6.1.1 Speeding up Using SRU

The comparison between "Conditional-NCM w/ LSTM" and "Conditional-NCM w/ SRU" indicates that the speeding up using SRU works well; SRU achieves higher relevance scores to LSTM. SRU used 53,539K parameters, whereas LSTM

---

[3] We used fastText embeddings trained by wikipedia-dump data. The size of vectors was 300.

[4] The accuracy of the classifier in the test-set was 0.8303.

Decoding	Models	Perplexity	Relevance				Controllability
			NIST	Average	Greedy	Extreme	
Beam search	Vanilla-NCM w/ LSTM	33.9076	0.0386	0.7603	0.5763	0.5079	-
	Conditional-NCM w/ LSTM	33.2739	0.0502	0.7804	0.5980	0.5319	0.8651
	Conditional-NCM w/ SRU	36.6614	0.0610	0.7850	0.5981	0.5380	0.8702
	Adversarial-Implicit	39.2864	0.0596	0.7773	**0.6041****	**0.5417****	0.8615
	Adversarial-Explicit	39.6993	0.0613	0.7824	**0.6034****	**0.5401***	**0.8946****
Sampling	Vanilla-NCM w/ LSTM	33.9076	0.0265	0.7746	0.5326	0.4662	-
	Conditional-NCM w/ LSTM	33.2739	0.0342	0.7867	0.5540	0.4849	0.8015
	Conditional-NCM w/ SRU	36.6614	0.0365	0.7917	0.5590	0.4905	0.8176
	Adversarial-Implicit	39.2864	**0.0401****	0.7853	**0.5641****	**0.5018****	0.8081
	Adversarial-Explicit	39.6993	**0.0411****	0.7907	**0.5687****	**0.5036****	**0.8531****

Table 1: Results in automatic evaluation: note that results of random sampling are an average of five decoding runs, each decoding is initialized with random seed. *: $p < 0.05$ and **: $p < 0.001$ indicate results of significance tests (vs. conditional-NCM w/ SRU).

required 82,924K parameters. These results support our experiments using SRU instead of LSTM. We will mainly focus on comparisons of SRU models in the following sections.

6.1.2 Qualities of Generated Responses

The "Vanilla-NCM w/ LSTM" scores show the difficulty of conversation modeling in Daily-Dialog corpus. By comparing these scores with scores of other conditional generation models, "Conditional-NCM" and "Adversarial", conditional generation models improved relevance scores even if they have controllability. This is probably because the dialogue act condition can be a training constrain to prevent dull responses. Generation methods using adversarial learning improved relevance scores than "Conditional-NCM w/ SRU".

6.1.3 Controllability of each Dialogue Act

By comparing "Controllability" scores, the proposed "Adversarial-Explicit" achieved best scores in both beam-search and sampling decoding. For a detailed analysis, we show a controllability score of "Adversarial-Explicit" for each dialogue act label in Table 2 and Table 3 (beam-search and sampling). Tables show precision, recall and their harmonic mean (F1) for each dialogue act, and the improvement from the score of "Conditional-NCM w/ SRU", which achieved the best controllability in baselines (**improv.**). The proposed "Adversarial-Explicit" achieved improvements for any classes, but in particular, it achieved large improvements on "Directives" and "Commissive"

Dialogue acts	Prec.	Recall	F1 (improv.)
Inform (46%)	0.8881	0.9291	0.9081 (**+0.0167**)
Questions (30%)	0.9693	0.9982	0.9836 (**+0.0060**)
Directives (16%)	0.9372	0.7164	0.8121 (**+0.0971**)
Commissive (8%)	0.6285	0.6921	0.6588 (**+0.0240**)
Weighted avg	0.8980	0.8946	0.8935 (**+0.0192**)

Table 2: Result for beam search decoding, controllability of each dialogue act (adversarial-explicit). The score in round brackets indicates the improvement from conditional-NCM w/ SRU.

Dialogue acts	Prec.	Recall	F1 (improv.)
Inform (46%)	0.8684	0.8973	0.8826 (**+0.0164**)
Questions (30%)	0.9243	0.9738	0.9484 (**+0.0281**)
Directives (16%)	0.7628	0.6652	0.7107 (**+0.1152**)
Commissive (8%)	0.6338	0.5579	0.5934 (**+0.0382**)
Weighted avg	0.8477	0.8531	0.8494 (**+0.0257**)

Table 3: Result for random sampling, controllability of each dialogue act (adversarial-explicit). The score in round brackets indicates the improvement from conditional-NCM w/ SRU.

tags. Our model generated more discriminative sentences even if these classes have similar attribute.

6.2 Results of Human-Subjective Evaluation

Table 4 and Table 5 show human evaluation results for naturalness and controllability, respectively. We used beam search (beam width of 5) for generating examples to be evaluated. Regarding the naturalness of responses (Table 4), models used adversarial learning produced a more acceptable response to the dialogue context. Regarding the controllability of response generation (Table 5), the adversarial-explicit model achieved the best performance among the compared models.

In summary, the proposed model based on

Models	+2	+1	+0
Conditional-NCM w/ SRU	0.06	0.43	0.51
Adversarial-Implicit	0.04	0.53	0.43
Adversarial-Explicit	0.06	0.51	0.42

Table 4: Response quality of each model. This table show the distribution of scores.

Models	Accuracy	Weighted-F1
Conditional-NCM w/ SRU	0.7432	0.7583
Adversarial-Implicit	0.7058	0.6810
Adversarial-Explicit	**0.7971**	**0.7868**

Table 5: Controllability of response generation. Table shows filtered results of contradicted responses. Weighted-F1 is a weighted average of F1 score of each dialogue act.

adversarial learning with multi-class objective achieved the best controllability, the main focus of this paper, even if it realized a comparable naturalness to existing methods.

7 Conclusion

In this paper, we introduced an extended framework of the generative adversarial network that is optimized by both conditioned generation and discrimination of dialogue act classes. Experimental results showed that our conditional response generation model improved both the response quality and controllability in neural conversation generation. In future works, we will examine the possibility of incorporating our adversarial framework in various generation approaches (Serban et al., 2017; Shen et al., 2017; Zhou and Wang, 2018) to build a more generalized conditional response generation model. We will also focus on different types of labels to be used as conditions.

Acknowledgements

This research and development work was supported by the JST PRESTO (JPMJPR165B) and JST CREST (JPMJCR1513).

References

Kristy Elizabeth Boyer, Eun Young Ha, Robert Phillips, Michael D Wallis, Mladen A Vouk, and James C Lester. 2010. Dialogue act modeling in a complex task-oriented domain. In *Proc. of SIG-DIAL*, pages 297–305.

Cameron B Browne, Edward Powley, Daniel Whitehouse, Simon M Lucas, Peter I Cowling, Philipp Rohlfshagen, Stephen Tavener, Diego Perez, Spyridon Samothrakis, and Simon Colton. 2012. A survey of monte carlo tree search methods. *IEEE Transactions on Computational Intelligence and AI in games*, 4(1):1–43.

Harry Bunt, Jan Alexandersson, Jae-Woong Choe, Alex Chengyu Fang, Koiti Hasida, Volha Petukhova, Andrei Popescu-Belis, and David R Traum. 2012. Iso 24617-2: A semantically-based standard for dialogue annotation. In *Proc. LREC*, pages 430–437.

George Doddington. 2002. Automatic evaluation of machine translation quality using n-gram co-occurrence statistics. In *Proceedings of the second international conference on Human Language Technology Research*, pages 138–145. Morgan Kaufmann Publishers Inc.

Sepp Hochreiter and Jürgen Schmidhuber. 1997. Long short-term memory. *Neural computation*, 9(8):1735–1780.

Chenyang Huang, Osmar Zaiane, Amine Trabelsi, and Nouha Dziri. 2018. Automatic dialogue generation with expressed emotions. In *Proc. of NAACL-HLT*, volume 2, pages 49–54.

Simon Keizer and Verena Rieser. 2017. Towards learning transferable conversational skills using multi-dimensional dialogue modelling. In *Proc. of SEM-DIAL*, pages 158–159.

Xiang Kong, Bohan Li, Graham Neubig, Eduard Hovy, and Yiming Yang. 2019. An adversarial approach to high-quality, sentiment-controlled neural dialogue generation. In *AAAI 2019 Workshop on Reasoning and Learning for Human-Machine Dialogues (DEEP-DIAL 2019)*, Honolulu, Hawaii.

Tao Lei, Yu Zhang, and Yoav Artzi. 2017. Training rnns as fast as cnns. *arXiv preprint arXiv:1709.02755*.

Tao Lei, Yu Zhang, Sida I Wang, Hui Dai, and Yoav Artzi. 2018. Simple recurrent units for highly parallelizable recurrence. In *Proc. of EMNLP*, pages 4470–4481.

Jiwei Li, Michel Galley, Chris Brockett, Georgios P. Spithourakis, Jianfeng Gao, and William B. Dolan. 2016. A persona-based neural conversation model. *CoRR*, abs/1603.06155.

Jiwei Li, Will Monroe, Tianlin Shi, Sébastien Jean, Alan Ritter, and Dan Jurafsky. 2017a. Adversarial learning for neural dialogue generation. In *Proc. of EMNLP*, pages 2157–2169.

Yanran Li, Hui Su, Xiaoyu Shen, Wenjie Li, Ziqiang Cao, and Shuzi Niu. 2017b. Dailydialog: A manually labelled multi-turn dialogue dataset. In *Proc. of IJCNLP*, volume 1, pages 986–995.

Ziming Li, Julia Kiseleva, and Maarten de Rijke. 2019. Dialogue generation: From imitation learning to inverse reinforcement learning. In *Proc. of AAAI*.

Chia-Wei Liu, Ryan Lowe, Iulian Serban, Mike Noseworthy, Laurent Charlin, and Joelle Pineau. 2016. How not to evaluate your dialogue system: An empirical study of unsupervised evaluation metrics for dialogue response generation. In *Proc. of EMNLP*, pages 2122–2132.

Toyomi Meguro, Ryuichiro Higashinaka, Yasuhiro Minami, and Kohji Dohsaka. 2010. Controlling listening-oriented dialogue using partially observable markov decision processes. In *Proc. of ACL*, pages 761–769.

Augustus Odena. 2016. Semi-supervised learning with generative adversarial networks. *arXiv preprint arXiv:1606.01583*.

Alice H Oh and Alexander I Rudnicky. 2000. Stochastic language generation for spoken dialogue systems. In *ANLP-NAACL 2000 Workshop: Conversational Systems*.

Iulian Vlad Serban, Alessandro Sordoni, Yoshua Bengio, Aaron C Courville, and Joelle Pineau. 2016. Building end-to-end dialogue systems using generative hierarchical neural network models. In *Proc. of AAAI*, pages 3776–3784.

Iulian Vlad Serban, Alessandro Sordoni, Ryan Lowe, Laurent Charlin, Joelle Pineau, Aaron Courville, and Yoshua Bengio. 2017. A hierarchical latent variable encoder-decoder model for generating dialogues. In *Thirty-First AAAI Conference on Artificial Intelligence*.

Xiaoyu Shen, Hui Su, Yanran Li, Wenjie Li, Shuzi Niu, Yang Zhao, Akiko Aizawa, and Guoping Long. 2017. A conditional variational framework for dialog generation. In *Proc. of ACL*, volume 2, pages 504–509.

Tomohide Shibata, Yusuke Egashira, and Sadao Kurohashi. 2016. Chat-like conversational system based on selection of reply generating module with reinforcement learning. In *Situated Dialog in Speech-Based Human-Computer Interaction*, pages 63–69. Springer.

Xiao Sun, Xinmiao Chen, Zhengmeng Pei, and Fuji Ren. 2018. Emotional human machine conversation generation based on seqgan. In *Proc. of ACII Asia*, pages 1–6. IEEE.

Xiao Sun, Xiaoqi Peng, and Shuai Ding. 2017. Emotional human-machine conversation generation based on long short-term memory. *Cognitive Computation*, 10:389–397.

Zhiliang Tian, Rui Yan, Lili Mou, Yiping Song, Yansong Feng, and Dongyan Zhao. 2017. How to make context more useful? an empirical study on context-aware neural conversational models. In *Proc. of ACL*, volume 2, pages 231–236.

Quan Hung Tran, Ingrid Zukerman, and Gholamreza Haffari. 2017. A hierarchical neural model for learning sequences of dialogue acts. In *Proc. of ACL*, volume 1, pages 428–437.

Yi-Lin Tuan and Hung-Yi Lee. 2019. Improving conditional sequence generative adversarial networks by stepwise evaluation. *IEEE/ACM Transactions on Audio, Speech, and Language Processing*.

Oriol Vinyals and Quoc V. Le. 2015. A neural conversational model. *CoRR*, abs/1506.05869.

Tsung-Hsien Wen, Milica Gasic, Nikola Mrkšić, Pei-Hao Su, David Vandyke, and Steve Young. 2015. Semantically conditioned lstm-based natural language generation for spoken dialogue systems. In *Proc. of EMNLP*, pages 1711–1721.

Ronald J Williams. 1992. Simple statistical gradient-following algorithms for connectionist reinforcement learning. *Machine learning*, 8(3-4):229–256.

Wei Xu and Alexander I Rudnicky. 2000. Task-based dialog management using an agenda. In *ANLP-NAACL 2000 Workshop: Conversational Systems*.

Koichiro Yoshino and Tatsuya Kawahara. 2015. Conversational system for information navigation based on pomdp with user focus tracking. *Computer Speech & Language*, 34(1):275–291.

Steve Young, Milica Gašić, Simon Keizer, François Mairesse, Jost Schatzmann, Blaise Thomson, and Kai Yu. 2010. The hidden information state model: A practical framework for pomdp-based spoken dialogue management. *Computer Speech & Language*, 24(2):150–174.

Lantao Yu, Weinan Zhang, Jun Wang, and Yong Yu. 2017. Seqgan: Sequence generative adversarial nets with policy gradient. In *Proc. of AAAI*, pages 2852–2858.

Tiancheng Zhao, Ran Zhao, and Maxine Eskenazi. 2017. Learning discourse-level diversity for neural dialog models using conditional variational autoencoders. In *Proc. of ACL*, volume 1, pages 654–664.

Hao Zhou, Minlie Huang, Tianyang Zhang, Xiaoyan Zhu, and Bing Liu. 2018. Emotional chatting machine: Emotional conversation generation with internal and external memory. In *Proc. of AAAI*.

Xianda Zhou and William Yang Wang. 2018. Mojitalk: Generating emotional responses at scale. In *Proc. ACL*, volume 1, pages 1128–1137.

Low-Level Linguistic Controls for Style Transfer and Content Preservation

Katy Ilonka Gero[b]*   **Chris Kedzie**[b]*   **Jonathan Reeve**[♯]   **Lydia B. Chilton**[b]

Columbia University

[b]Dept. of Computer Science, [♯]Dept. of English and Comparative Literature

katy@cs.columbia.edu, kedzie@cs.columbia.edu,
jpr2152@columbia.edu, chilton@cs.columbia.edu

Abstract

Despite the success of style transfer in image processing, it has seen limited progress in natural language generation. Part of the problem is that content is not as easily decoupled from style in the text domain. Curiously, in the field of stylometry, content does *not* figure prominently in practical methods of discriminating stylistic elements, such as authorship and genre. Rather, syntax and function words are the most salient features. Drawing on this work, we model style as a suite of low-level linguistic controls, such as frequency of pronouns, prepositions, and subordinate clause constructions. We train a neural encoder-decoder model to reconstruct reference sentences given only content words and the setting of the controls. We perform style transfer by keeping the content words fixed while adjusting the controls to be indicative of another style. In experiments, we show that the model reliably responds to the linguistic controls and perform both automatic and manual evaluations on style transfer. We find we can fool a style classifier 84% of the time, and that our model produces highly diverse and stylistically distinctive outputs. This work introduces a formal, extendable model of style that can add control to any neural text generation system.

1 Introduction

All text has style, whether it be formal or informal, polite or aggressive, colloquial, persuasive, or even robotic. Despite the success of style transfer in image processing (Gatys et al., 2015, 2016), there has been limited progress in the text domain, where disentangling style from content is particularly difficult.

To date, most work in style transfer relies on the availability of meta-data, such as sentiment, au-

thorship, or formality. While meta-data can provide insight into the style of a text, it often conflates style with content, limiting the ability to perform style transfer while preserving content. Generalizing style transfer requires separating style from the meaning of the text itself.

The study of literary style can guide us. For example, in the digital humanities and its subfield of stylometry, content doesn't figure prominently in practical methods of discriminating authorship and genres, which can be thought of as style at the level of the individual and population, respectively. Rather, syntactic and functional constructions are the most salient features.

In this work, we turn to literary style as a testbed for style transfer, and build on work from literature scholars using computational techniques for analysis. In particular we draw on stylometry: the use of surface level features, often counts of function words, to discriminate between literary styles. Stylometry first saw success in attributing authorship to the disputed Federalist Papers (Mosteller and Wallace, 2007), but is recently used by scholars to study things such as the birth of genres (Underwood, 2016) and the change of author styles over time (Reeve, 2019). The use of function words is likely not the way writers intend to express style, but they appear to be downstream realizations of higher-level stylistic decisions.

We hypothesize that surface-level linguistic features, such as counts of personal pronouns, prepositions, and punctuation, are an excellent definition of literary style, as borne out by their use in the digital humanities, and our own style classification experiments. We propose a controllable neural encoder-decoder model in which these features are modelled explicitly as decoder feature embeddings. In training, the model learns to reconstruct a text using only the content words and the linguistic feature embeddings. We can then

---

*Equal contribution.

Proceedings of The 12th International Conference on Natural Language Generation, pages 208–218,
Tokyo, Japan, 28 Oct - 1 Nov, 2019. ©2019 Association for Computational Linguistics

transfer arbitrary content words to a new style without parallel data by setting the low-level style feature embeddings to be indicative of the target style.

This paper makes the following contributions:

- A formal model of style as a suite of controllable, low-level linguistic features that are independent of content.

- An automatic evaluation showing that our model fools a style classifier 84% of the time.

- A human evaluation with English literature experts, including recommendations for dealing with the entanglement of content with style.

2 Related Work

2.1 Style Transfer with Parallel Data

Following in the footsteps of machine translation, style transfer in text has seen success by using parallel data. Jhamtani et al. (2017) use modern translations of Shakespeare plays to build a modern-to-Shakespearan model. Rao and Tetreault (2018) compile parallel data for formal and informal sentences, allowing them to successfully use various machine translation techniques. While parallel data may work for very specific styles, the difficulty of finding parallel texts dramatically limits this approach.

2.2 Style Transfer without Parallel Data

There has been a decent amount of work on this approach in the past few years (Zhao et al., 2018; Fu et al., 2018), mostly focusing on variations of an encoder-decoder framework in which style is modeled as a monolithic style embedding. The main obstacle is often to disentangle style and content. However, it remains a challenging problem.

Perhaps the most successful is Lample et al. (2019), who use a de-noising auto encoder and back translation to learn style without parallel data. Tikhonov and Yamshchikov (2018) outline the benefits of automatically extracting style, and suggest there is a formal weakness of using linguistic heuristics. In contrast, we believe that monolithic style embeddings don't capture the existing knowledge we have about style, and will struggle to disentangle content.

2.3 Controlling Linguistic Features

Several papers have worked on controlling style when generating sentences from restaurant meaning representations (Oraby et al., 2018; Deriu and Cieliebak, 2018). In each of these cases, the diversity in outputs is quite small given the constraints of the meaning representation, style is often constrained to interjections (like "yeah"), and there is no original style from which to transfer.

Ficler and Goldberg (2017) investigate using stylistic parameters and content parameters to control text generation using a movie review dataset. Their stylistic parameters are created using word-level heuristics and they are successful in controlling these parameters in the outputs. Their success bodes well for our related approach in a style transfer setting, in which the content (not merely content parameters) is held fixed.

2.4 Stylometry and the Digital Humanities

Style, in literary research, is anything but a stable concept, but it nonetheless has a long tradition of study in the digital humanities. In a remarkably early quantitative study of literature, Mendenhall (1887) charts sentence-level stylistic attributes specific to a number of novelists. Half a century later, Fucks (1952) builds on earlier work in information theory by Shannon (1948), and defines a literary text as consisting of two "materials": "the *vocabulary*, and some structural properties, the *style*, of its author."

Beginning with Mosteller and Wallace (2007), statistical approaches to style, or stylometry, join the already-heated debates over the authorship of literary works. A notable example of this is the "Delta" measure, which uses z-scores of function word frequencies (Burrows, 2002). Craig and Kinney (2009) find that Shakespeare added some material to a later edition of Thomas Kyd's *The Spanish Tragedy*, and that Christopher Marlowe collaborated with Shakespeare on *Henry VI*.

3 Models

3.1 Preliminary Classification Experiments

The stylometric research cited above suggests that the most frequently used words, e.g. function words, are most discriminating of authorship and literary style.[1] We investigate these claims using three corpora that have distinctive styles in

---

[1] Curiously, these are most often the kinds of words that are manually removed for text classification.

Style	Train Words/Sent	Dev Words/Sent	Test Words/Sent
Sci-fi	7.1M/344k	.9M/43k	.9M/43k
Phil	1.2M/120k	.15M/15k	.15M/15k
Gothic	.4M/74k	.05M/9k	.05M/9k

Table 1: The size of the data across the three different styles investigated.

Classifier	all	scifi	goth	phil
All	0.86	0.86	0.87	0.84
Content only	0.80	0.78	0.80	0.84
Ablated N	0.81	0.80	0.85	0.83
Ablated NV	0.80	0.83	0.77	0.72
Ablated NVA	0.75	0.73	0.72	0.80

Table 2: Accuracy of five classifiers trained using tri-grams with fasttext, for all test data and split by genre. Despite heavy ablation, the *Ablated NVA* classifier has an accuracy of 75%, suggesting synactic and functional features alone can be fully predictive of style.

Control	Source	Example
S	parse	n/a
SBAR	parse	n/a
ADVP	parse	n/a
FRAG	parse	n/a
conjunction	word list	and, or, yet, but
determiner	word list	the, an, this
3rdNeutralPer	word list	they, their, it
3rdFemalePer	word list	she, her
3rdMalePer	word list	he, his
1stPer	word list	I, my, we
2ndPer	word list	you, your
3rdPer	word list	they, she, he
helperVerbs	word list	be, am, could
negation	word list	no, not
simple prep	word list	for, despite
position prep	word list	above, down
punctuation	word list	, ; : - _ (

Table 3: All controls, their source, and examples. Punctuation doesn't include end punctuation.

the literary community: gothic novels, philosophy books, and pulp science fiction, hereafter sci-fi.

We retrieve gothic novels and philosophy books from Project Gutenberg[2] and pulp sci-fi from Internet Archive's Pulp Magazine Archive[3]. We partition this corpus into train, validation, and test sets the sizes of which can be found in Table 1.

In order to validate the above claims, we train five different classifiers to predict the literary style of sentences from our corpus. Each classifier has gradually more content words replaced with part-of-speech (POS) tag placeholder tokens. The *All* model is trained on sentences with all proper nouns replaced by 'PROPN'. The models *Ablated N, Ablated NV*, and *Ablated NVA* replace nouns, nouns & verbs, and nouns, verbs, & adjectives with the corresponding POS tag respectively. Finally, *Content-only* is trained on sentences with all words that are not tagged as NOUN, VERB, ADJ removed; the remaining words are not ablated.

We train the classifiers on the training set, balancing the class distribution to make sure there are the same number of sentences from each style. Classifiers are trained using fastText (Joulin et al., 2017), using tri-gram features with all other settings as default. Table 2 shows the accuracies of the classifiers.

The styles are highly distinctive: the *All* classifier has an accuracy of 86%. Additionally, even the *Ablated NVA* is quite successful, with 75% accuracy, even without access to any content words. The *Content only* classifier is also quite successful, at 80% accuracy. This indicates that these stylistic genres are distinctive at both the content level and at the syntactic level.

3.2 Formal Model of Style

Given that non-content words are distinctive enough for a classifier to determine style, we pro-

pose a suite of low-level linguistic feature counts (henceforth, controls) as our formal, content-blind definition of style. The style of a sentence is represented as a vector of counts of closed word classes (like personal pronouns) as well as counts of syntactic features like the number of SBAR nonterminals in its constituency parse, since clause structure has been shown to be indicative of style (Allison et al., 2013). Controls are extracted heuristically, and almost all rely on counts of predefined word lists. For constituency parses we use the Stanford Parser (Manning et al., 2014). Table 3 lists all the controls along with examples.

---

[2] www.gutenberg.org
[3] Specifically, Robin Sloan's OCR'ed corpus: https://archive.org/details/scifi-corpus

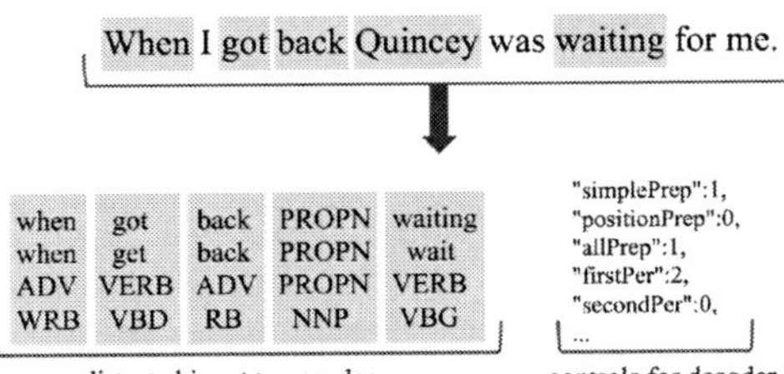

Figure 1: How a reference sentence from the dataset is prepared for input to the model. Controls are calculated heuristically, and then removed from the sentence. The remaining words, as well as their lemmatized versions and part-of-speech tags, are used as input separately.

3.2.1 Reconstruction Task

Models are trained with a reconstruction task, in which a distorted version of a reference sentence is input and the goal is to output the original reference.

Figure 1 illustrates the process. Controls are calculated heuristically. All words found in the control word lists are then removed from the reference sentence. The remaining words, which represent the content, are used as input into the model, along with their POS tags and lemmas.

In this way we encourage models to construct a sentence using content and style independently. This will allow us to vary the stylistic controls while keeping the content constant, and successfully perform style transfer. When generating a new sentence, the controls correspond to the counts of the corresponding syntactic features that we expect to be realized in the output.

3.3 Neural Architecture

We implement our feature controlled language model using a neural encoder-decoder with attention (Bahdanau et al., 2014), using 2-layer unidirectional gated recurrent units (GRUs) for the encoder and decoder (Cho et al., 2014).

The input to the encoder is a sequence of M content words, along with their lemmas, and fine and coarse grained part-of-speech (POS) tags,[4] i.e. $X_{\cdot,j} = (x_{1,j}, \ldots, x_{M,j})$ for $j \in \mathcal{T} = \{$word, lemma, fine-pos, coarse-pos$\}$. We embed each token (and its lemma and POS) before concatenating, and feeding into the encoder GRU to obtain encoder hidden states,

---

[4]We use the Penn Treebank (Marcus et al., 1994) and Universal Dependencies (de Marneffe et al.) tagsets for the fine and coarse-grained POS respectively.

$c_i = \text{gru}(c_{i-1}, [E_j(X_{i,j}), j \in \mathcal{T}]; \omega_{enc})$ for $i \in 1, \ldots, M$, where initial state c_0, encoder GRU parameters ω_{enc} and embedding matrices E_j are learned parameters.

The decoder sequentially generates the outputs, i.e. a sequence of N tokens $y = (y_1, \ldots, y_N)$, where all tokens y_i are drawn from a finite output vocabulary $\mathcal{V}$. To generate the each token we first embed the previously generated token y_{i-1} and a vector of K control features $z = (z_1, \ldots, z_K)$ (using embedding matrices E_{dec} and $E_{\text{ctrl-1}}, \ldots, E_{\text{ctrl-K}}$ respectively), before concatenating them into a vector ρ_i, and feeding them into the decoder side GRU along with the previous decoder state h_{i-1}:

$$\rho_i = [E_{dec}(y_{i-1}), E_{\text{ctrl-1}}(z_1), \ldots, E_{\text{ctrl-K}}(z_K)]$$
$$h_i = \text{gru}(h_{i-1}, \rho_i; \omega_{dec}),$$

where ω_{dec} are the decoder side GRU parameters.

Using the decoder hidden state h_i we then attend to the encoder context vectors c_j, computing attention scores $\alpha_{i,j}$, where

$$a_{i,j} = \nu^\mathsf{T} \tanh \left(W^\mathsf{T} \begin{bmatrix} c_j \\ h_i \end{bmatrix} \right)$$
$$\alpha_{i,j} = \frac{\exp\{a_{i,j}\}}{\sum_{j'} \exp\{a_{i,j'}\}},$$

before passing h_i and the attention weighted context $\bar{c}_i = \sum_{j=1}^{M} \alpha_{i,j} c_j$ into a single hidden-layer perceptron with softmax output to compute the next token prediction probability,

$$o_i = \tanh \left(U^\mathsf{T} \begin{bmatrix} h_i \\ \bar{c}_i \end{bmatrix} + u \right)$$
$$p(y_i|y_{<i}, X) \propto \exp\{V_{y_i}^\mathsf{T} o_i + v_{y_i}\}.$$

where W, U, V and u, v, ν are parameter matrices and vectors respectively.

Crucially, the controls z remain fixed for all input decoder steps. Each z_k represents the frequency of one of the low-level features described in subsection 3.2. During training on the reconstruction task, we can observe the full output sequence y, and so we can obtain counts for each control feature directly. Controls receive a different embedding depending on their frequency, where counts of 0-20 each get a unique embedding, and counts greater than 20 are assigned to the same embedding. At test time, we set the values of the controls according to procedure described in Section 3.3.3.

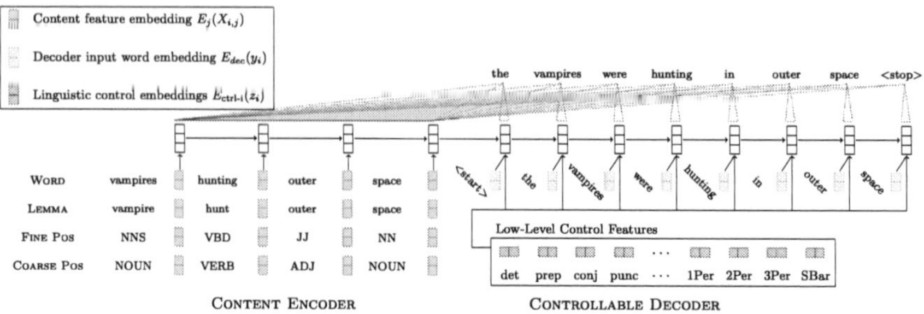

Figure 2: A schematic depiction of our style control model.

We use embedding sizes of 128, 128, 64, and 32 for token, lemma, fine, and coarse grained POS embedding matrices respectively. Output token embeddings E_{dec} have size 512, and 50 for the control feature embeddings. We set 512 for all GRU and perceptron output sizes. We refer to this model as the StyleEQ model.[5] See Figure 2 for a visual depiction of the model.[6]

3.3.1 Baseline Genre Model

We compare the above model to a similar model, where rather than explicitly represent K features as input, we have K features in the form of a genre embedding, i.e. we learn a genre specific embedding for each of the gothic, scifi, and philosophy genres, as studied in Fu et al. (2018) and Zhao et al. (2018). To generate in a specific style, we simply set the appropriate embedding. We use genre embeddings of size 850 which is equivalent to the total size of the K feature embeddings in the StyleEQ model.

3.3.2 Training

We train both models with minibatch stochastic gradient descent with a learning rate of 0.25, weight decay penalty of 0.0001, and batch size of 64. We also apply dropout with a drop rate of 0.25 to all embedding layers, the GRUs, and preceptron hidden layer. We train for a maximum of 200 epochs, using validation set BLEU score (Papineni et al., 2002) to select the final model iteration for evaluation.

3.3.3 Selecting Controls for Style Transfer

In the Baseline model, style transfer is straightforward: given an input sentence in one style, fix

the encoder content features while selecting a different genre embedding. In contrast, the StyleEQ model requires selecting the counts for each control. Although there are a variety of ways to do this, we use a method that encourages a diversity of outputs.

In order to ensure the controls match the reference sentence in magnitude, we first find all sentences in the target style with the same number of words as the reference sentence. Then, we add the following constraints: the same number of proper nouns, the same number of nouns, the same number of verbs, and the same number of adjectives. We randomly sample n of the remaining sentences, and for each of these 'sibling' sentences, we compute the controls. For each of the new controls, we generate a sentence using the original input sentence content features. The generated sentences are then reranked using the length normalized log-likelihood under the model. We can then select the highest scoring sentence as our style-transferred output, or take the top-k when we need a diverse set of outputs.

The reason for this process is that although there are group-level distinctive controls for each style, e.g. the high use of punctuation in philosophy books or of first person pronouns in gothic novels, at the sentence level it can understandably be quite varied. This method matches sentences between styles, capturing the natural distribution of the corpora.

4 Automatic Evaluations

4.1 BLEU Scores & Perplexity

In Table 4 we report BLEU scores for the reconstruction of test set sentences from their content and feature representations, as well as the model perplexities of the reconstruction. For both mod-

---

[5] We think of the suite of feature controls as knobs akin to a parametric equalizer (EQ) on a HiFi-stereo.

[6] Implementation code can be found at:
`https://github.com/kedz/styleeq`

Model	BLEU	Perplexity
Baseline	25.07	4.60
StyleEQ	**30.04**	**3.33**

Table 4: Test set reconstruction BLEU score and perplexity (in nats).

Control	Exact	Direction	Atomic
S	18.99	43.34	23.86
SBAR	24.22	41.41	18.16
ADVP	20.78	27.65	21.96
FRAG	24.47	26.60	19.71
conjunction	93.56	98.75	11.43
determiner	81.11	95.67	16.98
3rdNeutralPer	40.70	78.56	8.97
3rdFemalePer	32.77	65.53	12.62
3rdMalePer	36.20	75.72	9.27
1stPer	79.47	94.48	12.80
2ndPer	78.01	96.69	13.48
3rdPer	29.08	70.92	10.56
helperVerbs	69.92	90.23	12.30
negation	68.85	93.21	12.88
simple prep	49.32	77.74	19.86
position prep	47.18	79.42	19.42
punctuation	84.83	91.71	13.05

Table 5: Percentage rates of Exact, Direction, and Atomic feature control changes. See subsection 4.2 for explanation.

els, we use beam decoding with a beam size of eight. Beam candidates are ranked according to their length normalized log-likelihood. On these automatic measures we see that StyleEQ is better able to reconstruct the original sentences. In some sense this evaluation is mostly a sanity check, as the feature controls contain more locally specific information than the genre embeddings, which say very little about how many specific function words one should expect to see in the output.

4.2 Feature Control

Designing controllable language models is often difficult because of the various dependencies between tokens; when changing one control value it may effect other aspects of the surface realization. For example, increasing the number of conjunctions may effect how the generator places prepositions to compensate for structural changes in the sentence. Since our features are deterministically recoverable, we can perturb an individual control value and check to see that the desired change was realized in the output. Moreover, we can check the amount of change in the other non-perturbed features to measure the independence of the controls.

We sample 50 sentences from each genre from the test set. For each sample, we create a perturbed control setting for each control by adding δ to the original control value. This is done for $\delta \in \{-3, -2, -1, 0, 1, 2, 3\}$, skipping any settings where the new control value would be negative.

Table 5 shows the results of this experiment. The *Exact* column displays the percentage of generated texts that realize the exact number of control features specified by the perturbed control. High percentages in the *Exact* column indicate greater one-to-one correspondence between the control and surface realization. For example, if the input was "Dracula and Frankenstein and the mummy," and we change the conjunction feature by $\delta = -1$, an output of "Dracula, Frankenstein and the mummy," would count towards the *Exact* category, while "Dracula, Frankenstein, the mummy," would not.

The *Direction* column specifies the percentage of cases where the generated text produces a changed number of the control features that, while not exactly matching the specified value of the perturbed control, does change from the original in the correct direction. For example, if the input again was "Dracula and Frankenstein and the mummy," and we change the conjunction feature by $\delta = -1$, both outputs of "Dracula, Frankenstein and the mummy," and "Dracula, Frankenstein, the mummy," would count towards *Direction*. High percentages in *Direction* mean that we could roughly ensure desired surface realizations by modifying the control by a larger δ.

Finally, the *Atomic* column specifies the percentage of cases where the generated text with the perturbed control only realizes changes to that specific control, while other features remain constant. For example, if the input was "Dracula and Frankenstein in the castle," and we set the conjunction feature to $\delta = -1$, an output of "Dracula near Frankenstein in the castle," would not count as *Atomic* because, while the number of conjunctions did decrease by one, the number of simple preposition changed. An output of "Dracula, Frankenstein in the castle," would count as *Atomic*. High percentages in the *Atomic* column indicate this feature is only loosely coupled to the other features and can be changed without modifying other aspects of the sentence.

Controls such as *conjunction, determiner*, and *punctuation* are highly controllable, with *Exact* rates above 80%. But with the exception of the constituency parse features, all controls have high *Direction* rates, many in the 90s. These results indicate our model successfully controls these features. The fact that the *Atomic* rates are relatively low is to be expected, as controls are highly coupled – e.g. to increase *1stPer*, it is likely another pronoun control will have to decrease.

4.3 Automatic Classification

For each model we look at the classifier prediction accuracy of reconstructed and transferred sentences. In particular we use the *Ablated NVA* classifier, as this is the most content-blind one.

We produce 16 outputs from both the Baseline and StyleEq models. For the Baseline, we use a beam search of size 16. For the StyleEQ model, we use the method described in Section 3.3.3 to select 16 'sibling' sentences in the target style, and generated a transferred sentence for each.[7] We look at three different methods for selection: *all*, which uses all output sentences; *top*, which selects the top ranked sentence based on the score from the model; and *oracle*, which selects the sentence with the highest classifier likelihood for the intended style.

The reason for the third method, which indeed acts as an oracle, is that using the score from the model didn't always surface a transferred sentence that best reflected the desired style. Partially this was because the model score was mostly a function of how well a transferred sentence reflected the distribution of the training data. But additionally, some control settings are more indicative of a target style than others. The use of the classifier allows us to identify the most suitable control setting for a target style that was roughly compatible with the number of content words.

In Table 6 we see the results. Note that for both models, the *all* and *top* classification accuracy tends to be quite similar, though for the Baseline they are often almost exactly the same when the Baseline has little to no diversity in the outputs.

However, the *oracle* introduces a huge jump in accuracy for the StyleEQ model, especially compared to the Baseline, partially because the diversity of outputs from StyleEQ is much higher; often the Baseline model produces no diversity – the 16 output sentences may be nearly identical, save a single word or two. It's important to note that neither model uses the classifier in any way except to select the sentence from 16 candidate outputs.

What this implies is that lurking within the StyleEQ model outputs are great sentences, even if they are hard to find. In many cases, the StyleEQ model has a classification accuracy above the base rate from the test data, which is 75% (see Table 2).

5 Human Evaluation

Table 7 shows example outputs for the StyleEQ and Baseline models[8]. Through inspection we see that the StyleEQ model successfully changes syntactic constructions in stylistically distinctive ways, such as increasing syntactic complexity when transferring to philosophy, or changing relevant pronouns when transferring to sci-fi. In contrast, the Baseline model doesn't create outputs that move far from the reference sentence, making only minor modifications such changing the type of a single pronoun.

To determine how readers would classify our transferred sentences, we recruited three English Literature PhD candidates, all of whom had passed qualifying exams that included determining both genre and era of various literary texts.

5.1 Fluency Evaluation

To evaluate the fluency of our outputs, we had the annotators score reference sentences, reconstructed sentences, and transferred sentences on a 0-5 scale, where 0 was incoherent and 5 was a well-written human sentence.

Table 8 shows the average fluency of various conditions from all three annotators. Both models have fluency scores around 3. Upon inspection of the outputs, it is clear that many have fluency errors, resulting in ungrammatical sentences.

Notably the Baseline often has slightly higher fluency scores than the StyleEQ model. This is likely because the Baseline model is far less constrained in how to construct the output sentence,

---

[7]For each 'sibling' we used a beam search of size 8 and selected the top candidate according to length normalized log-likelihood.

[8]The outputs are manually selected from the set of 16 candidate output sentences.

Model	Method	all	scifi (s)			philosophy (p)			gothic (g)		
			s→s	s→p	s→g	p→s	p→p	p→g	g→s	g→p	g→g
Baseline	all	.424	.639	.344	.301	.242	.818	.140	.483	.422	.437
Baseline	top	.429	.666	.344	.301	.242	.819	.140	.483	.422	.400
Baseline	oracle	**.493**	.851	.344	.301	.242	.940	.140	.483	.422	.750
StyleEQ	all	.413	.561	.348	.322	.167	.803	.268	.378	.467	.426
StyleEQ	top	.382	.573	.307	.221	.201	.800	.165	.458	.430	.436
StyleEQ	oracle	**.841**	.804	.834	.947	.560	.926	.900	.866	.914	.679

Table 6: *Ablated NVA* classifier accuracy using three different methods of selecting an output sentence. This is additionally split into the nine transfer possibilities, given the three source styles. The StyleEQ model produces far more diverse outputs, allowing the oracle method to have a very high accuracy compared to the Baseline model.

Setting	StyleEQ output	Baseline output
reference	Her face had turned beet red.	Her face had turned beet red.
s→s	her face had turned thereto red.	his face had turned out of the dissolution of the red.
s→g	her face had turned to me, the realization red.	her face had turned, and, with a modesty of red.
s→p	in the face, had turned–that was, the realization red.	his face had turned, and, with a modesty of red.
reference	The desire for exclusive markets is one of the most potent causes of war.	The desire for exclusive markets is one of the most potent causes of war.
p→p	the desire of exclusive markets is one of the most potent causes of war.	the desire of exclusive markets is one of the most potent causes of war.
p→s	but his desire is an exclusive markets, one of the most potent causes of war.	the desire of the exclusive markets were one of the most potent causes of war.
p→g	i am a desire of your exclusive markets, and that you are one of the most potent causes of your war in me.	the desire of the exclusive markets were one of the most potent causes of war.
reference	a little while, and all this will appear a dream.	a little while, and all this will appear a dream.
g→g	but a little while, all this will appear a dream.	a little while all it would appear in a dream.
g→s	he wasn't a little while all he could appear in the dream.	a little while all it would appear in a dream.
g→p	a little while–all that would appear to do, dream.	a little while all will appear in a dream.

Table 7: Example outputs (manually selected) from both models. The StyleEQ model successfully rewrites the sentence with very different syntactic constructions that reflect style, while the Baseline model rarely moves far from the reference.

and upon inspection often reconstructs the reference sentence even when performing style transfer. In contrast, the StyleEQ is encouraged to follow the controls, but can struggle to incorporate these controls into a fluent sentence.

The fluency of all outputs is lower than desired. We expect that incorporating pre-trained language models would increase the fluency of all outputs without requiring larger datasets.

5.2 Human Classification

Each annotator annotated 90 reference sentences (i.e. from the training corpus) with which style they thought the sentence was from. The accuracy on this baseline task for annotators A1, A2, and A3 was 80%, 88%, and 80% respectively, giving us an upper expected bound on the human evaluation.

Sentence Type	Model	fluency		
		A1	A2	A3
Reference	none	4.94	4.47	4.82
Reconstruction	Baseline	3.48	3.09	4.13
	StyleEQ	3.60	2.93	3.96
Transferred	Baseline	3.36	4.17	3.30
	StyleEQ	3.22	3.86	3.00

Table 8: Fluency scores (0-5, where 0 is incoherent) of sentences from three annotators. The Baseline model tends to produce slightly more fluent sentences than the StyleEQ model, likely because it is less constrained.

Model	which-of-3			which-of-2		
	A1	A2	A3	A1	A2	A3
Baseline	.21	.17	.17	.57	.31	.58
StyleEQ	.24	.20	.17	.54	.51	.48

Table 9: Accuracy of three annotators in selecting the correct style for transferred sentences. In this evaluation there is little difference between the models.

In discussing this task with the annotators, they noted that content is a heavy predictor of genre, and that would certainly confound their annotations. To attempt to mitigate this, we gave them two annotation tasks: *which-of-3* where they simply marked which style they thought a sentence was from, and *which-of-2* where they were given the original style and marked which style they thought the sentence was transferred into.

For each task, each annotator marked 180 sentences: 90 from each model, with an even split across the three genres. Annotators were presented the sentences in a random order, without information about the models. In total, each marked 270 sentences. (Note there were no reconstructions in this annotation task.)

Table 9 shows the results. In both tasks, accuracy of annotators classifying the sentence as its intended style was low. In *which-of-3*, scores were around 20%, below the chance rate of 33%. In *which-of-2*, scores were in the 50s, slightly above the chance rate of 50%. This was the case for both models. There was a slight increase in accuracy for the StyleEQ model over the Baseline for *which-of-3*, but the opposite trend for *which-of-2*, suggesting these differences are not significant.

It's clear that it's hard to fool the annotators. Introspecting on their approach, the annotators expressed having immediate responses based on key words – for instance any references of 'space' implied 'sci-fi'. We call this the 'vampires in space' problem, because no matter how well a gothic sentence is rewritten as a sci-fi one, it's impossible to ignore the fact that there is a vampire in space. The transferred sentences, in the eyes of the *Ablated NVA* classifier (with no access to content words), did quite well transferring into their intended style. But people are not blind to content.

5.3 The 'Vampires in Space' Problem

Working with the annotators, we regularly came up against the 'vampires in space' problem: while syntactic constructions account for much of the distinction of literary styles, these constructions often co-occur with distinctive content.

Stylometrics finds syntactic constructions are great at fingerprinting, but suggests that these constructions are surface realizations of higher-level stylistic decisions. The number and type of personal pronouns is a reflection of how characters feature in a text. A large number of positional prepositions may be the result of a writer focusing on physical descriptions of scenes. In our attempt to decouple these, we create Frankenstein sentences, which piece together features of different styles – we are putting vampires in space.

Another way to validate our approach would be to select data that is stylistically distinctive but with similar content: perhaps genres in which content is static but language use changes over time, stylistically distinct authors within a single genre, or parodies of a distinctive genre.

6 Conclusion and Future Work

We present a formal, extendable model of style that can add control to any neural text generation system. We model style as a suite of low-level linguistic controls, and train a neural encoder-decoder model to reconstruct reference sentences given only content words and the setting of the controls. In automatic evaluations, we show that our model can fool a style classifier 84% of the time and outperforms a baseline genre-embedding model. In human evaluations, we encounter the 'vampires in space' problem in which content and style are equally discriminative but people focus more on the content.

In future work we would like to model higher-level syntactic controls. Allison et al. (2013) show that differences in clausal constructions, for instance having a dependent clause before an independent clause or vice versa, is a marker of style appreciated by the reader. Such features would likely interact with our lower-level controls in an interesting way, and provide further insight into style transfer in text.

Acknowledgements

Katy Gero is supported by an NSF GRF (DGE - 1644869). We would also like to thank Elsbeth Turcan for her helpful comments.

References

Sarah Allison, Marissa Gemma, Ryan Heuser, Franco Moretti, Amir Tevel, and Irena Yamboliev. 2013. *Style at the Scale of the Sentence*. Stanford Literary Lab.

Dzmitry Bahdanau, Kyunghyun Cho, and Yoshua Bengio. 2014. Neural machine translation by jointly learning to align and translate. *arXiv preprint arXiv:1409.0473*.

John Burrows. 2002. Delta: A Measure of Stylistic Difference and a Guide to Likely Authorship. 17(3):267–287.

Kyunghyun Cho, Bart van Merrienboer, Caglar Gulcehre, Dzmitry Bahdanau, Fethi Bougares, Holger Schwenk, and Yoshua Bengio. 2014. Learning phrase representations using rnn encoder–decoder for statistical machine translation. In *Proceedings of the 2014 Conference on Empirical Methods in Natural Language Processing (EMNLP)*, pages 1724–1734.

H. Craig and A.F. Kinney. 2009. *Shakespeare, Computers, and the Mystery of Authorship*. Cambridge University Press.

Jan Milan Deriu and Mark Cieliebak. 2018. Syntactic manipulation for generating more diverse and interesting texts. In *11th International Conference on Natural Language Generation (INLG 2018), Tilburg, The Netherlands, 05-08 November 2018*, pages 22–34. Association for Computational Linguistics.

Jessica Ficler and Yoav Goldberg. 2017. Controlling linguistic style aspects in neural language generation. *CoRR*, abs/1707.02633.

Zhenxin Fu, Xiaoye Tan, Nanyun Peng, Dongyan Zhao, and Rui Yan. 2018. Style transfer in text: Exploration and evaluation. In *Thirty-Second AAAI Conference on Artificial Intelligence*.

Wilhelm Fucks. 1952. On Mathematical Analysis of Style. 39(1/2):122–129.

Leon A Gatys, Alexander S Ecker, and Matthias Bethge. 2015. A neural algorithm of artistic style. *arXiv preprint arXiv:1508.06576*.

Leon A. Gatys, Alexander S. Ecker, and Matthias Bethge. 2016. Image style transfer using convolutional neural networks. In *The IEEE Conference on Computer Vision and Pattern Recognition (CVPR)*.

Harsh Jhamtani, Varun Gangal, Eduard H. Hovy, and Eric Nyberg. 2017. Shakespearizing modern language using copy-enriched sequence-to-sequence models. *CoRR*, abs/1707.01161.

Armand Joulin, Edouard Grave, Piotr Bojanowski, and Tomas Mikolov. 2017. Bag of tricks for efficient text classification. In *Proceedings of the 15th Conference of the European Chapter of the Association for Computational Linguistics: Volume 2, Short Papers*, pages 427–431. Association for Computational Linguistics.

Guillaume Lample, Sandeep Subramanian, Eric Smith, Ludovic Denoyer, Marc'Aurelio Ranzato, and Y-Lan Boureau. 2019. Multiple-attribute text rewriting. In *International Conference on Learning Representations*.

Christopher D. Manning, Mihai Surdeanu, John Bauer, Jenny Finkel, Steven J. Bethard, and David McClosky. 2014. The Stanford CoreNLP natural language processing toolkit. In *Association for Computational Linguistics (ACL) System Demonstrations*, pages 55–60.

Mitchell Marcus, Grace Kim, Mary Ann Marcinkiewicz, Robert MacIntyre, Ann Bies, Mark Ferguson, Karen Katz, and Britta Schasberger. 1994. The penn treebank: annotating predicate argument structure. In *Proceedings of the workshop on Human Language Technology*, pages 114–119. Association for Computational Linguistics.

Marie-Catherine de Marneffe, Timothy Dozat, Natalia Silveira, Katri Haverinen, Filip Ginter, Joakim Nivre, and Christopher D Manning. Universal dependencies: A cross-linguistic typology.

T. C. Mendenhall. 1887. The Characteristic Curves of Composition. 9(214):237–249.

Frederick Mosteller and David L. Wallace. 2007. *Inference and Disputed Authorship: The Federalist*. Center for the Study of Language and Information.

Shereen Oraby, Lena Reed, Shubhangi Tandon, Sharath T. S., Stephanie M. Lukin, and Marilyn A. Walker. 2018. Controlling personality-based stylistic variation with neural natural language generators. *CoRR*, abs/1805.08352.

Kishore Papineni, Salim Roukos, Todd Ward, and Wei-Jing Zhu. 2002. Bleu: a method for automatic evaluation of machine translation. In *Proceedings of the 40th annual meeting on association for computational linguistics*, pages 311–318. Association for Computational Linguistics.

Sudha Rao and Joel R. Tetreault. 2018. Dear sir or madam, may I introduce the YAFC corpus: Corpus, benchmarks and metrics for formality style transfer. *CoRR*, abs/1803.06535.

Jonathan Reeve. 2019. On early style: a stylochronometric critique of late style in literature. *Under Review at Digital Scholarship in the Humanities*.

Claude Elwood Shannon. 1948. A mathematical theory of communication. *Bell system technical journal*, 27(3):379–423.

Alexey Tikhonov and Ivan P. Yamshchikov. 2018. What is wrong with style transfer for texts? *CoRR*, abs/1808.04365.

Ted Underwood. 2016. The life cycles of genres.

Yanpeng Zhao, Wei Bi, Deng Cai, Xiaojiang Liu, Kewei Tu, and Shuming Shi. 2018. Language style transfer from sentences with arbitrary unknown styles. *CoRR*, abs/1808.04071.

Selecting Artificially-Generated Sentences for Fine-Tuning Neural Machine Translation

Alberto Poncelas and **Andy Way**
ADAPT Centre, School of Computing,
Dublin City University, Dublin, Ireland
{firstname.lastname}@adaptcentre.ie

Abstract

Neural Machine Translation (NMT) models tend to achieve best performance when larger sets of parallel sentences are provided for training. For this reason, augmenting the training set with artificially-generated sentence pairs can boost performance.

Nonetheless, the performance can also be improved with a small number of sentences if they are in the same domain as the test set. Accordingly, we want to explore the use of artificially-generated sentences along with data-selection algorithms to improve German-to-English NMT models trained solely with authentic data.

In this work, we show how artificially-generated sentences can be more beneficial than authentic pairs, and demonstrate their advantages when used in combination with data-selection algorithms.

1 Introduction

The data used for training Machine Translation (MT) models consist mainly of a set of parallel sentences (a set of sentence-pairs in which each sentence is paired with its translation). As Neural Machine Translation (NMT) models typically achieve best performance when using large sets of parallel sentences, they can benefit from the sentences created by Natural Language Generation (NLG) systems. Although artificial data is expected to be of lower quality than authentic sentences, it still can help the model to learn how to better generalize over the training instances and produce better translations.

A popular technique used to create artificial data is the back-translation technique (Sennrich et al., 2016a; Poncelas et al., 2018c). This consists of generating sentences in the source language by translating monolingual sentences in the target language. Then, these sentences in both languages are paired and can be used to augment the original parallel training set used to build better NMT models.

Nonetheless, if synthetic data are not in the same domain as the test set, it can also hurt the performance. For this reason, we explore an alternative approach to better use the artificially-generated training instances to improve NMT models. In particular, we propose that instead of blindly adding back-translated sentences into the training set they can be considered as candidate sentences for a data-selection algorithm to decide which sentence-pairs should be used to fine-tune the NMT model. By doing that, instead of increasing the number of training instances in a motivated manner, the generated sentences provide us with more chances of obtaining relevant parallel sentences (and still use smaller sets for fine-tuning).

As we want to build task-specific NMT models, in this work we explore two data-selection algorithms that are classified as Transductive Algorithms (TA): Infrequent N-gram Recovery (INR) and Feature Decay Algorithms (FDA). These methods use the test set S_{test} (the document to be translated) as the seed to retrieve sentences. In transductive learning (Vapnik, 1998) the goal is to identify the best training instances to learn how to classify a given test set. In order to select these sentences, the TAs search for those n-grams in the test set that are also present in the source side of the candidate sentences.

Although augmenting the candidate pool with more sentences should be beneficial, as the TAs select the sentences based on overlapping n-gram the mistakes produced by the model used for back-translation (which are those commonly addressed in NLG such as the generated word order or word choice) can be a disadvantage.

In this work, we explore whether TAs are more inclined to select authentic or artificial sentences. In addition, we propose three different methods of

Proceedings of The 12th International Conference on Natural Language Generation, pages 219–228,
Tokyo, Japan, 28 Oct - 1 Nov, 2019. ©2019 Association for Computational Linguistics

how they can be combined into a single hybrid set. Finally, we investigate whether the hybrid sets retrieved by TAs can be more useful than the authentic set of sentences to fine-tune NMT models.

2   Related Work

The work presented in this paper is based on two main concepts: the generation of synthetic sentences, and the selection of sentences from a set S of candidates.

2.1   Use of Artificially-Generated Data to Improve MT Models

The proposal of Sennrich et al. (2016a) showed that NMT models can be improved by back-translating a set of (monolingual) sentences in the target side into the source side using an MT model. Other uses of monolingual target-side sentences include building the parallel set by using a NULL token in the source side (Sennrich et al., 2016a) or creating language models to improve the decoder (Gülçehre et al., 2015).

Hoang et al. (2018) improve the model used for back-translation by training this model with increasing amounts of artificial sentences. They iteratively improve the models creating artificial sentences of better quality.

Similarly to this paper, the use of artificially-generated sentences to fine-tuned models has also been explored by Chinea-Rios et al. (2017) where they select monolingual authentic sentences in the source-side and translate them into the target language, or the work of Poncelas et al. (2019a) where they use back-translated sentences only to adapt the models.

2.2   Adaptation of NMT Models to the Test Set

The improvement of NMT models can be performed by fine-tuning (Luong and Manning, 2015; Freitag and Al-Onaizan, 2016), i.e. train the models for additional epochs using a small set of in-domain data. Alternatively, van der Wees et al. (2017) train models using smaller but more in-domain sentences in each epoch of the training process.

The use of the test set to retrieve relevant sentences for fine-tuning the model has been explored by Li et al. (2016), adapting a different model for each sentence in the test set, or Poncelas et al. (2018b, 2019b) where they adapt the model for the complete test set using transductive data-selection algorithms.

3   Transductive Algorithms

In this paper, the sentences used to fine-tune the model are retrieved using INR and FDA. These methods select sentences by scoring each sentence s from the candidate pool S, and adding that with the highest score to a selected pool L. This process is performed iteratively until the selected pool contains N sentences.

Infrequent n-gram Recovery (INR) (Parcheta et al., 2018; Gascó et al., 2012): This method selects those sentences that contain n-grams from the test set that are infrequent (ignoring frequent words such as stop words or general-domain terms). A candidate sentence $s \in S$ is scored according to the number of infrequent n-grams shared with the set of sentences of the test set S_{test}, computed as in (1):

$$score(s) = \sum_{ngr \in \{S_{test} \bigcap s\}} max(0, t - C_L(ngr))$$

(1)

where t is the threshold that indicates the number of occurrences of an n-gram to be considered infrequent. If the number of occurrences of ngr in the selected pool ($C_L(ngr)$) is above the threshold t, then the component $max(0, t - C_S(ngr))$ is 0 and so the n-gram does not contribute to scoring the sentence.

Feature Decay Algorithms (Biçici and Yuret, 2011; Biçici, 2013) also retrieve those sentences sharing the highest number of n-grams from the test set. However, in order to increase the variability and avoid selecting the same n-grams, those that have been selected are penalized is proportional to the number of occurrences in L. The score of a sentence is computed as in (2):

$$score(s, L) = \frac{\sum_{ngr \in S_{test}} 0.5^{C_L(ngr)}}{length(s)}$$

(2)

where $length(s)$ indicates the number of words in the sentence s. According to the equation, the more occurrences of ngr in L, the smaller the contribution is to the scoring of the sentence s.

3.1 Models Adapted with Hybrid Data

In order to fine-tune models with hybrid data, we propose three methods of creating these sets: *hybr*, *batch* and *online*. These methods can be classified depending on whether the combination is performed before or after the execution of the TA.

Combine Before Selection. This approach consists of selecting from a hybrid set (*hybr*). This involves concatenating both the authentic candidate S_{auth} and artificial S_{synth} sentences as a first step and then executing the TAs with the new candidate set $S_{auth+synth}$.

Combine After Selection. Another approach is to force the presence of both authentic and synthetic sentences by using different proportions of TA-selected authentic (L_{auth}) and synthetic (L_{synth}) sentence pairs. We concatenate the top-$(N * \gamma)$ sentences from the selected authentic set and the top-$(N * (1 - \gamma))$ from the synthetic set. The value of $\gamma \in [0, 1]$ indicates the proportion of authentic and synthetic sentences. For example, $\gamma = 0.75$ indicates that the 75% of sentences in the dataset are authentic and the remaining 25% are artificially generated.

The selected synthetic set L_{synth} can be obtained by executing the TAs on artificial candidate sentences S_{synth} (*batch*). This implies that the sentences will be retrieved by finding overlaps of *n*-grams between the test set and artificial sentences.

Alternatively, the retrieval may be carried by finding overlaps in the target-side (*online*) as they are human-produced sentences. However, as the test set is in the source language, we need to first generate an approximated translation of the test with a general-domain MT model (Poncelas et al., 2018a,d). Unlike in *batch*, the advantage of this approach is that it is not necessary to generate the source side of the whole set of monolingual sentences, but rather only those selected by the TA.

4 Experiments

4.1 Data and Models Settings

We build German-to-English NMT models using the following datasets:

- Training data: German-English parallel sentences provided in WMT 2015 (Bojar et al., 2015) (4.5M sentence pairs).

- Test sets: We evaluate the models with two test sets in different domains:
    - *BIO test set*: the Cochrane[1] dataset from the WMT 2017 biomedical translation shared task (Yepes et al., 2017).
    - *NEWS test set*: The test set provided in WMT 2015 News Translation Task.

All these data sets are tokenized, truecased, and Byte Pair Encoding (BPE) (Sennrich et al., 2016b) is applied using 89,500 merge operations.

The NMT models are built using the attentional encoder-decoder framework with OpenNMT-py[2] (Klein et al., 2017). We use the default values in the parameters: 2-layer LSTM (Hochreiter and Schmidhuber, 1997) with 500 hidden units. The size of the vocabulary is 50,000 words for each language.

In order to retrieve sentences, we use the TAs with default configuration (using *n*-grams of order 3 to find overlaps between the seed and the training data) to extract sets of 100K, 200K, and 500K sentences. We use a threshold of $t = 40$ for INR although this causes the INR to retrieve less than 500K sentences. Accordingly, the results shown for INR will include only 100K and 200K sentences.

4.2 Back-Translation Generation Settings

In order to generate artificial sentences, we use an NMT model (we refer to it as *BT model*) to back-translate sentences from the target language into the source language. This model is built by training a model with 1M sentences sampled from the training data and using the same configuration described above (but in the reverse language direction, English-to-German).

As we want to compare authentic and synthetic sentences, we back-translate the target-side of the training data using the BT model. By doing this we ensure both sets are comparable which allows us to perform a fair analysis of whether artificial sentences are more likely to be selected by a TA and which are more useful to fine-tune the models.

Note also that there are 1M sentences that have been generated by translating the same target-side sentences used in training. This could cause the generated sentences to be exactly the same as authentic ones. However, this is not always the case as we report in Section 5.2.

---

[1] http://www.himl.eu/test-sets
[2] https://github.com/OpenNMT/OpenNMT-py

5 Results

		BASE13	BASE12 + INR	BASE12 + FDA
	BIO			
100K lines	BLEU	33.14	**33.52***	**33.68***
	TER	46.79	**45.92***	**45.97***
	MET.	34.57	**34.77**	**34.71**
	CHRF3	59.08	**59.43**	**59.24**
200K lines	BLEU	33.14	**33.88***	**33.96***
	TER	46.79	**45.90***	**45.64***
	MET.	34.57	**34.94***	**35.01***
	CHRF3	59.08	**59.56**	**59.56**
500K lines	BLEU	33.14	-	**33.75***
	TER	46.79	-	**45.92***
	MET.	34.57	-	**34.92***
	CHRF3	59.08	-	**59.57**
	NEWS			
100K lines	BLEU	26.34	**26.49**	**26.49**
	TER	54.41	**54.19**	**54.21**
	MET.	30.09	**30.21***	**30.21***
	CHRF3	51.71	**51.78**	**51.80**
200K lines	BLEU	26.34	**26.44**	**26.55***
	TER	54.41	**54.35**	**54.17***
	MET.	30.09	**30.12**	**30.24***
	CHRF3	51.71	51.67	**51.89**
500K lines	BLEU	26.34	-	**26.40***
	TER	54.41	-	54.47
	MET.	30.09	-	**30.10***
	CHRF3	51.71	-	**51.71**

Table 1: Performance of the BASE13 model, and the models fine-tuned with subsets of the training data.

First of all, we present in Table 1 the performance of the model trained with all data for 13 epochs (BASE13), as this is when the model converges. We also show the performance of the model when fine-tuning the 12th epoch with the subset of (authentic) data selected by INR (*INR* column) and FDA (*FDA* column).

In order to evaluate the performance of the models, we present the following evaluation metrics: BLEU (Papineni et al., 2002), TER (Snover et al., 2006), METEOR (Banerjee and Lavie, 2005), and CHRF (Popovic, 2015). These metrics provide an estimation of the translation quality when the output is compared to a human-translated reference. Note that in general, the higher the score, the better the translation quality is. The only exception is TER which is an error metric and so lower results indicate better quality.

In addition, we indicate in bold those scores that show an improvement over the baseline (in Table 1 we use BASE13 as the baseline) and add an asterisk if the improvements are statistically significant at p=0.01 (using Bootstrap Resampling (Koehn, 2004), computed with multeval (Clark et al., 2011)).

In the table, we can see that using a small subset of data for training the 13th epoch can cause the performance of the model to improve. In the following experiments, we want to compare whether augmenting the candidate set with synthetic data can further boost these improvements. For this reason, we use *INR* and FDA *FDA* as baselines.

5.1 Results of Models Fine-tuned with Hybrid Data

		INR	INR HYBR
	BIO		
100K lines	BLEU	33.52	**33.87**
	TER	45.92	46.17
	METEOR	34.77	**35.01**
	CHRF3	59.43	**59.53**
200K lines	BLEU	33.88	33.70
	TER	45.90	46.33
	METEOR	34.94	**35.23**
	CHRF3	59.56	**60.03**
	NEWS		
100K lines	BLEU	26.49	**26.76**
	TER	54.19	54.36
	METEOR	30.21	**30.48***
	CHRF3	51.78	**52.35***
200K lines	BLEU	26.44	**26.80***
	TER	54.35	**54.34**
	METEOR	30.12	**30.51***
	CHRF3	51.67	**52.39***

Table 2: Results of the models built with different sizes of INR-selected hybrid data following the *hybr* approach. The results in bold indicate an improvement over INR. The asterisk means the improvement is statistically significant at p=0.01.

In the first set of experiments we explore the *hybr* approach, i.e. the TAs are executed on a mixture of authentic and synthetic data (combined before the execution of the TA). We present the results of the models trained with these sets in Table 2 (for INR) and Table 3 (for FDA). In the first column, we include as the baseline the fine-tuned models

		FDA	FDA HY-BR
	BIO		
100K lines	BLEU	33.68	**33.86**
	TER	45.97	46.20
	METEOR	34.71	**35.22***
	CHRF3	59.24	**59.89***
200K lines	BLEU	33.96	33.94
	TER	45.64	46.09
	METEOR	35.01	**35.29**
	CHRF3	59.56	**59.89**
500K lines	BLEU	33.75	**33.90**
	TER	45.92	46.34
	METEOR	34.92	**35.12**
	CHRF3	59.57	**59.80**
	NEWS		
100K lines	BLEU	26.49	**26.71**
	TER	54.21	54.31
	METEOR	30.21	**30.43***
	CHRF3	51.80	**52.30***
200K lines	BLEU	26.55	**26.78***
	TER	54.17	54.42
	METEOR	30.24	**30.51***
	CHRF3	51.89	**52.41***
500K lines	BLEU	26.40	**26.78***
	TER	54.47	**54.38**
	METEOR	30.10	**30.51***
	CHRF3	51.71	**52.38***

Table 3: Results of the models built with different sizes of FDA-selected hybrid data following the *hybr* approach. The results in bold indicate an improvement over FDA. The asterisk means the improvement is statistically significant at p=0.01.

presented in Table 1.

The results in the tables show that increasing the size of the candidate pool is beneficial. We see that most scores are better (marked in bold) than the model fine-tuned with only authentic data. However, the performance is also dependent on the domain. When comparing BIO and NEWS subtables we see that the models adapted for the latter domain tend to achieve better performances as most of the scores are statistically significant improvements.

When analyzing the selected dataset we find that the authentic sentences constitute slightly above half (between 51% and 64% of the sentences). This is an indicator that artificially-generated sentences contain *n*-grams that can be found by TA and are as useful as authentic sentences.

In addition, the amount of duplicated target-side sentences is very low (between 10% and 13%). This indicates that the MT-generated sentences contain *n*-grams that are different from the authentic counterpart, which increases the variety of the candidates that are useful for the TA to select.

In Table 4 and Table 5 we present the results of the models when fine-tuned with a combination of authentic and synthetic data following the *Combine Before Selection* approaches in Section 3.1. The tables are structured in two subtables showing the results of *batch* and *online* approaches. Each subtable present the results of three values of γ: 0.75, 0.50 and 0.25.

In these tables, we see that the performance of the models following the *batch* and *online* approaches is similar. These results are also in accord with those obtained following the *hybr* approach, as the improvements depend more on the domain (most evaluation scores in the NEWS test set indicate statistically significant improvements whereas for the BIO test set most of them are not) than the TA used, or the value of γ. Although the best scores tend to be when $\gamma = 0.50$ this is not always the case, and moreover we can find experiments in which using high amounts of synthetic sentences (i.e. $\gamma = 0.25$) achieve better results than using a higher proportion of authentic sentences. For instance, in BIO subtable of Table 4, using 100K sentences with the *online* $\gamma = 0.25$ approach, the improvements are statistically significant for two evaluation metrics whereas in the other experiments in that row they are not.

When analyzing the translations produced by these models we find several examples in which the translations of models fine-tuned with hybrid data are superior to those tuned with authentic sentences. An example of this is the sentence in the NEWS test set "nach Krankenhausangaben wurde ein Polizist verletzt." (in the reference, "according to statements released by the hospital, a police officer was injured.")

This sentence is translated by INR and FDA models (those fine-tuned with 100K authentic sentences) as "a policeman was injured after hospital information.". We see that these models translate the word "nach" with its literal meaning ("after") whereas in this context ("nach Krankenhausangaben") it should have been translated as "according

		INR	batch			online		
			$\gamma =$ 0.75	$\gamma =$ 0.50	$\gamma =$ 0.25	$\gamma =$ 0.75	$\gamma =$ 0.50	$\gamma =$ 0.25
BIO								
100K lines	BLEU	33.52	**33.88**	33.50	**33.67**	33.46	33.62	33.13
	TER	45.92	46.23	46.63	46.60	46.40	46.39	46.64
	METEOR	34.77	**35.03**	**35.13**	**35.13**	**34.90**	**34.96**	**35.12**
	CHRF3	59.43	**59.62**	**59.72**	**59.95**	**59.48**	**59.73**	59.92
200K lines	BLEU	33.88	33.85	33.70	33.51	33.69	33.52	33.39
	TER	45.90	46.43	46.14	46.80	46.40	46.46	46.62
	METEOR	34.94	**35.00**	**35.20**	**35.06**	**35.04**	**34.96**	**35.08**
	CHRF3	59.56	59.51	**59.95**	**59.93**	**59.61**	59.49	**59.91**
NEWS								
100K lines	BLEU	26.49	**26.81***	**26.59**	**26.75**	**26.77***	**26.73**	**26.75**
	TER	54.19	54.39	54.46	54.49	54.4	54.71	54.84
	METEOR	30.21	**30.45***	**30.51***	**30.65***	**30.54***	**30.51***	**30.64***
	CHRF3	51.78	**52.30***	**52.46***	**52.69***	**52.34***	**52.46***	**52.70***
200K lines	BLEU	26.44	**26.85***	**26.77***	**26.61**	**26.79***	**26.81***	**26.66**
	TER	54.35	54.37	54.43	54.70	54.4	54.67	54.67
	METEOR	30.12	**30.49***	**30.58***	**30.60***	**30.48***	**30.55***	**30.63***
	CHRF3	51.67	**52.35***	**52.55***	**52.60***	**52.25***	**52.57***	**52.69***

Table 4: Results of the models built with different sizes of INR-selected hybrid data following the *batch* and *online* approaches. The results in bold indicate an improvement over INR. The asterisk means the improvement is statistically significant at p=0.01.

to" as stated in the reference.

In the hybrid models, we see that the same sentence has been translated as "according to hospital information, a policeman was injured." (in this case the models fine-tuned with hybrid data have produced the same translations). The models tuned with hybrid data are capable of producing the *n*-gram "according to" which is the same as the reference.

In the selected data, the only sentence containing the *n*-gram "nach Krankenhausangaben" is the authentic sentence presented in the first row of Table 6 (selected by every execution of TA). As we see, this is a noisy sentence as the target-side does not correspond to an accurate translation (observe that in the source sentence we cannot find names such as "La Passione" or "Carlo Mazzacurati" that are present in the English side). Accordingly, using this sentence in the training of the NMT is harmful.

5.2 Analysis of Back-translated Sentences

We find many cases where artificially-generated data is more useful for NMT models than authentic translations. In Table 6 we show some examples.

In rows 1 and 2 we present sentences in which the artificial sentence (*German (synth)* column) is a better translation than the authentic counterpart. In addition to the example described previously (the example of the first row), we also see in row 2 that the authentic candidate pair is ("die Veranstalter haben viele Konzerte und Recitale geplant. Es wird für uns eine vorzügliche Gelegenheit sein Ihre Freizeit angenehm zu gestalten und Sie für die ernste Musik zu gewinnen.","every participant will play at least one programme.") whereas the synthetic counterpart is the pair ("jeder Teilnehmer wird mindestens ein Programm spielen.","every participant will play at least one programme."). In this case, it is preferable to use the synthetic sentence for training instead of the authentic as it is a more accurate translation (observe that the authentic German side consists of two sentences and it is longer than the English-side).

We also present a case in which both authentic and artificial sentences are not proper translations of the English sentence, so both sentences would hurt the performance of NMT if used for training. In row 3 there is a noisy sentence that should not

		FDA	batch			online		
			$\gamma = 0.75$	$\gamma = 0.50$	$\gamma = 0.25$	$\gamma = 0.75$	$\gamma = 0.50$	$\gamma = 0.25$
BIO								
100K lines	BLEU	33.68	33.56	33.48	33.3	33.39	33.41	33.45
	TER	45.97	46.51	46.49	46.93	46.33	46.58	46.7
	METEOR	34.71	**34.97**	**35.09***	**34.89**	**34.97**	**35.00**	**35.11***
	CHRF3	59.24	**59.48**	**59.62**	**59.59**	**59.45**	**59.55**	**59.83***
200K lines	BLEU	33.96	33.75	33.86	32.96	33.93	33.54	33.33
	TER	45.64	46.17	46.14	47.04	45.99	46.26	46.77
	METEOR	35.01	**35.08**	**35.08**	34.96	35.01	**35.09**	34.98
	CHRF3	59.56	**59.58**	**59.79**	**59.77**	**59.63**	**59.85**	**59.65**
500K lines	BLEU	33.75	33.72	33.74	33.13	33.75	**33.95**	33.46
	TER	45.92	46.32	46.13	46.90	46.12	46.14	46.85
	METEOR	34.92	**35.15**	**35.16**	34.87	**35.14**	**35.11**	**34.93**
	CHRF3	59.57	59.84	59.83	59.61	**59.83**	**60.00***	**59.77**
NEWS								
100K lines	BLEU	26.49	**26.58**	**26.61**	**26.60**	**26.51**	**26.59**	**26.54**
	TER	54.21	54.34	54.69	54.94	54.26	54.38	54.8
	METEOR	30.21	**30.36***	**30.43***	**30.51***	**30.33***	**30.49***	**30.49***
	CHRF3	51.80	**52.09***	**52.37***	**52.52***	**52.06***	**52.41***	**52.49***
200K lines	BLEU	26.55	**26.62**	**26.66**	**26.65**	**26.77***	**26.72**	**26.80***
	TER	54.17	54.36	54.52	54.70	54.29	54.48	54.55
	METEOR	30.24	**30.37***	**30.49***	**30.55***	**30.45***	**30.54***	**30.61***
	CHRF3	51.89	**52.14***	**52.49***	**52.55***	**52.35***	**52.56***	**52.75***
500K lines	BLEU	26.40	**26.70***	**26.92***	**26.73**	**26.68***	**26.94***	**26.98***
	TER	54.47	**54.29**	**54.37**	**54.63**	**54.13***	54.35	54.56
	METEOR	30.1	**30.44***	**30.59***	**30.59***	**30.42***	**30.58***	**30.68***
	CHRF3	51.71	**52.29***	**52.57***	**52.66***	**52.19***	**52.58***	**52.81***

Table 5: Results of the models built with different sizes of FDA-selected hybrid data following the *batch* and *online* approaches. The results in bold indicate an improvement over FDA. The asterisk means the improvement is statistically significant at p=0.01.

have been included as the target side is not English but French. The TAs search for n-grams in the source side, so as in this case the artificial sentence consists of a sequence of dots (the BT model has not been able to translate the French sentence) this prevents the TA from selecting it, whereas the authentic sentence-pair could be selected as it is a natural German sentence.

Surprisingly, this correction of inaccurate translations can also be seen on the set of sentences that have been used for training the BT model. As this model does not overfit, when it is provided with the same target sentence used for training, it is capable of generating different valid translations. For example, in row 4 of Table 6 we see the pair ("die Preise liegen zwischen 32.000 und 110.000 Won.","the first evening starts with a big parade of all participants through the city towards the beach.") which is one of the sentence pairs used for training the BT model. This is a noisy sentence (see, for instance, that the English-side does not include the numbers). However, the sentence generated by the BT model is "der erste Abend beginnt mit einer großen Parade aller Teilnehmer durch die Stadt zum Strand." which is a more accurate translation of than the sentence used for training the model that generates it.

6 Conclusion and Future Work

In this work, we have presented how artificially generated sentences can be used to augment a set of candidate sentences so data-selection algorithms have a wider variety of sentences to select from. The TA-selected sets have been evaluated

	German (auth)	German (synth)	English
1	nach Krankenhausangaben wurden zwei um die 50 Jahre alte Männer durch das Beben schwer verletzt. einer sei von einem herabfallenden Schornstein getroffen worden, der andere habe durch Glas Schnittwunden erlitten. außerdem seien mehrere Menschen durch herabstürzende Gegenstände in ihren Wohnungen leicht verletzt worden.	am Samstag wird es eine weitere Komödie, "La pasone"von Carlo Mazzacurati Italiens, geben, die die fruchtbare Silvio Orlando, die ein washed-up filmin der Toskana ist, in einer Nachbarkapelle aus dem 16. Jh.	Saturday will feature another comedy, "La Passione"by Carlo Mazzacurati of Italy starring the prolific Silvio Orlando, who plays a washed-up filmmaker who is forced to set his last-chance project in Tuscany after a plumbing disaster at his country home damages a 16th-century fresco in a neighbouring chapel.
2	die Veranstalter haben viele Konzerte und Recitale geplant. Es wird für uns eine vorzügliche Gelegenheit sein Ihre Freizeit angenehm zu gestalten und Sie für die ernste Musik zu gewinnen.	jeder Teilnehmer wird mindestens ein Programm spielen.	every participant will play at least one programme.
3	folglich übernimmt Informatic SA keine Gewährleistung für ihre Richtigkeit , ausser sie wurden vom Kunden schriftlich oder per E-Mail ausdrücklich für obligatorisch erklärt .	. . , ...	par conséquent, Informatic SA ne donne donc aucune assurance quant à leur exactitude à moins qu'elles n'aient été expressément déclarées obligatoires par écrit ou par e-mail par le client .
4	die Preise liegen zwischen 32.000 und 110.000 Won.	der erste Abend beginnt mit einer großen Parade aller Teilnehmer durch die Stadt zum Strand.	the first evening starts with a big parade of all participants through the city towards the beach.

Table 6: Examples of back-translated sentences

according to how useful they are for improving NMT models.

We have presented three methods of creating such hybrid data: (i) by allowing the TA decide whether to select authentic or synthetic data (*hybr*); (ii) by performing independent executions of the TA on authentic and synthetic sets (*batch*); and (iii) using an MT-generated seed to select monolingual sentences so only the extracted subset is back-translated (*online*).

The experiments showed that artificially-generated sentences can be as competitive as authentic data, as models built with different proportions of authentic and synthetic data achieve similar or even better performance than those fine-tuned with authentic pairs only. On one hand, those sentences whose target-sides could hurt the performance of NMT (such as sentences in a different language to that expected) causes the back-translated sentence to also contain unnatural *n*-grams and so TAs would not select them. On the other hand, if the source-side sentence is not an accurate translation of the target side (the problem of comparable corpus), the back-translated counterpart can be a better alternative to use as training data.

In the future, we want to explore other language pairs and other transductive algorithms. Another limitation of this work is that we have augmented the candidate pool with synthetic sentences generated by a single model. We propose to explore whether using several models for generating the synthetic sentences (including different approaches such as combining statistical and neural model (Poncelas et al., 2019c)) to augment the candidate pool can cause the selected data to further improve NMT models.

Acknowledgements

This research has been supported by the ADAPT Centre for Digital Content Technology which is funded under the SFI Research Centres Programme (Grant 13/RC/2106).

References

Satanjeev Banerjee and Alon Lavie. 2005. Meteor: An automatic metric for MT evaluation with improved correlation with human judgments. In *Proceedings of the ACL workshop on intrinsic and extrinsic evaluation measures for machine translation and/or summarization*, pages 65–72, Ann Arbor, Michigan.

Ergun Biçici. 2013. Feature decay algorithms for fast deployment of accurate statistical machine translation systems. In *Proceedings of the Eighth Work-*

shop on Statistical Machine Translation, pages 78–84, Sofia, Bulgaria.

Ergun Biçici and Deniz Yuret. 2011. Instance selection for machine translation using feature decay algorithms. In *Proceedings of the Sixth Workshop on Statistical Machine Translation*, pages 272–283, Edinburgh, Scotland.

Ondřej Bojar, Rajen Chatterjee, Christian Federmann, Barry Haddow, Matthias Huck, Chris Hokamp, Philipp Koehn, Varvara Logacheva, Christof Monz, Matteo Negri, Matt Post, Carolina Scarton, Lucia Specia, and Marco Turchi. 2015. Findings of the 2015 Workshop on Statistical Machine Translation. In *Proceedings of the Tenth Workshop on Statistical Machine Translation*, pages 1–46, Lisboa, Portugal.

Mara Chinea-Rios, Alvaro Peris, and Francisco Casacuberta. 2017. Adapting neural machine translation with parallel synthetic data. In *Proceedings of the Second Conference on Machine Translation*, pages 138–147, Copenhagen, Denmark.

Jonathan H. Clark, Chris Dyer, Alon Lavie, and Noah A. Smith. 2011. Better hypothesis testing for statistical machine translation: Controlling for optimizer instability. In *Proceedings of the 49th Annual Meeting of the Association for Computational Linguistics: Human Language Technologies (Volume 2: Short Papers)*, pages 176–181, Portland, Oregon.

Markus Freitag and Yaser Al-Onaizan. 2016. Fast domain adaptation for neural machine translation. *arXiv preprint arXiv:1612.06897*.

Guillem Gascó, Martha-Alicia Rocha, Germán Sanchis-Trilles, Jesús Andrés-Ferrer, and Francisco Casacuberta. 2012. Does more data always yield better translations? In *Proceedings of the 13th Conference of the European Chapter of the Association for Computational Linguistics*, pages 152–161, Avignon, France.

Çaglar Gülçehre, Orhan Firat, Kelvin Xu, Kyunghyun Cho, Loïc Barrault, Huei-Chi Lin, Fethi Bougares, Holger Schwenk, and Yoshua Bengio. 2015. On using monolingual corpora in neural machine translation. *arXiv preprint arXiv:1503.03535*.

Vu Cong Duy Hoang, Philipp Koehn, Gholamreza Haffari, and Trevor Cohn. 2018. Iterative back-translation for neural machine translation. In *Proceedings of the 2nd Workshop on Neural Machine Translation and Generation*, pages 18–24, Melbourne, Australia.

Sepp Hochreiter and Jürgen Schmidhuber. 1997. Long short-term memory. *Neural computation*, 9:1735–1780.

Guillaume Klein, Yoon Kim, Yuntian Deng, Jean Senellart, and Alexander M. Rush. 2017. Opennmt: Open-source toolkit for neural machine translation. In *Proceedings of the 55th Annual Meeting of the Association for Computational Linguistics-System Demonstrations*, pages 67–72, Vancouver, Canada.

Philipp Koehn. 2004. Statistical significance tests for machine translation evaluation. In *Proceedings of the 2004 Conference on Empirical Methods in Natural Language Processing*, pages 388–395, Barcelona, Spain.

Xiaoqing Li, Jiajun Zhang, and Chengqing Zong. 2016. One sentence one model for neural machine translation. *arXiv preprint arXiv:1609.06490*.

Minh-Thang Luong and Christopher D Manning. 2015. Stanford neural machine translation systems for spoken language domains. In *Proceedings of the International Workshop on Spoken Language Translation*, pages 76–79, Da Nang, Vietnam.

Kishore Papineni, Salim Roukos, Todd Ward, and Wei-Jing Zhu. 2002. Bleu: a method for automatic evaluation of machine translation. In *Proceedings of 40th Annual Meeting of the Association for Computational Linguistics*, pages 311–318, Philadelphia, Pennsylvania, USA.

Zuzanna Parcheta, Germán Sanchis-Trilles, and Francisco Casacuberta. 2018. Data selection for nmt using infrequent n-gram recovery. In *Proceedings of the 21st Annual Conference of the European Association for Machine Translation*, pages 219–227, Alacant, Spain.

Alberto Poncelas, Gideon Maillette de Buy Wenniger, and Andy Way. 2018a. Data selection with feature decay algorithms using an approximated target side. In *15th International Workshop on Spoken Language Translation*, pages 173–180, Bruges, Belgium.

Alberto Poncelas, Gideon Maillette de Buy Wenniger, and Andy Way. 2018b. Feature decay algorithms for neural machine translation. In *Proceedings of the 21st Annual Conference of the European Association for Machine Translation*, pages 239–248, Alacant, Spain.

Alberto Poncelas, Gideon Maillette de Buy Wenniger, and Andy Way. 2019a. Adaptation of machine translation models with back-translated data using transductive data selection methods. In *20th International Conference on Computational Linguistics and Intelligent Text Processing*, La Rochelle, France.

Alberto Poncelas, Gideon Maillette de Buy Wenniger, and Andy Way. 2019b. Transductive data-selection algorithms for fine-tuning neural machine translation. In *Proceedings of The 8th Workshop on Patent and Scientific Literature Translation*, pages 13–23, Dublin, Ireland.

Alberto Poncelas, Maja Popovic, Dimitar Shterionov, Gideon Maillette de Buy Wenniger, and Andy Way. 2019c. Combining SMT and NMT back-translated data for efficient NMT. In *Proceedings of Recent Advances in Natural Language Processing (RANLP)*, pages 922–931, Varna, Bulgaria.

Alberto Poncelas, Dimitar Shterionov, Andy Way, Gideon Maillette de Buy Wenniger, and Peyman Passban. 2018c. Investigating backtranslation in neural machine translation. In *21st Annual Conference of the European Association for Machine Translation*, pages 249–258, Alacant, Spain.

Alberto Poncelas, Andy Way, and Kepa Sarasola. 2018d. The ADAPT system description for the IWSLT 2018 Basque to English translation task. In *15th International Workshop on Spoken Language Translation*, pages 76–82, Bruges, Belgium.

Maja Popovic. 2015. chrF: character n-gram F-score for automatic MT evaluation. In *Proceedings of the Tenth Workshop on Statistical Machine Translation*, pages 392–395, Lisbon, Portugal.

Rico Sennrich, Barry Haddow, and Alexandra Birch. 2016a. Improving neural machine translation models with monolingual data. In *Proceedings of the 54th Annual Meeting of the Association for Computational Linguistics (Volume 1: Long Papers)*, pages 86–96, Berlin, Germany.

Rico Sennrich, Barry Haddow, and Alexandra Birch. 2016b. Neural machine translation of rare words with subword units. In *Proceedings of the 54th Annual Meeting of the Association for Computational Linguistics (Volume 1: Long Papers)*, volume 1, pages 1715–1725, Berlin, Germany.

Matthew Snover, Bonnie Dorr, Richard Schwartz, Linnea Micciulla, and John Makhoul. 2006. A study of translation edit rate with targeted human annotation. In *Proceedings of the 7th Conference of the Association for Machine Translation in the Americas*, pages 223–231, Cambridge, Massachusetts, USA.

Vladimir N. Vapnik. 1998. *Statistical Learning Theory*. Wiley-Interscience.

Marlies van der Wees, Arianna Bisazza, and Christof Monz. 2017. Dynamic data selection for neural machine translation. In *Proceedings of the 2017 Conference on Empirical Methods in Natural Language Processing*, pages 1400–1410, Copenhagen, Denmark.

Antonio Jimeno Yepes, Aurélie Névéol, Mariana Neves, Karin Verspoor, Ondrej Bojar, Arthur Boyer, Cristian Grozea, Barry Haddow, Madeleine Kittner, Yvonne Lichtblau, Pavel Pecina, Roland Roller, Rudolf Rosa, Amy Siu, Philippe Thomas, and Saskia Trescher. 2017. Findings of the WMT 2017 biomedical translation shared task. In *Proceedings of the Second Conference on Machine Translation*, pages 234–247, Copenhagen, Denmark.

Efficiency Metrics for Data-Driven Models:
A Text Summarization Case Study

Erion Çano
Institute of Formal and Applied
Linguistics, Charles University,
Prague, Czech Republic
cano@ufal.mff.cuni.cz

Ondřej Bojar
Institute of Formal and Applied
Linguistics, Charles University,
Prague, Czech Republic
bojar@ufal.mff.cuni.cz

Abstract

Using data-driven models for solving text summarization or similar tasks has become very common in the last years. Yet most of the studies report basic accuracy scores only, and nothing is known about the ability of the proposed models to improve when trained on more data. In this paper, we define and propose three data efficiency metrics: data score efficiency, data time deficiency and overall data efficiency. We also propose a simple scheme that uses those metrics and apply it for a more comprehensive evaluation of popular methods on text summarization and title generation tasks. For the latter task, we process and release a huge collection of 35 million abstract-title pairs from scientific articles. Our results reveal that among the tested models, the Transformer is the most efficient on both tasks.

1 Introduction

Text summarization is the process of distilling the most noteworthy information in a document to produce an abridged version of it. This task is earning considerable interest, since shorter versions of long documents are easier to read and save us time. There are two basic ways to summarize texts. Extractive summarization selects the most relevant parts of the source document and combines them to generate the summary. In this case, the summary contains exact copies of words or phrases picked from the source. Abstractive summarization, on the other hand, paraphrases the information required for the summary instead of copying it verbatim. This is usually better, but also more complex and harder to achieve.

There has been a rapid progress in ATS (Abstractive Text Summarization) over the last years. The vanilla encoder-decoder with bidirectional LSTMs (Hochreiter and Schmidhuber, 1997) is now enhanced with advanced mechanisms like attention (Bahdanau et al., 2014) which has been widely embraced. It allows the model to focus on various parts of the input during the generation phase and was successfully used by Rush et al. (2015) to summarize news articles. Pointing (copying) is another mechanism that helps to alleviate the problem of unknown words (Gulcehre et al., 2016; Gu et al., 2016). Moreover, coverage (Tu et al., 2016) and intra-attention (Paulus et al., 2017) were proposed and utilized to avoid word repetitions, producing more readable summaries. RL (Reinforcement Learning) concepts like policy gradient (Rennie et al., 2017) were recently combined into the encoder-decoder architecture, alleviating other problems like train/test inconsistency and exposure bias (Paulus et al., 2017; Chen and Bansal, 2018).

All these developments helped to boost the ATS ROUGE (Lin, 2004) scores from about 30 % in Rush et al. (2015) to about 41 % in Paulus et al. (2017). This is an increase of roughly 37 % in the last three years. Yet all the studies evaluate the methods using datasets of a fixed size. Doing so they tell us nothing about the expected performance[1] of the models when trained with more data. Moreover, training time is rarely reported. We believe that this evaluation practice of data-driven models is incomplete and data efficiency metrics should be computed and reported.

In this paper, we propose three data efficiency metrics, namely *data score efficiency*, *data time deficiency* and *overall data efficiency*. The first two represent the output quality gain and the training time delay of the model per additional data samples. The third is the ratio between them and reflects the overall efficiency of the models w.r.t the training data. We also suggest a simple scheme that considers several values for each of the above metrics, together with the basic accuracy score, in-

---

[1] We use "performance" solely for the output quality, not the time needed to train the model or obtain the output.

Proceedings of The 12th International Conference on Natural Language Generation, pages 229–239,
Tokyo, Japan, 28 Oct - 1 Nov, 2019. ©2019 Association for Computational Linguistics

stead of reporting only the latter. The proposed scheme and the metrics can be used for a more detailed evaluation of supervised learning models.

Using them, we examine various recently proposed methods in two tasks: text summarization using the popular CNNDM (CNN/Daily Mail, Nallapati et al., 2016) dataset and title generation of scientific articles using OAGS, a novel dataset of abstract-title pairs that we processed and released.[2] According to our results, the best-performing and fastest methods in the two datasets are those of Paulus et al. (2017) and Chen and Bansal (2018). Regarding score and time efficiency, Transformer (Vaswani et al., 2017) is distinctly superior. In the future, we will examine the Transformer model on more data with different parameter setups. Applying our evaluation scheme to related tasks such as MT (Machine Translation) could also be beneficial.

Overall, this work brings the following main contributions: (i) We define and propose three data efficiency metrics and a simple evaluation scheme that uses them for a more comprehensive evaluation of data-driven learning methods. (ii) We use the scheme and metrics to benchmark some of the most recently proposed ATS methods and discuss their training times, ROUGE, and data efficiency scores. (iii) Finally, a huge collection of about 35 million scientific paper abstracts and titles is prepared and released to the community. To our best knowledge, this is the largest data collection prepared for title generation experiments.

2 Data Efficiency Metrics

2.1 Related Work

Training data efficiency of the data-driven learning models is little considered in the literature. An early work is that of Lawrence et al. (1998) who investigate the generalization ability of neural networks with respect to the complexity of the approximation function, the size of the network and the degree of noise in the training data. In the case of latter factor, they vary the size of the training data and the levels of Gaussian noise added to those data concluding that ensemble techniques are more immune to the increased noise levels. Performance variations w.r.t the training data sizes are not considered, though.

Al-Jarrah et al. (2015) review the research literature focusing in the computational and energy efficiency of the data-driven methods. They particularly consider data-intensive application areas (e.g., big data computing) and how sustainable data models can help for a maximal learning accuracy with minimal computational cost and efficient processing of large volumes of data.

Boom et al. (2016) examine a character-level RNN (Recurrent Neural Network) used to predict the next character of a text given the previous input characters. They assess the evolution of the network performance (in terms of perplexity) in four train and prediction scenarios as a function of the training time and input training sequences. According to their results, the efficiency of the model is considerably influenced by the chosen scenario.

A similar experiment is conducted by Riou et al. (2019) who explore reinforcement learning concepts on the task of neural language generation. They compare different implementations reporting not only performance scores, but also their evolution as a function of the cumulated learning cost and the training data size.

The most relevant work we found is the one by Hlynsson. et al. (2019) who propose an experimental protocol for comparing the data efficiency of a CNN (Convolution Neural Network) with that of HiGSFA (Hierarchical information-preserving Graph-based Slow Feature Analysis). They give an informal definition of data efficiency considering it as *performance as a function of training set size*. Three character recognition challenges are defined and the two methods are trained on increasing amounts of data samples reporting the corresponding accuracy scores.

2.2 Proposed Data Efficiency Metrics

Despite the experimental results and insights they bring, the above studies are still task and method specific. Moreover, their computation schemes are not generic or transferable and no formalization of the data efficiency is given. In this section, we define three novel and useful data efficiency metrics.

Suppose we train a data-driven method $\mathbf{M}$ on dataset $\mathbf{D}$ to solve task $\mathbf{T}$ and we test it based on performance score $\mathbf{S}$. We also assume that the quality of the data samples in different intervals of $\mathbf{D}$ is homogeneous. In practice, this could be achieved by shuffling $\mathbf{D}$ before starting the experiments. For a certain training data size d, it takes t seconds to train the model m_d until convergence (i.e. until no further gains are observed with more

---

[2]http://hdl.handle.net/11234/1-3043

training time) and the score obtained by testing it on a standard and independent test dataset of a fixed size is s. We expect that for a certain increase Δd of training samples fed to $\mathbf{M}$, it will require an extra time Δt to converge, and the resulting model $m_{d+\Delta d}$ will attain an extra Δs score. We can thus define and compute *data score efficiency* (score gain per additional data samples) Σ of method $\mathbf{M}$ as:

$$\Sigma = \Delta s \,/\, \Delta d \tag{1}$$

It is a measure of how smartly or effectively $\mathbf{M}$ interprets the extra data samples, or how well its performance score scales w.r.t the training data. Similarly, *data time deficiency* (the inverse of *data time efficiency*) Θ of $\mathbf{M}$ will be:

$$\Theta = \Delta t \,/\, \Delta d \tag{2}$$

This measures how slowly or lazily $\mathbf{M}$ interprets the additional samples.[3] Given two train and test runs (original and enlarged datasets) characterized by the above measures (training data: d, $d + \Delta d$; training times: t, $t + \Delta t$; achieved scores: s, $s + \Delta s$), we define the *overall data efficiency* E as:

$$E = \Sigma \,/\, \Theta = \Delta s \,/\, \Delta t \tag{3}$$

It is a measure of how smartly and quickly the models of $\mathbf{M}$ utilizes the data of $\mathbf{D}$ on task $\mathbf{T}$.

In practice, using the absolute increments Δs, Δt, and Δd may produce small values of Σ which are hard to interpret and work with. Furthermore, Θ and E use training times which depend on the computing conditions (e.g., hardware setups). As a result, they are hardly reproducible across different computing environments. To overcome these limitations, we can instead use the relative increments $\Delta s/s$, $\Delta t/t$ and $\Delta d/d$, computing the corresponding *relative data efficiency metrics* as:

$$\sigma = \frac{\Delta s \,/\, s}{\Delta d \,/\, d} \tag{4}$$

$$\theta = \frac{\Delta t \,/\, t}{\Delta d \,/\, d} \tag{5}$$

$$\epsilon = \frac{\sigma}{\theta} = \frac{\Delta s \,/\, s}{\Delta t \,/\, t} \tag{6}$$

---

[3] Our *data time efficiency* ($\Delta d \,/\, \Delta t$) should not be confused with the *training throughput* as defined by Popel and Bojar (2018) for machine translation which reflects the time required for one model update given the additional data. Our Δt is the increase in the overall training time till convergence on the enlarged dataset in comparison with the original one.

These relative metrics and their values are practically easier to interpret and work with. Furthermore, they are transferable or reproducible in different computing setups which is important for cross-interpretation of the experimental results. We can express σ and θ values in percent and ϵ values as their ratio.

2.3 Assorted Remarks

The metrics presented above can be used to evaluate different data-driven methods or compare several parameter configurations of the same basic method (algorithm, neural network, etc.) and help us find the optimal one. In this sense, they are generic and task-independent. However, it is important to note that they do not represent "universal" or global attributes of method $\mathbf{M}$. They are instead linear approximations that can give us local characterizations of $\mathbf{M}$ in certain intervals of $\mathbf{D}$. In other words, high Σ (or σ) values of $\mathbf{M}$ in some intervals of $\mathbf{D}$ do not necessarily assure a decent generalization of $\mathbf{M}$.

It is also important not to confuse the data efficiency with performance or quality. In our daily intuition, we often tend to consider highly efficient machines, techniques or methods as well-performing ones. Instead, according to the above definitions, a model can perform poorly but still be highly efficient w.r.t the training data. This happens if its performance scores on increasing training data cuts are all very low, but grow very quickly from one assessment to the next. A model can also yield high scores which grow very slowly on increasing data sizes (thus relatively small Σ and σ values). In this case it is a well-performing (maybe even the best) model on those data, but not a data efficient one.

From the data efficiency viewpoint, the best models would obviously be those of higher *data score efficiency* and lower *data time deficiency*, or higher *overall data efficiency*. In practice, performance is generally the most desired characteristic. As a result, *data score efficiency* values (Σ, σ or both) should be more important and worthy to report in most of the cases. Since models are trained only once, θ and ϵ should be less relevant. Nevertheless, they might be useful from a technical or theoretical perspective. They can be used for comparing different methods, comparing different parameter configurations of a method, or for trying run time optimizations.

3 A Comprehensive Evaluation Scheme

Since the sizes of the predictive models and the utilized datasets are consistently growing, it becomes more difficult and costly to use human expertise for the evaluation. The typical approach is to test automatically by means of standard datasets and scoring metrics which are popular. For example, in the case of text summarization task, it is very common to find evaluations of proposed methods using the full set of CNNDM only (Table 1 in Paulus et al., Table 3 in Lin et al., Table 1 in See et al., and more).

We believe there are serious shortcomings in this evaluation practice. Testing only one model of a method trained on a fixed-size data split does not reveal anything about its score trend when fed with more data. It thus becomes hard to discern the overall best method (out of a few that are compared) in a fair and objective way, especially if the achieved scores are similar. Moreover, training time is rarely reported and nothing is known about the time efficiency of the models.

To overcome the above limitations, we propose a more detailed evaluation scheme that considers accuracy scores together with the data efficiency metrics defined in Section 2.2. Again, suppose we have a dataset D of size d with homogeneous training samples, a standard performance score S and two methods A and B that we want to compare. The typical practice trains two single models a and b from A and B on entire d and reports accuracy scores s^a and s^b from the standard test set.

Instead, we suggest to split d in n equal parts of size d/n and form n intervals d_1, d_2, ..., d_n of increasing sizes d/n, $2d/n$, ..., $(n-1)d/n$, d. This way we can train $2n$ models a_1, a_2, ..., a_n and b_1, b_2, ..., b_n on d_1, d_2, ..., d_n and compute their scores s_1^a, s_2^a, ..., s_n^a and s_1^b, s_2^b, ..., s_n^b from the same test set. From Equation 4, we also compute σ_1^a, σ_2^a, ..., σ_{n-1}^a using each two scores s_i^a and s_{i+1}^a of models a_i and a_{i+1}, together with σ_1^b, σ_2^b, ..., σ_{n-1}^b from the B models.

We can now report up to $2n$ score values and $2(n-1)$ relative data score efficiency values. For conciseness, we can limit in s_n^a and s_n^b of the two biggest models. Also, given the local nature of the efficiency metrics, it make sense to report values from dispersed data intervals like the leftmost (σ_1^a and σ_1^b), the middle ($\sigma_{n/2}^a$ and $\sigma_{n/2}^b$) and the rightmost (σ_{n-1}^a and σ_{n-1}^b) σ. The rightmost values

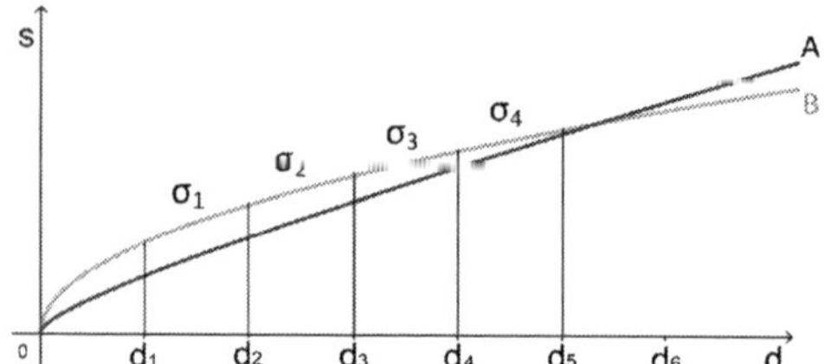

Figure 1: Illustration of the schema application

are probably more relevant for predicting the score trend on bigger training sizes. We can also compute and report the respective Σ values or even the θ and ϵ values in a similar fashion using the other equations of Section 2.2.

Getting back to A vs. B, we can first check s_n^a and s_n^b. If one of them is distinctly higher than the other, comparing the σ values may not be essential. The real worth comes when $s_n^a \approx s_n^b$, by contrasting the rightmost corresponding σ values (σ_{n-1}^a vs. σ_{n-1}^b). A significant difference of one against the other could suggest which of them will reach higher scores on a bigger training set.

To illustrate, we can see in Figure 1 two hypothetical graphs that approximate the variations of s^a and s^b over D. We have $n = 5$, training size $d = d_5$ and very similar performance scores ($s_5^a \approx s_5^b$). Obviously, s^b grows faster than s^a till d_2, but then the situation is reversed, since $\sigma_3^a > \sigma_3^b$ and $\sigma_4^a > \sigma_4^b$. We can thus expect $s^a > s^b$ for $d > d_5$ which is what actually happens in this example ($s_6^a > s_6^b$).

Using the traditional practice (computing s_5^a and s_5^b only) our verdict would be: *A and B perform (almost) the same on D.* Instead, using the above scheme we can conclude that: *A and B perform (almost) the same on D, but A will probably perform better than B if trained on more data.* The scheme can be used to evaluate data-driven methods with different scores, on different tasks. In Section 5 we show the results we obtained by applying it to assess several advanced ATS methods.

4 Text Summarization Datasets

The tendency towards data-driven methods based on neural networks has encouraged experiments with large text collections for various tasks. In the case of ATS, one of the first big datasets was the annotated English Gigaword (Napoles et al., 2012; Rush et al., 2015) with over nine million news articles and headlines processed using CoreNLP of

	Split	Rec	SrcL	TgtL	Voc	Used
CNNDM	Train1	96K	784	54	380K	49K
	Train2	192K	780	57	555K	49K
	Train3	287K	786	55	690K	49K
	Valid	13K	769	61	–	–
	Test	11K	787	58	–	–
OAGS	Train1	500K	183	9	1.2M	98K
	Train2	1M	205	10	2.1M	98K
	Train3	1.5M	211	11	2.8M	98K
	Valid	10K	231	13	–	–
	Test	10K	237	12	–	–

Table 1: Statistics of used datasets. For each split, it shows the number of records (Rec), average length of source and target texts in tokens (SrcL, TgtL), total vocabulary size (Voc), and the number of most frequent words that were used (Used).

Manning et al. (2014). Each headline was paired with the first sentence of the corresponding article to create the training base for the experiments. DUC-2004 is another dataset[4], mostly used as an evaluation baseline, given its small size. It consists of 500 document-summary pairs curated by human experts. Newsroom is a recent and heterogeneous bundle of about 1.3 million news articles (Grusky et al., 2018).

CNNDM has become the most popular dataset for text summarization (Nallapati et al., 2016). It provides a large set of news articles and the corresponding multi-sentence summaries, unlike the three above that contain one-sentence summaries only. It is thus more suitable for training and testing summarization models of longer texts.

Title generation task, on the other hand, requires data samples of shorter texts and one-sentence titles. Collections of abstracts and titles from scientific articles are well suited for exploring it. KP20k is a collection of 20K records of scientific paper metadata (title, abstract and keywords) presented by Meng et al. (2017). The metadata belong to articles of computer science from ACM Digital Library, ScienceDirect, and Web of Science.

The demand for more and more data has motivated initiatives that mine research articles from academic networks. One of them is ArnetMiner, a system that extracts researcher profiles from the Web and integrates the data into a unified network (Tang et al., 2008). A byproduct of that work is the OAG (Open Academic Graph) collection (Sinha et al., 2015).

To produce a big title generation dataset for our experiments, we started from OAG. First, *abstract*,

[4] https://duc.nist.gov/duc2004/

title, and *language* fields were extracted from each record where they were available. In many cases, abstract language did not match the *language* field. We ignored the latter and used a language identifier to remove records that were not in English. Duplicates were dropped and the texts were lowercased. Finally, Stanford CoreNLP tokenizer was used to split title and abstract texts. The resulting dataset (OAGS, released with this paper) contains about 35 million abstract-title pairs and can be used for title generation experiments.

We had a quick look at the content of OAGS and observed that most of the papers are from medicine. There are also many papers about social sciences, psychology, economics or engineering disciplines. Given its huge size and the topical richness, the value of OAGS is twofold: (i) It can be used to supplement existing datasets on title generation tasks when more training data are needed. (ii) It can be used for creating byproducts of specific scientific disciplines or domains.

5 Text Summarization Evaluation

In this section, we apply the relative metrics of Section 2.2 and the evaluation scheme of Section 3 to benchmark several advanced methods on text summarization of news articles and title generation of scientific papers. We first introduce the methods and their parameters, together with the experimental data. Later, we present and discuss the achieved accuracy and data efficiency scores.

5.1 Tested Summarization Methods

The ability of recurrent neural networks to represent and process variable-length sequences has created a tradition of applying them on sequence-to-sequence tasks such as ATS or MT. In the case of ATS, the goal is to process the source text producing a target text that is shorter but still meaningful and easy to read.

Rush et al. (2015) were probably the first to implement attention in a network dedicated to ATS. Their model (ABS in the following) uses an encoder that learns a soft alignment (attention) between the source and the target sequences producing the context vector. In the decoding phase, it uses a beam-search decoder (Dahlmeier and Ng, 2012) with a window of 10 candidate words in each target position. There are 256 and 128 dimensions in the hidden layer and word embedding layer respectively. The authors reported state-of-the-art results in the DUC-2004 testing dataset.

See et al. (2017) proposed Pointer-Generator (PCOV), a model that implements an attention based encoder for producing the context vector. The decoder is extended with a pointing/copying mechanism (Gulcehre et al., 2016; Gu et al., 2016) that is used in each step to compute a generation probability p_{gen} from the context vector, the decoder states, and the decoder output in that step. This generation probability is used as a switch to decide if the next word should be predicted or copied from the input. Another extension is the coverage mechanism (keeping track of decoder outputs) for avoiding word repetitions in the summary, a chronic problem of encoder-decoder summarizers (Tu et al., 2016). The method was implemented with word embeddings and hidden layer of sizes 128 and 256 respectively.

Lin et al. (2018) tried a partial use of convolutions in their model (GLOBEN) to avoid word repetitions and semantic irrelevance in the summaries. They couple the encoder with a convolutional gated unit which performs global encoding of the source context and uses it to filter certain n-gram features and refine the output of the encoder in each time step. GLOBEN is a very big network (about 68M parameters on CNNDM) with three layers in the encoder and other three in the decoder, each of 512 dimensions.

A taxonomy of the above (and more) sequence-to-sequence methods and added mechanisms can be found in Shi et al. (2018). Authors present a detailed review of problems and proposed solutions based on network structures, training strategies, and generation algorithms. Furthermore, they develop and release a library (NATS) that implements combinations of mechanisms like attention, pointing, and coverage, analyzing their effects in text summarization quality. NATS was implemented with the same network parameters as PCOV. Intra-decoder attention and weight sharing of embeddings were added in the decoder.

The introduction of the Transformer (TRANS) architecture that removes all recurrent or convolutional structures reduced computation cost and training time (Vaswani et al., 2017). Totally based on attention mechanism and primarily designed for MT, Transformer can also work for text summarization, since all it needs to do is to learn the alignments between the input (source) texts and the output (target) summaries. Positional encod-

ing is added to word embeddings to preserve the order of the input and output sequences. TRANS is the biggest model we tried, with four layers in both encoder and decoder, 512 dimensions in each layer, including the embedding layers, 200K training steps and 8000 warm-up steps.

Two observed problems in the encoder-decoder framework are the *exposure bias* and *train/test inconsistency* (Keneshloo et al., 2018). To overcome them, RL ideas have been recently applied. Paulus et al. (2017) use intra-attention to focus on different parts of the encoded sequence. This way it is less likely for their model (PGRL) to attend to the same parts of input in different decoding steps, and thus fewer word repetitions should appear in the summaries. To optimize for ROUGE or similar discrete evaluation metrics, they implement self-critical policy gradient training with reward function, a RL mechanism introduced by Rennie et al. (2017). PGRL was used with encoder and decoder of 256 dimensions and word embeddings of 128 dimensions.

Aiming for speed, Chen and Bansal (2018) developed an extractive-abstractive text summarizer (FASTRL) with policy-based reinforcement. It first uses an extractor agent to pick the most salient sentences or phrases, instead of encoding the entire input sequence which can be long. It then uses an encoder-decoder abstractor to rewrite (compress) the sentences in parallel. Actor-Critic policy gradient with reward function (Bahdanau et al., 2016) joins together the extractor and abstractor networks. Same as most models above, FASTRL uses 256 and 128 dimensions for the recurrent layer and the word embeddings.

In every experiment, no pretraining of word embeddings was performed. They were learned during the training of each model. Adam optimizer (Kingma and Ba, 2014) was used with $\alpha = 0.001$, $\beta_1 = 0.9$, $\beta_2 = 0.999$ and $\epsilon = 10^{-8}$. We chose mini-batches of size 16 in most of the cases (8 for GLOBEN and TRANS to avoid memory errors). All experiments were conducted on two NVIDIA GTX 1080Ti GPUs.

5.2 Used Data

To cope with limited computing resources, we used up to 1.5M records in our OAGS experiments. We also picked $n = 3$ for the scheme of Section 3 and created three splits of 500K, 1M and 1.5M samples each, together with the three

Authors	Model	CNNDM					OAGS				
		P	R_1	R_2	R_L	T_t	P	R_1	R_2	R_L	T_t
Rush et al.	ABS1	15M	26.66	8.81	24.46	135032	22M	24.75	10.05	21.84	48595
	ABS2	15M	28.56	10.42	25.57	185549	22M	26.6	11.5	23.33	61729
	ABS3	15M	29.64	11.55	26.32	243549	22M	27.86	12.15	24.48	73038
See et al.	PCOV1	14M	36.97	15.19	33.84	113110	21M	34.4	17.67	27.55	**30551**
	PCOV2	14M	38.56	16.03	35.09	138175	21M	35.18	18.06	28.83	42723
	PCOV3	14M	39.41	16.77	36.31	163744	21M	35.86	18.51	29.42	56538
Shi et al.	NATS1	15M	36.92	14.56	32.88	98791	–	–	–	–	–
	NATS2	15M	38.25	15.89	34.02	179689	–	–	–	–	–
	NATS3	15M	39.11	17.2	35.66	261794	–	–	–	–	–
Lin et al.	GLOBEN1	68M	36.53	14.9	34.11	658924	–	–	–	–	–
	GLOBEN2	68M	37.82	16.13	35.46	785622	–	–	–	–	–
	GLOBEN3	68M	38.67	16.94	36.25	875817	–	–	–	–	–
Vaswani et al.	TRANS1	81M	32.38	10.47	29.43	518924	129M	30.29	13.1	24.34	251802
	TRANS2	81M	36.76	14.54	33.82	579149	129M	34.17	17.49	28.46	269665
	TRANS3	81M	38.24	16.33	35.28	611359	129M	37.06	**19.44**	30.51	278602
Chen et al.	FASTRL1	–	36.95	14.89	34.69	**19601**	–	–	–	–	–
	FASTRL2	–	39.18	16.17	36.15	30485	–	–	–	–	–
	FASTRL3	–	40.02	**17.52**	37.24	52775	–	–	–	–	–
Paulus et al.	PGRL1	–	38.16	14.17	36.24	68942	–	35.52	16.81	28.65	43726
	PGRL2	–	39.88	15.31	37.89	81529	–	36.9	18.44	30.22	55324
	PGRL3	–	**40.83**	15.68	**38.73**	107179	–	**38.05**	19.23	**31.16**	74983

Table 2: Parameters, ROUGE F_1 scores and training times for each method on the splits of the two datasets

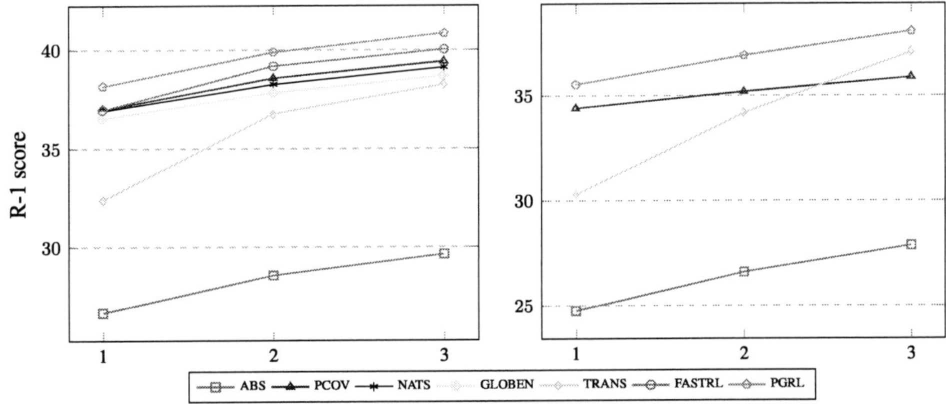

Figure 2: R_1 score trends of the three models of each method on CNNDM (left) and OAGS (right)

splits (one-third, two-thirds, and full) of CNNDM. Some statistics of the experimental data are shown in Table 1. Vocabulary sizes used in each experiment are shown in its last column.

The higher vocabulary sizes of OAGS splits cause a significant difference in parameters between the two corresponding models of each method. As we can see (Table 2), Transformer models grows from 81M in CNNDM to 129M in OAGS. Another difference between the two sets of experiments is in the maximal number of encoding and decoding steps (words in source and target texts). For CNNDM, we used 400 and 100 respectively. For OAGS, we chose 200 and 50, since paper abstracts and titles should not be longer.

5.3 Summarization Results

ROUGE scores and training times (in seconds) on CNNDM experiments are shown in the middle part of Table 2. The most accurate models are PGRL and FASTRL. They both implement policy-based training and optimize w.r.t ROUGE scores. The worst performer is ABS and the other four fall somewhere in between, reaching similar scores with each other.

The score differences between each third model and first one are usually small for all methods. We believe this has to do with the way ROUGE scores

Authors	Models	CNNDM						
		σ_1	σ_2	σ_L	θ	ϵ_1	ϵ_2	ϵ_L
Rush et al.	ABS12	7.13	18.27	4.54	37.41	0.19	0.45	0.12
	ABS23	7.64	21.92	5.93	63.10	0.12	0.35	0.094
See et al.	PCOV12	4.3	5.53	3.69	22.16	0.194	0.25	0.167
	PCOV23	4.46	9.33	7.03	37.4	0.119	0.249	0.188
Shi et al.	NATS12	3.6	9.13	3.47	81.89	0.044	0.112	0.042
	NATS23	4.53	16.6	9.74	92.35	0.049	0.18	0.106
Lin et al.	GLOBEN12	3.53	8.26	3.96	19.23	0.184	0.429	0.206
	GLOBEN23	4.54	10.15	4.50	23.2	0.196	0.437	0.194
Vaswani et al.	TRANS12	**13.53**	**38.87**	**14.92**	11.61	**1.166**	**3.34**	**1.285**
	TRANS23	8.14	24.88	8.72	**11.24**	0.724	2.214	0.776
Chen et al.	FASTRL12	6.04	8.6	4.21	55.53	0.109	0.155	0.067
	FASTRL23	4.33	16.87	6.09	147.78	0.029	0.114	0.041
Paulus et al.	PGRL12	4.51	8.05	4.55	18.26	0.247	0.441	0.249
	PGRL23	4.81	4.88	4.48	63.58	0.076	0.077	0.07

Table 3: Data efficiency scores of the models on CNNDM experiments. σ_X is computed based on the corresponding R_X score. Similarly, ϵ_X is computed based on σ_X and θ.

Authors	Models	OAGS						
		σ_1	σ_2	σ_L	θ	ϵ_1	ϵ_2	ϵ_L
Rush et al.	ABS12	7.47	14.43	6.82	27.03	0.277	0.534	0.252
	ABS23	9.47	11.3	9.86	36.64	0.259	0.309	0.269
See et al.	PCOV12	2.27	2.21	4.65	39.84	0.057	0.055	0.117
	PCOV23	3.87	5.04	4.09	64.67	0.06	0.077	0.063
Vaswani et al.	TRANS12	12.81	**33.51**	**16.93**	7.09	1.806	**4.724**	**2.386**
	TRANS23	**16.92**	22.3	14.41	**6.63**	**2.552**	3.364	2.173
Paulus et al.	PGRL12	3.89	9.7	5.48	26.52	0.146	0.366	0.207
	PGRL23	6.23	8.57	6.22	71.07	0.088	0.121	0.088

Table 4: Data efficiency scores of the models on OAGS experiments. σ_X is computed based on the corresponding R_X score. Similarly, ϵ_X is computed based on σ_X and θ.

are computed. A graphical representation of the R_1 trends for each method is depicted in Figure 2 (left). R_2 and R_L (not shown) behave similarly.

Results on OAGS are listed on the right side of Table 2. We could not run some of the models on OAGS data. The extractive part of FASTRL could not be easily adapted to perform word-level extraction of OAGS abstracts. Furthermore, NATS and GLOBEN ran out of memory very frequently. From the remaining four, PGRL is again the most accurate. TRANS follows and ABS is the weakest. R_1 score trends are shown in the Figure 2 (right).

Regarding training speed, on CNNDM we can see that FASTRL is absolutely the best, with a considerable difference from the second (PGRL). The slowest is GLOBEN with training times at least 17x higher than those of FASTRL. In fact, it took more than ten days to train GLOBEN on the full CNNDM data.

OAGS training times are lower than CNNDM ones, although OAGS data splits are 5.2 times bigger in number of training samples. This happens because OAGS source and target samples are actually much shorter. We see that PCOV is the fastest and TRANS is the slowest.

5.4 Efficiency Results

Using Equations 4, 5 and 6 of Section 2.2 we computed the relative efficiency metrics for every method. The values for CNNDM experiments are shown in Table 3. We see that TRANS is clearly the most efficient, with highest σ, lowest θ and highest ϵ. Its scores grow quickly (despite being relatively low) and training times grow slowly (despite being high) in both data intervals.

PCOV and GLOBEN manifest the slowest accuracy score gains (lowest σ), but GLOBEN comes second in time efficiency. NATS on the other hand, is very time inefficient, with highest θ and lowest ϵ. OAGS scores of Table 4 reflect a similar situation. TRANS leads and PCOV is again the worst. The values of the other two models appear somewhere in between.

It is not easy to explain the high score and time

efficiency of TRANS. GLOBEN is also time efficient but not score efficient. Both of them are the biggest (highest number of parameters) and deepest (many layers) networks we tried. The exclusive feature of TRANS is the lack of any recurrent structure. GLOBEN and the other five make use of at least one RNN in a certain phase. It is still hasty to infer that recurrent networks hinder score efficiency or that more attention boosts it.

An intuitive explanation could be the fact that in general, performance of deeper networks scales better with more data. It could also be that high-capacity networks are faster in interpreting large additions of training samples (thus low θ). In fact, using more layers and bigger training datasets is what has driven the progress of deep learning solutions in many application areas.

We plan to investigate this issue further in the future. One step could be to run more experiments on even bigger data sizes and smaller data intervals for checking at what point do accuracy scores keep growing. Transformer implementations with varying number of layers and other parameter setups can be further examined.

Investigating data efficiency of similar solutions to tasks like QA (Question Answering, Correia et al., 2018) with standard datasets such as SQuAD (Rajpurkar et al., 2018) could also be valuable.

6 Conclusions

In this paper, we defined three data efficiency metrics for a better evaluation of data-driven learning models. We also proposed a simple scheme for computing and reporting them, in addition to the basic accuracy scores. Text summarization and title generation tasks were chosen as a case study to see what insights the proposed scheme and metrics could reveal. For title generation, we also processed a dataset of about 35 million scientific titles and abstracts, released with this paper.

We applied seven recent ATS methods on the two tasks. According to our results, the two methods that mix RL concepts into the encoder-decoder framework are the fastest and the most accurate. A surprising result is the excellent efficiency of the popular Transformer model. As future work, we want to perform similar studies in analogous tasks like MT or QA. We would also like to investigate more in depth the Transformer model.

Acknowledgments

This research work was supported by the project No. CZ.02.2.69/0.0/0.0/16 027/0008495 (International Mobility of Researchers at Charles University) of the Operational Programme Research, Development and Education, the project no. 19-26934X (NEUREM3) of the Czech Science Foundation and ELITR (H2020-ICT-2018-2-825460) of the EU.

References

O. Y. Al-Jarrah, Paul D. Yoo, Sami Muhaidat, George K. Karagiannidis, and Kamal Taha. 2015. Efficient machine learning for big data: A review. *CoRR*, abs/1503.05296.

Dzmitry Bahdanau, Philemon Brakel, Kelvin Xu, Anirudh Goyal, Ryan Lowe, Joelle Pineau, Aaron Courville, and Yoshua Bengio. 2016. An actor-critic algorithm for sequence prediction. *arXiv e-prints*, abs/1607.07086.

Dzmitry Bahdanau, Kyunghyun Cho, and Yoshua Bengio. 2014. Neural machine translation by jointly learning to align and translate. *CoRR*, abs/1409.0473.

Cedric De Boom, Sam Leroux, Steven Bohez, Pieter Simoens, Thomas Demeester, and Bart Dhoedt. 2016. Efficiency evaluation of character-level RNN training schedules. *CoRR*, abs/1605.02486.

Yen-Chun Chen and Mohit Bansal. 2018. Fast abstractive summarization with reinforce-selected sentence rewriting. In *Proceedings of the 56th Annual Meeting of the Association for Computational Linguistics (Volume 1: Long Papers)*, pages 675–686. Association for Computational Linguistics.

Alvaro Henrique Chaim Correia, Jorge Luiz Moreira Silva, Thiago de Castro Martins, and Fábio Gagliardi Cozman. 2018. A fully attention-based information retriever. *CoRR*, abs/1810.09580.

Daniel Dahlmeier and Hwee Tou Ng. 2012. A beam-search decoder for grammatical error correction. In *Proceedings of the 2012 Joint Conference on Empirical Methods in Natural Language Processing and Computational Natural Language Learning*, EMNLP-CoNLL '12, pages 568–578, Stroudsburg, PA, USA. Association for Computational Linguistics.

Max Grusky, Mor Naaman, and Yoav Artzi. 2018. Newsroom: A dataset of 1.3 million summaries with diverse extractive strategies. In *Proceedings of the 2018 Conference of the North American Chapter of the Association for Computational Linguistics: Human Language Technologies*, pages 708–719. Association for Computational Linguistics.

Jiatao Gu, Zhengdong Lu, Hang Li, and Victor O.K. Li. 2016. Incorporating copying mechanism in sequence-to-sequence learning. In *Proceedings of the 54th Annual Meeting of the Association for Computational Linguistics (Volume 1: Long Papers)*, pages 1631–1640, Berlin, Germany. Association for Computational Linguistics.

Caglar Gulcehre, Sungjin Ahn, Ramesh Nallapati, Bowen Zhou, and Yoshua Bengio. 2016. Pointing the unknown words. In *Proceedings of the 54th Annual Meeting of the Association for Computational Linguistics (Volume 1: Long Papers)*, pages 140–149, Berlin, Germany. Association for Computational Linguistics.

Hlynur Davíð Hlynsson., Alberto N. Escalante-B.., and Laurenz Wiskott. 2019. Measuring the data efficiency of deep learning methods. In *Proceedings of the 8th International Conference on Pattern Recognition Applications and Methods - Volume 1: ICPRAM,*, pages 691–698. INSTICC, SciTePress.

Sepp Hochreiter and Jürgen Schmidhuber. 1997. Long short-term memory. *Neural computation*, 9(8):1735–1780.

Yaser Keneshloo, Tian Shi, Naren Ramakrishnan, and Chandan K. Reddy. 2018. Deep reinforcement learning for sequence to sequence models. *CoRR*, abs/1805.09461.

Diederik P. Kingma and Jimmy Ba. 2014. Adam: A method for stochastic optimization. Cite arxiv:1412.6980, Comment: Published as a conference paper at the 3rd International Conference for Learning Representations, San Diego, 2015.

Steve Lawrence, C Lee Giles, and Ah Chung Tsoi. 1998. What size neural network gives optimal generalization? convergence properties of backpropagation. Technical report.

Chin-Yew Lin. 2004. Rouge: A package for automatic evaluation of summaries. In *Proc. ACL workshop on Text Summarization Branches Out*, page 10.

Junyang Lin, Xu SUN, Shuming Ma, and Qi Su. 2018. Global encoding for abstractive summarization. In *Proceedings of the 56th Annual Meeting of the Association for Computational Linguistics (Volume 2: Short Papers)*, pages 163–169. Association for Computational Linguistics.

Christopher D. Manning, Mihai Surdeanu, John Bauer, Jenny Finkel, Steven J. Bethard, and David McClosky. 2014. The Stanford CoreNLP natural language processing toolkit. In *Association for Computational Linguistics (ACL) System Demonstrations*, pages 55–60.

Rui Meng, Sanqiang Zhao, Shuguang Han, Daqing He, Peter Brusilovsky, and Yu Chi. 2017. Deep keyphrase generation. In *Proceedings of the 55th Annual Meeting of the Association for Computational Linguistics*, pages 582–592. Association for Computational Linguistics.

Ramesh Nallapati, Bowen Zhou, Cicero dos Santos, Caglar Gulcehre, and Bing Xiang. 2016. Abstractive text summarization using sequence-to-sequence rnns and beyond. In *Proceedings of The 20th SIGNLL Conference on Computational Natural Language Learning*, pages 280–290. Association for Computational Linguistics.

Courtney Napoles, Matthew Gormley, and Benjamin Van Durme. 2012. Annotated gigaword. In *Proceedings of the Joint Workshop on Automatic Knowledge Base Construction and Web-scale Knowledge Extraction*, AKBC-WEKEX '12, pages 95–100, Stroudsburg, PA, USA. Association for Computational Linguistics.

Romain Paulus, Caiming Xiong, and Richard Socher. 2017. A deep reinforced model for abstractive summarization. *CoRR*, abs/1705.04304.

Martin Popel and Ondřej Bojar. 2018. Training Tips for the Transformer Model. *The Prague Bulletin of Mathematical Linguistics*, 110(1):43–70.

Pranav Rajpurkar, Robin Jia, and Percy Liang. 2018. Know what you don't know: Unanswerable questions for squad. In *Proceedings of the 56th Annual Meeting of the Association for Computational Linguistics (Volume 2: Short Papers)*, pages 784–789, Melbourne, Australia. Association for Computational Linguistics.

Steven J. Rennie, Etienne Marcheret, Youssef Mroueh, Jarret Ross, and Vaibhava Goel. 2017. Self-critical sequence training for image captioning. *2017 IEEE Conference on Computer Vision and Pattern Recognition (CVPR)*, pages 1179–1195.

Matthieu Riou, Bassam Jabaian, Stéphane Huet, and Fabrice Lefèvre. 2019. Reinforcement adaptation of an attention-based neural natural language generator for spoken dialogue systems. *Dialogue & Discourse*, 10:1–19.

Alexander M. Rush, Sumit Chopra, and Jason Weston. 2015. A neural attention model for abstractive sentence summarization. In *Proceedings of the 2015 Conference on Empirical Methods in Natural Language Processing*, pages 379–389. Association for Computational Linguistics.

Abigail See, Peter J. Liu, and Christopher D. Manning. 2017. Get to the point: Summarization with pointer-generator networks. In *Proceedings of the 55th Annual Meeting of the Association for Computational Linguistics*, pages 1073–1083. Association for Computational Linguistics.

Tian Shi, Yaser Keneshloo, Naren Ramakrishnan, and Chandan K. Reddy. 2018. Neural abstractive text summarization with sequence-to-sequence models. *CoRR*, abs/1812.02303.

Arnab Sinha, Zhihong Shen, Yang Song, Hao Ma, Darrin Eide, Bo-June (Paul) Hsu, and Kuansan Wang.

2015. An overview of microsoft academic service (mas) and applications. In *Proceedings of the 24th International Conference on World Wide Web*, WWW '15 Companion, pages 243–246, New York, NY, USA. ACM.

Jie Tang, Jing Zhang, Limin Yao, Juanzi Li, Li Zhang, and Zhong Su. 2008. Arnetminer: Extraction and mining of academic social networks. In *Proceedings of the 14th ACM SIGKDD International Conference on Knowledge Discovery and Data Mining*, KDD '08, pages 990–998, New York, NY, USA. ACM.

Zhaopeng Tu, Zhengdong Lu, Yang Liu, Xiaohua Liu, and Hang Li. 2016. Modeling coverage for neural machine translation. In *Proceedings of the 54th Annual Meeting of the Association for Computational Linguistics*, pages 76–85. Association for Computational Linguistics.

Ashish Vaswani, Noam Shazeer, Niki Parmar, Jakob Uszkoreit, Llion Jones, Aidan N Gomez, Ł ukasz Kaiser, and Illia Polosukhin. 2017. Attention is all you need. In I. Guyon, U. V. Luxburg, S. Bengio, H. Wallach, R. Fergus, S. Vishwanathan, and R. Garnett, editors, *Advances in Neural Information Processing Systems 30*, pages 5998–6008. Curran Associates, Inc.

An NLG System for Constituent Correspondence:
Personality, Affect, and Alignment

William Kolkey, Jian Dong, and Greg Bybee
nScribe Technologies
{will, jian, greg}@nscribe.tech

Abstract

Roughly 30% of congressional staffers in the United States report spending a "great deal" of time writing responses to constituent letters (Furnas, 2018). Letters often solicit an update on the status of legislation and a description of a congressman's vote record or vote intention — structurable data that can be leveraged by a natural language generation (NLG) system to create a coherent letter response. This paper describes how PoliScribe, a pipeline-architectured NLG platform, constructs personalized responses to constituents inquiring about legislation. Emphasis will be placed on adapting NLG methodologies to the political domain, which entails special attention to affect, discursive variety, and rhetorical strategies that align a speaker with their interlocutor, even in cases of policy disagreement.

1 Introduction

Recent work in the field of NLG has shifted from emphasizing the provision of information to aspects of tone and style. The shift follows from the increasing complexity of NLG systems themselves, which have evolved from vehicles of information delivery to sophisticated platforms aiming to persuade, engage, and even entertain. (Gatt and Krahmer, 2018). The trend holds particular relevance to the domain of political epistolography, in which qualities such as affect and personality are important for meeting the conventions of the genre.

This paper discusses these themes in the context of PoliScribe, an NLG system that is currently utilized by several dozen legislative offices across the United States, including federal and state representatives from California, Texas, and New York. To our knowledge, this is the first instance of an NLG platform that has been applied to constituent communications.

2 System Overview

PoliScribe is designed to respond to constituents who are advocating for or against legislation. At its core, the platform follows a Leveltian model of text generation, whereby letters are constructed according to a rules-based schema consisting of content and document planning, sentence planning, and surface realization (Levelt, 1989; Reiter and Dale, 1999).

PoliScribe works by inputting a bill number into the user interface (e.g., *H.R. 5*) and selecting the member's disposition toward the bill (e.g., *strongly support*, *undecided*, etc.). The system connects to public databases to identify the bill's title, description, vote history, committee assignments, and sponsorship information. These and other informational elements are expressed within PoliScribe as independent sentences, noun phrases, adjectives, or subordinate clauses, and are realized through a process of aggregation with a bias for sentence variation.

The output of this operation is a letter that explains where a bill is in the legislative process and how the elected official feels about the legislation. The system is versatile, supporting more than a billion letter variations, depending on factors that include the stylistic preferences of the user, the legislative stage of the bill, and the relationship of the constituent's policy views to that of their Representative's.

3 Letter Generation

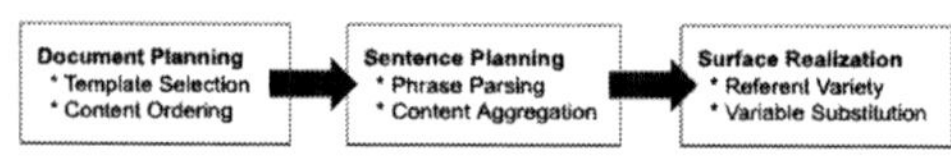

Figure 1: Schema for text generation.

Proceedings of The 12th International Conference on Natural Language Generation, pages 240–243,
Tokyo, Japan, 28 Oct - 1 Nov, 2019. ©2019 Association for Computational Linguistics

PoliScribe uses a rule-based schema (outlined in Figure 1) to ensure a predictable and consistent output, essential qualities for any NLG system applied to a professional environment. Though rule-based, this approach does allow for a high degree of flexibility.

During the document planning phase, the system selects from one of several dozen templates that determine the ordering of informational elements in the letter. The selection of a template is informed by (a) the level of agreement between the Representative and constituent (b) the bill's progress through the Legislature and (c) the stylistic preferences of the user, who can directly influence the properties of their letters though a *user settings* form on the system's frontend.

To fully accommodate a wide variety of user preferences, templates are further partitioned into smaller blocks of informational elements, whose ordering is also influenced by selections made in user settings.

During the sentence planning phase, elements of a template are aggregated to create fluid and stylistically varied sentences. A demonstration of this functionality is a sentence that informs a constituent of the following facts: that a bill has passed a House of the Legislature, that it will be considered in a committee of the opposite House, and that it remains eligible for amendments.

Initially, those elements would be expressed within a template as independent variables: *Vote Outcome + Bill Location + Amendment Eligibility.* The system inspects these variables to discern their string values, which (for the sake of example) we will assume correspond with the following text: *The bill has passed {{ last vote location }} by a vote of {{ last vote }}. + The bill is on its way to {{ next vote location }}. + The bill is eligible for amendments.*

The system parses their grammatical structures to determine how different elements can be combined. The first two sentences are identified as sharing similar syntax (noun phrase + verb phrase + prepositional phrase) and a common subject (*the bill*). According to the internal rules of the system, it is permissible to combine these sentences with a coordinating conjunction and to delete the second occurrence of the noun subject. Hence: *The bill has passed {{ last vote location }} by a vote of {{ last vote }} and is on its way to {{ next vote location }}.*

The system then attempts to aggregate the newly generated sentence with the sentence related to amendment eligibility. Though these sentences share a grammatical subject, the internal rules of the system prevent aggregation as a compound sentence, since the first sentence now employs a coordinating conjunction. Instead, the template opts to treat the second sentence as a relative clause, a hard-coded solution for this particular language combination. The result is as follows: *The bill has passed {{ last vote location }} by a vote of {{ last vote }} and is on its way to {{ next vote location }}, where the bill is eligible for amendments.*

During the surface realization phase, content placeholders are replaced with real values and redundant referents substituted. The example from the previous paragraph would be realized as follows: *The bill has passed the floor of the House by a vote of 417 to 38 and is now on its way to the Senate Judiciary Committee, where it is eligible for amendments.*

4   Navigating Affect and Style

How do you express support for legislation that is also supported by your constituent?
   A. I am also supportive of this bill.
   B. I share your support for this bill.
   C. I will be voting for this bill.
   D. None of the above. *(Write your own text here.)*

Figure 2: Onboarding question.

Since the objective of PoliScribe is to imitate the letter-writing style of a political officeholder, discursive features such as tone, personality, and affect are essential to engendering authenticity.

The system operates to imitate the stylistic tone of legislative offices by requiring users to fill out a language questionnaire prior to onboarding. An example of a typical onboarding question is given in Figure 2. Answers to questions influence both the system's lexicon and rules for aggregation.

In addition, PoliScribe maintains a cognitive model for how the constituent might feel about a legislative development, termed *constituent satisfaction*, which influences the emotive content of the letter response. If a bill supported both by the constituent and their Representative is defeated on the House floor, for example, the system might use language expressing disappointment: e.g., *Despite my best efforts, the bill failed on the House floor.* If that same bill was instead approved by the House, the system might say: *I am pleased to confirm the bill has passed the House of Representatives.*

5 Alignment Strategies

Just as important, PoliScribe takes into account the policy perspective of the constituent, so that letter-responses are framed around a shared vocabulary and political outlook. Such alignment strategies are common in dialogue and likewise pertain to epistolary correspondence, which are just another form of conversational act (Altman, 1982). They are also something that NLG systems are particularly well suited to perform, as shown by van der Lee's PASS system, which tailors summaries of football matches to audiences from opposing clubs (van der Lee et al., 2017).

Alignment is achieved by tagging bills with one of 220 topics appropriated from the Comparative Agendas Project (CAP), an organization that classifies legislation across democracies. Though CAP maintains a directory of coded bills, legislation can also be tagged independently through classification algorithms (Purpura and Hillard, 2006). PoliScribe next determines whether the bill is conservative, liberal, or bipartisan — primarily by considering the party affiliations of the bill's authors and cosponsors.

These efforts allow PoliScribe to employ issue-specific language that aligns with the policy perspective of the constituent. For example, a letter to a supporter of a *conservative* bill tagged *National Budget* might employ language emphasizing fiscal prudence. By contrast, a letter to a constituent supporting a *liberal* bill tagged *Labor Union* might employ language emphasizing fair labor practices. Issue-specific language can be edited and approved by user offices, ensuring that the system's rhetoric is consistent with their own policy outlook.

Tagging also enables PoliScribe to identify legislation that is related to bills that constituents write in about. This allows the system to educate the constituent about the Representative's vote record or emphasize areas of past agreement. Identifying related legislation is particularly useful for engendering a sense of alignment when the Representative disagrees with the constituent or has not yet taken a public position on a piece of pending legislation, but has voted for thematically similar legislation in the past.

For the sake of illustration, a letter generated by PoliScribe is produced below, with issue-specific language and related legislation emphasized in bold.

Thank you for contacting my office regarding your support for AB 129, a bill related to plastic microfibers.

This bill was introduced by Assemblymember Bloom on December 4th, and would reduce the amount of plastic that enters our drinking water, by banning fabric that is more than 50 percent polyester. I share your support for this legislation, but should note that the bill has died in the Assembly's Environmental Safety and Toxic Materials Committee before reaching me for a vote.

*Please know I am just as disappointed as you are with this result, and will keep your thoughts in mind as we continue to work on reforms that **promote healthy rivers and ensure a clean water supply.** If it is any consolation, you may be happy to know that I did vote for successful legislation last session **that would require all drinking water to be tested for plastic contamination.***

Thank you again for contacting my office, and please do keep in touch.

6 Conclusions

PoliScribe has been in use by legislative offices since the beginning of 2019, with users reporting in informal surveys that the system has improved response times and has enabled more detailed replies to constituent letters. Essential has been the ability to accommodate the various stylistic preferences and affectations of individual elected officials, a level of customizability no doubt fundamental for any NLG system operating on behalf of distinct and forceful personalities.

References

Janet Gurkin Altman. 1982. *Epistolarity: Approaches to a Form*. Ohio State University Press, Columbus, OH.

Alexander Furnas. 2018. Legislative staff are spending an increasing mount of time on constituent services. LegBranch.org. Accessed: 2 July 2019.

Albert Gatt and Emiel Krahmer. 2018. Survey of the State of the Art in Natural Language Generation: Core tasks, applications and evaluation. In *Journal of AI Research*, 6l: 65-170.

Willem J.M. Levelt. 1989. *Speaking: From Intention to Articulation*. MIT Press, Cambridge, MA.

Stephen Purpura and Dustin Hillard. 2006. Automated Classification of Congressional Legislation. In *Proceedings of the 2006 International Conference on Digital Government Research*: 219-225.

Ehud Reiter and Robert Dale. 1999. *Building natural language generation systems*. Cambridge University Press, New York, NY.

Chris van der Lee, Emiel Krahmer, and Sander Wubben. 2017. Pass: A Dutch data-to-text system for soccer, targeted towards specific audiences. *In Proceedings of the 10th International Conference on Natural Language Generation*: 95–104.

.

Margin Call: an Accessible Web-based Text Viewer with Generated Paragraph Summaries in the Margin

Naba Rizvi[1,2], Sebastian Gehrmann[2,3], Lidan Wang[2], Franck Dernoncourt[2]
[1]University of Toledo, [2]Adobe Research, [3]Harvard SEAS
`nabah.rizvi@rockets.utoledo.edu`, `gehrmann@seas.harvard.edu`,
`lidwang@adobe.com`, `franck.dernoncourt@adobe.com`

Abstract

We present Margin Call, an accessible web-based text viewer that automatically generates short summaries for each paragraph of the text and displays the summaries in the margin of the text next to the corresponding paragraph. On the back-end, the summarizer first identifies the most important sentence for each paragraph in the text file uploaded by the user. The selected sentence is then automatically compressed to produce the short summary. The resulting summary is a few words long. The displayed summaries can help the user understand and retrieve information faster from the text, while increasing the retention of information.

1 Introduction

Long documents can be difficult and time-consuming to read and comprehend, especially for people with reading or visual impairments. Before deciding whether to read a document or to find some information faster, it may be helpful to have an overview first. However, this is not possible with screen readers or without advanced skimming/reading skills. Moreover, it is easy to lose track of the overall story and message. Previous work showed that presenting a brief summary for each section of a text can help readers understand a text better (Kintsch and Van Dijk, 1978; Wiley and Rayner, 2000; Gehrmann et al., 2019), increase the reading speed (Bransford and Johnson, 1972) and improve the recall of content (Dooling and Lachman, 1971; Smith and Swinney, 1992).

To that end, we introduce in this work a web-based assistive text viewer that presents a document in an accessible way. The tool is accessible online at `https://github.com/Franck-Dernoncourt/margincall`.

2 Margin Call

Margin Call is an open-source web-based text viewer that provides the user with automatically generated summaries obtained from individual paragraphs in a text. It uses an extractive summarizer to obtain the best sentence for each paragraph, which is then compressed using a deletion-based sentence compressor.

2.1 Model

A common approach for text summarization uses information obtained from the content of a sentence to classify them as a whole (Cheng and Lapata, 2016; Dlikman and Last, 2016). This approach has limitations when using traditional hand-crafted feature functions and requires powerful sentence representations when applying a data-driven approach. Margin Call addresses this issue by scoring sentences on a word-level while still extracting full sentences. Margin Call uses the sentence extracted from the extractive summarizer and passes it to a deletion-based compressor. The compressor is based on a neural Semi-Markov Conditional Random Field, which decides whether a word should be included in the compressed output.

2.2 User Interface

Margin Call displays the generated summary next to each corresponding paragraph and highlights the sentence in the paragraph the summary was extracted from, as shown in Figure 1. This lets the user know which sentence in the paragraph was used to produce the summary.

2.3 Accessibility

Margin Call was developed to be accessible for users with various visual impairments. Research has shown color-blindness has an impact on the

Proceedings of The 12th International Conference on Natural Language Generation, pages 244–246,
Tokyo, Japan, 28 Oct - 1 Nov, 2019. ©2019 Association for Computational Linguistics

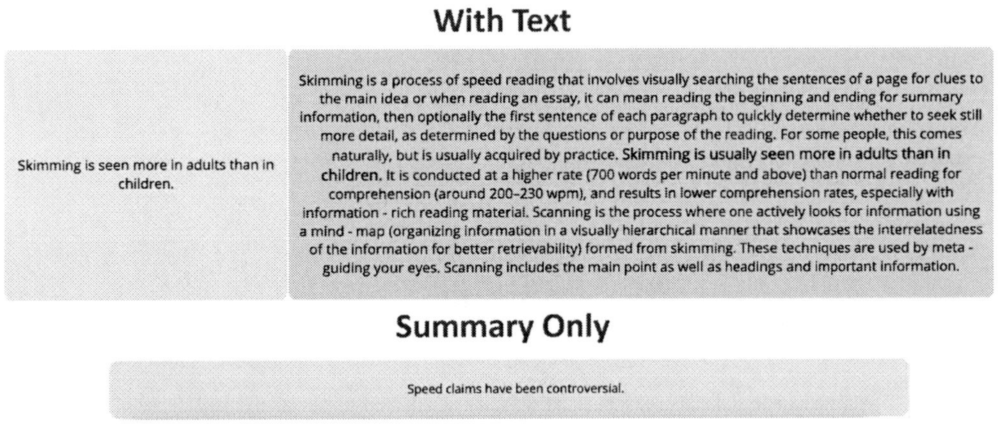

With Text

Summary Only

Figure 1: The interface of Margin Call displays summaries generated for each paragraph, allowing the user to decide to view the summary with the text it is generated from or by itself.

readability of web applications (Sparks, 2019). When developing the program, we decided to display the values in an HTML table to make the content easy for screen readers to interpret. The extension ChromeVox was used to test how a blind user would experience the website with the aid of a screen reader.

2.4 Implementation

The summarization models are implemented in PyTorch, the web interface relies on Flask, and the application is packaged as a Docker image.

3 Conclusion and Future Work

Margin Call is an easy-to-use and accessible web application that summarizes each paragraph of a text, thereby making state-of-the-art summarization techniques available to anyone. The summaries are displayed next to each paragraph, which help the reader understand, retrieve and memorize the information faster.

As extension of Margin Call, one could explore automatically segmenting text into paragraphs in case the text does not contain any paragraph, or if a paragraph is too long. Another improvement could be to allow the user to add some bias reflecting which aspect(s) of the text (e.g., "science" or "financial markets") they care the most about, so that the generated summaries reflect the user's interests.

References

John D Bransford and Marcia K Johnson. 1972. Contextual prerequisites for understanding: Some investigations of comprehension and recall. *Journal of verbal learning and verbal behavior*, 11(6):717–726.

Jianpeng Cheng and Mirella Lapata. 2016. Neural summarization by extracting sentences and words. *Proceedings of the 54th Annual Meeting of the Association for Computational Linguistics (Volume 1: Long Papers)*.

Alexander Dlikman and Mark Last. 2016. Using machine learning methods and linguistic features in single-document extractive summarization. *DMNLP@ PKDD/ECML*, page 18.

D James Dooling and Roy Lachman. 1971. Effects of comprehension on retention of prose. *Journal of experimental psychology*, 88(2):216.

Sebastian Gehrmann, Steven Layne, and Franck Dernoncourt. 2019. Improving human text comprehension through semi-Markov CRF-based neural section title generation. In *Proceedings of the 2019 Conference of the North American Chapter of the Association for Computational Linguistics: Human Language Technologies, Volume 1 (Long and Short Papers)*, pages 1677–1688, Minneapolis, Minnesota. Association for Computational Linguistics.

Teun A van DijkWalter Kintsch and TA Van Dijk. 1978. Cognitive psychology and discourse: Recalling and summarizing stories. *Current trends in textlinguistics*, page 61.

Edward E Smith and David A Swinney. 1992. The role of schemas in reading text: A real-time examination. *Discourse Processes*, 15(3):303–316.

Theresa Marie Sparks. 2019. The effects of color choice in web design on the usability for individuals with color-blindness.

Jennifer Wiley and Keith Rayner. 2000. Effects of titles on the processing of text and lexically ambiguous words: Evidence from eye movements. *Memory & Cognition*, 28(6):1011–1021.

Privacy-Aware Text Rewriting

Qiongkai Xu[1,2], Lizhen Qu[3], Chenchen Xu[1,2] and Ran Cui[1]
[1]The Australian National University, Canberra, Australia
[2]Data61 CSIRO, Canberra, Australia
[3]Monash University, Melbourne, Australia
{Qiongkai.Xu,Chenchen.Xu,Ran.Cui}@anu.edu.au, Lizhen.Qu@monash.edu

Abstract

Biased decisions made by automatic systems have led to growing concerns in research communities. Recent work from the NLP community focuses on building systems that make fair decisions based on text. Instead of relying on unknown decision systems or human decision-makers, we argue that a better way to protect data providers is to remove the trails of sensitive information before publishing the data. In light of this, we propose a new privacy-aware text rewriting task and explore two privacy-aware back-translation methods for the task, based on adversarial training and approximate fairness risk. Our extensive experiments on three real-world datasets with varying demographical attributes show that our methods are effective in obfuscating sensitive attributes. We have also observed that the fairness risk method retains better semantics and fluency, while the adversarial training method tends to leak less sensitive information.

1 Introduction

Abuse and unauthorized use of sensitive information, such as demographic data, have become an ethical issue in our society. Such information should not be taken into account when humans or automatic decision making systems determine insurance rates, screen applicants for employment, target customers for advertising, or bank loans. Concerns about the fairness of decisions made by machine learning systems have led to an increasing body of work on the algorithmic fairness problem (Pedreshi et al., 2008; Zemel et al., 2013; Hardt et al., 2016; Chouldechova and Roth, 2018). Existing work on fairness learning largely focused on unbiased decisions based on classification. The algorithms made decisions for data consumers (e.g., bank) based on input provided by data producers (e.g., loan applicants), with the

sensitive attributes (e.g., age, gender, and race) being exposed. Those algorithms acting as decision-makers are supposed to avoid discrimination on the basis of demographic groups of the individuals. In this case, the decision-makers are *trusted* to access sensitive attributes in a proper way.

However, we believe that it is doubtful that one can rely on algorithmic decision-makers to provide fair estimation. For example, discrimination by gender among job applicants has been reported (Calcagnini et al., 2015; Midtbøen, 2016). It was also reported that racial disparities pledged access to higher education (Farkas, 2003; Mickelson, 2003). Data producers are vulnerable to biased decisions. Therefore, we argue that data providers should also take the responsibility of protecting their own sensitive information. Although users may be allowed to conceal well-structured sensitive attributes such as age and gender, such sensitive information can still be predicted from unstructured text data (Blodgett et al., 2016; Mac Kim et al., 2017; Elazar and Goldberg, 2018; Voigt et al., 2018). As suppressing more sensitive information in text indicates more privacy, we propose a new research challenge, privacy-aware text rewriting, namely *protecting sensitive attributes in text data on behalf of data providers by rewriting the text*. A rephrased privacy-aware text should i) reduce the leakage of sensitive information; ii) retain as much semantic meaning of the original text; iii) be grammatically fluent.Compared with fair representation learning, our work focuses on text in string form.

Transforming text into a form with less sensitive information is challenging in two ways. The first challenge is that there is a trade-off between privacy preservation and semantic relevance or fluency during rewriting. For example, *"I am a software engineer with 18 years of working experience."* shows that the author is probably over 40

Proceedings of The 12th International Conference on Natural Language Generation, pages 247–257,
Tokyo, Japan, 28 Oct - 1 Nov, 2019. ©2019 Association for Computational Linguistics

years old. Replacing '18 years' with 'more than 10 years' altogether reduces the leakage of age information with slight shift of its semantic meaning. Removing '18 years of working experience' provides stronger privacy protection, while the semantic loss is greater at the same time. The data providers should leverage the trade-off depending on varying scenarios. Another challenge is that the indicators of such sensitive attributes are subtle. For example, *"I went to the restaurant with my boyfriend. The food is yummy!"* is a post from social media. *'boyfriend'* is an explicit indicator for female user, while *'yummy'* is an implicit indicator which can be ignored by humans and captured by machine learning models. Automatic text rewriting tools help people detect and modify the subtle indicators in their text.

To address the aforementioned problems, we propose to develop a tool that rewrites text into less sensitive ones. In this work, we design a privacy-aware text rewriting framework based on back-translation to reduce the leakage of sensitive information. The models are optimized according to the trade-off between a reconstruction loss and a privacy risk loss. The reconstruction loss focuses on semantic relatedness and grammatical fluency, and the privacy risk loss controls the leakage of sensitive information. We further explore two variants of the approach. The first method formulates the privacy risk as an adversarial loss derived from a text classifier. The second method derives an upper bound of an approximate fairness risk measurement on text data, which minimizes the discrepancy of generated text among different demographic groups. Finally, we conduct extensive experiments on three datasets with varying demographic groups (i.e. Politics, Gender, and Race). The results demonstrate the effectiveness of our methods in terms of reducing the leakage rates of sensitive information and retaining linguistic quality of the rewritten text. This work provides a novel framework for systematic research on privacy-aware text rewriting, including datasets, evaluation metrics and rewriting methods, which will promote the interest in privacy preservation in our research community.

The main contributions of this work are:

- To provide the first proposal for protecting sensitive attributes in text on behalf of data providers.

- To design a privacy-aware back-translation method for protecting sensitive information in rewritten text.

- To provide datasets and evaluation metrics for appropriate validation of method effectiveness.

2 Privacy-Aware Text Rewriting

Privacy-aware rewriting modifies text to obfuscate a sensitive attribute. The bespoke methodologies aim to minimize the loss of fluency as well as the change in the underlying semantics. We consider a setup in which we have a set of input text $\{X_1, ..., X_N\}$, where each text X_i is a word sequence $\langle x_1, ..., x_l \rangle$. Each text is associated with a sensitive attribute S, such as gender or race. The goal is to find a privacy-aware translator $f(X) : X \rightarrow Y$ to modify X into another word sequence $Y = \langle y_1, ..., y_l \rangle$, such that an attacker $g(Y) : Y \rightarrow S$ fails to predict the values of the sensitive attribute S from the translated text Y.

2.1 Privacy-aware Back-Translation Model

Privacy-aware rewriting can be regarded as a special monolingual machine translation (MT) task, which aims to remove sensitive information through rephrasing. In our experiment, there is no existing parallel corpus to learn the patterns of privacy-preserved rewriting. We use Back-Translation to obtain a meaning-preserving representation in the target language, and translate the sentences back to the source language (Prabhumoye et al., 2018). Since we aim to preserve sensitive information, we consider the risk from an attacker in the back-translation phase.

In our work, the source language is English and the target language is French. Let Z denote the space of target language, we build two translation models $\mathcal{T}_{en \rightarrow fr} : X \rightarrow Z$ and $\mathcal{T}_{fr \rightarrow en} : Z \rightarrow X$, respectively. We use the Transformer-based model (Vaswani et al., 2017) for each translation model. The back-translation procedure is formulated as,

$$f(X) = \mathcal{T}_{fr \rightarrow en}(\mathcal{T}_{en \rightarrow fr}(X)) \tag{1}$$

For each input text, the outcome of this model is a sequence of words in English.

The goal of learning privacy-aware back-translation is two-fold. Firstly, it aims to find an optimal predictor f^* that minimizes an expected reconstruction loss $\mathbb{E}_{X,Y}[\mathcal{L}(f(X), Y)]$

with $\mathcal{L}(f(X), Y)$: $\mathcal{X} \times \mathcal{Y} \rightarrow \mathbb{R}$, which measures the discrepancy between predicted sequences $f(X)$ and true target sequences Y. Secondly, the predictor should be reasonably fair to S by achieving a low risk loss with regard to privacy $\mathcal{R}(X, Y, S) : \mathcal{X} \times \mathcal{Y} \times \mathcal{S} \rightarrow \mathbb{R}$. Let $\mathcal{F}$ denote the space of all possible predictors, we find the optimal rewriting model f^* by

$$f^* = \arg\min_{f \in \mathcal{F}} \mathbb{E}_{X,Y}[\mathcal{L}(f(X), Y)] + \alpha \mathcal{R}(X, Y, S) \tag{2}$$

where α controls the degree of privacy protection.

2.2 Adversarial Classifier

Given an accurate classifier, the risk of privacy is able to be estimated by the negative classification loss on the sensitive information. Our target is finding the representations that are good at reconstructing the sentences, while poor in predicting sensitive labels. The setting is well-aligned with generative adversarial networks (Goodfellow et al., 2014). We construct the back-translation model as $f(X) = m(h(X))$, where $h(X)$ employs the two translators to map X into a sequence of hidden representations of decoded words in the source language. Then, $m(\cdot)$ maps the hidden representations into the corresponding words. An adversarial classifier $adv(h(X))$ is a linear classifier, which takes the mean of all hidden representations from $h(X)$ to predict S. The risk is formulated as adversarial classification loss $\mathcal{L}_c(adv(h(X)), S)$. The encoder $h(\cdot)$ is trained to fool the adversarial classifier $adv(\cdot)$ while optimizing the back-translation predication $f(X)$ in Eq.(4). Eq.(3) merely optimizes the adversarial classifier. The training is conducted by jointly optimizing the following two objectives:

$$\arg\min_{adv} \mathcal{L}_c(adv(h(X)), S) \tag{3}$$

$$\arg\min_{h,m} \mathcal{L}_g(m(h(X)), X) - \alpha \mathcal{L}_c(adv(h(X)), S) \tag{4}$$

where $\mathcal{L}_g$ is the cross entropy loss with Label Smoothing (Szegedy et al., 2016) for the transformer-based generator and L_c is the cross entropy loss for the adversarial classifier. The negative parameter $-\alpha$ is implemented by a gradient-reversal layer (GRL)(Ganin and Lempitsky, 2015) during back-propagation and α controls the intensity of adversarial training.

2.3 Fairness Risk Measurement

In this section, we define the privacy risk loss using fairness risk measurement. The perfect fairness for rewriting is a statement of conditional independence of generated text $Y \perp\!\!\!\perp S|X$. Holding such condition, the sensitive translator conduct similar generation results. Therefore, attackers will not be able to infer the dependent attributes. A *privacy-aware* translator $f(X)$ learns a distribution $P(Y|X)$, while $P(Y|X, S = a)$ denotes the distribution of a *subgroup* translator depending on a particular demographic group attribute S. The conditional independence is formulated as,

$$P(Y|X) = P(Y|X, S = a) \tag{5}$$

Agarwal et al. (2018) pointed out that given finite samples in training data, it is impossible to ensure perfect fairness on the test sample. An approximate formalism of fairness measurement is used to quantify the discrepancy of demographic parities, namely maximal deviation between subgroup predictions (MDSP) (Calmon et al., 2017).

$$\sup_{y,s,s'} |Pr(\hat{Y} = y|S = s) - Pr(\hat{Y} = y|S = s')| \tag{6}$$

where $\hat{Y}$ is a single variable.

Inspired by the single-variable MDSP, we define the sequential MDSP (SMDSP) for text rewriting as,

$$\sup_{a \in S} |\log P(Y|X) - \log P(Y|X, S = a)| \tag{7}$$

where Y is the generated sequences. We obfuscate the sensitive attribute by reducing the discrepancy between privacy-aware translator and the most different subgroup translator.

The challenge of using the SMDSP is that it is optimized on the whole sequences. However, the state-of-the-art encoder-decoder architecture (Vaswani et al., 2017; Klein et al., 2017) generate words in a word-by-word manner.We derive an upper bound of SMDSP by applying calculus on the sequential deviation

$$D(X, Y, S = a) \doteq |\log P(Y|X) - \log P(Y|X, S = a)|$$
$$= |\sum_{i=1}^{l} \log P(y_i|X, y_{<i}) - \sum_{i=1}^{l} \log P(y_i|X, y_{<i}, S = a)|$$
$$\leq \sum_{i=1}^{l} |\log P(y_i|X, y_{<i}) - \log P(y_i|X, y_{<i}, S = a)|$$
$$\doteq \mathcal{U}_a(X, Y)$$

The composition of MDSP for each word is an upper bound of SMDSP.

$$\mathcal{R}_u(X, Y, S) = \sup_{a \in S} \mathcal{U}_a(X, Y) \tag{8}$$

We replace the approximate fairness risk by its upper bound Eq.(8) and obtain a joint training objective.

$$\mathcal{L}_\alpha(X) = \mathcal{L}(f(X), X) + \alpha \mathcal{R}_u(X, Y, S) \tag{9}$$

In training, each subgroup translator is pre-trained beforehand with the training data labeled with the corresponding sensitive attribute value. Their parameters are kept fixed when minimizing the privacy-aware rewriting model.

3 Experimental Setup

3.1 Datasets

In this paper we conduct experiments on three tasks, which can lead to potential social-good applications, namely obfuscating gender, political slant and race of the authors. .

Gender (Reddy and Knight, 2016) is a dataset of reviews from Yelp annotated with the gender of the authors, either male or female. The sentences with low indication of gender (likelihood of gender lower than 0.7) is filtered out.

Politics (Voigt et al., 2018) is a dataset of comments on Facebook posts from 412 members from the United States Senate and House. Each comment is associated with the corresponding Congressperson's party affiliation as the sensitive attribute, $S \in \{democratic, republican\}$.

Race (Blodgett et al., 2016) is a dataset based on the dialectal tweets corpus (DIAL), including 59.2 million tweets. The tweets are categorized into African-American English (AAE) or Standard American English (SAE), which is highly correlated to the race of the author. The predictor takes into account both the content of the tweets and the geolocations of the the authors. We filter out the samples with predicted confidence lower than 80%, and tweets with less than 3 words. We consider race as sensitive information of the dataset. We also maintain the sentiment classification as a target task for this corpus to check if the sentiment information is still preserved after rewriting. The sentiment labels are derived from emojis which are associated with sentiments.

All the aforementioned corpora are split into four disjoint parts: **Class**, training corpus for sensitive attribute classifier; **Train**, training corpus

for privacy-aware text rewriting; **Valid**, validation set; and **Test**, test set. The number of sentences for each split of these datasets are listed in Table 1. The datasets are publicly available at `https://github.com/xuqiongkai/PATR`

Dataset	Class	Train	Valid	Test
Gender	2.6M	200K	4K	4K
Politics	80K	200K	4K	4K
Race	80K	100K	4K	4K

Table 1: Data splits of `Gender`, `Politics` and `Race`.

3.2 Models

We consider the following three models for privacy-aware text rewriting. **Back Trans** is the back translation model considered as baseline. **Adv** is the model using adversarial training. **SMDSP** model use Sequential Maximal Deviation between Subgroup Predictions. We also compare the quality of generated text of our systems with those of an open-domain **Paraphrase** generation system (Iyyer et al., 2018).

3.3 Implementation Details

We use Transformer (Vaswani et al., 2017) as the translation architecture in our experiments. We re-implement the transformer model based on Open-NMT (Klein et al., 2017). In our experiments, we use the same configurations, including 2 encoder and decoder layers, 256-dimensional word embedding and 256-dimensional hidden layers, drop out rate 0.1, label smoothing weight 0.1. All models use Beam Search decoding algorithm with beam size 5.

We train English-French machine translation (En-Fr) and French-English back-translation (Fr-En) using Europarl v7 from WMT15 (Bojar et al., 2015). The words are tokenized using Moses tokenizer (Koehn et al., 2007). Our translation system achieves the BLEU scores of 36.24% and 37.36% on En-Fr and Fr-En, respectively. The En-Fr model is used to generate the parallel corpus for all experiments.

3.4 Evaluation

The generated sentences are evaluated according to both linguistic quality of the sentences and obfuscation of the sensitive attribute. For each of these two aspects, we conduct automatic evaluation and human evaluation, respectively.

Linguistic Quality focuses on evaluating the quality of the results based on their semantic relevance to the original text and gramatical fluency of the generated sentences. We adopt four automatic evaluation metrics, BLEU, GLEU, METEOR and WMD. BLEU (Papineni et al., 2002) and GLEU (Wu et al., 2016) measure the n-gram matching between hypothesis and reference, where GLEU considers both precision and recall. METEOR (Banerjee and Lavie, 2005) further applies stemming and synonym matching. Word Mover Distance (WMD) (Kusner et al., 2015) calculates the optimal transport distance between word embedding in original and generated sentences[1]. Intuitively, BLEU and GLEU evaluate fluency of the sentence as they are based on the quality of n-grams, while WMD measures semantic relevance as words can be regarded as atom semantic components of sentences.

We also conduct human evaluation to judge the fluency and relevance of the results[2]. For each set of the results, two annotators are asked to judge the quality of the results between the scales of 1-5. The Kappa coefficients (McHugh, 2012) on `Gender`, `Politics` and `Race` are 0.45, 0.47 and 0.74, respectively.

Obfuscation evaluates the leakage of sensitive attributes of generated text. For automatic evaluation, we estimate the probability of sensitive attribute on generated sentences using a Logistic Regression with L2 regularization (Pedregosa et al., 2011). For all the experiments, we use top 3K frequent words as features. Based on the prediction of classifier $p_i = P(S = i|X)$, we propose to evaluate the obfuscation of the results using the following three metrics:

1. **Entropy** evaluates the averaged entropy ($\sum_i -p_i \log p_i$) of all predictions. Higher Entropy indicates better less sensitive information leakage.

2. **P-Acc**, prediction accuracy, calculates the portion of correct prediction of the sensitive attribute. In the case of binary classification, the score is better if it is closer to 50%.

3. **M-Acc**, modification accuracy, calculates the label probabilities of source and generated sentences. If the probability of the sensitive attribute decreases after rewriting, the modification is accepted. M-Acc counts the rate of accepted sentence modifications.

In human evaluation, annotators are asked to judge the sensitive attribute values of 300 sampled sentences in test set. We use accuracy to evaluation the awareness of sensitive information by human and automatic annotators. Due to the fact that human judgments underperform automatic judgments (see Table 4), we rely more on automatic metric to evaluate the rewriting results.

4 Results and Analysis

We first conduct human evaluation and discuss their relation to automatic evaluation metrics with regard to semantic relevance, grammatical fluency and obfuscation. Then, we compare our privacy-aware models according to linguistic quality and obfuscation. Later on, we test the semantic loss of our models on the target task. Finally, we provide some sample outputs for case study.

4.1 Human Evaluation

Firstly, we ask human annotators to evaluate linguistic quality of Back Trans, Adv ($\alpha = 1$) and SMDSP ($\alpha = 1$), based on the rewriting results from 300 test samples, with regard to fluency (Flu) and relevance (Rel)[3]. We calculate the Pearson Correlation between human and automatic evaluation metrics. Table 2 shows the correlation of semantic relevance between human and automatic evaluation. WMD is clear winner among all automatic metrics across the three datasets. According to Table 3, GLEU is the measure that most correlated to human judgement in terms of fluency, though METEOR falls slight short on the gender corpus. Unsurprisingly, the widely used BLEU is the relatively less correlated to human perception, which was also observed in machine translation (Wu et al., 2016; Callison-Burch et al., 2006).

Secondly, we compare the performance of predicting sensitive information between human annotators and automatic classifiers. We ask human annotators to classify the sensitive attributes of 300 original sentences in test set. The accuracy of the annotations are illustrated in Table 4.

---

[1] We use pre-trained word2vec model trained on Google News dataset from `https://code.google.com/archive/p/word2vec/`.

[2] We refer readers to Appendix A for more details about the annotation guideline.

[3] We refer readers to Appendix A with more details on annotation guideline.

Exp	BLEU	GLEU	METEOR	WMD
Gender(Adv)	0.489	0.557	0.559	**0.651**
Gender(SMDSP)	0.414	0.507	0.511	**0.645**
Politics(Adv)	0.372	0.460	0.496	**0.573**
Politics(SMDSP)	0.358	0.474	0.476	**0.563**
Race(Adv)	0.311	**0.545**	0.532	0.127
Race(SMDSP)	0.242	0.386	0.367	**0.382**

Table 2: Correlation between semantic relevance and automatic evaluation metrics on Gender, Politics and Race. The most correlated automatic metrics are **bold**.

Exp	BLEU	GLEU	METEOR	WMD
Gender(Adv)	0.265	**0.287**	0.222	**0.297**
Gender(SMDSP)	0.192	**0.231**	0.186	**0.361**
Politics(Adv)	0.180	**0.260**	**0.277**	0.200
Politics(SMDSP)	0.149	**0.236**	**0.236**	0.231
Race(Adv)	0.168	**0.403**	**0.433**	0.333
Race(SMDSP)	0.068	**0.150**	**0.124**	0.046

Table 3: Correlation between fluency and automatic evaluation metrics on Gender, Politics and Race. Top two correlated automatic metrics are **bold**.

To our surprise, human judgments are more than 10% worse than our classifiers on all the experiments. For Politics, we ask one more annotator for additional annotation and the accuracy of the annotation is still lower than 65%. After investigating the datasets, we found that a large proportion of samples are difficult for human annotators while our classifier can predict them correctly. For example, in Gender, human struggled in deciding whether "the food is delicious" and "the people were nice" are posted by male or female authors. For Politics, we observe several cases that human tends to annotate them with the opposite political slant when the sentences are in negative sentiment, while actually the speaker and the mentioned people support the same party, e.g., "Patty Murray couldn't be any more dishonest than this!". Other examples like "today is such a wonderful day!" and "God bless you guys" are neutral to our annotators. Correctly annotating these samples might require extensive background in American politics[4]. To sum up, human annotators fail to incorporate subtle indicators into their decision, however, the classifiers manage to detect them.

The human evaluation studies conclude that i) we can rely on sensitive attribute classifiers for obfuscation evaluation, and ii) we should look at WMD for semantic relevance and GLEU for flu-

---

	Gender	Politic	Race
Automatic	77.3	93.7	**82.7**
Human	66.0	60.3	71.0

Table 4: Comparison of human and automatic judgments on Gender, Politics and Race.

ency.

4.2 Adversarial Learning vs. SMDSP

We conduct automatic evaluation on text generated by Back Trans, Adv and SMDSP. The overall observations are i) Back Trans provides a preliminary baseline for our task; ii) both Adv and SMDSP are able to reduce the leakage of sensitive information; and iii) SMDSP retains better linguistic quality, while Adv manages to preserve sensitive information.

We first compare the linguistic quality of the results in Table 5. The Back Trans outperforms both Adv and SMDSP on average because it does not cope with sensitive attributes in training. The performance of Adv model with the highest α obtains less than half GLEU than that of Back Trans. Although SMDSP with higher α also shows performance reduction, the quality of generated text are still competitive with Back Trans, with less than 10% score reduction. In particular, SMDSP with ($\alpha = 1$) achieves even higher GLEU on both Politics and Race than the baseline. We attribute this to the regularization effect of SMDSP on language modeling. Results of human evaluation are coherent to automatic evaluation, in Table 7. SMDSP achieves highest fluency results and competitive relevance results.

Then, we show the obfuscation performance in Table 6. Back Trans is a competitive baseline that obfuscates the classifiers to some extent. Adv and SMDSP are able to further reduce the obfuscation score on all three datasets. Generally, models with higher α achieve better obfuscation performance. Adv tend to be more aggressive on privacy preservation than SMDSP. However, we observe that Adv acquires better privacy preservation by sacrificing the linguistic quality, e.g., Adv ($\alpha = 5$) basically chooses to 'keep silent' (produces almost no words) to protect the sensitive information on Politics[5]. We believe that generating totally non-sense sentences is too conservative for our task. On the other hand, SMDSP manages to protect sensitive attribute while keeping the semantic meaning as much as possible. For

---

[4]The top weighted words of male or female for Gender, democratic or republican for Politics, and SAE for Race are listed in Appendix B to show the difficulty for human annotators to capture subtle indicators.

[5]All the generated sentences are empty on test set.

Model	Gender			Politics			Race		
	GLEU	METEOR	WMD	GLEU	METEOR	WMD	GLEU	METEOR	WMD
Back Trans	**45.14**	**37.16**	**1.012**	37.29	**36.78**	**1.039**	23.09	26.94	1.460
Adv($\alpha = 1$)	44.11	36.76	1.023	29.44	33.55	1.125	12.94	18.07	**1.303**
Adv($\alpha = 2$)	40.29	34.34	1.117	23.20	26.82	1.261	12.75	18.39	1.430
Adv($\alpha = 5$)	22.98	23.32	1.561	N/A	N/A	N/A	9.67	17.03	2.242
SMDSP($\alpha = 1$)	44.17	36.69	1.031	**38.43**	36.59	1.044	**24.77**	**28.15**	1.483
SMDSP($\alpha = 2$)	43.10	35.84	1.062	38.01	36.36	1.056	23.95	27.49	1.501
SMDSP($\alpha = 10$)	41.54	35.09	1.101	36.40	35.96	1.069	23.10	26.99	1.531
SMDSP($\alpha = 100$)	40.90	34.64	1.122	36.84	35.64	1.082	22.74	26.81	2.242

Table 5: Automatic evaluation of linguistic quality on Gender, Politics and Race.

Model	Gender			Politics			Race		
	Entropy	P-Acc	M-Acc	Entropy	P-Acc	M-Acc	Entropy	P-Acc	M-Acc
Test(Ori)	0.5544	77.45	-	0.4873	93.05	-	0.3586	86.33	-
Back Trans	0.5617	72.45	48.90	0.5011	85.55	56.03	0.3960	74.68	62.35
Adv($\alpha = 1$)	0.5649	72.50	49.58	0.5026	84.90	57.25	0.4386	74.08	66.80
Adv($\alpha = 2$)	0.5644	70.23	52.73	0.5542	73.60	68.65	0.4623	73.40	69.13
Adv($\alpha = 5$)	0.5754	66.80	59.78	0.6931	50.00	93.15	0.5268	65.75	73.58
SMDSP($\alpha = 1$)	0.5711	71.80	50.18	0.5059	85.20	57.33	0.3989	74.85	62.48
SMDSP($\alpha = 2$)	0.5759	71.08	52.15	0.5066	84.95	58.35	0.4013	74.40	63.40
SMDSP($\alpha = 10$)	0.5768	70.88	53.05	0.5089	85.13	59.23	0.4007	74.08	63.65
SMDSP($\alpha = 100$)	0.5803	70.73	54.78	0.5129	85.08	59.90	0.4069	74.10	64.80

Table 6: Automatic evaluation of Obfuscation on Gender, Politics and Race.

Model	Gender		Politics		Race	
	Flu	Rel	Flu	Rel	Flu	Rel
Back Trans	4.68	4.09	**4.60**	**4.31**	4.31	3.88
Adv	4.66	4.13	4.42	4.01	3.84	3.53
SMDSP	**4.73**	**4.14**	**4.60**	4.21	**4.37**	**3.98**

Table 7: Human evaluation of fluency (Flu) and relevance (Rel) on Gender, Politics and Race based on the results of Back Trans, Adv ($\alpha = 1$) and SMDSP ($\alpha = 1$) with the scales of 1-5.

example, SMDSP ($\alpha = 1$) achieves both higher relevance score and better obfuscation score than Adv ($\alpha = 1$) on Gender and Politics.

Finally, we demonstrate the training stability of our models. The reconstruction losses of each model on validation set of Gender, Politics and Race are shown in Figure 1. We pre-train the back translation model for 10 epochs on Gender and 20 epochs on Politics and Race. Then, we train Adv model and SMDSP model based on the pre-trained model. We also include the pre-trained model with the same total number of training epochs in Black lines. After pre-training, Back-Trans models start to overfit and get slightly worse results on validation set. In most cases, the losses of Adv are higher than Transformer, and higher adversarial training intensity α decreases the performance of translation model. Adv ($\alpha = 5$) is not included in the plots, because their losses are out of the range. In contrast, SMDSP achieves better performance than Adv. The performance of SMDSP is even better than Back Trans on Gender and Race.

4.3 Target Task Performance

We evaluate sentiment classification (Sent) as the target task and racial (Race) as sensitive attribute on the Race. As shown in Table 8, the prediction performance of both Race and Sent using Adv models decrease as the hyperparameter α increases. Such trend shows that Adv improves privacy preservation by obfuscating the semantic meaning of the original text. In contrast, Risk models successfully decrease the accuracy on Race, while preserving the accuracy on Sent, showing the robustness of the model on preserving semantic meanings of the text.

4.4 Case Study

We demonstrate generated examples in Figure 2[6]. For Gender, Back Trans generates the words with clear tendency of gender, such as 'yummy' and 'girlfriend', while privacy-aware models use 'delicious', 'amazing' and 'friend' instead. For Politics, Adv and SMDSP skip the name after Sir to hide the political affiliation of the person. In the second example, Adv and SMDSP replace 'love you' with 'help' to reduce the political slant.

5 Related Work

Achieving fairness or preserving privacy through removing sensitive information from text has been explored by adversarial training (Li et al., 2018;

---

[6]Because the samples in Race are full of porny and violent words, they are excluded in the paper.

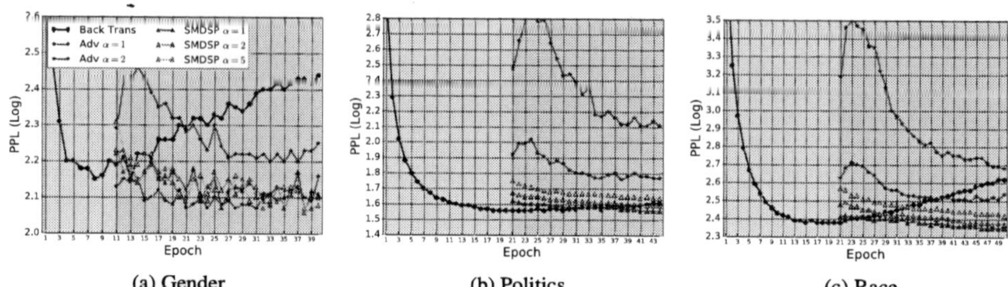

(a) Gender	(b) Politics	(c) Race

Figure 1: Log perplexity(PPL) on valid set of `Gender`, `Politics` and `Race`. Red areas indicate pre-training epochs and Blue areas represent the epochs for privacy-aware training.

Dataset	Original	Back Trans	Adv	SMDSP
Gender	food is always delicious ! (Female)	the food is always yummy !	the food is always delicious !	the food is always amazing !
Gender	I went with my girlfriend , and another couple . (Male)	I went with my girlfriend , and another couple .	I went with my friend , and another couple .	I went with my friend , and another couple .
Politics	Sir Scott , a limited attack will make any solution for Syria nearly impossible . (Republican)	Sir Scott , a limited attack will make almost impossible to Syria .	Sir , a limited attack will almost impossible attack Syria .	Sir , a limited attack will make almost impossible for Syria .
Politics	love you U.S. senator al franken (Democratic)	love you U.S. senator al franken	help U.S. senator al franken	help U.S. senator al franken

Figure 2: Sample of original text, with sensitive attribute labels, and corresponding rewritten text using Back Trans, Adv ($\alpha = 1$) and SMDSP ($\alpha = 1$) on `Gender` and `Politics`.

Model	Race	Sent
Test(Ori)	86.33	74.08
Back Trans	74.68	70.18
Adv($\alpha = 1$)	74.08	70.15
Adv($\alpha = 2$)	73.40	69.88
Adv($\alpha = 5$)	65.75	65.70
SMDSP($\alpha = 1$)	74.85†	69.88
SMDSP($\alpha = 2$)	74.40	70.23†
SMDSP($\alpha = 5$)	74.30	70.15†
SMDSP($\alpha = 10$)	74.08	70.60
SMDSP($\alpha = 100$)	74.10	70.83†

Table 8: Prediction accuracy (P-Acc) of classification results of race and sentiment classification task on `Race`. The results with higher accuracy than Back Trans are marked with daggers (†).

Elazar and Goldberg, 2018; Coavoux et al., 2018) and differential privacy (Fernandes et al., 2018). These work considers text classification as the target task and avoid data leakage by learning privacy-preserving latent representations. In contrast, our work aims to generate text in string form to protect sensitive information for data producers, which can be viewed as a special form of fair representation learning.

Paraphrase generation and text simplification are two tasks closely related to privacy-aware rewriting. Most models are based on monolingual machine translation (Ibrahim et al., 2003; Zhao et al., 2010; Wubben et al., 2012; Xu et al., 2012, 2016; Nisioi et al., 2017; Wang et al., 2016). Our work focuses on generating obfuscated text in order to conceal sensitive attribute.

There is a fast growing body of work on stylistic language generation, which focus on generating text with particular styles (e.g., humour or romantic) while trying to retain the meaning of text (Mathews et al., 2016; Fu et al., 2018; Su et al., 2018; Xu et al., 2019). Style transfer is also considered as text rewriting, which adds style information to text (Shen et al., 2017; Prabhumoye et al., 2018). In contrary, our work tries to eliminate the additional sensitive information.

6 Conclusion

In order to protect sensitive information in text, we propose a privacy-aware back-translation method for text rewriting. Adversarial training and fairness risk measurement based approaches are proposed to incorporate the privacy risk. We propose the evaluation metrics for the task to assess semantic relevance, fluency and obfuscation of the results. Our experimental results show that both methods reduce the leakage of sensitive information, and the fairness risk based method is able to better retain fluency and relevance than the adversarial one.

Acknowledgement

We gratefully acknowledge Philip Cohen for his insightful advice and encouragement on this project, as well as Alasdair Tran and Dawei Chen for their suggestions on the paper.

References

Alekh Agarwal, Alina Beygelzimer, Miroslav Dudík, John Langford, and Hanna Wallach. 2018. A reductions approach to fair classification. *arXiv preprint arXiv:1803.02453*.

Satanjeev Banerjee and Alon Lavie. 2005. Meteor: An automatic metric for mt evaluation with improved correlation with human judgments. In *Proceedings of the ACL workshop on Intrinsic and Extrinsic Evaluation Measures for Machine Translation and/or Summarization*, pages 65–72.

Su Lin Blodgett, Lisa Green, and Brendan O'Connor. 2016. Demographic dialectal variation in social media: A case study of african-american english. In *Proceedings of the 2016 Conference on Empirical Methods in Natural Language Processing*, pages 1119–1130.

Ondrej Bojar, Rajen Chatterjee, Christian Federmann, Barry Haddow, Matthias Huck, Chris Hokamp, Philipp Koehn, Varvara Logacheva, Christof Monz, Matteo Negri, Matt Post, Carolina Scarton, Lucia Specia, and Marco Turchi. 2015. Findings of the 2015 workshop on statistical machine translation. In *Proceedings of the 2015 Workshop on Statistical Machine Translation*.

Giorgio Calcagnini, Germana Giombini, and Elisa Lenti. 2015. Gender differences in bank loan access: an empirical analysis. *Italian Economic Journal*, 1(2):193–217.

Chris Callison-Burch, Miles Osborne, and Philipp Koehn. 2006. Re-evaluation the role of bleu in machine translation research. In *11th Conference of the European Chapter of the Association for Computational Linguistics*.

Flavio Calmon, Dennis Wei, Bhanukiran Vinzamuri, Karthikeyan Natesan Ramamurthy, and Kush R Varshney. 2017. Optimized pre-processing for discrimination prevention. In *Proceedings of Advances in Neural Information Processing Systems*, pages 3992–4001.

Alexandra Chouldechova and Aaron Roth. 2018. The frontiers of fairness in machine learning. *arXiv preprint arXiv:1810.08810*.

Maximin Coavoux, Shashi Narayan, and Shay B Cohen. 2018. Privacy-preserving neural representations of text. In *Proceedings of the 2018 Conference on Empirical Methods in Natural Language Processing*, pages 1–10.

Yanai Elazar and Yoav Goldberg. 2018. Adversarial removal of demographic attributes from text data. In *Proceedings of the 2018 Conference on Empirical Methods in Natural Language Processing*, pages 11–21.

George Farkas. 2003. Racial disparities and discrimination in education: What do we know, how do we know it, and what do we need to know? *Teachers College Record*, 105(6):1119–1146.

Natasha Fernandes, Mark Dras, and Annabelle McIver. 2018. Generalised differential privacy for text document processing. *arXiv preprint arXiv:1811.10256*.

Zhenxin Fu, Xiaoye Tan, Nanyun Peng, Dongyan Zhao, and Rui Yan. 2018. Style transfer in text: Exploration and evaluation. In *Proceedings of the 32nd AAAI Conference on Artificial Intelligence*.

Yaroslav Ganin and Victor Lempitsky. 2015. Unsupervised domain adaptation by backpropagation. In *Proceedings of International Conference on Machine Learning*, pages 1180–1189.

Ian Goodfellow, Jean Pouget-Abadie, Mehdi Mirza, Bing Xu, David Warde-Farley, Sherjil Ozair, Aaron Courville, and Yoshua Bengio. 2014. Generative adversarial nets. In *Advances in neural information processing systems*, pages 2672–2680.

Moritz Hardt, Eric Price, Nati Srebro, et al. 2016. Equality of opportunity in supervised learning. In *Proceedings of Advances in neural information processing systems*, pages 3315–3323.

Ali Ibrahim, Boris Katz, and Julie Qiaojin Lin. 2003. Extracting structural paraphrases from aligned monolingual corpora.

Mohit Iyyer, John Wieting, Kevin Gimpel, and Luke Zettlemoyer. 2018. Adversarial example generation with syntactically controlled paraphrase networks. In *Proceedings of the 2018 Conference of the North American Chapter of the Association for Computational Linguistics: Human Language Technologies, Volume 1 (Long Papers)*, pages 1875–1885.

Guillaume Klein, Yoon Kim, Yuntian Deng, Jean Senellart, and Alexander M. Rush. 2017. Opennmt: Open-source toolkit for neural machine translation. In *Proceedings of the 55th Annual Meeting of the Association for Computational Linguistics*.

Philipp Koehn, Hieu Hoang, Alexandra Birch, Chris Callison-Burch, Marcello Federico, Nicola Bertoldi, Brooke Cowan, Wade Shen, Christine Moran, Richard Zens, et al. 2007. Moses: Open source toolkit for statistical machine translation. In *Proceedings of the 45th Annual Meeting of the Association for Computational Linguistics Demo and Poster sessions*, pages 177–180.

Matt Kusner, Yu Sun, Nicholas Kolkin, and Kilian Weinberger. 2015. From word embeddings to document distances. In *International Conference on Machine Learning*, pages 957–966.

Yitong Li, Timothy Baldwin, and Trevor Cohn. 2018. Towards robust and privacy-preserving text representations. *arXiv preprint arXiv:1805.06093*.

Sunghwan Mac Kim, Qiongkai Xu, Lizhen Qu, Stephen Wan, and Cécile Paris. 2017. Demographic inference on twitter using recursive neural networks. In *Proceedings of the 55th Annual Meeting of the Association for Computational Linguistics*, pages 471–477.

Alexander Mathews, Lexing Xie, and Xuming He. 2016. Senticap: Generating image descriptions with sentiments. In *Proceedings of the 30th AAAI Conference on Artificial Intelligence*, pages 3574–3580.

Mary L McHugh. 2012. Interrater reliability: the kappa statistic. *Biochemia Medica*, 22(3):276–282.

Roslyn Arlin Mickelson. 2003. When are racial disparities in education the result of racial discrimination? a social science perspective. *Teachers College Record*.

Arnfinn H Midtbøen. 2016. Discrimination of the second generation: Evidence from a field experiment in norway. *Journal of International Migration and Integration*, 17(1):253–272.

Sergiu Nisioi, Sanja Štajner, Simone Paolo Ponzetto, and Liviu P Dinu. 2017. Exploring neural text simplification models. In *Proceedings of the 55th Annual Meeting of the Association for Computational Linguistics*, volume 2.

Kishore Papineni, Salim Roukos, Todd Ward, and Wei-Jing Zhu. 2002. Bleu: a method for automatic evaluation of machine translation. In *Proceedings of the 40th Annual Meeting on Association for Computational Linguistics*, pages 311–318.

Fabian Pedregosa, Gaël Varoquaux, Alexandre Gramfort, Vincent Michel, Bertrand Thirion, Olivier Grisel, Mathieu Blondel, Peter Prettenhofer, Ron Weiss, Vincent Dubourg, et al. 2011. Scikit-learn: Machine learning in python. *Journal of Machine Learning Research*, 12(Oct):2825–2830.

Dino Pedreshi, Salvatore Ruggieri, and Franco Turini. 2008. Discrimination-aware data mining. In *Proceedings of the 14th ACM SIGKDD International Conference on Knowledge Discovery and Data Mining*, pages 560–568.

Shrimai Prabhumoye, Yulia Tsvetkov, Ruslan Salakhutdinov, and Alan W Black. 2018. Style transfer through back-translation. In *Proceedings of the 56th Annual Meeting of the Association for Computational Linguistics*, pages 866–876.

Sravana Reddy and Kevin Knight. 2016. Obfuscating gender in social media writing. In *Proceedings of the First Workshop on NLP and Computational Social Science*, pages 17–26.

Tianxiao Shen, Tao Lei, Regina Barzilay, and Tommi Jaakkola. 2017. Style transfer from non-parallel text by cross-alignment. In *Proceedings of the 31st International Conference on Neural Information Processing Systems*, pages 6830–6841.

Jinyue Su, Jiacheng Xu, Xipeng Qiu, and Xuanjing Huang. 2018. Incorporating discriminator in sentence generation: a gibbs sampling method. In *Proceedings of the 32nd AAAI Conference on Artificial Intelligence*.

Christian Szegedy, Vincent Vanhoucke, Sergey Ioffe, Jon Shlens, and Zbigniew Wojna. 2016. Rethinking the inception architecture for computer vision. In *Proceedings of the IEEE Conference on Computer Vision and Pattern Recognition*, pages 2818–2826.

Ashish Vaswani, Noam Shazeer, Niki Parmar, Jakob Uszkoreit, Llion Jones, Aidan N Gomez, Łukasz Kaiser, and Illia Polosukhin. 2017. Attention is all you need. In *Proceedings of Advances in Neural Information Processing Systems*, pages 5998–6008.

Rob Voigt, David Jurgens, Vinodkumar Prabhakaran, Dan Jurafsky, and Yulia Tsvetkov. 2018. Rtgender: A corpus for studying differential responses to gender. In *Proceedings of the Eleventh International Conference on Language Resources and Evaluation*.

Tong Wang, Ping Chen, John Rochford, and Jipeng Qiang. 2016. Text simplification using neural machine translation. In *Proceedings of AAAI*.

Yonghui Wu, Mike Schuster, Zhifeng Chen, Quoc V Le, Mohammad Norouzi, Wolfgang Macherey, Maxim Krikun, Yuan Cao, Qin Gao, Klaus Macherey, et al. 2016. Googles neural machine translation system: Bridging the gap between human and machine translation. *arXiv preprint arXiv:1609.08144*.

Sander Wubben, Antal Van Den Bosch, and Emiel Krahmer. 2012. Sentence simplification by monolingual machine translation. In *Proceedings of the 50th Annual Meeting of the Association for Computational Linguistics*.

Qiongkai Xu, Chenchen Xu, and Lizhen Qu. 2019. Alter: Auxiliary text rewriting tool for natural language generation. *arXiv preprint arXiv:1909.06564*.

Wei Xu, Courtney Napoles, Ellie Pavlick, Quanze Chen, and Chris Callison-Burch. 2016. Optimizing statistical machine translation for text simplification. *Transactions of the Association for Computational Linguistics*, 4:401–415.

Wei Xu, Alan Ritter, William B. Dolan, Ralph Grishman, and Colin Cherry. 2012. Paraphrasing for style. In *Proceedings of the 24th International Conference on Computational Linguistics*.

Rich Zemel, Yu Wu, Kevin Swersky, Toni Pitassi, and Cynthia Dwork. 2013. Learning fair representations. In *Proceedings of the 30th International Conference on Machine Learning*, pages 325–333.

Shiqi Zhao, Haifeng Wang, Xiang Lan, and Ting Liu. 2010. Leveraging multiple mt engines for paraphrase generation. In *Proceedings of COLING*.

Personalized Substitution Ranking for Lexical Simplification

John Lee, Chak Yan Yeung
Department of Linguistics and Translation
City University of Hong Kong
jsylee@cityu.edu.hk, chak.yeung@my.cityu.edu.hk

Abstract

A lexical simplification (LS) system substitutes difficult words in a text with simpler ones to make it easier for the user to understand. In the typical LS pipeline, the Substitution Ranking step determines the best substitution out of a set of candidates. Most current systems do not consider the user's vocabulary proficiency, and always aim for the simplest candidate. This approach may overlook less-simple candidates that the user can understand, and that are semantically closer to the original word. We propose a personalized approach for Substitution Ranking to identify the candidate that is the closest synonym and is non-complex for the user. In experiments on learners of English at different proficiency levels, we show that this approach enhances the semantic faithfulness of the output, at the cost of a relatively small increase in the number of complex words.

1 Introduction

A lexical simplification (LS) system aims to make a text easier to understand for users such as language learners (Petersen and Ostendorf, 2007), children (Belder and Moens, 2010; Kajiwara et al., 2013), those with language disabilities (Devlin and Tait, 1998; Carroll et al., 1999; Rello et al., 2013), as well as those without the background needed for understanding the text in a specialized domain (Zeng et al., 2005; Elhadad, 2006). Given an input text, the system substitutes difficult words with simpler words or phrases, in such a way as to satisfy two requirements:

Semantic faithfulness The output text should preserve the meaning of the input as much as possible;

Word complexity The output text should minimize the number of complex words, i.e., words that the user cannot understand.

These two goals are often in conflict. To reduce word complexity, the system should make substitutions with the simplest words possible. However, when limited to simple words, it is more challenging to find a close synonym for the original word. In general, the larger the vocabulary pool, the better the simplified text can semantically approximate the original.

The trade-off between these two goals is best resolved with respect to the user's vocabulary knowledge. For example, to simplify the word "obnoxious", the word "offensive" would be the best substitution *if the user knows it*; otherwise, a looser synonym but simpler word such as "bad" should be preferred. Human editors follow this principle when composing graded versions of a text: they stick to simple substitutions ("bad") in basic versions, but allow more difficult words ("offensive") in more advanced versions, if these words better reflect the original meaning.

Current LS approaches do not mimic this strategy. The typical system offers the same substitutions, regardless of individual users' language proficiency, because it is trained on simple-complex text pairs that do not specify the target reader. With the notable exception of the Newsela corpus (Xu et al., 2015), annotators for LS corpora are not typically given precise guidelines on the vocabulary proficiency of the intended user, making it difficult to make optimal or consistent trade-off between semantic faithfulness and word complexity.

A possible solution is to use Newsela-style corpora to train systems to automatically generate multiple simplified versions, optimized for readers at different proficiency levels. The sheer amount of annotation required, however, would limit the granularity of the proficiency levels. This paper instead explores an alternative solution that leverages two existing subfields of computational

Word	User A	User B	User C
liberal	×	×	√
open	√	√	√
progressive	√	×	√
relaxed	√	√	√

Table 1: Example CWI model predictions on three users' vocabulary knowledge. Complex words are marked with a cross (×), and non-complex ones with a tick (√).

linguistics. We propose a novel, two-step Substitution Ranking algorithm for the LS pipeline, by combining lexical substitution (McCarthy and Navigli, 2009)[1] and personalized complex word identification (CWI) (Ehara et al., 2014). This algorithm first ranks the substitution candidates according to semantic proximity to the target word; it then selects as output the highest-ranked candidate that is non-complex for the user.

We make two main contributions. First, in terms of evaluation methodology, we present the first LS evaluation that explicitly takes into account the trade-off between semantic faithfulness and word complexity for users at different proficiency levels. Second, we show that our proposed Substitution Ranking algorithm leads to substitutions that are more meaning-preserving, with a relatively small increase in word complexity.

The goal of this paper is not to advance the state-of-the-art for lexical substitution or for CWI. Instead, we aim to show that, by combining existing methods in these two tasks, an LS system achieves superior trade-off between semantic faithfulness and word complexity, compared to the conventional approach of optimizing on word simplicity alone.

The rest of the paper is organized as follows. After a presentation of the general LS system architecture in the next section, Section 3 summarizes previous research in Substitution Ranking. Section 4 describes our proposed approach. Section 5 gives details on our datasets. Section 6 defines the evaluation metrics. Section 7 discusses the experimental set-up, and Section 8 presents experimental results. Finally, Section 9 concludes.

2 Background: LS pipeline

The most common LS architecture is a pipeline architecture with three steps: Complex Word Identification, Substitution Generation, and Substitution Ranking (Shardlow, 2014; Paetzold and Specia, 2016c).

2.1 Complex Word Identification (CWI)

CWI classifies each word in an input text as either "complex" (i.e., difficult to understand) or "non-complex" (i.e., not difficult to understand) (Paetzold and Specia, 2016c; Yimam et al., 2017). Complex words become *target words* for substitution in the rest of the pipeline.

Most CWI approaches adopt a generic definition of "complexity", without catering to variation in proficiency level among users. Some studies have begun to build personalized CWI models to predict whether a word can or cannot be understood by an individual user (Ehara et al., 2014; Lee and Yeung, 2018). For example, the top row in Table 1 shows the predictions for the word "liberal" for three users. Given these predictions, the system would attempt to simplify the word "liberal" in the sentence in Table 2 for Users A and B, but would not do so for User C.

2.2 Substitution Generation

For each target word, the Substitution Generation step identifies possible substitution candidates, without assessing the simplicity of the candidates.[2] In our running example in Table 2, the system generates three possible synonyms — "open", "progressive", and "relaxed" — as substitution candidates for "liberal".

2.3 Substitution Ranking

As the final step, Substitution Ranking chooses the best simplification among the generated candidates. The next section review previous research on this step, as well as previous work that we use as the basis for personalizing it.

3 Previous work

Substitution Ranking is "the task of ranking a set of selected substitutions for a target complex word with respect to their simplicity." (Paetzold and Specia, 2015). As this definition suggests, most

---

[1]In this paper, the abbreviation LS always refers to "Lexical Simplification", and not to "Lexical Substitution."

[2]Some systems take a separate Substitution Selection step to discard candidates that distort the meaning of the text or affect its grammaticality, and retain those that fit the context.

Input sentence: She is a product of a tremendously unorthodox family with *liberal* views toward sex, marriage, religion and child-rearing.		

Substitution Ranking algorithm	**User**	**Ranked substitution candidates for *liberal***
(a) Simplicity ranking	n/a	1. open 2. relaxed 3. progressive
(b) Similarity ranking	n/a	1. progressive 2. relaxed 3. open
(c) Personalized ranking	User A	1. progressive 2. relaxed 3. open
	User B	1. progressive 1. relaxed 2. open

Table 2: Gold ranking of substitution candidates for the target word "liberal" by optimizing on (a) lexical simplicity; (b) semantic similarity to the target word; (c) both user vocabulary knowledge (Table 1) *and* semantic similarity to the target word.

LS systems use simplicity, or word complexity, as the basis for ranking (Section 3.1). In contrast, we will propose an approach that takes into account both word complexity and semantic faithfulness, by building on previous research on ranking by semantic similarity (Section 3.2) and personalized CWI (Section 3.3).

3.1 Simplicity ranking

Various statistical models have been trained to rank substitution candidates by "simplicity", using a wide range of features including the number of syllables, word frequencies, n-gram language model scores, word embeddings, as well as relative frequencies in standard Wikipedia and Simple Wikipedia (Carroll et al., 1999; Ligozat et al., 2012; Horn et al., 2014; Glavaš and Štajner, 2015; Pavlick and Callison-Burch, 2016). Among the three candidates in our running example, "open" would be ranked first, and thus chosen to substitute for "liberal" (Table 2a).

Researchers have recognized that the "one-size-fits-all" approach does not adequately cater to users at different vocabulary proficiency levels, since they do not share the same notion of "simplicity". Some have begun to explore adaptation of the ranking through user feedback (Paetzold and Specia, 2016a; Yimam and Biemann, 2018). For example, the Lexi system asks the user whether the original word or a candidate substitution makes the sentence easier to understand, and then uses pairwise online logistic regression to adapt its simplicity ranking (Bingel et al., 2018).

3.2 Similarity ranking

Another possible criterion for ranking substitution candidates is their semantic similarity, or proximity, to the target word. On this criterion, "progres-

sive" would be ranked first among the three candidates in our running example (Table 2b).

Similarity ranking has been intensively studied for the task of lexical substitution (McCarthy and Navigli, 2009). To find the most appropriate paraphrases, PPDB uses a scoring model that estimates semantic distance between two words with WordNet, and also considers lexical overlap, distributional similarity, as well as cosine similarity of word embeddings (Pavlick et al., 2015). The SALSA system performs similarity ranking through latent semantic analysis, explicit semantic analysis and n-gram scores (Sinha and Mihalcea, 2014). It has been deployed in a reading assistance tool that displays synonyms for difficult words (Azab et al., 2015), but it does not attempt LS.

3.3 Personalized CWI

The first studies on personalized CWI were reported by Ehara et al. (2012; 2014). They proposed a graph-based active learning method, trained on word frequencies from various corpora, to select the most informative words for user annotation. A label propagation algorithm achieved an accuracy of 76.4% for English CWI on a 50-word training set (Ehara et al., 2014).

Lee and Yeung (2018) applied personalized CWI on LS. Their LS algorithm assumes a personal CWI model for each user. There were four possible CWI models, each corresponding to a vocabulary list. Each user is given the model that optimizes the F-measure on his or her small CWI training set. During ranking of the substitution candidates, candidates that are deemed complex for the user are rejected. Experimental results showed that this approach reduced both unnecessary simplification and the word complexity of the output text. Although their approach is similar to our CWI filtering step (Section 4), they did not incorporate similarity ranking or evaluate its effect on semantic faithfulness in the LS output.

4 Proposed Approach

In the Substitution Ranking step, the optimal candidate is often not the simplest one. A more pertinent criterion is whether the candidate is non-complex, i.e., whether it can be understood by the user. This is because a non-complex candidate that is more similar in meaning to the target word should be preferred, even if it is less simple. Our proposed algorithm selects the candidate that is semantically closest to the target word (to maximize semantic faithfulness), with the constraint that the candidate be non-complex for the user (to minimize word complexity). More concretely, it consists of two steps:

Similarity ranking Rank the substitution candidates according to semantic proximity, as a lexical substitution system would do.

CWI filtering Personalize the ranking by removing candidates that the user cannot understand, according to the prediction of the personalized CWI model.

Note that while CWI filtering employs the same CWI model as the one used in the first step in the LS pipeline (Section 2.1), it predicts user knowledge on the substitution candidates, rather than on the target word.

In our running example, for the word "liberal", the similarity ranking step would yield the ranked list "1. progressive; 2. relaxed; 3. open" (Table 2b), since "progressive" is semantically closest to the target word "liberal". The CWI filtering step then produces a personalized ranking for each user (Table 2c). Based on the personalized CWI model (Table 1), the ranked list for User A remains unchanged, since all three candidates are known to User A. The word "progressive" is removed from the ranked list for User B, however, since User B does not understand it. The second-best synonym, "relaxed", is instead offered to User B.

5 Data

Standard LS datasets, such as BenchLS (Paetzold and Specia, 2016b) and the Newsela corpus (Xu et al., 2015), are not suitable for evaluating our

proposed ranking approach (Section 4) since they do not offer human judgment on semantic similarity between target words and their substitutions. We instead took an existing paraphrase dataset as our starting point (Section 5.1), and then exploited a language learner dataset (Section 5.2) to construct personalized substitution rankings (Section 5.3).

5.1 Similarity rankings

During the development of PPDB 2.0 (Pavlick et al., 2015), human judgment on similarity was collected for 40,410 phrase pairs. Five human raters assigned a similarity score on a 5-point scale to each pair. For each target word, we computed the similarity ranking of its candidates according to their average score. While other lexical substitution corpora such as the 2007 English Lexical Substitution shared task (McCarthy and Navigli, 2009) and CoInCo (Kremer et al., 2014) could also serve as evaluation data, we chose PPDB because it offers a much larger number of substitution candidates per word, and thus facilitates a clear comparison between the simplicity-based approach and ours. We will refer to this dataset as "PPDB Set".

5.2 Personalization dataset

We used a personalized CWI dataset annotated by 15 learners of English as a foreign language (Ehara et al., 2010). Each learner rated their knowledge of 12,000 English words on a five-point scale. Following Ehara et al. (2014), we collapsed these five categories into either "complex" (score 1 through 4) or "non-complex" (score 5). For analysis purposes, we define the seven more advanced students as "high-proficiency", and the remaining students as "low-proficiency".

A disadvantage of this dataset is that it does not situate the target words in sentences. As a result, it is not possible to evaluate an in-context CWI model in this study. We decided to use this dataset because of its scale and wide representation: no other existing personalized CWI dataset approaches its size, with over 180K annotations by language learners spanning a wide range of proficiency levels.

5.3 Personalized rankings

We personalized the substitution candidate rankings in the PPDB Set (Section 5.1) for each of the 15 users in the personalized CWI dataset (Section 5.2), as follows:

- We excluded target words that are not present in the CWI dataset;

- We excluded target words that are annotated as non-complex for the user, since simplification is not needed;

- We removed substitution candidates from the ranked list if they are annotated as complex for the user, since they are not acceptable LS output for that user. For example, since User B does not understand the word "progressive" (Table 1), it is removed from his list and his optimal substitution becomes "relaxed".

Hence, each target word has 15 different personalized rankings of substitution candidates, derived from the original similarity ranking in the PPDB Set. These personalized rankings serves as the gold answer (Table 2c).

After these processing steps, our final dataset contains an average of 64.5 instances of word simplification for each of the 15 users; each target word has an average of 22.1 substitution candidates.

6 Evaluation metrics

Since the proposed algorithm aims to optimize the trade-off between word complexity and semantic faithfulness, we need to define metrics for both of these qualities.

6.1 Word complexity

We use the standard metric, Precision, to measure the simplicity of the output text.[3] Precision is defined as the ratio of correct simplifications out of all simplifications made by an LS system (Horn et al., 2014; Glavaš and Štajner, 2015). All candidates in the personalized ranking, without regard to its semantic faithfulness, are considered "correct". Thus, the higher the precision, the lower the word complexity of the output, i.e., fewer words are complex for the user.

We will rename Precision as Precision_{all} for reasons to be described in the next subsection.

---

[3] Another standard metric, accuracy, is defined as the ratio of correct simplifications out of all target words that should be simplified (Horn et al., 2014; Glavaš and Štajner, 2015) Since we are concerned only with Substitution Ranking, the system attempts to simplify all complex words. Therefore, accuracy is always the same as precision in our experiments.

6.2 Semantic faithfulness

It is not straightforward to draw a line on what suffices as a semantically "similar" substitution, or to specify the minimum level of semantic faithfulness. Extending the definition of Precision, we introduce the metric $\textbf{Precision}_r$ to express the degree of semantic similarity between the target word and its substitution, where the parameter r specifies the maximum position in the personalized ranking for the candidate to be considered "correct". More specifically, Precision_r is the percentage of substitutions made by the system that are ranked r or above. The larger the value of r, the less strict the metric is on semantic faithfulness.

As an illustration, consider User A in Table 2c. The $\textbf{Precision}_1$ metric (i.e., $r = 1$) counts as correct only the first-ranked substitution in the gold ranking, i.e., "progressive". In contrast, the $\textbf{Precision}_2$ metric (i.e., $r = 2$) counts both "progressive" and "relaxed" as correct.

In this context, then, the standard definition of Precision (Section 6.1) can be viewed as Precision_r where r is allowed to be any value. For clarity, we will refer to Precision as $\textbf{Precision}_{all}$ in the rest of this paper.

7 Experimental set-up

This section describes the experimental design to evaluate the two-step Substitution Ranking approach proposed in Section 4.

7.1 Ranking methods

In the first step, our proposed approach performs similarity ranking on the candidates:

Similarity Ranking (Automatic) We ranked the substitution candidates according to path similarity between the candidates and the target word using WordNet 3.0. The path similarity score denotes how similar two words are based on the shortest path that connects them. WordNet synsets have been found to be more coarse-grained, but consistent with lexical substitute sets (Kremer et al., 2014).

Similarity Ranking (Gold) This is derived from the gold similarity rankings in the PPDB Set (Section 5.1). This ceiling establishes the maximum performance of the proposed approach.

Our baseline ranks candidates with respect to simplicity, which is the prevalent approach in current LS systems:

Simplicity Ranking (Gold) We could not use the human judgement on simplicity collected during the construction of Simple PPDB (Pavlick and Callison-Burch, 2016), since it was performed on a set of word pairs that do not overlap with the gold similarity rankings in the PPDB Set. Instead, we derived the gold simplicity ranking from the personalization dataset (Section 5.2) by averaging the 15 subjects' annotations on each word.

Simplicity Ranking (Automatic) We ranked the substitution candidates according to their gold scores in the probabilistic track of the 2018 CWI shared task (Yimam and Biemann, 2018). The score is defined as the proportion of annotators who marked the word as "complex". The use of CWI gold scores, rather than an actual system output, ensured a strong baseline for comparison against our proposed approach.

7.2 CWI filtering methods

In the second step, the proposed approach uses a personalized CWI model to remove complex words from the ranked list. If all candidates are predicted to be complex, the first-ranked candidate is proposed as the substitution.

Gold Personalized CWI (Gold PCWI) This ceiling establishes the maximum performance of the proposed approach, by looking up the actual CWI annotation for each user (Section 5.2). In other words, the system can perfectly predict whether a particular user knows a particular word.

Automatic Personalized CWI (Auto PCWI) This model automatically predicts a word as complex or non-complex, based on graded vocabulary lists. We initially created four word lists with the 6,777 words covered by the New General Service List (NGSL).[4] Further, we split them into 222 groups of 25 words each, by sorting the words within each list according to frequency in the Google Web Trillion Word Corpus (Brants and Franz, 2006). Next, we constructed 222 CWI models corresponding to these groups: each model predicts the words in its group and the preceding ones to be "non-complex", and all other words to be "complex".

We then randomly selected 50 words as the training set.[5] For each user, we computed the precision and recall of each of the 222 CWI models on this training set, and then selected the model with the highest F-score.

Our baselines for CWI filtering are as follows[6]:

No CWI This baseline predicts all words to be non-complex; in other words, the system always returns the top-ranked candidate as output.

Generic CWI This baseline optimizes its prediction on the learner dataset (Section 5.2); in other words, it predicts a word to be complex if and only if a majority of the 15 users annotated it to be so. This baseline establishes the maximum performance of the generic, or user-independent CWI approach.

8 Experiments

We performed two experiments on the Substitution Ranking approach proposed in Section 4.

8.1 Results with gold similarity ranking

In this first experiment, the system used the gold similarity ranking and performed automatic CWI filtering only. This set-up is designed to provide a controlled contrast between similarity ranking and simplicity ranking by excluding noise from automatic semantic analysis. In the remainder of this subsection, please refer to the results in Table 3.

Word complexity. We first consider the Precision_{all} results. When assuming perfect prediction of users' vocabulary knowledge (Filtering="Gold PCWI"), all simplifications were by definition non-complex, resulting in 100% precision for both ranking methods.

With automatic prediction of the users' vocabulary knowledge (Filtering="Auto PCWI"), the use of similarity ranking led to more complex words

---

[4]The composition of these four lists followed the specifications in Lee and Yeung (2018).

[5]In actual deployment, this set-up means that each user would be required to annotate 50 words.

[6]We did not evaluate the model proposed by Ehara et al. (2014) since we were not able to get access to its system output.

Metric	Precision$_1$		Precision$_2$		Precision$_{all}$	
Ranking →	Gold Simplicity (Baseline)	Gold Similarity (Proposed)	Gold Simplicity (Baseline)	Gold Similarity (Proposed)	Gold Simplicity (Baseline)	Gold Similarity (Proposed)
↓ Filtering						
No CWI	17.74%	**30.08%** * (+12.34%)	37.53%	**72.44%** * (+34.91%)	**92.95%** *	72.44% (-20.51%)
Generic CWI	27.61%	**81.94%** * (+54.33%)	40.22%	**85.81%** * (45.59%)	**99.41%** *	87.00% (-12.41%)
Gold PCWI	28.13%	**100%** * (+71.87%)	40.74%	**100%** * (+59.26%)	100%	100% (same)
Auto PCWI	26.48%	**77.79%** * (+51.31%)	39.43%	**86.38%** * (+46.95%)	**99.00%** *	90.70% (-8.30%)
- low only	28.12%	**74.97%** * (+46.85%)	40.26%	**84.43%** * (+44.17%)	**98.43%** *	86.83% (-11.60%)
- high only	24.62%	**81.00%** * (+56.38%)	38.47%	**88.62%** * (+50.15%)	**99.65%** *	95.13% (-4.52%)

Table 3: LS performance using gold ranking and various CWI filtering methods on the dataset in Section 5.3. An asterisk means the improvement over the other ranking is significant ($p < 0.05$ by McNemar's test).

(-8.30% Precision$_{all}$) than simplicity ranking. The degradation is also observed for "No CWI" and "Generic CWI". This is because similarity ranking prioritizes semantically closer synonyms, which tend to be more difficult and therefore more likely to produce a complex output in the face of CWI error. In contrast, by always aiming for the simplest words, simplicity ranking reduced the chance of producing complex words in the output.

Semantic faithfulness. We next consider results with the Precision$_r$ metric. With perfect prediction of users' vocabulary knowledge (Filtering="Gold PCWI"), gold similarity ranking by definition chose the best non-complex synonym, hence achieving perfect semantic scores. In contrast, gold simplicity ranking rarely picked the best synonym (28.13% at Precision$_1$), and most of the time did not pick either of the top two synonyms (40.74% at Precision$_2$).

With automatic prediction of vocabulary knowledge (Filtering="Auto PCWI"), even gold similarity ranking was liable to selecting complex candidates. Its performance degraded to 77.79% for Precision$_1$, and 86.38% for Precision$_2$. It still outperformed gold simplicity ranking by large margins, with an absolute improvement of +51.31% for Precision$_1$ and +46.95% for Precision$_2$.

Impact of language proficiency. We now examine how language proficiency affects LS performance, using results obtained with automatic prediction of vocabulary knowledge (Filtering="Auto PCWI"). Overall, the similarity ranking method led to a 51.31% gain in semantic faithfulness (in terms of Precision$_1$), at the expense of a 8.3% increase in word complexity (i.e., a 8.3% loss in terms of Precision$_{all}$).

In terms of semantic faithfulness, high-proficiency users (as defined in Section 5.2) experienced a gain of 56.38% in Precision$_1$ (Fil-

tering="Auto PCWI - high only"), compared to a gain of only 46.85% for low-proficiency users (Filtering="Auto PCWI - low only"). This is because a larger vocabulary pool resulted in more instances where a non-complex and better synonym was available. The trend was similar for Precision$_2$, though the absolute gains were smaller for both groups of users.

In terms of word complexity, our proposed method also led to a smaller increase in unknown words for high-proficiency users than low-proficiency users. The former experienced a loss of 4.52% in Precision$_{all}$ (Filtering="Auto PCWI - high only"), while the latter suffered a loss of 11.60% (Filtering="Auto PCWI - low only"). This is because similarity ranking, being more aggressive in utilizing more difficult words, is less likely to produce a complex word for a higher-proficiency user.

Thus, generally speaking, the higher the users' language proficiency, the more they benefited from the proposed method. For more proficient users, the LS output shows increasing gain in semantic faithfulness and diminishing degradation in word complexity.

8.2 Fully automatic ranking

The second experiment adopted the realistic setting, with the system performing automatic processing for both steps in Substitution Ranking. Overall, results followed the same trends as observed in Section 8.1, but with lower performance in all settings. In the remainder of this subsection, please refer to the results in Table 4.

Word complexity. We first consider the results in Precision$_{all}$. Given perfect prediction of users' vocabulary knowledge (Filtering="Gold PCWI"), all simplifications were non-complex, resulting in 100% precision for both ranking methods.

For the same reasons as laid out in the previ-

Metric	$Precision_1$		$Precision_2$		$Precision_{all}$	
Ranking →	Automatic Simplicity	Automatic Similarity	Automatic Simplicity	Automatic Similarity	Automatic Simplicity	Automatic Similarity
↓ Filtering	(Baseline)	(Proposed)	(Baseline)	(Proposed)	(Baseline)	(Proposed)
No CWI	**22.92%**	22.13% (-0.79%)	**39.22%***	37.87% (-1.35%)	**90.21%***	77.71% (-12.50%)
Generic CWI	25.43%	**27.91%** (+2.48%)	37.26%	**46.15%*** (+8.89%)	**94.41%***	86.75% (-7.66%)
Gold PCWI	28.30%	**34.48%*** (+6.18%)	41.14%	**57.03%*** (+15.89%)	100%	100% (same)
Auto PCWI	25.09%	**34.47%*** (+9.38%)	36.63%	**50.79%*** (+14.16%)	**94.11%***	91.54% (-2.57%)
- low only	24.11%	**29.53%*** (+5.42%)	34.96%	**46.41%*** (+11.45%)	**91.78%***	86.96% (-4.82%)
- high only	26.21%	**40.10%*** (+13.89%)	38.54%	**55.79%*** (+17.25%)	96.77%	96.77% (same)

Table 4: LS performance using automatic ranking and various CWI filtering methods on the dataset in Section 5.3. An asterisk means the improvement over the other ranking is significant ($p < 0.05$ by McNemar's test).

ous experiment, when using automatic predictions of vocabulary knowledge, similarity ranking produced more complex words than simplicity ranking. The noise in ranking, however, reduced the performance gap between them. Similarity ranking trailed simplicity ranking by only -2.57% (Filtering="Auto PCWI"), compared to -8.30% in the first experiment in Table 3.

Semantic faithfulness. As can be expected, the use of automatic similarity ranking in this experiment led to a substantial drop in semantic faithfulness. With gold vocabulary knowledge prediction (Filtering="Gold PCWI"), the proposed method yielded 34.48% for $Precision_1$ and 57.03% for $Precision_2$. Even though similarity ranking was performed with a simple WordNet-based method, it still significantly outperformed a strong baseline of simplicity ranking; the absolute improvement was +6.18% for $Precision_1$ and +15.89% for $Precision_2$. When using automatic vocabulary knowledge prediction (Filtering="Auto PCWI"), performance degraded for both ranking methods, but similarity ranking continued to significantly outperform simplicity. It secured an absolute improvement of +9.38% for $Precision_1$ and +14.16% for $Precision_2$.

Impact of language proficiency. As seen from the results obtained with automatic prediction of vocabulary knowledge (Filtering="Auto PCWI"), the effect of language proficiency is similar to the trend observed in the first experiment. Overall, the similarity ranking method led to a +9.38% gain in semantic faithfulness (in terms of $Precision_1$), at the cost of a 2.57% increase in word complexity (i.e., a 2.57% loss in $Precision_{all}$).

In terms of semantic faithfulness, high-proficiency users (as defined in Section 5.2) experienced a gain of 13.89% in $Precision_1$ (Filtering="Auto PCWI - high only"), compared to a gain of only 5.42% for low-proficiency users (Fil-

tering="Auto PCWI - low only"). This gap also held for $Precision_2$.

In terms of word complexity, similarity ranking caused no degradation in $Precision_{all}$ for high-proficiency users (Filtering="Auto PCWI - high only"), but a 4.82% loss for low-proficiency users (Filtering="Auto PCWI - low only").

Thus, the overall impact of language proficiency remained the same with automatic ranking. Similar to the first experiment, the higher the users' language proficiency, the more they benefited from the proposed method. More advanced users generally experienced larger gains in semantic faithfulness, with a relatively small trade-off in word complexity. Both the gain and degradation are however smaller in magnitude.

9 Conclusion

We have proposed a novel, two-step Substitution Ranking algorithm that optimizes the trade-off between semantic faithfulness and word complexity for the lexical simplification (LS) task, by selecting the non-complex candidate that is the closest synonym to the target word. Experiments suggest that this algorithm leads to significantly enhanced semantic faithfulness in the LS system output, at the price of a relatively small increase in word complexity. For higher-proficiency users, this approach is especially beneficial because their larger vocabulary makes it more likely that the system can select a high-quality synonym that is more difficult but still known to them.

Acknowledgment

This work was partially supported by the Innovation and Technology Fund (Ref: ITS/132/15) of the Innovation and Technology Commission, the Government of the Hong Kong Special Administrative Region; and by the CityU Internal Funds for External Grant Schemes (#9678104).

References

Mahmoud Azab, Chris Hokamp, and Rada Mihalcea. 2015. Using Word Semantics To Assist English as a Second Language Learners. In *Proc. HLT-NAACL: Demonstrations*.

J. De Belder and M. F. Moens. 2010. Text Simplification for Children. In *Proc. SIGIR Workshop on Accessible Search Systems*.

Joachim Bingel, Gustavo H. Paetzold, and Anders Søgaard. 2018. Lexi: A Tool of Adaptive, Personalized Text Simplification. In *Proc. COLING*.

Thorsten Brants and Alex Franz. 2006. The google web 1t 5-gram corpus version 1.1. In *LDC2006T13*.

John Carroll, Guido Minnen, Darren Pearce, Yvonne Canning, Siobhan Devlin, and John Tait. 1999. Simplifying Text for Language-Impaired Readers. In *Proc. 9th EACL*.

Siobhan Devlin and John Tait. 1998. The Use of a Psycholinguistic Database in the Simplification of Text for Aphasic Readers. *Linguistic Databases*, pages 161–173.

Yo Ehara, Yusuke Miyao, Hidekazu Oiwa, Issei Sato, and Hiroshi Nakagawa. 2014. Formalizing Word Sampling for Vocabulary Prediction as Graph-based Active Learning. In *Proc. Conference on Empirical Methods in Natural Language Processing (EMNLP)*.

Yo Ehara, Issei Sato, Hidekazu Oiwa, and Hiroshi Nakagawa. 2012. Mining words in the minds of second language learners: learner-specific word difficulty. In *Proc. International Conference on Computational Linguistics (COLING)*.

Yo Ehara, Nobuyuki Shimizu, Takashi Ninomiya, and Hiroshi Nakagawa. 2010. Personalized Reading Support for Second-Language Web Documents by Collective Intelligence. In *Proc. 15th International Conference on Intelligent User Interfaces*, pages 51–60.

Noemie Elhadad. 2006. Comprehending technical texts: Predicting and defining unfamiliar terms. In *AMIA annual symposium proceedings*, volume 2006, page 239. American Medical Informatics Association.

Goran Glavaš and Sanja Štajner. 2015. Simplifying Lexical Simplification: Do We Need Simplified Corpora? In *Proc. ACL*.

Colby Horn, Cathryn Manduca, and David Kauchak. 2014. Learning a Lexical Simplifier Using Wikipedia. In *Proc. ACL*.

Tomoyuki Kajiwara, Hiroshi Matsumoto, and Kazuhide Yamamoto. 2013. Selecting Proper Lexical Paraphrase for Children. In *Proc. 25th Conference on Computational Linguistics and Speech Processing (ROCLING)*, pages 59–73.

Gerhard Kremer, Katrin Erk, Sebastian Padó, and Stefan Thater. 2014. What Substitutes Tell Us – Analysis of an "All-Words" Lexical Substitution Corpus. In *Proc. EACL*.

John Lee and Chak Yan Yeung. 2018. Personalizing Lexical Simplification. In *Proc. International Conference on Computational Linguistics (COLING)*.

Anne-Laure Ligozat, Anne Garcia-Fernandez, Cyril Grouin, and Delphine Bernhard. 2012. Annlor: A Naive Notation-System for Lexical Outputs Ranking. In *Proc. 6th International Workshop on Semantic Evaluation*.

Diana McCarthy and Roberto Navigli. 2009. The English Lexical Substitution Task. *Language Resources and Evaluation*, 43:139–159.

Gustavo H. Paetzold and Lucia Specia. 2015. LEXenstein: A Framework for Lexical Simplification. In *Proc. ACL-IJCNLP System Demonstrations*.

Gustavo H. Paetzold and Lucia Specia. 2016a. Anita: An Intelligent Text Adaptation Tool. In *Proc. COLING: System Demonstrations*.

Gustavo H. Paetzold and Lucia Specia. 2016b. Benchmarking Lexical Simplification Systems. In *Proc. LREC*.

Gustavo H. Paetzold and Lucia Specia. 2016c. SemEval 2016 Task 11: Complex Word Identification. In *Proc. 10th International Workshop on Semantic Evaluation (SemEval-2016)*.

Ellie Pavlick and Chris Callison-Burch. 2016. Simple PPDB: A Paraphrase Database for Simplification. In *Proc. ACL*.

Ellie Pavlick, Pushpendre Rastogi, Juri Ganitkevitch, Benjamin Van Durme, and Chris Callison-Burch. 2015. PPDB 2.0: Better Paraphrase Ranking, Fine-grained Entailment Relations, Word Embeddings, and Style Classification. In *Proc. ACL*.

Sarah E. Petersen and Mari Ostendorf. 2007. Text Simplification for Language Learners: A Corpus Analysis. In *Proc. SlaTE*.

Luz Rello, Ricardo Baeza-Yates, Stefan Bott, and Horacio Saggion. 2013. Simplify or Help? Text Simplification Strategies for People with Dyslexia. In *Proc. 10th International Cross-Disciplinary Conference on Web Accessibility*.

Matthew Shardlow. 2014. Out in the Open: Finding and Categorising Errors in the Lexical Simplification Pipeline. In *Proc. LREC*.

Ravi Sinha and Rada Mihalcea. 2014. Explorations in Lexical Sample and All-words Lexical Substitution. *Natural Language Engineering*, 20(1):99–129.

Wei Xu, Chris Callison-Burch, and Courtney Napoles. 2015. Problems in Current Text Simplification Research: New Data Can Help. *Transactions of the Association for Computational Linguistics*, 3:283–297.

Seid Muhie Yimam and Chris Biemann. 2018. Par4Sim — Adaptive Paraphrasing for Text Simplification. In *Proc. COLING*.

Seid Muhie Yimam, Sanja Stajner, Martin Riedl, and Chris Biemann. 2017. Multilingual and Cross-Lingual Complex Word Identification. In *Proc. Recent Advances in Natural Language Processing (RANLP)*.

Qing Zeng, Eunjung Kim, Jon Crowell, and Tony Tse. 2005. A Text Corpora-based Estimation of the Familiarity of Health Terminology. In *ISBMDA 2005, LNBI 3745*, pages 184–192.

Revisiting the Binary Linearization Technique for Surface Realization

Yevgeniy Puzikov[1], Claire Gardent[2], Ido Dagan[3], Iryna Gurevych[1]

[1] Ubiquitous Knowledge Processing Lab (UKP-TUDA) and Research Training Group AIPHES,
Department of Computer Science, Technische Universität Darmstadt, Germany
[2] CNRS / LORIA Nancy, France
[3] Department of Computer Science, Bar-Ilan University, Ramat-Gan, Israel
https://www.ukp.tu-darmstadt.de
gardent@loria.fr
dagan@cs.biu.ac.il

Abstract

End-to-end neural approaches have achieved state-of-the-art performance in many natural language processing (NLP) tasks. Yet, they often lack transparency of the underlying decision-making process, hindering error analysis and certain model improvements. In this work, we revisit the binary linearization approach to surface realization, which exhibits more interpretable behavior, but was falling short in terms of prediction accuracy. We show how enriching the training data to better capture word order constraints almost doubles the performance of the system. We further demonstrate that encoding both local and global prediction contexts yields another considerable performance boost. With the proposed modifications, the system which ranked low in the latest shared task on multilingual surface realization now achieves best results in five out of ten languages, while being on par with the state-of-the-art approaches in others. [1]

1 Introduction

Natural Language Generation (NLG) is the task of generating natural language utterances from various data representations. In this work we consider lemmatized dependency trees as input and focus on the process of transforming a dependency tree into a linearly-ordered grammatical string of morphologically inflected words – the setup which is most commonly known as surface realization (SR) (Langkilde-Geary, 2002; Belz et al., 2011).

Most surface realization approaches fall into two main groups: feature-based incremental generation pipelines and end-to-end neural approaches. To predict a correct token sequence, the former methods start with an empty hypothesis and extend it by ranking possible continuation candidates. These systems use manually-crafted feature sets and lack a principled way of incorporating global context. Neural models, on the other hand, usually encode the whole input to pass the information to the decoder which then generates the output sequence. The two main limitations of these approaches are their reliance on large amounts of training data and less interpretable behavior compared to feature-based methods.

This work builds upon BINLIN, a binary linearization technique proposed by Puzikov and Gurevych (2018). It is a hybrid approach which uses a feature-based neural word ordering module and a sequence-to-sequence morphological inflection component. In terms of prediction accuracy, BINLIN falls short compared to end-to-end neural approaches, but has an advantage of being more intuitive and interpretable. It also supports separate analysis of the syntactic ordering and morphological inflection steps of the surface linearization process. From a research perspective, this offers greater control over the problem-solving procedure.

In this work we extend BINLIN along two orthogonal directions. First, we propose a way to enrich the training data, which largely compensates for the small size of the datasets used in the task. Second, we propose a new input encoding strategy which incorporates both local and global prediction contexts. These modifications bridge the performance gap between BINLIN and end-to-end black-box approaches, while retaining its interpretability advantages.

---

[1] https://github.com/UKPLab/
inlg2019-revisiting-binlin

Proceedings of The 12th International Conference on Natural Language Generation, pages 268–278,
Tokyo, Japan, 28 Oct - 1 Nov, 2019. ©2019 Association for Computational Linguistics

Data split	Language									
	ar	cs	en	es	fi	fr	it	nl	pt	ru
Train	6,016	66,485	12,375	14,289	12,030	14,529	12,796	12,318	8,325	48,119
Dev	897	9,016	1,978	1,651	1,336	1,473	562	720	559	6,441
Test	676	9,876	2,061	1,719	1,525	416	480	685	476	6,366

Table 1: Number of sentences in SR'18 datasets (Mille et al., 2018).

2 Task Description

The NLP community organized two Surface Realization Shared Tasks (in 2011 and 2018) which aimed at developing a common representation that could be used by a variety of NLG systems as input (Belz et al., 2011). They used almost identical task definitions, but different datasets. We focus on the latest task (SR'18 (Mille et al., 2018)), because the former was confined to using English data only, while the latter included Arabic, Czech, Dutch, English, Finnish, French, Italian, Portuguese, Russian and Spanish Universal Dependencies (UD, version 2.0) treebanks. [2]

SR'18 offered two different input data representations:

Shallow Track: unordered dependency trees consisting of lemmatized nodes with part-of-speech (POS) tags and morphological information, as found in the UD annotations.

Deep Track: same as above, but having functional words and morphological features removed and syntactic edge labels mapped into predicate-argument semantic relation labels.

We focus on the Shallow Track, because it covers more languages than the Deep Track (only three), and is therefore more interesting to study the problem of word ordering and morphological inflection as two steps of the surface realization process. The task can be considered as operating under low-resource scenario: Table 1 shows that the treebanks are rather small, which poses a challenge for training complex neural models.

3 Related Work

The two best-performing approaches in the task of generating sentences from dependency trees have been feature-based incremental text generation (Bohnet et al., 2010; Liu et al., 2015; Puduppully et al., 2016; King and White, 2018) and

techniques performing more global input-output mapping (Castro Ferreira et al., 2018; Elder and Hokamp, 2018). The former approaches traverse the input tree, encode nodes using sparse manually defined feature sets as input representations and generate a sentence by extending a candidate hypothesis with an input word that has the highest score among other input words that have not yet been processed. These approaches rely on the observation that natural language production has a preference for shorter dependencies (Gibson, 2000; White and Rajkumar, 2012; King and White, 2018), which facilitates building sentences incrementally.

The second approach linearizes an input graph structure and treats the resulting sequence as the source string and the corresponding sentence as the target. Since the introduction of encoder-decoder (Cho et al., 2014) and sequence-to-sequence (seq2seq) (Sutskever et al., 2014) neural architectures, this line of work has gained a lot of popularity due to the method's simplicity: the input string is encoded into a dense vector and a sentence is being generated token-by-token from the encoded input representation. From an NLP perspective, one of the main research problems in this paradigm has become the choice of the graph encoding strategy. The most popular method is linearizing it into a sequence of tokens and encoding using a variant of a recurrent neural network (RNN) (Gardent et al., 2017; Castro Ferreira et al., 2017; Konstas et al., 2017). Another prominent approach is using graph-to-text neural networks (Song et al., 2018; Trisedya et al., 2018). These methods have shown good results across various tasks, but in the context of surface realization they produced somewhat mixed results: the former ones were successfully used only when being trained on large amounts of data (Elder and Hokamp, 2018), while the latter ones have been only evaluated on the SR'11 Deep Track data and, while performing better than RNN-type encoders, fell short behind feature-based methods (Marcheg-

---

[2] http://universaldependencies.org/

Property	Approaches	
	Neural	Feature-based
Data efficiency	✗	✓
Rich context representation	✓	✗
Interpretability	✗	✓
Language coverage	✓	✗

Table 2: High-level comparison of the two most prominent approaches to surface realization.

giani and Perez-Beltrachini, 2018).

Each of these approaches has their advantages and limitations (Table 2). Feature-based systems employ carefully crafted feature templates created using expert knowledge, which makes these approaches more interpretable and data efficient, but difficult to port to other domains or languages. The expressiveness of data representation in these systems is largely determined by the complexity of the feature set, which is another limitation of feature-based approaches. These systems are rather slow to train, since feature extraction is defined over a dynamically changing context.

Deep learning, on the other hand, offers a unified language-agnostic framework to train accurate models when abundant training data is available; they are also fast to train (although hyperparameter tuning routines can take a significant amount of time). However, neural models are less interpretable than their sparse-feature counterparts. Also, low-resource scenario still poses a great challenge to complex neural models. The ADAPT system that achieved the best results in SR'18 task on English data (Elder and Hokamp, 2018) used a data augmentation technique which allowed it to leverage 50 times more data than originally provided by the organizers of the workshop. The authors identified the lack of sufficient training data as the major obstacle to training high-performing neural models and mentioned that the system trained only on the original dataset failed to deliver sensible outputs. These results are supported by the work done in other NLP fields. For example, in the machine translation community researchers have found that neural models have a much slower learning curve with respect to the amount of training data, which usually manifests itself as worse quality in low-resource settings, but better performance in high-resource cases (Koehn and Knowles, 2017). In morphological inflection, when trained on small datasets, seq2seq models with additional external (noisy) alignments perform much better than similar systems which learn the alignment information from scratch (Aharoni and Goldberg, 2017).

The success of the encoder-decoder paradigm has given birth to a prominent research trend of finding various ways of utilizing the abundant data on the web. While looking for ways to acquire more data for training even larger models is a promising research topic, an orthogonal direction is pursuing the question of how to design and train more data-efficient models. Our work focuses on this latter point and attempts to address it via data analysis and algorithm design. Taking this into consideration, we build upon the work done by Puzikov and Gurevych (2018), and attempt to improve their method based on the results of our error analysis.

4 Approach Description

Before explaining our work, we briefly recap how BINLIN works. It is a pipeline system which generates a sentence from a dependency tree in two stages:

1. Syntactic ordering: convert dependency tree into a binary tree, then traverse the latter to obtain a sequence of lemmas.

2. Morphological inflection: conjugate each lemma into a surface form.

Figure 1 shows a schematic view of the first stage. It relies on the procedure which first runs a breadth-first search (BFS) algorithm on the input dependency tree to obtain *(head, children)* node groups, corresponding to subtrees of depth one. The head of each subtree is used to initialize a binary tree. Then a binary classifier is used to make decisions of positioning the child nodes to the right/left of the head node. Once all the children have been inserted, the construction of a binary tree for the subtree under consideration is finished and the algorithm moves on to the next subtree.

BINLIN uses a multi-layer perceptron model with a logistic regression function on top to predict the probability of node n_j being positioned to the right ($y = 1$) or left ($y = 0$) of node n_i in a binary tree:

$$p(y = 1) = g([\mathbf{x}_i; \mathbf{x}_j]; \theta) = \frac{1}{1 + e^{\theta \cdot [\mathbf{x}_i; \mathbf{x}_j]}} \quad (1)$$

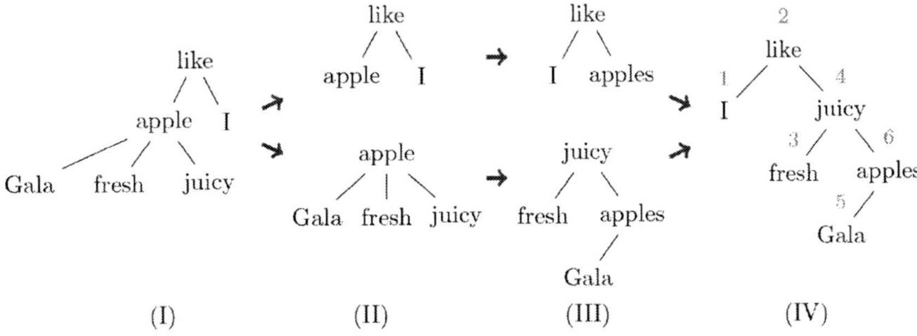

Figure 1: High-level overview of the BINLIN algorithm. Decompose the dependency tree (1) into subtrees of depth one (2), then convert subtrees into equivalent binary trees (3), and merge them. In-order traversal of the merged binary tree (4) produces a sequence of lemmas "I like fresh juicy Gala apple".

Here, $\mathbf{x}_i$ and $\mathbf{x}_j$ are feature representations of n_i and n_j, and θ denotes parameters of the neural network. The decision-making rule is defined by setting a threshold on the output of $g(\cdot)$:

$$
decision = \begin{cases} \text{right,} & \text{if } p(y = 1) \geq 0.5, \\ \text{left,} & \text{otherwise.} \end{cases}
$$

The algorithm converts local subtrees into binary trees in a bottom-up manner until it reaches the root node. At this point, all dependency nodes have been processed. The constructed local binary trees are merged and the resultant binary tree can be linearized by in-order traversal. Finally, a morphological inflection component, applying a character-level seq2seq model with a hard attention mechanism (Aharoni and Goldberg, 2017), is used to predict a surface form for each lemma in the sequence.

The error analysis of the system outputs provided in (Puzikov and Gurevych, 2018) has shown that the majority of BINLIN's mistakes are caused by the incorrect ordering of lemmas, which is why we focus on the syntactic ordering component and leave the morphological inflection module the same as in the original system.

We argue that there are several directions by which BINLIN could be improved: the way the training data is created and the input encoding schema. In what follows we describe the changes that we made to the original system; the corresponding performance improvements are reported in Section 5.

4.1 Modification 1: Training Data Preparation

The first modification we made was improving the way training data for the binary classifier is created. When making training examples, the BINLIN system considers (n_i, n_j) node pairs extracted from subtrees of depth one. For example, in the case of the "I like apple" subtree from Figure 1, one of the training examples the system would add is ("like", "I", *left*), since the word "I" in the sentence is positioned to the left of its head "like".

This procedure seems to be based on the assumption that the system learns position-invariant word order representations, i.e., if the system learns that node n_j should be positioned to the right of n_i, it will also be able to deduce that n_i should be inserted to the left of n_j. However, it is known that neural networks in general do not have this reasoning ability, and to circumvent this issue, researchers use various data augmentation techniques. For example, in the image processing domain it is common to create additional training images through random rotation, shifts, shear and flips, etc.

In a similar fashion, we propose to enrich the training set with training examples which we call "symmetric": for each $(n_i, n_j, label)$ triple originally considered by BINLIN, we add (n_j, n_i, op_label) with node positions flipped and having the opposite label. Reusing our previous example: in addition to ("like", "I", *left*), we would add the ("I", "like", *right*) triple to the training set. We run this procedure on all training examples, which effectively doubles the size of the training data.

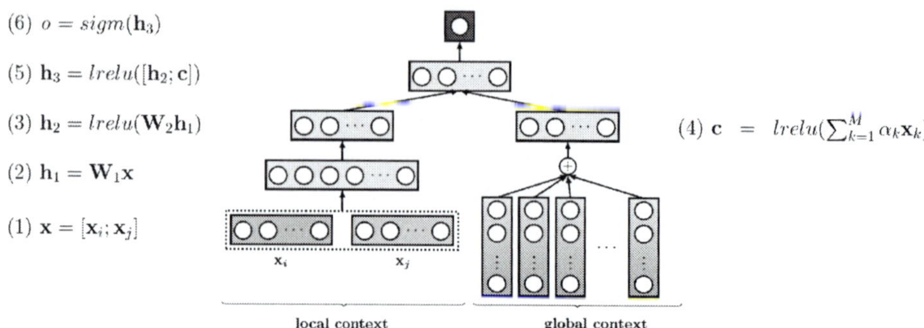

Figure 2: Schematic view of the neural network architecture used as a classifier for the syntactic ordering component of our system.

4.2 Modification 2: Encoding Strategy

Figure 2 shows the schematic view of the employed binary classifier; the original BINLIN system would consider the part marked as *local context*, while the remaining *global context* part is our proposed enhancement.

Given a pair of nodes (n_i, n_j), we first need to extract their features. BINLIN uses a local feature representation of each node, which includes the node itself and graph context in the close proximity – its head and an immediate child. Formally speaking, each node n_k is represented as a vector $\mathbf{x}_k \in \mathbb{R}^{Fd}$, where F denotes the number of extracted features and d is the embedding size. In other words, each dense node representation $\mathbf{x}_k$ is a concatenation of the embeddings for each feature in the feature set F. The embedding matrix is denoted as $\mathbf{E} \in \mathbb{R}^{d \times |V|}$, where V is the vocabulary of unique lemmas, POS tags and dependency edge labels, observed in the training data.

The extracted dense feature representations $\mathbf{x}_i$ and $\mathbf{x}_j$ for the two nodes are (1) concatenated to form the input to the classifier, (2) projected onto a lower-dimensional space via a linear transformation, (3) squeezed further via another linear transformation followed by applying the Leaky ReLu function (Maas et al., 2013). The last layer of the BINLIN classifier consists of one node, followed by the sigmoid function.

As mentioned in the previous subsection, in some cases knowing a wider context is crucial for making the correct decision. We decided to enrich the feature representation with a *global context* which encodes all the nodes in the subtree under consideration. We compute it as (4) a weighted sum of the feature representations of these nodes, similar to the attention mechanism of Bahdanau et al. (2015).

We also experimented with the feature set trying to figure out what provides a stronger supervision signal for the binary classifier. The best feature configuration is the same as in the original system with the exception of two additional node features: the number of the node's children and the length of the path from the node to the root of the dependency tree.

5 Experiments

The official SR'18 data preserved one-to-one correspondence between sentences and dependency trees, but the alignment between lemmas and surface word forms was omitted, which complicated extracting training data pairs.

Following BINLIN's authors, we used the original UD data files for training all our models (the files contain the same dependency trees as the shared task data, but the order of the tokens is not scrambled and each surface form is aligned with the respective lemma). For a fair comparison with other approaches, system evaluation was done using the official SR'18 data. We used English UD treebank for system development, the evaluation was done on all ten treebanks.

All neural network components were implemented using PyTorch (Paszke et al., 2017). No pretrained embedding vectors or other external resources were used for the experiments. The exact hyper-parameter values for each system component are provided in Appendix A.1.

The syntactic and morphological components were trained separately using the Adam (Kingma and Ba, 2015) optimizer with a learning rate of 0.001. We used a batch size of 600 for the syn-

		Language									
		ar	cs	en	es	fi	fr	it	nl	pt	ru
Left/right labels (%)		32/68	57/43	62/38	56/44	57/43	57/43	57/43	61/39	56/44	47/53
Node pair	head-dep	96.27	90.26	96.14	92.67	89.21	95.14	94.26	91.51	97.29	92.85
	dep-dep	82.81	82.78	87.64	83.85	81.43	85.12	84.98	82.52	85.6	85.56

Table 3: The distribution of left/right labels in the training data and the accuracy of predicting a node's relative position with the binary classifier. Two cases are considered: predicting the position of a dependent w.r.t. its head (*head-dep*), and a sibling (*dep-dep*).

	BLEU	EDIST	NIST
BINLIN	24.92	35.91	9.55
+ data enrichment	48.47	62.04	10.72
+ new encoder	50.67	64.05	10.82
+ new features	51.15	64.78	10.82
Upper bound	65.31	85.52	11.38

Table 4: Cumulative improvements from the modifications to the syntactic ordering procedure that we propose in this work, computed on the English portion of the SR'18 development set.

tactic component and 200 for the morphological component. Both modules were trained for a fixed number of epochs (ten for the syntactic component and 15 for the morphological one).

Since we left the morphological module intact, in Section 5.1 we report evaluation results only for the syntactic ordering component.

5.1 Syntactic Ordering

Before evaluating the syntactic ordering module, we conducted a preliminary study in which we tried to validate the dependency locality hypothesis and answer the following question: *Is it possible to accurately predict the relative position of a dependent with respect to its head?*

Table 3 shows the distribution of left/right target labels in the training data and the accuracy of predicting the node's relative position with our system's binary classifier (all proposed modifications applied), both for head-dependent and dependent-dependent node pairs. The latter pairs are relations between sibling nodes in the respective subtree, since at each prediction step the system operates on dependency subtrees of depth one. Note that modeling such relations is a harder task, since siblings in dependency trees do not directly share any grammatical information. However, the surrounding context seems to be enough to make high-accuracy predictions, which supports the depen-

dency locality hypothesis.

We trained the syntactic ordering component and performed its automatic metric evaluation by computing BLEU (Papineni et al., 2002)[3], NIST (Doddington, 2002) and normalized string edit distance (EDIST) scores between the references and system outputs. Note that system outputs contain ordered lemmas, not surface forms, while the references are correctly ordered sequences of inflected surface forms given in the CONLL file.

Table 4 shows the contribution of each of the modifications that we propose in this work; the results are computed on the English SR'18 development set. We also show the maximum metric scores that an ideal syntactic ordering component would get, i.e. an upper bound on its performance. We computed it by retrieving oracle lemma sequences and computing metric scores against the corresponding references. This evaluation was done on English data only, since it was used for system development.

5.2 Full Pipeline

We further add the morphological inflection component and evaluate the full pipeline on the SR'18 test data. Table 5 shows the metric scores achieved by the best SR'18 systems (OSU (King and White, 2018) and TILBURG (Castro Ferreira et al., 2018)), BINLIN and the version of BINLIN with the proposed modifications (BINLIN+). We excluded the scores achieved by the ADAPT system, since the system was only evaluated when trained with additional data and such a comparison would not be fair. In order to better assess the performance gains that we obtained from the proposed modifications, the syntactic ordering component of BINLIN+ was trained ten times with different random seeds; we report both the mean scores and standard deviation.

---

[3]Following the SR protocol, we use the smoothed version and report results using 4-grams (BLEU-4).

Metric	System	Language									
		ar	cs	en	es	fi	fr	it	nl	pt	ru
BLEU	OSU	25.65	–	**66.33**	**65.31**	**37.52**	38.24	–	25.52	–	–
	TILBURG	–	–	55.29	49.47	–	**52.03**	**44.46**	32.28	30.82	–
	BINLIN	18.20	23.03	13.00	31.15	20.96	20.60	27.66	23.60	24.50	34.34
	BINLIN+	**29.07 ± 0.20**	**54.49 ± 0.26**	64.70 ± 0.76	63.86 ± 0.50	37.38 ± 0.59	43.40 ± 1.33	41.17 ± 0.51	**50.28 ± 0.53**	**49.01 ± 0.60**	**62.88 ± 0.36**
NIST	OSU	7.15	–	12.02	**12.74**	9.56	8.0	–	7.33	–	–
	TILBURG	–	–	10.85	11.11	–	**9.85**	**9.11**	8.04	7.55	–
	BINLIN	6.94	10.74	9.53	10.19	9.34	7.21	7.6	8.63	7.52	13.05
	BINLIN+	**7.53 ± 0.01**	**13.65 ± 0.03**	**12.03 ± 0.05**	12.59 ± 0.03	**9.83 ± 0.06**	8.78 ± 0.11	8.63 ± 0.03	**10.30 ± 0.02**	**9.21 ± 0.05**	**14.43 ± 0.02**
EDIST	OSU	34.37	–	**68.59**	**59.75**	47.99	44.84	–	34.22	–	–
	TILBURG	–	–	60.32	48.47	–	**51.16**	46.67	37.20	40.75	–
	BINLIN	18.03	24.30	36.83	27.55	28.53	23.41	27.66	26.32	32.50	31.77
	BINLIN+	**38.11 ± 0.60**	**54.00 ± 0.34**	66.77 ± 0.77	59.00 ± 0.46	**49.58 ± 0.65**	45.17 ± 1.10	**48.50 ± 0.86**	**52.50 ± 0.65**	**59.70 ± 0.78**	**62.80 ± 0.54**

Table 5: Final results computed on the SR'18 test data. BINLIN+ results include mean scores and standard deviation (scores averaged across ten models trained with different random seed values). Cells with dashes denote cases for which the respective systems have not submitted any output in the shared task.

As can be seen from the table, our modifications bridge the gap between the top-scoring systems and BINLIN. BINLIN+ is the best-performing system for five out of ten languages.

6 Error Analysis

In order to better understand the most common errors made by the BINLIN+ system, we manually examined its predictions on the development set. We were focusing predominantly on the syntactic ordering component in its best configuration (i.e. with all the proposed modifications). In what follows we describe the most prominent error types.

Punctuation. Generally speaking, the position of punctuation marks is determined not by a specific dependency relation, but rather by discourse-level characteristics of the sentence, since their primary goal is to help the reader interpret text by means of delimiting the contents, dividing it into easy-to-process pieces. Oftentimes there are lexical markers ("so", "because", "although") which signal that, for example, a comma should be inserted before or after a phrase:

- I like chocolate, *because* it is sweet.

- Bryan, you're in, *right*?

However, in UD annotation punctuation marks are considered as dependents of the subtree root. The binary classifier fails to encode discourse information, since it mainly looks for local patterns in head-dependent relations. A more global technique of input encoding might alleviate this issue.

Contractions. Spanish, Czech, French, Portuguese, Arabic and Italian treebanks contain annotation of multi-word expressions (MWE). Table 6 shows the number of unique MWE encountered in the training portion of the UD treebanks.

Language					
ar	pt	it	es	cs	fr
3010	447	361	300	18	12

Table 6: Number of multi-word expressions (MWE) in UD treebanks for the languages included in the SR'18 task (only languages with MWE are shown).

The most common case marked as MWE in the UD treebanks is that of contractions which occur when two adjacent words are merged into one. For example, in French the article "les" contracts with the preposition "à" into a compound article "aux". English UD annotation does not contain contractions, which is why when developing BINLIN+ we did not encounter this issue.

Our system predicts the relative position of the contraction elements and attempts to conjugate them separately, but does not perform token merging. The following is an example of a contraction in French:

- Un autel à Jupiter est érigé à l'emplacement <u>de le</u> Temple.

- Un autel à Jupiter est érigé à l'emplacement <u>du</u> Temple.

The first line is what BINLIN+ would predict; the second is what the correct output should be. We suspect that this is the main reason for the performance gap that exists between BINLIN+ and the best-performing approaches on Spanish, French and Italian data.

A possible remedy to this limitation could be modeling syntactic ordering and morphological inflection jointly, but this exploration is out-of-scope for this work. As a quick fix, we added a

Metric	System	Language		
		cs	fr	it
BLEU	BinLin+	54.50	43.90	40.84
	- w/ MWE	**54.78**	**49.26**	**52.11**
NIST	BinLin+	13.63	8.85	8.61
	- w/ MWE	**13.67**	**9.46**	**9.78**
EDIST	BinLin+	54.00	46.20	47.57
	- w/ MWE	**54.07**	**49.45**	**53.25**

Table 7: The result of adding a post-processing step of merging MWE tokens for Czech, French and Italian SR'18 test data.

post-processing step to the outputs of our system [4], whereby we stitch adjacent contraction items into one token. We focused on Czech, French and Italian treebanks, since these languages have very simple contraction cases which we extracted without any knowledge of the respective grammar rules (see Appendix A.2).

Table 7 shows an improvement over all three languages, which suggests that this is indeed a promising direction to investigate in detail, and a more principled treatment of contractions would boost the performance of the system even further.

7 Limitations and Future Work

The proposed modifications increase the performance of the baseline BINLIN system significantly, closing the performance gap relative to the state-of-the-art methods to surface realization. Unlike feature-based approaches, the system does not require exhaustive enumeration of the feature templates and is much faster to train. On top of that, it follows a human-designed algorithm, relying on a neural model only to make binary classification decisions which are more transparent than the inner workings of end-to-end neural models. This offers an additional benefit of interpretability and easier debugging. Unlike seq2seq models that occasionally hallucinate content or generate incomprehensible outputs, our system remains faithful to its inputs, since it builds outputs by rearranging input elements and conjugating them.

However, the approach has its limitations. We outline them below and plan to address them in the future.

Zero-Markov assumption. The system does not rely on its past predictions when making a cur-

rent decision. This is a simplifying assumption that sped up system development, but at this point it is a constraint that limits the approach's potential.

Formalism specificity. Unlike seq2seq models which can process any input, the approach works only on tree inputs. When changing the input structure one would have to come up with a new graph-to-tree conversion technique. One reassuring fact is that as of now the annotation consistency of available meaning representations is rather low (considering inter-annotator agreement scores), which means that text-based representations like dependencies is the best option one could hope to use in real-life applications.

Dependent-dependent classification bottleneck. As can be seen from Table 3, ordering children nodes in a dependency tree is a much harder task, compared to deciding on the position of a child node w.r.t. its head. Most likely this is due to the fact that dependency annotation is not sufficient to make a correct decision, while predicting the order between children nodes might be easier if we change the optimization objective. The masked language modeling approach used in (Liu et al., 2015; King and White, 2018) is very promising in this regard and we plan to investigate it in the future.

8 Conclusion

In this work we extended the binary linearization technique for generating sentences from dependency trees. The modifications are motivated by the results of the error analysis of the baseline system and, when applied, significantly improve its accuracy. The resultant system reaches competitive performance in a multilingual setting, while preserving more interpretable behavior and higher data efficiency than the competitors.

Acknowledgments

This work was supported by the German Research Foundation through the German-Israeli Project Cooperation (DIP, grant DA 1600/1-1 and grant GU 798/17-1) and the DFG-funded research training group "Adaptive Preparation of Information form Heterogeneous Sources" (AIPHES, GRK 1994/1). The first author of the paper is supported by the FAZIT Foundation scholarship and the German Federal Ministry of Education and Research (BMBF) as part of the Software Campus program

---

[4]For the syntactic component that we trained with ten different random seeds, we chose one variant randomly.

under the promotional reference 01IS17050.

We thank Henry Elder and Anastasia Shimorina for the insightful discussions and our colleagues Michael Bugert, Yang Gao, Ji-Ung Lee and Jonas Pfeiffer who provided suggestions that greatly assisted our research.

References

Roee Aharoni and Yoav Goldberg. 2017. Morphological Inflection Generation with Hard Monotonic Attention. In *Proceedings of the 55th Annual Meeting of the Association for Computational Linguistics (Volume 1: Long Papers)*, pages 2004–2015, Vancouver, Canada.

Dzmitry Bahdanau, Kyunghyun Cho, and Yoshua Bengio. 2015. Neural machine translation by jointly learning to align and translate. In *Proceedings of the 3rd International Conference on Learning Representations (ICLR 2015)*, San Diego, CA, USA.

Anja Belz, Mike White, Dominic Espinosa, Eric Kow, Deirdre Hogan, and Amanda Stent. 2011. The First Surface Realisation Shared Task: Overview and Evaluation Results. In *Proceedings of the Generation Challenges Session at the 13th European Workshop on Natural Language Generation*, pages 217–226, Nancy, France.

Bernd Bohnet, Leo Wanner, Simon Mille, and Alicia Burga. 2010. Broad Coverage Multilingual Deep Sentence Generation with a Stochastic Multilevel Realizer. In *Proceedings of the 23rd International Conference on Computational Linguistics*, pages 98–106, Beijing, China.

Thiago Castro Ferreira, Iacer Calixto, Sander Wubben, and Emiel Krahmer. 2017. Linguistic realisation as machine translation: Comparing different MT models for AMR-to-text generation. In *Proceedings of the 10th International Conference on Natural Language Generation*, pages 1–10, Santiago de Compostela, Spain.

Thiago Castro Ferreira, Sander Wubben, and Emiel Krahmer. 2018. Surface realization shared task 2018 (SR18): The Tilburg university approach. In *Proceedings of the First Workshop on Multilingual Surface Realisation*, pages 35–38, Melbourne, Australia.

Kyunghyun Cho, Bart van Merrienboer, Caglar Gulcehre, Dzmitry Bahdanau, Fethi Bougares, Holger Schwenk, and Yoshua Bengio. 2014. Learning Phrase Representations Using RNN Encoder-decoder for Statistical Machine Translation. In *Proceedings of the 2014 Conference on Empirical Methods in Natural Language Processing (EMNLP)*, pages 1724–1734, Doha, Qatar.

George Doddington. 2002. Automatic Evaluation of Machine Translation Quality Using N-gram Co-occurrence Statistics. In *Proceedings of the Second International Conference on Human Language Technology Research*, pages 138–145, San Francisco, CA, USA.

Henry Elder and Chris Hokamp. 2018. Generating high-quality surface realizations using data augmentation and factored sequence models. In *Proceedings of the First Workshop on Multilingual Surface Realisation*, pages 49–53, Melbourne, Australia.

Claire Gardent, Anastasia Shimorina, Shashi Narayan, and Laura Perez-Beltrachini. 2017. The WebNLG challenge: Generating text from RDF data. In *Proceedings of the 10th International Conference on Natural Language Generation*, pages 124–133, Santiago de Compostela, Spain.

Edward Gibson. 2000. The dependency locality theory: a distance-based theory of linguistic complexity. *Image, Language, Brain: Papers from the First Mind Articulation Project Symposium*.

David King and Michael White. 2018. The OSU realizer for SRST '18: Neural sequence-to-sequence inflection and incremental locality-based linearization. In *Proceedings of the First Workshop on Multilingual Surface Realisation*, pages 39–48, Melbourne, Australia.

Diederik Kingma and Jimmy Ba. 2015. Adam: a method for stochastic optimization. In *Proceedings of the International Conference on Learning Representations (ICLR)*, San Diego, USA.

Philipp Koehn and Rebecca Knowles. 2017. Six challenges for neural machine translation. In *Proceedings of the First Workshop on Neural Machine Translation*, pages 28–39, Vancouver.

Ioannis Konstas, Srinivasan Iyer, Mark Yatskar, Yejin Choi, and Luke Zettlemoyer. 2017. Neural AMR: Sequence-to-sequence models for parsing and generation. In *Proceedings of the 55th Annual Meeting of the Association for Computational Linguistics (Volume 1: Long Papers)*, pages 146–157, Vancouver, Canada.

Irene Langkilde-Geary. 2002. An Empirical Verification of Coverage and Correctness for a General-purpose Sentence Generator. In *Proceedings of the 2nd International Natural Language Generation Conference*, pages 17–24, Harriman, New York, USA.

Yijia Liu, Yue Zhang, Wanxiang Che, and Bing Qin. 2015. Transition-based Syntactic Linearization. In *Proceedings of the 2015 Conference of the North American Chapter of the Association for Computational Linguistics: Human Language Technologies*, pages 113–122, Denver, Colorado.

Andrew L. Maas, Awni Y. Hannun, and Andrew Y. Ng. 2013. Rectifier Nonlinearities Improve Neural Network Acoustic Models. In *ICML Workshop on Deep Learning for Audio, Speech and Language Processing*, Atlanta, USA.

Diego Marcheggiani and Laura Perez-Beltrachini. 2018. Deep graph convolutional encoders for structured data to text generation. In *Proceedings of the 11th International Conference on Natural Language Generation*, pages 1–9, Tilburg University, The Netherlands.

Simon Mille, Anja Belz, Bernd Bohnet, Yvette Graham, Emily Pitler, and Leo Wanner. 2018. The first multilingual surface realisation shared task (SR'18): Overview and evaluation results. In *Proceedings of the First Workshop on Multilingual Surface Realisation*, pages 1–12, Melbourne, Australia.

Kishore Papineni, Salim Roukos, Todd Ward, and Wei-Jing Zhu. 2002. BLEU: a Method for Automatic Evaluation of Machine Translation. In *Proceedings of 40th Annual Meeting of the Association for Computational Linguistics*, pages 311–318, Philadelphia, Pennsylvania, USA.

Adam Paszke, Sam Gross, Soumith Chintala, Gregory Chanan, Edward Yang, Zachary DeVito, Zeming Lin, Alban Desmaison, Luca Antiga, and Adam Lerer. 2017. Automatic Differentiation in PyTorch. In *NIPS 2017 Workshop Autodiff*, Long Beach, California, USA.

Ratish Puduppully, Yue Zhang, and Manish Shrivastava. 2016. Transition-based Syntactic Linearization with Lookahead Features. In *Proceedings of the 2016 Conference of the North American Chapter of the Association for Computational Linguistics: Human Language Technologies*, pages 488–493, San Diego, California.

Yevgeniy Puzikov and Iryna Gurevych. 2018. BinLin: A simple method of dependency tree linearization. In *Proceedings of the First Workshop on Multilingual Surface Realisation*, pages 13–28, Melbourne, Australia.

Linfeng Song, Yue Zhang, Zhiguo Wang, and Daniel Gildea. 2018. A graph-to-sequence model for AMR-to-text generation. In *Proceedings of the 56th Annual Meeting of the Association for Computational Linguistics (Volume 1: Long Papers)*, pages 1616–1626, Melbourne, Australia.

Ilya Sutskever, Oriol Vinyals, and Quoc V Le. 2014. Sequence to Sequence Learning with Neural Networks. In Z. Ghahramani, M. Welling, C. Cortes, N. D. Lawrence, and K. Q. Weinberger, editors, *Advances in Neural Information Processing Systems 27*, pages 3104–3112. Curran Associates, Inc.

Bayu Distiawan Trisedya, Jianzhong Qi, Rui Zhang, and Wei Wang. 2018. GTR-LSTM: A triple encoder for sentence generation from RDF data. In *Proceedings of the 56th Annual Meeting of the Association for Computational Linguistics (Volume 1: Long Papers)*, pages 1627–1637, Melbourne, Australia.

Michael White and Rajakrishnan Rajkumar. 2012. Minimal dependency length in realization ranking. In *Proceedings of the 2012 Joint Conference on Empirical Methods in Natural Language Processing and Computational Natural Language Learning*, pages 244–255, Jeju Island, Korea.

A Appendix

A.1 Hyper-parameter Details

We did not perform any hyper-parameter tuning, all values were chosen based on our intuition and what we have observed in the research literature.

Morphological Component. The morphological inflection component was implemented using character-level LSTM networks, a two-layer bidirectional encoder and a one-layer unidirectional decoder with hidden layer sizes of 200. We used 200-dimensional randomly-initialized embeddings.

We did not lowercase the data, maintained a fixed size vocabulary of 250 characters, and for training used only sequences of maximum 30 characters long (both source and target sides).

Syntactic Ordering Component. The syntactic ordering component was implemented using feed-forward networks; the corresponding hidden layer sizes were fixed at 100 and 64 dimensions (weight matrices $\mathbf{W}_1$ and $\mathbf{W}_2$ from Figure 2). We used 200-dimensional randomly initialized word-level case-sensitive embeddings.

A.2 Contraction Rules

The following tables contain the contraction rules
we used as a post processing step described in
Section 6. The rules were created by extracting
lines with contractions in the UD CONLL files and
analyzing the contraction patterns.

à le → au	de lequel → duquel
à les → aux	de lesquels → desquels
à lequel → auquel	de lesquelles → desquelles
à lesquels → auxquels	en les → ès
à lesquelles → auxquelles	vois ci → voici
de le → du	vois là → voilà
de les → des	

Table 8: French contraction rules.

di il → del	a l' → all'
di lo → dello	a le → alle
di la → della	a i → ai
di l' → dell'	a gli → agli
di i → dei	su il → sul
di gli → degli	su la → sulla
di le → delle	su lo → sullo
a il → al	su gli → sugli
a lo → allo	con il → col
a la → alla	con i → coi

Table 9: Italian contraction rules.

aby by → aby	když by → kdyby
Aby by → Aby	Když by → Kdyby

Table 10: Czech contraction rules.

Head-First Linearization with Tree-Structured Representation

Xiang Yu, Agnieszka Falenska, Ngoc Thang Vu, Jonas Kuhn
Institut für Maschinelle Sprachverarbeitung
Universität Stuttgart, Germany
`firstname.lastname@ims.uni-stuttgart.de`

Abstract

We present a dependency tree linearization model with two novel components: (1) a tree-structured encoder based on bidirectional Tree-LSTM that propagates information first bottom-up then top-down, which allows each token to access information from the entire tree; and (2) a linguistically motivated head-first decoder that emphasizes the central role of the head and linearizes the subtree by incrementally attaching the dependents on both sides of the head. With the new encoder and decoder, we reach state-of-the-art performance on the Surface Realization Shared Task 2018 dataset, outperforming not only the shared tasks participants, but also previous state-of-the-art systems (Bohnet et al., 2011; Puduppully et al., 2016). Furthermore, we analyze the power of the tree-structured encoder with a probing task and show that it is able to recognize the topological relation between any pair of tokens in a tree.

1   Introduction

Surface realization is a natural language generation task that searches for the natural linear order of words given an unordered syntax tree. Often, the task is accompanied by predicting word inflection, as in two previous surface realization shared tasks (Belz et al., 2011, 2018). As morphological inflection prediction is in itself a separate task (Cotterell et al., 2016), we mainly focus on the linearization in this paper.

Syntactic linearization has been extensively studied in the literature. Earlier work mostly focuses on grammar-based approaches using different syntactic formalisms (Elhadad and Robin, 1992; Lavoie and Rainbow, 1997; Carroll et al., 1999). Recently, with the increasing availability of annotated treebanks, statistical methods gain popularity (Langkilde and Knight, 1998; Bangalore and Rambow, 2000; Filippova and Strube, 2009).

Among the most successful statistical linearization systems, Bohnet et al. (2010) employ the divide-and-conquer strategy and use beam search to incrementally find the best linearization for each subtree; Liu et al. (2015) propose a transition system akin to dependency parsing that produces a sentence that respects the given tree constraints, which is later improved by Puduppully et al. (2016) with look-ahead features. Both approaches rely on rich feature templates to capture the structural information from the input and score the (partial) output sequence, and use the perceptron to learn the parameters. Both linearizers achieve state-of-the-art performance on the Surface Realization Shared Task 2011 data (Belz et al., 2011) as part of a pipeline or joint system for the full task including deep semantic generation and word inflection (Bohnet et al., 2011; Puduppully et al., 2017). However, to the best of our knowledge, the two linearizers alone have never been directly compared. Also, they have not been tested on the data from the recent shared task (Belz et al., 2018), where they could have served as very strong baselines to put recent developments into context.

Song et al. (2018) are the first to use a neural model for syntactic linearization; they adapt the neural dependency parsing model by Chen and Manning (2014) to predict transitions for linearization, which essentially replaces the perceptron with an MLP for the transition system in Liu et al. (2015). However, their adoption of neural models only takes advantage of the token-level representation such as word embeddings, while the structural information is still not well modeled.

Recently, many neural models are proposed to represent graph structures, cf. Zhou et al. (2018) for an overview. Among them, Tree-LSTM, in particular the Child-Sum variation (Tai et al., 2015), has been proposed to model (unordered)

Proceedings of The 12th International Conference on Natural Language Generation, pages 279–289,
Tokyo, Japan, 28 Oct - 1 Nov, 2019. ©2019 Association for Computational Linguistics

dependency trees. It differs from the sequential LSTM (Hochreiter and Schmidhuber, 1997) in that it aggregates the hidden states of multiple dependents by summation. It is in turn improved by adding the attention mechanism to the hidden states (Zhou et al., 2016), so that each dependent influences the head representation to different degrees. Miwa and Bansal (2016) propose a bidirectional extension that traverses the tree both bottom-up and top-down to allow the tokens access information from their descendants as well as ancestors. We adopt and combine their proposed models to represent the tree structure in our task, while improving the bidirectional extension by using the output of the bottom-up pass as the input for the top-down pass, so that each token can access information from all other tokens.

In most linearization models, the incremental generation algorithm follows the left-to-right sequential order. However, in the linguistic study, the head position often plays a central role in describing the constraints and optimization of word orders (Gibson, 1998; Liu, 2010; Futrell et al., 2015). In the linearization models that employ left-to-right generation, such word order properties are only implicitly reflected in the features, if at all. Inspired by the above-mentioned study on head-oriented word order constraints, we adopt an improved linearization algorithm, in which we generate the sequence starting from the head and expanding to both directions. The head-first generation order can easily capture the constraints, since it naturally separates the decision into two aspects: (1) which side of the head to append the dependent and (2) which dependent to attach closer to the head, which exactly correspond to the two aspects of the word order constraints, namely (1) the direction of the dependent and (2) the distance of dependent to the head. The algorithm is somewhat similar to He et al. (2009), which also emphasizes the central role of the head by first predicting for each dependent which side of the head it is placed. However, they exhaustively score all permutations, which could be intractable for subtrees with too many dependents, while we use incremental beam-search to guarantee the efficiency.

In this context, our contribution in this work is threefold: (1) we incorporate the tree-based representation to the linearization models; (2) we improve the linearization algorithm with plausible linguistic intuition; and (3) we conduct a compre-

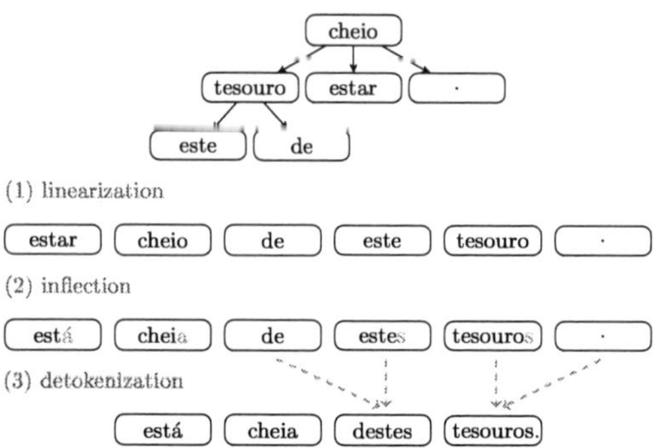

Figure 1: Overview of the pipeline and an example of the process from an unordered dependency tree to the final sentence.

hensive comparison with several strong baselines on the recent multilingual linearization shared task data, and achieve state-of-the-art performance.

2 Model

We use a pipeline system for the surface realization task, consisting of three steps: linearization (§2.1), inflection (§2.2), and detokenization (§2.3).

Figure 1 gives an overview of the pipeline along with an example from the input tree to output text. The input is an unordered dependency tree. We first linearize the tree to obtain an ordered sequence of tokens; then inflect each lemma into the corresponding word form given the morphological information; and finally contract some words into one token and remove the empty space around some punctuation marks, obtaining the output Portuguese text "está cheia destes tesouros." (*it is full of these treasures*).

To encode the tokens with tree-structured information, we use a bidirectional attentive Tree-LSTM model improved upon previous work (§2.1.1). We use a head-first decoding algorithm with beam search to order each subtree (§2.1.2), trained with latent generation order and augmented loss (§2.1.3). For the full surface realization task, we then use a hybrid rule-based and seq2seq model to inflect the word forms (§2.2). Finally, we construct an automaton to contract the tokens and use an off-the-shelf detokenizer to remove extra space in the text (§2.3).

In this paper, we mainly focus on the tree-based representation and the linearization algorithm; the inflection and detokenization models are rather simple, but also reasonably good.

2.1 Linearization

2.1.1 Tree-Structured Encoder

We first encode each individual token in the tree by concatenating the embeddings of the lemma, universal part-of-speech (UPOS) tag, and dependency label, denoted $\mathbf{v}^\circ$. We then encode the tree-level information so that each token is aware of other tokens in the tree.

To propagate the information bottom-up from the dependents to their heads, we use a Child-Sum Tree-LSTM model (Tai et al., 2015) that sums up the hidden states of the dependents and passes them to the head. To differentiate the importance of each dependent, we apply an attention on the hidden states following Zhou et al. (2016). The output of the LSTM is the bottom-up vector for each token, denoted as $\mathbf{v}^\uparrow$.

Following Miwa and Bansal (2016), we apply a top-down pass to propagate information from the head to the dependents. Since each dependent has only one head, unlike the bottom-up pass, we use a standard sequential LSTM to encode the paths from the root to each leaf node. For each node, we feed its bottom-up vector $\mathbf{v}^\uparrow$ into the hidden state of its head to obtain the hidden state for the current node, and the output is the top-down vector $\mathbf{v}^\downarrow$. Miwa and Bansal (2016) perform the two passes independently, i.e., both LSTMs take $\mathbf{v}^\circ$ as input and produce $\mathbf{v}^\uparrow$ and $\mathbf{v}^\downarrow$ as outputs, similar to the standard sequential bidirectional LSTM (Graves and Schmidhuber, 2005). However, two independent passes can not pass the information of all tokens to all other tokens in the tree, since each token only gets information from its ancestors and descendants, it is thus not aware of its siblings, which is crucial for the linearization.

Therefore, our model performs the bottom-up pass first, and uses its output $\mathbf{v}^\uparrow$ as the input for the top-down pass to obtain $\mathbf{v}^\downarrow$. In this way, all tokens in the tree can be accessed by other tokens, since any two tokens have a common ancestor, and the information of one token can be first passed up to the common ancestor, then down to the other token. Figure 2 illustrates the information flow of our bidirectional model, where the red dotted arrows indicate the bottom-up pass, and the blue dashed arrows indicate the top-down pass. We highlight how node 8 influences node 4. Its representation $\mathbf{v}_8^\circ$ is first propagated up to the lowest common ancestor $\mathbf{v}_2^\uparrow$, then goes down to $\mathbf{v}_4^\downarrow$.

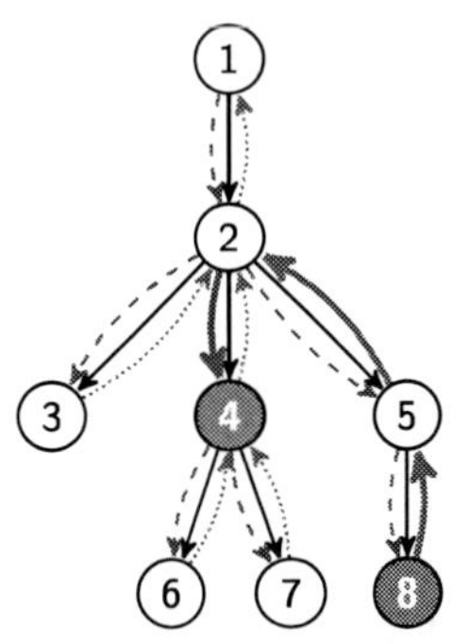

Figure 2: An illustration of the information flow in the encoder, where the red dotted arrows represent the bottom-up pass and the blue dashed arrows represent the top-down pass. The solid arrows illustrate the information flow from node 8 to node 4.

2.1.2 Head-First Decoder

We adopt the general *divide-and-conquer* strategy as in Bohnet et al. (2010), by first linearizing each subtree and then combining the ordered subtrees into a full sentence. Instead of generating the sequences from left to right as in Bohnet et al. (2010), we generate the sequence from inside out, i.e., we initialize the sequence with the head, and expand outwards by appending the dependents to the left or the right end of the sequence.

This new generation order is motivated by the linguistic research on word order constraints, which largely focuses on the relative direction and distance of the dependent to the head (Gibson, 1998; Liu, 2010; Gulordava, 2018).

Following Bohnet et al. (2010), we use beam search to find the best sequence for each subtree incrementally, see the pseudocode in Algorithm 1.

We initialize the agenda with a sequence which contains only the head (line 3-4). A sequence is represented by two LSTMs, both initialized with the head representation, which corresponds to the left expansion and right expansion of the sequence.

At each step, for each sequence in the agenda, we use a pointer network (Vinyals et al., 2015) to calculate the unnormalized attention score between the left LSTM state and all the remaining tokens as the scores of attaching each token to the left (ATTEND$_l$ in line 10[1], where $\mathbf{v}_t$ is the vector representation of the token t), and we do the same for the right (line 14). We then create a new se-

---

[1] We actually calculate all attachment scores in one go, we distribute them in the loop only for readability

quence for each possible attachment (line 9 and 13, where $\oplus$ denotes concatenation), and the score of each new sequence is incremented by the attachment score (line 10 and 14). We also update the corresponding LSTM state of that sequence by adding the representation of the attached dependent as input (line 11 and 15). The new sequences are then added into the agenda for the next step (line 12 and 16).

If the number of new sequences in the new agenda is larger than the beam size, we sort the sequences and keep only the highest scoring ones for further expansion (line 19-20), and we take the highest scoring full sequence as the linearization of the subtree (line 22). Finally, when each subtree is linearized, we combine them into a full sentence as the output (line 24).

Algorithm 1 Head-first linearization

```
1: for all h ∈ T do
2:      T_h = {h} ∪ dependents(h)         ▷ subtree of head h
3:      seq = [h]                          ▷ initial sequence
4:      agenda = [seq]                     ▷ initial agenda
5:      while |seq| < |T_h| do
6:          for all seq ∈ agenda do
7:              beam = []
8:              for all t ∈ T_h \ seq do   ▷ remaining tokens
9:                  seq_l = t ⊕ seq        ▷ attach left
10:                 seq_l.score_l += ATTEND_l(seq.state_l, v_t)
11:                 seq_l.state_l = seq.state_l.addInput(v_t)
12:                 beam.append(seq_l)
13:                 seq_r = seq ⊕ t        ▷ attach right
14:                 seq_r.score_r += ATTEND_r(seq.state_r, v_t)
15:                 seq_r.state_r = seq.state_r.addInput(v_t)
16:                 beam.append(seq_r)
17:             end for
18:         end for
19:         SORTBYSCORE(beam)
20:         agenda = N-BEST(beam, beam-size)
21:     end while
22:     S_h = N-BEST(agenda, 1)            ▷ best sequence for T_h
23: end for
24: S = COMBINESUBTREES(S_1, S_2, ..., S_n)
25: return S
```

We can easily modify the algorithm to left-to-right and right-to-left generation orders. Since the generation only goes in one direction, we only use one LSTM state to score the expansion, and the initial sequence is an empty sequence.

The three different decoders tend to make different mistakes, since they have different starting points and could prune off the correct path in different ways. Therefore it is beneficial to combine the three decoders to vote for the best sequence. Concretely, we first shift the scores of the sequences in each beam so that the minimum score is 0 (implying that the absent sequences have neg-

ative scores), then combine the sequences from the three beams by summing up the scores for identical sequences, and finally choose the highest scoring sequence in the combined beam as output.

2.1.3 Training with Beam Search

The head-first linearization introduces spurious ambiguity, since there may be two correct attachments (on the left or the right end of the sequence) at each step. Enforcing a canonical sequence of attachments would yield suboptimal performance. We view the order of attaching the dependents (i.e. whether to attach left or right dependent first) as latent variables, while the created sequence as the real target. We adopt the training method in Björkelund and Kuhn (2014): at every step after pruning the beam, we check if there is still at least one gold partial sequence in the beam. If not, then we calculate the hinge loss between the highest scoring gold sequence and *all* incorrect sequences in the beam[2].

We also follow the delayed LaSO strategy in Björkelund and Kuhn (2014): after all gold partial sequences fall out of the beam and a loss is incurred, we continue training by putting the gold sequence back into the beam, until reaching the full sequence. This is shown to be more sample efficient than the early-update strategy (Collins and Roark, 2004), since it allows the model to train on the full sequence, even if the gold path falls out of the beam early.

The standard hinge loss updates the gold sequence against the incorrect ones by enforcing a margin (typically 1), which punishes all incorrect sequences equally. However, not all incorrect sequences are equally bad in terms of the BLEU score, therefore, maintaining a larger margin for worse sequences could improve the performance.

We cannot directly use BLEU score as the margin, since it is calculated on the sentence level, while we are training on the subtree level, and the sequences in the training are often incomplete due to early-stop. Therefore, we use the inversion number as the surrogate loss for the BLEU score.

For a partial sequence, we first append the rest of the tokens to both ends of the sequence in the optimal way, then calculate the number of swaps in a bubble-sort to the gold sequence, and

---

[2]Perceptron-based training only updates against the highest scoring incorrect sequences, in contrast, we update against all incorrect sequences, which converged much faster and more stable in the preliminary experiments.

take the squared root as the loss[3]. For example, if we have a predicted partial sequence of $(1, 2, 4, 6, 7)$, and the remaining tokens are $\{3, 5\}$, then we first obtain the best available full sequence $(3, 1, 2, 4, 6, 7, 5)$, then calculate the number of swaps in a bubble-sort, which is 4, and the loss value is thus 2.

2.2 Inflection

We use a simple hybrid approach for the inflection task. We first extract all inflection patterns from the training data: given the combination of lemma, UPOS, and morphological features, if there is a word form appearing more than once and has over 99% certainty, then we keep it as a rule.

For the tokens not covered by the rules, we use a seq2seq model to predict the inflection similar to Kann and Schütze (2016), but with a major difference. Instead of the inflected word, we predict the edit script that modifies the lemma to the word as the output sequence. The alphabet of the edit script includes all the characters in the treebank and three special symbols: ✓ to copy one input character, ✗ to delete one input character, and \$ to finish generation. For example, to inflect the Portuguese verb "falar" to "falando", the output sequence is "✓✓✓✓✗ndo\$". The advantage of predicting edit scripts instead of words is that the copy action avoids the mistake of generating incorrect but similar characters.

The edit script is in a way also similar to Bohnet et al. (2010), but they predict the full edit scripts as one tag, which results in a very large tag set for many morphologically rich languages, and makes it difficult to learn and to generalize.

We use a bidirectional LSTM to encode the characters of the lemma and the morphological tags as a sequence. Each character embedding is concatenated with a binary feature that indicates whether the corresponding input character is currently the target of the edit operation. Initially, the indicator for the first character is set to 1 and the rest are 0. A decoder LSTM with attention is then used to predict the edit operations. The input to the decoder LSTM state is the concatenation of the tree-structured token representation as in §2.1.1, the attended input vector, and the embedding of the last produced character[4]. If the predicted ac-

tion is copy(✓) or delete(✗), the indicator on the input is then advanced by one step, and if the prediction is adding a character, the indicator does not move.

2.3 Detokenization

Since the surface realization shared task is evaluated on the generated text instead of tokens, a detokenization step is needed to compare with other participant systems. We first contract the tokenized words into one token, for example in Portuguese, the preposition "de" and determiner "estes" are contracted into one token "destes" in the text.

We extract the contraction cases from the training set, and construct an automaton to contract the tokens. Concretely, we read the tokens one by one, and when a token matches the initial state of the automaton, we store the token into a buffer and advance the automaton. If it reaches the end state, we replace the tokens in the buffer with the corresponding contracted token, otherwise we add the tokens in the buffer into the output sequence.

The final step is to remove the spaces surrounding certain punctuation marks, e.g., the period at the end of the sentence. We use a rule-based off-the-shelf tool MosesDetokenizer[5], which yields satisfactory results, compared to some other similar alternatives.

3 Experiments

3.1 Data and Baselines

We conduct the experiments on the datasets from the previous Surface Realization Shared Task 2018 (SR18) (Belz et al., 2018), which includes 10 (mostly European) languages from the Universal Dependencies (Nivre et al., 2016).

We compare our system with two state-of-the-art linearization systems Bohnet et al. (2010) and Puduppully et al. (2016), referred to as B10 and P16. We run their linearization systems *as is*, using lemma, UPOS and dependency labels as features. We also use the same features in our system for comparison. To evaluate the linearization step alone, we calculate BLEU score based on lemma.

We also compare to the best performing systems in the SR18, where the final BLEU score is reported on the detokenized text. We execute our

---

[3]Since the complexity of bubble-sort is $O(n^2)$, we make it linear to avoid unstable loss values.

[4]In the case of copy, we use the embedding of the copied character instead of the copy symbol ✓.

[5]https://pypi.org/project/mosestokenizer/

full pipeline of linearization, inflection, and detokenization and evaluate with the official evaluation script. We also apply our inflection and detokenization steps on the predicted linearization of B10 and P16, so that they can also be compared to other systems.

3.2 Implementation Details

Our model is implemented with the DyNet Library (Neubig et al., 2017), and is available at the first author's website[6]. We use the embedding sizes of 64, 32 and 32 for lemma, UPOS and dependency labels, respectively, and the dimension for the token representation is 128. The hidden states of both bottom-up and top-down encoder LSTMs, as well as the decoder LSTMs, have dimension of 128. The decoder beam size is 32. The linearizer is quite efficient among neural models, training a medium sized treebank takes about 2 hours on a single CPU core.

3.3 Linearization

We first compare each step in our pipeline to the available baselines. For linearization, we test our models with the same tree encoding and different decoding orders (left-to-right (L2R), right-to-left (R2L), head-first (H2LR), as well as voting among the three (Vote). The results are shown in Table 1.

Among the two baseline systems, B10 performs more than 4 BLEU points higher than P16, we believe the reason is that the subtree-level beam search in B10 allows it to explore almost all possible permutations for most of the subtrees[7], while P16 directly orders the full sentence, which can only explore a fraction of the full search space even with a very large beam size. Understandably, the P16 model is designed to linearize words with partial or even no syntactic information, therefore the knowledge of subtrees cannot be assumed. However, in the scenario with full syntactic information available, B10 is clearly a better model.

We then compare our model to B10. The L2R linearizer generates the hypothesis in the same way as B10, and it uses a much smaller beam with the size of 32. It achieves 1 BLEU point higher than B10, which demonstrates the advantage of the more expressive tree-based representation.

The H2LR order performs better than L2R and R2L, which could be explained in multiple aspects. One explanation is our motivation that generating from the head could better reflect word order constraints. The other explanation is that training with latent generation order allows the model to make easier decision first, similar to the easy-first parser by Goldberg and Elhadad (2010).

Finally, when combining the three decoders together by voting, it achieves 2 BLEU points higher than B10. There are two main reasons for this improvement: (1) multitask-style training helps regularize the parameters, and (2) different generation directions tend to prune the correct sequences at different locations, and the mistake in one direction might be saved by the other two.

	B10	P16	L2R	R2L	H2LR	Vote
ar	81.78	77.07	82.78	82.48	82.79	83.37
cs	74.74	70.93	73.52	71.89	74.16	75.17
en	82.83	78.80	84.92	83.95	84.01	85.48
es	81.84	74.33	82.82	82.53	82.99	83.69
fi	69.95	63.74	68.69	69.58	70.15	71.08
fr	84.38	81.74	85.04	85.24	85.45	85.66
it	82.60	77.41	83.03	83.28	82.66	84.51
nl	67.82	62.56	71.68	70.54	72.25	72.49
pt	80.46	76.52	81.48	81.13	82.10	81.80
ru	83.40	82.96	85.39	85.51	85.45	87.11
avg	78.98	74.61	79.94	79.61	80.20	81.04

Table 1: Linearization on the development set, where we compare different generation orders (L2R, R2L, H2LR and Voting) with Bohnet et al. (2010) and Puduppully et al. (2016).

3.4 Inflection

Table 2 shows the inflection performance with different models: the first model predicts edit script as a tag (EditTag); the second model predicts the character sequence of the inflected word (CharSeq); the third model predicts the edit scripts as sequences of actions (EditSeq); and the last one uses the same model as the third, but first applies the extracted rules if available (+rule). The results are compared to the reported inflection accuracy in Puzikov and Gurevych (2018) (P18), which is adapted from Aharoni and Goldberg (2017).

Among our first three models, EditTag performs the lowest, mainly because of the very large tag sets in many languages (the sizes vary from around 300 for English to over 10000 for Finnish and Russian), which prevents effective learning and generalization. The CharSeq model performs much

---

[7]They use beam size of 1000, which can cover all possible permutations of up to 6 tokens (6! = 720).

	P18	EditTag	CharSeq	EditSeq	+rule
ar	93.07	88.02	95.57	95.33	95.01
cs	99.53	97.52	97.01	97.98	98.92
en	98.11	98.57	97.95	98.33	98.51
es	99.59	98.11	98.59	99.27	99.47
fi	95.46	82.54	92.16	93.13	95.06
fr	95.56	90.83	95.85	97.39	97.78
it	97.44	92.87	96.84	98.05	98.49
nl	95.68	93.38	94.53	94.57	95.36
pt	99.30	93.05	98.45	98.71	99.22
ru	98.22	94.58	95.86	96.42	97.47
avg	97.20	92.95	96.28	96.92	97.53

Table 2: Inflection on the development set, where we compare our different models with Puzikov and Gurevych (2018): tagging edit scripts (EditTag), generating character sequences (CharSeq), generating edit script sequences (EditSeq), and apply the extracted rules (+rules).

better than the EditTag, especially on the languages with very large edit scripts tag sets. The EditSeq model performs better than the character seq2seq model, mainly because the copy mechanism avoids many noisy generation errors. Some typical mistakes by CharSeq we find in English are "traveling" → "braveling" and "children" → "thildren", where some characters in the input lemma are confused with a similar one. Some typical mistake by the EditSeq are "kidding" → "kiding" and "clashes" → "clashs", where some necessary characters in the output are omitted.

Finally, the combination of the EditSeq model and extracted rules performs the best. On the development sets, the token coverage of the rules ranges from about 60% to 90% for different languages, with over 99% accuracy, which means the majority of the inflection can be produced reliably and efficiently by simply looking up in a dictionary. The hybrid approach even outperforms the very strong baseline, although the seq2seq model alone is slightly weaker than the baseline, we believe this simple trick could also benefit other inflection models.

3.5 Detokenization

As the final step, we evaluate the performance of the detokenization, which includes contracting words and attaching punctuation. We use gold linearization and inflection as the input.

We separate the evaluation into two parts: for contraction, we evaluate the token-based BLEU score against the gold contraction on the UD development set; for the punctuation attachment, we use the gold contracted word and evaluate with the official text-based BLEU score. We also evaluate the combined results where both contraction and detokenization are predicted.

Table 3 shows the results of these four scenarios. The first column contains the results of simply separating all tokens with empty spaces. The BLEU score is around 55 even when the linearization and inflection are all correct, which shows the over-proportionally large impact of the detokenization in the shared task evaluation.

Our detokenizer works reasonably well for most of the languages, except for Arabic, where both contraction and detokenization results are rather poor. We will investigate this issue in the future work, it could potentially be addressed with a edit seq2seq model similar to the inflection task but on the sentence level.

contraction punctuation	None None	Pred Gold	Gold Pred	Pred Pred
ar	39.03	77.77	86.98	65.78
cs	59.85	99.81	97.39	97.38
en	63.71	99.15	91.38	91.38
es	66.97	99.23	99.65	98.95
fi	59.48	99.78	98.39	98.39
fr	51.12	99.92	98.53	98.46
it	44.66	96.96	98.82	95.31
nl	69.29	99.97	99.89	99.89
pt	43.95	96.84	94.35	91.26
ru	49.29	99.94	97.74	97.74
avg	54.74	96.94	96.31	93.45

Table 3: Detokenization on the development set, where the contraction and punctuation steps are gold, predicted, or not used.

3.6 Final Results

We choose the best variant for each step in the pipeline for the full experiment, where we compare with the results from other participants in the shared task, as well as the linearizers of Bohnet et al. (2010) and Puduppully et al. (2016) combined with our inflection and detokenization models as additional baselines for the shared task.

Table 4 shows the performance of the full pipeline on the test sets. B10 and P16 are the linearizers by Bohnet et al. (2010) and Puduppully et al. (2016) combined with our inflection and detokenization model, ST18 are the best results for each language in the shared task (King and White, 2018; Puzikov and Gurevych, 2018; Ferreira et al., 2018; Elder and Hokamp, 2018). The last column contains the results of our system.

It is apparent that both B10 and P16 have higher performance than the other systems by a large margin. The advantage of our linearizer also carries over to the full pipeline, it scores 2 BLEU points higher than the best baseline.

	B10	P16	ST18	Ours
ar	42.50	36.48	25.65	43.68
cs	64.75	58.87	25.05	65.42
en	70.75	65.86	69.14	72.67
es	74.75	56.50	65.31	77.77
fi	56.13	49.68	37.52	56.53
fr	66.62	52.12	52.03	68.75
it	69.09	47.14	44.46	71.98
nl	56.39	50.96	32.28	60.17
pt	66.13	49.34	30.82	66.16
ru	72.40	71.58	34.34	76.10
avg	63.95	53.85	41.66	65.92

Table 4: Final results on the test set, where we compare our model to two baselines (B10 and P16) and the best system in the shared task for each language (ST18).

4   Analysis

4.1   Relation Awareness

Our tree-based representation is theoretically able to propagate information from all other tokens in the tree. We now test whether it can really make use of such information.

We design a probing task to test whether the model can tell the relation between two tokens. Concretely, we pick two random tokens (t_1, t_2) in a tree, and their relation can be described as a tuple (d_1, d_2), which are the distances from t_1 and t_2 to their common ancestor. For example in Figure 2, the relation between token 4 and 8 is $(1, 2)$.

We build a simple MLP on the concatenation of the representations of both tokens to predict the relation as a classification task. To avoid data sparsity, we only predict d_1 and d_2 up to 3, and all relations beyond this distance is classified class "too far". There are in total $4 \times 4 = 16$ classes.

We test the token representations with and without tree encoding in two scenarios: (1) train all parameters which tests whether the encoder architecture is able to learn the relations and (2) only train the MLP which tests whether the parametrized encoder model actually captures such relation.

Table 5 shows the accuracy of the probing task. Clearly, the representation without tree encoding can not correctly classify the relation, its accuracy is higher than chance level because the lexical information allows it to guess to some extent. The

	Token	Tree
MLP	35.70	76.75
All	35.84	90.13

Table 5: Relation classification accuracy of the encoders with only token information (Token) vs. with tree information (Tree).

tree-structured encoder has much higher accuracy than the guessing baseline. Training on all parameters achieves higher accuracy than only training on the MLP, which suggests that the encoder architecture is able to memorize the relation of many tokens, but the linearization task does not actually require that much information.

4.2   Synergy between Encoder and Decoder

Our model uses the bidirectional Tree-LSTM to pass information both bottom-up and top-down. However, it is not yet clear whether having both directions is necessary, and how much it would influence the performance of different decoders.

Table 6 shows the average performance of the four decoders (H2LR, L2R, R2L, and combining all) combined with four possible encoders: both directions (Both), only bottom-up (BU), only top-down (TD), and only token representation without tree information (None).

When no bottom-up pass is performed (TD and None), the performance drops by a large margin, which means that the information about the dependents is very crucial for linearization. In contrast, skipping the top-down pass has much smaller influence on H2LR, while L2R and R2L also only have moderate performance drop.

Interestingly, the drop is much larger for L2R and R2L from only TD to None. The reason would be that L2R and R2L decoders treats each token equally and do not have any indication of the head if no structural information is used, while the H2LR decoder starts with the head and builds the sequence around it based on the head-oriented word order constraints. Therefore, even when there is no structural information, the prior in the H2LR decoder can still make better decisions. This also supports our intuition on the pivotal role of the head in the generation process.

Since skipping one of the passes would hurt the performances of L2R and R2L decoders, and thus also hurt the vote decoder, we use both passes for our final model, although the bottom-up pass alone suffices for the H2LR decoder.

	H2LR	L2R	R2L	Vote
Both	80.20	79.94	79.61	81.04
BU	80.17	79.31	79.47	80.64
TD	74.54	74.30	74.18	75.18
None	74.56	71.26	70.89	75.03

Table 6: Performance of combination of linearization orders and representations on the development set, averaged over 10 treebanks.

5   Conclusion

We present a dependency tree linearization model with tree-structured encoder and head-first decoder, which outperforms the previous state-of-the-art linearizers. Combined with our morphological inflection and detokenization model, it achieves the best performance on the Surface Realization Shared Task 2018 by a substantial margin. We also show that the previous work by Bohnet et al. (2010), which our decoding algorithm is based on, is still a very strong baseline.

As future work, we plan to extend the head-first linearization algorithm to (jointly) generate absent function words from the deep semantic representation. It corresponds to the deep track of the surface realization shared tasks, which is also a more realistic setting for natural language generation.

Acknowledgements

This work was in part supported by funding from the Ministry of Science, Research and the Arts of the State of Baden-Württemberg (MWK), within the CLARIN-D research project.

References

Roee Aharoni and Yoav Goldberg. 2017. Morphological Inflection Generation with Hard Monotonic Attention. In *Proceedings of the 55th Annual Meeting of the Association for Computational Linguistics (Volume 1: Long Papers)*, pages 2004–2015.

Srinivas Bangalore and Owen Rambow. 2000. Exploiting a Probabilistic Hierarchical Model for Generation. In *Proceedings of the 18th conference on Computational linguistics-Volume 1*, pages 42–48. Association for Computational Linguistics.

Anja Belz, Michael White, Dominic Espinosa, Eric Kow, Deirdre Hogan, and Amanda Stent. 2011. The First Surface Realisation Shared Task: Overview and Evaluation Results. In *Proceedings of the 13th European workshop on natural language generation*, pages 217–226. Association for Computational Linguistics.

Anya Belz, Bernd Bohnet, Emily Pitler, Leo Wanner, and Simone Mille. 2018. The First Multilingual Surface Realisation Shared Task (SR'18): Overview and Evaluation Results.

Anders Björkelund and Jonas Kuhn. 2014. Learning Structured Perceptrons for Coreference Resolution with Latent Antecedents and Non-Local Features. In *Proceedings of the 52nd Annual Meeting of the Association for Computational Linguistics (Volume 1: Long Papers)*, volume 1, pages 47–57.

Bernd Bohnet, Simon Mille, Benoît Favre, and Leo Wanner. 2011. StuMaBa: From deep representation to surface. In *Proceedings of the 13th European workshop on natural language generation*, pages 232–235.

Bernd Bohnet, Leo Wanner, Simon Mille, and Alicia Burga. 2010. Broad Coverage Multilingual Deep Sentence Generation with a Stochastic Multi-Level Realizer. In *Proceedings of the 23rd International Conference on Computational Linguistics*, pages 98–106. Association for Computational Linguistics.

John Carroll, Ann Copestake, Dan Flickinger, and Victor Poznanski. 1999. An Efficient Chart Generator for (Semi-) Lexicalist Grammars. In *Proceedings of the 7th European workshop on natural language generation (EWNLG99)*, pages 86–95.

Danqi Chen and Christopher Manning. 2014. A Fast and Accurate Dependency Parser Using Neural Networks. In *Proceedings of the 2014 conference on empirical methods in natural language processing (EMNLP)*, pages 740–750.

Michael Collins and Brian Roark. 2004. Incremental Parsing with the Perceptron Algorithm. In *Proceedings of the 42nd Annual Meeting on Association for Computational Linguistics*, page 111. Association for Computational Linguistics.

Ryan Cotterell, Christo Kirov, John Sylak-Glassman, David Yarowsky, Jason Eisner, and Mans Hulden. 2016. The SIGMORPHON 2016 Shared TaskMorphological Reinflection. In *Proceedings of the 14th SIGMORPHON Workshop on Computational Research in Phonetics, Phonology, and Morphology*, pages 10–22.

Henry Elder and Chris Hokamp. 2018. Generating High-Quality Surface Realizations Using Data Augmentation and Factored Sequence Models. In *Proceedings of the First Workshop on Multilingual Surface Realisation*, pages 49–53.

Michael Elhadad and Jacques Robin. 1992. Controlling Content Realization with Functional Unification Grammars. In *International Workshop on Natural Language Generation*, pages 89–104. Springer.

Thiago Castro Ferreira, Sander Wubben, and Emiel Krahmer. 2018. Surface Realization Shared Task 2018 (SR18): The Tilburg University Approach. In

Proceedings of the First Workshop on Multilingual Surface Realisation, pages 35–38.

Katja Filippova and Michael Strube. 2009. Tree Linearization in English: Improving Language Model Based Approaches. In *Proceedings of Human Language Technologies: The 2009 Annual Conference of the North American Chapter of the Association for Computational Linguistics, Companion Volume: Short Papers*, pages 225–228. Association for Computational Linguistics.

Richard Futrell, Kyle Mahowald, and Edward Gibson. 2015. Quantifying Word Order Freedom in Dependency Corpora. In *Proceedings of the third international conference on dependency linguistics (Depling 2015)*, pages 91–100.

Edward Gibson. 1998. Linguistic Complexity: Locality of Syntactic Dependencies. *Cognition*, 68(1):1–76.

Yoav Goldberg and Michael Elhadad. 2010. An Efficient Algorithm for Easy-First Non-Directional Dependency Parsing. In *Human Language Technologies: The 2010 Annual Conference of the North American Chapter of the Association for Computational Linguistics*, pages 742–750. Association for Computational Linguistics.

Alex Graves and Jürgen Schmidhuber. 2005. Framewise Phoneme Classification with Bidirectional LSTM and other Neural Network Architectures. *Neural networks*, 18(5-6):602–610.

Kristina Gulordava. 2018. *Word Order Variation and Dependency Length Minimisation: A Cross-Linguistic Computational Approach*. Ph.D. thesis, University of Geneva.

Wei He, Haifeng Wang, Yuqing Guo, and Ting Liu. 2009. Dependency Based Chinese Sentence Realization. In *Proceedings of the Joint Conference of the 47th Annual Meeting of the ACL and the 4th International Joint Conference on Natural Language Processing of the AFNLP: Volume 2-Volume 2*, pages 809–816. Association for Computational Linguistics.

Sepp Hochreiter and Jürgen Schmidhuber. 1997. Long Short-Term Memory. *Neural Comput.*, 9(8):1735–1780.

Katharina Kann and Hinrich Schütze. 2016. MED: The LMU system for the SIGMORPHON 2016 shared task on morphological reinflection. In *Proceedings of the 14th SIGMORPHON Workshop on Computational Research in Phonetics, Phonology, and Morphology*, pages 62–70.

David King and Michael White. 2018. The OSU Realizer for SRST '18: Neural Sequence-to-Sequence Inflection and Incremental Locality-Based Linearization. In *Proceedings of the First Workshop on Multilingual Surface Realisation*, pages 39–48.

Irene Langkilde and Kevin Knight. 1998. Generation that Exploits Corpus-based Statistical Knowledge. In *Proceedings of the 36th Annual Meeting of the Association for Computational Linguistics and 17th International Conference on Computational Linguistics-Volume 1*, pages 704–710. Association for Computational Linguistics.

Benoit Lavoie and Owen Rainbow. 1997. A Fast and Portable Realizer for Text Generation Systems. In *Fifth Conference on Applied Natural Language Processing*.

Haitao Liu. 2010. Dependency Direction as a Means of Word-Order Typology: A Method Based on Dependency Treebanks. *Lingua*, 120(6):1567–1578.

Yijia Liu, Yue Zhang, Wanxiang Che, and Bing Qin. 2015. Transition-Based Syntactic Linearization. In *Proceedings of the 2015 Conference of the North American Chapter of the Association for Computational Linguistics: Human Language Technologies*, pages 113–122.

Makoto Miwa and Mohit Bansal. 2016. End-to-End Relation Extraction using LSTMs on Sequences and Tree Structures. In *Proceedings of the 54th Annual Meeting of the Association for Computational Linguistics (Volume 1: Long Papers)*, pages 1105–1116.

Graham Neubig, Chris Dyer, Yoav Goldberg, Austin Matthews, Waleed Ammar, Antonios Anastasopoulos, Miguel Ballesteros, David Chiang, Daniel Clothiaux, Trevor Cohn, et al. 2017. Dynet: The Dynamic Neural Network Toolkit. *arXiv preprint arXiv:1701.03980*.

Joakim Nivre, Marie-Catherine De Marneffe, Filip Ginter, Yoav Goldberg, Jan Hajic, Christopher D Manning, Ryan McDonald, Slav Petrov, Sampo Pyysalo, Natalia Silveira, et al. 2016. Universal Dependencies v1: A Multilingual Treebank Collection. In *Proceedings of the Tenth International Conference on Language Resources and Evaluation (LREC 2016)*, pages 1659–1666.

Ratish Puduppully, Yue Zhang, and Manish Shrivastava. 2016. Transition-based Syntactic Linearization with Lookahead Features. In *Proceedings of the 2016 Conference of the North American Chapter of the Association for Computational Linguistics: Human Language Technologies*, pages 488–493.

Ratish Puduppully, Yue Zhang, and Manish Shrivastava. 2017. Transition-Based Deep Input Linearization. In *Proceedings of the 15th Conference of the European Chapter of the Association for Computational Linguistics: Volume 1, Long Papers*, volume 1, pages 643–654.

Yevgeniy Puzikov and Iryna Gurevych. 2018. BinLin: A Simple Method of Dependency Tree Linearization. In *Proceedings of the First Workshop on Multilingual Surface Realisation*, pages 13–28.

Linfeng Song, Yue Zhang, and Daniel Gildea. 2018. Neural Transition-based Syntactic Linearization. In *Proceedings of the 11th International Conference on Natural Language Generation*, pages 431–440, Tilburg University, The Netherlands. Association for Computational Linguistics.

Kai Sheng Tai, Richard Socher, and Christopher D Manning. 2015. Improved Semantic Representations From Tree-Structured Long Short-Term Memory Networks. In *Proceedings of the 53rd Annual Meeting of the Association for Computational Linguistics and the 7th International Joint Conference on Natural Language Processing (Volume 1: Long Papers)*, volume 1, pages 1556–1566.

Oriol Vinyals, Meire Fortunato, and Navdeep Jaitly. 2015. Pointer Networks. In *Advances in Neural Information Processing Systems*, pages 2692–2700.

Jie Zhou, Ganqu Cui, Zhengyan Zhang, Cheng Yang, Zhiyuan Liu, and Maosong Sun. 2018. Graph Neural Networks: A Review of Methods and Applications. *arXiv preprint arXiv:1812.08434*.

Yao Zhou, Cong Liu, and Yan Pan. 2016. Modelling Sentence Pairs with Tree-structured Attentive Encoder. In *Proceedings of COLING 2016, the 26th International Conference on Computational Linguistics: Technical Papers*, pages 2912–2922.

Let's FACE it. Finnish Poetry Generation with Aesthetics and Framing

Mika Hämäläinen
Department of Digital Humanities
University of Helsinki
mika.hamalainen@helsinki.fi

Khalid Alnajjar
Department of Computer Science (HIIT)
University of Helsinki
khalid.alnajjar@helsinki.fi

Abstract

We present a creative poem generator for the morphologically rich Finnish language. Our method falls into the master-apprentice paradigm, where a computationally creative genetic algorithm teaches a BRNN model to generate poetry. We model several parts of poetic aesthetics in the fitness function of the genetic algorithm, such as sonic features, semantic coherence, imagery and metaphor. Furthermore, we justify the creativity of our method based on the FACE theory on computational creativity and take additional care in evaluating our system by automatic metrics for concepts together with human evaluation for aesthetics, framing and expressions.

1 Introduction

This paper explores the topic of computational creativity in the case of poem generation in Finnish. Our work does not only aim to generate, but rather create poems automatically. We take the FACE model (Colton et al., 2011) for computational creativity as our definition of creativity. Through this model, we motivate and evaluate creativity exhibited by our system.

Methodologically, our work embraces the master-apprentice method (Alnajjar and Hämäläinen, 2018) used in the past for computationally creative tasks. This means using a creative genetic algorithm as a master to teach an apprentice which is sequence-to-sequence neural network model. This way the overall system can approximate creative autonomy (Jennings, 2010) if the apprentice was to be exposed to data originating from another source than the master. For further discussion on the topic of autonomy, see the original work establishing the master-apprentice method.

We pay special attention to evaluation of our system, and we motivate it through the FACE

model. A creative system should be evaluated in terms of what has actually been modelled rather than on an ad-hoc and unjustified fashion. Additionally, our contribution lies on the fact that the aesthetics of our system are motivated by existing non-computational literature in poetry analysis. Furthermore, our system is capable of adjusting its aesthetics based on existing poetry.

Our work sheds some more light into the nature of a master-apprentice system. Especially by seeking to answer the question of multiple masters raised in the original work on the topic (Alnajjar and Hämäläinen, 2018), which the authors left unanswered.

2 Related Work

While poetry generation has been tackled a number of times before by multiple authors (Gervás, 2001; Toivanen et al., 2012; Misztal and Indurkhya, 2014; Oliveira et al., 2017), and an excellent overview is provided by Oliveira (2017) on the recent state of the research, we dedicate this section in describing the most recent work conducted in the field after the aforementioned overview paper.

TwitSong (Lamb and Brown, 2019) mines a corpus for verses to be used in poetry based on how well they rhyme together. They score the verses in poems by four metrics (*meter, emotion, topicality* and *imagery*) and use a genetic algorithm to edit the worst scoring verse in the poem. However, they only assess poems on a verse level and their algorithm lacks poem level metrics (i.e. each verse is considered individually and not as a part of a whole). They base their evaluation on comparing generated poetry of different groups based on how the genetic algorithm was used. They use very broad questions such as *which poem is more creative* or *which poem has better imagery*. This

Proceedings of The 12th International Conference on Natural Language Generation, pages 290–300,
Tokyo, Japan, 28 Oct - 1 Nov, 2019. ©2019 Association for Computational Linguistics

is potentially problematic as broad questions open more room for subjective interpretation.

Last year, a myriad of work on generation of Chinese poetry with machine learning methods was conducted. Research ranging from mutual reinforcement learning (Yi et al., 2018) and conditional variational autoencoders (Li et al., 2018) to sequence-to-sequence Bi-LSTMs (Yang et al., 2018) was presented. However, none of these methods has been motivated from the point of view of computational creativity, but rather serve for a purely generative purpose.

The work conducted by Colton et al. (2012), although not recent, deserves special attention, as they had used the same FACE model as a basis in their poem generation. They take a template based approach to generating poems from current news articles. Unfortunately they do not provide an evaluation of the generated poetry, which makes meaningful comparison difficult.

The work presented by us in this paper has to deal with the rich morphosyntax of Finnish, which is an NLG problem far from solved. Hämäläinen (2018) presents a solution for this problem in their Finnish poem generator. However, their generator relies on predefined rule-based structures, whereas our aim is to have a system with more structural versatility, and yet the capability of coping with the morphosyntax.

3 Creativity

In order to separate our system from generative non-creative systems, we have to provide some justification as to why our system would exhibit creativity in the first place. For this reason, we follow the SPECS approach (Jordanous, 2012) that has been designed to evaluate creativity in a reasoned fashion. The approach requires creativity to be defined first on an abstract level, and then, following the abstract definition, creativity should be defined in the context of the creative task that is to be solved. After establishing these definitions, creativity of the system should then be evaluated based on the definitions.

3.1 Creativity in General

For an abstract level definition of creativity, we use FACE (Colton et al., 2011). The theory divides creative act into two categories, one is the ground level generative act of producing an artefact and the other is on the level of the process. Both of these categories are represented in the four aspects of creativity: framing, aesthetics, concept and expression.

Framing consists of outputting a framing for a creative artefact, and the process that generates this output. The framing should be an explanation in natural language, for instance, putting the created artefact into a historical and cultural context or describing the processes of creating the output artefact. In other words, framing can be used as an additional persuasive or explanatory message that is delivered to the human perceiving the artefact produced by a computational system.

Aesthetics consist of a function measuring the aesthetic quality of the output and/or the program producing it. On the process level, FACE takes into account how the aesthetic measures came to be in the system. The system should be able to assess its own work and rate its creations. This aesthetic measure can also be used to computationally assess artefacts produced by other systems or humans.

Concept is used to refer to the program that generates creative artefacts on the ground level. And on the process level it refers to how such a program was generated. Finally, the ground level expression is the creative output, or artefact, generated by the system, whereas the process level of expression describes the method for generating output for a given input.

3.2 Creativity for Our Poem Generator

As framing can exists in many different forms according to the original FACE model, we follow a more narrowed down notion of framing, which is the intention of the computer in creating artefacts (Charnley et al., 2012). In other words, the computer should be able to output a justification explaining what certain aspects of the poem mean. The importance of framing has recently been highlighted in the literature (Cook et al., 2019).

Framing does not have to be a creative act on its own. In our case, the process of coming up with a framing is a template based approach that conveys the intent of the creative program in producing the output poem. This intent, on the other hand is captured by the aesthetic function of the creative system. Therefore, the framing produced should explain the poem in terms of the aesthetic measures.

Poetry as a genre showcases a wide diversity in

terms of aesthetics; ranging from epic poetry following a strict meter to modern free form poetry. Even to a degree that the poetic genre has become fragmented ever since the 20th century (Juntunen, 2012). This diversity is not just limited to the level of structure, but is also reflected in meaning - some forms of poetry are meant to be read and interpreted literally, where as others rely on indirect communication such as symbolism and metaphors (see Kantokorpi et al., 1990). In our work, we are not aiming to model the poetic genre as a whole, but rather define a set of aesthetic functions that capture different aspects in poetry ranging from the structural to the meaning.

In terms of structure, our system should be able to assess rhyming in its various forms (alliteration, assonance, consonance and full rhymes) and the meter of the poetry as defined by poetic foot and syllable count.

For meaning, our system should be able appreciate the presence of metaphors, the semantic coherence of the words forming the poem and in especial the presence of words forming different semantic fields and the semantic difference of these fields as an indicator of tension built by the choice of words in a poem (cf. Lotman, 1974).

Certain poems paint a mental image in the mind of the reader; this qualia[1] provoking aspect of poetry is called *imagery*. As it is extremely difficult for a computer to assess such rich mental sensory phenomena provoked by poetry in humans, we have to reduce the aesthetics related to imagery to a more computationally manageable level, namely that of sentiment. Sentiments expressed in a poem can be indicators of the potential mood evoked by the sensory imagery in the poem. Another indicator of imagery is the use of concrete expressions (see Burroway, 2007).

Although the list of aesthetic measures is predefined, from the point of view of the process, our system should be able learn to adjust its aesthetic measures based on existing poetry. Furthermore, we aim towards a system that can learn aesthetics of its own on its own level of abstraction, hence the use of apprentice.

In our case, the system consists of two concepts. One of them is a genetic algorithm (master) that has been defined by us, the programmers. The role of the master is to produce expressions through a search informed by the aesthetic functions. These

expression are used to train the second concept, which is a sequence-to-sequence BRNN model (apprentice). This way, the overall system is given the capability of producing new concepts of its own.

The expressions output by the system are computationally created Finnish poems. Ultimately, we evaluate the expressions produced by the apprentice with real humans and by the master's aesthetic measures.

3.3 Data

We use the 6,189 Finnish poems that are available on Wikisources[2] as our poem corpus. We use the Finnish dependency parser (Haverinen et al., 2014) to parse the poems for morphological features, syntactic relations, part of speech and lemma for each word. The parsing is done on a verse-level. We split each poem into stanzas as divided in Wikisources. From now on we refer to a stanza of an existing poem simply as a poem. The reason for this is to have shorter poems to deal with in the generation step. This is especially important for the human evaluation as shorter poems can be evaluated more accurately, as longer poems have more room for unintentional characteristics that can be interpreted too positively by human judges, such as a perceivably deeper meaning that is due to the mere fact of having more context to read more into. After splitting the poems into stanzas, we have a total of 34,988 poems.

We use the word embeddings[3] that have been trained on the Finnish Internet Parsebank (Kanerva et al., 2014). We prefer this model for two reasons: first it has been trained on a 1.5 billion token corpus that is big on the Finnish scale and second it has been trained on lemmas, which is an important factor for a highly agglutinating language such as Finnish. In order to generate grammatical Finnish, the words need to be inflected. This step is easier if the replacement words are already in a lemmatized from.

4   Generating Poetry

The master-apprentice approach outlined in Alnajjar and Hämäläinen (2018) consists of a creative master, which is a genetic algorithm, and an apprentice, which is a sequence-to-sequence model.

---

[1] For more on the problem of qualia, see (Chalmers, 1995)

[2] https://fi.wikisource.org

[3] http://bionlp-www.utu.fi/fin-vector-space-models/fin-word2vec-lemma.bin

In this part of the paper, we describe how the aesthetics are implemented in the master and how it is used to generate poems for the apprentice to learn from.

In this paper, we experiment with two different masters, which will learn the weights for their aesthetic functions form poems of different eras. We use these masters to train one apprentice for each of them. In addition, we train one apprentice, which will learn from both of the masters.

4.1 Master

The master is a genetic algorithm following the implementation presented in Alnajjar et al. (2018). In practice, the algorithm takes in a random poem from the poem corpus and uses it to produce an initial population of 100 individuals. These individuals produce an offspring of another 100 individuals that go through mutation and crossover, and at the end of each generation the individuals are scored according to the aesthetic functions defined later in this section. The 100 fittest individuals are selected with NSGA-II algorithm (Deb et al., 2002) to survive to the next generation. This process is done for 50 generations.

All individuals in the initial population are based on a randomly selected poem and a randomly picked theme word. The theme is expanded into the 30 most semantically similar words to the theme word using word2vec (Mikolov et al., 2013). Each poem in the initial population is assigned a random theme out of the 30 semantically similar words to the theme. Additionally, we modify each poem in the initial population once by using the mutation function. This is applied to have more variety of poems in the initial population given that all of them are based on the same original poem from the corpus.

In mutation, a random content word is picked in the poem and it is replaced by a word related to the input theme (assigned to the poem) or by a word that is similar to the original one, while ensuring that the new replacement matches the original in terms of its part-of-speech. To obtain words that are related to the input theme, we build a semantic relatedness model following Xiao et al. (2016) using the flat 5-gram data provided by Kanerva et al. (2014) as the corpus. Regarding the semantic similarity to the original word, we utilize the word2vec word embeddings model. The space of candidate replacements consists of the top

1,000 and 300 (empirically chosen) semantically related and similar words, respectively. Out of these candidates, only words that match the part-of-speech of the original word, based on Uralic-NLP (Hämäläinen, 2019), are considered in the random selection.

In terms of the crossover, we employ a single-point crossover on a verse-level where one point in both individuals is selected at random and verses to the right of that point are swapped.

As mutations and crossovers are bound to break the morphosyntax of Finnish, the new words are always inflected to match the original morphology with UralicNLP and Omorfi (Pirinen et al., 2017). This will account for morphological agreement, but not for case government. In case government, the case of the complements of the verb depends on the verb itself. For this reason, we inflect words with an object relation with Syntax Maker (Hämäläinen and Rueter, 2018) to produce a grammatical surface form even if the predicate verb is changed.

4.1.1 Aesthetics

To assess the sonic structure of poetry the following rule-based aesthetic functions are defined on an inter-verse level: full rhyme, assonance and consonance. These count the number of rhyming words between verses of the poem. Alliteration is a metric calculated within a verse, as this type of rhyming occurs typically inside of a verse in Finnish poetry. As Finnish spelling is almost one to one mapping with phonology, we can do this on a character level without the need to approximate the pronunciation.

Meter is captured by two aesthetic functions: the number of syllables and the distribution of long and short syllables within a verse. These two functions are again solved by simple rules. The master rates higher the meter it has learned from its training corpus.

A previous attempt to capture imagery in the literature is by comparing the number of abstract and non-abstract words with the hypothesis that non-abstract words provoke more mental imagery (Kao and Jurafsky, 2012). However, this notion can be used only as a proxy to the quantity of imagery in poetry, but it tells nothing about the nature of the provoked imagery. For this reason, we have also decided to use sentiment as an indicator of the mood of the mental image painted by the poem.

For abstractness of words we use an existing

dataset for English that maps 40,000 common English words to an average concreteness score as annotated by humans on a 5-point Likert scale (Brysbaert et al., 2014). We translate this data in Finnish with a Wiktionary based online dictionary[4] in such a way that we consider the three topmost translations that are verbs, nouns or adjectives for each English word. To deal with polysemy, if multiple English words translate into one Finnish word, we take the average of the concreteness values of the English words for the Finnish word. If the concreteness value is greater or equal to 3, the word is considered concrete. The aesthetic function gives a ratio of concrete words over concrete and abstract words in the poem.

For sentiment, due to the lack of resources for Finnish, we use a recent state of the art method (Feng and Wan, 2019) that can learn sentiment prediction for English with annotated data and use the model for other languages by bilingual word embeddings. We train the model with sentiment annotated data for English from the OpeNER project (Agerri et al., 2013). We use their method to map the pretrained Finnish and English fasttext models from Grave et al. (2018) into a common space. This aesthetic measure will score sentiments on verse level and output their variance on the poem level.

Dividing words into semantic fields can be used as an auxiliary tool in poem analysis in literature studies as it can reveal tensions inside of a poem (c.f Lotman, 1974). By following this notion, we cluster the open class part of speech words based on their cosine similarity within a poem. For this clustering, we use affinity propagation (Frey and Dueck, 2007), which takes a similarity matrix as input and clusters the words based on the matrix. The number of clusters is not fixed and affinity propagation is free to divide the words in as many clusters as necessary.

The clustering aesthetic function looks at the number of clusters in a poem and the average semantic distances of the clusters. The distance between two clusters is calculated by counting a centroid for each cluster based on the word vectors of a cluster and then calculating the cosine distance of the centroids of the clusters. The values output by the aesthetic function will set standards to how semantically cohesive the words have to be with each other, and how distant can their meanings be.

Although words in different clusters might be distant *semantically*, they can be related *pragmatically*. Therefore, we want to reveal possible metaphorical interpretations of a given word in the poem. We represent each semantic cluster found in a poem by a single word. In doing so, we compute the centroid vector of words in each cluster and use the nearest word in the model's vocabulary to the centroid as the topic of the cluster. Thereafter, we iterate over all the possible combinations of having a certain topic as a tenor and another as a vehicle and measure the metaphoricity of the poem with respect to them. We measure that using the two metaphoriticy measurements defined by Alnajjar et al. (2018), one for measuring how a word in the poem relates to both concepts and the other for measuring how related a word is to the vehicle but not to the tenor[5]. The metaphoricity value is then represented by the mean of the two measurements in case both had a positive value, otherwise zero is returned. Using the metaphoricity value assigned to each tenor-vehicle combination, we define two metaphoricity aesthetics 1) the maximum metaphoricity value and 2) the number of metaphorical clusters (i.e. combinations where the metaphoricity value is above zero).

As having many objectives is difficult in practice to handle for the NSGA-II algorithm (see Tanigaki et al., 2014), we group the aesthetic functions into four fitness functions. Sonic (rhyme, alliteration, consonance, assonance, foot and syllable count), semantic (number of clusters and average and maximum distance between the clusters), imagerial (concrete word ratio and variance of sentiment) and metaphorical (the maximum score for metaphoricity and the number of metaphorical words) functions represent the four fitness functions used by the genetic algorithm. These fitness functions sum up the individual aesthetic functions when they are used to score a poem.

4.2 Learning the Aesthetics

We divide our corpus into centuries: the 19th and 20th century. We have two masters learn their aesthetics from either century making them specialized in that century in particular. We first learn weights for the individual aesthetic functions within the higher-level fitness function they belong to. We do this by training four random forest classifiers (Breiman, 2001), one for each of the four

---

[4]http://www.sanakirja.org/

[5]See (Richards, 1936) for more on tenor and vehicle

higher level fitness functions. The classifiers get the features produced by the aesthetic functions belonging to the fitness function in question. The classifiers are trained with the entire corpus to predict true for the desired century and false for other centuries.

The trained classifiers are only used for their weights for each individual feature. These weights are used in the genetic algorithm to multiply the output of each aesthetic function adjusting their importance for the century.

As the weights tell only little about the possible values the aesthetic functions can or should have within one century, we calculate a range of accepted values for each aesthetic function within a century. The 25th percentile of the values is set as the minimum boundary of an accepted value and the 75th percentile as the maximum boundary. If the value output by the aesthetic function is outside of this range, the output value is set to 0.

4.2.1 Master's liking

For the evaluation purposes of the apprentices, it is important to set standards to what is good poetry according to the master. The master likes a poem generated by the apprentice if the poem gets a positive value in each one of the four fitness functions. If any of the values is 0, the master is considered not liking the poems.

4.3 Apprentice

Apprentice is a sequence-to-sequence model that learns to produce creatively altered verses out of verses in existing poetry. To achieve this, we use a BRNN model with a copy attention mechanism by using OpenNMT (Klein et al., 2018). We use the default settings which are two layers for encoding and decoding and general global attention (Luong et al., 2015).

One apprentice is trained from the output of each master, and an additional one from the output of both of the masters. We train the apprentices for 90000 steps to produce poems one verse at a time, from the original poem to the master generated ones. The master for the 19th century produced 11903 poems and the 20th century one 11900 poems out of randomly picked initial poems from the entire corpus. These constitute the training data for the apprentices. The random seed used in training is the same for all apprentices to make intercomparison possible.

5 Results and Evaluation

Evaluation is one of the most important and difficult parts of computational creativity, however it is oftentimes overlooked and conducted in an ad-hoc manner with little to do with the actual problem being modelled (Lamb et al., 2018). In practice this means that a great deal of work is evaluated based on questions and metrics that have not been justified. This practice together with the issue expressed by Veale (2016) that people are ready to read more into the output if it has a suitable linguistic structure regardless of the actual underlying creative intent of the system, are things that should not go unnoticed when evaluating a computationally creative system.

> *Mutta hyökkäykset, jotka kestää sain,*
> *muistot, jotka rakkauden estää,*
> *esiin ilmentyy vihaa kasvattain.*
>
> But the attacks I was to endure,
> the memories that prevent love,
> emerge amplifying the ire

Above is an example poem output by the master in Finnish followed by its translation in English. The example is of a typical length of a poem produced by the system as the human authored poems were split into stanzas.

5.1 Concepts

The master as a concept is fixed and can only adjust its appreciation, but the apprentice is an entirely new concept that is created from the output of the master. In this section we evaluate the apprentices by evaluating their output by masters' liking. This is done only in an automatic fashion by having all 3 of the apprentices create output for 100 randomly picked poems from the poem corpus.

	master 1800	master 1900
apprentice 1800	28%	33%
apprentice 1900	36%	39%
apprentice both	47%	51%

Table 1: The percentage of the output of the two masters liked

Table 1 shows how many of the poems produced by the different apprentices the masters liked. It is clear from the results that the apprentices did not do too well in terms of learning the century specific aesthetics. Nevertheless, having both of the centuries in the training boosted the results in terms of the two masters liking the poems. This is probably due to the fact of having more training data available.

5.2 Framing and Aesthetics

In order to make it less likely that people read more into the poems than what is there, we evaluate the poems with people based on the framing produced by the system. The main purpose of this evaluation is not to evaluate how *good* the output poems are, but how often the aesthetic functions agree with human judgment. The framing consists of templates that the system fills based on its aesthetic functions. People are asked whether they agree or disagree with the statements expressed in the framing. In addition, people have the possibility of stating that they don't know whether to agree or disagree.

For the evaluation, we sampled 30 poems at random from the poetry generated by the two masters. We printed each poem 5 times, and we divided each set of 30 unique poems into 3 piles of 10 poems with their framing. Each pile was shuffled so that no pile contained exactly the same poems and no pile had the same order for the poems. The shuffling was done to decrease any potential bias introduced by the order of presentation of the poems.

Initially, we recruited 15 people, each one to go through one pile of 10 poems. However, 5 people found the task too time consuming and stopped after evaluating a few poems. The unevaluated poems from these piles were assigned to completely new reviewers. In the end, each unique poem was evaluated 5 times by different people and no individual evaluator evaluated more than 10 poems.

A framing was generated for each poem. The framing followed always the same structure. The first statements relating to rhyming were presented as questions whereas the rest of them were statements. The statements were formed in the following way (translated from Finnish):

1. Do the words written in italics have rhymes (e.g. **heikko peikko**)?

2. Do the words written in italics have assonance (e.g. **talo sano**)?

3. Do the words written in italics have consonance (e.g. **sakko sokka**)?

4. Does the poem have alliteration within a verse (e.g. **vanha vesi**)?

5. Verse number X and Y have the same meter

6. The poem has X semantic fields: [semantic cluster 1]... and [semantic cluster N]

7. The semantic fields [semantic cluster X] and [semantic cluster Y] are the closest to each other

8. The semantic fields [semantic cluster A] and [semantic cluster B] are the furthest away from each other

9. The following words in the poem [concrete words] are concrete concepts

10. The verse number X is positive

11. The verse number Y is negative

12. The following words in the poem [metaphorical words] can be understood metaphorically

13. The word X has a metaphorical connection to word Y

For the questions on rhyming, the system highlights in italics all the words that have one of the rhyming types. For the meter statement and negative and positive verse statements, random numbers are picked within the range of the length of the poem. For these questions, people agreeing does not produce the highest score, but rather if people's prediction is in line with the prediction of the aesthetic function. Also, if the poem didn't have any metaphorical words, random words were picked for the last two questions. Again, if people disagreed when random words were presented and agreed when actual metaphorical words were presented, the accuracy of the system based on the evaluation would go higher.

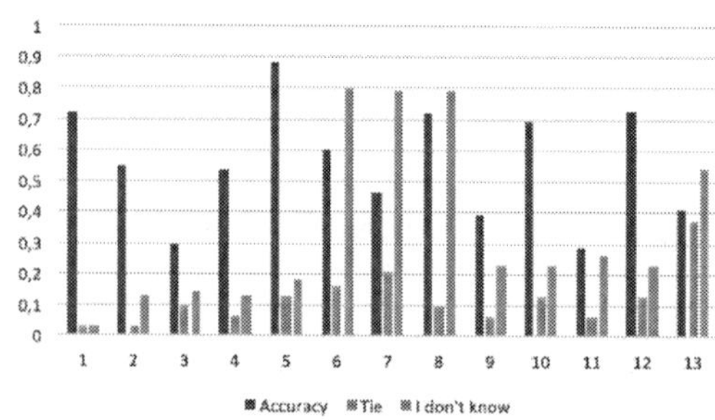

Figure 1: Evaluation results for aesthetics and framing

The accuracy reported in Figure 1 shows how often the prediction (agree/disagree) of the aesthetic functions matches that of the majority of the people out of all the times a majority decision could be reached per poem. The tie shown in the figure shows the percentage of time the statement received an equal number of agreeing and disagreeing opinions from people per poem. The data show by *I don't know* represents the number of times people stated they did not know over all the answers for the statement. Note that this is not calculated per poem but per statement.

The statements related to semantics were the most difficult ones for people to evaluate with around 80% of the time people saying they did not know whether to agree or not. Another difficult statement to judge was the last metaphorical statement including an interpretation for two words being metaphorically connected. This question also included the highest number of ties in people's judgments.

Interestingly, the accuracy was high only for the traditional rhyme types, but lower on the assonance and consonance. Even though our rules can easily and objectively measure the existence of these rhyming types, it is interesting to see that people's judgment deviates from the values output by the aesthetic functions. Especially revealing is the low accuracy on consonance. Our system sees consonance whenever two words have the same consonants in the same positions such as in *jo* (already) and *ja* (and) or *en* (I don't) and *on* (is). Even though these words do exhibit consonance, it seems that people do not find such consonance *perceivable*. This being said, the mere existence of rhyming is not enough, but it should also be perceivable. Just what this perceivability entails is an interesting question left for future research.

For semantics it is difficult to draw any meaningful conclusions as more often than not, people simply did not know whether to agree or not. However, the results do seem promising for the correctness semantic clusters (60 % of the time) and the furthest clusters (72% of the time). At any rate, semantics calls for further qualitative analysis in the future as it seems to be a difficult thing to assess for people.

In the case of imagery, it seems that people agreed on the concreteness 39% of the time, although the score might seem low, it is to remember that all the concrete words were presented as a list in the framing. If even one of the words was not perceived as concrete, people were likely to disagree. Sentiment, on the other hand, resulted in

mixed accuracies; the accuracy for positive sentiment was 69% whereas for negative sentiment the accuracy was 28%. As the sentiment analysis was based on an existing state-of-the-art method, this result is surprising. However, it is very likely the case that negativity in poetry is expressed in a very different way than in other text types. In other words, there is a need for a sentiment annotated corpus consisting of poetry and other literary texts for better predicting the sentiment in poems. All in all, the prediction for concrete words could also benefit from a dataset authored specifically for Finnish.

The accuracy for the metaphorical words was high, 73%. However, the interpretation provided for one of the metaphorical words gave inconclusive results, as people either did not know or had very mixed judgments. This part as well calls for qualitative analysis in the future.

5.3 Expressions

Finally we evaluate the expressions of the master and the apprentice in relation to each other. For this evaluation we treat both of the masters as one, and we evaluate the best apprentice according to the masters' liking. We sample randomly 10 poems from the corpus for which both the master and the apprentice had produced altered poems. We evaluate these poems by asking people which one of the generated poems from the same original one they prefer, that of the master or that of the apprentice. We present the two poems on the same page, shuffling their order for each printout. We also shuffle the order of the poems. We ask 10 people to rate the 20 poems, 10 master generated and 10 apprentice generated ones.

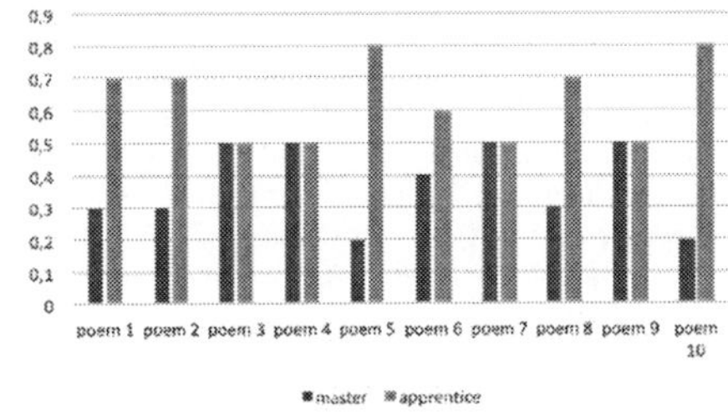

Figure 2: People's preference for each poem

Figure 2 shows the preference of the people per poem. The poetry generated by the apprentice was most often preferred by the judges. The master generated poetry did not reach to a majority in preference for any poem. The interesting question of what happens in the poems that result in a tie in people's preference calls for a future qualitative study to understand better the phenomenon of the evaluation.

6 Conclusions

We have shown our novel method for generating poetry in Finnish. With the help of the FACE model, we were able to conduct evaluation on the aesthetics and framing that was revealing of the shortcomings of our system. Framing made it possible to assess the core functionality better by minimizing the room for people reading more into the poem than what was there. Having the option for people to say that they do not know rather than forcing them to either agree or disagree revealed the difficulty of assessing semantics and metaphors even for people. We propose for the future to conduct evaluation on such high level features of language on a qualitative fashion to better understand how people perceive these in generated poetry.

As a vast majority of the NLP research focuses on English, we had to deal with the practical issue of the scarce annotated resources for Finnish to capture the high level features such as concreteness, sentiment and metaphor. As a result we ended up developing useful resources for the aesthetic functions which we have made publicly available on Github[6].

References

Rodrigo Agerri, Montse Cuadros, Sean Gaines, and German Rigau. 2013. Opener: Open polarity enhanced named entity recognition. *Procesamiento del Lenguaje Natural*, (51).

Khalid Alnajjar, Hadaytullah Hadaytullah, and Hannu Toivonen. 2018. "Talent, Skill and Support." A method for automatic creation of slogans. In *Proceedings of the 9th International Conference on Computational Creativity (ICCC 2018)*, pages 88–95, Salamanca, Spain. Association for Computational Creativity.

Khalid Alnajjar and Mika Hämäläinen. 2018. A master-apprentice approach to automatic creation of culturally satirical movie titles. In *Proceedings of the 11th International Conference on Natural Language Generation*, pages 274–283.

Leo Breiman. 2001. Random forests. *Machine learning*, 45(1):5–32.

Marc Brysbaert, Amy Beth Warriner, and Victor Kuperman. 2014. Concreteness ratings for 40 thousand generally known english word lemmas. *Behavior research methods*, 46(3):904–911

Janet Burroway. 2007. *Imaginative Writing: The Elements of Craft*. Pearson.

David J Chalmers. 1995. Absent qualia, fading qualia, dancing qualia. *Conscious experience*, pages 309–328.

John William Charnley, Alison Pease, and Simon Colton. 2012. On the notion of framing in computational creativity. In *ICCC*, pages 77–81.

Simon Colton, John William Charnley, and Alison Pease. 2011. Computational creativity theory: The FACE and IDEA descriptive models. In *ICCC*, pages 90–95.

Simon Colton, Jacob Goodwin, and Tony Veale. 2012. Full-FACE poetry generation. In *ICCC*, pages 95–102.

Michael Cook, Simon Colton, Alison Pease, and Maria Theresa Llano. 2019. Framing in computational creativity – a survey and taxonomy. In *The proceedings of the tenth international conference on computational creativity*, pages 156–163.

K. Deb, A. Pratap, S. Agarwal, and T. Meyarivan. 2002. A fast and elitist multiobjective genetic algorithm: Nsga-ii. *Trans. Evol. Comp*, 6(2):182–197.

Yanlin Feng and Xiaojun Wan. 2019. Learning bilingual sentiment-specific word embeddings without cross-lingual supervision. In *Proceedings of the 2019 Conference of the North American Chapter of the Association for Computational Linguistics: Human Language Technologies, Volume 1 (Long and Short Papers)*, pages 420–429, Minneapolis, Minnesota. Association for Computational Linguistics.

Brendan J Frey and Delbert Dueck. 2007. Clustering by passing messages between data points. *science*, 315(5814):972–976.

Pablo Gervás. 2001. An expert system for the composition of formal Spanish poetry. In *Applications and Innovations in Intelligent Systems VIII*, pages 19–32. Springer.

Edouard Grave, Piotr Bojanowski, Prakhar Gupta, Armand Joulin, and Tomas Mikolov. 2018. Learning word vectors for 157 languages. In *Proceedings of the International Conference on Language Resources and Evaluation (LREC 2018)*.

Mika Hämäläinen. 2018. Harnessing NLG to create Finnish poetry automatically. In *Proceedings of the Ninth International Conference on Computational Creativity*, pages 9–15.

Mika Hämäläinen. 2019. UralicNLP: An NLP library for Uralic languages. *Journal of Open Source Software*, 4(37):1345.

---

[6]https://github.com/mikahama/finmeter

Mika Hämäläinen and Jack Rueter. 2018. Development of an Open Source Natural Language Generation Tool for Finnish. In *Proceedings of the Fourth International Workshop on Computational Linguistics for Uralic Languages*, pages 51–58.

Katri Haverinen, Jenna Nyblom, Timo Viljanen, Veronika Laippala, Samuel Kohonen, Anna Missilä, Stina Ojala, Tapio Salakoski, and Filip Ginter. 2014. Building the essential resources for Finnish: the Turku dependency treebank. *Language Resources and Evaluation*, 48(3):493–531.

Kyle E. Jennings. 2010. Developing Creativity: Artificial Barriers in Artificial Intelligence. *Minds and Machines*, 20(4):489–501.

Anna Jordanous. 2012. A standardised procedure for evaluating creative systems: Computational creativity evaluation based on what it is to be creative. *Cognitive Computation*, 4(3):246–279.

Tuomas Juntunen. 2012. Kirjallisuudentutkimus. In *Genreanalyysi: tekstilajitutkimuksen käsikirja*, pages 528—536.

Jenna Kanerva, Juhani Luotolahti, Veronika Laippala, and Filip Ginter. 2014. Syntactic n-gram collection from a large-scale corpus of internet Finnish. In *Human Language Technologies-The Baltic Perspective: Proceedings of the Sixth International Conference Baltic HLT*, volume 268, pages 184–191.

Mervi Kantokorpi, Lyytikäinen Pirjo, and Viikari Auli. 1990. *Runousopin perusteet*. Gaudeamus.

Justine Kao and Dan Jurafsky. 2012. A computational analysis of style, affect, and imagery in contemporary poetry. In *Proceedings of the NAACL-HLT 2012 Workshop on Computational Linguistics for Literature*, pages 8–17.

Guillaume Klein, Yoon Kim, Yuntian Deng, Vincent Nguyen, Jean Senellart, and Alexander Rush. 2018. OpenNMT: Neural machine translation toolkit. In *Proceedings of the 13th Conference of the Association for Machine Translation in the Americas (Volume 1: Research Papers)*, pages 177–184, Boston, MA. Association for Machine Translation in the Americas.

Carolyn Lamb and Daniel G. Brown. 2019. TwitSong 3.0: towards semantic revisions in computational poetry. In *Proceedings of the Tenth International Conference on Computational Creativity*, pages 212–219.

Carolyn Lamb, Daniel G Brown, and Charles LA Clarke. 2018. Evaluating computational creativity: An interdisciplinary tutorial. *ACM Computing Surveys (CSUR)*, 51(2):28.

Juntao Li, Yan Song, Haisong Zhang, Dongmin Chen, Shuming Shi, Dongyan Zhao, and Rui Yan. 2018. Generating classical Chinese poems via conditional variational autoencoder and adversarial training.

In *Proceedings of the 2018 Conference on Empirical Methods in Natural Language Processing*, pages 3890–3900, Brussels, Belgium. Association for Computational Linguistics.

Juri Lotman. 1974. *Den poetiska texten*. Stockholm.

Minh-Thang Luong, Hieu Pham, and Christopher D Manning. 2015. Effective approaches to attention-based neural machine translation. *arXiv preprint arXiv:1508.04025*.

Tomas Mikolov, Ilya Sutskever, Kai Chen, Greg S Corrado, and Jeff Dean. 2013. Distributed representations of words and phrases and their compositionality. In *Advances in neural information processing systems*, pages 3111–3119.

Joanna Misztal and Bipin Indurkhya. 2014. Poetry generation system with an emotional personality. In *ICCC*, pages 72–81.

Hugo Gonçalo Oliveira. 2017. A survey on intelligent poetry generation: Languages, features, techniques, reutilisation and evaluation. In *Proceedings of the 10th International Conference on Natural Language Generation*, pages 11–20, Santiago de Compostela, Spain. Association for Computational Linguistics.

Hugo Gonçalo Oliveira, Raquel Hervás, Alberto Díaz, and Pablo Gervás. 2017. Multilingual extension and evaluation of a poetry generator. *Natural Language Engineering*, 23(6):929–967.

Tommi A Pirinen, Inari Listenmaa, Ryan Johnson, Francis M. Tyers, and Juha Kuokkala. 2017. Open morphology of finnish. LINDAT/CLARIN digital library at the Institute of Formal and Applied Linguistics, Charles University.

Ivor Armstrong Richards. 1936. *The Philosophy of Rhetoric*. Oxford University Press, London, United Kingdom.

Yuki Tanigaki, Kaname Narukawa, Yusuke Nojima, and Hisao Ishibuch. 2014. Preference-based nsga-ii for many-objective knapsack problems. In *2014 Joint 7th International Conference on Soft Computing and Intelligent Systems (SCIS) and 15th International Symposium on Advanced Intelligent Systems (ISIS)*, pages 637–642. IEEE.

Jukka Toivanen, Hannu Toivonen, Alessandro Valitutti, and Oskar Gross. 2012. Corpus-Based Generation of Content and Form in Poetry. In *Proceedings of the Third International Conference on Computational Creativity*.

Tony Veale. 2016. The shape of tweets to come: automating language play in social networks. *Multiple Perspectives on Language Play. Mouton De Gruyter, Language Play and Creativity series*, pages 73–92.

Ping Xiao, Khalid Alnajjar, Mark Granroth-Wilding, Kathleen Agres, and Hannu Toivonen. 2016.

Meta4meaning: Automatic metaphor interpretation using corpus-derived word associations. In *Proceedings of the 7th International Conference on Computational Creativity (ICCC 2016)*, Paris, France. Sony CSL, Sony CSL.

Cheng Yang, Maosong Sun, Xiaoyuan Yi, and Wenhao Li. 2018. Stylistic Chinese poetry generation via unsupervised style disentanglement. In *Proceedings of the 2018 Conference on Empirical Methods in Natural Language Processing*, pages 3960–3969, Brussels, Belgium. Association for Computational Linguistics.

Xiaoyuan Yi, Maosong Sun, Ruoyu Li, and Wenhao Li. 2018. Automatic poetry generation with mutual reinforcement learning. In *Proceedings of the 2018 Conference on Empirical Methods in Natural Language Processing*, pages 3143–3153, Brussels, Belgium. Association for Computational Linguistics.

Generation of Hip-Hop Lyrics with Hierarchical Modeling and Conditional Templates

Enrique Manjavacas[1], **Folgert Karsdorp**[2], and **Mike Kestemont**[1]

[1]Computational Linguistics and Psycholinguistics Research Center, University of Antwerp, Belgium
[2]Meertens Institute, Royal Netherlands Academy of Arts and Sciences, Amsterdam

Abstract

This paper addresses Hip-Hop lyric generation with conditional Neural Language Models. We develop a simple yet effective mechanism to extract and apply conditional templates from text snippets, and show—on the basis of a large-scale crowd-sourced manual evaluation—that these templates significantly improve the quality and realism of the generated snippets. Importantly, the proposed approach enables end-to-end training, targeting formal properties of text such as rhythm and rhyme, which are central characteristics of rap texts. Additionally, we explore how generating text at different scales (e.g. character-level or word-level) affects the quality of the output. We find that a hybrid form—a hierarchical model that aims to integrate Language Modeling at both word and character-level scales— yields significant improvements in text quality, yet surprisingly, cannot exploit conditional templates to their fullest extent. Our findings highlight that text generation models based on Recurrent Neural Networks (RNN) are sensitive to the modeling scale and call for further research on the observed differences in effectiveness of the conditioning mechanism at different scales.

1 Introduction

Neural Networks approaches to text generation have recently proliferated partly due to substantial progress made in Language Modeling. Being essentially a generative model, a Language Model (LM) is fit by definition to drive natural language generation systems. LMs based on Neural architectures, such as RNNs, ConvNets or self-attentive models such as Transformers, provide better fits to the underlying data distributions of the training material (currently holding the state-of-the-art on common benchmarks) and are also assumed to produce more realistic text than their count-based counterparts (Karpathy, 2016).

The end-to-end nature of such models and the ability to leverage out-of-domain data through pre-training have led to a broadening of domains in which text generation systems are being developed and applied. In particular, interest has emerged or increased in the generation of artistic text such as poetry (Zhang and Lapata, 2014; Yan, 2016), literature (Manjavacas et al., 2017), song lyrics (Watanabe et al., 2018) or cooking recipes (Kiddon et al., 2016), etc. In the present paper, we focus on generating Hip-Hop lyrics, a genre known for its relatively liberal formal properties (e.g. rhythm and rhyme) and topic specificity.

While full algorithmic modeling of the high-level creative process of song composition remains a challenge, we seek to improve the quality of the generated text by focusing on formal text properties. Typically, generating text with formal structure is done by applying constraints over the LM output distribution. By contrast, in this paper, we follow an end-to-end approach to generate text snippets that directly match the required structure. Our proposal makes use of templates based on sentence-level conditions (Ficler and Goldberg, 2017) that allow us to enforce rhyme and verse structure as it naturally occurs in training data. Our focus on Hip-Hop allows us to crowd-source an extensive collection of authenticity judgments through an online pseudo-Turing serious game. The evaluation shows the efficiency of the approach by bringing human guessing performance to chance-level.

Finally, while architectural improvements in Neural LMs target both character and word-level modeling, the application of LMs to artistic text generation has mostly focused on the word level. This situation is more likely the result of words being a central component of the creative process —e.g. topic, style and concepts are best modeled at the word level (Ghazvininejad et al., 2016;

Proceedings of The 12th International Conference on Natural Language Generation, pages 301–310,
Tokyo, Japan, 28 Oct - 1 Nov, 2019. ©2019 Association for Computational Linguistics

Yan, 2016)—, than a lack of generation capabilities of character-level LMs (Karpathy et al., 2015). Moreover, despite a few exceptions (Jagfeld et al., 2018), comparisons of LM-based generation systems at different scales are not common. To fill this gap, we explore the effects of modeling scale on text generation quality — including character-level, syllable-level and a hierarchical LM (HLM) — as well as the interplay between modeling scale and the proposed conditional template approach.

More specifically, we make the following contributions. (i) We introduce a simple approach to template-based generation, suitable for genres with a loose formal structure such as poetry or Hip-Hop. Crucially, this approach does not require search or constrained decoding to generate formally correct output. (ii) We present a comparison of unconstrained language generation with LMs at different scales and provide empirical evidence that hierarchical modeling produces more realistic output than both character-level and word-level modeling. (iii) We find that the success of the conditioning mechanism is dependent on the LM scale and the type of condition. In particular, we find that the gains from hierarchical modeling do not compound with the benefits obtained from the conditioning mechanism, which calls for further research on the matter.

2   Related Work

Much research has been devoted to poetry generation systems, and the field has reached a considerable degree of maturity (see (Gonçalo Oliveira, 2017)). A variety of approaches based on LMs have been proposed, including both Markov Models (Barbieri et al., 2012) and RNNs (Zhang and Lapata, 2014; Ghazvininejad et al., 2016; Yan, 2016; Hopkins and Kiela, 2017; Lau et al., 2018). In the literature on Hip-Hop lyric generation, besides an RNN-based LM (Potash et al., 2015), researchers have explored retrieval-based approaches where a Support Vector Machine is trained to select the continuing sentence based on formal properties of the text and global semantic coherence (Malmi et al., 2016). Moreover, various strategies have been proposed to generate text that matches specific verse structures. For example, Zhang and Lapata (2014) follow a generate-and-select approach that discards non-rhyming lines, and Ghazvininejad et al. (2016) use a finite-state-acceptor to decode lines that meet the desired out-

Songs	Artists	Words	Vocabulary
64,542	28,099	37,236,248	380,013

Table 1: Counts the total number of songs, artists and words collected from the *Original Hip-Hop (Rap) Lyrics Archive* (OHHLA).

Statistic	μ	σ
Words/Song	576.93	223.77
Songs/Artist	2.3	7.65
Words/Artist	1325.2	4223.2

Table 2: Statistics on the average number of (1) words per song, (2) songs per artist, and (3) words per artist.

put structure. Hopkins and Kiela (2017) compose a WFST with an RNN to enforce meter in the output text. Finally, Lau et al. (2018) use a rhyme detector jointly trained with a LM and discard non-rhyming line-ending words based on the models' confidence scores.

3   Dataset

The training data for this study was derived from the *Original Hip-Hop (Rap) Lyrics Archive* (OHHLA)[1], an online archive documenting Hip-Hop through since 1992 and offering a large collecting of Hip-Hop lyrics. A total of 64,542 songs were collected. The database contains almost exclusively English songs, although code-switching is common. The final corpus is the result of the following pre-processing steps. First, each text was tokenized using the Ucto tokenizer (Van Gompel et al., 2012). Second, all words were segmented into syllables using an in-house LSTM-based syllabifier trained on the CMU Pronouncing Dictionary (Lenzo, 2007). The syllabifier's segmentation accuracy is well over 99% on both a held-out development and test set, supporting confidence in its application to the lyric data. Finally, we applied the G2P toolkit[2] to extract phonological representations of words and corresponding stress patterns that will be exploited during training. The syllabified corpus consists of 43,531,133 syllables comprising 89,337 syllable types. A summary of overall corpus statistics is shown in Table 1 and Table 2.

---

[1] http://www.ohhla.com
[2] https://github.com/cmusphinx/
g2p-seq2seq

4 LM-based Text Generation

We generate text by sampling from a LM implemented on top of LSTM Networks (Hochreiter and Schmidhuber, 1997) trained to predict the next symbol y in the sequence given the history using the following definition:

$$P(y_1 \ldots y_n) = \prod_{t=1}^{n} P(y_t | y_{\ldots <t}) \qquad (1)$$

Regardless of the details of specific architectures, sampling is done in the following way. Let x_k be the activation for the kth vocabulary symbol at the penultimate layer (i.e. before the output softmax layer). At any given step, we sample from the multinomial distribution defined by:

$$P(y_k) = \frac{x_k/T}{\Sigma_{l \in V} x_l/T} \qquad (2)$$

where V refers to the vocabulary and T is a temperature parameter controlling the models confidence. We leave other sampling approaches such as Top-K Sampling (Fan et al., 2018) and Nucleus Sampling (Holtzman et al., 2019) for future work.

4.1 Hierarchical Language Model

LMs are typically trained at the character or word-level. Character-level modeling has the advantages of (i) reducing the vocabulary size and (ii) increasing the number of training examples available during model fitting, but it incurs the cost of enlarging the number of steps to account for a given dependency between any two given input words. Arguably, a hybrid approach that models language at the character level but also incorporates word-level information flow should provide a way out of such a trade-off (Karpathy et al., 2015).

Therefore, in the present paper, we compare text generation at three levels: character-level, syllable-level and a hierarchical LM (HLM) that integrates both levels. Note that we consider syllable-level instead of word-level based on two-fold reasoning: (i) similar to sub-word models — such as those induced through Byte-Pair-Encoding (Sennrich et al., 2016) or SentencePiece (Kudo and Richardson, 2018) —, syllable-level segmented input helps limiting the exploding vocabulary size of noisy corpora. (ii) Syllables play a more central role than words in a particularly rhythmic genre like Hip-Hop in which, moreover, a tendency towards monosyllabic words reduces the vocabulary differences for word-level modeling.

As mentioned above, the key idea behind HLM is to allow different layers to specialize in modeling the information flow at different scales. In order to achieve that, the HLM uses the chain-rule of probability to decompose the probability of a sentence into the product of the probabilities of words (exactly as in the word-level LM) but, furthermore, it decomposes the probability of each word into the product of the probabilities of its characters:[3]

$$P(w_{t+1} | w_{1 \ldots t}) = \prod_{i=1}^{|w_{t+1}|} P(c_{t+1}^i | c_{t+1}^{1 \ldots i-1}; w_{1 \ldots t}) \qquad (3)$$

We implement the HLM with LSTM layers at different scales. A first bidirectional LSTM_{inp} takes the input sequence of character embeddings of the current word w_t and produces word-level features concatenating the final activations of the forward and backward pass. Secondly, $\text{LSTM}_{\text{word}}$ takes word-level feature vector $\mathbf{w_t}$[4] and the recurrent state to generate sentence-level features $\mathbf{s_t} = \text{LSTM}_{\text{word}}(\mathbf{w_t}, \mathbf{s_{t-1}})$. Finally, LSTM_{out} computes the vector of scores x for the next character c_{t+1}^{i+1} of the target word w_{t+1} using the previously decoded character embedding $\mathbf{c_{t+1}^i}$, $\mathbf{s_t}$ and the recurrent state $\mathbf{h_{t+1}^i}$:

$$\mathbf{x_{t+1}^{i+1}} = W \cdot \text{LSTM}_{\text{out}}([\mathbf{c_{t+1}^i}; \mathbf{s_t}], \mathbf{h_{t+1}^i}) \qquad (4)$$

where W is a matrix that maps the LSTM output to the vocabulary space. HLM is a specific case of the Hierarchical Multi-scale LSTM by Chung et al. (2016) with the differences that HLM uses a fixed segmentation at syllable boundaries instead of implicitly learning a segmentation model, and that HLM only considers bottom-up information passing across layers. Interestingly, despite the simplification HLM achieves similar results on the Penn Treebank benchmark corpus (see Table 3).

4.2 Conditional Templates

Recent research has shown the effectiveness of a conditioning mechanism for controlled text generation (Ficler and Goldberg, 2017), which uses specific sentence-level information during training

---

[3] Note that while we discuss the HLM in terms of words, in practice, our implementation uses syllables following the argumentation at the beginning of the current section.

[4] We use bold to denote the feature vector (e.g., $\mathbf{w_t}$) corresponding to a particular input (e.g., word w_t).

Model	Parameters	BPC
HM-LSTM	NA	1.23
GHRNN	10.3M	1.223
2-layer LSTM	7.6M	1.275
HLM	7.5M	1.233

Table 3: A comparison of the proposed architecture with respect to a non-hierarchical deep character-level LSTM (2-later LSTM) and related hierarchical architectures on the Penn Treebank benchmark. Results correspond to bits-per-character (BPC). HM-LSTM corresponds to the Hierarchical Multiscale LSTM by Chung et al. (2016). GHRNN corresponds to the Gated Hierarchical RNN by Choi et al. (2018).

(e.g. tense, mood, sentiment or formal/informal style) to bias the generation towards text that reflects such conditions. Formally, such conditional information is encoded using condition embeddings and is fed into the LMs through vector concatenation. More formally, let c be a given condition with N_c assignments. For each c we allocate an embedding matrix $C_c \in \mathbb{R}^{N_c \times d}$. During training, each model input embedding is concatenated with a vector of condition embeddings $\mathbf{c} = [\mathbf{c_1}; \ldots; \mathbf{c_m}]$ representing the conditional information corresponding to the input sentence.

We deploy such conditioning mechanism in the form of *conditional templates* to the task of generating Hip-Hop lyrics. The idea behind conditional templates is to leverage the training material to bias the generation towards more realistic output. Consider the task of generating a verse consisting of m lines of Hip-Hop. In such a case, we sample a verse from the training corpus consisting of m lines and apply the corresponding conditions to a conditionally trained LM. The next question is what sentence-level information can be easily extracted and used to improve the quality and realism of the output. In the case of Hip-Hop, we focus on two formal characteristics that most typically represent Hip-Hop lyrics: *rhythm* and *rhyme* (Condit-Schultz, 2017).

Rhythm in Hip-Hop is characterized by a strict alignment between beat and stress with high correspondence between syntactic units and measures and a relatively stable ratio of number of syllables per beat (Adams, 2009). In order to approximate this stylistic feature[5], we condition our LMs

on a measure of verse length. In particular, we count the number of syllables of each line in the verse and bucket them according to the following ranges: < 10, $(10 - 15)$, $(15 - 20)$ and > 20.

Rhyme Hip-Hop employs liberal rhyme patterns in terms of placement — e.g., off-beat, syncopated rhyme, etc. — and often relies on imperfect matches (e.g. slant rhyme Adams, 2009). To mimic such rhyming style, we condition LMs on phonological endings, which we define, in alignment with a loose notion of rhyme, as the syllabic nucleus of the last stressed syllable followed by the syllabic nuclei of any following syllables. For example, the rhyme-based condition corresponding to the line 'unite around the corner' is AO1-ERO — i.e. the ARPABET representations corresponding to the stressed syllabic nuclei of 'cor-' and '-ner'.[6] Such a representation is then shared with other rhyming words such as 'daughter' or 'offer'. A successfully trained conditional LM can thus generate rhymes when the same phonological condition is passed to the networks for two consecutive lines. Similarly, templates from the corpus contain rhyming schemes and patterns (such as AABB, ABAB, etc.) that the conditional models can exploit for a more realistic effect. Table 4 shows example generations from conditional models at all three considered scales.

4.3 Model Training Details

We implement all models in PyTorch (Paszke et al., 2017), with the following parametrizations. Input and condition embedding layers have dimensionality of 100. Non-hierarchical models have 2 hidden LSTM layers with 640 units per layer. By definition the HLM has 2 LSTM layers in addition to the bidirectional LSTM layer that computes character-level word embeddings. For replication purposes, our implementation is available online.[7]

---

imented with conditioning on line-level stress patterns extracted through a cluster analysis but found the approach inconclusive. The difficulty stems from the fact that Hip-Hop artists commonly shift the word stress in order to align it to the underlying beat, and such misalignment cannot be recovered based on only text.

[6] We focus on generating rhyming in verse-final position, which represents the most abundant type. We extract a total of 430 such phonological endings in our corpus, from which only 270 involve an actual rhyme in the training corpus. Interestingly, however, we observed that the conditional models generalize so as to generate rhymes on phonological endings that have not been seen during training.

[7] Code can found in the following url https://www.github.com/emanjavacas/hierarchical-lm.

---

[5] The approximation lies in the fact that we ignore stress patterns in the template source. Initially, we experimented

"I Like It Like That" (by Hot Chelle Rae)			**Character-level Model**
I like it like that! Hey windows down	AW1	10–15	Now baby get the fuck out, check it out
Chillin with the radio on	AA1	<10	I be on top
I like it like that! Damn, the sun's so hot	AA1	10–15	I'll make some money what the fuck is goin' on

"Nothing to worry about" (by Peter Bjorn)			**Syllable-level Model**
C'mon everybody let's all get down, let's all get down, let's all get down	AW1	>20	We gon' shut'em down, if you wanna get down, don't fuck around
I've got nothin' to worry about	AW1	10–15	On the real, it's how it's goin' down
C'mon everybody let's all get down, let's all get down, let's all get down	AW1	>20	I'm trying to get this money right, you got to eat right now

"Lil like bic" (by Rae Sremmurd)			**Hierarchical Model**
Who said they got that stanky loud? I wanna smell it	IH1	10–15	Don't act like you ain't ready for this
You say you run your fuckin' town, I let you tell it	IH1	10–15	I never created this shit
Who really run the underground? I wanna meet you	UW1	10–15	You don't understand, it's all about you
I'm really tryna bite the style, you know we see you	UW1	10–15	Try to maintain, you know the rules

Table 4: Generated samples following the conditional templating approach. Left: the original snippet from which the template was extracted. Middle: Condition values extracted from the source text (phonological ending using the 2-letter ARPABET phoneset and the bucketed length in number of syllables). Right: generated text.

Scale	Conditional	Parameters	Result
Character		12.6M	1.65
Character	✓	12.9M	1.55
Syllable		29.8M	46.12
Syllable	✓	29.9M	33.43
HLM		14.M	1.38
HLM	✓	14.9M	1.27

Table 5: Model details. In agreement with the literature, the results correspond to perplexity for syllable-level models and bits per character (BPC) for character-level models.

We trained all models with a cross-entropy objective targeted at predicting the next symbol in the sequence. Parameter optimization was done using the Adam optimizer (Kingma and Ba, 2015) with default hyperparameters. Models are regularized using dropout (Srivastava et al., 2014) on the input embeddings, variational dropout (Gal and Ghahramani, 2016) on hidden recurrent layers, and default L2 penalty on model parameters. Finally, we stop training based on an early-stopping criterion computed after each epoch on held-out data. Table 5 shows total number model parameters and development perplexity per configuration.

5 Evaluation

Our first evaluation concerns the quality of the Hip-Hop snippets generated by each of the six architectures (three modeling scales, each with a conditioned variant). We focus on the effectiveness of the conditional template approach and hierarchical modeling. Evaluating artistic text generation poses additional challenges, mostly due to the absence of reference text against which a model output can be compared. While some authors rely on questionnaires addressing poetic properties of interest (e.g., "poeticness", "grammaticality", "meaningfulness") for evaluation (Das and Gambäck, 2014), we instead turn to a Turing-like setup that allowed us to crowd-source a large-scale pool of user authenticity judgments. In order to encourage user participation, we implemented a serious game where participants were shown Hip-Hop samples of lengths of 3 to 4 lines and were tasked to guess whether the displayed text was generated or real in 15 seconds.[8] Participants were motivated by being shown feedback immediately after each answer. Furthermore, the game entered a "sudden-death" phase after the first ten guesses, in which a wrong answer would finish the game. Finally, a leader-board was kept visible, showing the scores of the ten best performing participants. The resulting dataset underlying the present evaluation comprises 3,620 guesses by 670 participants.

In order to leverage the collected evaluations, we model guessing behavior using a Logistic Regression model (implemented in `brms`, Bürkner and others, 2017), taking into account user-specific variability through the inclusion of varying intercepts (i.e. for each participant, we use a unique intercept parameter). Our evaluation strategy contrasts with similar approaches in the literature — (e.g. Netzer et al., 2009) — which typically only provide raw empirical, single point estimates. Regularized estimates obtained from using a varying intercepts model provide more accurate estimates for individual user intercepts, enabling predictions about future behavior that are less prone to both over- and underfitting (cf. McElreath, 2015). Additionally, the interaction between generation scale and conditioning are modeled as fixed effects.

As shown in Figure 1, hierarchical modeling outperforms both character and syllable-level models in the unconditioned setup, with the median guessing accuracy dropping to 54.6%. Moreover, conditional templates push guessing accuracy further down for all models, with HLM and syllable-level achieving a median accuracy of 51.9% and 49.4%, respectively. Interestingly, the effect of the conditional templates differs across models. The smallest effect is observed for the hierarchical model (decrease of 2.6 points), followed by the character-level model (decrease of 6.7 points), while the effect on syllable-level model corresponds to a decrease of 13.4 points. The relatively high impact of conditioning on syllable-level generation contrasts sharply with the much smaller improvement on both character-level and HLM.

On first sight, this result seems to suggest that conditioning is more effective at higher modeling levels, perhaps hinting at optimization incompat-

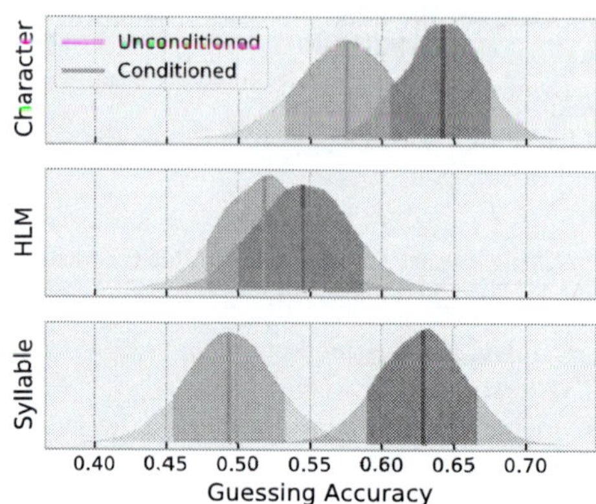

Figure 1: Results of crowd-sourced evaluation. Displayed results correspond to the full posterior predictive distributions of a logistic regression model, with (the interaction between) conditioning and generation scale as fixed effects, and participants as varying intercepts. For explanation purposes, median and 80% credible intervals are highlighted.

ibilities between sentence-level conditioning and character-level training objectives. Though, in order to better understand this result, we pursue the following two questions. First, why are conditional templates much more effective at a higher-level scale (i.e., syllable-level)? Second, what textual properties characterize text generated by different models, and can explain the better performance of the hierarchical model in particular?

5.1 Modeling scale and conditioning

To better understand the divergent effectiveness of conditioning at different scales, we investigate to what extent different models succeed at generating text that matches the conditions required by the template. Note that the benefits of a conditioned model might not be restricted to a model's ability to fulfill the target template conditions—for example, rhyme and rhythm information results in a better fit to the data as shown in Table 5. However, successfully replicating formal structures seen in the training data ensures a level of realism by definition and thus can be interpreted as an, at least partial, explanation for the observed differences in performance.

In order to quantify the ability of models to successfully generate the requested templates, we generate a dataset of lines exploring the space of possible templates. For each of the 2150 combinations (430 rhyming conditions by 5 length buck-

---

[8] Generated text was sampled at random from one of the six models.

ets), we sample 1000 lines. We then syllabify each of the lines using the same pre-processing pipeline described in Section 3. Subsequently, rhyme generation accuracy (`Acc`) can be quantified by the proportion of generated lines with the expected phonological ending. Moreover, we also quantify rhyme diversity (`H`) — i.e. the entropy of the distribution of successfully generated rhyme words. Finally, in order to quantify the ability to meet target verse length, we compute the average difference in syllables between the generated verse length and corpus-level average length per bucket (`Diff`).

The results in Table 6 show that syllable-level is, in fact, most accurate and diverse at generating rhyme by a large extent. The HLM achieves higher accuracy than the character-level but similar diversity. Overall, rhyme diversity is notably lower in generated text than in real text ($H =$ 1.669), a result that is in agreement with the expectations. In terms of rhythm, we observe a different picture: the character-level model generates lines much closer to the observed data than both HLM and syllable-level. From the last two, the HLM improves over syllable-level but both tend to produce shorter lines.

These results seem to suggest that character-level RNNs excel at modeling surface-level information responsible for estimating the current number of processed symbols, and can thus very accurately replicate the verse lengths observed in the training data. Moreover, it seems that the syllable-level model can derive a more substantial improvement from the conditional templates because rhyming patterns have an arguably more prominent impact on the perceived realism — however, we will leave an analysis of perceived realism for future work. Finally, it appears that in terms of conditioning, our hierarchical model does not succeed in exploiting the best of both worlds.

5.2 Modeling scale and text quality

We now turn to characterize the effect of modeling text at different scales as well as, more specifically, what textual properties single out hierarchically generated text. In order to approach this question, we utilize the unconditioned output from the main experiment and conduct a feature analysis across the following linguistic levels:

Prosody We quantify *rhyme* as the proportion of rhyming lines in the snippet, *assonance* as the proportion of the most frequent stressed syllable

Condition		Char	HLM	Syll
Rhyme	`Acc`	28.37	36.29	61.75
	`H`	0.861	0.836	1.077
Rhythm	`Diff`	0.09	-1.59	-2.59

Table 6: Effects of conditioning on model scale. The rhyme diversity (`H`) as observed in the training corpus for a sample of comparable size equals 1.669.

nucleus over total number of syllables, and *alliteration* as the proportion of consecutive words with equal consonant onset.

Morphology We approximate the morphological complexity of the text with the average *word-length* in syllables.

Lexical level *lexical diversity* is measured using entropy based on overall word distributions. Moreover, we also quantify the proportion of consecutive *word repetitions*, which represent a common artifact in LM-based text generation (Holtzman et al., 2019).

Syntax We approximate syntactic complexity based on the average *mean tree depth* from the corresponding dependency parse trees of the snippet lines. Parse trees are extracted using the dependency parser provided by AllenNLP[9] based on Dozat and Manning (2016) and trained on the PTB3.0 corpus.

Based on such features, we fit a Random Forest to classify the model underlying the corresponding text snippet. We resort to the machine learning library `scikit-learn` (Pedregosa et al., 2011) for the implementation and extract feature importance scores following the feature permutation approach detailed in Parr et al. (2018). Furthermore, in order to extract feature-class associations (i.e., which class each feature is mostly predictive of) odds-ratios are computed based on a linear model taking character-level as reference class. The resulting Random Forest achieves 91.7 out-of-bag accuracy, which provides certainty that the feature-set has sufficiently large coverage.

Figure 2 ranks features by importance scores. As we can see, word-length is by far the strongest predictor. The feature is most strongly associated with HLM and slightly less with syllable-level modeling. Following word-length, we encounter syntax (mean tree-depth) and lexical diversity, which again are mostly associated with HLM — with odds-ratios in favour of HLM amounting to

---

[9] `https://www.allennlp.org/models`

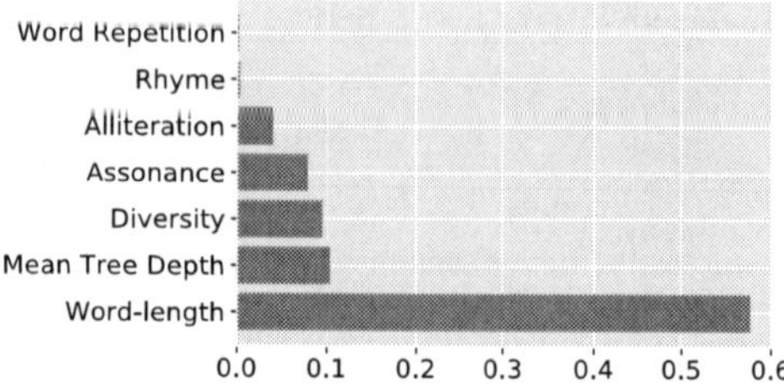

Figure 2: Feature importance analysis based on a Random Forest classifier trained to predict modeling scale.

3.8 and 2.4, respectively. Furthermore, prosodic features — in particular assonance — play a role in distinguishing character-level output from the other models. Finally, word repetition and rhyme density show near-zero importance scores.

Based on the present feature analysis, it can be inferred that one of the main advantages of hierarchical modeling relates to increased lexical diversity, which is further boosted by the ability to generate longer and more morphologically complex words. On the other hand, character-level modeling seems to be better characterized by surface-level prosodic features (in particular assonance). This analysis would connect with the interpretation advanced in Section 5.1, in which character-level modeling was shown to provide an accurate replication of a related surface-level textual property: rhythm as captured by verse length.

6   Discussion & Conclusion

Based on a large-scale evaluation involving hundreds of participants and authenticity judgments, we have shown that the modeling scale influences the quality of generated Hip-Hop lyrics. A feature analysis shows that hierarchically generated text displays morphologically and syntactically more complex output as well as higher lexical diversity. All such properties may help explain the better scores achieved by the hierarchical model in the absence of conditioning.

Furthermore, the proposed end-to-end approach to enforce formal structure in texts has similarly proved efficient. It reduces the human guessing accuracy of all models and is particularly efficient in the case of syllable-level modeling. Moreover, our analysis of the interplay between modeling scale and conditioning showed that syllable-level modeling displays much greater ability to exploit rhyme templates than the other lower-scale mod-

eling variants. This advantage can help to explain the more pronounced effect of conditional templates on syllable-level modeling when considering that rhyme patterns contribute arguably more strongly to the realism of a generated snippet.

And yet, character-level modeling scored much better than the other models at generating the requested verse lengths and was shown to be positively associated with prosodic features such as assonance by the feature analysis. Both results thus seem to suggest that character-level modeling has an edge at capturing surface-level information. The overall lower performance of the character-level model implies, however, that such an advantage does not translate in improved realism as perceived by the participants.

Finally, the evaluation shows that despite the already mentioned advantages of hierarchical modeling, the effects of conditional templates did not compound in this case. This result is somewhat discouraging, since the primary motivation of hierarchical modeling is to overcome deficiencies of both character and word-level modeling. The analysis in Section 5.1 shows that our implementation of the conditioned HLM scores in between the other two models. Future research might be able to overcome this drawback by carefully designing adaptive mechanisms that let the model decide to which layer in the hierarchy a particular type of sentence-level conditional embedding should be fed.

7   Future Work

Our study suggests several directions for future work. The most urgent issue, briefly touched upon above, concerns an investigation of improved hierarchical architectures that can exploit conditioning information better than either character-level and word-level models in isolation. Moreover, the positive results obtained for the hierarchical model in isolation encourage scaling up the modeling hierarchy, investigating the inclusion of higher scales such as stanza and document level. Furthermore, while we have only considered templates covering formal aspects of the text, the same approach can be extended to include content features such as keyword or stanza-level topic information. Finally, in this study, we have restricted ourselves to relatively short snippets of text, but future work should move on and consider an evaluation on more substantial text portions.

References

Kyle Adams. 2009. On the metrical techniques of flow in rap music. *Music Theory Online*, 15(5).

Gabriele Barbieri, Franois Pachet, Pierre Roy, and Mirko Degli Esposti. 2012. Markov Constraints for Generating Lyrics with Style. In *Ecai*, volume 242, pages 115–120.

Paul-Christian Bürkner and others. 2017. brms: An R package for Bayesian multilevel models using Stan. *Journal of Statistical Software*, 80(1):1–28.

Iksoo Choi, Jinhwan Park, and Wonyong Sung. 2018. Character-level Language Modeling with Gated Hierarchical Recurrent Neural Networks. *Proc. Interspeech 2018*, pages 411–415.

Junyoung Chung, Sungjin Ahn, and Yoshua Bengio. 2016. Hierarchical multiscale recurrent neural networks. *arXiv preprint arXiv:1609.01704*.

Nathaniel Condit-Schultz. 2017. MCFlow: A Digital Corpus of Rap Transcriptions. *Empirical Musicology Review*.

Amitava Das and Bjrn Gambäck. 2014. Poetic Machine: Computational Creativity for Automatic Poetry Generation in Bengali. In *ICCC*, pages 230–238.

Timothy Dozat and Christopher D Manning. 2016. Deep biaffine attention for neural dependency parsing. *arXiv preprint arXiv:1611.01734*.

Angela Fan, Mike Lewis, and Yann Dauphin. 2018. Hierarchical Neural Story Generation. In *Proceedings of the 56th Annual Meeting of the Association for Computational Linguistics (Volume 1: Long Papers)*, pages 889–898, Melbourne, Australia. Association for Computational Linguistics.

Jessica Ficler and Yoav Goldberg. 2017. Controlling Linguistic Style Aspects in Neural Language Generation. In *Proceedings of the Workshop on Stylistic Variation*, pages 94–104, Copenhagen, Denmark. Association for Computational Linguistics.

Yarin Gal and Zoubin Ghahramani. 2016. A theoretically grounded application of dropout in recurrent neural networks. In *Advances in neural information processing systems*, pages 1019–1027.

Marjan Ghazvininejad, Xing Shi, Yejin Choi, and Kevin Knight. 2016. Generating Topical Poetry. In *Proceedings of the 2016 Conference on Empirical Methods in Natural Language Processing*, pages 1183–1191, Austin, Texas. Association for Computational Linguistics.

Hugo Gonçalo Oliveira. 2017. A Survey on Intelligent Poetry Generation: Languages, Features, Techniques, Reutilisation and Evaluation. In *Proceedings of the 10th International Conference on Natural Language Generation*, pages 11–20. Association for Computational Linguistics.

Sepp Hochreiter and Jürgen Schmidhuber. 1997. Long Short-Term Memory. *Neural Computation*, 9(8):1735–1780.

Ari Holtzman, Jan Buys, Maxwell Forbes, and Yejin Choi. 2019. The curious case of neural text degeneration. *arXiv preprint arXiv:1904.09751*.

Jack Hopkins and Douwe Kiela. 2017. Automatically Generating Rhythmic Verse with Neural Networks. In *Proceedings of the 55th Annual Meeting of the Association for Computational Linguistics (Volume 1: Long Papers)*, pages 168–178. Association for Computational Linguistics.

Glorianna Jagfeld, Sabrina Jenne, and Ngoc Thang Vu. 2018. Sequence-to-Sequence Models for Data-to-Text Natural Language Generation: Word- vs. Character-based Processing and Output Diversity. In *Proceedings of the 11th International Conference on Natural Language Generation*, pages 221–232, Tilburg University, The Netherlands. Association for Computational Linguistics.

Andrej Karpathy. 2016. The Unreasonable Effectiveness of Recurrent Neural Networks.

Andrej Karpathy, Justin Johnson, and Li Fei-Fei. 2015. Visualizing and understanding recurrent networks. *arXiv preprint arXiv:1506.02078*.

Chlo Kiddon, Luke Zettlemoyer, and Yejin Choi. 2016. Globally Coherent Text Generation with Neural Checklist Models. In *Proceedings of the 2016 Conference on Empirical Methods in Natural Language Processing*, pages 329–339, Austin, Texas. Association for Computational Linguistics.

Diederik P. Kingma and Jimmy Lei Ba. 2015. Adam: a Method for Stochastic Optimization. *International Conference on Learning Representations 2015*, pages 1–15.

Taku Kudo and John Richardson. 2018. SentencePiece: A simple and language independent subword tokenizer and detokenizer for Neural Text Processing. *arXiv preprint arXiv:1808.06226*.

Jey Han Lau, Trevor Cohn, Timothy Baldwin, Julian Brooke, and Adam Hammond. 2018. Deep-speare: A joint neural model of poetic language, meter and rhyme. In *Proceedings of the 56th Annual Meeting of the Association for Computational Linguistics (Volume 1: Long Papers)*, pages 1948–1958. Association for Computational Linguistics.

Kevin Lenzo. 2007. The CMU pronouncing dictionary.

Eric Malmi, Pyry Takala, Hannu Toivonen, Tapani Raiko, and Aristides Gionis. 2016. DopeLearning: A computational approach to rap lyrics generation. In *Proceedings of the 22nd ACM SIGKDD International Conference on Knowledge Discovery and Data Mining*, pages 195–204. ACM.

Enrique Manjavacas, Folgert Karsdorp, Ben Burton shaw, and Mike Kestemont. 2017. Synthetic Literature: Writing Science Fiction in a Co-Creative Process. In *Proceedings of the Workshop on Computational Creativity in Natural Language Generation (CC-NLG 2017)*, pages 29–37, Santiago de Compostela, Spain. Association for Computational Linguistics.

Richard McElreath. 2015. *Statistical rethinking: A Bayesian course with examples in R and Stan*. Chapman and Hall/CRC.

Yael Netzer, David Gabay, Yoav Goldberg, and Michael Elhadad. 2009. Gaiku: Generating haiku with word associations norms. In *Proceedings of the Workshop on Computational Approaches to Linguistic Creativity*, pages 32–39. Association for Computational Linguistics.

Terence Parr, Kerem Turgutlu, Christopher Csiszar, and Jeremy Howard. 2018. Beware Default Random Forest Importances.

Adam Paszke, Sam Gross, Soumith Chintala, and Gregory Chanan. 2017. Pytorch: Tensors and dynamic neural networks in python with strong gpu acceleration. *PyTorch: Tensors and dynamic neural networks in Python with strong GPU acceleration*.

Fabian Pedregosa, Gal Varoquaux, Alexandre Gramfort, Vincent Michel, Bertrand Thirion, Olivier Grisel, Mathieu Blondel, Peter Prettenhofer, Ron Weiss, Vincent Dubourg, and others. 2011. Scikit-learn: Machine learning in Python. *Journal of machine learning research*, 12(Oct):2825–2830.

Peter Potash, Alexey Romanov, and Anna Rumshisky. 2015. GhostWriter: Using an LSTM for Automatic Rap Lyric Generation. *Proceedings of the 2015 Conference on Empirical Methods in Natural Language Processing*, (September):1919–1924.

Rico Sennrich, Barry Haddow, and Alexandra Birch. 2016. Neural Machine Translation of Rare Words with Subword Units. In *Proceedings of the 54th Annual Meeting of the Association for Computational Linguistics (Volume 1: Long Papers)*, pages 1715–1725, Berlin, Germany. Association for Computational Linguistics.

Nitish Srivastava, Geoffrey Hinton, Alex Krizhevsky, Ilya Sutskever, and Ruslan Salakhutdinov. 2014. Dropout: A Simple Way to Prevent Neural Networks from Overfitting. *Journal of Machine Learning Research*, 15:1929–1958.

Maarten Van Gompel, Ko Van Der Sloot, and Antal Van den Bosch. 2012. Ucto: Unicode Tokeniser Reference Guide. Technical report.

Kento Watanabe, Yuichiroh Matsubayashi, Satoru Fukayama, Masataka Goto, Kentaro Inui, and Tomoyasu Nakano. 2018. A Melody-Conditioned Lyrics Language Model. In *Proceedings of the 2018 Conference of the North American Chapter of the Association for Computational Linguistics: Human Language Technologies, Volume 1 (Long Papers)*, pages 163–172, New Orleans, Louisiana. Association for Computational Linguistics.

Rui Yan. 2016. i, Poet: Automatic Poetry Composition through Recurrent Neural Networks with Iterative Polishing Schema. In *IJCAI*, pages 2238–2244.

Xingxing Zhang and Mirella Lapata. 2014. Chinese Poetry Generation with Recurrent Neural Networks. In *Proceedings of the 2014 Conference on Empirical Methods in Natural Language Processing (EMNLP)*, pages 670–680. Association for Computational Linguistics.

Revisiting Challenges in Data-to-Text Generation with Fact Grounding

Hongmin Wang
University of California Santa Barbara
hongmin_wang@cs.ucsb.edu

Abstract

Data-to-text generation models face challenges in ensuring data fidelity by referring to the correct input source. To inspire studies in this area, Wiseman et al. (2017) introduced the `RotoWire` corpus on generating NBA game summaries from the box- and line-score tables. However, limited attempts have been made in this direction and the challenges remain. We observe a prominent bottleneck in the corpus where only about 60% of the summary contents can be grounded to the boxscore records. Such information deficiency tends to misguide a conditioned language model to produce unconditioned random facts and thus leads to factual hallucinations. In this work, we restore the information balance and revamp this task to focus on fact-grounded data-to-text generation. We introduce a purified and larger-scale dataset, `RotoWire-FG` (Fact-Grounding), with 50% more data from the year 2017-19 and enriched input tables, hoping to attract more research focuses in this direction. Moreover, we achieve improved data fidelity over the state-of-the-art models by integrating a new form of table reconstruction as an auxiliary task to boost the generation quality.

1 Introduction

Data-to-text generation aims at automatically producing descriptive natural language texts to convey the messages embodied in structured data formats, such as database records (Chisholm et al., 2017), knowledge graphs (Gardent et al., 2017a), and tables (Lebret et al., 2016; Wiseman et al., 2017). Table 1 shows an example from the `RotoWire`[1] (RW) corpus illustrating the task of generating document-level NBA basketball game summaries from the large box- and line-score tables[2]. It poses great challenges, requiring capabilities to select *what to say* (content selection) from two levels: what entity and which attribute, and to determine *how to say* on both discourse (content planning) and token (surface realization) levels.

Although this excellent resource has received great research attention, very few works (Li and Wan, 2018; Puduppully et al., 2019a,b; Iso et al., 2019) have attempted to tackle the challenges on ensuring data fidelity. This intrigues us to investigate the reason behind and we identify a major culprit undermining researchers' interests: the ungrounded contents in the human-written summaries impedes a model to learn to generate accurate fact-grounded statements and leads to possibly misleading evaluation results when the models are compared against each other.

Specifically, we observe that about 40% of the game summary contents cannot be directly mapped to any input boxscore records, as exemplified by Table 1. Written by professional sports journalists, these statements incorporate domain expertise and background knowledge consolidated from heterogeneous sources that are often hard to trace. The resulting information imbalance hinders a model to produce texts fully conditioned on the inputs and the uncontrolled randomness causes factual hallucinations, especially for the modern encoder-decoder framework (Sutskever et al., 2014; Cho et al., 2014). However, data fidelity is crucial for data-to-text generation besides fluency. In this real-world application, mistaken statements are detrimental to the document quality no matter how human-like they appear to be.

Apart from the popular BLEU (Papineni et al., 2002) metric for text generation, Wiseman et al.

---

[1] https://github.com/harvardnlp/boxscore-data

[2] Box- and line-score tables contain player and team statistics respectively. For simplicity, we call the combined input the *boxscore table* unless otherwise specified.

Proceedings of The 12th International Conference on Natural Language Generation, pages 311–322,
Tokyo, Japan, 28 Oct - 1 Nov, 2019. ©2019 Association for Computational Linguistics

TEAM	WIN	LOSS	PTS	FG_PCT	BLK	...
Rockets	18	5	108	44	7	
Nuggets	10	13	96	38	7	

PLAYER	H/A	PTS	RB	AST	MIN	...
James Harden	H	24	10	10	38	...
Dwight Howard	H	26	13	2	30	...
JJ Hickson	A	14	10	2	22	...

Column names :
H/A: home/away, PTS: points, RB: rebounds,
AST: assists, MIN: minutes, BLK: blocks,
FG_PCT: field goals percentage

An example hallucinated statement :
After going into halftime down by eight , the Rockets came out firing in the third quarter and out - scored the Nuggets 59 - 42 to seal the victory on the road

The **Houston Rockets (18-5)** defeated the **Denver Nuggets (10-13)** **108-96** on Saturday. **Houston** has won 2 straight games and 6 of their last 7. **Dwight Howard** returned to action Saturday after missing the Rockets ' last 11 games with a knee injury. He was supposed to be limited to 24 minutes in the game, but **Dwight Howard** persevered to play **30 minutes** and put up a monstrous double-double of 26 points and **13 rebounds**. Joining **Dwight Howard** in on the fun was **James Harden** with a triple-double of **24 points**, **10 rebounds** and **10 assists** in **38 minutes**. The **Rockets** ' formidable defense held the **Nuggets** to just **38 percent** shooting from the field. **Houston** will face the **Nuggets** again in their next game, going on the road to **Denver** for their game on Wednesday. **Denver** has lost 4 of their last 5 games as they struggle to find footing during a tough part of their schedule ... **Denver** will begin a 4 - game homestead hosting the San Antonio Spurs on Sunday.

Table 1: An example from the RotoWire corpus. Partial box- and line-score tables are on the top left. Grounded entities and numerical facts are in **bold**. Yellow sentences contain red ungrounded numerical facts, and team game schedule related statements. A system-generated statement with multiple hallucinations on the bottom left.

(2017) also formalized a set of post-hoc information extraction (IE) based evaluations to assess the data fidelity. Using the boxscore table schema, a sequence of (*entity*, *value*, *type*) records mentioned in a system-generated summary are extracted as the content plan. They are then validated for accuracy against the boxscore table and similarity with the one extracted from the human-written summary. However, any hallucinated facts may unrealistically boost the BLEU score while not penalized by the data fidelity metrics since no records can be identified from the ungrounded contents. Thus the possibly misleading evaluation results inhibit systems to demonstrate excellence on this task.

These two aspects potentially undermine people's interests in this data fidelity oriented table-to-text generation task. Therefore, in this work, we revamp the task emphasizing this core aspect to further enable research in this direction. First, we restore the information balance by trimming the summaries of ungrounded contents and replenish the boxscore table to compensate for missing inputs. This requires the non-trivial extraction of the latent gold standard content plans with high-quality. Thus, we take the efforts to design sophisticated heuristics and achieved an estimated 98% precision and 95% recall of the true content plans, retaining 74% of numerical words in the summaries. This yields better content plans as compared to the 94% precision, 80% recall by Puduppully et al. (2019b) and 60% retainment by Wiseman et al. (2017) respectively. Guided by the high-quality content plans, only fact-grounded contents are identified and retained as shown in Table 1.

Furthermore, by expanding with 50% more games between the years 2017-19, we obtain the more focused RotoWire-FG (RW-FG) dataset.

This leads to more accurate evaluations and collectively paves the way for future works by providing a more user-friendly alternative. With this refurbished setup, the existing models are then reassessed on their abilities to ensure data fidelity. We discover that by only purifying the RW dataset, the models can generate more precise facts without sacrificing fluency. Furthermore, we propose a new form of table reconstruction as an auxiliary task to improve fact grounding. By incorporating it into the state-of-the-art Neural Content Planning (NCP) (Puduppully et al., 2019a) model, we established a benchmark on the RW-FG dataset with a 24.41 BLEU score and 95.7% factual accuracy.

Finally, these insights lead us to summarize several fine-grained future challenges based on concrete examples, regarding factual accuracy and intra- and inter- sentence coherence.

Our contributions include:

1. We introduce a purified, enlarged and enriched new dataset to support the more focused fact-grounded table-to-text generation task. We provide high-quality summary facts to table records mappings (content plan) and a more user-friendly experimental setup. All codes and data are freely available[3].

2. We re-investigate existing methods with more insights, establish a new benchmark on this task, and uncover more fine-grained challenges to encourage future research.

---

[3]https://github.com/wanghm92/rw_fg

Type	His	Sch	Agg	Game	Inf
Count	69	33	9	23	23
Percent	43.9	21.0	5.7	14.7	14.7

Table 2: Types of ungrounded contents about statistics related to *His*: history (e.g. recent-game/career high/average) *Sch*: team schedule (e.g. what is next game); *Agg*: aggregation of statistics from multiple players (e.g. the duo of two stars combined scoring ...) ; *Game*: during the game (e.g. a game winning shot with 1 second left); *Inf*: inferred from aggregations (e.g. a player carried the team for winning)

2 Data-to-Text Dataset

This task requires models to take as inputs the NBA basketball game boxscore tables containing hundreds of records and generate the corresponding game summaries. A table can be view as a set of (*entity*, *value*, *type*) records where *entity* is the row name and *type* is the column name in Table 1. **Formally**: Let $\mathbb{E} = \{e_k\}_{k=1}^K$ be the set of entities for a game. $\mathbb{S} = \{r_j\}_{j=1}^S$ be the set of records where each r_j has a value r_j^m, an entity name r_j^e, a record type r_j^t and r_j^h indicating if the entity is the HOME or AWAY team. For example, a record has r_j^t = POINTS, r_j^e = Dwight Howard, r_j^m = 26, and r_j^h = HOME. The summary has T words: $\hat{y}_{1:T} = \hat{y}_1, \ldots, \hat{y}_T$. A sample is a $(\mathbb{S}, \hat{y}_{1:T})$ pair.

2.1 Looking into the `RotoWire` Corpus

To better understand what kind of ungrounded contents are causing the interference, we manually examine a set of 30 randomly picked samples[4] and categorize the sentences into 5 types whose counts and percentages are tabulated in Table 2.

The *His* type occupies the majority portion, followed by the game-specific *Game*, *Inf*, and *Agg* types, and the remaining goes to *Sch*. Specifically, the *His* and *Agg* types come from exponentially large number of possible combinations of game statistics, and the *Inf* type is based on subjective judgments. Thus, it is difficult to trace and aggregate the heterogeneous sources of origin for such statements to fully balance the input and output. The *Sch* and *Game* types require a sample from a large pool of non-numerical and time-related information, whose exclusion would not affect the nature of the fact-grounding generation task. On the other hand, these ungrounded contents misguide a system to generate hallucinated facts and

thus defeat the purpose of developing and evaluating models for fact-grounded table-to-text generation. Thus, we emphasize on this core aspect of the task by trimming contents not licensed by the boxscore table, which we show later still encompasses many fine-grained challenges awaiting to be resolved. While fully restoring all desired inputs is also an interesting research challenge, it is orthogonal to our focus and thus left for future explorations.

2.2 `RotoWire-FG`

Motivated by these observations, we perform purification and augmentation on the original dataset to obtain the new `RW-FG` dataset.

2.2.1 Dataset Purification

Purifying Contents: We aim to retain game summary contents with facts licensed by the boxscore records. The sports game summary genre is more descriptive than analytical and aims to concisely cover salient player or team statistics. Correspondingly, a summary often finishes describing one entity before shifting to the next. This fashion of topic shift allows us to identify the topic boundaries using sentences as units, and thus greatly narrows down the candidate boxscore records to be aligned with a fact. The mappings can then be identified using simple pattern-based matching, as also explored by Wiseman et al. (2017). It also enables resolving co-reference by mapping the singular and plural pronouns to the most recently mentioned players and teams respectively. A numerical value associated with an entity is licensed by the boxscore table if it equals to the record value of the desired type. Thus we design a set of heuristics to determine the types, such as mapping "Channing Frye furnished 12 points" to the (*Channing Frye, 12, POINTS*) record in the table. Finally, consecutive sentences describing the same entity is retained if any numerical value is licensed by the boxscore table.

This trimming process introduces negligible influences on the inter-sentence coherence for the summaries. We achieve a 98% precision and a 95% recall of the true content plans and align 74% of all numerical words in the summaries to records in the boxscore tables. The sequence of mapped records is extracted as the content plans and samples describing fewer than 5 records are discarded.

In between the labor-intensive yet imperfect manual annotation and the cheap but inaccu-

---

[4]For convenience, they are from the validation set and also used later for evaluation purposes.

Versions	Examples	Tokens	Vocab	Types	Avg Len
RW	4.9K	1.6M	11.3K	39	337.1
RW-EX	7.5K	2.5M	12.7K	39	334.3
RW-FG	7.3K	1.5M	8.8K	61	205.9

Table 3: Comparison between datasets. (RW-EX is the enlarged RW with 50% more games)

	Sents	Content Plans	Records	Num-only Records
RW-EX	14.0	27.2	494.2	429.3
RW-FG	8.6	28.5	519.9	478.3

Table 4: Dataset statistics by the average number of each item per sample.

rate lexical matching, we achieved better quality through designing the heuristics using similar efforts as training and assembling the IE models by Wiseman et al. (2017). Meanwhile, more accurate content plans provide better reliability during evaluation.

Normalization: To enhance accuracy, we convert all English number words into numerical values. As some percentages are rounded differently between the summaries and the boxscore tables, such discrepancies are rectified. We also perform entity normalization for players and teams, resolving mentions of the same entity to one lexical form. This makes evaluations more user-friendly and less prone to errors.

2.2.2 Dataset Augmentation

Enlargement: Similar to Wiseman et al. (2017), we crawl the game summaries from the *RotoWire Game Recaps*[5] between years 2017-19 and align the summaries with the official *NBA*[6] boxscore tables. This brings 2.6K more games with 56% more tokens, as tabulated in Table 4.

Line-score replenishment: Many team statistics in the summaries are missing in the line-score tables. We recover them by aggregating other boxscore statistics. For example, the number of shots attempted and made by the team for field goals, 3-pointers, and free-throws are calculated by summing their player statistics. Besides, we supplement a set of team point breakdowns as shown in Table 5. The replenishment boosts the recall on numerical values from 72% to 74% and augments the content plans by 1.3 records per sample.

Finalize: We conduct the same purification procedures described in section 2.2.1 after the augmen-

---

[5]https://www.RotoWire.com/basketball/game-recaps.php

[6]https://stats.nba.com/

	Quarters				Players	
Sums	1 to 2	1 to 3	2 to 3	2 to 4	bench	starters
	Halves		Quarters			
Diffs	1st	2nd	1	2	3	4

Table 5: Replenished line-score statistics. Each purple cell corresponds to a new record type, defined as applying the the operation in the row names (green) to the source of statistics in the column names (yellow). "Sums" operates on individual teams and "Diffs" is between the two teams. For example, the "1 to 2" cell in the second row means the summation of points scored by a team in the 1st and 2nd "Quarters", the "1st" cell in the fourth row means the difference between the two teams' 1st half points.

tations. More data collection details are included in Appendix A.

3 Re-assessing Models on Purified RW

3.1 Models

We re-assess three neural network based models on this task[7]. To feed the tables to the models, each record r_j has attribute embeddings for r_j^m, r_j^e, r_j^t, r_j^h and their concatenation is the input.

- ED-CC (Wiseman et al., 2017): This is an Encoder-Decoder (ED) (Sutskever et al., 2014; Cho et al., 2014) model with an 1-layer MLP encoder (Yang et al., 2017), and an LSTM (Hochreiter and Schmidhuber, 1997) decoder with the Conditional Copy (CC) mechanism (Gulcehre et al., 2016).

- NCP (Puduppully et al., 2019a): The Neural Content Planning (NCP) model employs a pointer network (Vinyals et al., 2015) to select a subset of records from the boxscore table and sequentially roll them out as the content plan. Then the summary is then generated only from the content plan using the ED-CC model with a Bi-LSTM encoder.

- ENT (Puduppully et al., 2019b): The ENTity memory network (ENT) model extends the ED-CC model with a dynamically updated entity-specific memory module to capture topic shifts in outputs and incorporate it into each decoder step with a hierarchical attention mechanism.

---

[7]Iso et al. (2019) was released after this work was submitted. It also altered the RW-FG dataset for experiments, so the results would not be directly comparable. The method is worth investigation for future works.

3.2 Evaluation

In addition to using BLEU (Papineni et al., 2002) as a reasonable proxy for evaluating the fluency of the generated summary, Wiseman et al. (2017) designed three types of metrics to assess if a summary accurately conveys the desired information.

Extractive Metrics: First, an ordered sequence of (*entity*, *value*, *type*) triples are extracted from the system output summary as the content plan using the same heuristics in section 2.2.1. It is then checked against the table for its accuracy (RG) and the gold content plan to measure how well they match (CS & CO). Specifically, let $cp = \{r_i\}$ and $cp' = \{r'_i\}$ be the gold and system content plan respectively, and $|.|$ denote set cardinality. We calculate the following measures:

- **Content Selection (CS)**:
    - Precision (**CSP**) = $|cp \cap cp'| / |cp'|$
    - Recall (**CSR**) = $|cp \cap cp'| / |cp|$
    - F1 (**CSF**) = $2PR/(P+R)$

- **Relation Generation (RG)**:
    - Count(#) = $|cp'|$
    - Precision (**RGP**) = $|cp' \cap \mathbb{S}| / |cp'|$

- **Content Ordering (CO)**:
    - **DLD**: normalized Damerau Levenshtein Distance (Brill and Moore, 2000) between cp and cp'

CS and **RG** measures the "what to say" and **CO** measures the "how to say" aspects.

3.3 Experiments

Setup: To re-investigate the existing three methods on the ability to convey accurate information conditioned on the input, we assess them by training on the purified RW corpus. To demonstrate the differences brought by the purification process, we keep all other settings unchanged and report results on the original validation and test sets after performing early stopping (Yao et al., 2007) based on the BLEU score.

Results: As shown in Table 6, we observe increase in Relation Generation Precision (RGP) and on-par performance for Content Selection

---

⁸For fair comparison, we report results of ENT model after fixing a bug in the evaluation script as endorsed by the author of Wiseman et al. (2017) at `https://github.com/harvardnlp/data2text/issues/6`

(CS) and Content Ordering (CO). In particular, Relation Generation Precision (RGP) is substantially increased by an average 2.7% for all models. The Content Selection (CS) and Content Ordering (CO) measures fluctuate above and below the references, with the biggest disparity on Content Selection Precision (CSP), Content Selection Recall (CSR) and Content Ordering (CO) for the ENT model. Since output length is a main independent variable for this set of experiments and a crucial factor in BLEU score as well, we report the breakdowns in Table 7. Specifically, the NCP model shows consistent improvements on all BLEU 1-4 scores, similarly for ENT on the validation set. Among all fluctuation around the references, nearly all models demonstrate an increase in BLEU-1 and BLEU-4 precision. Reflected on the BP coefficients, models trained on the purified summaries produces shorter outputs, which is the major reason for lower BLEU scores when using the un-purified summaries as the references.

3.4 How Purification Affects Performance

First, simply replacing with the purified training set leads to considerable improvements in the Relation Generation Precision (RGP). This is because removing the ungrounded facts (e.g. *His*, *Agg*, and *Game* types) alleviates their interference with the model while learning when and where to copy over a correct numerical value from the table. Besides, since the ungrounded facts do not contribute to the gold or system output content plan during the information extraction process, the other extractive metrics Content Selection (CS) and Content Ordering (CO) measures stay on-par.

One abnormality is the big difference in the Content Selection (CS) and Content Ordering (CO) measures from the ENT model. This is not that surprising after examining the outputs, which appear to collapse into template-like summaries. For example, 97.8% sentences start with the game points followed by a pattern "XX were the superior shooters" where XX represents a team. Tracing back to the model design, it is explicitly trained to model topic shifts on the token level during generation, which instead happens more often on the sentence level. As a result, it degenerates to remembering a frequent discourse-level pattern from the training data. We observe a similar pattern on the outputs from original outputs by Puduppully et al. (2019b), which is aggravated

315

Model	Dev						Test					
	RG		CS			CO	RG		CS			CO
	#	P%	P%	R%	F1%	DLD%	#	P%	P%	R%	F1%	DLD%
ED-CC	23.95	75.10	28.11	35.86	31.52	15.33	23.72	74.80	29.49	36.18	32.49	15.42
ED-CC(FG)	22.65	78.63	29.48	34.08	31.61	14.58	23.36	79.88	29.36	33.36	31.23	13.87
NCP	33.88	87.51	33.52	51.21	40.52	18.57	34.28	87.47	34.18	51.22	41.00	18.58
NCP(FG)	31.90	90.20	34.53	49.74	40.76	18.29	33.51	91.46	33.96	49.14	40.16	18.16
ENT[8]	21.49	91.17	40.50	37.78	39.09	19.10	21.53	91.87	42.61	38.31	40.34	19.50
ENT(FG)	30.08	93.74	30.43	48.64	37.44	16.53	30.66	93.09	32.40	41.69	36.46	16.44

Table 6: Comparison between models trained on RW and RW−FG

Model	Dev						Test					
	B1	B2	B3	B4	BP	BLEU	B1	B2	B3	B4	BP	BLEU
ED-CC	44.42	**18.16**	**9.40**	5.95	**1.00**	**14.57**	43.22	**17.64**	**9.16**	5.81	**1.00**	**14.19**
ED-CC(FG)	**46.61**	17.70	9.33	**6.21**	0.59	8.74	**45.75**	17.14	9.05	**5.98**	0.61	8.68
NCP	48.95	20.58	10.70	6.96	**1.00**	**16.19**	49.77	21.19	11.31	7.46	**0.96**	**16.50**
NCP(FG)	**56.63**	**24.15**	**12.45**	**8.13**	0.54	10.45	**56.33**	**23.92**	**12.42**	**8.11**	0.53	10.25
ENT	51.57	21.92	11.87	8.08	**0.88**	15.97	53.23	**23.07**	**12.78**	**8.78**	**0.84**	**16.12**
ENT(FG)	**56.08**	**23.29**	**12.29**	**8.16**	0.44	8.92	**55.03**	21.86	11.38	7.38	0.57	10.17

Table 7: Breakdown of BLEU scores for models trained on RW and RW−FG

when trained on the purified dataset. On the other hand, the NCP model decouples the content selection and planning on the discourse level from the surface realization on the token level, and thus generalizes better.

4 A New Benchmark on RW−FG

With more insights about the existing methods, we take a step further to achieve better data fidelity. Wiseman et al. (2017) achieved improvements on the ED with Joint Copy (JC) (Gu et al., 2016) model by introducing an reconstruction loss (Tu et al., 2017) during training. Specifically, the decoder states at each time step are used to predict record values in the table to enable broader input information coverage.

However, we take a different point of view: one key mechanism to avoid reference errors is to ensure that the set of numerical values mentioned in a sentence belongs to the correct entity with the correct record field type. While the ED-CC model is trained to achieve such alignments, it should also be able to accurately fill the numbers back to the correct cells in an empty table. This should be done by only accessing the column and row information of the cells without explicitly knowing the original cell values. Further leveraging on the planner output of the NCP model, the candidate cells to be filled can be reduced to the content plan cells selected by the planner. With this intuition, we devise a new form of table reconstruction (TR) task incorporated into the NCP model.

Specifically, each content plan record has at-tribute embeddings for r_j^e, r_j^t, and r_j^h, excluding its value, and we encode them using a 1-layer MLP (Yang et al., 2017). We then employ the Luong et al. (2015) attention mechanism at each $\hat{y}_t$ if it is a numerical value with the encoded content plan as the memory bank. The attention weights are then viewed as probabilities of selecting each cell to fill the number $\hat{y}_t$. The model is additionally trained to minimize the negative log-likelihood of the correct cell.

4.1 Experiments

Setup: We assess models on the RW−FG corpus to establish a new benchmark. Following Wiseman et al. (2017), we split all samples into train (70%), validation (15%), and test (15%) sets, and perform early stopping (Yao et al., 2007) using BLEU (Papineni et al., 2002). We adapt the template-based generator by Wiseman et al. (2017) and remove the ungrounded end sentence since they are eliminated in RW−FG.

Results: As shown in Table 8, the template model can ensure high Relation Generation Precision (RGP) but is inflexible as shown by other measures. Different from Puduppully et al. (2019b), the NCP model is superior on all measures among the baseline neural models. The ENT model only outperforms the basic ED-CC model but surprisingly yields lower Content Selection (CS) measures. Our NCP+TR model outperforms all baselines except for slightly lower Content Selection Precision (CSP) compared to the NCP model.

Model	Dev							Test						
	RG		CS			CO	BLEU	RG		CS			CO	BLEU
	#	P%	P%	R%	F1%	DLD%		#	P%	P%	R%	F1%	DLD%	
TMPL	51.81	99.09	23.78	43.75	30.81	10.06	11.91	51.80	98.89	23.98	43.96	31.03	10.25	12.09
WS17	30.47	81.51	36.15	39.12	37.57	18.56	21.31	30.28	82.16	35.84	38.40	37.08	18.45	20.80
ENT	35.56	93.30	40.19	50.71	44.84	17.81	21.67	35.69	93.72	39.04	49.29	43.57	17.50	21.23
NCP	36.28	94.27	**43.31**	55.96	48.91	24.08	24.49	35.99	94.21	**43.31**	55.15	48.52	23.46	23.86
NCP+TR	**37.04**	**95.65**	43.09	**57.24**	**49.17**	**24.75**	**24.80**	**37.49**	**95.70**	42.90	**56.91**	**48.92**	**24.47**	**24.41**

Table 8: Performances of models on RW-FG

Model	Total(#)	RP(%)	WC(%)	UG(%)	IC(%)
NCP	246	9.21	11.84	3.07	5.26
NCP+TR	228	3.66	8.94	3.25	2.03

Table 9: Error types of manual evaluation. *Total*: number of sentences; *RP*: Repetition; *WC*: Wrong Claim; *UG*: Ungrounded sentence; *IC*: Incoherent sentence

4.2 Discussion

We observe that the ED-CC model produces the least number of candidate records, and correspondingly achieves the lowest Content Selection Recall (CSR) compared to the gold standard content plans. As discussed in section 3.4, the template-like discourse pattern produced by the ENT model noticeably deteriorates its performance. It is completely outperformed by the NCP model and even achieves lower CO-DLD than the ED-CC model. Finally, as supported by the extractive evaluation metrics, employing table reconstruction as an auxiliary task indeed boosts the decoder to produce more accurate factual statements. We discuss in more detail as follows.

4.2.1 Manual Evaluation

To gain more insights into how exactly NCP+TR improves from NCP in terms of factual accuracy, we manually examined the outputs on the 30 samples. We compare the two systems after categorizing the errors into 4 types. As shown in Table 9, the largest improvement comes from reducing repeated statements and wrong fact claims, where the latter involves referring to the wrong entity or making the wrong judgment of the numerical value. The NCP+TR generally produces more concise outputs with a reduction in repetitions, consistent with the objective for table reconstruction.

4.2.2 Case study

Table 10 shows a pair of outputs by the two systems. In this example, the NCP+TR model can correct wrong the player name "*Jahlil Okafor*"

by "*Joel Embiid*", while keeping the statistics intact. It also avoids repeating on "*Channing Frye*" and the semantically incoherent expression about "*Kevin Love*" and "*Kyrie Irving*". Nonetheless, this NCP output selects more records to describe the progress of the game. This shows how the NCP+TR trained with more constraints behaves more accurately but conservatively.

5 Errors and Challenges

Having revamped the task with better focus, reassessed existing and improved models, we discuss 3 future directions in this task with concrete examples in Table 11:

Content Selection: Since writers are subjective in choosing *what to say* given the boxscore, it is unrealistic to force a model to mimic all kinds of styles. However, a model still needs to learn from training to select both the salient (e.g. surprisingly high/low statistics for a team/player) and the popular (e.g. the big stars) statistics. One potential direction is to involve multiple human references to help reveal such saliency and make Content Ordering (CO) and Content Selection (CS) measures more interpretive. This is particularly applicable for the sports domain since a game can be uniquely identified by the teams and date but mapped to articles from different sources. Besides, multi-reference has been explored for evaluating data-to-text generation systems (Novikova et al., 2017) and for content selection and planning (Gehrmann et al., 2018). It has also been studied in machine translation for evaluation (Dreyer and Marcu, 2012) and training (Zheng et al., 2018).

Content Planning: Content plans have been extracted by linearly rolling out the records and topic shifts are modeled as sequential changes between adjacent entities. However, this fashion does not reflect the hierarchical discourse structures of a document and thus ensures neither intra- nor inter-sentence coherence. As shown by the errors in (1)

The **Cleveland Cavaliers** defeated the **Philadelphia 76ers** , 102 - 101 , at Wells Fargo Center on Monday evening . **LeBron James** led the way with a **25 - point** , **14 - assist** double double that also included **8 rebounds** , **2 steals** and **1 block** . **Kevin Love** followed with a **20 - point** , **11 - rebound** double double that also included **1 assist** and **1 block** . **Channing Frye** led the bench with **12 points** , **2 rebounds** , **2 assists** and **2 steals** **Kyrie Irving** managed **8 points** , **7 rebounds** , **2 assists** and **2 steals** . ... Joel Embiid 's 22 points led the Sixers , a total he supplemented with **6 rebounds** , **2 assists** , **4 blocks** and **1 steal** ...

The **Cleveland Cavaliers** defeated the **Philadelphia 76ers** , 102 - 101 , at Wells Fargo Center on Friday evening . The Cavaliers came out of the gates hot , jumping out to a **34 - 15** lead after 1 quarter . However , the **Sixers** (**0 - 5**) stormed back in the second to cut the deficit to just **2 points** by halftime . However , the light went on for Cleveland at intermission , as they built a **9 - point** lead by halftime . **LeBron James** led the way for the Cavaliers with a **25 - point** , **14 - assist** double double that also included **8 rebounds** , **2 steals** and **1 block** . Kyrie Irving followed Kevin Love with a **20 - point** , **11 - rebound** double double that also included **1 assist** and **1 block** . **Channing Frye** furnished **12 points** , **2 rebounds** , **2 assists** and **2 steals** ... **Channing Frye** led the bench with **12 points** , **2 rebounds** , **2 assists** and **2 steals** . Jahlil Okafor led the Sixers with 22 points, 6 rebounds, 2 assists, 4 blocks and 1 steal ... **Jahlil Okafor** managed **14 points** , **5 rebounds** , **3 blocks** and **1 steal** .

Table 10: Case study comparing NCP+TR (above) and NCP (below). The records identified are in **bold**. The pair of sentences in orange shows an referring error to **Jahlil Okafor** is corrected above to **Joel Embiid**, where all the trailing statistics actually belong to **Joel Embiid**, and **Jahlil Okafor**'s actual statistics are described at the end. The yellow sentences repeats on the same player. The green sentences actually shows some more contents selected by the NCP model. The blue sentence is a tricky one, where it should describe **Kyrie Irving**'s statistics but actually describing **Kevin Love**'s but the summary above does not have this issue.

in Table 11, the links between entities and their numerical statistics are not strictly monotonic and switching the order results in errors.

On the other hand, autoregressive training for creating such content plans limits the model to capture frequent sequence patterns rather than allowing diverse arrangements. Moryossef et al. (2019) demonstrates isolating the content planning from the joint end-to-end training and employing multiple valid content plans during testing. Although the content plan extraction heuristics are dataset-dependent, it is worth exploring for data in a closed domain like RW.

Surface Realization: Although the NCP+TR model has achieved nearly 96% Relation Gen-

(1) Intra-sentence coherence:

- The **Lakers** were the *superior shooters* in this game , going **48 percent** from the field and 24 percent from the three point line , while the **Jazz** went **47 percent** from the floor and just 30 percent from beyond the arc.
- The **Rockets** got off to a quick start in this game, *out scoring* the **Nuggets** 21-31 right away in the 1st quarter.

(2) Inter-sentence coherence:

- **LeBron James** was the lone bright spot for the **Cavaliers** , as he led the team with **20 points** . **Kevin Love** was *the only Cleveland starter in double figures* , as he tallied **17 points** , **11 rebounds** and **3 assists** in the loss.
- *Dirk Nowitzki led the Mavericks in scoring* , finishing with **22 points** (7 - 13 FG , 3 - 5 3PT , 5 - 5 FT) , **5 rebounds** and **3 assists** in **37 minutes**. *He* 's had a very strong stretch of games , scoring **17 points** on 6 - for - **13** shooting from the field and 5 - for - **10** from the three point line . *JJ Barea finished with 32 points* (**13 - 21 FG , 5 - 8 3PT**) and **11 assists** ...

(3) Incorrect claim:

- The **Heat** were able to force 20 turnovers from the **Sixers**, which may have been the difference in this game.

Table 11: Cases for three major types of system errors

eration Precision (RGP), it is still paramount to keep on improving data accuracy since one single mistake is destructive to the whole document. The challenge is more with the evaluation metrics. Specifically, all extractive metrics only validate if an extracted record maps to the true entity and type but disregards the semantics of its contexts. For example (2) in Table 11, even assuming the linear ordering of records, their context still causes inter-sentence incoherence. In particular, both LeBron and Kevin scored double digits and JJ Barea leads the scores rather than Dirk. For another example (3), the 20 turnovers records are selected to be Heat's but expressed falsely as Sixers'. As pointed out by Wiseman et al. (2017), this may require the integration of semantic or reference-based constraints during generation. The number magnitudes should be incorporated. For example, Nie et al. (2018) has devised an interesting idea to implicitly improve coherence by supplementing the input with pre-computed results from algebraic operations on the table. Moreover, Qin et al. (2018) proposed to automatically align the game summary with the record types in the input table on the phrase level. It can potentially be combined with the operation results to correct incoherence errors and improve the generations.

6 Related Works

Various forms of structured data has been used as input for data-to-text generation tasks, such as tree (Belz et al., 2011; Mille et al., 2018), graph (Konstas and Lapata, 2012), dialog moves (Novikova et al., 2017), knowledge base (Gardent et al., 2017b; Chisholm et al., 2017), database (Konstas and Lapata, 2012; Gardent et al., 2017a; Wang et al., 2018), and table (Wiseman et al., 2017; Lebret et al., 2016). The RW corpus we studied is from the sports domain which has attracted great interests (Chen and Mooney, 2008; Mei et al., 2016; Puduppully et al., 2019b). However, unlike generating the one-entity descriptions (Lebret et al., 2016; Wang et al., 2018) or having the output strictly bounded by the inputs (Novikova et al., 2017), this corpus poses additional challenges since the targets contain ungrounded contents. To facilitate better usage and evaluation of this task, we hope to provide a refined alternative, similar to the purpose by Castro Ferreira et al. (2018).

7 Conclusion

In this work, we study the core fact-grounding aspect of the data-to-text generation task and contribute a purified, enlarged, and enriched RotoWire-FG corpus with a more fair and reliable evaluation setup. We re-assess existing models and found that the more focused setting helps the models to express more accurate statements and alleviate fact hallucinations. Improving the state-of-the-art model and setting a benchmark on the new task, we reveal fine-grained unsolved challenges hoping to inspire more research in this direction.

Acknowledgments

Thanks for the generous and valuable feedback from the reviewers. Special thanks to Dr. Jing Huang and Dr. Yun Tang for their unselfish guidance and support.

References

Anja Belz, Mike White, Dominic Espinosa, Eric Kow, Deirdre Hogan, and Amanda Stent. 2011. The first surface realisation shared task: Overview and evaluation results. In *ENLG*.

Eric Brill and Robert C. Moore. 2000. An improved error model for noisy channel spelling correction. In *Proceedings of the 38th Annual Meeting of the Association for Computational Linguistics*, pages 286–293, Hong Kong. Association for Computational Linguistics.

Thiago Castro Ferreira, Diego Moussallem, Emiel Krahmer, and Sander Wubben. 2018. Enriching the WebNLG corpus. In *Proceedings of the 11th International Conference on Natural Language Generation*, pages 171–176, Tilburg University, The Netherlands. Association for Computational Linguistics.

David L. Chen and Raymond J. Mooney. 2008. Learning to sportscast: a test of grounded language acquisition. In *Machine Learning, Proceedings of the Twenty-Fifth International Conference (ICML 2008), Helsinki, Finland, June 5-9, 2008*, pages 128–135.

Andrew Chisholm, Will Radford, and Ben Hachey. 2017. Learning to generate one-sentence biographies from Wikidata. In *Proceedings of the 15th Conference of the European Chapter of the Association for Computational Linguistics: Volume 1, Long Papers*, pages 633–642, Valencia, Spain. Association for Computational Linguistics.

Kyunghyun Cho, Bart van Merrienboer, Dzmitry Bahdanau, and Yoshua Bengio. 2014. On the properties of neural machine translation: Encoder-decoder approaches. In *Proceedings of SSST@EMNLP 2014, Eighth Workshop on Syntax, Semantics and Structure in Statistical Translation, Doha, Qatar, 25 October 2014*, pages 103–111.

Markus Dreyer and Daniel Marcu. 2012. HyTER: Meaning-equivalent semantics for translation evaluation. In *Proceedings of the 2012 Conference of the North American Chapter of the Association for Computational Linguistics: Human Language Technologies*, pages 162–171, Montréal, Canada. Association for Computational Linguistics.

Claire Gardent, Anastasia Shimorina, Shashi Narayan, and Laura Perez-Beltrachini. 2017a. Creating training corpora for NLG micro-planners. In *Proceedings of the 55th Annual Meeting of the Association for Computational Linguistics (Volume 1: Long Papers)*, Vancouver, Canada. Association for Computational Linguistics.

Claire Gardent, Anastasia Shimorina, Shashi Narayan, and Laura Perez-Beltrachini. 2017b. The webnlg challenge: Generating text from RDF data. In *Proceedings of the 10th International Conference on Natural Language Generation, INLG 2017, Santiago de Compostela, Spain, September 4-7, 2017*, pages 124–133.

Sebastian Gehrmann, Falcon Z. Dai, Henry Elder, and Alexander M. Rush. 2018. End-to-end content and plan selection for data-to-text generation. In *Proceedings of the 11th International Conference on Natural Language Generation, Tilburg University, The Netherlands, November 5-8, 2018, pages 46–56.*

Jiatao Gu, Zhengdong Lu, Hang Li, and Victor O.K. Li. 2016. Incorporating copying mechanism in sequence-to-sequence learning. In *Proceedings of the 54th Annual Meeting of the Association for Computational Linguistics (Volume 1: Long Papers)*, pages 1631–1640, Berlin, Germany. Association for Computational Linguistics.

Caglar Gulcehre, Sungjin Ahn, Ramesh Nallapati, Bowen Zhou, and Yoshua Bengio. 2016. Pointing the unknown words. In *Proceedings of the 54th Annual Meeting of the Association for Computational Linguistics (Volume 1: Long Papers)*, pages 140–149, Berlin, Germany. Association for Computational Linguistics.

Sepp Hochreiter and Jürgen Schmidhuber. 1997. Long short-term memory. *Neural Computation*, 9(8):1735–1780.

Hayate Iso, Yui Uehara, Tatsuya Ishigaki, Hiroshi Noji, Eiji Aramaki, Ichiro Kobayashi, Yusuke Miyao, Naoaki Okazaki, and Hiroya Takamura. 2019. Learning to select, track, and generate for data-to-text. In *Proceedings of the 57th Annual Meeting of the Association for Computational Linguistics*, pages 2102–2113, Florence, Italy. Association for Computational Linguistics.

Ioannis Konstas and Mirella Lapata. 2012. Concept-to-text generation via discriminative reranking. In *The 50th Annual Meeting of the Association for Computational Linguistics, Proceedings of the Conference, July 8-14, 2012, Jeju Island, Korea - Volume 1: Long Papers*, pages 369–378.

Rémi Lebret, David Grangier, and Michael Auli. 2016. Neural text generation from structured data with application to the biography domain. In *Proceedings of the 2016 Conference on Empirical Methods in Natural Language Processing*, pages 1203–1213, Austin, Texas. Association for Computational Linguistics.

Liunian Li and Xiaojun Wan. 2018. Point precisely: Towards ensuring the precision of data in generated texts using delayed copy mechanism. In *Proceedings of the 27th International Conference on Computational Linguistics, COLING 2018, Santa Fe, New Mexico, USA, August 20-26, 2018*, pages 1044–1055.

Thang Luong, Hieu Pham, and Christopher D. Manning. 2015. Effective approaches to attention-based neural machine translation. In *Proceedings of the 2015 Conference on Empirical Methods in Natural Language Processing*, pages 1412–1421, Lisbon, Portugal. Association for Computational Linguistics.

Hongyuan Mei, Mohit Bansal, and Matthew R. Walter. 2016. What to talk about and how? selective generation using LSTMs with coarse-to-fine alignment. In *Proceedings of the 2016 Conference of the North American Chapter of the Association for Computational Linguistics: Human Language Technologies*, pages 720–730, San Diego, California. Association for Computational Linguistics.

Simon Mille, Anja Belz, Bernd Bohnet, Yvette Graham, Emily Pitler, and Leo Wanner. 2018. The first multilingual surface realisation shared task (SR'18): Overview and evaluation results. In *Proceedings of the First Workshop on Multilingual Surface Realisation*, pages 1–12, Melbourne, Australia. Association for Computational Linguistics.

Amit Moryossef, Yoav Goldberg, and Ido Dagan. 2019. Step-by-step: Separating planning from realization in neural data-to-text generation. In *Proceedings of the 2019 Conference of the North American Chapter of the Association for Computational Linguistics: Human Language Technologies, Volume 1 (Long and Short Papers)*, pages 2267–2277, Minneapolis, Minnesota. Association for Computational Linguistics.

Feng Nie, Jinpeng Wang, Jin-Ge Yao, Rong Pan, and Chin-Yew Lin. 2018. Operation-guided neural networks for high fidelity data-to-text generation. In *Proceedings of the 2018 Conference on Empirical Methods in Natural Language Processing*, pages 3879–3889, Brussels, Belgium. Association for Computational Linguistics.

Jekaterina Novikova, Ondrej Dusek, and Verena Rieser. 2017. The E2E dataset: New challenges for end-to-end generation. In *Proceedings of the 18th Annual SIGdial Meeting on Discourse and Dialogue, Saarbrücken, Germany, August 15-17, 2017*.

Kishore Papineni, Salim Roukos, Todd Ward, and Wei-Jing Zhu. 2002. Bleu: a method for automatic evaluation of machine translation. In *Proceedings of the 40th Annual Meeting of the Association for Computational Linguistics, July 6-12, 2002, Philadelphia, PA, USA.*, pages 311–318.

Ratish Puduppully, Li Dong, and Mirella Lapata. 2019a. Data-to-text generation with content selection and planning. In *The Thirty-Third AAAI Conference on Artificial Intelligence, AAAI 2019, The Thirty-First Innovative Applications of Artificial Intelligence Conference, IAAI 2019, The Ninth AAAI Symposium on Educational Advances in Artificial Intelligence, EAAI 2019, Honolulu, Hawaii, USA, January 27 - February 1, 2019.*, pages 6908–6915.

Ratish Puduppully, Li Dong, and Mirella Lapata. 2019b. Data-to-text generation with entity modeling. In *Proceedings of the 57th Annual Meeting of the Association for Computational Linguistics*, pages 2023–2035, Florence, Italy. Association for Computational Linguistics.

Guanghui Qin, Jin-Ge Yao, Xuening Wang, Jinpeng Wang, and Chin-Yew Lin. 2018. Learning latent semantic annotations for grounding natural language to structured data. In *Proceedings of the 2018 Conference on Empirical Methods in Natural Language Processing*, pages 3761–3771, Brussels, Belgium. Association for Computational Linguistics.

Ilya Sutskever, Oriol Vinyals, and Quoc V. Le. 2014. Sequence to sequence learning with neural networks. In *Advances in Neural Information Processing Systems 27: Annual Conference on Neural Information Processing Systems 2014, December 8-13 2014, Montreal, Quebec, Canada*, pages 3104–3112.

Zhaopeng Tu, Yang Liu, Lifeng Shang, Xiaohua Liu, and Hang Li. 2017. Neural machine translation with reconstruction. In *Proceedings of the Thirty-First AAAI Conference on Artificial Intelligence, February 4-9, 2017, San Francisco, California, USA.*, pages 3097–3103.

Oriol Vinyals, Meire Fortunato, and Navdeep Jaitly. 2015. Pointer networks. In *Advances in Neural Information Processing Systems 28: Annual Conference on Neural Information Processing Systems 2015, December 7-12, 2015, Montreal, Quebec, Canada*, pages 2692–2700.

Qingyun Wang, Xiaoman Pan, Lifu Huang, Boliang Zhang, Zhiying Jiang, Heng Ji, and Kevin Knight. 2018. Describing a knowledge base. In *Proceedings of the 11th International Conference on Natural Language Generation*, pages 10–21, Tilburg University, The Netherlands. Association for Computational Linguistics.

Sam Wiseman, Stuart Shieber, and Alexander Rush. 2017. Challenges in data-to-document generation. In *Proceedings of the 2017 Conference on Empirical Methods in Natural Language Processing*, pages 2253–2263, Copenhagen, Denmark. Association for Computational Linguistics.

Zichao Yang, Phil Blunsom, Chris Dyer, and Wang Ling. 2017. Reference-aware language models. In *Proceedings of the 2017 Conference on Empirical Methods in Natural Language Processing*, pages 1850–1859, Copenhagen, Denmark. Association for Computational Linguistics.

Yuan Yao, Lorenzo Rosasco, and Andrea Caponnetto. 2007. On early stopping in gradient descent learning. *Constructive Approximation*, 26(2):289–315.

Renjie Zheng, Mingbo Ma, and Liang Huang. 2018. Multi-reference training with pseudo-references for neural translation and text generation. In *Proceedings of the 2018 Conference on Empirical Methods in Natural Language Processing*, pages 3188–3197, Brussels, Belgium. Association for Computational Linguistics.

A Appendices

A.1 Data Collection Details

- We use the text2num[9] package to convert all English number words into numerical values

- We first get the summary title, date, and the contents from *RotoWire Game Recaps*. The title contains the home and visiting team. Together with the date, this game is uniquely identified with a *GAME_ID*. Then we use the *nba_api*[10] package to query the *stats.nba.com* by *NBA.com*[11] to obtain the game boxscore and line scores. Wiseman et al. (2017) used the *nba_py*[12] package , which unfortunately has become obsolete due to lack of maintenance. To obtain the line scores with the same set of column types as the original RotoWire dataset, we collectively used two APIs, *BoxScoreTraditionalV2* and *BoxScoreSummaryV2*.

---

[9] https://github.com/ghewgill/text2num/blob/master/text2num.py
[10] https://github.com/swar/nba_api
[11] www.nba.com; https://stats.nba.com/
[12] https://github.com/seemethere/nba_py

Controlling Contents in Data-to-Document Generation with Human-Designed Topic Labels

Kasumi Aoki[b♠]   Akira Miyazawa[◇♡♠]   Tatsuya Ishigaki[♠♠]   Tatsuya Aoki[♠♠]   Hiroshi Noji[♠]
Keiichi Goshima[♯♠]   Ichiro Kobayashi[b♠]   Hiroya Takamura[♠♠]   Yusuke Miyao[b♠]

[b]Ochanomizu University   [♠]National Institute of Advanced Industrial Science and Technology
[◇]The Graduate University for Advanced Studies   [♡]National Institute of Informatics
[♠]Tokyo Institute of Technology   [♯]Waseda University   [b]The University of Tokyo

{g1120501, koba}@is.ocha.ac.jp   miyazawa-a@nii.ac.jp   {aoki, ishigaki}@lr.pi.titech.ac.jp
hiroshi.noji@aist.go.jp   keiichi.goshima@aoni.waseda.jp   takamura@pi.titech.ac.jp   yusuke@is.s.u-tokyo.ac.jp

Abstract

We propose a data-to-document generator that can easily control the contents of output texts based on a neural language model. Conventional data-to-text model is useful when a reader seeks a global summary of data because it has only to describe an important part that has been extracted beforehand. However, since it differs from users to users what they are interested in, it is necessary to develop a method to generate various summaries according to users' requests. We develop a model to generate various summaries and to control their contents by providing the explicit targets for a reference to the model as controllable factors. In the experiments, we used five-minute or one-hour charts of 9 indicators (e.g., Nikkei 225), as time-series data, and daily summaries of Nikkei Quick News as textual data. We conducted comparative experiments using two pieces of information: human-designed topic labels indicating the contents of a sentence and automatically extracted keywords as the referential information for generation. Experiments show both models using additional information of target document achieved higher performance in terms of BLEU and human evaluation. We found that human-designed topic labels are superior to extracted keywords in terms of controllability.

1 Introduction

Data-to-text is one of the challenging tasks in natural language generation, which aims to generate summaries of input data such as statistics from sports games (Robin, 1995; Barzilay and Lapata, 2005; Wiseman et al., 2017), financial data (Murakami et al., 2017; Aoki et al., 2018), and database records (Reiter and Dale, 1997; Liang et al., 2009; Mei et al., 2016; Lebret et al., 2016; Novikova et al., 2017; Liu et al., 2018; Wiseman et al., 2017).

Over the past several years, end-to-end neural language generation models have successfully been applied to versatile data-to-text tasks, because they can generate fluent texts without task-specific knowledge and resources.

However, it has also been pointed out that texts generated by neural models suffer from low diversity in expressions (Yang et al., 2019). Especially on the data-to-text tasks, since they are developed under the assumption that the important contents could be uniquely determined, previous methods did not focus on controlling the contents in terms of user's interests.

However, each user may expect different contents in a summary depending on what they are interested in, and thus it is appealing to develop a method to generate various summaries which reflect user's interests.

This paper investigates a method for guiding data-to-document generation in the finance domain, by referring to a sequence of additional information for input financial data. Generating documents consisting of multiple sentences involves an inherent challenge in content selection and ordering (Reiter and Dale, 1997), because one can produce a large variety of documents for specific input data, depending on a focus, intent, readers' interest, etc. Therefore, it is essential for document generation systems to have an additional mechanism to select and order the contents to be represented.

We introduce and empirically compare two types of topic labels, both of which are intended to denote clause-level contents and their orders. One is topical keywords automatically extracted from domain texts (Rose et al., 2010), which was applied for the story generation by using as the contents of the story (Yao et al., 2018).

The other is manually defined topic labels. As our target domain is finance, major topics mentioned in documents are restricted to market indices such as Dow Jones Industrial Average (DJI), Nikkei 225, or foreign exchange rates, etc. We devised a

Proceedings of The 12th International Conference on Natural Language Generation, pages 323–332,
Tokyo, Japan, 28 Oct - 1 Nov, 2019. ©2019 Association for Computational Linguistics

closed set of domain-specific labels by investigating financial news articles. In the experiments on generating daily summaries of financial markets, we will empirically show the effectiveness of topic labels and potential advantages/disadvantages of this approach.

2 Related study

Controllability of text generation has been an intensive research focus recently. Examples include suggestive content control such as tense, sentiment, gender, or automatically learned hidden states (Hu et al., 2017; Zhao et al., 2018; Juraska and Walker, 2018; Bau et al., 2019). Another series of work is focused on controlling surface textual features such as length, descriptiveness and politeness (Li et al., 2016; Sennrich et al., 2016; Kikuchi et al., 2016; Ficler and Goldberg, 2017; Shen et al., 2017; Prabhumoye et al., 2018). The target of these previous methods is on controlling generic content-independent features of texts. That is, they aim at varying surface strings while preserving main information content. Wiseman et al. (2018) proposed a neural model that generates diverse texts by learning templates. They control diversity through templates rather than contents or the order of them. The present work is more closely related to methods for controlling topical content by using automatically extracted or human-designed keywords (Wang et al., 2016; Yao et al., 2017, 2018; Miao et al., 2018). Our method resembles the idea of using keywords to control topics of sentences and their orders, but it primarily focuses on describing given data and uses topic labels as auxiliary information. We will empirically attest added effects of introducing topic labels in the data-to-document scenario.

Besides, Gkatzia et al. (2017) and Portet et al. (2009) proposed non-neural language generation models for the data-to-text task with higher controllability on the output. They assumed that the important contents and their descriptions are determined primarily by experts, and their models do not allow users to select the contents directly.

To the best of our knowledge, no previous research tackled a problem with controllability of the content in the data-to-document task.

We believe that the contribution of this paper is the followings: First, we propose explicitly content-controllable data-to-document generator that uses additional clause information. Ex-

periments show the fluency and fidelity of the generated document in terms of BLEU and human-evaluation. Secondly, compared the generated documents between with human-designed labels and automatically extracted keywords, human-designed labels are more useful as the ease of understanding.

3 Generation of Market Comments

Our task is to generate summaries of financial markets. The input is a set of financial time-series data, such as DJI, Nikkei 225, and JPY/USD exchange rate. The output is a sequence of sentences describing movements of the financial data and their relationships.

The overview of our model is illustrated in Figure 1. In the following, we first describe our design of topic labels, then describe our data-to-text model with topic labels.

3.1 Topic Labels

Topic labels are defined as clause-level topics for aiming to guide a sequence of contents to be output. We empirically compare two methods to obtain topic labels: automatically extracted keywords and human-designed labels.

Automatically extracted keywords

This is a straightforward strategy to obtain the labels as the topic of sentences. We use RAKE (Rose et al., 2010) algorithm, which builds document graphs and weights the importance of each word combining several word-level and graph-level criteria to extract the keywords. Using such an automatic keywords extraction system has an advantage on the cost of human annotation while the extracted keywords sometimes do not express writers' intent. For example, RAKE often outputs the word "market" or "observation" as keywords, but they are not appropriate as the topic labels because of the lack of precise information—a system would be unable to understand which market, e.g., Nikkei or DJI, or what kinds of observations, e.g., the growth rate of stock prices or the trends of investments, when generating a text considering these labels.

Human-designed topic labels

We devised a set of topic labels by observing target sentences in the training data and what they often refer to, especially for *Nikkei Quick News* (NQN).

A topic label denotes the objects mentioned in documents and is defined as a triple, each element

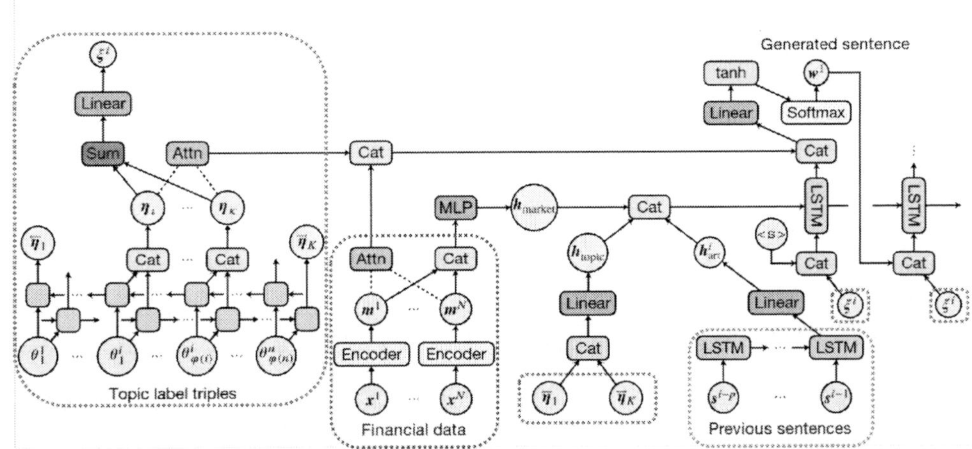

Figure 1: The neural-network architecture of our model with topic labels. The model generates each sentence $s^i = (w_t^1, w_t^2, \ldots)$ separately with document topic labels $\Theta = (\theta_1^1, \ldots, \theta_1^i, \ldots)$, financial data $X = (x^1, \ldots, x^N)$ and also previous sentences s^{i-p} to s^{i-1}. Topic labels are encoded to capture both of the document-level and sentence-level information. We denote concatenation as *Cat*, 3-layer MLP as *MLP*. In addition, *Attn* denotes the attention with the hidden states of the decoder.

of which indicates *target, actuals or futures*, and *trade or movement*. The latter two are subcategories of *target*; for example, [US Market]-[Actuals]-[Movement] denotes a topic about the movement of actuals of the US market, while [Nikkei 225]-[Futures]-[Trade] means the trading activity of the futures market of Nikkei 225. [Others] is given when these subcategories do not apply.

Table 1 shows all atomic labels, and Table 2 illustrates an example of sentence and its topic labels. Note that a topic label is given to a clause, which means one sentence may have multiple topic labels. On the annotated data, the average number of labels for each sentence is 2.0.

We designed the topic labels aiming to make it easy for a user to control the contents. News articles often refer to trends of each market indices and also their relationships focusing on the general market movements. This means that sometimes the generated summary would not contain the contents expected by the user, especially when the markets attended by the user are not common ones. Therefore, we developed *topic labels* with the concrete names of market indices. The *topic labels* help a user to generate articles which have sufficient content by inputting market names as their interest.

Besides, the granularity of topics is an important factor to design the topic labels. Too rough topics could lead the vagueness of meaning of the topic while too detailed topics would be difficult for some

users and take time to annotate. We designed our topic labels in a hierarchical structure to make them adaptive to different levels of granularity.

Human-designed labels are inferior in terms of construction cost, but expected to be superior to automatically extracted keywords in terms of interpretability as discussed later.

3.2 Encoder–Decoder with Topic Labels

Our model is an extended encoder–decoder that conditions on a document topic label sequence and previous sentences, in addition to financial data consisting of multiple numerical sequences. To make learning and generation simpler, our decoder generates each sentence separately, by encoding the sentence that was generated last. The entire neural-network architecture of our encoder–decoder model is shown in Figure 1.

Assume that we have generated $i-1$ sentences in an article and generate the next i-th sentence. Let $s^j = (w_t^j)_{t=1}^T$ $(j = 1, \ldots, n)$ be the j-th sentence in an article, where each w_t^j is a word. We also use $\boldsymbol{w}_t^j$ to denote embedding of w_t^j. In addition, in the following, W_* and b_* are a weight matrix and bias terms in the model parameters, respectively.

3.2.1 Encoders

We employ three encoders for encoding financial indices, previous generated sentences, and topic labels. To generate a next sentence s^i, from these

Topic Labels

Target: [Nikkei 225], [Individual stock (Japan)], [Narrow-based stock indices (Japan)], [TSE1] (First section of Tokyo Stock Exchange), [TSE2] (Second section of Tokyo Stock Exchange), [TOPIX], [US Market], [Individual stock (US)], [Narrow-based stock indices (US)], [DJI] (Dow Jones Industrial Average), [Hong Kong Market], [Market (Other countries)], [Individual stock (Other countries)], [Narrow-based stock indices (Other countries)], [JPY], [JPY/USD], [JPY/EUR], [JPY/AUD], [JPY Others], [USD], [AUD], [EUR], [HKD], [JGB] (Japanese government bond), [JGB (5–10 years)], [JGB (2–3 years)], [US Treasury securities], [US Treasury Notes (5–10 years)], [US Treasury Notes (2–3 years)], [TIBOR], [JPY interest rate], [Economic Index], [Events], [Lack of information for making a decision], [Investors], [Buying operation], [Statement of prominent person], [Others]
Actuals or Futures: [Actuals], [Futures], [N/A]
Trade or Movement: [Trade], [Movement], [N/A]

Table 1: Full set of human-designed atomic topic labels. Each topic is a tuple of values from three categories.

Topic labels	Segments of a sentence
[US Market]-[Actuals]-[Movement]	Observing the US stock markets fell during the year-end and New Year holiday, 年末年始の米株式相場の下落を受けて
[Investors]-[N/A]-[N/A]	investors got slightly risk-averse, 投資家のリスク回避姿勢がやや強まり、
[Nikkei 225]-[Actuals]-[Trade]	and selling pressure prevailed in the (Japanese stock) markets. 売りが優勢だった。

Table 2: Example of a sentence and its topic labels. One sentence may have multiple topic labels as in this example.

encoders we first obtain three vectors, $\boldsymbol{h}_{\text{market}}$, $\boldsymbol{h}^i_{\text{art}}$, and $\boldsymbol{h}_{\text{topic}}$, which encode financial data, previous sentences, and all topic labels on the article, respectively. Note that $\boldsymbol{h}_{\text{topic}}$ encodes a sequence of all topics on the article. We also obtain a vector encoding the topic labels of the current sentence, denoted by $\boldsymbol{\xi}^i$, from the topic labels encoder.

Financial data encoder

As the encoder of financial data, we follow Murakami et al. (2017). Given L numerical sequences $\boldsymbol{x}^1, \ldots, \boldsymbol{x}^L$, which are numerical sequences of financial indicators (e.g., Nikkei stock average and the foreign exchange rate of Japanese yen). We concatenate these vectors and feed it to a 3-layer MLP to obtain a single vector $\boldsymbol{h}_{\text{market}}$:

$$\boldsymbol{h}_{\text{market}} = \text{MLP}([\boldsymbol{m}^1 ; \ldots ; \boldsymbol{m}^L]).$$

We use different MLPs to convert numerical sequences into vectors. Note that $\boldsymbol{x}^l$ consists of $\boldsymbol{x}^l_{\text{short}}$ and $\boldsymbol{x}^l_{\text{long}}$, which are short-term and long-term normalized data of $\boldsymbol{x}^l$. $\boldsymbol{x}^l_{\text{short}}$ is composed of the previous prices within one trading day and $\boldsymbol{x}^l_{\text{long}}$ is composed of the closing prices of the seven preceding trading days.

$$\boldsymbol{m}^l = \boldsymbol{W}_l([\boldsymbol{x}^l_{\text{short}} ; \boldsymbol{x}^l_{\text{long}} ; \\ \text{MLP}(\boldsymbol{x}^l_{\text{short}}) ; \text{MLP}(\boldsymbol{x}^l_{\text{long}})]) + b_l.$$

Previous sentences encoder

The hidden state $\boldsymbol{h}^i_{\text{art}}$ representing previous sentences of s^i is obtained from p preceding sentences, $s^{i-p}, \ldots, s^{i-1}$. We input embeddings $\boldsymbol{w}^{i-p}_1, \ldots, \boldsymbol{w}^{i-p}_{|s^{i-p}|}, \ldots, \boldsymbol{w}^{i-1}_1, \ldots, \boldsymbol{w}^{i-1}_{|s^{i-1}|}$ to long short-term memory (LSTM) cells and obtain $\boldsymbol{h}_{\text{art}^i}$ after passing its terminal hidden state to a linear layer, where $|s^j|$ denotes the number of tokens in s^j.

Topic label encoder

The outputs of this encoder are $\boldsymbol{h}_{\text{topic}}$, which encodes the topic sequence of the article, and $\boldsymbol{\xi}^i$, corresponding to the embedding of topics assigned to the target (i-th) sentence s^i. The reason why we encode the document-level topic sequence, rather than sentence topics only, is to make $\boldsymbol{\xi}^i$ context-sensitive, by which we expect the output sentence, conditioned on $\boldsymbol{\xi}^i$, to reflect the position of sentence topics on the entire document topics.

We use a bidirectional LSTM network (see the left part of Figure 1) to encode the sequence of document topics. As an input, we first concatenate all

326

topic labels of sentences with a token </s>. Then h_{topic} is obtained from the outputs of this LSTM, by concatenating the outputs at the end tokens of both directions. These are denoted by $\overrightarrow{\eta}_K$ and $\overleftarrow{\eta}_1$ in Figure 1, where $K = \sum_j \varphi(j)$, the length of the document-level topic sequence. $\varphi(j)$ denotes the length of assigned topics for s^j, including the last topic label </s>.

We then extract topic embedding corresponding to the topic labels of s^i as *topic embedding* ξ^i. We do this by summing all outputs of LSTMs in a span corresponding to the current sentence *excluding* </s>. Let θ^i_k be the k-th topic in s^i. The bi-LSTM introduced above transforms this input into a vector $\eta_t = [\overleftarrow{\eta}_t ; \overrightarrow{\eta}_t]$, by concatenating the outputs of LSTMs of both directions. Then ξ^i is obtained by summing the outputs in the span, followed by a linear layer:

$$\xi^i = W_\xi \left(\sum_{t=\iota}^{\kappa} \eta_t \right) + b_\xi,$$

in which ι and κ are the indices corresponding to θ^i_1 and $\theta^i_{\varphi(i)-1}$, the start and end topic labels for the i-th sentence. Formally, $\iota = \sum_{j=1}^{i-1} \varphi(j) + 1$ and $\kappa = \iota + \varphi(i) - 1$.

3.2.2 Decoder

Our decoder is another LSTM conditioned on the outputs of three encoders introduced above. To initialize the decoder, we first concatenate three outputs of encoders and apply a linear layer:

$$H^i_0 = W_H[h_{\text{topic}} ; h_{\text{market}} ; h^i_{\text{art}}] + b_H. \quad (1)$$

Note that h_{topic} encodes the entire document-level topics, not the topics for the target sentence only. To make the output sentence more relevant to those target topics, we feed ξ^i to the input of the decoder at every step, by concatenating it with the original input vector w^j_t.

While this would allow the contents of output sentence to follow the given local topics, the sentence should also reflect the information of global topic sequence, e.g., the relative position of the target sentence in the article. A natural way to encode such context in the decoder is the attention mechanism (Luong et al., 2015), which we apply to the outputs of topic label encoder η_t, as well as the outputs of financial data encoder m_l, to capture the important resources relevant to the current sentence.

We obtain the context vectors c^{market}_t and c^{topic}_t for attending the financial data and topic labels from the output of decoder LSTM, and concatenate them before the softmax layer:

$$w_t \sim \text{softmax}(\tanh(W_c[c^{\text{topic}}_t ; c^{\text{market}}_t ; H^i_t] + b_c)).$$

The context vector c^{market}_t is obtained by a bilinear attention (Luong et al., 2015):

$$c^{\text{market}}_t = \sum_{l=1}^{L} \alpha^{\text{market}}_t(l) m_l,$$

$$\alpha^{\text{market}}_t(l) \propto \exp (H^{i\top}_t W^{\text{market}}_a m_l).$$

c^{topic}_t is obtained similarly:

$$c^{\text{topic}}_t = \sum_{k=1}^{K} \alpha^{\text{topic}}_t(k) \eta_k,$$

$$\alpha^{\text{topic}}_t(k) \propto \exp (H^{i\top}_t W^{\text{topic}}_a \eta_k).$$

4 Experimental Settings

Each example in our dataset is a pair of aligned time-series data and a corresponding document. We obtained documents by retrieving daily summaries from NQN, which describes market trends in Japanese, as well as aligned time-series data, from Thomson Reuters DataScope Select[1]. Dividing by periods, we obtained 864, 122, and 124 documents (9,337, 1,215, and 1,237 sentences) for train/valid/test sets, respectively. The vocabulary size was 3,025. As topic labels, we used 91 human-designed topic labels and 818 kinds of extracted keywords by the RAKE algorithm. We preprocessed each indicator following Aoki et al. (2018), and used the same parameters for the financial data encoder. Other parameters were tuned by document-level BLEU scores on the validation set.

We compared five different documents; a document written by human writer (GOLD), a document generated by our model without topic labels (NOTOPICLABEL) and three documents respectively generated by our models using topic labels:

- HDTAG3: Human-designed topic labels.

- HDTAG1: Simplified Human-designed topic labels (only target of Table 1) to see the importance of other factors.

- RAKE: Two keywords extracted by RAKE.

---

[1] We retrieved five-minute or one-hour charts of 9 indicators (Nikkei 225, TOPIX, DJI, HKHSI, USD/JPY, USD/EUR, JGB (2 years), JGB (10 years), US Treasury Notes (10 years).

Method	BLEU (doc)	BLEU (sent)
NoTopicLabel	21.19±1.16	14.69±0.39
HDTag3	29.21±0.29	22.77±0.40
HDTag1	27.92±0.37	21.25±0.57
RAKE	29.53±0.25	23.35±0.40

Table 3: Result of evaluation in terms of BLEU. Scores were averaged over 5 runs. The values after ± are the standard deviations. We report both the averaged BLEU scores over all the documents (**BLEU (doc)**) and sentences (**BLEU (sent)**).

We conducted both an automatic evaluation with BLEU score in words and a human-evaluation. The human evaluation focused on the fluency and the fidelity and the correctness of each approach. For human evaluation, we sample 15 instances from the test dataset. For each of the 15 instances, evaluators are presented with 5 documents that are respectively generated by a human writer (Gold), NoTopicLabel, HDTag3, HDTag1, and RAKE. Note that NoTopicLabel does not use topic labels, while HDTag3, HDTag1, and RAKE use topic labels. The evaluators are asked to rate the documents on a 1–3 scale with respect to fidelity, correctness and fluency. **Fidelity** measures whether each document reflects the given topic labels. **Correctness** measures whether each document is faithful to the given financial data. **Fluency** measures the fluency of each document without regard to input data. Since the evaluation of **Correctness** is a complicated process which requires the reference to input numerical data, the evaluators are supposed to evaluate only the sentences that satisfy the following two conditions: (i) the sentence starts with "Nikkei stock average" or "The exchange rate of the Japanese yen"[2], (ii) the sentence is labeled with only [Nikkei 225/ Actuals/ Movement] or [JPY//Movement]. Additionally, the evaluators are also asked to conduct sentence-level evaluation of fluency, in which they are presented with 5 sentences generated by the 5 methods including Gold. All the evaluations are conducted by two evaluators, and we compute the average scores for each approach.

<hr>

[2]The original Japanese phrases are "日経平均株価は (Nikkei stock average)" and "円相場は (The exchange rate of the yen)".

5 Results

Table 3 shows the BLEU scores of different approaches. The models with label information (HDTag3, HDTag1, and RAKE) achieved higher performances in terms of BLEU. RAKE achieved a slightly higher BLEU score than HDTag3, but the difference was not statistically significant. HDTag3 achieved a higher BLEU score than HDTag1. This result suggests that more informative topic labels improved the quality of generated text. In other words, careful design of topic labels helps high-quality generation, although it requires more human cost. It is also encouraging that HDTag3 is comparable to RAKE, in spite of the fact that the labels in the latter are extracted from words in the reference.

The results of human-evaluation are shown in Table 4. There was no statistically-significant difference among the sentence-level fluency scores of all methods. This means that the neural-network based method has the ability to generate a fluent text at least at the sentence level. The methods with topic-label information showed a better document-level fluency than the one without topic labels.

Meanwhile, there was a significant difference between the document-level fluency scores of generated sentences and human-written sentences. We considered it is caused by not considering relationships among topic-labels and also by weak consideration of generated sentences. Specifically, our model possibly generates almost the same content repeatedly as the content of previously generated sentences which are not treated as input resource, and moreover our model could generate different movement descriptions about the same indicator within a document. An example is shown in Table 5, where two sentences describing the same movement of the exchange rate state the contradictory things; *dropped* and *rose*. To solve the above problems, the implementation of additional memories to keep tracking which topics have been mentioned and how topics have been mentioned is interesting avenue for future work.

Besides, we observed the correctness of RAKE is higher than that of the other models. It is not surprising, because topic labels of RAKE are words in the target documents, and the topic labels like *continuously fall* or *rebound* would directly deliver the characteristics of the input data. In comparison between the methods with human-designed labels, HDTag3 is superior to HDTag1. This result is

Method	Fidelity	Correctness	Fluency (doc)	Fluency (sent)
Gold	–	2.80	2.90	2.93
NoTopicLabel	–	1.70	1.13	2.86
HDTag3	2.70	2.23	1.70	2.90
HDTag1	2.60	1.93	1.86	2.86
RAKE	1.96	2.53	1.76	2.93

Table 4: Result of human-evaluation. Scores range in [1,3]. **Fidelity** measures whether each document reflects the given topic labels. **Correctness** measures whether each document is faithful to the given financial data. **Fluency** measures the fluency of each document or sentence without regard to input data. **Fluency (doc)** is the document-level fluency, while **Fluency (sent)** is the sentence-level fluency.

Method	Topic label	Text
Gold		..., </s>, "The yen exchange rates rose for four days in a row.", </s>, "There were movements to sell the yen along with the rise of Nikkei 225, but they soon calmed down.", </s>, "In the afternoon, the yen rose and hit a high of around 108.5 yen against the dollar, which was the highest in about three weeks.", </s>, ..., </s>, "円相場は4日続伸した。", </s>, "日経平均の上昇と歩調を合わせて円を売る動きがあったが、勢いは続かなかった。", </s>, "午後に1ドル=108円台半ばまで上昇し、約3週間ぶりの高値を付ける場面があった。", </s>, ...
HDTag3	..., </s>, [JPY]-[N/A]-[Movement], </s>, [Nikkei]-[Actual]-[Movement],[JPY]-[N/A]-[Trade], [JPY]-[N/A]-[Movement], </s>, [JPY/USD]-[N/A]-[Movement], </s>, ...	..., </s>, "The yen exchange rates dropped.", </s>, "Observing the steady rise of Nikkei 225, traders started to sell the yen regarding it as a low-risk currency, and it did not rise constantly.", </s>, "The yen exchange rate rose against the dollar.", </s>, ..., </s>, "円相場は反落。", </s>, "日経平均株価が堅調に推移したことで、「低リスク通貨」とされる円を売る動きが出て、円の上値は重かった。", </s>, "円は対ドルで上昇した。", </s>, ...

Table 5: Sentences generated by HDTag3.

consistent with the result of BLEU scores.

Moreover, both models with human-designed topic labels show higher fidelity, which means the generated documents reflect the given topic labels. We speculate that the lower fidelity of RAKE is caused by the ambiguity of extracted keywords as discussed through examples in the next paragraph.

We then provide a qualitative comparison of RAKE and human-designed topic labels. Table 6 shows some output examples. As we mentioned, we found that RAKE keywords are often more ambiguous than the human-designed topic labels. This is mainly because the granularity of keywords is not properly defined. Table 6(a) shows an example, where RAKE keywords contain "high", which however does not tell which quantity is high, resulting in the wrong contents in the generated sentence. The human-designed topic labels have a higher interpretability, and the sentences generated with such topic labels are well-controlled.

The quantitative and qualitative evaluations above suggest that human-designed topic labels

contribute to a better controllability backed up by high fidelity and interpretability.

Although our approach has the advantage of the controllability in generating sentences, we also found complication in terms of topic design, in particular, the definition of granularity of the topics. We found that the system often generates a wrong description when the topic labels contain a general label, such as Others and Events. These labels tend to be used as catch-all labels, resulting in diverse contents. Table 6(b) shows an example that Others leads to a longer sentence with wrong contents.

To demonstrate that we can control the contents given the same financial data, in Table 6(c), we show how a generated sentence varies by giving topic labels that are different from the actual topic labels (HDTag3Unseen). We can see that a generated sentence properly changes its contents so that it reflects the new topic labels.

(a) Sentences generated by HDTAG3 and HDTAG1, RAKE, for which the topic labels by RAKE are ambiguous.

Method	Topic label	Text
GOLD		..., </s>, "Then, Nikkei 225 significantly rose, and traders sold the yen expecting investors to get risk-appetite and regarding yen as a 'low-risk currency'.", </s>, ..., </s>, "その後、日経平均株価が大幅高となり、投資家のリスク選好意欲が強まるとみた市場参加者が「低リスク通貨」とされる円の売りを増やした。", </s>, ...
HDTAG1	..., </s>, [Nikkei 225], [Investors], [JPY], </s>, ...	..., </s>, "A rise of Nikkei 225 improved investor sentiment and prompted traders to buy the yen regarding it as a low-risk currency.", </s>, ..., </s>, "日経平均株価が上昇したことで投資家心理が改善し、低リスク通貨とされる円を買う動きが優勢だった。", </s>, ...
HDTAG3	..., </s>, [Nikkei 225]-[Actuals]-[Movement], [Investors]-[N/A]-[N/A], [JPY]-[N/A]-[Trade], </s>, ...	..., </s>, "A significant rise of Nikkei 225 also improved investor sentiment and prompted traders to buy the yen.", </s>, ..., </s>, "日経平均株価が大幅に上昇したことも投資家心理の改善につながり、円買いを誘った。", </s>, ...
RAKE	..., </s>, high, preference, </s>, ...	..., </s>, "However, traders bought the yen and sold the dollars to adjust the position in advance of the Fed's Interest-Rate Announcement.", </s>, ..., </s>, "ただ、米連邦公開市場委員会 (FOMC) の結果発表を控え、持ち高調整の円買い・ドル売りが入った。", </s>, ...

(b) Sentences generated by HDTAG3 with [Others].

Method	Topic label	Text
GOLD		..., </s>, "Speculation that the Bank of Japan purchased exchange-traded funds was positive for the markets." </s>, ..., </s>, "日銀が株価指数連動型上場投資信託 (ETF) 買いを入れたとの思惑も相場を支えた。", </s>, ...
HDTAG3	..., </s>, [Others]-[N/A]-[N/A], [Investors]-[N/A]-[N/A], [Nikkei 225]-[Actuals]-[Movement], </s>, ...	..., </s>, "On alert against the debt problem in Europe, stock prices continued to decline while bonds continued to rise." </s>, ..., </s>, "もっとも、欧州債務問題への警戒感から株安・債券高が進んだ。", </s>, ...

(c) Sentences generated by HDTAG3 and HDTAG3UNSEEN.

Method	Topic label	Text
GOLD		<d>, "Nikkei 225 rebounded greatly.", </s>, "It was the fourth largest leap in this year.", </s> ...... <d>, </s>, "日経平均株価は大幅に反発した。", </s>, "上げ幅は今年 4 番目の大きさとなった。"</s> ...
HDTAG3	<d>, [Nikkei 225]-[Actual]-[Movement], </s>, [Nikkei 225]-[Actual]-[Movement], </s>, ...	<d>, "Nikkei 225 rebounded greatly.", </s>, "The closing price was the highest since <month/> <day/>.", </s> ... <d>, </s>, "日経平均株価は大幅反発した。", </s>, "終値は<month/><day/>以来約<months/>ぶりの高値を付けた。"</s> ...
HDTAG3UNSEEN	<d>, [Nikkei 225]-[Actual]-[Movement], </s>, [US Market]-[Actual]-[Movement], [Nikkei 225]-[Actual]-[Trade], </s>, </d>	<d>, "Nikkei 225 rebounded greatly.", </s>, "Observing the rise in the US stock markets yesterday, traders tended to buy stocks from this morning.", </s>, </d> <d>, </s>, "日経平均株価は大幅反発した。", </s>, "前日の米株式相場の上昇を受けて朝方から買いが先行した。", </s>, </d>

Table 6: Examples of generated sentences.

6 Conclusion

We proposed a data-to-document generator which can be controlled by a sequence of topic labels. We compared two topic labels, the human-designed topic label and automatically extracted keywords, and conducted experiments with a financial dataset. Our experiments empirically showed that the model using topic label information achieved higher performance in terms of BLEU and human-evaluation. Furthermore, the model using the human-designed topic labels has an advantage on controllability of the output documents without reducing BLEU scores. In addition, experiments showed that the granularity of topic labels influences the generation quality.

As future work, we will employ the network architectures which have additional memories to keep tracking which topics have been mentioned and how topics have been mentioned for high topical coherence in the sentences. In addition, future work should include reducing the inconsistency between a generated text and the actual movement of input financial indicators because even one conflict could be fatal to the reliability of the generated text.

Topic labels should also be easy to handle for human users, who actually use the system to generate a document. We also need to evaluate topic labels in terms of the easiness of use.

Acknowledgements

This paper is based on results obtained from a project commissioned by the New Energy and Industrial Technology Development Organization (NEDO).

References

Tatsuya Aoki, Akira Miyazawa, Tatsuya Ishigaki, Kei-ichi Goshima, Kasumi Aoki, Ichiro Kobayashi, Hiroya Takamura, and Yusuke Miyao. 2018. Generating market comments referring to external resources. In *Proc. of INLG 2018*, pages 135–139.

Regina Barzilay and Mirella Lapata. 2005. Collective content selection for concept-to-text generation. In *Proceedings of the Conference on Human Language Technology and Empirical Methods in Natural Language Processing*, HLT '05, pages 331–338, Stroudsburg, PA, USA. Association for Computational Linguistics.

Anthony Bau, Yonatan Belinkov, Hassan Sajjad, Nadir Durrani, Fahim Dalvi, and James Glass. 2019. Identifying and controlling important neurons in neural machine translation. In *International Conference on Learning Representations*.

Jessica Ficler and Yoav Goldberg. 2017. Controlling linguistic style aspects in neural language generation. In *Proceedings of the Workshop on Stylistic Variation*, pages 94–104. Association for Computational Linguistics.

Dimitra Gkatzia, Oliver Lemon, and Verena Rieser. 2017. Data-to-text generation improves decision-making under uncertainty. *IEEE Computational Intelligence Magazine*, 12:10–17.

Zhiting Hu, Zichao Yang, Xiaodan Liang, Ruslan Salakhutdinov, and Eric P. Xing. 2017. Toward controlled generation of text. In *Proceedings of the 34th International Conference on Machine Learning*, volume 70 of *Proceedings of Machine Learning Research*, pages 1587–1596, International Convention Centre, Sydney, Australia. PMLR.

Juraj Juraska and Marilyn Walker. 2018. Characterizing variation in crowd-sourced data for training neural language generators to produce stylistically varied outputs. In *Proceedings of the 11th International Conference on Natural Language Generation*, pages 441–450, Tilburg University, The Netherlands. Association for Computational Linguistics.

Yuta Kikuchi, Graham Neubig, Ryohei Sasano, Hiroya Takamura, and Manabu Okumura. 2016. Controlling output length in neural encoder-decoders. In *Proceedings of the 2016 Conference on Empirical Methods in Natural Language Processing*, pages 1328–1338, Austin, Texas. Association for Computational Linguistics.

Rémi Lebret, David Grangier, and Michael Auli. 2016. Neural text generation from structured data with application to the biography domain. In *Proceedings of the 2016 Conference on Empirical Methods in Natural Language Processing*, pages 1203–1213. Association for Computational Linguistics.

Jiwei Li, Michel Galley, Chris Brockett, Georgios Spithourakis, Jianfeng Gao, and Bill Dolan. 2016. A persona-based neural conversation model. In *Proceedings of the 54th Annual Meeting of the Association for Computational Linguistics (Volume 1: Long Papers)*, pages 994–1003, Berlin, Germany. Association for Computational Linguistics.

Percy Liang, Michael Jordan, and Dan Klein. 2009. Learning semantic correspondences with less supervision. In *Proceedings of the Joint Conference of the 47th Annual Meeting of the ACL and the 4th International Joint Conference on Natural Language Processing of the AFNLP*, pages 91–99, Suntec, Singapore. Association for Computational Linguistics.

Tianyu Liu, Kexiang Wang, Baobao Chang Lei Sha, and Zhifang Sui. 2018. Table-to-text generation by structure-aware seq2seq learning. In *Proc. of the Thirty-Second AAAI Conference on Artificial Intelligence*.

Thang Luong, Hieu Pham, and Christopher D. Manning. 2015. Effective approaches to attention-based neural machine translation. In *Proceedings of Empirical Methods in Natural Language Processing (EMNLP)*, pages 1412–1421.

Hongyuan Mei, Mohit Bansal, and Matthew R. Walter. 2016. What to talk about and how? selective generation using lstms with coarse-to-fine alignment. In *Proceedings of the 2016 Conference of the North American Chapter of the Association for Computational Linguistics: Human Language Technologies*, pages 720–730, San Diego, California. Association for Computational Linguistics.

Ning Miao, Hao Zhou, Lili Mou, Rui Yan, and Lei Li. 2018. CGMH: constrained sentence generation by metropolis-hastings sampling. *CoRR*, abs/1811.10996.

Soichiro Murakami, Akihiko Watanabe, Akira Miyazawa, Keiichi Goshima, Toshihiko Yanase, Hiroya Takamura, and Yusuke Miyao. 2017. Learning to generate market comments from stock prices. In *Proc. of ACL 2017*, pages 1374–1384.

Jekaterina Novikova, Ondřej Dušek, and Verena Rieser. 2017. The e2e dataset: New challenges for end-to-end generation. In *Proceedings of the 18th Annual SIGdial Meeting on Discourse and Dialogue*, pages 201–206, Saarbrcken, Germany. Association for Computational Linguistics.

Francois Portet, Ehud Reiter, Albert Gatt, Jim Hunter, Somayajulu Sripada, Yvonne Freer, and Cindy Sykes. 2009. Automatic generation of textual summaries from neonatal intensive care data. *Artificial Intelligence*, 173(7-8):789–816.

Shrimai Prabhumoye, Yulia Tsvetkov, Ruslan Salakhutdinov, and Alan W Black. 2018. Style transfer through back-translation. In *Proceedings of the 56th Annual Meeting of the Association for Computational Linguistics (Volume 1: Long Papers)*, pages 866–876, Melbourne, Australia. Association for Computational Linguistics.

Ehud Reiter and Robert Dale. 1997. Building applied natural language generation systems. *Nat. Lang. Eng.*, 3(1):57–87.

Jacques Pierre Robin. 1995. *Revision-based Generation of Natural Language Summaries Providing Historical Background: Corpus-based Analysis, Design, Implementation and Evaluation*. Ph.D. thesis, New York, NY, USA. UMI Order No. GAX95-33653.

Stuart Rose, Dave Engel, Nick Cramer, and Wendy Cowley. 2010. Automatic keyword extraction from individual documents. In *Text Mining. Applications and Theory*, pages 1–20.

Rico Sennrich, Barry Haddow, and Alexandra Birch. 2016. Controlling politeness in neural machine translation via side constraints. In *Proceedings of the 2016 Conference of the North American Chapter of the Association for Computational Linguistics: Human Language Technologies*, pages 35–40. Association for Computational Linguistics.

Tianxiao Shen, Tao Lei, Regina Barzilay, and Tommi Jaakkola. 2017. Style transfer from non-parallel text by cross-alignment. In I. Guyon, U. V. Luxburg, S. Bengio, H. Wallach, R. Fergus, S. Vishwanathan, and R. Garnett, editors, *Advances in Neural Information Processing Systems 30*, pages 6830–6841. Curran Associates, Inc.

Zhe Wang, Wei He, Hua Wu, Haiyang Wu, Wei Li, Haifeng Wang, and Enhong Chen. 2016. Chinese poetry generation with planning based neural network. In *Proceedings of COLING 2016, the 26th International Conference on Computational Linguistics: Technical Papers*, pages 1051–1060. The COLING 2016 Organizing Committee.

Sam Wiseman, Stuart Shieber, and Alexander Rush. 2017. Challenges in data-to-document generation. In *Proceedings of the 2017 Conference on Empirical Methods in Natural Language Processing*, pages 2253–2263, Copenhagen, Denmark. Association for Computational Linguistics.

Sam Wiseman, Stuart Shieber, and Alexander Rush. 2018. Learning neural templates for text generation. In *Proceedings of the 2018 Conference on Empirical Methods in Natural Language Processing*, pages 3174–3187, Brussels, Belgium. Association for Computational Linguistics.

Pengcheng Yang, Lei Li, Fuli Luo, Tianyu Liu, and Xu Sun. 2019. Knowledgeable writer: Enhancing topic-to-essay generation with external commonsense knowledge. In *Proc. of ACL 2019*.

Lili Yao, Nanyun Peng, Ralph Weischedel, Kevin Knight, Dongyan Zhao, and Rui Yan. 2018. Plan-and-write: Towards better automatic storytelling.

Lili Yao, Yaoyuan Zhang, Yansong Feng, Dongyan Zhao, and Rui Yan. 2017. Towards implicit content-introducing for generative short-text conversation systems. In *Proceedings of the 2017 Conference on Empirical Methods in Natural Language Processing*, pages 2190–2199, Copenhagen, Denmark. Association for Computational Linguistics.

Junbo Zhao, Yoon Kim, Kelly Zhang, Alexander Rush, and Yann LeCun. 2018. Adversarially regularized autoencoders. In *Proceedings of the 35th International Conference on Machine Learning*, volume 80 of *Proceedings of Machine Learning Research*, pages 5902–5911, Stockholmsmä ssan, Stockholm Sweden. PMLR.

A Large-Scale Multi-Length Headline Corpus for Analyzing Length-Constrained Headline Generation Model Evaluation

Yuta Hitomi[1]   Yuya Taguchi[1]   Hideaki Tamori[1]   Ko Kikuta[*2]   Jiro Nishitoba[2]

Naoaki Okazaki[3]   Kentaro Inui[4]   Manabu Okumura[3]

[1] The Asahi Shimbun Company, [2] Retrieva, Inc., [3] Tokyo Institute of Technology

[4] Tohoku University, RIKEN Center Advanced Intelligence Project

{hitomi-y1, taguchi-y2, tamori-h}@asahi.com, kikutakou@gmail.com

jiro.nishitoba@retrieva.jp, okazaki@c.titech.ac.jp

inui@ecei.tohoku.ac.jp, oku@pi.titech.ac.jp

Abstract

Browsing news articles on multiple devices is now possible. The lengths of news article headlines have precise upper bounds, dictated by the size of the display of the relevant device or interface. Therefore, controlling the length of headlines is essential when applying the task of headline generation to news production. However, because there is no corpus of headlines of multiple lengths for a given article, previous research on controlling output length in headline generation has not discussed whether the system outputs could be adequately evaluated without multiple references of different lengths. In this paper, we introduce two corpora, which are Japanese News Corpus (JNC) and JApanese MUlti-Length Headline Corpus (JAMUL), to confirm the validity of previous evaluation settings. The JNC provides common supervision data for headline generation. The JAMUL is a large-scale evaluation dataset for headlines of three different lengths composed by professional editors. We report new findings on these corpora; for example, although the longest length reference summary can appropriately evaluate the existing methods controlling output length, this evaluation setting has several problems.

1 Introduction

The news media publish newspapers in print form and in electronic form. In the electric form, articles might be read on various types of devices using any application; thus, news media companies have an increasing need to produce multiple headlines for the same news article based on what would be most appropriate and most compelling on an array of devices. All devices and applications used for viewing articles have strict upper bounds regarding the number of characters

This work was done at Retrieva, Inc. within Project.

Article:	トヨタ自動車は18日、エンジン車だけの車種を2025年ごろまでにゼロにすると発表した。…ハイブリッド車 (HV)やプラグインハイブリッド車 (PHV)、燃料電池車 (FCV)も加えた「電動車」を、すべての車種に設定する。…
	On the 18th, Toyota announced that it would set the model of only engine cars to zero by about 2025.... They set "electric vehicle" which is Hybrid Vehicle (HV), Plug-in Hybrid Vehicle (PHV), and Fuel Cell Vehicle (FCV) to all models....
Headline for print media:	トヨタ、全車種に電動車 25年ごろまでに　HVやFCV含め
	All Toyota models will contain electric vehicles including HV and FCV by about 2025.
Multi-length headlines for digital media:	
9 chars	全車種に「電動車」
(10char-ref)	"Electric cars" for all models
13 chars	トヨタ、全車種に「電動車」
(13char-ref)	"Electric cars" for all Toyota's models
24 chars	トヨタ、エンジン車だけの車種ゼロへ　2025年ごろ
(26char-ref)	Toyota sets the number of models with only engine cars to zero by about 2025.

Table 1: An example of four headlines for the same article that were created by professional editors. In this example, '電動車'(Electric cars) and '全'(all) are represented by red letters and are not included in the 24-character headline. These tokens cannot be evaluated by 24-character headlines. The blue tokens are not included in 9- and 13-character headlines. These tokens should not be included in shorter headlines.

allowed because of limitations in the space where the headline appears. The technology of automatic headline generation has the potential to contribute greatly to this domain, and the problems of news headline generation have motivated a wide range of studies (Wang et al., 2018; Chen et al., 2018; Kiyono et al., 2018; Zhou et al., 2018; Cao et al., 2018; Wang et al., 2019).

Table 1 shows sample headlines in three different lengths written by professional editors of a media company for the same news article: The length of the first headline for the digital media is restricted to 10 characters, the second to 13 characters, and the third to 26 characters. From a practical perspective, headlines must be generated under a rigid length constraint.

The first study to consider the length of system outputs in the encoder-decoder framework was Rush et al. (2015). This study controlled the length of an output sequence by reducing the score of the end-of-sentence token to $-\infty$ until the method generated the desired number of words. Subsequently, Kikuchi et al. (2016) and Fan et al. (2018) proposed mechanisms for length control; however, these studies produced summaries of 30, 50, and 75 bytes, and the studies evaluated the summaries by using the reference summaries of a single length (approximately 75 bytes long) in DUC 2004[1]. In addition, Takase and Okazaki (2019) proposed the mechanism for length control and evaluated their method with part of the test set which is consisted by summaries satisfying some length constraints in Annotated English Gigaword corpus (AEG) (Napoles et al., 2012).

Thus, some questions can be posed: (1) Can previous evaluation settings adequately evaluate system outputs in headline generation task? (2) What type of problem should we solve in this task according to the target length? (3) How well do systems solve the problems? In this study, we present novel corpora to investigate these research questions. The contributions of this study are threefold.

1. We release the **J**apanese **N**ews **C**orpus (JNC)[2], which includes 1.93 million pairs of headlines and the lead three sentences of Japanese news articles. We expect this corpus to provide common supervision data for headline generation.

2. We build the **JA**panese **MU**lti-**L**ength Headline Corpus (JAMUL)[2] for the evaluation of headlines of different lengths. In this novel dataset, each news article is associated with multiple headlines of three different lengths.

3. We report new findings for the JAMUL; for example, although the longer reference seems to be able to evaluate the short system output, we also found a problem with this evaluation setting. Additionally, we clarified that the existing methods could not capture

[1] https://duc.nist.gov/duc2004/
[2] https://cl.asahi.com/api_data/
jnc-jamul-en.html

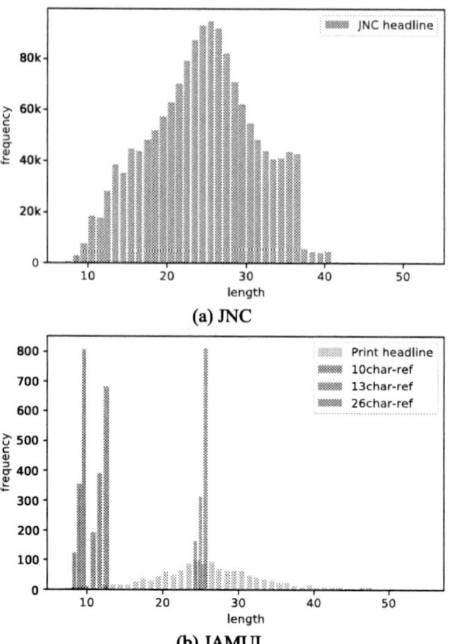

Figure 1: Length distributions of headlines in (a) the JNC and (b) the JAMUL.

what must be changed according to the specified length.

2 JNC and JAMUL

2.1 Headlines Composed by a Media Company

Before describing the JNC and the JAMUL in detail, we explain the process where a Japanese media company composes headlines for a news article. We describe the process of The Asahi Shimbun Company, a Japanese newspaper company. First, reporters write an article and submit it to the editorial department. The editorial department picks up some articles to publish in the newspaper and writes a headline for the article dedicated to print media. We call these headlines *print headlines* or *length-insensitive headlines* hereafter.

In addition to print headlines, digital media editors, who are typically not the same editors for print, pick up the articles they want to distribute on digital media from the articles dedicated to digital media and compose three different headlines. The first headline for the digital signage and audio media has a limit of up to 10 characters. This type of headline is appended to the beginning of a concise summary of the article so that readers can understand the news at first glance. The second type of headline is produced for mobile phones with small LCDs and small areas on the website sidebar (e.g., the access ranking); the upper limit of the number of characters is 13. The third type of headline is produced for desktop computer news websites, and the upper limit of the number of characters is 26. This limit is derived from the layout of the news site. We refer to the three types of headlines as *10char-ref*, *13char-ref*, and *26char-ref* (refer to Table 1 for examples). We collectively call these headlines *length-sensitive headlines*.

Table 1 presents an example of headlines written for an article by the professional editors. We extract the JNC and the JAMUL from the news production process of The Asahi Shimbun Company; therefore, they can be considered representative of contemporary editorial practice.

2.2 JNC

The JNC is a collection of 1,932,398 pairs of the three lead sentences[2] of articles and their print headlines published by The Asahi Shimbun Company from 2007 to 2016. Figure 1 (a) depicts the distribution of the headline lengths in the JNC. The headline lengths in the JNC are diverse because almost all headlines are not restricted by length limitations.

The JNC is useful for training headline generation models because it has many training instances. Furthermore, the corpus is suitable for training a model for variable-length headline generation because of the variety of the headline lengths.

2.3 JAMUL

The JAMUL is a corpus containing 1,489 full-text news articles and their length-insensitive headlines for print media and length-sensitive headlines of 10 characters, 13 characters, and 26 characters for digital media. We just extract these articles and headlines from the company database. All the articles and headlines were published by The Asahi Shimbun Company between September 2017 and March 2018. The volume of the news articles may be insufficient for training a headline generation model. However, as Figure 1 (b) shows, the JAMUL includes length-sensitive headlines that strictly preserve the length requirements. This novel characteristic of the JAMUL is suitable for the test set to adapt headline generation to business practice. In this paper, we use the first three

System	Reference	Precision	Recall
JAMUL Article	Paper headline	11.26	72.91
	10char-ref	5.42	85.02
	13char-ref	7.10	85.74
	26char-ref	13.26	77.38
AEG Article	AEG headline	17.74	62.03

Table 2: ROUGE-1 precision and recall scores when comparing article and length-insensitive/sensitive headlines.

System	Reference	Precision	Recall
Print headline	10char-ref	27.95	71.28
	13char-ref	37.70	74.48
	26char-ref	61.78	60.56

Table 3: ROUGE-1 precision and recall scores when comparing length-insensitive and -sensitive headlines.

sentences of the article as input because of fitting in the JNC corpus. But we publish the full edition of the article. No overlap of articles between the JNC and the JAMUL was confirmed.

2.4 Comparing of Headlines with Article Bodies

What type of operation which includes extractive and abstractive operations did the editors perform to create length-sensitive and length-insensitive headlines in the JAMUL? To clarify this question, we analyzed the proportions of the number of extractive and abstractive operations. Specifically, we reported ROUGE-1 precision and recall scores (Lin, 2004) in Table 2, assuming that articles are "system" summaries and that 10char-ref, 13char-ref, and 26char-ref headlines are "reference" summaries. Notably, we removed blank spaces, which were the most common token in longer headlines. The relatively high recall score indicates that the operations most often required to generate headlines are extractive, and the abstractive operation is about 15–27% of the total. In addition, we explored the proportions of each operation in AEG[3], which has been used in many studies for English headline generation tasks. From the relatively high recall score, we observed that Japanese headlines tend to be more extractive.

2.5 Comparing of Length-sensitive Headlines with Print headlines

How similar are the headlines used for training (length-insensitive) and for evaluation (length-

---

[3] We obtained this dataset by applying the pre-processing script at https://github.com/facebookarchive/NAMAS

Table 4: A typical example for comparing length-insensitive and -sensitive headlines

sensitive)? We estimated the appropriateness of length-insensitive headlines as a "seed" for producing length-sensitive headlines. More concretely, we report ROUGE-1 precision and recall scores in Table 3, assuming that length-insensitive headlines are "system" summaries, and that 10char-ref, 13char-ref and 26char-ref headlines are "reference" summaries. The relatively high recall scores indicate that the training and evaluation data were not very distant. Additionally, we found that the editors used a moderate number of words that did not appear in print headlines when composing length-sensitive headlines. Table 4 is an example of the typical differences between the length-insensitive and length-sensitive headlines. Comparing the 26-character headline with the print headline, the choices of contents are different; for example, the print headline reports the reason for the record profit, but the 26-character headline describes the topic regarding the increasing number of personnel. Next, comparing the 7-character (10char-ref) headline with the print headline, we observe that the choices of words are different; the print headline uses "Facebook," which is changed to "FB" in the 7-character headline.

System	Reference	P	R
26char ref	10char-ref	30.22	81.77
26char-ref	13char-ref	43.59	90.75
First 10 chars in 26char-ref	10char-ref	44.30	29.42
First 13 chars in 26char-ref	13char-ref	67.01	44.34

Table 5: Difference between 26char-ref headlines and shorter headlines. P and R denote ROUGE-1 precision and recall scores, respectively.

2.6 Comparing of Length-sensitive Headlines

How similar is the composition of headlines for a news article of different lengths? How good are 26char-ref headlines as "seeds" for generating 10char-ref or 13char-ref headlines? Is the simple strategy of trimming 26char-ref headlines to 10 or 13 characters sufficient? To answer these questions, we computed word-level precision and recall scores, assuming that 26char-ref headlines are "system" summaries and that 10char-ref and 13char-ref headlines are "reference" summaries.

The first and second rows of Table 5 represent the situation when we used 26char-ref headlines as they are, and without preserving the length constraint. Although this setting was unrealistic, we could estimate how similar the contents were among the length-sensitive headlines. The high recall scores indicate that 26char-ref headlines mostly cover the words included in the 10char-ref and 13char-ref headlines. From this result, we consider the contents among length-sensitive headlines are comparably similar. The third and fourth rows of Table 5 correspond to the strategy where we generated headlines in 10 and 13 characters from the first 10 and 13 characters of the 26char-ref headlines. This strategy achieved moderate success for generating headlines in 13 characters, but did not work well for headlines in 10 characters. In other words, we observed large differences between the 10char-ref and the first 10 characters of the 26char-ref headlines. Therefore, we need to re-generate the shorter headline, as well as the longest one.

In sum, we found similarities in headlines of different lengths in the JAMUL. However, the simple strategy of trimming a longer headline into a shorter headline is insufficient. Table 1 is an example of the typical differences among length-sensitive headlines. There is a little overlap between longer and shorter headlines because the 9- and 13-character headlines extract the shorter phrases which have the nearly same meaning as the 24-character headline. Focusing on "車種" (models), the words are in the latter half of the 24-character headline, and we could confirm that important keywords are not always included at the beginning of the headlines.

3 Comparing of Headline Generation Methods on the JAMUL

In this section, we explore a question about evaluation: How reliable is the two conventional evaluation method; the first is the method that uses a single length summary for measuring the quality of summaries of different lengths; the second is the method that uses the specified length headlines which are extracted from the dataset constructed by length-insensitive headlines, for measuring the quality of each length summary. To answer this question, we generated multiple summaries of different lengths by using the existing methods, and measured the correlation between the performance values computed by the conventional evaluation methods and those computed on the JAMUL.

3.1 Headline-generation Methods with the Mechanism to Control the Output Length

In this study, we explored four methods for headline generation that can control the output length. The first two methods, *LenEmb* and *LenInit*, were proposed by Kikuchi et al. (2016).

LenEmb provides the decoder with output length information in the form of the length embedding. *LenInit* controls the output length by multiplying the initial state of the decoder's memory cell of long short-term memory (Hochreiter and Schmidhuber, 1997) by the desired length.

Fan et al. (2018) also proposed a length-controllable method for a convolutional sequence-to-sequence (ConvS2S) model (Gehring et al., 2017). Their method added special tokens indicating the range of the output length at the beginning of an input sequence. In our experiment, we used a special token to specify an output length[4] and called this method *SP-token*.

We also considered the *LC* method (Liu et al., 2018), which extends ConvS2S and multiplies the initial state of the residual connection (He et al., 2016) by the desired number of output tokens. In the experiment, we set the desired number of characters instead of that of tokens.

	Seq2Seq	ConvS2S	Transformer
Num of Layer	2	8	6
Dropout Rate	0.3	0.1	0.3
Grad Clipping	[-5.0, 5.0]	[-0.1, 0.1]	-
Learning Rate	0.001	0.2	0.001
Optimizer	Adam	NAG	Adam

Table 6: Parameters of each encoder-decoder model.

In addition to these four methods, we combined *SP-token* not only on ConvS2S but also on Seq2Seq and Transformer (Vaswani et al., 2017). Eventually, we examined six combinations in total: (1) Seq2Seq + *LenEmb*, (2) Seq2Seq + *LenInit*, (3) Seq2Seq + *SP-token*, (4) ConvS2S + *SP-token*, (5) ConvS2S + *LC*, and (6) Transformer + *SP-token*.

3.2 Datasets and the Evaluation Protocol

We trained the six methods for headline generation on the JNC. We removed instances that were duplicated or unsuitable for training a headline generation model[5]. The filtering step obtained 1,554,558 pairs of newspaper articles and headlines. We randomly selected 98% of the instances (1,523,468 pairs) as a training set, selected 1% of the instances (15,545 pairs) as a validation set, and used the remainder (15,545 pairs) as a test set. As for the JNC test set, we additionally extracted the length-restricted test set to evaluate the length control methods. Specifically, we extracted 303, 1,436, and 4,289 headlines which are 8-10, 11-13, and 24-26 characters long, respectively, and corresponding articles from the JNC, similar to the 10char-ref, 13char-ref, and 26char-ref in the JA-MUL. We call them the *length-restricted JNC test set*. We also filtered the JAMUL by setting lower bounds for the length of the headlines[6]. We set each lower bound to 8 for 10char-ref, to 11 for 13char-ref, and to 24 for 26char-ref. Finally, we achieved 1,288 instances for the JAMUL test set.

We used SentencePiece[6] (Kudo and Richardson, 2018) for tokenization. We set the merge operation to 8,000. Finally, we obtained 10,868 tokens for the source side and 9,556 tokens for the target side. When training a model, we set the length of each reference headline to the model. When generating headlines in the evaluation, we set the output lengths to 10, 13, and 26 char-

---

[4]Fan et al. (2018) also included special tokens for entities, but we did not use them in the experiments.

[5]The filtering script is available at:
https://github.com/asahi-research/Gingo
[6]https://github.com/google/
sentencepiece

	10 characters			13 characters			26 characters		
Models	R-1	R-2	R-L	R-1	R-2	R-L	R-1	R-2	R-L
(1) Seq2Seq + *LenEmb*	34.62	15.02	33.54	39.31	18.14	37.07	43.65	19.73	36.03
(2) Seq2Seq + *LenInit*	36.14	16.88	35.15	41.39	19.55	38.83	46.30	21.33	37.79
(3) Seq2Seq + *SP-token*	38.01	17.16	36.72	42.03	19.83	39.56	46.62	21.47	38.29
(4) ConvS2S + *SP-token*	39.20	18.66	38.07	42.63	20.00	40.38	47.41	21.47	38.04
(5) ConvS2S + *LC*	34.93	15.52	34.02	38.80	17.21	36.68	42.59	19.34	35.41
(6) Transformer + *SP-token*	41.21	19.16	39.91	44.84	21.62	42.09	49.66	23.69	40.65

Table 7: ROUGE scores of each model on the JAMUL. The specified lengths are 10, 13, and 26 characters. R-1, R-2, and R-L represent ROUGE-1, ROUGE-2, and ROUGE-L, respectively. Note that (1) to (6) in Table 8 and after that represent models (1) to (6) of this table.

	10 characters			13 characters		
Models	R-1	R-2	R-L	R-1	R-2	R-L
(1)	$21.58_{[+0]}$	$8.73_{[+1]}$	$19.56_{[+0]}$	$27.47_{[-1]}$	$11.82_{[+0]}$	$24.20_{[-1]}$
(2)	$22.17_{[+0]}$	$9.14_{[+1]}$	$20.12_{[+0]}$	$28.93_{[+1]}$	$12.98_{[+2]}$	$25.35_{[+1]}$
(3)	$22.80_{[+1]}$	$9.51_{[+1]}$	$20.59_{[+1]}$	$28.78_{[-1]}$	$12.64_{[-1]}$	$25.14_{[-1]}$
(4)	$22.53_{[-1]}$	$9.04_{[-2]}$	$20.47_{[-1]}$	$29.23_{[+0]}$	$12.82_{[-1]}$	$25.58_{[+0]}$
(5)	$21.60_{[+0]}$	$8.55_{[-1]}$	$19.63_{[+0]}$	$27.63_{[+1]}$	$11.72_{[+0]}$	$24.34_{[+1]}$
(6)	$24.36_{[+0]}$	$10.32_{[+0]}$	$21.97_{[+0]}$	$30.84_{[+0]}$	$13.85_{[+0]}$	$26.98_{[+0]}$
τ	0.867	0.600	0.867	0.733	0.733	0.733

Table 8: ROUGE scores of the system outputs in 10 and 13 characters evaluated by 26char-ref headlines as the references. Note that [] denote the change of the rank when we compare the rank in Table 7; + and - denote the rank up and rank down, respectively.

acters; each output was evaluated by the reference that had the same length in the JAMUL and JNC test sets. To generate summaries, we follow standard practice in disallowing repetition of the same trigram (Paulus et al., 2018). We evaluated all models by using three variants of ROUGE recall metric[7]: ROUGE-1, ROUGE-2, and ROUGE-L. Headlines exceeding the length limits were trimmed for a fair evaluation.

3.3 Implementation

We employed OpenNMT[8] (Klein et al., 2017) for Seq2Seq, and fairseq[9] (Ott et al., 2019) for ConvS2S and Transformer. We extended the implementations to realize *LenEmb, LenInit*, and *LC*. We set the dimensions for the token and length embeddings to 512, those for hidden states to 512, and the beam width to 5. These parameters are common in all the models. Table 6 summarizes other parameters specific to each sequence-to-sequence model. We used Nesterov's accelerated gradient method (NAG) (Sutskever et al., 2013) with a momentum of 0.99 in ConvS2S. In Transformer, we set the number of attention heads to 8, the dimensions for the feed-forward network to 2,048, Adam's β to 0.98, the warm-up steps to

4,000, and label smoothing to 0.1.

3.4 Evaluation of Multi-length Headlines Generated by Methods on the JAMUL

Table 7 presents ROUGE scores of each method on the JAMUL test set. Transformer + *SP-token* was the clear winner in all length and evaluation metrics. Additionally, the three methods with *SP-token* outperformed the others.

What if we do not have multiple headlines of different lengths to evaluate the methods? To answer this question, we followed the evaluation setup of the previous studies on DUC 2004: The reference summaries of 75 bytes were used even when evaluating summaries of 30 and 50 bytes. Table 8 reports ROUGE scores for the system outputs in 10 and 13 characters evaluated based on the 26char-ref headlines. This evaluation setup reduced the performance differences between the methods. Although Transformer + *SP-token* remained the clear winner, the ranking in ROUGE scores of the other methods are flipped. We also computed rank correlation coefficients (Kendall's τ) to assess the discrepancy in the ranking among the methods presented in Table 7 and Table 8. The last row of Table 8 reveals that the rank correlation is not perfect (lower than one) but moderate. We understand that τ is maintained high to some extent because of two reasons: (1) Most of the

---

[7]We used MeCab (Kudo et al., 2004) to tokenize the system outputs.

[8]https://github.com/OpenNMT/OpenNMT-py

[9]https://github.com/pytorch/fairseq

	10 characters			13 characters			26 characters		
Models	R-1	R-2	R-L	R-1	R-2	R-L	R-1	R-2	R-L
(1)	$37.95_{[+0]}$	$19.97_{[+1]}$	$36.54_{[+0]}$	$41.54_{[+1]}$	$21.60_{[+1]}$	$39.41_{[+1]}$	$33.97_{[+0]}$	$13.54_{[-1]}$	$27.66_{[+0]}$
(2)	$38.35_{[-1]}$	$20.71_{[+1]}$	$37.04_{[-1]}$	$41.52_{[-1]}$	$21.13_{[-1]}$	$39.05_{[-1]}$	$35.50_{[+0]}$	$14.18_{[+1]}$	$28.64_{[+0]}$
(3)	$41.35_{[+1]}$	$21.95_{[+1]}$	$39.93_{[+1]}$	$43.62_{[+1]}$	$22.51_{[+0]}$	$40.89_{[+1]}$	$35.66_{[+0]}$	$14.14_{[-1]}$	$28.80_{[+0]}$
(4)	$39.33_{[-1]}$	$20.47_{[-2]}$	$37.46_{[-2]}$	$40.38_{[-4]}$	$20.47_{[-4]}$	$37.53_{[-4]}$	$36.84_{[+0]}$	$14.42_{[+0]}$	$29.21_{[+0]}$
(5)	$39.21_{[+2]}$	$19.59_{[-1]}$	$37.69_{[+2]}$	$42.99_{[+3]}$	$22.94_{[+4]}$	$40.53_{[+3]}$	$33.36_{[+0]}$	$13.55_{[+1]}$	$27.59_{[+0]}$
(6)	$45.14_{[+0]}$	$26.35_{[+0]}$	$43.70_{[+0]}$	$47.09_{[+0]}$	$25.80_{[+0]}$	$43.95_{[+0]}$	$37.86_{[+0]}$	$15.68_{[+0]}$	$30.46_{[+0]}$
τ	0.733	0.600	0.600	0.067	-0.067	0.067	1.000	0.733	1.000

Table 9: ROUGE scores of each model on the length-restricted JNC test set.

swaps occur in adjacent ranks, and (2) there are not many samples of the method in this analysis. Then, we focus on the samples flipped in this evaluation setup, as shown in Table 8. We observed that the rankings are swapped even if there is a difference of 1.0 or more (these differences are well observed in state-of-the-art competition) in Table 7. For example, we can show this issue between (3) and (4) in 10 characters of R-1 score, (2) and (4) in 10 characters of R-2 score, and (3) and (4) in 10 characters setting of R-L score in Table 7.

What if we do not have strict length headlines to evaluate the methods? To answer this question, we followed the evaluation setup of previous studies : The reference summaries of each target length were extracted from the JNC test set. Table 9 reports ROUGE scores for the system outputs in 10, 13, and 26 characters evaluated in the length-restricted JNC test set. In this evaluation setup, Transformer + *SP-token* remained the clear winner, but the performances of the other methods were flipped. We also calculated τ in this case. The last row of Table 9 reveals that the 13 character setting considerably lost correlation with the JAMUL evaluation result. We guess this inconsistency is brought about by using the different content test sets among each length setting. Depending on the target length which is specified by the evaluation setting, this evaluation protocol might not evaluate the methods adequately.

4 Analysis

4.1 Performance of Word Selection According to the Output Length

How well do the existing methods change the word selection depending on the output length? As shown in the first and second rows of Table 5, the 10char-ref and 13char-ref headlines contain words that are not included in the 26char-ref headlines. In other words, the selection of words in the generated headline should be changed in response to the length restriction. To confirm this question, we computed ROUGE-1 recall scores for the system outputs generated by each method, assuming that the groups of the words included in the 10char-ref or 13char-ref but not in the 26char-ref headlines are the "reference" summaries. For instance, the red words in Table 1 are the "reference" summaries in this experiment.

We report this result in Figure 2. The low recall score indicates that each system cannot select the words tailored to the length constraints. However, (4) ConvS2S + *SP-token* shows the highest performance. Taking this into account, Transformer + *SP-token* improves the important words in all lengths setting, but ConvS2S + *SP-token* may improve the change of words according to the target length.

4.2 Performance of Managing Extractive and Abstractive Tasks

In Table 2, we reported the proportion of the number of extractive and abstractive operations in the JAMUL. We analyze how the existing methods can reflect extractive and abstractive operations in generating summaries.

First, to observe extractive operations, we computed ROUGE-1 recall scores for the system outputs generated by each system, measuring the number of overlapping words between an article as "system" summaries and 10char-ref, 13char-ref, and 26char-ref headlines as "reference" summaries. The group of bars which contained *ext* in its name in Figure 3 reports the result. The relatively high recall score indicates that the length control method succeeds in managing extractive operations.

Next, we examine whether the length control methods could perform abstractive operations. We adopted the words included in 10char-ref, 13char-ref, or 26char-ref headlines but not included in an article as "reference" summaries, and computed the ROUGE-1 recall scores for the system outputs.

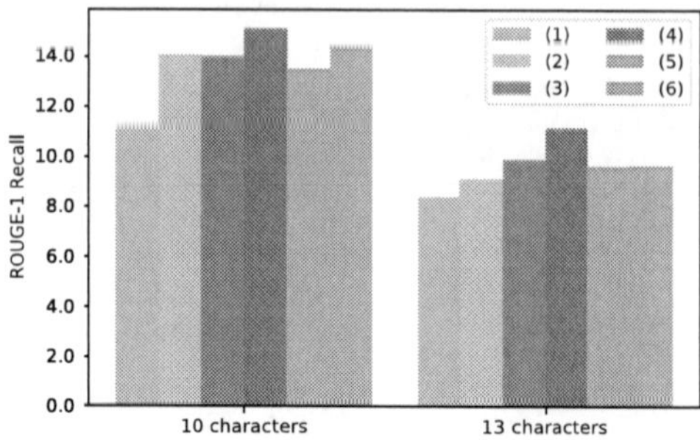

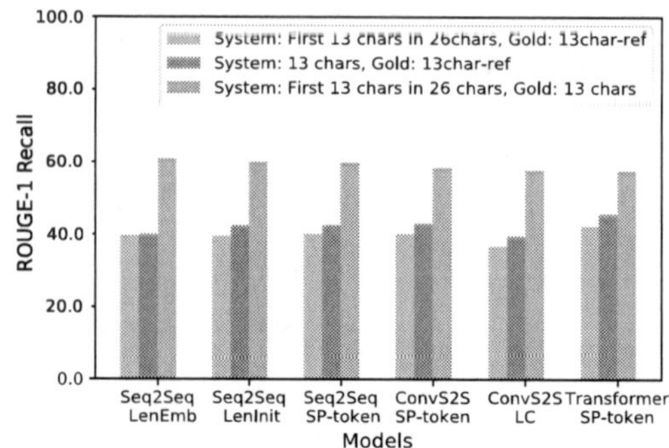

Figure 2: ROUGE-1 recall scores when comparing system outputs and the groups of the words included in 10char-ref or 13char-ref but not included in 26char-ref.

Figure 4: ROUGE-1 recall scores to assess the similarity of headlines generated for different lengths.

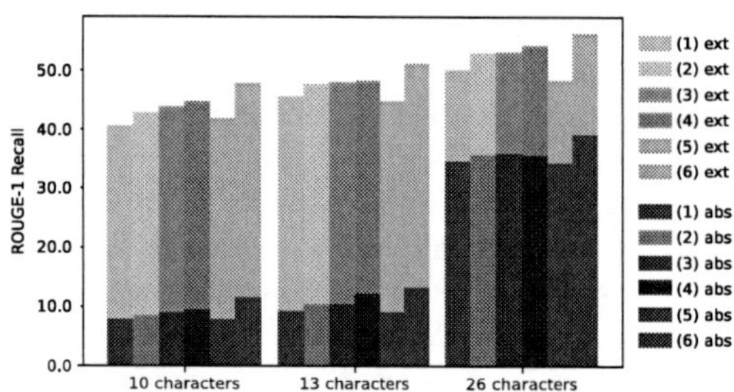

Figure 3: ROUGE-1 recall scores when comparing system outputs and the groups of the words which are extractive and abstractive.

The group of bars which contained *abs* in its name in Figure 3 reports the result. Regarding the outputs targeting 26 characters, the recall scores of around 30 point imply that each model can manage abstractive operations to some extent. In contrast, the low recall scores for the outputs targeting 10 and 13 characters revealed that all length control methods could not perform well on abstractive operations under the severe length constraint.

4.3 How Do Length Control Mechanisms Work?

We wondered whether a method that could control the output length would produce similar headlines even for different lengths for the same news article. To confirm this suspicion, we reported ROUGE-1 recall scores in Figure 4 with three different configurations: (a) evaluating the first 13 characters of headlines generated to be 26 characters long on 13char-ref headlines (blue); (b) evaluating headlines generated to be 13 characters long on 13char-ref headlines (pink); and setting (c) is the same as setting (a) but evaluated on the headline generated to be 13 characters long (green).

Setting (a) corresponds to the strategy where we trimmed headlines of different lengths to 13 characters long. This setting was worse than setting (b), where a method tailored headlines to the desired length. However, the difference in ROUGE scores between (a) and (b) was not very large, indicating that the existing methods do not drastically change the content for 13 characters long and 26 characters long. This tendency was also verified by setting (c), which assessed how much the first 13 characters of headlines generated to be 26 characters long covered the content of those generated to be 13 characters long. These facts suggest that we should explore in further research a method not only trained by generic supervision data (print headlines) but also tuned for the desired length.

5 Related Work

Rush et al. (2015) created the first approach to neural abstractive summarization. They generated a headline from the first sentence of a news article in the AEG (Napoles et al., 2012), which contains an enormous number of pairs of headlines and articles. After their study, a number of researchers addressed this task: For example, Chopra et al. (2016) used the encoder-decoder framework (Sutskever et al., 2014; Bahdanau et al., 2015) and Nallapati et al. (2016) incorporated additional features into the model, such as parts-of-speech tags and named entities. Suzuki and Nagata (2017) proposed word-frequency estimation to reduce the repeated phrases being generated. Zhou et al. (2017) proposed a gating mechanism (*sGate*) to ensure that important information is selected at each decoding step.

Furthermore, attempts to control the output

length in neural abstractive summarization have been gradually increasing. Shi et al. (2016) reported that hidden states in recurrent neural networks in the encoder-decoder framework could implicitly model the length of the output sequences. Kikuchi et al. (2016) was the first to propose the idea of controlling the output length in the encoder-decoder framework. Their approach inserts length information for the output length into the decoder. Additionally, Fan et al. (2018) reported that output lengths could be controlled by embedding special tokens given to an input sequence. These two studies used DUC 2004 (Over et al., 2007), which comprises only 75-byte summaries, to evaluate the outputs in multiple lengths. Liu et al. (2018) also proposed a method for controlling the number of output tokens in the ConvS2S model. In Transformer (Vaswani et al., 2017), Takase and Okazaki (2019) proposed two length control methods by extending positional embedding. They additionally evaluated the system outputs by using the reconstructed test set of AEG which consists of the fixed length headlines. Makino et al. (2019) proposed a global optimization method under a length constraint.

Sun et al. (2019) examined how to compare summarizers by considering the length bias of generated summaries in the test set that includes various length summaries. However, no previous work built a dataset for evaluating headlines of multiple lengths or reported an in-depth perspective on this task during the process of new production in the real world. However, a single length reference that could appropriately evaluate multiple length summaries in multiple document summarization was reported (Shapira et al., 2018). In that study, the authors confirmed the correlation coefficient of ROUGE scores between the scores using a single length reference and multiple (gold) length references in the evaluation. The present research differed in that we examined what kind of problems occurred and studied headline generation domain, which requires stricter keyword selection.

6 Conclusion

In this paper, we presented two new corpora: The JNC contains a large number of pairs of news articles and their headlines, and the JAMUL includes headlines of three different lengths (10, 13, and 26 characters long) written by professional editors.

This study is the first to analyze the characteristics of multiple headlines of different lengths, and to evaluate existing approaches for length control based on the reference headlines composed for different lengths. We found that Transformer model with a special length token (*SP-token*) outperformed the other methods on the JAMUL. Additionally, although we confirmed that single length (the longest) references could adequately evaluate multiple length system outputs, the rankings were swapped even if there is a difference of 1.0 or more in the ROUGE scores. We also confirmed the length-restricted test set, which was extracted from length-insensitive headlines and corresponding articles, could not adequately evaluate the multiple length system outputs depending on the specified length. In the analysis, the existing methods could not take into account the word selection according to length constraint. We also found it difficult to evaluate methods to controlling output length, because headlines of different lengths are written based on different goals, and because the training data does not necessarily reflect the goal of the headlines of a specific length. In the future, we plan to explore an approach to adapt a model trained on print headlines to those which dedicated to a different length.

References

Dzmitry Bahdanau, Kyunghyun Cho, and Yoshua Bengio. 2015. Neural machine translation by jointly learning to align and translate. In *International Conference on Learning Representations (ICLR 2015)*.

Ziqiang Cao, Wenjie Li, Sujian Li, and Furu Wei. 2018. Retrieve, rerank and rewrite: Soft template based neural summarization. In *Proceedings of the 56th Annual Meeting of the Association for Computational Linguistics (ACL 2018)*, pages 152–161.

Wenhu Chen, Guanlin Li, Shuo Ren, Shujie Liu, Zhirui Zhang, Mu Li, and Ming Zhou. 2018. Generative bridging network for neural sequence prediction. In *Proceedings of the 2018 Conference of the North American Chapter of the Association for Computational Linguistics: Human Language Technologies (NAACL-HLT 2018)*, pages 1706–1715.

Sumit Chopra, Michael Auli, and Alexander M. Rush. 2016. Abstractive sentence summarization with attentive recurrent neural networks. In *Proceedings of the 2016 Conference of the North American Chapter of the Association for Computational Linguistics (NAACL 2016)*, pages 93–98.

Angela Fan, David Grangier, and Michael Auli. 2018. Controllable abstractive summarization. In *Pro-*

ceedings of the 2nd Workshop on Neural Machine Translation and Generation (WNMT 2018), pages 45–54.

Jonas Gehring, Michael Auli, David Grangier, Denis Yarats, and Yann N. Dauphin. 2017. Convolutional sequence to sequence learning. In *Proceedings of the 34th International Conference on Machine Learning, (ICML 2017)*, pages 1243–1252.

Kaiming He, Xiangyu Zhang, Shaoqing Ren, and Jian Sun. 2016. Deep residual learning for image recognition. In *2016 IEEE Conference on Computer Vision and Pattern Recognition, (CVPR 2016)*, pages 770–778.

Sepp Hochreiter and Jürgen Schmidhuber. 1997. Long short-term memory. *Neural Computation*, 9(8):1735–1780.

Yuta Kikuchi, Graham Neubig, Ryohei Sasano, Hiroya Takamura, and Manabu Okumura. 2016. Controlling output length in neural encoder-decoders. In *Proceedings of the 2016 Conference on Empirical Methods in Natural Language Processing (EMNLP 2016)*, pages 1328–1338.

Shun Kiyono, Sho Takase, Jun Suzuki, Naoaki Okazaki, Kentaro Inui, and Masaaki Nagata. 2018. Unsupervised token-wise alignment to improve interpretation of encoder-decoder models. In *Proceedings of the 2018 EMNLP Workshop BlackboxNLP: Analyzing and Interpreting Neural Networks for NLP (BlackboxNLP 2018)*, pages 74–81.

Guillaume Klein, Yoon Kim, Yuntian Deng, Jean Senellart, and Alexander Rush. 2017. OpenNMT: Open-source toolkit for neural machine translation. In *Proceedings of ACL 2017, System Demonstrations (ACL 2017)*, pages 67–72.

Taku Kudo and John Richardson. 2018. Sentence-Piece: A simple and language independent subword tokenizer and detokenizer for neural text processing. In *Proceedings of the 2018 Conference on Empirical Methods in Natural Language Processing: System Demonstrations (EMNLP 2018)*, pages 66–71.

Taku Kudo, Kaoru Yamamoto, and Yuji Matsumoto. 2004. Applying conditional random fields to japanese morphological analysis. In *Proceedings of the 2004 Conference on Empirical Methods in Natural Language Processing (EMNLP 2004)*, pages 230–237.

Chin-Yew Lin. 2004. ROUGE: A package for automatic evaluation of summaries. In *Text Summarization Branches Out: Proceedings of the ACL-04 Workshop*, pages 74–81.

Yizhu Liu, Zhiyi Luo, and Kenny Zhu. 2018. Controlling length in abstractive summarization using a convolutional neural network. In *Proceedings of the 2018 Conference on Empirical Methods in Natural Language Processing (EMNLP 2018)*, pages 4110–4119.

Takuya Makino, Tomoya Iwakura, Hiroya Takamura, and Manabu Okumura. 2019. Global optimization under length constraint for neural text summarization. In *Proceedings of the 57th Conference of the Association for Computational Linguistics, (ACL 2019)*, pages 1039–1048.

Ramesh Nallapati, Bowen Zhou, Cícero Nogueira dos Santos, Çaglar Gülçehre, and Bing Xiang. 2016. Abstractive text summarization using sequence-to-sequence rnns and beyond. In *Proceedings of the 20th SIGNLL Conference on Computational Natural Language Learning, (CoNLL 2016)*, pages 280–290.

Courtney Napoles, Matthew Gormley, and Benjamin Van Durme. 2012. Annotated Gigaword. In *Proceedings of the Joint Workshop on Automatic Knowledge Base Construction and Web-scale Knowledge Extraction (AKBC-WEKEX 2012)*, pages 95–100.

Myle Ott, Sergey Edunov, Alexei Baevski, Angela Fan, Sam Gross, Nathan Ng, David Grangier, and Michael Auli. 2019. fairseq: A fast, extensible toolkit for sequence modeling. In *Proceedings of the 2019 Conference of the North American Chapter of the Association for Computational Linguistics: Human Language Technologies, Demonstrations (NAACL-HLT 2019)*, pages 48–53.

Paul Over, Hoa Dang, and Donna Harman. 2007. DUC in context. *Information Processing and Management*, 43(6):1506–1520.

Romain Paulus, Caiming Xiong, and Richard Socher. 2018. A deep reinforced model for abstractive summarization. In *6th International Conference on Learning Representations (ICLR 2018)*.

Alexander M. Rush, Sumit Chopra, and Jason Weston. 2015. A neural attention model for abstractive sentence summarization. In *Proceedings of the 2015 Conference on Empirical Methods in Natural Language Processing (EMNLP 2015)*, pages 379–389.

Ori Shapira, David Gabay, Hadar Ronen, Judit Bar-Ilan, Yael Amsterdamer, Ani Nenkova, and Ido Dagan. 2018. Evaluating multiple system summary lengths: A case study. In *Proceedings of the 2018 Conference on Empirical Methods in Natural Language Processing (EMNLP 2018)*, pages 774–778.

Xing Shi, Kevin Knight, and Deniz Yuret. 2016. Why neural translations are the right length. In *Proceedings of the 2016 Conference on Empirical Methods in Natural Language Processing (EMNLP 2016)*, pages 2278–2282.

Simeng Sun, Ori Shapira, Ido Dagan, and Ani Nenkova. 2019. How to compare summarizers without target length? pitfalls, solutions and reexamination of the neural summarization literature. In *Proceedings of the Workshop on Methods for Optimizing and Evaluating Neural Language Generation (NeuralGen 2019)*, pages 21–29.

Ilya Sutskever, James Martens, George E. Dahl, and Geoffrey E. Hinton. 2013. On the importance of initialization and momentum in deep learning. In *Proceedings of the 30nd International Conference on Machine Learning (ICML 2013)*, pages 1139–1147.

Ilya Sutskever, Oriol Vinyals, and Quoc V. Le. 2014. Sequence to sequence learning with neural networks. In *Proceedings of the 27th International Conference on Neural Information Processing Systems (NIPS 2014)*, pages 3104–3112.

Jun Suzuki and Masaaki Nagata. 2017. Cutting-off redundant repeating generations for neural abstractive summarization. In *Proceedings of the 15th Conference of the European Chapter of the Association for Computational Linguistics (EACL 2017)*, pages 291–297.

Sho Takase and Naoaki Okazaki. 2019. Positional encoding to control output sequence length. In *Proceedings of the 2019 Conference of the North American Chapter of the Association for Computational Linguistics: Human Language Technologies (NAACL-HLT 2019)*, pages 3999–4004.

Ashish Vaswani, Noam Shazeer, Niki Parmar, Jakob Uszkoreit, Llion Jones, Aidan N. Gomez, Lukasz Kaiser, and Illia Polosukhin. 2017. Attention is all you need. In *Advances in Neural Information Processing Systems 30: Annual Conference on Neural Information Processing Systems 2017 (NIPS 2017)*, pages 6000–6010.

Kai Wang, Xiaojun Quan, and Rui Wang. 2019. Biset: Bi-directional selective encoding with template for abstractive summarization. In *Proceedings of the 57th Conference of the Association for Computational Linguistics (ACL 2019)*, pages 2153–2162.

Li Wang, Junlin Yao, Yunzhe Tao, Li Zhong, Wei Liu, and Qiang Du. 2018. A reinforced topic-aware convolutional sequence-to-sequence model for abstractive text summarization. In *Proceedings of the Twenty-Seventh International Joint Conference on Artificial Intelligence, (IJCAI 2018)*, pages 4453–4460.

Qingyu Zhou, Nan Yang, Furu Wei, and Ming Zhou. 2017. Selective encoding for abstractive sentence summarization. In *Proceedings of the 55th Annual Meeting of the Association for Computational Linguistics (ACL 2017)*, pages 1095–1104.

Qingyu Zhou, Nan Yang, Furu Wei, and Ming Zhou. 2018. Sequential copying networks. In *Proceedings of the Thirty-Second AAAI Conference on Artificial Intelligence, (AAAI 2018)*, pages 4987–4995.

Agreement is overrated:
A plea for correlation to assess human evaluation reliability

Jacopo Amidei and **Paul Piwek** and **Alistair Willis**
School of Computing and Communications
The Open University
Milton Keynes, UK
{jacopo.amidei, paul.piwek, alistair.willis}@open.ac.uk

Abstract

Inter-Annotator Agreement (IAA) is used as a means of assessing the quality of NLG evaluation data, in particular, its reliability. According to existing scales of IAA interpretation – see, for example, Lommel et al. (2014), Liu et al. (2016), Sedoc et al. (2018) and Amidei et al. (2018a) – most data collected for NLG evaluation fail the reliability test. We confirmed this trend by analysing papers published over the last 10 years in NLG-specific conferences (in total 135 papers that included some sort of human evaluation study). Following Sampson and Babarczy (2008), Lommel et al. (2014), Joshi et al. (2016) and Amidei et al. (2018b), such phenomena can be explained in terms of irreducible human language variability. Using three case studies, we show the limits of considering IAA as the only criterion for checking evaluation reliability. Given human language variability, we propose that for human evaluation of NLG, correlation coefficients and agreement coefficients should be used together to obtain a better assessment of the evaluation data reliability. This is illustrated using the three case studies.

1   Introduction

Data reliability plays a pivotal role in human annotation efforts. Krippendorff (1980) delineates three types of reliability, which are *stability*, *accuracy* and *reproducibility*.

Stability or intra-coder agreement is generally measured by the test-retest strategy, which is based on the resubmission, after some time, of some items to the original annotators. That is, annotators are asked to re-assess the same items after some time has elapsed. Comparing the annotations of the same items provides a measure of the annotator's consistency.

Accuracy is measured calculating the deviations from a given gold standard.

Reproducibility is a measure of the extent to which different annotators arrive at the same annotation when working independently. If different annotators[1], when independently performing the annotation task, consistently make the same annotation decision, then we have strong support for the belief that the phenomena to be annotated are well understood and shared across the annotators. The reproducibility of the annotation is dependent on a well-defined coding scheme and clear annotation guidelines. With these, different annotators can perform the same annotation task reaching equivalent (or very similar) results. As shown in Artstein (2017), Finlayson and Erjavec (2017), Hovy and Lavid (2010) and Pustejovsky and Stubbs (2013), where general rules for annotation design are developed, this idea of reliability as reproducibility has become the predominant reliability concept used in any Computational Linguistics (CL) annotation task. Accordingly, guidelines and good practice descriptions for applying IAA in CL annotation tasks have been developed (for example, Lombard et al. (2002); Artstein and Poesio (2008); LeBreton and Senter (2008); Kottner et al. (2011)). An assumption behind such good practice is the existence of a gold standard, which although true in many annotation tasks, for example speech tagging, may not always be the case. Such an assumption falls short in the case of NLG. Indeed, in the case of NLG, where the existence of a gold standard is mostly not available – for example, criteria such as ambiguity, relevance, usefulness or overall quality – the concept of reliability as reproducibility can hide some pitfalls.

For this paper we analysed papers published in

---

[1] In Section 4 we will refer to annotators as judges. We chose such terminology to emphasize the evaluation aim of the annotation.

Proceedings of The 12th International Conference on Natural Language Generation, pages 344–354,
Tokyo, Japan, 28 Oct - 1 Nov, 2019. ©2019 Association for Computational Linguistics

NLG specialist conferences over the last ten years (135 in total) in order to check how IAA is used in the human evaluation of NLG systems. In order to carry out our survey, we selected the papers from the Special Interest Group on Natural Language Generation (SIGGEN) webpage hosted by the ACL Anthology website[2]. We examined the papers with a publication date between the years 2008 to 2018. To select the papers, we decided to use the following criteria: 1) the paper should include a study with human annotators or judges; 2) the study should be an evaluation study (we did not take into account other tasks involving human annotation) 3) the study should allow for measurement of the IAA (for example, we did not take into account papers in which the human evaluation was done with open questions, nor papers whose human evaluation consisted of an author manually inspecting outputs. Likewise, we did not take into account papers that use extrinsic evaluation methodology. However, we did include papers whose extrinsic evaluation methodology was followed by a survey which allows the study of the IAA, for example, surveys done with Likert scale questions.[3]

Our analysis highlights that there is little use of reliability studies in the evaluation phase and a lack of common practice in the use of IAA. More interestingly, we confirm a trend already suggested in Craggs and Wood (2005), Lommel et al. (2014), Liu et al. (2016), Sedoc et al. (2018), Amidei et al. (2018a) and the supplementary material of Reiter (2018): according to existing scales of IAA interpretation – see for example Table 1 and Table 2 – most data collected for NLG evaluation fail the reliability test.

Following Craggs and Wood (2005), Sampson and Babarczy (2008), Lommel et al. (2014), Joshi et al. (2016) and Amidei et al. (2018b) such phenomena can be explained with variability in language interpretation and quality judgement, particularly for semantic or pragmatic language aspects – such as for instance concepts such as text usability, fluency, comprehensibility etc. Human language processing and understanding are fundamental aspects of the human language. Given their subjectivity, they are exposed to high variability.

As noted in Craggs and Wood (2005), Sampson and Babarczy (2008), Lommel et al. (2014), Joshi et al. (2016) and Amidei et al. (2018b) annotators diverge in language annotation tasks due to a range of inelimable factors such as background knowledge, preconceptions about language and general educational level. Such divergence or variability is what makes human language so broad in its use, interpretation and understanding. For this reason, this divergence and variability should not be eliminated from NLG generation tasks. If evaluation results have to inform generation system developers of the extent to which they can improve the communicative power of their systems, levelling the human language interpretation and use divergences is in danger of biasing system developers towards ignoring important aspects of human language. However, the concept of reliability as reproducibility goes in the direction of levelling human languages divergences. This raises the need of a better understanding of reliability of human evaluations.

Given the human language variability that NLG systems have to take into account, we propose the use of correlation coefficients[4] alongside the Kappa statistic[5] in order to obtain a more faithful picture of the evaluation reliability.

2 Related work

The use of IAA in corpus annotation tasks has been widely studied. To our knowledge, less attention has been paid to the use of IAA in human evaluation for NLG systems. Our paper tries to fill this gap.

Regarding the use of IAA in corpus annotation tasks, and more specifically the task of linguistic annotation, we refer to Palmer and Xue (2005) and Pustejovsky and Stubbs (2013). Both provide extensive theoretical descriptions of how to perform

---

[2]https://aclweb.org/anthology/venues/inlg/

[3]Further information about the paper selection can be found in the supplementary materials, at: https://bit.ly/2lKL516.

[4]Some examples of correlation coefficients are Kendall's τ, Pearson's r, Spearman's ρ and Goodman and Kruskall's Gamma.

[5]In CL, since Carletta (1996)'s paper, the standard measure to calculate human agreement in annotation efforts is some variation of the *kappa* coefficient of agreement, which Carletta collectively refers to as the name of *Kappa statistic*. Following the notation used in Carletta (1996), the Kappa statistic K can be expressed in the following general formulation: $K = P(A) - P(E)/1 - P(E)$ where $P(A)$ is the proportion of times the annotators agree, whereas $P(E)$ is the proportion of times the annotators would be expected to agree by chance. Some example of the Kappa statistic are Cohen's κ (Cohen, 1960) and Fleiss' κ (Fleiss, 1971). Krippendorff's α coefficient (Krippendorff, 1980) is expressed in a similar way but in terms of disagreement.

an annotation task. For human evaluation of NLG systems, we refer to Krahmer and Theune (2010) and Gatt and Krahmer (2018). Both devote an entire section to evaluation. In particular, Section 7 of Gatt and Krahmer's paper gives a helpful description of the methodologies used in NLG for the purpose of evaluation, alongside examples and a discussion of the relevant problems.

A very helpful survey paper for understanding IAA in CL is presented by Artstein and Poesio (2008), who give a deep analysis of the kappa agreement measures. The authors discuss the mathematics and interpretation of these coefficients and their use in several computational linguistic tasks.

Regarding the basic statistics concepts and statistical analysis we refer to Witte and Witte (2017). More specifically, regarding the use of correlation coefficients in annotation tasks we refer to Stemler and Tsai (2008), LeBreton and Senter (2008) and Gisev et al. (2013). A brief introduction to some of the statistical concepts used in this paper, as well as a complete list of the papers we examined, can be found at `https://bit.ly/21KL516`.

3 10 years of IAA in evaluation of NLG systems

The main findings of our analysis are: (1) little use of reliability studies in the evaluation phase, (2) shortcomings and oversights in reporting the IAA studies, and consequent lack of a common practice in the use of IAA, (3) generally a low value of IAA.

Point 1: Use of reliability studies

The first thing that stands out in our analysis is the small number of papers which compute IAA in order to validate the evaluation results. Indeed, of the 135 papers in our study, just 18% (24 papers) report information about the IAA. Among these, four papers use two different coefficients to measure the IAA. The other 20 use just one coefficient. In 67% of the papers (16 papers) the IAA was reported in papers published between the 2016 and the 2018. This fact shows an improving trend, in reporting the IAA values, in the area.

Point 1 underlines a shortcoming of NLG human evaluation tasks. When human evaluations are performed, it is good practice to verify the reliability of the evaluations. Without a reliability study there are no solid reasons to accept the conclusions from an evaluation. In Section 4 we suggest that to assess reliability, correlation should play a central role.

Point 2: Reporting IAA studies

With regard to point 2, much has been said in previous works. Because presenting a detailed report of those works is beyond the scope of this paper, we refer to Krippendorff (1980), Lombard et al. (2002), Artstein and Poesio (2008), LeBreton and Senter (2008), Kottner et al. (2011) and Artstein (2017), where guidelines and good practice descriptions for applying IAA have been developed. Based on our research, the following shortcomings have been identified. Papers often:

- do not report the names of the coefficients used;

- do not report sufficient details about the experiments used to collect the data;

- use a coefficient that is not suitable for the data collected;

- do not report the number of items on which the IAA study is performed;

- do not report whether the annotators were performing the evaluation independently or not;

- do not report the scale used to interpret the IAA values, and when reported do not discuss the results accurately.

More specifically, between the papers that report the IAA, 37% of the papers (9 works) use a IAA coefficient that is not suitable for the data collected. For example, the use of Fleiss' κ coefficient for data whose level of measurement is interval. Related to this point, we note that often the researchers do not report in sufficient detail the experiment used to collect the data, which can also give information about the data level of measurement – that is whether the data are nominal, ordinal, intervals or ratios. Across the papers we studied, such information had to be deduced from the statistic used for analysing the data.[6]

---

[6] We note that this is an imperfect, although sometimes the only possible, way to deduce the data level of measurement. Indeed, researchers can use the wrong statistic to analyse the data, which results in a distorted image of the data level of measurement.

From Table 3 we can see that although discouraged by previous work – see for example Krippendorff (1980), Craggs and Wood (2005) and Artstein and Poesio (2008) – percent agreement is the coefficient used the most. Indeed it is applied in 25% of the works (7 papers). It is followed by Krippendorff's α (Krippendorff, 1980) and Fleiss's κ (Fleiss, 1971). Both coefficients were used in 5 papers each. Three papers do not report the name of the Kappa statistic used. Because each metric is different, reporting the exact coefficient used in the analysis would help the readers to better understand the data reliability and the evaluation results.

Few papers discuss the interpretation of the IAA for their evaluation. Between the papers that report the IAA, just 20% of the papers (5 works) make implicit or explicit reference to the interpretation scales used. The IAA interpretation scales reported by these papers are the Krippendorff scale (Krippendorff, 1980, see Table 1) and the Landis and Koch scale (Landis and Koch, 1977, see Table 2).

IAA value	IAA interpretation
IAA < 0.67	Discard
$0.67 \leq$ IAA < 0.8	Tentative
$0.8 \leq$ IAA ≤ 1	Good

Table 1: Krippendorff (1980).

IAA value	IAA interpretation
IAA < 0	Poor
$0 \leq$ IAA ≤ 0.2	Slight
$0.2 <$ IAA ≤ 0.4	Fair
$0.4 <$ IAA ≤ 0.6	Moderate
$0.6 <$ IAA ≤ 0.8	Substantial
$0.8 <$ IAA ≤ 1	Almost Perfect

Table 2: Landis and Koch (1977).

In almost every paper we analysed, the number of items used for the IAA studies was not reported. Likewise, there were few cases in which it was reported whether or not the annotators worked independently.

Finally, we also note that the terminology used is not shared across the analysed papers. Some examples are: reliability, agreement, inter-evaluator agreement, pair-wise agreement, inter-annotator agreement, inter-assessor agreement, inter-rater reliability and inter-coder agreement.

Point 3: Low IAA values

Table 3 shows a tendency also found in other work; see for example Craggs and Wood (2005), Lommel et al. (2014), Liu et al. (2016), Sedoc et al. (2018) and Amidei et al. (2018a) and the supplementary material of Reiter (2018).[7] The trend is that in human evaluation of NLG systems the IAA values reached are relatively low. Following the Krippendorff scale of IAA interpretation (Krippendorff, 1980) – which considers the threshold 0.67 as the minimum to be reached in order to get a reliable set of data (see Table 1) – the majority of the evaluations should be discarded. The problem of how to interpret IAA values is an

Coefficient	# used	Average	Min.	Max.
Percent agreement	7	0.69	0.44	0.94
Cohen's κ	4	0.40	0.10	0.88
Krippendorff's α	5	0.62	0.37	0.90
Fleiss's κ	5	0.53	0.29	0.78
Pearson's r	2	0.42	0.20	0.71
Kendall's W	1	0.61	0.47	0.76
Weighted κ	1	0.07	0.07	0.07
κ no better specified	3	0.57	0.32	0.77

Table 3: Average, minimal and maximum IAA value per coefficient. *# used* means the number of times that a coefficient was used in total across the papers. In each paper each coefficient was used to measure the annotator's agreement about one or more questions or criteria.

intriguing and complicated one. Artstein and Poesio (2008) describe this as "the most serious problem with current practice in reliability testing". As noted by Krippendorff (1980, 2004), Craggs and Wood (2005) and Hovy and Lavid (2010), the choice of IAA interpretation scale is arbitrary and task-dependent. The reduction of a statistical test interpretation to a simple number, whilst common, can be arbitrary and accordingly give us little information[8]. For example, Artstein (2017) show that a single label is not sufficient to give a deep understanding of the reliability of an annotation. In this paper, we do not face the problem of how to interpret IAA, rather, we try to tackle the prob-

---

[7]We note that for the κ coefficients which are "no better specified" the average measure is not appropriate. Indeed, they could be different κ coefficients. However, we chose to report the average for uniformity reasons. It worth saying that such a choice does not affect the theoretical point here presented.

[8]Lately, this point has been raised also for the $p - value$. See for example the special issue *Statistical Inference in the 21st Century: A World Beyond* $p < 0.05$ (Wasserstein et al., 2019) published by The American Statistician.

lem of data reliability by suggesting that correlation coefficients and agreement coefficients should be used together to obtain a better assessment of the evaluation data reliability.

Point 3 also reveals a big issue in the area. Indeed, the main purpose of IAA is to check the reliability of the annotated data. Following the existing scales of IAA interpretation, for example those of Krippendorff (1980) and Landis and Koch (1977), the majority of the evaluations should be discarded because they are unreliable. However, Sampson and Babarczy (2008), Lommel et al. (2014), Joshi et al. (2016) and Amidei et al. (2018b) suggest that a low level of IAA can be explained with human language variability. Arguably such a property, which must be preserved by NLG systems, makes strict agreement unsuitable for testing the reliability of human evaluations. This raises the problem of how to improve the analysis of reliability of human evaluation datasets. In Section 4 we argue that to assess reliability, correlation coefficients should play a central role.

4 The use of correlation coefficients for NLG human evaluation tasks

Correlation coefficients are generally considered inappropriate for measuring the reliability of annotated data; see for example, Lombard et al. (2002), Krippendorff (2004) and Artstein and Poesio (2008). The main concern about the use of correlation coefficient for reliability studies is well expressed by the following quotation:

> [Correlation coefficients, for example Pearson's r] measure the extent to which two logically separate interval variables, say X and Y, covary in a linear relationship of the form $Y = a + bX$. They indicate the degree to which the values of one variable predict the values of the other. Agreement coefficients, in contrast, must measure the extent to which $Y = X$. (Krippendorff, 1980, p. 244)

Indeed, the rationale behind agreement coefficients, such as the Kappa statistic, is to catch the extent to which judges rank a given item equally. When judges rank a given item in the same way, it is assumed that the judges share the same interpretation and understanding of the schema and guideline used in the annotation task. When this happens, given the fact that the annotation is reached

with judges that work independently, the concept of reliability as reproducibility suggests that the same annotation can be reached with other judges. This makes the annotation repeatable and consequently reliable.

Although such a concept of reliability as reproducibility is well-founded in cases where the phenomenon under investigation has some objective meaning, for example in the case of many CL annotation tasks where the gold standard is available, it falls short in the case of NLG evaluation tasks. As we argued in the introduction, in the case of NLG the concept of IAA as reproducibility can hide some pitfalls. For evaluation tasks that aim to evaluate semantic or pragmatic language aspects – such as for instance concepts such as text usability, fluency, comprehensibility etc. – two people can entertain different, although equally valid, opinions. In cases such as these, given the variability of human language – specifically variability in language interpretation and quality judgement – expecting judges to always arrive at exactly the same judgement may be both unrealistic and over-constrained. Variation in language interpretation and use makes strict agreement unsuitable for measuring human evaluation reliability.

It is arguable that, from an evaluation point of view, what is important, more than the fact that judges have the same interpretation of the phenomena studied, is to know whether the judges are consistent relative to each other. A possible first step to test this is checking judges' relative consistency, that is checking whether the judges follow a systematic pattern in their assessments.

A feasible strategy to frame this problem is the following. Expecting judges to always arrive at exactly the same judgement may be unrealistic. For instance, one judge may be stricter than another one. However, in such situations the judgements would still covary. In other words, we can ask: Is it possible to predict J_a's judgements based on J_b's judgements, where J_a and J_b are two judges who are judging the same set of sentences?

Correlation coefficients can be used to answer this question. Such coefficients measure to what extent a variable changes, in a way not expected by chance alone, in relation to the change of another variable. That is, they measure the covariation of two variables. The change can be either in the same (positive correlation) or in the opposite (negative correlation) direction. In the presence of correlation, given a judges' annotation, it is mostly possible to predict the annotation of another judge. Correlation coefficients, measuring the judges' relative covariance, can give an insight into to the extent different judges are consistent relative to each other when annotating the data, even when their individual interpretations of the phenomena are not identical but following a consistent pattern, see for example (Stemler and Tsai, 2008, page 38) and (Gisev et al., 2013, page 331).

To test such an interpretation of correlation coefficients, we use data collected in a previous pilot study, and extend the analysis to two publicly available datasets with human evaluation: the QG-STEC[9] (Rus et al., 2010) and the Flickr-8k (Elliott and Keller, 2014) [10].

The pilot study was an attempt to define annotation guidelines for an Atumatic Question Generation task[11]. The methodology we used was that of refining the criteria chosen through several iterations of discussions and pilot evaluations. During these iterations we noticed that regardless of how many changes we made, there remained a divergence in the judgements that we could not reduce by modifying the guidelines. Nevertheless, we realized that such divergences showed an interesting degree of consistency, due to the fact that the judges were consistent in following their interpretation of the criteria in play. The pilot study we use in this paper, although consisting only of ten items, helps to formalize the problem and makes it clear from a visual point of view. Indeed, the use of ten items allows a clear visualization of the data. Although judgements are different in values, they show a clear pattern – see Figure 5 and Figure 1. Once we test the use of correlation coefficients in the pilot study we scale the experiment by the use of larger datasets, QG-STEC and Flickr-8k, that allow more stronger statistical conclusions.

4.1 Datasets analysis

Following Siegel and Castellan (1988) and Singh (2007) we use Goodman and Kruskal's Gamma as

a correlation coefficient (Goodman and Kruskal, 1954) and Fleiss' κ (Fleiss, 1971) to measure the IAA. Goodman and Kruskals Gamma is the most adequate coefficient for ordinal data with many ties which is exactly our case[12]. Fleiss' κ is a measure for nominal or ordinal data annotated from two or more judges. To measure Fleiss' κ we used the implementation supplied in the nltk library.[13] Goodman and Kruskal's Gamma was measured with the *GoodmanKruskalGamma* function supplied by the R software.[14] In order to interpret the values obtained in the analysis, we use the Krippendorff scale of interpretation for IAA (Krippendorff, 1980) (see Table 1) and the interpretation for non-parametric correlation coefficient introduced in Rosenthal (1996) (see Table 4). Since Carletta (1996), the Krippendorff scale of interpretation has become the standard for CL annotation tasks.

For a nonparametric correlation coefficient we chose the Rosenthal (1996) scale because it extends Cohen's popular scale (Cohen, 1988). More precisely, it allows a more fine grained value distinction for the interval $[0.50, 1]$ – in particular, Rosenthal's scale specifies Cohen's "large" interval $[0.50, 1]$ into the two intervals "large" $[0.50, 0.7]$ and "very large" $[0.70, 1]$. Because Goodman and Kruskal's Gamma tends to give higher values than other correlation coefficients, such a choice allows a finer-grained analysis.

Correlation value	Value interpretation
$[0, - 0.1] \setminus [0, 0.1]$	Negligible
$[-0.1, - 0.3] \setminus [0.1, 0.3]$	Small
$[-0.3, - 0.5] \setminus [0.3, 0.5]$	Medium
$[-0.5, - 0.7] \setminus [0.5, 0.7]$	Large
$[-0.7, - 1] \setminus [0.7, 1]$	Very large

Table 4: Rosenthal (1996).

---

[9]The dataset is available at: `https://github.com/Keith-Godwin/QG-STEC-plus/blob/master/Export-Subsets.zip`.

[10]The dataset is available at: `https://github.com/elliottd/compareImageDescriptionMeasures`. For the original dataset detail we refer to (Hodosh et al., 2013).

[11]Given a text T as an input, the task was to generate a question which can be used, for example, to verify the respondents knowledge about T.

[12]Ties data are data with value repetition. In the case of the pilot dataset we use categorical questions (yes/no) and rating graphical scale. Likewise, the QG-STEC evaluation was performed with rating graphical scale, see Rus et al. (2012).

[13]The documentation for the agreement metric can be found at: `https://www.nltk.org/_modules/nltk/metrics/agreement.html`.

[14]The documentation for this function can be found at: `https://www.rdocumentation.org/packages/DescTools/versions/0.99.19/topics/GoodmanKruskalGamma`.

Interpretation of correlation coefficients case studies

Pilot: The pilot dataset was created taking random input paragraphs and questions from the SQuAD dataset (Rajpurkar et al., 2016). Seven judges engaged in the annotation task. Out of the seven judges, three were native speakers of English. The other four were proficient in English. The criteria measured were: i) Pertinence, ii) Grammaticality, iii) Comprehensibility, and iv) Fluency. The Pertinence criterion is ranked on a scale from 0 to 3, whereas the other criteria use a binary scale. Further detail about the dataset can be found in Amidei et al. (2018b)[15].

Table 5 reports the result for the pilot study. As we can note the native English speakers get the better IAA value and correlation results. Quite interestingly, although IAA value is below 0.4, for the fluency criterion they get a perfect correlation, which is 0.73 bigger than the correlation reached from non-native English speakers. This can be an indication that native judges have a different but strong interpretation of the concept of fluency[16]. Figure 1, which depicts the evaluation of question

Criteria	Coefficients	Dataset		
		All	Native	Non-native
Syntactic	Fleiss' kappa	0.36	0.59	0.21
	Goodman and Kruskal's Gamma	0.56	0.86	0.37
Comprehensibility	Fleiss' kappa	0.55	0.63	0.48
	Goodman and Kruskal's Gamma	0.92	1	0.91
Fluency	Fleiss' kappa	0.30	0.39	0.17
	Goodman and Kruskal's Gamma	0.56	1	0.27
Pertinence	Fleiss' kappa	0.20	0.22	0.07
	Goodman and Kruskal's Gamma	0.57	0.47	0.48
Average	Fleiss' kappa	0.35	0.45	0.23
	Goodman and Kruskal's Gamma	0.65	0.83	0.50

Table 5: Results of Fleiss' κ and Goodman and Kruskal's Gamma in the pilot dataset. *All, Native* and *Non-native* indicate the measure performed respectively over the seven judges, over the three English native speaker judges and over the four no English native speaker judges.

fluency, can help to better understand this phenomenon. Judge 5 systematically ranks with a value that is equal or less than the value given by judges 6 and 7. In contrast, the ranks provided by non-native English speakers lack systematicity.

It is also worth noticing that for the cases of comprehensibility and pertinence, in the case of non-native English speakers, there is an interest-

---

[15]The evaluation guideline and the actual evaluation can be found via: `https://bit.ly/2lKL516`.

[16]It is worth noticing that in the case of No English native speaker, the Goodman Kruskal's Gamma measured on triple of judges reached the following values: 0.54, 0.29, 0.12, 0.12.

ing gap (more than 0.4) between IAA and correlation value. Figure 2 shows the annotators'

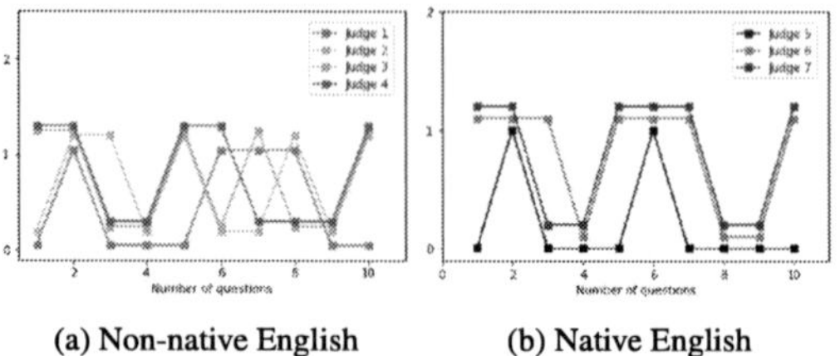

(a) Non-native English   (b) Native English

Figure 1: Plots of the evaluation of question fluency. Non-native English speakers (a) and native English speakers (b). For better readability, the scores are shifted upward slightly.

ranks are different in value, which explain a medium/low, for comprehensibility, and very low, for pertinence, IAA. However, there is systematicity in the annotators' ranks – it is really clear in the case of compressibility, and less accentuated in the case of pertinence.

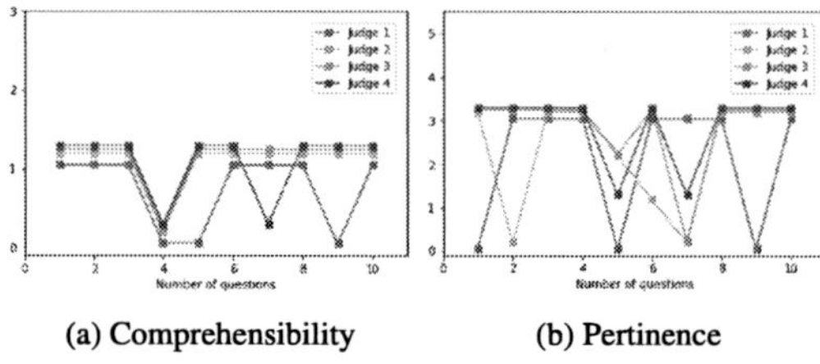

(a) Comprehensibility   (b) Pertinence

Figure 2: Plots of the evaluation of question comprehensibility (a) and question pertinence (b) in the case of non-native English speakers. For better readability, the scores were shifted upward.

The average score in Table 5 can be used to attempt a conclusion about the reliability of the dataset. Following the Krippendorff scale of interpretation (Krippendorff, 1980), the evaluation data should be discarded because the IAA is below the threshold of 0.67. However, following the scale of interpretation for non-parametric correlation coefficients introduced in Rosenthal (1996), the data reach a large correlation, and a very large correlation in the case of native English speakers.

Taking into account the interpretation we gave in the previous section, although the annotators use different values in the evaluation, their interpretations are constant with each other: they judgements covary systematically with each other. This interpretation suggests that the data are reliable.

Flickr-8k: The Flickr-8K dataset contains quality judgements for 5,822 sentences[17] (Elliott and Keller, 2014)[18]. Each sentence was a description of an image. The annotation was carried out by 3 human experts who judged the sentence semantic correctness in a scale from 1 to 4.

Because we don't have the information about how the data were collected, in order to decide which kind of analysis to carry out on the Flickr-8k dataset we plot the distribution of the categories used by the judges. Figure 3 suggests that the data do not have a normal distribution, and so we opt for the use of nonparametric statistics. As in the previous case we used Goodman and Kruskal's Gamma and Fleiss' κ to carry out our analysis. For Goodman and Kruskal's Gamma, we report the average results of the pairwise measure between the annotators. This method is suggested by Siegel and Castellan (1988) for the case of Kendall τ correlation coefficient, which is a variant of the Goodman and Kruskal's Gamma.

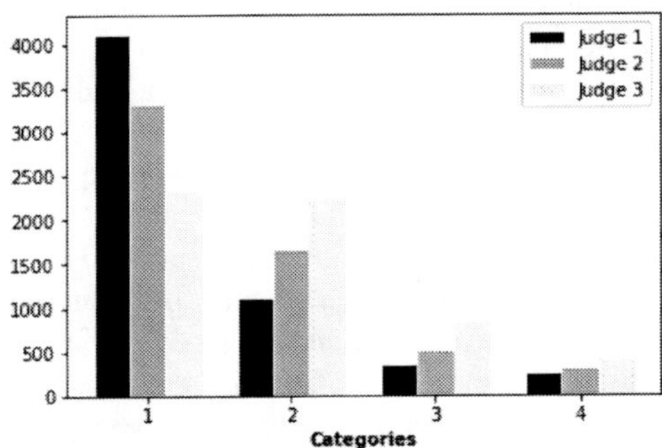

Figure 3: Distribution of the categories used by the judges in the Flickr-8k dataset.

The measurements give a Fleiss' value of 0.52 and a Gamma value of 0.98. Following the Krippendorff interpretation of IAA, the annotation has to be considered not reliable. However, the annotation achieves a very high correlation, which suggests a high relative consistency between the judges. Indeed, when they are in disagreement, judge 2 ranks systematically higher than judge 1, and judge 3 ranks systematically higher than judge 2. Although judges rank the items with different magnitude their judgement covary systematically.

Also in this case, the correlation coefficient suggests the evaluation data are reliable and justifies a deeper analysis of the data quality. For example, following (Bayerl and Paul, 2007), the use of Generalizability Theory (Brennan, 2001), which allows a deeper analysis of the factors that influence annotation quality.

Use of correlation coefficients, an application

QG-STEC: The QG-STEC dataset is composed of questions generated from four systems that participated in the QG-STEC (Rus et al., 2010) Task B, that is the task to generate a question from an input sentence. Each question is evaluated based on five criteria: Relevance (on a scale from 1-4), Question Type (on a scale from 1 to 2), Syntactic Correctness and Fluency (on a scale from 1-4), Ambiguity (on a scale from 1-3) and Variety (on a scale from 1-3). Six judges took part in the evaluation. They judged batches of sentences independently. Table 6 shows the batch of questions judged and independent judges for that batch.

Judges	Batches of question
J1 and J2	80
J1 and J3	67
J1 and J4	81
J1 and J5	7
J1 and J6	106
J2 and J5	158
J3 and J5	125
J4 and J5	142
J5 and J6	129

Table 6: Batches of question with independent judges assigned to them. For $i = 1, \ldots, 6$, J_i means judge i.

Table 7 shows the result of the analysis carried out for the QG-STEC dataset. Also in this case an interesting discrepancy between the IAA values and the correlation values is measured. The average result, shows that, although IAA values are low, annotators reach large, and in two cases, very large Gamma correlation values.[19]

As in the previous cases, the Gamma coefficient suggests that all the batches are annotated by judges that shows a relative consistency and suggest data reliability.

Each pair of annotators evaluated different batches of questions, which were generated from

---

[17]The dataset is available at: `https://github.com/elliottd/compareImageDescriptionMeasures`.

[18]For the original dataset detail we refer to (Hodosh et al., 2013).

[19]We note that in the case of judge 1 and 3 the Gamma value is low due to the negative, although perfect, correlation reached in the question type criteria. If the average was done with absolute value the average gamma value would be 0.72.

Criteria	Coefficients	Coefficients values for pair of judges							
		J1 and J2	J1 and J3	J1 and J4	J1 and J6	J2 and J5	J3 and J5	J4 and J5	J5 and J6
Ambiguity	Fleiss' kappa	0.06	0.17	0.29	0.08	0.45	0.14	0.17	0.22
	Goodman and Kruskal's Gamma	0.33	0.33	0.61	0.21	0.84	0.51	0.39	0.75
Correctness	Fleiss' kappa	0.31	0.31	0.31	-0.00013	0.20	0.32	0.28	0.13
	Goodman and Kruskal's Gamma	0.67	0.67	0.71	0.39	0.57	0.62	0.57	0.38
QuestionType	Fleiss' kappa	0.32	-0.05	0.2	0.34	1	0.14	0.15	0.52
	Goodman and Kruskal's Gamma	0.91	-1	1	0.89	1	0.45	0.80	0.95
Relevance	Fleiss' kappa	0.13	0.16	0.13	0.08	0.15	0.28	0.19	0.01
	Goodman and Kruskal's Gamma	0.41	0.63	0.67	0.76	0.58	0.79	0.63	1
Variety	Fleiss' kappa	0.35	0.89	0.10	0.08	0.52	0.36	0.29	0.35
	Goodman and Kruskal's Gamma	0.81	0.99	0.08	0.15	0.82	0.73	0.43	0.54
Average	Fleiss' kappa	0.23	0.29	0.20	0.11	0.46	0.24	0.21	0.24
	Goodman and Kruskal's Gamma	0.62	0.32	0.61	0.48	0.76	0.62	0.56	0.72

Table 7: Fleiss' κ and Goodman and Kruskal's Gamma values reached in the QG-STEC dataset. For $i = 1, \ldots, 6$, J_i means judge i.

4 different systems. Consequently, given the variance in question quality, a deeper analysis is complicated. However, we can see that judge 5 gets good correlation in any batch, which is also the case for judge 2. This fact allows us to consider the batch they annotated together as the more reliable one. This is confirmed by the k and Gamma values reached.

We can also notice that regarding the variety criterion, it is arguable that judge 4 and judge 6 miss a sound interpretation of the variety criterion. Indeed, both of them get low correlation with judge 1. Judge 1, on the other hand, gets really high correlation with both judge 3 and judge 2. At the same time, judge 5 gets high correlation with both judge 2 and judge 3 and lower correlation with judge 4 and judge 6. This evidence suggests that, in the case of the variety criterion, care must be taken with the data collected by judge 4 and 6.

Following the same analysis we can notice that judge 2 may be inconsistent for the relevance criteria. Indeed, it is lower than the correlation value reached by judge 1 and judge 5.

5 Conclusion

Based on an analysis of papers published over the last 10 years in NLG-specific conferences (in total 135 papers), we presented a snapshot of the use of IAA in NLG human evaluation tasks. One of the main points that stands out is the low level of IAA reached, and how few reliability studies there are. From our study, the problem of human evaluation reliability stands up.

Using three case studies, we show the limitations of using the IAA as the only criterion for checking the reliability of an evaluation. Given the variability of human language, we suggest that in human evaluation of NLG, correlation coefficients and agreement coefficients, such as for example the Kappa statistic, can be used together to have a better picture of the evaluation data reliability. Agreement coefficients can be used both in pilot studies to improve annotation schemes and guidelines, and for data analysis to give a picture of how distant the annotators' interpretation of the phenomena is. Correlation coefficients can instead tell us to what extent annotators are consistent with each other. As we have seen in Section 4, a low agreement coefficient value can hide a consistent pattern in the annotation which is captured by high value for the correlation coefficient. Although judges have different opinions about the quality of a generated text, which is a result of the language variability, they entertain consistent relative interpretations. Consequently, their judgments may still be considered reliable, although ideally further investigation, for example test-retest annotation (Krippendorff, 1980) and where possible the use of internal coefficient as Cronbach's alpha (Cronbach, 1951), should be carried out. Regarding test-retest evaluation and Cronbach's alpha, it is important to note that they have to be considered in the evaluation design.

Our aim with this paper is to enhance, in the NLG community, awareness about the need to handle the problem of human evaluation reliability. This problem is much more relevant nowadays given the growing use of crowdsourced workers in the evaluation phase. Indeed, in our analysis, we found that of the 29 papers that used crowdsourced workers, 23 were published in the last three years.

Acknowledgments

We warmly thank the anonymous reviewers for their helpful suggestions.

References

J. Amidei, P. Piwek, and A. Willis. 2018a. Evaluation methodologies in automatic question generation 2013-2018. In *Proceedings of the 11th International Conference on Natural Language Generation*, pages 307–317.

J. Amidei, P. Piwek, and A. Willis. 2018b. Rethinking the agreement in human evaluation tasks. In *Proceedings of the 27th International Conference on Computational Linguistics*, pages 3318–3329.

R. Artstein. 2017. *Inter-annotator agreement.* in Handbook of Linguistic Annotation, (Eds.) Nancy Ide and James Pustejovsky, pages 297-313. Springer, Dordrecht.

R. Artstein and M. Poesio. 2008. Inter-coder agreement for computational linguistics. *Computational Linguistics*, 34(4):555–596.

P. S. Bayerl and K. I. Paul. 2007. Identifying sources of disagreement: Generalizability theory in manual annotation studies. *Computational Linguistics*, 33(1):3–8.

RL Brennan. 2001. *Generalizability theory.* New York: Springer-Verlag.

J. Carletta. 1996. Assessing agreement on classification tasks: The kappa statistic. *Computational Linguistics*, 22(2):249–254.

J. Cohen. 1960. A coefficient of agreement for nominal scales. *Educational and psychological measurement*, 20(1):37–46.

J. Cohen. 1988. *Statistical power analysis for the behavioral sciences.* West Publishing Company, USA.

R. Craggs and M. M. Wood. 2005. Evaluating discourse and dialogue coding schemes. *Computational Linguistics*, 3(3):289–296.

L. J. Cronbach. 1951. Coefficient alpha and the internal structure of tests. *psychometrika*, 16(3):297–334.

D. Elliott and F. Keller. 2014. Comparing automatic evaluation measures for image description. In *Proceedings of the 52nd Annual Meeting of the Association for Computational Linguistics (Volume 2: Short Papers)*, volume 2, pages 452–457.

M. A. Finlayson and T. Erjavec. 2017. *Overview of Annotation Creation: Processes and Tools.* in Handbook of Linguistic Annotation, (Eds.) Nancy Ide and James Pustejovsky, pages 167-911. Springer, Dordrecht.

J. L. Fleiss. 1971. Measuring nominal scale agreement among many raters. *Psychological bulletin*, 76(5):378.

A. Gatt and E. Krahmer. 2018. Survey of the state of the art in natural language generation: Core tasks, applications and evaluation. *Journal of Artificial Intelligence Research*, 61:65–170.

N. Gisev, J. S. Bell, and T. F. Chen. 2013. Interrater agreement and interrater reliability: key concepts, approaches, and applications. *Research in Social and Administrative Pharmacy*, 9(3):330–338.

L. A. Goodman and W. H. Kruskal. 1954. Measures of association for cross classifications. *Journal of the American Statistical Association*, 49(268):732–764.

M. Hodosh, P. Young, and J. Hockenmaier. 2013. Framing image description as a ranking task: Data, models and evaluation metrics. *Journal of Artificial Intelligence Research*, 47:853–899.

E. Hovy and J Lavid. 2010. Towards a 'science' of corpus annotation: A new methodological challenge for corpus linguistics. *International Journal of Translation Studies*, 22(1):13–36.

A. Joshi, P. Bhattacharyya, M. Carman, J. Saraswati, and R. Shukla. 2016. How do cultural differences impact the quality of sarcasm annotation?: A case study of indian annotators and american text. In *Proceedings of the 10th SIGHUM Workshop on Language Technology for Cultural Heritage, Social Sciences, and Humanities*, pages 95–99.

J. Kottner, L. Audigé, S. Brorson, A. Donner, B. J. Gajewski, A. Hróbjartsson, C. Roberts, M. Shoukri, and D. L. Streiner. 2011. Guidelines for reporting reliability and agreement studies (grras) were proposed. *International journal of nursing studies*, 48(6):661–671.

E. Krahmer and M. Theune. 2010. *(Eds.) Empirical Methods in Natural Language Generation.* Springer-Verlag, Berlin Heidelberg.

K. Krippendorff. 1980. *Content Analysis: An Introduction to Its Methodology.* Sage Publications, Beverly Hills, CA.

K. Krippendorff. 2004. Reliability in content analysis: Some common misconceptions and recommendations. *Human Communication Research*, 30(3):411–433.

J. R. Landis and G. G.. Koch. 1977. The measurement of observer agreement for categorical data. *Biometrics*, 33(1):159–174.

J. M. LeBreton and J. L. Senter. 2008. Answers to 20 questions about interrater reliability and interrater agreement. *Organizational research methods*, 11(4):815–852.

C. W. Liu, R. Lowe, I. V. Serban, M. Noseworthy, L. Charlin, and J. Pineau. 2016. How not to evaluate your dialogue system: An empirical study of unsupervised evaluation metrics for dialogue response generation. *arXiv preprint arXiv:1603.08023*.

M. Lombard, J. Snyder-Duch, and C. C. Bracken. 2002. Content analysis in mass communication: Assessment and reporting of intercoder reliability. *Human communication research*, 28(4):587–604.

A. Lommel, M. Popović, and A. Burchardt. 2014. Assessing inter-annotator agreement for translation error annotation. *In Proceedings of the Ninth International Conference on Language Resources and Evaluation (LREC), 26-31 May. Reykjavik, Iceland.*

M. Palmer and N. Xue. 2005. Linguistic annotation. *Computational Linguistics*, 31(1):71–106.

J. Pustejovsky and A. Stubbs. 2013. *Natural Language Annotation for Machine Learning*, volume 1. Published by OReilly Media, Gravenstein Highway North, Sebastopol, CA.

P. Rajpurkar, J. Zhang, K. Lopyrev, and P. Liang. 2016. Squad: 100,000+ questions for machine comprehension of text. *arXiv preprint arXiv:1606.05250.*

E. Reiter. 2018. A structured review of the validity of bleu. *Computational Linguistics*, 44(3):393–401.

J. A. Rosenthal. 1996. Qualitative descriptors of strength of association and effect size. *Journal of social service Research*, 21(4):37–59.

V. Rus, B. Wyse, P. Piwek, M. Lintean, S. Stoyanchev, and C. Moldovan. 2010. The first question generation shared task evaluation challenge. *In: Proceedings of the Sixth International Natural Language Generation Conference (INLG 2010), 7-9 Jul 2010, Trim Castle, Ireland.*

V. Rus, B. Wyse, P. Piwek, M. Lintean, S. Stoyanchev, and C. Moldovan. 2012. A detailed account of the first question generation shared task evaluation challenge. *Dialogue & Discourse*, 3(2):177–204.

G. Sampson and A. Babarczy. 2008. Definitional and human constraints on structural annotation of english. *Natural Language Engineering*, 14(4):471–494.

J. Sedoc, D. Ippolito, A. Kirubarajan, J. Thirani, L. Ungar, and C. Callison-Burch. 2018. Chateval: A tool for the systematic evaluation of chatbots. In *Proceedings of the Workshop on Intelligent Interactive Systems and Language Generation (2IS&NLG)*, pages 42–44.

S. Siegel and N. J. Jr. Castellan. 1988. *Nonparametric statistics for the behavioral sciences*. McGraw-hill, New York.

K. Singh. 2007. *Quantitative social research methods*. Sage, New Delhi.

S. E. Stemler and J. Tsai. 2008. Best practices in interrater reliability: Three common approaches. *In, Osborne, J. W., (ed.) Best practices in quantitative methods*, pages 29–49. Sage, California.

R. L. Wasserstein, A. Schirm, and Lazar N. A. 2019. *Statistical Inference in the 21st Century: A World Beyond $p < 0.05$*, volume 73. Taylor & Francis.

R. S. Witte and J. S. Witte. 2017. *Statistics, Eleventh Edition*. John Wiley & Sons, Inc., LaVergne, Tennessee, USA.

A complete list of the papers we examined can be found at: `https://bit.ly/2lKL516`.

Best practices for the human evaluation of automatically generated text

Chris van der Lee
Tilburg University
c.vdrlee@uvt.nl

Albert Gatt
University of Malta
albert.gatt@um.edu.mt

Emiel van Miltenburg
Tilburg University
c.w.j.vanmiltenburg@uvt.nl

Sander Wubben
Tilburg University
s.wubben@uvt.nl

Emiel Krahmer
Tilburg University
e.j.krahmer@uvt.nl

Abstract

Currently, there is little agreement as to how Natural Language Generation (NLG) systems should be evaluated, with a particularly high degree of variation in the way that human evaluation is carried out. This paper provides an overview of how human evaluation is currently conducted, and presents a set of best practices, grounded in the literature. With this paper, we hope to contribute to the quality and consistency of human evaluations in NLG.

1 Introduction

Even though automatic text generation has a long tradition, going back at least to Peter (1677) (see also Swift, 1774; Rodgers, 2017), human evaluation is still an understudied aspect. Such an evaluation is crucial for the development of Natural Language Generation (NLG) systems. With a well-executed evaluation it is possible to assess the quality of a system and its properties, and to demonstrate the progress that has been made on a task, but it can also help us to get a better understanding of the current state of the field (Mellish and Dale, 1998; Gkatzia and Mahamood, 2015; van der Lee et al., 2018). The importance of evaluation for NLG is itself uncontentious; what is perhaps more contentious is the way in which evaluation should be conducted. This paper provides an overview of current practices in human evaluation, showing that there is no consensus as to how NLG systems should be evaluated. As a result, it is hard to compare the results published by different groups, and it is difficult for newcomers to the field to identify which approach to take for evaluation. This paper addresses these issues by providing a set of best practices for human evaluation in NLG. A further motivation for this paper's focus on human evaluation is the recent discussion on the (un)suitability of automatic measures for

the evaluation of NLG systems (see Ananthakrishnan et al., 2007; Novikova et al., 2017; Sulem et al., 2018; Reiter, 2018, and the discussion in Section 2).

Previous studies have also provided overviews of evaluation methods. Gkatzia and Mahamood (2015) focused on NLG papers from 2005-2014; Amidei et al. (2018a) provided a 2013-2018 overview of evaluation in question generation; and Gatt and Krahmer (2018) provided a more general survey of the state-of-the-art in NLG. However, the aim of these papers was to give a structured overview of existing methods, rather than discuss shortcomings and best practices. Moreover, they did not focus on human evaluation.

Following Gkatzia and Mahamood (2015), Section 3 provides an overview of current evaluation practices, based on papers from INLG and ACL in 2018. Apart from the broad range of methods used, we also observe that evaluation practices have changed since 2015: for example, there is a significant decrease in the number of papers featuring extrinsic evaluation. This may be caused by the current focus on smaller, decontextualized tasks, which do not take users into account.

Building on findings from NLG, but also statistics and the behavioral sciences, Section 4 provides a set of recommendations and best practices for human evaluation in NLG. We hope that our recommendations can serve as a guide for newcomers in the field, and can otherwise help NLG research by standardizing the way human evaluation is carried out.

2 Automatic versus human evaluation

Automatic metrics such as BLEU, METEOR, and ROUGE are increasingly popular; Gkatzia and Mahamood's (2015) survey of NLG papers from 2005-2014 found that 38.2% used automatic met-

Proceedings of The 12th International Conference on Natural Language Generation, pages 355–368,
Tokyo, Japan, 28 Oct - 1 Nov, 2019. ©2019 Association for Computational Linguistics

rics, while our own survey (described more fully in Section 3) shows that 80% of the empirical papers presented at the ACL track on NLG or at the INLG conference in 2018 reported on automatic metrics. However, the use of these metrics for the assessment of a system's quality is controversial, and has been criticized for a variety of reasons. The two main points of criticism are:

Automatic metrics are uninterpretable. Text generation can go wrong in different ways while still receiving the same scores on automated metrics. Furthermore, low scores can be caused by correct, but unexpected verbalizations (Ananthakrishnan et al., 2007). Identifying what can be improved therefore requires an error analysis. Automatic metric scores can also be hard to interpret because it is unclear how stable the reported scores are. With BLEU, for instance, libraries often have their own BLEU score implementation, which may differ from one another, thus affecting the scores (this is recently addressed by Post, 2018). Reporting the scores accompanied by confidence intervals, calculated using bootstrap resampling (Koehn, 2004), may increase the stability and therefore interpretability of the results. However, such statistical tests are not straightforward to perform.

Automatic metrics do not correlate with human evaluations. This has been repeatedly observed (e.g. Belz and Reiter, 2006; Reiter and Belz, 2009; Novikova et al., 2017).[1] In light of this criticism, it has been argued that automated metrics are not suitable to assess linguistic properties (Scott and Moore, 2007), and Reiter (2018) discouraged the use of automatic metrics as a (primary) evaluation metric. The alternative is to perform a human evaluation.

There are arguably still good reasons to use automatic metrics: they are a cheap, quick and repeatable way to approximate text quality (Reiter and Belz, 2009), and they can be useful for error analysis and system development (Novikova et al., 2017). We would not recommend using

human evaluation for every step of the development process, since this would be costly and time-consuming. Furthermore, there may be automatic metrics that reliably capture some qualitative aspects of NLG output, such as fluency or stylistic compatibility with reference texts. But for a general assessment of overall system quality, human evaluation remains the gold standard.

3 Overview of current work

This section provides an overview of current human evaluation practices, based on the papers published at INLG (N=51) and ACL (N=38) in 2018. We did not observe noticeable differences in evaluation practices between INLG and ACL, which is why they are merged for the discussion of the bibliometric study.[2]

3.1 Intrinsic and extrinsic evaluation

Human evaluation of natural language generation systems can be done using intrinsic and extrinsic methods (Sparck Jones and Galliers, 1996; Belz and Reiter, 2006). Intrinsic approaches aim to evaluate properties of the system's output, for instance, by asking participants about the fluency of the system's output in a questionnaire. Extrinsic approaches aim to evaluate the impact of the system, by investigating to what degree the system achieves the overarching task for which it was developed. While extrinsic evaluation has been argued to be more useful (Reiter and Belz, 2009), it is also rare. Only three papers (3%) in the sample of INLG and ACL papers presented an extrinsic evaluation. This is a notable decrease from Gkatzia and Mahamood (2015), who found that nearly 25% of studies contained an extrinsic evaluation. Of course, extrinsic evaluation is the most time- and cost-intensive out of all possible evaluations (Gatt and Krahmer, 2018), which might explain the rarity, but does not explain the decline in (relative) frequency. That might be because of the set-up of the tasks we see nowadays. Extrinsic evaluations require that the system is embedded in its target use context (or a suitable simulation thereof), which in turn requires that the system addresses a specific purpose. In practice, this often means the system follows the 'traditional' NLG

---

[1]In theory this correlation might increase when more reference texts are used, since this allows for more variety in the generated texts. However, in contrast to what this theory would predict, both Doddington (2002) and Turian et al. (2003) report that correlations between metrics and human judgments in machine translation do not improve substantially as the number of reference texts increases. Similarly, Choshen and Abend (2018) found that reliability issues of reference-based evaluation due to low-coverage reference sets cannot be overcome by attainably increasing references.

[2]For the ACL papers, we focused on the following tracks: Machine Translation, Summarization, Question Answering, and Generation. See Supplementary Materials for a detailed overview of the investigated papers and their evaluation characteristics

Criterion	Total	Criterion	Total
Fluency	13	Manipulation check	3
Naturalness	8	Informativeness	3
Quality	5	Correctness	3
Meaning preservation	5	Syntactic correctness	2
Relevance	5	Qualitative analysis	2
Grammaticality	5	Appropriateness	2
Overall quality	4	Non-redundancy	2
Readability	4	Semantic adequacy	2
Clarity	3	Other criteria	25

Table 1: Criteria used for human evaluation from all papers. Separate counts for ACL and INLG 2018 are in the appendix.

Scale	Count
Likert (5-point)	14
Preference	10
Likert (2-point)	6
Likert (3-point)	5
Other Likert (4,7,10-point)	5
Rank-based Magnitude Estimation	5
Free text comments	1

Table 2: Types of scales used for human evaluation

pipeline (Reiter and Dale, 2000), encompassing many of these pipeline sub-tasks to go from input data to complete output texts (Mellish et al., 2006; Gatt and Krahmer, 2018). Such systems were a mainstay of NLG literature until recently (e.g., Harris, 2008; Gatt and Portet, 2010; Reiter et al., 2003), but the field has shifted towards focusing on only one or a few of the sub-tasks from the NLG pipeline (e.g. text planning, surface realization, referring expression generation), with a concomitant focus on text output quality, for which an intrinsic evaluation may be sufficient. However, we are starting to see a swing back towards a full pipeline approach with separate neural modules handling sub-tasks (Castro Ferreira et al., 2019), which may also cause a resurgence of extrinsic evaluation.

3.2 Properties of text quality

Many studies take some notion of 'text quality' as their primary evaluation measure, but this goal is not easy to assess, since text quality criteria differ across tasks (see Section 4.1 for further discussion). This variety, suggesting a lack of agreement, is clear from Table 1. Except for fluency, and for naturalness and quality which were used for a shared task, most criteria are infrequent; the numerous 'other criteria' are those which are used only once. At the same time, there is probably significant overlap. For instance, naturalness is sometimes linked to fluency, and informativeness to adequacy (Novikova et al., 2018). In short, there is no standard evaluation model for NLG. Furthermore, there is significant variety in naming conventions.

3.3 Sample size and demographics

When looking at sample size, it is possible to distinguish between expert-focused and reader-focused evaluation. 14 papers (28%) used an expert-focused approach, meaning that between 1 and 4 expert annotators evaluated system output. 13 papers (26%) employed a larger-scale reader-focused method in which 10 to 60 readers judged the generated output. We found a median of 4 annotators. However, these numbers might not reflect reality: only 55% of papers specified the number of participants and an even smaller number (18%) reported the demographics of their sample. Only 12.5% of the papers with a human evaluation reported inter-annotator agreement, using Krippendorff's α, Fleiss' κ, Weighted κ or Cohen's κ. Agreement in most cases ranged from 0.3 to 0.5, but given the variety of metrics and the thresholds used to determine acceptable agreement, this range should be treated with caution.

3.4 Design

Apart from participant sample size, an important issue that impacts statistical power is the number of items (e.g. generated sentences) used in an evaluation. Among papers that reported these numbers, we observed a median of 100 items used for human evaluation in INLG and ACL papers. The number of items however ranged between 2 and 5,400, illustrating a sizable discrepancy. In 83% of papers that reported these figures, all annotators saw all examples. Only 12.5% of papers reported other aspects of evaluation study design, such as the order in which items were presented, randomisation and counterbalancing methods used (e.g. a latin square design), or whether criteria were measured at the same time or separately.

3.5 Number of questions and types of scales

In addition to the diversity in criteria used to measure text quality (see Section 3.2), there is a wide range of rating methods that are used to measure those criteria. Do note that Likert and rating scales are treated indistinctly here (for a distinction, see Amidei et al., 2019). The 5-point Likert scale is the most popular option, but preference ratings are a close second (see Table 2). Other types of rating methods are much less common. Rank-based Magnitude Estimation, a continuous metric, was only found among shared task papers, and only one paper reported using free-text comments.

We also investigated the number of ratings used to measure a single criterion (e.g. a paper may use two ratings to measure two different aspects of fluency). Only 34% of papers with a human evaluation reported the number of ratings to measure a criterion. These numbers ranged from 1 to 4 ratings for a criterion, with 1 rating being the most common.

3.6 Statistics and data analysis

A minority (33%) of papers report one or more statistical analyses for their human evaluation to investigate if findings are statistically significant. The types of statistical analyses vary greatly: there is not one single test that is the most common. Examples of tests found are Student's T test, Mann-Whitney U test, and McNemar's test. Theoretically, such statistical tests should be performed to test a specific hypothesis (Navarro, 2019). However, not all papers using a statistical test report their hypotheses. And conversely, some papers reporting hypotheses do not perform a statistical test. 19% of all papers explicitly state their hypotheses or research questions.

4 Best practices

This section provides best practices for carrying out and reporting human evaluation in NLG. We (mostly) restrict ourselves to intrinsic evaluation.

4.1 Text quality and criteria

Renkema (2012, p. 37) defines text quality in terms of whether the writer (or: NLG system) succeeds in conveying their intentions to the reader. He outlines three requirements for this to be achieved: (i) the writer needs to achieve their goal while meeting the reader's expectations; (ii) linguistic choices need to match the goal; and (iii) the text needs to be free of errors.

If successfully conveying communicative intention is taken to be the main overarching criterion for quality, then two possibilities arise. One could treat quality as a primitive, as it were, evaluating it directly with users. Alternatively—and more in line with current NLG evaluation practices—one could take text quality to be contingent on individ-ual dimensions or criteria (for various studies of such criteria, see Dell'Orletta et al., 2011; Falkenjack et al., 2013; Nenkova et al., 2010; Pitler and Nenkova, 2008, *inter alia*).

The choice between these two options turns out to be a point of contention. Highly correlated scores on different quality criteria suggest that human annotators find them hard to distinguish (Novikova et al., 2017). For this reason, some researchers directly measure the overall quality of a text. However, Hastie and Belz (2014) note that an overall communicative goal is often too abstract a construct to measure directly. They argue against this practice and in favour of identifying separate criteria, weighted according to their importance in contributing to the overall goal.

The position taken by Hastie and Belz (2014) implies that, to the extent that valid and agreed-upon definitions exist for specific quality criteria, these should be systematically related to overall communicative success. Yet, this relationship need not be monotonic or linear. For example, two texts might convey the underlying intention (including the intention to inform) equally successfully, while varying in fluency, perhaps as long as some minimal level of fluency is satisfied by both. In that case, the relationship would not be monotonic (higher fluency may not guarantee success beyond a point). A further question is how the various criteria interact. For instance, it is conceivable that under certain conditions (e.g. summarising high-volume, heterogeneous data in a short span of text), readability and adequacy are mutually conflicting goals beyond a certain point (e.g. because adequately conveying all information will result in more convoluted text which is harder to understand).

Ultimately, the criteria to be considered will depend on the task. For example, in style transfer, manipulation checks are important to determine whether the style has been transferred correctly, while also ensuring meaning preservation. These criteria are not necessarily important for a system that generates weather reports from numerical data, where accuracy, fluency, coherence and genre compatibility might be more prominent concerns. By contrast, coherence and fluency would not be important criteria for the PARRY chatbot (Colby et al., 1971) which attempts to simulate the speech of a person with paranoid schizophrenia.

As we have shown, the criteria used for NLG

evaluation are usually treated as subjective (as in the case of judgments of fluency, adequacy and the like). It is also conceivable that these criteria can be assessed using more objective measures, similar to existing readability measures (e.g., Ambati et al., 2016; Kincaid et al., 1975; Pitler and Nenkova, 2008; Vajjala and Meurers, 2014), where objective text metrics (e.g. average word length, average parse tree height, average number of nouns) are used in a formula, or as features in a regression model, to obtain a score for a text criterion. Similarly, it may be possible to use separate subjective criteria as features in a regression model to calculate overall text quality scores. This would also provide information about the importance of the subjective criteria for overall text quality judgments. However, such research on the relationship between subjective criteria and objective measures is currently lacking for NLG.

One obstacle to addressing the difficulties identified in this section is the lack of a standardised nomenclature for different text quality criteria. This presents a practical problem, in that it is hard to compare evaluation results to previously reported work; but it also presents a theoretical problem, in that different criteria may overlap or be inter-definable. As Gatt and Belz (2010) and Hastie and Belz (2014) suggest, common and shared evaluation guidelines should be developed for each task, and efforts should be made to standardise criteria and naming conventions. In the absence of such guidelines, care should be taken to explicitly define the criteria measured and highlight possible overlaps between them.

4.2 Sample size, demographics and agreement

Expert- versus reader-focused Section 3.3 made a distinction between expert-focused and reader-focused evaluation. With an expert-focused design, a small number of expert annotators is recruited to judge aspects of the NLG system. A reader-focused design entails a typically larger sample of (non-expert) participants. Lentz and De Jong (1997) found that these two methods can be complementary: expert problem detection may highlight textual problems that are missed by general readers. However, this strength is mostly applicable when a more qualitative analysis is used, whereas most expert-focused evaluations in our sample of papers used closed-ended questions

with Likert scales.

Evidence suggests that expert readers approach evaluation differently from general readers, injecting their own opinions and biases (Amidei et al., 2018b). This might be troublesome if a system is meant for the general population, as expert opinions and biases might not be representative for those of non-experts. This is corroborated by Lentz and De Jong (1997), who found that expert judgments only predict the outcomes of reader-focused evaluation to a limited extent. Experts are also susceptible to considerable variance, so that automatic metrics are sometimes more reliable (Belz and Reiter, 2006). Thus, the conclusion of Belz and Reiter (2006) in favour of large-scale reader-focused studies, rather than expert-focused ones, seems well-taken.

An additional factor to consider is the types of 'general' or 'expert' populations that are accessible to NLG researchers. It is not untypical for evaluations to be carried out with students, or fellow researchers (recruited, for instance, via SIGGEN or other mailing lists). This may introduce sampling biases of the kind that have been critiqued in psychology in recent years, where experimental results based on samples of WEIRD (Western, Educated, Industrialised, Rich and Developed) populations may well have given rise to biased models (see, for example, Henrich et al., 2010).

Evaluator agreement The varying opinions of judges are also reflected in low Inter-Annotator Agreement (IAA), where adequate thresholds also tend to be open to interpretation (Artstein and Poesio, 2008). Amidei et al. (2018b) argue that, given the variable nature of natural language, it is undesirable to use restrictive thresholds, since an ostensibly low IAA score could be due to a host of factors, including personal bias. The authors therefore suggest reporting IAA statistics with confidence intervals. However, narrower confidence intervals (suggesting a more precise IAA score) would normally be expected with large samples (e.g., 1000 or more comparisons McHugh, 2012), which are well beyond most sizes reported in our overview (§ 3.4).

When the goal of an evaluation is to identify potential problems with output texts, a low IAA, indicating variety among annotators, can be highly informative (Amidei et al., 2018b). On the other hand, low IAA in evaluations of text quality can also suggest that results should not be extrapolated to a broader reader population. An additional consideration is that some statistics (such as κ; see McHugh, 2012) make overly restrictive assumptions, though they have the advantage of accounting for chance agreement. Thus, apart from reporting such statistics, it is advisable to also report percentage agreement, which is easily interpretable (McHugh, 2012).

Sample size For expert-focused evaluations, good advice is provided by Van Enschot et al. (2017): difficult coding tasks (which most NLG evaluations are) require three or more annotators (though preferably more; see Potter and Levine-Donnerstein, 1999), more straightforward tasks can do with two to three. In the case of large-scale studies, Brysbaert (2019) recently stated that most studies with less than 50 participants are underpowered and that for most designs and analyses 100 or more participants are needed. With the introduction of crowdsourcing such numbers are obtainable, at least for widely-spoken languages (though see van Miltenburg et al. 2017 for a counterexample). Furthermore, the number of participants necessary can be decreased by having multiple observations per condition per participant (i.e., having participants perform more judgments).

Whatever the sample size, a minimum good practice guideline is to always report participant numbers, with relevant demographic data (i.e., gender, nationality, age, fluency in the target language, academic background, etc), in order to enhance replicability and enable readers to gauge the meaningfulness of the results.

4.3 Number of questions and types of scales

As shown in Section 3.5, Likert scales are the prevalent rating method for NLG evaluation, 5-point scales being the most popular, followed by 2-point, and 3-point scales. While the most appropriate number of response points may depend on the task itself, 7-point scales (with clear verbal anchoring) seem best for most tasks. Most of the experimental literature's findings found that 7-point scales maximise reliability, validity and discriminative power (for instance, Miller, 1956; Green and Rao, 1970; Jones, 1968; Cicchetti et al., 1985; Lissitz and Green, 1975; Preston and Colman, 2000). These studies discourage smaller scales, and adding more response points than 7 also does not increase reliability according to these studies.

While Likert scales are the most popular scale

within the NLG domain (and probably in many other domains), the use of this scale has been receiving more and more criticism. Recent studies have found that participant ratings are more reliable, consistent, and are less prone to order effects when they involve ranking rather than Likert scales (Martinez et al., 2014; Yannakakis and Martínez, 2015; Yannakakis and Hallam, 2011). Similarly, for the development of an automatic metric for NLG, Chaganty et al. (2018) found that annotator variance decreased significantly when using post-edits as a metric instead of a Likert scale survey. Finally, Novikova et al. (2018) compared Likert scales for NLG system evaluation to two continuous scales: a vanilla magnitude estimation measure and a rank-based magnitude estimation measure. The researchers found that both magnitude estimation scales delivered more reliable and consistent text evaluation scores.

All these studies seem to suggest that ranking-based methods (combined with continuous scales) are the preferred method. However, there are two critical remarks to be made on this. Firstly, a drawback of ranking-based methods is that the number of judgments increases substantially as more systems are compared. To mitigate this, Novikova et al. (2018) illustrated that the TrueSkill^{TM} algorithm (Herbrich et al., 2007) can be implemented. This algorithm uses binary comparisons to reliably rank systems, which greatly reduces the amount of data needed for multiple-system comparisons.

Another point of criticism is that studies comparing Likert scales to other research instruments mostly look at single-rating constructs, that is, experiments where a single judgment is elicited on a given criterion. While constructs measured with one rating are also the most common in NLG research, this practice has been criticized. It is unlikely that a complex concept (e.g. fluency or adequacy) can be captured in a single rating (McIver and Carmines, 1981). Furthermore,a single Likert scale often does not provide enough points of discrimination: a single 7-point Likert question has only 7 points to discriminate on, while 5 7-point Likert questions have $5 * 7 = 35$ points of discrimination. A practical objection against single-item scales is that no reliability measure for internal consistency (e.g., Cronbach's alpha) can be calculated for a single item. At least two items or more are necessary for this. In light of these concerns, Diamantopoulos et al. (2012) advocate great caution in the use of single-item scales, unless the construct in question is very simple, clear and one-dimensional. Under most conditions, multi-item scales have much higher predictive validity. Using multiple items may well make the reliability of Likert scales on a par with that of ranking tasks; this, however, has not been empirically tested. Also, do note that the use of multiple-item scales versus single-item scales affects the type of statistical testing needed (for an overview and explanation, see Amidei et al., 2019).

In sum, we advise to use either multiple-item 7-point Likert scales, or a (continuous) ranking task. The latter should be used in combination with TrueSkill[TM] when multiple systems are compared. As Aroyo and Welty (2014) note, disagreement in the responses can be due to three factors: the item, the worker, and the task. Therefore, it is necessary to pilot the rating task before deploying it more widely, and to analyze disagreement on the annotator level, to see whether individual annotators are causing discrepancies in the ratings for different items.

Alternative evaluation instruments should not be ruled out either. Ever since a pilot in 2016 (Bojar et al., 2016a), recent editions of the Conference on Machine Translation (WMT), have used Direct Assessment, whereby participants compare an output to a reference text on a continuous (0-100) scale (Graham et al., 2017; Bojar et al., 2016b), similar to Magnitude Estimation (Bard et al., 1996). Zarrieß et al. (2015) used a mouse contingent reading paradigm in an evaluation study of generated text, finding that features recorded using this paradigm (e.g. reading time) provided valuable information to gauge text quality levels. It should also be noted that most metrics used in NLG are reader-focused. However, in many real-world scenarios, especially 'creative' NLG applications, NLG systems and human writers work alongside each other in some way (see Maher, 2012; Manjavacas et al., 2017). With such a collaboration in mind, it makes sense to also investigate writer-focused methods. Having participants edit generated texts. Then processing these edits using post-editing distance measures like Translation Edit Rate (Snover et al., 2006), might be a viable method to investigate the time and cost associated with using a system. While more commonly seen in Machine Translation, authors have explored the use of such metrics in

NLG (Bernhard et al., 2012; Han et al., 2017; Sripada et al., 2005).

Finally, some remarks on qualitative evaluation methods are in order. Reiter and Belz (2009) note that free-text comments can be beneficial to diagnose potential problems of an NLG system. Furthermore, Sambaraju et al. (2011) argue the added value of content analysis and discourse analysis for evaluation. Such qualitative analyses can find potential blind spots of quantitative analyses. At the same time, the subjectivity that is often inherent in studies based on discourse analysis, such as Sambaraju et al. (2011) would need to be offset by data from larger-scale, quantitative studies.

4.4 Design

Few papers report exact details of the design of their human evaluation experiments, although most indicate that multiple systems were compared and annotators were shown all examples. This suggests that within-subjects designs are a common practice.

Within-subjects designs are susceptible to order effects: over the course of an experiment, annotators can change their responses due to fatigue, practice, carryover effects or other (external) factors. If the order in which the output of systems are presented is fixed, differences found between systems may be due to order effects rather than differences in the output itself. To mitigate this, researchers can implement measures in the task design. Practice effects can be reduced with a practice trial in which examples of both very good (fluent, accurate, grammatical) and very bad (disfluent, inaccurate, ungrammatical) outputs are provided before the actual rating task. This allows for the participants to calibrate their responses, before starting with the actual task. Carryover effects can be reduced by increasing the amount of time between presenting different conditions (Shaughnessy et al., 2006). Fatigue effects can be reduced by shortening the task, although this also means more participants are necessary since fewer observations per condition per participant means less statistical power (Brysbaert, 2019). Another way to tackle fatigue effects sometimes seen in research is to remove all entries with missing data, or to remove participants that failed 'attention checks' (or related checks e.g. instructional manipulation checks, or trap questions) from the sample. However, the use of attention checks is subject to debate, with some researchers pointing out that after such elimination procedures, the remaining cases may be a biased subsample of the total sample, thus biasing the results (Anduiza and Galais, 2016; Bennett, 2001; Berinsky et al., 2016). Experiments show that excluding participants that failed attention checks introduces a demographic bias, and attention checks actually induce low-effort responses or socially desirable responses (Clifford and Jerit, 2015; Vannette, 2016).

Order effects can also be reduced by presenting the conditions in a systematically varied order. Counterbalancing is one such measure. With counterbalancing, all examples are presented in every possible order. While such a design is the best way to reduce order-effects, it quickly becomes expensive. When annotators judge 4 examples, $4! = 24$ different orders should be investigated (this, however, can be partially mitigated by grouping items randomly into sets, and counterbalancing the order of sets rather than individual items). In most cases, randomising the order of examples should be sufficient. Another possibility is to use a between-subjects design, in which the subjects only judge the (randomly ordered) outputs of one system. When order effects are expected and a large number of conditions are investigated, such a design is preferable (Shaughnessy et al., 2006).

Novikova et al. (2018) found that the presentation of questions matters. When evaluating text criteria, answers to questions about different criteria tend to correlate when they are presented simultaneously for a given item. When participants are shown an item multiple times and questioned about each text criterion separately, this correlation is reduced.

4.5 Statistics and data analysis

Within behavioral sciences, it is standard to evaluate hypotheses based on whether findings are statistically significant or not (typically, in published papers, they are), although a majority of NLG papers do not report statistical tests (see Section 3.6). However, there is a growing awareness that statistical tests are often conducted incorrectly, both in NLP (Dror et al., 2018) and in behavioral sciences more generally (e.g., Wagenmakers et al., 2011). Moreover, one may wonder whether standard null-hypothesis significance testing (NHST) is applicable or helpful in human NLG evaluation.

In a common scenario, NLG researchers may want to compare various versions of their own novel system (e.g. with or without output variation, or relying on different word embedding models, to give just two more or less random examples) to compare them to each other, to some other ('state-of-the-art') systems, and/or with respect to one or more baselines. Notice that this quickly gives rise to a rather complex statistical design with multiple factors and multiple levels. Ironically, with every system or baseline that is added to the evaluation, the comparison becomes more interesting but the statistical model becomes more complex, and power issues become more pressing (Cohen, 1988; Button et al., 2013). However, statistical power—the probability that the statistical test will reject the null hypothesis (H0) when the alternative hypothesis (H1, e.g., that your new NLG system is the best) is true—are seldom (if ever) discussed in the NLG literature.

A related issue is that clear hypotheses are often not stated (see Section 3.6). Of course, researchers generally assume that their system will be rated higher than the comparison systems. But they will not necessarily assume that they will perform better on all dependent variables. Moreover, they may have no specific hypotheses about which variant of their own system will perform best.

In fact, in the scenario sketched above there may be multiple (implicit) hypotheses: new system better than state-of-the-art, new system better than baseline, etcetera. When testing multiple hypotheses, the probability of making at least one false claim (incorrectly rejecting a H0) increases (such errors are known as false positives or Type I errors). Various remedies for this particular problem exist, one being an application of the simple Bonferroni correction, which amounts to lowering the significance threshold α—commonly .05, but see for example Benjamin et al. (2018) and Lakens et al. (2018)—to α/m, where m is the number of hypotheses tested. This procedure is not systematically applied in NLG, although the awareness of the issues with multiple comparisons is increasing.

Finally, statistical tests are associated with assumptions about their applicability. One is the independence assumption (especially relevant for t-tests and ANOVAs, for example), which amounts to assuming that the value of one observation obtained in the experiment is unaffected by the value of other observations. This assumption is difficult to guarantee in NLP research (Dror et al., 2018),

Topic	Best practice
General	Always conduct a human evaluation (if possible).
Criteria	Use separate criteria rather than an overall quality assessment. Properly define the criteria that are used in the evaluation.
Sampling	Preferably use a (large-scale) reader-focused design rather than a (small-scale) expert-focused design. Always recruit sufficiently many participants. Report (and motivate) the sample size and the demographics.
Annotation	For a qualitative analysis, recruit multiple annotators (at least 2, more is better) Report the Inter-Annotator Agreement score with confidence intervals, plus a percentage agreement.
Measurement	For a quantitative study, use multiple item 7-point (preferably) Likert scales, or (continuous) ranking.
Design	Reduce order- and learning effects by counterbalancing/random ordering, and properly report this.
Statistics	If the evaluation study is exploratory, only report exploratory data analysis. If the study is confirmatory, consider preregistering and conduct appropriate statistical analyses.

Table 3: List of best practices for human evaluation of automatically generated text.

if only because different systems may rely on the same training data. In view of these issues, some have argued that NHST should be abandoned (Koplenig, 2017; McShane et al., 2019).

In our opinion, the distinction between exploratory and confirmative (hypothesis) testing should be taken more seriously within NLG. Much human evaluation of NLG could better be approached from an exploratory perspective, and instead of full-fledged hypothesis testing it would be more appropriate to analyse findings with exploratory data analysis techniques (Tukey, 1980; Cumming, 2013). When researchers do have clear hypotheses, statistical significance testing can be a powerful tool (assuming it is applied correctly). In these cases, we recommend preregistering the hypotheses and analysis plans before conducting the actual evaluation.[3]

Preregistration is still uncommon in NLG and other fields of AI (with a few notable exceptions, like for instance Vogt et al., 2019), but it addresses an important issue with human evaluations. Conducting and analysing a human experiment is like entering a garden of forking paths (Gelman and Loken, 2013): along the way researchers have many choices to make, and even though each choice may be small and seemingly innocuous, collectively they can have a substantial effect on the outcome of the statistical analyses, to the extent that it becomes possible to present virtually every finding as statistically significant (Simmons et al., 2011; Wicherts et al., 2016). In human NLG evaluation, choices may include for instance, termination criteria (when does the data collection stop?), exclusion criteria (when is a participant removed from the analysis?), reporting of variables

(which dependent variables are reported?), etc. By being explicit beforehand (i.e., by preregistering), any flexibility in the analysis (be it intentional or not) is removed. Preregistration is increasingly common in medical and psychological science, and even though it is not perfect (Claesen et al., 2019) at least it has made research more transparent and controllable, which has a positive impact on the possibilities to replicate earlier findings.

Finally, alternative statistical models deserve more attention within NLG. For example, within psycholinguistics it is common to look both at participant and item effects (Clark, 1973). This would make a lot of sense in human NLG evaluations as well, because it might well be that a new NLG system works well for one kind of generated item (short active sentences, say) and less well for another kind (complex sentences with relative clauses). Mixed effects models capture such potential item aspects very well (e.g., Barr et al., 2013), and deserve more attention in NLG. Finally, Bayesian models are worth exploring, because they are less sensitive to the aforementioned problems with NHST (e.g., Gelman et al., 2006; Wagenmakers, 2007).

5   Conclusion

We have provided an overview of the current state of human evaluation in NLG, and presented a set of best practices, summarized in Table 3. This is a broad topic, and for reasons of space we were not able to cover all aspects of human evaluation in detail. Nevertheless, we hope that this overview will serve as a useful reference for NLG practitioners, and in future work we aim to provide a more extensive set of best practices for carrying out human evaluations in Natural Language Generation.

---

[3]For example at `osf.io` or `aspredicted.org`

Acknowledgements

We received support from RAAK-PRO SIA (2014-01-51PRO) and The Netherlands Organization for Scientific Research (NWO 360-89-050), which is gratefully acknowledged. We would also like to thank the anonymous reviewers for their valuable and insightful comments.

References

Bharat Ram Ambati, Siva Reddy, and Mark Steedman. 2016. Assessing relative sentence complexity using an incremental CCG parser. In *Proceedings of the 2016 Conference of the North American Chapter of the Association for Computational Linguistics*, pages 1051–1057, San Diego, California, USA. Association for Computational Linguistics.

Jacopo Amidei, Paul Piwek, and Alistair Willis. 2018a. Evaluation methodologies in Automatic Question Generation 2013-2018. *INLG 2018*, page 307.

Jacopo Amidei, Paul Piwek, and Alistair Willis. 2018b. Rethinking the agreement in human evaluation tasks. In *Proceedings of the 27th International Conference on Computational Linguistics*, pages 3318–3329.

Jacopo Amidei, Paul Piwek, and Alistair Willis. 2019. The use of rating and Likert scales in Natural Language Generation human evaluation tasks: A review and some recommendations. In *Proceedings of the 12th International Conference on Natural Language Generation*, Tokyo, Japan. Association for Computational Linguistics.

R Ananthakrishnan, Pushpak Bhattacharyya, M Sasikumar, and Ritesh M Shah. 2007. Some issues in automatic evaluation of English-Hindi MT: More blues for BLEU. *ICON*.

Eva Anduiza and Carol Galais. 2016. Answering without reading: IMCs and strong satisficing in online surveys. *International Journal of Public Opinion Research*, 29(3):497–519.

Lora Aroyo and Chris Welty. 2014. The three sides of crowdtruth. *Journal of Human Computation*, 1:31–34.

Ron Artstein and Massimo Poesio. 2008. Inter-coder agreement for computational linguistics. *Computational Linguistics*, 34(4):555–596.

Ellen Gurman Bard, Dan Robertson, and Antonella Sorace. 1996. Magnitude estimation of linguistic acceptability. *Language*, pages 32–68.

Dale J Barr, Roger Levy, Christoph Scheepers, and Harry J Tily. 2013. Random effects structure for confirmatory hypothesis testing: Keep it maximal. *Journal of Memory and Language*, 68(3):255–278.

Anja Belz and Ehud Reiter. 2006. Comparing automatic and human evaluation of NLG systems. In *11th Conference of the European Chapter of the Association for Computational Linguistics*, pages 313–320. Association for Computational Linguistics.

Daniel J Benjamin, James O Berger, Magnus Johannesson, Brian A Nosek, E-J Wagenmakers, Richard Berk, Kenneth A Bollen, Björn Brembs, Lawrence Brown, Colin Camerer, et al. 2018. Redefine statistical significance. *Nature Human Behaviour*, 2(1):6.

Derrick A Bennett. 2001. How can I deal with missing data in my study? *Australian and New Zealand Journal of Public Health*, 25(5):464–469.

Adam J Berinsky, Michele F Margolis, and Michael W Sances. 2016. Can we turn shirkers into workers? *Journal of Experimental Social Psychology*, 66:20–28.

Delphine Bernhard, Louis De Viron, Véronique Moriceau, and Xavier Tannier. 2012. Question generation for french: Collating parsers and paraphrasing questions. *Dialogue & Discourse*, 3(2):43–74.

Ondřej Bojar, Rajen Chatterjee, Christian Federmann, Yvette Graham, Barry Haddow, Matthias Huck, Antonio Jimeno Yepes, Philipp Koehn, Varvara Logacheva, Christof Monz, Matteo Negri, Aurélie Névéol, Mariana Neves, Martin Popel, Matt Post, Raphael Rubino, Carolina Scarton, Lucia Specia, Marco Turchi, Karin Verspoor, and Marcos Zampieri. 2016a. Findings of the 2016 conference on machine translation. In *Proceedings of the First Conference on Machine Translation: Volume 2, Shared Task Papers*, pages 131–198, Berlin, Germany. Association for Computational Linguistics.

Ondrej Bojar, Christian Federmann, Barry Haddow, Philipp Koehn, Matt Post, and Lucia Specia. 2016b. Ten years of WMT evaluation campaigns: Lessons learnt. In *Proceedings of the LREC 2016 Workshop Translation Evaluation From Fragmented Tools and Data Sets to an Integrated Ecosystem*, pages 27–34.

Marc Brysbaert. 2019. How many participants do we have to include in properly powered experiments? A tutorial of power analysis with reference tables. *Journal of Cognition*, 2(1):1–38.

Katherine S Button, John PA Ioannidis, Claire Mokrysz, Brian A Nosek, Jonathan Flint, Emma SJ Robinson, and Marcus R Munafò. 2013. Power failure: Why small sample size undermines the reliability of neuroscience. *Nature Reviews Neuroscience*, 14(5):365.

Thiago Castro Ferreira, Chris van der Lee, Emiel van Miltenburg, and Emiel Krahmer. 2019. Neural data-to-text generation: A comparison between pipeline and end-to-end architectures. In *Proceedings of the 2019 Conference on Empirical Methods in Natural Language Processing*, Hong Kong, SAR. Association for Computational Linguistics.

Arun Chaganty, Stephen Mussmann, and Percy Liang. 2018. The price of debiasing automatic metrics in natural language evaluation. In *Proceedings of the 56th Annual Meeting of the Association for Computational Linguistics (Volume 1: Long Papers)*, pages 643–653.

Leshem Choshen and Omeri Abend. 2018. Inherent biases in reference-based evaluation for grammatical error correction and text simplification. In *Proceedings of 56th Annual Meeting of the Association for Computational Linguistics*, pages 632–642, Melbourne, Australia. Association for Computational Linguistics.

Domenic V Cicchetti, Donald Shoinralter, and Peter J Tyrer. 1985. The effect of number of rating scale categories on levels of interrater reliability: A Monte Carlo investigation. *Applied Psychological Measurement*, 9(1):31–36.

Aline Claesen, Sara Lucia Brazuna Tavares Gomes, Francis Tuerlinckx, et al. 2019. Preregistration: Comparing dream to reality. *PsyArXiv*.

Herbert H Clark. 1973. The language-as-fixed-effect fallacy: A critique of language statistics in psychological research. *Journal of verbal learning and verbal behavior*, 12(4):335–359.

Scott Clifford and Jennifer Jerit. 2015. Do attempts to improve respondent attention increase social desirability bias? *Public Opinion Quarterly*, 79(3):790–802.

Jacob Cohen. 1988. *Statistical power analysis for the behavioral sciences*. Routledge.

Kenneth Mark Colby, Sylvia Weber, and Franklin Dennis Hilf. 1971. Artificial paranoia. *Artificial Intelligence*, 2(1):1–25.

Geoff Cumming. 2013. *Understanding the new statistics: Effect sizes, confidence intervals, and meta-analysis*. Routledge.

Felice Dell'Orletta, Simonetta Montemagni, and Giulia Venturi. 2011. READ-IT: Assessing readability of Italian texts with a view to text simplification. In *Proceedings of the Second Workshop on Speech and Language Processing for Assistive Technologies*, pages 73–83. Association for Computational Linguistics.

Adamantios Diamantopoulos, Marko Sarstedt, Christoph Fuchs, Petra Wilczynski, and Sebastian Kaiser. 2012. Guidelines for choosing between multi-item and single-item scales for construct measurement: A predictive validity perspective. *Journal of the Academy of Marketing Science*, 40(3):434–449.

George Doddington. 2002. Automatic evaluation of machine translation quality using n-gram co-occurrence statistics. In *Proceedings of the Second International Conference on Human Language Technology Research*, pages 138–145. Morgan Kaufmann Publishers Inc.

Rotem Dror, Gili Baumer, Segev Shlomov, and Roi Reichart. 2018. The hitchhikers guide to testing statistical significance in natural language processing. In *Proceedings of the 56th Annual Meeting of the Association for Computational Linguistics (Volume 1: Long Papers)*, pages 1383–1392.

Johan Falkenjack, Katarina Heimann Mühlenbock, and Arne Jönsson. 2013. Features indicating readability in Swedish text. In *Proceedings of the 19th Nordic Conference of Computational Linguistics (NODAL-IDA 2013)*, pages 27–40.

Albert Gatt and Anja Belz. 2010. Introducing shared tasks to NLG: The TUNA shared task evaluation challenges. In *Empirical Methods in Natural Language Generation*, pages 264–293. Springer.

Albert Gatt and Emiel Krahmer. 2018. Survey of the state of the art in natural language generation: Core tasks, applications and evaluation. *Journal of Artificial Intelligence Research*, 61:65–170.

Albert Gatt and François Portet. 2010. Textual properties and task based evaluation: Investigating the role of surface properties, structure and content. In *Proceedings of the 6th International Natural Language Generation Conference*, pages 57–65. Association for Computational Linguistics.

Andrew Gelman and Eric Loken. 2013. The garden of forking paths: Why multiple comparisons can be a problem, even when there is no fishing expedition or p-hacking and the research hypothesis was posited ahead of time. *Unpublished Manuscript*.

Andrew Gelman et al. 2006. Prior distributions for variance parameters in hierarchical models (comment on article by Browne and Draper). *Bayesian analysis*, 1(3):515–534.

Dimitra Gkatzia and Saad Mahamood. 2015. A snapshot of NLG evaluation practices 2005-2014. In *Proceedings of the 15th European Workshop on Natural Language Generation (ENLG)*, pages 57–60. Association for Computational Linguistics.

Yvette Graham, Timothy Baldwin, Alistair Moffast, and Justin Zobel. 2017. Can machine translation systems be evaluated by the crowd alone. *Natural Language Engineering*, 23(1):330.

Paul E Green and Vithala R Rao. 1970. Rating scales and information recovery: How many scales and response categories to use? *Journal of Marketing*, 34(3):33–39.

Bo Han, Will Radford, Anaïs Cadilhac, Art Harol, Andrew Chisholm, and Ben Hachey. 2017. Post-edit analysis of collective biography generation. In *Proceedings of the 26th International Conference on World Wide Web Companion*, pages 791–792, Perth, Australia. International World Wide Web Conferences Steering Committee.

Mary Dee Harris. 2008. Building a large-scale commercial NLG system for an EMR. In *Proceedings of the Fifth International Natural Language Generation Conference (INLG '08)*, pages 157–160, Morristown, NJ, USA. Association for Computational Linguistics.

Helen Hastie and Anja Belz. 2014. A comparative evaluation methodology for NLG in interactive systems. In *Proceedings of the Ninth International Conference on Language Resources and Evaluation (LREC-2014)*.

Joseph Henrich, Steven J Heine, and Ara Norenzayan. 2010. The weirdest people in the world? *The Behavioral and Brain Sciences*, 23:61–83; discussion 83–135.

Ralf Herbrich, Tom Minka, and Thore Graepel. 2007. TrueSkill^{TM}: A Bayesian skill rating system. In *Advances in Neural Information Processing Systems*, pages 569–576.

Richard R Jones. 1968. Differences in response consistency and subjects preferences for three personality inventory response formats. In *Proceedings of the 76th Annual Convention of the American Psychological Association*, volume 3, pages 247–248. American Psychological Association Washington, DC.

J Peter Kincaid, Robert P Fishburne Jr, Richard L Rogers, and Brad S Chissom. 1975. Derivation of new readability formulas (Automated Readability Index, FOG count and Flesch reading ease formula) for navy enlisted personnel. *Research Branch Report*, 8(75).

Philipp Koehn. 2004. Statistical significance tests for machine translation evaluation. In *Proceedings of the 2004 Conference on Empirical Methods in Natural Language Processing*, pages 388–395, Barcelona, Spain. Association for Computational Linguistics, Association for Computational Linguistics.

Alexander Koplenig. 2017. Against statistical significance testing in corpus linguistics. *Corpus Linguistics and Linguistic Theory*.

Daniel Lakens, Federico G Adolfi, Casper J Albers, Farid Anvari, Matthew AJ Apps, Shlomo E Argamon, Thom Baguley, Raymond B Becker, Stephen D Benning, Daniel E Bradford, et al. 2018. Justify your alpha. *Nature Human Behaviour*, 2(3):168.

Chris van der Lee, Bart Verduijn, Emiel Krahmer, and Sander Wubben. 2018. Evaluating the text quality, human likeness and tailoring component of PASS: A Dutch data-to-text system for soccer. In *Proceedings of the 27th International Conference on Computational Linguistics*, pages 962–972.

Leo Lentz and Menno De Jong. 1997. The evaluation of text quality: Expert-focused and reader-focused methods compared. *IEEE transactions on professional communication*, 40(3):224–234.

Robert W Lissitz and Samuel B Green. 1975. Effect of the number of scale points on reliability: A Monte Carlo approach. *Journal of Applied Psychology*, 60(1):10.

Mary Lou Maher. 2012. Computational and collective creativity: Who's being creative? In *Proceedings of the 3rd International Conference on Computer Creativity*, pages 67–71, Dublin, Ireland. Association for Computational Linguistics.

Enrique Manjavacas, Folgert Karsdorp, Ben Burtenshaw, and Mike Kestemont. 2017. Synthetic literature: Writing science fiction in a co-creative process. In *Proceedings of the Workshop on Computational Creativity in Natural Language Generation (CC-NLG 2017)*, pages 29–37, Santiago de Compostela, Spain. Association for Computational Linguistics.

Hector P Martinez, Georgios N Yannakakis, and John Hallam. 2014. Don't classify ratings of affect; rank them! *IEEE transactions on affective computing*, 5(3):314–326.

Mary L McHugh. 2012. Interrater reliability: The kappa statistic. *Biochemia Medica*, 22(3):276–282.

John McIver and Edward G Carmines. 1981. *Unidimensional scaling*. 24. Sage.

Blakeley B McShane, David Gal, Andrew Gelman, Christian Robert, and Jennifer L Tackett. 2019. Abandon statistical significance. *The American Statistician*, 73(sup1):235–245.

Chris Mellish and Robert Dale. 1998. Evaluation in the context of natural language generation. *Computer Speech & Language*, 12(4):349–373.

Chris Mellish, Donia Scott, Lynne Cahill, Daniel Paiva, Roger Evans, and Mike Reape. 2006. A reference architecture for natural language generation systems. *Natural Language Engineering*, 12(01):1–34.

George A Miller. 1956. The magical number seven, plus or minus two: Some limits on our capacity for processing information. *Psychological Review*, 63(2):81.

Emiel van Miltenburg, Desmond Elliott, and Piek Vossen. 2017. Cross-linguistic differences and similarities in image descriptions. In *Proceedings of the 10th International Conference on Natural Language Generation*, pages 21–30, Santiago de Compostela, Spain. Association for Computational Linguistics.

Daniel Navarro. 2019. *Learning statistics with R: A tutorial for psychology students and other beginners: Version 0.6.1*. University of Adelaide.

Ani Nenkova, Jieun Chae, Annie Louis, and Emily Pitler. 2010. Structural features for predicting the linguistic quality of text. In *Empirical Methods in Natural Language Generation*, pages 222–241. Springer.

Jekaterina Novikova, Ondřej Dušek, Amanda Cercas Curry, and Verena Rieser. 2017. Why we need new evaluation metrics for NLG. In *Proceedings of the 2017 Conference on Empirical Methods in Natural Language Processing*, pages 2241–2252.

Jekaterina Novikova, Ondřej Dušek, and Verena Rieser. 2018. RankME: Reliable human ratings for Natural Language Generation. In *Proceedings of the 2018 Conference of the North American Chapter of the Association for Computational Linguistics: Human Language Technologies, Volume 2 (Short Papers)*, pages 72–78.

John Peter. 1677. *Artificial Versifying, or the Schoolboys Recreation*. John Sims, London, UK.

Emily Pitler and Ani Nenkova. 2008. Revisiting readability: A unified framework for predicting text quality. In *Proceedings of the conference on empirical methods in natural language processing*, pages 186–195. Association for Computational Linguistics.

Matt Post. 2018. A call for clarity in reporting BLEU scores. In *Proceedings of the Third Conference on Machine Translation: Research Papers*, pages 186–191, Belgium, Brussels. Association for Computational Linguistics.

W James Potter and Deborah Levine-Donnerstein. 1999. Rethinking validity and reliability in content analysis. *Journal of Applied Communication Research*, 27:258–284.

Carolyn C Preston and Andrew M Colman. 2000. Optimal number of response categories in rating scales: reliability, validity, discriminating power, and respondent preferences. *Acta Psychologica*, 104(1):1–15.

Ehud Reiter. 2018. A structured review of the validity of BLEU. *Computational Linguistics*, pages 1–12.

Ehud Reiter and Anja Belz. 2009. An investigation into the validity of some metrics for automatically evaluating natural language generation systems. *Computational Linguistics*, 35(4):529–558.

Ehud Reiter and Robert Dale. 2000. *Building Natural Language Generation Systems*. Cambridge University Press, Cambridge, UK.

Ehud Reiter, Roma Robertson, and Liesl M Osman. 2003. Lessons from a failure: Generating tailored smoking cessation letters. *Artificial Intelligence*, 144(1-2):41–58.

Jan Renkema. 2012. *Schrijfwijzer*, 5 edition. SDU Uitgevers, Den Haag, The Netherlands.

Johannah Rodgers. 2017. The genealogy of an image, or, what does literature (not) have to do with the history of computing?: Tracing the sources and reception of Gullivers 'Knowledge Engine. *Humanities*, 6(4):85.

Rahul Sambaraju, Ehud Reiter, Robert Logie, Andy McKinlay, Chris McVittie, Albert Gatt, and Cindy Sykes. 2011. What is in a text and what does it do: Qualitative evaluations of an NLG system –the BT-Nurse– using content analysis and discourse analysis. In *Proceedings of the 13th European Workshop on Natural Language Generation*, pages 22–31. Association for Computational Linguistics.

Donia Scott and Johanna Moore. 2007. An NLG evaluation competition? Eight reasons to be cautious. In *Proceedings of the Workshop on Shared Tasks and Comparative Evaluation in Natural Language Generation*, pages 22–23.

JJ Shaughnessy, EB Zechmeister, and JS Zechmeister. 2006. *Research methods in psychology*. McGraw-Hill.

Joseph P Simmons, Leif D Nelson, and Uri Simonsohn. 2011. False-positive psychology: Undisclosed flexibility in data collection and analysis allows presenting anything as significant. *Psychological science*, 22(11):1359–1366.

Matthew Snover, Bonnie Dorr, Richard Schwartz, Linnea Micciulla, and John Makhoul. 2006. A study of translation edit rate with targeted human annotation. In *Proceedings of Association for Machine Translation in the Americas*, pages 223–231, Cambridge, MA, USA. Association for Machine Translation in the Americas.

Karen Sparck Jones and Julia R. Galliers. 1996. *Evaluating Natural Language Processing Systems: An Analysis and Review*. Springer, Berlin and Heidelberg.

Somayajulu Sripada, Ehud Reiter, and Lezan Hawizy. 2005. Evaluation of an NLG system using post-edit data: Lessons learnt. In *Proceedings of the 10th European Workshop on Natural Language Generation*, pages 133–139, Aberdeen, Scotland. Association for Computational Linguistics.

Elior Sulem, Omri Abend, and Ari Rappoport. 2018. BLEU is not suitable for the evaluation of text simplification. *arXiv preprint arXiv:1810.05995*. Accepted for publication as a short paper at EMNLP 2018.

Jonathan Swift. 1774. *Travels Into Several Remote Nations of the World: In Four Parts. By Lemuel Gulliver. First a Surgeon, and Then a Captain of Several Ships...*, volume 1. Benjamin Motte, London, UK.

John W Tukey. 1980. We need both exploratory and confirmatory. *The American Statistician*, 34(1):23–25.

Joseph P Turian, Luke Shen, and I Dan Melamed. 2003. Evaluation of machine translation and its evaluation. In *Proceedings of MT Summit IX*.

Sowmya Vajjala and Detmar Meurers. 2014. Assessing the relative reading level of sentence pairs for text simplification. In *Proceedings of the 14th Conference of the European Chapter of the Association for Computational Linguistics*, pages 288–297, Gothenburg, Sweden. Association for Computational Linguistics.

Renske Van Enschot, Wilbert Spooren, Antal van den Bosch, Christian Burgers, Liesbeth Degand, Jacqueline Evers-Vermeul, Florian Kunneman, Christine Liebrecht, Yvette Linders, and Alfons Maes. 2017. Taming our wild data: On intercoder reliability in discourse research. *Unpublished Manuscript*, pages 1–18.

David L Vannette. 2016. Testing the effects of different types of attention interventions on data quality in web surveys. Experimental evidence from a 14 country study. In *71st Annual Conference of the American Association for Public Opinion Research*.

Paul Vogt, Rianne van den Berghe, Mirjam de Haas, Laura Hoffman, Junko Kanero, Ezgi Mamus, Jean-Marc Montanier, Cansu Oranc, Ora Oudgenoeg-Paz, Daniel Hernandez Garcia, , Fotios Papadopoulos, Thorsten Schodde, Josje Verhagen, Christopher Wallbridge, Bram Willemsen, Jan de Wit, Tony Belpaeme, Tilbe Göksun, Stefan Kopp, Emiel Krahmer, Aylin Küntay, Paul Leseman, and Amit Kumar Pandey. 2019. Second language tutoring using social robots: A large-scale study. In *2019 14th ACM/IEEE International Conference on Human-Robot Interaction (HRI)*. IEEE.

Eric-Jan Wagenmakers. 2007. A practical solution to the pervasive problems of p values. *Psychonomic bulletin & review*, 14(5):779–804.

Eric-Jan Wagenmakers, Ruud Wetzels, Denny Borsboom, and Han van der Maas. 2011. Why psychologists must change the way they analyze their data: the case of psi: Comment on Bem (2011). *Journal of personality and social psychology*, 100(3):426.

Jelte M Wicherts, Coosje LS Veldkamp, Hilde EM Augusteijn, Marjan Bakker, Robbie Van Aert, and Marcel ALM Van Assen. 2016. Degrees of freedom in planning, running, analyzing, and reporting psychological studies: A checklist to avoid p-hacking. *Frontiers in psychology*, 7:1832.

Georgios N Yannakakis and John Hallam. 2011. Ranking vs. preference: A comparative study of self-reporting. In *International Conference on Affective Computing and Intelligent Interaction*, pages 437–446. Springer.

Georgios N Yannakakis and Héctor P Martínez. 2015. Ratings are overrated! *Frontiers in ICT*, 2:13.

Sina Zarrieß, Sebastian Loth, and David Schlangen. 2015. Reading times predict the quality of generated text above and beyond human ratings. In *Proceedings of the 15th European Workshop on Natural Language Generation*, pages 38–47, Brighton, UK. Association for Computational Linguistics.

Automatic Quality Estimation for Natural Language Generation: Ranting (Jointly Rating and Ranking)

Ondřej Dušek, * **Karin Sevegnani,**[†] **Ioannis Konstas**[†] and **Verena Rieser**[†]

*Charles University, Faculty of Mathematics and Physics, Prague, Czechia

[†]Heriot-Watt University, MACS, The Interaction Lab, Edinburgh, Scotland, UK

`odusek@ufal.mff.cuni.cz`, `{ks85,i.konstas,v.t.rieser}@hw.ac.uk`

Abstract

We present a recurrent neural network based system for automatic quality estimation of natural language generation (NLG) outputs, which jointly learns to assign numerical *ratings* to individual outputs and to provide pairwise *rankings* of two different outputs. The latter is trained using pairwise hinge loss over scores from two copies of the rating network.

We use learning to rank and synthetic data to improve the quality of ratings assigned by our system: we synthesise training pairs of distorted system outputs and train the system to rank the less distorted one higher. This leads to a 12% increase in correlation with human ratings over the previous benchmark. We also establish the state of the art on the dataset of relative rankings from the E2E NLG Challenge (Dušek et al., 2019), where synthetic data lead to a 4% accuracy increase over the base model.

1 Introduction

While automatic output quality estimation (QE) is an established field of research in other areas of NLP, such as machine translation (MT) (Specia et al., 2010, 2018), research on QE in natural language generation (NLG) from structured meaning representations (MR) such as dialogue acts is relatively recent (Dušek et al., 2017; Ueffing et al., 2018) and often focuses on output fluency only (Tian et al., 2018; Kann et al., 2018). In contrast to traditional metrics, QE does not rely on gold-standard human reference texts (Specia et al., 2010), which are expensive to obtain, do not cover the full output space, and are not accurate on the level of individual outputs (Novikova et al., 2017; Reiter, 2018). Automatic QE for NLG has several possible use cases that can improve NLG quality and reliability. For example, rating individual NLG outputs allows to ensure a minimum output quality and engage a backup, e.g., template-based NLG

system, if a certain threshold is not met. Relative ranking of multiple NLG outputs can be used directly within a system to rerank n-best outputs or to guide system development, selecting optimal system parameters or comparing to state of the art.

In this paper, we present a novel model that jointly learns to perform both tasks—rating individual outputs as well as pairwise ranking. We show that this leads to performance improvements over previously published results (Dušek et al., 2017). Our model is portable, since we do not assume any specific input schema and only rely on ratings of the text output, which are relatively easy to obtain, e.g. through crowdsourcing for a small number of outputs of an initial NLG system. The model learns to rank or rate according to any criterion annotated in the data, such as adequacy, fluency, or overall quality (see e.g., Wen et al., 2015; Manishina et al., 2016; Novikova et al., 2017). Our main contributions are as follows:

- A novel, domain- and input representation-agnostic, and conceptually simple model for NLG QE, which jointly learns ratings and pairwise rankings. It is able to seamlessly switch between the two and is directly applicable for n-way ranking (see Section 3). Crucially, it does not require human-authored references during inference.

- An original methodology for synthetically generating training instances for pairwise ranking based on introducing errors (see Section 4).

- A significant, 12% relative improvement in Pearson correlation with human ratings over results previously published on the dataset of Novikova et al. (2017), as well as the first pairwise ranking results for NLG QE on the E2E ranking dataset of Dušek et al. (2019), with significant improvements over the baseline due to synthetic training instance generation (see Sections 5 and 6).

Proceedings of The 12th International Conference on Natural Language Generation, pages 369–376,
Tokyo, Japan, 28 Oct - 1 Nov, 2019. ©2019 Association for Computational Linguistics

Both datasets are freely available, and we release our experimental code on GitHub.[1]

2 The Task(s)

The task of NLG QE for *ratings* is to assign a numerical score to a single NLG output, given its input MR, such as a dialogue act (consisting of the main intent, attributes and values). The score can be e.g. on a Likert scale in the 1-6 range (Novikova et al., 2017). In a pairwise *ranking* task, the QE system is given two outputs of different NLG systems for the same MR, and decides which one has better quality (see Figure 1).

As opposed to automatic word-overlap-based metrics, such as BLEU (Papineni et al., 2002) or METEOR (Lavie and Agarwal, 2007), no human reference texts for the given MR are required. This widens the scope of possible applications – QE systems can be used for previously unseen MRs.

3 Model

Our model is a direct extension of the freely available RatPred system (Dušek et al., 2017). The original RatPred model assigns numerical ratings to single outputs and is a dual-encoder (Lu et al., 2017), consisting of two GRU-based recurrent neural networks (Cho et al., 2014) encoding the MR and the system output, followed by fully connected layers and a final linear layer providing the score. The system is trained using squared error loss, and it uses dropout over embeddings (Hinton et al., 2012).

We make RatPred's encoders bidirectional and add a novel extension to allow pairwise ranking—a second copy of the system output encoder plus the fully connected layers and linear layer (Figure 2). All network parameters are shared among the two copies. This way, the network is able to rate two NLG outputs at once. We add a simple difference operator on top of this; the pairwise rank is computed as the difference between the two predicted scores. In addition to the squared loss for rating, we incur pairwise hinge loss for ranking. The final loss function looks as follows:

$$\mathcal{L} = (1 - I) \cdot (\hat{y} - y)^2 + I \cdot \max(0, 1 - (\hat{y} - \hat{y}'))$$

I indicates if the current instance is a ranking-based one (value of 1 for ranking and 0 for rating, effectively a mask to only incur the correct loss). y denotes the true score for a NLG output, $\hat{y}$ and $\hat{y}'$ denote scores assigned by the model for (up to) two NLG outputs.[2] Note that $\hat{y}'$ is ignored in rating instances, while a true score y is ignored for ranking. This way, the same network performs ranking and rating jointly, and it can be exposed to training instances of both types in any order. Our model is also directly applicable to n-way rankings—using it to score a group of NLG outputs and comparing the scores is equivalent to comparing the pairwise ranking.

Jointly learning to rank and rate was first introduced by Sculley (2010) for support vector machines and similar approaches have been applied for image classification (Park et al., 2017; Liu et al., 2018) as well as audio classification (Lee et al., 2016), However, we argue that the application for text classification/QE is novel, as is the implementation as a single neural network with two parts that share parameters, capable of training from mixed ranking/rating instances with masking to incur the proper loss.

4 Synthetic Training Data Generation

We use RatPred's code to generate synthetic rating instances from both NLG outputs and human-authored texts by distorting the text and lowering its score (i.e., randomly removing or adding words; cf. Dušek et al. (2017) and Figure 3 for details). We also create synthetic training pairs by using the same NLG output/human-authored text under two different levels of distortion (e.g., one vs. two artificially introduced errors). The system is then trained to rank higher the version of the text with fewer errors (see Figure 3 for an example). This novel approach can be used to generate synthetic training data for both ranking and rating tasks—in a rating task, the generated ranking instances are simply mixed among the original training instances for rating, and the model uses both kinds for training. Note that synthetic data are never used for validation or testing in any of our setups.

---

[1] The datasets can be downloaded under the following links: https://github.com/jeknov/EMNLP_17 submission, http://www.macs.hw.ac.uk/InteractionLab/E2E/. Our code is available at https://github.com/tuetschek/ratpred.

[2] Since the ranking result is a difference of two scores assigned by copies of the same network, we can assume without loss of generality that $\hat{y}$ ranks higher than $\hat{y}'$.

	Instance	Rating/Rank
MR	inform_only_match(name='hotel drisco', area='pacific heights')	4
RNNLG output	the only match i have for you is the hotel drisco in the pacific heights area.	
MR	inform(name='The Cricketers', eat_type='coffee shop', rating=high, family_friendly=yes, near='Café Sicilia')	
ZHANG output	The Cricketers is a children friendly coffee shop near Café Sicilia with a high customer rating .	*better*
TR2 output	The Cricketers can be found near the Café Sicilia. Customers give this coffee shop a high rating. It's family friendly.	*worse*

Figure 1: Examples for NLG output quality rating (top, from the NEM dataset) and ranking (bottom, from the E2E rankings dataset); RNNLG, ZHANG and TR2 are NLG systems. See Section 5.1 for details on the datasets.

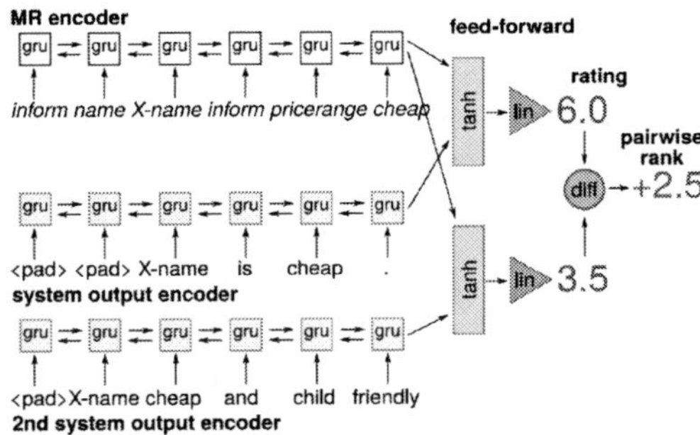

Figure 2: Schematic of our NLG QE model. Components sharing weights are shaded with the same colour.

5 Experimental Setup

5.1 Datasets

We experiment on the following two datasets, both in the restaurant/hotel information domain:

- NEM[3] (Novikova et al., 2017) – Likert-scale rated outputs (scores 1–6) of 3 NLG systems over 3 datasets, totalling 2,460 instances.

- E2E system rankings (Dušek et al., 2019) – outputs of 21 systems on a single NLG dataset with 2,979 5-way relative rankings.

We choose these two datasets because they contain human-assessed outputs from a variety of NLG systems. Another candidate is the WebNLG corpus (Gardent et al., 2017), which we leave for future work due to MR format differences.

Although both selected datasets contain ratings for multiple criteria (informativeness, naturalness and quality for NEM and the latter two for E2E), we follow Dušek et al. (2017) and focus on the overall quality criterion in our experiments as it takes both semantic accuracy and fluency into account.

We use RatPred's preprocessing, synthetic data generation, and 5-way cross-validation split on the NEM dataset. In addition, we generate synthetic training pairs as described in Section 4. We convert the 5-way rankings from the E2E set to pairwise rankings (Sakaguchi et al., 2014) (leaving out ties), which produces 15,001 instances. We split the data into training, development and test sections in an 8:1:1 ratio, ensuring that each section contains NLG outputs for different MRs (Lampouras and Vlachos, 2016).[4] In addition to the human-assessed NLG outputs themselves, human-authored training data for the NLG systems are also available and are used for synthetic instances. We use a partial delexicalisation (replacing names with placeholders).[5]

5.2 Model Settings

We evaluate our model in several configurations, with increasing amounts of synthetic training data. Note that even setups using *training* human references (i.e. additional in-domain data) are still "referenceless"—they do not use human references for test MRs. Setups using human references for validation and *test* MRs ("reference-aided"; marked with "*" in Table 1) are not referenceless and are mainly shown for comparison with Dušek et al. (2017).

We use the same network parameters for all setups, selected based on a small-scale grid search on the development data of both sets, taking training speed into consideration.[6] As a result, we use a network with fewer parameters than Dušek et al. (2017), which makes our base setup worse-performing than the original base setup, despite our use of bidirectional encoders (cf. Section 6). On

---

[3]While the dataset authors did not give it a name, we use "NEM" as an acronym for "New Evaluation Metrics", which comes from the title of the paper.

[4]We first split the data according to MRs, then assign different MRs with all corresponding system outputs into different sections.

[5]See Table 3 in the Supplementary for details.

[6]See Table 4 in the Supplementary for details.

MR	inform(name='house of nanking',food=chinese)
RNNLG output (0 errors)	house of nanking serves chinese food .
1 error	house of nanking <u>restaurant</u> chinese food .
2 errors	house of nanking serves <u>food</u> chinese food <u>cheaply</u> .
3 errors	<u>food</u> house of nanking <u>house of nanking</u> serves chinese <u>chinese</u> food .

Figure 3: Synthetic data generation example.

Synthesising errors: The original NLG output is distorted by introducing errors (underlined) of the following types: Words in the texts are removed or duplicated at original or random positions, random words from a dictionary learned from training data are used to replace current words or added at random positions. Other words are preferred over articles and punctuation in making the changes (see Dušek et al., 2017 for details).

Rating instances: We use the same settings as Dušek et al. (2017) for synthetic individual rating instances – generating up to 4 errors and lowering the target rating by 1 each time (lowering by 2 if the original value was 6). We are able to generate more synthetic rating instances since Dušek et al. (2017) did not use all available NLG system outputs due to a bug in their code (cf. Table 1).

Ranking Instances: Following our new method, pairs of outputs with a different number of errors (e.g., 0-1, 1-3) are then sampled as synthetic training instances for ranking. In our setting, we introduce up to 4 errors and create instances for all numbers of errors against the original (0-1 through 0-4), plus a set of 5 other, randomly chosen instances (e.g. 1-3, 2-4). We use both rating and ranking synthetic instances for NEM data and only ranking synthetic instances for E2E data.

the other hand, training runs several times faster. We use Adam (Kingma and Ba, 2015) for training, evaluating on the validation set after each epoch and selecting the best-performing configuration. Synthetic data are removed after 50 (out of 100) epochs. Following Dušek et al. (2017), we run all experiments with 5 different random initializations of the networks and report averaged results.

5.3 Evaluation Metrics

On the NEM data, we follow Dušek et al. (2017) to compare with their results. We use Pearson correlation of system-provided ratings with human ratings as our primary evaluation metric; we also measure Spearman rank correlation, mean absolute error (MAE) and root mean squared error (RMSE). On the E2E data, we use pairwise ranking accuracy (or Precision@1), a common ranking metric. We also measure mean ranking loss, i.e., mean score difference in wrongly rated instances.

6 Results and Discussion

The results on the NEM dataset in Table 1 show that our improved synthetic data generation methods bring significant improvements in correlation.[7] On the other hand, they worsen MAE and RMSE scores slightly, probably due to missing supervision on the exact rating in synthetic ranking instances. Compared to Dušek et al. (2017), we get a 12%

increase in Pearson correlation on the best referenceless configurations; our best referenceless system method outperforms even Dušek et al. (2017)'s reference-aided system. Note that the absolute correlations, while still not ideal, are much higher than those achieved by word-overlap-based metrics such as BLEU, which stay well below 0.1.

Our reference-aided setup did not improve with synthetic ranking pairs. Probably this is because there are already enough training data for the domain. Furthermore, this system is more prone to overfit the validation set (exploiting validation references during training). The intra-class correlation coefficient (ICC) of 0.45 measuring rater agreement on the NEM data as reported by Novikova et al. (2017) ('moderate agreement') also suggests that a certain level of noise may hinder further improvements on this dataset.

Table 2 shows our results on the E2E data. Here, all configurations perform well above random chance (i.e. accuracy of 0.5). Using the synthesised ranking pairs brings a small but statistically significant[8] improvement over the base model (3% using only NLG system outputs, additional 1% if also human references from NLG system training data are used for synthetic pairs generation).

We also explored training the system using data from both sets; however, this did not bring performance improvements, probably due to different text styles in the two datasets – the NEM data in-

---

[7]We used the Williams (1959) test to assess significant differences in correlation, following Graham and Baldwin (2014) and Kilickaya et al. (2017).

[8]We used pairwise bootstrap resampling (Koehn, 2004) to assess significance in ranking accuracy.

System	Training insts	Pearson	Spearman	MAE	RMSE
Constant	-	-	-	1.013	1.233
BLEU* (Papineni et al., 2002)	-	0.074	0.061	2.264	2.731
METEOR* (Lavie and Agarwal, 2007)	-	0.095	0.099	1.820	2.129
ROUGE-L* (Lin, 2004)	-	0.079	0.072	1.312	1.674
CIDEr* (Vedantam et al., 2015)	-	0.061	0.058	2.606	2.935
RatPred (Dušek et al., 2017) base system	1,476	0.273	0.260	0.948	1.258
+ generated data based on training system outputs	3,937	0.283	0.268	0.948	1.273
+ generated data based on training human references	45,137	0.330	0.274	0.914	1.226
+ generated data based on test human references*	80,522	0.354	0.287	0.909	1.208
Our base system	1,476	0.253	0.252	0.917	1.221
+ generated data based on training system outputs	8,856	**0.332**	**0.308**	0.924	1.241
+ generated pairs for ranking	22,140	**0.347**	**0.320**	0.936	1.261
+ generated data based on training human references	59,436	0.343	0.278	0.922	1.238
+ generated pairs for ranking	163,764	**0.369**	0.295	0.925	1.250
+ generated data based on test human references*	85,441	0.344	0.265	0.925	1.249
+ generated pairs for ranking*	236,578	0.345	0.256	0.944	1.277

Table 1: Results on the NEM ratings dataset; the number of training instances includes synthetic data (cf. Sections 4 and 5.1, Figure 3). Boldface denotes configurations of our system that are significantly better than all previous ones according to the Williams (1959) test ($p < 0.01$). Values for baseline metrics and the original RatPred system are taken over from Dušek et al. (2017). Configurations marked with "*" use human references for test instances (this includes word-overlap-based metrics such as BLEU).

System	Training insts	Accuracy	Avg. loss
Our base system	11,921	0.708	0.173
+ generated pairs based on training system outputs	50,324	0.732[†]	0.158
+ generated pairs based on training human references	428,873	**0.740**	0.153

Table 2: Results on the E2E rankings dataset. Boldface denotes significant improvements over previous configurations according to pairwise bootstrap resampling (Koehn, 2004) ($p < 0.05$; $^\dagger = p < 0.01$).

clude requests, confirmations, etc., while the E2E data only contain informative statements.

7 Related Work

QE has been an active topic in many NLP tasks—image captioning (Anderson et al., 2016), dialogue response generation (Lowe et al., 2017), grammar correction (Napoles et al., 2016) or text simplification (Martin et al., 2018)—with MT being perhaps the most prominent area (Specia et al., 2010; Avramidis, 2012; Specia et al., 2018). QE for NLG recently saw an increase of focus in various subtasks, such as title generation (Ueffing et al., 2018; Camargo de Souza et al., 2018) or content selection and ordering (Wiseman et al., 2017). Furthermore, several recent studies focus on predicting NLG fluency only, e.g., (Tian et al., 2018; Kann et al., 2018).

However, apart from our work, (Dušek et al., 2017) is the only general NLG QE system to our knowledge, which aims to predict the overall quality of a generated utterance, where quality includes both fluency and semantic coverage of the MR. Note that the correct semantic coverage of MRs is a problem for many neural NLG approaches (Gehrmann et al., 2018; Dušek et al., 2019; Nie et al., 2019). Compared to Dušek et al. (2017), our model is able to jointly rate and rank NLG outputs and includes better synthetic training data creation methods.

Our approach to QE is similar to adversarial evaluation—distinguishing between human- and machine-generated outputs (Goodfellow et al., 2014). This approach is employed in generators for random text (Bowman et al., 2016) and dialogue responses (Kannan and Vinyals, 2016; Li et al., 2017; Bruni and Fernandez, 2017). We argue that our approach is more explainable with users being able to reason with the ordinal output score.

Acknowledgments

This research received funding from the EPSRC projects DILiGENt (EP/M005429/1) and MaDrIgAL (EP/N017536/1) and Charles University project PRIMUS/19/SCI/10.

References

Peter Anderson, Basura Fernando, Mark Johnson, and Stephen Gould. 2016. Spice: Semantic propositional image caption evaluation. In *Proceedings* of the European Conference on Computer Vision, pages 382–398, Amsterdam, The Netherlands.

Eleftherios Avramidis. 2012. Comparative quality estimation: Automatic sentence-level ranking of multiple machine translation outputs. In *Proceedings of the International Conference on Computational Linguistics*, pages 115–132, Mumbai, India.

Samuel R Bowman, Luke Vilnis, Oriol Vinyals, Andrew M Dai, Rafal Jozefowicz, and Samy Bengio. 2016. Generating sentences from a continuous space. In *Proceedings of the SIGNLL Conference on Computational Natural Language Learning*, Berlin, Germany.

Elia Bruni and Raquel Fernandez. 2017. Adversarial evaluation for open-domain dialogue generation. In *Proceedings of the 18th Annual SIGdial Meeting on Discourse and Dialogue*, pages 284–288, Saarbrücken, Germany.

Kyunghyun Cho, Bart van Merrienboer, Caglar Gulcehre, Dzmitry Bahdanau, Fethi Bougares, Holger Schwenk, and Yoshua Bengio. 2014. Learning Phrase Representations using RNN Encoder-Decoder for Statistical Machine Translation. In *Proceedings of the Conference on Empirical Methods in Natural Language Processing*, pages 1724–1734, Doha, Qatar.

Ondřej Dušek, Jekaterina Novikova, and Verena Rieser. 2017. Referenceless Quality Estimation for Natural Language Generation. In *Proceedings of the Workshop on Learning to Generate Natural Language*, Sydney, Australia. arXiv:1708.01759.

Ondřej Dušek, Jekaterina Novikova, and Verena Rieser. 2019. Evaluating the State-of-the-Art of End-to-End Natural Language Generation: The E2E NLG Challenge. *Computer Speech & Language*, 59:123–156. arXiv:1901.07931.

Claire Gardent, Anastasia Shimorina, Shashi Narayan, and Laura Perez-Beltrachini. 2017. The WebNLG Challenge: Generating Text from RDF Data. In *Proceedings of the International Conference on Natural Language Generation*, pages 124–133, Santiago de Compostela, Spain.

Sebastian Gehrmann, Falcon Z. Dai, Henry Elder, and Alexander M. Rush. 2018. End-to-End Content and Plan Selection for Data-to-Text Generation. In *Proceedings of the International Conference on Natural Language Generation*, Tilburg, The Netherlands.

Ian Goodfellow, Jean Pouget-Abadie, Mehdi Mirza, Bing Xu, David Warde-Farley, Sherjil Ozair, Aaron Courville, and Yoshua Bengio. 2014. Generative adversarial nets. In *Proceedings of the Advances in Neural Information Processing Systems*, pages 2672–2680, Montréal, Canada.

Yvette Graham and Timothy Baldwin. 2014. Testing for Significance of Increased Correlation with Human Judgment. In *Proceedings of the Conference on Empirical Methods in Natural Language Processing*, pages 172–176, Doha, Qatar.

Geoffrey E Hinton, Nitish Srivastava, Alex Krizhevsky, Ilya Sutskever, and Ruslan R. Salakhutdinov. 2012. Improving neural networks by preventing co-adaptation of feature detectors. *arXiv:1207.0580*.

Katharina Kann, Sascha Rothe, and Katja Filippova. 2018. Sentence-Level Fluency Evaluation: References Help, But Can Be Spared! In *Proceedings of the Conference on Computational Natural Language Learning*, pages 313–323, Brussels, Belgium.

Anjuli Kannan and Oriol Vinyals. 2016. Adversarial evaluation of dialogue models. In *NIPS Workshop on Adversarial Training*, Barcelona, Spain. arXiv:1701.08198.

Mert Kilickaya, Aykut Erdem, Nazli Ikizler-Cinbis, and Erkut Erdem. 2017. Re-evaluating Automatic Metrics for Image Captioning. In *Proceedings of the Conference of the European Chapter of the ACL*, pages 199–209, Valencia, Spain.

Diederik Kingma and Jimmy Ba. 2015. Adam: A Method for Stochastic Optimization. In *Proceedings of the International Conference on Learning Representations*, San Diego, CA, USA. arXiv:1412.6980.

Philipp Koehn. 2004. Statistical significance tests for machine translation evaluation. In *Proceedings of the Conference on Empirical Methods in Natural Language Processing*, pages 388–395, Barcelona, Spain.

Gerasimos Lampouras and Andreas Vlachos. 2016. Imitation learning for language generation from unaligned data. In *Proceedings of the International Conference on Computational Linguistics: Technical Papers*, pages 1101–1112, Osaka, Japan.

Alon Lavie and Abhaya Agarwal. 2007. Meteor: An Automatic Metric for MT Evaluation with High Levels of Correlation with Human Judgments. In *Proceedings of the Workshop on Statistical Machine Translation*, pages 228–231, Prague, Czech Republic.

Hung-Shin Lee, Yu Tsao, Chi-Chun Lee, Hsin-Min Wang, Wei-Cheng Lin, Wei-Chen Chen, Shan-Wen Hsiao, and Shyh-Kang Jeng. 2016. Minimization of Regression and Ranking Losses with Shallow Neural Networks on Automatic Sincerity Evaluation. In *Proceedings of InterSpeech*, pages 2031–2035, San Francisco, CA, USA.

Jiwei Li, Will Monroe, Tianlin Shi, Sébastien Jean, Alan Ritter, and Dan Jurafsky. 2017. Adversarial learning for neural dialogue generation. In *Proceedings of the Conference on Empirical Methods in Natural Language Processing*, pages 2157–2169, Copenhagen, Denmark.

Chin-Yew Lin. 2004. ROUGE: A package for automatic evaluation of summaries. In *Text summarization branches out: Proceedings of the ACL-04 workshop*, pages 74–81, Barcelona, Spain.

Xiaobai Liu, Qian Xu, Jingjie Yang, Jacob Thalman, Shuicheng Yan, and Jiebo Luo. 2018. Learning Multi-Instance Deep Ranking and Regression Network for Visual House Appraisal. *IEEE Transactions on Knowledge and Data Engineering*, 30(8):1496–1506.

Ryan Lowe, Michael Noseworthy, Iulian V. Serban, Nicolas Angelard-Gontier, Yoshua Bengio, and Joelle Pineau. 2017. Towards an automatic Turing test: learning to evaluate dialogue responses. In *Proceedings of Annual Meeting of the ACL*, pages 1116–1126, Vancouver, Canada.

Yichao Lu, Phillip Keung, Shaonan Zhang, Jason Sun, and Vikas Bhardwaj. 2017. A practical approach to dialogue response generation in closed domains. *arXiv:1703.09439*.

F. Mairesse, M. Gašić, F. Jurčíček, S. Keizer, B. Thomson, K. Yu, and S. Young. 2010. Phrase-based statistical language generation using graphical models and active learning. In *Proceedings of the Annual Meeting of the ACL*, pages 1552–1561, Uppsala, Sweden.

Elena Manishina, Bassam Jabaian, Stéphane Huet, and Fabrice Lefevre. 2016. Automatic Corpus Extension for Data-driven Natural Language Generation. In *Proceedings of the Tenth International Conference on Language Resources and Evaluation (LREC 2016)*, pages 3624–3631, Portorož, Slovenia.

Louis Martin, Samuel Humean, and Pierre-Emmanuel Mazare. 2018. Reference-less Quality Estimation of Text Simplification Systems. In *Proceedings of the 1st Workshop on Automatic Text Adaption*, Tilburg, The Netherlands.

Courtney Napoles, Keisuke Sakaguchi, and Joel Tetreault. 2016. There's No Comparison: Reference-less Evaluation Metrics in Grammatical Error Correction. In *Proceedings of the Conference on Empirical Methods in Natural Language Processing*, pages 2109–2115, Austin, TX, USA.

Feng Nie, Jin-Ge Yao, Jinpeng Wang, Rong Pan, and Chin-Yew Lin. 2019. A Simple Recipe towards Reducing Hallucination in Neural Surface Realisation. In *Proceedings of the 57th Annual Meeting of the Association for Computational Linguistics*, pages 2673–2679, Florence, Italy.

Jekaterina Novikova, Ondřej Dušek, Amanda Cercas Curry, and Verena Rieser. 2017. Why We Need New Evaluation Metrics for NLG. In *Proceedings of the Conference on Empirical Methods in Natural Language Processing*, pages 2243–2253, Copenhagen, Denmark.

Kishore Papineni, Salim Roukos, Todd Ward, and Wei-Jing Zhu. 2002. BLEU: a method for automatic evaluation of machine translation. In *Proceedings of the Annual Meeting of the ACL*, pages 311–318, Philadelphia, PA, USA.

Kayoung Park, Seunghoon Hong, Mooyeol Baek, and Bohyung Han. 2017. Personalized Image Aesthetic Quality Assessment by Joint Regression and Ranking. In *IEEE Winter Conference on Applications of Computer Vision*, pages 1206–1214, Santa Rosa, CA, USA.

Ehud Reiter. 2018. A Structured Review of the Validity of BLEU. *Computational Linguistics*, 44(3):1–8.

Keisuke Sakaguchi, Matt Post, and Benjamin Van Durme. 2014. Efficient elicitation of annotations for human evaluation of machine translation. In *Proceedings of the Workshop on Statistical Machine Translation*, pages 1–11, Baltimore, MD, USA.

D. Sculley. 2010. Combined regression and ranking. In *Proceedings of the International Conference on Knowledge Discovery and Data Mining*, pages 979–988, Washington, DC, USA.

José G. Camargo de Souza, Michael Kozielski, Prashant Mathur, Ernie Chang, Marco Guerini, Matteo Negri, Marco Turchi, and Evgeny Matusov. 2018. Generating E-Commerce Product Titles and Predicting their Quality. In *Proceedings of the International Conference on Natural Language Generation*, pages 233–243, Tilburg, The Netherlands.

Lucia Specia, Dhwaj Raj, and Marco Turchi. 2010. Machine translation evaluation versus quality estimation. *Machine Translation*, 24(1):39–50.

Lucia Specia, Carolina Scarton, and Gustavo Henrique Paetzold. 2018. *Quality Estimation for Machine Translation*. Number 39 in Synthesis Lectures on Human Language Technologies. Morgan & Claypool.

Ye Tian, Ioannis Douratsos, and Isabel Groves. 2018. Treat the system like a human student: Automatic naturalness evaluation of generated text without reference texts. In *Proceedings of the International Conference on Natural Language Generation*, pages 109–118, Tilburg, The Netherlands.

Nicola Ueffing, José G. C. de Souza, and Gregor Leusch. 2018. Quality Estimation for Automatically Generated Titles of eCommerce Browse Pages. In *Proceedings of the Conference of the North American Chapter of the ACL*, pages 52–59, New Orleans, LA, USA.

Ramakrishna Vedantam, C. Lawrence Zitnick, and Devi Parikh. 2015. CIDEr: Consensus-Based Image Description Evaluation. In *Proceedings of the IEEE Conference on Computer Vision and Pattern Recognition*, pages 4566–4575, Boston, MA, USA. arXiv:1411.5726.

Tsung-Hsien Wen, Milica Gasic, Nikola Mrkšić, Pei-Hao Su, David Vandyke, and Steve Young. 2015. Semantically Conditioned LSTM-based Natural Language Generation for Spoken Dialogue Systems. In *Proceedings of the Conference on Empirical Methods in Natural Language Processing*, pages 1711–1721, Lisbon, Portugal.

Evan James Williams. 1959. *Regression analysis*. Wiley, New York, NY, USA.

Sam Wiseman, Stuart M Shieber, and Alexander M Rush. 2017. Challenges in data-to-document generation. In *Proceedings of the Conference on Empirical Methods in Natural Language Processing*, pages 2243–2253, Copenhagen, Denmark.

Improving Quality and Efficiency
in Plan-based Neural Data-to-Text Generation

Amit Moryossef[†] **Ido Dagan**[†] **Yoav Goldberg**[†‡]

`amitmoryossef@gmail.com, {dagan,yogo}@cs.biu.ac.il`

[†]Bar Ilan University, Ramat Gan, Israel
[‡]Allen Institute for Artificial Intelligence

Abstract

We follow the step-by-step approach to neural data-to-text generation we proposed in Moryossef et al. (2019), in which the generation process is divided into a text-planning stage followed by a plan-realization stage. We suggest four extensions to that framework: (1) we introduce a trainable neural planning component that can generate effective plans several orders of magnitude faster than the original planner; (2) we incorporate typing hints that improve the model's ability to deal with unseen relations and entities; (3) we introduce a verification-by-reranking stage that substantially improves the faithfulness of the resulting texts; (4) we incorporate a simple but effective referring expression generation module. These extensions result in a generation process that is faster, more fluent, and more accurate.

1 Introduction

In the data-to-text generation task (D2T), the input is data encoding facts (e.g., a table, a set of tuples, or a small knowledge graph), and the output is a natural language text representing those facts.[1] In neural D2T, the common approaches train a neural end-to-end encoder-decoder system that encodes the input data and decodes an output text. In recent work (Moryossef et al., 2019) we proposed to adopt ideas from "traditional" language generation approaches (i.e. Reiter and Dale (2000); Walker et al. (2007); Gatt and Krahmer (2017)) that separate the generation into a *planning* stage that determines the order and structure of the expressed facts, and a *realization* stage that maps the plan to natural language text. We show that by breaking the task this way, one can achieve the same fluency

of neural generation systems while being able to better control the form of the generated text and to improve its correctness by reducing missing facts and "hallucinations", common in neural systems.

In this work we adopt the step-by-step framework of Moryossef et al. (2019) and propose four independent extensions that improve aspects of our original system: we suggest a new plan generation mechanism, based on a trainable-yet-verifiable neural decoder, that is orders of magnitude faster than the original one (§3); we use knowledge of the plan structure to add typing information to plan elements. This improves the system's performance on unseen relations and entities (§4); the separation of planning from realizations allows the incorporation of a simple output verification heuristic that drastically improves the correctness of the output (§5); and finally we incorporate a post-processing referring expression generation (REG) component, as proposed but not implemented in our previous work, to improve the naturalness of the resulting output (§6).

2 Step-by-step Generation

We provide a brief overview of the step-by-step system. See Moryossef et al. (2019) for further details. The system works in two stages. The first stage (planning) maps the input facts (encoded as a directed, labeled graph, where nodes represent entities and edges represent relations) to text plans, while the second stage (realization) maps the text plans to natural language text.

The text plans are a sequence of sentence plans—each of which is a tree— representing the ordering of facts and entities within the sentence. In other words, the plans determine the separation of facts into sentences, the ordering of sentences, and the ordering of facts and entities within each sentence. This stage is *completely verifiable*:

---

[1] In this paper, we focus on a setup where the desired output represents *all* and *only* the facts expressed in the dataset. Other variants also involve content selection, allowing the process to select which subset of the facts to express.

Proceedings of The 12th International Conference on Natural Language Generation, pages 377–382,
Tokyo, Japan, 28 Oct - 1 Nov, 2019. ©2019 Association for Computational Linguistics

the text plans are guaranteed to faithfully encode all and only the facts from the input. The realization stage then translates the plans into natural language sentences, using a neural sequence-to-sequence system, resulting in fluent output.

3 Fast and Verifiable Planner

The data-to-plan component in Moryossef et al. (2019) exhaustively generates all possible plans, scores them using a heuristic, and chooses the highest scoring one for realization. While this is feasible with the small input graphs in the WebNLG challenge (Colin et al., 2016), it is also very computationally intensive, growing exponentially with the input size. We propose an alternative planner which works in linear time in the size of the graph and remains verifiable: generated plans are guaranteed to represent the input faithfully.

The original planner works by first enumerating over all possible splits into sentences (subgraphs), and for each sub-graph enumerating over all possible undirected, unordered, Depth First Search (DFS) traversals, where each traversal corresponds to a sentence plan. Our planner combines these into a single process. It works by performing a series of what we call *random truncated DFS traversals*. In a DFS traversal, a node is visited, then its children are visited recursively in order. Once all children are visited, the node "pops" back to the parent. In a *random truncated traversal*, the choice of which children to visit next, as well as whether to go to the next children or to "pop", is non-deterministic (in practice, our planner decides by using a neural-network controller). Popping at a node before visiting all its children truncates the DFS: further descendants of that node will not be visited in this traversal. It behaves as a DFS on a graph where edges to these descendants do not exist. Popping the starting node terminates the traversal.

Our planner works by choosing a node with a non-zero degree and performing a truncated DFS traversal from that node. Then, all edges visited in the traversal are removed from the input graph, and the process repeats (performing another truncated DFS) until no more edges remain. Each truncated DFS traversal corresponds to a sentence plan, following the DFS-to-plan procedure of Moryossef et al. (2019): the linearized plan is generated incrementally at each step of the traversal. This process is linear in the number of edges in the graph.

At training time, we use the plan-to-DFS mapping to perform the correct sequence of traversals, and train a neural classifier to act as a controller, choosing which action to perform at each step. At test time, we use the controller to guide the truncated DFS process. This mechanism is inspired by transition based parsing (Nivre and McDonald, 2008). The action set at each stage is dynamic. During traversal, it includes the available children at each stage and POP. Before traversals, it includes a *choose-i* action for each available node n_i. We assign a score to each action, normalize with softmax, and train to choose the desired one using cross-entropy loss. At test time, we either greedily choose the best action, or we can sample plans by sampling actions according to their assigned probabilities.

Feature Representation and action scoring. Each graph node n_i corresponds to an entity x_{n_i}, and has an associated embedding vector $\mathbf{x_{n_i}}$. Each relation r_i is associated with an embedding vector $\mathbf{r_i}$. Each labeled input graph edge $e_k = (n_i, r_\ell, n_j)$ is represented as a projected concatenated vector $\mathbf{e_k} = \mathbf{E}(\mathbf{x_{n_i}}; \mathbf{r_\ell}; \mathbf{x_{n_j}})$, where $\mathbf{E}$ is a projection matrix. Finally, each node n_i is then represented as a vector $\mathbf{n_i} = \mathbf{V}[\mathbf{x_{n_i}}; \sum_{e_j \in \pi(i)} \mathbf{e_j}; \sum_{e_j \in \pi^{-1}(i)} \mathbf{e_j}]$, where $\pi(i)$ and $\pi^{-1}(i)$ are the incoming and outgoing edges from node n_i. The traverse-to-child-via-edge-e_j action is represented as $\mathbf{e_j}$, choose-node-i is represented as $\mathbf{n_i}$ and pop-to-node-i is represented as $\mathbf{n_i} + \mathbf{p}$ where $\mathbf{p}$ is a learned vector. The score for an action a at time t is calculated as a dot-product between the action representation and the LSTM state over the symbols generated in the plan so far. Thus, each decision takes into account the immediate surrounding of the node in the graph, and the plan structure generated so far.

Speed On a 7 edges graph, the planner of Moryossef et al. (2019) takes an average of 250 seconds to generate a plan, while our planner takes 0.0025 seconds, 5 orders of magnitude faster.

4 Incorporating typing information for unseen entities and relations

In Moryossef et al. (2019), the sentence plan trees were linearized into strings that were then fed to a neural machine translation decoder (Open-NMT) (Klein et al., 2017) with a copy mechanism. This linearization process is lossy, in the sense that the linearized strings do not explicitly distinguish between symbols that represent *entities* (e.g., BARACK_OBAMA) and symbols that represent *relations* (e.g., works-for). While this information can be deduced from the position of the symbol within the structure, there is a benefit in making it more explicit. In particular, the decoder needs to act differently when decoding relations and entities: entities are copied, while relations need to be verbalized. By making the typing information explicit to the decoder, we make it easier for it to generalize this behavior distinction and apply it also for *unseen* entities and relations. We thus expect the typing information to be especially useful for the unseen part of the evaluation set.

We incorporate typing information by concatenating to the embedding vector of each input symbol one of three embedding vectors, **S**, **E** or **R**, where **S** is concatenated to structural elements (opening and closing brackets), **E** to entity symbols and **R** to relation symbols.

5 Output verification

While the plan generation stage is guaranteed to be faithful to the input, the translation process from plans to text is based on a neural seq2seq model and may suffer from known issues with such models: hallucinating facts that do not exist in the input, repeating facts, or dropping facts. While the clear mapping between plans and text helps to reduce these issues greatly, the system in Moryossef et al. (2019) still has 2% errors of these kinds.

Existing approaches: soft encouragement via neural modules. Recent work in neural text generation and summarization attempt to address these issues by trying to map the textual outputs back to structured predicates, and comparing these predicates to the input data. Kiddon et al. (2016) uses a neural checklist model to avoid the repetition of facts and improve coverage. Agarwal et al. (2018) generate k-best output candidates with beam search, and then try to map each candidate output back to the input structure using a reverse seq2seq model trained on the same data. They then select the highest scoring output candidate that best translates back to the input. Mohiuddin and Joty (2019) reconstructs the input in training time, by jointly learning a back-translation model and enforcing the back-translation to re-construct the input. Both of these approaches are "soft" in the sense that they crucially rely on the internal dynamics or on the output of a neural network module that may or may not be correct.

Our proposal: explicit verification. The separation between planning and realization provided by the step-by-step framework allows incorporating a robust and straightforward *verification step*, that does not rely on brittle information extraction procedures or trust neural network models.

The plan-to-text generation handles each sentence individually and translates entities as copy operations. We thus have complete knowledge of the generated entities and their locations. We can then assess the correctness of an output sentence by comparing[2] its sequence of entities to the entity sequence in the corresponding sentence plan, which is guaranteed to be complete.

We then decode k-best outputs and rerank them based on their correctness scores, tie-breaking using model scores. We found empirically that, with a beam of size 5 we find at least one candidate with an exact match to the plan's entity sequence in 99.82% of the cases for seen entities and relations compared to 98.48% at 1-best, and 72.3% for cases of unseen entities and relations compared to 58.06% at 1-best. In the remaining cases, we set the system to continue searching by trying other plans, by going down the list of plans (when using the exhaustive planner of Moryossef et al. (2019)) or by sampling a new plan (when using the linear time planner suggested in this paper).

6 Referring Expressions

The step-by-step system generates entities by first generating an indexed entity symbols, and then lexicalizing each symbol to the string associated with this entity in the input structure (i.e., all occurrences of the entity *11TH MISSISSIPPI IN-FANTRY MONUMENT* will be lexicalized with the full name rather than "*it*" or "*the monument*"). This results in correct but somewhat unnatural structures. In contrast, end-to-end neural generation systems are trained on text that includes referring expressions, and generate them naturally as part of the decoding process, resulting in natural looking text. However, the generated referring expressions are sometimes incorrect. Moryossef et al. (2019) suggests the possibility of handling

---

[2]We use Levenshtein-distance (Levenshtein, 1966).

this with a post-processing referring-expression generation step (REG). Here, we propose a concrete REG module and demonstrate its effectiveness. One option is to use a supervised REG module (Ferreira et al., 2018), that is trained to lexicalize in-context mentions. Such an approach is suboptimal for our setup as it is restricted to the entities and contexts it seen in training, and is prone to error on unseen entities and contexts.

Our REG solution lexicalizes the first mention of each entity as its associated string and attempts to generate referring expressions to subsequent mentions. The generated referring expressions can take the form "PRON", "X" or "THE X" where PRON is a pronoun[3], and X is a word appearing in the entity's string (allowing, e.g., *John*, or *the monument*). We also allow referring to its entity with its entire associated string. We restrict the set of allowed pronouns for each entity according to its type (male, female, plural-animate, unknown-animate, inanimate).[4] We then take, for each entity mention individually, the referring expression that receives the best language model score in context, using a strong unsupervised neural LM (BERT (Devlin et al., 2018)). The system is guaranteed to be correct in the sense that it will not generate wrong pronouns. It also has failure modes: it is possible for the system to generate ambiguous referring expressions (e.g., *John is Bob's father. He works as a nurse.*), and may lexicalize *Boston University* as *Boston*. We find that the second kind of mistake is rare as it is handled well by the language model. It can also be controlled by manually restricting the set of possible referring expression to each entity. Similarly, it is easy to extend the system to support other lexicalizations of entities by extending the sets of allowed lexicalizations (for example, supporting abbreviations, initials or nicknames) either as user-supplied inputs or using heuristics.

7 Evaluation and Results

We evaluate each of the introduced components separately. Tables listing their interactions are available in the appendix. The appendix also lists some qualitative outputs. The main trends that we observe are:

- The new planner causes a small drop in BLEU, but is orders of magnitude faster (§7.1).

- Typing information causes a negligible drop in BLEU overall, but improves results substantially for the *unseen* portion of the dataset (§7.2).

- The verification step is effective at improving the faithfulness of the output, practically eliminating omitted and overgenerated facts, reducing the number of wrong facts, and increasing the number of correctly expressed facts. This is based on both manual and automatic evaluations. (§7.3).

- The referring expression module is effective, with an intrinsic correctness of 92.2%. It substantially improves BLEU scores. (§7.4).

Setup We evaluate on the WebNLG dataset (Colin et al., 2016), comparing to the step-by-step systems described in Moryossef et al. (2019), which are state of the art. Due to randomness inherent in neural training, our reported automatic evaluation measures are based on an average of 5 training runs of each system (neural planner and neural realizer), each run with a different random seed.

7.1 Neural Planner vs Exhaustive Planner

We compare the exhaustive planner from Moryossef et al. (2019) to our neural planner, by replacing the planner component in the Moryossef et al. (2019) system. Moving to the neural planner exhibits a small drop in BLEU (46.882 dropped to 46.506). However, figure 1 indicates 5 orders of magnitude (100,000x) speedup for graphs with 7 edges, and a linear growth in time for number of edges compared to exponential time for the exhaustive planner.

7.2 Effect of Type Information

We repeat the coverage experiment in (Moryossef et al., 2019), counting the number of output texts that contain all the entities in the input graph, and, of these text, counting the ones in which the entities appear in the exact same order as the plan. Incorporating typing information reduced the number of texts not containing all entities by 18% for the *seen* part of the test set, and 16% for the unseen part. Moreover, for the text containing all

---

[3]One of *he, his, him, himself, she, her, hers, herself, they, them, theirs, it, its, itself.*

[4]We extract the types from DBPedia pages for the entities. In case we cannot deduce a type, we do not allow any pronoun.

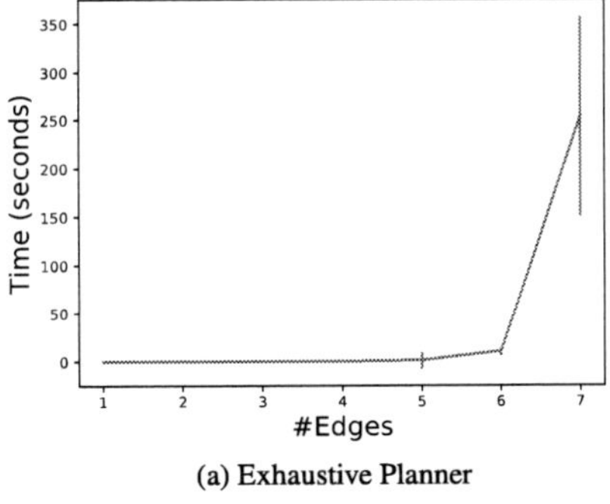

(a) Exhaustive Planner

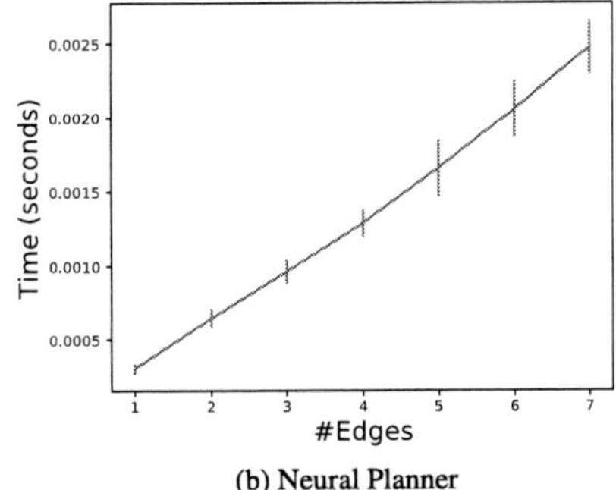

(b) Neural Planner

Figure 1: Average (+std) planning time (seconds) for different graph sizes, for exhaustive vs neural planner.

	Moryosef et al StrongNeural	Moryosef et al BestPlan	Exhaustive +Verify	Neural +Verify
Expressed	360	417	**426**	405
Omitted	41	6	**0**	2
Wrong	39	17	**14**	30
Over-generation	29	3	**0**	4
Wrong REG	-	-	**0**	3

Table 1: Manual correctness analysis comparing our systems with the ones from Moryossef et al. (2019).

entities, the number of texts that did not follow the plan's entity order is reduced by 46% for the *seen* part of the test set, and by 35% for the *unseen* part. We also observe a small drop in BLEU scores, which we attribute to some relations being verbalized more freely (though correctly).

7.3 Effect of Output Verification

The addition of output verification resulted in negligible changes in BLEU, reinforcing that automatic metrics are not sensitive enough to output accuracy. We thus performed manual analysis, following the procedure in Moryossef et al. (2019). We manually inspect 148 samples from the seen part of the test set, containing 440 relations, counting expressed, omitted, wrong and over-generated (hallucinated) facts.[5] We compare to the **StrongNeural** and **BestPlan** systems from Moryossef et al. (2019). Results in Table 1 indicate that the effectiveness of the verification process in ensuring correct output, reducing the already small number of ommited and overgenerated facts to 0 (with the exhaustive planner) and keeping it small (with the fast neural planner).

---

[5]A wrong fact is one in which a fact exists between the two entities, but the text implies a different fact from the graph, while over-generated is either repeating facts or inventing new facts.

7.4 Referring Expression Module

Intrinsic evaluation of the REG module. We manually reviewed 1,177 pairs of entities and referring expressions generated by the system. We find that 92.2% of the generated referring expressions refer to the correct entity.

From the generated expressions, 325 (27.6%) were pronouns, 192 (16.3%) are repeating a one-token entity as is, and 505 (42.9%) are generating correct shortening of a long entity. In 63 (5.6%) of the cases the system did not find a good substitute and kept the entire entity intact. Finally, 92 (7.82%) are wrong referrals. Overall, 73.3% of the non-first mentions of entities were replaced with suitable shorter and more fluent expressions.

Effect on BLEU scores. As can be seen in Table 2, using the REG module increases BLEU scores for both the exhaustive and the neural planner.

	-	**REG**
Exhaustive Planner	46.882	47.338
Neural Planner	46.506	47.124

Table 2: Effect of the REG component on BLEU score

8 Conclusions

We adopt the planning-based neural generation framework of Moryossef et al. (2019) and extend it to be orders of magnitude faster and produce more correct and more fluent text. We conclude that these extensions not only improve the system of Moryossef et al. (2019) but also highlight the flexibility and advantages of the step-by-step framework for text generation.

Acknowledgements

This work was supported in part by the German Research Foundation through the German-Israeli Project Cooperation (DIP, grant DA 1600/1-1) and by a grant from Reverso and Theo Hoffenberg.

References

Shubham Agarwal, Marc Dymetman, and Eric Gaussier. 2018. Char2char generation with reranking for the e2e nlg challenge. *arXiv preprint arXiv:1811.05826*.

Emilie Colin, Claire Gardent, Yassine Mrabet, Shashi Narayan, and Laura Perez-Beltrachini. 2016. The webnlg challenge: Generating text from dbpedia data. In *Proceedings of the 9th International Natural Language Generation conference*, pages 163–167.

Jacob Devlin, Ming-Wei Chang, Kenton Lee, and Kristina Toutanova. 2018. Bert: Pre-training of deep bidirectional transformers for language understanding. *arXiv preprint arXiv:1810.04805*.

Thiago Castro Ferreira, Diego Moussallem, Ákos Kádár, Sander Wubben, and Emiel Krahmer. 2018. Neuralreg: An end-to-end approach to referring expression generation. *arXiv preprint arXiv:1805.08093*.

Albert Gatt and Emiel Krahmer. 2017. Survey of the state of the art in natural language generation: Core tasks, applications and evaluation. *CoRR*, abs/1703.09902.

Chloé Kiddon, Luke Zettlemoyer, and Yejin Choi. 2016. Globally coherent text generation with neural checklist models. In *Proceedings of the 2016 Conference on Empirical Methods in Natural Language Processing*, pages 329–339.

Guillaume Klein, Yoon Kim, Yuntian Deng, Jean Senellart, and Alexander M Rush. 2017. Opennmt: Open-source toolkit for neural machine translation. *arXiv preprint arXiv:1701.02810*.

Vladimir I Levenshtein. 1966. Binary codes capable of correcting deletions, insertions, and reversals. In *Soviet physics doklady*, volume 10, pages 707–710.

Tasnim Mohiuddin and Shafiq Joty. 2019. Revisiting adversarial autoencoder for unsupervised word translation with cycle consistency and improved training. *arXiv preprint arXiv:1904.04116*.

Amit Moryossef, Yoav Goldberg, and Ido Dagan. 2019. Step-by-step: Separating planning from realization in neural data-to-text generation. *arXiv preprint arXiv:1904.03396*.

Joakim Nivre and Ryan McDonald. 2008. Integrating graph-based and transition-based dependency parsers.

Kishore Papineni, Salim Roukos, Todd Ward, and Wei-Jing Zhu. 2002. Bleu: a method for automatic evaluation of machine translation. In *Proceedings of the 40th annual meeting on association for computational linguistics*, pages 311–318. Association for Computational Linguistics.

Ehud Reiter and Robert Dale. 2000. *Building natural language generation systems*. Cambridge university press.

Marilyn A Walker, Amanda Stent, François Mairesse, and Rashmi Prasad. 2007. Individual and domain adaptation in sentence planning for dialogue. *Journal of Artificial Intelligence Research*, 30:413–456.

Toward a Better Story End: Collecting Human Evaluation with Reasons

Yusuke Mori[1] **Hiroaki Yamane**[2,1] **Yusuke Mukuta**[1,2] **Tatsuya Harada**[1,2]
[1]The University of Tokyo, [2]RIKEN
{mori, mukuta, harada}@mi.t.u-tokyo.ac.jp
hiroaki.yamane@riken.jp

Abstract

Creativity is an essential element of human nature used for many activities, such as telling a story. Based on human creativity, researchers have attempted to teach a computer to generate stories automatically or support this creative process. In this study, we undertake the task of story ending generation. This is a relatively new task, in which the last sentence of a given incomplete story is automatically generated. This is challenging because, in order to predict an appropriate ending, the generation method should comprehend the context of events. Despite the importance of this task, no clear evaluation metric has been established thus far; hence, it has remained an open problem. Therefore, we study the various elements involved in evaluating an automatic method for generating story endings. First, we introduce a baseline hierarchical sequence-to-sequence method for story ending generation. Then, we conduct a pairwise comparison against human-written endings, in which annotators choose the preferable ending. In addition to a quantitative evaluation, we conduct a qualitative evaluation by asking annotators to specify the reason for their choice. From the collected reasons, we discuss what elements the evaluation should focus on, to thereby propose effective metrics for the task.

1 Introduction

Creativity is vital to human nature, and storytelling is among the most important representations of human creativity. Humans use stories for entertainment and practical purposes, such as teaching lessons and creating advertisements. Stories are deeply rooted in our lives.

In computer science, understanding how humans read and create a story, and imitating these activities with a computer, is a major challenge. Mostafazadeh et al. (2016) proposed *Story Cloze Test* (SCT) as a reading comprehension task and released a large-scale corpus *ROCStories*. SCT presents four sentences, where the last sentence is excluded from a story comprising five sentences. A system must select an appropriate sentence from two choices that complement the missing 5th sentence. Among the two options is "right ending", i.e., the appropriate one to complete the story, and the other is "wrong ending".

Herein, we consider *story ending generation* (SEG) (Guan et al., 2019; Li et al., 2018; Zhao et al., 2018). This is a relatively new task inspired by SCT, and it is designed to be generation-oriented. In SEG, the last sentence of a given incomplete story is generated automatically. This is challenging because the system should comprehend the context to generate an appropriate ending.

Despite the importance of this task, no clear evaluation metric has been established thus far. To serve as a reference for future proposals of the evaluation metrics, we conduct human evaluations and study the various elements involved in evaluating an automatic SEG method.

The main contributions of this paper are:

- In order to show how well a baseline method performs and what drawbacks it has for SEG, we conducted a pairwise comparison against human-written right endings.

- Besides a quantitative evaluation, we conducted a qualitative evaluation by asking annotators to specify the reason for their choice. From the collected reasons, we explored the elements that the evaluation should focus on, to thus propose effective metrics for SEG.

2 Related Work

Automatic evaluation metrics that measure word matching are not effective in text generation, espe-

Proceedings of The 12th International Conference on Natural Language Generation, pages 383–390,
Tokyo, Japan, 28 Oct - 1 Nov, 2019. ©2019 Association for Computational Linguistics

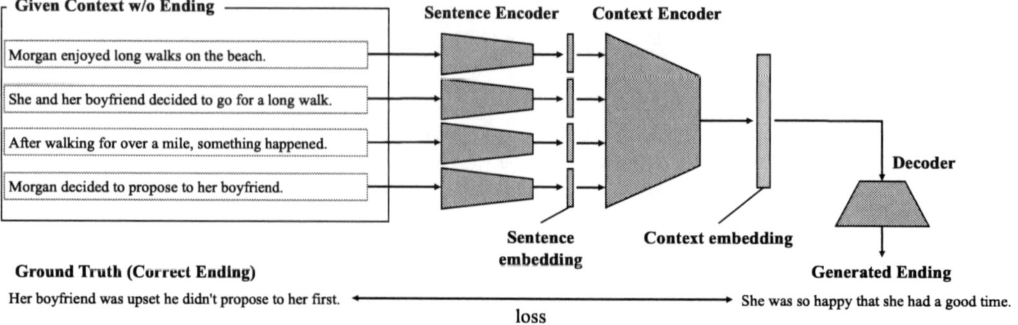

Figure 1: Given stories where the last sentence has been excluded, a method is required to generate an appropriate ending to complete the story. Our baseline method has two steps: sentence encoder and context encoder. The first encoder processes each sentence and generates corresponding sentence embeddings. These sentence embeddings are input to the second encoder, which calculates a representation of the context. The recurrent neural network (RNN) decoder receives the context embedding and generates a sentence to complete the story.

cially in dialog generation (Liu et al., 2016). Further, in story generation, it seems difficult to evaluate text generation methods with conventional automatic evaluation metrics.

As SEG is a relatively new task, metrics for human evaluation have also not been established. Zhao et al. (2018) defined two criteria, *Consistency* and *Readability*, to implement human evaluation. For each criterion, human assessors rated endings on a scale of 0 to 5. Li et al. (2018) assigned four levels to each ending (Bad (0), Relevant (1), Good (2), and Perfect (3)). Three judgement criteria were provided to annotators: *Grammar and Fluency*, *Context Relevance*, and *Logic Consistency*. They also conducted a direct comparison of the story endings generated by their baseline and their proposed approach. Guan et al. (2019) defined two metrics, *Grammar* and *Logicality*, for human evaluation. For each metric, the score 0/1/2 was applied.

In order to measure the distance from the goal of "a system writing story endings like humans", it is useful to compare the generated endings directly with human-written endings. Therefore, we conducted a pairwise comparison against human-written "right endings". To show what elements of stories humans focus on, we conducted a qualitative evaluation by asking annotators to specify the reasons for their choices.

3 Baseline Method for SEG

We define $S = \{s_1, s_2, ..., s_n\}$ as a story consisting of n sentences. In SEG, $S' = \{s_1, s_2, ..., s_{n-1}\}$ is given as an input. Then, a method is required to generate an appropriate ending s_n. We refer to S' as "context".

A hierarchical approach is useful for generating a long text (Liu et al., 2018), and also effective in story generation (Fan et al., 2018; Ravi et al., 2018). Using the "sequence-to-sequence" (Seq2seq) model (Sutskever et al., 2014) as a point of departure, we introduce a baseline method that handles input text hierarchically. This refers to the conventional method using a hierarchical structure for document modeling (Li et al., 2015) and query suggestion (Sordoni et al., 2015).

To be more precise, we use a two-step encoder. The first encoder receives $\{s_1, s_2, ..., s_{n-1}\}$ as a word-level input and outputs the sentence embeddings $\{v_1, v_2, ..., v_{n-1}\}$. Then, the second encoder receives the sentence embeddings as a sentence-level input and generates a distributed representation of the entire context. We named the first encoder "sentence encoder", and the second encoder "context encoder". We refer to this method as "Hierarchical Seq2seq" (H-Seq2seq). An overview of the method is shown in Figure 1.

Sentence Encoder: As a sentence encoder, we apply the pre-trained "InferSent" model, a bi-directional long-short term memory (Bi-LSTM) network with max pooling, trained with a natural language inference task (Conneau et al., 2017). InferSent was devised as a supervised universal sentence embedding model and demonstrated good performance with various tasks.

Context Encoder: Using the sentence embeddings obtained with the sentence encoder, we applied another embedding layer for context embedding $v_{context}$ for the entire input sequence S'. We use a gated recurrent unit (GRU) (Cho et al., 2014), for the context encoder to consider the sentences as a time series. A batch normalization layer (Ioffe and Szegedy, 2015) followed.

Then, we input $v_{context}$ to the RNN decoder.

Compared with tasks like translation, current datasets for story generation are relatively small. We believe that techniques for avoiding overfitting become more effective in such a situation. We use "word dropout", which drops words from input sentences according to a Bernoulli distribution (Iyyer et al., 2015). As an association from word dropout, we also introduced dropout at the sentence-level. When obtaining sentence embeddings, sentence-level dropout drops some elements randomly according to a given probability ratio and scales the remaining elements.

4 Experiment

4.1 Methods

H-Seq2seq As explained in Section 3, pre-trained InferSent was applied as the sentence encoder.

Seq2seq As a particularly simple method, we used basic Seq2seq for comparison. To examine the strength of the hierarchical approach, non-hierarchical basic Seq2seq is useful. The series of input words was handled collectively without considering sentence-level information.

Human Right Ending We used the human-written "right ending" in SCT as the ground truth. Two candidates in SCT are written by a person that did not write the original story (Mostafazadeh et al., 2016). Therefore, we can consider the "right ending" as the answer if SEG is solved by humans.

Note that while H-Seq2seq uses pre-trained embeddings, Seq2seq does not. For Seq2seq, we randomly initialized the word embeddings because we intended to simplify the implementation of Seq2seq. The results with and without the pre-trained embeddings should be compared for more accurate evaluation. Different parameters should also be examined. However, in story generation, it is difficult to evaluate methods with conventional automatic evaluation metrics. On the other hand, conducting all evaluations with humans is unrealistic. Therefore, we focused on investigating how much a baseline model can solve SEG and discuss how to conduct human evaluation. Although there are more sophisticated methods for SEG already proposed (Guan et al., 2019; Li et al., 2018; Zhao

ROCStories (training data)	98,161
Story Cloze validation set, Spring 2016	1,871
Story Cloze test set, Spring 2016	1,871

Table 1: The size of the dataset for our experiment.

et al., 2018), they are beyond the scope of this study. We leave it as a future work to apply the evaluation method discussed in this paper to more advanced models.

4.2 Dataset

Refer to the setting of SCT competition in SemEval-2017 (Mostafazadeh et al., 2017), we used "Spring 2016 release" and "Winter 2017 release" from *ROCStories* for training and "Spring 2016 release" validation and test sets from SCT for validation and testing (Table 1).

4.3 Quantitative Evaluation with MTurk

As a story is created on the premise that a human will read it, evaluation by human readers is considered to be the most accurate evaluation. We conducted human evaluation with help from Amazon Mechanical Turk (MTurk) workers. We evaluated the performance of the model depending on whether the generated ending correctly considers the context and properly completes the story. MTurk workers were given a four-sentence incomplete story and two options for an ending (5th sentence), and they were asked to indicate the best ending among them. We instructed workers that the given stories originally consisted of five sentences but the 5th sentence is lost, and they are required to choose the 5th sentence to complete each story. The workers were given four choices: option A is more appropriate (A), option B is more appropriate (B), both options are equally appropriate (both A and B), and neither options are suitable (neither A nor B). For each pair, we used 200 stories from the SCT test set for comparison. Five MTurk workers evaluated each story and its corresponding candidate endings. The most popular answer among the five workers was considered as agreement among the workers. The results are shown in Table 2.

4.4 Qualitative Evaluation with MTurk

We conducted another experiment similar to that in Section 4.3, where workers were required to write the reason they chose the answer. We focused on comparing H-Seq2seq against humans

H-Seq2seq VS. Human Right Ending			
H-Seq2seq	Human	both	neither
3	180	16	1

Seq2seq VS. Human Right Ending			
Seq2seq	Human	both	neither
1	194	5	0

H-Seq2seq VS. Seq2seq			
H-Seq2seq	Seq2seq	both	neither
30	18	5	147

Table 2: Human evaluation results in a pair-wise experiment. The most frequently chosen answers were considered as an agreement among the five workers.

and used 50 stories for evaluation. Five workers provided responses to each question. Examples from the results are shown in Table 3. Similar to Table 2, the agreement among five workers was counted: H-Seq2seq = 0, Human = 42, both = 5, neither = 3 (total of 50 stories). The collected reasons are publicly available[1].

4.5 Sentiment Analysis

Regarding SCT, when crowdsourced workers write the "right ending" and "wrong ending" without constraints, the "right ending" tended to be more positive (Sharma et al., 2018). Referring to this finding, we analyzed the endings in SCT, *ROCStories*, and 1,871 endings generated by H-Seq2seq. To calculate sentiment, we used the VADER sentiment analyzer (Hutto and Gilbert, 2014). The results are shown in Table 4.

Focusing on the difference of sentiment between "right ending" and "wrong ending" in SCT, Sharma et al. (2018) aim to improve SCT as a reading comprehension task. In order to eliminate the bias, they apply constraints when they have crowdsourced workers write new "right ending" and "wrong ending". On the other hand, our goal is to clarify what sentiment bias exists when humans freely write the story (SCT "right ending" and ROCStories), and how this sentiment bias is reproduced in SEG as a generation task. As the task of story generation aims to imitate the story that humans write freely, our focus is not on setting constraints when humans write.

5 Discussion

In quantitative evaluation with MTurk, H-Seq2seq beat Seq2seq in 30 stories out of 200. As this exceeds the number of stories in which Seq2seq beat H-Seq2seq (18 stories), it can be concluded that H-Seq2seq performs better than Seq2seq. Comparing H-Seq2seq with Human Right Ending, H-Seq2seq is far from generating endings that mirror those written by humans. However, 20 stories were evaluated to be equal to or better than an ending written by humans.

To clarify the characteristic of the endings generated with H-Seq2seq, we analyzed the qualitative evaluation results. Table 3 shows that endings containing positive emotions are frequently generated. This tendency is also supported by sentiment analysis (Table 4). Considering the human-written endings, the mean score of the endings from *ROCStories* is 0.119. This value is significantly different from 0 ($p < 0.05$). Hence, if we have crowdsourced workers write short stories on everyday life, they tend to write stories with happy endings.

We then analyzed the 250 reasons for the choices (five answers for each of the 50 stories). Some examples are shown in Table 3. To identify important elements of the reasons, we tried topic modeling with latent Dirichlet allocation (LDA) (Blei et al., 2003). However, the elements that characterize the topics depended on the content of the story (such as eating or going somewhere), and it was not clear what elements of the reasons were important for the choice. Therefore, we instead used word frequency to analyze 250 reasons. The most frequent 20 words among the 250 reasons are shown in Figure 2. Using this word frequency as a reference, we checked all 250 reasons to determine what was the important factor. "Logical" is a frequently used word; some reasons insisted on the importance of logicality. "Make" and "sense" are both frequently-used words because the idiom "make sense" was commonly used. When a word unrelated to the context was generated, annotators evaluated the generated ending as bad, saying "no mention". As mentioned earlier, an ending is often emotionally biased toward being positive. Therefore, the reasons also included references to emotions, such as "happy". The example in Table 3 shows that an immoral story seems to be disliked. Even the human-written ending was considered as inappropriate. Moreover, there were cases where a choice was made based on common sense, such

Context	Howard is a senior. He feels a lot of bittersweet thoughts. He holds a senior party with all of his friends. They all enjoyed it and drank a lot.	
Human	Howard liked socializing.	
H-Seq2seq	He is happy that he has a good time.	

Answers with Reasons (A: Human, B: H-Seq2seq)		
	Human (A)	he was sad about leaving his friends
	both	Both make sense, even if B has a tad more detail.
	both	Either ending will work for the story. A might be a bit better.
	both	Both fit, he might have a bittersweet feeling but he would likely be happy at the end of the party, esp if they all enjoyed themselves.
	both	He wanted to interact with his friends, and they "all enjoyed it", so he was happy.

Context	Lily and Pam were popular girls in school. They invited Joy to a diner after school. Joy was not popular and Lily and Pam knew it. They invited her just to bully her when they got there!	
Human	Joy had brought a gun and shot both the bullies in the face.	
H-Seq2seq	They had a great time at the party.	

Answers with Reasons (A: H-Seq2seq, B: Human)		
	Human (B)	B is morbid, but it fits.
	Human (B)	People who are bullied sometimes use guns on others.
	neither	I don't think she would have a good time with the bully there
	Human (B)	a terrible story which shows that bullying is risky; sometimes very risky.
	neither	Neither, they certainly didn't have a great time, and why would she shoot them?

Table 3: Examples of contexts and endings, followed by answers and reasoning provided by MTurk workers.

	mean	# of Positive	# of Negative
Right	0.146	1,652 (44.1%)	715 (19.1%)
Wrong	0.011	997 (26.6%)	1,016 (27.2%)
ROCStories	0.119	39,368 (40.1%)	20,558 (20.9%)
H-Seq2seq	0.457	1,337 (71.46%)	81 (4.33%)

Table 4: Sentiment of endings calculated with VADER.

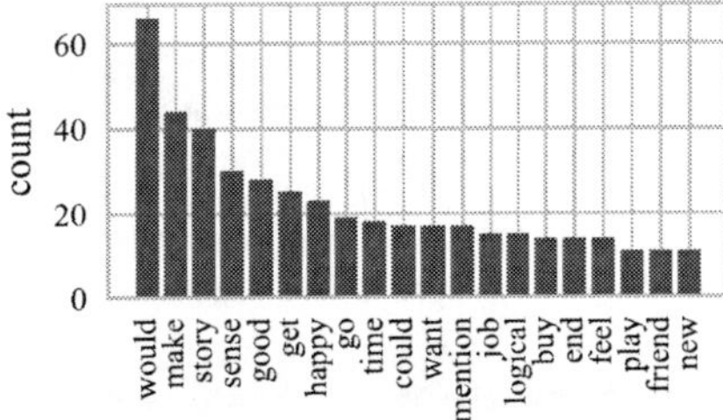

Figure 2: Frequency of words appearing in the reasons written by annotators for their choice.

as "dogs do love to play in the snow." There was a "neither" case involving grammar. For example, an annotator explained that "trying to buy a car" implies that it was not successful; therefore, the human-written ending implying buying a car is considered inappropriate. Thus, it would be desirable that the evaluation metric be designed by considering that annotators are conscious of emotions, morals, and common sense, in addition to logic and grammar.

6 Conclusion

We undertook an SEG task, and examined how to make manual evaluation more effective. As a baseline method, we introduced a hierarchical sequence-to-sequence model. Our focus is not on proposing a better model, but on discussing how to conduct human evaluation. Through quantitative and qualitative evaluations, we showed how well a baseline model performs and what drawbacks it has. To examine the qualities of the generated endings, we asked crowdsourced workers to provide reasons for their choice. This qualitative evaluation illustrates the characteristics of our baseline method. The analysis indicated that the evaluation metric should be designed by considering that workers are conscious of emotions, morals, and common sense when they evaluate story endings. Although the amount of analyzed data is limited, we believe that the findings obtained by human-reasoned evaluation would contribute to suggest metrics for story generation in future research.

Acknowledgements

This work was partially supported by JST CREST Grant Number JPMJCR1403, Japan.

References

Steven Bird, Ewan Klein, and Edward Loper. 2009. *Natural Language Processing with Python*, 1st edition. O'Reilly Media, Inc.

David M. Blei, Andrew Y. Ng, and Michael I. Jordan. 2003. Latent dirichlet allocation. *J. Mach. Learn. Res.*, 3:993–1022.

Kyunghyun Cho, Bart van Merriënboer, Çağlar Gülçehre, Dzmitry Bahdanau, Fethi Bougares, Holger Schwenk, and Yoshua Bengio. 2014. Learning phrase representations using rnn encoder–decoder for statistical machine translation. In *Proceedings of the 2014 Conference on Empirical Methods in Natural Language Processing (EMNLP)*, pages 1724–1734, Doha, Qatar. Association for Computational Linguistics.

Alexis Conneau, Douwe Kiela, Holger Schwenk, Loïc Barrault, and Antoine Bordes. 2017. Supervised learning of universal sentence representations from natural language inference data. In *Proceedings of the 2017 Conference on Empirical Methods in Natural Language Processing*, pages 670–680, Copenhagen, Denmark. Association for Computational Linguistics.

Angela Fan, Mike Lewis, and Yann Dauphin. 2018. Hierarchical neural story generation. In *Proceedings of the 56th Annual Meeting of the Association for Computational Linguistics (Volume 1: Long Papers)*, pages 889–898, Melbourne, Australia. Association for Computational Linguistics.

Jian Guan, Yansen Wang, and Minlie Huang. 2019. Story ending generation with incremental encoding and commonsense knowledge. In *Proceedings of the Thirty-Third AAAI Conference on Artificial Intelligence (AAAI-19)*, volume abs/1808.10113.

Matthew Honnibal and Ines Montani. 2017. spacy 2: Natural language understanding with bloom embeddings, convolutional neural networks and incremental parsing. *To appear.*

Clayton J. Hutto and Eric Gilbert. 2014. VADER: A parsimonious rule-based model for sentiment analysis of social media text. In *International AAAI Conference on Web and Social Media*, pages 216–225. The AAAI Press.

Sergey Ioffe and Christian Szegedy. 2015. Batch normalization: Accelerating deep network training by reducing internal covariate shift. In *Proceedings of the 32nd International Conference on Machine Learning*, volume 37 of *Proceedings of Machine Learning Research*, pages 448–456, Lille, France. PMLR.

Mohit Iyyer, Varun Manjunatha, Jordan Boyd-Graber, and Hal Daumé III. 2015. Deep unordered composition rivals syntactic methods for text classification. In *Proceedings of the 53rd Annual Meeting of the Association for Computational Linguistics and the 7th International Joint Conference on Natural Language Processing (Volume 1: Long Papers)*, pages 1681–1691, Beijing, China. Association for Computational Linguistics.

Jiwei Li, Thang Luong, and Dan Jurafsky. 2015. A hierarchical neural autoencoder for paragraphs and documents. In *Proceedings of the 53rd Annual Meeting of the Association for Computational Linguistics and the 7th International Joint Conference on Natural Language Processing (Volume 1: Long Papers)*, pages 1106–1115, Beijing, China. Association for Computational Linguistics.

Zhongyang Li, Xiao Ding, and Ting Liu. 2018. Generating reasonable and diversified story ending using sequence to sequence model with adversarial training. In *Proceedings of the 27th International Conference on Computational Linguistics*, pages 1033–1043, Santa Fe, New Mexico, USA. Association for Computational Linguistics.

Chia-Wei Liu, Ryan Lowe, Iulian Serban, Mike Noseworthy, Laurent Charlin, and Joelle Pineau. 2016. How not to evaluate your dialogue system: An empirical study of unsupervised evaluation metrics for dialogue response generation. In *Proceedings of the 2016 Conference on Empirical Methods in Natural Language Processing*, pages 2122–2132, Austin, Texas. Association for Computational Linguistics.

Peter J. Liu, Mohammad Saleh, Etienne Pot, Ben Goodrich, Ryan Sepassi, Lukasz Kaiser, and Noam Shazeer. 2018. Generating wikipedia by summarizing long sequences. In *International Conference on Learning Representations*.

Nasrin Mostafazadeh, Nathanael Chambers, Xiaodong He, Devi Parikh, Dhruv Batra, Lucy Vanderwende, Pushmeet Kohli, and James Allen. 2016. A corpus and cloze evaluation for deeper understanding of commonsense stories. In *Proceedings of the 2016 Conference of the North American Chapter of the Association for Computational Linguistics: Human Language Technologies*, pages 839–849, San Diego, California. Association for Computational Linguistics.

Nasrin Mostafazadeh, Michael Roth, Annie Louis, Nathanael Chambers, and James Allen. 2017. Lsdsem 2017 shared task: The story cloze test. In *Proceedings of the 2nd Workshop on Linking Models of Lexical, Sentential and Discourse-level Semantics*, pages 46–51, Valencia, Spain. Association for Computational Linguistics.

Jeffrey Pennington, Richard Socher, and Christopher Manning. 2014. GloVe: Global vectors for word representation. In *Proceedings of the 2014 Conference on Empirical Methods in Natural Language Processing (EMNLP)*, pages 1532–1543, Doha, Qatar. Association for Computational Linguistics.

Hareesh Ravi, Lezi Wang, Carlos Muniz, Leonid Sigal, Dimitris Metaxas, and Mubbasir Kapadia. 2018.

Show me a story: Towards coherent neural story illustration. In *The IEEE Conference on Computer Vision and Pattern Recognition (CVPR)*, pages 7613–7621.

Radim Řehůřek and Petr Sojka. 2010. Software Framework for Topic Modelling with Large Corpora. In *Proceedings of the LREC 2010 Workshop on New Challenges for NLP Frameworks*, pages 45–50, Valletta, Malta. ELRA. http://is.muni.cz/publication/884893/en.

Rishi Sharma, James Allen, Omid Bakhshandeh, and Nasrin Mostafazadeh. 2018. Tackling the story ending biases in the story cloze test. In *Proceedings of the 56th Annual Meeting of the Association for Computational Linguistics (Volume 2: Short Papers)*, pages 752–757, Melbourne, Australia. Association for Computational Linguistics.

Alessandro Sordoni, Yoshua Bengio, Hossein Vahabi, Christina Lioma, Jakob Grue Simonsen, and Jian-Yun Nie. 2015. A hierarchical recurrent encoder-decoder for generative context-aware query suggestion. In *Proceedings of the 24th ACM International on Conference on Information and Knowledge Management*, CIKM '15, pages 553–562, New York, NY, USA. ACM.

Ilya Sutskever, Oriol Vinyals, and Quoc V. Le. 2014. Sequence to sequence learning with neural networks. In *Proceedings of the 27th International Conference on Neural Information Processing Systems - Volume 2*, NIPS'14, pages 3104–3112, Cambridge, MA, USA. MIT Press.

Seiya Tokui, Kenta Oono, Shohei Hido, and Justin Clayton. 2015. Chainer: a next-generation open source framework for deep learning. In *Proceedings of Workshop on Machine Learning Systems (LearningSys) in The Twenty-ninth Annual Conference on Neural Information Processing Systems (NIPS)*.

Yan Zhao, Lu Liu, Chunhua Liu, Ruoyao Yang, and Dong Yu. 2018. From plots to endings: A reinforced pointer generator for story ending generation. In *Proceedings of Natural Language Processing and Chinese Computing (NLPCC)*, volume abs/1901.03459.

A   Supplemental Material

A.1   Training details

H-Seq2seq Pre-trained InferSent was applied as the sentence encoder. Pre-trained word embeddings "GloVe" (Pennington et al., 2014) is used in InferSent. The sentence encoder is not fine-tuned during training. We used a 1-layer GRU for each context encoder and decoder and set the number of hidden layer units to 256. We set the dropout ratio to 0.3 for word-dropout and to 0.5 for sentence-level dropout. We used Adam optimization with

parameters $\alpha = 0.001, \beta_1 = 0.9, \beta_2 = 0.999, \epsilon = 1e - 08$. The results obtained from 15 epochs were used for evaluation.

We implemented the method with Chainer, a Python-based deep learning framework (Tokui et al., 2015).

Seq2seq The series of input words were handled collectively by Seq2seq without considering sentence-level information. We used a 2-layer LSTM encoder and 2-layer LSTM decoder. Each hidden layer contained 512 units. We used the results from 15 epochs.

A.2   Human Evaluation with MTurk

We conducted the quantitative evaluation and the qualitative evaluation with help from MTurk workers. In Figure A.1, we show the snippet of the instruction and the question we used in the qualitative evaluation. In the quantitative evaluation, the reason for the choice was not asked.

Each story was evaluated by five workers. Workers chose their answer from "A", "B", "both A and B", and "neither A nor B". Among the five answers obtained for each story, The most frequently chosen answers were considered as an agreement among the workers. We should note that we had to handle exceptions if multiple answers were most popular. If "A" and "B" received two votes each, we considered the agreement among workers to be "both". Similarly, if "A" and "both" received two votes each, we considered the agreement among workers to be "A". Similarly, if "B" and "both', then "B"; if "A" and "neither', then "A"; if "B" and "neither', then "B"; if "both" and "neither", then "both".

A.3   Sentiment Analysis

According to the original paper on VADER, We count an ending as positive if the score ≥ 0.05 and count it as negative if ≤ -0.05.

A.4   Pre-processing for Word Frequency

Pre-processing of word frequency was done as below. First, we used Gensim (Řehůřek and Sojka, 2010) for converting sentences into lists of lowercase tokens. Second, we removed stop words with NLTK (Bird et al., 2009). Then, we lemmatized the words with spaCy (Honnibal and Montani, 2017). We used the words with part-of-speech (pos) tags 'NOUN,' 'ADJ,' 'VERB,' and 'ADV.' After the pre-processing process, we counted the number of tokens.

Pick the right endings to complete unfinished stories.

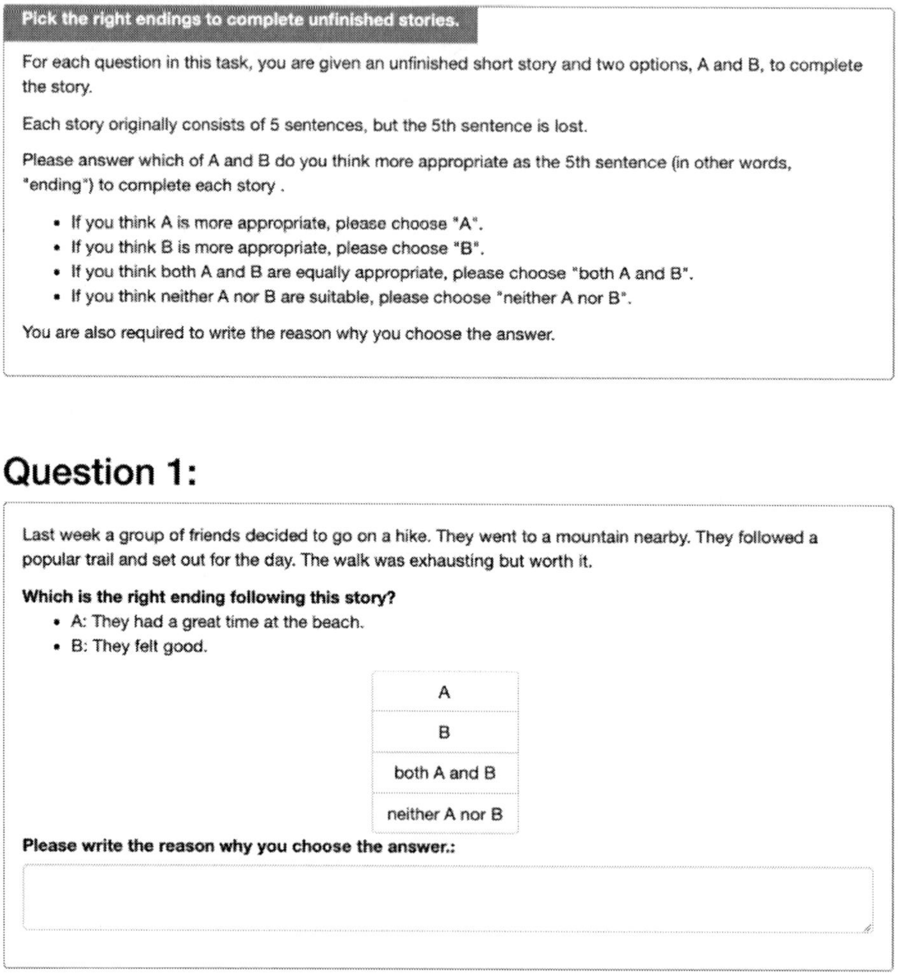

For each question in this task, you are given an unfinished short story and two options, A and B, to complete the story.

Each story originally consists of 5 sentences, but the 5th sentence is lost.

Please answer which of A and B do you think more appropriate as the 5th sentence (in other words, "ending") to complete each story .

- If you think A is more appropriate, please choose "A".
- If you think B is more appropriate, please choose "B".
- If you think both A and B are equally appropriate, please choose "both A and B".
- If you think neither A nor B are suitable, please choose "neither A nor B".

You are also required to write the reason why you choose the answer.

Question 1:

Last week a group of friends decided to go on a hike. They went to a mountain nearby. They followed a popular trail and set out for the day. The walk was exhausting but worth it.

Which is the right ending following this story?

- A: They had a great time at the beach.
- B: They felt good.

A

B

both A and B

neither A nor B

Please write the reason why you choose the answer.:

Figure A.1: The instruction and the question snippet we used in the qualitative evaluation.

Hotel Scribe: Generating High Variation Hotel Descriptions

Saad Mahamood
trivago N.V.
Düsseldorf, Germany
saad.mahamood@trivago.com

Maciej Zembrzuski
trivago N.V.
Düsseldorf, Germany
maciej.zembrzuski@trivago.com

Abstract

This paper describes the implementation of the Hotel Scribe system. A commercial Natural Language Generation (NLG) system which generates descriptions of hotels from accommodation metadata with a high level of content and linguistic variation in English. It has been deployed live by *trivago* for the purpose of improving coverage of accommodation descriptions and for Search Engine Optimisation (SEO). In this paper, we describe the motivation for building this system, the challenges faced when dealing with limited metadata, and the implementation used to generate the highly variate accommodation descriptions. Additionally, we evaluate the uniqueness of the texts generated by our system against comparable human written accommodation description texts.

1 Introduction

The hotel search business is a highly competitive market in which websites attempt to align the accommodation needs of a given user with the available marketplace of prices/deals offered by hoteliers and other accommodation providers. It is imperative that users are able to find the type of accommodation they are seeking and find relevant information associated to a given accommodation in the form of images, text, maps, and infographics.

One key piece of textual information is an *accommodation description*, which provides a given user with detailed information about the accommodation and the facilities that it offers for their guests. Within *trivago* these descriptions have been typically written manually by humans either with the use of freelancers or the hotelier providing a description themselves. As the global market size of hotels has continuously grown over the past few years this has meant an ever increasing inventory of accommodations requiring a description. Other problems such as the cost of employing freelancers across multiple languages, the lack of consistency, and the time-lag in providing updated descriptions for accommodations meant that an automated solution for generating accommodation descriptions was needed. Finally, with the importance of SEO for consumers searching for a specific accommodation from a search engine, there was also a need to generate accommodation descriptions with a high level of content and linguistic variation to make generated description as distinct as possible.

In this paper, we will describe relevant past work that has been done using NLG for commercial applications and the use of variation in NLG. In later sections we will describe our approach for generating accommodation descriptions with variation, our methodology for evaluating the effectiveness of the implemented system, and discuss the results that we have obtained. In the final section we conclude the paper based upon the findings we have obtained.

2 Background

2.1 Commercial NLG

Over the past 5-10 years there has been a substantial increase in the number of commercial based NLG solutions (Dale, 2019). Commercial NLG applications have appeared in differing domains such as Weather (Sripada et al., 2014), Automated Journalism (Caswell and Dörr, 2018), Oil & Gas Industry (Reiter, 2017), Healthcare (Harris, 2008), and Financial reporting (Danlos et al., 2011). This increase has been in part due to the rise of companies such as *Narrative Science, Automated Insights, Arria NLG, Yesop,* and *Ax Semantics*. Whilst there has been some interest among these companies in exploring aspects of

Proceedings of The 12th International Conference on Natural Language Generation, pages 391–396,
Tokyo, Japan, 28 Oct - 1 Nov, 2019. ©2019 Association for Computational Linguistics

multimodality (Mahamood et al., 2014), referring expression generation (REG) (Reiter, 2017), and morphology inflection (Madsack et al., 2018), the majority of these commercial NLG offerings leverage little-to-no rich linguistic concepts such as aggregation and REG that have been developed by the research community (Dale, 2019). Preferring instead an approach of using 'smart templates' to generate routine texts from data (Dale, 2019), which in some domains the actual implementation can be "embarrassingly simple" (Graefe, 2016).

Building commercial NLG systems can introduce a set of challenges that may not be found in typical academic implementations. These challenges can range from issues with ensuring reliability/accuracy of the output text generated (to minimise legal liability) (Harris, 2008), reusability & configurability (Sripada et al., 2014; Reiter, 2017), absence of appropriate data (Caswell and Dörr, 2018), and finally the need for scalability in generating large volumes of output (Harris, 2008). Additionally challenges can be found during the corpus analysis phase with target corpora not being available entirely (Sripada et al., 2014), access issues due to data privacy (Harris, 2008), or a lack of consistency in style due the corpora being authored by multiple authors (Sripada et al., 2004). The totality of these numerous challenges means that for some commercial applications there is a need to focus on simplicity rather than implement cutting-edge techniques (Harris, 2008).

2.2 NLG & Textual Variation

Variation in NLG systems is the process in which there is a variance in content and/or lexical expressions chosen by a given system when generating textual output. Traditionally, output texts created through the use of 'canned text' rules tended to be fairly simplistic and show almost no variation (Theune et al., 2001). Systems, however, must be built with variation as part of their core-design specification. This can be achieved with the use of probabilistic variation and/or through the use of more parametrised variation, which adapts the type of variation based on a given context (van Deemter et al., 2005).

The desirability of having variation in the generated output text very much depends on the nature of the application. Systems where users are only likely to read at most a single generated text have less need for variation than compared to applications where users are expected to read many generated text over a period time (Reiter and Sripada, 2002). However, in such systems where there is lexical variation there should also be consistency in terminology to avoid confusing readers with differing definitions (Reiter and Sripada, 2002). Work by Foster et al. (2007) has shown that when texts containing variation are evaluated they are strongly preferred and appreciated by human evaluators.

2.3 NLG for Hotel & Restaurant Descriptions

There has been very examples of NLG systems for generating descriptions about hotels. The only recent example is the SuRe system (Tien et al., 2015). The SuRe system generated an abstractive summary that summarised the positive and negative factors for a given accommodation solely from user reviews. Factors such as whether users thought in aggregate that the accommodation's location, food, etc. was a positive aspect or not. Like many applied NLG systems, it used a standard data-to-text pipeline architecture, but with the key difference being the need to first identify and aggregate opinions from user reviews about features within the given accommodation before performing pipeline based text generation with a surface realiser. However, a majority of the human evaluators found that the system have low levels of grammar quality and the output to be repetitious.

In contrast generating descriptions of restaurants has garnered far more interest within the NLG research community. There has been a considerable amount of past work in generating descriptions or recommendations of restaurants with effort also applied to generating recommendations with stylistic variations (Oraby et al., 2017). The most recent work in this domain has been due to the E2E shared task utilising a crowdsourced dataset of 50k meaning representation instances in the restaurant domain (Novikova et al., 2017). This shared task had brought about the training and construction of a number of systems using either machine learning (ML), rule-based, or template-based approaches to generating short one to three sentence descriptions of a given restaurant. Whilst ML approaches outperformed rule or template based approaches several issues were identified such as hallucinations in the output text, short output length, and low levels of output diversity and syntactic complexity (Dušek et al., 2020).

3 Corpus Analysis

Before deciding on the implementation approach for our system, we first conducted a corpus analysis by examining five existing human written accommodation descriptions (example shown in Table 1) chosen at random. The purpose of this exercise was to gain a better understanding of possible gaps or shortcomings with the available accommodation metadata. Each fact within the human authored corpora is checked to see if there was underlying data present to generate the same or a similar statement as well using an automatic approach.

Overall there were two main issues that were identified after analysing the human authored corpora: The *first* was the lack of specificity in accommodation metadata and the *second* was incomplete data coverage.

The lack of specificity was a significant challenge. Whilst the human authored corpora might mention the name of an in-house hotel restaurant, the actual metadata for a given accommodation would only have binary data points, which indicate the presence of a hotel restaurant and/or café. The encoding of hotel amenities as binary information meant that the metadata would lack details that make it challenging to describe accommodation facilities with significant detail. The second main issue was the incompleteness in data coverage. The analysis of the corpora showed that the corpora contained details that were not represented within the accommodation metadata. This lack of data coverage also affected transportation and places of interest (POI) data as well. In particular, there were issues in regards to the lack of data coverage for nearby transportation stations and a lack of data on nearby POIs for a given accommodation.

As we were building an initial first version of the Hotel Scribe system these data quality issues were not addressed prior to implementation.

4 System Implementation

The Hotel Scribe system was implemented using a standard Data-to-Text NLG pipeline architecture (Reiter, 2007), using SimpleNLG (Gatt and Reiter, 2009) for English surface realisation. Data is read by the system from a database and is mapped onto ontological concepts which represents a taxonomical structure of the hotel accommodation domain. The taxonomical structure of the ontology was devised manually with the assistance of a domain ex-

pert and specifies with increasing levels of granularity all the possible types of entities that can exist in the accommodation domain. For example a Casa Rural *is a* form of self catering which *is a* form of accommodation type.

The key difference from a standard NLG Data-to-Text application was how the Document Planner and Microplanner components of the pipeline functioned. Both of these modules incorporated several variation strategies to help increase the amount of variation in the generated output texts. These strategies included the following types:

- Semantic variation – Varying what content to talk about.

- Content ordering variation – Varying the order of how content is placed.

- Aggregation variation – Varying how and when concepts should be aggregated in a single sentence or not.

- Linguistic variation – Variation in how the concepts are expressed in language.

All four of these variation strategies were executed in both the Document Planner and Microplanner probabilistically. Linguistic variation included variation at a phrase/word level and also REG variation such as varying how an accommodation is referred to in the generated text (e.g. "Hilton Hotel London", "Hilton", "accommodation", "hotel"), which was specified in the 31 syntactic rule specification files to lexicalise the ontological concepts. The combination of these strategies enabled a high level of output variation. For example, the sentence generated by the system to describe 24 hour front desk check-in/check-out services has over *6,000* unique variants.

In addition to implementing the variation strategies the secondary challenge for this system was to make it scalable to generate a large number of texts in a short period of time. This was addressed by making the system multi-threaded therefore capable of generating a number of texts in parallel from a single request. The system was also made scalable and could be deployed to multiple machines at the same time, through the deployment onto scalable cloud computing resources. This in turn allowed many multiple text generation requests to be processed simultaneously. These two optimisations allowed the system to generated up to

Hotel Scribe Text	Freelancer Text
Located in London, the four-star Park Plaza Victoria London is near to Victoria Station. Parents of children should note that there are a number of child friendly amenities including childcare facilities and baby cribs. Meal options are accessible in this hotel through an on-site café and a restaurant. Express check-in/check-out can be done at the 24 hour service counter from 14:00 for check-ins and as late as 12:00 for check-out. In terms of water based facilities this residence includes a pool for guests. Parking amenities comprises of a close by car park, with valet parking. There is complimentary Wifi connectivity within the hotel in both public and in-room hotel areas. For guests travelling on business, this residence features a business centre and conference/meeting rooms. Rooms within this accommodation feature facilities such as a hairdryer, desk, minibar and a telephone. In-room entertainment is available for guests, which is provided by cable TV. Additionally, some rooms come with views of the city.	Situated in the heart of London, just a three-minute walk from Apollo Victoria Theatre, Park Plaza Victoria London boasts a modern, fully equipped fitness centre. A 49-inch flat-screen TV with cable channels, tea and coffee-making facilities, and a desk are provided in each room at Park Plaza Victoria London. The standard apartments boast a kitchenette with a microwave and fridge, while the larger apartments include a balcony. Park Plaza Victoria London offers guests a range of business services. The executive lounge boasts free Wi-Fi and daily newspapers, while the 24-hour front desk offers concierge services and luggage storage. Venetian-Italian dishes are prepared in the on-site TOZI Restaurant, while cocktails can be sipped at Lounge Bar. This hotel also serves breakfast daily, and allows guests to order room service 24 hours a day. Guests staying at here are just a 14-minute walk away from Buckingham Palace, and five minutes' walk from bustling Victoria Station. This hotel is just over a kilometre from Tate Britain.

Table 1: Text examples for the same hotel between the Hotel Scribe and a freelancer written description.

600,000+ accommodation description texts within a matter of a few days.

5 Evaluation

To better understand the effectiveness and value of the texts generated by the Hotel Scribe we undertook an evaluation of the system. We compared the texts generated by the Hotel Scribe system against accommodation descriptions written from three different sources. The first was accommodation descriptions written by freelancers, the second was from those written directly by the hoteliers, and the third was descriptions written by a direct commercial competitor[1]. Corpora for the commercial competitor were collected by automatically scraping accommodation description texts from their website across a random set of cities.

To make the comparison between these four different sources of corpora we used two different evaluation metrics. The first metric was the use of a commercial anti-plagiarism software[2] to measure the amount of repetition and thus the amount of variation between the four types of corpora. For each source we selected at random around a 1,000 different texts into a private index. Next we selected at random another 200 texts which were used to compute the average "percentage matched" metric for each text against the given private index.

Similarly, we calculated the Levenshtein edit distance between each of the 200 randomly selected texts and the documents in the private index and we select the lowest edit distance for each of the 200 texts. The calculated average of the minimal edit distances was also a proxy metric for estimating the level of text variation. This evaluation approach is similar to the one undertaken by Foster et al. (2007) to measure the level of texutal variation.

Given the level of variation implemented in the Hotel Scribe system, the system was also evaluated for the level of factual correctness as part of a general quality assurance check. This was done with a team of seven human evaluators with each evaluating 13 different accommodation descriptions that were chosen at random to make an evaluated total of 91 descriptions. For each description, the evaluator would count the total number of facts present in the given description and then check to see if the same corresponding fact was also present in the corresponding accommodation webpage. From this a count of the number of *incorrect* and *correct* facts could be derived for each annotator for each of the 91 accommodation descriptions. These counts of *incorrect* and *correct* facts enabled the calculation of an accuracy score at a per accommodation description level and also an average accuracy score for over all descriptions.

---

[1] Anonymous due to commercial sensitivity.

[2] Copyscape – https://www.copyscape.com/

Text Source Type	Avg. Copyscale "percent matched" (lower is better)	Avg. Levenshtein edit distance (higher is better)
Freelancer Descriptions	4.09 (σ 10.66)	647.88 (σ 69.79)
Hotelier Descriptions	0.842 (σ 6.26)	602.48 (σ 341.64)
Competitor Descriptions	32.43 (σ 25.81)	345.35 (σ 150.68)
Hotel Scribe Descriptions	44.02 (σ 11.39)	296.25 (σ 104)

Table 2: Results for both Copyscale and Levenshtein edit distance metrics. Standard deviation is shown in brackets.

6 Results

The results are shown above in table 2. From the results obtained it's sufficiently clear that the accommodation descriptions written by the Freelancers and Hoteliers contain considerably more variation than texts generated by the Hotel Scribe system and those written by the commercial competitor. This is not unexpected as both Freelancers and Hoteliers were unconstrained from limiting themselves from writing their descriptions from only the database accommodation metadata and were free to use external information resources. Therefore resulting in descriptions that are much richer in detail and more unique in comparison to the automatically generated texts.

What was interesting is the finding showing the near-comparable performance between the Hotel Scribe system and the direct commercial competitor. Whilst texts from the commercial competitor out-performed our system for both the Copyscape and Levenshtein edit distance metrics the difference is small. This is a considerable result given the limitations in data as described in section 3 and the short development time of only a few months. However, the large gap in performance between the commercial competitor and the texts written by humans (Freelancer and Hoteliers) may possibly indicate that they are also using an automated approach to generate their texts or a hybrid approach with humans post-editing the texts. However, this cannot be known for certain.

The Hotel Scribe system was also evaluated for factual correctness and the average score between the seven judges was 84%. Some of the discrepancies were due to errors in the input data and others were due to software bugs in system, which were subsequently fixed in later revisions of the system.

7 Conclusion

In this paper we described an approach for generating accommodation descriptions with a large number of textual variations and evaluated this against other types of corpora. Whilst, the system does not have the level of performance as human written corpora in terms of uniqueness and variation the fact that it has a near-comparable performance to a direct competitor is highly encouraging.

The discrepancy in performance between our system and human written corpora indicates a greater need to have more detailed accommodation metadata with greater *breadth* and *depth*, which will enable our system to generate more unique descriptions about the amenities/facilities found in a given accommodation. We have put our system into production to cover accommodations that have no existing human written description as shown in figure 1. Going forward, we will continue to refine its capabilities and performance in the future.

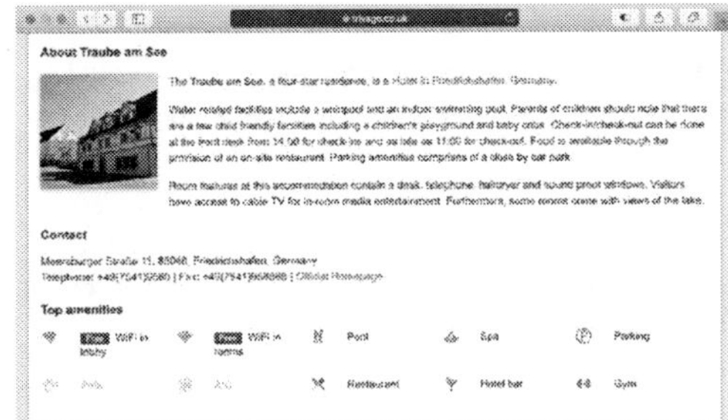

Figure 1: A live example of an accommodation description displayed on the trivago website.

Acknowledgements

Many thanks for the following people who provided considerable help and support during the development of this project: *Annachiara Foschi, Anja Klassen, Doreh Taghavidinani, Janine Cushnie, Allyson Clark, Agata Abram, Roman Orishko,* and *Nick Dale.*

References

David Caswell and Konstantin Dörr. 2018. Automated Journalism 2.0. Event-driven narratives. *Journalism Practice*, 12(4):477–496.

Robert Dale. 2019. NLP commercialisation in the last 25 years. *Natural Language Engineering*, 25(3):419–426.

Laurence Danlos, Frédéric Meunier, and Vanessa Combet. 2011. EasyText: an Operational NLG System. In *ENLG 2011 - 13th European Workshop on Natural Language Generation*.

Kees van Deemter, Emiel Krahmer, and Mariët Theune. 2005. Real versus Template-Based Natural Language Generation: A False Opposition? *Computational Linguistics*, 31(1):15–23.

Ondřej Dušek, Jekaterina Novikova, and Verena Rieser. 2020. Evaluating the state-of-the-art of end-to-end natural language generation: The E2E NLG Challenge. *Computer Speech & Language*, 59:123–156.

Mary Ellen Foster and Michael White. 2007. Avoiding repetition in generated text. In *Proceedings of the Eleventh European Workshop on Natural Language Generation*, pages 33–40. Association for Computational Linguistics.

Albert Gatt and Ehud Reiter. 2009. SimpleNLG: A realisation engine for practical applications. In *Proceedings of the 12th European Workshop on Natural Language Generation (ENLG 2009)*, pages 90–93.

Andreas Graefe. 2016. Guide to Automated Journalism. *Tow Center for Digital Journalism*.

Mary Dee Harris. 2008. Building a large-scale commercial NLG system for an EMR. In *Proceedings of the Fifth International Natural Language Generation Conference*, pages 157–160.

Andreas Madsack, Alessia Cavallo, Johanna Heininger, and Robert Weißgraeber. 2018. AX Semantics' Submission to the CoNLL-SIGMORPHON 2018 Shared Task. In *Proceedings of the CoNLL SIGMORPHON 2018 Shared Task: Universal Morphological Reinflection*, pages 43–47.

Saad Mahamood, William Bradshaw, and Ehud Reiter. 2014. Generating Annotated Graphs using the NLG Pipeline Architecture. In *Proceedings of the 8th International Natural Language Generation Conference (INLG)*, pages 123–127.

Jekaterina Novikova, Ondřej Dušek, and Verena Rieser. 2017. The E2E dataset: New challenges for end-to-end generation. In *Proceedings of the 18th Annual SIGdial Meeting on Discourse and Dialogue*, pages 201–206, Saarbrücken, Germany. Association for Computational Linguistics.

Shereen Oraby, Sheideh Homayon, and Marilyn Walker. 2017. Harvesting creative templates for generating stylistically varied restaurant reviews. In *Workshop on Stylistic Variation at EMNLP 2017*.

Ehud Reiter. 2007. An architecture for data-to-text systems. In *Proceedings of the 11th European Workshop on Natural Language Generation (ENLG'07)*.

Ehud Reiter. 2017. A Commercial Perspective on Reference. In *Proceedings of the 10th International Conference on Natural Language Generation*, pages 134–138.

Ehud Reiter and Somayajulu Sripada. 2002. Human Variation and Lexical Choice. *Computational Linguistics*, 28:545–553.

Somayajulu Sripada, Neil Burnett, Ross Turner, John Mastin, and Dave Evans. 2014. A case study: NLG meeting weather industry demand for quality and quantity of textual weather forecasts. In *Proceedings of the 8th International Natural Language Generation Conference (INLG)*, pages 1–5.

Somayajulu G Sripada, Ehud Reiter, Ian Davy, and Kristian Nilssen. 2004. Lessons from deploying NLG technology for marine weather forecast text generation. In *Proceedings of the 16th European Conference on Artificial Intelligence*, pages 760–764.

M. Theune, E. Klabbers, J. Odijk, J.R. de Pijper, and E. Krahmer. 2001. From Data to Speech: A General Approach. *Natural Language Engineering*, 7(1):47–86.

Minh Tien, François Portet, and Cyril Labbé. 2015. Hypertext Summarization for Hotel Review.

The use of rating and Likert scales in Natural Language Generation human evaluation tasks: A review and some recommendations

Jacopo Amidei and **Paul Piwek** and **Alistair Willis**
School of Computing and Communications
The Open University
Milton Keynes, UK
{jacopo.amidei, paul.piwek, alistair.willis}@open.ac.uk

Abstract

Rating and Likert scales are widely used in evaluation experiments to measure the quality of Natural Language Generation (NLG) systems. We review the use of rating and Likert scales for NLG evaluation tasks published in NLG specialized conferences over the last ten years (135 papers in total). Our analysis brings to light a number of deviations from good practice in their use. We conclude with some recommendations about the use of such scales. Our aim is to encourage the appropriate use of evaluation methodologies in the NLG community.

1 Introduction

Rating and Likert scales are popular tools used in surveys to estimate feeling, opinions or attitudes of responders. Although both instruments are widely used, their nature and their appropriate statistical analysis remain a matter of controversy. In particular, it can be controversial whether rating and Likert scales should be considered as ordinal or interval scales; see for example Knapp (1990), Jamieson (2004), Pell (2005), Carifio et al. (2008), Norman (2010) and Sullivan and Artino (2013). However, this distinction is of capital importance because it determines whether the statistical tool to be used on the collected data is parametric or nonparametric. Guidelines and good practice descriptions for the use and analysis of rating and Likert scales have been developed; see for example Knapp (1990), Kuzon et al. (1996), Pell (2005), Carifio et al. (2008), De Winter and Dodou (2010), Sullivan and Artino (2013), Harpe (2015), Joshi et al. (2015) and Johnson and Morgan (2016).

For this paper we analysed 135 papers published in NLG specialist conferences.[1] Our anal-

ysis brings to light common deviations from good practice in the use of rating and Likert scales. The aim of the present paper is to enhance awareness about the use of these scales in the NLG community. Indeed, both rating and Likert scales are widely used in evaluation experiments to measure the quality of NLG systems.

2 Related work

Our paper follows the path started by Robertson (2012), which highlights deviations from statistical good practice in the area of Human Computer Interaction (HCI) and computer science education.

Regarding the basic statistics concepts and statistical analyses we refer to Witte and Witte (2017) and Johnson and Morgan (2016). A detailed description of Likert scales and their analysis is given in Joshi et al. (2015). Regarding the recommendations on the use of rating and Likert scales we refer to Knapp (1990), Kuzon et al. (1996), Pell (2005), Carifio et al. (2008), De Winter and Dodou (2010), Sullivan and Artino (2013), Harpe (2015), Joshi et al. (2015), Johnson and Morgan (2016).

A complete list of the papers we examined can be found via the following link https://bit.ly/2lKL516.

3 Rating and Likert scales

In this section we use illustrative examples to underline the differences between rating and Likert scales. We use the term *scale* with the following two meanings:

- Given a statement, the term *scale* is the group of points making up the options offered to respondents. We refer to the combination of the statement and the scale as an *item*.

- In the case of an aggregate scale[2], such as the

---

[1] Further information about the paper selection can be found in the supplementary material via the following link https://bit.ly/2lKL516.

[2] An aggregate or summated scale is a set of rating scales.

Proceedings of The 12th International Conference on Natural Language Generation, pages 397–402,
Tokyo, Japan, 28 Oct - 1 Nov, 2019. ©2019 Association for Computational Linguistics

Likert scale, we use the term *scale* to indicate a collection of items.

Rating scales: Rating scales are items used in surveys to estimate feeling, opinions or attitudes of responders. The data collected through a rating scale can be interpreted both as ordinal and interval. A rating scale is composed of an n-point scale. Scales with 3, 5, 7, 10 or 11 points are used most often. Rating scales can be both numerical and verbal.

In a *numerical rating scale*, a number is associated with each point. A variation of a numerical scale uses label words at the extreme values and leaves the intermediate values with a numerical label, as for example shown in Figure 1. A rat-

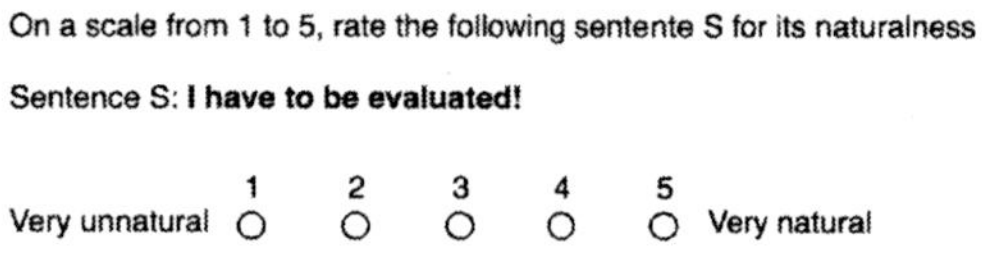

Figure 1: Example of a numerical rating scale.

ing scale that uses words as labels for the points is named a *graphic rating scale*[3]. An example of this kind of rating scale is pictured in Figure 2. Some-

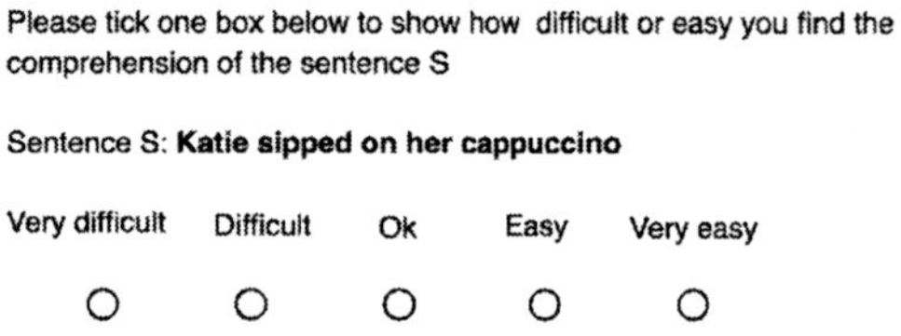

Figure 2: Example of a graphic rating scale.

times the points of a graphic rating scale can also be labelled with numbers. Another sort of rating scale is the *comparative rating scale*. This kind of scale is used to ask respondents to answer a question in terms of a comparison. An example of a comparative rating scale is given in Figure 3.

Likert scale: A Likert scale is an aggregate scale. The items that make a Likert scale are

---

In other words, it is a composite of items which are summed or averaged all together to get an overall positive or negative orientation towards the object under examination in the survey.

[3]Sometimes a graphic rating scale is called *Likert item* or *Likert-style scale*. However, Likert items and Likert-style scale are particular cases of graphic rating scales.

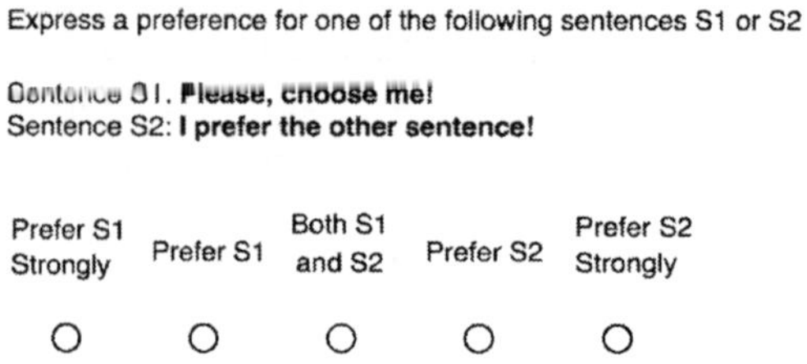

Figure 3: Example of a comparative rating scale.

graphic rating scales. In this context, each graphic rating scale is called a *Likert item*. Likert scales are usually expressed in terms of agreement and disagreement. An example of a Likert scale is shown in Figure 4. The items that make a Lik-

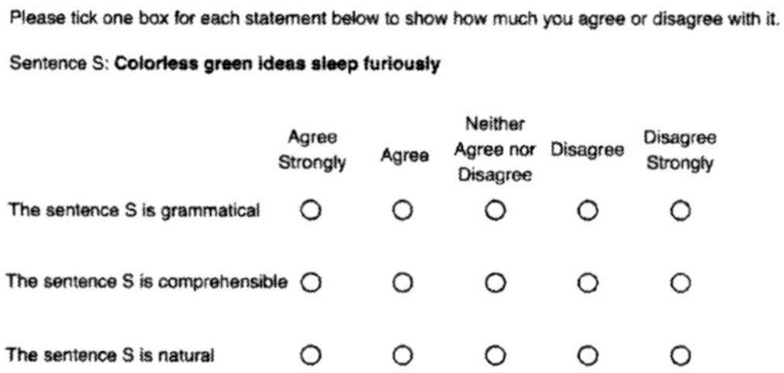

Figure 4: Likert scale example.

ert scales are designed to collectively capture the phenomenon under analysis. Accordingly, they shouldn't be considered in isolation and they should be summed or averaged to produce a total score. However, individual items by themselves are often considered as a single scale. Because of this ambivalent use of the Likert scale and its items, the nature of the Likert scale is highly controversial. Researchers are split between who consider it an interval scale and those who consider it an ordinal scale; see for example Jamieson (2004), Pell (2005), Norman (2010).

The confusion generated by the ambivalent use of the Likert scale and its items is well illustrated and explained in Joshi et al. (2015), where an image similar to Figure 5 is introduced. Likert scales are built in such a way that respondents express their level of agreement or disagreement with the sentences expressed by the Likert items. Because all the items are presented all together and with the same point labels, it is assumed that each respondent gives the same interpretation to the answer points – that is, as suggested by Likert, the

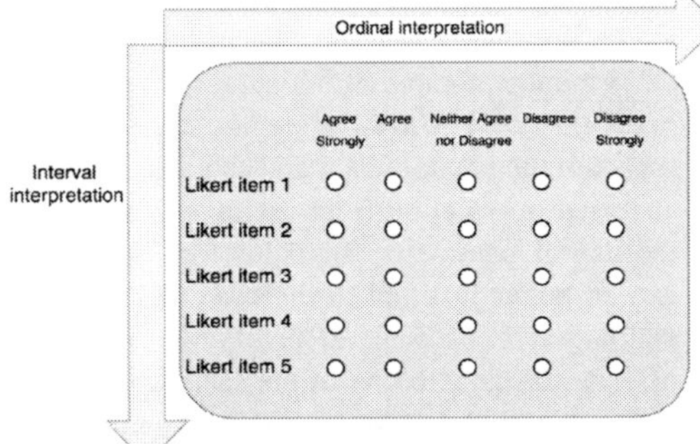

Figure 5: Likert scale interpretations.

distances between the points in the scale can be considered equal.[4] This assumption licenses use of the scale as an interval scale. Consequently, adding or averaging the items annotated by the same respondent is justified. This raises the interval interpretation, depicted by the vertical arrow of Figure 5.

Otherwise, an item-by-item analysis – that is a separate analysis of a single item extracted from an aggregate scale – cannot justify the assumption that the difference between adjacent points is equal. Indeed, we cannot assume that different respondents perceive the difference between adjacent label points as being of equal distance. The difference between "agree" and "strongly agree" can be perceived differently from one respondent to another. Consequently, the addition or the average of the items extracted from an aggregate scale is not justified. In such cases, the median or mode can be used as the measure of central tendency. This follows the ordinal interpretation, depicted by the horizontal arrow of Figure 5.

Unfortunately, in many cases there is not a clear understanding of the difference between the horizontal and the vertical direction of the aggregate scale. It is common to see item-by-item analysis (that is the horizontal direction) that makes use of parametric statistics without a justification of this choice. Indeed, as shown in Section 4, the interpretation of Likert items as interval scales has become a common practice. This particularly applies to the use of the mean for measuring the central tendency for the analysis of Likert items.

---

[4]Some authors, for example Jamieson (2004), do not accept such an assumption and do not consider the points as equally distant. In this case the Likert scales themselves, and not only the Likert items, are considered ordinal.

4 The use of rating and Likert scales in NLG evaluation tasks

In this section we present our analysis of 135 NLG papers.

First of all, it is important to note that several papers report the evaluation study in a very succinct manner that makes it difficult to understand and interpret the authors' conclusions.

From this observation follow two recommendations. First, researchers should be careful in the way they report the evaluation study. For instance, readers can benefit from examples and graphical and/or tabular presentation of data. Second, for the purpose of reproducibility, it is essential that evaluation guidelines and data are shared.

# Papers	# Rating	# Likert	# Others
135	48	37	50

Table 1: *# Papers*: Number of papers used in the study. *# rating*: Number of papers that use rating scales. *# Likert*: Number of papers that use Likert scales. *# Others*: Number of papers that use different kinds of human evaluation methodologies.

Table 1 shows that 63% of the papers used either a rating scale or a Likert scale. Between these papers, rating scales are used 56% of the time whereas Likert scales 44% of the time.

Because the majority of the papers we analysed report the evaluation study in an approximate manner, it is impossible to provide a statistic for the type of rating or Likert scale used. We found that in 64 papers, either it was not stated whether the rating or Likert scale was used, or the rating or Likert scale name used was imprecise. However, we can go as far as to say that the graphic scales and Likert item are the preferred rating scales used.

We found that the favourite scale dimension both for rating and Likert scales was the 5-point scale. Indeed, 31 papers use 5-point rating scales, and 23 papers use 5-point Likert scales.

Table 2 shows how the rating or Likert scales are interpreted. 16% of rating scales are interpreted as ordinal, whereas the 77% are interpreted as interval.[5] Likewise 16% of Likert scales are interpreted as ordinal, whereas the 84% are interpreted as interval. Table 2 shows the predom-

---

[5]7% of the papers do not give enough information to determine the interpretation used.

	Rating	Likert
Ordinal	8	6
Interval	37	31
(?)	3	0

Table 2: Number of rating and Likert scales which are considered Ordinal or Interval scales. The symbol (?) means we cannot determine the scale interpretation from the information given in the paper. We classified scales as ordinal or interval based on the statistic that was reported in the paper, i.e., whether the statistic used was parametric or nonparametric.

inant use of parametric statistics over nonparametric statistics in the papers we analysed.

Between the 68 papers (37 rating and 31 Likert) that interpret the data as interval, only 3 papers justify such an interpretation (2 rating and 1 Likert).

Regarding the use of Likert scales, we note that only one paper uses the Likert scale suitably, that is as an aggregate scale. All the other papers used Likert scales in order to perform item-by-item analysis.

For statistical significance testing, we found that ANOVA and the t-test are the preferred parametric statistics. Among nonparametric statistics the most commonly used are χ^2 and the Mann-Whitney U test.

5 Conclusion

From our analysis the following two main deviations from good practice in the use of rating and Likert scales in NLG evaluation tasks emerge:

1. Many studies confuse Likert scales and Likert items. Often Likert scales are used for an item-by-item analysis.

2. Scales are often analysed with parametric statistics without a justification.[6]

Regarding 1: Aggregate scales such as Likert scales are created to estimate the overall opinion of a responder about some phenomenon by the use of aggregate items. Indeed, the design of a Likert scale is aimed at reaching an overall opinion by analysing together the answers given by the responder about the single items. Accordingly, items extracted from an aggregate scale reveal one aspect of the phenomenon and can lose meaning if analysed in isolation from the other items. Also, the use of parametric statistics for Likert scales can be better justified in the case of item aggregation. It is difficult to justify the assumption of equal distance between the scale points across different responders when doing an item-by-item analysis. If researchers are interested in performing parametric statistics using Likert items, or better graphic rating scales, we refer to Harpe (2015) for some recommendations. It is important to decide the scale as part of the experimental design and not at the time of analysis[7]. In case one Likert scale is used, because the items are considered as pieces of a bigger picture, it is important to check their internal consistency. To this end Cronbach's α[8], Revelle's β, McDonald's ω_h, ω_{Total} or Kuder-Richardson 20 can be used. A review of different measures of internal consistency can be found in Revelle and Zinbarg (2009) and McNeish (2018).

Finally, it is important to use appropriate language to avoid confusion and allow the readers to form a better understanding of the results. For example, one should avoid using the term Likert scale to refer to a graphic rating scale or Likert items, especially if Likert items are analysed in isolation.

Regarding 2: Although there is no right way to interpret rating and aggregate scales, such as Likert scales, it is good practice to justify the scale interpretation and the choice of the statistic used in their analysis. As proved by previous studies, see for example Norman (2010), the use of parametric statistics is quite robust with ordinal data. Generally, is not clear whether authors are aware of the controversy about scale interpretations, and many do not provide an argument for using one interpretation rather than another.

Due to the fact that using parametric statistics for ordinal data can lead to unwanted conse-

---

[6]We note that the use of parametric statistics without a justification is also present for evaluation methodologies other than rating and Likert scales (for instance ranking experiments). This is in general true also for nonparametric statistics. Although nonparametric methods do not require assumptions about the distribution of the population probability, they do require assumptions such as randomness and independence of the samples. This suggests that in general researchers have to pay more attention to the statistics use in their evaluation studies.

[7]Decisions about the levels of measurement and the choice of analysis method should be made at the design stage (for example, whether to use ordinal or interval scale, or by using descriptive or inferential statistics). This way, the researchers can create a survey compatible with the chosen methodology.

[8]Although the use of Cronbach's α was recently criticized in McNeish (2018).

quences, sometimes substantial and sometimes inconsequential, the use of parametric statistics on data which are not interval should be clearly justified. Liddell and Kruschke (2018) present several problematic cases where parametric statistic were used for ordinal data. Liddell and Kruschke, for instance, discuss examples with low correct detection rates, risk of inflated Type I and Type II error rates and distorted effect size estimates. The first problem reduces statistical power. The second can result in a false positive conclusion or false negative conclusion.[9] Finally, the last problem can lead to either overestimating or underestimating the size of the difference between two groups.

Without a preliminary verification of the parametric statistic assumptions, the use of such a statistic is controversial. Although parametric statistics allow more powerful and nuanced data analyses than nonparametric statistics, sometimes the use of nonparametric statistics is enough. If the data collected fails to satisfy the conditions required from the parametric statistic, it does not mean that the data lost statistical importance. Indeed, the use of percentages or central tendency measures such as mode or median as well as statistical significance such as Mann-Whitney U Test, Kruskal-Wallis, χ^2 etc., can give a good picture of the generative abilities of a NLG system. Furthermore, recent advances in statistics have introduced new options for ordinal data which are worth to be taken into account, for example ordinal regression models (Bürkner and Vuorre, 2019) or generalized mixed effect models (Faraway, 2016) which are able to work with several different data distributions.

To our knowledge, there is currently a lack of robustness studies in the NLG area. Such studies would be greatly valuable for the discussion of the use of parametric and nonparametric statistics as well as the use of ordinal regression models and generalized mixed effect models.

Acknowledgments

We warmly thanks the anonymous reviewers for their helpful suggestions.

---

[9]Type I error is the rejection of the null hypothesis when it is true. Type II error is the failure to reject the null hypothesis when it is false.

References

P. C. Bürkner and M. Vuorre. 2019. Ordinal regression models in psychology: a tutorial. *Advances in Methods and Practices in Psychological Science*, 2(1):77–101.

L. Carifio, R. Perla, and P. Giraux. 2008. Resolving the 50-year debate around using and misusing likert scales. *Med Educ.*, 42(12):1150–1152.

J. CF De Winter and D. Dodou. 2010. Five-point likert items: t test versus mann-whitney-wilcoxon. *Practical Assessment, Research & Evaluation*, 15(11):1–12.

J. J. Faraway. 2016. *Extending the linear model with R: generalized linear, mixed effects and nonparametric regression models*. Chapman and Hall/CRC, Boca Raton, FL.

S. E. Harpe. 2015. How to analyze likert and other rating scale data. *Currents in Pharmacy Teaching and Learning*, 7(6):836–850.

S. Jamieson. 2004. Likert scales: how to (ab)use them. *Med Educ.*, 38(12):1217–1218.

R. L. Johnson and G. B. Morgan. 2016. *Survey Scales. A Guide to Development, Analysis, and Reporting*. The Guilford Press, New York, NY.

A. Joshi, S. Kale, S. Chandel, and D. K. Pal. 2015. Likert scale: Explored and explained. *British Journal of Applied Science & Technology*, 7(4):396–403.

T. R. Knapp. 1990. Treating ordinal scales as interval scales: an attempt to resolve the controversy. *Nurs Res.*, 39:121–123.

W. Kuzon, M. Urbanchek, and S. McCabe. 1996. The seven deadly sins of statistical analysis. *Annals of plastic surgery*, 37:265–272.

T. M. Liddell and J. K. Kruschke. 2018. Analyzing ordinal data with metric models: What could possibly go wrong? *Journal of Experimental Social Psychology*, 79:328–348.

R. Likert. A technique for the measurement of attitudes. *Archives of Psychology*, 22:1–55.

D. McNeish. 2018. Thanks coefficient alpha, well take it from here. *Psychological Methods*, 23(3):412.

G. Norman. 2010. Likert scales, levels of measurement and the "laws" of statistics. *Adv Health Sci Educ Theory Pract.*, 15(10):625–632.

G. Pell. 2005. Uses and misuses of likert scales. *Med Educ.*, 39(9):970.

W. Revelle and R. E. Zinbarg. 2009. Coefficients alpha, beta, omega, and the glb: Comments on sijtsma. *Psychometrika*, 74(1):145.

J. Robertson. 2012. Likert-type scales, statistical methods, and effect sizes. *Commun. ACM*, 55(5):6–7.

G. M. Sullivan and A. R. Artino. 2013. Analyzing and interpreting data from likert-type scales. *Journal of Graduate Medical Education*, pages 541–542.

R. S. Witte and J. S. Witte. 2017. *Statistics, Eleventh Edition*. John Wiley & Sons, Inc., LaVergne, Tennessee, USA.

A complete list of the papers we examined can be found via the following link `https://bit.ly/21KL516`.

On task effects in NLG corpus elicitation:
A replication study using mixed effects modeling

Emiel van Miltenburg   **Merel van de Kerkhof**
Ruud Koolen   **Martijn Goudbeek**   **Emiel Krahmer**
Tilburg center for Cognition and Communication (TiCC), Tilburg University

C.W.J.vanMiltenburg@uvt.nl   merelvdkerkhof@hotmail.com
R.M.F.Koolen@uvt.nl   M.B.Goudbeek@uvt.nl   E.J.Krahmer@uvt.nl

Abstract

Task effects in NLG corpus elicitation recently started to receive more attention, but are usually not modeled statistically. We present a controlled replication of the study by Van Miltenburg et al. (2018b), contrasting spoken with written descriptions. We collected additional written Dutch descriptions to supplement the spoken data from the DIDEC corpus, and analyzed the descriptions using mixed effects modeling to account for variation between participants and items. Our results show that the effects of modality largely disappear in a controlled setting.

1 Introduction

Natural Language Generation (NLG) systems are increasingly trained on the basis of datasets of human-produced examples, for example in the recent E2E-challenge (Dušek et al., 2018), or in automatic image description (Bernardi et al., 2016). The quality of the system output depends to a large extent on the quality of the data that is used to train the system, which in turn depends on the way that data is collected. A recent trend in NLG is to study task effects in the creation of corpora for natural language generation (Baltaretu and Castro Ferreira, 2016; van Miltenburg et al., 2017; Ilinykh et al., 2018). However, there does not seem to be an established methodology to investigate whether differences in task design lead to any significant differences in the output. This paper uses a tightly controlled approach to study task effects in NLG.

As a case study, we look at the effects of modality in an image description task. In their exploratory study, Van Miltenburg et al. (2018b) found that spoken and written descriptions differ in several ways, with the main result being that speakers have a greater tendency to show themselves through the use of 'egocentric language' (Akinnaso, 1982). The problem with this study is that it did not use

matched corpora (containing exactly the same images) and their experiment did not control for the demographics of the participants. Therefore this paper presents a controlled replication of the study by Van Miltenburg et al. (2018b), to see if its findings are robust.

We carried out a between-subjects study where participants were assigned either to the SPOKEN or the WRITTEN condition. All participants were asked to describe the same images. For the former condition, we used the data from the Dutch Image Description and Eye-tracking Corpus (DIDEC; van Miltenburg et al. 2018a). For the latter condition, we collected additional data using a similar sample of participants. We analyzed the effects of modality on the elicited descriptions using mixed-effects models, controlling for variation in participants and images used to elicit the descriptions. We only found a significant effect for prepositions (used more in written descriptions); other effects disappear in a controlled setting.

This paper contributes to our understanding of the linguistic aspects of image descriptions (e.g., Ferraro et al. 2015; van Miltenburg et al. 2016; Alikhani and Stone 2019). Still, the main takeaway from our study is methodological: for studying task effects in elicitation tasks, we should control for individual variation and the effects of the stimuli used in the experiment. We hope that this study can serve as an example for the use of mixed effects modeling in natural language generation.[1]

2 The original study

Van Miltenburg et al. (2018b) aimed to identify

---

[1] All our code and data is publicly available online. The interface for the written descriptions is available through: https://github.com/evanmiltenburg/DIDEC-written. The data analysis is available through: https://github.com/evanmiltenburg/SpokenWritten-INLG More information on the DIDEC website.

Feature	Terms
Consciousness-of-projection	*Lijkt, waarschijnlijk, misschien, duidelijk, mogelijk, zeker, vermoedelijk, eigenlijk*
Negations	*Geen, niet, niemand, nergens, noch, nooit, niets*
Positive allness	*Alle, elke, iedere, iedereen*
Pseudo-quantifiers	*Veel, vele, weinig, enkele, een paar, een hoop, grote hoeveelheid, kleine hoeveelheid*
Self-reference	*Ik, me, mij*

Table 1: Terms that were used for each feature. We added *vermoedelijk* ('presumably'), and *eigenlijk* ('actually').

differences between spoken and written image descriptions in both English and Dutch. Since our replication is carried out in Dutch, we will focus on the Dutch part of the original experiment.

Data. For the written sample, Van Miltenburg et al. used crowdsourced Dutch descriptions for the Flickr30K validation split (1000 images, 5 descriptions per image, collected by van Miltenburg et al. 2017). For the spoken descriptions, they used the Dutch Image Description and Eye-tracking Corpus (DIDEC; van Miltenburg et al. 2018a). This dataset contains 307 different images from the MS COCO dataset, with 14–16 spoken descriptions per image. The authors measured the following kinds of dependent variables:

LENGTH: Token length (in syllables or in characters), description length (in tokens). Both are measured after tokenizing the text.

PART-OF-SPEECH: (Attributive) adjectives, adverbs, prepositions. These are detected using a part-of-speech tagger (SpaCy 2.0.4).

SEMANTIC CATEGORIES: negations (*no, not*), pseudo-quantifiers (*few, lots*), consciousness-of-projection terms (*seem, appear, maybe*, positive allness terms (*all, every*), and self-reference terms (*I, me, my*) are detected by matching word tokens with a word list. Table 1 provides an overview.

OTHER: Propositional Information Density (PID; Turner and Greene 1977), which corresponds to the average number of propositional ideas per word in a text, and is computed through an external tool (Marckx, 2017). Mean-segmental type-token ratio (MSTTR; Johnson 1944), which is a measure of diversity (the average number of types per segment).

Findings. Van Miltenburg et al. (2018b) found no consistent differences between spoken and written descriptions for token length, MSTTR, PID, or the use of adjectives or prepositions. The authors did find that spoken descriptions are longer, and contain more adverbs, negations, positive allness terms, self-reference terms, pseudo-quantifiers, and consciousness-of-projection terms. This led them to conclude that speakers have a greater tendency to show themselves through the use of 'egocentric language' (Akinnaso, 1982). What the authors mean by this is that spoken descriptions are not just neutral and detached, but that they also tend to communicate something about the observer who generated the description. For example, if a participant says that some entity X *looks like* or *might be* a sheep (i.e., describing the entity using consciousness-of-projection terms), then their description also signals their uncertainty about whether X is a sheep or not. Written descriptions typically avoid this kind of language (Akinnaso, 1982).

Limitations. The original study did not control for the content of the images, or for the demographics of the participants. Furthermore, it did not control for the setting: the DIDEC dataset was collected in a laboratory setting, whereas the written sample was collected through a crowdsourcing task. This makes it hard to determine whether the results were actually due to the difference in modularity, and not due to any other difference. Hence we set out to provide a controlled replication.

3 The current study

The current study was set up to provide a more controlled comparison between spoken and written image descriptions. We collected written descriptions for the images from the Dutch Image Description and Eye-tracking Corpus, so that we could compare these written descriptions to the existing spoken data. We used a different sample of participants from the exact same population (the Tilburg University participant pool) to generate the descriptions, so that we could isolate the effect of modality on the generated descriptions.

Participants. Our participants were 48 Dutch students (33 women, 15 men, with a mean age of 21.6) who earned course credits for their participation. Our study followed standard ethical procedures. We obtained IRB approval for this study, and all participants were asked for their informed consent. Participants were allowed to quit the experiment at any stage and still earn credits.

Materials. We used the same 307 images (originally from MS COCO) that were used for the creation of the DIDEC dataset. In the original task, participants provided spoken descriptions for 102 or 103 images in one session. However, written language is typically slower to produce than spoken language; data from Van Miltenburg et al. (2017) shows that the median time for crowdworkers to write 5 descriptions is 294 seconds. Extrapolating from this, we expect that it would take 49 minutes to write descriptions for 50 images. To ensure that participants are able to finish the experiment within one hour (and to avoid fatigue), we shortened the lists to 51 or 52 images.

Design. We used a single-factor (modality) between-subjects design, where the participants who took part in the DIDEC study serve as the SPOKEN group, and we collect additional responses for the WRITTEN condition. Because both sets of participants are sampled from the same population, we can compare their descriptions for the same images to examine the effect of modality. However, we do note that a within-subjects design would have more statistical power, since we would also have information about the effects of modality for each participant.[2] Our choice for a between-subjects design was motivated by economic reasons: it would have been very time-consuming to build a new corpus of spoken image descriptions.

Procedure. The elicitation task is similar to the one carried out by Van Miltenburg et al. (2018a) for the DIDEC dataset. We implemented the task using Qualtrics,[3] so as to have a simple web interface. The participants sat in a computer room with 20 computers. They were not allowed to communicate with each other. After reading the instructions and signing the consent form, participants first carried out a practice trial, after which they could ask clarification questions. For the main task, participants were presented with a list of images, and asked to describe each of the images in one short but complete sentence.

Dependent variables. Our dependent variables are almost the same as in the original study; we ignore MSTTR for reasons of space.[4] We modified

---

	Spoken	Written
Number of participants	45	48
Number of descriptions	4604	2547
Descriptions per image	14–16	7–9

Table 2: General statistics for the two datasets. Spoken data comes from the DIDEC dataset (van Miltenburg et al., 2018a), written data was collected for this paper.

the original (public) scripts to prepare the results for our analysis. Whereas the original study reported average results over the aggregated data (per 1000 tokens or per description), we measure the variables for each individual description.

4 Statistical analysis

In addition to the effects of modality (SPOKEN and WRITTEN), our observations (the individual descriptions) are influenced by two other factors; namely PARTICIPANT and IMAGE. To capture the random effects of both participants and images, we use a linear mixed effect model (Baayen et al. 2008; see Winter 2013 for a tutorial). We used the `lme4` package (Bates et al., 2015) to build our models in R (R Core Team, 2017) and the `lmertest` package (Kuznetsova et al., 2017) to provide p-values for linear mixed effect models. We created a separate model for each dependent variable and assessed the effect of modality for significance.[5] When significant, the null hypothesis of no difference between the means of the written and spoken condition is rejected (implying there is a task effect). For each model, we specify the relevant type of distribution. We model sentence length, token length, and propositional idea density as continuous data, and assume a standard Gaussian distribution. The other variables correspond to count data, modeled using the Poisson distribution (through the `glmer` function).

5 Results

We collected 2457 descriptions from 48 participants. Table 2 provides general statistics about the spoken and written descriptions. Descriptive statistics are provided in Table 3. Compared to the spoken descriptions, written descriptions are longer, have longer tokens, and (with the exception

---

[2]This is the set-up of Drieman (1962), who asked participants to describe different paintings using either spoken or written language. However, they did not use mixed effects models, and could not investigate stimulus effects.

[3]An online survey platform: https://www.qualtrics.com

[4]MSTTR should be analyzed using a t-test, since we cannot analyze diversity at the item level. We can only aggregate the descriptions for each participant, compute the MSTTR

scores (one per participant) and see whether there is a significant difference in the scores between the two conditions.

[5]We use the traditional significance level of $\alpha = 0.05$, and correct for multiple comparisons using the Bonferroni method: $\alpha' = 1 - (1 - \alpha)^{1/k}$. With k=12 models, α=0.00427.

#	Variable	Expectation	μ_{spoken}	μ_{diff}	Data type	β_{written}	SE	Statistic	p
1.	Sentence length	s>w	12.621	+2.632	Continuous	2.630	0.993	t: 2.648	0.010
2.	Token length (characters)	s=w	4.679	+0.003	Continuous	0.005	0.046	t: 0.111	0.912
3.	Token length (syllables)	s=w	1.519	+0.001	Continuous	0.001	0.014	t: 0.087	0.931
4.	Propositional idea density	s=w	0.443	+0.003	Continuous	0.002	0.006	t: 0.367	0.714
5.	Attributive adjectives	s=w	0.495	+0.071	Count	0.151	0.105	z: 1.434	0.152
6.	Adverbs	s>w	0.648	+0.070	Count	0.092	0.127	z: 0.726	0.468
7.	Prepositions	s=w	1.810	+0.821	Count	0.260	0.069	z: 3.768	<0.001
8.	Negations	s>w	0.010	+0.005	Count	0.438	0.288	z: 1.520	0.128
9.	Pseudo-quantifiers	s>w	0.050	+0.024	Count	0.459	0.201	z: 2.288	0.022
10.	Consciousness-of-projection	s>w	0.031	−0.018	Count	−0.852	0.364	z: −2.339	0.019
11.	Self-reference	s>w	0.145	+0.072	Binary	−2.291	1.010	z: −2.268	0.023
12.	Positive allness	s>w	0.004	+0.001	Binary			Failed to converge.	

Table 3: All models with their dependent variables, whether we expect a difference (less/greater than: difference, equals: no difference), the mean results for the spoken descriptions, difference between written and spoken descriptions (w–s), the data type used in our analysis, the fixed effect (β) of the written modality on the outcome, the standard error, statistic, and the p-value for the model.

of consciousness-of-projection terms) contain more terms from each category. The direction of these differences is surprising, because they are opposite to our expectations (again with the exception of consciousness-of-projection terms). For example, we expected spoken descriptions to be longer than written ones, indicated as 's>w' in Table 3.

To assess whether these observed differences generalize outside of this particular dataset, we assessed their statistical significance using the linear mixed effect models described earlier.

Model convergence. Initially, the models for token length (syllables), self-reference, and allness terms failed to converge (i.e. find stable estimates of the effects). We addressed this issue in two ways: 1. For the token length model, we used a different optimizer (bobyqa); 2. For self-reference and allness terms, we modeled the presence or absence of the relevant terms with a binomial distribution. After this, only the model for positive allness failed to converge; likely because only 30 out of 7,056 descriptions contained positive allness terms —not enough positive examples.

Main results. The last four columns of Table 3 show the effect of modality on the dependent variables (full models are in the supplementary materials). We only found a significant effect of modality on the use of prepositions: written descriptions use more prepositions than spoken ones.

We found no significant effect of modality on any of the other dependent variables. (Note that this is partly due to the Bonferroni correction we applied earlier. If we had not corrected for multiple comparisons, we would have judged the models for sentence length, pseudo-quantifiers, consciousness-of-projection terms, and self-reference terms to be significant at $\alpha = 0.05$.) This means that while those models may capture general tendencies in the data, there are no consistent differences between spoken and written language for these variables.

Model interpretation. Although most of our analyses do not show significant differences, we can still interpret the way they capture the overall distribution of the data. The strongest non-significant effect is observed for sentence length; on average, written descriptions are β=2.6 words longer than spoken ones.

6 Discussion

We will now briefly summarize and explain our results, before discussing their implications.

6.1 Summary of the results

We aimed to replicate the findings by van Miltenburg et al. (2018b), who looked at modality effects in the elicitation of NLG corpus data. Like the original authors, we found no significant difference for token length, PID, or the use of adjectives. While Van Miltenburg et al. did not find a consistent difference in the use of prepositions for both English and Dutch prepositions, we replicate their finding that written Dutch descriptions contain more prepositions than spoken ones. This is in line with earlier findings by Drieman (1962) and Chafe and Danielewicz (1987).

All other effects disappear in a controlled setting. This is not to say that there is no effect of modality, but that the effect is smaller than can be detected with these variables and this elicitation method. We are unsure how the original effects emerged, but a likely explanation lies in the differences between the datasets used in the original study (which contain different images, and were collected in a different setting, with less comparable participants). This shows the importance of setting up a controlled study, where such differences are minimized, and we can isolate the factor that we are interested in (here: modality).

6.2 Rarity and the need for guidelines

One other factor contributing to the difficulty of finding statistically significant effects for modality is that many of the phenomena under investigation are low-frequent. Positive allness terms are the most extreme case, occurring in 0.4% of all spoken descriptions. But attributive adjectives, negations, pseudo-quantifiers, consciousness-of-projection terms, and self-reference terms also occur in less than half of the spoken descriptions.

It appears that only changing the modality is not enough to observe a (strong) task effect. If we want participants to produce different kinds of descriptions, they will probably need guidelines, with explicit instructions to change their behavior. But this raises the next issue: what should those guidelines look like?

6.3 Usefulness of different modalities

One of the reasons cited by van Miltenburg et al. (2018b) to look at spoken image descriptions is that they might provide more natural examples of how people generally talk about images. After all: speech is a more primary form of language (cf. Biber 1988, Chapter 1). Their naturalness would make spoken descriptions more suitable for training voice-operated image description systems.

Our results show that changing the modality of the elicitation task does not necessarily yield qualitatively different descriptions, let alone more natural descriptions. Importantly, our study does not say anything about the *usefulness* of typical features of spoken language. User studies may still find that emulating the spoken style (as presented in the literature) positively/negatively affects users' appreciation of the output. After establishing desirable properties that image descriptions should have, we can define guidelines for what image descriptions should look like. We may then be able to alter the elicitation task in such a way that participants provide suitable descriptions. Here, the question arises: how do you know whether the elicitation task is successful? This brings us to our next point.

6.4 Statistics as a manipulation check

Our failure to replicate the effects of modality for all variables (except the use of prepositions) suggests that (at least for those other variables) it does not matter in which modality you collect the descriptions; they will look more or less the same. In other words, our study served as a *manipulation check*, to see if the manipulation (changing the modality of the elicitation task) had the desired effect (changing the style of the descriptions). In this case, the manipulation turned out to be unsuccessful. We hope that our study provides a good example for showing (or refuting) the robustness of different task effects in NLG. Note that, for a check like this to be possible, one needs to establish a metric or set of metrics that can be used to quantify the phenomenon that you're interested in.

7 Conclusion

We presented a controlled study to evaluate task effects in an NLG elicitation task, namely image description. We used mixed effects models to filter out the effects of participants and individual stimuli. Using these models, we learned that modality alone has a minimal effect on the content of the descriptions. Thus, a stronger manipulation is needed to obtain different kinds of descriptions. The methodology used in this paper is suitable for running pilot studies to check whether task manipulations are successful. We hope that future studies will adopt this methodology, so as to ensure fruitful data collection.

8 Acknowledgments

This study is based on the MA thesis of the second author. The design was approved by the Research Ethics and Data Management Committee at Tilburg University, reference: REC #2018/56.

References

F Niyi Akinnaso. 1982. On the differences between spoken and written language. *Language and speech*, 25(2):97–125.

Malihe Alikhani and Matthew Stone. 2019. "caption" as a coherence relation: Evidence and implications. In *Proceedings of the Second Workshop on Shortcomings in Vision and Language*, pages 58–67, Minneapolis, Minnesota. Association for Computational Linguistics.

R Harald Baayen, Douglas J Davidson, and Douglas M Bates. 2008. Mixed-effects modeling with crossed random effects for subjects and items. *Journal of memory and language*, 59(4):390–412.

Adriana Baltaretu and Thiago Castro Ferreira. 2016. Task demands and individual variation in referring expressions. In *Proceedings of the 9th International Natural Language Generation conference*, pages 89–93, Edinburgh, UK. Association for Computational Linguistics.

Douglas Bates, Martin Mächler, Ben Bolker, and Steve Walker. 2015. Fitting linear mixed-effects models using lme4. *Journal of Statistical Software*, 67(1):1–48.

Raffaella Bernardi, Ruket Cakici, Desmond Elliott, Aykut Erdem, Erkut Erdem, Nazli Ikizler-Cinbis, Frank Keller, Adrian Muscat, and Barbara Plank. 2016. Automatic description generation from images: A survey of models, datasets, and evaluation measures. *Journal of Artificial Intelligence Research*, 55:409–442.

Douglas Biber. 1988. *Variation across speech and writing*. Cambridge University Press.

Wallace Chafe and Jane Danielewicz. 1987. Properties of spoken and written language. In R. Horowitz and F.J. Samuels, editors, *Comprehending oral and written language*. New York: Academic Press.

Gerard HJ Drieman. 1962. Differences between written and spoken language: An exploratory study, I. quantitative approach. *Acta Psychologica*, 20:36–57.

Ondřej Dušek, Jekaterina Novikova, and Verena Rieser. 2018. Findings of the E2E NLG challenge. In *Proceedings of the 11th International Conference on Natural Language Generation*, pages 322–328, Tilburg University, The Netherlands. Association for Computational Linguistics.

Francis Ferraro, Nasrin Mostafazadeh, Lucy Vanderwende, Jacob Devlin, Michel Galley, Margaret Mitchell, et al. 2015. A survey of current datasets for vision and language research. In *Proceedings of the 2015 Conference on Empirical Methods in Natural Language Processing*, pages 201–213.

Nikolai Ilinykh, Sina Zarrieß, and David Schlangen. 2018. The task matters: Comparing image captioning and task-based dialogical image description. In *Proceedings of the 11th International Conference on Natural Language Generation*, pages 397–402, Tilburg University, The Netherlands. Association for Computational Linguistics.

Wendell Johnson. 1944. I. a program of research. *Psychological Monographs*, 56(2):1.

Alexandra Kuznetsova, Per B. Brockhoff, and Rune H. B. Christensen. 2017. lmerTest package: Tests in linear mixed effects models. *Journal of Statistical Software*, 82(13):1–26.

Silke Marckx. 2017. Propositional idea density in patients with alzheimer's disease: An exploratory study. Master's thesis, Universiteit Antwerpen.

Emiel van Miltenburg, Desmond Elliott, and Piek Vossen. 2017. Cross-linguistic differences and similarities in image descriptions. In *Proceedings of the 10th International Conference on Natural Language Generation*, pages 21–30, Santiago de Compostela, Spain. Association for Computational Linguistics.

Emiel van Miltenburg, Ákos Kádar, Ruud Koolen, and Emiel Krahmer. 2018a. DIDEC: The Dutch Image Description and Eye-tracking Corpus. In *Proceedings of COLING 2018, the 27th International Conference on Computational Linguistics*. Resource available at https://didec.uvt.nl.

Emiel van Miltenburg, Ruud Koolen, and Emiel Krahmer. 2018b. Varying image description tasks: spoken versus written descriptions. In *Proceedings of the Fifth Workshop on NLP for Similar Languages, Varieties and Dialects (VarDial)*.

Emiel van Miltenburg, Roser Morante, and Desmond Elliott. 2016. Pragmatic factors in image description: The case of negations. In *Proceedings of the 5th Workshop on Vision and Language*, pages 54–59, Berlin, Germany. Association for Computational Linguistics.

R Core Team. 2017. *R: A Language and Environment for Statistical Computing*. R Foundation for Statistical Computing, Vienna, Austria.

Althea Turner and Edith Greene. 1977. *The construction and use of a propositional text base*. Institute for the Study of Intellectual Behavior, University of Colorado Boulder.

Bodo Winter. 2013. Linear models and linear mixed effects models in r with linguistic applications. *arXiv preprint arXiv:1308.5499*.

Procedural Text Generation from a Photo Sequence

Taichi Nishimura[1], Atsushi Hashimoto[2], Shinsuke Mori[3]
[1]Graduate School of Informatics, Kyoto University
[2]OMRON SINIC X Corporation
[3]Academic Center for Computing and Media Studies, Kyoto University
`nishimura.taichi.43x@st.kyoto-u.ac.jp`
`atsushi.hashimoto@sinicx.com`
`forest@i.kyoto-u.ac.jp`

Abstract

Multimedia procedural texts, such as instructions and manuals with pictures, support people to share how-to knowledge. In this paper, we propose a method for generating a procedural text given a photo sequence allowing users to obtain a multimedia procedural text. We propose a single embedding space both for image and text enabling to interconnect them and to select appropriate words to describe a photo. We implemented our method and tested it on cooking instructions, i.e., recipes. Various experimental results showed that our method outperforms standard baselines.

1 Introduction

A multimedia procedural text, e.g. instruction sentences with photos, inspires users to learn a new skill. Some web services, such as Cookpad and Instructables, capitalize on this characteristics allowing users to submit photos or video clips in addition to instruction sentences to explain procedures better. An automatic system outputting instruction sentences given a photo sequence supports authors of such services.

In this paper, we propose a method for generating a procedural text from a photo sequence. As shown in Figure 1, given a photo sequence, it outputs a step consisting of some instruction sentences for each photo. Among various kinds of procedural texts, we take the cooking domain for example because cooking is daily activity and recipe is one of the most familiar procedural texts.

Our task may resemble visual storytelling (Huang et al., 2016) sharing the input. The main difference is, however, that the output of our task is a procedural text that should be concise and concrete allowing its readers to execute it. In cooking domain the output, a recipe consisting of multiple sentences, should have necessary and sufficient foods, tools, and actions in the correct or-

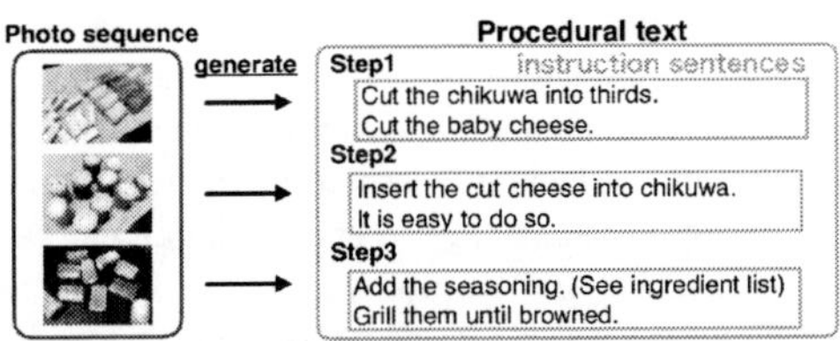

Figure 1: An overview of our task. The input is a photo sequence (left). The task is to output a step consisting of instruction sentences (right) for each photo.

der. For this reason procedural text generation seemed to be difficult and was initially solved by formulating it as a retrieval task (Salvador et al., 2017; Zhu et al., 2019; Chen and Ngo, 2016). Another similar task setting is recipe generation from a photo of the final dish using ingredient predictor (Salvador et al., 2019). This setting may be, however, very difficult or even impossible because a single photo of the final dish does not contain sufficient information for its production procedure.

In this background, we focus on procedural text generation from a photo sequence and, as a solution, we propose to incorporate a retrieval method into a generation model. Our method generates a procedural text in two phases. First given a photo sequence, it retrieves relating steps using a joint embedding model, which has been pre-trained on a large amount of image/step pairs available in the Web. Then it generates word sequences referring to these retrieved steps.

We conducted experiments to evaluate our method in comparison with existing methods in BLEU, ROUGE-L, and CIDEr-D. The results showed the effectiveness of the proposed method. However, as often pointed out, these metrics are not perfect because they ignore importance of each token. Thus we investigated the ratios of correctly verbalized important terms, i.e., foods, tools, and

Proceedings of The 12th International Conference on Natural Language Generation, pages 409–414,
Tokyo, Japan, 28 Oct - 1 Nov, 2019. ©2019 Association for Computational Linguistics

actions in the recipe case. The result showed that
the proposed method verbalizes them more correctly. Some qualitative analyses also suggested
that the proposed method generates a suitable procedural text for a given photo sequence.

2 Related Work

Some researchers have been tackling problems to
generate a procedural text from various inputs.
In cooking domain, Salvador et al. (2019) tried to
generate a recipe from an image of a complete
dish. Bosselut et al. (2018) and Kiddon et al. assumed a title and ingredients as the input. It may
be, however, almost impossible to generate a good
recipe due to lack of information on mesomorphic
states of ingredients. Mori et al. (2014a) generated
a procedural text from a meaning representation
taking intermediate states into account. Close look
at these studies suggests the importance of the information on intermediate processes for a procedural text generator to be practical.

Thus we assume a photo sequence as the input.
Since authors of multimedia procedural texts at
least take a photo at each important step, this setting is realistic. Sharing the input and output media the most similar task may be the visual storytelling (Huang et al., 2016). Liu et al. (2017) proposed a joint embedding model for image and text
to interconnect them. Contrary to this, we propose
to generate sentences directly from the vectors in
this shared space.

3 Procedural Text Generation

Figure 2 shows an overview of our method. (i)
We pre-train the joint embedding model using im-
age/text pairs. Then, given a photo sequence, our
method repeats the following procedures for each
photo: (ii) retrieve the top K nearest steps to the
photo in the embedding space, (iii) compute the
vector by the encorder from the input photo and
the average of the K vectors of the retrieved steps,
and (iv) decode a step represented by the photo.

3.1 Joint embedding model

First, (i) we train a joint embedding model based
on the two branch networks (Wang et al., 2016),
which transform different modality representations, i.e., text and image, into a common feature
space using multiple layer perceptrons with non-
linear functions. With the resulting joint embedding model we can calculate similarity between

a step and an image. In our preliminary experiment, the original networks did not achieve a good
performance because there are many omissions in
procedural texts (Malmaud et al., 2014). To solve
this problem, we propose to insert a bi-directional
LSTM (biLSTM) to the textual encoder to refer
to the preceding and following steps in addition to
the current one.

3.2 Procedural text generation assisted by vector retrieval

The input is a photo sequence $(v_1, v_2, \ldots, v_N)$.
Each photo v_n is converted into an image embedding vector $\hat{v}_n$ through the image encoder of the
joint embedding model. For each photo we execute the following procedures.

Image vector enhancement (ii): We retrieve the
top K nearest vectors $R = (r_1, r_2, \ldots, r_K)$
among those converted from the steps in the training dataset for the embedding space. Then we calculate their average

$$\bar{r}_n = \frac{1}{K} \sum_{k=1}^{K} r_k, \tag{1}$$

and concatenate it to the image embedding vector
for the photo to have $u_n = (\hat{v}_n, \bar{r}_n)$.

Encoding (iii): We provide the enhanced image
embedding vector to a biLSTM

$$o_n = \text{biLSTM}(u_n). \tag{2}$$

Decoding (iv): We provide an LSTM with the output of the encoder o_n as the initial vector. It decodes repeatedly outputting a token in the vocab-
ulary including period, beginning of step ($\langle \text{step} \rangle$),
and its ending ($\langle /\text{step} \rangle$) to form a step consisting of
multiple sentences. We also use the general atten-
tion mechanism (Luong et al., 2015), which helps
the model to generate important terms by reciev-
ing feedback from retrieved step embedding vectors. Based on a hidden vector h_t at decoding t-th
token and the series of retrieved step embedding
vectors R, we calculate the attention weight of k-
th step a_k^t at t-th token decoding as follows:

$$a_k^t = \frac{\exp(r_k W_a h_t)}{\sum_{j=1}^{K} \exp(r_j W_a h_t)} \tag{3}$$

$$c_t = \sum_{k=1}^{K} a_k^t r_k \tag{4}$$

$$\tilde{h}_t = \tanh(W_c(c_t, h_t)), \tag{5}$$

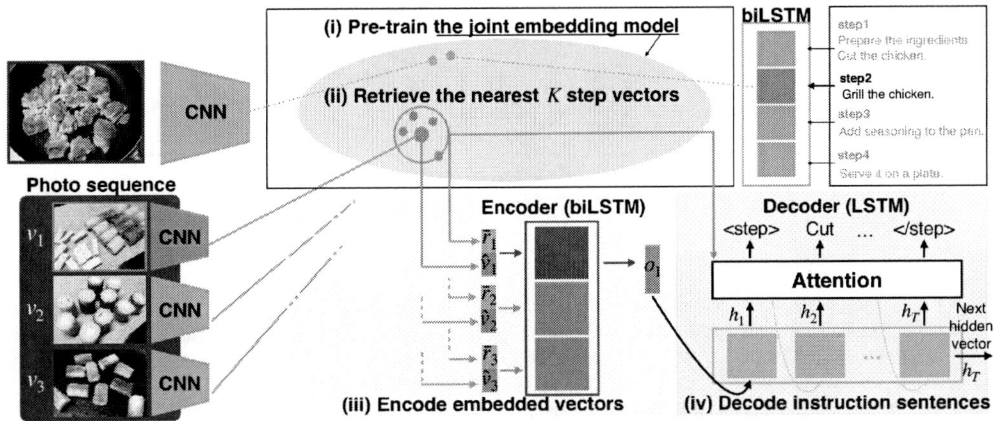

Figure 2: The outline of the proposed method.

where $\boldsymbol{W}_a$ and $\boldsymbol{W}_c$ are trainable parameters. The probability distribution of the output tokens $p(y_t|y_{<t}, \boldsymbol{o}_n)$ is calculated as follows:

$$p(y_t|y_{<t}, \boldsymbol{o}_n) = \mathrm{softmax}(\boldsymbol{W}_o\tilde{\boldsymbol{h}}_t + \boldsymbol{b}_o), \quad (6)$$

where $\boldsymbol{W}_o$ is the weight matrix to transform the size of the vector $\tilde{\boldsymbol{h}}_t$ into the vocabulary size and $\boldsymbol{b}_o$ is a bias weight. In the test phase the model outputs the token of the highest probability. After decoding, the last hidden state of the decoder is reset to the initial state of the decoder to get ready to generate the next step.

In the training phase, we minimize the sum of the negative log likelihood over all the tokens in the training set

$$L(\boldsymbol{\theta}) = -\sum_{\mathcal{D}}\sum_{t=1}^{T} \log p(y_t|y_{<t}, \boldsymbol{o}_n; \boldsymbol{\theta}), \quad (7)$$

where $\mathcal{D}$ is the entire training dataset and $\boldsymbol{\theta}$ is all the parameters and T is the length of target instruction sentences.

4   Evaluation

In order to evaluate our method, we implemented it and tested it in the cooking domain.

4.1   Parameter setting

We employed ResNet-50 (He et al., 2016) trained with ImageNet (Deng et al., 2009) as the image encoder of the joint embedding model. We removed only its last softmax layer. Thus the dimension of the output vector is 2,048. In the joint embedding model, we set the dimension of the hidden

		train	valid	test
D_{emb}	# recipes	162,463	18,059	20,104
	# steps	5.65	5.57	5.66
	# tokens	24.51	24.51	24.40
	vocabulary		24,152	
D_{gen}	# recipes	21,039	2,281	2,598
	# steps	8.09	8.10	8.10
	# tokens	19.35	19.51	19.32
	vocabulary		11,091	

Table 1: Dataset statistics.

	image2step	step2image
w/o biLSTM	23	24
w/ biLSTM	**6**	**6**

Table 2: MedR results.

layer of biLSTM to 1,024, hence the dimension of the output vector is its doubble (2,048) because the bi-directional output vectors are concatenated. Training procedure is the same as the two branch networks (Wang et al., 2016). In our generation model, we set the dimension size of the hidden vector to 512 in both of the biLSTM encoder and the LSTM decoder. To train the model, we freeze the joint embedding weights and all other weights were optimized by Adam (Kingma and Ba, 2015) with the initial value $\alpha = 0.001$. The number of retrieved steps K was set to ten.

4.2   Dataset

To prepare the dataset we selected all recipes (in Japanese) from the Cookpad Image Dataset (Harashima et al., 2017) under the condition that

Baseline

1: Prepare ingredients.
2: Slice up the onion.
3: Slice up the onion.
4: Slice up the onion.
5: Add water and consommé, and turn off the heat when boiled.
6: Serve it on a plate.
7: Add shichimi if you want.
8: Add shichimi if you want.

Proposed method

1: Cut the **carrot** into thin strips.
2: Slice up the **cucumber** and add salt.
3: Cut the vegetables.
4: Cut the bacon.
5: Add the egg and mix them.
6: Add the pasta and **cover it with the olive oil.**
7: Add olive oil and salt.
8: **Serve it on a plate.**

Reference

1: Cut the **carrot** into thin strips.
2: Slice up the **cucumber** and onion.
3: Squeeze them with salt.
4: Cut the ham.
5: Add boiled water and salt, and boil the macaroni and carrot.
6: Drain it using a strainer, and **cover it with the olive oil.**
7: Add dressings and salt.
8: **Serve it on a plate.**

Figure 3: Output examples. Word sequences in bold green are correct instructions, while those in underlined red are incorrect ones. Those double underlined are correctly verbalized ingredients.

		BLEU1	BLEU4	ROUGE-L	CIDEr-D
Baseline	Image	27.3	4.2	18.3	13.2
	Image + Title	28.6	5.4	17.6	13.1
	Image + Title + Ingredient	28.8	6.1	19.4	14.6
Proposed method w/o biLSTM	Image embedding + top1 step embedding	26.7	4.1	17.7	13.8
	Image embedding + top$K$ step embedding	31.4	6.8	21.5	11.7
Proposed method w/ biLSTM	Image embedding	31.0	6.5	21.6	14.9
	Image embedding + top1 step embedding	32.9	6.7	**21.8**	**16.4**
	Image embedding + top$K$ step embedding	**33.4**	**7.2**	20.7	14.9

Table 3: Results of overlap metrics for generated procedural texts by the models and the baselines.

an image is attached to all the steps in a recipe[1]. To obtain reliable results, we extracted recipes consisting of reasonable length (7-10 steps), which are denoted by D_{gen}, for text generation test. We used the rest, D_{emb}, as the training set for the joint embedding model. The size of D_{gen} is not enough to train the joint embedding model and generation model jointly, thus we train each model using D_{gen} and D_{emb} independently. All tokens appearing less than three times were replaced with the unknown word symbol. Table 1 shows statistics of the datasets.

4.3 Effect on the joint embedding space

First we check the effect of the biLSTM insertion. We calculated the cosine similarity in the common space for ranking the relevant steps and relevant

images and measured image2step and step2image retrieval performance in median rank (MedR). Table 2 shows the results on a subset of randomly selected 1,000 step-image pairs from the test set. From this result, we see that the insertion of the biLSTM improves the original two branch networks enabling to refer to the context.

4.4 Results and Discussion

To evaluate our method, we measured overall generation qualities as well as ratios of important terms. We also present some generated examples.

4.4.1 Overlap metrics

To evaluate the proposed method, we calculated BLEU1, BLEU4, ROUGE-L, and CIDEr-D scores over all the recipes in the test set. As the baselines, we train the model to output texts using an LSTM from multiple images (Huang et al., 2016) and mean word vectors of a title and ingredients,

---

[1]Cookpad Image Dataset contains 3.10 million images and steps, but some steps lack images.

		F	T	Ac	Total
Baseline	Recall	7.9	22.6	19.2	14.8
	Precision	12.3	15.8	17.0	15.4
	F1	9.6	18.6	18.0	15.1
Top1 w/ biLSTM	Recall	18.5	24.7	31.6	25.2
	Precision	23.8	21.0	21.1	21.9
	F1	20.8	22.7	25.3	23.4
Top$K$ w/ biLSTM	Recall	40.5	29.8	35.9	37.2
	Precision	43.6	26.8	32.4	36.1
	F1	**42.0**	**28.2**	**34.0**	**36.6**

Table 4: The verbalization ratios of important terms.

which are calculated by word2vec (Mikolov et al., 2013). The results, Table 3, show that the proposed method achieves a higher performance than the baselines in these metrics.

4.4.2 Important term verbalization

Traditional overlap metrics do not measure verbalization of important terms in the generated procedural text. In the cooking domain, they are foods (F), tools (T), and actions (Ac) as the statistics on the flow graph corpus (Mori et al., 2014b) indicate. Thus we calculated the ratios of correctly verbalized ones in these categories. Although this is more important than the ordinary overlap metrics, synonyms and spelling variants prevent us from automatic calculation. Therefore we selected 50 generated recipes randomly from the test set and manually counted numbers of important terms occurring in the generated recipes, in their references, and both. Table 4 shows the results. We see that clearly Top1 retrieval outperforms the baseline and Top$K$ is far better than top1 for all the term categories, showing advantages of our image vector enhancement in procedural text generation.

4.4.3 Qualitative analysis

In Figure 3 we present example generated sentences by the baseline, those by the proposed method, and their reference. It can be seen that the proposed method is capable of generating recipes which contain the ingredients really shown in the photos, while the baseline tends to just enumerate frequent ingredients in the training set.

5 Conclusion

In this paper, we proposed a method for generating a procedural text from a photo sequence and tested it in the cooking domain. Our main ideas are (1) biLSTM to overcome omissions in the text side for the joint embedding space, (2) image vector enhancement by top K retrieval, and (3) overall design for procedural text generation from a photo sequence. Various analyses on experimental results, which are also important contributions of this paper, showed that our method outperforms standard baselines and each one of our ideas contributes to it.

The generated sentences have the correspondence to the source photos allowing us to generate multimedia procedural texts as a natural extension of our method.

Acknowledgments

We would like to be grateful to Mr. Hirokuni Maeta, Prof. Yoko Yamakata, and Cookpad Inc. for supporting our work. We also thank anonymous reviewers for useful comments that greatly improved the manuscript.

References

Antoine Bosselut, Asli Celikyilmaz, Xiaodong He, Jianfeng Gao, Po-Sen Huang, and Yejin Choi. 2018. Discourse-aware neural rewards for coherent text generation. In *Proceedings of the 2018 Conference of the North American Chapter of the Association for Computational Linguistics: Human Language Technologies*, pages 173–184.

Jingjing Chen and Chong-Wah Ngo. 2016. Deep-based ingredient recognition for cooking recipe retrieval. In *Proceedings of the 24th ACM international conference on Multimedia*, pages 32–41.

Jia Deng, Wei Dong, Richard Socher, Li-Jia Li, Kai Li, and Li Fei-Fei. 2009. Imagenet: A large-scale hierarchical image database. In *Proceedings of the Conference on Computer Vision and Pattern Recognition*, pages 248–255.

Jun Harashima, Yuichiro Someya, and Yohei Kikuta. 2017. Cookpad image dataset: An image collection as infrastructure for food research. In *Proceedings of the 40th International ACM SIGIR Conference on Research and Development in Information Retrieval*, pages 1229–1232.

Kaiming He, Xiangyu Zhang, Shaoqing Ren, and Jian Sun. 2016. Deep residual learning for image recognition. In *Proceedings of the Conference on Computer Vision and Pattern Recognition*, pages 770–778.

Ting-Hao Kenneth Huang, Francis Ferraro, Nasrin Mostafazadeh, Aishwarya Agrawal Ishan Misra, Jacob Devlin, Ross Girshick, Xiaodong He, Pushmeet Kohli, Dhruv Batra, C. Lawrence Zitnick, Devi Parikh, Lucy Vanderwende, Michel Galley, and

Margaret Mitchell. 2016. Visual storytelling. In *Proceedings of the 2016 Conference of the North American Chapter of the Association for Computational Linguistics: Human Language Technologies*, pages 1233–1239.

Chloé Kiddon, Luke Zettlemoyer, and Yejin Choi. Globally coherent text generation with neural checklist models. In *Proceedings of the Conference on Empirical Methods in Natural Language Processing*, pages 329–339.

Diederik P. Kingma and Jimmy Ba. 2015. Adam: A method for stochastic optimization. In *Proceedings of the International Conference for Learning Representations*.

Yu Liu, Jianlong Fu, Tao Mei, and Chang Wen Chen. 2017. Let your photos talk: Generating narrative paragraph for photo stream via bidirectional attention recurrent neural networks. In *Proceedings of the Thirty-First AAAI Conference on Artificial Intelligence*, pages 1445–1452.

Thang Luong, Hieu Pham, and Christopher D. Manning. 2015. Effective approaches to attention-based neural machine translation. In *Proceedings of the Conference on Empirical Methods in Natural Language Processing*, pages 1412–1421.

Jonathan Malmaud, Earl J. Wagner, Nancy Chang, and Kevin Murphy. 2014. Cooking with semantics. In *Proceedings of the ACL Workshop on Semantic Parsing*, pages 33–38.

Tomas Mikolov, Ilya Sutskever, Kai Chen, Greg Corrado, and Jeffrey Dean. 2013. Distributed representations of words and phrases and their compositionality. In *In Advances in Neural Information Processing Systems*.

Shinsuke Mori, Hirokuni Maeta, Tetsuro Sasada, Koichiro Yoshino, Atsushi Hashimoto, Takuya Funatomi, and Yoko Yamakata. 2014a. Flowgraph2text: Automatic sentence skeleton compilation for procedural text generation. In *Proceedings of the 8th International Natural Language Generation Conference*, pages 118–122.

Shinsuke Mori, Hirokuni Maeta, Yoko Yamakata, and Tetsuro Sasada. 2014b. Flow graph corpus from recipe texts. In *Proceedings of the 9th International Conference on Language Resources and Evaluation*, pages 2370–2377.

Amaia Salvador, Michal Drozdzal, Xavier Giro i Nieto, and Adriana Romero. 2019. Inverse cooking: Recipe generation from food images. In *Proceedings of the IEEE Conference on Computer Vision and Pattern Recognition*, pages 10453–10462.

Amaia Salvador, Nicholas Hynes, Yusuf Aytar, Javier Marin, Ferda Ofli, Ingmar Weber, and Antonio Torralba. 2017. Learning cross-modal embeddings for cooking recipes and food images. In *Proceedings of the IEEE Conference on Computer Vision and Pattern Recognition*, pages 3020–3028.

Liwei Wang, Yin Li, Jing Huang, and Svetlana Lazebnik. 2016. Learning two-branch neural networks for image text matching tasks. In *Proceedings of the Conference on Computer Vision and Pattern Recognition*, pages 5005–5013.

Bin Zhu, Chong-Wah Ngo, Jingjing Chen, and Yanbin Hao. 2019. R2GAN: cross-modal recipe retrieval with generative adversarial network. In *Proceedings of the IEEE Conference on Computer Vision and Pattern Recognition*, pages 11477–11486.

SimpleNLG-DE: Adapting SimpleNLG 4 to German

Daniel Braun
Department of Informatics
Technical University of Munich
`daniel.braun@tum.de`

Kira Klimt
Department of Informatics
Technical University of Munich
`kira.klimt@tum.de`

Daniela Schneider
Allianz SE
`daniela.schneider1@allianz.com`

Florian Matthes
Department of Informatics
Technical University of Munich
`matthes@tum.de`

Abstract

SimpleNLG is a popular open source surface realiser for the English language. For German, however, the availability of open source and non-domain specific realisers is sparse, partly due to the complexity of the German language. In this paper, we present SimpleNLG-DE, an adaption of SimpleNLG to German. We discuss which parts of the German language have been implemented and how we evaluated our implementation using the TIGER Corpus and newly created data-sets.

1 Introduction

More than 20 years after it was first published, the three-stage architecture for Natural Language Generation (NLG) systems described by Reiter (1994) is still frequently cited. According to his architecture, most NLG systems of the time consisted of a pipeline with three steps: Content Determination, Sentence Planning, and Surface Realisation (or Surface Generation). Today, stochastic approaches to NLG are very popular, which often use a black box approach instead of a modular pipeline (cf. e.g. Dušek et al. (2018)).

Nevertheless, rule-based systems still play a crucial role, especially in application contexts, because they provide advantages like higher controllability. SimpleNLG, developed by Gatt and Reiter (2009) is arguably the most popular open source realisation engine. It is implemented in Java and its current Version (4.4.8) is available under the Mozilla Public License (MPL).[1]

Since it was published in 2009, SimpleNLG was adapted to seven other languages, these are (in chronological order): German (Bollmann, 2011), French (Vaudry and Lapalme, 2013), Italian (Mazzei et al., 2016), Spanish (Ramos-Soto et al.,

2017), Dutch (de Jong and Theune, 2018), Mandarin (Chen et al., 2018), and Galician (Cascallar-Fuentes et al., 2018).

Unfortunately, the German version of SimpleNLG[2] is not maintained anymore and is based on the outdated third version of SimpleNLG, which used a more restrictive license that prohibited commercial use. (Bollmann, 2019) Moreover, the existing German version also comes with a very limited lexicon, consisting of just around 100 lemmata. It also does not automatically recognise and handle separable verbs like "abfahren" ("to depart") or "einkaufen" ("to purchase"). The only openly available alternative is a German grammar for OpenCCG (Vancoppenolle et al., 2011), which is even more limited with regard to both grammatical coverage and its lexicon.

Therefore, we decided to develop SimpleNLG-DE, a new German version of SimpleNLG, implemented from scratch, based on SimpleNLG 4.4.8 and the MPL. SimpleNLG-DE comes with a standard lexicon containing more than 100,000 lemmata and is available from `https://github.com/sebischair/SimpleNLG-DE`.

2 German Language

As also acknowledged by Bollmann (2011), the German language has its specificities, which pose special challenges for the task of surface realisation.

2.1 Word Order

Many different possible word orders can exist for the same sentence in German. "Ohne Pause in den Hof tragen konnten die Kiste nur zwei kräftige Männer." ("Only two strong men could carry the

---

[1] `https://github.com/simplenlg/simplenlg`

[2] `https://marcel.bollmann.me/software/simplenlg.html`

Proceedings of The 12th International Conference on Natural Language Generation, pages 415–420,
Tokyo, Japan, 28 Oct - 1 Nov, 2019. ©2019 Association for Computational Linguistics

box into the yard without a break.") can also be expressed by shuffling the sentence constituents, resulting in "Die Kiste in den Hof tragen konnten, ohne Pause, nur zwei kräftige Männer.", "In den Hof tragen konnten die Kiste, ohne Pause, nur zwei kräftige Männer.", or "Nur zwei kräftige Männer konnten die Kiste ohne Pause in den Hof tragen.". The German language is thus seen as a "partially free constituent order language" (Vancoppenolle et al., 2011), whereas the shuffling of constituents is called "scrambling" (Eisenberg et al., 2016, p. 881). Moreover, depending on the sentence type, the verb of a sentence must be placed at different positions. The finite verb has to be positioned either in second place, in the first place or in the last place (Eisenberg et al., 2016, pp. 875-878).

2.2 Inflection

Manifold inflection rules are another major reason why the German language is, from a surface realisation perspective, more complex than e.g. English. For the English language, table look-ups for inflected forms can be performed reasonably. This is not feasible for German.

Whereas in the English language "the" as definite article and "a" / "an" as indefinite articles suffice, in German, "der", "die", and "das" as definite articles and "ein" and "eine" as indefinite articles exist. In the German language, additionally, all articles and pronouns must be inflected according to gender, number, person and grammatical case (nominative, genitive, dative, accusative). This results in more article forms, for instance for indefinite articles in "einen", "einem", "einer", "eines". (Eisenberg et al., 2016, p. 341)

Inflection of nouns is dependent on the noun's gender, the grammatical case the noun is in, and the number (singular or plural). (Eisenberg et al., 2016, pp. 146-228) Adjectives can be attributive, predicative, adverbial or nominalized. (Eisenberg et al., 2016, pp. 345-372) In most cases, attributive adjectives are inflected and change with the grammatical case, the number and the gender of the corresponding noun. The following examples illustrate the inflection:

- Inflection according to the case: "das große Haus" ("the big house"), in dative "dem großen Haus"

- Inflection according to the number: "das große Haus", in plural "die großen Häuser"

- Inflection according to the gender: "ein großes Haus" ("a big house", neutral), "die große Frau" ("a tall women", feminine)

Finally, verb conjugation reflects person, number, tense, voice, and mood. (Eisenberg et al., 2016, p. 395) German verbs can be grouped into strong and weak verbs, depending on their inflection pattern in past tense and participle II. (Eisenberg et al., 2016, pp. 440-466) Weak verbs build their past tense forms with a syllable introducing t-suffix, e.g. "lachte" ("laughed"), "redete" ("talked") and their participle II form with "-t"/"-et", e.g. "gelacht", "geredet". Normally, the stem vocal of weak verbs does not change. Strong verbs, in contrast, do not build their past tense forms with a suffix, but with an alteration of the stem vocal (ablaut), e.g. "rufen - rief" ("to call - called") or "finden - fand" ("to find - found"). Participle II forms are built with the suffix "-en" and, in some cases, with an ablaut: "singen - sang" ("to sing - sang"). Furthermore, there are some verbs with strong-weak mixed conjugation, or other irregularities, for example some modal verbs, auxiliary verbs, or the verb "wissen" ("to know").

2.3 Separable Verbs

Separable verbs (e.g. "losfahren" / "moving off"), also referred to as particle verbs, contain a prefix which can be separated. The order of the prefix ("los") and the verb ("fahren") can be reversed in some conjugated forms (Eisenberg et al., 2016, pp. 705-714). The verb "hinausgehen" ("to step out", "to leave"), for instance, consists of the adverb "hinaus" ("out"), and the verb "gehen" ("to go"). When "hinausgehen" is conjugated, the first person in the present tense is "ich gehe hinaus" ("I step out"), where the prefix is separated from the verb. Prefix types range from prepositional, to adverbial, adjective or substantive particles. "Preis" ("price") in "preisgeben" ("to reveal") contains a substantive particle, whereas "widerspiegeln" ("to reflect"), contains a preposition as prefix. Separable verbs also exist in other languages like Dutch. (de Jong and Theune, 2018)

2.4 Compound Words

Compounds are complex linguistic constructs consisting of several words. Subjective and adjective compounds can be built by combining two or more words into a compound, for example, "Wunderkind" ("prodigy child"), or "rubinrot" ("ruby red"). The last component of a compound word dominates the word, i.e., a "Wunderkind" is a "Kind" ("child") rather than a "Wunder" ("prodigy"). Internally, compound words can e.g. be inflected with a genitive ending, like in "Kapitänsmütze" ("captain's head"). The grammatical characteristics of the whole word, like the gender or the inflection type, are determined by the last component. Compound words are the most important way of building words in the German language. (Elsen, 2009)

So-called word group lexemes are similar to compound words. They are fixed phrases of at least two separately written words. "Erste Hilfe" ("first aid"), "Europäische Union" ("European Union"), or "Vereinigte Arabische Emirate" ("United Arab Emirates") are examples for word group lexemes. (Elsen, 2009) In contrast to compound words, word group lexemes are internally inflected. "Vereinigte Arabische Emirate" ("United Arab Emirates") is inflected in the dative case to "[aus den] Vereinigten Arabischen Emiraten" ("from the United Arab Emirates").

3 Grammatical Coverage

In this section, we describe which parts of the grammar of the German language are implemented in the first version of SimpleNLG-DE. In Section 5, we will discuss which important parts are not yet covered.

3.1 Syntax

The handling of the word order in SimpleNLG-DE is implemented according to the topological model of the "Duden" (Eisenberg et al., 2016, pp. 874 - 880). The library currently supports two types of clauses, declarative clauses and questions. The word order for declarative clauses without a frontmodifier is *subject - finite verb - objects - other verb forms*. Unlike the previous implementation of SimpleNLG for German, SimpleNLG-DE detects separable verbs automatically and changes the word order to *subject - finite verb - objects - separable particle* (e.g. "Alice räumt das Auto ein." / "Alice is loading the car."). The handling of separable words is similar to the implementation in the Dutch version of SimpleNLG (de Jong and Theune, 2018). Separable verbs are marked as separable in the lexicon and the lexicon entry includes their prefix as a separate entry. Initiated subordinate clauses which contain a separable

verb have to be treated with care. As an example, the complex sentence "Florian geht einkaufen, Alex räumt sein Zimmer auf." ("Florian goes shopping, Alex cleans his room.") can be changed to "Florian geht einkaufen, während Alex sein Zimmer aufräumt." ("Florian goes shopping, while Alex cleans his room."), with the second sentence added as initiated subordinate clause to the first. In the second sentence, besides the changed word oder, the verb conjugation changes too. The separable verb is separated in the first clause ("räumt auf" / "tidies up"), but stays together in the second clause ("aufräumt"). (Agbaria, 2009) For all initiated subordinate clauses, SimpleNLG-De does not split separable verbs.

Moreover, SimpleNLG-DE can produce five different kinds of questions: yes/no questions and questions about the subject and object of a sentence for both people ("wer" / "who") and things ("was" / "what").

Beyond the main clauses, SimpleNLG-DE can handle compound sentences connected with "und" ("and") or comma ("Der Hund bellt und die Katze miaut." / "The dog barks and the cat mews."), temporal, causal, conditional, consecutive, concessive, modal, comparative, final, and adversative subordinate clauses ("Die Sonne scheint, während es regnet." / "The sun shines while it is raining."), appositions ("SAP, eine deutsche Firma, ..." / "SAP, a German company, ..."), and enumerations ("SAP, Bayer und EON" / "SAP, Bayern, and EON").

3.2 Morphology

Morphology in SimpleNLG-DE is based on a combination of rules for regular inflections, extracted from Eisenberg et al. (2016) and Agbaria (2009), and a lexicon covering 100,000 unique lemmata ($\sim$ 78,000 nouns, 10,000 verbs, 11,000 adjectives, 1,000 adverbs), which was extracted from Wiktionary[3]. Like Wiktionary itself, the lexicon is licensed under the Creative Commons Attribution-ShareAlike 3.0 Unported (CC BY-SA 3.0)[4] license. The lexicon does not contain all conjugated forms for all persons in all tenses but covers a set of forms big enough to create all inflected forms with additional rules. If a verb is not in the lexicon, it is conjugated regularly.

---

[3] https://de.wiktionary.org/
[4] https://creativecommons.org/licenses/by-sa/3.0/deed.en

Verb conjugation currently covers present, past, perfect, and future tense, passive in present and past, modal verbs in present, as well as the handling of separable verbs. Adjectives are declined according to the case, number, and article. Moreover, comparative and superlative for adjectives and adverbs can be generated. Nouns can be inflected based on the case and number and their articles according to the case, number, and gender, for both, definite and indefinite articles. Word group lexemes can also be inflected according to the case and number. Additionally, SimpleNLG-DE is able to automatically detect the contraction of prepositions and inflect adjectives correctly in cases like "in dem großen Haus" which can be contracted to "im großen Haus" ("in the big house").

3.3 Orthography

The orthography processor of SimpleNLG-DE handles terminating declarative clauses with ".", questions with "?", capitalising the first character in a sentence, and comma rules. If a sentence is set as a complement to another sentence, and both of them do not add a complementiser, or the complementiser is in a list of conjunctions which requires a comma, the complement is added with a preceding comma. For sentences added with the complementiser "und", no comma is added. Appositions have a comma added before and after them, no matter if "und" is contained in the apposition or not. Enumerations are connected by adding a comma between the first constituents, and separating the last one with "und", for instance in "A, B und C" ("A, B, and C").

4 Evaluation

Evaluating a surface realiser is in many aspects a difficult task. There are two facets which we tried to evaluate: First, how robust and correct is the implementation of the grammatical features described in Section 3 and second, how much of everyday language can be covered with the current implementation of SimpleNLG-DE. The first aspect can be evaluated relatively easy by manually creating special test cases for the different grammatical features that have been implemented. Evaluating the coverage of a language is far more complex. The best, yet flawed, approach is choosing an existent corpus which is believed to be somewhat representative of the language as a whole. This approach was also chosen by the authors of other versions of SimpleNLG. Bollmann (2011), for example, used five Wikipedia articles with 152 sentences in total to evaluate the coverage and achieved 75.66%. Unfortunately, the test data was not published, therefore, we can not compare the new implementation directly with the previous version on this dataset. Many other versions, like the Spanish and Mandarin versions, used translations of the 144 test sentences from the original SimpleNLG version. However, it should be noted that these sentences were merely meant to be an "indication of efficiency" test (Gatt and Reiter, 2009) and not an evaluation of the coverage.

We used more than 3,800 test sentences to evaluate the correct implementation of the grammatical features described in Section 3. These tests cover e.g. the inflection of verbs (2,436 sentences), the inflection of adjectives (1,002 sentences), and the inflection of nouns (390 sentences), but also other features like question generation. SimpleNLG-DE was able to generate all of these sentences correctly. The sentences were implemented manually and partially based on sentences from documents from the financial domain and partially written by the authors for testing purposes.

In order to get an estimate how much of the German language is covered, we used the TIGER Corpus (Brants et al., 2004). It contains 50,000 sentences of German newspaper articles taken from the "Frankfurter Rundschau". As newspaper text can contain rather complex phrase structures, it is considered suitable test data for a German language realiser. Annotations in TIGER corpus include semi-automatically generated POS-tags as well as syntactic structure, morphological and lemma information. The TIGER corpus is freely available for research and evaluation purposes.

Since writing the code to generate a sentence is a very time consuming task, we could not test our implementation on the whole corpus. Instead, we randomly chose 100 declarative sentences from the TIGER corpus (i.e. interrogative, imperative, and exclamatory sentences were excluded) and implemented them using SimpleNLG-DE. We used the annotations from the TIGER corpus to semi-automatically create the code for the tests, however all sentences were manually checked and adapted before they were added to the test set.

84% of all sentences could be generated correctly using the library. Counted as correct are only sentences which are equal to their corresponding sentence in the corpus. The main reasons for wrongly realised sentences include problems with the pluralisation of irregular compound nouns which are not part of the lexicon and of verbs in cases where the corresponding noun is a number (e.g. "Im Schnitt waren es seit 1980 jedoch nur 4 208." / "On average, however, since 1980 it has been only 4 208.").

Since the code for the tests is only compatible with SimpleNLG version 4, we were not able to directly compare the performance of the old and new version of SimpleNLG on the TIGER corpus. For license reasons, the tests generated from the TIGER corpus are not published alongside the code of SimpleNLG-DE, however, all other tests are part of the repository.

5   Limitations

SimpleNLG-DE covers a subset of the German language. Some grammar parts are left for future work, due to the complexity of German language, its manifold inflected words and rules, and its diverse word order possibilities with a large number of exceptions. Indications on how to extend the library in the future, according to its current limitations, are given in this section.

Tenses currently not covered by SimpleNLG-DE are future II ("Ich werde es gekauft haben." / "I will have bought it.") and plusquamperfect tense ("Sie hatte Fußball gespielt." / "She had played football."). Furthermore, passive currently only works for present and preterite tenses, and modal verbs only work for present active. Phrases such as "soll verursacht sein" ("shall be caused"), for instance, are not covered. Only indicative mood is integrated. Conjunctive and imperative are not yet implemented.

Compound words (cf. Section 2.4) are currently only correctly handled if they are part of the lexicon. While there are existing approaches on how to automatically split compound words into their respective parts (e.g. by Baroni et al. (2002), Koehn and Knight (2003), Daiber et al. (2015), Sugisaki and Tuggener (2018), and Weller-Di Marco (2017)), the problem is far from being trivial and is not yet addressed by the implementation.

For some German verbs, there are several correct ways to conjugate them. The verb "senden" ("to send"), for instance, in the third person past tense can either be conjugated to "sendete" or to "sandte", without changing the meaning. Such subtleties are currently not covered by the library. While in the previous example, this is merely a question of style, some verbs actually change their meaning. The verb "wachsen" in third person present tense in its irregular form is "er wächst" meaning "he is growing", whereas the regular form "er wachst" means "he waxes (sth.)". In future, an option for the user to set the desired meaning should be given.

6   Conclusion

In this paper, we presented SimpleNLG-DE, an adaption of the open source surface realiser SimpleNLG for the German language which is licensed under the MPL. The current implementation covers the most important basic features of the German language and comes with a lexicon covering more than 100,000 lemmata.

The implementation was validated by testing for grammatical functionality, e.g. verb conjugation, and language coverage on real-world newspaper articles from the TIGER corpus. SimpleNLG-DE was able to correctly reproduce 84% of the selected sentences from the TIGER corpus.

In the future, we would like to enhance the implementation by addressing the limitations mentioned in Section 5. Furthermore, we would like to test SimpleNLG-DE in different application domains with specific language, like the legal domain (cf. e.g. Braun et al. (2019)).

Acknowledgments

This work has been sponsored by the German Federal Ministry of Education and Research (BMBF) grant A-SUM 01IS17049 and Allianz SE.

References

Evelyn Agbaria. 2009. *PONS die deutsche Rechtschreibung*, volume 1. PONS GmbH, Stuttgart.

Marco Baroni, Johannes Matiasek, and Harald Trost. 2002. Predicting the components of german nominal compounds. In *ECAI 2002: 15th European Conference on Artificial Intelligence*, pages 470–474.

Marcel Bollmann. 2011. Adapting SimpleNLG to German. In *Proceedings of the 13th European Work-

shop on Natural Language Generation, pages 133–138, Nancy, France. Association for Computational Linguistics.

Marcel Bollmann. 2019. Simplenlg for german. `https://marcel.bollmann.me/software/simplenlg.html`. Last accessed 2019-09-10.

Sabine Brants, Stefanie Dipper, Peter Eisenberg, Silvia Hansen-Schirra, Esther König, Wolfgang Lezius, Christian Rohrer, George Smith, and Hans Uszkoreit. 2004. Tiger: Linguistic interpretation of a german corpus. *Research on language and computation*, 2(4):597–620.

Daniel Braun, Elena Scepankova, Patrick Holl, and Florian Matthes. 2019. Consumer protection in the digital era: The potential of customer-centered legaltech. In *INFORMATIK 2019: 50 Jahre Gesellschaft für Informatik - Informatik für Gesellschaft*, pages 407–420, Bonn. Gesellschaft für Informatik e.V.

Andrea Cascallar-Fuentes, Alejandro Ramos-Soto, and Alberto Bugarín Diz. 2018. Adapting SimpleNLG to Galician language. In *Proceedings of the 11th International Conference on Natural Language Generation*, pages 67–72, Tilburg University, The Netherlands. Association for Computational Linguistics.

Guanyi Chen, Kees van Deemter, and Chenghua Lin. 2018. SimpleNLG-ZH: a linguistic realisation engine for Mandarin. In *Proceedings of the 11th International Conference on Natural Language Generation*, pages 57–66, Tilburg University, The Netherlands. Association for Computational Linguistics.

Joachim Daiber, Lautaro Quiroz, Roger Wechsler, and Stella Frank. 2015. Splitting compounds by semantic analogy. In *Proceedings of the 1st Deep Machine Translation Workshop*, pages 20–28, Praha, Czechia. ÚFAL MFF UK.

Ondřej Dušek, Jekaterina Novikova, and Verena Rieser. 2018. Findings of the E2E NLG challenge. In *Proceedings of the 11th International Conference on Natural Language Generation*, pages 322–328, Tilburg University, The Netherlands. Association for Computational Linguistics.

Peter Eisenberg, Jörg Peters, Peter Gallmann, Cathrine Fabricius-Hansen, Damaris Nübling, Irmhild Barz, Thomas A Fritz, Reinhard Fiehler, and Mathilde Henning. 2016. *Duden - Die Grammatik. Unentbehrlich für richtiges Deutsch*. Dudenverlag, Mannheim.

Hilke Elsen. 2009. Komplexe komposita und verwandtes. *Germanistische Mitteilungen: Zeitschrift für Deutsche Sprache, Literatur und Kultur*, (69):57–71.

Albert Gatt and Ehud Reiter. 2009. Simplenlg: A realisation engine for practical applications. In *Proceedings of the 12th European Workshop on Natural Language Generation*, ENLG '09, pages 90–93, Stroudsburg, PA, USA. Association for Computational Linguistics.

Ruud de Jong and Mariët Theune. 2018. Going Dutch: Creating SimpleNLG-NL. In *Proceedings of the 11th International Conference on Natural Language Generation*, pages 73–78, Tilburg University, The Netherlands. Association for Computational Linguistics.

Philipp Koehn and Kevin Knight. 2003. Empirical methods for compound splitting. In *Proceedings of the Tenth Conference on European Chapter of the Association for Computational Linguistics - Volume 1*, EACL '03, pages 187–193, Stroudsburg, PA, USA. Association for Computational Linguistics.

Alessandro Mazzei, Cristina Battaglino, and Cristina Bosco. 2016. SimpleNLG-IT: adapting SimpleNLG to Italian. In *Proceedings of the 9th International Natural Language Generation conference*, pages 184–192, Edinburgh, UK. Association for Computational Linguistics.

Alejandro Ramos-Soto, Julio Janeiro-Gallardo, and Alberto Bugarín Diz. 2017. Adapting SimpleNLG to Spanish. In *Proceedings of the 10th International Conference on Natural Language Generation*, pages 144–148, Santiago de Compostela, Spain. Association for Computational Linguistics.

Ehud Reiter. 1994. Has a consensus nl generation architecture appeared, and is it psycholinguistically plausible? In *Proceedings of the Seventh International Workshop on Natural Language Generation*, pages 163–170. Association for Computational Linguistics.

Kyoko Sugisaki and Don Tuggener. 2018. German compound splitting using the compound productivity of morphemes. In *14th Conference on Natural Language Processing-KONVENS 2018*, pages 141–147. Austrian Academy of Sciences Press.

Jean Vancoppenolle, Eric Tabbert, Gerlof Bouma, and Manfred Stede. 2011. A german grammar for generation in open ccg. In *Multilingual resources and multilingual applications: Proceedings of the Conference of the German Society for Computational Linguistics and Language Technology (GSCL)*, pages 145–150. Citeseer.

Pierre-Luc Vaudry and Guy Lapalme. 2013. Adapting SimpleNLG for bilingual English-French realisation. In *Proceedings of the 14th European Workshop on Natural Language Generation*, pages 183–187, Sofia, Bulgaria. Association for Computational Linguistics.

Marion Weller-Di Marco. 2017. Simple compound splitting for German. In *Proceedings of the 13th Workshop on Multiword Expressions (MWE 2017)*, pages 161–166, Valencia, Spain. Association for Computational Linguistics.

Semantic Noise Matters for Neural Natural Language Generation

Ondřej Dušek*
Charles University
Faculty of Mathematics and Physics
Prague, Czech Republic
odusek@ufal.mff.cuni.cz

David M. Howcroft* & **Verena Rieser**
The Interaction Lab, MACS
Heriot-Watt University
Edinburgh, Scotland, UK
{d.howcroft,v.t.rieser}@hw.ac.uk

Abstract

Neural natural language generation (NNLG) systems are known for their pathological outputs, i.e. generating text which is unrelated to the input specification. In this paper, we show the impact of semantic noise on state-of-the-art NNLG models which implement different semantic control mechanisms. We find that cleaned data can improve semantic correctness by up to 97%, while maintaining fluency. We also find that the most common error is omitting information, rather than hallucination.

1 Introduction

Neural Natural Language Generation (NNLG) is promising for generating text from Meaning Representations (MRs) in an 'end-to-end' fashion, i.e. without needing alignments (Wen et al., 2015, 2016; Dušek and Jurčíček, 2016; Mei et al., 2016). However, NNLG requires large volumes of in-domain data, which is typically crowdsourced (e.g. Mairesse et al., 2010; Novikova et al., 2016; Wen et al., 2015, 2016; Howcroft et al., 2017), introducing noise. For example, up to 40% of the E2E Generation Challenge[1] data contains omitted or additional information (Dušek et al., 2019).

In this paper, we examine the impact of this type of semantic noise on two state-of-the-art NNLG models with different semantic control mechanisms: TGen (Dušek and Jurčíček, 2016) and SC-LSTM (Wen et al., 2015). In particular, we investigate the systems' ability to produce fact-accurate text, i.e. without omitting or hallucinating information, in the presence of semantic noise.[2] We find that:

- training on cleaned data reduces slot-error rate up to 97% on the original evaluation data;
- testing on cleaned data is challenging, even for models trained on cleaned data, likely due to increased MR diversity in the cleaned dataset; and
- TGen performs better than SC-LSTM, even when cleaner training data is available. We hypothesise that this is due to differences in how the two systems handle semantic input and the degree of delexicalization that they expect.

In addition, we release our code and a cleaned version of the E2E data with this paper.[3]

2 Mismatched Semantics in E2E Data

The E2E dataset contains input MRs and corresponding target human-authored textual references in the restaurant domain. MRs here are sets of attribute-value pairs (see Figure 1). Most MRs in the dataset have multiple references (8.1 on average). These were collected using crowdsourcing, leading to noise when crowd workers did not verbalise all attributes or added information not present in the MR. According to Dušek et al. (2019), the multiple references should help NLG systems abstract from the noise. However, most NLG systems in the E2E challenge in fact produced noisy outputs, suggesting that they were unable to learn to ignore noise in the training input.

Problems with the semantic accuracy in training data is not unique to the E2E dataset. Howcroft et al. (2017) collected a corpus of paraphrases differing with respect to information density for use in training NLG systems and found that subjects' paraphrases dropped about 5% of the slot-value pairs from the original texts and changed the val-

---

*Denotes equal contribution.

[1] http://www.macs.hw.ac.uk/InteractionLab/E2E/

[2] Also see https://ehudreiter.com/2018/11/12/hallucination-in-neural-nlg/

[3] Data cleaning scripts, the resulting cleaned data and links to code are available at https://github.com/tuetschek/e2e-cleaning.

Proceedings of The 12th International Conference on Natural Language Generation, pages 421–426,
Tokyo, Japan, 28 Oct - 1 Nov, 2019. ©2019 Association for Computational Linguistics

Original MR: name[Cotto], eatType[coffee shop], food[English], priceRange[less than £20], customer_rating[low], area[riverside], near[The Portland Arms]

Human reference 1 (accurate): At the riverside near The Portland Arms, Cotto is a coffee shop that serves English food at less than £20 and has low customer rating.

HR 2: Located near The Portland Arms in riverside, the Cotto coffee shop serves English food with a price range of £20 and a low customer rating.
Corrected MR: name[Cotto], eatType[coffee shop], food[English], customer_rating[low], area[riverside], near[The Portland Arms]
(removed price range)

HR 3: Cotto is a coffee shop that serves English food in the city centre. They are located near the Portland Arms and are low rated.
Corrected MR: name[Cotto], eatType[coffee shop], food[English], customer_rating[low], area[city centre], near[The Portland Arms]
(removed price range, changed area)

HR 4: Cotto is a cheap coffee shop with one-star located near The Portland Arms.
Corrected MR: name[Cotto], eatType[coffee shop], priceRange[less than £20], customer rating[low], near[The Portland Arms]
(removed area)

Figure 1: MR and references from the E2E corpus. The first reference is accurate and verbalises all attributes, but the remaining ones contain inaccuracies. Corrected MRs were automatically produced by our slot matching script (see Section 3). Note that HR 2 is not fixed properly since the script's patterns are not perfect.

Dataset	Part	MRs	Refs	SER(%)
	TRAIN	4,862	42,061	17.69
Original	DEV	547	4,672	11.42
	TEST	630	4,693	11.49
	TRAIN	8,362	33,525	(0.00)
Cleaned	DEV	1,132	4,299	(0.00)
	TEST	1,358	4,693	(0.00)

Table 1: Data statistics comparison for the original E2E data and our cleaned version (number of distinct MRs, total number of textual references, SER as measured by our slot matching script, see Section 3).

ues for approximately 10% of the slot-value pairs. As a result of these changes and the insertion of new facts, only 61% of the corpus contained all and only the intended propositions. This is similar to what Eric et al. (2019) found in their work on the MultiWOZ 2.0 dataset: correcting the dialogue state annotations resulted in changes to about 40% of the dialogue turns in their dataset. These findings suggest that efforts to create more accurate training data—whether through stricter crowdsourcing protocols, conducting follow-up annotations (cf. Eric et al., 2019), or automated cleanup heuristics like we report here—are likely necessary in the NLG and dialogue systems communities.

3 Cleaning the Meaning Representations

To produce a cleaned version of the E2E data, we used the original human textual references, but paired them with correctly matching MRs.[4] To this end, we reimplemented the slot matching script of Reed et al. (2018), which tags MR slots and values using regular expressions. We tuned our expressions based on the first 500 instances from the E2E development set and ran the script on the full dataset, producing corrected MRs for all human references (see Figure 1). The differences against the original MRs allow us to compute the *semantic/slot error rate* (SER; Wen et al., 2015; Reed et al., 2018; Dušek et al., 2019):

$$\text{SER} = \frac{\#\text{added} + \#\text{missing} + \#\text{wrong value}}{\#\text{slots}}$$

To guarantee the integrity of the test set, we removed instances from the TRAIN (training) and DEV (development) sets that overlapped the TEST set. This resulted in 20% reduction for TRAIN and ca. 8% reduction for DEV in terms of references (see Table 1). On the other hand, the number of distinct MRs rose sharply after reannotation; the MRs also have more variance in the number of attributes. This means that the cleaned dataset is more complex overall, with fewer references per MR and more diverse MRs.

We manually evaluated 200 randomly chosen instances from the cleaned TRAIN set to check the accuracy of the slot matching script. We found that the slot matching script itself has a SER of 4.2%, with 39 instances (19.5%) not 100% correctly rated. This is much lower than the E2E dataset authors' own manual assessment of ca. 40% noisy instances (Dušek et al., 2019) and the script's rating of the whole dataset (mean SER: 16.37%),and comparable to the slot matching script of Juraska et al. (2018) evaluated on the same data.[5]

4 Evaluating the Impact on Neural NLG

We chose two recent neural end-to-end NLG systems, which represent two different approaches to semantic control and have been widely used and extended by the research community.

---

[4]Note that this can be done automatically, unlike fixing the references to match the original MRs.

[5]Juraska et al. (2018)'s script reaches 6.2% SER and 60 instances with errors, most of which is just omitting the *eatType[restaurant]* value. If we ignore this value, it gets 1.9% SER and 20 incorrect instances. We did not use this script as it was not available to us until very shortly before the camera-ready deadline. The script is now accessible under `https://github.com/jjuraska/slug2slug`. We plan to further improve our slot matching script based on errors found during the manual evaluation and comparison to Juraska et al. (2018).

4.1 TGen

TGen (Dušek and Jurčíček, 2016) is the baseline system used in the E2E challenge.[6] TGen is in essence a vanilla sequence-to-sequence (seq2seq) model with attention (Bahdanau et al., 2015) using LSTM cells where input MRs are encoded as sequences of triples in the form (dialogue act, slot, value).[7] TGen adds to the standard seq2seq setup a reranker that selects the output with the lowest SER from the decoder output beam (n-best list). SER is estimated based on a classifier trained to identify the MR corresponding to a given text. We use the default TGen parameters for the E2E data, experimenting with three variants:

- **TGen without reranker:** a vanilla seq2seq model with attention (TGen$-$);
- **TGen with default reranker:** the same augmented with an LSTM encoder and binary classifier for individual slot-value pairs;
- **TGen with oracle reranker:** directly uses the slot matching script to compute SER (TGen$+$).

We fixed the parameters of the main seq2seq generator to see the direct influence of each reranker, without the added effect of random initialization.

4.2 SC-LSTM

In contrast to seq2seq architecture used by TGen, the Semantically Controlled LSTM (SC-LSTM, Wen et al., 2015) uses a learned gating mechanism to selectively express parts of the MR during generation. We use the SC-LSTM model provided as part of the RNNLG repository[8] with minor changes to improve comparability to TGen. Most importantly, we incorporate the tokenization and normalization used by TGen into RNNLG. Since the word embeddings provided with RNNLG only cover about half of the tokens in the E2E dataset, we use randomly initialised word embeddings (dimension 50; same as TGen).

5 Evaluation and Results

To measure the effect of noisy data, we compare systems trained on the original data against systems trained using cleaned TRAIN and validation (=DEV) sets; we perform the comparisons both on the original and the cleaned TEST sets. Note that only scores on the same test set are directly comparable as the cleaned TEST set has more diverse MRs and fewer references per MR (i.e. numbers in Tables 2 and 3 cannot be compared across tables; cf. Section 3).

5.1 Automatic Metrics

We use freely available word-overlap-based evaluation metrics (WOM) scripts that come with the E2E data (Dušek et al., 2019),[9] supporting BLEU (Papineni et al., 2002), NIST (Doddington, 2002), ROUGE-L (Lin, 2004), METEOR (Lavie and Agarwal, 2007) and CIDEr (Vedantam et al., 2015). In addition, we use our slot matching script for SER (cf. Section 3). We also show detailed results for the percentages of added and missed slots and wrong slot values.[10]

The results in Table 2 (top half) for the original setup confirm that the ranking mechanism for TGen is effective for both WOMs and SER, whereas the SC-LSTM seems to have trouble scaling to the E2E dataset. We hypothesise that this is mainly due to the amount of delexicalisation required. However, the main improvement of SER comes from training on cleaned data with up to 97% error reduction with the ranker and 94% without.[11] In other words, just cleaning the training data has a much more dramatic effect than just using a semantic control mechanism, such as the reranker (0.97% vs. 4.27% SER). WOMs are slightly lower for TGen trained on the cleaned data, except for NIST, which gives more importance to matching less frequent n-grams. This suggests better preservation of content at the expense of slightly lower fluency.

The results for testing on cleaned data (Table 3, top half) confirm the positive impact of cleaned training data and also show that the cleaned test data is more challenging (cf. Section 3), as reflected in the lower WOMs. This raises the question whether the improved results from clean training data are due to seeing more challenging examples at training time. However, the improved results for training and testing on clean data (i.e. seeing equally challenging examples at training and test time), suggest the increase in performance can be attributed to data accuracy rather than diversity.

Looking at the detailed results for the number of

---

[6] https://github.com/UFAL-DSG/tgen

[7] The dialogue act is constant/ignored for the E2E dataset since it's not part of the MRs there.

[8] https://github.com/shawnwun/RNNLG

[9] https://github.com/tuetschek/e2e-metrics

[10] Absolute numbers of errors and number of completely correct instances are shown in Table 5 in the Supplementary.

[11] $\frac{0.12}{4.27} = 0.028$ and $\frac{0.97}{15.94} = 0.061$

TRAIN	TEST	System	BLEU	NIST	METEOR	ROUGE-L	CIDEr	Add	Miss	Wrong	SER
Original		TGen−	63.37	7.7188	41.99	68.53	1.9355	00.06	15.77	00.11	15.94
		TGen	66.41	8.5565	45.07	69.17	2.2253	00.14	04.11	00.03	04.27
		TGen+	67.06	8.5871	45.83	69.73	2.2681	00.04	01.75	00.01	01.80
		SC-LSTM	39.11	5.6704	36.83	50.02	0.6045	02.79	18.90	09.79	31.51
Cleaned	Original	TGen−	65.87	8.6400	44.20	67.51	2.1710	00.20	00.56	00.21	00.97
		TGen	66.24	8.6889	44.66	67.85	2.2181	00.10	00.02	00.00	00.12
		TGen+	65.97	8.6630	44.45	67.59	2.1855	00.02	00.00	00.00	00.03
		SC-LSTM	38.52	5.7125	37.45	48.50	0.4343	03.85	17.39	08.12	29.37
Cleaned missing		TGen−	66.28	8.5202	43.96	67.83	2.1375	00.14	02.26	00.22	02.61
		TGen	67.00	8.6889	44.97	68.19	2.2228	00.06	00.44	00.03	00.53
		TGen+	66.74	8.6649	44.84	67.95	2.2018	00.00	00.21	00.03	00.24
Cleaned added		TGen−	64.40	7.9692	42.81	68.87	2.0563	00.01	13.08	00.00	13.09
		TGen	66.23	8.5578	45.12	68.87	2.2548	00.04	03.04	00.00	03.09
		TGen+	65.96	8.5238	45.49	68.79	2.2456	00.00	01.44	00.00	01.45

Table 2: Results evaluated on the original test set (averaged over 5 runs with different random initialisation). See Section 5.1 for explanation of metrics. All numbers except NIST and ROUGE-L are percentages. Note that the numbers are *not* comparable to Table 3 as the test set is different.

TRAIN	TEST	System	BLEU	NIST	METEOR	ROUGE-L	CIDEr	Add	Miss	Wrong	SER
Original		TGen−	36.85	5.3782	35.14	55.01	1.6016	00.34	09.81	00.15	10.31
		TGen	39.23	6.0217	36.97	55.52	1.7623	00.40	03.59	00.07	04.05
		TGen+	40.25	6.1448	37.50	56.19	1.8181	00.21	01.99	00.05	02.24
		SC-LSTM	23.88	3.9310	32.11	39.90	0.5036	07.73	17.76	09.52	35.03
Cleaned	Cleaned	TGen−	40.19	6.0543	37.38	55.88	1.8104	00.17	01.31	00.25	01.72
		TGen	40.73	6.1711	37.76	56.09	1.8518	00.07	00.72	00.08	00.87
		TGen+	40.51	6.1226	37.61	55.98	1.8286	00.02	00.63	00.06	00.70
		SC-LSTM	23.66	3.9511	32.93	39.29	0.3855	07.89	15.60	08.44	31.94
Cleaned missing		TGen−	40.48	6.0269	37.26	56.19	1.7999	00.43	02.84	00.26	03.52
		TGen	41.57	6.2830	37.99	56.36	1.8849	00.37	01.40	00.09	01.86
		TGen+	41.56	6.2700	37.94	56.38	1.8827	00.21	01.04	00.07	01.31
Cleaned added		TGen−	35.99	5.0734	34.74	54.79	1.5259	00.02	11.58	00.02	11.62
		TGen	40.07	6.1243	37.45	55.81	1.8026	00.05	03.23	00.01	03.29
		TGen+	40.80	6.2197	37.86	56.13	1.8422	00.01	01.87	00.01	01.88

Table 3: Results evaluated on the cleaned test set (cf. Table 2 for column details; note that the numbers are *not* comparable to Table 2 as the test set is different).

Training data	Add	Miss	Wrong	Disfl
Original	0	22	0	14
Cleaned added	0	23	0	14
Cleaned missing	0	1	0	2
Cleaned	0	0	0	5

Table 4: Results of manual error analysis of TGen on a sample of 100 instances from the original test set: total absolute numbers of errors we found (added, missed, wrong values, slight disfluencies).

added, missing, and wrong-valued slots (Add, Miss, Wrong), we observe more deletions than insertions, i.e. the models more often fail to realise part of the MR, rather than hallucinating additional information. To investigate whether this effect stems from the training data, we partially cleaned the data of missing or added information only.[12] However, the results in bottom halves of Tables 2 and 3 do not support our hypothesis: we observe the main effect on SER from cleaning the missed slots, reducing both insertions and deletions. Again, one possible explanation is that cleaning the missing slots provided more complex training examples.

5.2 Manual Error Analysis

We carried out a detailed manual error analysis of selected systems to confirm the automatic metrics results, performing a blind annotation of semantic and fluency errors (not a human preference rating). We evaluated a sample of 100 outputs on the original test set produced by TGen with the default reranker trained using all four cleaning settings (original data, cleaned missing slots, cleaned added slots, fully cleaned). The results in Table 4 confirm the findings of the automatic metrics: systems trained on the fully cleaned set or the set with cleaned missing slots have near-perfect per-

---

[12] We only performed these experiments on TGen because of the low performance of SC-LSTM in general.

formance, with the fully-cleaned one showing a few more slight disfluencies than the other. The systems trained on the original data or with cleaned added slots clearly perform worse in terms of both semantic accuracy and fluency. All fluency problems we found were very slight and no added or wrong-valued slots were found, so missed slots are the main problem.

The manual error analysis also served to assess the accuracy of the SER measuring script on system outputs. Since NNLG tends to use more frequent phrasing, we expected better performance than on the dataset itself, and this proved true: we only found 2 errors in the 400 system outputs (i.e. 99.5% of instances and 99.93% of slots were matched correctly). This confirms that the automatic SER numbers reflect the semantic accuracy of individual systems very closely.

6 Discussion and Related Work

We present a detailed study of semantic errors in NNLG outputs and how these relate to noise in training data. We found that even imperfectly cleaned input data significantly improves semantic accuracy for seq2seq-based generators (up to 97% relative error reduction with the reranker), while only causing a slight decrease in fluency.

Contemporaneous with our work is the effort of Nie et al. (2019), who focus on automatic data cleaning using a NLU iteratively bootstrapped from the noisy data. Their analysis similarly finds that omissions are more common than hallucinations. Correcting for missing slots, i.e. forcing the generator to verbalise all slots during training, leads to the biggest performance improvement. This phenomenon is also observed by Dušek et al. (2018, 2019) for systems in the E2E NLG challenge, but stands in contrast to work on related tasks, which mostly reports on hallucinations (i.e. adding information not grounded in the input), as observed for image captioning (Rohrbach et al., 2018), sports report generation (Wiseman et al., 2017), machine translation (Koehn and Knowles, 2017; Lee et al., 2019), and question answering (Feng et al., 2018). These previous works suggest that the most likely case of hallucinations is an over-reliance on language priors, i.e. memorising 'which words go together'. Similar priors could equally exist in the E2E data for omitting a slot; this might be connected with the fact that the E2E test set MRs tend to be longer than training MRs (6.91 slots on av-erage for test MRs vs. 5.52 for training MRs) and that a large part of them is 'saturated', i.e. contains all possible 8 attributes.

Furthermore, in accordance with our observations, related work also reports a relation between hallucinations and data diversity: Rohrbach et al. (2018) observe an increase for "novel compositions of objects at test time", i.e. non-overlapping test and training sets (cf. Section 3); whereas Lee et al. (2019) reports data augmentation as one of the most efficient counter measures. In future work, we plan to experimentally manipulate these factors to disentangle the relative contributions of data cleanliness and diversity.

Acknowledgments

This research received funding from the EP-SRC projects DILiGENt (EP/M005429/1) and MaDrIgAL (EP/N017536/1) and Charles University project PRIMUS/19/SCI/10. The authors would also like to thank Prof. Ehud Reiter, whose blog[13] inspired some of this research.

References

Dzmitry Bahdanau, Kyunghyun Cho, and Yoshua Bengio. 2015. Neural Machine Translation by Jointly Learning to Align and Translate. In *3rd International Conference on Learning Representations (ICLR2015)*, San Diego, CA, USA. arXiv:1409.0473.

George Doddington. 2002. Automatic evaluation of machine translation quality using n-gram co-occurrence statistics. In *Proceedings of the Second International Conference on Human Language Technology Research*, pages 138–145, San Diego, CA, USA.

Ondřej Dušek and Filip Jurčíček. 2016. Sequence-to-Sequence Generation for Spoken Dialogue via Deep Syntax Trees and Strings. In *Proceedings of the 54th Annual Meeting of the Association for Computational Linguistics (Volume 2: Short Papers)*, pages 45–51, Berlin, Germany. arXiv:1606.05491.

Ondřej Dušek, Jekaterina Novikova, and Verena Rieser. 2018. Findings of the E2E NLG Challenge. In *Proceedings of the 11th International Conference on Natural Language Generation*, pages 322–328, Tilburg, The Netherlands. arXiv:1810.01170.

Ondřej Dušek, Jekaterina Novikova, and Verena Rieser. 2019. Evaluating the State-of-the-Art of End-to-End Natural Language Generation: The E2E NLG Challenge. *Computer Speech & Language*, 59:123–156. arXiv:1901.07931.

---

[13] https://ehudreiter.com/

Mihail Eric, Rahul Goel, Shachi Paul, Abhishek Sethi, Sanchit Agarwal, Shuyag Gao, and Dilek Hakkani-Tur. 2019. MultiWOZ 2.1: Multi-Domain Dialogue State Corrections and State Tracking Baselines. arXiv:1907.01669.

Shi Feng, Eric Wallace, Alvin Grissom II, Mohit Iyyer, Pedro Rodriguez, and Jordan Boyd-Graber. 2018. Pathologies of Neural Models Make Interpretations Difficult. In *Proceedings of the 2018 Conference on Empirical Methods in Natural Language Processing*, pages 3719–3728, Brussels, Belgium.

David M. Howcroft, Dietrich Klakow, and Vera Demberg. 2017. The Extended SPaRKy Restaurant Corpus: Designing a Corpus with Variable Information Density. In *Proceedings of Interspeech 2017*, pages 3757–3761, Stockholm, Sweden.

Juraj Juraska, Panagiotis Karagiannis, Kevin K. Bowden, and Marilyn A. Walker. 2018. A Deep Ensemble Model with Slot Alignment for Sequence-to-Sequence Natural Language Generation. In *Proceedings of the 2018 Conference of the North American Chapter of the Association for Computational Linguistics: Human Language Technologies, Volume 1 (Long Papers)*, pages 152–162, New Orleans, LA, USA.

Philipp Koehn and Rebecca Knowles. 2017. Six Challenges for Neural Machine Translation. In *Proceedings of the First Workshop on Neural Machine Translation*, pages 28–39, Vancouver, Canada.

Alon Lavie and Abhaya Agarwal. 2007. Meteor: An Automatic Metric for MT Evaluation with High Levels of Correlation with Human Judgments. In *Proceedings of the Second Workshop on Statistical Machine Translation*, pages 228–231, Prague, Czech Republic.

Katherine Lee, Orhan Firat, Ashish Agarwal, Clara Fannjiang, and David Sussillo. 2019. Hallucinations in neural machine translation. OpenReview.

Chin-Yew Lin. 2004. ROUGE: A package for automatic evaluation of summaries. In *Text summarization branches out: Proceedings of the ACL-04 workshop*, pages 74–81, Barcelona, Spain.

F. Mairesse, M. Gašić, F. Jurčíček, S. Keizer, B. Thomson, K. Yu, and S. Young. 2010. Phrase-based statistical language generation using graphical models and active learning. In *Proceedings of the 48th Annual Meeting of the Association for Computational Linguistics*, page 1552–1561, Uppsala, Sweden.

Hongyuan Mei, Mohit Bansal, and Matthew R. Walter. 2016. What to talk about and how? Selective Generation using LSTMs with Coarse-to-Fine Alignment. In *Proceedings of the 2016 Conference of the North American Chapter of the Association for Computational Linguistics: Human Language Technologies*, pages 720–730, San Diego, CA, USA. arXiv:1509.00838.

Feng Nie, Jin-Ge Yao, Jinpeng Wang, Rong Pan, and Chin-Yew Lin. 2019. A simple recipe towards reducing hallucination in neural surface realisation. In *Proceedings of the 57th Conference of the Association for Computational Linguistics Volume 1: Long Papers*, pages 2673–2679, Florence, Italy.

Jekaterina Novikova, Oliver Lemon, and Verena Rieser. 2016. Crowd-sourcing NLG Data: Pictures Elicit Better Data. In *The 9th International Natural Language Generation conference INLG*, Edinburgh, Scotland, UK. arXiv: 1608.00339.

Kishore Papineni, Salim Roukos, Todd Ward, and Wei-Jing Zhu. 2002. BLEU: a method for automatic evaluation of machine translation. In *Proceedings of the 40th Annual Meeting of the Association for Computational Linguistics*, pages 311–318, Philadelphia, PA, USA.

Lena Reed, Shereen Oraby, and Marilyn Walker. 2018. Can Neural Generators for Dialogue Learn Sentence Planning and Discourse Structuring? In *Proceedings of the 11th International Conference on Natural Language Generation*, pages 284–295, Tilburg, The Netherlands. arXiv:1809.03015.

Anna Rohrbach, Lisa Anne Hendricks, Kaylee Burns, Trevor Darrell, and Kate Saenko. 2018. Object hallucination in image captioning. In *Proceedings of the 2018 Conference on Empirical Methods in Natural Language Processing*, pages 4035–4045, Brussels, Belgium.

Ramakrishna Vedantam, C. Lawrence Zitnick, and Devi Parikh. 2015. CIDEr: Consensus-based image description evaluation. In *Proceedings of the 2015 IEEE Conference on Computer Vision and Pattern Recognition (CVPR)*, pages 4566–4575, Boston, MA, USA.

Tsung-Hsien Wen, Milica Gasic, Nikola Mrksic, Lina M. Rojas-Barahona, Pei-Hao Su, David Vandyke, and Steve Young. 2016. Multi-domain Neural Network Language Generation for Spoken Dialogue Systems. In *Proceedings of the 2016 Conference of the North American Chapter of the Association for Computational Linguistics: Human Language Technologies*, pages 120–129, San Diego, CA, USA. arXiv: 1603.01232.

Tsung-Hsien Wen, Milica Gasic, Nikola Mrkšić, Pei-Hao Su, David Vandyke, and Steve Young. 2015. Semantically Conditioned LSTM-based Natural Language Generation for Spoken Dialogue Systems. In *Proceedings of the 2015 Conference on Empirical Methods in Natural Language Processing*, pages 1711–1721, Lisbon, Portugal.

Sam Wiseman, Stuart M. Shieber, and Alexander M. Rush. 2017. Challenges in Data-to-Document Generation. In *Proceedings of the 2017 Conference on Empirical Methods in Natural Language Processing*, pages 2243–2253, Copenhagen, Denmark. arXiv:1707.08052.

Can Neural Image Captioning be Controlled via Forced Attention?

Philipp Sadler, Tatjana Scheffler and David Schlangen
Department of Linguistics
Research Focus Cognitive Sciences
University of Potsdam, Germany
`{name.surname}@uni-potsdam.de`

Abstract

Learned dynamic weighting of the conditioning signal (attention) has been shown to improve neural language generation in a variety of settings. The weights applied when generating a particular output sequence have also been viewed as providing a potentially explanatory insight into the internal workings of the generator. In this paper, we reverse the direction of this connection and ask whether through the control of the attention of the model we can control its output. Specifically, we take a standard neural image captioning model that uses attention, and fix the attention to predetermined areas in the image. We evaluate whether the resulting output is more likely to mention the class of the object in that area than the normally generated caption. We introduce three effective methods to control the attention and find that these are producing expected results in up to 27.43% of the cases.

1 Introduction

Sequential deep learning language models with an attention mechanism are able to use not only the immediately previous inputs, but can involve context by "attending to" select parts of the whole input sequence at each time step. This has first been shown to be helpful for neural machine translation, which operates on sequences of words. Here, deep learning networks with attention are capable to jointly learn the alignment and translation of languages (Bahdanau et al., 2014; Luong et al., 2015).

From the beginning, the dynamics of the attention while generating output sequences has been seen as providing insight into the workings of the models, if only qualitatively. This is in particular applicable to the interdisciplinary fields of natural language processing and computer vision like image captioning. For example, Xu et al. (2015)

Figure 1: A caption generated by an image captioning model. The attention is pixelated and summed up over all time steps. In addition, the dog and the bicycle are framed with the corresponding bounding boxes.

overlay the attention weights over the input image and show how it shifts while generating the image caption step by step. We show a variant of this visualisation type in Figure 1. The implicit argument at least seems to be that this is informative, because there is a causal relation between where the attention is placed and what is being produced, which has been critically discussed recently (Serrano and Smith, 2019; Jain and Wallace, 2019).

In this paper, we address the question of whether this assumed connection can be used to assert additional control over the generation process. We train a caption generation model with spatial attention in the usual way, but then at test time override its attention mechanism and force it to attend to pre-determined parts of the image. Does this cause the generated output to be different from what would otherwise have been produced, in predictable ways? Our results show that this expectation is partially supported.

Proceedings of The 12th International Conference on Natural Language Generation, pages 427–431,
Tokyo, Japan, 28 Oct - 1 Nov, 2019. ©2019 Association for Computational Linguistics

2   Related Work

There have been several attempts to achieve more control over neural language generation. Anderson et al. (2017) control the output of a captioning model at test time with an enhanced beam search. An external system is generating image tags as a control signal at the decoder level. They show that adding the additional hints for the generation process actually improves the performance for out-of-domain captioning. Although this approach works, there is no attention effecting mechanism involved. Zarrieß and Schlangen (2018) evaluate a "trainable decoding" approach that inserts task-specific concerns into the decoding process.

Interfering with the attention mechanism after training, however, has to our knowledge been tried less often. Cornia et al. (2018) train a captioning model not only to learn the distribution for images and sentences, but also for bounding boxes and noun chunks. In addition, the model has to learn when to switch between boxes. As a result, the captioning model is controllable by a bounding box sequence provided as an input to the network at test time. Although this approach has been shown to work well, here the model is explicitly designed to be controllable.

In contrast to the previous approaches, we assume that an attention-aware captioning model is inherently controllable by its spatial attention. In such a sense, our approach is an inverse of the visual grounding task. In one of their experiments, Rohrbach et al. (2016) try to localize phrases within an image by deriving bounding boxes from the spatial attention of a specially trained model. We try to reverse this direction and fix the attention to manually chosen parts of the image after training to generate captions about that region.

3   An Attentive Image Captioning Model

We implement a standard neural image captioning architecture that uses spatial attention, which has shown to correlate objects within the image with spatial attention (Xu et al., 2015). As a modification, we use the image features of the pooling layer in the fifth convolutional block like Yang et al. (2015). This modification lead to higher BLEU scores for our setup.

The network is trained on the training split of the MSCOCO dataset for the *Captioning Challenge 2015*. This split provides five ground-truth captions for each of the 82,783 images. The

dataset images are resized to 448x448 pixels *not* keeping the aspect ratio. We apply only basic tokenization on the captions. Then the captions of the dataset are prepared to contain only captions that have a maximal length of 16 words. Furthermore, the vocabulary is constrained to the 10,000 most common words and we discard captions that are containing words not included in this vocabulary. The caption-image pairs are shuffled randomly before training. As in the work of Xu et al. (2015), we apply dropout and use the Adam optimizer to minimize the loss function

$$L = -log(P(y|x)) + \lambda \sum_{i}^{L} (1 - \sum_{t}^{C} \alpha_{it})^2 \quad (1)$$

with the alpha-regularizer λ, L as the number of image features, C as the caption length and α_{it} as the spatial attention for an image feature at a specific time-step. The alpha-regularizer λ constraints the caption generator to distribute the spatial attention more equally among the image areas during the whole generation process. Xu et al. (2015) noted that this regularizer is important for the resulting overall BLEU score, but they did not mention the exact value to be chosen. Therefore we tried $0.001, 0.005, 0.010$ and found that $\lambda = 0.005$ produces the best scores.

Our best model achieves 69.8, 51.8, 37.2, 26.6 in BLEU-1,2,3,4, respectively. Thus we were able to partially increase on the reported scores on the same validation split. Xu et al. (2015) reported 70.7, 49.2, 34.4, 24.3, so our model is worse by -0.9 in BLEU-1 scores, but better by $+2.6$, $+2.8$, $+2.3$ in the other scores.

4   Methods

Assuming that a sufficiently well trained captioning system is capable of talking about a variety of objects and object configurations, we expect that the caption generation process is controllable when forcing the attention to specific parts in the image. We create a dataset for this specific captioning task using the MSCOCO validation split for the *Detection Challenge 2015*, which provides one or more bounding boxes for each of the 40,504 images (Lin et al., 2014). The boxes frame distinct (but possibly overlapping) objects in the images that are each labelled with one of 80 categories.

4.1 Constructing Spatial Attention Vectors

The distinct objects in the images are framed with bounding boxes which are rectangles defined by their width, height and the xy-coordinates of the left upper corner. We discard all bounding boxes that are smaller than the median size, because the model less likely attends to small objects in the images. From the remaining boxes we derive the spatial attention vectors for the experiments.

To construct a spatial attention vector, we define a matrix $Z \in \mathbb{Z}^{W \times H}$ with $W \times H$ as the according image size and a box coordinate space $B \in \mathbb{Z}^2$ with each point that falls into the box. Given these we set the values in the matrix as the following:

$$\alpha_{xy} = \begin{cases} 255 \text{ if } (x, y) \in B \\ 0 \text{ otherwise} \end{cases} \quad (2)$$

We use 255 as the attention values to align to RGB format, so that we can easily present the maps along with the their images. We resize the matrix to 14×14 using nearest neighbor downsampling not keeping the aspect ratio. Finally, the matrix is flattened to a 196-dimensional vector and the softmax function is applied, so that $\sum \alpha_i = 1$ and $\alpha \in [0, 1]$ is guaranteed like in the implementation of Xu et al. (2015). An important detail is that no value is actually zero. The model is still allowed to include image aspects outside the boxes for the caption generation. In addition, when using 255 as an initial attention value, we found that we need to interpolate for each vector the pixels values following $[0, 255] \rightarrow [0, 1]$, because otherwise the softmax results in too much weight on individual spatial areas and leads to qualitative worse captions e.g. the model is referring to polar bear for the dog on the ground.

4.2 Forcing the Spatial Attention

The trained image captioning model has to produce what we call a *box caption* for each constructed attention vector. That is, the spatial attention is derived from the bounding box like in section 4.1 and applied to the model in one of the following ways.

(a) **Unlimited step-wise fixed attention.** For this experiment, we feed the spatial attention vector at each time step to the model for the whole caption generation process. The model's own predicted attention is dismissed.

	Sensitivity	
	general (diff)	method (diff)
unlimited	88.68 (0.55)	**52.65** (0.54)
limited-3	85.23 (0.55)	35.20 (0.55)
limited-6	87.90 (0.56)	46.49 (0.55)
limited-9	**88.88** (0.55)	51.81 (0.54)
additive-1	85.51 (0.54)	33.43 (0.51)
additive-2	87.26 (0.54)	41.25 (0.53)
additive-3	85.49 (0.54)	44.29 (0.52)

Table 1: The degree of sensitivity as the percentage of 117,798 box captions which deviate from the control (method sens.) or self-attending (general sens.) caption in at least a single word. The differentness for the according subset is given in parentheses as WER scores.

(b) **Limited step-wise fixed attention.** We feed the spatial attention vector for the first $i = \{3, 6, 9\}$ time steps which are empirically chosen. After the t_i time step, the model is again "free to choose" the spatial attention depending on its state and the previous word.

(c) **Step-wise additive attention.** At each time step, the spatial attention vector is added to the one predicted by the model. We introduce a factor to control the weight of the externally induced attention and divide by the according term plus 1.

5 Results

For the test image shown in Figure 1, the model produces the caption "a dog is laying down on the street" with unlimited fixed attention on the dog, whereas when forcing the attention on the bicycle: "a bicycle parked in front of a bicycle".

Likewise, when forcing the attention on the bike, the model is producing bike related captions "a bicycle parked in front of a building" for our limited step-wise configurations. In contrast to that, additive attention in this case leads to dog related captions "a dog is sitting on the sidewalk next to a bike" for lower weights up to two and bike related captions "a bicycle parked in front of a building" for weights higher than two. More examples can be found in the supplementary material.

5.1 Quantitative Analysis: Sensitivity

The qualitative results show that the model is capable to react to changes in its spatial attention. As a measurement for this capability, we suggest the *degree of sensitivity*. Here, we quantify how

	Controllable		and distinct	
	k@1	k@5	k@1	k@5
unlimited	**28.56**	**58.17**	**9.00**	**21.39**
limited-3	26.36	50.84	6.89	15.21
limited-6	27.69	52.75	8.21	17.86
limited-9	27.32	52.94	7.85	18.03
additive-1	25.86	52.89	6.27	17.23
additive-2	26.98	52.28	7.26	16.70
additive-3	27.35	53.83	7.33	18.69

Table 2: The degree of controllability as the percentage of box captions containing their category in relation to all 117,798 box captions. The degree for the distinct share is based on 87,033 (k@1) or 58,407 (k@5) box captions with before unmentioned categories.

often the resulting box captions deviate from the normally generated caption for an image. In the following, we call the normally generated caption a *self-attending caption*, because the attention is "freely chosen" by the model.

As shown in Table 1, the model has the highest general sensitivity for the limited-9 fixed attention method where 88.88% of the box captions differ from the self-attending caption in at least a single word. We also compute the WER scores for these subsets and see that on average the box captions are changed in every second word in comparison to the self-attending caption.

In addition, we indicate whether the model's changes in caption generation are related to specific attention forcing methods or a method unrelated phenomenon. To do so, we let the model produce a *control caption* where the fixed spatial attention has been distributed uniformly over the whole image. This makes it possible to study the effect of the individual forcing methods.

The highest degree of method specific sensitivity is measured for the unlimited fixed attention method as depicted in Table 1. Here, 52.65% of the box captions differ to the control caption in at least one word. This indicates that among the presented methods, the unlimited spatial fixation is the most effective attention induction method.

5.2 Quantitative Analysis: Controllability

Finally, we expect that the produced box captions are referring to objects in the bounding boxes from which the spatial attention vectors are constructed. Thus we evaluate the *degree of controllability* of our forcing methods by checking that the box cap-

tions include the according box categories (k@1).[1]

Table 2 shows the highest degree of controllability for the unlimited configuration, which results in 28.56% of the cases in a box caption that includes its according box category. As the set of COCO categories is rather restrictive, and e.g. only states "person" where a caption might say "woman" or "man", we also check for the five nearest neighbors in cosine distance of the model's learned word embedding space (k@5). Still, the limited-6 configuration results in the highest score with 55.58%, in which, for example, the box caption contains the category name "person" or one of its neighbors ("man", "woman", "guy" or "girl").

Furthermore, we compute the degree of controllability within the more interesting *distinct* subset. In cases where the model already refers to objects within the bounding box, because they include the main objects of an image, we cannot conclude whether the forcing methods have a controllable impact on the resulting captions. Thus, for the distinct subset we discard bounding boxes from the evaluation, which have categories attached that are already included in the standardly produced caption (nearest neighbors accordingly).

Table 2 shows for the distinct subset that in 9.00% of the cases the resulting caption includes the box category, when the spatial attention is focusing on something new (not mentioned before) in the image using the unlimited fixed attention method. The unlimited configuration has also the highest degree with 21.39%, when we also allow the five nearest neighbors to be included.

6 Discussion and further work

The results show that a caption generation model with spatial attention is controllable by the presented forcing methods. The forced model produces predictable results in up to 28.56% of the cases. These results provide evidence that the model is inherently learning to react to changes in the spatial attention, although the learning task is a more general one. Therefore these results show that specific types of attention like spatial attention might be useful control mechanisms.

The evaluation is difficult, because we use a general purpose dataset in MSCOCO. For example, the most common category in the dataset is

---

[1]The defined metric provides a lower boundary on the performance of attention control, since we compare freely generated captions with a restricted list of classes. We leave a manual evaluation for future work.

"person", which is also the most diverse one. We tried to tackle this problem by also looking for the nearest neighbors of the categories and achieved up to 21.39% matches in the relevant subset.

Future work will include building and using cleaner and more balanced datasets for the proposed evaluation task. The model's performance is expected to improve when trained on a larger dataset like Visual Genome (Krishna et al., 2016). We think that modifying the spatial attention of a standard neural image captioning model introduces an interesting new research direction for natural language generation, which will allow researchers to handle and understand the complexities of these models more easily.

References

Peter Anderson, Basura Fernando, Mark Johnson, and Stephen Gould. 2017. Guided Open Vocabulary Image Captioning with Constrained Beam Search. In *Proceedings of the 2017 Conference on Empirical Methods in Natural Language Processing*, pages 936–945, Copenhagen, Denmark. Association for Computational Linguistics.

Dzmitry Bahdanau, Kyunghyun Cho, and Yoshua Bengio. 2014. Neural Machine Translation by Jointly Learning to Align and Translate. *arXiv:1409.0473 [cs, stat]*. ArXiv: 1409.0473.

Marcella Cornia, Lorenzo Baraldi, and Rita Cucchiara. 2018. Show, Control and Tell: A Framework for Generating Controllable and Grounded Captions. *arXiv:1811.10652 [cs]*. ArXiv: 1811.10652.

Sarthak Jain and Byron C. Wallace. 2019. Attention is not Explanation. *arXiv:1902.10186 [cs]*. ArXiv: 1902.10186.

Ranjay Krishna, Yuke Zhu, Oliver Groth, Justin Johnson, Kenji Hata, Joshua Kravitz, Stephanie Chen, Yannis Kalantidis, Li-Jia Li, David A. Shamma, Michael S. Bernstein, and Fei-Fei Li. 2016. Visual Genome: Connecting Language and Vision Using Crowdsourced Dense Image Annotations. *arXiv:1602.07332 [cs]*. ArXiv: 1602.07332.

Tsung-Yi Lin, Michael Maire, Serge Belongie, Lubomir Bourdev, Ross Girshick, James Hays, Pietro Perona, Deva Ramanan, C. Lawrence Zitnick, and Piotr Dollár. 2014. Microsoft COCO: Common Objects in Context. *arXiv:1405.0312 [cs]*. ArXiv: 1405.0312.

Jiasen Lu, Jianwei Yang, Dhruv Batra, and Devi Parikh. 2016. Hierarchical Question-image Co-attention for Visual Question Answering. In *Proceedings of the 30th International Conference on Neural Information Processing Systems*, NIPS'16, pages 289–297, USA. Curran Associates Inc. Event-place: Barcelona, Spain.

Thang Luong, Hieu Pham, and Christopher D. Manning. 2015. Effective Approaches to Attention-based Neural Machine Translation. In *Proceedings of the 2015 Conference on Empirical Methods in Natural Language Processing*, pages 1412–1421, Lisbon, Portugal. Association for Computational Linguistics.

Anna Rohrbach, Marcus Rohrbach, Ronghang Hu, Trevor Darrell, and Bernt Schiele. 2016. Grounding of Textual Phrases in Images by Reconstruction. *arXiv:1511.03745 [cs]*, 9905:817–834. ArXiv: 1511.03745.

Sofia Serrano and Noah A. Smith. 2019. Is Attention Interpretable? *arXiv:1906.03731 [cs]*. ArXiv: 1906.03731.

Kelvin Xu, Jimmy Lei Ba, Ryan Kiros, Kyunghyun Cho, Aaron Courville, Ruslan Salakhutdinov, Richard S. Zemel, and Yoshua Bengio. 2015. Show, Attend and Tell: Neural Image Caption Generation with Visual Attention. In *Proceedings of the 32Nd International Conference on International Conference on Machine Learning - Volume 37*, ICML'15, pages 2048–2057, Lille, France. JMLR.org.

Zichao Yang, Xiaodong He, Jianfeng Gao, Li Deng, and Alex Smola. 2015. Stacked Attention Networks for Image Question Answering. *arXiv:1511.02274 [cs]*. ArXiv: 1511.02274.

Sina Zarrieß and David Schlangen. 2018. Decoding Strategies for Neural Referring Expression Generation. In *Proceedings of the International Conference on Natural Language Generation (INLG)*.

Towards a Metric for Automated Conversational Dialogue System Evaluation and Improvement

Jan Deriu
Zurich University of Applied Sciences
deri@zhaw.ch

Mark Cieliebak
Zurich University of Applied Sciences
ciel@zhaw.ch

Abstract

We present "AutoJudge", an automated evaluation method for conversational dialogue systems. The method works by first generating dialogues based on self-talk, i.e. dialogue systems talking to itself. Then, it uses human ratings on these dialogues to train an automated judgement model. Our experiments show that AutoJudge correlates well with the human ratings and can be used to automatically evaluate dialogue systems, even in deployed systems. In a second part, we attempt to apply AutoJudge to improve existing systems. This works well for re-ranking a set of candidate utterances. However, our experiments show that AutoJudge cannot be applied as reward for reinforcement learning, although the metric can distinguish good from bad dialogues. We discuss potential reasons, but state here already that this is still an open question for further research.

1 Introduction

Conversational dialogue systems (also referred to as chatbots, social bots, or non-task-oriented dialogue systems) allow for a natural conversation between computer and humans. Research on these dialogue systems has recently reemerged due to the availability of large dialogue corpora, (Serban et al., 2018) as well as the popularization of deep learning (Sordoni et al., 2015; Vinyals and Le, 2015; Serban et al., 2016b).

One major challenge in developing high-quality dialogue systems is the evaluation process. Ideally, an evaluation method should be automated, have a high correlation to human judgements and be able to discriminate between different dialogue strategies. Most common techniques to evaluate conversational dialogue systems rely on crowd-sourcing, where human judges are asked to rate the *appropriateness* (or *quality*) of a generated response given a context. Although this procedure allows to discriminate between different strategies, it has several drawbacks: it is time and cost intensive, it has to be redone for every change in dialogue strategy, and the results cannot be used to improve the system.

On the other hand, the automated evaluation is usually performed by applying word-overlap metrics borrowed from the machine translation or text summarization community, which have been shown to correlate poorly to human judgements on the utterance level (Liu et al., 2016).

Trained Metrics. Recently, the notion of *trained metrics* was introduced for conversational dialogue systems (Lowe et al., 2017). The main idea is that humans rate the generated response of a dialogue system in relation to a given context (i.e. the dialogue history). Based on these ratings, a regression model is trained which models the human judges. For this, the context, the candidate response, and the gold-standard response are used as input and the judgement is predicted. This approach correlates well with human judgements on the turn level as well as on the system level.

However, these metrics rely on a gold-standard and work on static contexts, which is problematic for two reasons. First, as the context is written by humans it does not reflect the behaviour of the dialogue system. Second, it cannot be used in deployed systems where no gold-standard is available. Dynamic context evaluation (Gandhe and Traum, 2016), on the other hand, usually requires human-computer interaction, which is costly, and puts an additional cognitive strain on the users if they are to rate live during the conversation (Schmitt and Ultes, 2015).

Contribution. In this work we propose to automatically generate the dialogues relying on *self-talk*, which is derived from *AlphaGo* self-play (Silver et al., 2016). Dialogues are generated by two

Proceedings of The 12th International Conference on Natural Language Generation, pages 432–437,
Tokyo, Japan, 28 Oct - 1 Nov, 2019. ©2019 Association for Computational Linguistics

instances of the same system conversing with each other. Then the automatically generated dialogues are rated by human judges. That is, the judges read the dialogues and rate it on the turn level. Based on these ratings, we train a regression model which learns to predict the ratings of the human judges. Our results show that this method, which we refer to as *AutoJudge*, achieves high correlation to human judgements. Thus, it can be applied to fully automatically assess the quality of a dialogue system without being dependent on gold standard responses.

Applications. Since our approach is fully automatic and requires no humans in the loop, we want to go one step further and apply it to *improve* the dialogue system at hand. More precisely we attempt to apply the metric in two different ways: (i) response ranking similar to (Shalyminov et al., 2018; Hancock et al., 2019), and (ii) reward for reinforcement learning. It turns out that only the re-ranking shows promising results, whereas the metric is not useful as a reward function. This is very surprising, since the trained metric correlates well to human judgements, and it can discriminate between good and bad utterances. Why this happens, and how it can be resolved, is an open research question, which we discuss towards the end of this paper.

2 Experimental Setup

Our experimental pipeline follows three phases. First, the data generation phase, where we let the dialogue systems generate dialogues automatically. Second, the data annotation phase, where we rely on crowdsouring to rate the dialogues on the turn level. Third, the improvement phase, where we train an automated judgement model on the annotated data and apply this model to improve the dialogue system.

2.1 Dialogue Systems

For our experiments we relied on the following state-of-the-art dialogue systems (the training details are in Appendix A):

Seq2Seq. The Sequence-to-Sequence model as proposed by (Vinyals and Le, 2015) consists of an encoder and a decoder. Both modules are based on Long Short-Term Memory cells (LSTM) (Hochreiter and Schmidhuber, 1997), where the encoder consumes the last utterance and produces a hidden representation, which is passed as initial state to the decoder to condition the generation process.

HRED. The Hierarchical Recurrent Encoder-Decoder (HRED) model proposed by (Serban et al., 2016a) enhances the Seq2Seq model by a hierarchical encoding procedure. Here, the context-turns are encoded by first encoding each turn separately and then by applying a recurrent encoder over the hidden states of the turns. The decoding procedure is conditioned on the hidden state produced by the context encoder.

VHRED. The Hierarchical Latent Variable Encoder-Dcoder model (VHRED) (Serban et al., 2017a) enhances the aforementioned HRED model by introducing a stochastic latent variable at the utterance level. This stochastic variable aims to inject variability at the utterance level, which in turn increases the variety of responses a model generates.

MrRNN. The Multi-resolution Recurrent Neural Ntwork (MrRNN) (Serban et al., 2017b) enhances the HRED model by introducing an abstraction layer. More precisely, the dialogue is modelled by processing the inputs and outputs at various level of abstractions (e.g. at the level of meaning bearing words and the usual word-level).

DE. The Dual Encoder (DE) (Lowe et al., 2015) is a selection based model, which differs from the generation based approaches of the aforementioned models. The DE encodes both the context and a candidate response (using the same encoder as the VHRED model) and then classifies if the candidate is a valid response to the given context.

2.2 Turn-Level Annotation

We apply *self-talk* to automatically generate dialogues. For this, we sample 100 different contexts randomly from a set of unseen contexts and let the dialogue system generate a dialogue starting from this context, which consist of 10 turns each. For the annotation process, we use Amazon Mechanical Turk (AMT) [1] and follow the procedure outlined by (Lowe et al., 2017), i.e. the judges rated the *overall quality* of each turn on a scale from 1 (low quality) to 5 (high quality). Each turn is annotated by three different judges. We required the AMT workers to be from an english speaking country (USA, UK, Ireland or Australia)

---

[1] https://www.mturk.com/

in order to ensure that they are native speakers, since the generated messages are highly colloquial and make heavy usage of slang. For each annotation, we paid 15 cents, where we assumed that each annotation takes between 60 to 90 seconds. For the selection of the final turn-label, we apply the MACE procedure (Hovy et al., 2013), which learns confidence scores for the annotators. Our final dataset consists of a total of 500 annotated dialogues, which amounts to 5000 annotated pairs of contexts and responses.

2.3 AutoJudge

Similarly to the *ADEM* procedure proposed by (Lowe et al., 2017), we train a regression model on the annotated data. For this, we use the pre-trained context and response encoder from the VHRED model. Unlike *ADEM*, our dialogues are generated automatically, thus, we do not have access to a gold-standard response. For this reason, we use the following scoring function: $score(c, r) = (c^T M r - \alpha)/\beta$ where $M \in \mathbb{R}^{d \times d}$ is a learned similarity matrix, α, β are scalar constants, and c, r are the context and response embeddings respectively. The model is optimized to minimize the mean squared error between the predicted ratings and the human judgements.

2.4 Improving Dialogue Systems

Since *AutoJudge* is fully automated, we apply it to improve the existing dialogue systems. For this, we implemented the following two applications: as reward for reinforcement learning (RL), and as re-ranking candidate utterances.

Re-Ranking. Given a list of responses from the five aforementioned dialogue systems for a given context, *AutoJudge* re-ranks them by their predicted score. In our experiments, we use the dialogue systems, which we trained for the self-talk experiment, i.e. we re-rank the outputs of the five aforementioned dialogue systems. Thus, the re-ranker serves as a meta-selection module.

Reinforcement Learning Reward. We apply the predicted ratings as reward in the RL framework. For this, we apply the Policy Gradient formulation, as done in (Li et al., 2016), which is defined as follows: $\nabla J_{RL}(\theta) = \sum_i \nabla \log p(r_i|c_i) \times \sum_i R(r_i, c_i)$, where r_i and c_i are the response and context in the ith turn, $R(r_i, c_i)$ is the predicted reward by *AutoJudge*, and $\sum_i \log p(r_i|c_i)$ is the reconstruction error.

3 Results and Discussion

In our experiments we use the Twitter Dialogue Corpus (Ritter et al., 2011)[2]. The Twitter Dialogue Corpus provides social interactions, which we believe to be a good basis for being annotated via crowdsouring.

Data Aggregation. The turn-level ratings provide us with 5000 annotated pairs of context and responses. The distribution over the labels is balanced (i.e. each class is represented between 19% and 21% of the cases). However, the agreement scores among the human judges is rather low: the median pairwise Spearman correlation between two judges is only at 0.403. Furthermore, the MACE procedure reports on the confidence score (between 0 and 1) of single judges, which is used as basis for selecting the final label. The average confidence is at only 0.15. We assume that these problems stem from the high degree of subjectivity of the problem.

	Pearson Corr	Spearman's Rho	MAE
CONVO SPLIT	0.573	0.577	0.928
SYSTEM SPLIT	0.544	0.53	0.984

Table 1: Average correlations between the judgements predicted by AutoJudge and the human judgement. CONVO SPLIT denotes the cross-validation split according to the contexts and SYSTEM SPLIT denotes the cross-validation split according to the dialogue system.

AutoJudge. We train *AutoJuge* using k-fold cross validation. There are two ways of splitting the data into folds, in order to ensure that all turns of the same dialogue are in the same fold. First, we group the 100 contexts into 10 folds, thus, each fold consists of 50 dialogues (i.e. 10 contexts times the number of dialogue systems), this is denoted as CONVO SPLIT. The second option is to split the data according to the system which created the conversation, which evaluates the performance of *AutoJuge* in rating dialogues of unseen dialogue systems. We denote this as SYSTEM SPLIT. In Table 1, we report the average Pearson correlation, Spearman's rho and mean absolute error (MAE) over all folds for the *conversation split* and the *system split*. With moderate correlations of 0.573 on the dialogue level, we get results which are comparable to (Lowe et al., 2017),

---

[2]We use the IDs provided by (Serban et al., 2017a), which can be found here: www.iulianserban.com/Files/TweetIDs.zip

where ADEM achieves a Pearson correlation of 0.436. Note that we cannot directly compare our results to BLEU score and ADEM, since these base their predictions on gold standards, which we do not have in our setting. An interesting result is the *System Split*, i.e. that our approach is able to maintain a high correlation (0.544) with the ratings of a dialogue system when removing the data of that system from the training, which is not the case in (Lowe et al., 2017) where the correlation for a different system dropped significantly.

Answer Selection. In order to evaluate the improvements achieved by the re-ranking method, we sample a disjoint set of 100 new contexts and apply *self-talk* to generate conversations. Then, we use AMT to let humans judge the automatically generated conversations on the dialogue level (i.e. a rating for the entire dialogue as opposed to turn-based ratings). We compare the performance of the five base dialogue systems to the performance of the re-ranking strategy. Table 2 shows the average scores for each dialogue system. Our results show that the *re-ranking* approach works very well. It raises the score to 3.47, which is 0.16 points higher than the best base-system (i.e. SEQ2SEQ).

Systems	Dialogue Level Rating
SEQ2SEQ	*3.31*
HRED	2.78
VHRED	3.20
MRRNN	2.37
DUAL ENCODER	2.02
RE-RANKING	**3.47**

Table 2: Human judgements on the dialogue level for each dialogue system. For this, a each dialogue system (the five base-systems and the re-ranking system) generate 100 dialogues using self-talk, which human judges rated on the dialogue level. Here we see the average ratings for each system.

Reinforcement Learning. When we apply *AutoJudge* as reward resulted in suboptimal dialogues. Although the return increases over time (from 21.74 to 37.41 over 80 episodes), the dialogues which the policy generates are often incoherent or completely useless. This seems counterintuitive when taking into account the aforementioned high correlation scores. We believe that the main reason for the suboptimal behaviour is that *AutoJudge* does not have enough coverage during training. Thus, very bad responses (e.g. empty responses, repeating responses, convergence to a single universal response) tend to receive high scores, since the training data for *AutoJudge* does not include these kinds of responses. However, it is not clear how to stabilize *AutoJudge* to handle these cases. For instance, by artificially enhancing the training data for *AutoJudge* with negative examples, the Pearson correlation score drops to 0.50 without any impact on the reinforcement learning.

4 Conclusion

Our results show that *AutoJudge* correlates well to human judgements and it is useful to measure the progress of a dialogue system, as it is able to discriminate among different strategies. Furthermore, it generalizes well to unseen strategies for the same domain. Since *AutoJudge* is independent of a gold-standard it can be applied to deployed systems where gold-standards are not available. Finally, it shows promising results when applied as answer selection module. As a next step, we intend to apply *AutoJudge* onto human-computer dialogues to measure the viability of *AutoJudge* in a real-world setting.

In this work we tried to use *AutoJudge* as a reward for reinforcement learning, which resulted in suboptimal dialogues. The main reason seems to be that *AutoJudge* cannot properly handle the bad utterance that are generated during the initial phase of reinforcement learning. This is surprising, since *AutoJudge* is able to distinguish good and bad utterances of fully-trained systems. This seems to indicate that there are different types of "bad" utterances, and we need to adapt the training mechanism of *AutoJudge* if we want to apply it not only to evaluation, but also to improving dialogue systems. Our results indicate that trained metrics suffer from instabilities, which might be caused by the size of the dataset.

One major issue is that it is not clear which aspects *AutoJudge* captures. Although the correlation between the human judgements and the outputs of *AutoJudge* are high, we cannot make any statement about what aspects of the context or the response are relevant for the predicted rating. This is a fundamental problem with the evaluation of conversational dialogue systems, as there is no clear definition for "adequate" responses. Thus, an important future work problem is the investigation into the definition of "adequacy" for conversational dialogue systems.

We conjecture that this might apply also to other automated metrics, thus, this is an important research question that needs to be addressed if we want to understand how to better train and optimize dialogue systems.

5 Acknowledgements

This paper has been partially funded by the LIH-LITH project, supported by ERA-NET CHIST-ERA and Swiss National Science Foundation (20CH21_174237).

References

Sudeep Gandhe and David Traum. 2016. *A Semi-automated Evaluation Metric for Dialogue Model Coherence*, pages 217–225. Springer International Publishing, Cham.

Braden Hancock, Antoine Bordes, Pierre-Emmanuel Mazare, and Jason Weston. 2019. Learning from dialogue after deployment: Feed yourself, chatbot! *arXiv preprint arXiv:1901.05415*.

Sepp Hochreiter and Jürgen Schmidhuber. 1997. Long short-term memory. *Neural computation*, pages 1735–1780.

Dirk Hovy, Taylor Berg-Kirkpatrick, Ashish Vaswani, and Eduard Hovy. 2013. Learning whom to trust with mace. In *Proceedings of the 2013 Conference of the North American Chapter of the Association for Computational Linguistics: Human Language Technologies*, pages 1120–1130. Association for Computational Linguistics.

Diederik P Kingma and Jimmy Ba. 2014. Adam: A method for stochastic optimization. *arXiv preprint arXiv:1412.6980*.

Jiwei Li, Will Monroe, Alan Ritter, Dan Jurafsky, Michel Galley, and Jianfeng Gao. 2016. Deep reinforcement learning for dialogue generation. In *Proceedings of the 2016 Conference on Empirical Methods in Natural Language Processing*, pages 1192–1202. Association for Computational Linguistics.

Chia-Wei Liu, Ryan Lowe, Iulian Serban, Mike Noseworthy, Laurent Charlin, and Joelle Pineau. 2016. How NOT To Evaluate Your Dialogue System: An Empirical Study of Unsupervised Evaluation Metrics for Dialogue Response Generation. In *Proceedings of the 2016 Conference on Empirical Methods in Natural Language Processing*, pages 2122–2132. Association for Computational Linguistics.

Ryan Lowe, Michael Noseworthy, Iulian Vlad Serban, Nicolas Angelard-Gontier, Yoshua Bengio, and Joelle Pineau. 2017. Towards an Automatic Turing Test: Learning to Evaluate Dialogue Responses. In *Proceedings of the 55th Annual Meeting of the Association for Computational Linguistics (Volume 1: Long Papers)*, pages 1116–1126. Association for Computational Linguistics.

Ryan Lowe, Nissan Pow, Iulian Serban, and Joelle Pineau. 2015. The ubuntu dialogue corpus: A large dataset for research in unstructured multi-turn dialogue systems. In *Proceedings of the 16th Annual Meeting of the Special Interest Group on Discourse and Dialogue*, pages 285–294, Prague, Czech Republic. Association for Computational Linguistics.

Tomas Mikolov, Edouard Grave, Piotr Bojanowski, Christian Puhrsch, and Armand Joulin. 2018. Advances in pre-training distributed word representations. In *Proceedings of the International Conference on Language Resources and Evaluation (LREC 2018)*.

Alan Ritter, Colin Cherry, and William B. Dolan. 2011. Data-driven Response Generation in Social Media. In *Proceedings of the Conference on Empirical Methods in Natural Language Processing*, EMNLP '11, pages 583–593, Stroudsburg, PA, USA. Association for Computational Linguistics.

Alexander Schmitt and Stefan Ultes. 2015. Interaction Quality: Assessing the quality of ongoing spoken dialog interaction by expertsAnd how it relates to user satisfaction. *Speech Communication*, 74:12 – 36.

Iulian V. Serban, Alessandro Sordoni, Yoshua Bengio, Aaron Courville, and Joelle Pineau. 2016a. Building End-to-end Dialogue Systems Using Generative Hierarchical Neural Network Models. In *Proceedings of the Thirtieth AAAI Conference on Artificial Intelligence*, AAAI'16, pages 3776–3783. AAAI Press.

Iulian V. Serban, Alessandro Sordoni, Ryan Lowe, Laurent Charlin, Joelle Pineau, Aaron Courville, and Yoshua Bengio. 2017a. A Hierarchical Latent Variable Encoder-Decoder Model for Generating Dialogues. In *Thirty-First AAAI Conference on Artificial Intelligence*, page 1583.

Iulian Vlad Serban, Tim Klinger, Gerald Tesauro, Kartik Talamadupula, Bowen Zhou, Yoshua Bengio, and Aaron C. Courville. 2017b. Multiresolution Recurrent Neural Networks: An Application to Dialogue Response Generation. In *Proceedings of the Thirty-First AAAI Conference on Artificial Intelligence, February 4-9, 2017, San Francisco, California, USA.*, pages 3288–3294.

Iulian Vlad Serban, Ryan Lowe, Laurent Charlin, and Joelle Pineau. 2016b. Generative deep neural networks for dialogue: A short review. *arXiv preprint arXiv:1611.06216*.

Iulian Vlad Serban, Ryan Lowe, Peter Henderson, Laurent Charlin, and Joelle Pineau. 2018. A Survey of Available Corpora for Building Data-Driven Dialogue Systems: The Journal Version. *Dialogue & Discourse*, 1(9).

Igor Shalyminov, Ondřej Dušek, and Oliver Lemon. 2018. Neural response ranking for social conversation: A data-efficient approach. In *Proceedings of the 2018 EMNLP Workshop SCAI: The 2nd International Workshop on Search-Oriented Conversational AI*, pages 1–8, Brussels, Belgium. Association for Computational Linguistics.

David Silver, Aja Huang, Chris J Maddison, Arthur Guez, Laurent Sifre, George Van Den Driessche, Julian Schrittwieser, Ioannis Antonoglou, Veda Panneershelvam, Marc Lanctot, et al. 2016. Mastering the game of go with deep neural networks and tree search. *nature*, 529(7587):484.

Alessandro Sordoni, Michel Galley, Michael Auli, Chris Brockett, Yangfeng Ji, Margaret Mitchell, Jian-Yun Nie, Jianfeng Gao, and Bill Dolan. 2015. A Neural Network Approach to Context-Sensitive Generation of Conversational Responses. In *Proceedings of the 2015 Conference of the North American Chapter of the Association for Computational Linguistics: Human Language Technologies*, pages 196–205. Association for Computational Linguistics.

Oriol Vinyals and Quoc Le. 2015. A neural conversational model. *arXiv preprint arXiv:1506.05869*.

Generating Paraphrases with Lean Vocabulary

Tadashi Nomoto
National Institute of Japanese Literature
10-3 Midori Tachikawa Tokyo, 190-0014, Japan
nomoto@acm.org

Abstract

In this work, we examine whether it is possible to achieve the state of the art performance in paraphrase generation with reduced vocabulary. Our approach consists of building a convolution to sequence model (Conv2Seq) partially guided by the reinforcement learning, and training it on the subword representation of the input. The experiment on the Quora dataset, which contains over 140,000 pairs of sentences and corresponding paraphrases, found that with less than 1,000 token types, we were able to achieve performance that exceeded that of the current state of the art.

1 Introduction and Background

The past few years have seen the surge of interest among NLP researchers in applying deep learning to the end-to-end generation of paraphrases: where the goal is to create a sentence semantically close to but distinct in style from the source sentence, without a recourse to some linguistically motivated devices as was often the case with the work a decade ago (Barzilay and Lee, 2003; Power and Scott, 2005; Duboué and Chu-Carroll, 2006; Zhao et al., 2009).

Among the more recent efforts that are of relevance to this work are (Gupta et al., 2017; Iyyer et al., 2018; Wieting et al., 2017; Li et al., 2018), each of which employs the deep learning one way or another to address particular aspects of paraphrase generation. (Iyyer et al., 2018) was concerned with generating paraphrases in a controlled fashion so that the outputs adhere to a certain syntactic requirement specified by the user. (Wieting et al., 2017), meanwhile, worked on creating a high quality paraphrase corpus through backtranslation and argued that they brought the quality of paraphrases close to that of those manually written. (Gupta et al., 2017) was the first attempt to bring the variational auto-encoder (VAE),

wildly popular in computer vision, to bear on the current issue. The idea is to cast paraphrase generation as a problem of sampling a hidden encoding from VAE that retains some similarity to the input sentence. (Li et al., 2018) is a paper most closely related to this one. It features Monte Carlo policy gradient and Inverse Reinforcement Learning, which achieved record setting results on the Quora dataset. Broadly, this paper falls in line with (Li et al., 2018), except that we aim at pushing their results even further by letting reinforcement learning work with the lean vocabulary enabled by the subword encoding.

2 Approach

While we work with a convolution to sequence architecture as provided by Facebook at Github (Fairseq),[1] we made a few changes to the criterion (loss) part of the model in order to accommodate the policy gradient variety of reinforcement learning (PRL). What it does is to allow the model to *randomly* explore the vocabulary space for each decoded output of the model, in search of a word sequence that results in a higher BLEU score. The goal of PRL is to nudge the model toward words that lead to a higher cumulative gain over a long run in terms of BLEU, not just those that result in an immediate reward in the form of the cross entropy. Formally, PRL aims to maximize the following quantity:

$$U(\theta) = \log \pi(\tau; \theta) R(\tau)$$

i.e., an expected return from taking a trajectory τ (word sequence) under π, a policy parameterized with θ. Note that a policy here is understood as a stochastic function that indicates how

---

[1] In particular, one called 'fconv iwslt de en,' which is part of fconv.py found at https://github.com/pytorch/fairseq

Proceedings of The 12th International Conference on Natural Language Generation, pages 438–442,
Tokyo, Japan, 28 Oct - 1 Nov, 2019. ©2019 Association for Computational Linguistics

likely a particular word occurs following the previous one, which is equivalent to a language model $P(w_t \mid w_0, \ldots, w_{t-1})$. $R(\tau)$ is a reward function that determines how much reward will be given for a particular path pursued.

Formally, R is defined as:

$$R(\tau) = \sum_t^T R_t(w_t) \quad \text{where:}$$
$$R_t(w_t) = r_t + \sum_{i=t+1}^{T-1} \lambda R_i(w_i)$$

t represents a time step at which each word appears in the trajectory of length T. r_t represents a reward for the entire trajectory τ against the target, and λ a decay coefficient, which is set at 1.0 for our case. Note that $U(\theta)$ amounts to an expected reward under the policy π. Importantly, we do not use a baseline for R, as we did not find it much of use in our experiment, which is consonant with (Wu et al., 2018), who reported that its use led to no improvement in neural machine translation. Crucially, however, we will make use of multiple reinforcement objectives: a bigram based BLEU and **seqratio**, a string similarity metric based on Levenshtein distance.[2]

The loss function for the present model now looks like:

$$\mathcal{L} = \mathcal{V}(f(u), t) + R(\tau) * \mathcal{V}(f(u), \tau)$$

where $\mathcal{V}$ is a cross-entropy loss, $f(u)$ is an output of Conv2Seq applied to the input u, and t a target. In training, R *alternates* between BLEU and **seqratio**[3] as it moves from one mini-batch to another. Of note is that we have not employed any particular scheduling tactic for training, in contrast to (Ranzato et al., 2015), who initially trained the model on the ground truth and let it slowly deviate from the optimal policy. More in line with the present approach is (Paulus et al., 2017), who worked with a mixed learning objective which attempts to maximize the probability of generating a target given the input, while searching for an optimal policy, except that they rewarded actions that would encourage the generation of fluent text, not those that might improve an evaluation metric such as BLEU.

Another important idea that underlies the current approach is the notion of *subword*, whose members include anything from a single letter or symbol to a full-fledged word. When reviewing errors incurred in an earlier experiment, we came to realize that the majority of them were caused by the model's inability to handle out-of-vocabulary words (OOVs). The observation led us to explore the use of subword as a way to represent text, which turned out to be quite effective, reducing OOVs, and boosting the over-all performance. A particular approach we adopt here is one by (Kudo, 2018). It works by replacing a sentence with a string of reasonably likely textual fragments (or subwords), which may or may not correspond to a meaningful linguistic expression. Under the subword scheme, OOVs are less likely to occur because any word that is not part of the vocabulary will be broken up into or replaced with those that are part of the dictionary. If anything, one can revert to representing a word as a string of alphabets which are always kept in the dictionary (Kudo, 2018).

To recap, two key ideas that drive the current approach are: the adoption of a learning objective informed by multiple reinforcement objectives in addition to the ground truth and the use of subwords to ensure that the model knows every word it sees in the input. For the sake of convenience, we refer to the present approach as RIPER (Reduced InPut Model Enhanced with Reinforcement Learning).

3 Experiment Setup

In the experiment, we made use of the Quora duplicate dataset (QRA), which contains 404,302 pairs of questions and their near duplicates that appeared on the Quora's online forum,[4] out of which we extracted some 140,000 pairs marked as a duplicate for use in training and testing. We follow the same setup as one used in (Li et al., 2018), which involves dividing the corpus into 100K for training, 3K for validation and 30K for testing. In addition to QRA, we tested the approach on the ParaNMT-50M dataset (Wieting and Gimpel, 2017) (PMT).[5] PMT is a fairly large corpus built by back-translating what is translated into Czech with machine translation, into English again using machine translation. We report all the results

---

[2] `https://github.com/ztane/`
`python-Levenshtein.git`

[3] It is the averaged sum of lengths of common substrings, with the range of 0 (least similar) to 1 (most similar).

[4] `https://www.kaggle.com/c/`
`quora-question-pairs`

[5] The corpus we used here contains paraphrase pairs randomly sampled from one of its variants called Para-nmt-5m-processed where staggering 5,370,128 pairs of sentences are found.

Table 1: Corpus Statistics (in sentences)

	TRAIN	VALID	TEST
PMT	600,000	5,000	5,000
QRA	100,000	3,000	30,000

Table 2: Results on PMT and QRA in BLEU.

VOC.	MODEL	PMT	QRA
subword	V8K	**0.414**	0.447
	V8K$^-$	0.411	0.444
	V4K	0.412	0.448
	V4K$^-$	0.397	0.448
	V1K	0.392	**0.453**
	V1K$^-$	0.391	0.442
word	BSE$^+$	0.312	0.295
	BSE	0.395	0.406
	VAE	0.154	0.295
	R-RL	–	0.418
	NMT	0.328	0.399
	RbM-SL	–	0.435
	RbM-IRL	–	0.431

in the bigram based BLEU which we used for reinforcement learning. We also looked at how the present framework would fare against some of the prior approaches tackling the same problem. In this work, we are focusing on some of the more recent attempts, VAE-SVG-eq (Gupta et al., 2017), RbM-SL and its variant, RbM-IRL (Li et al., 2018), along with other more conventional approaches. The former is based on the variational auto-encoder (Kingma and Welling, 2013) while RbM-SL draws essentially on Monte Carlo Policy Gradient, enhanced with reward reshaping (Ng et al., 1999). RbM-IRL differs from RbM-SL in that it makes use of *inverse reinforcement learning* whose goal is to reconstruct a reward function by directly exposing the model to the optimal state/action transition taken by human.

We report results for VAE-SVG-eq from running the third party implementation.[6] As for the latter models (RbM-SL/IRL). we repeat what was published as there is no code available to reproduce runs. We note that for the subword encoding, we have taken advantage of the code published as a part of (Kudo, 2018) on Github.[7]

---

[6]https://github.com/ale3otik/
paraphrases-generator
[7]https://github.com/google/
sentencepiece

4   Results and Discussion

Table 2 summarizes major results. To start, V8K, V4K and V1K are all RIPER models that feed on subwords with dictionaries of sizes 8,000, 4,000, and 1,000, respectively. Note that all of them are derived from the Conv2Seq model, which we call BSE and serves as a baseline.[8] To see the effect of reinforcement, we created some variations on RIPER which differed from the originals in that they were decoupled from the reinforcement capability. To highlight the difference, we mark them with a minus sign. Thus 'V1K$^-$' denotes a V1K with the reinforcement removed. Similarly for V4K and V8K. Furthermore, we had another model, created by extending BSE with the reinforcement, denoted here by BSE$^+$, which works at the word level. VAE is a third party implementation of VAE-SVG-eq. NMT is another baseline derived from OpenNMT-py, a sequence to sequence machine translation model,[9] which we used with the default settings.[10] R-RL corresponds to a pointer generator network empowered with reinforcement learning based on ROUGE (Ranzato et al., 2015). We took its score on QRA from (Li et al., 2018). VOC. indicates the kind of vocabulary the models use: 'word' means that they use tokens as identified by a tokenizer while 'subword' indicates that they work on word fragments as produced by (Kudo, 2018). In the following, we take RbM-SL as the state of the art (SOTA).

In QRA, we see that RIPERs are doing well across the board, beating all the rest, which includes the SOTA. It is remarkable that V1K outruns others, with as little as 1K tokens. On PMT, V8K comes out a winner. The fact that RIPERs did well on two reasonably large datasets and even outperformed the SOTA, drives home the utility of vocabulary reduction through the subword trick. The results also show that reinforcement learning benefitted to some degree from the reduced vocabulary, a point underscored by the fact that BSE$^+$ fell visibly behind BSE both on PMT and on QRA, which can only be explained as the result of having a large action space it had to deal with. By contrast, the use of subwords, with the concomitant reduction in search space, led V1K to reach

---

[8]Refer to footnote 1 for details
[9]https://github.com/OpenNMT/OpenNMT-py
[10]In particular, we enabled options related to the copying functionality, -copy_attn and -reuse_copy_attn

Table 3: Generated Paraphrases (V8K/PMT)

source	target	generated
she staggered , went to one knee , and was up again almost at once .	she staggered , dropped to her knee , but she got up again .	she staggered , went to one knee and stood up again .
i stopped by your room , you know , because i recognized your name .	yes , i was in your room because i know your name and ...	i stopped by your room because i recognized your name .
moving to his command post , he barked , " get me visual ! "	he headed for his command post and barked , " let go of the picture ! "	he 's moving to his command post , he barked , " get me visual ! "
at the point when we were developing this , nobody knew that there were drugs over there .	by the time we torched it , no one knew there were drugs in it .	at the point when we got this , no one knew there were drugs .

Table 4: Generated Paraphrases (V1K/QRA)

source	target	generated
why there is a ban of 500 and 1000 notes ?	what are the pros and cons of banning 500 and 1000 rupee notes in india ?	what are the ill effects of demonetization of 500 and 1000 rupees notes ?
what is ultimate purpose of life ?	what purpose do you find in life ?	what is the purpose of life if not money ?
what can i do to improve my english speaking ?	how can i improve my english pronunciation ?	how can i improve my english pronunciation ?
what is the best laptop in 50000 in india ?	what could be the best laptop in budget upto 50k ?	which is the best laptop to buy under rs 50000 ?
why were the 500 and 1000 rupee notes demonetized ?	what is the logic behind scrapping of 500 and 1000 rupee notes by the indian government ?	why did the indian government demonetize the current 500 and 1000 rupee notes ?

Table 5: The number of tokens in the vocabulary

	PMT	QRA
V8K	7,981 (4.8%)	7,992 (27.9%)
V4K	3,983 (2.3%)	3,994 (14.0%)
V1K	994 (0.5%)	995 (3.5%)
BSE	166,899	28,615

as high as 0.453 on QRA while leaving behind its word based cousin at 0.295. Across the results, there is a general tendency for the subword based models to improve through reinforcement, while those dependent on words suffer the steep decline.

Table 5 shows how much reduction is achieved through the subwording. V1K on QRA works with less than 4% of the vocabulary used by BSE, and on PMT as little as 0.5%. One thing we should point out is that on PMT, we have the maximum score with V4K, while on QRA, the best result comes from V1K. Its performance appears to peak when run on 3 to 5% of the vocabulary. The question of how broadly the observation holds is an interesting one, though it is not clear what the answer would be at this point.

We conclude the section by leaving the reader with some paraphrases RIPERs generated (Table 4), to give an intuitive sense of how we are doing.

5   Conclusions

In this paper, we introduced a fairly straightforward yet novel approach to paraphrase generation we call RIPER, which leverages a recent development in the subword encoding and a policy gradient variety of reinforcement learning. The experiments with two large datasets PMT and QRA have shown unequivocally that RIPER works. One key takeaway is the idea of coupling the subword encoding with reinforcement learning (RL). The application of RL to NLP has been generally perceived as a difficult one (Irpan, 2018). One reason is the enormity of search space due to ever growing vocabulary the model works with. The subword encoding is a nice trick which may mitigate the problem, and could lead to a wider adoption of RL in NLP.

6   Acknowledgement

The present work was partly funded by the Microsoft Core Fellowship for 2018-2019.

References

Regina Barzilay and Lillian Lee. 2003. Learning to paraphrase. An unsupervised approach using multiple-sequence alignment. *CoRR*, cs.CL/0304006.

Pablo Ariel Duboué and Jennifer Chu-Carroll. 2006. Answering the question you wish they had asked: The impact of paraphrasing for question answering. In *Human Language Technology Conference of the North American Chapter of the Association of Computational Linguistics, Proceedings, June 4-9, 2006, New York, New York, USA*.

Ankush Gupta, Arvind Agarwal, Prawaan Singh, and Piyush Rai. 2017. A deep generative framework for paraphrase generation. *CoRR*, abs/1709.05074.

Alex Irpan. 2018. Deep reinforcement learning doesn't work yet. https://www.alexirpan.com/2018/02/14/rl-hard.html.

Mohit Iyyer, John Wieting, Kevin Gimpel, and Luke Zettlemoyer. 2018. Adversarial example generation with syntactically controlled paraphrase networks. *CoRR*, abs/1804.06059.

Diederik P Kingma and Max Welling. 2013. Auto-encoding variational bayes. *CoRR*, https://arxiv.org/abs/1312.6114.

Taku Kudo. 2018. Subword regularization: Improving neural network translation models with multiple subword candidates. *CoRR*, abs/1804.10959.

Zichao Li, Xin Jiang, Lifeng Shang, and Hang Li. 2018. Paraphrase generation with deep reinforcement learning. In *Proceedings of the 2018 Conference on Empirical Methods in Natural Language Processing*, pages 3865–3878. Association for Computational Linguistics.

Andrew Y. Ng, Daishi Harada, and Stuart J. Russel. 1999. Policy invariance under reward transformations: Theory and application to reward shaping. In *ICML '99 Proceedings of the Sixteenth International Conference on Machine Learning*, pages 278–287. Morgan Kaufmann.

Romain Paulus, Caiming Xiong, and Richard Socher. 2017. A deep reinforced model for abstractive summarization. *CoRR*, abs/1705.04304.

Richard Power and Donia Scott. 2005. Automatic generation of large-scale paraphrases. In *Proceedings of the Third International Workshop on Paraphrasing (IWP2005)*.

Marc'Aurelio Ranzato, Sumit Chopra, Michael Auli, and Wojciech Zaremba. 2015. Sequence level training with recurrent neural networks. *CoRR*, abs/1511.06732.

John Wieting and Kevin Gimpel. 2017. Pushing the limits of paraphrastic sentence embeddings with millions of machine translations. *CoRR*, abs/1711.05732.

John Wieting, Jonathan Mallinson, and Kevin Gimpel. 2017. Learning paraphrastic sentence embeddings from back translated bitext. *CoRR*, abs/1706.01847.

Lijun Wu, Fei Tian, Tao Qin, Jianhuang Lai, and Tie-Yan Liu. 2018. A study of reinforcement learning for neural machine translation. *CoRR*, abs/1808.08866.

Shiqi Zhao, Xiang Lan, Ting Liu, and Sheng Li. 2009. Application-driven statistical paraphrase generation. In *Proceedings of the Joint Conference of the 47th Annual Meeting of the ACL and the 4th International Joint Conference on Natural Language Processing of the AFNLP: Volume 2 - Volume 2*, ACL '09, pages 834–842, Stroudsburg, PA, USA. Association for Computational Linguistics.

A Personalized Data-to-Text Support Tool for Cancer Patients

Saar Hommes
TiCC, Tilburg University
s.hommes@uvt.nl

Chris van der Lee
TiCC, Tilburg University
c.vdrlee@uvt.nl

Felix Clouth
Tilburg University
f.j.clouth@uvt.nl

Jeroen Vermunt
Tilburg University
j.k.vermunt@uvt.nl

Xander Verbeek
Netherlands Comprehensive
Cancer Organization (IKNL)
x.verbeek@iknl.nl

Emiel Krahmer
TiCC, Tilburg University
e.j.krahmer@uvt.nl

Abstract

In this paper, we present a novel data-to-text system for cancer patients, providing information on quality of life implications after treatment, which can be embedded in the context of shared decision making. Currently, information on quality of life implications is often not discussed, partly because (until recently) data has been lacking. In our work, we rely on a newly developed prediction model, which assigns patients to scenarios. Furthermore, we use data-to-text techniques to explain these scenario-based predictions in personalized and understandable language. We highlight the possibilities of NLG for personalization, discuss ethical implications and also present the outcomes of a first evaluation with clinicians.

1 Introduction

Data-to-text generation systems are increasingly used in the health domain (Pauws et al., 2019). They can, for example, be used for automation of health reports, clinical decision support, encourage behavioural change, ensure patient engagement or assist patients with making health decisions (Pauws et al., 2019). The tool we present here focuses on the latter two in the context of shared decision making (SDM) (Elwyn et al., 2017) for colorectal cancer patients. Since patients are increasingly encouraged to have an active role in treatment decision making (Pieterse et al., 2008), patients need to be accurately informed about their treatment options. Next to information on incidence and survival, patients also want to consider how a treatment is going to affect their quality of life (QoL) (Zafar et al., 2009). Since survival rates for colorectal cancer patients are increasing (Mols et al., 2013), the relevance of QoL becomes more prominent and patients are more likely to consider, for example, how treatments will impact their social life, ability to go

to work, or emotional well-being. Importantly, in recent years, a dedicated effort has started to collect data on such QoL dimensions. However, this information is often not communicated to the patient, or is generic and difficult to understand (Brundage et al., 2005). In this paper, we describe the design and implementation of a new patient support tool that is able to communicate QoL information to individual patients in an understandable and personalized way. Additionally, ethical issues are considered and results of an initial evaluation with clinicians are discussed.

2 Background

To explain health data in a clear way and assist patients with making treatment decisions, so called 'decision aids' are developed. These are tools that explain health information and lay out the benefits and risks of treatments to patients. A recent systematic review concluded that "[...] people exposed to decision aids feel more knowledgeable, better informed, and clearer about their values, and they probably have a more active role in decision making and more accurate risk perceptions" (Stacey et al., 2017). Vromans et al. (2019a,b) looked at the content and communication styles of such decision aids in more detail. The authors found that information communicated in such tools is often generic (based on the general population instead of the individual patient), which seems to undermine the potential effects of decision aids since understanding personalized risks (rather than generic risks) is easier and more relevant for patients (Thorne et al., 2005).

Many patients are unable to benefit from this generic health information, because these documents fail to communicate crucial information that influences the patient's understanding of these materials (e.g. the patient's individual risks, con-

Proceedings of The 12th International Conference on Natural Language Generation, pages 443–452,
Tokyo, Japan, 28 Oct - 1 Nov, 2019. ©2019 Association for Computational Linguistics

cerns and values) (Acharya et al., 2019). Tailoring health communication to individual patients seems a fruitful solution. And although such personalized health information can be effective (Kreuter and Wray, 2003), it is not without challenges. Personalizing health information manually is time consuming, costly and the outputs are often inconsistent (Pauws et al., 2019). Natural language generation (NLG) techniques can tackle these problems, and are therefore increasingly used in the health domain (Di Eugenio and Green, 2010; Pauws et al., 2019). A leading example of tailored health information using NLG is the BabyTalk-system developed by Gatt et al. (2009). This system generates personalized hospital stay summaries for parents of babies in a neonatal intensive care unit. Not all tailored NLG information is successful. Reiter et al. (2003) created 'STOP', a system aimed at generating tailored smoking cessation letters. However, the non-tailored letters were just as effective as the tailored letters. For our system, we do not need to change health behavior, but rather inform patients in the best way in order to assist them with decision making.

Some NLG health applications have already been developed to facilitate shared decision making to some degree. PIGLIT (Binsted et al., 1995; Cawsey et al., 2000), for example, was developed to generate explanations of patient records to help patients make sense of their prognosis. Additionally, Gkatzia et al. (2014) use NLG techniques to generate textual summaries of medical sensory data and personalize the presentation format of these summaries.

To date however, no tool has been developed to communicate personalized Quality of Life outcomes, which is the aim of the current tool. By deploying data-to-text techniques, the tool can communicate QoL data in a personal, relevant, understandable and consistent way. What follows is a description of how the tool is able to do so.

3 The system

3.1 Clinical setting

For the current tool, we focus on colorectal cancer as the health subject. Colorectal cancer is the third most common cancer in the world (American Cancer Society, 2019; World Cancer Research Fund, 2019). It is expected that in 2020, 17.000 people will suffer from colorectal cancer in the Nether-

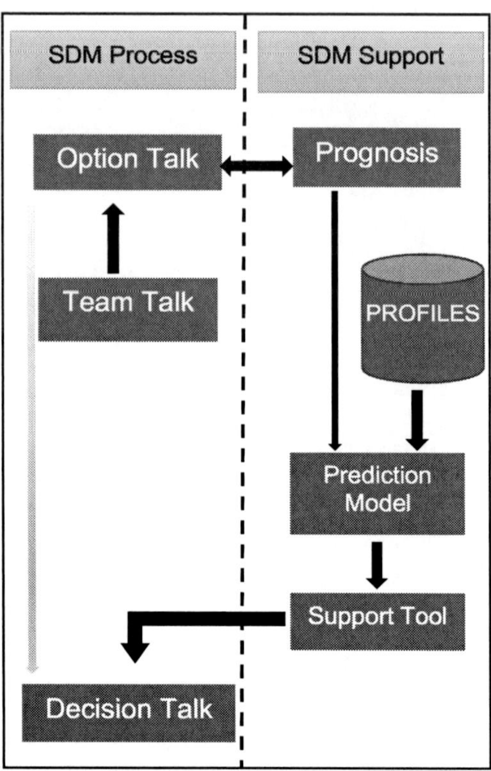

Figure 1: The support tool within the three-talk shared decision model (Elwyn et al., 2017).

lands alone (KWF Kankerbestrijding, 2019). At the same time, survival rates are improving (Mols et al., 2013). This means that increasingly, people with colorectal cancer will have to face the long-term effects of the treatments they underwent. Partly because of this, patients want to be involved in treatment decision making (Shay and Elston Lafata, 2015). In order to take part in these treatment decisions, however, patients need to have access to the relevant quality of life data. Providing patients this access is the aim of the system we developed.

3.2 Shared decision making

Figure 1 shows the system's ecosystem within the context of shared decision making. Elwyn et al. (2017) identified three different kinds of talks in the SDM process, which can be supported by a decision support tool. Shared decision making begins with the 'Team Talk'. Here, patient and clinician work together as a team and explore the choices and goals of different treatment options.

Secondly, the clinician and patient discuss the different treatment options in the 'Option Talk'. Within this talk, data become important since patient and clinician need to discuss risks and benefits of the options. Therefore, they can decide to use decision aid support (or directly go to the decision talk without interference of a decision support tool).

When a decision support tool is used, the SDM-support stage is entered (see Figure 1). Within this stage, it is essential that treatments are explained and in order to do so, data are required. For our support tool, there are two different kinds of input data. The first is a registry data set called "PRO-FILES" (Patient Reported Outcomes Following Initial treatment and Long term Evaluation of Survivorship (van de Poll-Franse et al., 2011). This is a dataset that consists of over 21.000 Dutch cancer patients who have reported on health-related quality of life measures within the Netherlands Cancer Registry (NCR). Of those patients, 1.631 were colorectal cancer patients. The questionnaire-based data are acquired via the European Organisation for Research and Treatment of Cancer (EORTC) Quality of Life Questionnaire (QLQ) C30 (version 3.0) which assesses health-related quality of life (HRQOL) (Mols et al., 2013). The QoL measures include: physical functioning, role functioning, emotional functioning, cognitive functioning, social functioning, global health status, fatigue, nausea/vomiting, pain, dyspnea, insomnia, appetite loss, constipation, diarrhea, and financial impact.

The second form of input data are based on the individual patient prognosis data (gender, age, tumor stage, comorbidities, examined lymph nodes, differentiation grade, topography and histology). This information is put into the system by the patient's clinician.

Both kinds of data feed into the prediction model that assigns patients to different outcome scenarios. The model has been developed by statisticians (Clouth et al., 2019), and uses latent class analysis (Vermunt and Magidson, 2002). The model clusters patients, from the PROFILES registry, into five latent classes (or scenarios as we call them here). That is, patients in the same outcome class have a comparable combination of answers on EORTC items. Based on the clinical information from the NCR, the model predicts class membership. This way, we can predict QoL outcome scenarios for new patients with unknown

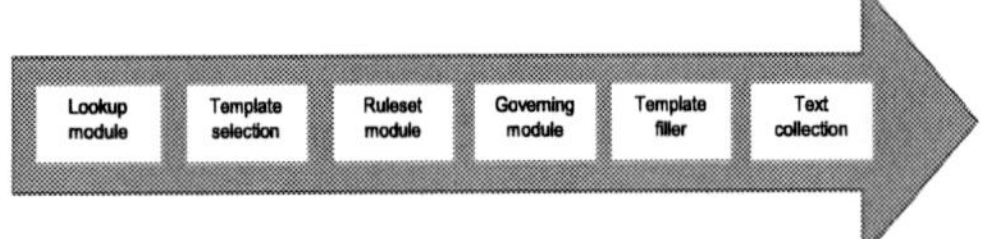

Figure 2: Module selection of the system.

scores on the EORTC questionnaire. More precisely, we estimate the probability of an individual patient as belonging to one of the five latent classes assuming treatment is known. See 4.1 for more.

In turn, the different data inputs and the prediction model output feed the support tool. See 3.3 for a more detailed explanation of the current support tool. The decision support tool can assist patients and clinicians within the 'Decision Talk', where patient and clinician discuss the preferences for treatment.

3.3 Module selection

Figure 2 is an overview of the system's module selection. The system is rule- and template-based. Contrary to neural approaches, rule- and template-based systems ensure precise and consistent communication without room for new or incorrect interpretations of the data. Since the current system communicates sensitive health data, this approach is essential. The module selection framework is based on van der Lee et al. (2017) who developed a system called 'PASS'. PASS automatically generates soccer reports (from soccer data) and tailors these texts based on the receiver's club preference. Similarly, the current support system translates medical data into texts and personalizes that information based on relevance.

As van der Lee et al. (2017) argue, a major advantage of such a modular approach is the flexibility of such a system. One can easily add modules. For the current system, this means that we plan on adding other cancer types and treatments, but also expand the personalization techniques used.

The modules used for the system are derived from PASS, although some modules were modified or omitted. For instance, modules that present references and information in a varied way were suitable for PASS, since the system's goal was to generate enjoyable and varied output, but these goals are not appropriate for the current system for which effective communication of sensitive health data is most salient.

After data is obtained using the prediction

model and the two input data types (PROFILES and individual patient prognosis data), the data-to-text system is initiated. The system starts with loading the patient's prognosis data and activating the *lookup module*. This module opens the template database and retrieves all the different templates that can be used to describe the medical information for the patient.

After collecting these templates within the *template selection module, the governing module* will walk through all topics that need to be discussed one by one, and send all the templates pertaining to the topic to the template selection module. Since patients have the option to choose if they want to receive (more) information on a QoL measure (see 4.1), this governing module will continuously update the topics based on the patient's information preference.

In the template selection module, a template is selected for a topic based on the *ruleset module*, which checks which template is most appropriate based on the input data as well as personalization condition (see 4.2). After choosing a template, the empty slots in the template are filled out with the corresponding data using the *template filler module*. Finally, the filled out templates are ordered within the *text collection module*, and a personalized text is generated. Next, we will discuss which personalization techniques are used specifically.

4 Personalization techniques

The most salient personalization technique used is based on communicating the relevant health information to the individual patient by generating personalized predictions. Although it may seem evident that patients need information based on their own personal information, most patient education materials or decision aids are not tailored towards specific patient outcomes (Vromans et al., 2019a,b). By using the output of the prediction model as a starting point, the current system is able to do so since it can identify different quality of life outcome scenarios. What follows is a brief description of these scenarios and how textual output is tailored towards them.

4.1 Scenarios

Based on latent class analysis, patients are predicted to belong to one of five different scenarios. Broadly speaking, patients can (1) have good outcomes on all quality of life outcomes, (2) have

good outcomes for physical dimensions, but relatively poor outcomes for mental dimensions, (3) perform average across all dimensions, (4) perform well on mental dimension, but poorly on physical outcomes and (5) perform poorly across all dimensions.

When patients have a better indication of how treatment will impact their specific lives, they can make better treatment decisions. For patients belonging to scenario 5 for example (who perform badly across all dimensions), it seems essential to know that treatment is going to affect your quality of life greatly. For patients in scenario 1 however, knowing that a particular treatment is not going to have a huge impact on your quality of life might be a relief. All in all, knowing which scenario is most applicable can help the patient to plan better for their life with and after treatment.

In total, patients can view 15 QoL outcomes (see the QoL outcomes mentioned in 3.2). Text 1 and Text 2 give an overview of how patients within the different scenarios are informed about their general personal QoL outcomes.

[Fixed text]:
This tool calculated how chemotherapy will probably affect your quality of life. It did this by comparing how your personal medical information relates to the medical information of other colorectal cancer patients who also underwent chemotherapy.

[Scenario 1]:
[s1] Overall, patients like you have good to very good outcomes on quality of life. [s2] This means that chemotherapy will probably not have a major effect on your quality of life afterwards. [s3] Do keep in mind that these outcomes are probabilities, so real life can be different.

[Scenario 2]:
[s4] Overall, patients like you experience few to very few physical problems. [s5] Overall, mental problems are quite common for patients like you. [s6] You might benefit from talking to a therapist or going to meetings with other colorectal cancer patients. [s7] Also, keep in mind that these results are probabilities, so your real life can be different from these outcomes.

[Scenario 3]:
[s8] Overall, patients like you could experience several problems relating to quality of life. [s9] There are a lot of things that could help you with possible problems you might experience. [s7].

Text 1: Patients in different scenarios (1, 2 and 3) receive different explanations of QoL outcomes. All patients receive the fixed texts. Some sentences overlap between scenarios (sentence s7).

[Scenario 4]:
[s10] Overall, patients like you experience few to very few mental problems. [s11] Overall, physical problems are quite common for patients like you. [s12] You might benefit from going to a physical therapist or taking medication. [s7]

[Scenario 5]:
[s13] Overall, patients like you do experience problems relating to quality of life. [s14] This means that chemotherapy could have a big impact on your quality of life afterwards. [s9] [s7]

[Fixed text]:
Click on the different outcomes to see a more detailed description of your risk, examples of how it can affect your life and the things you can do to help you manage.

Text 2: Patients in different scenarios (4 and 5) receive different explanations of QoL outcomes. All patients receive the fixed texts. Some sentences overlap between scenarios (sentence s7 and s9).

After viewing the general explanation of the personal QoL outcome scenario (Text 1 and Text 2), patients can click on specific QoL outcomes they would like to view. For example, if a patient clicks on physical functioning (one of the QoL measures), Text 3 shows an example of how information presentation is done for a patient within scenario 2 (good on physical dimensions), and Text 4 shows this for a patient within scenario 5 (poor outcomes overall).

Most patients like you have **excellent** physical functioning.

This means that **most patients** like you have **no difficulty** with dressing themselves, eating or washing up. Also, patients like you can **easily** lift a heavy suitcase.

If you **do** have physical problems, a physical therapist could help you.

Text 3: Information on physical functioning for patients in scenario 2. Bold text is personalized based on scenario outcomes.

A vast majority of patients like you have **difficulty with** physical functioning.

This means that **most patients** like you have **difficulty** with dressing themselves, eating or washing up. Also, patients like you **might have difficulty with** lifting a heavy suitcase.

If you have physical problems, a physical therapist could help you.

Text 4: Information on physical functioning for patients in scenario 5. Bold text is personalized based on scenario outcomes.

Note that individual patients only get information based on their own scenario. This way, patients in scenario 5 are not confronted with the better outcomes in other scenarios (which is the case for health materials not tailored towards the individual patient). Also, patients can opt for the QoL outcomes they want to view, so they do not have to view all the information. Finally, patients can choose whether they want the personal information based on scenarios, or general information based on the whole colorectal cancer population (e.g. "In general, about half of the colorectal cancer patients have difficulty with physical functioning. This means that half of the patients have difficulty with dressing themselves, eating or washing up. Also, half of the patients have difficulty with lifting a heavy suitcase. If you have physical problems, a physical therapist could help you.").

4.2 Experimentation with personalization

Understanding statistical information about the risks and benefits of treatment, or QoL outcomes, is difficult to interpret for many patients (Gigerenzer et al., 2007) . Gigerenzer et al. (2007) even state that there is a "collective statistical illiteracy" (p.53). At the same time, when communicating health information, statistical information is inevitable. That is why within the current tool a 'statistical module' is included. Within this module, textual output can vary based on the statistic that is used, for example:

"Most patients like you/ about 80% of patients like you/ 8 out of 10 patients like you experience X"

One of the strengths of NLG is that the textual output is consistent. Since research has shown that patients have a strong preference for the presentation of statistical information (e.g. Brundage et al. (2005)), but studies also show that patients vary in their preferences (e.g. Hagerty et al. (2004)), the current system could help investigate which patterns underlie these statistical preferences.

Another module that is built in in the current system is the 'framing-module'. Some research indicates that "the framing effect" occurs when delivering messages (Akl et al., 2011). That is, that the intended message depends on how it is formulated. For example, "there is a 10% chance of dying" statistically means the same as "there is a 90% chance of surviving". Arguably though, the information and acceptance of that information can be interpreted differently by the patient. Since a neutral way of presenting health related quality of life information is essential in this case, the tool can assist with determining the most appropriate way of phrasing the information. This may depend on personal preferences, but might also have to do with the scenarios patients are in.

4.3 Affective NLG

Although clinicians sometimes fear that patients cannot handle poor outcomes (de Haes and Koedoot, 2003), other research indicates that patients prefer to know all the information, even when this information is upsetting (Kehl et al., 2015). In any case, when dealing with delivering this sensitive information, it is crucial to think about the context in which such information is delivered. Earlier evaluation studies of NLG-systems, such as Mahamood and Reiter (2011), showed that all patients – regardless of their stress level – prefer affective texts over neutral ones. That is why affective language is used in all scenarios. For example, possible solutions such as ("if you experience physical problems, a physical therapist might help you") are included in all scenarios. Also, fixed texts convey messages such as "getting a cancer diagnosis may be overwhelming". Patient evaluation will reveal how such texts are received within this context.

5 Ethical considerations

Since sensitive data are being used, some ethical considerations need to be discussed. More so than systems such as PASS, NLG-systems within the health domain need to be accurate since generation mistakes can have severe implications for patients. That is why, while designing the support tool, the ethical checklist of Smiley et al. (2017) is kept in mind. Smiley et al. (2017) give a 12-item checklist relating to human consequences, data issues, generation issues and provenance. Next, these items are discussed in light of the current support tool.

5.1 Human consequences

The questions relating to human consequences are (1) "are there any ethical objections to building the application", (2) "how could a user be disadvantaged by the system" and (3) "does the system use any personally identifiable information". With re-

spect to the first two questions, it should be noted that patients should always have the choice not to receive the information, if they prefer not to be informed. For the current system, we think it is best if the clinician and patient jointly decide whether they want to use the support system at all. Also, patients can choose the option to only receive general information (not based on their own medical situation). Additionally, personal identifiers such as names, residence or specific birth dates are not asked so data is anonymized (question 3).

5.2 Data issues

For data issues, Smiley et al. (2017) identified four questions: (1) "how accurate is the underlying data", (2) "are there any misleading rankings given", (3) "are there (automatic) checks for missing data" and (4) "does the data contain any outliers". The quality of the data used for the support tool is excellent. The information on QoL outcomes of patients is based on a representative sample of colorectal cancer survivors in the Netherlands (van de Poll-Franse et al., 2011) and all clinical information is registry based data from the NCR. With regard to the second question, patients need to be informed about the probabilities of belonging to a certain outcome scenario. The system provides patients with a personalized text that explains what the scenarios are, how the tool is able to get these scenarios and that the information communicated are probabilities so that real life outcomes can still differ. For patients that have a relatively negative outcome (scenario 5), the system generates a more detailed explanation of how probabilities can differ from reality (see Text 2). Patient evaluation will demonstrate if people are satisfied with these explanations.

Questions 3 and 4 refer to the quality of the data. Both the PROFILES and NCR data are rigorously and manually checked for missing of implausible values to ensure high quality of the data. Further, latent class analysis is particularly suited for dealing with missing data and robust methods are used to ensure accurate predictions. Mistakes could be made with the clinical information the clinician puts in. That is why the system prints the patient data so both patient and clinician can check this during the Decision Talk (Figure 1). When a mistake was made, the clinician can adjust the data accordingly. The patient does not have this access to ensure that he or she only receives accurate information and cannot inadvertently introduce mistakes.

5.3 Generation issues

For generation issues, three questions are formulated: (1) "can you defend how the story is written", (2) "does the style of the automated report match your style" and (3) "who is watching the machines". Questions 1 and 2 will be kept in mind while doing patient evaluation. Because the underlying data is NCR data, governance of the data is ensured.

5.4 Provenance

Finally, (1) "will you disclose your methods" and (2) "will you disclose the underlying data sources" concludes the provenance section. Both of these questions are answered with a 'yes' for the current system. Patients have the option to click on "more information" sections, which will explain how the data and probabilities are acquired (in fixed text). Patient evaluation will reveal how this will be communicated specifically to ensure that patients understand these explanations.

6 Evaluation with clinicians

As Mahamood and Reiter (2012) point out, involving clinicians in an early stage of the development of NLG systems can "significantly enhance the quality of many NLG systems" (p.100). Therefore, as an initial iteration, the tool was evaluated with two clinicians (both colorectal cancer surgeons). Two individual semi-structured interviews were conducted and both conversations lasted about 30 minutes. The goals of the interviews were to assess (1) what clinicians thought of the clinical information that was used, (2) how the tool should be implemented, (3) whether they thought the outcomes of the tool are relevant, (4) what they thought of the interpretation of the outcomes and (5) what the general aim of the tool is. Outcomes of the evaluation are discussed next.

6.1 Clinical information

Initially, names of the patients were also inserted into the system. Both clinicians agreed however, that working with anonymized data would be best to ensure safety. This way, clinicians could also access the tool without a password, as they both agreed remembering login information is not ideal. As for all the other clinical information

(gender, age, tumour stage, comorbidities, examined lymph nodes, differentiation grade, topography and histology), the clinicians agreed that this information is readily available for them and does not take up too much time to enter.

6.2 Implementation of the tool

When asked about where in the consultation the tool could be implemented best, both clinicians agreed that they were able to reserve limited time for this during consultation. The patient can then access his or her information at home and results can be discussed during the next consultation with an oncologist (cf. the Option Talk and the Decision Talk, see Figure 1).

6.3 Relevance of outcomes

Both clinicians agreed that knowing how treatment is going to impact the quality of life for specific patients is valuable information and that this information is currently lacking in clinical practice. They agreed that when communicating QoL outcomes, patients may know better what to expect and clinicians can provide better care. However, one clinician noted that not all quality of life measures should be communicated in the same way. For example, the effect of chemotherapy on financial issues was communicated as in Text 5.

About half of the patients like you (5 out of 10) experience financial issues.

Financial issues mean for example that you cannot pay the bills on time.

When you experience financial issues, you can contact a financial expert.

Text 5: Financial issues communicated before evaluation with clinicians.

One clinician noted however that predicting how treatment is going to affect your financial status is dependent on many external factors (such as current financial status, whether or not patients are (self-)employed, what sort of job they have, et cetera). In order to make more valid predictions, patients would have to answer a lot of questions beforehand and even then, predictions could easily be wrong. That is why we choose to communicate financial issues in a more general way (Text 6).

Depending on your own financial situation, there are some patients who experience financial issues.

Financial issues mean for example that you cannot pay the bills on time.

When you experience financial issues, you can contact a financial expert.

Text 6: Financial issues communicated after evaluation with clinicians.

Furthermore, both clinicians agreed that including examples of how quality of life is going to affect the lives of patients is very useful (e.g. "you will probably have difficulty lifting a heavy suitcase", "you might feel lonely at times", "most patients like you do not have difficulty falling asleep").

6.4 Interpretation issues

Before evaluation, the different scenarios were called "profiles". Both clinicians agreed however, that interpretation of these profiles is hard. That is why, after evaluation, profiles are not mentioned and patients only receive information on scenarios with the phrase "patients like you" instead of "patients belonging to your profile".

6.5 Aim of the tool

Both clinicians noted that it would be nice to also include information on survival outcomes and how this is affected by chemotherapy. In a next phase, we plan on incorporating such data if our data-set permits this. Also, data on QoL outcomes for patients who haven't had chemotherapy will be included, as both clinicians noted that this is important information for the decision making process. Incorporating both survival outcomes and QoL outcomes for non-chemotherapy patients, the tool would be able to support patients and clinicians with shared decision making even more.

7 Conclusios & future work

In the current paper, a personalized data-to-text support system for colorectal cancer patients was described. The tool is aimed at communicating quality of life outcomes in an understandable, personalized, relevant and consistent way. As a starting point, the system was evaluated with two clinicians and yielded positive results. Both clinicians were convinced of the relevance of communicating quality of life information in a more person-alized manner. As the support tool will be implemented in a clinical setting, several ethical issues should be kept in mind when developing the system further. The next step is therefore to evaluate the tool with patients.

For the development of this tool, we build on the PASS data-to-text system (van der Lee et al., 2017), which was originally developed for the tailored generation of soccer reports. Building on an analysis of existing decision aids (Vromans et al., 2019a,b), templates were defined with different framing policies relating to different outcome scenarios. Dedicated modules were developed for, among other things, generating descriptions of personalized probabilities. In this way, it becomes possible to generate descriptions for personalized, individual tailored predictions in many different ways, something which would never be possible for a traditional decision aid (which typically is generic).

The main aim of this prototype was to come up with medically relevant information for patients in a personalized manner. We are aware that this undermines the linguistic variation of the textual output. However, as we plan on adding more modules (for example include relevant patient testimonials), linguistic variability will increase. Furthermore, decision support tools in current practice are very static because they almost never take into account personalized information from the patient (Vromans et al., 2019a,b). Our support tool is therefore an important contribution to ensure personalized medicine. We hope to have shown that personalized treatment decision aids are both a new and interesting practical application of NLG-techniques, as well as an exciting testbed for the development of new NLG techniques.

Acknowledgements

We received support from The Netherlands Organization for Scientific Research (NWO Data2Person 628.011.030), for which we are grateful. We would also like to thank the clinicians for their expert opinions during the evaluation of the data-to-text support tool, and the anonymous reviewers for their helpful comments.

References

Sabita Acharya, Andrew Boyd, Richard Cameron, Karen Lopez, Pamela Martyn-Nemeth, Carolyn Dickens, Amer Ardati, and Barbara Di Eugenio.

2019. Incorporating personalization features in a hospital-stay summary generation system. In *Proceedings of the 52nd Hawaii International Conference on System Sciences*, pages 4175–4184.

Elie Akl, Andrew Oxman, Jeph Herrin, Gunn Vist, Irene Terrenato, Francesca Sperati, Cecilia Costiniuk, Diana Blank, and Holger Schünemann. 2011. Framing of health information messages. *Cochrane Database of Systematic Reviews*, (12).

American Cancer Society. 2019. Key statistics for colorectal cancer.

Kim Binsted, Alison Cawsey, and Ray Jones. 1995. Generating personalised patient information using the medical record. In *Conference on Artificial Intelligence in Medicine in Europe*, pages 29–41. Springer.

Michael Brundage, Deb Feldman-Stewart, Ann Leis, Andrea Bezjak, Lesley Degner, Karima Velji, Lisa Zetes-Zanatta, Dongsheng Tu, Paul Ritvo, and Joseph Pater. 2005. Communicating quality of life information to cancer patients: A study of six presentation formats. *Journal of Clinical Oncology*, 23(28):6949–6956.

Alison Cawsey, Ray Jones, and Janne Pearson. 2000. The evaluation of a personalised health information system for patients with cancer. *User Modeling and User-Adapted Interaction*, 10(1):47–72.

Felix Clouth, Gijs Geleijnse, Lonneke van de Poll-Franse, Steffen Pauws, and Jeroen Vermunt. 2019. Quality of life profiles of colon cancer survivors: A three-step latent class analysis. In *Abstract from IFCS, Thessaloniki, Greece*.

Barbara Di Eugenio and Nancy Green. 2010. Emerging applications of natural language generation in information visualization, education and health-care. In Nitin Indurkhya and Fred J. Damerau, editors, *Handbook of Natural Language Processing*, volume 2, chapter 23, pages 557–575. CRC Press, Taylor and Francis Group.

Glyn Elwyn, Nan Cochran, and Michael Pignone. 2017. Shared decision making—the importance of diagnosing preferences. *JAMA internal medicine*, 177(9):1239–1240.

Albert Gatt, Francois Portet, Ehud Reiter, Jim Hunter, Saad Mahamood, Wendy Moncur, and Somayajulu Sripada. 2009. From data to text in the neonatal intensive care unit: Using NLG technology for decision support and information management. *AI Communications*, 22(3):153–186.

Gerd Gigerenzer, Wolfgang Gaissmaier, Elke Kurz-Milcke, Lisa Schwartz, and Steven Woloshin. 2007. Helping doctors and patients make sense of health statistics. *Psychological science in the public interest*, 8(2):53–96.

Dimitra Gkatzia, Verena Rieser, Alexander McSporran, Alistair McGowan, Alasdair Mort, and Michaela Dewar. 2014. Generating verbal descriptions from medical sensor data: A corpus study on user preferences. *BCS Health Informatics Scotland. Glasgow, UK*.

Hanneke de Haes and Nelleke Koedoot. 2003. Patient centered decision making in palliative cancer treatment: a world of paradoxes. *Patient education and counseling*, 50(1):43–49.

Rebecca Hagerty, Phyllis Butow, Peter Ellis, Elizabeth Lobb, Susan Pendlebury, Natasha Leighl, David Goldstein, Sing Kai Lo, and Martin Tattersall. 2004. Cancer patient preferences for communication of prognosis in the metastatic setting. *Journal of clinical oncology*, 22(9):1721–1730.

Kenneth Kehl, Mary Landrum, Neeraj Arora, Patricia Ganz, Michelle van Ryn, Jennifer Mack, and Nancy Keating. 2015. Association of actual and preferred decision roles with patient-reported quality of care: shared decision making in cancer care. *JAMA oncology*, 1(1):50–58.

Matthew Kreuter and Ricardo Wray. 2003. Tailored and targeted health communication: Strategies for enhancing information relevance. *American journal of health behavior*, 27(1):227–232.

KWF Kankerbestrijding. 2019. Kanker in nederland tot 2020. Trends en prognoses.

Chris van der Lee, Emiel Krahmer, and Sander Wubben. 2017. Pass: A dutch data-to-text system for soccer, targeted towards specific audiences. In *Proceedings of the 10th International Conference on Natural Language Generation*, pages 95–104.

Saad Mahamood and Ehud Reiter. 2011. Generating affective natural language for parents of neonatal infants. In *Proceedings of the 13th European Workshop on Natural Language Generation*, pages 12–21.

Saad Mahamood and Ehud Reiter. 2012. Working with clinicians to improve a patient-information nlg system. In *Proceedings of the Seventh International Natural Language Generation Conference*, pages 100–104. Association for Computational Linguistics.

Floortje Mols, Tonneke Beijers, Valery Lemmens, Corina van den Hurk, Gerard Vreugdenhil, and Lonneke van de Poll-Franse. 2013. Chemotherapy-induced neuropathy and its association with quality of life among 2-to 11-year colorectal cancer survivors: Results from the population-based PROFILES registry. *Journal of Clinical Oncology*, 31(21):2699–2707.

Steffen Pauws, Albert Gatt, Emiel Krahmer, and Ehud Reiter. 2019. Making effective use of healthcare data using data-to-text technology. In *Data Science for Healthcare*, pages 119–145. Springer.

Arwen Pieterse, Monique Baas-Thijssen, Corrie Marijnen, and Anne Stiggelbout. 2008. Clinician and cancer patient views on patient participation in treatment decision-making: A quantitative and qualitative exploration. *British Journal of Cancer*, 99(6):875–882.

Lonneke van de Poll-Franse, Nicole Horevoorts, Mies van Eenbergen, Johan Denollet, Jan Anne Roukema, Neil Aaronson, Ad Vingerhoets, Jan Willem Coebergh, Jolanda de Vries, and Marie-Louise Essink-Bot. 2011. The patient reported outcomes following initial treatment and long term evaluation of survivorship registry: scope, rationale and design of an infrastructure for the study of physical and psychosocial outcomes in cancer survivorship cohorts. *European Journal of Cancer*, 47(14):2188–2194.

Ehud Reiter, Roma Robertson, and Liesl Osman. 2003. Lessons from a failure: Generating tailored smoking cessation letters. *Artificial Intelligence*, 144(1-2):41–58.

Aubree Shay and Jennifer Elston Lafata. 2015. Where is the evidence? A systematic review of shared decision making and patient outcomes. *Medical Decision Making*, 35(1):114–131.

Charese Smiley, Frank Schilder, Vassilis Plachouras, and Jochen Leidner. 2017. Say the right thing right: Ethics issues in natural language generation systems. In *Proceedings of the First ACL Workshop on Ethics in Natural Language Processing*, pages 103–108.

Dawn Stacey, France Légaré, Krystina Lewis, Michael Barry, Carol Bennett, Karen Eden, Margaret Holmes-Rovner, Hilary Llewellyn-Thomas, Anne Lyddiatt, Richard Thomson, and Lyndal Trevena. 2017. Decision aids for people facing health treatment or screening decisions. *Cochrane Database of Systematic Reviews*, (4).

Sally Thorne, Barry Bultz, and Walter Baile. 2005. Is there a cost to poor communication in cancer care? a critical review of the literature. *Psycho-oncology*, (14):875–884.

Jeroen Vermunt and Jay Magidson. 2002. Latent class cluster analysis. *Applied latent class analysis*, 11:89–106.

Ruben Vromans, Mies van Eenbergen, Steffen Pauws, Gijs Geleijnse, Henk van der Poel, Lonneke van de Poll-Franse, and Emiel Krahmer. 2019a. Communicative aspects of decision aids for localized prostate cancer treatment–A systematic review. In *Urologic Oncology: Seminars and Original Investigations*, 37, pages 409–429.

Ruben Vromans, Kim Tenfelde, Steffen Pauws, Mies van Eenbergen, Ingeborg Mares-Engelberts, Galina Velikova, Lonneke van de Poll-Franse, and Emiel Krahmer. 2019b. Assessing the quality and communicative aspects of patient decision aids for early-stage breast cancer treatment: A systematic review. In *Breast Cancer Research and Treatment*.

World Cancer Research Fund. 2019. Colorectal cancer statistics.

Yousuf Zafar, Stewart Alexander, Kevin Weinfurt, Kevin Schulman, and Amy Abernethy. 2009. Decision making and quality of life in the treatment of cancer: a review. *Supportive Care in Cancer*, 17(2):117–127.

Natural Language Generation at Scale:
A Case Study for Open Domain Question Answering

Alessandra Cervone[1]*, Chandra Khatri[2]†, Rahul Goel[3]‡ Behnam Hedayatnia[4],
Anu Venkatesh[4], Dilek Hakkani-Tür[4], Raefer Gabriel[4]
[1]Signals and Interactive Systems Lab, University of Trento, Italy
[2]Uber AI, [3]Google, [4]Amazon Alexa AI
alessandra.cervone@unitn.it, chandrak@uber.com,
{behnam, anuvenk, hakkanit, raeferg}@amazon.com,
goelrahul@google.com

Abstract

Current approaches to Natural Language Generation (NLG) for dialog mainly focus on domain-specific, task-oriented applications (e.g. restaurant booking) using limited ontologies (up to 20 slot types), usually without considering the previous conversation context. Furthermore, these approaches require large amounts of data for each domain, and do not benefit from examples that may be available for other domains. This work explores the feasibility of applying statistical NLG to scenarios requiring larger ontologies, such as multi-domain dialog applications or open-domain question answering (QA) based on knowledge graphs. We model NLG through an Encoder-Decoder framework using a large dataset of interactions between real-world users and a conversational agent for open-domain QA. First, we investigate the impact of increasing the number of slot types on the generation quality and experiment with different partitions of the QA data with progressively larger ontologies (up to 369 slot types). Second, we perform multi-task learning experiments between open-domain QA and task-oriented dialog, and benchmark our model on a popular NLG dataset. Moreover, we experiment with using the conversational context as an additional input to improve response generation quality. Our experiments show the feasibility of learning statistical NLG models for open-domain QA with larger ontologies.

1 Introduction

In dialog literature Natural Language Generation (NLG) is framed as the task of generating natural language responses that faithfully convey the semantic information given by a Meaning Representation (MR). A MR is typically a structure consisting of a Dialog Act (DA) and a list of associated slots. While the DA (Stolcke et al., 2000; Mezza et al., 2018) expresses the intent of the utterance to be generated (e.g. "inform" in Table 1), the slots, organized as slot type-slot value pairs (e.g. *food*:'french' in Table 1), represent the information which has to be conveyed in the generated text.

So far statistical NLG for dialog has mainly been investigated in research for task-oriented applications (e.g. restaurant reservation, bus information) in narrow, controlled environments with limited ontologies, i.e. considering a small set of DAs and slot types (respectively 12 and 8 in the popular San Francisco restaurant dataset (SFX) (Wen et al., 2015), 8 and 1 in the recent E2E NLG challenge (Novikova et al., 2017)). Furthermore, most datasets consider MRs in isolation (Novikova et al., 2017) i.e., they lack con-

	Input		Output
	context	**MR**	**Text**
Task Oriented	-	**inform** *name*: 'fringale' *food*: 'french'	'fringale is a french restaurant' 'fringale serves french food'
QA	'when was kentucky founded'	**inform** *timepoint*: '1792' *objStr*: 'kentucky' *claStr*: 'state' *relStr*: 'founded'	'1792' 'kentucky formed in 1792' 'kentucky founded in 1792'

Table 1: Examples of input-output pairs from a task-oriented (Task) NLG (SFX (Wen et al., 2015)) and a Question-Answering (QA) dataset. In NLG the input is typically a Meaning Representation (MR) and the output is its textual realization (Text). Each MR is composed of a Dialog Act (bold) and a list of slot type (italic)-value pairs. Compared to most NLG datasets, our QA corpus also has the previous question (context) as input. While in the task-oriented setting we observe a one-to-one relation between slots in the input and the ones realized in the text, the same is not true for QA.

---

* Work done during internship at Amazon Alexa AI.
† Work done while working at Amazon Alexa AI.
‡ Work done while working at Amazon Alexa AI.

versational context, even though the previous utterances in the dialog have been shown to improve the performance of task-oriented NLG (Dušek and Jurcicek, 2016). These characteristics of current approaches to NLG can be linked to the fact that a vast majority of dialog NLG research is tested on a single domain where the dialog agent performs simple tasks such as giving information about a restaurant, with few exceptions (Wen et al., 2016).

However, with the rise of conversational agents such as Amazon Alexa and Google Assistant, there is an increasing interest in complex multi-domain tasks. These systems typically rely on hand-crafted NLG, but this approach cannot scale to the complex ontologies which may be required in real-world applications (e.g. booking a trip).

In this work we explore the applicability of current NLG models for task-oriented dialog, based on a MR-to-text framework using Encoder-Decoder architectures, to open-domain QA. This allows us to investigate the performance of current NLG research in an environment with (1) much larger numbers of slot types, and (2) a different application compared to task-oriented dialog. We generate the QA datasets for our experiments using as source a large corpus of open-domain QA pairs from interactions between real-world users and a conversational agent. For evaluation, we utilize both objective metrics and human judgment. We observe that NLG for open-domain QA poses its own challenges compared to task-oriented dialog, since correct answers to the same question do not necessarily convey all slot types in the MR (see Table 1).

In particular, in our first set of experiments, we investigate the effect of using increasingly larger ontologies with regards to slot types on the performance of our NLG models for QA. We find that, notwithstanding the larger ontologies and the noisiness of our dataset, models' performance does not degrade significantly in terms of naturalness of generated text and efficiency in encoding the MR information (i.e. Slot Error Rate). Interestingly, we find it improves for some of the human evaluation metrics. We also observe that using conversational context improves the quality of generated responses. In our second set of experiments, we investigate whether jointly training NLG models for task-oriented dialog and QA improves performances. To this end, we experiment with learning NLG models in a multi-task setting between

our QA data and SFX. Our experiments show that learning models in a multi-task setting lead to better performances in terms of naturalness of the generated output for both tasks.

This work has several contributions:

1. We apply the MR-to-text framework (typical of NLG for task-oriented dialog) to a open-domain QA application.

2. We explore the importance of adding the previous conversational context to improve the quality of the generated output.

3. We investigate the possibility of learning NLG models using a MR-to-text approach with increasingly larger ontologies in terms of slot types.

4. We experiment with multi-task learning for NLG between open-domain QA and task-oriented dialog.

5. Finally we also propose new evaluation metrics (see Section 5) to capture the variability of output in open-domain QA compared to NLG for task-oriented dialog.

2   Related work

While classical approaches to NLG involve a pipeline of modules such as content selection, planning, and surface realization (Gatt and Krahmer, 2018), recently a large part of the literature investigated end-to-end neural approaches to NLG. The tasks tackled include dialog, text, and QA. While these tasks share some similarities, each comes with its own set of challenges and requires specific solutions.

NLG for dialog   State of the art NLG models for dialog (Dušek and Jurcicek, 2016; Juraska et al., 2018) mostly use end-to-end neural Encoder-Decoder approaches with attention (Bahdanau et al., 2014) and re-ranking (Dušek et al., 2018). Ensembling is another technique employed to boost model performance (Juraska et al., 2018). Using delexicalization (Henderson et al., 2014), i.e., the process of substituting slot values with slot types in the generated text, has also shown improvements in many settings. However, recent work also depicted the disadvantages of delexicalization (Nayak et al., 2017). In our work, we compare and combine both delixecalized and lexicalized inputs for the NLG system.

NLG for dialog has been mostly tested in controlled environments using task-oriented, single domain datasets with limited ontologies (Wen et al., 2015; Novikova et al., 2017; Balakrishnan et al., 2019). Although Wen et al. (2016) perform multi-domain task-oriented NLG experiments, the ontologies used are still limited for such settings. Finally, while research has shown how encoding the previous utterance leads to better performances (Dušek and Jurcicek, 2016), most settings consider the turns in isolation (Wen et al., 2015; Novikova et al., 2017).

In our work, we perform open-domain NLG with significantly larger ontologies and also evaluate the impact of adding the context to the input.

NLG for text and QA   Recent work around NLG for text involves generating text using structured data using the encoder-decoder networks (Mei et al., 2016). Similarly to dialog, NLG for text has also been addressed in controlled environments such as weather forecast (Liang et al., 2009) with few exceptions (Lebret et al., 2016).

In the literature for QA, most approaches retrieve answers directly or generate answers jointly with the retrieval, and answers are usually entities or lists of entities (Dodge et al., 2015). On the contrary, in NLG we assume the answer has already been retrieved, and the goal is to generate text matching it. The field of QA which most strictly relates to our work is answer generation, where current approaches are also based on encoder-decoder networks encoding information directly from a knowledge base (Yin et al., 2016; He et al., 2017; Wei and Zhang, 2019). An additional challenge to answer generation is that there are no publicly available datasets for this task (Fu and Feng, 2018).

Our approach differs from answer generation in that we structure the task as in NLG dialog literature with a MR-to-text approach.

3   Datasets

3.1   Question Answering

Source data   Our source for generating the MR-text pairs are thousands of open-domain factual question-answer pairs from commercial data. The domains covered in this data are manifold, including geography (e.g. 'is canada bigger than united states' in Table 7), history (e.g. 'when was kentucky founded' in Table 1), present-day

	Size	Slots	DAs	Words	Domain	Context
E2E	51k	8	1	2453	restaurant	no
SFX	5k	12	8	438	restaurant	no
QA.1	6k	147	1	702	open	yes
QA.2	16k	210	1	1528	open	yes
QA.3	67k	369	1	2963	open	yes

Table 2: Our QA NLG datasets compared to popular (task-oriented) NLG datasets: San Francisco restaurant (SFX) and the NLG E2E challenge (E2E). We report the full size of datasets in terms of MR-text pairs, the number of slot types, DAs, words (computed after delexicalization), domain and whether the dataset comprises the previous utterance or not.

knowledge (e.g. 'will ferrell's wife' in Table 7), grammar ('is there a plural form of pegasus') and even mathematics ('what is one modulo seven'). Pairs are grouped according to the type of question asked. Each group consists of a list of specific questions (e.g. "who is the wife of barack obama", "tell me the wives of henry the viii") of the same type (e.g. "who is the wife of") asked by real users to a conversational agent. Each specific question additionally has: (1) the answer to the question (e.g. "michelle obama is obama's wife") generated by the NLG of the conversational system, either using information retrieval or a knowledge base search coupled with templates; (2) relevant noun and verb phrases (e.g. "michelle obama", "barack obama", "wife") used by the system to generate the answer, including the ones from the question. Noun phrases are tagged according to their semantic type (examples of semantic types are *timepoint* and *human being*), while verb phrases are tagged as "relation" types (see "founded" tagged as *relStr* in Table 1).

The answers in the source data are varied, and range from a simple entity to a fully formed answer, as in Table 1 example where valid answers to the question "when was kentucky founded" can be "1792" or "kentucky formed in 1792". This shows an interesting difference between our QA data and task-oriented NLG datasets. While for task-oriented NLG all valid responses for a single MR have the same slot types (i.e., the ones in the input MR), in our dataset this is not always true.

QA NLG datasets   We generate the NLG input-output pairs for QA from our source data. In order to perform cross-application experiments, we maintain the same MR-text format as task-oriented dialog NLG. The target output is the text

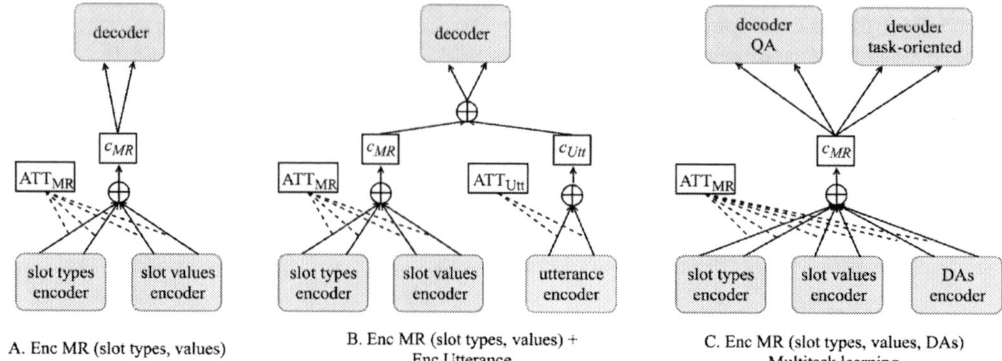

Figure 1: Our baseline model (A) and the models with the previous utterance (B) and for multi-task learning (C). While our baseline model Enc MR (slot types, values) is composed by two encoders for the MR, one for slot types and one for slot values; our model in subfigure B extends this baseline by adding an encoder for the previous utterance. In the multitask learning setting, on the hand, where we do not have the previous context but might have different Dialog Acts (DAs), we add a corresponding encoder (see subfigure C).

of the answers in the source data. To generate the input MRs we assumed only one DA across all answers, i.e. "inform"; for the slots, we used the semantic types and relations for noun phrases and verb phrases in the source data as slot types, while the actual entity or verb was used as the corresponding slot value. [1] On top of the generated MR we use, as additional input, the previously asked question as context.

Answers are delexicalized (Henderson et al., 2014) to improve generalization. Since we do not have alignment between entities in the input and the generated text, we use a heuristic-based aligner which we also use to filter out data that could not be appropriately aligned. All noun phrases are delexicalized while verb phrases are not. Furthermore, similar to (Juraska et al., 2018), we use delexicalization for data augmentation. We generate additional references for each MR, besides the original one, by considering all delexicalized answers in the question group as candidate template answers for each specific question in the group and then substituting (where possible) slots values which are already available in the input. The text of the previous question is also delexicalized.

Finally, to investigate performances across different ontology sizes, we generate 3 different partitions of the data (QA.1, 2 and 3 in Table 2) with a progressively larger number of slot types. Each

QA partition was split in train, test and development set (using a 80-10-10 split) according to the type of question asked. We ensured there was no overlap between the different sets to test if models generalize to previously unseen questions.

3.2 Task-oriented Dialog

As a task-oriented NLG corpus for our multi-task learning experiments we use the popular San Francisco restaurants (SFX; Wen et al. (2015)) dataset. Statistics about the dataset is shown in Table 2. Although SFX is not large (6k examples), compared to the E2E NLG corpus it presents more variation for DA (although less in style). For all our datasets, we use the TGEN library [2] (Dušek and Jurcicek, 2016) to delexicalize all slot types except binary values.

4 Model and Architectures

In this section we present the variety of different architectures used in our experiments. Although all our models are based on the Encoder-Decoder framework, we investigate architectures with different number of Encoders (up to 3). Given this variety, for clarity, we follow a template Enc <Encoder type> for naming our different models. The type of Encoder, in particular, can be of Meaning Representation (MR) type, when we encode parts of the MR, such as slot types, values or Dialog Act; or it can be of Utterance type, when we encode the previous utterance context.

---

[1] Although we use the original tags of the source data, a similar representation could be produced by tagging noun phrases with their Named Entity type and verb phrases with a "relation" slot type.

[2] https://github.com/UFAL-DSG/tgen

Encoder-Decoder with Attention Following recent state-of-the-art approaches to NLG for dialog (Juraska et al., 2018; Balakrishnan et al., 2019), our models are based on the Encoder-Decoder with Attention framework. In particular, we use bidirectional Gated Recurrent Units (GRU) and Luong general attention (Luong et al., 2015) as our baseline. While we also experimented with other types of architectures, such as using Long-Short-Term Memory Units (Hochreiter and Schmidhuber, 1997) instead of GRUs and different types of attention (including Bahdanau attention (Bahdanau et al., 2014) and Luong dot attention (Luong et al., 2015), this combination gave us the best results for our setting. Depending on the encoder used, either slot type or slot value, we refer to this model as Enc MR (slot types) or Enc MR (slot values).

Multi-Encoder, Single Decoder: We expand the baseline (Enc MR) models using multiple inputs from the MR (slot types, values, DAs), each encoded by a different encoder. The attention is performed on their concatenated output to produce the MR context vector c_{MR}. Figure 1 A shows an example of such an architecture using two encoders, one for slot types and one for slot values. Furthermore, we experimented with adding the previous utterance as input with an additional encoder (Enc Utterance). In this case, the context vector for the previous utterance c_{Utt} is produced by an independent attention mechanism and the outputs of both attentions (c_{MR} and c_{Utt}) are concatenated (see Figure 1 B).

Multi-Encoder, Multi-Decoder: We also performed multi-task learning, jointly training the models for both QA and task-oriented NLG. As shown in Figure 1 C, we shared the encoders and corresponding input layers across multiple tasks while we maintained multiple decoders for individual tasks. We alternated between mini-batches from various data sources to perform multitasking.

5 Evaluation

As word overlap metrics may not have a good correlation with human judgment for NLG output evaluation (Stent et al., 2005), we use both objective metrics and human evaluation.

Objective metrics Besides the standard BLEU score (obtained using the official E2E NLG chal-

lenge evaluation script [3]), we report different types of Slot Error Rate (SER). In dialog NLG approaches SER shows the number of correct slots in the output compared to the input MR. We refer to this metric as SER_{mr} to differentiate it from its modified versions we introduce next. The formula (Wen et al., 2015) is:

$$SER_{mr} = \frac{p_{mr} + q_{mr}}{N_{mr}} \quad (1)$$

where N_{mr} is the total number of slots in the input MR and p_{mr} , q_{mr} are respectively the number of missing and redundant slots in the output. This formula works well for task-oriented NLG approaches, but it assumes a one-to-one relationship between the slots in the input MR and the output text. We found this assumption might not hold for our QA datasets where not all slots in the input MR need to be realized for the output to be correct. An example of this is shown in Table 1, where the first QA reference text ('1792') would be penalized with 3 missing slots, while still being correct.

In order to capture this different behaviour we designed additional NLG metrics tailored for QA. Slot Error Rate Target (SER_{trg}) is a modification of SER_{mr} where we simply substitute the MR with the main reference text:

$$SER_{trg} = \frac{p_{trg} + q_{trg}}{N_{trg}} \quad (2)$$

SER_{trg} is designed to penalize both missing and redundant slots compared to the target sentence. Hence, using SER_{trg} the first QA reference text in Table 1 would not be penalized.

Slot Error Rate MultiTarget (SER_{mtrg}), on the other hand, penalizes redundant slots that did not appear in any of the references:

$$SER_{mtrg} = \frac{p_{mtrg}}{N_{mtrg}} \quad (3)$$

where N_{mtrg} are all slots appearing in any reference and p_{mtrg} are the slots in the output that did not appear in any reference sentence. To compute SER_{mtrg} for the model output "kentucky formed in 1792" given the QA MR in Table 1 we assume to have two references "1792" and "kentucky formed in 1792". In this case, SER_{mtrg} would consider the output correct as all of its slots appear in at least one of the references.

---

[3]We do not report other word overlap metrics (e.g., METEOR) computed by the E2E evaluation scripts due to space limitations and correlation with the BLEU score.

	QA.1				QA.2				QA.3			
	BLEU	SER$_{mr}$	SER$_{trg}$	SER$_{mtrg}$	BLEU	SER$_{mr}$	SER$_{trg}$	SER$_{mtrg}$	BLEU	SER$_{mr}$	SER$_{trg}$	SER$_{mtrg}$
Enc MR (slot types, values)	0.85	**0.42**	0.21	0.023	0.77	0.44	0.3	0.057	0.66	**0.43**	0.37	**0.05**
+ Enc Utterance delex	0.90	0.44	0.19	0.011	0.83	**0.43**	0.33	**0.026**	0.7	0.45	0.33	0.051
+ Enc Utterance lex	**0.95**	0.46	**0.15**	**0.012**	**0.89**	0.47	**0.19**	0.03	**0.72**	0.46	**0.28**	0.067

Table 3: Objective metrics results on three QA NLG datasets with increasingly larger ontologies. The models under comparison are a baseline with two encoders, for slot types and slot values, and its extensions with a delexicalised or lexicalised previous utterance. While for BLEU score the higher the better, for all types of Slot Error Rate (SER) the lower the better.

	QA.1				QA.2				QA.3			
	Nat.	*Inf.*	*Conv.*	*Ans.*	*Nat.*	*Inf.*	*Conv.*	*Ans.*	*Nat.*	*Inf.*	*Conv.*	*Ans.*
Enc MR (slot types, values)	3.73	3.8	3.96	0.36	3.88	3.78	4.57	0.38	4.29	4.37	4.40	0.73
+ Enc Utterance delex	4.61	4.63	**4.59**	0.67	4.64	4.32	**4.88**	0.5	4.52	4.47	**4.51**	0.79
+ Enc Utterance lex	**4.7**	**4.69**	4.48	**0.78**	**5.15**	**4.88**	4.85	**0.67**	**4.57**	**4.57**	4.45	**0.80**

Table 4: Human evaluation results on three QA NLG datasets with increasingly larger ontologies. The models reported are a baseline with two encoders, for slot types and slot values, and its extensions with a delexicalised or lexicalised previous utterance. We report averages of Naturalness (*Nat.*), Informativeness (*Inf.*), and how conversational the response was judged (*Conv.*) on a scale of 1 to 6. Additionally, we report the average of whether responses could be considered an answer to the given question (*Ans.*), given to annotators as a binary choice.

	Dataset	BLEU	SER$_{mr}$	SER$_{trg}$	SER$_{mtrg}$
baseline	SFX	0.727	**0.40**	-	-
+ QA.3		**0.74**	0.413	-	-
baseline	QA.3	0.659	**0.429**	0.37	**0.05**
+ SFX		**0.673**	0.44	**0.368**	0.07

Table 5: Objective metrics of multitask learning experiments combining QA (QA.3) and task-oriented dialog (SFX) NLG. For all Slot Error Rate (SER) metrics the lower the better.

	Dataset	*Nat.*	*Inf.*	*Conv.*	*Ans.*
baseline	SFX	4.69	**5.50**	-	-
+ QA.3		**5.11**	5.40	-	-
baseline	QA.3	4.29	4.33	4.40	**0.73**
+SFX		**4.43**	**4.38**	**4.5**	0.72

Table 6: Results of multitask learning experiments combining NLG for QA (on QA.3) and task-oriented dialog (on SFX) according to human evaluation.

Human evaluation In all experiments, for each dataset, we selected a sample of 100 MR-text pairs from the test set. Pairs were randomly selected among those where all models under comparison in the experiment had generated different output text. Data for all reported experiments were annotated by 2 human annotators, and final ratings were averaged between the two. In all experiments annotators, presented with MR and all outputs of the systems under comparison, were asked to rate the *naturalness* and *informativeness* of the generated output using a 1-6 Likert score, as in previous NLG dialog evaluations (Gatt and Krahmer,

2018). Additionally, for the QA datasets annotators had also the previous question as context. Moreover, for the QA datasets annotators were asked to rate how *conversational* the output was, on the same Likert scale, and whether or not the output could ultimately be considered an answer to the question (*answer*), as a binary choice.

6 Experimental setup

The hyperparameters chosen for our models were empirically determined through various experiments. Both encoder and decoder in all our models had only one layer, as we noticed additional layers did not give improvements. All embeddings were trained from scratch with a fixed dimension of 50. Models were trained using a cross-entropy loss function and the Adam (Kingma and Ba, 2014) optimizer with a learning rate of 0.001, for 1000 epochs, with early stopping on the validation set. We used mini-batches of size 32.

For the NLG models for QA, experiments on QA.1 (not reported due to space limitations) with different encoders combinations showed that the best performances were achieved using all input types (slot type, value, and previous context) with lexicalized (+ Enc Utterance lex) or delexicalized (+ Enc Utterance delex) previous context in terms of all metrics, except SER$_{trg}$. On this metric, the architecture with slot types and values, but without the previous context (Enc MR (slot types, values)) achieved the best performance (cf. Table 3). For this reason, we chose to report the performances of these architectures in our QA experiments.

7 Results

Open domain QA In our first batch of experiments we test various Encoder-Decoder architectures on our 3 different partitions of QA NLG data.

As we can see from Table 3, in general, the best performances across all QA datasets for both BLEU and SER_{trg} are achieved by the model using as additional input the lexicalized previous question, followed by the model with the delexicalized one. However, SER_{mr} results show the opposite picture, where the baseline with only slot types and values performs better (except for QA.2 where the score is close to the model with the delexicalized input) and the model with the lexicalized previous utterance is the worst. SER_{mtrg} shows, on the other hand, that the context might slightly degrade performances with bigger ontologies in terms of all text references.

Human evaluation, on the other hand, seems in line with the picture depicted by BLEU and SER_{trg}. Table 4 shows the model with the lexicalized context is regarded as the best, closely followed by the model with the delexicalized one in every metric except for *conversational*, where delexicalized is better. This confirms our hypothesis that SER_{mr} might be a less reliable metric to evaluate NLG QA output. Moreover, although we notice a consistent but not drastic degradation in terms of BLEU and SER_{trg} in correlation with bigger ontologies, human evaluation shows an even more gentle degradation between QA.1 and 3 for many metrics. Interestingly, it seems the ability of all models to give a proper answer to the question (*answer*) increases from QA.1 to 3.

Multitask learning In our multitask learning experiments we combine the biggest QA dataset, QA.3, with a task-oriented corpus, SFX. We aim to investigate the possibility of transferring knowledge across different NLG systems, notwithstanding the diversity of the data in terms of domain, ontology size, DAs, application (QA vs. task-oriented). Since context is not available in SFX, the model we use has 3 MR Encoders (slot types, values, DAs) and 2 Decoders (one for each task).

Our experiments show that the NLG QA task improves the fluency on SFX both in terms of objective metrics (in Table 5) and human evaluation (in Table 6). However, training with QA seems to slightly degrade the model efficiency in generating

the correct slots. This is to be expected given the difference in the relation between slots in MR and output (one-to-one in SFX, variable in QA.3). As for QA.3 results, it seems the task-oriented NLG task improves QA NLG performances in terms of fluency (BLEU and *Naturalness*) and slot errors (SER_{trg} and *Informativeness*). SER_{mr} and SER_{mtrg}, however, show a slight degradation. We observe task-oriented NLG also makes QA NLG more conversational, however slightly reducing its probability of being an answer to the posed question as well.

Finally, comparing all experiments on QA.3, we notice that although multi-task learning helps, the previous context (either lexicalized or delexicalized) plays a critical role in improving the overall performance.

8 Qualitative analysis

In this section we report the qualitative analysis we performed on the human annotated testset. Table 7 reports some output examples from different models given the same input MR. In particular, we are interested on the impact of adding various features and multi-tasking.

QA According to our qualitative analysis on the QA datasets, the baseline model is the one with most grammatical errors (e.g. "will ferrell 's 's wife is viveca paulin", "no , canada is not the bigger than united states ."), while in general adding "delex" and "lex" features generates more grammatical responses. This observation was confirmed from both the objective (in terms of BLEU score) and subjective (*naturalness*) evaluations performed.

We also notice how lexicalizing the previous question helps in producing generally correct (e.g. 'unilever.') however shorter answers, which can be regarded as less conversational. Delexicalizing the input, on the other hand, produces more conversational (e.g. 'popsicle's manufacturer is unilever') but also more factually incorrect answers. These observations seem also in line with the subjective evaluation results, which on average reported the best scores for the model with lexicalized previous context (+ Enc Utterance lex) on whether the generated text could be considered an answer to the given question (*answer*), except for the metric rating how *conversational* the output was, for which the model with delexicalized previous context (+ Enc Utterance delex) was regarded

Dataset	Input		baseline	+delex	+lex	multitask
	context	MR				
QA.1	'sing your song writer'	*human being*: 'vic ruggiero' *a*:'sing your song' *b*:'writer'	'sing your song ' song is vic ruggiero .'	'sing your song ' writer is vic ruggiero .'	'vic ruggiero .'	-
QA.1	'did abraham lincoln have a dad'	*true*:'positive polarity', *lp*:'dad' *ro*:'abraham lincoln'	'yes . abraham lincoln has at least one dad .'	'yes , abraham lincoln had a mother.'	'yes , abraham lincoln had a father.'	-
QA.1	'what is the masters starting date'	*timepoint*:'1999', *a*:'the masters' *b*:'starting date'	'1999 's starting date point is 1999 .'	'the the masters 's starting date point is 1999 .'	'the masters was created on 1999 .'	-
QA.3	'is canada bigger than united states'	*false*:'negative polarity', *r*:'bigger than', *y*:'united states', *x*:'canada'	'no , canada is not the bigger than united states .'	'no , canada is not bigger than united states .'	'no , canada is not bigger than united states .'	'no , canada is not bigger than united states .'
QA.3	'will ferrell's wife'	*human being*: 'viveca paulin', *a*:"will ferrell 's", *b*:'wife'	'will ferrell 's 's wife is viveca paulin .'	'will ferrell 's 's wife is viveca paulin .'	'viveca paulin .'	'will ferrell 's wife is viveca paulin .'
QA.3	'popsicle maker'	*business*:'unilever', *a*:'popsicle' *b*:'maker'	'popsicle 's maker is unilever .'	'popsicle 's manufacturer is unilever .'	'unilever .'	popsicle 's maker is unilever .'
SFX	-	**inform** (*name*:'sanjalisco', *kidsallowed*:'yes')	sanjalisco allows kid -s and is located	-	-	sanjalisco allows kid -s
SFX	-	**inform** (*name*:'red door cafe', *area*:'cathedral hill') *goodformeal*:'breakfast') *kidsallowed*:'no')	red door cafe is a nice restaurant in the cathedral hill does not allow kid -s and is good for breakfast	-	-	red door cafe is a nice restaurant in cathedral hill that is good for breakfast and does not allow kid -s
SFX	-	**inform** (*name*:'darbar restaurant', *food*:'pakistani') *goodformeal*:'lunch') *kidsallowed*:'yes')	darbar restaurant is a pakistani restaurant that allows kid -s and is good for lunch	-	-	darbar restaurant is a nice restaurant that serves pakistani food and allows kid -s

Table 7: Examples of different outputs from our models when given the same input Meaning Representation (and previous context when available) on two of our Question-Answering datasets (QA.1, QA.3) and on a task-based (SFX) dataset.

as the best one across all QA partitions.

Multitask Looking at the output of the models trained in a multi-task learning setting, we observe that the baseline tends to be more prone to grammatical errors compared to models jointly trained with another task (e.g. in Table 7 'sanjalisco allows kid-s and is located'). Due to multi-tasking the models generate more grammatically correct and natural responses for both SFX and QA.3.

9 Conclusions

In this work, we apply the traditional dialog MR-to-text approach to NLG to an open-domain QA setting, with sensibly larger ontologies compared to current task-oriented dialog approaches. Our goal was to test the reliability of current approaches to NLG for dialog in an environment where the number of slots could be substantial, a requirement that is critical to meet if we want to move towards an integrated NLG module across different domains.

The experiments presented show the feasibility of learning a NLG module for QA using a MR-to-text approach. NLG models performances on datasets with progressively bigger ontologies reported a continuous but not drastic decline for most metrics. Moreover, our multitask learning experiments showed that learning NLG models jointly for QA and task-oriented dialog improves single tasks performances in terms of fluency. Results across different experimental settings also point towards the vital role played by the previous utterance context (delexicalized and especially lexicalized) to improve NLG models for open-domain QA.

While we envision our approach as a first step towards an integrated statistical NLG module for a dialog system, still much remains to be done in order to achieve such a challenge. In this work, for example, we saw the importance of adapting approaches to NLG typical of task-oriented dialog when moving to an open-domain QA setting. This is important not only in terms of modelling (the essential role of the previous utterance), but also in terms of evaluation (designing metrics able to capture the relative importance of some slots in a given answer compared to others).

As our future work, we would like to expand our multi-task learning experiments to novel NLG datasets, for example recently proposed datasets of reviews (Oraby et al., 2019). Another possibility would be to explore transfer learning, rather than multi-task learning for NLG in the MR-to-text approach. Additionally, another interesting research direction would be the investigation of evaluation metrics for NLG in a QA setting, for example to better capture the centrality of some slots (or entities) compared to others when answering a given question.

References

Dzmitry Bahdanau, KyungHyun Cho, and Yoshua Bengio. 2014. Neural machine translation by jointly learning to align and translate. *arXiv preprint arXiv:1409.0473*.

Anusha Balakrishnan, Jinfeng Rao, Kartikeya Upasani, Michael White, and Rajen Subba. 2019. Constrained decoding for neural nlg from compositional representations in task-oriented dialogue. *arXiv preprint arXiv:1906.07220*.

Jesse Dodge, Andreea Gane, Xiang Zhang, Antoine Bordes, Sumit Chopra, Alexander Miller, Arthur Szlam, and Jason Weston. 2015. Evaluating prerequisite qualities for learning end-to-end dialog systems. *arXiv preprint arXiv:1511.06931*.

Ondřej Dušek and Filip Jurcicek. 2016. A context-aware natural language generator for dialogue systems. In *Proceedings of the 17th Annual Meeting of the Special Interest Group on Discourse and Dialogue*, pages 185–190.

Ondrej Dušek and Filip Jurcıcek. 2016. Sequence-to-sequence generation for spoken dialogue via deep syntax trees and strings. In *The 54th Annual Meeting of the Association for Computational Linguistics*, page 45.

Ondřej Dušek, Jekaterina Novikova, and Verena Rieser. 2018. Findings of the e2e nlg challenge. In *Proceedings of the 11th International Conference on Natural Language Generation*, pages 322–328.

Yao Fu and Yansong Feng. 2018. Natural answer generation with heterogeneous memory. In *Proceedings of the 2018 Conference of the North American Chapter of the Association for Computational Linguistics: Human Language Technologies, Volume 1 (Long Papers)*, volume 1, pages 185–195.

Albert Gatt and Emiel Krahmer. 2018. Survey of the state of the art in natural language generation: Core tasks, applications and evaluation. *Journal of Artificial Intelligence Research*, 61:65–170.

He He, Anusha Balakrishnan, Mihail Eric, and Percy Liang. 2017. Learning symmetric collaborative dialogue agents with dynamic knowledge graph embeddings. In *Proceedings of the 55th Annual Meeting of the Association for Computational Linguistics (Volume 1: Long Papers)*, volume 1, pages 1766–1776.

Matthew Henderson, Blaise Thomson, and Steve Young. 2014. Robust dialog state tracking using delexicalised recurrent neural networks and unsupervised adaptation. In *Spoken Language Technology Workshop (SLT), 2014 IEEE*, pages 360–365. IEEE.

Sepp Hochreiter and Jürgen Schmidhuber. 1997. Long short-term memory. *Neural computation*, 9(8):1735–1780.

Juraj Juraska, Panagiotis Karagiannis, Kevin Bowden, and Marilyn Walker. 2018. A deep ensemble model with slot alignment for sequence-to-sequence natural language generation. In *Proceedings of the 2018 Conference of the North American Chapter of the Association for Computational Linguistics: Human Language Technologies, Volume 1 (Long Papers)*, volume 1, pages 152–162.

Diederik P Kingma and Jimmy Ba. 2014. Adam: A method for stochastic optimization. *arXiv preprint arXiv:1412.6980*.

Rémi Lebret, David Grangier, and Michael Auli. 2016. Neural text generation from structured data with application to the biography domain. In *Proceedings of the 2016 Conference on Empirical Methods in Natural Language Processing*, pages 1203–1213.

Percy Liang, Michael I Jordan, and Dan Klein. 2009. Learning semantic correspondences with less supervision. In *Proceedings of the Joint Conference of the 47th Annual Meeting of the ACL and the 4th International Joint Conference on Natural Language Processing of the AFNLP: Volume 1-Volume 1*, pages 91–99. Association for Computational Linguistics.

Thang Luong, Hieu Pham, and Christopher D Manning. 2015. Effective approaches to attention-based neural machine translation. In *Proceedings of the 2015 Conference on Empirical Methods in Natural Language Processing*, pages 1412–1421.

Hongyuan Mei, TTI UChicago, Mohit Bansal, and Matthew R Walter. 2016. What to talk about and how? selective generation using lstms with coarse-to-fine alignment. In *Proceedings of NAACL-HLT*, pages 720–730.

Stefano Mezza, Alessandra Cervone, Evgeny Stepanov, Giuliano Tortoreto, and Giuseppe Riccardi. 2018. Iso-standard domain-independent dialogue act tagging for conversational agents. In *Proceedings of the 27th International Conference on Computational Linguistics*, pages 3539–3551.

Neha Nayak, Dilek Hakkani-Tur, Marilyn Walker, and Larry Heck. 2017. To plan or not to plan? discourse planning in slot-value informed sequence to sequence models for language generation. In *Proc. of Interspeech*.

Jekaterina Novikova, Ondřej Dušek, and Verena Rieser. 2017. The e2e dataset: New challenges for end-to-end generation. In *Proceedings of the 18th Annual SIGdial Meeting on Discourse and Dialogue*, pages 201–206.

Shereen Oraby, Vrindavan Harrison, Abteen Ebrahimi, and Marilyn Walker. 2019. Curate and generate: A corpus and method for joint control of semantics and style in neural nlg. *arXiv preprint arXiv:1906.01334*.

Amanda Stent, Matthew Marge, and Mohit Singhai. 2005. Evaluating evaluation methods for generation in the presence of variation. In *International Conference on Intelligent Text Processing and Computational Linguistics*, pages 341–351. Springer.

Andreas Stolcke, Klaus Ries, Noah Coccaro, Elizabeth Shriberg, Rebecca Bates, Daniel Jurafsky, Paul Taylor, Rachel Martin, Carol Van Ess-Dykema, and Marie Meteer. 2000. Dialogue act modeling for automatic tagging and recognition of conversational speech. *Computational linguistics*, 26(3):339–373.

Mengxi Wei and Yang Zhang. 2019. Natural answer generation with attention over instances. *IEEE Access*, 7:61008–61017.

Tsung-Hsien Wen, Milica Gašic, Nikola Mrkšic, Lina M Rojas-Barahona, Pei-Hao Su, David Vandyke, and Steve Young. 2016. Multi-domain neural network language generation for spoken dialogue systems. In *Proceedings of NAACL-HLT*, pages 120–129.

Tsung-Hsien Wen, Milica Gasic, Nikola Mrksic, Pei-Hao Su, David Vandyke, and Steve Young. 2015. Semantically conditioned lstm-based natural language generation for spoken dialogue systems. In *Conference Proceedings-EMNLP 2015: Conference on Empirical Methods in Natural Language Processing*, pages 1711–1721.

Jun Yin, Xin Jiang, Zhengdong Lu, Lifeng Shang, Hang Li, and Xiaoming Li. 2016. Neural generative question answering. In *Proceedings of the Twenty-Fifth International Joint Conference on Artificial Intelligence*, pages 2972–2978. AAAI Press.

Using NLG for speech synthesis of mathematical sentences

Alessandro Mazzei
Università degli Studi di Torino
`alessandro.mazzei@unito.it`

Michele Monticone
Università degli Studi di Torino
`michele.monticone@edu.unito.it`

Cristian Bernareggi
Università degli Studi di Torino
`cristian.bernareggi@google.com`

Abstract

People with sight impairments can access to
a mathematical expression by using its LaTeX
source. However, this mechanisms have several drawbacks: (1) it assumes the knowledge
of the LaTeX, (2) it is slow, since LaTeX is verbose and (3) it is error-prone since LaTeX is
a typographical language. In this paper we
study the design of a natural language generation system for producing a *mathematical sentence*, i.e. a natural language sentence expressing the semantics of a mathematical expression. Moreover, we describe the main results
of a first human based evaluation experiment
of the system for Italian language.

1 Introduction

The recent progress of computational linguistic
techniques and frameworks had a deep impact
in the field of the assistive technologies. For
instance, the recent development of commercial
platforms for building speech dialogue systems,
which are designed for not-impaired people, can
also help people with disabilities in daily activities. For example a vocal command can be used
to unlock a door in a house. However, for more
specialized activities one needs to understand the
necessity of specific communities in specific domains.

In the case of mathematical domain, blind people can access to a mathematical expression by using its LaTeX source. However, this process have
several drawbacks. First of all, it assumes the
knowledge of the LaTeX. Second, listening LaTeX
is slow, since LaTeX is verbose. Finally, it is error-
prone since LaTeX is a typographical language, that
is a language designed for specifying the details
of typographical visualization rather than for efficiently communicate the semantics of a mathematical expression. For instance, the simple LaTeX expression $f(x)$ is just a typographical description

and so it represents both the function application
of f to x, and the multiplication of the constant f
for the constant x surrounded by parenthesis.

In this paper we study the design of a natural language generation (NLG) system for producing a *mathematical sentence*, that is a natural
language sentence containing the semantics of a
mathematical expression. Indeed, humans, when
have to orally communicate mathematical expressions, use their most sophisticated communication
technology, that is natural language. However,
with respect to other domains, the mathematical
domain has a number of peculiarities for speech
that needed to be accounted for (see Section 4).

We have three main research goals in this paper. The first goal is answering to the question:
*what is the linguistic status of a mathematical ex-
pression?* In other words, we want to investigate
about the possibility to use the standard notions
of linguistics, primarily syntax, for mathematical
sentences. The second goal concerns the *possibility to use a standard NLG architecture*, that is a
sentence planner and a realizer, for the production
of a mathematical sentence. The third goal concerns *the possibility to simplify the listening of a
mathematical expression by using speech features*
during the speech synthesis. Indeed, in contrast
with other fields, the mathematical domain is essentially a spoken domain (Chang, 1983). Indeed,
by only listening the audio format of mathematical sentence, that is without accessing to its written form, the standard precedence of the mathematical operators are hardly recognizable. In other
words, speech features, as pauses and prosody, can
modify the perceived structure of the mathematical sentence in a peculiar way.

The schematic architecture of the developed
framework is designed in Figure 1. The schema
follows the well-known approach of the *interlin-
gua* of rule-based machine translation (Hutchins

Proceedings of The 12th International Conference on Natural Language Generation, pages 463–472,
Tokyo, Japan, 28 Oct - 1 Nov, 2019. ©2019 Association for Computational Linguistics

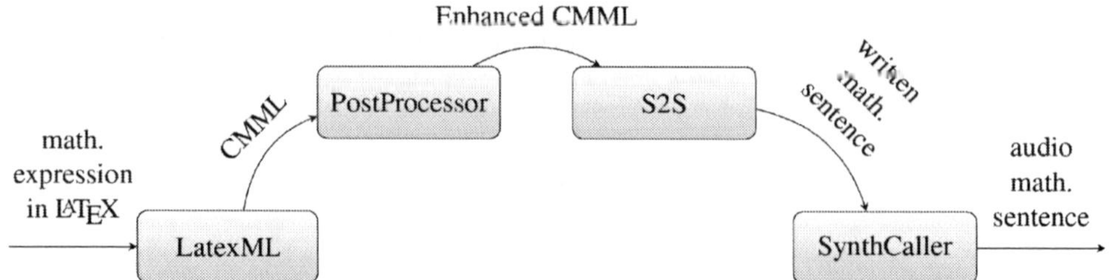

Figure 1: The software architecture for the generation of mathematical sentences. The information flow starts from (1) the LaTeX representation of the expression, (2) its translation in CMML, (3) enhancement of CMML, (4) generation of the written form of the mathematical sentence, (5) production of the audio form of the mathematical sentence.

and Somer, 1992). The process of generating a mathematical expression from its LaTeX source is a two-step algorithm. In the first step the LaTeX is analyzed and its semantics is represented in *Content MathML* (CMML henceforth), a W3C standard[1] for the syntax and semantics of mathematical expressions. In the second step, the CMML representation is used as input of the S2S (Semantics to Speech) module, that is a NLG module, to generate the mathematical sentence and, after the introduction of parenthesis or pauses, its audio format encoding.

The paper is structured as follows. In Section 2 we give a short review of the accessibility problem of mathematical expressions for visually impaired people. In Section 3 we describe the first step of the algorithm, that is the process to extract the CMML representation from its LaTeX representation. In Section 4 we describe our assumptions about the syntactic structures associated to mathematical operators. In Section 5 we describe the second step of the algorithm, that is the NLG of the mathematical expression from its CMML representation. In Section 6 we describe a first human-based evaluation of the system for Italian language performed by four blind people. Finally, Section 7 closes the paper with some considerations and pointing to future work.

2   Related work

Research to enable people with sight impairments to access mathematical notation has been conducted in two main directions. On one hand, different techniques have been investigated to preserve mathematical notation in a source format, that can be processed by a screen reader, through-

out the whole workflow of a scientific document. In particular, nowadays it is possible to embed mathematical expressions in web pages not only as images, which cannot be processed by screen readers, but through MathML or MathJax (Cervone, 2012) and in PDF documents produced from LaTeX through the LaTeX package Axessibility (Ahmetovic et al., 2018). On the other side, many research works have investigated how people with sight impairments can read and understand mathematical notation, along two directions: conversion into Braille and speech reading. Since Braille is not a universal standard, different converters have been developed. The most widespread include conversion from LaTeX to Japanese Braille (Hara et al., 2000), to Nemeth code mostly used in English speaking countries (Papasalouros and Tsolomitis, 2015), to Marburg code mostly used in German speaking countries (Murillo-Morales et al., 2016) and from MathML to Spanish, French and Italian Braille codes (Soiffer, 2016). Nonetheless, Braille cannot support all the notations that can be expressed through LaTeX or presentation MathML (e.g., category theory, computational logic) and it has not a mechanism to introduce new notations hence the converters have a number of limitations. For what concerns speech reading, different techniques have been investigated. First, the most common approach transforms LaTeX or MathML expressions into a readable sentence by mapping a sequence of mathematical symbols to an aural equivalent for English (Raman, 1996), Spanish, German and French (Soiffer, 2007), Polish (Bier and Sroczynski, 2015) and Thai (Boonprakong et al., 2017). This approach is totally unambiguous, but it is very verbose (e.g. multiple nested parentheses can be hardly retained). Moreover, only a limited number of mathematical contexts are managed. Second, in addition to se-

---

[1] https://www.w3.org/TR/MathML3/
chapter4.html

```
<m:apply>
    <m:eq/>
    <m:ci>y</m:ci>
    <m:apply>
        <m:times/>
        <m:ci>f</m:ci>
        <m:ci>x</m:ci>
    </m:apply>
</m:apply>
```

```
<apply>
    <eq/>
    <ci>y</ci>
    <apply>
        <ci>f</ci>
        <ci>x</ci>
    </apply>
</apply>
```

Figure 2: On the left the CMML generated by LatexML. On the rigth the enhanced CMML obtained after the preprocessing phase and .

quential speech reading, hierarchical exploration of the mathematical expression is provided (Soiffer, 2007; Sorge et al., 2014). This approach reduces the mental workload to retain the chunks of the expression. Third, speech reading is generated in a controlled environment such as a mathematical editor (Waltraud Schweikhardt, 2006; Raman and Gries, 1994). The context is defined by the author, hence the speech reading can be more accurate with respect to the semantics.

The idea to use mathematical sentences for improving the accessibility of mathematical expressions has been previously presented and experimented in (Ferres and Fuentes Sepúlveda, 2011; Fuentes Sepúlveda and Ferres, 2012) for Spanish language. However, in contrast to (Ferres and Fuentes Sepúlveda, 2011; Fuentes Sepúlveda and Ferres, 2012), we use a linguistic-based NLG architecture rather than a template-based one. In particular, by using the SimpleNLG realization engine for Italian, we allow both (i) for portability of the system to other languages, and (ii) a major and simple customization of the mathematical sentences. Indeed, the linguistic nature of the SimpleNLG input format allow for a very simple implementation of linguistic operations, as coordination or punctuation insertion (e.g. parenthesis. Cf. (van Deemter et al., 2005) for a discussion on the advantages and limitations of the template-based approach).

3 From LaTeX to CMML

The first step of our algorithm is the generation of CMML associated to a LaTeX formula. We based this step on an external tool named *LatexML* (Miller, 2007). However, the CMML obtained from this tool needed to be enhanced by a postprocessing procedure for two distinct reasons.

1. We decided to clean the CMML obtained from LatexML since we wanted to remove some extra characters in the tag names (e.g. the suffix m:). With the same aim, we replaced all non standard characters from the tag values, e.g. some variable names which are written by the LatexML with italics font. Moreover, in certain cases LatexML generate some tags with the *open math* standard, as the case of conditional-set, that is converted by using the csymbol tag. For the sake of generality, in order to simplify the generation step of the system, we decided to uniform these cases to their corresponding *pure CMML* tag.

2. There are case in which the typographical origin of the LaTeX creates ambiguity that cannot always correctly solved by LatexML. If $y = f(x)$ is the LaTeX representation of formula $y = f(x)$, LatexML cannot autonomously decide the correct relation between the symbols f and x. One could force its interpretation as a function application (i.e. f is a function and x is his argument) or in alternative could force its interpretation as a multiplication (i.e. both f and x are just variables). Indeed, by default LatexML always assumes latter option. As a consequence, we had to fix it by hand in a number of cases.

The output of LatexML and the enhanced version with the hand fix applied are shown in Figure 2.

4 The (linguistic) Syntactic Structure of the Mathematical Expressions

Mathematical notation has been conceived with the aim of representing mathematical concepts using a specific written symbolic language. However, it is used in speech as *standard* language where usual syntactic notions, as number agreement, have to be accounted. For example the, ut-

Category	Operators	Construction
relational	$>, \geq, \gg, <, \leq, \ll, =, \neq, \sqsubseteq, \not\sqsubseteq, \subseteq, \not\subseteq$	Copula
arithmetic, algebraic, set	$+, -, *, /, \circ, [x]^{[n]}, \in, \notin, \cap, \cup, \backslash, \times$	Declarative
logical connectives	$\wedge, \vee, \neg, \Longrightarrow, \Longleftrightarrow$	Coordination
elementary functions	$\sin, \cos, \tan, \arcsin, \arccos, \arctan, \lvert \ldots \rvert, \sqrt[r]{x}, n!, f^{-1}$	Noun Phrase
sequence	$\displaystyle\sum_{[x=a]}^{[b]} [f(x)], \prod_{[x=a]}^{[b]} [f(x)], \lim_{[x \to a]} [f(x)]$	Noun Phrase
calculus	$\displaystyle\int_{[a]}^{[b]} f(x)\,\mathrm{d}x, f^{(n)}(x), \frac{\mathrm{d}^n f(x)}{\mathrm{d}x^n}$	Noun Phrase
conditional set	$\{[vars] \mid conditions\}$	Reduced Relative
pair	$([x], [y])$	Reduced Relative

Table 1: In this table are shown all operators considered in our work, divided in category by the same linguistic structure.

terance $2/3$ can be pronounced as `two thirds`. Establishing what are the similarities between mathematical language and natural language is important for theoretical and practical considerations since this would imply the existence of linguistic structures which could be exploited for language generation. Also very simple mathematical expression can often be pronunced in different ways which underlay different mathematical sentences and so different syntactic structures, as $2/3$ that can also be pronunced with the sentence `two over three` (Chang, 1983). In contrast, there are cases in which the parsing of a mathematical expression unambiguously conducts to a specific mathematical sentence and to a unambiguous syntactic structure. For example, the mathematical expression $|x|$, that corresponds to the mathematical sentence *the absolute value of x* seems obviously to be a noun phrase modified both by an adjective and by a propositional phrase. In contrast, for the mathematical sentence `x belongs to A`, the most natural syntactic analysis seems to be a declarative sentence. However, there are many cases where the syntactic structure of a mathematical sentence is not so simple to represent. For example, `x plus three` could be analyzed as composed by the subject `x` and the object `three`, but this declarative representation of the sentence clashes with the impossibility to assign the part of speech verb to the word `plus` in the standard language.

As working hypothesis, we decided to assume a "specialized" syntactic analysis for a number of mathematical objects. For instance, `x plus three` indicates the action of adding one quantity to another, so it can be represented as a declarative structure. As a consequence, `plus` can be analysed as verb and this assumption can be extended to all the mathematical sentences.

In this paper we considered only the mathematical structures belonging to the subfield of the mathematical analysis. In particular we considered all the mathematical expressions in an Italian analysis book (Pandolfi, 2013). By using this corpus of expressions and by assuming that all numbers and variables can be treated as nouns and that all arithmetic operators can be treated as verbs, we found eight additional categories for representing all complex mathematical expressions and we defined a specific syntactic construction for each category. We reported these eight categories in Table 1.

We decided to analyse the mathematical sentences of relational operators as copula sentences (`a is greater than b`), algebraic operators as declarative sentences (`a cartesian product b`), logical operators as conjunctions (`a or b`), elementary operators (e.g. radical sign), sequence (e.g. limit), calculus (e.g. integral) as noun phrases (`the square root of x`), pairs and conditional sets as reduced relatives (`the set of x such that x is less than 3`). It is worth noting that our syntactic representations for mathematical operators in the analysis domain could have alternative representations or could be specialized in a more refined classification (c.f. (Chang, 1983)). However, we decided to use only eight category for the sake of simplicity.

5 Building Mathematical Sentences with NLG

Traditional NLG architectures split the generation process into three distinct phases, that are *document planning, sentence planning* and *realization* (Reiter and Dale, 2000; Gatt and Krahmer, 2018). In particular document planning decides *what* to say and sentence planning and realization decides *how* to say it. In this project the content of the communication is specified by the input mathematical expression, so the content selection phase is not necessary at all.

In Section 5.1 we will give some details on the rule-based sentence planner designed for managing mathematical sentences and in Section 5.2 we will describe the use of the SimpleNLG-it realizer (Mazzei et al., 2016) for the case of mathematical domain.

5.1 Building a Sentence Planner for Mathematical Sentences

The input of the sentence planner is a mathematical expression in the form of enhanced CMML, that is a sort of linguistic semantic tree for the mathematical expression. In order to associate a *sentence plan*, that is a sort of under-specified tree-based syntactic structure, we devised a recursive algorithm that traverses top-down the CMML structure.

We classified all the mathematical expressions into a number of predefined categories, as discussed in the Section 4 (see Table 1). In particular, for each category we designed a prototypical sentence plan that will be used in the recursive process. Each prototype builds a specific linguistic construction (e.g. *copula, reduced relative* etc.), that is designed for giving syntactic roles to the arguments of the specific mathematical construction. For instance, on the left of the Figure 3, we reported the prototypical sentence plan for the *conditional set* mathematical structure and on the right of we reported an example of its instantiation. Note that in the produced structures: (1) the leaves of the sentence plan are lemmas rather than words, (2) the syntactic relations among the nodes are expressed using both dependency relations (e.g. subj, complement) as well as constituency nodes (e.g. Prepositional Phrase, PP). This peculiar representation is typical of some re-

alization engines. and will be exploited in the next step of the generation.

In order to build a sentence plan for a mathematical sentence, there are two important issues: (i) the perception of precedence of the arithmetic operator and (ii) its most economical non ambiguous representation.

(i) Listening mathematics has some peculiarities with respect to reading it. For instance, division is granted a higher precedence than addition, and during the reading process the expression $a+b/c$ is parsed as $a+\frac{b}{c}$ without ambiguities. A different result arises if one listens the equivalent mathematical sentence `a plus b divided by c` without reading the expression: we experimented that the most frequent perceived parse is $\frac{a+b}{c}$. After a limited number of experiments in listening arithmetic expressions with distinct (blind and not blind) people, we decided to state as working hypothesis that *the precedence of the arithmetic operators are perceived in the reverse order when one listens a mathematical expressions without reading it.* We are aware that this speculation should be supported by specific experimental studies but, at the best of our knowledge, we have not been able to find them.

(ii) A different problem concerns the most efficient way to represent the *correct* precedence of a mathematical expression. In other words, how we can build a mathematical sentence unambiguously equivalent to $a + \frac{b}{c}$? A trivial but effective solution is to use parenthesis, that is to produce the mathematical sentence `a plus open parenthesis b divided by c close parenthesis`. However, the drawback of this solution is the length of the sentence that, for very complex expressions, can augment substantially.

In order to account for the problem of the precedence of the operators and its representation, we modified the sentence planner in two ways. First, we decided to model parenthesis as *first-class citizens* in the sentence plan, that is we considered *open-parenthesis* and *closed-parenthesis* as two new lexical items of the SimpleNLG lexicon which can be used as pre-modifier and post-modifier of a mathematical sentence respectively.

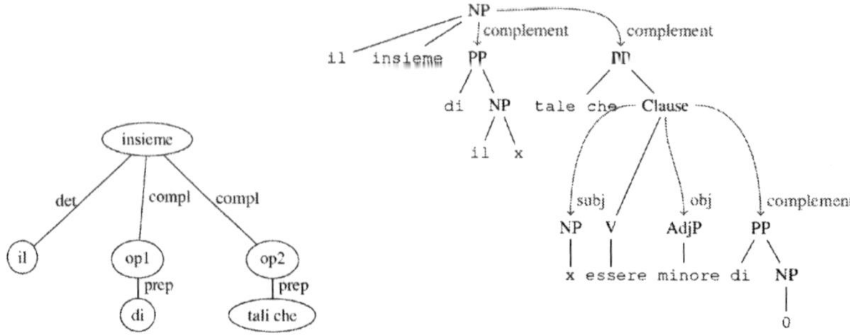

Figure 3: The prototypical sentence plan for the *conditional set* mathematical structure (left), and its fulfillment producing the sentence L'insieme degli x tali che x è minore di 0 (rigth, *the set of all x such that x is lesser than 0*).

Second, similar to (Fuentes Sepúlveda and Ferres, 2012), we allowed to use a *speech pause* as a synonymous of open/closed-parenthesis items.

In order to experiment the pros and cons of using parentheses and pauses in the understanding of a mathematical sentence, we decided to implement three distinct parenthesization strategies, called *parenthesis*, *pause*, and *smart*.

1. In the *parenthesis strategy*, all the necessary parentheses are inserted in the sentence plan. Note that a parenthesis has to be considered necessary with respect to the inverted precedence order hypothesis stated above.

2. In the *pause strategy*, all the necessary pauses are inserted in the sentence plan.

3. In the *smart strategy*, all the necessary parentheses are inserted in the higher nodes of the sentence plan, and the necessary pauses are inserted close to the leaves of the sentence plan. This is a hybrid strategy that combines parentheses and pauses in order to have a less verbose mathematical sentence.

The evaluation of the performance of these parenthesization strategies is one of the goal of the experimentation described in the Section 6.

5.2 Using SimpleNLG for spoken mathematics

In order to produce a spoken mathematical sentences in Italian with the SimpleNLG-it realizer (Mazzei et al., 2016), we needed to account for the construction of a domain specific lexicon for the field of the mathematical analysis.

SimpleNLG-it is the Italian porting of the SimpleNLG realizer, that was originally designed only for English (Gatt and Reiter, 2009). As default Italian lexicon, SimpleNLG-it uses a basic vocabulary of around 7000 words, that is a *simple* lexicon studied to be perfectly understood by most Italian people (Mazzei, 2016). However, for this specific project we needed to augment the basic lexicon with a mathematical specialized lexicon, that contains both new lexical entries (as arcotangente, *arctangent*), than new associated value for lexical entry that are yet in the basic lexicon (as the *noun* value for the part of speech of the lemma integrale, *integral*). This specialized lexicon contains 113 entries that are mostly categorized as nouns (e.g. logaritmo, *logarithm*), verbs (e.g. intersecare, *intersect*), adjective (e.g. iperbolico, *hyperbolic*). In the lexicon, there are only two new instances of adverbs (that are relativamente and propriamente, *relative, properly*), and only one instance of "prepositional locution" (that is tale che, *such that*). Finally, we added specific lexical items to realize both parenthesis (that are parentesi aperta and parentesi chiusa, *open/closed parenthesis*) and speech pause. This latter item will be finally realized by using the SSML (Speech Synthesis Markup Language) tag <break/>, that can be processed by many speech synthesis engines[2]. An example of written mathematical sentence generated for the mathematical expression $\sqrt[n]{x} = x^{1/n}$ is <break time="1000ms"/>La radice n-esima di x è uguale a x elevato a <break time="500ms"/> 1 diviso n (*the n-th root of x is equal to x raised to 1 divided by n*).

---

[2]https://www.w3.org/TR/speech-synthesis11/

Simple formulas	Complex Formula
$A \times B = \{(x,y) \mid x \in A, y \in B\}$	$\lim\limits_{x \to x_0} \left\{ \dfrac{f(x) - f(x_0)}{x - x_0} - f'(x_0) \right\} = 0$
$g^{-1}(y) = f^{-1}\left((y-b)/a\right)$	$y = f(a) + \dfrac{f(b) - f(a)}{b - a}(x - a)$
$\displaystyle\int_b^c a\,\mathrm{d}x = a(c - b)$	$\displaystyle\int \dfrac{1}{\sqrt{m^2 - x^2}}\mathrm{d}x = \arcsin\dfrac{x}{m} + c$
$x > b \implies \|f(x)\| < M$	$\displaystyle\sum_{k=0}^{n} \dfrac{f^{(k)}(x_0)}{k!}(x - x_0)^k$
$\sqrt[n]{x} = x^{1/n}$	$\lim \left(1 + \dfrac{1}{n}\right)^n = e$

Table 2: On the left are shown the simple formulas. On the right the complex ones.

The actual version of the mathematical sentence generator has been interfaced with two speech synthesis engines, that are the web service provided by the IBM-Watson framework[3] (*W-engine* henceforth), and the Espeak API[4] (*E-engine* henceforth). W-engine is a commercial, closed software based on deep learning, while E-engine is a free, open-source software based on formant synthesis algorithms. Note that for not visual impaired people W-engine sounds more fluent but for visual impaired people sounds more familiar since it is used by the free NVDA screen reader.

6 Evaluation

In order to have a first evaluation of the generation system, we wanted to test the hypothesis that the system produces mathematical sentences which are understandable by visually impaired people. So, we built a web-based test explicitly designed for this class of users. We designed a questionnaire composed by a 6 multiple choices questions concerning personal data, a core of 25 open questions each one concerning the listening of a mathematical sentence and its comprehensibility, 1 Likert-scale question globally comparing LaTeX and system comprehensibility, 1 open question for free comments.

The 25 core questions have a all the same schema: there is a audio file encoding a mathematical sentence and there is a open form for transcribing it. In the compilation instructions, we asked the users to fill this section by using "LaTeX or with other non ambiguous formal representation". The mathematical expressions obtained have been manually translated to CMML

for evaluation. We implemented the questionnaire by using the Google Form framework, that was preliminarily judged accessible by a blind person.

We have built the 25 core questions by using 10 mathematical expressions belonging to the analysis book used for developing the generation module (Pandolfi, 2013) (see Table 2). We have selected simple 5 expressions (less than 15 nodes in their *MathML* representation) and 5 complex expressions (more than 15 nodes). By varying (i) the synthesis engines (W-engine and E-engine), and (ii) the parenthesization strategies (*parentheses*, *pauses* and *smart*), we instantiate 25 possible mathematical sentences of the 10 mathematical expressions in the questionnaire.

In order to score the comprehension of the user we used two distinct metrics on the CMML expressions, that are *Exact Match* and *SPICE* (Anderson et al., 2016) metrics. The exact match returns 1 (or 0) value if the starting CMML tree and the perceived CMML are equals (or not). The SPICE score is a tree similarity measure previously used in the context of automatic caption generation. SPICE is obtained by computing the F-score of the overlap between two trees: the overlap is measured by decomposing trees in typed elementary substructures, that are operands, operators and their relations. For instance, the expression $x - 1$ is decomposed as $\{1, x, minus, (\text{op: } minus, \text{first: } x), (\text{op: } minus, \text{second: } 1)\}$ (cf. (Anderson et al., 2016) for more details).

For the experimentation, we recruited 4 visually impaired people with personal invitation without any rewards. All users are Italian mother tongue, have a good knowledge of mathematical analysis and have a bachelor degree (only one related to mathematics). We believe that for a preliminary evaluation of the system, 4 blind people is a valu-

---

[3] https://www.ibm.com/watson/services/text-to-speech/

[4] http://espeak.sourceforge.net

able number. Indeed, note that all the users found the complete experimentation quite tiring and they spend around one hour to complete it. Note that in previous work on the generation mathematical sentences (Ferres and Fuentes Sepúlveda, 2011; Fuentes Sepúlveda and Ferres, 2012), the evaluations have been performed without blind people[5]. So, in our knowledge, this is the first NLG study on mathematical sentence with a realistic users' test-set.

We also submitted the questionnaire to a not visually impaired analysis teacher. She found the task of understanding mathematical sentence only by listening extremely hard. We did not report her (very low) scores since it is outside of the main goal of the experimentation, but this poor results show the different perception difficulty among different kind of users.

6.1 Results and Error Analysis

In Table 3 and in Table 4 are reported the scores obtained by the users for Exact Match and SPICE measures.   From the first column of Table 3

U	All (25)	Simple (7)	Comp. (18)
1	13	5	8
2	18	5	13
3	13	5	8
4	14	5	9
Tot.	58 (58%)	20 (71%)	38 (53%)

Table 3: The Exact Match measure for all mathematical sentences (25 instances), only simple (7 instances), only complex (18 instances).

U	All (25)	Simple (7)	Comp. (18)
1	0.92 (0.11)	0.95 (0.1)	0.91 (0.11)
2	0.96 (0.06)	0.98 (0.05)	0.97 (0.07)
3	0.93 (0.09)	0.90 (0.14)	0.94 (0.06)
4	0.95 (0.07)	0.97 (0.09)	0.94 (0.07)
Avg.	0.94 (0.08)	0.95 (0.01)	0.94 (0.08)

Table 4: The averaged SPICE measure and standard deviations for all mathematical sentences (25 instances), only simple (7 instances), only complex (18 instances).

we can see that score variation seems strongly depend by the user. Indeed, User 2 is the only one with a Master Degree related to mathematics. A possible comparison can be done with

---

[5](Ferres and Fuentes Sepúlveda, 2011) used automatic evaluation for the coverage and (Fuentes Sepúlveda and Ferres, 2012) recruited "20 engineers and engineering students" for the correctness.

(Fuentes Sepúlveda and Ferres, 2012), where a user group of 20 not-blind engineers have been exposed to 15 mathematical sentences generated from mathematical formulas obtained from Wikipedia. (Fuentes Sepúlveda and Ferres, 2012) obtained a final score for the exact match between $76 - 79\%$, that is comparable with the results of Table 3.

The SPICE scores in Table 4 confirms the dependence from the user of the results and evidences that only small portions of the mathematical expressions have been misunderstood. A manual inspection of the results showed that most of misunderstood sentence have structural errors in the perceived tree (11 errors), while are less frequent erroneous symbols (6 errors). For instance, a common mistake regarded the perception of the derivation operator, that is `la derivata di f di x` (*the derivative of f of x*).

By considering the Simple and Complex columns of the Table 3 is evident that, not surprisingly, the complexity of the expression have a strong impact on the comprehension and the t-test returns a value of 0.01 (two-tailed p-value). However, the application of t-test to the SPICE values for Simple and Complex expression do not consider them significantly different (0.75 two-tailed p-value).

In Table 5 we reported the averaged values of SPICE for three distinct categorizations of the mathematical expressions, that are parenthesization strategy, synthesis engine and *fame*. This last category expresses that the last two complex expressions in Table 2 are two well-known mathematical definitions and this fact could affect their comprehension.

With respect to the main goal of searching for specific strategy for simplify the listening of a mathematical expression, we note that the statistical analysis of the values in Table 5 concerning category parenthesization did not suggest any significant variations among the strategies. For instance, by comparing with t-test the SPICE scores of parenthesis and pauses strategies, we obtain a not significant value (0.75 two-tailed p-value). In contrast we could assert as posthoc hypotheses that both synthesis engine and fame have a significant effect on the performance of the system: by applying the t-test we obtained for both 0.02 two-tailed p-value. However, new experiments with more users are necessary to confirm these conclu-

Cat.	U1	U2	U3	U4
Par.	0.87 (0.16)	0.98 (0.06)	0.93 (0.06)	0.93 (0.08)
Pause	0.95 (0.04)	0.95 (0.11)	0.96 (0.04)	0.96 (0.04)
Smart	0.93 (0.10)	0.98 (0.04)	0.92 (0.11)	0.95 (0.09)
W-eng.	0.91 (0.11)	0.97 (0.07)	0.92 (0.09)	0.94 (0.08)
E-eng.	0.99 (0.03)	0.99 (0.03)	0.97 (0.04)	0.97 (0.04)
Famous	1.00 (0.00)	0.96 (0.10)	1.00 (0.00)	1.00 (0.00)
NFamous	0.89 (0.11)	0.97 (0.05)	0.90 (0.09)	0.93 (0.08)

Table 5: The averaged SPICE measures and standard deviations for different categorizations of the mathematical expressions.

sions.

7 Conclusion

In this paper we have presented a study on the generation of mathematical sentences, i.e. sentences in natural language expressing mathematical expressions[6].

We have described the peculiarities of the mathematical domain with respect to the task of NLG. In particular, we have considered the practical problem of analysing the semantics expressed by a mathematical expression in LaTeX, and its speech production in Italian language by using the SimpleNLG-it realizer and two distinct synthesis engines. We have proposed three different strategies for parenthesization of ambiguous mathematical expressions based on both parenthesis and pauses in speech. Finally, we have conducted a human-based evaluation of the system by using a tree-based measures of similarity. The results of the experimentation suggests (1) a preference for formant-based synthesizer with respect to NN-based synthesizer, (2) the performances on simple expressions are good, but (3) on more structurally complex expressions need improvements

In future work we intend to expand the lexicon in order to use English language and so to perform evaluation with a larger number of users and with more complex procedures of parenthesization. In particular, we want to experiment the use of acoustic signals for represents the opening and the closure of nested parentheses. Moreover, we intend to integrate the system into a dialogue system architecture with the idea to allow user to ask for repetition and clarification in the case of very complex expressions.

---

[6]The open-source licensed software can be downloaded at `https://bitbucket.org/tesimagistralemonticone/formula-to-speech/`

References

Dragan Ahmetovic, Tiziana Armano, Cristian Bernareggi, Michele Berra, Anna Capietto, Sandro Coriasco, Nadir Murru, Alice Ruighi, and Eugenia Taranto. 2018. Axessibility: A latex package for mathematical formulae accessibility in pdf documents. In *Proceedings of the 20th International ACM SIGACCESS Conference on Computers and Accessibility*, ASSETS '18, pages 352–354, New York, NY, USA. ACM.

Peter Anderson, Basura Fernando, Mark Johnson, and Stephen Gould. 2016. SPICE: semantic propositional image caption evaluation. *CoRR*, abs/1607.08822.

Agnieszka Bier and Zdzislaw Sroczynski. 2015. Adaptive math-to-speech interface. In *Proceedings of the Mulitimedia, Interaction, Design and Innnovation*, MIDI '15, pages 7:1–7:9, New York, NY, USA. ACM.

Nattapat Boonprakong, Patcharida Pudpadee, Thanarat H. Chalidabhongse, and Proadpran Punyabukkana. 2017. Reading mathematical expression in thai. In *Proceedings of the 11th International Convention on Rehabilitation Engineering and Assistive Technology*, i-CREATe 2017, pages 9:1–9:3, Kaki Bukit TechPark II,, Singapore. Singapore Therapeutic, Assistive & Rehabilitative Technologies (START) Centre.

Davide Cervone. 2012. Mathjax: A platform for mathematics on the web. *Notices of the American Mathematical Society*, 59.

Lawrence A. Chang. 1983. Handbook for spoken mathematics (larry's speakeasy). *Lawrence Livermore Laboratory, The Regents of the University of California*.

Leo Ferres and José Fuentes Sepúlveda. 2011. Improving accessibility to mathematical formulas: the wikipedia math accessor. In *Proceedings of the International Cross-Disciplinary Conference on Web Accessibility, W4A 2011, Hyderabad, Andhra Pradesh, India, March 28-29, 2011*, page 25.

José Fuentes Sepúlveda and Leo Ferres. 2012. Improving accessibility to mathematical formulas: The wikipedia math accessor. *New Rev Hypermedia Multimedia*, 18(3):183–204.

Albert Gatt and Emiel Krahmer. 2018. Survey of the state of the art in natural language generation: Core tasks, applications and evaluation. *J. Artif. Intell. Res.*, 61:65–170.

Albert Gatt and Ehud Reiter. 2009. SimpleNLG: A Realisation Engine for Practical Applications. In *Proceedings of the 12th European Workshop on Natural Language Generation*, ENLG '09, pages 90–93, Stroudsburg, PA, USA. Association for Computational Linguistics.

Shunsuke Hara, Nobuyuki Ohtake, Mika Higuchi, Noriko Miyazaki, Ayako Watanabe, Kanako Kusunoki, and Hiroshi Sato. 2000. Mathbraille; a system to transform latex documents into braille. *SIGCAPH Comput. Phys. Handicap.*, (66):17–20.

W. John Hutchins and Harold L. Somer. 1992. *An Introduction to Machine Translation*. London: Academic Press.

Alessandro Mazzei. 2016. Building a computational lexicon by using SQL. In *Proceedings of Third Italian Conference on Computational Linguistics (CLiC-it 2016) & Fifth Evaluation Campaign of Natural Language Processing and Speech Tools for Italian. Final Workshop (EVALITA 2016), Napoli, Italy, December 5-7, 2016.*, volume 1749, pages 1–5. CEUR-WS.org.

Alessandro Mazzei, Cristina Battaglino, and Cristina Bosco. 2016. SimpleNLG-IT: adapting SimpleNLG to Italian. In *Proceedings of the 9th International Natural Language Generation conference*, pages 184–192, Edinburgh, UK. Association for Computational Linguistics.

Bruce Miller. LaTeXML: A LaTeX to XML converter [online]. 2007.

Tomas Murillo-Morales, Klaus Miesenberger, and Reinhard Ruemer. 2016. A latex to braille conversion tool for creating accessible schoolbooks in austria. volume 9758, pages 397–400.

Luciano Pandolfi. 2013. *ANALISI MATEMATICA 1*. Dipartimento di Scienze Matematiche "Giuseppe Luigi Lagrange", Politecnico di Torino.

Andreas Papasalouros and Antonis Tsolomitis. 2015. A direct tex-to-braille transcribing method. In *Proceedings of the 17th International ACM SIGACCESS Conference on Computers & Accessibility*, ASSETS '15, pages 373–374, New York, NY, USA. ACM.

T. V. Raman. 1996. Emacspeak—direct speech access. In *Proceedings of the Second Annual ACM Conference on Assistive Technologies*, Assets '96, pages 32–36, New York, NY, USA. ACM.

T. V. Raman and David Gries. 1994. Interactive audio documents. In *Proceedings of the First Annual ACM Conference on Assistive Technologies*, Assets '94, pages 62–68, New York, NY, USA. ACM.

Ehud Reiter and Robert Dale. 2000. *Building Natural Language Generation Systems*. Studies in Natural Language Processing. Cambridge University Press.

Neil Soiffer. 2007. Mathplayer v2.1: Web-based math accessibility. In *Proceedings of the 9th International ACM SIGACCESS Conference on Computers and Accessibility*, Assets '07, pages 257–258, New York, NY, USA. ACM.

Neil Soiffer. 2016. A study of speech versus braille and large print of mathematical expresisons. In *Lecture Notes in Computer Science*, volume 9758, Berlin. Springer.

Volker Sorge, Charles Chen, T. V. Raman, and David Tseng. 2014. Towards making mathematics a first class citizen in general screen readers. In *Proceedings of the 11th Web for All Conference*, W4A '14, pages 40:1–40:10, New York, NY, USA. ACM.

Kees van Deemter, Emiel Krahmer, and Mariet Theune. 2005. Real versus template-based natural language generation: a false opposition? *Computational linguistics*, 31(1):15–23. Imported from HMI.

Nadine Jessel Benoit Encelle Margaret Gut Waltraud Schweikhardt, Cristian Bernareggi. 2006. Lambda: A european system to access mathematics with braille and audio synthesis. In *Lecture Notes in Computer Science*, volume 4061, Berlin. Springer.

Teaching FORGe to Verbalize DBpedia Properties in Spanish

Simon Mille
Universitat Pompeu Fabra
Barcelona, Spain
simon.mille@upf.edu

Stamatia Dasiopoulou
Independent Researcher
Barcelona, Spain
stamatia.dasiopoulou@gmail.com

Beatriz Fisas
Universitat Pompeu Fabra
Barcelona, Spain
beatriz.fisas@upf.edu

Leo Wanner
ICREA and Universitat Pompeu Fabra
Barcelona, Spain
leo.wanner@upf.edu

Abstract

Statistical generators increasingly dominate the research in NLG. However, grammar-based generators that are grounded in a solid linguistic framework remain very competitive, especially for generation from deep knowledge structures. Furthermore, if built modularly, they can be ported to other genres and languages with a limited amount of work, without the need of the annotation of a considerable amount of training data. One of these generators is FORGe, which is based on the Meaning-Text Model. In the recent WebNLG challenge (the first comprehensive task addressing the mapping of RDF triples to text) FORGe ranked first with respect to the overall quality in human evaluation. We extend the coverage of FORGE's open source grammatical and lexical resources for English, so as to further improve the English outcome, and port them to Spanish, to achieve a comparable quality. This confirms that, as already observed in the case of SimpleNLG, a robust universal grammar-driven framework and a systematic organization of the linguistic resources can be an adequate choice for NLG applications.

1 Introduction

The origins of Natural Language Generation (NLG) are in rule-based sentence/text generation from numerical data or deep semantic structures. With the availability of large scale syntactically annotated corpora and the lack of publicly available knowledge repositories, the focus had shifted to statistical surface generation. However, thanks to Semantic Web (SW) initiatives such as the *W3C Linking Open Data Project*,[1]

---

[1] https://www.w3.org/wiki/SweoIG/
TaskForces/CommunityProjects/
LinkingOpenData

a tremendous amount of structured knowledge has been made publicly available as language-independent triples; the Linked Open Data (LOD) cloud currently contains over one thousand inter-linked datasets (e.g., DBpedia, Wikidata), which cover a large range of domains and amount to billions of different triples. The verbalization of LOD triples, i.e., their mapping onto sentences in natural languages, has been attracting a growing interest in the past years, as shown by the organization of dedicated events such as the WebNLG 2016 workshop (Gardent and Gangemi, 2016) and the 2017 WebNLG challenge (Gardent et al., 2017b). As a result, a variety of new NLG systems designed specifically for handling structured data have emerged, most of them statistical, as seen in the 2017 WebNLG challenge, although a number of rule-based generators have also been presented. All systems focus on English, mainly because no training data other than for English are available as yet. Given the high cost for the creation of training data, this state of affairs is likely to persist for some time. Therefore, the question on the competitiveness of rule-based generators arises.

One of the rule-based generators presented at WebNLG was FORGe (Mille and Dasiopoulou, 2017), which ranked first with respect to over-all quality in the human evaluation. FORGe is grounded in the linguistic model of the Meaning-Text Theory (Mel'čuk, 1988). The multistratal nature of this model allows for a modular organization of blocks of graph-transduction rules, from blocks that are universal, i.e., multilingual, to blocks that are language-specific. The graph-transduction framework MATE (Bohnet and Wanner, 2010) furthermore facilitates a systematic hierarchical rule writing and testing. SimpleNLG

Proceedings of The 12th International Conference on Natural Language Generation, pages 473–483,
Tokyo, Japan, 28 Oct - 1 Nov, 2019. ©2019 Association for Computational Linguistics

(Gatt and Reiter, 2009) demonstrated that a well
defined generation infrastructure, along with a
transparent, easy to handle rule and structure format, is a key for its take up and use for creation
of generation modules for multiple languages. In
what follows, we aim to demonstrate that the
FORGe generator can also well serve as a multilingual portable text generator for verbalization of
structured data and that its lexical and grammatical
resources can be easily extended to reach a higher
coverage of linguistic constructions. For this, we
extend its publicly available resources for English,
so as to improve the quality of the English texts
and port the resources to Spanish with a comparable output quality.

In the next section, we summarize the related
work. Section 3 introduces FORGe. In Section
4, we outline our work on the extension of the
available English resources and on the adaptation
of FORGe to Spanish. Section 5 presents the results of the automatic evaluation of the extended
system, and Section 6 a qualitative evaluation of
the outputs in both languages. Section 7, finally,
draws some conclusions and presents the future
work.

2 Related work

The most prominent recent illustration of the
portability of a generation framework is SimpleNLG. Originally developed for generation of
English in practical applications (Gatt and Reiter, 2009), in the meantime it has been ported to
generate, among others, in Brasilian Portuguese
(De Oliveira and Sripada, 2014), Dutch (de Jong
and Theune, 2018), German (Bollmann, 2011),
Italian (Mazzei et al., 2016), and Spanish (Soto
et al., 2017). However, while SimpleNLG is a
framework for surface generation, usually with a
limited coverage, we are interested in a portable
multilingual framework for large scale text generation from structured data, more precisely, from
DBpedia properties (Lehmann et al., 2015).

Although most existing NLG generators combine different techniques, there are three main approaches to generating texts from an input sequence of structured data (Bouayad-Agha et al.,
2014; Gatt and Krahmer, 2018): (i) filling slot
values in predefined sentence templates (Androutsopoulos et al., 2013), (ii) applying grammars
(rules) that encode different types of linguistic
knowledge (Wanner et al., 2010), and (iii) predict-

ing statistically the most appropriate output (Gardent et al., 2017b; Belz et al., 2011). Template-
based systems are very robust, but also limited in
terms of portability since new templates need to
be defined for every new domain, style, language,
etc. Statistical systems have the best coverage, but
the relevance and the quality of the produced texts
cannot be ensured. Furthermore, they are fully dependent on the available (still scarce and mostly
monolingual) training data. The development of
grammar-based systems is time-consuming and
they usually have coverage issues. However, they
do not require training material, allow for a greater
control over the outputs (e.g. for mitigating errors or tuning the output to a desired style), and
the linguistic knowledge used for one domain or
language can be reused for other domains and languages. In addition to these, a number of systems
actually address the whole sequence as one step,
by combining approaches (i) and (iii) and filling
the slot values of pre-existing templates using neural network techniques (Nayak et al., 2017).

In the WebNLG challenge (Gardent et al.,
2017a), systems of types (ii) and (iii) have been
presented. The task consisted in generating texts
from up to 7 DBpedia triples from 15 categories,
covering in total 373 distinct DBpedia properties.
Nine categories appeared in the training data ('As-
tronaut', 'Building', 'University', etc.), i.e., were
"seen", and five categories were "unseen", i.e.,
they did not appear in the training data ('Athlete',
'Artist', etc.). At the time of the challenge, the
WebNLG dataset contained about 10K distinct inputs and 25K data-text pairs; a sample data-text
pair is shown in Figure 1. The neural generator ADAPT (Elder et al., 2018) performed best on
seen data, and FORGe on unseen data and overall. In what follows, we aim to improve the performance of FORGe on seen data for English and
furthermore port it to Spanish.

3 Overview of FORGe

FORGe is an open-source generator implemented
in terms of graph transducers; it covers the last
two typical NLG tasks (text planning and linguistic generation). Following the Meaning-Text Theory (Mel'čuk, 1988), FORGe is based on the notion of linguistic dependencies, that is, the semantic, syntactic and morphological relations between
the components of the sentence. Input predicate-
argument structures are mapped onto sentences by

```
<originaltripleset>
<otriple> Antwerp_International_Airport | city | Antwerp </otriple>
<otriple> Belgium | leader | Charles_Michel </otriple>
<otriple> Antwerp| country | Belgium </otriple>
<otriple> Belgium| language| German </otriple>
</originaltripleset>
```

Reference 1: Charles Michel is the leader of Belgium where the German language is spoken. Antwerp is located in the country and served by Antwerp International airport.

Reference 2: Antwerp International Airport serves the city of Antwerp which is a popular tourist destination in Belgium. One of the languages spoken in Belgium is German, and the leader is Charles Michel.

Figure 1: Sample pair of data (subject-property-object) and human-produced texts (*references*).

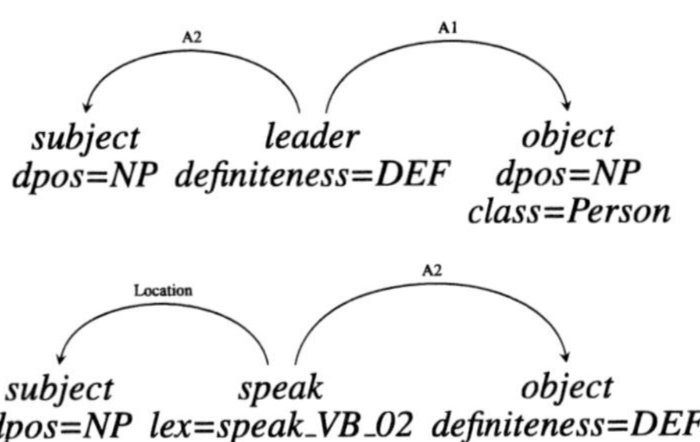

Figure 2: Sample PredArg templates corresponding to the *leader* (top) and *language* (bottom) properties.

applying a series of rule-based graph transducers. The generator handles Semantic Web inputs by means of introducing abstract predicate-argument (PredArg) templates and micro-planning grammars before the core linguistic generation module (Mille and Dasiopoulou, 2017).

3.1 Mapping properties to PredArg templates

Predicate-argument templates in a PropBank (Kingsbury and Palmer, 2002; Babko-Malaya, 2005) fashion were defined taking into account the property as well as the type of the subject and object values.[2] Thus, each of the properties found in the evaluation triples was associated to one of these templates. Parts of speech (e.g., NP –proper noun), grammatical features (e.g., verbal tense or nominal definiteness), or information from DBpedia (e.g., classes), for instance, can be specified in the template.[3] Figure 2 shows sample PredArg templates for the DBpedia properties *leader* and *language* respectively;[4] 318 templates were used for the 373 properties of WebNLG.

3.2 Population of the templates

Using the aforementioned mappings, each input triple is transformed into a respective PredArg structure. This involves two main steps. First, the cleaning of the object, including the extraction of value/unit information from datatype fillers and distinct values from list-like fillers. Second, if different from the template, the assignment of

pertinent subject/object class labels, which are geared to the subsequent linguistic generation steps and currently include 'Person', 'Location', 'Time' (further distinguishing between date, year, month), and 'Literal' (i.e. datatype values). During this step, cardinality and number information labels are also assigned. Last, in the case of multiple triple inputs, the triples are ordered (as a preliminary step for the subsequent aggregation) based on the number of appearances of their subjects and on whether a subject of a triple serves also as an object in another triple. For the population of the templates of Figure 2, the subject and object placeholders are simply replaced by the corresponding subjects and objects of Figure 1, without cleaning or further modification.

3.3 Aggregation of PredArg structures

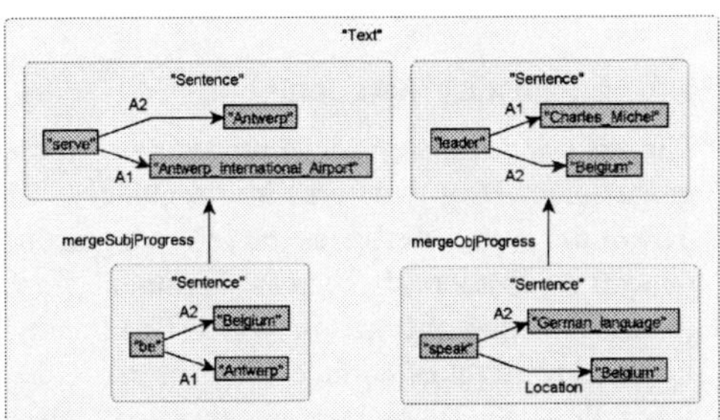

Figure 3: Aggregation of populated templates (step 2)

In order to group triples into complex sentences, a graph-transduction module that performs aggregation in two steps was developed. First, shared predicate–object argument pairs in the populated templates are targeted: if the object arguments have the same relation with their respective predicates, they will be coordinated (e.g., $Jazz_S$

---

[2]Inspection of subject and object types was needed as some properties denoted more than one meaning and corresponded to different templates.

[3]Unspecified values are assigned later in the process.

[4]Note that is possible to refer to a particular PropBank class in the PredArg graphs as, e.g., *speak_VB_02*, which corresponds to the second meaning of *speak* in ProbBank; if no class is indicated (e.g. *leader*), the first PropBank sense is assigned by default.

influenced$_P$ funk$_{O1}$ and afrobeat$_{O2}$,); if the relations are different, the objects become siblings under the first occurrence of the predicate (e.g. *[Alan Bean]$_S$ [was born]$_P$ [in Wheeler (Texas)]$_{O1}$ [on March 15]$_{O2}$.*); the duplicated nodes are removed. What is targeted in the second place is an argument of a predicate that appears further down in the ordered list of PredArg structures. If identified, the PredArg structures are merged by fusing the common argument; see e.g. Antwerp and Belgium in Figure 3, which are merged at the end of the process, c.f. Figure 4. During linguistic generation, this results in the introduction of post-nominal modifiers such as relative and participial clauses or appositions (see next section). In order to avoid the formation of heavy nominal groups, at most one aggregation is allowed per argument.

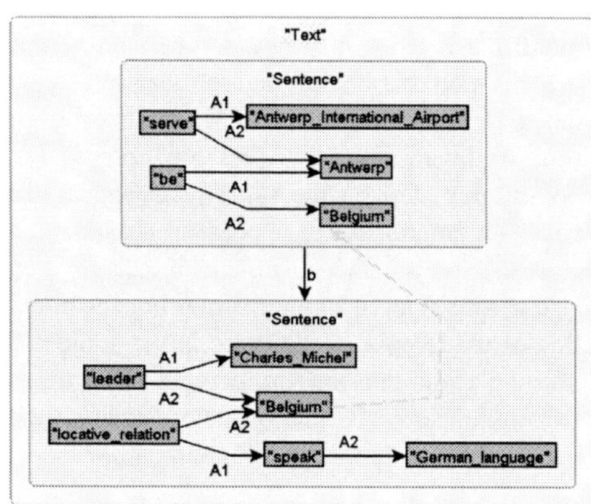

Figure 4: Aggregated PredArg structures

3.4 Linguistic generation

The next and last step is the rendering of the aggregated PredArg structures into sentences. This part of the system performs the following actions: (i) syntacticization of predicate-argument graphs; (ii) introduction of function words; (iii) linearization and retrieval of surface forms. First, a deep-syntactic (DSynt) structure is generated: missing parts of speech are assigned, the syntactic root of the sentence is chosen, and from there a syntactic tree over content words is built node by node; see Figure 5.[5] Then, as shown in Figure 6, functional words (prepositions, auxiliaries, determiners, etc.) are introduced and fine-grained surface-syntactic (SSynt) labels are established, using a subcate-

[5]Note that the node brought together during the previous step are not necessarily split up at this level.

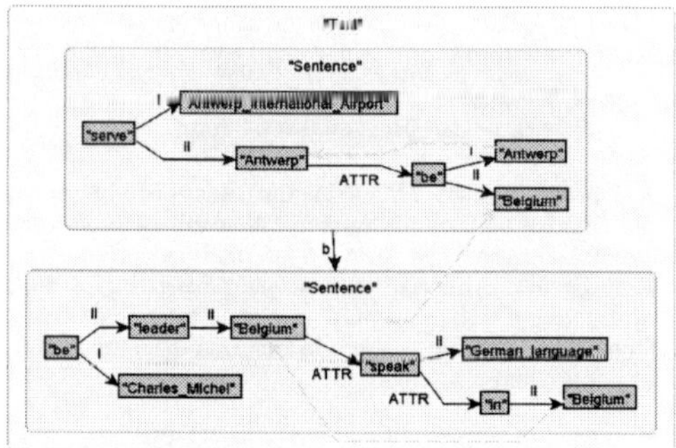

Figure 5: Deep-syntactic structures

gorisation lexicon. For this purpose, lexical resources derived from PropBank (Kingsbury and Palmer, 2002), NomBank (Meyers et al., 2004) or VerbNet (Schuler, 2005) are used; see (Mille and Wanner, 2015; Lareau et al., 2018). Personal and relative pronouns are introduced using the coreference relations (dotted arrows) and the *class* feature, which allows for distinguishing between human and non-human antecedents. Finally, morpho-syntactic agreements are resolved, the syntactic tree is linearized through the ordering of (i) governor/dependent and (ii) dependents with each other, and the surface forms are retrieved. Post-processing rules are then applied: upper casing, replacement of underscores by spaces, etc.

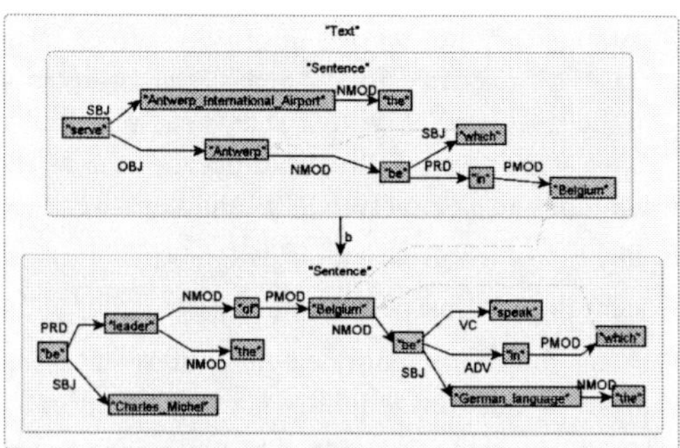

Figure 6: Surface-syntactic structures

Consider for instance the *leader* property of Figure 2 and selected phenomena: (i) the support verb *be* is established as the root (Fig. 5), (ii) the preposition *of* is introduced below *leader* (Fig. 6), and the *SBJ* relation is introduced between *be* and *Charles_Michel*, which (iii) causes the verb to be placed after the noun and get morphological agreement features from it (third person singular), while *NMOD* towards a preposition causes the opposite order and no agreement, etc.: *Charles_Michel$_{3sg}$ > is$_{3sg}$ > the > leader >of >Belgium*. The final sentence generated for the four triples is *The Antwerp International Airport serves Antwerp, which is in Belgium. Charles Michel is the leader of Belgium, in which the German language is spoken.*

4 Multilingual extension of FORGe

FORGe was developed primarily for English generation, and in order to port it to Spanish, four main aspects had to be addressed: (i) the PredArg templates, (ii) the grammatical resources, (iii) the lexical resources, and (iv) the translation of the Subject and Object values from the original DBpedia triples, in which English is used.

4.1 Adaptation of the PredArg templates

130 out of the 217 templates that cover all the WebNLG seen dataset were left unchanged, and 87 of them had to be adapted to Spanish (all templates stay in English). The adaptation of the templates consisted of two major modifications: on the one hand, some predicates were changed, such as the English predicate *parent_company*, which was modified to *daughter_company*, more idiomatic in Spanish (28 cases); and on the other hand, some predicate-argument relations have been updated in order to match the entries in the Spanish lexicon (50 cases).[6] The other modifications include: a change in the definiteness of a noun (7 cases, e.g. *chickens$_{INDEF}$* in *Chickens belong to the class "bird"* would be rendered as *el$_{DEF}$ pollo* in Spanish) or the tense or aspect of a verb (6 cases), or the addition of a new predicate (1 case)[7].

4.2 Adapting the rules to Spanish

The most important rules added for Spanish are (i) rules introducing the surface-syntactic relations, based on which linear order and morphological agreements are resolved, (ii) rules for gender and number agreements in noun groups and auxiliary constructions, and (iii) word ordering rules. Note that the rules for Spanish also apply to other Romance languages with similar features (e.g. French, Italian, etc.).

For designing the rules, we followed the approach of AnCora-UPF (Mille et al., 2013), a Spanish dataset in which each dependency relation is associated with a set of syntactic properties. For instance, a *subject* is characterized by being linearized to the left of its governing verb (by default), by being removable, by triggering the number and person agreements on the verb, etc. During the linguistic generation stage, 27 out of the 47 relations proposed in AnCora-UPF [8] are currently supported.

In order to generalize the ordering rules across languages, the dependencies were introduced in the lexicon with details about how they are linearized with respect to their governor (*vertical* ordering). Generic linearization rules also apply. For instance, for the *copul* dependency (such as between *be* and *retired*), pronominal dependents are linearized BEFORE the finite verb, and the other dependents AFTER it. If several dependents end up at the same height with respect to their governor, they need to be ordered with each other. 21 rules were added to manage these *horizontal* orderings. They facilitate the ordering of, for instance, determiners before the adjectives, or small adverbial groups before the objects. Finally, 18 rules for resolving the agreements between verb and subject, adjective/determiner and noun, copulatives and subjects, etc. were implemented. For instance, in the structure *Joana$_{3-FEM-SING}$ ←subj estar copul → jubilado*, will be linearized and inflected as follows: *Juana está jubilada* (lit. 'Joana is$_{3-SING}$ retired$_{FEM-SING}$').

4.3 Crafting the Spanish dictionaries

Several types of dictionaries are needed for generation: (i) a dictionary that maps the input meanings/concepts onto lexical units of a particular language (called *concepticon*), (ii) a dictionary that contains the combinatorial properties of each lexical unit (*lexicon*), (iii) a dictionary with the full forms of the words (called *morphologicon*). Some other information, such as linearization properties of dependencies (see Section 4.2) are also better stored in the lexicon in order to allow for more generic (hence less numerous) rules.

As explained in Section 3.1, the DBpedia properties are mapped to PredArg structures. For the

---

[6] The mismatch between the relations in English and Spanish is simply practical; it originates from a detail in the implementation of the mapping of the arguments in both languages, so a unification of the rule design would solve it.

[7] More than one change can happen in one template.

[8] adjunct, adv, agent, analyt_fut, analyt_pass, analyt_perf, analyt_progr, aux_phras, appos, attr, compar, coord, coord_conj, copul, det, dobj, iobj, modal, modif, obl_compl, obl_obj, prepos, punc, quant, relat, sub_conj, and subj.

WebNLG challenge, English was the only language to generate, so the labels of the nodes in the PredArg templates were in English. In order to take advantage of the templates developed for FORGe in 2017, we also use these structures with English vocabulary as input to the generator. Thus, we manually crafted the concepticon (255 entries), in which the keys are the predicates from the templates, and the values are lexical units in Spanish; for instance, the predicate *locate* is mapped to the Spanish verb *estar_VB_04* ("to be").

In the lexicon, lexical units such as *estar_VB_04* are described; this fourth entry for *estar* corresponds to a verb that has two arguments, the second being an adverb or a prepositional group. *estar_VB_01* is the simple copula, *estar_VB_02* is the existential *be*, which has only one argument, and *estar_VB_03* is the auxiliary. Each lexical unit contained in the concepticon is a key in the lexicon. The lexicon has been crafted manually for the experiments in this paper, but we are developing an automatic conversion of AnCora-Verb (Aparicio et al., 2008) to obtain a large scale resource. Finally, in order to store the surface forms of the inflected words, we crafted a very small morphological dictionary of about 450 entries to cover the needed forms in the experiments.

4.4 Obtaining Spanish property values

The DBpedia project uses the Resource Description Framework (RDF) as a data model for representing and publishing on the Web structured information that has been extracted from Wikipedia. Each DBpedia entity (*resource*) is directly tied to a Wikipedia article and denoted using a de-referenceable URI or IRI. Until DBpedia release 3.6, data were extracted from non-English Wikipedia pages only if an equivalent English page existed, in order to ensure that each entity is uniquely identified by a single de-referenceable URI of the form `http://dbpedia.org/resource/Name` (e.g., `http://dbpedia.org/page/Switzerland`), where *Name* is derived from the URL of the source (English) Wikipedia article. As of DBpedia release 3.7, localized datasets are provided that contain data from all Wikipedia pages in a specific language, using IRIs and language-specific namespaces of the form `http://xx.dbpedia.org/resource/Name`, where 'xx' is the Wikipedia language code and 'Name' is now derived from the respective language-specific

Wikipedia URL, e.g., `http://es.dbpedia.org/page/Suiza`; inter-language links from the different Wikipedia editions are also extracted and the `owl:sameAs` property is used to link the localized DBpedia IRI to its equivalent in English DBpedia edition URI.

Thus, whenever an inter-language link between a non-English Wikipedia page and its English equivalent exists, by querying the `owl:sameAs` property links of the English DBpedia entity and filtering them using the language code, respective language-specific names can be obtained. However, not every English Wikipedia page has an equivalent page in every non-English Wikipedia edition; moreover, even if an equivalent non-English page exists, the respective `owl:sameAs` link does not necessarily pertain to the English DBpedia entity at hand (as for example, in the case of the Spanish entity `http://es.dbpedia.org/page/Galleta` that can be accessed only when starting from the English resource `http://es.dbpedia.org/page/Biscuit`, but not from `http://es.dbpedia.org/page/Cookie`). Further complications may still arise, as sometimes the obtained language-specific name corresponds to the most rigorously rather than commonly used name, which, in the context of NLG, can affect the fluency of the resulting verbalization; for example, starting from the English entity *Chicken*, the Spanish value is *Gallus gallus domesticus*, instead of *Gallo*. Moreover, sometimes datatype values (i.e., raw data) rather than entities are used as object values (e.g., `Bakewell_pudding` ‖ *ingredientName* ‖ `‘‘Ground almond, jam, butter, eggs’’`).

4.5 Improving language-independent rules

FORGe received good evaluation marks at the WebNLG challenge, especially in the human assessments, according to which it was close to the quality of human-written text. However, after an error analysis of FORGe's outputs, we found a series of general problems impairing the quality of the generated texts in terms of contents and grammaticality. In particular: (i) some properties were not verbalized due to the failure to produce relative clauses in some specific cases; (ii) the aggregations were at times excessive, erroneously merging verbs with different tenses (e.g. *X created Y, which was created by Z*, instead of *X and Z created Y*), failing to merge (e.g. *X is the headquarters of Y. Z is the headquarters of Y*), or leading to an ungrammatical outcome, with for instance the presence of several *also*; (iii) the construction of some relative clauses were faulty, as e.g. *X can a variation of which be Y*, instead of *X, which can be a variation of Y*; (iv) the referring expression module was applying excessively, resulting in ambiguous pronouns, and sometimes incorrectly pronominalizing non-human entities with *he*; (v) some agreements were not solved (e.g. *the main ingredient are*); (vi) some determiners were erroneously introduced, and some others not in the correct form (*a* instead of *an*). And for English in particular, (vii) some templates were mixed up (e.g. runway name with runway number), and some were incorrect, with present instead of past tense.

Many occurrences of these issues were fixed in the grammars, by modifying and adding rules, and some new features were added, as for instance, new aggregation and pronominalization types in order to improve the fluency of the outputs, and new rules to cover more cases of embedded clauses generation. For developing the grammars, we used the 6 and 7 triple inputs from the WebNLG training data, and the whole development set. A qualitative evaluation of the new outputs is provided in Section 6.

As a result, the extended version of the DBpedia generator comprises 971 active rules. 73% of the rules (702) are language-independent, 19% are for English, and 8% for Spanish.[9] For instance, all (82/82) of the aggregation rules and most (365/395) of the sentence structuring rules, which map PredArg graph onto Deep-Syntactic graphs, apply for both languages. When getting closer to the surface, the rules are less language-independent, representing about half of the DSynt-SSynt rules (108/239) and of the linearization and agreement resolution rules (66/129).

5 Evaluation

In this section, we detail how we built a new dataset for evaluating the outputs, and describe the results of the automatic evaluations.

5.1 Selection of triples for evaluation

For evaluation purposes, we compiled a benchmark dataset of 200 inputs, i.e., sets of DBpedia triples, with sizes ranging from 1 to 7 triples, using as reference pool the WebNLG challenge test set. The reason for using as reference basis the WebNLG challenge dataset is that it is the most recent and comprehensive dataset with respect to text generation from RDF data that has been specifically designed to promote data and text variety (Perez-Beltrachini et al., 2016). Moreover, it allows the direct comparison with the generators that participated in the challenge. In order to ensure future comparisons with machine learning-based systems in terms of their best obtained performance, only the seen categories subset of the original test set has been considered, i.e., only inputs with entities that belonged to DBpedia categories that were contained in the training data.

The compilation methodology for our benchmark dataset implements a twofold goal. On one hand, we want to ensure that all properties appearing in the seen categories subset are included. On the other hand, and unlike the WebNLG human evaluation test set, we aim towards a more balanced number of inputs of different sizes. In practice, since the inputs of size 6 and 7 in the original seen categories subset of the WebNLG test set are 24 and 21 respectively, we chose to include them all in the benchmark; 31 inputs for each of the remaining input sizes were subsequently added.

5.2 Reference sentences

The English reference texts are taken from the WebNLG dataset, for which there could be more than one reference per triple set. For Spanish, one single reference text was produced for each triple set, with natural and grammatical constructions containing all and only the entities and relations in the triples. The reference texts were written by one of the authors, a native Spanish speaker, having at hand the English references from the WebNLG challenge to serve as a potential model.

5.3 Automatic evaluation

The predicted outputs in English and Spanish were compared to the reference sentences in the corresponding language; three metrics were used: BLEU (Papineni et al., 2002), which matches exact words, METEOR (Banerjee and Lavie, 2005), which matches also synonyms, and TER (Snover et al., 2006), which reflects the amount of edits needed to transform the predicted output into the reference output. Table 1 shows the results of the automatic evaluation on the English and Spanish

---

[9]Note that we exclude from the count all rules than simply transfer individual attributes at each level, which amount to about 250. There are more English-specific rules simply because the coverage of the English generator is higher.

extensions proposed in this paper using for each input its corresponding reference text(s). The first two rows show that in terms of automatic metrics, the extended FORGe and the 2017 FORGe have almost exactly the same scores on the English data (which are also very close to the WebNLG scores: 40.88, 0.40, 0.55). In other words, the quality improvements in English are not reflected by these metrics. To compare English and Spanish results, we calculated the scores using one sentence as reference (only one reference per text is available in Spanish). The English scores drop (third row) due to the way the scores are calculated by the individual metrics.[10] In the last row of the table, the scores of the Spanish generator look contradictory: the BLEU is 10 points below the English BLEU with the same number of reference (1), but METEOR is 8 points above, that is, the predicted outputs do not match the exact word forms, but they do match similar words. One reason for the low BLEU score could be the higher morphological variation in Spanish. However, the METEOR score is surprisingly high, actually even higher than the highest METEOR score at WebNLG, obtained by ADAPT and calculated with multiple references (0.44).

Reference set	BLEU	METEOR	TER
EN (All$_{FORGe-2017}$)	39.87	0.40	0.58
EN (All$_{FORGe-Ext}$)	39.33	0.40	0.58
EN (1$_{FORGe-Ext}$)	29.18	0.38	0.65
ES (1$_{FORGe-Ext}$)	18.68	0.46	0.77

Table 1: English and Spanish scores according to BLEU, METEOR and TER, with 1 and All references on the 200-triples test set.

6 Qualitative analysis of the results

In the 200 outputs of the 2017 generator, 275 errors were detected, compared to 166 in the current one in English (170 in Spanish), and 26.5% of the texts were error-free, as opposed to 43.5% now (45.5% in Spanish). In this section, we report on the examination of both English and Spanish outputs, in order to identify the main issues of the grammars in both languages.[11]

6.1 English

The qualitative analysis of the generated English texts showed that the resulting texts are of a higher

---

[10]BLEU matches n-grams in all candidate references, and METEOR and TER consider the best scoring reference.

[11]Outputs are available as supplementary material below.

grammaticality and fluency than the 2017 ones. Below, we discuss the observed remaining errors and their respective causes.

Determiners: Definite determiners are missed with the property `language`, when referring to the language of a written work. The reason of this error lies in the discrepancy between the respective PredArg template that was defined based on the premise that the object value of this property is a language name (i.e., English, Italian), hence not admitting a determiner, and the form of the DBpedia language entities that in practice concatenate the language name with the word *language* (cf., *English_language*); this type of error is the most frequent, being found about 65 times in the test set and representing about 40% of the total amount of errors (166). This underlies the need for further normalization of the DBpedia property values, so that during the PredArg templates instantiation, consistent linguistic features will be ensured for argument values of the same type.

Tense: Errors are observed with respect to the verb tense selection (6% of the errors). More specifically, in some cases the present tense is used instead of the past, as, e.g., in *Alan Shepard, who graduated from NWC in 1957 with a M.A., is deceased. [...] He is a test pilot.* This is a direct consequence of the fact that in the current implementation, tense selection does not take into account the temporal context as defined by the rest of the input triples.

Aggregations: Another type of error relates to the generation of unintuitive, yet still grammatical, constructs when aggregating the contents of more than one triple when certain properties are involved (11% of the errors). More specifically, when the property `occupation` is selected to be expressed as a relative clause, it fails to append the occupation information to the referring entity as shown in *Alan Bean, born in wheeler (Texas) on March 15, 1932, is from the United States (test pilot)*; a similar behaviour has been observed with the property `category`. This is a result of the current implementation of aggregation that takes place in a single step and tries to avoid orphan clauses by attaching them to the closest reference head; introducing iterative aggregation steps and incorporating semantic coherence information would mitigate such effects.

A related issue is, for instance, the way location information is verbalized in the presence of multiple subdivision references (15% of the errors), as, for example, in *the Acharya Institute of Technology is in Bangalore, Karnataka and India*, where the three involved location-denoting properties, namely `city`, `state` and `country` have been aggregated in a semantics-agnostic manner. Navigating DBpedia and obtaining information about their interrelations would enable more fluent verbalizations. Fluency and meaning accuracy are also impacted when the input triples capture in practice n-ary relations. This is the case with the `leader` and `leaderTitle` properties, which in the absence of any semantic preprocessing before the instantiation of the PredArg templates, result in verbalizations such as *the leaders of Romania are the prime minister of Romania and Klaus Iohannis*, which does not communicate the fact that Klaus Iohannis is the prime minister.

Subject/Object values: Last, a number of disfluent verbalizations is the direct result of idiosyncrasies in the involved DBpedia properties and/or the respective subject and object values (4% of the errors). There are properties that although meant to capture different types of information are not used consistently, thus impacting the resulting verbalizations; the properties `mainIngredient(s)` and `ingredient(s)` are such an example, e.g. in an input about the dish *Ayam Penyet*, which is described as having as main ingredient the fried chicken and as a further ingredient chicken. Some minor errors such as unnatural word ordering (11%) or lexicalizations (8%) were also detected.

6.2 Spanish

The aforementioned errors listed for English are mostly independent of the language and thus also apply to Spanish, except from the first aggregation error, which does not appear due to a difference in the templates. The determiner error represents 30% of the total number of detected errors (51/170), the location aggregation 12%, the values and word choices 7%, the ordering 6%, the verbal tense 5%. However, despite its overall good quality, Spanish has some additional specific issues.

English words: There are some not-translated nouns (*52 minutes*) or phrases (*está dedicado a Ottoman army soldiers killed in the battle of Baku*), which in addition of not being understandable, may produce subsequent morphological errors (21% of the errors).

Morphology: Morphological errors, mainly gen-

der (invisible in English) and number disagreements, are found in the Spanish texts (5% of the errors). For example, in *Dianne Feinstein es un senador de california*, (lit. 'Dianne Feinstein is a$_{MASC}$ senator$_{MASC}$ of California'), both *a* and *senator* should be feminine, but there is no information that D. Feinstein is a woman in the input.

Complex relative clauses: The main syntactic error is related to the genitive relatives with *cuyo* ('of which'), in particular when the antecedent is a location (5% of the errors). For example, in the sentence *Alba Iulia , en el cual está el 1 Decembrie 1918 University*, lit. 'Alba Iulia, in the which is the 1 Decembrie 1918 University', the proper pronoun should be *donde* 'where' instead of *en el cual*. Even when gramatically correct, sentences with these relative clauses tend to lack naturalness.

Other series of errors that produce sub-optimal Spanish constructions include: occasional choice of a relative clause instead of a past participle modifier, and various other constructions that lack naturalness (10% of the errors).

7 Conclusions and future work

This paper reports on the extension of the FORGe system for verbalizing DBpedia triples, which results in a better quality of English texts, and the adaption of FORGe to Spanish. The qualitative evaluation of both English and Spanish texts showed that overall, the grammaticality and fluency of the resulting verbalizations was high, but could be further improved, in particular by getting more information about the subject and object entities. The next step is to run a large-scale human assessment of the outputs in terms of quality of language and contents. Furthermore, the DBpedia cross-language overlap is not sufficiently high to obtain property values in languages other English by using only inter-language links; in our evaluation, it approximated 55%, but this percentage can vary, depending on how well-known the referred entities are, thus requiring complementary investigations. Another objective is to port FORGe to other languages.

Acknowledgements.

This work has been partly supported by the European Commission (H2020 Programme) under the contract numbers 700475-IA, 700024-RIA, 779962-RIA, 786731-RIA and 825079-ICT-STARTS. We thank Anastasia Shimorina and the reviewers for their valuable help and feedback.

References

Ion Androutsopoulos, Gerasimos Lampouras, and Dimitrios Galanis. 2013. Generating natural language descriptions from owl ontologies: the naturalowl system. *Journal of Artificial Intelligence Research*, 48:671–715.

Juan Aparicio, Mariona Taulé, and M Antònia Martí. 2008. Ancora-verb: Two large-scale lexicons for catalan and spanish. In *Proceedings of the XIII Euralex International Congress*. Institut Universitari de Lingüística Aplicada, UPF.

Olga Babko-Malaya. 2005. *Propbank Annotation Guidelines*.

Satanjeev Banerjee and Alon Lavie. 2005. Meteor: An automatic metric for mt evaluation with improved correlation with human judgments. In *Proceedings of the acl workshop on intrinsic and extrinsic evaluation measures for machine translation and/or summarization*, pages 65–72.

Anja Belz, Mike White, Dominic Espinosa, Eric Kow, Deirdre Hogan, and Amanda Stent. 2011. The first Surface Realisation Shared Task: Overview and evaluation results. In *Proceedings of the Generation Challenges Session at the 13th European Workshop on Natural Language Generation (ENLG)*, pages 217–226, Nancy, France.

Bernd Bohnet and Leo Wanner. 2010. Open soucre graph transducer interpreter and grammar development environment. In *Proceedings of the 7th International Conference on Language Resources and Evaluation (LREC)*, Valletta, Malta.

M. Bollmann. 2011. Adapting SimpleNLG to German. In *Proceedings of the 13th European Workshop on Natural Language Generation (ENLG 2011)*, pages 133–138.

Nadjet Bouayad-Agha, Gerard Casamayor, and Leo Wanner. 2014. Natural language generation in the context of the semantic web. *Semantic Web*, 5(6):493–513.

R. De Oliveira and S. Sripada. 2014. Adapting SimpleNLG for Brazilian Portuguese realisation. In *Proceedings of the 8th International Natural Language Generation Conference*, pages 93–94.

Henry Elder, Sebastian Gehrmann, Alexander OConnor, and Qun Liu. 2018. E2e nlg challenge submission: Towards controllable generation of diverse natural language. In *Proceedings of the 11th International Conference on Natural Language Generation*, pages 457–462.

Claire Gardent and Aldo Gangemi. 2016. Proceedings of the 2nd international workshop on natural language generation and the semantic web (webnlg 2016). In *Proceedings of the 2nd International Workshop on Natural Language Generation and the Semantic Web (WebNLG 2016)*.

Claire Gardent, Anastasia Shimorina, Shashi Narayan, and Laura Perez-Beltrachini. 2017a. Creating training corpora for micro-planners. In *Proceedings of the 55th Annual Meeting of the Association for Computational Linguistics (Volume 1: Long Papers)*, Vancouver, Canada. Association for Computational Linguistics.

Claire Gardent, Anastasia Shimorina, Shashi Narayan, and Laura Perez-Beltrachini. 2017b. The WebNLG challenge: Generating text from RDF data. In *Proceedings of the 10th International Conference on Natural Language Generation*, pages 124–133.

A. Gatt and E. Reiter. 2009. SimpleNLG: A realisation engine for practical applications. In *Proceedings of the 12th European Workshop on Natural Language Generation*, pages 90–93.

Albert Gatt and Emiel Krahmer. 2018. Survey of the state of the art in natural language generation: Core tasks, applications and evaluation. *Journal of Artificial Intelligence Research*, 61:65–170.

R. de Jong and M. Theune. 2018. Going Dutch: Creating SimpleNLG-NL. In *Proceedings of the 11th International Natural Language Generation Conference*, pages 73–78.

Paul Kingsbury and Martha Palmer. 2002. From TreeBank to PropBank. In *Proceedings of the 3rd International Conference on Language Resources and Evaluation (LREC)*, pages 1989–1993, Las Palmas, Canary Islands, Spain.

François Lareau, Florie Lambrey, Ieva Dubinskaite, Daniel Galarreta-Piquette, and Maryam Nejat. 2018. Gendr: A generic deep realizer with complex lexicalization. In *Proceedings of the 11th International Conference on Language Resources and Evaluation (LREC)*, pages 3018–3025, Miyazaki, Japan.

Jens Lehmann, Robert Isele, Max Jakob, Anja Jentzsch, Dimitris Kontokostas, Pablo N Mendes, Sebastian Hellmann, Mohamed Morsey, Patrick Van Kleef, Sören Auer, et al. 2015. Dbpedia–a large-scale, multilingual knowledge base extracted from wikipedia. *Semantic Web*, 6(2):167–195.

A. Mazzei, C. Battaglino, and C. Bosco. 2016. SimpleNLG-IT: Adapting SimpleNLG to Italian. In *Proceedings of the 9th International Natural Language Generation Conference*, pages 184–192.

Igor Mel'čuk. 1988. *Dependency Syntax: Theory and Practice*. State University of New York Press, Albany.

Adam Meyers, Ruth Reeves, Catherine Macleod, Rachel Szekely, Veronika Zielinska, Brian Young, and Ralph Grishman. 2004. The NomBank Project: An interim report. In *Proceedings of the Workshop on Frontiers in Corpus Annotation, Human Language Technology Conference of the North American Chapter of the Association for Computational Linguistics (HLT/NAACL)*, pages 24–31, Boston, MA, USA.

Simon Mille, Alicia Burga, and Leo Wanner. 2013. AnCora-UPF: A multi-level annotation of Spanish. In *Proceedings of the 2nd International Conference on Dependency Linguistics (DepLing)*, pages 217–226, Prague, Czech Republic.

Simon Mille and Stamatia Dasiopoulou. 2017. *FORGe at WebNLG 2017*. Technical report, Dept. of Engineering and Information and Communication Technologies, Universitat Pompeu Fabra, Barcelona, Spain.

Simon Mille and Leo Wanner. 2015. Towards large-coverage detailed lexical resources for data-to-text generation. In *Proceedings of the First International Workshop on Data-to-text Generation*, Edinburgh, Scotland.

Neha Nayak, Dilek Hakkani-Tür, Marilyn A Walker, and Larry P Heck. 2017. To plan or not to plan? discourse planning in slot-value informed sequence to sequence models for language generation. In *Proceedings of INTERSPEECH*, pages 3339–3343, Stockholm, Sweden.

Kishore Papineni, Salim Roukos, Todd Ward, and Wei-Jing Zhu. 2002. Bleu: a method for automatic evaluation of machine translation. In *Proceedings of the 40th annual meeting on association for computational linguistics*, pages 311–318. Association for Computational Linguistics.

Laura Perez-Beltrachini, Rania Sayed, and Claire Gardent. 2016. Building rdf content for data-to-text generation. In *Proceedings of the 26th International Conference on Computational Linguistics (COLING)*.

Karin Kipper Schuler. 2005. *VerbNet: A broad-coverage, comprehensive verb lexicon*. Ph.D. thesis, University of Pennsylvania.

Matthew Snover, Bonnie Dorr, Richard Schwartz, Linnea Micciulla, and John Makhoul. 2006. A study of translation edit rate with targeted human annotation. In *Proceedings of association for machine translation in the Americas*, volume 200.

Alejandro Ramos Soto, Julio Janeiro Gallardo, and Alberto Bugarín Diz. 2017. Adapting simplenlg to spanish. In *Proceedings of the 10th International Natural Language Generation Conference (INLG)*, pages 144–148.

Leo Wanner, Bernd Bohnet, Nadjet Bouayad-Agha, Francois Lareau, and Daniel Nicklaß. 2010. MARQUIS: Generation of user-tailored multilingual air quality bulletins. *Applied Artificial Intelligence*, 24(10):914–952.

A   Supplementary Material

Sample sentences with no detected problems.
ES: Antioch (California), cuya población total es 102372, tiene una diferencia horaria UTC de -7. Su código de área es 925. La superficie total de Antioch (California) es 753 kilómetros cuadrados.
EN$_{Ext}$: Antioch, California, the total population of which is 102372, has a UTC offset of -7. Its area code is 925. The total area of Antioch, California is 753 square kilometers.
EN$_{2017}$: Antioch, California, the total population of which is 102372, has a UTC offset of -7. The area code of Antioch, California is 925. The total area of Antioch, California is 753 square kilometers.

Sample sentences with a missing translation and unnatural word ordering (ES).
ES: 1634: The Ram Rebellion se publica en Estados Unidos. Barack Obama es el líder de Estados Unidos, en el cual viven americans. La capital de Estados Unidos, un grupo étnico del cual es afroamericanos, es Washington D.C..
EN$_{Ext}$: 1634: The Ram Rebellion is published in the United States. Barack Obama is the leader of the United States, in which Americans live. the capital of the United States is Washington (D.C.). An ethnic group of the United States are African Americans.
EN$_{2017}$: 1634: The Ram Rebellion is published in the United States. Barack Obama is the leader of the United States, Americans live in which. The capital of the United States is Washington (D.C.). An ethnic group of the United States are African Americans.

Sample sentences with a missing translation (ES) and determiner error (EN, ES).
ES: Asilomar Conference Grounds, que fue incorporado al National Register of Historic Places el 27 de febrero de 1987, está en Pacific Grove. Su número de referencia en registro nacional de sitios históricos es 87000823. Asilomar conference grounds se construyó en 1913.
EN$_{Ext}$: Asilomar Conference Grounds, which was added to the National Register of Historic Places on February 27 (1987), is in Pacific Grove (California). The reference number in the National Register of Historic places of Asilomar Conference Grounds, built in 1913, is 87000823.
EN$_{2017}$: Asilomar Conference Grounds, the reference number in the National Register of Historic Places of which is 87000823, is in Pacific Grove (California) in added to the National Register of Historic Places on February 27 (1987). It was built in 1913.

Generating Justifications for Norm-related Agent Decisions

Daniel Kasenberg*, Antonio Roque, Ravenna Thielstrom,
Meia Chita-Tegmark, and Matthias Scheutz
Human-Robot Interaction Laboratory
Tufts University
*dmk@cs.tufts.edu

Abstract

We present an approach to generating natural language justifications of decisions derived from norm-based reasoning. Assuming an agent which maximally satisfies a set of rules specified in an object-oriented temporal logic, the user can ask factual questions (about the agent's rules, actions, and the extent to which the agent violated the rules) as well as "why" questions that require the agent comparing actual behavior to counterfactual trajectories with respect to these rules. To produce natural-sounding explanations, we focus on the subproblem of producing natural language clauses from statements in a fragment of temporal logic, and then describe how to embed these clauses into explanatory sentences. We use a human judgment evaluation on a testbed task to compare our approach to variants in terms of intelligibility, mental model and perceived trust.

1 Introduction

Recent research has enabled artificial agents (such as robots) to work closely with humans, sometimes as team-mates, sometimes as independent decision-makers. For these agents to be trusted by the humans they interact with, they must be able to follow human **norms**: expected standards of behavior and social interaction. Crucially, agents must be able to *explain* the norms they are following and how those norms have guided their decisions. Because these explanations may occur in task settings, agents need to be able to make these explanations in natural language dialogue that humans will easily understand.

The field of *explainable planning* (Fox et al., 2017) emphasizes, as we do, rendering the behaviors of a particular agent explainable to human interactants. Our approach embodies a form of Questions 1 to 3 as described by Fox et al, applying "why did you do that" (Question 1) to general queries representable in temporal logic, and

applying "why is what you propose [superior] to something else" (Question 3) by appealing to the agent's rules. Our approach operationalizes Langley (2019)'s definition of *justified agency* for an intelligent system as "follow[ing] society's norms and explain[ing] its activities in those terms" by providing natural language explanations which appeal to temporal logic rules which may represent moral or social norms. Further relevant recent papers in explainable planning include Vasileiou et al. (2019), who formulate a logic-based approach; Krarup et al. (2019), who like us employ contrastive explanations; and Kim et al. (2019), who construct temporal logic specifications which demonstrate the differences between plans. While the latter work has in common with ours a focus on explainable planning and temporal logic, we are interested in justifying the agent's choice of plan, whereas they seek to succinctly describe the difference between two plans. None of the above approaches are concerned with providing natural language explanations.

Natural language explanations *are* provided by Chiyah Garcia et al. (2018), who develop an approach to providing system explainability by having a human expert "speak aloud" while watching system videos, and turning that explanation into tree form. Our approach is similar in that we provide explanations of agent behavior in natural language, but in our case the content is provided not by human experts but by the agent's reasoning.

In that respect, our approach is similar to the tradition of generating natural language explanations of mathematical proofs. Horacek (2007) describes the differences between proof explanations as required by humans, as opposed to proof explanations as produced by Automated Theorem Provers. Fiedler (2001b) provides a survey (pgs 10-12) of early research in developing explanations that allow the output of Automated Theorem Provers to be intelligible to humans, and describes

Proceedings of The 12th International Conference on Natural Language Generation, pages 484–493,
Tokyo, Japan, 28 Oct - 1 Nov, 2019. ©2019 Association for Computational Linguistics

a system that includes a user model to guide the production of explanations of more or less abstraction. This work is summarized by Fiedler (2001a). Recent work focusing on the more general problem of generating text from formal or logical structures includes Manome et al. (2018)'s generation of sentences from logical formulas using a sequence-to-sequence approach, and Pourdamghani et al. (2016)'s generation of sentences from Abstract Meaning Representations by linearizing and using Phrase Based Machine Translation approaches. Where our approach differs is that rather than aiming to justify logical conclusions via proofs or specify natural language translations of arbitrary logical forms, our approach justifies the decisions of autonomous agents (governed by principles *specified* in logic) in a way that is understandable to human users. More similar in this vein is the work of (Kutlak and van Deemter, 2015), who provide natural language descriptions of the pre- and post-conditions of planner actions.

Our approach provides two main contributions. First, we construct explanations for the behavior of an agent governed by temporal logic rules acting in a deterministic relational Markov decision process (RMDP) , including questions about the agent's rules and actions and "why" queries requiring a contrastive explanation (Elzein, 2019) appealing to the temporal logic rules (*content generation*; section 3). Second, we convert these explanation structures into natural language, constructing natural language clauses from statements belonging to a fragment of our temporal logic, and embedding these into general response templates (*surface representation generation*; section 4). We evaluate the outputs of our approach in a testbed domain against baselines, and find that our approach shows increased performance in terms of the agent's intelligibility, the user's mental model of the agent, and trust in the agent's ability to obey norms in a principled way (section 5). We conclude with a summary and discussion of our contributions (section 6).

2 Generating agent behavior

2.1 Test scenario

To illustrate the workings of our approach, we will allude to a test scenario chosen to be simple while highlighting some of the virtues of our approach. Our approach may be applied to other domains as well; we describe the assumptions our approach makes about the agent's environment and norms in section 4.1.1.

The scenario is as follows: a robot has just gone shopping on behalf of a human user to a store that sells a pair of glasses and a watch. The human user wants the glasses and the watch, and the robot has a rule for buying everything that the human wants. However, the robot can only afford one of these items. The robot is able to pick up items and walking out of the store without paying for them, but it also has a rule against doing so (i.e. against stealing), and this rule is the stronger of the two.

After acting in this environment, the robot is asked about its rules, its actions, and why it made the decisions it did. The types of utterances that are needed at this point are shown in Dialogues 1-5.

2.2 Agent environment

We consider agents operating in RMDPs, where an RMDP assumes that each state of the world $s \in S$ can be decomposed into the states $s_{o_1}, \cdots, s_{o_k}$ of a set of objects $o_1, o_2, \cdots, o_k$, where each o_i belongs to one of a finite set of object classes $C_1, \cdots, C_\ell$, as well as a "residual state" not corresponding to any objects, $s_{\backslash o}$. Agents may perform actions in the world, where each action may be parameterized by zero or more of these objects. Actions performed in the environment change the state according to a transition function, which we here assume to be deterministic. We will further assume a set of *atomic predicates* Π which take in zero or more objects as arguments, and which can be true or false in a particular state.

In our example domain, the state consists of the states of the objects $glasses$ and $watch$, both members of the object class $ForSaleItem$, as well as separate environment variables such as whether the agent is in the store. At each time step the agent can perform the actions $pickup(o)$, $putdown(o)$, or $buy(o)$ where $o \in glasses, watch$, or can perform the non-object action $leave$. (The agent may only put down or buy an object which it has picked up.) Predicates include whether object o has been previously bought ($bought(o)$), whether the agent is currently holding o ($holding(o)$), and whether o is currently on the shelf ($onShelf(o)$) as well as whether the agent has left the store ($leftStore$). Each of the agent actions also corresponds to a predicate which indicates whether that action is performed in the corresponding time step.

2.3 Violation enumeration language (VEL)

We generate justifications for an agent acting with respect to a set of rules expressible in temporal logic. In particular we represent the rules that the agent is to follow in an object-oriented temporal logic fragment which we refer to as *violation enumeration language* (VEL). VEL is based on linear temporal logic (LTL), and thus incorporates temporal operators roughly encoding the concepts of "always" ($\mathbf{G}$), "eventually" ($\mathbf{F}$), "in the next time step" ($\mathbf{X}$), and "until" ($\mathbf{U}$) as well as the standard operators in propositional logic ($\neg, \vee, \wedge, \rightarrow$).

The main difference between VEL and LTL is that in VEL atomic propositions have been replaced by atomic predicates of the sort found in the RMDP environment. The arguments to these predicates may be particular objects in the agent's environment, or may be object variables. Each object variable is existentially ($\exists$) or universally ($\forall$) quantified, or declared "costly" . Costly variables are those for which the cost of violating the rule depends on the number of bindings that violate the rule; where a formula has multiple costly variables, the cost depends on the number of violating tuples of bound variables. The costly variables of a VEL formula are listed, enclosed in angle brackets ($\langle, \rangle$) to the left of the formula.

In our example domain, we assume that the agent must attempt to satisfy two VEL rules:

$$\langle o \rangle.\mathbf{G}\neg(leave \wedge holding(o) \wedge \neg bought(o)) \qquad (1)$$
$$\langle o \rangle.\mathbf{F}(leave \wedge holding(o)) \qquad (2)$$

These VEL rules correspond to the injunction never leave the store while holding an object that has not been bought (shoplifting; the agent is penalized for each such object) and to leave while holding as many objects as possible.

2.4 Calculating and minimizing violation cost

The agent acts in its environment so as to maximally satisfy its VEL objectives, by minimizing a *violation cost*. We define the violation cost of an agent trajectory with respect to a VEL formula as the number of bindings of the costly variables such that the formula fails to hold for those bindings. To compute an aggregate violation cost for a set of rules, each rule is assigned a *weight* $w \in \mathbb{R}_{\geq 0}$ and a priority $z \in \mathbb{N}_{\geq 0}$. VEL rules with the same priority may be traded off (the agent minimizes

HUMAN: What rules do you follow?
ROBOT: **I must not leave the store while holding anything which I have not bought, and I must leave the store while holding everything.**
HUMAN: What did you do?
ROBOT: **I picked up the glasses, bought the glasses and left the store.**
HUMAN: What rules did you break?
ROBOT: **I did not leave the store while holding the watch.**

Dialogue 1: Questions about rules, actions, and violations.

HUMAN: Why didn't you buy anything?
ROBOT: **I bought the glasses.**

Dialogue 2: "Why" query with false premise.

the weighted sum of the violation costs for these rules), while rules with different priorities cannot (no amount of satisfying rules of lesser priority may justify violating a rule of a greater priority).

Given a set of VEL rules and their corresponding weight/priority values and an environment (where we assume the agent knows the environmental dynamics), the agent can compute an optimal policy that minimizes the violation cost with respect to those rules (e.g., using value iteration). For the purposes of the paper, we assume that the agent generating justifications has done precisely this process and has executed this optimal policy.

In our example domain, we assume that rule 1 has a priority of 1 and that rule 2 has a priority of 0, so that they are incomparable (and thus the weights of each are irrelevant). In order to maximally satisfy these rules, the agent picks up the glasses, buys the glasses, and leaves the store.

3   Content Generation

This section describes how content of explanations is generated; section 4 describes how utterances are constructed from this content.[1]

We have developed an algorithm which produces raw (non-NL) explanations from queries which contain VEL statements. We do not dis-

---

[1] Because our contribution relates to natural language *generation*, we assume the existence of a parser that processes input sentences such as the Human utterances in Dialogues 1-5. Such a parser is not one of this paper's contributions.

cuss this process in detail in this work; it is described in a separate forthcoming paper. In this work, we leverage this algorithm to support the following types of queries from the user and their corresponding responses:

1. The user may ask the agent for the contents of its *rules*. The response will be a list of the VEL rules that the agent attempts to follow.
2. The user may ask the agent for the sequence of actions it actually performed. The response will be a list of such actions.
3. The user may ask the agent which VEL rules it violated in the observed trajectory. The result is a list of such rules, which list will be non-empty only if the rules are not all mutually satisfiable. (This and the previous two query types are depicted in Dialogue 1).
4. The user may ask the agent "why ϕ", where ϕ is a VEL statement (where the statement may involve quantification, but not costly variables): why did the agent act in such a way as to make ϕ true? The response to this question can take one of three forms:
   - The agent could determine that ϕ is not entailed by the agent's trajectory (the premise of the question is false). Here the algorithm simply returns $\neg\phi$ (with existentially quantified variables bound to a particular counterexample where appropriate). Dialogue 2 shows a question-response pair of this type.
   - The agent may determine that ϕ holds over the agent's trajectory *and over all other trajectories* (ϕ cannot be false in the given RMDP). Here the generated response takes the form "$\neg\phi$ is impossible". Dialogue 3 shows a question-response pair of this type.
   - If there *is* an alternate (counterfactual) trajectory over which ϕ is not satisfied, our system constructs such a trajectory, and then considers the relative preference of those trajectories with respect to the VEL rules.
   If the trajectories are equally preferable, then we state that equivalence, such as in the dialogue in Dialogue 4. If the real trajectory is preferable to the counterfactual, then we produce a statement to that effect, as in Dialogue 5 (due to our assumption that the agent behaves optimally with respect to its rules, the agent does not consider the case that the counterfactual trajectory is preferable).
   As Dialogues 4 and 5 indicate, in either case

HUMAN: Why didn't you buy everything?
ROBOT: **It was impossible for me to buy everything.**

Dialogue 3: "Why" query with impossibility.

HUMAN: Why did you buy the glasses?
ROBOT: **I could have avoided buying the glasses and that would not have broken more important rules.**
HUMAN: How would you have done that?
ROBOT: **I would have picked up the watch, bought the watch, and left the store.**
HUMAN: What rules would you have broken?
ROBOT: **I would not have left the store while holding the glasses.**

Dialogue 4: "Why" query for equally preferable counterfactual.

the user may ask follow-up questions asking about the specific content of the counterfactual trajectory, including the agent's action sequence and the rules it would have violated. If the real trajectory is preferable, the user may also ask the agent to elaborate about why the counterfactual would have been worse, to which the answer is a minimal list of (bound) rules violated by the counterfactual trajectory with violation cost exceeding that of the actual trajectory.

4   Surface Representation Generation

The primary challenge to constructing utterances based on the output of our explanation generator is the need to construct natural-sounding expressions of VEL statements. Once this problem is solved, we may use SimpleNLG (Gatt and Reiter, 2009) to plug the resulting clauses into template sentences corresponding to each of the outputs we are interested in producing.

4.1   Translating VEL to natural language

We here discuss how to construct clauses corresponding to individual VEL formulae, a critical subtask of generating natural language justifications for the behavior of agents with VEL rules. Due to the difficulty of the task, rather than attempt to handle every possible VEL formula, we will work with a small fragment which nevertheless can express a large number of the plausible agent rules/queries. (We are confident that many

HUMAN: Why did you not leave the store while holding everything?

ROBOT: **I could have left the store while holding everything but that would have broken more important rules.**

HUMAN: How would you have done that?

ROBOT: **I would have picked up the glasses, picked up the watch, bought the watch and left the store.**

HUMAN: What rules would you have broken?

ROBOT: **I would have left the store while holding the glasses which I had not bought.**

HUMAN: How would that have been worse?

ROBOT: **Leaving the store while holding the glasses which I have not bought is worse than not leaving the store while holding the watch.**

Dialogue 5: "Why" query for "worse" counterfactual.

more sentences will ultimately be representable, although we are not convinced that it is possible to express *every* VEL formula in coherent English.)

4.1.1 Key assumptions

Our assumptions about the structure of the VEL statements we will convert are as follows:

- The statements have the form $\mathbf{G}\phi$ or $\mathbf{F}\phi$, possibly with quantification and costly variables, where ϕ is a (possibly negated) conjunction of (possibly negated) predicates with no temporal operators (e.g. $p_1(o_1) \wedge p_2(o_1) \wedge \neg p_3$). Not all predicates in the conjunction are negated.

- Each predicate, with the exception of those corresponding to the agent's action set, corresponds to a parameterized English sentence where either the subject is not the agent, or the subject is the agent and the verb is in the progressive or perfect tense (corresponding to actions or processes currently in progress, or which have finished in the past, respectively). For example, in the shopping domain the predicate $bought(o)$ corresponds to "I have bought o", while $holding(o)$ corresponds to "I am holding o" and $onShelf(o)$ corresponds to "o is on the shelf". Actions also correspond to present-tense English sentences: $buy(o)$ corresponds to "I buy o".

- While predicates may take multiple objects as parameters, at most one of these may

be quantified in a rule/query (and the rest must refer to specific objects within the domain). The rule "$\forall x \exists y. \neg injures(x, y)$" is not permissible under this assumption, though "$\forall x. \neg injures(bob, x)$" is if bob is a particular object in the environment.

- Each specific object in the environment corresponds to a particular referring expression in English; e.g. *glasses* to "the glasses" and *watch* to "the watch". Each object class also corresponds to an English referring expression; e.g. $ForSaleItem$ to "thing".

4.1.2 VEL clause construction pipeline

The process of constructing a clause suitable for embedding in a sentence from a VEL statement (given the assumptions outlined in section 4.1.1) is as follows. In particular, we construct a predicate form based on the statement which is processed by a separate NLG component within our robotic architecture (which in turn calls SimpleNLG to perform realization). For simplicity, we will show the realization of the predicate form instead of the predicate representation itself.

1. If the formula has costly variables, these are treated for the purposes of natural language generation as universal quantifiers.[2]

2. If the conjunction of predicates is negated (e.g. $\neg(p_1(o_1) \wedge \cdots)))$, this negation is pushed outward beyond the temporal operators and quantifiers. This will negate the main verb of the resulting clause.

3. Next the conjunction itself is processed into a clause containing "which" and "while" subclauses. Section 4.1.3 describes this process.

4. Existential and universal variable quantifiers are removed and replaced by determiners on the first instance of the variable in the main clause. If the quantification is universal, the determiner "every" is used; if existential, "a" is used (or "any", if the formula is negated). The names of particular objects are substituted for the corresponding referring expressions; the names of object variables are substituted for the referring expression of the corresponding object class.

5. Finally, if the formula contains $\mathbf{F}$ ("eventually"), this is dropped in the clause representation (since this is usually implicit in English; e.g. "I did not buy the watch" generally means

---

[2]Costly variables could alternately be handled using some form of "as little as possible", but we chose not to do this as it would make the resulting sentences needlessly complex.

"I did not eventually buy the watch"). If the clause has a remaining negation ($\neg$), the resulting clause is negated.

Figure 1 outlines this process of constructing a clause from the agent's rule against shoplifting in the example domain.

4.1.3   Processing a conjunction of predicates

Because processing a conjunction of (possibly negated) predicates is the most non-straightforward part of our clause construction process, we now explain how this is done.

Throughout the process, we maintain the list of unused conjunction arguments $unusedArgs$; the algorithm is finished when this list is empty.

We first sort predicates on three criteria, in decreasing order of importance: (1) whether the predicate is negated (non-negated first); (2) whether the predicate corresponds to an action in the RMDP, or a sentence with the agent as subject and a verb in progressive (first) or perfect (second) tense, or whether the predicate does not feature the agent as subject; and (3) which objects and variables appear in the predicate (those without objects first; then those with variables; then those with specific objects). Sorting predicates in this order will help to ensure that the main verb of the resulting clause is as similar to an action the agent is performing as possible ("I leave the store while having bought" instead of "I have bought while leaving the store"), while minimizing the likelihood of a double negation in the sentence ("I do not *not* leave the store while holding...").

Once predicates are sorted in this order, the first predicate becomes the primary verb of the clause (and is removed from $unusedArgs$). If this predicate has an object/variable as an argument, a "which" clause is constructed for that argument.[3]

A "which" clause is built for an object/variable o by isolating each predicate in $unusedArgs$ which contains that object/variable as a parameter (if o is the name of a particular object, all predicates which also contain quantified object variables are excluded from this list: they will be handled in the "which" statement for that object variable). These are sorted in a slightly different order: predicates with the agent as subject ("agent-subject"), first perfect then progressive tense; then those in which the object/variable is subject ("object-subject") and finally those with another subject entirely ("other-subject"). Within each of these classes, the corresponding sentences are conjoined by "and", and in the "object-subject" class the subject is elided. Then the individual "which" statements are conjoined by "and". Each predicate in the "which" statement is removed from $unusedArgs$. For example, if the main predicate is $putdown(t)$ and the other arguments are $\neg bought(t)$, $\neg onShelf(t)$, and $holding(t)$, the result is "put down t, which I have bought and I am holding and which is not on the shelf".

Once the first verb has been processed (and potentially modified with its "which" clause), remaining predicates are handled by adding "while" statements. If these have the agent as subject, the subject is elided and the verb conjugated into present participle form ("I leave the store while holding...").[4] Predicates without the agent as subject are added in separate while clauses, joined by "and". For example, the clause $leave \wedge holding(glasses) \wedge bought(glasses) \wedge onShelf(watch)$ would correspond to the phrase "I leave the store while holding the glasses, which I have bought, and while the watch is on the shelf". Predicates handled in such a way are removed from $unusedArgs$, and again "which" clauses are constructed for them. Once $unusedArgs$ is empty, the algorithm terminates.

4.2   Embedding VEL clauses into response templates

Listing rules, actions, or violations: When the user asks about the rules the agent follows or about the complete list of actions performed or rules violated by either the actual or the counterfactual trajectory, the response returned is a conjunction of the converted clauses using "and". In the case of rules, each such clause is modalized with "must" (and each rule for which the agent is not the subject of the clause is prefaced with "make sure that"); for actions or violations, the sentences are transformed into the past tense and (for the counterfactual trajectory) modalized with "would".

Rejecting the "why" premise: When responding to "why ϕ?" by asserting $\neg\phi$ (perhaps with a variable binding), the agent simply constructs the VEL clause corresponding to $\neg\phi$ and converts it into the past tense, e.g. "I did not ϕ".

---

[3]If the argument in question is a universally-quantified object variable, we swap "which" for "all of which" because "which" is not semantically accurate.

[4]With perfect-tense predicates with the agent as subject the auxiliary 'have' is converted into participle form, e.g. "while having bought...".

$$\textbf{Input: } (o).\mathbf{G}\,\neg(leave \wedge holding(o) \wedge \neg bought(o))$$
$$\downarrow \text{Costly variables to universal quantification}$$
$$\forall o.\mathbf{G}\neg(leave \wedge holding(o) \wedge \neg bought(o))$$
$$\downarrow \text{Push negation outward}$$
$$\neg(\exists t.\mathbf{F}(leave \wedge holding(o) \wedge \neg bought(o)))$$
$$\downarrow \text{Process conjunction (see section 4.1.3)}$$
$$\neg\exists t.\text{``I eventually leave the store while holding t which I have not bought''}$$
$$\downarrow \text{Replace quantifiers with determiners; add ref. expressions}$$
$$\neg\text{``I eventually leave the store while holding any thing which I have not bought''}$$
$$\downarrow \text{Drop ``eventually'' and apply outermost ``}\neg\text{'' to clause}$$
$$\textbf{Output: ``I do not leave the store while holding any thing which I have not bought''}$$

Figure 1: Converting a VEL statement into an English clause.

Query cannot be false: When the response to "why ϕ?" is that it is not possible for it to be otherwise, the VEL clause is converted into infinitive form in a sentence of the form "it was impossible for (subject) (not?) to (VP-infinitive)".

Counterfactual explanations: When a counterfactual trajectory is constructed to explain "why ϕ?", the VEL clause for $\neg\phi$ is computed. If this clause is negated (e.g. "I do not leave the store"), then the negation is removed, and the verb "avoid" added as an auxiliary, e.g. "I avoid leaving the store". Regardless, the clause is modalized with "could" and put into the past tense, and a canned subordinate clause is added depending on whether the real trajectory was preferable ("...but that would have violated more important rules") or equivalent ("...and that would not have broken more important rules").

Comparing real and counterfactual violations: When elaborating on the counterfactual explanation for "why ϕ" by outputting a set of rules violated by the counterfactual trajectory sufficient to exceed the violation cost of the rules violated by the actual trajectory, each such rule is negated and converted into its corresponding VEL clause, each of which are converted into gerund form. The resulting sentence takes the form "X is worse than Y" where X is the set of counterfactual violations conjoined by "and", and Y is the set of actual violations, also conjoined by "and".

5 Evaluation

We conducted a preliminary evaluation to quantify the human attitudes towards our approach in terms of trust, mental model, and intelligibility of response.

We hypothesized that the explanations provided by our approach would provide better performance than both baselines in terms of mental model and trust, and better than the surface representation baseline in terms of intelligibility.

90 participants were recruited through Amazon Mechanical Turk; 1 participant's data was removed because of technical failure delivering transcripts. A total of 89 participants (Male: 54, Female: 32, Other: 2, No answer: 1) provided usable data. The mean age was 35.4 years (SD: 11.4).

5.1 Conditions

Each participant was shown 5 text transcripts of human-robot dialogue containing natural language explanations, one at a time. Each explanation was one of three conditions as described below. We further discuss these conditions in section 6.

In the **content generation baseline** the system produces a high-level statement indicating that it compared the outcome to other reasons, without fully explaining what alternatives it considered and how they would be worse (and with no attempt to translate the agent's norms). These sentences were hand-crafted by the authors. The purpose of this baseline is to test for any improvements that our content generation system produces. Dialogue 6 is an example of this.

In the **surface representation generation baseline** the system produces explanations with the same content as our approach, but directly translating VEL formulas (without our surface representation) and inserting them into canned sentences. The purpose of this baseline is to test for any improvements that our surface generation system produces. Dialogue 7 is an example of this.

Our **experimental explanation baseline** uses our content generation and surface generation approaches to provide a brief explanation subdialogue. Dialogues 1 through 5 give the dialogues appearing in this condition, where the Robot utterances are the actual output of our system.

HUMAN: Why didn't you buy any thing?
ROBOT: **The assumption of the question is false.**

HUMAN: Why didn't you buy every thing?
ROBOT: **The alternative was impossible.**

HUMAN: Why did you buy the glasses?
ROBOT: **For no rule-related reason; the alternative would have broken no more important rules.**

HUMAN: Why did you not leave the store while holding every thing?
ROBOT: **The alternative would have broken more important rules.**

Dialogue 6: Examples of Content Generation Baseline.

5.2 Measures

Along with each dialogue interaction the subjects were prompted to provide three ratings on a 5-point Likert scale. In all three cases the labels of the Likert scale were: Strongly agree, Agree, Neutral, Disagree, Strongly disagree.

The first rating was designed to measure the **intelligibility** of the system giving the explanation. The wording of the explanation was: "I understand what the robot is trying to communicate."

The second rating was designed to measure the human subject's perceived **mental model** of the system giving the explanation. The wording of the explanation was: "I understand how the robot makes decisions."

The third rating was designed to measure the subject's **trust** in the system giving the explanation. The wording was: "I trust this robot's ability to obey norms in a principled way."

5.3 Results

To investigate whether the type of explanations had an effect on people's comprehension of what the robot was trying to communicate (intelligibility), people's model of the robot's decision-making process (mental model) and how much the

HUMAN: Why did you not leave the store while holding every thing?
ROBOT: **I could have made "For every thing, eventually leave the store and holding thing" false but that would have broken more important rules.**
HUMAN: How would you have done that?
ROBOT: **I would pick up the glasses, pick up the watch, buy the watch, and leave the store.**
HUMAN: What rules would you have broken?
ROBOT: **I would have broken the rule "For every thing, always not leave the store and holding thing and not bought thing".**
HUMAN: How would that have been worse?
ROBOT: **Breaking the rule "always not leave the store and holding the glasses and not bought the glasses" is worse than breaking the rule "eventually leave the store and holding the watch".**

Dialogue 7: Examples of Surface Representation Baseline.

robot was trusted (trust) we conducted three one-way ANOVAs. For each model we used the following measures as dependent variables respectively: a) *intelligibility* b) *mental model* and c) *trust*. For all models we used *condition* (experimental, content and surface) as the independent variable. We found a main effect of condition on *intelligibility*, $F(2, 86) = 14.26$, $p < .001$, $\eta_p^2 = .25$, pairwise comparisons revealing that people perceived explanations in the experimental condition as more intelligible than in both the surface ($p < .001$) and content ($p < .001$) conditions. The *condition* variable also significantly impacted people's formation of a *mental model*, $F(2, 86) = 16.82, p < .001, \eta_p^2 = .28$, the experimental condition leading to better understanding (more agreement with the statement) than both the surface ($p < .001$) and content ($p = .001$) conditions. Finally, we found a main effect of *condition* on *trust*, $F(2, 86) = 5.70$, $p = .005$, $\eta_p^2 = .12$. Pairwise comparisons showed that the robot was trusted significantly more in the experimental condition than in the surface condition ($p = .004$). The comparison between the experimental condition and the content condition with regards to trust approached significance but did not pass the 95% CI threshold ($p = .000$). Throughout, we found no significant differences between the baseline conditions, surface and content.

6 Discussion and Conclusion

In terms of content generation, our primary contribution is an algorithm that constructs explanations for the behavior of an agent governed by rules specified in violation enumeration language (VEL) acting in an RMDP. The system can answer queries about the rules themselves, how the observed trajectory violates these rules, and "why" queries which invite reasoning about counterfactual trajectories. Here the assumption that the environment is deterministic is restrictive. Introducing nondeterministic environments raises the possibility that not one but many counterfactual trajectories would need be generated in describing why an agent made a particular decision. Furthermore, how to construct reasonable explanations when a bad outcome occurs due to environmental stochasticity is a topic for empirical research.

From the perspective of generating surface representations, our contribution is in a method for constructing clauses corresponding to VEL statements, which we then embed into response sentence templates. One limitation is that we restrict the set of statements from which we can construct clauses to a small fragment of VEL. We note that the algorithmic (rule-based) approach we employ to translating VEL statements to English may require significant revision to be applicable to broader categories of statements. Relaxing a few of our assumptions (such as allowing disjunctions) is likely fairly straightforward; others (such as complex combinations of temporal operators) would be significantly more involved even if it is possible to express these sentences in a succinct way that humans can understand.

As mentioned in section 2.1, we chose the shopping robot domain for its simplicity rather than for realism. In principle, the system may operate on any RMDP and set of VEL norms that meet the assumptions set out in section 4.1.1. Nevertheless, implementing our approach on a physical robot operating in a real environment is a topic for future work.

The study confirmed our hypotheses that the explanations provided by our approach would provide better performance than both baselines we selected in terms of mental model and trust, and better than the surface realization baseline in terms of intelligibility. Comparison to these provide some evidence for our approach's value in terms of both content generation and surface representation generation.

Our results corroborate Lim et al. (2009)'s finding that explanations increase trust. Our results also complement Chiyah Garcia et al. (2018)'s finding that mental models can in some cases increase the mental model of an agent: in their case by varying the soundness and completeness, and in our case through our approach to content generation and surface representation generation.

Our evaluation demonstrates that explaining behavior in terms of norms translated from VEL to English can facilitate trust and improve mental models versus naive methods for explaining the agent's behavior that (a) do not directly reference the agent's norms, or (b) translate those norms in the most naive possible way. We do not compare our approach to other approaches to constructing English text from formulae, e.g. in first-order logic (Kutlak and van Deemter, 2015; Flickinger, 2016). These approaches solve a slightly different problem than our approach does, and would likely require significant adaptation to solve the problem of explaining norm-related agent decisions. Nevertheless, comparison with these methods (and with state-of-the-art deep learning methods such as in Manome et al., 2018) is a fruitful topic for future work.

By enabling agents to craft natural language explanations of behavior governed by temporal logic rules, our approach provides an early step towards systems which can not only explain their behavior, but also engage in model reconciliation (Chakraborti et al., 2019), updating their understanding of both the rules and their relative importance and the dynamics of the environment by interacting with human users while informing those users about the way the system operates.

7 Acknowledgements

This project was supported in part by ONR MURI grant N00014-16-1-2278 and NSF IIS grant 1723963.

References

Tathagata Chakraborti, Sarath Sreedharan, Sachin Grover, and Subbarao Kambhampati. 2019. Plan explanations as model reconciliation. In *2019 14th ACM/IEEE International Conference on Human-Robot Interaction (HRI)*, pages 258–266. IEEE.

Francisco Javier Chiyah Garcia, David A. Robb, Xingkun Liu, Atanas Laskov, Pedro Patron, and Helen Hastie. 2018. Explainable autonomy: A study of explanation styles for building clear mental models. In *Proceedings of the 11th International Conference on Natural Language Generation*, pages 99–108, Tilburg University, The Netherlands. Association for Computational Linguistics.

Nadine Elzein. 2019. The demand for contrastive explanations. *Philosophical Studies*, 176(5):1325–1339.

Armin Fiedler. 2001a. Dialog-driven adaptation of explanations of proofs. In *International Joint Conference on Artificial Intelligence*, volume 17, pages 1295–1300.

Armin Fiedler. 2001b. *User-adaptive proof explanation*. Ph.D. thesis, Universitat des Saarlandes.

Dan Flickinger. 2016. Generating English paraphrases from logic. In *From Semantics to Dialectometry*, pages 99–107.

Maria Fox, Derek Long, and Daniele Magazzeni. 2017. Explainable planning. In *Proceedings of the IJCAI 2017 Workshop on Explainable AI*.

Albert Gatt and Ehud Reiter. 2009. SimpleNLG: A realisation engine for practical applications. In *Proceedings of the 12th European Workshop on Natural Language Generation (ENLG 2009)*, pages 90–93.

Helmut Horacek. 2007. How to build explanations of automated proofs: A methodology and requirements on domain representations. In *Proceedings of AAAI ExaCt: Workshop on Explanation-aware Computing*, pages 34–41.

Joseph Kim, Christian Muise, Ankit Shah, Shubham Agarwal, and Julie Shah. 2019. Bayesian inference of temporal specifications to explain how plans differ. In *Proceedings of the ICAPS 2019 Workshop on Explainable Planning (XAIP)*.

Benjamin Krarup, Michael Cashmore, Daniele Magazzeni, and Tim Miller. 2019. Model-based contrastive explanations for explainable planning. In *Proceedings of the ICAPS 2019 Workshop on Explainable Planning (XAIP)*.

Roman Kutlak and Kees van Deemter. 2015. Generating Succinct English Text from FOL Formulae. In *Procs. of First Scottish Workshop on Data-to-Text Generation*.

Pat Langley. 2019. Explainable, normative, and justified agency. In *Proceedings of the Thirty-Third AAAI Conference on Artificial Intelligence*.

Brian Y Lim, Anind K Dey, and Daniel Avrahami. 2009. Why and why not explanations improve the intelligibility of context-aware intelligent systems. In *Proceedings of the SIGCHI Conference on Human Factors in Computing Systems*, pages 2119–2128. ACM.

Kana Manome, Masashi Yoshikawa, Hitomi Yanaka, Pascual Martínez-Gómez, Koji Mineshima, and Daisuke Bekki. 2018. Neural sentence generation from formal semantics. In *Proceedings of the 11th International Conference on Natural Language Generation*, pages 408–414, Tilburg University, The Netherlands. Association for Computational Linguistics.

Nima Pourdamghani, Kevin Knight, and Ulf Hermjakob. 2016. Generating English from abstract meaning representations. In *Proceedings of the 9th International Natural Language Generation conference*, pages 21–25, Edinburgh, UK. Association for Computational Linguistics.

Stylianos Loukas Vasileiou, William Yeoh, and Tran Cao Son. 2019. A general logic-based approach for explanation generation. In *Proceedings of the ICAPS 2019 Workshop on Explainable Planning (XAIP)*.

Towards Generating Math Word Problems from Equations and Topics

Qingyu Zhou[*]
Harbin Institute of Technology
qyzhou@hit.edu.cn

Danqing Huang[*]
Microsoft Research
dahua@microsoft.com

Abstract

A math word problem is a narrative with a specific topic that provides clues to the correct equation with numerical quantities and variables therein. In this paper, we focus on the task of generating math word problems. Previous works are mainly template-based with pre-defined rules. We propose a novel neural network model to generate math word problems from the given equations and topics. First, we design a fusion mechanism to incorporate the information of both equations and topics. Second, an entity-enforced loss is introduced to ensure the relevance between the generated math problem and the equation. Automatic evaluation results show that the proposed model significantly outperforms the baseline models. In human evaluations, the math word problems generated by our model are rated as being more relevant (in terms of solvability of the given equations and relevance to topics) and natural (i.e., grammaticality, fluency) than the baseline models.

1 Introduction

A math word problem is a narrative which describes a story under a specific topic. Moreover, it provides clues to the correct equation interpreting mathematical relations of numerical quantities and variables. The two example problems in Table 1 belong to two different topics (ticket selling, land purchase) respectively. Meanwhile they share the same equation template interpreting the underlying mathematical relations between numbers and variables. To generate a math word problem, a system needs to produce a *topic*-specific story while maintaining the underlying *equation*.

There is a surge of interest in automatic math word problem generation (K. and Elliot, 2002; Deane and Sheehan, 2013; Polozov et al., 2015;

Koncel-Kedziorski et al., 2016). Previous attempts are mainly based on templates. Polozov et al. (2015) consider several components (e.g., event graph construction, surface text realization), each with manual defined templates and rules. Koncel-Kedziorski et al. (2016) generate math problems by revising existing problems into a new topic. They use a problem as the verbal template and simply replace nouns and verbs with suitable words from the new topic. The generation of template-based systems is based directly on existing items with high coherence. However, they have clear limitations. As templates are fixed, the possible outputs are limited to follow template patterns without too many grammatical and lexical options. Additionally, they require manual effort to construct domain-specific templates.

Recently, neural network approaches to automatic generation of questions (Du et al., 2017; Zhou et al., 2017) and stories (Fan et al., 2018) have shown promising results. Despite their success, they cannot be directly applied to math word problem generation, since generation of math word problems need to maintain the underlying mathematical operations between quantities and variables, while at the same time ensuring the relevance of the output problem and a given topic.

In this paper, we propose a novel neural network model for *Ma*th word Problem *Gen*eration from *E*quations and *T*opics (**MAGNET**). The proposed model consists of three main components: an equation encoder, a topic encoder and a math problem decoder. The equation encoder is implemented with a bidirectional recurrent neural networks (RNN) which takes the equation tokens as input and produces a sequence of hidden vectors. The topic encoder maps the given topic words into continuous word representations. The decoder is a single directional RNN with dual-attention mechanism, which can dynamically extract information

---

[*] Equal contribution.

Proceedings of The 12th International Conference on Natural Language Generation, pages 494–503,
Tokyo, Japan, 28 Oct - 1 Nov, 2019. ©2019 Association for Computational Linguistics

Equation Template:
$x + y = [num0]$ $[num1] * x + [num2] * y = [num3]$
Problem 1:   Tickets to local movie were sold at \$4.00 for adults and \$2.50 for students. If 267 tickets were sold for a total of \$1042.50, how many adult tickets were sold?   **Topic:** ticket selling   **Equation:** $x + y = 267, 4 * x + 2.5 * y = 1042.5$
Problem 2:   A farmer bought 100 acres of land, part at \$300 an acre and part at \$450, paying for the whole \$42,200. How much land was there in each part?   **Topic:** land purchase   **Equation:** $x + y = 100, 370 * x + 450 * y = 42200$

Table 1: Math word problems of the same equation template but with different topics.

from equations and topic words. To leverage both the equation and topic information, we design an equation-topic fusion mechanism to enable the decoder to choose which information to use. Furthermore, to ensure that the generated math word problem is highly related to the given equations, we introduce a novel entity-enforced loss function which considers the correspondence between variables in the given equations and entities in the output problem.

Large-scale annotated math problem datasets play a crucial role in developing neural math problem generation systems. We propose to adapt Dolphin18K (Huang et al., 2016) as the training, development and test sets, since it is one of the current largest math problem datasets with diverse problem types. It contains 18,460 elementary math problems from Yahoo! Answers[1], with annotation of equations and answers.

Extensive experiments are conducted on the Dolphin18K dataset. We first propose three baseline methods: 1) a retrieve-based model that find the closest math problems in the training set; 2) a sequence-to-sequence model which takes only the equation as input (Equ2Math); 3) a neural decoder model conditioned on topic words

---

[1] https://answers.yahoo.com/

(Topic2Math). We use three commonly used automatic evaluation metrics in recent text generation works, i.e., BLEU (Papineni et al., 2002), ROUGE (Lin, 2004) and METEOR (Denkowski and Lavie, 2014). Evaluation results on all three metrics show that our MAGNET model outperforms the baseline methods. To further examine the quality of generated math word problems, we also conduct human evaluations. Human evaluation results show that our MAGNET model performs better than the baseline systems on three aspects, i.e., 1) solvability to the given equation; 2) relevance to the given topic and 3) grammaticality and fluency of language.

Our contributions are three-folds:

1. We propose a novel end-to-end neural network model MAGNET to generate math word problems based on given equations and topics.
2. We introduce an Equation-Topic Fusion mechanism which helps the decoder incorporate both the information from the equation and the topic.
3. We design an entity-enforced loss function to improve the relevance between the generated math word problem and the given equations.

2 Related Work

Automatic question generation from text aims to generate questions taking text as input, which has the potential value of education purpose (Heilman, 2011). Previous question generation works focus on generating natural language questions from a given piece of text. Heilman (2011) employs a syntactic parser to parse the input text into a tree and extract answer candidates. Then a rule-based system transforms the tree into the corresponding question. Recently, generative neural network methods are also applied to this area since large-scale manually annotated passage-question pairs become available. Du et al. (2017) and Zhou et al. (2017) propose to use SQuAD (Rajpurkar et al., 2016) question answering dataset as the training data of question generation. In SQuAD dataset, the given passage is a piece of text from Wikipedia and the answer is a sub-span in it. Du et al. (2017) use a sequence-to-sequence model on the passage-question pair to generate questions. Their model takes the passage text as input to generate a question from it. Different from Du et al. (2017), they add the answer position to the model input as BIO tagging features, However, these methods cannot directly applied to math word problem generation.

There are previous approaches specifically targeting math problem generation. Most of them are template based, such as natural language schemas (K. and Elliot, 2002) and semantic frames of conceptual structures (Deane and Sheehan, 2013). Polozov et al. (2015) propose a pipeline including equation generation, plot generation and surface text realization, which requires manually defined ontology and templates. These approaches are ensured to maintain highly-coherent story, but with the manual cost of template construction, which is difficult to extend to more domains. Recently, Koncel-Kedziorski et al. (2016) propose a rewrite-based approach. They generate new problems by simply replacing noun phrases and verbs in the existing math problems with words in the target topic. However, they do not consider global optimization of the whole problem that results in semantic incoherence.

Math problem solving, which can be formatted as learning the mapping from math problem to equations, is also related to our work. In this paper, we adapt a math problem dataset Dolphin18K for development. Dolphin18K (Huang et al., 2016) is constructed from Yahoo! Answer containing over 18,000 math problems. Previous to that, there are several datasets with size less than 2,000, such as VERB-375 (Hosseini et al., 2014), ALG514 (Kushman et al., 2014) and Dolphin1878 (Shi et al., 2015).

3 Problem Statement

Given an equation template and a target topic, our goal is to generate a math word problem in natural language. In this section, we first define the equation template and the topic, and then give the formal introduction of our task.

3.1 Equation Template

Equation template, introduced in Kushman et al. (2014), is a unique form of an equation system. For example, given an equation system as follows:

$$x + y = 20; x - 4 = y$$

We replace the numbers with tokens and generalize the equations as the following template:

$$x + y = [num0]; x - [num1] = y$$

Equation is a solution for a specific math problem, while an equation template can correspond to several math problems. Therefore, an equation template can be seen as an abstraction of a set of equations.

3.2 Topic

As pointed out in Koncel-Kedziorski et al. (2016), math problems are coherent stories with different topics (e.g., ticket selling or land purchase). In one math problem, there are words that act as topic indicators. For the problems in Table 1, the corresponding topic indicators are:
Problem 1: {*tickets, movie, adults, students, sold*}
Problem 2: {*farmer, bought, dollar, land, pay*}

Therefore, we extract the keywords of a math problem as its topic words for representing the topic. The details of topic words extraction will be described in Section 3.4.

3.3 Math Problem Generation

Now we can formally define the task of math word problem generation. Given an equation template E and a set of topic words T as input, the goal is to generate a math word problem P, satisfying:
(1) P is a piece of natural language text whose topic is T;
(2) P maintains the mathematical operations between numerical quantities and variables in the equation template E.

3.4 Dataset Creation

We create the math word problem generation dataset based on the Dolphin18K (Huang et al., 2016) dataset. Specifically, we construct (E, T, P) triple where E is an equation, T is a set of topic words, and P is the corresponding math word problem. In the Dolphin18K dataset, the equation E and math word problem P are given. Therefore, we need to extract the topic words from the text of P.

There are previous studies on the task of topic word extraction, such as simple counting of word frequency and LDA topic model (Blei et al., 2003). We practically observe that the TF-IDF method is effective which satisfies our needs. We calculate the scores of the words as follows:

$$tf_{ij} = \frac{n_{ij}}{\sum_k n_{kj}} \qquad (1)$$

$$idf_i = \log\frac{|P|}{|j : t_i \in P_j| + 1} \qquad (2)$$

$$score_{ij} = tf_{ij} * idf_i \qquad (3)$$

where tf_{ij} is the term frequency of word i in problem P_j, and idf_i is the inverse document frequency of word i. We sort the score of each word i in P_j, and keep the **top** n_{tp} words as the problem's topic words.

4 MAGNET

As shown in Figure 1, our MAGNET model consists of three main parts, namely, the topic encoder, the equation encoder and the math word problem decoder. The topic encoder and equation decoder are used to map topic words and equations to continuous vectors. The decoder is a single directional recurrent neural network equipped with dual-attention mechanism which leverages by the equation-topic fusion mechanism.

4.1 Topic Encoder

The input topic T contains a set of keywords $\{t_1, t_2, \ldots, t_{n_{tp}}\}$. Considering the fact that these topic words do not have sequential or temporal relationships, we represent them as a set of word embeddings $\{tp_1, tp_2, \ldots, tp_{n_{tp}}\}$ as shown in the upper-left part of Figure 1. Specifically, the topic encoder is a lookup table which maps input topic words to the corresponding real-valued vectors.

4.2 Equation Encoder

The encoder is implemented as a single-layer bidirectional GRU (Cho et al., 2014) (BiGRU). We concatenate all the equations together with a special delimiter "," (indicates the end of an equation). The BiGRU reads the input equation tokens one-by-one, producing a sequence of hidden states $h_i = [\vec{h}_i; \overleftarrow{h}_i]$ with:

$$\vec{h}_i = \text{GRU}(x_i, \vec{h}_{i-1}) \qquad (4)$$

$$\overleftarrow{h}_i = \text{GRU}(x_i, \overleftarrow{h}_{i+1}) \qquad (5)$$

The initial states of the BiGRU are set to zero vectors, i.e., $\vec{h}_1 = 0$ and $\overleftarrow{h}_n = 0$.

4.3 Math Word Problem Decoder

At each time-step t, the decoder GRU holds its previous hidden state s_{t-1}, the embedding of previous output word y_{t-1} and the previous context vector c_{t-1}. With these previous states, the decoder GRU updates its states as given by Equation 6. To initialize the GRU hidden state, we use a linear layer with the last backward encoder hidden state $\overleftarrow{h}_1$ of equation as input:

$$s_t = \text{GRU}(w_{t-1}, c_{t-1}, s_{t-1}) \qquad (6)$$

$$s_0 = \tanh(\mathbf{W}_d\overleftarrow{h}_1 + b) \qquad (7)$$

Then the decoder first generates a readout state r_t and passes it through a maxout hidden layer (Goodfellow et al., 2013) to predict the next word with a softmax layer over the output vocabulary.

$$r_t = \mathbf{W}_r w_{t-1} + \mathbf{U}_r c_t + \mathbf{V}_r s_t \qquad (8)$$

$$r'_t = [\max\{r_{t,2j-1}, r_{t,2j}\}]^\top_{j=1,\ldots,d} \qquad (9)$$

$$p(y_t|y_{<t}) = \text{softmax}(\mathbf{W}_o r'_t) \qquad (10)$$

where $\mathbf{W}_r$, $\mathbf{U}_r$, $\mathbf{V}_r$ and $\mathbf{W}_o$ are weight matrices. w_{t-1} is the word embedding of the previously generated word y_{t-1}. The readout state r_t is a $2d$-dimensional vector, and the maxout layer (Equation 9) picks the max value for every two numbers in r_t and produces a d-dimensional maxout vector r'_t. We then apply a linear transformation on r'_t to get a target vocabulary size vector and predict the next word y_t with the softmax operation.

4.4 Equation-Topic Fusion

To incorporate both the information of equation and topic, we propose the Equation-Topic fusion mechanism. Intuitively, the Equation-Topic Fusion mechanism enables the decoder to pay different portions of attention to the equation templates and topic words. For instance, when the decoder is generating descriptive words about the story, it should pay more attention to the topic words. Vice versa, the decoder should pay more attention to the equation if it is generating numbers or variables in the equation. In detail, the context vector c_t in Equation 6 and 8 is a fused vector of equation and topic. We employ two attention modules to produce the corresponding context vectors of equa-

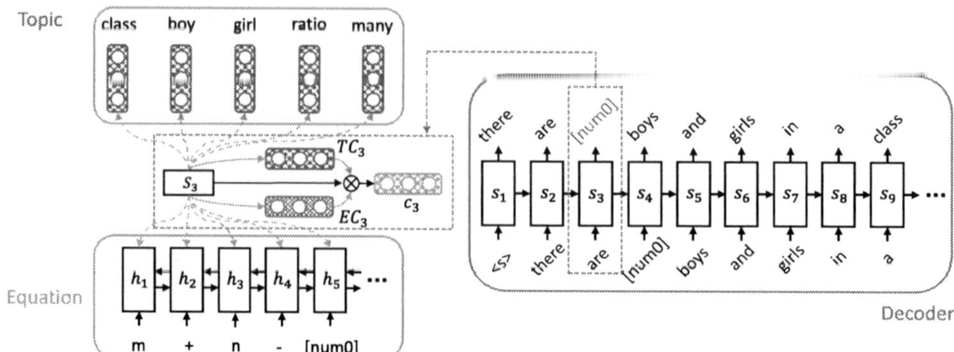

Figure 1: The overview diagram of MAGNET. For simplicity, we omit some units and connections. This figure shows the detail that the decoder is generating the third word by fusing the information from both the input equation and topic words.

tion and topic :

$$e_{t,i} = v_a^\top \tanh(\mathbf{W}_a s_t + \mathbf{U}_a \text{repr}(\cdot)_i) \tag{11}$$

$$\alpha_{t,i} = \frac{\exp(e_{t,i})}{\sum_{i=1}^n \exp(e_{t,i})} \tag{12}$$

$$c(\cdot)_t = \sum_{i=1}^n \alpha_{t,i} \text{repr}(\cdot)_i \tag{13}$$

where $\text{repr}(\cdot)_i$ represents the vector of encoded equation tokens or topic words, which can be h_i or tp_i. The $v_a^\top$, $\mathbf{W}_a$ and $\mathbf{U}_a$ are learnable parameters. Since the equation and topic information are of different types, we use two sets of these parameters for equation and topic attention modules.

We represent the equation context vector $c(\text{equation})_t$ and topic context vector $c(\text{topic})_t$ as EC_t and TC_t respectively. To fuse EC_t and TC_t together, we predict a fusion coefficient g_t using an MLP:

$$g_t = \text{sigmoid}(\mathbf{W}_f s_t + b) \tag{14}$$

$$c_t = g_t \cdot EC_t + (1 - g_t) \cdot TC_t, \tag{15}$$

where g_t is the fusion gate. Therefore, the context vector c_t is the combination of equation template and topic which is determined by the current decoding state s_t.

4.5 Entity-Enforced Loss

As we mention before, the generated math problems should be highly relevant to the given equation template. The *entities* in the generated math problem should correspond to the *variables* in the equations (e.g., m, n, $[num0]$). To ensure high

relevance of equation template and the generated math problem, we propose an entity-enforced loss:

$$acc_e = \sum_{t=1}^L g_t \alpha_{t,e} \tag{16}$$

$$\mathcal{L}_e = \sum_{\forall e \in \text{equation}} \text{ReLU}(1 - acc_e) \tag{17}$$

where L is the length of output problem, and ReLU is rectifier function defined as:

$$\text{ReLU}(x) = \max(0, x) \tag{18}$$

The intuition behind the entity-enforced loss is that the model needs to attend to the entities in the given equations. In Equation 16, we accumulate the attention scores of variables in the equation for all the decoding time steps. Then a ReLU function is applied on $(1 - acc_e)$ to ensure that the entity e is attended for at least one time during decoding.

4.6 Objective Function

Given a training dataset with n equation-topic-question triples $\mathcal{D} = \{(E^{(1)}, T^{(1)}, P^{(1)}), \ldots, (E^{(n)}, T^{(n)}, P^{(n)})\}$, the training objective is to minimize the negative log likelihood loss $\mathcal{L}$ with respect to the model parameter θ:

$$\mathcal{L} = -\sum_i^n \log p(P^i | E^i, T^i; \theta) + \lambda \mathcal{L}_e \tag{19}$$

where λ is a hyper-parameter that controls the contribution of entity-enforced in the loss.

5 Experiment

In this section, we evaluate our model with both automatic and human evaluations.

5.1 Datasets

We conduct our experiments on the Dolphin18K dataset[2]. Since we need equation templates as input to generate math problems, we use its subset with equation annotation, which sums up to 10,644 problems with 5,738 equation templates. The average sentence length of a problem is 2.70. The average number of words in a problem is 32.72. We train on 8,515 examples and evaluate on 2,129 test examples, following the split setting in Huang et al. (2016).

As pre-processing, we obtain equation template and topic words for each problem as their input. We extract at most $n_{tp} = 10$ words with highest TF-IDF scores as the topic words in our experiments. According to the statistic, the average number of extracted topic words are 7.7 and 7.5 in the training and testing datasets respectively.

5.2 Baselines

We provide three baselines of math word problem generation, considering the input of equation template and topic words respectively[3].

KNN finds the closest problem in the training set given the input topic words. It first narrows down training problems to those with the same input equation template. Then a TF-IDF vector for topic words was created and KNN is applied to retrieve the nearest training problem.

Topic2Math generates math problems only given the input of topic words. Topics words are encoded by Topic Encoder component described in Section 4.1.

Equ2Math generates math problems only given the input of equation template. Equation template is encoded by Equation Encoder component described in Section 4.2.

---

[2] Other datasets are small and biased on problem types, which can be seen as subsets of the dataset we used.

[3] Previous works are not comparable: 1) The rules used in Polozov et al. (2015) are not publicly available; 2) Koncel-Kedziorski et al. (2016) have a different input from us, that their system needs a full math word problem and then rewrite it. While our system tries to generate a problem from scratch.

5.3 Implementation Details

The dimension of encoder/decoder hidden state and embedding are set to 512. The hyper-parameter λ in Equation 19 is 0.7. Dropout rate is set to 0.6. All model parameters are initialized using a Gaussian distribution with Xavier scheme (Glorot and Bengio, 2010). We use the Adam (Kingma and Ba, 2015) optimizer with its hyper-parameters set as: learning rate $\alpha = 0.001$, momentum parameters $\beta_1 = 0.9$ and $\beta_1 = 0.999$, and $\epsilon = 10^{-8}$. We also apply gradient clipping (Pascanu et al., 2013) with range $[-5, 5]$. The beam size is set to 3 in the decoding stage. We release the source code at an anonymous URL for blind review.

5.4 Automatic Evaluation

Though the automatic evaluation methods have their limitations in natural language generation evaluation, we use them as important evaluation methods since they are easily reproducible. Furthermore, in the task of math word problem generation, retaining some key information such as the quantities and entities can be well measured by the automatic evaluation methods.

5.4.1 Evaluation Metrics

We evaluate the performance of our model using three evaluation metrics following recent text generation works (Du et al., 2017; Zhou et al., 2017; Fan et al., 2018):

BLEU (Papineni et al., 2002) is a widely used evaluation method in machine translation and text generation.

ROUGE (Lin, 2004) is commonly to evaluate n-gram overlap of summaries with gold-standard sentences.

METEOR (Denkowski and Lavie, 2014) is provided following previous work (Koncel-Kedziorski et al., 2016).

5.4.2 Evaluation Results

Table 2 shows the evaluation results on automatic metrics. From the table, we can see that MAG-NET significantly outperforms the baseline models on all metrics. On one hand, our model obtains a large improvement compared to the Equ2Math model (+19.24 ROUGE-1, +17.08 ROUGE-2, +14.02 ROUGE-L). On the other hand, compared to the Topic2Math model, our model has a (+1.15

Models	BLEU	ROUGE-1	ROUGE-2	ROUGE-L	METEOR
KNN	11.97	43.93	23.08	36.14	16.78
Equ2Math	5.00	35.88	12.94	29.56	13.51
Topic2Math	12.26	53.97	28.79	42.19	23.90
MAGNET w/o Entity	12.28	54.28	28.77	42.88	24.73
MAGNET	**12.47**	**55.12**	**30.02**	**43.58**	**24.76**

Table 2: Automatic evaluation results on Dolphin18K. MAGNET w/o Entity indicates the ablation model without entity-enforced loss.

Models	Equation Relevance		Topic Relevance		Solvability		Language Fluency	
	score	Kappa	score	Kappa	score	Kappa	score	Kappa
KNN	1.65	0.75	1.80	0.90	**2.07**	0.90	**2.92**	0.80
Equ2Math	1.97	0.68	1.58	0.85	1.98	0.80	2.62	0.75
Topic2Math	1.63	0.58	2.88	0.85	1.50	0.55	1.98	0.52
MAGNET w/o Entity	1.85	0.40	**2.90**	0.90	1.73	0.65	2.35	0.50
MAGNET	**2.08**	0.43	**2.90**	0.90	**2.07**	0.65	2.57	0.77

Table 3: Human evaluation results: the average scores from the three annotators together (ranged from 1 to 3, higher is better).

ROUGE-1, +1.23 ROUGE-2, +1.39 ROUGE-L) relative gain respectively. The improvement over the baselines demonstrates the usefulness of both equation and topic input. Moreover, without the entity-enforced loss, the performance drops on all metricsthe, which shows its effectiveness.

5.5 Human Evaluation

To better evaluate the performance of our system, we recruit three human annotators to judge the quality of the generated math problems, in addition to the automatic metrics. We randomly select 50 instances in the test set, and show the equation template and topic words with generated math problems from different models. We then ask the annotators to rate the outputs with scores ranged 1 to 3 from the following four aspects (detailed guidelines attached in supplementary):

1. Equation Relevance: the generated problem is relevant to the given equation;

2. Topic Relevance: the generated problem is relevant to the given topic words;

3. Solvability: the generated problem can be solved by an (given) equation;

4. Language Fluency: the generated problem is grammatical and fluent.

Table 3 reports the human evaluation results. As we can see, MAGNET has the highest scores across the three criteria of equation relevance (2.08), topic relevance (2.9), solvability (2.07), outperforming all the baselines and the ablation test. KNN performs the best in terms of language fluency, since as a retrieval-based method its outputs are existing problems in the training data. The Kappa (Randolph, 2005) values on all models range from 0.4 to 0.9, indicating relatively intermediate to excellent agreement among annotators. The human evaluation result is consistent with the automatic evaluation.

6 Discussion

To better understand the model, we show the attention visualization and qualitative analysis with some examples.

6.1 Effect of Model Fusion

To illustrate how MAGNET leverages both inputs, we visualize the output fusion coefficient g (top), and attention of topic words (middle) and equation template (bottom) in Figure 2.

We can see MAGNET generates a reasonable math problem. When generating the words such as "product", "decreased" in the output, the fusion module is concentrated on the topic words;

Equation Template: $m = [num0]/[num1]/60$
Topic words: sun approximately light kilometer planet travels travel rate take minute
KNN: what is [num0] of [num1] ?
Equ2Math: if i ran [num0] mile in [num1] minute , what is my meter per hour ?
Topic2Math: find the speed of the light [num0] kilometer in [num1] minute [num2] minute .
MAGNET-Entity: a light travels [num0] kilometer at [num1] kilometer per h. how far would it take to travel [num2] kilometer ?
MAGNET: if a man travels [num0] kilometer in [num1] minute , what is the speed in kilometer per h ?
Ground truth: the sun is approximately [num0] kilometer from the planet saturn , and light from the sun travels to saturn at the rate of approximately [num1] kilometer per second. approximately how many minute does it take for light to travel from the sun to saturn?

Table 4: An example of generated math word problems.

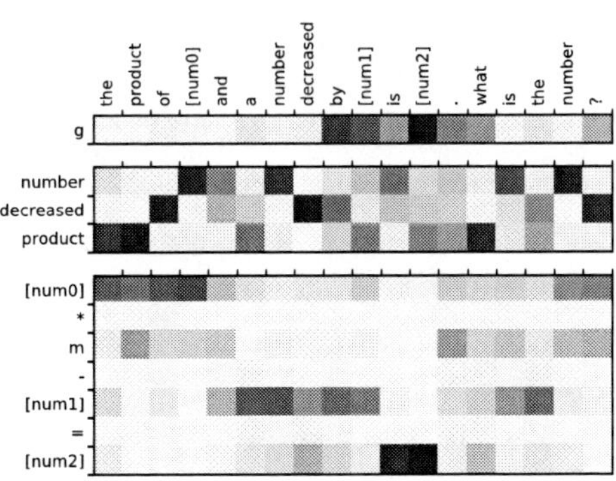

Figure 2: Fusion coefficient g and attention visualization example.

while the attention is focused on the equation template when generating the corresponding numbers ([num0], [num1], ...).

6.2 Qualitative Results

Table 4 shows an example case from the test set. We can see that MAGNET generates a more reasonable math problem, with respect to equation solvability and topic relevance. Please note that the equation template does not exist in the training data. Surprisingly, MAGNET has captured the constant "60" in the equation template and generates "kilometer per h" as unit conversion of minute to hour. The ablation model MAGNET-Entity does not generate reasonable problem as well as the baselines, while MAGNET generates "speed" word problem, perfectly describing the division of two numbers. This further demonstrates the effectiveness of the entity-enforced loss which encour-

ages the relevance between the equation template and the output problem. Due to space limit, we attach more examples in the supplementary.

6.3 Error Analysis

Furthermore, we observe two main types of errors by our model (examples shown in Supplementary): (1) Problem soundness. The generated problem lacks semantic coherence. For example, the model generates "plants $[num0]$ feet of fence to build a fence" that is non-comprehensive; (2) Equation matchness. The input equation template is partially correlated to the output, but not an exact solution of it. This is somewhat expected, since we use the entity-enforced loss only as a soft constraint to ensure the relevance with equation.

7 Conclusion

In this work, we present MAGNET, a novel model for math word problem generation. It considers the input of both equations and topics using a fusion module. Additionally, an entity-enforced loss is introduced to ensure the relevance of equation and the problem during training. Experiments on a large-scale math problem dataset demonstrated our model can produce fluent math word problems that are highly relevant to the given equations and topics.

Future work could incorporate language models to improve the language fluency, and design more fine-grained models to improve the semantic coherence by employing harder constrains of equation template. Furthermore, we would like to extend to more diverse topics with external resources.

8 Acknowledgements

We would like to thank the annotators for their efforts in the evaluation process. Thanks to the anonymous reviewers for their helpful comments and suggestions.

References

David M. Blei, Andrew Y. Ng, and Michael I. Jordan. 2003. Latent dirichlet allocation. *J. Mach. Learn. Res.*, 3:993–1022.

Kyunghyun Cho, Bart van Merrienboer, Caglar Gulcehre, Dzmitry Bahdanau, Fethi Bougares, Holger Schwenk, and Yoshua Bengio. 2014. Learning phrase representations using rnn encoder–decoder for statistical machine translation. In *Proceedings of the EMNLP 2014*, pages 1724–1734, Doha, Qatar. Association for Computational Linguistics.

Paul Deane and Kathleen Sheehan. 2013. Automatic item generation via frame semantics: Natural language generation of math word problems. In *Proceedings of the Annual Meeting of the National Council on Measurement in Education*, Chicago, America.

Michael Denkowski and Alon Lavie. 2014. Meteor universal: Language specific translation evaluation for any target language. In *Proceedings of the EACL 2014 Workshop on Statistical Machine Translation*.

Xinya Du, Junru Shao, and Claire Cardie. 2017. Learning to ask: Neural question generation for reading comprehension. In *Proceedings of the 55th ACL*, pages 1342–1352, Vancouver, Canada. Association for Computational Linguistics.

Angela Fan, Mike Lewis, and Yann Dauphin. 2018. Hierarchical neural story generation. In *Proceedings of the 56th ACL*, pages 889–898. Association for Computational Linguistics.

Xavier Glorot and Yoshua Bengio. 2010. Understanding the difficulty of training deep feedforward neural networks. In *Aistats*, volume 9, pages 249–256.

Ian J Goodfellow, David Warde-Farley, Mehdi Mirza, Aaron C Courville, and Yoshua Bengio. 2013. Maxout networks. *ICML (3)*, 28:1319–1327.

Michael Heilman. 2011. *Automatic factual question generation from text*. Ph.D. thesis, Carnegie Mellon University.

Mohammad Javad Hosseini, Hannaneh Hajishirzi, Oren Etzioni, and Nate Kushman. 2014. Learning to solve arithmetic word problems with verb categorization. In *Proceedings of the 2014 Conference on Empirical Methods in Natural Language Processing*.

Danqing Huang, Shuming Shi, Chin-Yew Lin, Jian Yin, and Wei-Ying Ma. 2016. How well do computers solve math word problems? large-scale dataset construction and evaluation. In *Proceedings of the 52nd Annual Meeting of the Association for Computational Linguistics*.

Singley Mark K. and Bennett Randy Elliot. 2002. Item generation and beyond: Applications of schema theory to mathematics assessment. In *Irvine, Sidney H.; Kyllonen, Patrick C. (eds.) Item Generation for Test Development. Mahwah, NJ: Lawrence Erlbaum Associates.*

Diederik Kingma and Jimmy Ba. 2015. Adam: A method for stochastic optimization. In *Proceedings of 3rd International Conference for Learning Representations*, San Diego.

Rik Koncel-Kedziorski, Ioannis Konstas, Luke Zettlemoyer, and Hannaneh Hajishirzi. 2016. A theme-rewriting approach for generating algebra word problems. In *Proceedings of the 2016 Conference on Empirical Methods in Natural Language Processing*, pages 1617–1628, Austin, Texas. Association for Computational Linguistics.

Nate Kushman, Yoav Artzi, Luke Zettlemoyer, and Regina Barzilay. 2014. Learning to automatically solve algebra word problems. In *Proceedings of the 52nd Annual Meeting of the Association for Computational Linguistics*.

Chin-Yew Lin. 2004. Rouge: A package for automatic evaluation of summaries. In *Text summarization branches out: Proceedings of the ACL-04 workshop*, volume 8. Barcelona, Spain.

Kishore Papineni, Salim Roukos, Todd Ward, and Wei-Jing Zhu. 2002. Bleu: a method for automatic evaluation of machine translation. In *Proceedings of the 40th annual meeting on association for computational linguistics*, pages 311–318. Association for Computational Linguistics.

Razvan Pascanu, Tomas Mikolov, and Yoshua Bengio. 2013. On the difficulty of training recurrent neural networks. *ICML (3)*, 28:1310–1318.

Oleksandr Polozov, Eleanor O'Rourke, Adam M. Smith, Luke Zettlemoyer, Sumit Gulwani, and Zoran Popović. 2015. Personalized mathematical word problem generation.

Pranav Rajpurkar, Jian Zhang, Konstantin Lopyrev, and Percy Liang. 2016. Squad: 100,000+ questions for machine comprehension of text. In *Proceedings of the 2016 Conference on Empirical Methods in Natural Language Processing*, pages 2383–2392, Austin, Texas. Association for Computational Linguistics.

Justus J Randolph. 2005. Free-marginal multirater kappa (multirater k [free]): An alternative to fleiss' fixed-marginal multirater kappa. *Online submission.*

Shuming Shi, Wang Yuehui, Chin-Yew Lin, Xiaojiang Liu, and Yong Rui. 2015. Automatically solving number word problems by semantic parsing and reasoning. In *Proceedings of the 2015 Conference on Empirical Methods in Natural Language Processing*.

Qingyu Zhou, Nan Yang, Furu Wei, Chuanqi Tan, Hangbo Bao, and Ming Zhou. 2017. Neural question generation from text: A preliminary study. *arXiv preprint arXiv:1704.01792*.

DISSIM: A Discourse-Aware Syntactic Text Simplification Framework for English and German

Christina Niklaus[13], Matthias Cetto[1], André Freitas[2], and **Siegfried Handschuh[13]**

[1] University of St.Gallen

{christina.niklaus, matthias.cetto, siegfried.handschuh}@unisg.ch

[2] University of Manchester

andre.freitas@manchester.ac.uk

[3] University of Passau

{christina.niklaus, siegfried.handschuh}@uni-passau.de

Abstract

We introduce DISSIM, a discourse-aware sentence splitting framework for English and German whose goal is to transform syntactically complex sentences into an intermediate representation that presents a simple and more regular structure which is easier to process for downstream semantic applications. For this purpose, we turn input sentences into a two-layered semantic hierarchy in the form of core facts and accompanying contexts, while identifying the rhetorical relations that hold between them. In that way, we preserve the coherence structure of the input and, hence, its interpretability for downstream tasks.

1 Introduction

We developed a syntactic text simplification (TS) approach that can be used as a preprocessing step to facilitate and improve the performance of a wide range of artificial intelligence (AI) tasks, such as Machine Translation, Information Extraction (IE) or Text Summarization. Since shorter sentences are generally better processed by natural language processing (NLP) systems (Narayan et al., 2017), the goal of our approach is to **break down a complex source sentence into a set of minimal propositions**, i.e. a sequence of sound, self-contained utterances, with each of them presenting a minimal semantic unit that cannot be further decomposed into meaningful propositions (Bast and Haussmann, 2013).

However, any sound and coherent text is not simply a loose arrangement of self-contained units, but rather a logical structure of utterances that are semantically connected (Siddharthan, 2014). Consequently, when carrying out syntactic simplification operations without considering discourse implications, the rewriting may easily result in a disconnected sequence of simplified sentences that lack important contextual information, making the text harder to interpret. Thus, in order to **preserve the coherence structure** and, hence, the interpretability of the input, we developed a discourse-aware TS approach based on Rhetorical Structure Theory (RST) (Mann and Thompson, 1988). It establishes a contextual hierarchy between the split components, and identifies and classifies the semantic relationship that holds between them. In that way, a complex source sentence is turned into a so-called discourse tree, consisting of a **set of hierarchically ordered and semantically interconnected sentences that present a simplified syntax** which is easier to process for downstream semantic applications and may support a faster generalization in machine learning tasks.

2 System Description

We present DISSIM, a discourse-aware sentence splitting approach for English and German that creates a semantic hierarchy of simplified sentences.[1] It takes a sentence as input and performs a recursive transformation process that is based upon a small set of 35 hand-crafted grammar rules for the English version and 29 rules for the German approach.[2] These patterns were heuristically determined in a comprehensive linguistic analysis and encode syntactic and lexical features that can be derived from a sentence's parse tree.[3] Each rule

---

[1] The source code of our framework is available under https://github.com/Lambda-3/DiscourseSimplification.

[2] For reproducibility purposes, the complete set of transformation patterns is available under https://github.com/Lambda-3/DiscourseSimplification/tree/master/supplemental_material.

[3] For the English version, we use Stanford's pre-trained lexicalized parser (Socher et al., 2013) to create a sentence's phrasal parse tree. For the German approach, we apply dependency parse structures generated by the spaCy parser (https://spacy.io/).

Proceedings of The 12th International Conference on Natural Language Generation, pages 504–507,
Tokyo, Japan, 28 Oct - 1 Nov, 2019. ©2019 Association for Computational Linguistics

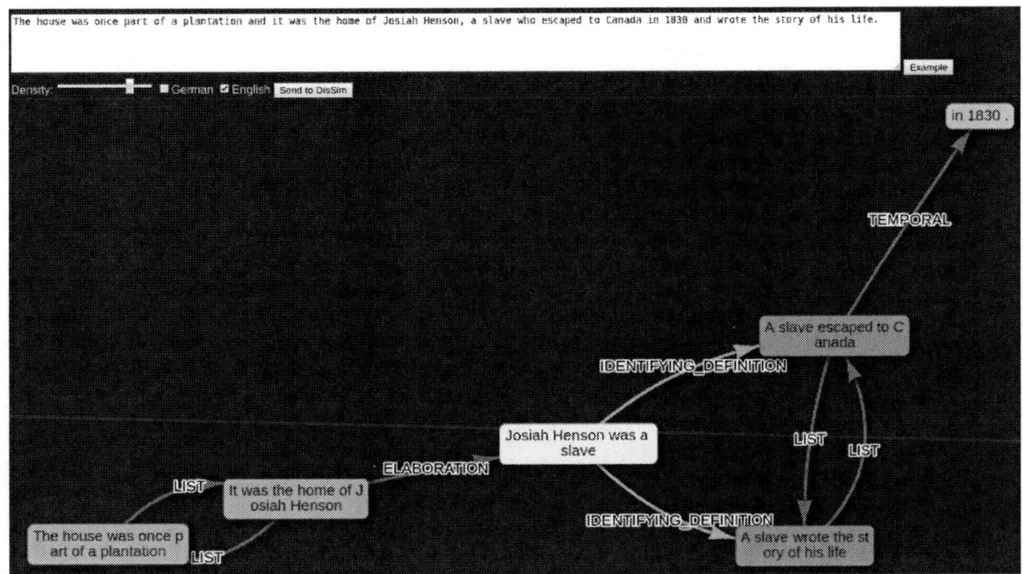

Figure 1: DISSIM's browser-based user interface. The simplified output is displayed in the form of a directed graph where the split sentences are connected by arrows whose labels denote the semantic relationship that holds between a pair of simplified sentences and whose direction indicates their contextual hierarchy. The colors signal different context layers. In that way, a semantic hierarchy of minimal, self-contained propositions is established.

specifies (1) how to *split up and rephrase* the input into structurally simplified sentences and (2) how to *set up a semantic hierarchy* between them. They are recursively applied on a given source sentence in a top-down fashion. When no more rule matches, the algorithm stops and returns the generated discourse tree.

2.1 Split into Minimal Propositions

In a first step, source sentences that present a complex linguistic form are turned into clean, compact structures by decomposing clausal and phrasal components. For this purpose, the transformation rules encode both the splitting points and rephrasing procedure for reconstructing proper sentences.

2.2 Establish a Semantic Hierarchy

Each split will create two or more sentences with a simplified syntax. To establish a semantic hierarchy between them, two subtasks are carried out:

Constituency Type Classification. First, we set up a contextual hierarchy between the split sentences by connecting them with information about their hierarchical level, similar to the concept of nuclearity in RST. For this purpose, we distinguish core sentences (*nuclei*), which carry the key infor-

mation of the input, from accompanying contextual sentences (*satellites*) that disclose additional information about it. To differentiate between those two types of constituents, the transformation patterns encode a simple syntax-based approach where subordinate clauses/phrases are classified as context sentences, while superordinate as well as coordinate clauses/phrases are labelled as core.

Rhetorical Relation Identification. Second, we aim to restore the semantic relationship between the disembedded components. For this purpose, we identify and classify the rhetorical relations that hold between the simplified sentences, making use of both syntactic features, which are derived from the input's parse tree structure, and lexical features in the form of cue phrases. Following the work of Taboada and Das (2013), they are mapped to a predefined list of rhetorical cue words to infer the type of rhetorical relation.

3 Usage

DISSIM can be either used as a Java API, imported as a Maven dependency, or as a service which we provide through a command line interface or a REST-like web service that can be deployed via docker. It takes as input NL text in the form of a

```
Input sentence:
A fluoroscopic study known as an upper gastrointestinal series is typically the next step in management,
although if volvulus is suspected, caution with non water soluble contrast is mandatory as the usage of
barium can impede surgical revision and lead to increased post operative complications.

Supervised-OIE (alone):
(1)  (A fluoroscopic study; known; as an upper gastrointestinal series)
(2)  (caution with non water soluble contrast; is; mandatory as the usage of barium)
(3)  (as the usage; of barium can impede; surgical revision and lead)
(4)  ( ; to increased; post operative complications)

Supervised-OIE (using discourse-aware TS framework for preprocessing):
(5) #1 0 (A fluoroscopic study; is; typically, the next step in management)
(5a)         L:ELABORATION    #2
(5b)         L:CONTRAST       #3
(6) #2 1 (This; fluoroscopic study is known; as an upper gastrointestinal series)
(7) #3 0 (Caution with non water soluble; is; mandatory)
(7a)         L:CONTRAST       #1
(7b)         L:CONDITION      #7
(7c)         L:BACKGROUND     #4
(7d)         L:BACKGROUND     #5
(7e)         L:BACKGROUND     #6
(8) #4 1 (The usage of barium; can impede; surgical revision)
(8a)         L:LIST           #5
(8b)         L:LIST           #6
(9) #5 1 (The usage of barium; can lead; to increased post operative complications)
(9a)         L:LIST           #4
(9b)         L:LIST           #6
(10) #6 1 (The usage of barium; to increased; post operative complications)
(10a)         L:LIST          #4
(10b)         L:LIST          #5
(11) #7 1 (Volvulus; is suspected; )
```

Figure 2: Comparison of the propositions extracted by Supervised-OIE (Stanovsky et al., 2018) *with* (5-11) and *without* (1-4) using our discourse-aware TS approach as a preprocessing step.

single sentence. Alternatively, a file containing a sequence of sentences can be loaded. The result of the transformation process is either written to the console or stored in a specified output file in JSON format. We also provide a browser-based user interface, where the user can directly type in sentences to be processed (see Figure 1).[4]

4   Experiments

For the English version, we performed both a thorough manual analysis and automatic evaluation across three commonly used TS datasets from two different domains in order to assess the performance of our framework with regard to the sentence splitting subtask. The results show that our proposed sentence splitting approach outperforms the state of the art in structural TS, returning fine-grained simplified sentences that achieve a high level of grammaticality and preserve the meaning of the input. The full evaluation methodology and detailed results are reported in Niklaus et al. (2019). In addition, a comparative analysis with the annotations contained in the RST Discourse Treebank (Carlson et al., 2002) demonstrates that we are able to capture the contextual hierarchy between the split sentences with a precision of almost 90% and reach an average precision of approximately 70% for the classification of the rhetorical relations that hold between them. The evaluation of the German version is in progress.

5   Application in Downstream Tasks

An extrinsic evaluation was carried out on the task of Open IE (Banko et al., 2007). It revealed that when applying DISSIM as a preprocessing step, the performance of state-of-the-art Open IE systems can be improved by up to 346% in precision and 52% in recall, i.e. leading to a lower information loss and a higher accuracy of the extracted relations. For details, the interested reader may refer to Niklaus et al. (2019).

Moreover, most current Open IE approaches output only a loose arrangement of extracted tuples that are hard to interpret as they ignore the context under which a proposition is complete and correct and thus lack the expressiveness needed for a proper interpretation of complex assertions (Niklaus et al., 2018). As illustrated in Figure 2, with the help of the semantic hierarchy generated by our discourse-aware sentence splitting approach the output of Open IE systems can be easily enriched with contextual information that allows to restore the semantic relationship between a set of propositions and, hence, preserve their interpretability in downstream tasks.

6   Conclusion

We developed and implemented a discourse-aware syntactic TS approach that recursively splits and rephrases complex English or German sentences into a semantic hierarchy of simplified sentences. The resulting lightweight semantic representation can be used to facilitate and improve a variety of AI tasks.

---

[4]A demonstration video is available online: `https://streamable.com/08clo`.

References

Michele Banko, Michael J. Cafarella, Stephen Soderland, Matt Broadhead, and Oren Etzioni. 2007. Open information extraction from the web. In *Proceedings of the 20th International Joint Conference on Artifical Intelligence*, pages 2670–2676, San Francisco, CA, USA. Morgan Kaufmann Publishers Inc.

Hannah Bast and Elmar Haussmann. 2013. Open information extraction via contextual sentence decomposition. In *2013 IEEE Seventh International Conference on Semantic Computing*, pages 154–159. IEEE.

Lynn Carlson, Mary Ellen Okurowski, and Daniel Marcu. 2002. *RST discourse treebank*. Linguistic Data Consortium, University of Pennsylvania.

William C Mann and Sandra A Thompson. 1988. Rhetorical structure theory: Toward a functional theory of text organization. *Text-Interdisciplinary Journal for the Study of Discourse*, 8(3):243–281.

Shashi Narayan, Claire Gardent, Shay B. Cohen, and Anastasia Shimorina. 2017. Split and rephrase. In *Proceedings of the 2017 Conference on EMNLP*, pages 606–616. ACL.

Christina Niklaus, Matthias Cetto, André Freitas, and Siegfried Handschuh. 2018. A survey on open information extraction. In *Proceedings of the 27th International Conference on Computational Linguistics*, pages 3866–3878, Santa Fe, New Mexico, USA. Association for Computational Linguistics.

Christina Niklaus, Matthias Cetto, André Freitas, and Siegfried Handschuh. 2019. Transforming complex sentences into a semantic hierarchy. In *Proceedings of the 57th Annual Meeting of the Association for Computational Linguistics*, pages 3415–3427, Florence, Italy. Association for Computational Linguistics.

Advaith Siddharthan. 2014. A survey of research on text simplification. *ITL-International Journal of Applied Linguistics*, 165(2):259–298.

Richard Socher, John Bauer, Christopher D. Manning, and Andrew Y. Ng. 2013. Parsing With Compositional Vector Grammars. In *ACL*.

Gabriel Stanovsky, Julian Michael, Luke Zettlemoyer, and Ido Dagan. 2018. Supervised open information extraction. In *Proceedings of the 2018 Conference of the North American Chapter of the Association for Computational Linguistics: Human Language Technologies, Volume 1 (Long Papers)*, volume 1, pages 885–895.

Maite Taboada and Debopam Das. 2013. Annotation upon annotation: Adding signalling information to a corpus of discourse relations. *D&D*, 4(2):249–281.

Real World Voice Assistant System for Cooking

Takahiko Ito, Shintaro Inuzuka, Yoshiaki Yamada, Jun Harashima
Cookpad Inc.
Yebisu Garden Place Tower 12F, 4-20-3 Ebisu, Shibuya-ku, Tokyo, 150-6012, Japan
{takahi-i, shintaro-inuzuka, yoshiaki-yamada, jun-harashima}@cookpad.com

Abstract

This study presents a voice assistant system to support cooking by utilizing smart speakers in Japanese. This system not only speaks the procedures written in recipes point by point but also answers the common questions from users for the specified recipes. The system applies machine comprehension techniques to millions of recipes for answering the common questions in cooking such as "人参はどうしたらよいですか (How should I cook carrots?) ". Furthermore, several machine-learning techniques are applied to generate better responses to users.

1 Introduction

Smart speakers, such as Google Home and Amazon Echo, have drawn attention due to their crucial applications in recent times. Many voice assistant applications that support users have been released in the smart speaker platforms. There are different technologies associated with smart speakers; one of the most important tasks of smart speakers is machine comprehension. In this regard, many studies have been conducted, including (Pranav et al., 2016) and (Yagcioglu et al., 2018).

This study presents a voice assistant system, which supports cooking, in Japanese. This system not only speaks the procedures written in specified recipes point by point but also applies machine comprehension techniques to answer common questions in cooking on particular recipes. The system supports millions of recipes stored on a recipe sharing service. To instantly handle questions from users, we build a *knowledge base* to support the generation of the answer sentences.

2 Voice Assistant System for Cooking

This section describes the basic usage of the voice assistant system. Figure 1 depicts the interaction between the voice assistant system for cooking and the users.

The voice assistant system speaks the procedures (steps) point by point in a recipe specified by the users. In addition, when users ask questions regarding the recipe at any time, the system answers the question in an arbitrary time. To reduce the time of response, we build a knowledge base by which the voice assistant system seeks to generate answers to the questions from users. The knowldege base contains the resources used by the voice assistant to speak each of the procedures and answer the questions from users.

3 Knowledge Base to Support Cooking

The knowledge base contains structured resources, which are dependent on each recipe. The resources contain the title, procedures, ingredients and answers to common questions on recipes. The following sections show the features of the developed kdnowledge for cooking.

3.1 Machine Cmprehension

To make the voice assistant answer the questions, we build a set of resources required to answer the common questions on the target recipes.

In the sequel, we shall describe the processes involved in extracting the resources to answer the questions.

3.1.1 Description of the Related Procedures on Particular Ingredients

When we cook after studying a recipe, we sometimes do not remember the details of the procedures or the quantity of ingredients in the recipe. In this case, users ask a question such as "how should I process potatoes?" Then, our voice assistant replies stating that "the recipe said that you should boil the potatoes and then mush them."

Proceedings of The 12th International Conference on Natural Language Generation, pages 508–509,
Tokyo, Japan, 28 Oct - 1 Nov, 2019. ©2019 Association for Computational Linguistics

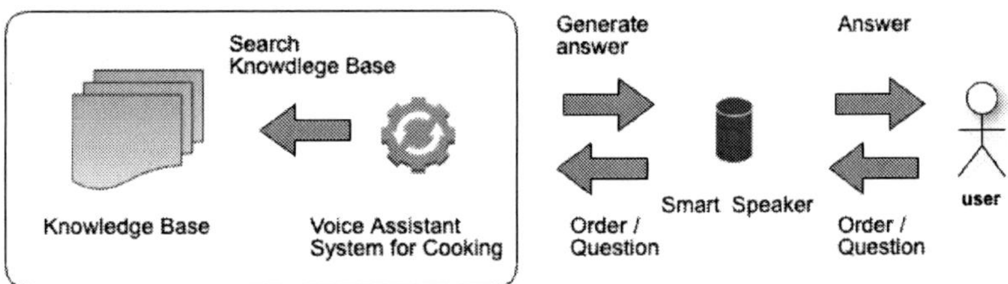

Figure 1: Interaction with a voice assistant system.

The system automatically extracts the procedures of processing each ingredient in the target recipe with simple pattern matching ingredient names and procedures.

3.1.2 Extract other expressions

In addition to the extraction of the related procedures on each ingredient, the system extracts other pieces of knowledge in cooking.

Quantitative expressions Recipes contain quantitative expressions such as temperature or the time range of processing ingredients. For example, when the procedure of a recipe says "heat potatoes for 10 min using a microwave," the system automatically extracts the time and temperature with respect to the cooking instruments.

Seasonings Our voice assistant system extracts the required quantity of the specified ingredients. In addition, it automatically detects whether each ingredient requires seasoning.

3.2 Detect Fake Procedures

In consideration of the recipe data in sharing services, users publish recipes in the form of a series of procedures. Some "procedures" are not actually part of the cooking process but fake. Fake procedures include the advertisements of the recipes themselves or comments. These fake procedures cause problems when they are given by the voice assistant systems.

Therefore, we constructed a LSTM based discriminator that distinguishes fake procedures or those that do not follow the procedures (Inuzuka et al., 2018).

3.3 Normalize the Ingredient Names

Recipes have a list of a blocks containing ingredient names with their quantities. When an ingreident name inserted from the voice assistant system

does not match the name in the target recipe, the voice assistant system is not able to return the answer.

Therefore, we apply two types of normalization methods to ingredient names. The first applied method is based on a dictionary. The dictionary contains the ingredient names with different variations and the canonical form. The second applied method is a character-based encoder-decoder model described in (Harashima and Yamada, 2018).

4 Summary and Future Work

This study presented the voice assistant system deployed in smart speakers. We build knowledge base to answer the common questions from users. Practical machine learning techniques are applied to generate better responses to questions from users.

The machine comprehension for recipe is currently implemented with simple matching. In the future we will apply modern deep neural network methods such as BERT.

References

Jun Harashima and Yoshiaki Yamada. 2018. Two-step Validation in Character-based Ingredient Normalization. In *CEA*.

Shintaro Inuzuka, Takahiko Ito, and Jun Harashima. 2018. Step or Not: Discriminator for The Real Instructions in User-generated Recipes. In *W-NUT*.

Rajpurkar Pranav, Zhang Jian, Lopyrev Konstantin, and Liang Percy. 2016. SQuAD: 100,000+ questions for machine comprehension of text. In *EMNLP*.

Semih Yagcioglu, Aykut Erdem, Erkut Erdem, and Nazli Ikizler-Cinbis. 2018. RecipeQA: A Challenge Dataset for Multimodal Comprehension of Cooking Recipes. In *EMNLP*.

VAE-PGN based Abstractive Model in Multi-stage Architecture for Text Summarization

Hyungtak Choi[1], Lohith Ravuru[1], Tomasz Dryjański[2], Seonghan Ryu[1], Donghyun Lee[1], Hojung Lee[1] and Inchul Hwang[1]

[1] Samsung Research, Samsung Electronics Co. Ltd., Seoul, Korea

[2] Samsung R&D Institute, Warsaw, Poland

```
{ht777.choi, loki.ravuru, t.dryjanski, seonghan.ryu,
dh.semko.lee, hojung76.lee, inc.hwang}@samsung.com
```


Abstract

This paper describes our submission to the TL;DR challenge. Neural abstractive summarization models have been successful in generating fluent and consistent summaries with advancements like the copy (Pointer-generator) and coverage mechanisms. However, these models suffer from their extractive nature as they learn to copy words from the source text. In this paper, we propose a novel abstractive model based on Variational Autoencoder (VAE) to address this issue. We also propose a Unified Summarization Framework for the generation of summaries. Our model eliminates non-critical information at a sentence-level with an extractive summarization module and generates the summary word by word using an abstractive summarization module. To implement our framework, we combine submodules with state-of-the-art techniques including Pointer-Generator Network (PGN) and BERT while also using our new VAE-PGN abstractive model. We evaluate our model on the benchmark Reddit corpus as part of the TL;DR challenge and show that our model outperforms the baseline in ROUGE score while generating diverse summaries.

1 Introduction

Text summarization is the task of producing an accurate summary by preserving essential information from a long text document. This is a challenging and significant task, as it can be applied to many real-world applications such as summarizing news articles, social media, web pages, blogs or long text documents. Many approaches have been proposed to solve the text summarization problem (See et al., 2017; Liu, 2019b; Gehrmann et al., 2018). Extractive summarization generates a summary by selecting important phrases or sentences from the source text. This approach mainly uses ranking the importance of phrases or sentences to select only important information (Liu, 2019b). Whereas the abstractive approach generates entirely new phrases or sentences that capture the meaning of the source text. In this paper, we focus on a few challenges that need to be addressed in generating an abstractive summarization of a given text.

The first challenge comes from the difficulty in preserving the contents of a large source text in the generated summary. The state-of-the-art models for abstractive summarization use a sequence-to-sequence attention model with a copy mechanism (Gu et al., 2016; See et al., 2017), to select the relevant content of the source text. But these models suffer from their extractive nature of generating summaries due to the copy mechanism (Boutkan et al., 2019; Chawla et al., 2019). We introduce a VAE-based PGN model to overcome this extractive nature. Another challenge is to eliminate non-critical information from the source text. Gehrmann et al. (2018) employ a word-level content selection model to focus on only critical information, but handling critical information at word-level is difficult in long sentences because of the repetition of many common words. Our approach handles the critical information by using a multi-stage model with a sentence-level selection (extractive) and abstractive summarization modules.

First, we use a fine-tuned BERT-based extractive model named BERTSUM (Liu, 2019b) to eliminate less important sentences by scoring each sentence in the source text. Second, an abstractive summary is generated on the basis of the extracted sentences by the extractive model. This combination of VAE and PGN mechanisms brings diversity to abstractive summaries. This sequential multi-stage processing improves performance compared to using single-stage abstraction models. We found that the proposed model performs well, achieving the best result compared to our

Proceedings of The 12th International Conference on Natural Language Generation, pages 510–515,
Tokyo, Japan, 28 Oct - 1 Nov, 2019. ©2019 Association for Computational Linguistics

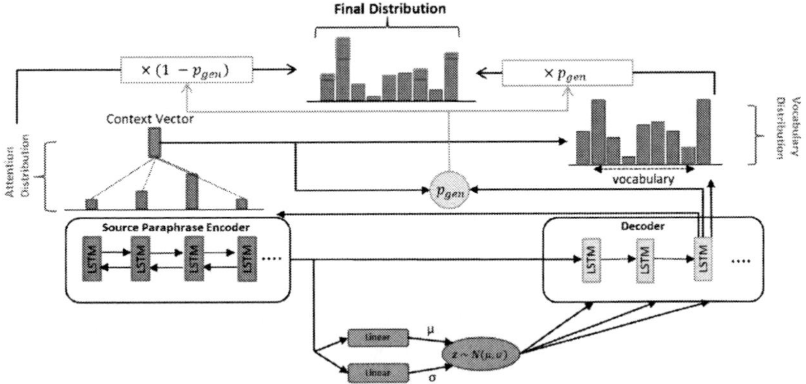

Figure 1: Overview of VAE-PGN, combining a pointer-generator network based encoding for copying the content related words and a VAE-based encoding for generating the variations.

baselines on this task.

The contributions of our work are as follows:

- We develop VAE-based PGN to address the diversity issue and generate abstractive summaries.
- We propose a new architecture that excludes less important information at the first stage.

2 Related Work

2.1 Extractive Summarization

Zhang et al. (2018) use a latent variable extractive model where sentences are viewed as latent variables and sentences with activated variables are used to infer gold summaries. Dong et al. (2018) utilize a policy gradient reinforcement learning algorithm to select a sequence of sentences that maximize ROUGE scores. Zhou et al. (2018) use a novel end-to-end neural network framework for extractive document summarization by jointly learning to score and select sentences. Motivated by BERT (Devlin et al., 2018), which has achieved state-of-the-art performance on multiple NLP tasks, Liu (2019b) use a fine-tuned BERT model to score the sentences. This model is used by our work for extractive summarization module.

2.2 Abstractive Summarization

The work on attention-based encoder-decoder models (Rush et al., 2015; Chopra et al., 2016) created a surge of research interest in text generation approaches. Recent abstractive summarization models adopt the attention mechanism (Bahdanau et al., 2015), and a pointer-network to copy

infrequent words and entities to the target sentence (See et al., 2017; Gülçehre et al., 2016; Nallapati et al., 2016; Gu et al., 2016). Gehrmann et al. (2018) use content selector that can be used for a bottom-up attention that restricts the ability of abstractive summarizers to copy words from the source text.

2.3 Diversity

In this work, the diversity of summarization refers to generating words that are different from the source text. VAEs have become more and more popular (Hu et al., 2017; Shen et al., 2017) in generating diverse sentences through learning a high-level latent variable representation of the context. Bowman et al. (2015) points out that generating sentences from a continuous space like VAE is of higher grammatical quality compared to other techniques such as Beam Search.

3 Proposed Architecture

In this section, we explain the proposed architecture to resolve the problems discussed above.

3.1 VAE-PGN Model

As illustrated in Figure 1, the proposed model is based on two main components, the pointer-generator network, and the VAE mechanism. We incorporate the vanilla VAE to learn a representation of source text that captures the complex semantic structures underlying the text. The latent representation from the VAE component is combined with the pointer-generator component to generate the summary at the decoder.

An LSTM encoder encodes source text. From the final state of the encoder, we sample a latent variable over a Gaussian distribution. An LSTM decoder is used to generate the summary. Each decoding step uses the latent variable from the encoder and an attention mechanism to generate a probability distribution over the vocabulary. A pointer-generator network is used in tandem to aid in copying words from the source text.

Now we define the notations used in the rest of the paper. We represent the training data as $\{s_i, t_i\}_{i=1}^{N}$. It contains N content-summary pairs. $s = (w_1^s, w_2^s, ..., w_p^s)$ represents source text of length p, and $t = (w_1^t, w_2^t, ..., w_q^t)$ represents the target summary of length q. The source and target embeddings of a word w_i, are represented as $e_{w_i}^s$ and $e_{w_i}^t$ respectively.

The embeddings of words from the source text are encoded by a bidirectional LSTM Encoder.

$$h^s = ENC_e^s(e_{w_1}^s, e_{w_2}^s, e_{w_3}^s, ..., e_{w_p}^s) \quad (1)$$

where ENC_e^s is the bidirectional LSTM encoder and h^s is the final encoder state of the source text. Since we use a bi-directional encoder, the hidden states of forward and backward encoder are concatenated, and passed through a feed-forward network to get h^s. The final state of encoder is passed through two feed-forward layers to get μ and σ respectively.

$$\mu = Linear_1(h^s) \text{ and } \sigma = Linear_2(h^s) \quad (2)$$

Although $Linear_1$,$Linear_2$ layers are both feed-forward layers, they are labelled separately here to reflect that the weights are updated differently during backpropagation. The latent variable which encodes the representation of the source sentence is modelled as a one-dimensional tensor whose dimensions is a hyperparameter. We set this hyperparameter is initialized to dimensions of the encoder and decoder. A random variable from the $N(0, I)$ normal distribution is sampled and is transformed to the required $N(\mu, \sigma)$ distribution.

$$z' \sim N(0, I) \longrightarrow z \sim N(\mu, \sigma) \quad (3)$$

The LSTM decoder is initialized with the final state of the encoder h^s. The input to the decoder at every time step is $z \oplus e_{w_t}$, which is a concatenation of the latent variable z and embeddings of the previous word (e_{w_t}). During training, e_{w_t} is the embedding of the previous word of target paraphrase

and while testing, it is embedding of the word generated by the decoder at step t-1.

The loss function is the sum of the cross-entropy loss calculated between the target and the generated summary, the Coverage loss, and the Kullback-Leibler Divergence (KL-D) loss calculated between the N(0, I) distribution and the generated $N(\mu, \sigma)$ distribution. The loss function can be formalized as follows:

$$L(\theta, \phi; x^s, x^t) = E_{q_\phi(z|x^s)}[log p_\theta(x^t|z, x^s)]$$
$$+\lambda \sum_i min(a_i^t, c_i^t) - KL(q_\phi(z|x^s)||p(z)) \quad (4)$$

3.2 Multi-Stage Architecture

Gehrmann et al. (2018) studies the effect of eliminating duplicate or insignificant words by performing a word-level content selection. Motivated by the content selection, we use a sentence level selection before generating an abstractive summary as described by the Algorithm 1.

Algorithm 1 Multi-Stage Architecture

1: Train two language models, one using BERT-SUM for extractive summarization and the other using PGN or VAE-PGN for abstractive summarization.
2: Get scores for sentences from the source text using BERTSUM
3: Reorder the sentences using Algorithm 2
4: Generate abstractive summary using the Abstractive model (PGN or VAE-PGN)

We obtain a score for each sentence through a high-performance extractive summarization model based on fine-tuned BERT called BERT-SUM (Liu, 2019b). The scored sentences are then reordered using the Algorithm 2. Also, the number of input sentences for the abstractive summary was selected dynamically according to the parameter min_words in Algorithm 2. This hyperparameter is tuned based on the average target summary length of a given dataset. As a result, abstractive summarization can be performed with the filtered input in which the unimportant sentences are removed.

4 Experiments

4.1 Datasets and Experimental Setup

TL;DR Reddit corpus (Völske et al., 2017): This is the dataset for the TL;DR challenge. They pro-

Algorithm 2 Order Preserving Selection

1: $A = list(< sentence, id, score >)$
2: **procedure** REORDER(A)
3:     $sortedA = sortByScore(A)$
4:     $maxcount = getmax(sortedA)$
5:     $trimA = sortedA[0 : maxcount]$
6:     $reorderedA = sortById(trimA)$
7:     **return** $reorderdA$
8: **end procedure**
9: **procedure** GETMAX(A)
10:     **for** $< sentence, id, score >$ in A **do**
11:         $words$ += no. of words in $sentence$
12:         $maxcount$ += 1
13:         **if** $words > min\_words$ **then**
14:             **break**
15:         **end if**
16:     **end for**
17:     **return** $maxcount$
18: **end procedure**

---

vide a corpus consisting of approximately 3 million content-summary pairs mined from Reddit. The competition organizers split the dataset into training, validation and test datasets.

CNN/Daily Mail corpus (Hermann et al., 2015; Nallapati et al., 2016): We use the non-anonymized version (See et al., 2017) of the dataset which contains pairs of online news articles and their summaries. The dataset contains approximately 287,000 training pairs, 13,368 validation pairs, and 11,490 testing pairs.

The VAE implementation of paper Bowman et al. (2015), Gavrilov (2017) and the PGN implementation of paper See et al. (2017), Kumar (2019) are used as references for abstractive module. The BERTSUM implementation of paper Liu (2019b), Liu (2019a) is used as a reference for the extractive module.

Extractive Summarization and Abstractive Summarization modules are finetuned on each datasets for obtaining respetive results. Apart from the minimum words generated, we borrow all hyperparameters from baseline code implementations. The min_words parameter is tuned by setting it to the average target summary length and doing to a grid-search based fine-tuning around the initialized value.

4.2 Metrics and Baselines

ROUGE (Lin, 2004) metric is used as an automatic evaluation metric. Rouge-N (R-n) scores refer to the n-gram overlap between the generated and the reference summary. Rouge-L (R-L) score refers to the Longest Common Subsequence based overlap score. All scores are calculated using the virtual machine provided by competition (2018) on the TIRA platform that uses the tagucci (2019) project to calculate the scores. We compared models using a validation set, choose the best scored models and then evaluated them on the official test set due to resource and time constraints.

PGN is the pointer-generator model with copy and coverage mechanism. **VAE-PGN** is the VAE-based pointer-generator model with copy and coverage mechanism as shown in Figure 1. **Unified PGN** and **Unified VAE-PGN** refer to the Unified Architecture with PGN and VAE-PGN models used for respective abstractive summarization modules.

4.3 Results

Table 1: Results on CNN-DM test dataset

Model	R-1	R-2	R-L
PGN	38.86	16.70	35.38
VAE-PGN	39.06	16.93	**35.61**
Unified PGN	39.00	16.65	29.08
Unified VAE-PGN	**39.32**	**17.07**	29.43

The results on the test set of CNN/Daily Mail dataset are presented in Table 1. The results show that VAE-PGN model performs better than the PGN model by achieving higher ROUGE scores. Although the unified model increases the R-1 and R-2 scores on both the abstractive models, there is a reduction in R-L score. We expect this decline to be caused by using different tokenization techniques used in the abstractive model (uses Stanford NLP tokenizer) and the extractive model (uses BERT tokenizer).

Table 2: Results on Reddit data validation set

Model	R-1	R-2	R-L
PGN	18	3	13
VAE-PGN	18	3	12
Unified PGN	19	4	**15**
Unified VAE-PGN	**20**	4	14

Table 3: Results on Reddit data test set

Model	R-1	R-2	R-L
Unified PGN	19	4	15
Unified VAE-PGN	19	4	15

The results on the validation set and the test set are presented in Table 2 and Table 3 respectively. The results show that the unified architecture model outperforms the abstractive model on both VAE and VAE-PGN based models and also the Unified VAE-PGN model gets a better R-1 score than Unified PGN on the validation set. But Unified PGN and Unified VAE-PGN model perform almost similarly on the test set.

5 Conclusions

In this paper, we propose a Unified VAE-PGN model and an effective multi-stage architecture for abstractive summarization. Our model eliminates non-critical information at sentence-level and also generates diverse summaries using a continuous space representation of the information. We evaluate our models on the benchmark Reddit datasets as part of the TL;DR challenge and show that our proposed models outperform the baseline models. We plan to include content selection, eliminating word-level non-critical information in the multi-stage architecture in future work.

Acknowledgments

The authors would like to thank Katarzyna Beksa and Katarzyna Podlaska for their helpful review and suggestions.

References

Dzmitry Bahdanau, Kyunghyun Cho, and Yoshua Bengio. 2015. Neural machine translation by jointly learning to align and translate. In *ICLR*.

Freek Boutkan, Jorn Ranzijn, David Rau, and Eelco van der Wel. 2019. Point-less: More abstractive summarization with pointer-generator networks. *CoRR*, abs/1905.01975.

Samuel R. Bowman, Luke Vilnis, Oriol Vinyals, Andrew M. Dai, Rafal Józefowicz, and Samy Bengio. 2015. Generating sentences from a continuous space. *CoRR*, abs/1511.06349.

Kushal Chawla, Kundan Krishna, and Balaji Vasan Srinivasan. 2019. Improving generation quality of pointer networks via guided attention. *CoRR*, abs/1901.11492.

Sumit Chopra, Michael Auli, and Alexander M. Rush. 2016. Abstractive sentence summarization with attentive recurrent neural networks. In *Proceedings of the 2016 Conference of the North American Chapter of the Association for Computational Linguistics: Human Language Technologies*, pages 93–98, San Diego, California. Association for Computational Linguistics.

TL;DR competition. 2018. Tl;dr the abstractive summarization challenge.

Jacob Devlin, Ming-Wei Chang, Kenton Lee, and Kristina Toutanova. 2018. BERT: pre-training of deep bidirectional transformers for language understanding. *CoRR*, abs/1810.04805.

Yue Dong, Yikang Shen, Eric Crawford, Herke van Hoof, and Jackie Chi Kit Cheung. 2018. Banditsum: Extractive summarization as a contextual bandit. *CoRR*, abs/1809.09672.

Daniil Gavrilov. 2017. pytorch_rvae.

Sebastian Gehrmann, Yuntian Deng, and Alexander M. Rush. 2018. Bottom-up abstractive summarization. *CoRR*, abs/1808.10792.

Jiatao Gu, Zhengdong Lu, Hang Li, and Victor O. K. Li. 2016. Incorporating copying mechanism in sequence-to-sequence learning. *CoRR*, abs/1603.06393.

Çaglar Gülçehre, Sungjin Ahn, Ramesh Nallapati, Bowen Zhou, and Yoshua Bengio. 2016. Pointing the unknown words. *CoRR*, abs/1603.08148.

Karl Moritz Hermann, Tomás Kociský, Edward Grefenstette, Lasse Espeholt, Will Kay, Mustafa Suleyman, and Phil Blunsom. 2015. Teaching machines to read and comprehend. *CoRR*, abs/1506.03340.

Zhiting Hu, Zichao Yang, Xiaodan Liang, Ruslan Salakhutdinov, and Eric P. Xing. 2017. Controllable text generation. *CoRR*, abs/1703.00955.

Atul Kumar. 2019. pytorch_rvae.

Chin-Yew Lin. 2004. ROUGE: A package for automatic evaluation of summaries. In *Text Summarization Branches Out*, pages 74–81, Barcelona, Spain. Association for Computational Linguistics.

Yang Liu. 2019a. Bertsum.

Yang Liu. 2019b. Fine-tune BERT for extractive summarization. *CoRR*, abs/1903.10318.

Ramesh Nallapati, Bing Xiang, and Bowen Zhou. 2016. Sequence-to-sequence rnns for text summarization. *CoRR*, abs/1602.06'023.

Alexander M. Rush, Sumit Chopra, and Jason Weston. 2015. A neural attention model for abstractive sentence summarization. *CoRR*, abs/1509.00685.

Abigail See, Peter J. Liu, and Christopher D. Manning. 2017. Get to the point: Summarization with pointer-generator networks. *CoRR*, abs/1704.04368.

Tianxiao Shen, Tao Lei, Regina Barzilay, and Tommi Jaakkola. 2017. Style transfer from non-parallel text by cross-alignment. In I. Guyon, U. V. Luxburg, S. Bengio, H. Wallach, R. Fergus, S. Vishwanathan, and R. Garnett, editors, *Advances in Neural Information Processing Systems 30*, pages 6830–6841. Curran Associates, Inc.

tagucci. 2019. pythonrouge.

Michael Völske, Martin Potthast, Shahbaz Syed, and Benno Stein. 2017. TL;DR: Mining Reddit to learn automatic summarization. In *Proceedings of the Workshop on New Frontiers in Summarization*, pages 59–63, Copenhagen, Denmark. Association for Computational Linguistics.

Xingxing Zhang, Mirella Lapata, Furu Wei, and Ming Zhou. 2018. Neural latent extractive document summarization. *CoRR*, abs/1808.07187.

Qingyu Zhou, Nan Yang, Furu Wei, Shaohan Huang, Ming Zhou, and Tiejun Zhao. 2018. Neural document summarization by jointly learning to score and select sentences. *CoRR*, abs/1807.02305.

Generating Abstractive Summaries with Finetuned Language Models

Sebastian Gehrmann*
Harvard SEAS

Zachary M. Ziegler*
Harvard SEAS

Alexander M. Rush
Harvard SEAS

`{gehrmann@seas,zziegler@g,srush@seas}.harvard.edu`

Abstract

Neural abstractive document summarization is commonly approached by models that exhibit a mostly extractive behavior. This behavior is facilitated by a copy-attention which allows models to copy words from a source document. While models in the mostly extractive news summarization domain benefit from this inductive bias, they commonly fail to paraphrase or compress information from the source document. Recent advances in transfer-learning from large pretrained language models give rise to alternative approaches that do not rely on copy-attention and instead learn to generate concise and abstractive summaries. In this paper, as part of the TL;DR challenge, we compare the abstractiveness of summaries from different summarization approaches and show that transfer-learning can be efficiently utilized without any changes to the model architecture. We demonstrate that the approach leads to a higher level of abstraction for a similar performance on the TL;DR challenge tasks, enabling true natural language compression.

1 Introduction

Abstractive summarization, the challenge of generating text that captures the content of a longer document, has been successfully approached by many recent deep learning systems (e.g., Rush et al., 2015; Nallapati et al., 2016). However, the most common testbed for such methods, news summarization, provides mostly extractive reference summaries which reuse long phrases from the source document. This property gave rise to extensions of neural summarization models that extract text from a source document in addition to generating new words (Vinyals et al., 2015; Gu et al., 2016). As a side-effect, many of the abstractive summarization models have an inductive bias to almost always extract text from the source document verbatim instead of paraphrasing it.

To encourage research on models that can generate summaries that are not extractive, Völske et al. (2017) developed the TL;DR corpus which comprises over three million posts and associated user-written summaries from reddit. Because of the social media nature of the dataset, the user-written summaries copy long sequences from the source much less frequently than common news summarization corpora, resulting in a truly abstractive dataset. This dataset offers the opportunity to investigate the performance of common summarization models in an abstractive setting.

In this work, which is part of the TL;DR challenge, we evaluate and analyze a number of common summarization approaches on both the standard news summarization corpus CNN-DM and the TL;DR dataset. We investigate whether the ability to copy from the source document leads to the same learned extractive behavior, even when the target summaries are mostly abstractive. We additionally evaluate whether neural summarization models can take advantage of pretrained language representation to generate more abstractive text. To measure the abstractiveness of generated summaries, we identify a general "abstractiveness" metric and compare the approaches to the ground truth data for both datasets.

Our results demonstrate that the ability to copy leads to improvements in terms of automated performance evaluation even on the TL;DR dataset, even though it leads to a significantly lower level of abstractiveness. Furthermore, we find that *all* models without pretraining exhibit a significantly higher level of extractiveness than the reference summaries, while language model pretraining allows for more abstractive behavior. Overall, these results suggest that standard summarization approaches learn an easier extractive shortcut than true natural language compression, and that this phenomena occurs even in highly abstractive data.

Proceedings of The 12th International Conference on Natural Language Generation, pages 516–522,
Tokyo, Japan, 28 Oct - 1 Nov, 2019. ©2019 Association for Computational Linguistics

2 Problem and Related Work

Throughout this study, we consider the supervised summarization problem, which aims to compress a source document of tokens $x_1, \ldots, x_m$ of length m. The aligned summary $y_1, \ldots, y_n$ has a length $n \ll m$, and aims to convey a compressed version of the source document.

Sequence-to-sequence models (S2S, Sutskever et al., 2014) are the de-facto standard for neural abstractive summarization (Rush et al., 2015; Nallapati et al., 2016). The development of models that incorporate a copy-attention mechanism for models to copy word from source documents, has further improved the performance (Gu et al., 2016; Vinyals et al., 2015; See et al., 2017).

However, most summarization tasks use data from news domains which have mostly extractive summaries. Among others, See et al. (2017) and Gehrmann et al. (2018) found that models learn to replicate this latent extraction behavior, and that the resulting summaries of copy-attention based models are over 95% extractive. To address this issue, related approaches have used reinforcement learning objectives to prevent the model from reusing longer phrases from the input and to be more concise (Paulus et al., 2017; Chen and Bansal, 2018; Li et al., 2018). However, these methods often suffer from ungrammatical output or much slower training while also requiring task-specific loss functions. To avoid this problem, Kim et al. (2018) and Völske et al. (2017) created reddit-based corpora with more abstractive target summaries that enable the evaluation of supervised models instead.

Since the generation of abstractive summaries requires a powerful representation of language, we investigate the use of transfer learning. Large language models based on the neural Transformer architecture (Vaswani et al., 2017) have shown promising results in language understanding tasks (Houlsby et al., 2019; Devlin et al., 2018; Chronopoulou et al., 2019), but so far have had limited success in generation tasks (Zhang et al., 2019). Most recently, the pseudo-self attention method for fine-tuning language models to generation tasks has been introduced which may allow the application of transfer-learning to abstractive summarization (Ziegler et al., 2019). In this work, we compare this approach to strong baselines that rely on minor modifications of the Transformer (Gehrmann et al., 2018).

3 Methods

3.1 Models

We consider the following models for neural abstractive summarization. All models are sequence-to-sequence models with attention (Bahdanau et al., 2014), but differ in architecture, use of a copy mechanism, and language model pretraining.

LSTM As a baseline we consider a bidirectional LSTM encoder and uni-directional LSTM decoder with attention from Luong et al. (2015).

LSTM+Copy We additionally consider the same LSTM model equipped with the copy attention mechanism from See et al. (2017). At each time step the approach reuses the normal alignment distribution as a distribution over source words to copy. This copy distribution is combined with the standard target vocabulary distribution from the decoder via a binary switch z_t that is predicted at each time step t.

Transformer(+Copy) For the transformer baselines, we replace the LSTM architecture in the encoder and decoder with transformers (Vaswani et al., 2017). As in the LSTM case we consider version with and without the copy mechanism. Similarly to Gehrmann et al. (2018), we randomly select one of the attention heads as the source of the copy distribution and otherwise follow the same procedure as for the LSTM+Copy.

Transformer+Pretrain Pretrained language models lead to significant performance improvements across a wide range of natural language understanding tasks (Devlin et al., 2018). The recently introduced pseudo self attention method (Ziegler et al., 2019) has also demonstrated strong performance across different generation tasks. The pseudo self attention model follows the same architecture as the original transformer, with minor modifications to inject the context information into the decoder while keeping the structure of the decoder similar to that of an unconditional language model. Most importantly, on the decoder side the context-attention block is removed and the self-attention block is modified to use the source information via pseudo self attention. The normal transformer self-attention computation from Vaswani et al. (2017) can be written most generally as

$$\text{SA}(Y) = \text{softmax}\left((YW_q)(YW_k)^\top\right)(YW_v)$$

where $Y \in T \times D$ is the input and $W_k, W_v, W_q \in D \times D'$ are parameters. In comparison, the pseudo self attention computation is

$$\text{PSA}(X, Y) =$$
$$\text{softmax}\left((YW_q)\begin{bmatrix}XU_k\\YW_k\end{bmatrix}^\top\right)\begin{bmatrix}XU_v\\YW_v\end{bmatrix}$$

where $X \in S \times D$ is the output of the transformer encoder representing the source document and $U_k, U_v \in D \times D'$ are additional parameters.

As in Ziegler et al. (2019), We use the "small" GPT-2 (Radford et al., 2019) as a pretrained unidirectional transformer-based language model. All parameters of the decoder, including the input embeddings, self-attention weights W_k, W_v, W_q for each head and layer, feed forward weights, and layer normalization weights are initialized with the weights from the pretrained language model. The rest of the weights, including those that make up the encoder and the context projections U_k, U_v for each head and layer are randomly initialized. The model is then trained end-to-end on the supervised dataset without fixing any parameters.

Compared to a fully randomly initialized model, the pretrained model has a strong inductive bias towards abstractive generation. Whereas the decoder in a randomly initialized model can learn a generative procedure that largely extracts sequences from the source, the pseudo self attention decoder is initialized with a decoder that already generates coherent language. It may thus be easier for the model to learn to use the source as "inspiration" for the generated text, rather than to learn an entirely different extractive generative procedure. Our experiments aim to quantify this intuition.

3.2 Metric

% novel n-grams One metric used in the literature as a proxy for abstractiveness is the percent of n-grams in the summary that are not found in the source document (See et al., 2017). We report this metric for comparison to previous work.

n-gram abstractiveness While % novel n-grams approximately captures the correct trend, it is poorly normalized: consider a source document

The dog runs around. A cat jumps up. The brown horse stands and the corresponding summary *The dog runs around. The brown horse stands.* The 4-gram novelty score would identify 4-grams such as *around. The brown horse* as novel, yielding a 4-gram novelty score of 60% even though the summary is composed entirely of copied 4-grams (i.e. a true novelty score should measure 0%). To remedy this, we propose an alternate metric denoted "n-gram abstractiveness":

$$\text{n-gram abstractiveness} =$$
$$1 - \frac{\text{\# summary words part of n-gram copied}}{\text{total \# summary words}}$$

To calculate this, we first generate the set of n-grams in the source and summary. All words in the summary which are part of n-grams in the intersection of the two sets are counted as "# summary words part of n-gram copied". Since this (normalized) quantity gives an indication of the fraction of the summary that is copied in n-grams from the source, 1 minus this quantity gives an indication for the abstractiveness of the summary at the n-gram level.

4 Experiments

We compare the presented methods on the nonanonymized CNN-DM dataset (Hermann et al., 2015) and the TL;DR challenge dataset (Völske et al., 2017). CNN-DM comprises roughly 290,000 training examples, which are pruned at a maximum length of 400 words. The corpus is highly extractive, as only 14.0% of tokens in the output do not appear in the corresponding input. Even when we ignore all stopwords, only 17.7% of tokens are novel.

The TL;DR challenge dataset is composed of over three million examples, mined from comments across reddit. We apply the same 400 word pruning to the dataset.The corpus exhibits a much more abstractive behavior, as 53.6% of tokens in the target are novel. After excluding stopwords, this number increases to over 71.4%. That means that this dataset requires a much better text-generating model than CNN-DM.

First baseline models trained on the TL;DR data exhibited a problem that is commonly seen in conversational models in that it defaults to the most simple answer. The simplest answers were a combination of *This is not a problem; edit: thank*

Model	CNN-DM			TL;DR		
	R1	R2	RL	R1	R2	RL
LSTM	30.8	11.8	28.5	16	4	13
LSTM+Copy	39.0	16.8	35.7	20	5	15
Transformer	**39.9**	**17.8**	36.6	21	**6**	16
Transformer+Copy	**39.9**	17.7	**37.1**	**22**	**6**	**17**
Transformer+Pretrain	30.5	7.2	28.0	**22**	5	**17**

Table 1: The ROUGE results on the CNN-DM test set and the blind TL;DR test set.

you for the gold; and a number of insults. We thus filtered the dataset by excluding examples in which the target included the following phrases in any capitalization and including common misspellings: *I don't know*; *edit:*; *good idea*; *what I am talking about*; *worth it*; *upvote*; *downvote*; *you'll be fine*; *source:*; and ten different profanities. We further excluded all examples in which the target was shorter than 25 characters to bias the model towards longer generated texts. In total, this procedure excluded 516,000 examples.

Consistent with previous work (Paulus et al., 2017; See et al., 2017; Gehrmann et al., 2018), we find that the LSTM baselines are strongly biased towards short and repetitive summaries. To avoid this, we apply the inference-time loss functions suggested by Gehrmann et al. (2018); a coverage penalty, a length penalty, and a mechanism that prevents repetition of trigrams. We additionally set the minimum length for TL;DR to 25 tokens, which we found to works best on the validation set[1] It is not necessary to apply the same mechanisms to the Transformer-based models. For a better comparison, we only set the minimum length of TL;DR to 25.

5 Automated Evaluation

Table 1 presents the ROUGE scores on the test set for each model on the two datasets[2]. For the LSTM, adding the copy mechanism significantly improves the performance on both the CNN-DM and TL;DR datasets across R1, R2, and RL. Despite the added inference-time loss functions, the LSTM models consistently perform worse than the Transformer models. For the Transformer model, adding the copy mechanism yields a nearly identical performance on CNN-DM and slightly improved performance on TL;DR. Thus, even though the TL;DR dataset is inherently abstractive, copy-attention still improves or is at least no worse in terms of empirical performance.

Using the pretrained representations in the form of pseudo self attention without copy-attention hurts performance considerably on CNN-DM, but slightly improves performance on TL;DR. We hypothesize that this effect can be explained by the abstractiveness of the dataset. Since CNN-DM is mostly extractive, it benefits from the extractive approaches. At the same time, the inductive copying bias has only a minor positive effect on the ROUGE score of the abstractive TL;DR dataset and, thus, a more fluent abstractive summary leads to better performance. Note that here, for the sake of simplicity, we do not consider the Transformer with pseudo self attention and a copy mechanism which was reported to give strong performance in Ziegler et al. (2019).

6 Analysis

To validate our hypothesis that pretraining leads to higher abstractiveness, we evaluate the two abstractiveness metrics described in Section 3.2. The results are presented in Figure 1 for all models and the ground truth data on both CNN-DM and TL;DR.

Metric comparison Comparing the overall results for all datasets and models between the proposed n-gram abstractiveness metric and the % novel n-gram metric we find that both metrics present identical trends. The major difference is that the n-gram abstractiveness accounts for the increase in % novel n-grams as n increases, which reduces the noise and leads to a more interpretable

---

[1] We note that an increased length of generated summaries has been found to increase ROUGE scores which make comparison to other systems with different length outputs challenging (Sun et al., 2019).

[2] The TIRA system (Potthast et al., 2019) used for evaluating the TL;DR task presents scores only with the presented precision.

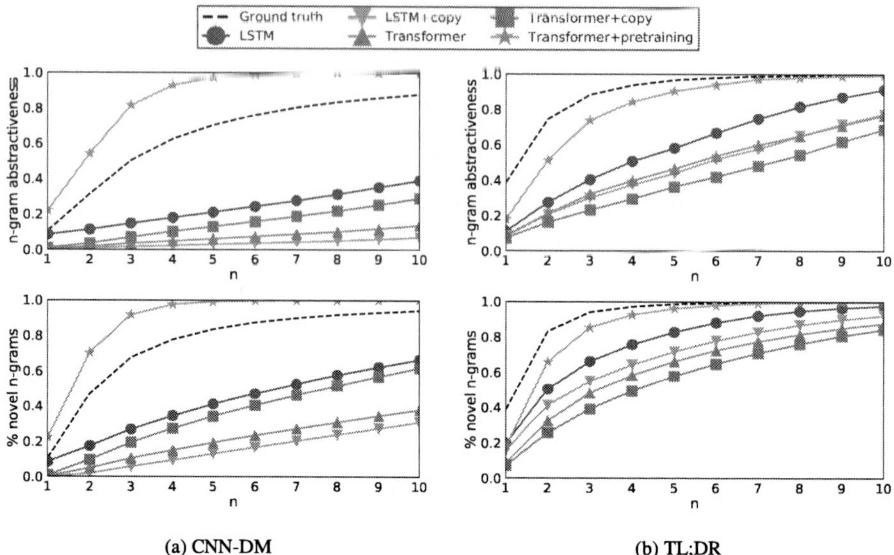

(a) CNN-DM   (b) TL;DR

Figure 1: The n-gram abstractiveness and % novel n-gram metrics for increasing n show the gap between standard abstractive approaches and the human references. For both corpora, our approach closes this gap.

result. The rest of the analysis will thus focus on the n-gram abstractiveness.

Dataset comparison Comparing the abstractiveness metrics for the reference data between the two datasets provides further evidence that TL;DR is a more abstractive dataset than CNN-DM. While the 4-gram abstractiveness of CNN-DM is only 63%, for example, the 4-gram abstractiveness of TL;DR is 94%. Still, at the higher n-gram levels CNN-DM becomes more than 80% abstractive, suggesting that less than 20% of tokens are part of very long sequences that were copied verbatim.

Randomly-initialized models All randomly initialized models show considerably more extractive behavior than the reference data, for all values of n. This trend exists even for the variants without an explicit copy mechanism and is found in both datasets. This pattern suggests that models trained from scratch may exploit an extractive shortcut which is easier to learn than abstractive data compression.

The addition of a copy mechanism decreases the abstractiveness for all pairs studied expect for the Transformer on CNN-DM. This general trend aligns with the intuition that an explicit copy mechanism allows the model to exploit this easier-to-learn extractive behavior.

Pretraining Compared to the other models, the pseudo self attention pretraining approach leads to a much higher level of abstractiveness. This provides evidence that unlike the randomly initialized models which learn an extractive shortcut, the pretrained model has a strong inductive bias toward abstractive behavior. It is unclear whether this is an artifact of the specific pseudo self attention method or a more general consequence of pretraining for conditional generation.

7 Conclusion

In this paper we study the summarization performance and abstractiveness of summarization models with and without copy attention and pretraining. Combining these two sets of evidence, we find that often the models which perform better are less abstractive, even when the dataset itself is highly abstractive. It is thus challenging to attribute value to abstractiveness when a model is evaluated purely based on its ROUGE score. Our results suggest that if the goal is solely summarization performance, perhaps more extractive models are well suited for this task. Importantly, however, our study emphasizes that despite the performance, we should not be fooled into believing that state-of-the-art summarization models are learning true semantic natural language compression.

Acknowledgements

SG is supported by a Siebel Scholarship. AMR and ZMZ are support by NSF 1845664 and Intel research.

References

Dzmitry Bahdanau, Kyunghyun Cho, and Yoshua Bengio. 2014. Neural machine translation by jointly learning to align and translate. *CoRR*, abs/1409.0473.

Yen-Chun Chen and Mohit Bansal. 2018. Fast abstractive summarization with reinforce-selected sentence rewriting. *arXiv preprint arXiv:1805.11080.*

Alexandra Chronopoulou, Christos Baziotis, and Alexandros Potamianos. 2019. An Embarrassingly Simple Approach for Transfer Learning from Pretrained Language Models.

Jacob Devlin, Ming-Wei Chang, Kenton Lee, and Kristina Toutanova. 2018. BERT: Pre-training of Deep Bidirectional Transformers for Language Understanding.

Sebastian Gehrmann, Yuntian Deng, and Alexander Rush. 2018. Bottom-up abstractive summarization. In *Proceedings of the 2018 Conference on Empirical Methods in Natural Language Processing*, pages 4098–4109.

Jiatao Gu, Zhengdong Lu, Hang Li, and Victor OK Li. 2016. Incorporating copying mechanism in sequence-to-sequence learning. *arXiv preprint arXiv:1603.06393.*

Karl Moritz Hermann, Tomas Kocisky, Edward Grefenstette, Lasse Espeholt, Will Kay, Mustafa Suleyman, and Phil Blunsom. 2015. Teaching machines to read and comprehend. In *Advances in Neural Information Processing Systems*, pages 1693–1701.

Neil Houlsby, Andrei Giurgiu, Stanislaw Jastrzebski, Bruna Morrone, Quentin de Laroussilhe, Andrea Gesmundo, Mona Attariyan, and Sylvain Gelly. 2019. Parameter-Efficient Transfer Learning for NLP.

Byeongchang Kim, Hyunwoo Kim, and Gunhee Kim. 2018. Abstractive summarization of reddit posts with multi-level memory networks. *arXiv preprint arXiv:1811.00783.*

Piji Li, Lidong Bing, and Wai Lam. 2018. Actor-critic based training framework for abstractive summarization. *arXiv preprint arXiv:1803.11070.*

Thang Luong, Hieu Pham, and Christopher D Manning. 2015. Effective approaches to attention-based neural machine translation. In *Proceedings of the 2015 Conference on Empirical Methods in Natural Language Processing*, pages 1412–1421.

Ramesh Nallapati, Bowen Zhou, Caglar Gulcehre, Bing Xiang, et al. 2016. Abstractive text summarization using sequence-to-sequence rnns and beyond. *arXiv preprint arXiv:1602.06023.*

Romain Paulus, Caiming Xiong, and Richard Socher. 2017. A deep reinforced model for abstractive summarization. *arXiv preprint arXiv:1705.04304.*

Martin Potthast, Tim Gollub, Matti Wiegmann, and Benno Stein. 2019. TIRA Integrated Research Architecture. In Nicola Ferro and Carol Peters, editors, *Information Retrieval Evaluation in a Changing World - Lessons Learned from 20 Years of CLEF*. Springer.

Alec Radford, Jeffrey Wu, Rewon Child, David Luan, Dario Amodei, and Ilya Sutskever. 2019. Language Models are Unsupervised Multitask Learners.

Alexander M Rush, Sumit Chopra, and Jason Weston. 2015. A neural attention model for abstractive sentence summarization. *arXiv preprint arXiv:1509.00685.*

Abigail See, Peter J Liu, and Christopher D Manning. 2017. Get to the point: Summarization with pointer-generator networks. *arXiv preprint arXiv:1704.04368.*

Simeng Sun, Ori Shapira, Ido Dagan, and Ani Nenkova. 2019. How to compare summarizers without target length? pitfalls, solutions and re-examination of the neural summarization literature. In *Proceedings of the Workshop on Methods for Optimizing and Evaluating Neural Language Generation*, pages 21–29.

Ilya Sutskever, Oriol Vinyals, and Quoc V Le. 2014. Sequence to sequence learning with neural networks. In *Advances in neural information processing systems*, pages 3104–3112.

Ashish Vaswani, Noam Shazeer, Niki Parmar, Jakob Uszkoreit, Llion Jones, Aidan N Gomez, Łukasz Kaiser, and Illia Polosukhin. 2017. Attention is all you need. In *Advances in Neural Information Processing Systems*, pages 6000–6010.

Oriol Vinyals, Meire Fortunato, and Navdeep Jaitly. 2015. Pointer networks. In *Advances in Neural Information Processing Systems*, pages 2692–2700.

Michael Völske, Martin Potthast, Shahbaz Syed, and Benno Stein. 2017. TL;DR: Mining Reddit to Learn Automatic Summarization. In *EMNLP 2017 Workshop on New Frontiers in Summarization*, pages 59–63. Association for Computational Linguistics.

Haoyu Zhang, Yeyun Gong, Yu Yan, Nan Duan, Jianjun Xu, Ji Wang, Ming Gong, and Ming Zhou. 2019. Pretraining-Based Natural Language Generation for Text Summarization.

Zachary M Ziegler, Luke Melas-Kyriazi, Sebastian Gehrmann, and Alexander M Rush. 2019. Encoder-agnostic adaptation for conditional language generation. *arXiv preprint arXiv:1908.06938.*

Towards Summarization for Social Media

Results of the TL;DR Challenge

Shahbaz Syed[a]   Michael Völske[b]   Nedim Lipka[c]   Benno Stein[b]   Hinrich Schütze[d]   Martin Potthast[a]

[a]Leipzig University   [b]Bauhaus-Universität Weimar   [c]Adobe Research   [d]LMU Munich

Abstract

With most summarization research focused on the news domain and scientific papers, little is known about the capabilities of the state of the art at summarizing more informal text. Today, the vast majority of text on the web is informally written on social media, and staying on top of the fast-paced stream of posts originating from one's subscriptions and followees is a burden to many. The TL;DR challenge marks a first step towards developing new summarization technology for social media, focusing on abstractive summarization. This paper reports the results of the challenge and describes our manual evaluation of the submissions. Finally, we discuss the expected properties of a good summary after analyzing the comments provided by human annotators.

1 Introduction

Current research on abstractive summarization focuses primarily on the genre of news. This can be attributed to the ease of obtaining large amounts of news articles alongside suitable summary ground truth, greatly simplifying the corpus construction. However, the summaries found in the currently widely used corpora are either only highlights directly extracted from news articles, offering little abstraction and no coherent text, or headlines, which are short and not necessarily summaries, albeit occasionally abstractive. Furthermore, the common structure of news articles[1] introduces bias, since the lead paragraph usually already captures the most relevant information (Kedzie et al., 2018).

To foster the development of robust summarization technology, we need to venture off the beaten track and explore more diverse domains. In this regard, the recently published Webis-TLDR-17 corpus (Völske et al., 2017) provides for the first English summarization corpus from the domain of social media, consisting of 3 million posts alongside so-called TL;DR summaries.[2] The summaries found in this corpus are true summaries provided by the authors of a post, they often abstract over a subject matter, and they cover a much wider range of topics than generally found in news articles. Table 1 shows a comparison of the nature of ground truth summaries in the news and the social media domain. With permission from its creators, we used this corpus to organize the TL;DR challenge (Syed et al., 2018), inviting summarization researchers to test existing models as well as new ones. To ensure reproducibility as well as blind and semi-automatic evaluation, we adopted the cloud-based evaluation platform TIRA (Potthast et al., 2019). In addition to the automatic ROUGE metrics, we evaluate the submissions manually for summary effectiveness and text quality via crowdsourcing. In this paper, we report our findings, discuss what annotators consider when scoring summaries, and outline future directions for abstractive summarization research.

2 Related Work

Shared tasks on automatic summarization were first introduced at the Document Understanding Conferences (DUC).[3] In addition to new summarization technology, equal emphasis was given to formulating strong evaluation measures. Methods such as basic elements (Hovy et al., 2006), pyramid (Nenkova and Passonneau, 2004), and ROUGE (Lin, 2004) were introduced for automatically evaluating the content selection capabilities of the participating systems. Furthermore, Dang (2005) presented the first guideline for manually judging summary quality. In 2008, DUC became a summarization track at the Text Analysis Conference

---

[1]https://en.wikipedia.org/wiki/News_style

[2]TL;DR, short for "too long; didn't read", is a cliché reply bemoaning a post's excessive length, and has given rise to a practice of adding a summary at the end of long posts, introduced by that same letter sequence or variants thereof.
[3]https://www-nlpir.nist.gov/projects/duc/index.html

Proceedings of The 12th International Conference on Natural Language Generation, pages 523–528,
Tokyo, Japan, 28 Oct - 1 Nov, 2019. ©2019 Association for Computational Linguistics

Example - CNN/DailyMail Corpus

Article

NASA will launch Space Shuttle Endeavour on February 7, which will be the first of five launches this year before the shuttle fleet is retired. Endeavour will blast off from the Kennedy Space Center in Florida on a 13-day mission to the international space station. The mission will include three spacewalks, NASA said. The shuttle will also deliver the final U.S. portion of the space station. This portion will provide more room for crew members. NASA plans to retire its space shuttles Discovery, Endeavour and Atlantis later this year. The space agency has been looking for places, such as museums, to house the shuttles after they are retired. Space Shuttle Discovery will be transferred to the Smithsonian National Air and Space Museum in Washington. The privilege of showing off a shuttle won't be cheap – about $29 million, NASA said.

Highlights

- This will be first of five launches this year before the shuttle fleet is retired

- NASA is scheduled to launch Space Shuttle Endeavour on February 7.

- Shuttle will deliver final U.S. portion of the international space station

- NASA has been looking for places to house the shuttles once they are retired

Example- Webis-TLDR-17 Corpus

Post

I'm so upset at myself. My boyfriend surprised me with an amazing, fancy dinner for our one year anniversary yesterday. I already wasn't feeling well when he told me we were going to dinner but when I saw what he planned I didn't have the heart to tell him I wasn't that hungry. In the end I pushed myself to eat the fixed menu he ordered for us and the bill was over 500, I couldn't handle it and after dessert I ended up going to the bathroom and throwing it all up.

I can't believe I wasted so much of his money and am so disappointed in myself for not speaking up and simply saying I didn't feel well. I feel like I've wasted the effort he put into planning this. I also feel like I missed out on some amazing food that we would usually never splurge for. He doesn't know I threw it up and I just told him I loved it because regardless of how I felt health wise I loved that he put in so much effort to make sure I felt special. But I can't stop stewing in my own feelings. Help.

TL;DR

my boyfriend is amazing and bought us an expensive anniversary dinner. Threw it all up, he doesn't know. Feel horrible guilt and FOMO

Table 1: Comparison of summary styles from the CNN/DailyMail and the Webis-TLDR-17 corpus. Emphasized text shows the extractive nature of the summary (highlights) for the news domain. The highlights are concatenated and used as the target summary for training summarization models. In contrast, the example from the Webis-TLDR-17 corpus exhibits higher abstraction, abbreviations and composition of multiple facts into single phrases.

(TAC)[4] with evaluation as an independent task (Automatically Evaluating Summaries of Peers, AESOP). Most of these efforts were limited to extractive summarization on comparably small datasets from specific domains, such as biomedical records, newswire articles, and opinions, since neural text generation had not yet become mainstream, rendering abstractive summarization much more difficult.

The first attempt at abstractive summarization was presented by Rush et al. (2015), which resulted in a subsequent surge in neural summarization research yielding promising results—we refer to Shi et al. (2018) for a comprehensive review. However, as most recent models have been evaluated exclusively on news corpora, our knowledge of their full capabilities is still superficial. Through the TL;DR challenge, we hope to close this gap.

3 Survey of Submissions

Out of 16 registered participants, we received 5 submissions from 3 participants (2 from industry). In addition, we provided a `seq2seq-baseline` model with 2 layers, bi-LSTM, 256 hidden units and no attention. Participants trained models at their own premises and deployed them to a virtual machine on TIRA. Via TIRA's web interface, scripts were configured to generate summaries for a hidden test set and then remotely executed. Multiple runs were allowed for each participant.[5] Each run was fed to an automatic evaluator script to compute ROUGE scores. Each software and evaluator run on the test set was manually reviewed by organizers for errors and data leakage. After a successful review,

---

[4]https://tac.nist.gov/

[5]Evaluating models on TIRA using ROUGE was allowed even after the submission deadline. Thus, a participant's technical paper may have a variation of the same model with different ROUGE scores, but was not manually evaluated.

the scores were shared on a public leaderboard.[6] Two participants provided their system descriptions. We did not receive any description for the `tldr-bottom-up` model.

Gehrmann et al. (2019) leveraged fine-tuned language models to generate abstractive summaries. They argue that excessive copying facilitated by the copy-attention mechanism hinders paraphrasing and information compression (abstraction). As part of the TL;DR challenge, they compared two summarization approaches (`pseudo-self-attn` and `transf-seq2seq`) demonstrating the effectiveness of transfer learning at generating abstractive summaries. Our manual evaluation confirms that these models generate concise and coherent summaries.

Tackling the same problem of excessive copying in pointer-generator models, Choi et al. (2019) proposed using Variational Autoencoder (VAE) in combination with an extractive summarization model. The `unified-pgn` model uses a BERT-based extractive model that is fine-tuned to select important sentences, which are then summarized using a pointer-generator network. In order to introduce diversity, the `unified-vae-pgn` model uses a VAE for generating summaries of the extracted important sentences. This multi-stage architecture preserves a substantial amount of key information while generating acceptable summaries as revealed in our manual evaluation. We refer readers to the system description papers for further details.

4 Evaluation

Summarization evaluation measures based on the n-gram overlap between an automatically generated summary and a ground truth summary give good approximations of a summarizer's content selection capabilities. They are thus widely adopted and the de facto standard for the evaluation of extractive summarization technology. For lack of better alternatives, however, these measures have also been directly applied to abstractive summarization, where higher n-gram overlap does not necessarily indicate higher quality in terms of abstraction. In general, the measures employed to date also fail to capture situations where generated summaries are better than the corresponding ground truth summaries, since the latter must be considered only one of many possible alternative summarizations. Therefore, besides computing a standard measure, we also carry out a series of manual assessments

via crowdsourcing to evaluate both the sufficiency and the text quality of a generated abstractive summary. Below, after reviewing both approaches, we report on the results of the participating systems.

4.1 Automatic Evaluation

We begin with a novelty analysis as per See et al. (2017), calculating the fraction of n-grams in the summary that are absent from the text as its novelty (Table 2). The ground truth has the highest novelty, underlining the abstractive nature of self-authored summaries. Next, we used ROUGE (Lin, 2004) for automatic evaluation and report the F1-scores.[7] From Table 2 it is difficult to draw any conclusions just by looking at ROUGE scores. Furthermore, a key issue of ROUGE is that it does not provide any upper bounds for the quality of a summarization system (Schluter, 2017), thus warranting an extensive manual evaluation of the systems.

Model	ROUGE			Novelty (n-grams)				Len.
	1	2	L	1	2	3	4	
unified-pgn	19	4	**15**	0.80	5.15	8.67	11.42	33.5
unified-vae-pgn	19	4	**15**	0.86	5.04	8.90	11.92	32.8
transf-seq2seq	19	**5**	14	0.82	4.28	6.44	7.54	14.5
pseudo-self-attn	18	4	13	1.49	7.21	9.54	9.98	12.1
tldr-bottom-up	**20**	4	**15**	1.90	5.29	8.32	10.73	37.3
seq2seq-baseline	3	0	2	0.00	2.27	2.47	2.05	4.9
ground truth	–	–	–	**9.48**	**21.94**	**24.86**	**25.20**	26.1

Table 2: ROUGE-1, 2, and L scores and novelty analysis for 1 to 4-grams of the generated summaries along with their average lengths in words.

4.2 Manual Evaluation

Using Amazon Mechanical Turk, we crowdsourced our manual evaluation within two tasks: preference scoring and quality scoring. One hundred randomly selected examples from the test set were scored in both tasks, where each HIT (Human Intelligence Task) was assigned to 3 workers. We employed master workers with a minimum approval rate of 95% and at least 10,000 approved HITs.[8]

Preference scoring. The DUC guidelines for manually evaluating summaries by Dang (2005) were designed for experts. Gillick and Liu (2010) reported that Mechanical Turk workers were unable

---

[6] https://www.tira.io/task/tldr-generation/

[7] https://github.com/pltrdy/rouge; we intentionally rounded off the scores in our evaluation script in order to show differences of at least one point on the ROUGE metric.

[8] We paid $0.80 per HIT for preference scoring and $0.20 for quality scoring at an average hourly rate of $8 and $825 total.

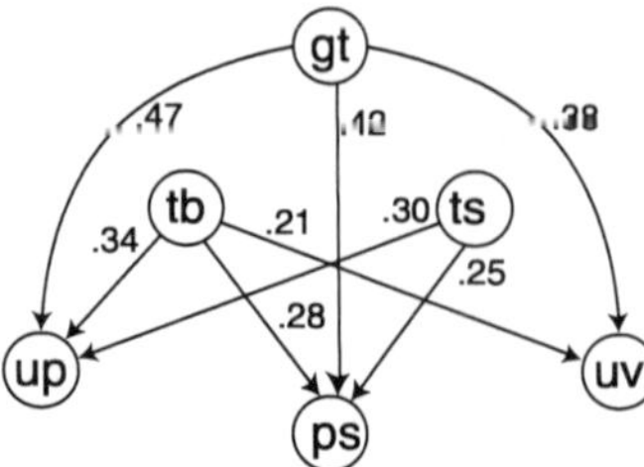

Figure 1: Summary of the preference scoring task: directed edges denote significantly higher scores ($p <$ 0.001), and are annotated with effect sizes. The baseline model is much worse in comparison and hence not included. Key: **gt**: ground truth, **tb**: tldr-bottom-up, **ps**: pseudo-self-attn, **up**: unified-pgn, **ts**: transf-seq2seq, **uv**: unified-vae-pgn.

Model	Sufficiency				Text quality			
	1	2	3	Avg.	1	2	3	Avg.
unified-pgn	2	38	60	2.11	6	68	26	1.78
unified-vae-pgn	4	30	66	2.13	9	62	29	1.78
transf-seq2seq	4	27	69	2.20	0	5	95	**2.70**
pseudo-self-attn	12	35	53	1.97	2	8	90	**2.67**
tldr-bottom-up	2	25	73	2.30	1	28	71	2.29
seq2seq-baseline	79	14	7	1.11	73	21	6	1.11
ground truth	2	8	90	**2.52**	0	15	85	2.57

Table 3: Sufficiency and text quality score distribution in the majority category.

to provide expert-like scores and had strong disagreements. Therefore, we kept the task as simple as possible: "Given a text and its summaries from all models (and the ground truth), score each summary for how well it summarizes the given text." We employed a four-point Likert scale ((1) very bad, (2) bad, (3) good, and (4) very good), since (Bishop, 1987) showed that presenting a middle alternative causes many people to choose it to escape uncertainty. Moreover, we asked for a written justification for each score. The scores collected reflect the summaries' overall quality, combining all aspects of summary quality relative to all other summaries, as perceived by the workers. Note that the summaries were shown in random order to prevent order effects. The score justifications required the workers to reflect about their judgments, and at the same time, they provide for an error analysis (see Section 4.3 for details). Moreover, the justifications allowed for double-checking whether workers actually read the summaries while scoring. Figure 1 shows which pairs of systems have significant differences along with effect sizes.[9]

Quality Scoring. Our second evaluation task was to independently assess a model's summaries across two specific qualitative dimensions. We adopt the term *sufficiency* to group multiple properties of a summary, such as informativeness, relevance, and focus. Similarly, *text quality* groups properties independent of the content, such as structure, coherence, grammar, and readability. In contrast to the first task, this gives workers specific goals and helps us to better differentiate between

the models. Furthermore, it may help to identify if non-expert annotators can still produce reliable judgments without a guideline. Gillick and Liu (2010) cautioned that workers have difficulties distinguishing the content of a summary from its text quality. With that in mind, we devised two orthogonal three-level rating scales. With respect to *sufficiency*, workers could rate a summary as *insufficient* (incomplete and unrelated to the source text), as *barely acceptable* (missing the main point, but capturing relevant secondary information), or as *sufficient* (capturing the main point of the text). In terms of *text quality*, we distinguished the levels *badly written* (incoherent or major errors), *needs improvement* (minor errors breaking the flow, but understandable), and *well written* (no errors, coherent, and understandable).

Table 3 shows the score distribution for both dimensions in the majority category. For text quality, multiple models perform well compared to `ground truth`. Models with longer summaries (see Table 2), require further improvement in terms of text quality despite having a similar number of sufficient summaries. To compute significance, we assign the score of a summary to be the average of sufficiency and quality score. Figure 2 shows which pairs of systems had significant differences in scores along with effect sizes.

4.3 Error Analysis: Score Justifications

We manually reviewed all 2100 justifications given during the preference scoring task, and identified the summary aspects that most frequently influenced the scores. We further categorize these reasons under the two dimensions of sufficiency and text quality as shown in Table 4. These justifications may help the participants in improving their systems, and also aid the development of new models and evaluation methodologies. Moreover, com-

---

[9]We use Mann-Whitney U for pairwise comparison using Bonferroni correction.

Sufficiency

Missing context (MC)	The summary does not provide any context, misses primary information or captures only secondary information.
Wrong sentiment (WS)	The overall sentiment of the post is either flipped or neutralized due to wrong negations.
Factually incorrect (FI)	Entities, such as names, locations, dates are wrongly reproduced, making the summary factually incorrect.
Overly simplistic (OS)	Summary lacks reasoning and necessary details making it too generic.

Text quality

Bad grammar (BG)	A bad summary contains incorrect punctuations, wrong connectives, or formatting errors.
Incoherence (IC)	Improper flow of text which renders the summary meaningless.
Repetition (RP)	Excessive repetition of tokens.
Bad continuity (BC)	Summary starts off well but later culminates to gibberish text.

Table 4: Categories of worker criticism; the score of a summary was in many cases influenced by a combination of these aspects.

Model	Sufficiency				Text quality				Pos.
	MC	WS	FI	OS	BG	IC	RP	BC	
unified-pgn	94	12	11	6	40	81	22	10	56
unified-vae-pgn	52	6	21	9	39	61	12	8	100
transf-seq2seq	102	5	15	23	2	23	1	–	128
pseudo-self-attn	106	15	38	29	1	28	4	–	83
tldr-bottom-up	61	1	25	6	20	43	1	7	137
seq2seq-baseline	–	–	–	–	–	221	68	–	0
ground truth	69	1	11	14	10	12	0	3	178

Table 5: Distribution of summary aspects obtained from error analysis. The last column (positive) is the number of judgments (out of 300) where workers found no major problems with the summary .

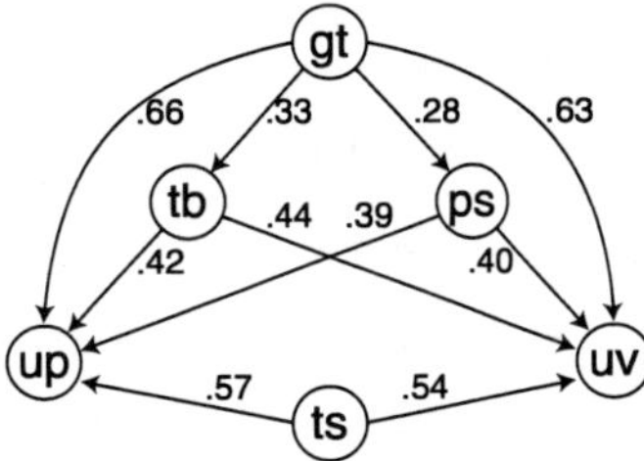

Figure 2: Summary of the quality scoring task: directed edges denote significantly higher scores ($p < 0.001$), and are annotated with effect sizes. The baseline model is much worse in comparison and hence not included. Key: **gt**: ground truth, **tb**: tldr-bottom-up, **ps**: pseudo-self-attn, **up**: unified-pgn, **ts**: transf-seq2seq, **uv**: unified-vae-pgn.

paring the ordering of systems in Figure 1 and Figure 2, we see that master workers could differentiate the systems reasonably well without a guideline in the preference scoring task.

Table 5 shows the distribution of summary aspects for each model. *Missing context (MC)* was a key concern across all models where summaries failed to either capture enough details, or provide a proper reasoning, rendering them as *partial summaries* instead. This was prominent in the transf-seq2seq and pseudo-self-attn models, which produce shorter summaries that either lack relevant details or are overly simplistic *(OS)*. However, these models generate the most coherent and readable summaries with very few cases of incoherence *(IC)* and no repetition *(RP)*, obtaining an overall positive feedback. In contrast, the tldr-bottom-up and unified-vae-pgn models with much longer summaries preserved more information, but with issues in grammar *(BG)* or continuity *(BC)*, leading to higher numbers of incoherent summaries.

5 Conclusion

Both transf-seq2seq and pseudo-self-attn generated the highest-quality text, but especially the latter often lacked information; tldr-bottom-up generated the most informative summaries (with acceptable text quality), followed by transf-seq2seq. We found that, in the absence of a guideline, master workers provided reliable judgments by identifying influential summary aspects as seen in Table 4. All models struggled with capturing sufficient context spread throughout the posts, further aggravated by the casual writing style. Nevertheless, we observed encouraging results in terms of text quality. We envision that summarization will benefit from including formalisms of importance, argumentation, and reasoning into the models, while striking a balance between summary length and text quality. In the next edition of this task, we will foster corresponding contributions.

References

George F Bishop. 1987. Experiments with the middle response alternative in survey questions. *Public Opinion Quarterly*, 51(2):220–232.

Hyungtak Choi, Lohith Ravuru, Tomasz Dryjanski, Sunghan Rye, Donghyun Lee, Hojung Lee, and Inchul Hwang. 2019. Vae-pgn based abstractive model in multi-stage architecture for text summarization. In *TL;DR Challenge System Descriptions*.

Hoa Trang Dang. 2005. Overview of duc 2005. In *Proceedings of the document understanding conference*, volume 2005, pages 1–12.

Sebastian Gehrmann, Zachary Ziegler, and Alexander Rush. 2019. Generating abstractive summaries with finetuned language models. In *TL;DR Challenge System Descriptions*.

Dan Gillick and Yang Liu. 2010. Non-expert evaluation of summarization systems is risky. In *Proceedings of the 2010 Workshop on Creating Speech and Language Data with Amazon's Mechanical Turk, Los Angeles, USA, June 6, 2010*, pages 148–151.

Eduard Hovy, Chin-Yew Lin, Liang Zhou, and Junichi Fukumoto. 2006. Automated summarization evaluation with basic elements. In *Proceedings of the Fifth Conference on Language Resources and Evaluation (LREC 2006)*, pages 604–611. Citeseer.

Chris Kedzie, Kathleen McKeown, and Hal Daume III. 2018. Content selection in deep learning models of summarization. In *Proceedings of the 2018 Conference on Empirical Methods in Natural Language Processing*, pages 1818–1828.

Chin-Yew Lin. 2004. Rouge: A package for automatic evaluation of summaries. *Text Summarization Branches Out*.

Ani Nenkova and Rebecca Passonneau. 2004. Evaluating content selection in summarization: The pyramid method. In *Proceedings of the human language technology conference of the north american chapter of the association for computational linguistics: Hlt-naacl 2004*.

Martin Potthast, Tim Gollub, Matti Wiegmann, and Benno Stein. 2019. TIRA Integrated Research Architecture. In Nicola Ferro and Carol Peters, editors, *Information Retrieval Evaluation in a Changing World - Lessons Learned from 20 Years of CLEF*. Springer.

Alexander M. Rush, Sumit Chopra, and Jason Weston. 2015. A neural attention model for abstractive sentence summarization. In *Proceedings of the 2015 Conference on Empirical Methods in Natural Language Processing, EMNLP 2015, Lisbon, Portugal, September 17-21, 2015*, pages 379–389.

Natalie Schluter. 2017. The limits of automatic summarisation according to ROUGE. In *Proceedings of the 15th Conference of the European Chapter of the Association for Computational Linguistics, EACL 2017, Valencia, Spain, April 3-7, 2017, Volume 2: Short Papers*, pages 41–45.

Abigail See, Peter J. Liu, and Christopher D. Manning. 2017. Get to the point: Summarization with pointer-generator networks. In *Proceedings of the 55th Annual Meeting of the Association for Computational Linguistics, ACL 2017, Vancouver, Canada, July 30 - August 4, Volume 1: Long Papers*, pages 1073–1083.

Tian Shi, Yaser Keneshloo, Naren Ramakrishnan, and Chandan K. Reddy. 2018. Neural abstractive text summarization with sequence-to-sequence models. *CoRR*, abs/1812.02303.

Shahbaz Syed, Michael Völske, Martin Potthast, Nedim Lipka, Benno Stein, and Hinrich Schütze. 2018. Task proposal: The tl;dr challenge. In *Proceedings of the 11th International Conference on Natural Language Generation, Tilburg University, The Netherlands, November 5-8, 2018*, pages 318–321.

Michael Völske, Martin Potthast, Shahbaz Syed, and Benno Stein. 2017. Tl; dr: Mining reddit to learn automatic summarization. In *Proceedings of the Workshop on New Frontiers in Summarization*, pages 59–63.

Generating Quantified Descriptions of Abstract Visual Scenes

Guanyi Chen[†], Kees van Deemter[†‡], Chenghua Lin[*]
[†]Department of Information and Computing Sciences, Utrecht University
[‡]Department of Computing Science, University of Aberdeen
[*]Department of Computer Science, University of Sheffield
{g.chen, c.j.vandeemter}@uu.nl, c.lin@sheffield.ac.uk

Abstract

Quantified expressions have always taken up a central position in formal theories of meaning and language use. Yet quantified expressions have so far attracted far less attention from the Natural Language Generation community than, for example, referring expressions. In an attempt to start redressing the balance, we investigate a recently developed corpus in which quantified expressions play a crucial role; the corpus is the result of a carefully controlled elicitation experiment, in which human participants were asked to describe visually presented scenes. Informed by an analysis of this corpus, we propose algorithms that produce computer-generated descriptions of a wider class of visual scenes, and we evaluate the descriptions generated by these algorithms in terms of their correctness, completeness, and human-likeness. We discuss what this exercise can teach us about the nature of quantification and about the challenges posed by the generation of quantified expressions.

1 Introduction

A long tradition of research in formal semantics studies the question how speakers express quantification. Much of this work starts from the idea that the prime function of Noun Phrases (NPs) is to express quantitative relations between sets of individuals. Obvious examples are akin to the universal and existential quantifier of First Order Predicate logic, as in *"all A are B"* and *"Some A B"*. Crucially, researchers observed that NPs permit much more variation in terms of the relations expressed: not only can we say things like *"between 2 and 5 A are B"* (where *"between 2 and 5 A"* is a noun phrase), but also things like *"most A are B"* and *"Few A are B"*, which are not even expressible in First-Order Predicate Logic. For this reason, this research are, is known as the study of Generalised Quantifiers, often regarded as starting from Mostowski (1957); the link with natural language was more fully established with Barwise and Cooper (1981) and further elaborated in Keenan and Moss (1985); Van Benthem et al. (1986); Peters et al. (2006).

Though the main focus of this work has been on mathematical logic, there is a growing body of empirical work. For example, there is some psycholinguistic work on the human use of vague quantifiers (Moxey and Sanford, 1993), and work that investigates the links between quantifiers' logical types and the human processing of quantified expressions (Szymanik and Zajenkowski, 2010; Szymanik et al., 2016, QEs). Sorodoc et al. (2016) looked at speakers' choice between *all*, *some*, and *no* (see also Grefenstette (2013) and Herbelot and Vecchi (2015)). However, there has been no attempt to find out how the wider class of all ("generalised") quantifiers are used by human speakers.

In a simple version of the problem, consider a table with two black tea cups and four coffee cups, three of which are red while the remaining one is white. Each of (a)-(d) describes the scene truthfully (though not necessarily optimally):

(a) *There are some red cups.*
(b) *At least three cups are red.*
(c) *Fewer than four cups are red.*
(d) *All the red objects are coffee cups.*

The computational challenge is to design an NLG algorithm that chooses the "best" statement, choosing from all the ones above and many others. In more complicated situations, which cannot be adequately described by one single quantified pattern, the algorithm should generate a sequence of sentences. This is a difficult *computational modelling* challenge to which the present paper makes a contribution.

In section 2, we discuss a strand of work in

NLG that provided inspiration for this enterprise. Section 3 proposes a computational mechanism, which will show up some surprising commonalities between the task of the present paper – Quantified Description Generation (QDG) – and the Referring Expressions Generation (REG). Section 4 details our evaluation experiment and section 5 discusses implications and future work. Code for the proposed QDG algorithms can be found at: `https://github.com/a-quei/quantified-description-generation`.

2   Background

An early investigation of the choice between patterns (a)-(d) above rested on the idea that the generator should always choose the logically strongest statement that holds true in the situation described (Creaney, 1996). Thus, statement (b) was always preferred over (a). However, this attractive idea ran into difficulties over pairs of statements that are logically independent of each other, such as (b) and (c), or also (b) and (d), where each of the two statements conveys some information that the other one does not. Clearly, other computational mechanisms are called for. The present paper proposes and evaluates a family of such mechanisms.

A body of work that is indirectly relevant concerns the generation of *referring* NPs (Krahmer and van Deemter, 2012; van Deemter, 2016). One strand of this work focusses on corpora of referring expressions (REs) that were elicited under experimentally controlled conditions (e.g., the TUNA corpus (Gatt et al., 2007; van Deemter et al., 2012); such corpora were used in evaluation campaigns where computer-generated referring expressions were compared with the corpus gold standard (Gatt and Belz, 2010). This comparison allowed researchers to know which algorithms worked best, and to develop new algorithms that match human language production even more closely. These evaluation campaigns created a tradition of NLG "generation challenges", consistent with the broader tradition of evaluation campaigns in Machine Translation (Barrault et al., 2019), parsing (Buchholz and Marsi, 2006), and other areas of Computational Linguistics.

Focusing on a far wider class of NPs, a series of elicitation experiments was recently conducted, called here the QTUNA experiments (Q stands for quantification). We will summarise the main findings from these experiments before proposing and

experimentally comparing algorithms that seek to mimic the aforementioned corpus. More details can be found in Chen et al. (2019) [1].

The QTUNA experiment was set up in order to study how speakers use sequences of QEs to describe a visual scene. Participants were asked to describe a series of abstract visual scenes. Participants were told that their descriptions should allow readers to *reconstruct* the scene *modulo* their location. Each scene contained n objects, which is either a circle or a square and either blue or red. To chart how domain size n influences human production of QEs, QTUNA conducted 3 experiments, with n of 4, 9, and 20 respectively.

The experiment was conducted on a total of 187 subjects, producing a total of 1414 multi-sentence descriptions for the resulting QTUNA corpus. Each description was annotated with its meaning representation: following Barwise and Cooper (1981), each quantifier was cast as a relation between 2 or more set-denoting arguments. For example, *"Half of the objects are blue"* was represented as Half(O, B). [2] To represent plurality, (as in *"Some blue squares ..."*, as opposed to *"Some blue square ..."*) the suffix *-s* was appended. Examples with their corresponding meaning representations are shown in Table 1.

Analysis of this corpus (see Chen et al. (2019)) taught us the following lessons: 1) Speakers use more vague quantifiers (e.g., *most, few*) as domain size increases; 2) Speakers also use more under-specifications in larger domains, describing large domain "with a broad brush"; 3) The average length of quantified descriptions is not significantly larger in larger domains than in smaller ones; 4) Speakers tends to start describing the high level information of the whole scene, before going into detail about parts; 5) Speakers tend to mention shape before the colour.

Quantified Expression Generation. Previous computational models of speakers' choice of quantifiers focus on the choice between a limited number of candidate quantifiers (Grefenstette, 2013; Yildirim et al., 2013; Herbelot and Vecchi, 2015; Sorodoc et al., 2016; Castillo-Ortega et al., 2009; Barr et al., 2013; Ramos-Soto et al., 2016). Barr et al. (2013) studies the use of quantifiers that

---

[1] The dataset can be found at: `https://github.com/a-quei/qtuna`

[2] O, S, C, R, C are property representations representing object, square, circle, red, and circle, respectively. BS means blue square, and so on.

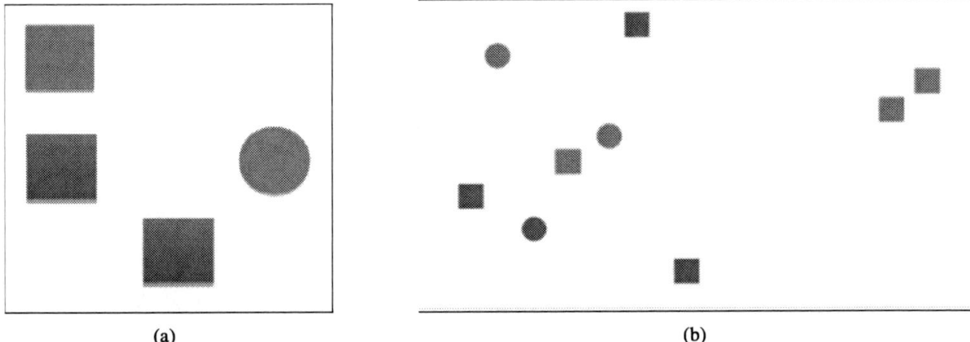

(a)   (b)

Figure 1: Examples from (a) the $n = 4$ experiment; (b) the $n = 9$ experiment.

n	Description	Meaning
4	*There are 4 squares. All objects are blue.*	$\exists_{=4}(S_s) \wedge \mathrm{All}(O_s, B_s)$
9	*Most of the items are red circles, but there are a couple of blue squares.*	$\mathrm{Most}(O_s, RC_s) \wedge \exists_{=2}(BS_s)$
20	*All the objects in the picture are circles and majority of them is blue.*	$\mathrm{All}(O_s, C_s) \wedge \mathrm{Majority}(O_s, B_s)$

Table 1: List of example descriptions from QTUNA corpus; n indicates domain size.

are part of a referring expression. The present papers models how human speakers use quantifiers as part of a wider task, namely the task of describing a complicated visual scene.

3 Quantified Description Generation

The aim of our generator is to perform the same task as was given to the human participants in the QTUNA experiments, but unlike those experiments, we would like our algorithm to succeed in domains of any reasonable size – including the sizes 4, 9, and 20 of those experiments and all sizes in between. Domains with fewer than 4 objects, and those in which there are many more objects than can be counted in a few seconds, are beyond the scope of this work. Participants in the QTUNA experiments were asked to make the generated descriptions correct (i.e., truthful) and complete (i.e., giving as much information as can reasonably be expected). Our generator endeavours to do the same and will therefore be evaluated using these same two criteria, plus an additional criterion that asks more explicitly how human-like the generated descriptions are. We start by introducing the general framework of our QDG system, which is a pipeline including a pre-processor, a QDG algorithm, and a surface realiser. Second,

we introduce two pre-defined knowledge bases that will be used by the QDG system. Third, we propose and sketch two QDG algorithms.

3.1 General Framework

Our explanation will make use of the following formalisation. Given a target scene s with its domain knowledge $\mathcal{K}_d$ (for details see §3.2), the generator constructs a set S containing all possible scenes in the same domain as s. The generator then calls a QDG algorithm to construct a description $\mathcal{D}$ containing a set of L QEs $\{q_l(v)\}_{l=1}^{L}$. We use $q(\cdot)$ to represent a quantified pattern, for instance $\mathrm{All}(\cdot, \cdot)$. Furthermore, v is a property tuple. If v is capable of filling in the slots of a quantified pattern, we say that the pattern *accepts* v, and we write $q(v)$. The QE $q(v)$ is a logical form, as introduced in §2. The algorithm selects from a set of candidate patterns $\mathcal{Q}$, based on the common knowledge $\mathcal{K}_c$ (for details see §3.2) defined on $\mathcal{Q}$ by mimicking how human beings did so in the experiment. Finally, a simple template-based surface realiser is called to map $\mathcal{D}$ into natural language text. The architecture of the generator is shown in Figure 2.[3]

---

[3] In the future, a Sequentialiser will put the QEs in an optimal order, but the algorithms in this section will realise the

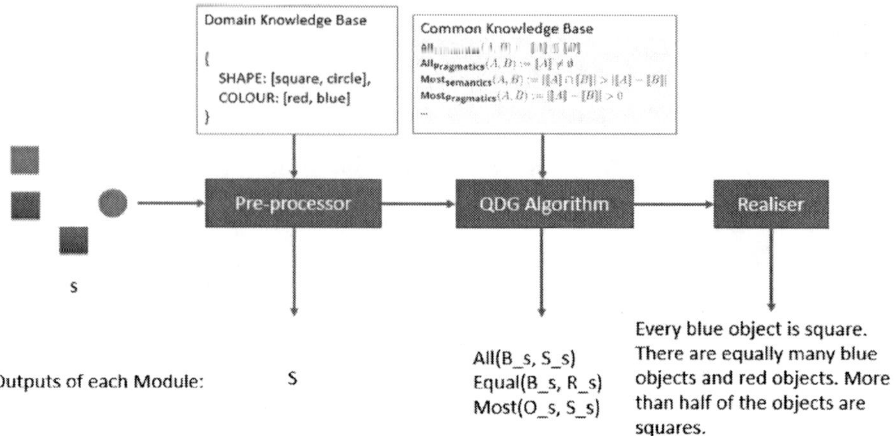

Figure 2: Sketch of the Quantified Description Generation System.

3.2 Knowledge Bases for QDG Algorithms

Domain Knowledge $\mathcal{K}_d$. This is the list of possible attributes with their possible values, represented as a set of key-value pairs. For example, matching the experimental setting of QTUNA, its domain knowledge is $\{$SHAPE $:$ $[square, circle], $COLOUR$: [red, blue]\}$.

Common Knowledge $\mathcal{K}_c$. This is a body of knowledge that corresponds to the quantified patterns in Q. For a quantified pattern $q(\cdot)$, this knowledge includes the meaning of the quantified pattern, and a list of possible property tuples that could be assigned to v. The list of supported patterns can be found in the supplementary materials.

The meaning of a quantified pattern has two parts: its semantics and its pragmatics. For example, the *semantics* of All(A, B) asserts that $[[A]] \subseteq [[B]]$. The *pragmatics* says that $[[A]]$ is not empty. Determining the semantics and pragmatics of each English quantifier term can be tricky, but the QTUNA corpus allowed us to choose definitions that match majority usage in that corpus.

3.3 An Incremental QDG Algorithm

Looking at the QTUNA dataset, some quantifier patterns are more frequent than others, and some choices of properties to fill a given pattern are more frequent than others. Therefore, to mimic people's production of quantified descriptions, a natural idea is to maintain a sequence of properties and a sequence of fillers, which the algorithm

---

QEs in the order in which they were selected.

can then make use of to determine in what order to consider the different types of statements for inclusion in the generated description:

- **Quantifier Sequence.** Inspired by our finding that humans tend to start describing the scene as a whole, QEs such as *all*, *half*, and *most* have high priority.

- **Property Sequence.** Informal inspection of QTUNA suggested that, for patterns of the form All(A, B), the first argument, A, is more often a SHAPE property, whereas B is more often a COLOUR. For example, the algorithm should check the property tuple (S, R) before (R, S).

The algorithm generates the description by considering possible quantifiers and properties one by one, starting at the top of the sequence, working its way down. Because of its similarity with the Incremental algorithm of Dale and Reiter (1995), we call this algorithm the *Incremental QDG algorithm* (abbreviated QDG-IA). Likewise, we allude to the "Preference Order" of properties employed by Dale and Reiter's REG algorithm by speaking of the Quantifier Preference Order (instead of Quantifier Sequence) and the Property Preference Order (instead of Property Sequence). Algorithm 1 shows the detailed QDG-IA.

Given the inputs listed in Algorithm 1, the QDG-IA will go through all the quantified patterns in Q in the order of the quantifier preference order. In each iteration, for the selected quantified pattern

Algorithm 1 The Incremental Algorithm for Generating Quantified Descriptions

---

Input: A target scene s, a set S of all possible scenes, a set of quantified patterns $\mathcal{Q}$, the common knowledge $\mathcal{K}_c$ defined on $\mathcal{Q}$, a Quantifier Preference Order defined on $\mathcal{Q}$, a set of all possible property tuples in the domain $\mathcal{V}$, and a property preference order defined on $\mathcal{V}$.

Output: A quantified description $\mathcal{D}$ of s that uses conjunctions of single or multiple $q(v)$s.

1: $\mathcal{D} := \{\}$
2: **for** each q in $\mathcal{Q}$ (in order of the Quantifier Preference Order) **do**
3:     **for** each v in $\mathcal{V}$ such that q accepts v (in order of the Property Preference Order) **do**
4:         $q(v) := \texttt{pluralise}(q(v), s)$
5:         **if** $q(v)$ is true for s, and $\mathcal{D} \not\models q(v)$ **then**
6:             $\mathcal{D} := \mathcal{D} \cup \{q(v)\}$
7:             $S := \{s' \in S : q(v) \text{ is true for } s'\}$
8:     Until $S = \{s\}$ or $|\mathcal{D}| \geq \delta$

$q(\cdot)$, QDG-IA will test all possible property tuples accepted by $q(\cdot)$, in the order of property preference order. (Recall that the information which $q(\cdot)$ accepts which property tuples can be found in the common knowledge $\mathcal{K}_c$.) The algorithm then calls the `pluralise` function on the QE, where the `pluralise` assigns a plural suffix on properties that appear multiple times in the target scene s.

In step 5, the algorithm will first validate whether $q(v)$ is correct as a QE for s. The validation is performed by using both the semantics and pragmatics of $q(v)$, in a somewhat unexpected manner. The semantics of a QE $q(v)$ is the same as the semantics of the pattern $q(\cdot)$, but the pragmatics takes issues such as plurality into account.

For example, consider $Few(O, S)$. The semantics says that fewer than n O are S; the pragmatics of this QE says that there exist *at least two* O. Consequently, the QE will not be included in the description unless there exist two O (and if it is included, this information is taken into account when scenes are removed from S in line 7).

Subsequently, step 5 ensures that $q(v)$ *does not follow* from the generated description $\mathcal{D}$, ensuring that $q(v)$ rules out one or more further scenes. Crucially, this validation is performed by using only the semantics of $q(v)$, not the pragmatics. To see why, consider QE $Few(O, S)$ again: if the pragmatics of this QE (which says that at least 2 O are S) were taken into account during validation, then the algorithm would end up adding this QE to a description $\mathcal{D}$ *even* in cases where the QE's only contribution to $\mathcal{D}$ is the (pragmatic) requirement that at least 2 O are S (because other QEs, previously added to $\mathcal{D}$, already ensure that fewer than n O are S). This would tend to lead to unwieldy descriptions, some of whose constituent QEs contribute very little to the description of the scene.

Once the above two conditions have been validated, $q(v)$ is appended at the end of the description and the scenes for which $q(v)$ is not true are removed from S. Both semantics and pragmatics are used for removing such "distractor" scenes. The generation terminates when all the distractors are removed from S or the length of D reaches an upper bound δ. The idea of setting a upper bound comes from the observation that, in QTUNA, descriptions were remarkably constant across domain sizes. As for the design of preference orders, we started with testing the following settings, once again based on analysis of the corpus: 1) the quantifier preference order is a linear preference order, which starts with All $\succ$ Half $\succ$ Most [4] (A $\succ$ B means A following B in the preference order); 2) the property preference order was designed by following some constraints, e.g., SHAPE properties have higher priorities in the first argument place of a quantified pattern, whereas COLOUR properties have higher priority in order argument places. The preference order was designed and refined based on the data from the pilot experiments and the n=4 QTUNA experiment.

When we ran the algorithm, we found that some quantified patterns that have low preference will never be chosen by the algorithm, so the generated descriptions used only a very limited set of patterns. For example, the pattern $All(\cdot, \cdot)$ has higher preference than the pattern $Everything(\cdot)$, and consequently the latter is *never* chosen, because its meaning is covered by the former. To increase the variety of quantifier patterns in the descriptions generated, we introduced a probability θ, with which the QDG-IA can perform a one-off move of a quantified pattern with low preference into a higher preference order. Since quantified patterns with low preference order should not appear frequently, the value θ should not be high. For

---

[4] A full linear quantifier preference order can be found in the supplementary materials.

Algorithm 2 The Greedy Algorithm for Generating Quantified Descriptions

---

Input: A target scene s, a set S of all possible scene, a set of quantified patterns Q, the common knowledge $\mathcal{K}_c$ defined on Q, a set of all possible property tuples V

Output: A quantified description $\mathcal{D}$ of s that uses conjunctions of single or multiple $q(v)$s.

1: $\mathcal{D} := \{\}$
2: **while** $S \neq \{s\}$, and $|\mathcal{D}| < \delta$ **do**
3:     $q(v) := \texttt{FindBestQE}(s, S, Q, V, \mathcal{K}_c)$
4:     **if** $\mathcal{D} \not\models q(v)$ **then**
5:         $\mathcal{D} := \mathcal{D} \cup \{q(v)\}$
6:         $S := \{s' \in S : q(v) \text{ is true for } s'\}$

---

the work reported in this paper, we set θ to 0.1. A list of quantified patterns that have high meaning overlap with each other (so the use of one tends to preclude the use of the other) can be found in the supplementary material.

3.4 A Greedy QDG Algorithm

The QDG task can be viewed as a search problem, searching for the best set of QEs that can single out a scene s from its distractors. From this perspective, another natural idea is to use a greedy algorithm, which selects a QE that singles out the largest number of distractors in each iteration.

We propose a greedy algorithm for QDG (abbreviated QDG-GREEDY), as in Algorithm 2. In each iteration, the algorithm calls the function `FindBestQE` to choose the QE that rules out the most distractors from all possible QEs. Specifically, for each QE $q(v)$, it first pluralises the $q(v)$, as in step 4 of Algorithm 1, and check whether it is true for the target scene using $q(v)$'s semantics and pragmatics. Then it calculates the number of distractors that can be removed by only using $q(v)$'s semantics. The number of distractors that $q(v)$ can remove is called $q(v)$'s discriminatory power. At last, the `FindBestQE` will return the QE that has the highest discriminatory power.

In line 4, the algorithm ensures that the discriminatory power of the selected $q(v)$ is not zero. If it passes this test, $q(v)$ is added to $\mathcal{D}$, and distractor scenes are removed from S. The stop criterion of QDG-GREEDY is the same as the one of QDG-IA.

In order to increase the variation in the generated quantified descriptions, the `FindBestQE` function returns all the best QE that has the same discriminatory power. In step 5, one of these is randomly selected and appended to $\mathcal{D}$.

3.5 Realisation

Since our main focus was on quantifier choice (not wording), the QDG system uses a simple template based surface realiser. For each quantified pattern, there is a specific template. When filling the slots with chosen properties, some simple syntactic and morphological operations are employed. For example, if a COLOUR property takes the first place of a quantified pattern, a noun is appended to package it into a NP (e.g., *red* → *red object*). If a property has a plural suffix, the surface form of the property is mapped into its plural form. A number of further constraints, specific to particular quantifier patterns, were also coded in the realiser.

3.6 Comparing QDG with REG

The two algorithms presented above (1) start out from the set S of all possible scenes, (2) accumulate, one by one, quantified statements $q(v)$ that are true for the target scene and false for some other elements of S, (3) remove from S all scenes for which $q(v)$ is false (4) until the target scene is the only remaining element of S or some other stopping condition is met.

Quantification is not normally seen as a reference problem. Yet our approach resembles the classic algorithms for Referring Expressions Generation (REG) originally discussed in Dale and Reiter (1995), where a referring expression is constructed by accumulating properties (e.g., colours, sizes) one by one, each of which is thought to "remove" from consideration a set of "distractor objects" (i.e., potential referents that differ from the target referent in one or more respects). We have emphasised this similarity throughout, by using terms familiar from REG (e.g., "target", "(removing) distractors", "preference order", and so on).

One difference is that, in REG: (1) a set of potential *referents* takes the place of the set of all possible *scenes*, and (2) properties (such as "red") take the place of quantified statements. These differences have important consequences. Quantified statements are much more complicated than properties, hence the distinction between choosing a pattern $q(\cdot)$ (line 2 of Algorithm 1) and instantiating the pattern by choosing a value v (line 3). And, unlike the set of all possible referents in REG, the set S of all possible scenes is not a given but needs to be computed from the properties that are given (e.g., red, blue, circle, square). Furthermore, our algorithms have had to find a way to take both the semantics and the pragmatics of a quantifier pattern into account. Finally, the QTUNA experiments have taught us that, except in very small domains (such as the QTUNA one where n=4), vague quantifiers (such as *many*, *most*) are highly frequent, and hence need to be taken into account by any QDG algorithm. By contrast, REG has been able to disregard vague properties for a long time, because in domains consisting of simple objects (such as the TUNA furniture domains, and those of Dale and Viethen (2009), where all properties were crisp and well defined,) they did not play an important role. A related difference is that, for larger domains, it is typically not feasible to produce a description that identifies the target scene completely. This different in REG, where except in very complicated situations (e.g., van Deemter (2016, Chapters 11-15)), producing a distinguishing description (i.e., one that singles out its referent) is par for the course.

4 Evaluation by Human Judgements

Although our algorithms were informed by extensive elicitation experiments, we wanted to gain additional insights into the quality of the generated descriptions. We were curious how humanlike these descriptions were perceived to be; at a more detailed level, we wanted to know how correct and informative these descriptions were thought to be.

Note that these are not things that could easily be measured automatically. Consider the example of the QE $Few(O, S)$ once again. Suppose 5 out of 20 O are S, then is it correct to say that $Few(O, S)$, or does this underestimate the number of O are S? And if $Few(O, S)$ is all that is said about the proportion of O that are S, is this sufficiently informative or not quite? We are not aware of any existing metric or algorithm that would give us a reliable answer.

To get an insight into these difficult issues, we recruited 4 academics from Utrecht University, none of whom had been involved in our research. Two were young lecturing staff in computational linguistics and two were senior lecturing staff in computational logic and formal argumentation. We divided the experiment into experiment A and experiment B. For A, we randomly selected 3 or 4 scenes (10 in total) from each of the 3 sub-corpora of QTUNA, each of which was

paired with 3 descriptions: one by QDG-IA, one by QDG-GREEDY, and one selected at random from our corpus. A number of example scenes paired with their descriptions produced by human beings, QDG-IA, and QDG-GREEDY are listed in Table 3.

As for experiment B, to test the generality of our algorithms, we focused on two new domain sizes, namely n=6 and n=16. For each of these we sampled 6 scenes, each of which was paired with 2 descriptions: one by QDG-IA[5], and one by QDG-GREEDY. (Human-generated descriptions were not available in these new domains.) All these 66 scene-description pairs were put together and randomly allocated to our four "judges". Each judged 33 scene-description pairs. Thus, each scene-description pair was judged by two judges. Judges were asked three questions in each case:

- Q1 (Naturalness): On a scale of 1-5, how likely do you think it might be that this description was uttered by a human? [1=very unlikely, 5=very likely]

- Q2 (Informativity): On a scale of 1-5, do you believe the description is as informative as it can be expected to be? [1= description isnt even nearly informative enough, 5= description gives as much information as is possible]

- Q3 (Correctness): On a scale of 1-5, how correct do you consider this description to be? [1= the description is not at all correct, 5=everything the description says is correct.]

The words Naturalness, Informativity, and Correctness were not seen by the judges. Our instructions to them added, "Please note that were mainly interested in the 'logic' of how people describe the scene, and less in the details of the wording, so please disregard minor syntax errors and typos."

Because in Experiment A, question Q1 was asked about a human-produced description as well as two computer-generated descriptions, this setup allowed us to perform what is essentially a **Turing test**.The other two questions offered invaluable formative evaluation.

We formulated a number of hypotheses: 1) humans perform better at naturalness than QDG-IA and QDG-GREEDY; 2) both algorithms perform better at informativity and correctness than humans, because both of them were explicitly

---

[5]The preference order used in all 3 experiments of this paper was the same.

	Model	Naturalness	Informativity	Correctness
Experiment A	Human	3.45	4.05	4.6
	QDG-IA	2.85	3.95	4.55
	QDG-GREEDY	3.45	3.8	4.8
Experiment B	QDG-IA	3.7	3.8	4.83
	QDG-GREEDY	3.46	4.2	4.83

Table 2: Average scores for each algorithm and for human-produced descriptions, by naturalness, informativity, and correctness as annotated by our four human judges.

designed to optimise informativity and correctness; 3) QDG-IA performs better at naturalness than QDG-GREEDY. We reasoned that, in REG, the incremental algorithm offered greater human-likeness than the greedy algorithm, so why should things be different this time?

Table 2 shows the scores from the judges. Both algorithms performed well, scoring well over 3 in all except one cell, confirming our impression that the descriptions were of respectable quality.

Remarkably, the first hypothesis was rejected; in terms of naturalness, QDG-GREEDY gained the exact same score as the human speakers. QDG-IA had a slightly lower score, but there was no significant difference (tested by a paired t-test). Though "no difference" results always need to be approached with caution, this might be seen as a case of an NLG algorithm passing a Turing test (focussing on a limited type of language use of course, rather than real conversation).

In an effort to understand the low naturalness performance of QDG-IA, we investigated the cases where QDG-IA had particularly low scores. We found that these were almost always descriptions that contain vague quantifiers (e.g., *few*, *most*), where we know that our semantic and pragmatic definitions were especially tentative. What confirmed this suspicion was the observation that vague quantifiers are used disproportionally often in the scenes of Experiment A (where some scenes for $n = 9$ and $n = 20$ were chosen to find out how vague quantifiers are used), and far less in the scenes of Experiment B (which were generated at random); accordingly, the QDG-IA scored much better on naturalness in Experiment B.

Our analysis of the second hypothesis shows some of the hidden difficulties of the description task that our algorithms solve. All quantified descriptions performed similarly in terms of informativity and correctness. To understand why, we

decided to separately calculate the average informativity score for those descriptions in experiment B that were *logically complete* (i.e., the algorithm stopped when $S = \{s\}$). For this reduced set of descriptions, the average scores for QDG-IA and QDG-GREEDY were a mere 3.88 and 4.1, instead of 5 (as one might expect). One possible cause is the fact that our algorithms judged the logical completeness of these descriptions by taking both their semantics and their pragmatics into account, which is something our judges may have disagreed with. Similar things may have happened when they were judging correctness.

The last hypothesis was rejected, as there was no significant difference between the naturalness performance of QDG-IA and QDG-GREEDY. This may be caused by the fact that the preference order that we proposed for quantified patterns has much higher complexity than that of properties (or attributes) in REG. In particular, the number quantifiers is considerable, and our preference order of quantifiers was not linear (as discussed in §3.3). And although our preference orders were informed by a study of the QTUNA corpus, this step was far from water tight, and further improvements to these preference orders are likely, for example if they can be learnt automatically.

5 Discussion and Future Work

We have investigated Generation of Quantified Descriptions of abstract scenes that are populated by a limited number (4-20) of simple objects, and given that this task is full of hidden complexities, our algorithms performed remarkably well. We're curious whether the essence of the findings reported in this paper will stand up when more naturalistic scenes are described. Naturalistic scenes permit many more than 2 attributes (in our experiment: COLOUR and SHAPE), each of which will tend to have more than 2 values. Furthermore, in

Scene	Model	Description
BS:2 RS:2 BC:0 RC:0	Human	All the objects are squares and half of them is blue.
	QDG-IA	Every object is square. There are equally many blue squares and red squares.
	QDG-GREEDY	Half of the objects are blue squares, the rest are red squares.
BS:2 RS:2 BC:5 RC:0	Human	Two objects are red squares. Two objects are blue squares and the remainder is blue.
	QDG-IA	Every circle is blue. Half of the squares are blue. More than half of the objects are blue circles.
	QDG-GREEDY	Half of the squares are red, the rest are blue. Most of the objects are blue circles.
BS:1 RS:6 BC:2 RC:0	Human	Two thirds of the objects are red squares. The remaining objects are blue, of which two are circles.
	QDG-IA	All of the circles are blue. There are more red squares than blue circles. There are more red objects than blue objects. More than half of the blue objects are circles.
	QDG-GREEDY	More than half of the objects are red squares. There is only one blue square. Some objects are blue circles. All of the circles are blue.
BS:9 RS:2 BC:8 RC:1	Human	There is a mixture of squares and circles. Most of them are blue. Some of them are red.
	QDG-IA	All possible objects are shown. A minority of the objects are red squares. Less then half of the objects are blue circles. Less then half of the objects are blue squares. Less then half of the objects are circles.
	QDG-GREEDY	All possible objects are shown. A minority of the objects are red squares. Less then half of the objects are blue circles. Less then half of the objects are blue squares. Less then half of the objects are circles.

Table 3: Examples of quantified descriptions produced by humans, QDG-IA, and QDG-GREEDY. The numbers after each type of object represents the number of that object in the input scene.

real life, it may often be difficult to state what the set S of all possible scenes is, which played such a key role in our algorithms.

Suppose, for instance, you want to describe the people in a football stadium, saying *"About half the people were wearing a hat"*. It is then unclear what were all the possibilities that your description is trying to rule out, since it is difficult to determine all the things people *might* be wearing. A possible solution is to abandon the idea of starting from the set of *all* possible scenes, starting instead from a suitably sized *sample* of possible scenes, possibly gleaned from other football matches in the same stadium, proceeding as before in other ways (e.g., terminating when all distractor scenes from the sample have been ruled out). An added advantage of this approach would be that it would be sensitive to constraints and statistical regularities that the speaker and hearer are attuned to. For instance, the sample would tend to bear out the regularity that if one's left shoe is brown then so is one's right shoe.

We have seen that our algorithms for the generation of quantified descriptions bear some striking resemblances with existing algorithms designed for a very different problem, namely REG. We plan to look at some recent advances of REG algorithms, such as those of Ramos-Soto et al. (2016); Monroe and Potts (2015); Li et al. (2018); van Gompel et al. (2019) to see how they can inspire improvements of our QDG models.

Acknowledgements

We thank the reviewers for their helpful comments. We thank Larry Moss, Jakub Szymanik, and Camilo Thorne for suggestions that helped shape our work. Guanyi Chen is supported by China Scholarship Council (No.201907720022).

References

Dale Barr, Kees van Deemter, and Raquel Fernández. 2013. Generation of quantified referring expressions: Evidence from experimental data. In *Proceedings of the 14th European Workshop on Natural Language Generation*, pages 157–161, Sofia, Bulgaria. Association for Computational Linguistics.

Loïc Barrault, Ondřej Bojar, Marta R. Costa-jussà, Christian Federmann, Mark Fishel, Yvette Graham, Barry Haddow, Matthias Huck, Philipp Koehn, Shervin Malmasi, Christof Monz, Mathias Müller, Santanu Pal, Matt Post, and Marcos Zampieri. 2019. Findings of the 2019 conference on machine translation (WMT19). In *Proceedings of the Fourth Conference on Machine Translation (Volume 2: Shared Task Papers, Day 1)*, pages 1–61, Florence, Italy. Association for Computational Linguistics.

Jon Barwise and Robin Cooper. 1981. Generalized quantifiers and natural language. In *Philosophy, language, and artificial intelligence*, pages 241–301. Springer.

Sabine Buchholz and Erwin Marsi. 2006. CoNLL-x shared task on multilingual dependency parsing. In *Proceedings of the Tenth Conference on Computational Natural Language Learning (CoNLL-X)*, pages 149–164, New York City. Association for Computational Linguistics.

Rita Castillo-Ortega, Nicolás Marín, and Daniel Sánchez. 2009. Fuzzy quantification-based linguistic summaries in data cubes with hierarchical fuzzy partition of time dimension. In *International Conference on Intelligent Data Engineering and Automated Learning*, pages 578–585. Springer.

Guanyi Chen, Kees van Deemter, Silvia Pagliaro, Louk Smalbil, and Chenghua Lin. 2019. QTUNA: a corpus for understanding how speakers use quantification. In *Proceedings of the 12th International Conference on Natural Language Generation*.

Norman Creaney. 1996. An algorithm for generating quantifiers. In *Eighth International Natural Language Generation Workshop*.

Robert Dale and Ehud Reiter. 1995. Computational interpretations of the gricean maxims in the generation of referring expressions. *Cognitive science*, 19(2):233–263.

Robert Dale and Jette Viethen. 2009. Referring expression generation through attribute-based heuristics. In *Proceedings of the 12th European Workshop on Natural Language Generation (ENLG 2009)*, pages 58–65, Athens, Greece. Association for Computational Linguistics.

Kees van Deemter. 2016. *Computational models of referring: a study in cognitive science*. MIT Press.

Kees van Deemter, Albert Gatt, Ielka van der Sluis, and Richard Power. 2012. Generation of referring expressions: Assessing the incremental algorithm. *Cognitive science*, 36(5):799–836.

Albert Gatt and Anja Belz. 2010. Introducing shared tasks to nlg: The tuna shared task evaluation challenges. In *Empirical methods in natural language generation*, pages 264–293. Springer.

Albert Gatt, Ielka van der Sluis, and Kees van Deemter. 2007. Evaluating algorithms for the generation of referring expressions using a balanced corpus. In *Proceedings of the Eleventh European Workshop on Natural Language Generation (ENLG 07)*, pages 49–56, Saarbrücken, Germany. DFKI GmbH.

Roger van Gompel, Kees van Deemter, Albert Gatt, Rick Snoeren, and Emiel Krahmer. 2019. Conceptualization in reference production: Probabilistic modeling and experimental testing. *Psychological review*, 126(3):345.

Edward Grefenstette. 2013. Towards a formal distributional semantics: Simulating logical calculi with tensors. In *Second Joint Conference on Lexical and Computational Semantics (*SEM), Volume 1: Proceedings of the Main Conference and the Shared Task: Semantic Textual Similarity*, pages 1–10, Atlanta, Georgia, USA. Association for Computational Linguistics.

Aurélie Herbelot and Eva Maria Vecchi. 2015. Building a shared world: mapping distributional to model-theoretic semantic spaces. In *Proceedings of the 2015 Conference on Empirical Methods in Natural Language Processing*, pages 22–32, Lisbon, Portugal. Association for Computational Linguistics.

Edward L Keenan and Lawrence S Moss. 1985. Generalized quantifiers and the expressive power of natural language. In *Generalized quantifiers in natural language*, volume 4, pages 73–124. Foris Dordrecht.

Emiel Krahmer and Kees van Deemter. 2012. Computational generation of referring expressions: A survey. *Computational Linguistics*, 38(1):173–218.

Xiao Li, Kees van Deemter, and Chenghua Lin. 2018. Statistical NLG for generating the content and form of referring expressions. In *Proceedings of the 11th International Conference on Natural Language Generation*, pages 482–491, Tilburg University, The Netherlands. Association for Computational Linguistics.

Will Monroe and Christopher Potts. 2015. Learning in the rational speech acts model. *CoRR*, abs/1510.06807.

Andrzej Mostowski. 1957. On a generalization of quantifiers. *Fundamenta Mathematicae*, 44(2):12–36.

Linda M Moxey and Anthony J Sanford. 1993. *Communicating quantities: A psychological perspective*. Lawrence Erlbaum Associates, Inc.

Stanley Peters, Dag Westerstahl, and Dag Westerståhl. 2006. *Quantifiers in language and logic*. Oxford University Press.

Alejandro Ramos-Soto, Alberto Bugarín, and Senén Barro. 2016. Fuzzy sets across the natural language generation pipeline. *Progress in artificial intelligence*, 5(4):261–276.

Ionut Sorodoc, Angeliki Lazaridou, Gemma Boleda, Aurélie Herbelot, Sandro Pezzelle, and Raffaella Bernardi. 2016. "look, some green circles!": Learning to quantify from images. In *Proceedings of the 5th Workshop on Vision and Language*, pages 75–79, Berlin, Germany. Association for Computational Linguistics.

Jakub Szymanik and Marcin Zajenkowski. 2010. Comprehension of simple quantifiers: Empirical evaluation of a computational model. *Cognitive Science*, 34(3):521–532.

Jakub Szymanik et al. 2016. *Quantifiers and cognition: Logical and computational perspectives*, volume 96. Springer.

JFAK Van Benthem et al. 1986. *Essays in logical semantics*. Springer.

Ilker Yildirim, Judith Degen, Michael K. Tanenhaus, and T. Florian Jaeger. 2013. Linguistic variability and adaptation in quantifier meanings. In *Proceedings of the 35th Annual Meeting of the Cognitive Science Society*.

What Goes Into A Word: Generating Image Descriptions With Top-Down Spatial Knowledge

Mehdi Ghanimifard   **Simon Dobnik**
Centre for Linguistic Theory and Studies in Probability (CLASP)
Department of Philosophy, Linguistics and Theory of Science (FLoV)
University of Gothenburg, Sweden
{mehdi.ghanimifard,simon.dobnik}@gu.se

Abstract

Generating grounded image descriptions requires associating linguistic units with their corresponding visual clues. A common method is to train a decoder language model with attention mechanism over convolutional visual features. Attention weights align the stratified visual features arranged by their location with tokens, most commonly words, in the target description. However, words such as spatial relations (e.g. *next to* and *under*) are not directly referring to geometric arrangements of pixels but to complex geometric and conceptual representations. The aim of this paper is to evaluate what representations facilitate generating image descriptions with spatial relations and lead to better grounded language generation. In particular, we investigate the contribution of four different representational modalities in generating relational referring expressions: (i) (pre-trained) convolutional visual features, (ii) spatial attention over visual features, (iii) top-down geometric relational knowledge between objects, and (iv) world knowledge captured by contextual embeddings in language models.

1 Introduction

Spatial recognition and reasoning are essential bases for visual understanding. Automatically generating descriptions of scenes involves both recognising objects and their spatial configuration. This project follows up on recent attempts to improve language generation and understanding in terms of using spatial modules in the fusion of vision and language (Xu et al., 2015; Johnson et al., 2016; Lu et al., 2017; Hu et al., 2017; Anderson et al., 2018) (see also Section 6).

Generating spatial descriptions is an important part of the image description task which requires several types of knowledge obtained from different modalities: (i) invariant visual clues for object identification, (ii) geometric configuration of the scene representing relations between objects relative to the size of the environment (iii) object-specific functional relations that capture interaction between them and are formed by our knowledge of the world for example *an umbrella is over a man* is true if the referring umbrella serves its function, protecting the man from the rain (Coventry et al., 2001), and (iv) for projective relations (e.g. "to the left of" and "above") but not topological relations (e.g. "close" and "at"), the frame of reference which can be influenced from other modalities such as scene attention and dialogue interaction (Dobnik et al., 2015). Work in cognitive psychology (Logan, 1994, 1995) argues that while object identification may be pre-attentive, identification of spatial relations is not and is accomplished by a top-down mechanisms of attention after the objects have been identified. It is also the case that we do not identify all possible relations between objects but only those that are attended by such top-down mechanisms considering different kinds of high-level knowledge.

Experiments on training neural recurrent language models in a bottom-up fashion from data[1] demonstrated that spatial relations are frequently not learned to be grounded in visual inputs (Lu et al., 2017; Tanti et al., 2018a; Ghanimifard and Dobnik, 2018) which has been attributed to the design choices of these models that primarily focus on identification of objects (Kelleher and Dobnik, 2017). Therefore, targeted integration of different modalities is required to capture the properties from (i) to (iv). We can do this top-down (Anderson et al., 2018; Hu et al., 2017; Liu et al., 2017). However, it is not immediately obvious *what* kind of top-down spatial knowledge will benefit the bottom-up models most. Therefore, in this paper we investigate the integration of different kind of

---

[1] A bottom-up learning acquires higher level representations from examples of local features rather than using an external procedure to extract them. See also Section 6.

Proceedings of The 12th International Conference on Natural Language Generation, pages 540–551,
Tokyo, Japan, 28 Oct - 1 Nov, 2019. ©2019 Association for Computational Linguistics

⟨ "teddy bear", "partially under", "go cart"⟩

Figure 1: ⟨TARGET, RELATION, LANDMARK⟩ annotation of bounding boxes in VisualGenome 2318741[a]

[a]RaSeLaSeD_Il_Pinguino (2008): CC BY-SA 2.0.

top-down spatial knowledge beyond object localisation represented as features with the bottom-up neural language model.

The paper is organised as follows. In Section 2, we discuss how spatial descriptions are constructed and what components are required to generate descriptions. In Section 3, the neural networks' design is explained. In Section 4, we explain what dataset is used for this study, what pre-processing was applied on it and how the models are trained. Then the experiments and evaluation results are presented in Section 5. The related work in relation to our methods and findings is discussed in Section 6. The conclusion is given in Section 7.

2 Generating Spatial Descriptions

When describing a scene, there are several ways to construct spatial descriptions referring to objects and places and their relation with each other. A spatial description has three parts: a TARGET and a LANDMARK referring to objects or places and a RELATION denoting the location of the target in relation to the landmark (Logan and Sadler, 1996).[2] These are in the example in Figure 1 as follows: There is *a teddy bear* *partially under* *a go cart*.

TARGET   RELATION   LANDMARK

Therefore generating such description requires (a) identification of objects and their locations: the target is what we want to describe and the landmark is what we will relate the target to; the salience of the landmark is important for the hearer. (b) Grounding of the relation in geomet-

---

[2]Sometimes these are also known as *referent* and *relatum* (Miller and Johnson-Laird, 1976), *figure* and *ground* (Talmy, 1983) or *the located object* and *the reference object* (Herskovits, 1986; Gapp, 1994; Dobnik, 2009).

ric space: the spatial relation is expressed relative to the landmark which grounds a 3-dimensional coordinate system; furthermore, for projective relations, the coordinate system is aligned with the orientation of the external viewpoint which determines the frame of reference (Maillat, 2003). (Viewpoint may also be the landmark object itself in which case the coordinate system is oriented in the same way as the landmark). (c) Grounding in function: a spatial relation may be selected also based on the functional properties between target and landmark objects, e.g. the difference between *"the teapot is over the cup"* and *"the teapot is above the cup"* (Coventry et al., 2001).

Generating spatial descriptions requires knowing the intended target object and how we want to convey its location to the listener. The bottom-up approach in image captioning is focused on learning the salience of objects and events to generate captions expressed in the dataset (e.g. Xu et al. (2015)). The combination of bottom-up and top-down approaches for generating descriptions use modularisation in order to improve the generation of descriptions of different kind (e.g. You et al. (2016)). However, as we have seen in the preceding discussion, the generation of spatial descriptions requires a highly specific geometric knowledge. How is this knowledge approximated by the bottom-up models? To what degree can we integrate this knowledge with the top-down models? In this paper, we investigate these questions in a language generation task by comparing different variations of included top-down spatial knowledge. More specifically, for each image, we generate a description for every pair of objects that are localised in the image. We consider a variety of top-down spatial knowledge representations about objects as inputs to the model: (a) explicit object localisation and extraction of visual features; (b) explicit identification of the target-landmark by specifying their order in the feature vector; and (c) explicit geometric representation of objects in a 2D image. We investigate the contribution of each of these sets of features to generation of image descriptions.

3 Neural Network Design

Our method is to add step-by-step modules and configurations to the network providing different kind of top-down knowledge in Section 2 and investigating the performance of such configurations. There are several design choices with small effects on the performance but costly in terms of parameter size (Tanti et al., 2018b). Therefore, if there is no research question related to that choice, we take the simplest choice as reported in the previous work such as (Lu et al., 2017; Anderson et al., 2018). We use the following configurations:

1. Simple bottom-up encoder-decoder;
2. Bottom-up object localisation with attention;
3. Top-down object annotated localisation;
4. Top-down target and landmark assignment;
5. Two methods of top-down representation of geometric features (s-features).

These five configurations give us 10 variations of the model design as shown in Table 1. A detailed definition of each module is given in the Appendix A in the supplementary material.

Generative language model We use a simple forward recurrent neural model with cross-entropy loss in all model configurations.

Simple encoder-decoder An encoder-decoder architecture without spatial attention shown in Figure 3a and similar to (Vinyals et al., 2015) is the simplest baseline for fusing vision and language. The input to the model is an image and the start symbol $< s >$ of a description and the output is produced by the language model decoder. The embeddings are randomly initialised and learned as a parameter set of the model. The visual vectors are produced by a pre-trained ResNet50 (He et al., 2016). A multi-layer perceptron module (F_v in Figure 2) is used to fine-tune the visual features.

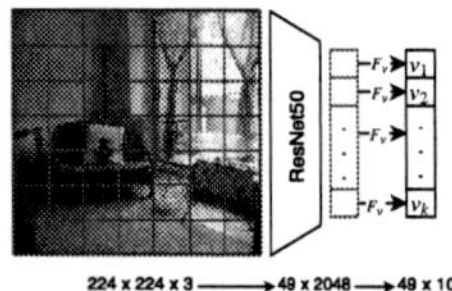

Figure 2: Visual features are obtained from the pre-trained ResNet50, then translated to a low dimensional vector with a dense layer F_v.

Bottom-up localisation With visual feature representing all regions of the image as in Figure 2, the attention mechanism is used as a localisation module. We generalised the adaptive attention introduced in (Lu et al., 2017) to be able to fuse the modalities. As shown in Figure 3b, the interaction between the attention mechanism and the language model is more similar to (Anderson et al., 2018): two layers of stacked LSTM, the first stack ($LSTM_u$) to produce the features for the attention model and the second stack ($LSTM_l$) to produce contextualised linguistic features which are fused with the attended visual features. This design is easier to extend with additional top-down vectors.

Top-down localisation Unlike the bottom-up unsupervised localisation, the top-down method includes a provision of a list regions of interest (ROI) from external procedures. For example, the region proposals can come from another bottom-up task as in (Anderson et al., 2018; Johnson et al., 2016) which use a Faster R-CNN (Ren et al., 2015) to extract possible regions of interest from the ConvNets regions in Figure 2. Here, as shown in Figure 4 we use the bounding box annotations of objects in images as the top-down localisation knowledge and then extract ResNet50 visual features from these regions. In the first stage the top-down visual representation only proposes visual vectors of the two objects in a random order without their spatial role as targets and landmarks in the descriptions. The model is shown in Figure 3d.

Top-down target-landmark assignment In the second iteration of the top-down localisation module we assign semantic roles to regions as targets and landmarks. This is directly related to localisation as spatial relations are asymmetric. We encode this top-down knowledge by fixing the order of the regions in the feature vector. The first object is the target and the second object is the landmark. Otherwise, the model is the same as in the previous iteration shown in Figure 3d.

Top-down geometric features The localisation procedure of objects discussed previously does not provide any geometric information about the relation between the two regions. However, top-down geometric features are required for grounding spatial relations where the location of the target object is expressed relative to the landmark. For example, a simple (but by no means sufficient) geometric relation between two bounding boxes can be represented by an arrow from the centre of one bounding box to the centre of the other and by ordering the information about bounding boxes in the feature vector as in the previous model to encode target-landmark asymmetry. The network architecture of the model with top-down geometric features expressing relations between the objects is shown in Figure 3e. We consider two different rep-

Model name	Regions Of Interest	TARGET-LANDMARK	s-features	Architecture
simple	-	-	-	Figure 3a
*bu*49	Bottom-up (7×7 grid)	Bottom-up attention	-	Figure 3b
*bu*49 + *mask*	Bottom-up (7×7 grid)	Bottom-up attention	Multi-hot 98	Figure 3c
*bu*49 + *VisKE*	Bottom-up (7×7 grid)	Bottom-up attention	Dense 11	Figure 3c
td	Top-down (2 bbox)	Bottom-up attention	-	Figure 3d
td + *mask*	Top-down (2 bbox)	Bottom-up attention	Multi-hot 98	Figure 3e
td + *VisKE*	Top-down (2 bbox)	Bottom-up attention	Dense 11	Figure 3e
td order	Top-down (2 bbox)	Top-down assignment	-	Figure 3d
td order + *mask*	Top-down (2 bbox)	Top-down assignment	Multi-hot 98	Figure 3e
td order + *VisKE*	Top-down (2 bbox)	Top-down assignment	Dense 11	Figure 3e

Table 1: The 10 variations of the neural network model after incrementally adding modules and features.

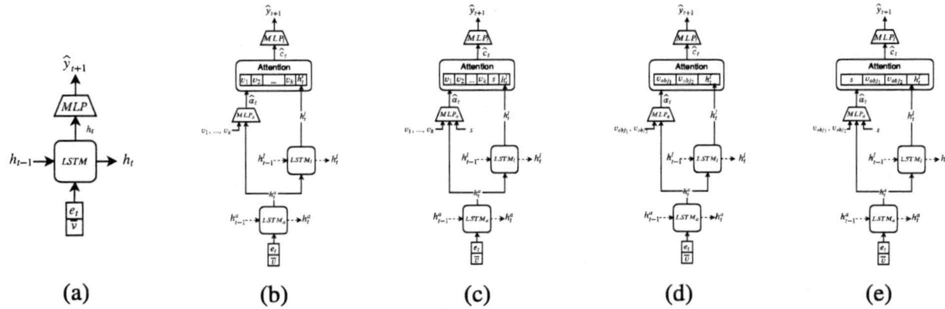

(a) (b) (c) (d) (e)

Figure 3: Five architectures: (a) simple encoder-decoder (*simple*). (b) bottom-up localisation with adaptive attention on 49 regions (*bu*49). (c) bottom-up localisation with explicit spatial vectors of the bounding boxes *bu*49 + *mask*/*bu*49 + *VisKE*. (d) top-down localisation with attentions on two bounding boxes (*td*). (e) top-down localisation augmented with explicit spatial vectors of the bounding boxes (*td* + *mask*/*td* + *VisKE*).

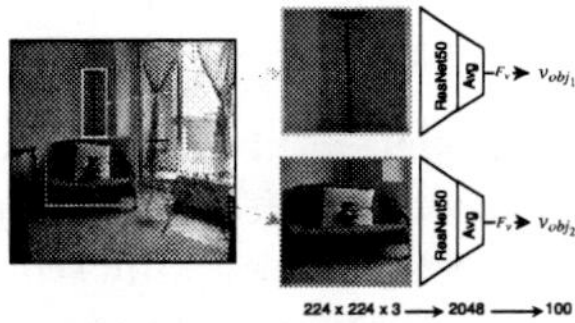

Figure 4: Top-down localisation of objects with bounding boxes whose visual features are extracted and translated to lower dimensions with F_v.

resentations of the top-down geometric features shown in Figure 5: Multi-hot mask over 49 vectors independently for target and landmark (*Mask*) over 49 locations (Figure 5a) and *VisKE* (Sadeghi et al., 2015) dense representations with 11 geometric features (Figure 5b) where dx, dy are changes in the coordinates of the centres, ov, ov_1, ov_2 the overlapping areas (total, relative to the first, and the second bounding box), h_1, h_2 heights, w_1, w_2 widths and a_1, a_2 areas. Note that *Mask* features provide geometric information about the size and the location of objects relative to the picture frame and *VisKE* feature provide more detailed geometric information that expresses the relation between the objects. The latter therefore more closely match the features that were identified in spatial cognitive models. A feed-forward network with

two layers (F_s) is used to project geometric features into a vector with the same dimensionality as the F_v outputs so that different modalities are comparable in weighted sum model of attention.

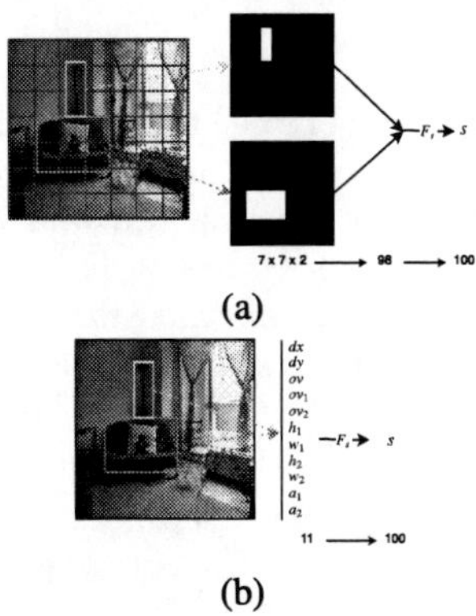

(a)

(b)

Figure 5: (a) Each bounding box is converted to a mask of multi-hot vector on 49 regions. (b) The geometric relation between the two bounding boxes are represented with features from (Sadeghi et al., 2015).

4 Dataset and Training

We use the relationship dataset in Visual Genome (Krishna et al., 2017) which is a collection of referring expressions represented as triplets

⟨subject, predicate, object⟩ on 108K images. Unlike image captioning datasets such as MSCOCO (Chen et al., 2015) and Flickr30K (Plummer et al., 2015) where only 5 captions are given for each image, each image in this dataset is annotated with 50 phrases. The annotators were asked to annotate relations between two given bounding boxes of subject and object by freely writing the text for each of the three parts of the annotation. The bounding boxes produced by another annotation procedure which detected objects in the images. In total, there are $2,316,104$ annotations of $664,805$ unique triplets, $35,744$ unique labels of subjects and $21,299$ unique labels of objects most of which consist of multiple tokens. We omit all repetitions of triplets on each image, this leaves total $1,614,055$ annotations.[3]

Spatial relations Based on the lists of spatial prepositions in (Landau, 1996) and (Herskovits, 1986), we have created a dictionary of spatial relations and their possible multi-word variants including their composite forms. This dictionary contains $7,122$ entries of 235 relations (e.g. *right* to represent both *on the right hand side of* and *to the right of*). Of these only 202 are found in Visual Genome dataset covering 79 spatial relations. $328,966$ unique triplets in Visual Genome are based on exactly one of these terms which covers 49.4% of all possible relationships.[4]

Bounding boxes Each bounding box is a tuple of 4 numbers (x, y, w, h). We normalise the numbers to the range of $(0, 1)$ relative to the image size to create geometric feature vectors (Section 3). The image is split into a grid with 7x7 cells to which bounding boxes are mapped, one bounding box potentially covering more than one cell. With this bounding box granularity, there are exactly $308,330$ possible bounding boxes. However, only $151,974$ are observed in the relationships dataset.

The spatial distribution of paired objects reflects how natural pictures are framed and how related objects are understood by annotators.

Pre-processing We first removed duplicate triplets describing the same image. Then we converted each triplet into a word sequence by concatenating the strings and de-tokenising them with the white space separator. This produced a corpus with a vocabulary of $26,530$ types with a maximum sequence length of 16 tokens and on average 15 referring expressions per image. We use 95% of the descriptions for training and 5% for validation and testing (5,230 images with 80,231 triplets).

Training We use Keras (Chollet et al., 2015) with TensorFlow backend (Abadi et al., 2015) to implement and train all of the neural network architectures in Section 3. The models are trained with the Adam optimiser (Kingma and Ba, 2014) ($\alpha = 0.001$, $\beta_1 = 0.9$, $\beta_2 = 0.999$) with a batch size of 128 and 15 epochs.

5 Evaluation

All implementations are available online[5].

5.1 Qualitative Examples

Figure 6 shows generated descriptions for two examples of unseen pictures from the test dataset by five models. The generated word sequence is that with the lowest loss using beam search with $k = 5$. The first example shows exactly how top-down localisation of objects is important especially if the goal is to refer to specific objects in the scene. In the second example, the visual features inside the bounding box are confusing for all 5 models. More examples are in Figure 13 in the Appendix.

5.2 Overall Model Performance

Hypothesis Top-down spatial knowledge improves the model performance. We consider three categories of top-down spatial knowledge: (i) top-down localisation of regions of interest; (ii) top-down assignment of semantic roles to regions; and (iii) two kinds of geometric feature vectors.

Method After training the models we evaluate them by calculating the average word level cross-entropy loss on held out instances in the test set[6].

---

[3]The repetitions include reflexive expressions (e.g. *horse next to horse*), annotations of several objects of the same type (e.g. *cup on table*), and repetitions due to several bounding box annotations of the same objects with different sizes.

[4]Other triplets in Visual Genome also have spatial content. Some of them include modifiers such as *partially under* as in Figure 1 and some of them are descriptions of an event or an action such as *sitting on* and *jumping over*. Some annotated relationships are verbs such as *flying* with less obvious spatial denotation. The spatial bias in the dataset was studied in (Collell et al., 2018). The most frequent spatial relation in the dataset is "*on*" (over 450K instances), the second place is "*in*" (150K instances), then "*with*", variations of "*behind*", "*near*", "*top*", "*next*", "*under*", "*front*", and "*by*" (less than 10K instances each).

[5]https://gu-clasp.github.io/generate_spatial_descriptions/

[6]Equivalent to log-perplexity of the language model.

⟨ "bat", "over", "shoulder"⟩
simple	player
*bu*49	man wearing shirt
td	bat in hand
td order	bat in hand
td order + VisKE	bat in hand

⟨ "hood", "above", "oven"⟩
simple	window
*bu*49	pot on stove
td	oven has door
td order	vent above sink
td order + VisKE	cabinet has door

Figure 6: From VisualGenome: 2412051[a] 2413282[b]

---

[a]Herholz (2005): CC BY-SA 2.0.

[b]juanjogasp (2013): CC BY-NC-SA 2.0.

We also calculate the loss on descriptions containing specific spatial relations for qualitative understanding of the effects of each type of top-down knowledge.

Results The overall loss of each model on the unseen descriptions of images is shown in Figure 7. The fully bottom-up model with no spatial attention (*simple*) has the highest loss. The loss in the variations of the model with bottom-up localisation in *bu*49 is higher than the one in the models with top-down localisation. The models with the top-down assignment of TARGET-LANDMARK achieves the best results. The effect of top-down geometric features is not significant.

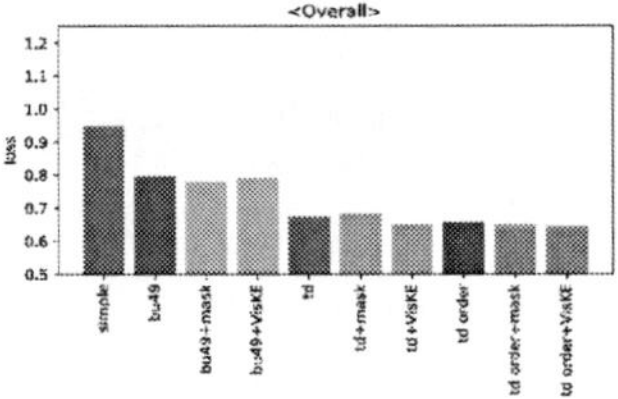

Figure 7: Cross-entropy loss of different model configurations on evaluation data.

Figure 8 shows the performance of the models on a selection spatial relations.

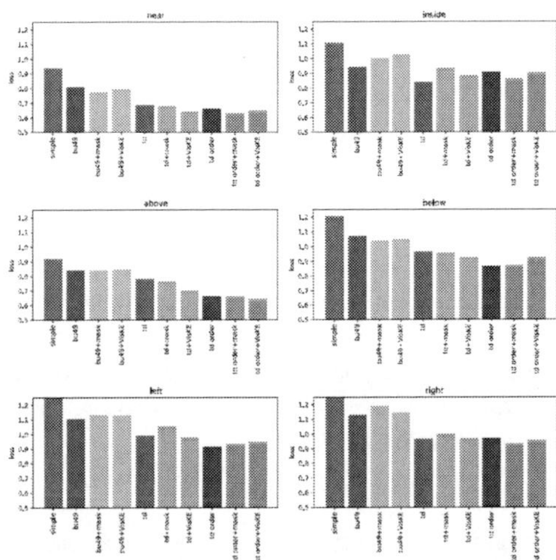

Figure 8: Cross-entropy loss of different model configurations on 40 descriptions for each relation: *near*, *inside*, *above* and *below*.

Discussion The top-down localisation (*td*) certainly improves the performance of the language models compared to purely bottom-up representations. However, additional top-down assignment of TARGET-LANDMARK (*td order*) and their additional geometric arrangement of bounding box features (*mask* and *VisKe*) has a small positive effect on overall performance. The overall performance is not a representative of how these configurations effect the grounding of spatial relations. More specifically, the imbalance of certain groups of relations (especially a generally lower proportion of geometrically biased relations such as "left" and "right" in this dataset and the presence of relations with a minimum spatial content such as *has, wearing*) makes it harder to make conclusions about overall performance of the models. We further examine two groups of some frequent spatial relations. The relations such as *inside* and *near* represent one group and *above* and *below* represent the other. Some top-down knowledge (as represented by our features) is less informative for the first group but is informative for the second group. For example *near* does not require the assignment of TARGET-LANDMARK roles. We observe that *td order* is not performing better than *td*. On the other hand, *inside* is sensitive to TARGET-LANDMARK assignment. However, since the relation is also restricted by a choice of objects (only certain objects can be inside others) their TARGET-LANDMARK assignment may already be inferred without such top-down knowledge from a language model. For the second group, the top-down knowledge about the semantic role of objects is important. However, *left* and *right* are among the least frequent relations in the dataset which is demonstrated by the fact that their descriptions have a higher loss than *above* and *below*. For these relations the loss of the *simple* model is much higher than other configurations. It can be seen that *td* is performing better than *bu* and *td order* is contributing over *td* but geometric features have a lesser effect than identification of semantic roles (*td order*).

5.3 Grounding in features

Hypotheses With the aim to evaluate *what* top-down information contributed to grounding of words we examine the following hypotheses:

H1 *s*-features contribute to predicting spatial relation words.

H2 Without top-down TARGET-LANDMARK role assignments to each region, attention is uniformly distributed over region choices at the beginning of a sequence generation.

Method In order to check the contribution of each feature from different modalities in prediction of each word, we look at the adaptive attention on each feature at the point of predicting the word[7]. Since feature vectors are not normalised against the number of features of each modality, we first multiply each attention measure with the magnitude of the feature vector, and then we normalised it to sum to 1 again:

$$\beta_{t,f_i} = \frac{\alpha_{t,f_i}\|f_i\|}{\sum_j \alpha_{t,f_j}\|f_j\|} \qquad (1)$$

where t refers to the time in the word sequence, and f_i is the feature the attention of which α_{t,f_i} is applied to it. We report the average β_{t,f_i} over the instances in the validation dataset.

Figure 9 shows β on two examples in three models. For each word, the bar chart is divided between four features (in Figure 3e): (1) target v_{obj_1} (2) landmark v_{obj_2} (3) *s*-features for bounding boxes (4) contextualized embeddings h^l.

---

[7]In this experiment, we do not check if the estimated likelihood for the correct word is the highest predicted score. The generated descriptions may still be acceptable with an alternative spatial relation. Furthermore, in the following analysis we report the attention over semantic roles and not individual words.

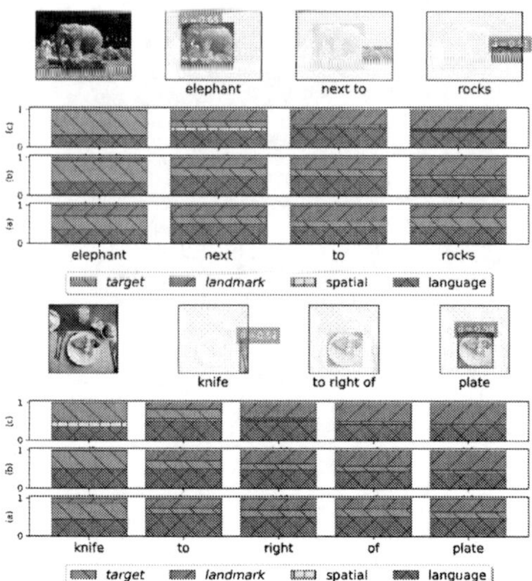

Figure 9: β is plotted in bar charts for each word. (a) *td order + VisKE* (b) *td + VisKE* (c) *td*. The values of β for each word that constitute description referring to each bounding box region is given in images.

After measuring the normalised attention on each feature according to Equation 1, we report the average of attentions on each token at that time step of the word sequence. We also group the tokens based on their semantic role in the triplets and report the average β on these tokens for a given role.

Results The average of attentions over triplets of tokens is plotted in Figure 10. The behaviour of attentions on word sequences in the four models in given in Figure 11.

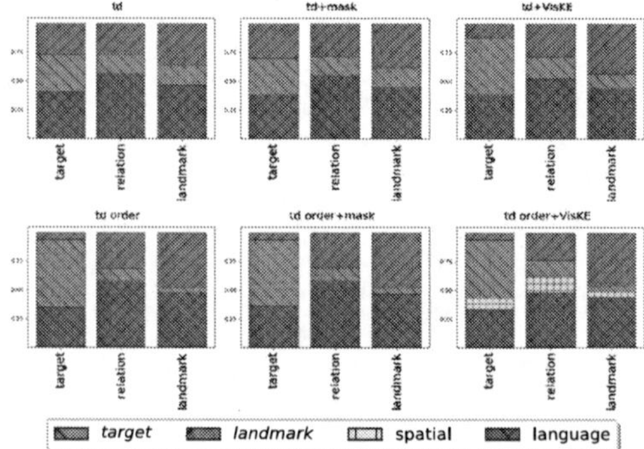

Figure 10: The overall average of β on tokens of each semantic role (target, relation, landmark) on all examples of the test dataset, for 6 variations of the top-down knowledge about regions of interest (ROI): location of objects and their order as target and landmark.

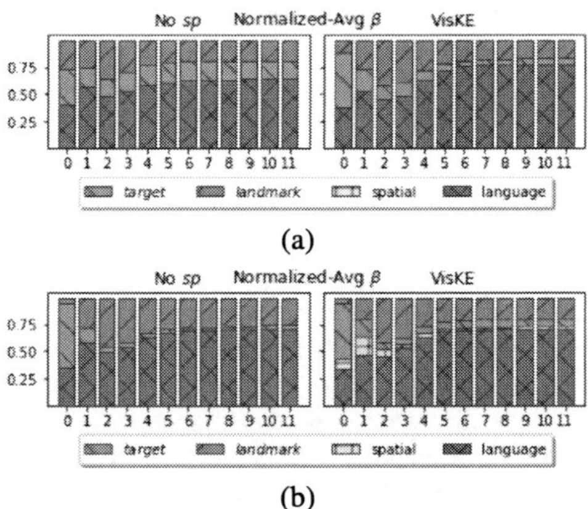

Figure 11: The average of β attentions of top-down models over sequences of words $1 \ldots 11$ (a) comparing *td* and *td + VisKE* and (b) comparing *td order* and *td order + VisKE*.

Discussion The comparison of 6 models in Figure 10 shows that geometric *mask s*-features are not contributing as well as dense *VisKE s*-features. In the models without top-down semantic role assignment only the model with *+VisKE* features has the expected attention on target and landmark, but there is no attention on the *s*-features. In the models with top-down semantic role assignment, the model with *VisKE s*-features has higher attention on *s*-features when predicting a relation word (H1). A similar situation is observable over word sequences in Figure 11. Without prior semantic role assignment the model is more confused how to attend target or landmark (H2). Finally, note that geometric *VisKE s*-features help predicting the TARGET-LANDMARK roles when these are not assigned top-down.

6 Related Work

Generating referring expressions Generating locative expressions is part of the general field of generating referring expressions (Dale and Reiter, 1995; Krahmer and van Deemter, 2011) with applications such as describing scenes (Viethen and Dale, 2008) and images (Mitchell et al., 2012). The research on describing visible objects (Mitchell et al., 2013) and human-robot dialogue (Kelleher and Kruijff, 2006) raised question about grounding relations in hierarchical representation of context. Application of neural language models and using convolutional neural networks for encoding visual features is an open question in interactive GRE tasks.

Encoder-decoder models with attention Recently several methods focused on finding better neural architectures for generating image descriptions based on pre-trained convolutional neural networks have been introduced. Karpathy and Fei-Fei (2015) align descriptions with images. Vinyals et al. (2015) introduce an encoder-decoder framework. Xu et al. (2015) improve this approach with spatial attention. Lu et al. (2017) introduce adaptive attention that balances language and visual embeddings. The attention measure provides an explanation of encoder-decoder architectures on how each modality contributes to language generation. Based on the attended features the performance of these models can be examined (Liu et al., 2017; Ghanimifard and Dobnik, 2018). In our paper, we develop a model similar to the adaptive attention which exploits its expressive aspects as a degree of grounding in different features.

Outputs of external models as top-down features In another line of work, the output of the bottom-up visual understanding is used as top-down features for language generation. For example, an object detection pipeline is combined explicitly with language generation. This procedure was previously used in template-based language generation (Elliott and Keller, 2013; Elliott and de Vries, 2015). There have been attempts to combine this process with neural language models with attention. For example, You et al. (2016) extract candidate semantic attributes from images (e.g. a list of objects in the scene), then the attention mechanism is used to learn to attend on them when generating tokens of image descriptions. Instead of semantic attributes, Anderson et al. (2018) use a region proposal network from a pre-trained object detection model to extract the generated bounding box regions as possible locations of visual clues. Then, the attention model learns to attend on the visual features associated with these regions. The idea of using an object detection module is also used in Johnson et al. (2016) where Faster R-CNN (Ren et al., 2015) is used to find regions of interest. Instead of assigning one object class to each region, a full description is generated for each proposed region. In all of these models, an image understanding module extracts some proposed representations and then this knowledge is used as a top-down representation of the scene to generate an image description. In this paper, we investigate the extent to which different spatial information is facilitating as a top-down knowledge to generate descriptions of scenes with neural language models.

Modular design Our paper examines strategies that can demonstrate language grounding within a neural architecture. The studies of neural architectures such as (Tanti et al., 2018b) provide analytical insight on differences between multimodal architectures for language generation. The modular design is mostly used in language parsing tasks such as (Hu et al., 2017) where object recognition, localisation and relation recognition are separate modules for grounding different parts of image descriptions in images in order to solve tasks such as visual question answering. In our paper, the modularity of the neural architecture is not focused on parsing text but used to incrementally demonstrate the contribution of each introduced modality to language generation.

Multimodal embeddings There are related studies on learning multimodal embeddings (Kiros et al., 2014; Lazaridou et al., 2015) to represent vision and language in the same semantic space. The focus of our paper is to investigate how these different modalities complement each other in neural language generation. In our models, the semantic representations of spatial relations are considered as a separate modality extending both the language and visual embeddings. There are related studies on encoding spatial knowledge in feature space in order to predict spatial prepositions (Ramisa et al., 2015) or on prepositional embeddings which can predict regions in space (Collell and Moens, 2018). In our paper, we investigate the degree in which each embedding contributes to language generation within the neural language model.

7 Conclusions

We explored the effects of encoding top-down spatial knowledge in a bottom-up trained generative neural language model for the image description task. The findings of the experiments in this paper are as follows:

(1) Overall, integration of top-down knowledge has a positive effect on grounded neural language models for this task. (2) When combining bottom-up language grounding with top-down knowledge representation as different features, different types of top-down knowledge have different contribution to grounded language models. The general picture is further complicated by the fact that different spatial relations have different bias to different knowledge. (3) The performance gain from the geometric features extracted from bounding boxes (s-features) is smaller than initially expected, with two possible explanations related to the nature of the corpora of image descriptions: (i) The corpus contains images of typical scenes where the relation of objects with each other is predictable from the description and therefore is captured in the language model; (ii) As annotators are focused on describing "what is in the image" rather "where things are spatially in relation to each other", descriptions of geometric spatial relations which refer to the locational information are rare in the corpus. (4) The majority of attention is placed on the language model which demonstrates that this provides significant information when generating spatial descriptions. While this may be a confounding factor if the visual features are ignored, the language model also encodes useful information about spatial information as discussed in (Kulkarni et al., 2011; Dobnik et al., 2018).

The results open several questions about grounded language models. Firstly, the degree to which the system is using each modality can be affected by dataset biases and this should be taken into account in the forthcoming work. Given this bias, learning a single common language model for descriptions of spatial scenes is insufficient as different kinds of knowledge may come to focus in different interactional scenarios. This further supports the idea that top-down integration of knowledge is required where we hope that the models will learn to attend to the appropriate features. Secondly, our investigation leaves open the question whether the representations both visual and geometric that we use are good representations for learning spatial relations. Further work will include a focused investigation of what kind of geometric relations they encode.

Acknowledgements

The research reported in this paper was supported by a grant from the Swedish Research Council (VR project 2014-39) for the establishment of the Centre for Linguistic Theory and Studies in Probability (CLASP) at the University of Gothenburg.

References

Martín Abadi, Ashish Agarwal, Paul Barham, Eugene Brevdo, Zhifeng Chen, Craig Citro, Greg S. Corrado, Andy Davis, Jeffrey Dean, Matthieu Devin, Sanjay Ghemawat, Ian Goodfellow, Andrew Harp, Geoffrey Irving, Michael Isard, Yangqing Jia, Rafal Jozefowicz, Lukasz Kaiser, Manjunath Kudlur, Josh Levenberg, Dandelion Mané, Rajat Monga, Sherry Moore, Derek Murray, Chris Olah, Mike Schuster, Jonathon Shlens, Benoit Steiner, Ilya Sutskever, Kunal Talwar, Paul Tucker, Vincent Vanhoucke, Vijay Vasudevan, Fernanda Viégas, Oriol Vinyals, Pete Warden, Martin Wattenberg, Martin Wicke, Yuan Yu, and Xiaoqiang Zheng. 2015. TensorFlow: Large-scale machine learning on heterogeneous systems. Software available from tensorflow.org.

Peter Anderson, Xiaodong He, Chris Buehler, Damien Teney, Mark Johnson, Stephen Gould, and Lei Zhang. 2018. Bottom-up and top-down attention for image captioning and visual question answering. *CVPR*, 3(5):6.

Xinlei Chen, Hao Fang, Tsung-Yi Lin, Ramakrishna Vedantam, Saurabh Gupta, Piotr Dollár, and C Lawrence Zitnick. 2015. Microsoft coco captions: Data collection and evaluation server. *arXiv preprint arXiv:1504.00325*.

François Chollet et al. 2015. Keras. `https://keras.io`.

Michael Coghlan. 2011. Tony cook. VisualGenome image id 2413371.

Guillem Collell and Marie-Francine Moens. 2018. Learning representations specialized in spatial knowledge: Leveraging language and vision. *Transactions of the Association of Computational Linguistics*, 6:133–144.

Guillem Collell, Luc Van Gool, and Marie-Francine Moens. 2018. Acquiring common sense spatial knowledge through implicit spatial templates. In *Thirty-Second AAAI Conference on Artificial Intelligence*.

Kenny R Coventry, Merce Prat-Sala, and Lynn Richards. 2001. The interplay between geometry and function in the comprehension of over, under, above, and below. *Journal of memory and language*, 44(3):376–398.

Robert Dale and Ehud Reiter. 1995. Computational interpretations of the Gricean maxims in the generation of referring expressions. *Cognitive science*, 19(2):233–263.

Simon Dobnik. 2009. *Teaching mobile robots to use spatial words*. Ph.D. thesis, University of Oxford: Faculty of Linguistics, Philology and Phonetics and The Queen's College, Oxford, United Kingdom.

Simon Dobnik, Mehdi Ghanimifard, and John D. Kelleher. 2018. Exploring the functional and geometric bias of spatial relations using neural language models. In *Proceedings of the First International Workshop on Spatial Language Understanding (SpLU 2018) at NAACL-HLT 2018*, pages 1–11, New Orleans, Louisiana, USA. Association for Computational Linguistics.

Simon Dobnik, Christine Howes, and John D. Kelleher. 2015. Changing perspective: Local alignment of reference frames in dialogue. In *Proceedings of goDIAL – Semdial 2015: The 19th Workshop on the Semantics and Pragmatics of Dialogue*, pages 24–32, Gothenburg, Sweden.

Desmond Elliott and Frank Keller. 2013. Image description using visual dependency representations. In *Proceedings of the 2013 Conference on Empirical Methods in Natural Language Processing*, pages 1292–1302.

Desmond Elliott and Arjen de Vries. 2015. Describing images using inferred visual dependency representations. In *Proceedings of the 53rd Annual Meeting of the Association for Computational Linguistics and the 7th International Joint Conference on Natural Language Processing (Volume 1: Long Papers)*, volume 1, pages 42–52.

Klaus-Peter Gapp. 1994. Basic meanings of spatial relations: computation and evaluation in 3D space. In *Proceedings of the twelfth national conference on Artificial Intelligence (AAAI'94)*, volume 2, pages 1393–1398, Menlo Park, CA, USA. American Association for Artificial Intelligence, AAAI Press/MIT Press.

Mehdi Ghanimifard and Simon Dobnik. 2018. Knowing when to look for what and where: Evaluating generation of spatial descriptions with adaptive attention. In *Proceedings of the 1st Workshop on Shortcomings in Vision and Language (SiVL'18), ECCV, 2018*.

Kaiming He, Xiangyu Zhang, Shaoqing Ren, and Jian Sun. 2016. Deep residual learning for image recognition. In *Proceedings of the IEEE conference on computer vision and pattern recognition*, pages 770–778.

Dave Herholz. 2005. Wide stance. VisualGenome image id 2412051.

Annette Herskovits. 1986. *Language and spatial cognition: an interdisciplinary study of the prepositions in English*. Cambridge University Press, Cambridge.

Sepp Hochreiter and Jürgen Schmidhuber. 1997. Long short-term memory. *Neural computation*, 9(8):1735–1780.

Ronghang Hu, Marcus Rohrbach, Jacob Andreas, Trevor Darrell, and Kate Saenko. 2017. Modeling relationships in referential expressions with compositional modular networks. In *Proceedings of the IEEE Conference on Computer Vision and Pattern Recognition*, pages 1115–1124.

Justin Johnson, Andrej Karpathy, and Li Fei-Fei. 2016. Densecap: Fully convolutional localization networks for dense captioning. In *Proceedings of the IEEE Conference on Computer Vision and Pattern Recognition*, pages 4565–4574.

juanjogasp. 2013. Baltic trip. VisualGenome image id 2413282.

Andrej Karpathy and Li Fei-Fei. 2015. Deep visual-semantic alignments for generating image descriptions. In *Proceedings of the IEEE conference on computer vision and pattern recognition*, pages 3128–3137.

John D. Kelleher and Simon Dobnik. 2017. What is not where: the challenge of integrating spatial representations into deep learning architectures. In *Proceedings of the Conference on Logic and Machine Learning in Natural Language (LaML 2017), Gothenburg, 12 –13 June*, volume 1 of *CLASP Papers in Computational Linguistics*, pages 41–52, Gothenburg, Sweden. Department of Philosophy, Linguistics and Theory of Science (FLOV), University of Gothenburg, CLASP, Centre for Language and Studies in Probability.

John D. Kelleher and Geert-Jan M. Kruijff. 2006. Incremental generation of spatial referring expressions in situated dialog. In *Proceedings of the 21st International Conference on Computational Linguistics and 44th Annual Meeting of the Association for Computational Linguistics*, pages 1041–1048, Sydney, Australia. Association for Computational Linguistics.

Diederik P Kingma and Jimmy Ba. 2014. Adam: A method for stochastic optimization. *arXiv preprint arXiv:1412.6980*.

Ryan Kiros, Ruslan Salakhutdinov, and Rich Zemel. 2014. Multimodal neural language models. In *International Conference on Machine Learning*, pages 595–603.

Emiel Krahmer and Kees van Deemter. 2011. Computational generation of referring expressions: A survey. *Computational Linguistics*, 38(1):173–218.

Ranjay Krishna, Yuke Zhu, Oliver Groth, Justin Johnson, Kenji Hata, Joshua Kravitz, Stephanie Chen, Yannis Kalantidis, Li-Jia Li, David A Shamma, et al. 2017. Visual genome: Connecting language and vision using crowdsourced dense image annotations. *International Journal of Computer Vision*, 123(1):32–73.

Girish Kulkarni, Visruth Premraj, Sagnik Dhar, Siming Li, Yejin Choi, Alexander C Berg, and Tamara L Berg. 2011. Baby talk: Understanding and generating image descriptions. In *Proceedings of the 24th CVPR*. Citeseer.

Barbara Landau. 1996. Multiple geometric representations of objects in languages and language learners. *Language and space*, pages 317–363.

Angeliki Lazaridou, Marco Baroni, et al. 2015. Combining language and vision with a multimodal skip-gram model. In *Proceedings of the 2015 Conference of the North American Chapter of the Association for Computational Linguistics: Human Language Technologies*, pages 153–163.

Chenxi Liu, Junhua Mao, Fei Sha, and Alan Yuille. 2017. Attention correctness in neural image captioning. In *Thirty-First AAAI Conference on Artificial Intelligence*.

Gordon D Logan. 1994. Spatial attention and the apprehension of spatial relations. *Journal of Experimental Psychology: Human Perception and Performance*, 20(5):1015.

Gordon D Logan. 1995. Linguistic and conceptual control of visual spatial attention. *Cognitive psychology*, 28(2):103–174.

Gordon D. Logan and Daniel D. Sadler. 1996. A computational analysis of the apprehension of spatial relations. In Paul Bloom, Mary A. Peterson, Lynn Nadel, and Merrill F. Garrett, editors, *Language and Space*, pages 493–530. MIT Press, Cambridge, MA.

Jiasen Lu, Caiming Xiong, Devi Parikh, and Richard Socher. 2017. Knowing when to look: Adaptive attention via a visual sentinel for image captioning. In *Proceedings of the IEEE Conference on Computer Vision and Pattern Recognition (CVPR)*, volume 6.

Didier Maillat. 2003. *The semantics and pragmatics of directionals: a case study in English and French*. Ph.D. thesis, University of Oxford: Committee for Comparative Philology and General Linguistics, Oxford, United Kingdom.

George A. Miller and Philip N. Johnson-Laird. 1976. *Language and perception*. Cambridge University Press, Cambridge.

Margaret Mitchell, Kees van Deemter, and Ehud Reiter. 2013. Generating expressions that refer to visible objects. In *Proceedings of the 2013 Conference of the North American Chapter of the Association for Computational Linguistics: Human Language Technologies*, pages 1174–1184, Atlanta, Georgia. Association for Computational Linguistics.

Margaret Mitchell, Xufeng Han, Jesse Dodge, Alyssa Mensch, Amit Goyal, Alex Berg, Kota Yamaguchi, Tamara Berg, Karl Stratos, and Hal Daumé III. 2012. Midge: Generating image descriptions from computer vision detections. In *Proceedings of the 13th Conference of the European Chapter of the Association for Computational Linguistics*, pages 747–756. Association for Computational Linguistics.

Bryan A Plummer, Liwei Wang, Chris M Cervantes, Juan C Caicedo, Julia Hockenmaier, and Svetlana Lazebnik. 2015. Flickr30k entities: Collecting region-to-phrase correspondences for richer image-to-sentence models. In *Proceedings of the IEEE international conference on computer vision*, pages 2641–2649.

Arnau Ramisa, JK Wang, Ying Lu, Emmanuel Dellandrea, Francesc Moreno-Noguer, and Robert Gaizauskas. 2015. Combining geometric, textual and visual features for predicting prepositions in image descriptions. In *Proceedings of the 2015 Conference on Empirical Methods in Natural Language Processing*, pages 214–220. Association for Computational Linguistics.

RaSeLaSeD_Il_Pinguino. 2008. Killer bear. VisualGenome image id 2318741.

Shaoqing Ren, Kaiming He, Ross Girshick, and Jian Sun. 2015. Faster r-cnn: Towards real-time object detection with region proposal networks. In *Advances in neural information processing systems*, pages 91–99.

Fereshteh Sadeghi, Santosh K Kumar Divvala, and Ali Farhadi. 2015. Viske: Visual knowledge extraction and question answering by visual verification of relation phrases. In *Proceedings of the IEEE conference on computer vision and pattern recognition*, pages 1456–1464.

Jared Schmidt. 2010. Desk 2010-08-08. VisualGenome image id 2413204.

Leonard Talmy. 1983. How language structures space. In Herbert L. Pick Jr. and Linda P. Acredolo, editors, *Spatial orientation: theory, research, and application*, pages 225–282. Plenum Press, New York.

Marc Tanti, Albert Gatt, and Kenneth P Camilleri. 2018a. Quantifying the amount of visual information used by neural caption generators. In *Proceedings of the European Conference on Computer Vision (ECCV)*, pages 0–0.

Marc Tanti, Albert Gatt, and Kenneth P Camilleri. 2018b. Where to put the image in an image caption generator. *Natural Language Engineering*, 24(3):467–489.

Jette Viethen and Robert Dale. 2008. The use of spatial relations in referring expression generation. In *Proceedings of the Fifth International Natural Language Generation Conference*, pages 59–67. Association for Computational Linguistics.

Oriol Vinyals, Alexander Toshev, Samy Bengio, and Dumitru Erhan. 2015. Show and tell: A neural image caption generator. In *Computer Vision and Pattern Recognition (CVPR), 2015 IEEE Conference on*, pages 3156–3164. IEEE.

Kelvin Xu, Jimmy Ba, Ryan Kiros, Kyunghyun Cho, Aaron Courville, Ruslan Salakhudinov, Rich Zemel, and Yoshua Bengio. 2015. Show, attend and tell: Neural image caption generation with visual attention. In *International Conference on Machine Learning*, pages 2048–2057.

Brian Yap. 2008. New england highway. VisualGenome image id 2417890.

Quanzeng You, Hailin Jin, Zhaowen Wang, Chen Fang, and Jiebo Luo. 2016. Image captioning with semantic attention. In *Proceedings of the IEEE Conference on Computer Vision and Pattern Recognition*, pages 4651–4659.

Semi-Supervised Neural Text Generation by Joint Learning of Natural Language Generation and Natural Language Understanding Models

Raheel Qader[1]   François Portet[2]   Cyril Labbé[2]
Univ. Grenoble Alpes, LIG
38000 Grenoble, France
[1]`raheel.qader@univ-grenoble-alpes.fr`
[2]`{francois.portet, cyril.labbe}@imag.fr`

Abstract

In Natural Language Generation (NLG), End-to-End (E2E) systems trained through deep learning have recently gained a strong interest. Such deep models need a large amount of carefully annotated data to reach satisfactory performance. However, acquiring such datasets for every new NLG application is a tedious and time-consuming task. In this paper, we propose a semi-supervised deep learning scheme that can learn from non-annotated data and annotated data when available. It uses an NLG and a Natural Language Understanding (NLU) sequence-to-sequence models which are learned jointly to compensate for the lack of annotation. Experiments on two benchmark datasets show that, with limited amount of annotated data, the method can achieve very competitive results while not using any preprocessing or re-scoring tricks. These findings open the way to the exploitation of non-annotated datasets which is the current bottleneck for the E2E NLG system development to new applications.

1 Introduction

Natural Language Generation (NLG) is an NLP task that consists in generating a sequence of natural language sentences from non-linguistic data. Traditional approaches of NLG consist in creating specific algorithms in the consensual NLG pipeline (Gatt and Krahmer, 2018), but there has been recently a strong interest in End-to-End (E2E) NLG systems which are able to jointly learn sentence planning and surface realization (Dušek and Jurcícek, 2016; Agarwal et al., 2018; Juraska et al., 2018; Gehrmann et al., 2018). Probably the most well known effort of this trend is the E2E NLG challenge (Novikova et al., 2017b) whose task was to perform sentence planing and realization from dialogue act-based Meaning Representation (MR) on *unaligned* data. For instance, Fig-

---

Source sequence (MR):
name[The Eagle], eatType[coffee shop], food[French], priceRange[moderate], customerRating[3/5], area[riverside], kidsFriendly[yes], near[Burger King]
Target sequence (natural language):
The three star coffee shop, The Eagle, gives families a mid-priced dining experience featuring a variety of wines and cheeses. Find The Eagle near Burger King.

Figure 1: Example of Meaning Representation (MR) and one of its paired possible text realizations. This is a excerpt of the E2E NLG challenge dataset.

ure 1 presents, on the upper part, a meaning representation and on the lower part, one possible textual realization to convey this meaning. Although the challenge was a great success, the data used in the challenge contained a lot of redundancy of structure and a limited amount of concepts and several reference texts per MR input (8.1 in average). This is an ideal case for machine learning but is it the one that is encountered in all E2E NLG real-world applications?

In this work, we are interested in learning E2E models for real world applications in which there is a low amount of annotated data. Indeed, it is well known that neural approaches need a large amount of carefully annotated data to be able to induce NLP models. For the NLG task, that means that MR and (possibly many) reference texts must be *paired* together so that supervised learning is made possible. In NLG, such paired datasets are rare and remains tedious to acquire (Novikova et al., 2017b; Gardent et al., 2017; Qader et al., 2018). On the contrary, large amount of *unpaired* meaning representations and texts can be available but cannot be exploited for supervised learning.

In order to tackle this problem, we propose a semi-supervised learning approach which is able to benefit from unpaired (non-annotated) dataset which are much easier to acquire in real life applications. In an unpaired dataset, only the input data

Proceedings of The 12th International Conference on Natural Language Generation, pages 552–562,
Tokyo, Japan, 28 Oct - 1 Nov, 2019. ©2019 Association for Computational Linguistics

is assumed to be representative of the task. In such case, autoencoders can be used to learn an (often more compact) internal representation of the data. Monolingual word embeddings learning also benefit from unpaired data. However, none of these techniques are fit for the task of generating from a constrained MR representation. Hence, we extend the idea of autoencoder which is to regenerate the input sequence by using an NLG and an NLU models. To learn the NLG model, the input text is fed to the NLU model which in turn feeds the NLG model. The output of the NLG model is compared to the input and a loss can be computed. A similar strategy is applied for NLU. This approach brings several advantages: 1) the learning is performed from a large unpaired (non-annotated) dataset and a small amount of paired data to constrain the inner representation of the models to respect the format of the task (here MR and abstract text); 2) the architecture is completely differentiable which enables a fully joint learning; and 3) the two NLG and NLU models remain independent and can thus be applied to different tasks separately.

The remaining of this paper gives some background about seq2seq models (Sec 2) before introducing the joint learning approach (Sec 3). Two benchmarks, described in Sec 4, have been used to evaluate the method and whose results are presented in Sec 5. The method is then positioned with respect to the state-of-the-art in Sec 6 before providing some concluding remarks in Sec 7.

2   Background: E2E systems

E2E Natural Language Generation systems are typically based on the Recurrent Neural Network (RNN) architecture consisting of an encoder and a decoder also known as seq2seq (Sutskever et al., 2014). The encoder takes a sequence of source words $\mathbf{x} = \{x_1, x_2, ..., x_{T_x}\}$ and encodes it to a fixed length vector. The decoder then decodes this vector into a sequence of target words $\mathbf{y} = \{y_1, y_2, ..., y_{T_y}\}$. Seq2seq models are able to treat variable sized source and target sequences making them a great choice for NLG and NLU tasks.

More formally, in a seq2seq model, the recurrent unit of the encoder, at each time step t receives an input word x_t (in practice the embedding vector of the word) and a previous hidden state $h_t - 1$

then generates a new hidden state h_t using:

$$h_t = f(h_{t-1}, x_t), \tag{1}$$

where the function f is an RNN unit such as Long Short-Term Memory (LSTM) (Hochreiter and Schmidhuber, 1997) or Gated Recurrent Unit (GRU) (Cho et al., 2014). Once the encoder has treated the entire source sequence, the last hidden state h_{T_x} is passed to the decoder. To generate the sequence of target words, the decoder also uses an RNN and computes, at each time step, a new hidden state s_t from its previous hidden state s_{t-1} and the previously generated word y_{t-1}. At training time, y_{t-1} is the previous word in the target sequence (teacher-forcing). Lastly, the conditional probability of each target word y_t is computed as follows:

$$P(y_t|\mathbf{y}_{<t}, \mathbf{x}) = softmax(W[s_t, c_t]+b), \tag{2}$$

where W and b are a trainable parameters used to map the output to the same size as the target vocabulary and c_t is the context vector obtained using the sum of hidden states in the encoder, weighted by its attention (Bahdanau et al., 2014; Luong et al., 2015). The context is computed as follow:

$$c_t = \sum_{i=1}^{T_x} \alpha_i^t h_i \tag{3}$$

Attention weights α_i^t are computed by applying a softmax function over a score calculated using the encoder and decoder hidden states:

$$\alpha_i^t = softmax(e_i^t) \tag{4}$$

$$e_i^t = score(s_t, h_i) \tag{5}$$

The choice of the score adopted in this papers is based on the *dot attention* mechanism introduced in (Luong et al., 2015). The attention mechanism helps the decoder to find relevant information on the encoder side based on the current decoder hidden state.

3   Joint NLG/NLU learning scheme

The joint NLG/NLU learning scheme is shown in Figure 2. It consists of two seq2seq models for NLG and NLU tasks. Both models can be trained separately on paired data. In that case, the NLG task is to predict the text $\hat{y}$ from the input MR x

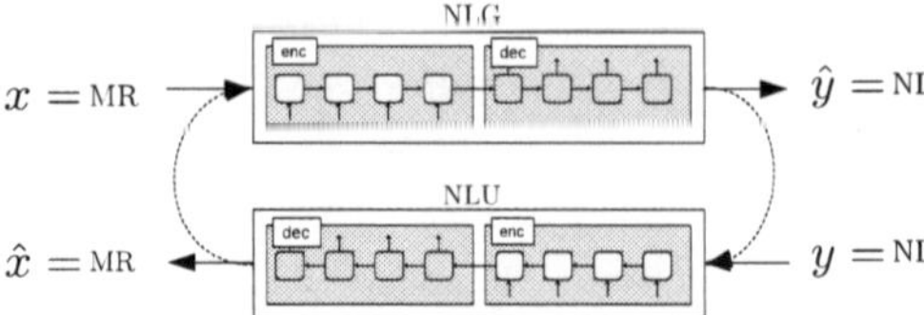

Figure 2: The joint NLG/NLU learning scheme. Dashed arrows between NLG and NLU models show data flow in the case of learning with unpaired data.

while the NLU task is to predict the MR $\hat{x}$ from the input text y. On unpaired data, the two models are connected through two different loops. In the first case, when the unpaired input source is text, y is provided to the NLU models which feeds the NLG model to produce $\hat{y}$. A loss is computed between y and $\hat{y}$ (but not between $\hat{x}$ and x since x is unknown). In the second case, when the input is only MR, x is provided to the NLG model which then feeds the NLU model and finally predicts $\hat{x}$. Similarly, a loss is computed between x and $\hat{x}$ (but not between $\hat{y}$ and y since y is unknown). This section details these four steps and how the loss is backpropagated through the loops.

Learning with Paired Data:

The NLG model is a seq2seq model with attention as described in section 2. It takes as input a MR and generates a natural language text. The objective is to find the model parameters θ^{nlg} such that they minimize the loss which is defined as follows:

$$\mathcal{L}_p^{nlg} = -\frac{1}{T_y} \sum_{t=1}^{T_y} log P(y_t|\mathbf{x}; \theta^{nlg}) \qquad (6)$$

The NLU model is based on the same architecture but takes a natural language text and outputs a MR and its loss can be formulated as:

$$\mathcal{L}_p^{nlu} = -\frac{1}{T_x} \sum_{t=1}^{T_x} log P(x_t|\mathbf{y}; \theta^{nlu}) \qquad (7)$$

Learning with Unpaired Data:

When data are unpaired, there is also a loop connection between the two seq2seq models. This is achieved by feeding MR to the NLG model in order to generate a sequence of natural language text $\hat{y}$ by applying an argmax over the probability distribution at each time step ($\hat{y}_t =$

$argmax P(y_t|\mathbf{x}; \theta^{nlg})$). This text is then fed back into the NLU model which in turn generates an MR. Finally, we compute the loss between the original MR and the reconstructed MR:

$$\mathcal{L}_u^{nlu} = -\frac{1}{T_x} \sum_{t=1}^{T_x} log P(x_t|\mathbf{x}; \theta^{nlg}, \theta^{nlu}) \qquad (8)$$

The same can be applied in the opposite direction where we feed text to the NLU model and then the NLG model reconstructs back the text. This loss is given by:

$$\mathcal{L}_u^{nlg} = -\frac{1}{T_y} \sum_{t=1}^{T_y} log P(y_t|\mathbf{y}; \theta^{nlg}, \theta^{nlu}) \qquad (9)$$

To perform joint learning, all four losses are summed together to provide the uniq loss $\mathcal{L}$ as follows:

$$\mathcal{L} = \alpha \cdot \mathcal{L}_p^{nlg} + \beta \cdot \mathcal{L}_p^{nlu} + \gamma \cdot \mathcal{L}_u^{nlg} + \delta \cdot \mathcal{L}_u^{nlu} \qquad (10)$$

The weights α, β, δ and $\gamma \in [0, 1]$ are defined to fine tune the contribution of each task and data to the learning or to bias the learning towards one specific task. We show in the experiment section the impact of different settings.

Since the loss functions in Equation 6 and 7 force the model to generate a sequence of words based on the target and the losses in Equation 9 and 8 force the model to reconstruct back the input sequence, this way the model is encouraged to generate text that is supported by the facts found in the input sequence. It is important to note that the gradients based on $\mathcal{L}_p^{nlg}$ and $\mathcal{L}_p^{nlu}$ can only backpropagate through their respective model (i.e., NLG and NLU), while $\mathcal{L}_u^{nlg}$ and $\mathcal{L}_u^{nlu}$ gradients should backpropagate through both models.

Straight-Through Gumbel-Softmax:

A major problem with the proposed joint learning architecture in the unpaired case is that the model is not fully differentiable. Indeed, given the input x and the intermediate output $\hat{y}$, the $\mathcal{L}_u^{nlu}$ and the NLG parameter θ_{nlg}, the gradient is computed as:

$$\frac{\partial \mathcal{L}_u^{nlu}}{\partial \theta_{nlg}} = \sum_t^{T} \left(\frac{\partial \mathcal{L}_u^{nlu}}{\partial \hat{y}_t} + \frac{\partial \hat{y}_t}{\partial p_{y_t}} + \frac{\partial p_{y_t}}{\partial \theta_{nlg}} \right) \qquad (11)$$

At each time step t, the output probability p_{y_t} is computed trough the softmax layer and $\hat{y}_t$ is obtained using $\hat{y}_t = onehot(argmax_w p_{y_t}[w])$ that is the word index w with maximum probability at time step t. To address this problem, one solution is to replace this operation by the identity matrix $\frac{\partial \hat{y}_t}{\partial p_{y_t}} \approx \mathbb{1}$. This approach is called the Straight-Through (ST) estimator, which simply consists of backpropagating through the argmax function as if it had been the identity function (Bengio et al., 2013; Yin et al., 2019).

A more principled way of dealing with the non-differential nature of argmax, is to use the Gumbel-Softmax which proposes a continuous approximation to sampling from a categorical distribution (Jang et al., 2017). Hence, the discontinuous argmax is replaced by a differentiable and smooth function. More formally, consider a k-dimensional categorical distribution u with probabilities $\pi_1, \pi_2, ..., \pi_k$. Samples from u can be approximated using:

$$y_i = \frac{\exp((\log(\pi_i) + g_i)/\tau)}{\sum_{j=1}^{k} \exp((\log(\pi_j) + g_j)/\tau)} \quad (12)$$

$$g_i = -\log(-\log(u_i)) \quad (13)$$

$$u_i \sim \text{Uniform}(0, 1), \quad (14)$$

where g_i is the Gumbel noise drawn from a uniform distribution and τ is a temperature parameter. The sample distribution from the Gumbel-Softmax resembles the argmax operation as $\tau \rightarrow 0$, and it becomes uniform when $\tau \rightarrow \infty$.

Although Gumbel-Softmax is differentiable, the samples drawn from it are not adequate input to the subsequent models which expect a discrete values in order to retrieve the embedding matrix of the input words. So, instead, we use the Straight-Through (ST) Gumbel-Softmax which is basically the discrete version of the Gumbel-Softmax. During the forward phase, ST Gumbel-Softmax discretizes y in Equation 12 but it uses the continuous approximation in the backward pass. Although the Gumbel-Softmax estimator is biased due to the sample mismatch between the backward and forward phases, many studies have shown that ST Gumbel-Softmax can lead to significant improvements in several tasks (Choi et al., 2018; Gu et al., 2018; Tjandra et al., 2018).

4   Dataset

The models developed were evaluated on two datasets. The first one is the E2E NLG challenge dataset (Novikova et al., 2017b) which contains 51k of annotated samples. The second one is the Wikipedia Company Dataset (Qader et al., 2018) which consists of around 51K of noisy MR-abstract pairs of company descriptions.

4.1   E2E NLG challenge Dataset

The E2E NLG challenge Dataset has become one of the benchmarks of reference for end-to-end sentence-planning NLG systems. It is still one of the largest dataset available for this task. The dataset was collected via crowd-sourcing using pictorial representations in the domain of restaurant recommendation.

Although the E2E challenge dataset contains more than 50k samples, each MR is associated on average with 8.1 different reference utterances leading to around 6K unique MRs. Each MR consists of 3 to 8 slots, such as *name*, *food* or *area*, and their values and slot types are fairly equally distributed. The majority of MRs consist of 5 or 6 slots while human utterances consist mainly of one or two sentences only. The vocabulary size of the dataset is of 2780 distinct tokens.

4.2   The Wikipedia Company Dataset

The wikipedia company dataset (Qader et al., 2018), is composed of a set of company data from English Wikipedia. The dataset contains 51k samples where each sample is composed of up to 3 components: the Wikipedia article abstract, the Wikipedia article body, and the infobox which is a set of attribute–value pairs containing primary information about the company (*founder*, *creation date* etc.). The infobox part was taken as MR where each attribute–value pair was represented as a sequence of string `attribute [value]`. The MR representation is composed of 41 attributes with 4.5 attributes per article and 2 words per value in average. The abstract length is between 1 to 5 sentences. The vocabulary size is of 158464 words.

The Wikipedia company dataset contains much more lexical variation and semantic information than the E2E challenge dataset. Furthermore, company texts have been written by humans within the Wikipedia ecosystem and not during a controlled experiment whose human en-

gagement was unknown. Hence, the Wikipedia
dataset seems an ecological target for research in
NLG. However, as pointed out by the authors, the
Wikipedia dataset is not ideal for machine learning. First, the data is not controlled and each
article contains only one reference (vs. 8.1 for
the E2E challenge dataset). Second the abstract,
the body and the infobox are only loosely correlated. Indeed, the meaning representation coverage is poor since, for some MR, none of the information is found in the text and vice-versa. To give
a rough estimate of this coverage, we performed
an analysis of 100 articles randomly selected in
the test set. Over 868 total slot instances, 28% of
the slots in the infobox cannot be found in their
respective abstract text, while 13% are missing in
the infobox.

Despite these problems, we believe the E2E and
the Wikipedia company datasets can provide contrasted evaluation, the first being well controlled
and lexically focused, the latter representing the
kind of data that can be found in real situations
and that E2E systems must deal with in order to
percolate in the society.

5   Experiments

The performance of the joint learning architecture was evaluated on the two datasets described
in the previous section. The joint learning model
requires a paired and an unpaired dataset, so each
of the two datasets was split into several parts.

E2E NLG challenge Dataset: The training set
of the E2E challenge dataset which consists of
42K samples was partitioned into a 10K paired and
32K unpaired datasets by a random process. The
unpaired database was composed of two sets, one
containing MRs only and the other containing natural texts only. This process resulted in 3 training
sets: paired set, unpaired text set and unpaired MR
set. The original development set (4.7K) and test
set (4.7K) of the E2E dataset have been kept.

The Wikipedia Company Dataset: The
Wikipedia company dataset presented in Section 4.2 was filtered to contain only companies
having abstracts of at least 7 words and at most
105 words. As a result of this process, 43K companies were retained. The dataset was then divided into: a training set (35K), a development set
(4.3K) and a test set (4.3K). Of course, there was
no intersection between these sets.

The training set was also partitioned in order to

obtain the paired and unpaired datasets. Because
of the loose correlation between the MRs and
their corresponding text, the paired dataset was
selected such that it contained the infobox values
with the highest similarity with its reference
text. The similarity was computed using "difflib"
library[1], which is an extension of the Ratcliff
and Obershelp algorithm (Ratcliff and Metzener,
1988). The paired set was selected in this way
(rather than randomly) to get samples as close as
possible to a carefully annotated set. At the end
of partitioning, the following training sets were
obtained: paired set (10.5K), unpaired text set
(24.5K) and unpaired MR set (24.5K).

The way the datasets are split into paired and
unpaired sets is artificial and might be biased particularly for the E2E dataset as it is a rather easy
dataset. This is why we included the Wikipedia
dataset in our study since the possibility of having such bias is low because 1) each company
summary/infobox was written by different authors
at different time within the wikipedia eco-system
making this data far more natural than in the E2E
challenge case, 2) there is a large amount of variation in the dataset, and 3) the dataset was split
in such a way that the paired set contains perfect
matches between the MR and the text, while re-
serving the least matching samples for the the unpaired set (i.e., the more representative of real-life
Wikipedia articles). As a result, the paired and
unpaired sets of the Wikipedia dataset are different from each other and the text and MR unpaired
samples are only loosely correlated.

5.1   Evaluation with Automatic Metrics

For the experiments, each seq2seq model was
composed of 2 layers of Bi-LSTM in the encoder
and two layers of LSTM in the decoder with 256
hidden units and *dot attention* trained using Adam
optimization with learning rate of 0.001. The embeddings had 500 dimensions and the vocabulary
was limited to 50K words. The Gumbel-Softmax
temperature τ was set to 1. Hyper-parameters tuning was performed on the development set and
models were trained until the loss on the development set stops decreasing for several consecutive
iterations. All models were implemented with Py-
Torch library.

---

[1] https://docs.python.org/2/library/
difflib.html#difflib.SequenceMatcher

					NLG			NLU		
System	α	β	γ	δ	BLEU	Rouge-L	Meteor	Precision	Recall	F-score
Paired	-	-	-	-	0.60	0.64	0.42	0.74	**0.83**	0.78
Paired + Unpaired	0.25	0.25	1	1	**0.64**†	0.66†	0.43	0.73	0.78	0.76
	0.1	0.1	1	1	**0.64**†	**0.67**†	0.42	0.73	0.74	0.74
	1	0.1	1	1	0.63†	**0.67**†	0.43†	0.72	0.78	0.75
	1	0.1	1	0.1	**0.64**†	**0.67**†	**0.45**†	**0.77**	**0.83**	**0.80**

Table 1: Results on the test set of E2E dataset. † indicates t-test $p < 0.001$ against the paired NLG results.

					NLG			NLU		
System	α	β	γ	δ	BLEU	Rouge-L	Meteor	Precision	Recall	F-score
Paired	-	-	-	-	0.08	0.24	0.11	**0.20**	0.33	0.25
Paired + Unpaired	0.25	0.25	1	1	0.02†	0.15†	0.07†	**0.20**	**0.43**	**0.27**
	0.1	0.1	1	1	0.04†	0.18†	0.08†	0.08	0.22	0.12
	1	0.1	1	1	0.08	**0.26**†	**0.12**†	0.18	0.42	0.25
	1	0.1	1	0.1	**0.09**†	**0.26**†	**0.12**†	**0.20**	0.35	0.26

Table 2: Results on the test set of Wikipedia company dataset. † indicates t-test $p < 0.001$ against the Paired NLG results.

Results of the experiment on the E2E challenge data are summarized Table 1 for both the NLG and the NLU tasks. BLEU, Rouge-L and Meteor were computed using the E2E challenge metrics script[2] with default settings. NLU performances were computed at the slot level. The model learned using paired+unpaired methods shows significant superior performances than the paired version. Among the paired+unpaired methods, the one of last row exhibits the highest balanced score between NLG and NLU. This is achieved when the weights α and γ favor the NLG task against NLU ($\beta = \delta = 0.1$). This setting has been chosen since the NLU task converged much quicker than the NLG task. Hence lower weight for NLU during the learning avoided over-fitting. This best system exhibits similar performances than the E2E challenge winner for ROUGE-L and METEOR whereas it did not use any pre-processing (delexicalisation, slot alignment, data augmentation) or re-scoring and was trained on far less annotated data.

Results of the experiment on Wikipedia company dataset are summarized Table 2 for both the NLG and the NLU tasks. Due to noise in the dataset and the fact that only one reference is available for each sample, the automatic metrics show very low scores. This is in line with (Qader et al., 2018) for which the best system obtained BLEU= 0.0413, ROUGE-L= 0.266 and METEOR= 0.1076. Contrary to the previous results, the paired method brings one of the best performance. However, the best performing system is the one of the last row which again put more emphasis on the NLG task than on the NLU one. Once again, this system obtained performances comparable to the best system of (Qader et al., 2018) but without using any pointer generator or coverage mechanisms.

In order to further analyze the results, in Table 3 we show samples of the generated text by different models alongside the reference texts. The first two examples are from the model trained on the E2E NLG dataset and the last two are from the Wikipedia dataset. Although on the E2E dataset the outputs of paired and paired+unpaired models seem very similar, the latter resembles the reference slightly more and because of this it achieves a higher score in the automatic metrics. This resemblance to the reference could be attributed to the fact that we use a reconstruction loss which forces the model to generate text that is only supported by facts found in the input. As for the Wikipedia dataset examples, we can see that the model with paired+unpaired data is less noisy and the outputs are generally shorter. The model with only paired data generates unnecessarily longer text with lots of unsupported facts and repetitions. Needless to say that both models are doing lots of mistakes and this is because of all the noise contained in

[2] https://github.com/tuetschek/e2e-metrics

Input	name[the punter], eattype[restaurant], food[indian], pricerange[moderate], customer_rating[1 out of 5], area[city centre], familyfriendly[no], near[express by holiday inn]
Reference	the punter is a restaurant providing indian food in the moderate price range. it is located in the city centre. it is near express by holiday inn. its customer rating is 1 out of 5.
Paired model	the punter is a moderately priced indian restaurant in the city centre near express by holiday inn. it has a customer rating of 1 out of 5.
Paired+unpaired model	the punter is a restaurant providing indian food in the moderate price range. it is located in the city centre. it is near express by holiday inn. its customer rating is 1 out of 5.
Input	name[the cricketers], eattype[restaurant], food[chinese], pricerange[less than 20], customer_rating[low], area[city centre], familyfriendly[no], near[all bar one]
Reference	the cricketers is a restaurant providing chinese for under 20. it has a low customer rating. it is located in the city center. it is not family friendly. it is near all bar one.
Paired model	the cricketers is a chinese restaurant located in the city centre near all bar one that is not family friendly and has a low customer rating and a price range of less than 20.
Paired+unpaired model	the cricketers is a restaurant providing chinese food in the less than 20 price range. it is located in the city centre. it is near all bar one. its customer rating is low.
Input	name1[sedgwick group], headquarters1[london], founded1[1998], industry1[insurance], key_people1[sax riley (chairman)], key_people2[rob whitecooper (ceo)], defunct1[1998]
Reference	sedgwick group plc was a very large british insurance broker . it was listed on the london stock exchange and was a constituent of the ftse 100 index . however it was acquired by marsh & mclennan in 1998 .
Paired model	the porton group was a british insurance company . it was founded in 1998 by former mckinsey and entrepreneur erik muir . it was the first property manager until it was acquired by the saatchi group in 1998 .
Paired+unpaired model	sedgwick group plc was a british insurance company based in london . it was listed on the london stock exchange and was once a constituent of the ftse 100 index .
Input	name1[federal realty investment trust], founded1[1962], industry1[real estate investment trust], key_people1[joseph s vassalluzzo chairman], key_people2[donald c wood ceo president], key_people3[daniel guglielmone cfo], products1[shopping centers], founder1[samuel j gorlitz]
Reference	federal realty investment trust is a real estate investment trust that invests in shopping centers in the northeastern united states , the mid-atlantic states , california , and south florida .
Paired model	city capital trust trust , inc. is a real estate investment trust and investment trust . it was founded in 1962 by robert c. smith , and is based in new york city , and is headquartered in cleveland , connecticut . the company is headquartered in cleveland , florida , and has offices in new york city , new york , and geneva .
Paired+unpaired model	the federal realty investment trust , is a real estate investment trust that invests in shopping centers in the united states . it was founded in 1962 by robert duncan , jr. and john epstein .

Table 3: Sample of generated text from the E2E and Wikipedia test sets using our systems along with the reference text.

	cover.	non-redun.	semant.	gramm.
reference	3.42	4.25	4.19	4.13
paired	2.26	**3.67**	3.28	**4.11**
unpaired	**2.87**[†]	3.63	**3.67**	3.96

Table 4: Results of the human evaluation per system on the Wikipedia corpus using the best unpaired system. [†] indicates wilcoxon $p < 0.05$ against the paired results.

the training data.

5.2 Human Evaluation

It is well know that automatic metrics in NLG are poorly predictive of human ratings although they are useful for system analysis and development (Novikova et al., 2017a; Gatt and Krahmer,

2018). Hence, to gain more insight about the generation properties of each model, a human evaluation with 16 human subjects was performed on the Wikipedia dataset models. We set up a web-based experiment and used the same 4 questions as in (Qader et al., 2018) which were asked on a 5-point Lickert scale: How do you judge the Information Coverage of the company summary? How do you judge the Non-Redundancy of Information in the company summary? How do you judge the Semantic Adequacy of the company summary? How do you judge the Grammatical Correctness of the company summary?

For this experiment, 40 company summaries were selected randomly from the test set. Each participant had to treat 10 summaries by first read-

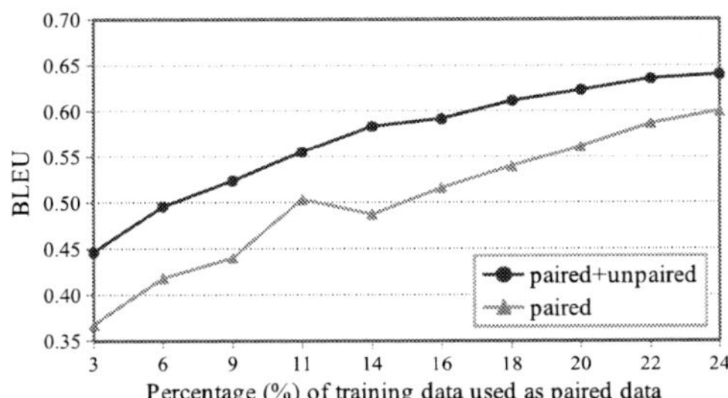

Figure 3: BLEU score as a function of percentage of paired data in the training set on the E2E dataset.

α	β	γ	δ	BLEU	Rouge-L	Meteor
1	0.1	1	0.1	**0.64**	**0.67**	**0.45**
0	0.1	1	0.1	0.62	0.66	0.42
1	0	1	0.1	0.63	0.67	0.42
1	0.1	0	0.1	0.50	0.58	0.36
1	0.1	1	0	0.63	0.66	0.44

Table 5: Effect of loss weights on the performance of the NLG model on the E2E dataset.

α	β	γ	δ	Precision	Recall	F-score
1	0.1	1	0.1	**0.77**	**0.83**	**0.80**
0	0.1	1	0.1	0.74	0.79	0.76
1	0	1	0.1	0.74	0.71	0.73
1	0.1	0	0.1	0.68	0.73	0.70
1	0.1	1	0	0.75	0.73	0.74

Table 6: Effect of loss weights on the performance of the NLU model on the E2E dataset.

ing the summary and the infobox, then answering the aforementioned four questions.

Results of the human experiment are reported in Table 4. The first line reports the results of the reference (i.e., the Wikipedia abstract) for comparison, while the second line is the model with paired data, and the last line is the model trained on paired+unpaired data with parameters reported in the last row of Table 2, i.e., $\alpha = \gamma = 1$ and $\beta = \delta = 0.1$. It is clear from the coverage metric that no system nor the reference was seen as doing a good job at conveying the information present in the infobox. This is in line with the corpus analysis of section 4. However, between the automatic methods, the unpaired models exhibit a clear superiority in coverage and in semantic adequacy, two measures that are linked. On the other side, the model learned with paired data is slightly more performing in term of non-redundancy and grammaticality. The results of the unpaired model with coverage and grammaticality are equivalent to best models of Qader et al. (2018) but for non-redundancy and semantic adequacy the result are slightly below. This is probably because the authors have used a pointer generator mechanism (See et al., 2017), a trick we avoided and which is subject of further work.

These results express the difference between the learning methods: on the one hand, the unpaired learning relaxes the intermediate labels which are noisy so that the model learns to express what is really in the input (this explain the higher result for coverage) while, on the other hand, the paired learning is only constrained by the output text (not also with the NLU loss as in the unpaired case) which results in slightly more grammatical sentence to the expense of semantic coverage.

5.3 Ablation Study

In this section, we further discuss different aspects of the proposed joint learning approach. In particular we are interested in studying the impact of: 1) having different amounts of paired data and 2) the weight of each loss function on the overall performance. Since only the E2E dataset is non-noisy and hence provide meaningful automatic metrics, the ablation study was performed only on this dataset.

To evaluate the dependence on the amount of paired data, the best model was re-trained by changing the size of the paired data ranging from 3% of the training data (i.e., 1K) up to 24% (i.e., 10K). The results are shown in Figure 3. The figure reveals that regardless of the amount of paired data, the joint learning approach: 1) always improves over the model with only paired data and 2) is always able to benefit from supplementary paired data. This is particularly true when the amount of paired data is very small and the difference seems to get smaller as the percentage of the paired data increases.

Next, to evaluate which of the four losses contribute most to the overall performance, the best model was re-trained in different settings. In short, in each setting, one of the weights was set to zero while the others three weights were kept similar as in the best case. The results are presented in Table 5 and Table 6 for NLG and NLU tasks respectively. In these table the first line if the best model as reported in Table 1. It can be seen that all the four losses are important since setting any of the weights to zero leads to a decrease in performance. However, the results of both tables show that the most important loss is the NLG unpaired loss $\mathcal{L}_u^{nlg}$ since setting γ to zeros leads to a significant reduction in the performance for both NLU and NLG.

6 Related Work

The approach of joint learning has been tested in the literature in other domains than NLG/NLU for tasks such machine translation (Cheng et al., 2016; He et al., 2016; Tu et al., 2017) and speech processing (Tjandra et al., 2017, 2018; Liu et al., 2018). In (Tu et al., 2017) an encoder-decoder-reconstructor for MT is proposed. The reconstructor, integrated to the NMT model, rebuilds the source sentence from the hidden layer of the output target sentence, to ensure that the information in the source side is transformed to the target side as much as possible. In (Tjandra et al., 2018), a joint learning architecture of Automatic Speech Recognition (ASR) and Text-To-Speech (TTS) is proposed which leverages unannotated data. In the unannotated case, during the learning, ASR output is fed to the TTS and the TTS output is compared with the original ASR signal input to compute a loss which is back-propagated through both modules. Regarding NLU, joint learning of NLU with other tasks remain scarce. In (Yang et al., 2017), an NLU model is jointly learned with a system action prediction (SAP) model on supervised dialogue data. The NLU model is integrated into the sequence-to-sequence SAP model so that three losses (intent prediction, slot prediction and action prediction) are used to backpropagate through both models. The paper shows that this approach is competitive against the baselines.

To the best of our knowledge, the idea of joint NLG/NLU learning has not been tested previously in NLG. In NLG E2E models (Dušek and Jurcícek, 2016; Juraska et al., 2018), some approaches have learned a concept extractor (which is close to but simpler than an NLU model), but this was not integrated in the NLG learning scheme and only used for output re-scoring. Probably the closest work to our is (Chisholm et al., 2017) in which a seq2seq auto-encoder was used to generate biographies from MR. In this work, the generated text of the 'forward' seq2seq model was constrained by a 'backward' seq2seq model, which shared parameters. However, this works differs from ours since their model was not completely differentiable. Furthermore, their NLU backward model was only used as a support for the forward NLG. Finally, the shared parameters, although in line with the definition of an auto-encoder, make each model impossible to specialize.

7 Conclusion and Further Work

In this paper, we describe a learning scheme which provides the ability to jointly learn two models for NLG and for NLU using large amount of unannotated data and small amount of annotated data. The results obtained with this method on the E2E challenge benchmark, show that the method can achieve a similar score of the winner of the challenge (Juraska et al., 2018) but with far less annotated data and without using any pre-processing (delexicalisation, data augmentation) or re-scoring tricks. Results on the challenging Wikipedia company dataset shows that highest score can be achieve by mixing paired and unpaired datasets. These results are at the state-of-the-art level (Qader et al., 2018) but without using any pointer generator or coverage mechanisms. These findings open the way to the exploitation of unannotated data since the lack of large annotated data source is the current bottleneck of E2E NLG systems development for new applications.

Next steps of the research include, replacing the ST Gumbel-Softmax with reinforcement learning techniques such as policy gradient. This is particularly interesting as with policy gradient we will be able do design reward functions that better suit the problem we are trying to solve. Furthermore, it would be interesting to evaluate how pointer generator mechanism (See et al., 2017) and coverage mechanism (Tu et al., 2016) can be integrated in the learning scheme to increase the non-redundancy and coverage performance of the generation.

Acknowledgments

This project was partly funded by the IDEX Université Grenoble Alpes innovation grant (AI4I-2018-2019) and the Région Auvergne-Rhône-Alpes (AISUA-2018-2019).

References

Shubham Agarwal, Marc Dymetman, and Eric Gaussier. 2018. Char2char generation with reranking for the e2e nlg challenge. In *Proceedings of INLG*, pages 451–456.

Dzmitry Bahdanau, Kyunghyun Cho, and Yoshua Bengio. 2014. Neural machine translation by jointly learning to align and translate. In *Proceedings of ICLR*.

Yoshua Bengio, Nicholas Léonard, and Aaron Courville. 2013. Estimating or propagating gradients through stochastic neurons for conditional computation. *arXiv preprint arXiv:1308.3432*.

Yong Cheng, Wei Xu, Zhongjun He, Wei He, Hua Wu, Maosong Sun, and Yang Liu. 2016. Semi-supervised learning for neural machine translation. In *Proceedings of ACL*, pages 1965–1974.

Andrew Chisholm, Will Radford, and Ben Hachey. 2017. Learning to generate one-sentence biographies from wikidata. In *Proceedings of EACL*, pages 633–642.

Kyunghyun Cho, Bart van Merrienboer, Caglar Gulcehre, Dzmitry Bahdanau, Fethi Bougares, Holger Schwenk, and Yoshua Bengio. 2014. Learning phrase representations using rnn encoder–decoder for statistical machine translation. In *Proceedings of EMNLP*, pages 1724–1734.

Jihun Choi, Kang Min Yoo, and Sang-goo Lee. 2018. Learning to compose task-specific tree structures. In *Proceedings of AAAI*.

Ondřej Dušek and Filip Jurcícek. 2016. Sequence-to-sequence generation for spoken dialogue via deep syntax trees and strings. In *Proceedings of ACL*, pages 45–51.

Claire Gardent, Anastasia Shimorina, Shashi Narayan, and Laura Perez-Beltrachini. 2017. Creating training corpora for micro-planners. In *Proceedings of ACL*.

Albert Gatt and Emiel Krahmer. 2018. Survey of the state of the art in natural language generation: Core tasks, applications and evaluation. *Journal of AI Research*, pages 65–170.

Sebastian Gehrmann, Falcon Dai, Henry Elder, and Alexander Rush. 2018. End-to-end content and plan selection for data-to-text generation. In *Proceedings of INLG*, pages 46–56.

Jiatao Gu, Daniel Jiwoong Im, and Victor OK Li. 2018. Neural machine translation with gumbel-greedy decoding. In *Proceedings of AAAI*.

Di He, Yingce Xia, Tao Qin, Liwei Wang, Nenghai Yu, Tie-Yan Liu, and Wei-Ying Ma. 2016. Dual learning for machine translation. In *Proceedings of NIPS*, pages 820–828.

Sepp Hochreiter and Jürgen Schmidhuber. 1997. Long short-term memory. *Neural computation*, 9:1735–1780.

Eric Jang, Shixiang Gu, and Ben Poole. 2017. Categorical reparameterization with gumbel-softmax. In *Proceedings of ICLR*.

Juraj Juraska, Panagiotis Karagiannis, Kevin Bowden, and Marilyn A. Walker. 2018. A deep ensemble model with slot alignment for sequence-to-sequence natural language generation. In *Proceedings of NAACL-HLT*, pages 152–162.

Da-Rong Liu, Chi-Yu Yang, Szu-Lin Wu, and Hung-Yi Lee. 2018. Improving unsupervised style transfer in end-to-end speech synthesis with end-to-end speech recognition. In *Proceedings of SLT*, pages 640–647.

Thang Luong, Hieu Pham, and Christopher D Manning. 2015. Effective approaches to attention-based neural machine translation. In *Proceedings of EMNLP*, pages 1412–1421.

Jekaterina Novikova, Ondřej Dušek, Amanda Cercas Curry, and Verena Rieser. 2017a. Why we need new evaluation metrics for nlg. In *Proceedings of EMNLP*, pages 2241–2252.

Jekaterina Novikova, Ondřej Dušek, and Verena Rieser. 2017b. The E2E dataset: New challenges for end-to-end generation. In *Proceedings of SIGDIAL*, pages 201–206.

Raheel Qader, Khoder Jneid, François Portet, and Cyril Labbé. 2018. Generation of Company descriptions using concept-to-text and text-to-text deep models: dataset collection and systems evaluation. In *Proceedings of INLG*.

John W Ratcliff and David E Metzener. 1988. Pattern-matching-the gestalt approach. *Dr Dobbs Journal*, pages 46–51.

Abigail See, Peter J Liu, and Christopher D Manning. 2017. Get to the point: Summarization with pointer-generator networks. In *Proceedings of ACL*, pages 1073–1083.

Ilya Sutskever, Oriol Vinyals, and Quoc V Le. 2014. Sequence to sequence learning with neural networks. In *Proceedings of NIPS*, pages 3104–3112.

Andros Tjandra, Sakriani Sakti, and Satoshi Nakamura. 2017. Listening while speaking: Speech chain by deep learning. In *Proceedings of ASRU*, pages 301–308.

Andros Tjandra, Sakriani Sakti, and Satoshi Nakamura. 2018. End-to-end feedback loss in speech chain framework via straight-through estimator. *arXiv preprint arXiv:1810.13107*.

Zhaopeng Tu, Yang Liu, Lifeng Shang, Xiaohua Liu, and Hang Li. 2017. Neural machine translation with reconstruction. In *Proceedings of AAAI*.

Zhaopeng Tu, Zhengdong Lu, Yang Liu, Xiaohua Liu, and Hang Li. 2016. Modeling coverage for neural machine translation. In *Proceedings of ACL*, pages 76–85.

X. Yang, Y. Chen, D. Hakkani-Tr, P. Crook, X. Li, J. Gao, and L. Deng. 2017. End-to-end joint learning of natural language understanding and dialogue manager. In *Proceedings of ICASSP*, pages 5690–5694.

Penghang Yin, Jiancheng Lyu, Shuai Zhang, Stanley J. Osher, Yingyong Qi, and Jack Xin. 2019. Understanding straight-through estimator in training activation quantized neural nets. In *Proceedings of ICLR*.

Neural Generation for Czech: Data and Baselines

Ondřej Dušek and **Filip Jurčíček**
Charles University, Faculty of Mathematics and Physics
Institute of Formal and Applied Linguistics
Prague, Czech Republic
{odusek,jurcicek}@ufal.mff.cuni.cz

Abstract

We present the first dataset targeted at end-to-end NLG in Czech in the restaurant domain, along with several strong baseline models using the sequence-to-sequence approach. While non-English NLG is under-explored in general, Czech, as a morphologically rich language, makes the task even harder: Since Czech requires inflecting named entities, delexicalization or copy mechanisms do not work out-of-the-box and lexicalizing the generated outputs is non-trivial.

In our experiments, we present two different approaches to this this problem: (1) using a neural language model to select the correct inflected form while lexicalizing, (2) a two-step generation setup: our sequence-to-sequence model generates an interleaved sequence of lemmas and morphological tags, which are then inflected by a morphological generator.

1 Introduction

While most current neural NLG systems do not explicitly contain language-specific components and are thus capable of multilingual generation in principle, there has been little work to test these capabilities experimentally. This goes hand in hand with the scarcity of non-English training datasets for NLG – the only data-to-text NLG set known to us is a small sportscasting Korean dataset (Chen et al., 2010),[1] which only contains a limited number of named entities, reducing the need for their inflection.

Since most generators are only tested on English, they do not need to handle grammar complexities not present in English. A prime example is the delexicalization technique used by most current generators (e.g., Oh and Rudnicky, 2000; Mairesse et al., 2010; Wen et al., 2015a,b; Juraska

et al., 2018): It is generally assumed that attribute (slot) values from the input meaning representation (MR) can be replaced by placeholders during generation and inserted into the output verbatim. Delexicalization or an analogous technique, such as a copy mechanism (Gu et al., 2016; Gehrmann et al., 2018), is required for most generation scenarios to allow generalization to unseen entity names: sets of entities are open (potentially infinite and subject to change) while training data is scarce. However, the verbatim insertion assumption does not hold for languages with extensive noun inflection – attribute values need to be inflected here to produce fluent outputs (see Figure 1).

This paper presents the following contributions:

- We create a novel dataset for Czech delexicalized generation; this extends the typical task of data-to-text NLG by requiring attribute value inflection (Section 2). We choose Czech as an example of a morphologically complex language (Cotterell et al., 2018) with a large set of NLP tools readily available (e.g. Popel and Žabokrtský, 2010; Straková et al., 2014; Straka and Straková, 2017).

- We present baseline models based on the TGen sequence-to-sequence (seq2seq) system (Dušek and Jurčíček, 2016), with two novel extensions to the model for our task (Section 3):

  - A model for lexicalization, i.e., selecting the correct inflected surface form for a slot value, based on a recurrent neural network language model (RNN LM);

  - A new generation mode, where the seq2seq generator produces interleaved sequences of lemmas (base word forms) and morphological tags that are postprocessed using a morphological generator.

- Using both automatic and manual evaluation in Section 4, we show that our extensions improve

---

[1] http://www.cs.utexas.edu/users/ml/clamp/sportscasting/

Proceedings of The 12th International Conference on Natural Language Generation, pages 563–574,
Tokyo, Japan, 28 Oct - 1 Nov, 2019. ©2019 Association for Computational Linguistics

?confirm(good_for_meal=breakfast)

needs accusative noun

snídani

Hledáte **vhodnou restauraci na X-good_for_meal ?**
Do-you-look-for a-suitable restaurant for [breakfast]

needs a verb in 2nd person plural future

nasnídáte

Chcete **najít restauraci, kde se dobře X-good_for_meal ?**
Do-you-want to-find a-restaurant where yourself well [you-will-have-breakfast]

snídaně	NNFS1-----A----	snídaňový	AAMS1----1A----	snídat	Vf--------A----
snídaně	NNFP1-----A----	snídaňový	AATS1----1A----	nasnídáta	VB P RP AA
snídaně	NNFS2-----A----	snídaňová	AAFS1----1A----	nasnídat	Vf--------A----
snídaní	NNFP2-----A----	snídaňové	AANS1----1A----	nasnídali	VpMP---XR-AA---
snídani	NNFS3-----A----	snídaňoví	AAMP1----1A----	posnídáte	VB-P---2P-AA---
snídaním	NNFP3-----A----	snídaňové	AATP1----1A----	posnídat	Vf--------A----
snídaní	NNFS4-----A----	(37 more…)		posnídali	VpMP---XR-AA---
snídaně	NNFP4-----A----	snídaňového	AAIS2----1A----		
snídani	NNFS6-----A----	snídaňové	AAFS2----1A----		
snídaních	NNFP6-----A----	snídaňového	AANS2----1A----		
snídaní	NNFS7-----A----	snídaňových	AAMP2----1A----		
snídaněmi	NNFP7-----A----	snídaňovými	AANP7----1A----		

inform(name='Baráčnická rychta', area='Malá Strana')

Baráčnická rychta

needs nominative

X-name **je na X-area .**
[Baráčnická rychta] is in [Malá Strana]

Baráčnickou rychtu

needs accusative

X-name **najdete v oblasti X-area .**
[Baráčnická rychta] you-find in the-area [of-Malá Strana]

Malé Straně

needs locative

Malé Strany

needs genitive

Baráčnická rychta	NNFS1-----A----
Baráčnické rychty	NNFS2-----A----
Baráčnické rychtě	NNFS3-----A----
Baráčnickou rychtu	NNFS4-----A----
Baráčnické rychtě	NNFS6-----A----
Baráčnickou rychtou	NNFS7-----A----

Malá Strana	NNFS1-----A----
Malé Strany	NNFS2-----A----
Malé Straně	NNFS3-----A----
Malou Stranu	NNFS4-----A----
Malé Straně	NNFS6-----A----
Malou Stranou	NNFS7-----A----

Figure 1: Example of delexicalized generation in Czech. Input MRs are shown in bold blue, corresponding target (delexicalized) outputs in bold black, with "X-" marking slot value placeholders. English glosses are shown below each word in gray. Appropriate inflected forms to be filled into slot placeholders are shown in bold green, with lists of all possible forms along with their morphological tags (Hajič, 2004). Note that the surface form for "X-good_for_meal" can even have different parts-of-speech (left column: noun, middle: adjective, right: verb forms).

over the base model, but do not solve the task completely.

We propose improvements for future work in Section 6. Our dataset and all experimental code are released on GitHub.[2]

2 Dataset

Our goal was to create a dataset comparable in size and domain to existing English data-to-text NLG datasets used in experiments with neural systems. Since there are few to none Czech speakers on crowdsourcing platforms (Pavlick et al., 2014; Dušek et al., 2014), we were not able to use them for data collection. Recruiting freelance translators seemed easier than training annotators; therefore, we turned to localizing and translating an existing dataset instead of creating a new one from scratch. We chose the restaurant dataset of Wen et al. (2015b) due to its manageable, yet non-trivial size and the familiarity of the domain (cf. Mairesse et al., 2010; Dušek et al., 2019). The original dataset contains 5,192 MR-sentence pairs, where MRs come in the form of dialogue acts (DAs). A DA consists of DA type (e.g., *request, confirm, inform*) and a list of slots (attributes) and their values (e.g., *name, price_range, address, area*). There are 8 different DA types and 12 slots in the dataset. All slots except the binary *kids_allowed* are delexicalized during generation (cf. Figure 1).

Ananta — feminine noun, inflected (nom: *Ananta*, gen: *Ananty*, dat, loc: *Anantě*, acc: *Anantu*, inst: *Anantou*)

BarBar — masculine inanimate noun, inflected (nom, acc: *BarBar*, gen, dat, loc: *BarBaru*, inst: *BarBarem*)

Café Savoy — neuter noun, not inflected

Místo — neuter noun, inflected (nom, acc: *Místo*, gen: *Místa*, dat: *Místu*, loc: *Místě*, inst: *Místem*)

U Konšelů — prepositional phrase, not inflected

Figure 2: Examples of restaurant names from the localized data with different morphosyntactic behavior (*nom* = nominative, *gen* = genitive, *dat* = dative, *acc* = accusative, *loc* = locative, *inst* = instrumental).

2.1 Localizing the Data

We first needed to localize the dataset, replacing the original setting of San Francisco with a Czech one. In particular, we aimed at using domestic entity names (DA slot values) that need to be inflected since foreign names are often kept uninflected in Czech, using less fluent and conspicuous grammatical constructions to avoid inflection.[3]

We localized the following slots in both DAs and texts from the dataset: restaurant names, areas, food types, street addresses, and landmarks. We

---

[2]Dataset: `https://github.com/UFAL-DSG/cs_restaurant_dataset`, code: `https://github.com/UFAL-DSG/tgen`.

[3]This is not to say that we avoided using any foreign words in the localization process. Since foreign restaurant names are quite common in Czechia, we also included some of them in the localized data.

used a list of randomly chosen restaurant names from the Prague city center as well as lists of Prague neighborhoods, streets, and landmarks. The resulting sentences contain mostly factually inaccurate, yet meaningful utterances about restaurants in Prague.

The localized lists are quite short, with just 15 different restaurant names and a similar number of landmarks, streets, and neighborhoods. While much longer lists would be needed for a real-world scenario, this is sufficient to cover most common classes of names with different inflection patterns and/or syntactic behavior (see Figure 2).

2.2 Translation

We recruited six translators and asked them to translate all unique texts in the localized dataset. They were given the following instructions:

- translate the utterances in isolation,

- use fluent, spoken-style Czech,

- strive to preserve the facts but not necessarily all nuances of the original,

- use varying synonyms (as long as they belong to casual, fluent Czech), including for entity names or slot values (such as price ranges or meal types),

- inflect entity names as needed,

- use formal address (or plural) when addressing the user, and use the female form in the first person for self-references.[4]

All rules but the last one aim at obtaining a varied and fluent dataset; the last rule strives for consistency. Note that the translators were not given the input DAs – these carry no more information than the corresponding English sentences, and we assume that they would only confuse the translators and could hurt the fluency of the results.

2.3 Consistency Checks and Deduplication

We checked the translated Czech texts for the presence of all required slot values. We took the following iterative, partially automatic approach:

1. Create a list of possible inflected surface forms for all slot values in the dataset. We used

the morphological generator of Straková et al. (2014) to inflect the surface forms automatically and manually checked for errors.

2. Given a DA and a translated sentence, check (using an automatic script) that the sentence contains surface forms for all slots in the DA.

3. Given a sentence found by the script to miss a value, check if it contains an alternative surface form not included in the list from Step 1. If so, add this alternative surface form to the list.

4. If the translated sentence does not contain any mention of the DA value, fix the translation.

5. Repeat from Step 2 until there are no missing DA value mentions in the whole set.

Note that these checks result not only in greater consistency of the dataset, but also in a list of possible surface realizations for all slot values in the dataset. We store this list including morphological information provided by the tagger (with manually corrected errors), and we use it for lexicalization (see Section 3).[5]

2.4 Duplicate Sentence Handling

If the exact lexicalization is not taken into account, the original dataset of Wen et al. (2015b) contains a lot of duplicate texts – the total number of DA-text pairs is 5,192, but only 2,648 are unique. Therefore, we chose to only translate unique texts, in order to speed up the translation process and lower the costs, albeit at a cost of a lower-quality result. We ensured that the translations preserve the same number of unique sentences by modifying any duplicate translations, manually replacing selected words or phrases with synonyms.

After the dataset was translated, we expanded it to obtain the same number of instances and the same distribution of different DAs as in the original. Given a delexicalized DA, a list of corresponding translated sentences, and the target number of corresponding sentences to match the original set, we sampled additional copies of the existing translations to match the number of originals. To estimate probabilities of the individual translations for the sampling, we used a 5-gram LM[6] trained on lemmatized and delexicalized translations (see Figure 3 for details). We obtained LM scores for all

---

[4]Czech grammar requires a selection between formal an informal address whenever using a verb in the 2nd person (Naughton, 2005, p. 134ff.). For verbs with past tense or conditional and in any person, gender must be selected (Naughton, 2005, p. 140ff.). Here we opted for a feminine form whenever the system addresses itself, and formal address (mostly homonymous with plural) when addressing the user.

[5]We treat multiword slot values as single tokens in our surface form list. We assign them a morphological tag that fits the whole expression best, e.g., a noun tag for noun phrases.

[6]We used the implementation in the KenLM toolkit (Heafield, 2011).

mít   pro   ty   vhodný   restaurace . jeho název být X-name   a   moci   se   dát   X-food kuchyně .
Mám   pro   Vás   vhodnou   restauraci . Její   název je Kočár z Vídně a   můžete si   dát   českou kuchyni .
I have for   you   a suitable restaurant . Its   name   is Kočár z Vídně and   you can yourself give Czech   cuisine .

'I have a suitable restaurant for you. Its name is Kočár z Vídně and you can have Czech cuisine.'

Figure 3: Lemmatized and delexicalized form of the translations for LM scoring. Top: lemmatized and delexicalized Czech used for the LM; middle: original Czech sentence including lexicalization; bottom: English word-by-word gloss. An English translation is shown below the example.

	English	Czech
Number of instances	5,192	5,192
Unique delexicalized instances	2,648	2,752
Unique delexicalized DAs	248	248
Unique lemmas (in delexicalized set)	399	532
Unique word forms (in delexicalized set)	455	962
Average lexicalizations per slot value	1	3.84

Table 1: Statistics of our translated Czech dataset and a comparison to the English original of Wen et al. (2015b). The average lexicalizations per slot value shows the number of different surface lexical forms per slot value, as it appears in the dataset. Numerals were disregarded when computing this value.

Part	Train	Dev	Test
Unique delexicalized DAs	144	51	53
Total number of instances	3,569	781	842

Table 2: Dataset split statistics.

translations, used softmax to obtain a probability distribution, and sampled additional copies from this distribution. This ensures that translations using more frequent phrasing are more likely to be used multiple times in the set.

We then relexicalized the sampled copies: We randomly changed DA slot values and replaced their surface forms in the text using the surface forms list, checking for roughly corresponding morphology. Since the morphological information used by this approach was rather crude (e.g., noun/adjective gender was not taken into account), disfluencies ensued in some cases. Therefore, we manually corrected all relexicalized sentences, changing inflection or wording where needed.

2.5 Dataset Statistics

The final Czech set contains the same number of instances as the English original, copies the DA distribution of the original, and contains a slightly higher number of unique delexicalized sentences due to post-expansion corrections (see Section 2.4). A statistics of the dataset size is shown in Table 1, with a comparison to the original English set. We can see that while the number of unique word lemmas (disregarding restaurant and place names) is slightly higher in the Czech set, the number of unique inflected word forms is more than twice as

high. It is also clear that using slot values verbatim in the text is not possible in the Czech set as the number of possible lexical realizations for each value is much higher than one.

2.6 Data Split

The original dataset of Wen et al. (2015b), which used a sequential 3:1:1 split into training, development and test parts, suffered from a lot of overlap in terms of delexicalized DAs between the sections. This means that a system can perform quite well on this dataset and still be unable to generalize to unseen DAs (Lampouras and Vlachos, 2016). To make testing systems' generalization capabilities possible on our Czech dataset, we opted for a different data split. We roughly keep the same 3:1:1 size proportion (see Table 2), but we make sure no delexicalized DA appears in two different parts. On the other hand, we ensure that most DA types (*inform, confirm* etc.) are represented in all data parts, so the system has access to all general types of sentences during training.[7]

3   Model

We use TGen (Dušek and Jurčíček, 2016) in our experiments, which is a freely available NLG system based on the seq2seq model with attention (Bahdanau et al., 2015).

The seq2seq model consists of the encoder, the decoder, and the attention model. Both the encoder and decoder are recurrent neural networks (RNN)

---

[7]This is impossible to achieve for the *goodbye* and *?reqmore* DA types (i.e., goodbyes and asking if the user needs anything else). These DA types never appear with slots and thus only have one corresponding DA. We keep the corresponding instances in the training set.

with LSTM cells (Hochreiter and Schmidhuber, 1997). The encoder takes the input DA as a sequence of triples "DA type – slot – value"[8] and produces a sequence of hidden states. The last hidden state is used to initialize the decoder, all hidden states serve as input into the attention model. The attention model produces their weighted combination for each decoder step using a 1-layer fully connected network. The decoder generates output tokens one-by-one using the previously generated token and the attention model as inputs.

In addition to the basic seq2seq model, TGen adds beam search and a reranker for the candidate outputs on the generation beam that checks if the input semantics is preserved. The reranker encodes a candidate output using an LSTM RNN and produces a binary classification of DA types and slot-value pairs present. The number of differences against the input DA is used as penalty.

3.1 Basic Extensions

We added two features fairly standard in seq2seq-based models but absent from TGen:

- Bidirectional encoder (Bahdanau et al., 2015) – the input sequence is encoded in both directions and the resulting hidden states are joined. We added this for both the main seq2seq generator and the reranker.

- Dropout (Hinton et al., 2012) – this zeroes out certain connections within the network with a given probability during the training process; it serves as regularization feature. We use this in the main generator only.

We use these extensions in all our setups as they improved results in our preliminary experiments.

3.2 Lemma-tag Generation Mode

Dušek and Jurčíček (2016) experiment with generating syntactic trees and realizing them using an external surface realizer; they report slightly worse performance than generating tokens directly.

In order to fight data sparsity coming from the rich morphology of Czech, we decided to explore the middle ground between syntactic trees and full word-form generation: generating base forms (lemmas) and morphological tags that indicate how the form should be inflected. We train TGen to simply generate an interleaved sequence of lemmas and tags (see Figure 4), which are then postprocessed

---

[8]DA type is repeated for each slot-value pair.

using the dictionary-based morphological generator of Straková et al. (2014) to obtain the inflected word forms.

In the lemma-tag mode, the set of possible output tokens is reduced compared to direct token generation, but the postprocessing step is much simpler than using a full syntactic surface realizer. Moreover, the generated morphological tags following slot placeholders can be used to limit the scope of possible surface forms during lexicalization (see Section 3.3).

This approach is inspired by similar approaches in phrase-based MT (Bojar, 2007; Toutanova et al., 2008; Fraser, 2009) and was developed in parallel to recent similar experiments with two-step neural MT (Nadejde et al., 2017; Tamchyna et al., 2017). We compare the lemma-tag generation mode against the TGen default direct word-form generation mode in our experiments.

3.3 Lexicalization

We experiment with three different approaches for selecting the surface form for a DA slot value placeholder from a set of applicable ones – two very straightforward baselines requiring no training and our proposed solution based on a neural LM:

- *Random baseline.* This selects a surface form at random. This approach is certainly not suitable for a real application, we only use it for comparison.

- *Most frequent baseline.* Here, the applicable surface form that occurs overall most frequently in the training data is selected. This represents a stronger baseline than the random method.

- *RNN-based language model.* Our main solution attempts to choose the best surface form using a bidirectional LSTM RNN-based LM (Mikolov et al., 2010), trained to predict a token probability distribution given all previous and all following tokens. During decoding, the RNN LM estimates the probabilities of all applicable surface forms, and we select the most probable surface form for the output.

When selecting a surface form during direct word-form generation, all possible forms for the given slot value are considered. In the lemma-tag mode (Section 3.2), only forms matching the morphological tag following the slot placeholder are considered (cf. Figure 4) – first the ones matching perfectly, with backoffs to coarse part-of-speech or all possible forms.

hledat VB-P---2P-AA---   *vhodný* AAFS4----1A----   *restaurace* NNFS4-----A----
search   verb, 2nd person present formal   suitable adjective, fem sg acc   restaurant   noun, fem sg acc

na RR--4----------   *X good_for_meal* NNFS4-----A----   ? Z:-------------
for   preposition, acc   slot placeholder   noun, fem sg acc   ? final punctuation

Figure 4: Example interleaved lemma-tag sequence for the input DA *?confirm(good_for_meal=breakfast)*, the first output from Figure 1 (acc = accusative, fem = feminine, sg = singular; cf. (Hajič, 2004) for tagset details). Note that the morphological tag for the slot placeholder is included and can be used during lexicalization (cf. Section 3.3).

3.4 Lexicalized Input DAs

Some slot values in our dataset may require certain morphosyntactic structure of their neighborhood. This is the case for restaurant counts: Czech cardinal numerals 2-4 behave as adjectives, while higher numerals behave as nouns and take the counted quantity as genitive object. The correct nominative forms when counting restaurants are then "2 restaurac*e*", but "5 restaurac*í*" (Naughton, 2005, p. 113ff.). Another example are area names requiring different prepositions for location – the correct form for "in Malá Strana" is "*na* Malé Straně", but for "in Karlín", it is "*v* Karlíně" (Naughton, 2005, p. 202).

Therefore, inspired by Sharma et al. (2017), we test using fully lexicalized input DAs with the main generator to check if it learns to produce more appropriate structure for concrete values (while still producing delexicalized output).[9] We compare this setup against the default with delexicalized DAs.

4 Experiments

4.1 Experimental Setup

We test all combinations of the features described in Section 3:

- Direct token vs. lemma-tag generation

- Random / most-frequent / RNN LM lexicalizer

- Delexicalized vs. lexicalized input DAs

We train the resulting 12 model variants using the Adam optimizer (Kingma and Ba, 2015) to minimize cross entropy on the training set; this approach is used for all parts of the system: the main seq2seq generator, the reranker, and the RNN LM lexicalizer. After each training data pass, we validate the models and keep the best-performing parameters. We use BLEU score (Papineni et al., 2002), classification error, and LM perplexity as the respective validation criteria. We set hyperparameters based on TGen defaults for other datasets and a few experiments on the development set.[10]

Training the baseline lexicalizers is trivial: the random baseline does not require any training, it simply uses the list of possible surface forms; the most frequent baseline just memorizes surface form frequencies in the training data.

To reduce the effect of random initialization, we train five runs using different random seeds and use results of all of them for evaluation. In addition, we fix the random seeds so that identical seq2seq generators and rerankers are used in setups that only differ in the lexicalization method.

4.2 Metrics

We use the suite of word-overlap-based automatic metrics from the E2E NLG Challenge (Dušek et al., 2019),[11] supporting BLEU (Papineni et al., 2002), NIST (Doddington, 2002), ROUGE-L (Lin, 2004), METEOR (Lavie and Agarwal, 2007) and CIDEr (Vedantam et al., 2015). Although multiple texts often correspond to the same delexicalized DA, we treat each instance individually both in training and testing since the particular slot values influence the shape of the whole sentence (see Sections 2.4 and 3.4). This means that only a single reference output per instance is available to be used with automatic metrics (see Section 4.3).

---

[9] We exploit the fact that the number of possible values for different slots in the dataset is relatively small (cf. Section 2); morphosyntactic classes of the values would need to be used if the number of values was higher.

[10] The main generator uses embedding and LSTM cell size 200, learning rate 0.005, dropout rate 0.5, and batch size 20. At least 50 and up to 1000 training data passes are used, with early stopping if the top 10 validation BLEU scores do not change for 50 passes. Beam size 20 is used for decoding.

The reranker uses embedding and LSTM cell size 50, no dropout, learning rate 0.001, and batch size 20. Training runs for 100 passes, performance is validated starting with pass 10. The reranker is validated both on training and development data; classification error on the development set is given 10 times more weight than training set error.

The RNN LM lexicalizer uses the same parameters as the reranker, with training for 50 passes maximum and validation (on development data only) starting after the first pass.

[11] https://github.com/tuetschek/e2e-metrics

Input DAs	Generator mode	Lexicalizer	BLEU	NIST	METEOR	ROUGE-L	CIDEr	SER
Delexicalized	Word forms	Random	15.51‡	3.7352	18.60	35.00	1.3922	**00.70**
		Most frequent	20.28‡	4.5192	22.69	40.92	1.9399	**00.70**
		RNN LM	20.74*	4.5096	22.61	40.72	1.9924	**00.70**
	Lemma-tag	Random	19.66†	4.4884†‡	22.19	41.42	1.8844	01.85
		Most frequent	21.21†‡	4.6900†‡	23.07	42.62	2.0983	01.85
		RNN LM	**21.96***†‡	**4.7720***†‡	**23.32**	**42.95**	**2.1783**	01.85
Lexicalized	Word forms	Random	14.70	3.7595	18.29	35.64	1.3712	02.30
		Most frequent	19.73	4.5618	22.45	41.71	1.9473	02.30
		RNN LM	20.48*	4.6060*‡	22.55	41.66	2.0192	02.30
	Lemma-tag	Random	18.92†	4.3501†	21.76	40.55	1.8014	03.08
		Most frequent	19.44	4.4453	22.22	41.26	1.8801	03.08
		RNN LM	20.42*	4.5460*	22.56	41.73	1.9796	03.08

Table 3: Automatic metrics results. See Section 4.2 for metrics; scores are averaged over 5 different random initializations, all scores except for NIST and CIDEr are percentages. * = significantly better than the corresponding most frequent baseline lexicalizer, † = significantly better than the corresponding word forms mode, ‡ = significantly better than the corresponding (de)lexicalized input DAs. Significance was assessed using pairwise bootstrap resampling (Koehn, 2004), $p < 0.01$.

Input DAs	Generator mode	Lexicalizer	S	R	F	I	L	F+I+L	Σ
Delexicalized	Word forms	Most frequent	**8**	**0**	**5**	11	57	73	81
		RNN LM	**8**	**0**	**5**	11	25	41	49
	Lemma-tag	Most frequent	12	2	**5**	11	45	61	75
		RNN LM	12	2	**5**	11	6	22	36
Lexicalized	Word forms	Most frequent	14	5	14	6	34	54	73
		RNN LM	14	5	14	6	10	30	49
	Lemma-tag	Most frequent	15	4	6	**4**	34	44	63
		RNN LM	15	4	6	**4**	**4**	**14**	**33**

Table 4: Manual evaluation results on 100 sampled sentences – absolute numbers of different types of errors (S = semantic errors, R = repetition, F = fluency problems except lexicalization, I = impossible to lexicalize correctly with the given value, L = lexicalization errors). All error types are exemplified in Figure 5.

In addition to word-overlap metrics, we use the slot error rate (SER; Wen et al., 2015b) to evaluate semantic accuracy of the outputs. This metric counts slot placeholders in the output before lexicalization and compares them to slots in the input DA. It reliably measures the amount of missed/added content in all delexicalized slots (cf. Section 2), but the non-delexicalized binary *kids_allowed* slot is ignored.

4.3 Results

The automatic metrics scores for all setups are shown in Table 3. In terms of generator mode, using lemma-tag generation significantly[12] improves word-overlap metrics over direct token generation in the delexicalized input setting. However, it also leads to an increased SER. The RNN LM brings a significant[12] improvement over both baselines in all setups; the very low performance of the random baseline only documents that inflection indeed matters for slot values. The lexicalized input DAs did not bring improvement over the delexicalized set-

ting – lexicalized setups seem to perform slightly worse in terms of both word-overlap metrics and SER.

4.4 Manual Error Analysis

To obtain a deeper insight into the results and account for automatic metrics' inaccuracy (Novikova et al., 2017; Reiter, 2018), we performed a detailed manual error analysis on a sample of 100 outputs produced by all systems except the ones with random baseline lexicalizers, which clearly perform poorly. This was a blind annotation of semantic and fluency errors; it is not a preference rating. We categorized multiple error types; the results are shown in Table 4.

The analysis confirmed that lexicalized input DAs cause more semantic errors (both missed slots and repetition). On the other hand, the outputs were more fluent in this setting, which is not apparent with automatic metrics. Lemma-tag generation also improves fluency overall, at the cost of increasing the number of semantic errors. The RNN LM lexicalizer leads to significant reduction of lexicalization errors compared to the most frequent

---

[12]BLEU and NIST differences are statistically significant ($p < 0.01$) according to bootstrap resampling (Koehn, 2004).

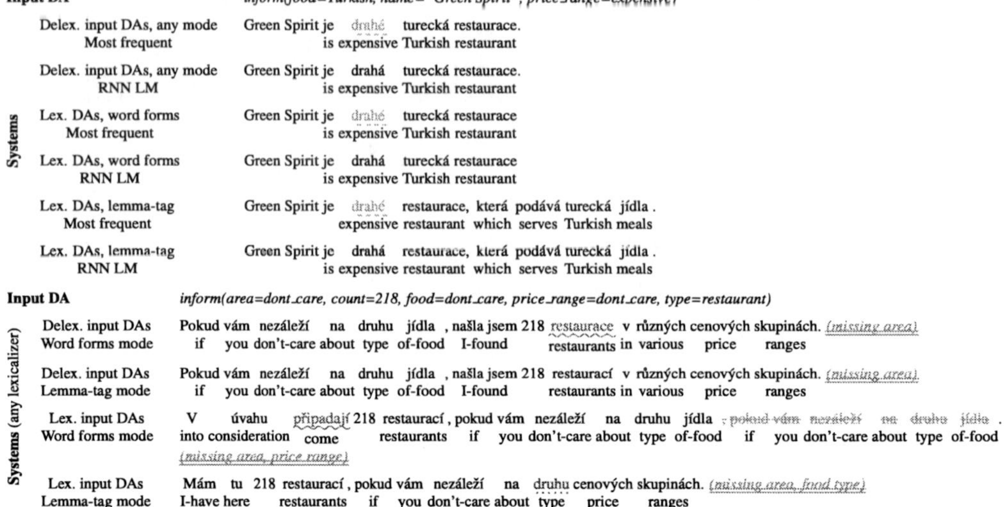

Figure 5: Examples from manual error analysis. Errors are marked with color and underlining: *semantic errors*, repetition, fluency, impossible to lexicalize correctly, lexicalization (cf. Table 4). In the top example, the RNN LM lexicalizer is able to select the correct feminine singular form, while the most frequent baseline selects a neuter form. In the bottom example, systems with lexicalized input DAs make more semantic errors. The lemma-tag mode is able to select a more appropriate syntactic structure for the numeral 218.

baseline, especially in combination with lemma-tag generation (see top example in Figure 5). None of the systems produce perfect output; they seem to struggle especially with DAs that are very different from the ones found in the training set and/or occur less frequently (see bottom example in Figure 5, cf. Section 2.6). We believe that an increased amount of training data could improve the situation.

5 Related Work

NLG experiments for non-English languages are relatively rare and fully trainable approaches even rarer. Our work is, to our knowledge, the first application of neural NLG to a non-English language for data-to-text generation.

Most works concerned with multiple languages focus on surface realization. There have been a few approaches using handcrafted grammars (Bateman, 1997; Allman et al., 2012). The procedural SimpleNLG realizer (Gatt and Reiter, 2009) has also been ported into multiple languages (Bollmann, 2011; Vaudry and Lapalme, 2013; de Oliveira and Sripada, 2014; Mazzei et al., 2016; Ramos-Soto et al., 2017; Cascallar-Fuentes et al., 2018; Chen et al., 2018; de Jong and Theune, 2018). Further works using multilingual rule-based surface realiza-

tion pipelines were developed in the context of machine translation (Aikawa et al., 2001; Žabokrtský et al., 2008; Dušek et al., 2015). Bohnet et al. (2010) created the first statistical multilingual realizer based on a pipeline of SVMs, the recent surface realization challenge (Mille et al., 2018) then features further fully trainable realizers tested on multiple languages, including neural models.

In data-to-text generation, the recent work of Moussallem et al. (2018) is applied to Portuguese, but is largely rule-based. The works of Chen et al. (2010) and Kim and Mooney (2010) represent the only data-to-text end-to-end NLG system with multilingual experiments known to us; they generate English and Korean sport commentary sentences using an inverted (non-neural) semantic parser. Our dataset is ca. 2.5 times larger and more complex, given the slot value inflection.

Other works on neural non-English NLG solve in fact different tasks from ours: Chinese poetry generation (Zhang and Lapata, 2014; Yi et al., 2017; Wang et al., 2016), non-task-oriented response generation in chatbots (Xing et al., 2016, 2017), or morphological inflection (e.g. Faruqui et al., 2016; Kann and Schütze, 2016).

6 Conclusions and Future Work

We presented the first dataset targeted at end-to-end neural non-English NLG, containing Czech texts from the restaurant domain. We show that the task of data-to-text NLG here is harder as slot values require morphological inflection. We apply to our data the freely available, state-of-the-art TGen NLG system (Dušek and Jurčíček, 2016) based on the seq2seq architecture, and we implement two extensions for Czech: (1) an RNN LM model to select the correct inflected surface form for slot values and (2) lemma-tag generation mode, where the generator produces an interleaved sequences of base form and morphological tags, which are postprocessed by a morphological generator. We also experiment with lexicalized and delexicalized slot values in generator inputs. Using both automatic metrics and manual analysis, we show that the RNN LM brings clear benefits. The lemma-tag mode and lexicalized inputs improve fluency but hurt semantic accuracy of the outputs. We release our dataset dataset and all experimental code on GitHub.[13]

In future work, we will collect a large unannotated dataset and pretrain the generator (Chen et al., 2019). We believe that this will lead to increased output fluency and accuracy. We are also considering using machine translation to obtain more synthetic training data points.

Acknowledgments

This research was supported by the Charles University project PRIMUS/19/SCI/10 and by the Ministry of Education, Youth and Sports of the Czech Republic under the grant agreement LK11221. This work used using language resources distributed by the LINDAT/CLARIN project of the Ministry of Education, Youth and Sports of the Czech Republic (project LM2015071).

References

T. Aikawa, M. Melero, L. Schwartz, and A. Wu. 2001. Generation for multilingual MT. In *Proceedings of the MT-Summit*, pages 9–14, Santiago de Compostela, Spain.

T. Allman, S. Beale, and R. Denton. 2012. Linguist's Assistant: A Multi-Lingual Natural Language Generator based on Linguistic Universals, Typologies, and Primitives. In *INLG 2012 Proceedings of the Seventh International Natural Language Generation Conference*, pages 59–66, Utica, IL, USA.

Dzmitry Bahdanau, Kyunghyun Cho, and Yoshua Bengio. 2015. Neural Machine Translation by Jointly Learning to Align and Translate. In *3rd International Conference on Learning Representations (ICLR2015)*, San Diego, CA, USA. arXiv:1409.0473.

J. A. Bateman. 1997. Enabling technology for multilingual natural language generation: the KPML development environment. *Natural Language Engineering*, 3(1):15–55.

B. Bohnet, L. Wanner, S. Mille, and A. Burga. 2010. Broad coverage multilingual deep sentence generation with a stochastic multi-level realizer. In *Proceedings of the 23rd International Conference on Computational Linguistics*, pages 98–106, Beijing, China.

Ondřej Bojar. 2007. English-to-Czech factored machine translation. In *Proceedings of the Second Workshop on Statistical Machine Translation – StatMT '07*, pages 232–239, Prague, Czech Republic.

M. Bollmann. 2011. Adapting SimpleNLG to German. In *Proceedings of the 13th European Workshop on Natural Language Generation*, pages 133–138, Nancy, France.

Andrea Cascallar-Fuentes, Alejandro Ramos-Soto, and Alberto Bugarín Diz. 2018. Adapting SimpleNLG to Galician language. In *Proceedings of the 11th International Conference on Natural Language Generation*, pages 67–72, Tilburg, The Netherlands.

David L. Chen, Joohyun Kim, and Raymond J. Mooney. 2010. Training a multilingual sportscaster: Using perceptual context to learn language. *Journal of Artificial Intelligence Research*, 37:397–435.

Guanyi Chen, Kees van Deemter, and Chenghua Lin. 2018. SimpleNLG-ZH: a Linguistic Realisation Engine for Mandarin. In *Proceedings of the 11th International Conference on Natural Language Generation*, pages 57–66, Tilburg, The Netherlands.

Zhiyu Chen, Harini Eavani, Yinyin Liu, and William Yang Wang. 2019. Few-shot NLG with Pretrained Language Model. *arXiv:1904.09521 [cs]*.

Ryan Cotterell, Sebastian J. Mielke, Jason Eisner, and Brian Roark. 2018. Are All Languages Equally Hard to Language-Model? In *Proceedings of the 2018 Conference of the North American Chapter of the Association for Computational Linguistics: Human Language Technologies, Volume 2 (Short Papers)*, pages 536–541, New Orleans, LA, USA.

George Doddington. 2002. Automatic Evaluation of Machine Translation Quality Using N-gram Co-occurrence Statistics. In *Proceedings of the Second International Conference on Human Language*

---

[13]Dataset: `https://github.com/UFAL-DSG/cs_restaurant_dataset`, code: `https://github.com/UFAL-DSG/tgen`.

Technology Research, HLT '02, pages 138–145, San Francisco, CA, USA.

Ondřej Dušek, Ondřej Plátek, Lukáš Žilka, and Filip Jurčíček. 2014. Alex: Bootstrapping a Spoken Dialogue System for a New Domain by Real Users. In *Proceedings of the 15th Annual Meeting of the Special Interest Group on Discourse and Dialogue*, pages 79–83, Philadelphia, PA, USA.

Ondřej Dušek, Luís Gomes, Michal Novák, Martin Popel, and Rudolf Rosa. 2015. New Language Pairs in TectoMT. In *Proceedings of the 10th Workshop on Machine Translation*, pages 98–104, Lisbon, Portugal.

Ondřej Dušek and Filip Jurčíček. 2016. Sequence-to-Sequence Generation for Spoken Dialogue via Deep Syntax Trees and Strings. In *Proceedings of the 54th Annual Meeting of the Association for Computational Linguistics (Volume 2: Short Papers)*, pages 45–51, Berlin. arXiv:1606.05491.

Ondřej Dušek, Jekaterina Novikova, and Verena Rieser. 2019. Evaluating the State-of-the-Art of End-to-End Natural Language Generation: The E2E NLG Challenge. *Computer Speech & Language*, 59:123–156. arXiv:1901.07931.

Manaal Faruqui, Yulia Tsvetkov, Graham Neubig, and Chris Dyer. 2016. Morphological Inflection Generation Using Character Sequence to Sequence Learning. In *Proceedings of the 2016 Conference of the North American Chapter of the Association for Computational Linguistics: Human Language Technologies*, pages 634–643, San Diego, CA, USA. arXiv:1512.06110.

Alexander Fraser. 2009. Experiments in Morphosyntactic Processing for Translating to and from German. In *Proceedings of the Fourth Workshop on Statistical Machine Translation*, pages 115–119, Athens, Greece.

A. Gatt and E. Reiter. 2009. SimpleNLG: A realisation engine for practical applications. In *Proceedings of the 12th European Workshop on Natural Language Generation*, pages 90–93.

Sebastian Gehrmann, Falcon Z. Dai, Henry Elder, and Alexander M. Rush. 2018. End-to-End Content and Plan Selection for Data-to-Text Generation. In *Proceedings of the 11th International Conference on Natural Language Generation*, Tilburg, The Netherlands. arXiv:1810.04700.

Jiatao Gu, Zhengdong Lu, Hang Li, and Victor O. K. Li. 2016. Incorporating Copying Mechanism in Sequence-to-Sequence Learning. In *Proceedings of the 54th Annual Meeting of the Association for Computational Linguistics*, pages 1631–1640, Berlin, Germany. arXiv:1603.06393.

Ian Hajič. 2004. *Disambiguation of rich inflection. computational morphology of Czech*. Karolinum, Praha.

Kenneth Heafield. 2011. KenLM: Faster and smaller language model queries. In *Proceedings of the Sixth Workshop on Statistical Machine Translation*, pages 187–197, Edinburgh, Scotland, UK.

Geoffrey E. Hinton, Nitish Srivastava, Alex Krizhevsky, Ilya Sutskever, and Ruslan R. Salakhutdinov. 2012. Improving neural networks by preventing co-adaptation of feature detectors. *arXiv:1207.0580 [cs]*.

Sepp Hochreiter and Jürgen Schmidhuber. 1997. Long short-term memory. *Neural computation*, 9(8):1735–1780.

Ruud de Jong and Mariët Theune. 2018. Going Dutch: Creating SimpleNLG-NL. In *Proceedings of the 11th International Conference on Natural Language Generation*, pages 73–78, Tilburg, The Netherlands.

Juraj Juraska, Panagiotis Karagiannis, Kevin K. Bowden, and Marilyn A. Walker. 2018. A Deep Ensemble Model with Slot Alignment for Sequence-to-Sequence Natural Language Generation. In *NAACL*, New Orleans, LA, USA. arXiv:1805.06553.

Katharina Kann and Hinrich Schütze. 2016. Single-Model Encoder-Decoder with Explicit Morphological Representation for Reinflection. In *Proceedings of the 54th Annual Meeting of the Association for Computational Linguistics (Volume 2: Short Papers)*, pages 555–560, Berlin, Germany. arXiv:1606.00589.

Joohyun Kim and Raymond J. Mooney. 2010. Generative Alignment and Semantic Parsing for Learning from Ambiguous Supervision. In *Proceedings of the 23rd International Conference on Computational Linguistics: Posters*, pages 543–551, Beijing, China.

Diederik Kingma and Jimmy Ba. 2015. Adam: A Method for Stochastic Optimization. In *Proceedings of the 3rd International Conference on Learning Representations*, San Diego, CA, USA. arXiv:1412.6980.

Philipp Koehn. 2004. Statistical significance tests for machine translation evaluation. In *Proceedings of the 2004 Conference on Empirical Methods in Natural Language Processing*, pages 388–395.

Gerasimos Lampouras and Andreas Vlachos. 2016. Imitation learning for language generation from unaligned data. In *Proceedings of COLING 2016, the 26th International Conference on Computational Linguistics: Technical Papers*, pages 1101–1112, Osaka, Japan.

Alon Lavie and Abhaya Agarwal. 2007. Meteor: An Automatic Metric for MT Evaluation with High Levels of Correlation with Human Judgments. In *Proceedings of the Second Workshop on Statistical Machine Translation*, pages 228–231, Prague, Czech Republic.

Chin-Yew Lin. 2004. ROUGE: A package for automatic evaluation of summaries. In *Text summarization branches out: Proceedings of the ACL-04 workshop*, pages 74–81. Barcelona, Spain.

F. Mairesse, M. Gašić, F. Jurčíček, S. Keizer, B. Thomson, K. Yu, and S. Young. 2010. Phrase-based statistical language generation using graphical models and active learning. In *Proceedings of the 48th Annual Meeting of the Association for Computational Linguistics*, page 1552–1561, Uppsala, Sweden.

Alessandro Mazzei, Cristina Battaglino, and Cristina Bosco. 2016. SimpleNLG-IT: Adapting SimpleNLG to Italian. In *The 9th International Natural Language Generation conference*, pages 184–192, Edinburgh, Scotland, UK.

Tomáš Mikolov, Martin Karafiát, Lukáš Burget, Jan Černocký, and Sanjeev Khudanpur. 2010. Recurrent neural network based language model. In *Interspeech*, pages 1045–1048, Makuhari, Japan.

Simon Mille, Anja Belz, Bernd Bohnet, Yvette Graham, Emily Pitler, and Leo Wanner. 2018. The First Multilingual Surface Realisation Shared Task (SR'18): Overview and Evaluation Results. In *Proceedings of the First Workshop on Multilingual Surface Realisation*, pages 1–12, Melbourne, Australia.

Diego Moussallem, Thiago Castro Ferreira, Marcos Zampieri, Maria Claudia Cavalcanti, Geraldo Xexéo, Mariana Neves, and Axel-Cyrille Ngonga Ngomo. 2018. RDF2pt: Generating Brazilian Portuguese Texts from RDF Data. In *Proceedings of the Eleventh International Conference on Language Resources and Evaluation (LREC-2018)*, Miyazaki, Japan. arXiv:1802.08150.

Maria Nadejde, Siva Reddy, Rico Sennrich, Tomasz Dwojak, Marcin Junczys-Dowmunt, Philipp Koehn, and Alexandra Birch. 2017. Predicting Target Language CCG Supertags Improves Neural Machine Translation. In *Proceedings of the Second Conference on Machine Translation*, pages 68–79, Copenhagen, Denmark.

James Naughton. 2005. *Czech : an essential grammar*. Routledge, London.

Jekaterina Novikova, Ondřej Dušek, Amanda Cercas Curry, and Verena Rieser. 2017. Why We Need New Evaluation Metrics for NLG. In *Proceedings of the 2017 Conference on Empirical Methods in Natural Language Processing*, pages 2243–2253, Copenhagen, Denmark. arXiv:1707.06875.

A. H. Oh and A. I. Rudnicky. 2000. Stochastic language generation for spoken dialogue systems. In *Proceedings of the 2000 ANLP/NAACL Workshop on Conversational systems-Volume 3*, page 27–32, Seattle, WA, USA.

Rodrigo de Oliveira and Somayajulu Sripada. 2014. Adapting SimpleNLG for Brazilian Portuguese realisation. In *Proceedings of the 8th International Natural Language Generation Conference (INLG)*, pages 93–94, Philadelphia, PA, USA.

Kishore Papineni, Salim Roukos, Todd Ward, and Wei-Jing Zhu. 2002. BLEU: a method for automatic evaluation of machine translation. In *Proceedings of the 40th annual meeting of the Association for Computational Linguistics*, pages 311–318.

Ellie Pavlick, Matt Post, Ann Irvine, Dmitry Kachaev, and Chris Callison-Burch. 2014. The language demographics of Amazon Mechanical Turk. *Transactions of the Association for Computational Linguistics*, 2:79–92.

Martin Popel and Zdeněk Žabokrtský. 2010. TectoMT: modular NLP framework. In *Proceedings of IceTAL, 7th International Conference on Natural Language Processing*, pages 293–304, Reykjavík, Iceland.

Alejandro Ramos-Soto, Julio Janeiro-Gallardo, and Alberto Bugarín Diz. 2017. Adapting SimpleNLG to Spanish. In *Proceedings of the 10th International Conference on Natural Language Generation*, pages 144–148, Santiago de Compostela, Spain.

Ehud Reiter. 2018. A Structured Review of the Validity of BLEU. *Computational Linguistics*, 44(3):1–8.

Shikhar Sharma, Jing He, Kaheer Suleman, Hannes Schulz, and Philip Bachman. 2017. Natural Language Generation in Dialogue using Lexicalized and Delexicalized Data. In *ICLR Workshop Track*, Toulon, France. arXiv:1606.03632.

Milan Straka and Jana Straková. 2017. Tokenizing, POS Tagging, Lemmatizing and Parsing UD 2.0 with UDPipe. In *Proceedings of the CoNLL 2017 Shared Task: Multilingual Parsing from Raw Text to Universal Dependencies*, pages 88–99, Vancouver, Canada.

Jana Straková, Milan Straka, and Jan Hajič. 2014. Open-Source Tools for Morphology, Lemmatization, POS Tagging and Named Entity Recognition. In *Proceedings of 52nd Annual Meeting of the Association for Computational Linguistics: System Demonstrations*, pages 13–18, Baltimore, MD, USA.

Aleš Tamchyna, Marion Weller-Di Marco, and Alexander Fraser. 2017. Modeling Target-Side Inflection in Neural Machine Translation. In *Proceedings of the Conference on Machine Translation (WMT), Volume 1: Research Papers*, Copenhagen, Denmark. arXiv:1707.06012.

Kristina Toutanova, Hisami Suzuki, and Achim Ruopp. 2008. Applying morphology generation models to machine translation. In *Proceedings of ACL-08: HLT*, pages 514–522, Columbus, OH, USA.

Pierre-Luc Vaudry and Guy Lapalme. 2013. Adapting SimpleNLG for bilingual English-French realisation. In *Proceedings of the 14th European Workshop on Natural Language Generation*, pages 183–187, Sofia, Bulgaria.

Ramakrishna Vedantam, C. Lawrence Zitnick, and Devi Parikh. 2015. CIDEr: Consensus-Based Image Description Evaluation. In *Proceedings of the IEEE Conference on Computer Vision and Pattern Recognition*, pages 4566–4575, Boston, MA, USA. arXiv:1411.5726.

Zhe Wang, Wei He, Hua Wu, Haiyang Wu, Wei Li, Haifeng Wang, and Enhong Chen. 2016. Chinese Poetry Generation with Planning based Neural Network. In *Proceedings of COLING 2016, the 26th International Conference on Computational Linguistics: Technical Papers*, pages 1051–1060, Osaka, Japan. arXiv:1610.09889.

Tsung-Hsien Wen, Milica Gasic, Dongho Kim, Nikola Mrksic, Pei-Hao Su, David Vandyke, and Steve Young. 2015a. Stochastic Language Generation in Dialogue using Recurrent Neural Networks with Convolutional Sentence Reranking. In *Proceedings of the 16th Annual Meeting of the Special Interest Group on Discourse and Dialogue*, pages 275–284, Prague, Czech Republic.

Tsung-Hsien Wen, Milica Gasic, Nikola Mrkšić, Pei-Hao Su, David Vandyke, and Steve Young. 2015b. Semantically Conditioned LSTM-based Natural Language Generation for Spoken Dialogue Systems. In *Proceedings of the 2015 Conference on Empirical Methods in Natural Language Processing*, pages 1711–1721, Lisbon, Portugal.

Chen Xing, Wei Wu, Yu Wu, Jie Liu, Yalou Huang, Ming Zhou, and Wei-Ying Ma. 2016. Topic Augmented Neural Response Generation with a Joint Attention Mechanism. *arXiv:1606.08340 [cs]*.

Chen Xing, Wei Wu, Yu Wu, Jie Liu, Yalou Huang, Ming Zhou, and Wei-Ying Ma. 2017. Topic Aware Neural Response Generation. In *Proceedings of the Thirty-First AAAI Conference on Artificial Intelligence (AAAI-17)*, pages 3351–3357, San Francisco, CA, USA.

Xiaoyuan Yi, Ruoyu Li, and Maosong Sun. 2017. Generating Chinese Classical Poems with RNN Encoder-Decoder. In *Chinese Computational Linguistics and Natural Language Processing Based on Naturally Annotated Big Data*, pages 211–223, Nanjing, China. arXiv:1604.01537.

Xingxing Zhang and Mirella Lapata. 2014. Chinese poetry generation with recurrent neural networks. In *Proceedings of the 2014 Conference on Empirical Methods in Natural Language Processing (EMNLP)*, pages 670–680, Doha, Qatar.

Z. Žabokrtský, J. Ptáček, and P. Pajas. 2008. TectoMT: highly modular MT system with tectogrammatics used as transfer layer. In *Proceedings of the Third Workshop on Statistical Machine Translation*, pages 167–170, Columbus, OH, USA.

Modeling Confidence in Sequence-to-Sequence Models

Jan Niehues
Department of Data Science
and Knowledge Engineering (DKE)
Maastricht University
jan.niehues@maastrichtuniversity.nl

Ngoc-Quan Pham
Institute of Anthropomatics
Karlsruhe Initute of Technology
ngoc.pham@kit.edu

Abstract

Recently, significant improvements have been achieved in various natural language processing tasks using neural sequence-to-sequence models. While aiming for the best generation quality is important, ultimately it is also necessary to develop models that can assess the quality of their output.

In this work, we propose to use the similarity between training and test conditions as a measure for models' confidence. We investigate methods solely using the similarity as well as methods combining it with the posterior probability. While traditionally only target tokens are annotated with confidence measures, we also investigate methods to annotate source tokens with confidence. By learning an internal alignment model, we can significantly improve confidence projection over using state-of-the-art external alignment tools. We evaluate the proposed methods on downstream confidence estimation for machine translation (MT). We show improvements on segment-level confidence estimation as well as on confidence estimation for source tokens. In addition, we show that the same methods can also be applied to other tasks using sequence-to-sequence models. On the automatic speech recognition (ASR) task, we are able to find 60% of the errors by looking at 20% of the data.

1 Introduction

Deep learning methods have significantly increased the quality of natural language generation tasks such as Machine Translation (MT). However, when deployed in a production environment, understanding the model's confidence and how well it correlates with output quality is as important as training the best models.

While humans are often capable of estimating whether their decisions are sensible or produced by random guesses, it is often not possible to know how confident deep learning models are with respect to their output (Gal, 2016). However, information regarding confidence can be essential in production scenarios. In cases with a human-in-the-loop, confidence can be used to identify the parts of the machine output that require human intervention, e.g. in post-editing for machine translation or to guide reformulation of the original input to simplify the task for sequence-to-sequence models.

Intuitively, models should have higher confidence towards data points that are similar to their training data. Motivated by this, our first contribution is an autoencoder network that is applied as an extension to the sequence-to-sequence models to measure the training-testing discrepancy. In contrast to methods that directly compare the test and training data to generate confidence scores, we do not need to store the whole training data, thereby enabling our method to scale to larger datasets and tasks.

Motivated by the successful application of posterior probabilities for confidence estimation in statistical machine translation (SMT) (Ueffing and Ney, 2007) and traditional ASR systems (Siu and Gish, 1999), our second contribution is a combination our approach with this prior approach.

Traditionally, confidence estimation has been defined as a task of assessing the quality of the whole sequence of words in the target sentence. Especially when evaluating translations, there are also several cases when it can be very beneficial to estimate how well the source words are translated beyond coverage. For example, a person only speaking the source language might be able to reformulate the source sentence, if he knows that the system has difficulties with certain words. As our third contribution, we present a method to estimate the alignment between source and target

Proceedings of The 12th International Conference on Natural Language Generation, pages 575–583,
Tokyo, Japan, 28 Oct - 1 Nov, 2019. ©2019 Association for Computational Linguistics

tokens in complex sequence-to-sequence models. We can show that this strongly outperforms external state-of-the-art alignment methods.

Our experiments shows that in machine translation, the posterior probabilities can be competitive with automatic metrics in terms of correlation with human evaluation. For speech recognition, we are able to find 60% of the errors by looking at 20% of the data.

2 Confidence Estimation Task

Depending on the use case, there are different ways to define the task of confidence estimation. Furthermore, there is no clear separation between confidence estimation and quality estimation. A first important dimension is the granularity of the predictions. We investigate three different use cases in this work, described in the next three subsections in greater detail.

Previous methods differ in whether they predicting continuous values or discrete labels. In this work, we will predict continuous values, but evaluate against gold standard labels. In Section 5, we describe in detail how we map continuous predictions to discrete labels.

In addition, previous methods differ in whether they can be trained on gold standard labels or if no annotated training data is available. Training data is a particular challenge in confidence estimation since annotations are associated with the output of a particular model. Therefore, this raises the question whether the task is to estimate the quality of *any* model, or of a particular one. This has implications for whether we can use model internal information or not. In this work, we focus on the situation where we want to estimate the confidence of a particular model, using internal information. Since in a realistic real-world scenario we are not able to collect annotated data for each model we are interested in, we further do not use any labeled training data.

2.1 Granularity

First, the confidence of the whole output sequence can be estimated. Given an input sequence $X = x_1 \ldots x_{I_w}$ and an output sequence $Y = y_1 \ldots y_{J_w}$, the model estimates quality c for the whole sequence. We will present several methods that calculate a sequence of confidence estimations $c'_1, ..., c'_L$. Therefore, we need an additional aggregation function for the sequence confidence es-

timates. In all our experiments, we are using the minimum as the aggregation function.

In some use cases, it is important to get more fine-grained quality estimation. To be specific, we aim at estimating the confidence of every target token x_j instead of one single score for the sequence. Given an input sequence $X = x_1 \ldots x_{I_w}$ and an output sequence $Y = y_1 \ldots y_{J_w}$, the output will be a sequence of quality estimations $C = c_1 \ldots c_{J_w}$. One additional challenge is that we might be interested in the confidence using a different granularity than the predicted by the model $c'_1, ..., c'_L$ (with $L \neq J_w$). For example, the user is interested in word-based confidence, while the system uses subword units. In this case, we assume to have a mapping m between the positions $1 \ldots J_w$ and $1 \ldots L$. In the example of subwords, this is straightforward because segmentation is recoverable. Then, we also need an additional aggregation function for the confidence estimates. We estimate the confidence c_j by $agg_{m(l)=j}(c_l)$. For this type of aggregation we also use the minimum.

In machine translation, it is not only the confidence at the output level that is of interest, but also how adequately each individual source token is translated. From an application point of view, when the machine translation is used in an interactive scenario, this feature for example enables the user to reformulate the source sentence in order to avoid phrases that the system is not able to handle.

Formally, given an input sequence $X = x_1 \ldots x_{I_w}$ and an output sequence $Y = y_1 \ldots y_{J_w}$, the model estimates a sequence of confidence measures $C = c_1 \ldots c_{I_w}$. Therefore, in this case, given the estimation of the model $c'_1, ..., c'_L$, we need a mapping m between the positions $1 \ldots I_w$ and $1 \ldots L$.

2.2 Posterior Probabilities

As a baseline for our experiments, we use the posterior probabilities. The intuition behind this technique is that the model will distribute the probability mass over several outputs in low-confidence situations. In contrast, if the model is confident about its prediction, it should assign a high probability to the prediction.

Formally, given an input sequence $X = x_1 \ldots x_{I_w}$ and an output sequence $Y = y_1 \ldots y_{J_w}$, we first define the input tokens $X' = x'_1 \ldots x'_{I_y}$

and an output sequence $Y' = y'_1 \ldots y'_{J_t}$ (e.g. by using subwords). The encoder will first calculate a sequence of hidden states $E = e_1, \ldots e_{I_t} = ENC(X')$. Secondly, we predict the target hidden states $D = d_1, \ldots d_{J_t} = DEC(E, Y')$. Finally, we can use the posterior probabilities $P = p_1, \ldots, p_{J_t}$ calculated by:

$$p_i = softmax(FF(d_i))[y'_i] \tag{1}$$

where FF is a linear transformation and $[k]$ indicates the k-th element of the vector. By using P for C' as described in Section 2.1, we can calculate now a sequence confidence or an output confidence.

3 Training similarity

The similarity between test input and the examples seen in training is an important indication for the model's performance. Intuitively, models should be better at predicting examples similar to their training data than examples very different from the training data.

3.1 Approaches to measure similarity

Two sentences can be similar in many ways. Therefore, there are also many ways to estimate the similarity between sentences. For our use case, it is important how similar the sentence representation generated by the translation systems is. Hence, we use the internal representations of the neural machine translation model to measure the similarity of the sentences.

In an NMT system, there are different representation levels which can be used to measure the similarity of the sentence. For example, we can use the final encoder hidden states, the final decoder hidden states, or the context vectors. As motivated in the introduction, one interesting use case for using confidence is to find difficult source segments, so that the user can rewrite them. For this case, we concentrate on the encoder hidden states.

We measure the training-test similarity as follows: First, we run the encoder on the source side of the training data and store the encoder hidden representation (top layer) for every sentence k ($E^k = e_1^k, \ldots, e_{I_t^k}^k$). Second, we calculate the hidden representations of the test sentences ($E^{tst} = e_1^{tst}, \ldots, e_{I_t^{tst}}^{tst}$) and used approximate k-nearest neighbor search (implemented in

the Annoy[1] toolkit).

We investigated two methods to estimate the similarity, one on the sentence level and one on token level. First, we use the distance to the overall most similar training sentence by using the average vector of the encoder hidden states for the training as well as for the test data. Formally:

$$s = \min_{k \in train} L^2(avg(e_1^k, \ldots, e_{I_k}^k), avg(e_1^{tst}, \ldots, e_{I_{tst}}^{tst})) \tag{2}$$

Then we use s directly as the sequence confidence c from Section 2.1.

The second method is to estimate the confidence for each source token. This is achieved by finding the nearest neighbor for each hidden encoder state e_i^{tst}.

$$s_i \min_{k \in train; i_k \in 1, \ldots, I_k} L^2(e_{i_k}^k, e_i^{tst}) \tag{3}$$

By using $S = s_1 \ldots s_{I^{tst}}$ as C' in Section 2.1, we can calculate a sequence confidence or an confidence for each input token.

3.2 Similarity estimation

The main disadvantage of aforementioned method is that we need to calculate and store the hidden representation of all training examples. Such storage consumption is non-trivial even for small datasets like the TED corpus and it is infeasible for large-scale sequence-to-sequence models.

Therefore, we also investigate methods to approximate the distance without storing the hidden states for the whole training data. Here we propose to approximate this distance by using autoencoders. The autoencoder will be able to reconstruct typical hidden states seen in the training data, while the reconstruction of unusual hidden states will be less exact.

As shown in Figure 1, we are using an autoencoder with a single hidden layer. In our experiments, we investigate different hidden sizes of the autoencoder. Afterwards, we apply the sigmoid activation function before predicting the output.

Next, we then can use the quality of the reconstruction as a measure of the model's confidence in its predictions. We found that it is possible to get the confidence qualitatively by measuring the L^2-distance between the hidden representation and its reconstruction.

$$s_i^e = L2(e_i, Auto(e_i)) \tag{4}$$

---

[1] https://github.com/spotify/annoy

As for the direct measurement, we can use $S^e = s_1^e \ldots s_{j\ldots}^e$ as C' to calculate the confidence of the sequence or for each input token. Furthermore, by using the decoder states D instead of the encoder states E, we can calculate S^d accordingly and use it to estimate the sequence or target token confidence.

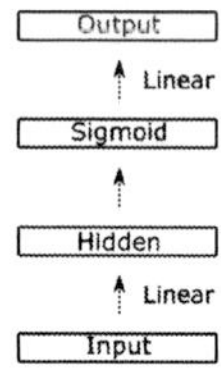

Figure 1: Architecture of the autoencoder

3.3 Combining both approaches

While using similarity measurements is able to estimate the quality of the whole sequence as well as of parts of the sequence, it also has two drawbacks: First, in the L^2-norm all dimensions are equally important, while this might not be the case for the final prediction of the words. Second, we are only looking at the similarity between training and test condition, but ignoring that some outputs might be inherently more difficult to predict than others.

Therefore, we combine both techniques and thereby minimize their respective drawbacks. To do so, the hidden representation is first replaced by the reconstruction generated by the autoencoder. After that, we calculate the probabilities based on these reconstructed hidden representations. If we use the autoencoder on the decoder states, Equation 1 needs to be modified to:

$$p_i^s = softmax(FF(Auto(d_i)))[y_i'] \quad (5)$$

By using P^s for C as described in Section 2.1, we can calculate now a sequence confidence or an output confidence. Similarly, we can replace $Auto(d_i)$ by d_i' with $D' = DEC(Auto(E), Y')$ to use the autoencoders on the encoder hidden states. It is important to note, that the similarity approximated by the encoder hidden states can be used for source token confidence estimation, while the combination of autoencoders on the source hidden state and posterior probabilities can only be used for target token confidence estimation. One advantage of this combination is that no additional parameters are introduced.

4   Alignment

While the previously presented models are all able to generate confidence measures for each target token, only the distance-based similarity measures are able to also generate scores for the source tokens. In order to generate source token confidence qualitatively, a straightforward approach is to use word alignment to map the confidence score from the target side to the source.

Our baseline for these experiments uses the IBM4 GIZA alignment model (Och and Ney, 2003) to map the posterior probabilities and the combined approach's confidence estimations from target to source tokens. If several target tokens align to the same source token, we again use the minimal confidence.

Motivated by our autoencoding approach to measure similarity between training and test data, we investigate similar approaches to model the alignment between source and target tokens. In this case, we used a model to predict a target hidden state d_j given a source state e_i. If a source word aligns to a target word, it should be possible to predict this target word primarily based on this source word. Therefore, we choose the same architecture as for the autoencoder. We use the source hidden state to predict a target hidden state. Then, we compare the predicted hidden state to all decoder hidden states and describe the alignment strength between the source and target hidden state using the cosine similarity between the predicted hidden state and the target hidden state. Let $NN()$ be the neural network-based predictor. We then calculate the alignment by:

$$a_{ij}' = \cos sim(NN(e_i), d_j) \quad (6)$$

Based on the alignment scores, we created an alignment matrix by aligning each source word to the target word with the strongest link according to Equation 7.

$$a(i) = \min_{j \in 1,\ldots,J} a_{ij}' \quad (7)$$

Since there are not confidence labels with aligned source and target words available, we cannot simply train the neural network. Inspired by the GIZA model, we utilize the EM algorithm for training. Given an alignment $a*$, we can train our model using the following MSE-based loss function:

$$MSE(NN(e_i), d_{a*_i}) \quad (8)$$

This can be extended for soft alignments a to:

$$MSE(NN(e_i), \sum_j a_{ij} d_j) \qquad (9)$$

This corresponds to the M-Step in the EM algorithm. To be able to train the model using this loss function, we need to estimate an alignment a in the E-step. Given the source representation $e_1, \dots e_I$ of a sentence, we use the predictor to calculate the prediction $p_1, \dots p_I$. Based on this, we calculate the alignment similarities a'_{ij} based on cosine similarities between p_i and the decoder hidden states d_j. In order to prevent the model from learning to collapse into aligning all source words to the most obvious words e.g. the period at the end of the sentence, we normalize them to probabilities for each target word. ($a'_{ij} = a_{ij} / \sum_{i'=1}^{I} (a_{i'j})$).

5 Evaluation

In this work, we evaluate the ability of sequence-to-sequence models to estimate their confidence in their own output on two different tasks: MT and ASR.

It is necessary to define a gold standard for the evaluation. For ASR, there is only one ground truth. Accordingly, we can label each output word from the model as correct/substitution/deletion/insertion. Our confidence measurement is then done on he word level (predicting whether the word is correct or not) [2].

For machine translation, a single correct translation for each source sentence does not exist. To account for this, our experiments are carried out in the following way: We collected annotations with incorrectly translated source words for 1177 sentence pairs, resulting in 39.93% of the source sentences containing mistranslated words. We were not able to test our methods on existing quality estimation data sets, as we cannot access internal model information for this data.

Given the reference labels, the next step is to measure the quality of the confidence measures. In our experiments, we use four different measures. The first possible scenario is that, we assume that the user has a fixed amount of time and wants to maximize the improvements. Therefore, we calculate the confidence score for all the test data and look at the 10% and 20% of the test data that the model has given the lowest confidences. Then,

we measure what percentage of errors according to the reference are found in this part of the data.

In another scenario, we want to dynamically correct as many sentences as would be beneficial. This can be measured using the F-Score. Since we need to map the confidence scores to labels, we have the additional challenge of finding a good threshold for when to assign the label "high confidence" or "low confidence" to an output sentence/word. Therefore, we report oracle F-Scores using an optimal threshold found on the test data. Furthermore, we evaluate an approach to find this threshold in an unsupervised manner: While our baseline system uses beam search with beam=8, we also perform greedy decoding. We assume that the model is not confident if the beam search leads to a different outcome from the greedy decoding, and create pseudo-labels where each segment or token is labeled wrong if the results of beam search and greedy search differ. Then, we select the optimal threshold based by comparing the predict scores and these pseudo-labels and evaluate the approach on the real labels.

6 Experiments

The sequence-to-sequence models in our work are based on the state-of-the-art Transformer architecture (Vaswani et al., 2017). We followed the model configuration with the learning rate schedule from the *Base* configuration in the original work. The number of layers is adapted for each task for the best performance possible and will be reported respectively. The autoencoders are implemented on top of the Transformer (with PyTorch (Paszke et al., 2017)) using one hidden layer with different sizes and sigmoid activation function. [3] The MT model is a 12-layer Transformer trained on the German-English TED corpus (Cettolo et al., 2012) with the development set and test set from the IWSLT 2017 evaluation campaign. The data is preprocessed with Moses tokenization, true-casing and segmented with byte-pair encoding (Sennrich et al., 2016) with 40K codes. The model achieves a BLEU score of 28.82 on the development set and 30.63 on the test data.

We conducted further ASR experiments on the Switchboard-1 Release 2 (LDC97S62) corpus, which contains over 300 hours of speech. The Hub5'00 evaluation data (LDC2002S09) was used as our test set. On this set, we are especially inter-

---

[2]If a word in the reference was deleted, we marked the previous and next word also as an erroneous word.

[3]https://github.com/isl-mt/NMTGMinor

ested in the influence of the model performance on the quality estimation. Therefore, we trained 4 different models with 4,8,12 and 24 layers. These models achieve a WER of 20.8, 14.8, 13.0 and 12.1 on the Switchboard test set respectively, and 33.2, 25.5, 23.9 and 23.0 on the Callhome set.

6.1 Machine translation results

The first concern in the experiments is the performance on segment-level quality estimation for machine translation. The results are summarized in Table 1.

Two baseline systems are presented in this experiment. To measure the difficulty of the task, we use the BEER evaluation metric as comparison, which has been performing competitively in the WMT Metric evaluations (Stanojevic and Simaan, 2014). It is important to note that the metric has access to the reference translation, while the confidence measure do not. Even with this advantage, the metric does not clearly outperform a random baseline, showing the difficulty of the task. Using the model's posterior probability, we can improve on all four types of confidence measure. Among the 10% of the sentences with the lowest confidence, this method was able to find 17.66% of the sentences with errors. For this task, this is further the best performance. This confirms our hypothesis that the posterior probabilities can be reliable for modelling the system's confidence.

Proceeding to experiments shown in the next two lines, we evaluate the ability of using the similarity between test and training data as a measure for confidence. Although not performing as well as the posterior probabilities, the data difference is a good estimator for the task difficulty and the confidence of the model. When comparing a single sentence representation (Enc Sent Distance) and the token representation (Enc Distance) in the next line, the second one outperforms the first one, except for the top 10%. Therefore, it seems to be important to measure the distance of each individual token and not only of the whole sentence.

Motivated by these results, we trained the autoencoders on the individual tokens and not on the whole sentence and used the autoencoder networks on the source hidden representation to estimate the performance. We analyze the influence of the size of the bottleneck of the autoencoder. The network with bottleneck size of 256 (Enc Auto 256), which is half the size of the input size, managed to get the best performance in all measures. While we see a drop in performance due to the approximation, e.g. from 32.77% to 29.57% when looking at 20% of the data, this is still better than BEER.

We performed the same experiment using the target hidden representations. Again, we investigated the influence of the bottleneck size and achieved the best performance with a bottleneck size of 256 (Dec Auto 256). Reasonably, the target hidden states contain more information about the sequence-to-be-generated than the source states.

Finally, when combining the output probability with the decoder hidden states (Dec Auto 256 + Prob), we are able to achieve the best performance. Again, it is better to use the autoencoder on the decoder hidden state than on the encoder hidden state. It is worth noting that the pseudo-labels perform very well when including the posterior probabilities. Interestingly, we see a clear drop in performance between oracle and pseudo-labels when not using the posterior probabilities.

Moreover, we evaluated methods to identify source words with low confidence. The results for these experiments are summarized in Table 2. In this case the baseline is to map the posterior probabilities to the source sentence using a GIZA (Och and Ney, 2003) alignment. Again, we evaluate the approach with the same four scores. As shown in the first two lines, the Giza alignment from source to target performance clearly better than the one from target to source. Therefore, in the remaining experiments, we only evaluate approaches using the source to target alignment.

By using the training-test distance approximated by the autoencoder on the encoder states (Enc Auto 256), we directly have an estimate on the source side and so do not need to map target estimates to the source side. In this case, we see improvements over using the posterior probabilities. Again, the pseudo labels perform not as well without using the posterior probabilities. Next, we map the other three measures, decoder hidden states and the combination of encoder or decoder states and output probabilities, using the Giza alignment to the source. Interestingly, this time, solely using the approximation of the training-test similarity is even better than the combination with the output probabilities. The best system is achieved by the autoencoder of the decoder states (Dec Auto 256). We see improvements by 3% and 10% over the

Model	10%	20%	Oracle	Pseudo-label
BEER	10.43	24.68	61.24	61.10
Prob	**17.66**	33.19	64.66	63.96
Enc Sent Distance	17.02	31.91	62.95	61.73
Enc Distance	16.81	32.77	63.66	62.64
Enc Auto 128	13.62	25.74	60.13	59.64
Enc Auto 256	14.47	29.57	61.94	61.37
Enc Auto 512	13.62	25.74	60.50	59.61
Dec Auto 128	15.11	30.00	62.87	61.63
Dec Auto 256	16.17	31.91	63.96	61.43
Dec Auto 512	15.11	31.28	62.92	60.31
Enc Auto 256 + Prob	16.38	**34.04**	64.48	64.15
Dec Auto 256 + Prob	17.02	**34.04**	**65.92**	**65.54**

Table 1: Segment-level confidence estimation for MT. First two columns: Percentage of found errors when selecting 10% and 20% of the data; Final two columns: F-score when using oracle threshold and thresholds optimized on pseudo-labels

Model	Alignment	10%	20%	Oracle	Pseudo-label
Prob	Giza DE-EN	25.15	34.09	19.33	17.73
Prob	Giza EN-DE	28.90	39.86	22.58	21.18
Enc Auto 256		28.78	49.58	23.54	16.31
Dec Auto 256	Giza EN-DE	32.21	49.51	24.85	19.49
Enc Auto 256 + Prob	Giza EN-DE	29.75	40.44	22.97	22.37
Dec Auto 256 + Prob	Giza EN-DE	32.21	47.38	24.54	24.37
Prob	256	32.34	44.59	25.16	24.25
Prob	512	32.79	44.91	25.45	24.39
Prob	2048	32.27	44.91	24.98	23.85
Prob	8192	33.38	46.34	25.63	24.33
Dec Auto 256	8192	33.89	53.27	26.23	21.65
Dec Auto 256 + Prob	8192	**35.58**	**52.62**	**27.21**	**27.02**

Table 2: Source word confidence for MT. First two columns: Percentage of found errors when selecting 10% and 20% of the data; Final two columns: F-score when using oracle threshold and thresholds optimized on pseudo-labels

posterior probabilities when looking at 10% and 20% of the data. Finally, we tried to use an internal alignment instead of the Giza alignment. Therefore, we predict the decoder hidden states based on the encoder hidden states as described in Section 4. Again, we investigated different sizes for the hidden states used to map the posterior probabilities. As shown in Table 2, all the models perform better than the GIZA alignment. We can further improve the quality by using a larger hidden layer. Since we need to learn a very complex mapping from source to target hidden states, a larger layer is better. The best performance is achieved using a layer of 8192 hidden units.

In the end, we also used the same model to map the autoencoder predictions. The combination of all three methods leads to the best results (Dec Auto 256 + Prob, 8192). By looking only at 10% of the words, we are able to find more than 35% of the errors and for 20% of the words we identify more than half of the errors.

6.2 Speech recognition results

The ASR results for this task are summarized in Table 3. We present the percentage of found errors when looking at 10 and 20 percent of the data. In each column, we estimate the quality of one output generated by the different models. Each row represents the results when using one model to estimate the quality of the different outputs.

Generation		4 layer		8 layer		12 layer		24 layer	
		SWB	CH	SWB	CH	SWB	CH	SWB	CH
	WER	20.8	33.2	14.8	25.5	13.0	23.9	12.1	23.0
Layer	Methods	10%	20%	10%	20%	10%	20%	10%	20%
4	prob	23.29	43.63	26.46	46.89	26.60	48.12	27.63	48.96
4	auto+prob	23.50	43.87	26.45	46.96	26.67	48.14	27.64	49.00
8	prob	30.00	53.08	29.37	51.83	32.65	54.76	32.46	55.02
8	auto+prob	30.00	53.20	29.67	53.80	32.63	57.10	32.43	57.87
12	prob	30.09	54.80	34.59	56.44	31.13	54.71	34.67	56.61
12	auto+prob	30.97	54.87	34.62	58.61	31.37	57.09	34.70	59.31
24	prob	31.21	55.40	35.34	57.29	35.91	57.54	31.95	55.30
24	auto+prob	31.65	57.26	36.05	61.15	36.73	60.97	37.42	60.77

Table 3: Confidence estimation on ASR using different ASR systems for output predictions and confidence estimation: Found errors when selection 10% and 20% of the data

Here we evaluated four different models with increasing transcription quality. The only difference between the models are the number of hidden layers. We investigated models using $4, 8, 12$ and 24 layers. In this task, the test set consists of two subsets. The best model achieves a word error rate of 12.1 and 23.0 on the two subsets, respectively.

Again, we use the output probabilities as well as the combination of the autoencoder and the output probabilities. We again use half the input size for the bottleneck size. Firstly, as shown in the MT experiments, we can improve the quality estimation by combining the posterior probabilities and the autoencoder approach. In all configurations, the combination performs better or similar than the posterior probability.

Secondly, the better models are able to better estimate the confidence on the same output. In most cases, the performance can be improved by using a more complex model to estimate the confidence. One exception is the estimation of its own output.

Finally, the estimation of the distance between training and test data mainly helps when using stronger models, both for the generation of the output and for confidence estimation. Furthermore, this method also removes the effect of models performing worse than their own output.

7   Related Work

Prior work has investigated confidence measurement for speech recognition models (Siu and Gish, 1999), and statistical machine translation models using either word-level posteriors (Ueffing and Ney, 2007) or external models (Gandrabur and Foster, 2003). Deep learning models have also received attention on uncertainty and confidence measurement recently: (Gal and Ghahramani, 2016) formulate neural network models with dropout as Bayesian models to obtain uncertainty based on sampling methods. Specifically, for neural machine translation models or other sequence-to-sequence models, quality estimation has remained as a topic of concern. While most prior research focused on developing confidence measures for a general system using external features (Specia et al., 2018), this works concentrates on estimating the confidence of a specific system by making use of the information available in the internal representation of the network.

8   Conclusion

In this work, we investigated the ability of sequence-to-sequence models to model their confidence in their decisions. We performed experiments using these models for two tasks: machine translation and speech recognition.

We analyzed the influence of train-test mismatch on quality estimation. By approximating this mismatch using an autoencoder and combining it with the posterior probabilities, we are able to improve confidence estimation over a strong baseline. We showed that it is better to measure the mismatch on the decoder hidden states than on the encoder hidden states.

Secondly, we also investigated methods to predict how well each individual source token is translated by a given model. In this case, measuring the train-test mismatch was even more important. Furthermore, we present an approach to infer the internal alignment of complex sequence-to-sequence models. Using this alignment instead of a state-of-the-art external alignment for mapping target confidence measure to source tokens clearly improved the quality of the confidence measure for source words

Acknowledgments

The project ELITR leading to this publication has received funding from the European Unions Horizon 2020 Research and Innovation Programme under grant agreement № 825460. We thank Elizabeth Salesky for the constructive comments.

References

Mauro Cettolo, Christian Girardi, and Marcello Federico. 2012. Wit^3: Web inventory of transcribed and translated talks. In *Proceedings of the 16th Conference of the European Association for Machine Translation (EAMT)*, pages 261–268, Trento, Italy.

Yarin Gal. 2016. *Uncertainty in Deep Learning*. Ph.D. thesis, University of Cambridge.

Yarin Gal and Zoubin Ghahramani. 2016. A theoretically grounded application of dropout in recurrent neural networks. In *Advances in Neural Information Processing Systems 29 (NIPS)*.

S. Gandrabur and G. Foster. 2003. Confidence estimation for translation prediction. In *Proceedings of the Seventh Conference on Natural Language Learning at HLT-NAACL 2003 - Volume 4*, CONLL '03, pages 95–102, Stroudsburg, PA, USA. Association for Computational Linguistics.

Franz Josef Och and Hermann Ney. 2003. A Systematic Comparison of Various Statistical Alignment Models. *Computational Linguistics*, 29(1):19–51.

Adam Paszke, Sam Gross, Soumith Chintala, Gregory Chanan, Edward Yang, Zachary DeVito, Zeming Lin, Alban Desmaison, Luca Antiga, and Adam Lerer. 2017. Automatic differentiation in pytorch.

Rico Sennrich, Barry Haddow, and Alexandra Birch. 2016. Neural machine translation of rare words with subword units. *Proceedings of the 54th Annual Meeting of the Association for Computational Linguistics (Volume 1: Long Papers)*.

M. Siu and H. Gish. 1999. Evaluation of word confidence for speech recognition systems. *Computer Speech & Language*, 13(4):299 – 319.

L. Specia, F. Blain, V. Logacheva, R. Astudillo, and A. F. T. Martins. 2018. Findings of the wmt 2018 shared task on quality estimation. In *Proceedings of the Third Conference on Machine Translation, Volume 2: Shared Task Papers*, pages 702–722, Belgium, Brussels. Association for Computational Linguistics.

Milos Stanojevic and Khalil Simaan. 2014. Beer: Better evaluation as ranking. In *Proceedings of the Ninth Workshop on Statistical Machine Translation*, pages 414–419.

N. Ueffing and H. Ney. 2007. Word-level confidence estimation for machine translation. *Computational Linguistics*, 33:9–40.

Ashish Vaswani, Noam Shazeer, Niki Parmar, Jakob Uszkoreit, Llion Jones, Aidan N Gomez, Łukasz Kaiser, and Illia Polosukhin. 2017. Attention is all you need. In *Advances in Neural Information Processing Systems*, pages 5998–6008.

A Good Sample is Hard to Find: Noise Injection Sampling and Self-Training for Neural Language Generation Models

Chris Kedzie
Columbia University
Department of Computer Science
kedzie@cs.columbia.edu

Kathleen McKeown
Columbia University
Department of Computer Science
kathy@cs.columbia.edu

Abstract

Deep neural networks (DNN) are quickly becoming the de facto standard modeling method for many natural language generation (NLG) tasks. In order for such models to truly be useful, they must be capable of correctly generating utterances for novel meaning representations (MRs) at test time. In practice, even sophisticated DNNs with various forms of semantic control frequently fail to generate utterances faithful to the input MR. In this paper, we propose an architecture agnostic self-training method to sample novel MR/text utterance pairs to augment the original training data. Remarkably, after training on the augmented data, even simple encoder-decoder models with greedy decoding are capable of generating semantically correct utterances that are as good as state-of-the-art outputs in both automatic and human evaluations of quality.

1 Introduction

Deep neural network (DNN) architectures have become the standard modeling method for a host of language generation tasks. When data is plentiful, the sequence-to-sequence framework proves to be incredibly adaptable to a variety of problem domains. Recent evaluations of end-to-end trained DNNs for dialogue generation have shown that they are capable of learning very natural text realizations of formal meaning representations (MRs), i.e. dialogue acts (DAs) with slot-filler type attributes (see Figure 1 for an example). In many cases, they beat rule and template based systems on human and automatic measures of quality (Dušek et al., 2019).

However, this powerful generation capability comes with a cost; DNN language models are notoriously difficult to control, often producing quite fluent but semantically misleading outputs. In order for such models to truly be useful, they

---

Inform   name[The Golden Curry]
          near[The Six Bells]
          familyFriendly[yes]

Training Reference Utterance
Near The Six Bells is a venue that is children friendly named The Golden Curry.

Figure 1: Example MR for the Inform DA with example human reference utterance.

must be capable of correctly generating utterances for novel MRs at test time. In practice, even with delexicalization (Dušek and Jurčíček, 2016; Juraska et al., 2018), copy and coverage mechanisms (Elder et al., 2018), and overgeneration plus reranking (Dušek and Jurčíček, 2016; Juraska et al., 2018), DNN generators still produce errors (Dušek et al., 2019).

In this work, rather than develop more sophisticated DNN architectures or ensembles, we explore the use of simpler DNNs with self-training. We train a bare-bones unidirectional neural encoder-decoder with attention (Bahdanau et al., 2014) as our base model from which we sample novel utterances for MRs not seen in the original training data. We obtain a diverse collection of samples using noise injection sampling (Cho, 2016). Using an MR parser, we add novel utterances with valid MRs to the original training data. Retraining the model on the augmented data yields a language generator that is more reliable than the sophisticated DNNs that have been recently developed, in some cases reducing test set semantic errors to zero, without sacrificing linguistic quality.

In this paper we make the following contributions. 1) We propose a general method of data augmentation for natural language generation (NLG) problems using noise injection sampling and self-

Proceedings of The 12th International Conference on Natural Language Generation, pages 584–593,
Tokyo, Japan, 28 Oct - 1 Nov, 2019. ©2019 Association for Computational Linguistics

training. 2) We show a reduction of attribute realization errors across several dialog generation datasets, while achieving competitive automatic and human quality evaluation scores. 3) Finally, we show that these results hold even when the MR parser is noisy or we use fully lexicalized generation models.[1]

2 Datasets and Problem Defintion

We ground our experiments in three recent dialogue generation datasets, the E2E Challenge Dataset (Dušek et al., 2019), and the Laptops and TVs datasets (Wen et al., 2016). We only briefly review them here. Each dataset consists of dialog act MRs paired with one or more reference utterances (see Figure 1 for an example from the E2E dataset). The structure of each MR is relatively simple, consisting of the dialog act itself, (e.g. *inform, recommend, compare*, etc.) and a variable number of attribute slots which need to be realised in the utterance. All attribute values come from a closed vocabulary. If an attribute is not present in the MR it should not be realized in the corresponding utterance.

The three datasets also represent different training size conditions; there are 42,061, 7,944, and 4,221 training examples in E2E, Laptops, and TVs datasets respectively.

The NLG task for all three datasets is to produce an utterance for a given MR such that all attributes in the MR are realized naturally and correctly.

E2E Model Input Following previous sequence-to-sequence approaches for the E2E dataset (Juraska et al., 2018), we treat the MRs as a linear sequence of tokens $x = (x_1, \ldots, x_8)$ where each of the 8 positions represents the value of a corresponding attribute. If an attribute is not specified in the MR we assign it an attribute specific *n/a* token. In the E2E dataset there is only one dialog act type, *Inform*, so we do not represent it in x.

Prior work often delexicalizes the *Name* and *Near* attributes (i.e. replaces verbalizations of attribute values with a placeholder token), which can later be replaced with the original attribute value in a post-processing step. For example, the delexicalized version of the utterance in Figure 1 would be "Near NEAR is a venue that is children friendly named NAME." *Name* and *Near* have

a relatively large vocabulary of valid slot fillers, some of which are only seen infrequently in the training data; it can be difficult for fully lexicalized models to produce some of the rarer location names for these attributes.

However, since delexicalization might be difficult or impossible in other domains, we implement both delexicalized and lexicalized versions of the generation models on the E2E dataset to more fully evaluate the self-training method.[2]

Laptops and TVs Model Inputs The Laptops and TVs datasets have a more diverse set of dialog acts and can have repeated attributes (with different values) in some cases, so we abandon our fixed length, fixed position encoding, and represent each MR as a initial dialog act token and then a variable length sequence of tokens for each of the specified attributes. The evaluation script for these datasets uses delexicalization to evaluate attribute realization error, and so we use it here to be consistent with prior work, delexicalizing all possible attributes. See Appendix B for example input sequences for all datasets.

3 Generation Model

We treat the generation task as a sequence-to-sequence transduction problem, where we learn a probabilistic mapping p from the linearized MR x to a sequence of N tokens $y = (y_1, \ldots, y_N)$ consituting the utterance. The model p is implemented using a two-layer unidirectional[3] encoder-decoder architecture with gated recurrent units (Cho et al., 2014) and feed-forward style attention (Bahdanau et al., 2014) as this is a canonical recurrent architecture for sequence-to-sequence modeling. We use 512 dimensions for all embeddings and GRU states.

We fit the model parameters θ by minimizing the negative log likelihood of the training set $\mathcal{D}$, i.e. $\mathcal{L}(\theta) = -\sum_{(x,y)\in\mathcal{D}} \log p(y|x;\theta)$ using stochastic gradient descent. Going forward we omit θ for clarity.

3.1 Generating from p

Deterministic Decoding Given an arbitrary MR x, we can generate an utterance $\tilde{y}$ using greedy decoding, i.e. $\tilde{y}_i = \arg\max_{y_i} p(y_i|\tilde{y}_{<i}, x)$.

---

[1] Code and data for this paper can be found at
https://github.com/kedz/noiseylg

[2] Additional preprocessing details can be found in Appendix A.

[3] In initial experiments, we found the unidirectional encoder to perform better than a bidirectional one.

To produce an "n-best" list of outputs, we can also use beam decoding where n candidate utterances are maintained during each decoding step. Both greedy and beam decoding are known to produce somewhat homogeneous outputs (Serban et al., 2016). Diversifying beam outputs often involves careful tuning of secondary search objectives which trade off fluency (Li et al., 2015).

Moreover, when training fully lexicalized models we found that we could often *not* produce certain *Name* and *Near* attribute values. For example, we constructed a novel MR with *near[Burger King]* and fed it into our base generator. Even with an impractically large beam size of 512, we could not produce an utterance with "Burger King" in it. This failure mode makes beam search a relatively unuseable method for producing utterances for MRs under-represented in the training data.[4]

To overcome this limitation we explored several sampling methods for generating these rarer utterances, namely ancestral and noise injection sampling.

Stochastic Decoding Ancestral sampling (i.e. drawing a random token from $p(Y_i|y_{<i}, x)$ at each decoder step) is another option for generating diverse outputs, but the outputs can be of lower fluency and coherence. Producing rare tokens often involves tuning a temperature parameter to flatten the output distribution, but this again can hurt fluency.

As an alternative, we can obtain diverse samples from greedy decoding by injecting Gaussian noise into the decoder hidden states following Cho (2016). Under our model, the probability $p(y_i|y_{<i}, x) = f(x, h_i)$ of the i-th token is a function of the encoder inputs x and the decoder hidden state $h_i \in \mathbb{R}^D$. When peforming noise injection sampling, we replace h_i with a noisy state $\tilde{h}_i = h_i + \epsilon_i$ where ϵ_i is drawn from a D-dimensional Gaussian distribution $\mathcal{N}(0, \sigma_i^2 I)$ with variance $\sigma_i^2 = \frac{\sigma_0^2}{i}$. The base variance σ_0^2 is a a hyperparameter. Effectively, the first few steps allow the decoder to reach a novel hidden state space, while the gradually diminishing noise allows the decoder to produce fluent outputs.

Generating Rare Values Remarkably, the samples obtained by noise injection maintain fluency

---

[4]The MR in this case had three attributes. *near[Burger King]* only occurs in size eight MRs in the training data.

and valid syntactic structure. At the same time they often hallucinate or drop attributes. For example, see the last noise injection sample in Table 1 where the attribute *near[The Bakers]* is hallucinated. This kind of error is actually useful because, as long as we have a reliable MR parser, we can recover the MR of the sample and we now have a totally valid extra datapoint that we could use for training. Syntactic errors of the kind produced by ancestral sampling (see the last ancetral sampling example in Table 1), on the other hand, are not good to train on because they damage the fluency of the decoder.

Returning to the "Burger King" example, with noise injection sampling we were able to produce over 10,000 novel instances of it. See Appendix D for more samples.

4 MR Parsing Model

Given a novel utterance $\tilde{y}$ sampled from p, we need to reliably parse the implied MR, i.e. $\tilde{x} = q(\tilde{y})$, where q is our parsing model. We have two things going for us in our experimental setting. First, even with noise injection sampling, model outputs are fairly patterned, reducing the variability of the utterances we need to parse in practice.

Second, the MRs in this study are flat lists of attributes that are somewhat independent of each other. We only need to detect the presence of each attribute and its value. For the Laptops and TVs datasets we also need to recover the dialog act but these also are signaled by a fairly limited repertoire of cues, e.g. "we recommend." Given this, we experiment with both hand crafted regular expression rules and learned classifiers to predict the value of an attribute if present or that it is missing.

Rule-based parser $q_{\mathfrak{R}}$ We design hand-crafted regular expression based rules to match for the presence of key phrases for each of the attributes and DAs in the datasets while also checking to make sure that there is only one match per attribute.

To construct the rules, we look through both the training data references as well as the generation model outputs as this is what the rules will be operating on in practice. For each lexicalized attribute (and DA) we develop a list of regular expressions such as, `/is (family|kid|child) friendly/` $\Rightarrow$ *familyFriendly[yes]*. For the delexicalized attributes, we simply check for the presence of the placeholder token.

Input MR
Inform(name[The Cambridge Blue], eatType[Restaurant], customerRating[high], food[Italian])
Ancestral Sampling
The Cambridge Blue is an Italian restaurant with a high customer rating.
The Cambridge Blue is an Italian restaurant with high ratings.
*Italian restaurant, the Cambridge Blue, has a high customer rating. (Phrase fragments, not fluent.)
Noise Injection Sampling
The Cambridge Blue is a restaurant that serves Italian food. it has a high customer rating.
*The Cambridge Blue is a highly rated restaurant. (Drops *food[Italian]*.)
*The Cambridge Blue is a restaurant located near the Bakers. (Hallucinates *near[The Bakers]*.)

Table 1: Examples of ancestral sampling and noise injection sampling ($\sigma_0 = 1.0$). * indicates output that is either not grammatical or is not correct with respect to the input MR. Text in parentheses explains the details of the error in either case.

We design these rules to be high precision, as it is safer to miss out on more obscure varieties of utterance to avoid adding incorrectly parsed data points. However, in many cases the rules are also high recall as well. The average F-score on the E2E validation set is 0.93.

Classifier-based parser q_ϕ It is perhaps too optimistic to believe we can construct reasonable rules in all cases. Rule creation quickly becomes tedious and for more complex MRs this would become a bottleneck. To address these concerns, we also study the feasibility of using learned classifiers to predict the presence and value of the attributes. For each attribute in the E2E dataset, we trained a separate convolutional neural network (CNN) classifier to predict the correct attribute value (or *n/a* if the attribute is not present). The CNN architecture follows that of Kim (2014) and is trained with gradient descent on the original training data. See Appendix C for full architecture and training details. The average E2E validation F-score is 0.94.

5   Self-Training Methodology

Our approach to self-training is relatively straightforward and invariant to the choices of whether or not to use delexicalization, and rule vs. classifier based parser. There are minor differences depending on the dataset and we elaborate on those below. There are three main steps to our self-training approach. Starting with an initially empty augmented dataset $\mathcal{A}$, we

1. Train a base generator model p_0 on the original training data $\mathcal{D}$.

2. Repeat many times:

   (a) Sample a random MR $x \sim \mathcal{X}$.
   (b) Sample K utterances $\tilde{y}^{(i)} \sim p_0(\cdot|x, \epsilon)$
   (c) Parse MR, $\tilde{x}^{(i)} = q(\tilde{y}^{(i)})$, discarding any samples with invalid parses, and adding the survivors to $\mathcal{A}$.

3. Train a new generator p_1 on the combined dataset $\mathcal{D} \cup \mathcal{A}$.

Steps 1 and 3 are identical, the generators p_0 and p_1 have the same architecture and training setup, ony the dataset, $\mathcal{D}$ vs. $\mathcal{D} \cup \mathcal{A}$, is different. We now discuss step 2 in detail.

Step 2: E2E Dataset To sample a novel MR with S attributes, we sample a combination of $S - 1$ attributes uniformly at random (always appending the *name* attribute since every MR contains it). We then sample attribute values for each slot inversely proportional to their empirical frequency in the training set so as to increase the likelihood of creating a novel or under-represented MR.

After obtaining such a sample x we then perform noise injection sampling, generating 200 samples $\tilde{y}^{(i)} \sim p_0(\cdot|x, \epsilon^{(i)})$ in parallel and discarding all but the top 20 samples by average log likelihood according to p_0. We also discard any utterances that have previously been generated.

We then apply the parser to the sampled utterances, to obtain its predicted MR, $\tilde{x}^{(i)} = q(\tilde{y}^{(i)})$. If using the rule based parser $q_{\mathfrak{R}}$ and $\tilde{x} = \emptyset$, i.e. the utterance does not have a valid parse, we discard it. Similarly, when using the classifier based parser, q_ϕ, if any attribute value is predicted with less than 50% probability we discard it. All surviving $(\tilde{x}^{(i)}, \tilde{y}^{(i)})$ pairs are added to $\mathcal{A}$. We repeat this process 25,000 times for each valid MR size S. See Table 8 for statistics on the total sample sizes after filtering.

Step 2: Laptops and TVs On the Laptops and TVs dataset, for each DA and legal number of attributes S we draw S random attributes (modulo any required attributes like *Name*; not all DAs require it).[5]

We then perform noise injection sampling, generating 200 samples $\tilde{y}^{(i)} \sim p_0(\cdot|x, \epsilon^{(i)})$ under the same settings as the E2E dataset. We repeat this process 25,000 times for each DA and DA size. We obtain 373,468 and 33,478 additional samples for the Laptops and TVs datasets respectively.

6 Experiments

6.1 E2E Self-Training

We train base generators p_0 on the original training data $\mathcal{D}$, with and without delexicalizing the *Name* and *Near* attributes. We train for 500 epochs with gradient descent. We use a batch size of 128, with a learning rate of 0.25, weight decay penalty of 0.0001, and a dropout probability of 0.25. We select the best model iteration using validation set BLEU score[6].

Using the self-training method outlined in section 5, we create augmented datasets using either $q_{\mathfrak{R}}$ or q_ϕ, which we refer to as $\mathcal{A}_{q_{\mathfrak{R}}}$ and $\mathcal{A}_{q_\phi}$ respectively (q_ϕ is only in the delexicalized setting).

For both $\mathcal{D} \cup \mathcal{A}_{q_{\mathfrak{R}}}$ and $\mathcal{D} \cup \mathcal{A}_{q_\phi}$ we train new generators p_1 using the same training setting as above (although we terminate training after 50 epochs because the models converge much faster with the additional data).

Results Table 2 shows the automatic quality measurements on the E2E test set using BLEU, ROUGE-L, and METEOR. We show results for both greedy and beam decoding with beam size 8 under p_0 and p_1 models. We compare our models to the best sequence-to-sequence DNN model, Slug (Juraska et al., 2018), the best grammar rule based model, DANGNT (Nguyen and Tran, 2018), and the best template based model, TUDA

---

[5]A number of attributes S is "legal" if we observe a DA instance with that many attributes in the original training data.

[6]We use the official shared task script to compute automatic quality metrics on the E2E dataset.

	Model	BLEU	R.-L	MET.
	Slug	66.19	67.72	44.54
	DANGNT	59.90	66.34	43.46
	TUDA	56.57	66.14	45.29
delex. p_0	greedy	66.91	68.27	44.95
	beam	**67.13**	**68.91**	45.15
$p_1\ q_{\mathfrak{R}}$	greedy	65.57	67.71	45.56
	beam	66.28	68.08	**45.78**
q_ϕ	greedy	63.76	67.31	44.94
	beam	64.23	67.54	45.17
lex. p_0	greedy	60.35	64.51	41.82
	beam	61.81	65.83	42.69
$p_1\ q_{\mathfrak{R}}$	greedy	64.74	68.21	44.46
	beam	64.81	67.83	44.39

Table 2: BLEU, ROUGE-L, and METEOR metrics on the E2E test set. Baseline methods all rely on at least partial delexicalization, puting our delexicalized models at a relative disadvantage.

(Puzikov and Gurevych, 2018), as determined during the shared task evaluation (Dušek et al., 2019).

Surprisingly, p_0 using greedy decoding surpases all of the baseline systems. This is quite shocking as the Slug model ensembles three different sequence-to-sequence models producing 10 outputs each using beam search and reranking based on slot alignment to select the final generation output. The $p_1/q_{\mathfrak{R}}$ model remains competitive with Slug, again even using greedy decoding. The p_1/q_ϕ starts underperforming Slug on BLEU score but remains competitive on ROUGE-L and METEOR again when using greedy decoding. Overall the augmented training data tends to hurt generation quality. In this regard, the added noise of the trained classifier exacerbates things as it reduces quality more than the rule-based filtering.

In the lexicalized setting, p_0 produces lower quality output than the Slug system. However, the augmented training procedure increases the quality of the lexicalized p_1 model which beats Slug on ROUGE-L.

The automatic quality evaluations are somewhat limited, however. To gain more insight into model performance we apply our rule based parser to estimate attribute realization error for all system outputs on the test set, similarly to (Dušek et al., 2019) (e.g., if the MR specifies *food[French]*, we check to make sure the generated utterance says so). The results of this evaluation are shown in

	Model		Name	Near	Family Friendly	Area	Customer Rating	Food	Price Range	Eat Type	All
		Slug	0	0	6	1	6	10	35	9	67
		DANGNT	0	0	18	0	0	0	0	58	76
		TUDA	0	0	0	0	0	0	0	0	**0**
delex.	p_0	greedy	0	0	23	23	16	26	27	0	115
		beam	0	0	60	3	9	3	8	0	83
	p_1 $q_{\Re}$	greedy	0	0	0	0	0	0	0	0	**0**
		beam	0	0	0	0	0	0	0	0	**0**
	q_ϕ	greedy	0	0	1	0	8	1	9	0	19
		beam	0	0	0	0	3	0	0	0	3
lex.	p_0	greedy	145	141	14	15	2	14	2	0	333
		beam	155	124	62	0	0	0	0	0	341
	p_1 $q_{\Re}$	greedy	0	0	2	0	0	125	0	0	127
		beam	0	2	0	0	0	119	0	0	121

Table 3: Attribute realization errors on the E2E test set. The Slug model and our delexicalized models delexicalize the NAME and NEAR slots, thus making 0 errors on these attributes. DANGNT and TUDA models perform complete delexicalization.

Table 3. Immediately, it is revealed that p_0 is far worse than the baseline methods making 115 and 83 errors using greedy and beam decoding respectively.

The $p_1/q_{\Re}$ model achieves zero test set errors even when using the greedy decoding. The p_1/q_ϕ model is slightly worse (in agreement with the automatic quality measurements), but its greedy search is still superior to the more sophisticated Slug decoder, achieving 19 total test set errors compared to Slug's 67 errors.

The lexicalized p_0 model has especially high error rates, particularly on the *Name* and *Near* attributes. With augmented data training, the p_1 model reduces these errors to zero when using greedy search and 2 with beam search. Unfortunately, the augmented training is more unstable in the lexicalized setting, as it produces a large spike in *food* attribute errors, although the p_1 models still have lower overall error than p_0.

6.2 Laptops and TVs Self-Training

We perform similar experiments on the Laptops and TVs datasets. We train a separate p_0 model for each dataset for 300 epochs with a learning rate of 0.1 for Laptops and 0.25 for TVs. The weight decay penalty was 0.0001 and dropout probability was 0.25. Best model iteration is determined by validation set BLEU score. As in the E2E experiments, we create an augmented dataset for both the Laptops and TVs dataset using the method outlined in section 5. We then train new generators p_1 on the union of original training data and the augmented dataset.

Results We automatically evaluate our models using the evaluation script of Wen et al. (2016), which computes BLEU scores, as well as slot alignment error rate (since this dataset is almost fully delexicalized, it simply checks for the presence of the correct attribute placeholders according to the MR). We compare again to the Slug model as well as the Semantically Conditioned LSTM (SCLSTM) (Wen et al., 2015) which report state-of-the-art results on these datasets.

The results are more mixed here. Our BLEU scores are about 15 points below the baselines on the Laptops dataset and 20 points below the baselines on the TVs dataset. Upon examing the evaluation script in detail we see that BLEU score is calculated using 5 model outputs which Juraska et al. (2018) and Wen et al. (2016) do. We only produce the 1-best output at test time, perhaps explaining the difference.

Looking through our model outputs we see mostly good utterances, often nearly exactly matching the references. Our models outperform the state of the art models on errors. The best state of the art models make errors by generating sentences that do not match the input representation

Model	Laptops		TVs	
	BLEU	Err.	BLEU	Err.
SCLSTM	51.16	0.79%	**52.65**	2.31%
Slug	**52.38**	1.55%	52.26	1.67%
p_0 beam	37.13	0.72%	32.63	0.72%
p_1 greedy	37.21	**0.13%**	32.43	0.28%
beam	37.19	0.14%	32.59	**0.20%**

Table 4: BLEU and automatic attribute error on the Laptops and TVs datasets.

0.79% and 1.67% of the time on the Laptops and TVs datasets respectively. Our p_1 model reduces that error to only 0.13% and 0.20%.

6.3 Experiment 4: Human Evaluation

E2E Dataset We had two undergraduate students not involved with the research look at 100 random test set utterances for six of our model variants. They were shown both the Slug output and one of our model outputs and asked to select which output was of better linguistic quality and correctness or indicate that they were equally good. We resolved disagreements in favor of the baseline, i.e. if any annotator thought the baseline was better we considered it so. If an annotator marked one of our systems as better and the other marked it as equal, we considered it equal to the baseline. Inter-annotator agreement was high, with 92% agreement on correctness and 88% agreement on quality.

Table 5 shows the results of the evaluation. We find that the p_1 model outputs are indistinguishable from the Slug model in terms of linguistic quality, regardless of the setting. In terms of correctness, the lexicalized p_1 model is as good as or better than the Slug model 98% of the time. When using the delexicalized models, we don't even need beam search. The delexicalized p_1 greedy decoder is as good as or better than Slug 100% of the time.

Laptops Dataset We had the same annotators look at 100 random *Inform* DAs from the Laptops test set since they are the majority DA type and we could use the same annotator guidelines from the E2E experiment. We do not have access to the Slug or SCLSTM outputs on this dataset, so we compared to one of the two test set reference sentences (picking at random) vs. the $p_1/q_\Re$ with greedy decoding. Table 6 shows the results. De-

Model	Correct.			Quality		
	>	=	<	>	=	<
delex. p_0 b	7	89	4	1	96	3
delex. p_1 $q_\Re$ g	7	93	0	0	100	0
delex. p_1 $q_\Re$ b	7	93	0	0	100	0
delex. p_1 q_ϕ g	5	95	0	0	100	0
delex. p_1 q_ϕ b	8	92	0	0	100	0
lex. p_1 $q_\Re$ g	8	90	2	0	100	0

Table 5: Human correctness and quality judgments (%). Comparisons are better than (>), equal to (=), and worse than (<) the baseline Slug model. (g) and (b) indicate greedy and beam decoding respectively.

Model	Correct.			Quality		
	>	=	<	>	=	<
delex. p_1 $q_\Re$ g	0	100	0	2	91	7

Table 6: Human correctness and quality judgments (%). Comparisons are better than (>), equal to (=), and worse than (<) the test set references.

spite the low BLEU scores, we find our outputs to be of comparable quality to references 91% of the time. Moreover, they are equally as correct as the human references 100% of the time. Annotators agreed 99% and 87% of the time on correctness and quality respectively.

7 Sample Analysis and Discussion

We hypothesize that self-training improves the correctness of outputs by sacrificing some expressivity of the model. For example, p_1 BLEU scores on the E2E dataset drop by at least 0.8 as compared to p_0 with beam search. We see a similar pattern on the TVs dataset. Self-training increases automatic metrics in the lexicalized setting, but this could be attributable to reductions in *Name* and *Near* realization errors, which are orthogonal to the syntactic diversity of generation.

To better quantify these effects we report the average length in words, average number of sentences, and average revised Developmental Level (D-Level) score according to the D-Level analyser (Lu, 2009). The D-Level analyser automatically categorizes the syntactic complexities of an utterance into one of eight categories, with eight being the most complex, based on the revised Developmental Level scale (Rosenberg and Abbeduto, 1987; Covington et al., 2006).

Model	Words	Sents	MDL
Human Refs.	24.06	1.76	**2.25**
Slug	24.20	1.86	1.39
lex. p_0 greedy	25.73	2.18	**1.84**
lex. p_0 beam	26.00	2.20	1.50
lex. p_1 $q_{\Re}$ greedy	26.01	2.20	1.39
lex. p_1 $q_{\Re}$ beam	26.04	2.17	1.45
delex. p_0 greedy	24.83	2.10	1.79
delex. p_0 beam	24.51	2.03	1.48
delex. p_1 $q_{\Re}$ greedy	26.50	2.29	1.74
delex. p_1 $q_{\Re}$ beam	26.46	2.28	1.74
delex. p_1 q_ϕ greedy	25.33	1.76	1.77
delex. p_1 q_ϕ beam	25.49	1.75	**1.87**

Table 7: Words/sentences per utterance and mean D-Level score of model outputs on the E2E dataset.

$\mathcal{A}$	Size	Words	Sents	MDL
delex. $\mathcal{A}_{q_\phi}$	384,436	22.5	2.0	1.77
delex. $\mathcal{A}_{q_{\Re}}$	501,909	22.7	2.1	1.76
lex. $\mathcal{A}_{q_{\Re}}$	1,591,778	23.2	2.1	1.69

Table 8: E2E augmented dataset statistics: total utterances, words per utterance, sentences per utterance, and mean D-Level score.

Table 8 shows the statistics for the E2E test set outputs. In the lexicalized setting, the mean D-level results support our hypothesis; syntactic complexity of test set outputs decreases from p_0 to p_1. In the delexicalized setting this is somewhat true; three of the p_1 models have lower mean D-level scores than p_0 with greedy decoding. Curiously, p_1/q_ϕ with beam search has the highest overall syntactic complexity of any our model variants, at odds with our hypothesis. No models are as syntactically complex as the human references, but our models come closest, with a mean D-Level category of 1.87 using the delex. p_1/q_ϕ model with beam decoder.

We also see that $p_1/q_{\Re}$ models are over two sentences in length on average while the human references are under two sentences, suggesting they are more often falling back to simple but reliable ways to realize attributes (e.g., appending "It is a family-friendly venue.").

That our simple models with greedy search and no semantic control mechanisms can perform as reliably as more sophisticated models suggest that in standard training regimes we are often not fully learning from all information available in the training data. Via sampling we can uncover novel recombinations of utterances that are only implied by the provided references. The gains of self-training also suggest that additional research into active learning for this task might bear fruit.

One curious observation about the self-training procedure is that it leads to a convergence in output complexity of greedy and beam decoding. The differences between mean D-level score on the p_0 models is 0.34 and 0.31 in the lexicalized and delexicalized settings respectively. This shrinks to 0.0 and 0.1 in the delexicalized p_1 settings and 0.06 for lexicalized p_1, suggesting that the model probability distributions are sharpening around a smaller set of output structures.

8 Related Work

Neural encoder-decoder models, are a popular choice for dialog generation (Mei et al., 2015; Dušek and Jurčíček, 2016; Chen et al., 2018; Juraska et al., 2018; Elder et al., 2018). However, the quality can vary significantly, with relatively similar architectures yielding both poor and competitve performance (Dušek et al., 2019). All of the cited work on the E2E or Laptops and TVs datasets uses beam search to achieve competitive performance. In addition, they often employ reranking to ensure that all attributes are realized (Dušek and Jurčíček, 2016; Juraska et al., 2018; Wen et al., 2015). (Elder et al., 2018) employ pointer generators to directly copy attribute values, while also using coverage penalties on the attention weights to ensure that all attribute slots are attended to. Unlike these approaches, we do not require beam search, reranking, or other specialized attention mechanisms or loss functions to obtain low error rates. Instead we use data-augmentation to obtain a more reliable but simpler model.

Data augmentation has also been used by prior neural generation models. Juraska et al. (2018) breaks multi-sentence utterances into separate training instances. They also try training on more complex sentences alone but this model was less reliably able to realize all attributes correctly. They also do not generate new utterance/MR pairs for training as we do.

Our method is in some ways similar to the reconstructor setting of Shen et al. (2019), where a base speaker model S_0 produces utterances and a listener model L reconstructs the input MR. In the framework of rational speech acts (RSA) (Monroe and Potts, 2015), a rational speaker model is obtained by composing the base speaker and listener, i.e. $S_1(y|x) = L(x|y) \cdot S_0(y|x)$. While we do not directly compose our parser q and p_0, the p_1 model is learning from the composition of the two. The theoretical commitments of RSA are somewhat orthogonal to our approach. It would be interesing to combine both methods, by incorporating self-training into the RSA framework.

9 Conclusion

We present a novel self-training methodology for learning DNN-based dialogue generation models using noise injection sampling and a MR parser. Even with relatively simple architectures and greedy decoding we are able to match the performance of state-of-the-art baselines on automatic measures of quality while also achieving superior semantic correctness. These findings hold under a human evaluation as well. On automatic measures of syntactic complexity we also find our approach is closer to matching human authored references than prior work. In future work, we intend to explore methods of self-training that futher improve syntactic diversity.

10 Acknowledgements

The authors would like to thank the anonymous reviewers for their valuable feedback, as well as Thomas Effland, Katy Ilonka Gero, and Christopher Hidey for their comments during the drafting of this paper.

This research is based upon work supported in part by the Office of the Director of National Intelligence (ODNI), Intelligence Advanced Research Projects Activity (IARPA), via contract #FA8650-17-C-9117. The views and conclusions contained herein are those of the authors and should not be interpreted as necessarily representing the official policies, either expressed or implied, of ODNI, IARPA, or the U.S. Government. The U.S. Government is authorized to reproduce and distribute reprints for governmental purposes notwithstanding any copyright annotation therein.

References

Dzmitry Bahdanau, Kyunghyun Cho, and Yoshua Bengio. 2014. Neural machine translation by jointly learning to align and translate. *arXiv preprint arXiv:1409.0473*.

Mingje Chen, Gerasimos Lampouras, and Andreas Vlachos. 2018. Sheffield at e2e: structured prediction approaches to end-to-end language generation. *E2E NLG Challenge System Descriptions*.

Kyunghyun Cho. 2016. Noisy parallel approximate decoding for conditional recurrent language model. *arXiv preprint arXiv:1605.03835*.

Kyunghyun Cho, Bart van Merrienboer, Caglar Gulcehre, Dzmitry Bahdanau, Fethi Bougares, Holger Schwenk, and Yoshua Bengio. 2014. Learning phrase representations using rnn encoder–decoder for statistical machine translation. In *Proceedings of the 2014 Conference on Empirical Methods in Natural Language Processing (EMNLP)*, pages 1724–1734.

Michael A Covington, Congzhou He, Cati Brown, Lorina Naci, and John Brown. 2006. How complex is that sentence? a proposed revision of the rosenberg and abbeduto d-level scale.

Ondřej Dušek and Filip Jurčíček. 2016. Sequence-to-sequence generation for spoken dialogue via deep syntax trees and strings. *arXiv preprint arXiv:1606.05491*.

Ondřej Dušek, Jekaterina Novikova, and Verena Rieser. 2019. Evaluating the state-of-the-art of end-to-end natural language generation: The e2e nlg challenge. *arXiv preprint arXiv:1901.07931*.

Henry Elder, Sebastian Gehrmann, Alexander OConnor, and Qun Liu. 2018. E2e nlg challenge submission: Towards controllable generation of diverse natural language. In *Proceedings of the 11th International Conference on Natural Language Generation*, pages 457–462.

Juraj Juraska, Panagiotis Karagiannis, Kevin K Bowden, and Marilyn A Walker. 2018. Slug2slug: A deep ensemble model with slot alignment for sequence-to-sequence natural language generation.

Yoon Kim. 2014. Convolutional neural networks for sentence classification. In *Proceedings of the 2014 Conference on Empirical Methods in Natural Language Processing (EMNLP)*, pages 1746–1751.

Jiwei Li, Michel Galley, Chris Brockett, Jianfeng Gao, and Bill Dolan. 2015. A diversity-promoting objective function for neural conversation models. *arXiv preprint arXiv:1510.03055*.

Xiaofei Lu. 2009. Automatic measurement of syntactic complexity in child language acquisition. *International Journal of Corpus Linguistics*, 14(1):3–28.

Hongyuan Mei, Mohit Bansal, and Matthew R Walter. 2015. What to talk about and how? selective generation using lstms with coarse-to-fine alignment. *arXiv preprint arXiv:1509.00838*.

Will Monroe and Christopher Potts. 2015. Learning in the rational speech acts model. *arXiv preprint arXiv:1510.06807*.

Dang Tuan Nguyen and Trung Tran. 2018. Structure-based generation system for e2e nlg challenge. *E2E NLG Challenge System Descriptions*.

Yevgeniy Puzikov and Iryna Gurevych. 2018. E2e nlg challenge: Neural models vs. templates. In *Proceedings of the 11th International Conference on Natural Language Generation*, pages 463–471.

Sheldon Rosenberg and Leonard Abbeduto. 1987. Indicators of linguistic competence in the peer group conversational behavior of mildly retarded adults 1. *Applied Psycholinguistics*, 8(1):19–32.

Iulian V Serban, Alessandro Sordoni, Yoshua Bengio, Aaron Courville, and Joelle Pineau. 2016. Building end-to-end dialogue systems using generative hierarchical neural network models. In *Thirtieth AAAI Conference on Artificial Intelligence*.

Sheng Shen, Daniel Fried, Jacob Andreas, and Dan Klein. 2019. Pragmatically informative text generation. *arXiv preprint arXiv:1904.01301*.

Tsung-Hsien Wen, Milica Gašić, Nikola Mrkšić, Lina M Rojas-Barahona, Pei-Hao Su, David Vandyke, and Steve Young. 2016. Multi-domain neural network language generation for spoken dialogue systems. In *Proceedings of the 2016 Conference of the North American Chapter of the Association for Computational Linguistics: Human Language Technologies*, pages 120–129.

Tsung-Hsien Wen, Milica Gasic, Nikola Mrkšić, Pei-Hao Su, David Vandyke, and Steve Young. 2015. Semantically conditioned lstm-based natural language generation for spoken dialogue systems. In *Proceedings of the 2015 Conference on Empirical Methods in Natural Language Processing*, pages 1711–1721.

A Stable Variational Autoencoder for Text Modelling

Ruizhe Li♠, Xiao Li♠, Chenghua Lin♡, Matthew Collinson♠ and Rui Mao♠
♠Department of Computing Science, University of Aberdeen, UK
{r02rl17, x.li, matthew.collinson, r03rm16}@abdn.ac.uk
♡Department of Computer Science, University of Sheffield, UK
c.lin@sheffield.ac.uk

Abstract

Variational Autoencoder (VAE) is a powerful method for learning representations of high-dimensional data. However, VAEs can suffer from an issue known as latent variable collapse (or KL loss vanishing), where the posterior collapses to the prior and the model will ignore the latent codes in generative tasks. Such an issue is particularly prevalent when employing VAE-RNN architectures for text modelling (Bowman et al., 2016). In this paper, we present a simple architecture called holistic regularisation VAE (HR-VAE), which can effectively avoid latent variable collapse. Compared to existing VAE-RNN architectures, we show that our model can achieve much more stable training process and can generate text with significantly better quality.

1 Introduction

Variational Autoencoder (VAE) (Kingma and Welling, 2013) is a powerful method for learning representations of high-dimensional data. However, recent attempts of applying VAEs to text modelling are still far less successful compared to its application to image and speech (Bachman, 2016; Fraccaro et al., 2016; Semeniuta et al., 2017). When applying VAEs for text modelling, recurrent neural networks (RNNs)[1] are commonly used as the architecture for both encoder and decoder (Bowman et al., 2016; Xu and Durrett, 2018; Dieng et al., 2019). While such a VAE-RNN based architecture allows encoding and generating sentences (in the decoding phase) with variable-length effectively, it is also vulnerable to an issue known as latent variable collapse (or KL loss vanishing), where the posterior collapses to the prior and the model will ignore the latent codes in generative tasks.

---

[1]NB: here we refer RNN to any type of recurrent neural architectures including LSTM and GRU.

Various efforts have been made to alleviate the latent variable collapse issue. Bowman et al. (2016) uses KL annealing, where a variable weight is added to the KL term in the cost function at training time. Yang et al. (2017) discovered that there is a trade-off between the contextual capacity of the decoder and effective use of encoding information, and developed a dilated CNN as decoder which can vary the amount of conditioning context. They also introduced a loss clipping strategy in order to make the model more robust. Xu and Durrett (2018) addressed the problem by replacing the standard normal distribution for the prior with the von Mises-Fisher (vMF) distribution. With vMF, the KL loss only depends on the concentration parameter which is fixed during training and testing, and hence results in a constant KL loss. In a more recent work, Dieng et al. (2019) avoided latent variable collapse by including skip connections in the generative model, where the skip connections enforce strong links between the latent variables and the likelihood function.

Although the aforementioned works show effectiveness in addressing the latent variable collapse issue to some extent, they either require carefully engineering to balance the weight between the reconstruction loss and KL loss (Bowman et al., 2016; Sønderby et al., 2016), or resort to designing more sophisticated model structures (Yang et al., 2017; Xu and Durrett, 2018; Dieng et al., 2019).

In this paper, we present a simple architecture called holistic regularisation VAE (HR-VAE), which can effectively avoid latent variable collapse. In contrast to existing VAE-RNN models for text modelling which merely impose a standard normal distribution prior on the last hidden state of the RNN encoder, our HR-VAE model imposes regularisation for all hidden states of the RNN encoder. Another advantage of our model is that it

Proceedings of The 12th International Conference on Natural Language Generation, pages 594–599,
Tokyo, Japan, 28 Oct - 1 Nov, 2019. ©2019 Association for Computational Linguistics

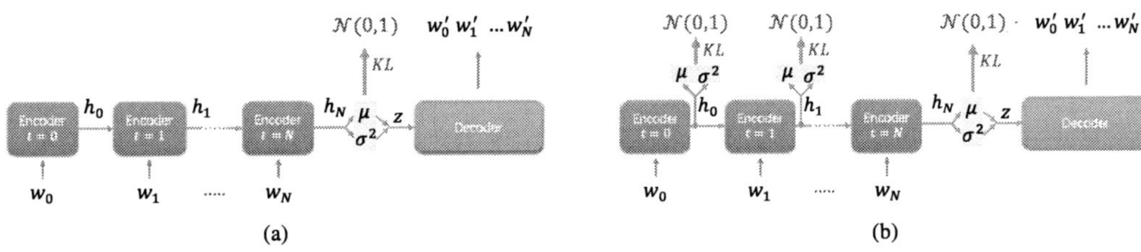

Figure 1: (a) The typical architecture of RNN-based VAE; (b) the proposed HR-VAE architecture.

is generic and can be applied to any existing VAE-RNN-based architectures.

We evaluate our model against several strong baselines which apply VAE for text modelling (Bowman et al., 2016; Yang et al., 2017; Xu and Durrett, 2018). We conducted experiments based on two public benchmark datasets, namely, the Penn Treebank dataset (Marcus and Marcinkiewicz) and the end-to-end (E2E) text generation dataset (Novikova et al., 2017). Experimental results show that our HR-VAE model not only can effectively mitigate the latent variable collapse issue with a stable training process, but also can give better predictive performance than the baselines, as evidenced by both quantitative (e.g., negative log likelihood and perplexity) and qualitative evaluation. The code for our model is available online[2].

2 Methodology

2.1 Background of VAE

A variational autoencoder (VAE) is a deep generative model, which combines variational inference with deep learning. The VAE modifies the conventional autoencoder architecture by replacing the deterministic latent representation $\mathbf{z}$ of an input $\mathbf{x}$ with a posterior distribution $P(\mathbf{z}|\mathbf{x})$, and imposing a prior distribution on the posterior, such that the model allows sampling from any point of the latent space and yet able to generate novel and plausible output. The prior is typically chosen to be standard normal distributions, i.e., $P(\mathbf{z}) = \mathcal{N}(\mathbf{0}, \mathbf{1})$, such that the KL divergence between posterior and prior can be computed in closed form (Kingma and Welling, 2013).

To train a VAE, we need to optimise the marginal likelihood $P_\theta(\mathbf{x}) = \int P(\mathbf{z})P_\theta(\mathbf{x}|\mathbf{z})d\mathbf{z}$, where the log likelihood can take following form:

$$\log P_\theta(\mathbf{x}) = \mathcal{L}(\theta, \phi; \mathbf{x}) + \mathrm{KL}\left(Q_\phi(\mathbf{z}|\mathbf{x})\|P_\theta(\mathbf{z}|\mathbf{x})\right) \tag{1}$$

$$\mathcal{L}(\theta, \phi; \mathbf{x}) = \mathbb{E}_{Q_\phi(\mathbf{z}|\mathbf{x})}[\log P_\theta(\mathbf{x}|\mathbf{z})] \\ - \mathrm{KL}\left(Q_\phi(\mathbf{z}|\mathbf{x})\|P(\mathbf{z})\right) \tag{2}$$

Here $Q_\phi(\mathbf{z}|\mathbf{x})$ is the variational approximation for the true posterior $P_\theta(\mathbf{z}|\mathbf{x})$. Specifically, $Q_\phi(\mathbf{z}|\mathbf{x})$ can be regarded as an encoder (a.k.a. the recognition model) and $P_\theta(\mathbf{x}|\mathbf{z})$ the decoder (a.k.a. the generative model). Both encoder and decoder are implemented via neural networks. As proved in (Kingma and Welling, 2013), optimising the marginal log likelihood is essentially equivalent to maximising $\mathcal{L}(\theta, \phi; \mathbf{x})$, i.e., the evidence lower bound (ELBO), which consists of two terms. The first term is the expected reconstruction error indicating how well the model can reconstruct data given a latent variable. The the second term is the KL divergence of the approximate posterior from prior, i.e., a regularisation pushing the learned posterior to be as close to the prior as possible.

2.2 Variational Autoendoder with Holistic Regularisation

In this section, we discuss the technical details of the proposed holistic regularisation VAE (HR-VAE) model, a general architecture which can effectively mitigate the KL vanishing phenomenon.

Our model design is motivated by one noticeable defect shared by the VAE-RNN based models in previous works (Bowman et al., 2016; Yang et al., 2017; Xu and Durrett, 2018; Dieng et al., 2019). That is, all these models, as shown in Figure 1a, only impose a standard normal distribution prior on the last hidden state of the RNN encoder, which potentially leads to learning a suboptimal representation of the latent variable and results in model vulnerable to KL loss vanishing. Our hypothesis is that to learn a good representation of

---

[2]https://github.com/ruizheliUOA/HR-VAE

data and a good generative model, it is crucial to impose the standard normal prior on all the hidden states of the RNN-based encoder (see Figure 1b), which allows a better regularisation of the model learning process.

We implement the HR-VAE model using a two-layer LSTM for both the encoder and decoder. However, one should note that our architecture can be readily applied to other types of RNN such as GRU. For each time stamp t (see Figure 1b), we concatenate the hidden state $\mathbf{h}_t$ and the cell state $\mathbf{c}_t$ of the encoder. The concatenation (i.e., $[\mathbf{h}_t; \mathbf{c}_t]$) is then fed into two linear transformation layers for estimating $\boldsymbol{\mu}_t$ and $\boldsymbol{\sigma}_t^2$, which are parameters of a normal distribution corresponding to the concatenation of $\mathbf{h}_t$ and $\mathbf{c}_t$. Let $Q_{\phi_t}(\mathbf{z}_t|\mathbf{x}) = \mathcal{N}(\mathbf{z}_t|\boldsymbol{\mu}_t, \boldsymbol{\sigma}_t^2)$, we wish $Q_{\phi_t}(\mathbf{z}_t|\mathbf{x})$ to be close to a prior $P(\mathbf{z}_t)$, which is a standard Gaussian. Finally, the KL divergence between these two multivariate Gaussian distributions (i.e., Q_{ϕ_t} and $P(\mathbf{z}_t)$) will contribute to the overall KL loss of the ELBO. By taking the average of the KL loss at each time stamp t, the resulting ELBO takes the following form

$$\mathcal{L}(\theta, \phi; \mathbf{x}) = \mathbb{E}_{Q_\phi(\mathbf{z}_N|\mathbf{x})}[\log P_\theta(\mathbf{x}|\mathbf{z}_N)]$$
$$- \frac{1}{N} \sum_{t=0}^{N} \mathrm{KL}(Q_{\phi_t}(\mathbf{z}_t|\mathbf{x}) \| P(\mathbf{z}_t)).$$
$$(3)$$

As can be seen in Eq. 3, our solution to the KL collapse issue does not require any engineering for balancing the weight between the reconstruction term and KL loss as commonly the case in existing works (Bowman et al., 2016; Sønderby et al., 2016). The weight between these two terms of our model is simply $1:1$.

3 Experimental Setup

3.1 Datasets

We evaluate our model on two public datasets, namely, Penn Treebank (PTB) (Marcus and Marcinkiewicz) and the end-to-end (E2E) text generation corpus (Novikova et al., 2017), which have been used in a number of previous works for text generation (Bowman et al., 2016; Xu and Durrett, 2018; Wiseman et al., 2018; Su et al., 2018). PTB consists of more than 40,000 sentences from Wall Street Journal articles whereas the E2E dataset contains over 50,000 sentences

of restaurant reviews. The statistics of these two datasets are summarised in Table 1.

3.2 Implementation Details

For the PTB dataset, we used the train-test split following (Bowman et al., 2016; Xu and Durrett, 2018). For the E2E dataset, we used the train-test split from the original dataset (Novikova et al., 2017) and indexed the words with a frequency higher than 3. We represent input data with 512-dimensional word2vec embeddings (Mikolov et al., 2013). We set the dimension of the hidden layers of both encoder and decoder to 256. The Adam optimiser (Kingma and Ba, 2014) was used for training with an initial learning rate of 0.0001. Each utterance in a mini-batch was padded to the maximum length for that batch, and the maximum batch-size allowed is 128.

3.3 Baselines

We compare our HR-VAE model with three strong baselines using VAE for text modelling:

VAE-LSTM-base[3]: A variational autoencoder model which uses LSTM for both encoder and decoder. KL annealing is used to tackled the latent variable collapse issue (Bowman et al., 2016);

VAE-CNN[4]: A variational autoencoder model with a LSTM encoder and a dilated CNN decoder (Yang et al., 2017);

vMF-VAE[5]: A variational autoencoder model using LSTM for both encoder and decoder where the prior distribution is the von Mises-Fisher (vMF) distribution rather than a Gaussian distribution (Xu and Durrett, 2018).

4 Experimental Results

We evaluate our HR-VAE model in two experimental settings, following the setup of (Bowman et al., 2016; Xu and Durrett, 2018). In the *standard setting*, the input to the decoder at each time stamp is the concatenation of latent variable $\mathbf{z}$ and the ground truth word of the previous time stamp. Under this setting, the decoder will be more powerful because it uses the ground truth word as input, resulting in little information of the training data captured by latent variable $\mathbf{z}$. The *inputless setting*, in contrast, does not use the previous ground truth word as input for the decoder. In other words,

---

[3]https://github.com/timbmg/Sentence-VAE
[4]https://github.com/kefirski/contiguous-succotash
[5]https://github.com/jiacheng-xu/vmf_vae_nlp

Dataset	Training	Development	Testing	Avg. sent. length	Vocab.
PTB	42,068	3,370	3,761	21.1	10K
E2E	42,061	4,672	4,693	22.67	2.8K

Table 1: The statistics of the PTB and E2E datasets.

Model	PTB				E2E			
	Standard		Inputless		Standard		Inputless	
	NLL	PPL	NLL	PPL	NLL	PPL	NLL	PPL
VAE-LSTM-base	$101^{\dagger}$ $(2^{\dagger})$	$119^{\dagger}$	$125^{\dagger}$ $(15^{\dagger})$	$380^{\dagger}$	50 (1.88)	5.77	101 (5.48)	34.70
VAE-CNN	99 (3.1)	113	121 (16.2)	323	41 (3.02)	4.23	82 (5.95)	17.81
vMF-VAE	$96^{\dagger}$ $(5.7^{\dagger})$	$98^{\dagger}$	$117^{\dagger}$ $(18.6^{\dagger})$	$262^{\dagger}$	34 (7.63)	3.29	61 (19.58)	8.52
HR-VAE (Ours)	**79 (10.4)**	**43**	**85 (17.32)**	**54**	**20 (5.37)**	**2.02**	**38 (7.78)**	**3.74**

Table 2: Language modelling results on the PTB and E2E datasets. † indicates the results which are reported from the prior publications. KL loss is shown in the parenthesis.

the decoder needs to predict the entire sequence with only the help of the given latent variable $\mathbf{z}$. In this way, a high-quality representation abstracting the information of the input sentence is much needed for the decoder, and hence enforcing $\mathbf{z}$ to learn the required information.

Overall performance. Table 2 shows the language modelling results of our approach and the baselines. We report negative log likelihood (NLL), KL loss, and perplexity (PPL) on the test set. As expected, all the models have a higher KL loss in the inputless setting than the standard setting, as $\mathbf{z}$ is required to encode more information about the input data for reconstruction. In terms of overall performance, our model outperforms all the baselines in both datasets (i.e., PTB and E2E). For instance, when comparing with the strongest baseline vMF-VAE in the standard setting, our model reduces NLL from 96 to 79 and PPL from 98 to 43 in PTB, respectively. In the inputless setting, our performance gain is even higher, i.e., NLL reduced from 117 to 85 and PPL from 262 to 54. A similar pattern can be observed for the E2E dataset. These observations suggest that our approach can learn a better generative model for data.

Loss analysis. To conduct a more thorough evaluation, we further investigate model behaviours in terms of both reconstruction loss and KL loss, as shown in Figure 2. These plots were obtained based on the E2E training set using the inputless setting.

We can see that the KL loss of VAE-LSTM-base, which uses Sigmoid annealing (Bowman et al., 2016), collapses to zero, leading to a poor generative performance as indicated by the high reconstruction loss. The KL loss for both VAE-CNN and vMF-VAE are nonzero, where the former mitigates the KL collapse issue with a KL loss clipping strategy and the latter by replacing the standard normal distribution for the prior with the vMF distribution (i.e., with the vMF distribution, the KL loss only depends on a fixed concentration parameter, and hence results in a constant KL loss). Although both VAE-CNN and vMF-VAE outperform VAE-LSTM-base by a large margin in terms of reconstruction loss as shown in Figure 2, one should also notice that these two models actually overfit the training data, as their performance on the test set is much worse (cf. Table 2). In contrast to the baselines which mitigate the KL collapse issue by carefully engineering the weight between the reconstruction loss and KL loss or choosing a different choice of prior, we provide a simple and elegant solution through holistic KL regularisation, which can effectively mitigate the KL collapse issue and achieve a better reconstruction error in both training and testing.

Sentence reconstruction. Lastly, we show some sentence examples reconstructed by vMF-VAE (i.e., the best baseline) and our model in the inputless setting using sentences from the E2E test set as input. As shown in Table 3, the sentences generated by vMF-VAE contain repeated words in quite a few cases, such as *'city city area'* and *'blue spice spice'*. In addition, vMF-VAE also tends to generate unnecessary or unrelated words at the end of sentences, making the generated sentences ungrammatical. The sentences reconstructed by our model, in contrast, are more grammatical and more similar to the corresponding ground truth sentences than vMF-VAE.

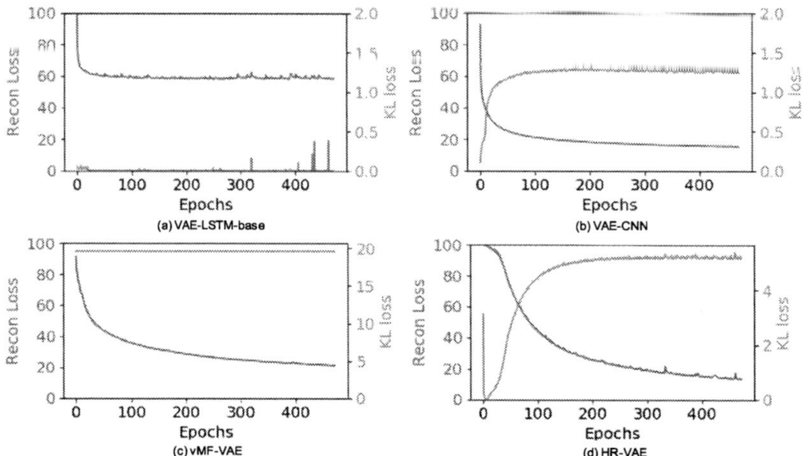

Figure 2: Training curves of reconstruction loss and KL loss of (a) VAE-LSTM-base, (b) VAE-CNN, (c) vMF-VAE, and (d) our model, based on the E2E training set using the inputless setting.

Input	1. blue spice is a coffee shop in city centre .
	2. giraffe is a coffee shop found near the bakers .
	3. a pub in the city centre area called blue spice
	4. pub located near café sicilia called cocum with a high customer rating
	5. the cricketers is a one star coffee shop near the ranch that is not family friendly .
vMF-VAE	1. blue spice is a coffee in city centre . it is not , and
	2. cotto is a coffee shop located near the bakers . . is 5 out of
	3. a coffee in the city city area is blue spice spice . the is is
	4. located located near café rouge , cotto has a high customer rating and a customer
	5. the cricketers is a low rated coffee shop near the bakers that is a star , is is
Ours	1. blue spice is a coffee shop in city centre .
	2. giraffe is a coffee shop located near the bakers .
	3. a restaurant in the city centre called blue spice italian
	4. located place near café sicilia called punter has a high customer rating
	5. the cricketers is a one star coffee shop near ranch ranch that is not family friendly .

Table 3: Example input sentences from the E2E test dataset (top); sentences reconstructed by vMF-VAE (middle); sentences reconstructed by our model (bottom).

5 Conclusion

In this paper, we present a simple and generic architecture called holistic regularisation VAE (HR-VAE), which can effectively avoid latent variable collapse. In contrast to existing VAE-RNN models which merely impose a standard normal distribution prior on the last hidden state of the RNN encoder, our HR-VAE model imposes regularisation on all the hidden states, allowing a better regularisation of the model learning process. Empirical results show that our model can effectively mitigate the latent variable collapse issue while giving a better predictive performance than the baselines.

Acknowledgment

This work is supported by the award made by the UK Engineering and Physical Sciences Research Council (Grant number: EP/P011829/1).

References

Philip Bachman. 2016. An architecture for deep, hierarchical generative models. In *Advances in Neural Information Processing Systems*, pages 4826–4834.

Samuel Bowman, Luke Vilnis, Oriol Vinyals, Andrew M Dai, Rafal Jozefowicz, and Samy Bengio. 2016. Generating sentences from a continuous space. In *Proceedings of the Twentieth Conference on Computational Natural Language Learning (CoNLL)*.

Adji B Dieng, Yoon Kim, Alexander M Rush, and David M Blei. 2019. Avoiding latent variable collapse with generative skip models. In *The 22nd International Conference on Artificial Intelligence and Statistics*, pages 2397–2405.

Marco Fraccaro, Søren Kaae Sønderby, Ulrich Paquet, and Ole Winther. 2016. Sequential neural models with stochastic layers. In *Advances in neural information processing systems*, pages 2199–2207.

Diederik P Kingma and Jimmy Ba. 2014. Adam: A method for stochastic optimization. *arXiv preprint arXiv:1412.6980*.

Diederik P Kingma and Max Welling. 2013. Auto-encoding variational bayes. *arXiv preprint arXiv:1312.6114*.

Mitchell P Marcus and Mary Ann Marcinkiewicz. Building a large annotated corpus of english: The penn treebank. *Computational Linguistics*, 19(2).

Tomas Mikolov, Ilya Sutskever, Kai Chen, Greg S Corrado, and Jeff Dean. 2013. Distributed representations of words and phrases and their compositionality. In *Advances in neural information processing systems*, pages 3111–3119.

Jekaterina Novikova, Ondřej Dušek, and Verena Rieser. 2017. The e2e dataset: New challenges for end-to-end generation. In *Proceedings of the 18th Annual SIGdial Meeting on Discourse and Dialogue*, pages 201–206.

Stanislau Semeniuta, Aliaksei Severyn, and Erhardt Barth. 2017. A hybrid convolutional variational autoencoder for text generation. In *Proceedings of the 2017 Conference on Empirical Methods in Natural Language Processing*, pages 627–637.

Casper Kaae Sønderby, Tapani Raiko, Lars Maaløe, Søren Kaae Sønderby, and Ole Winther. 2016. How to train deep variational autoencoders and probabilistic ladder networks. In *33rd International Conference on Machine Learning (ICML 2016)*.

Shang-Yu Su, Kai-Ling Lo, Yi Ting Yeh, and Yun-Nung Chen. 2018. Natural language generation by hierarchical decoding with linguistic patterns. In *Proceedings of the 2018 Conference of the North American Chapter of the Association for Computational Linguistics: Human Language Technologies, Volume 2 (Short Papers)*, pages 61–66.

Sam Wiseman, Stuart Shieber, and Alexander Rush. 2018. Learning neural templates for text generation. In *Proceedings of the 2018 Conference on Empirical Methods in Natural Language Processing*, pages 3174–3187.

Jiacheng Xu and Greg Durrett. 2018. Spherical latent spaces for stable variational autoencoders. In *Proceedings of the 2018 Conference on Empirical Methods in Natural Language Processing*, pages 4503–4513.

Zichao Yang, Zhiting Hu, Ruslan Salakhutdinov, and Taylor Berg-Kirkpatrick. 2017. Improved variational autoencoders for text modeling using dilated convolutions. In *Proceedings of the 34th International Conference on Machine Learning-Volume 70*, pages 3881–3890. JMLR. org.

Association for Computational Linguistics
209 N. Eighth Street
Stroudsburg, Pennsylvania 18360